STAFFORDSHIRE POTTERS

1781-1900

STAFFORDSHIRE POTTERS

1781-1900

A Comprehensive List Assembled from Contemporary Directories with Selected Marks

R.K. Henrywood

ANTIQUE COLLECTORS' CLUB

ISBN 1 85149 370 0

British Library Cataloguing-in-Publication Data
A catalogue record for this book is available from the British Library

Printed in England
by the Antique Collectors' Club Ltd.,
Woodbridge, Suffolk IP12 4SD

Frontispiece: *Scene titled "The Kilns where the ware is fired", from an early-20th century postcard.*

Title page: *Printed pre-Victorian royal arms mark with unattributed maker's initials BB from a Willow pattern meat dish.*

ANTIQUE COLLECTORS' CLUB

The Antique Collectors' Club was formed in 1966 and quickly grew to a five figure membership spread throughout the world. It publishes the only independently run monthly antiques magazine, *Antique Collecting*, which caters for those collectors who are interested in widening their knowledge of antiques, both by greater awareness of quality and by discussion of the factors which influence the price that is likely to be asked. The Antique Collectors' Club pioneered the provision of information on prices for collectors and the magazine still leads in the provision of detailed articles on a variety of subjects.

It was in response to the enormous demand for information on 'what to pay' that the price guide series was introduced in 1968 with the first edition of *The Price Guide to Antique Furniture* (completely revised 1978 and 1989), a book which broke new ground by illustrating the more common types of antique furniture, the sort that collectors could buy in shops and at auctions rather than the rare museum pieces which had previously been used (and still to a large extent are used) to make up the limited amount of illustrations in books published by commercial publishers. Many other price guides have followed, all copiously illustrated, and greatly appreciated by collectors for the valuable information they contain, quite apart from prices. The Price Guide Series heralded the publication of many standard works of reference on art and antiques. *The Dictionary of British Art* (now in six volumes), *The Pictorial Dictionary of British 19th Century Furniture Design, Oak Furniture* and *Early English Clocks* were followed by many deeply researched reference works such as *The Directory of Gold and Silversmiths,* providing new information. Many of these books are now accepted as the standard work of reference on their subject.

The Antique Collectors' Club has widened its list to include books on gardens and architecture. All the Club's publications are available through bookshops world wide and a full catalogue of all these titles is available free of charge from the addresses below.

Club membership, open to all collectors, costs little. Members receive free of charge *Antique Collecting*, the Club's magazine (published ten times a year), which contains well-illustrated articles dealing with the practical aspects of collecting not normally dealt with by magazines. Prices, features of value, investment potential, fakes and forgeries are all given prominence in the magazine.

Among other facilities available to members are private buying and selling facilities and the opportunity to meet other collectors at their local antique collectors' clubs. There are over eighty in Britain and more than a dozen overseas. Members may also buy the Club's publications at special pre-publication prices.

As its motto implies, the Club is an organisation designed to help collectors get the most out of their hobby: it is informal and friendly and gives enormous enjoyment to all concerned.

For Collectors — By Collectors — About Collecting

ANTIQUE COLLECTORS' CLUB
Sandy Lane, Old Martlesham, Woodbridge Suffolk, IP12 4SD
Tel: (01394) 389950 Fax: (01394) 389999
Email: sales@antique-acc.com
Website: www.antique-acc.com
or
Market Street Industrial Park, Wappingers' Falls, NY 12590, USA
Tel: (845) 297 0003 Fax (845) 297 0068
ORDERS: (800) 252 5231
Email: info@antiquecc.com
Website: www.antiquecc.com

Dedicated to the memory of

Jack Hacking

A giant of a man whose love of pots and generosity to fellow collectors knew no bounds. His enthusiasm for this book was an inspiration and his encouragement played a great part in the completion of the project.

CONTENTS

ACKNOWLEDGEMENTS

It would never be possible to assemble a book of this nature without considerable assistance, and I should like to express my thanks to the librarians and staff at the Central Reference Libraries or Local Studies Libraries at Barnstaple, Birmingham, Bristol, Cardiff, Exeter, Kensington, Leamington Spa, Newcastle-under-Lyme, Plymouth, Salisbury, Stoke-on-Trent (Hanley), Taunton, Trowbridge, Westminster (Victoria), Winchester, Wolverhampton and Worcester, and also at the Institute of Historical Research (University of London), the Guildhall Library (City of London), and the William Salt Library (Stafford).

The marks illustrated have been selected from private collections, examples in the Potteries Museum & Art Gallery at Hanley (including a few from the Godden reference collection), and many from items which have passed through auction sales held by Dreweatt Neate at Newbury. I am indebted to Clive Stewart-Lockhart for encouragement and particularly to Dave Pincott for taking so many excellent photographs while still processing his day-to-day workload.

Considerable thanks for specific help, information or access to marks are due to Victoria Bergesen, David Bromwich, Janet Coysh, Tony Curnock, Geoffrey Godden, the late Jack Hacking, Pat Halfpenny, Rodney and Eileen Hampson, Tom Jones, Barry Lamb, Griselda Lewis and the late John Lewis, Martin Pulver, Deborah Skinner, Margo and Ken Swift, Lavinia Walbridge, and Helen Williams.

I would also like to thank my wife Melanie and our children Ross and Verity. Writing books is a time-consuming task and they deserve much credit for their support.

BIBLIOGRAPHY

Cushion, John P., and Honey, W.B., *Handbook of Pottery and Porcelain Marks.* Faber, London, 1956. Fourth revised edition 1980.

Godden, Geoffrey A., *Encyclopaedia of British Pottery and Porcelain Marks.* Herbert Jenkins, London, 1964. Revised edition Barrie & Jenkins 1991.

Godden, Geoffrey A., *Encyclopaedia of British Porcelain Manufacturers.* Barrie & Jenkins, London, 1988.

Goss, Charles W.F., *The London Directories 1677-1855. A Bibliography with Notes on their Origin and Development.* Denis Archer, London, 1932.

Jewitt, Llewellynn, *The Ceramic Art of Great Britain.* Virtue & Co., London, 1878. Second revised edition in a single volume, 1883 (reprinted 1971 by Paul P.B. Minet, Chicheley)

Norton, Jane E., *Guide to the National and Provincial Directories of England and Wales, excluding London, Published before 1856.* Royal Historical Society, London, 1950, 1984.

Shaw, Gareth, and Tipper, Allison, *British Directories: A Bibliography and Guide to Directories published in England and Wales (1850-1950) and Scotland (1773-1950).* Leicester University Press, 1989.

Shaw, Simeon, *History of the Staffordshire Potteries.* Hanley, 1829 (reprinted 1970 by David & Charles, Newton Abbot, and S.R. Publishers, Wakefield).

Thomas, John, *The Rise of the Staffordshire Potteries.* Adams & Dart, Bath, 1971.

Ward, John, *The Borough of Stoke-upon-Trent.* W. Lewis & Son, London, 1843 (reprinted 1969 by S.R. Publishers, Wakefield, and 1984 by Webberly, Stoke-on-Trent).

Yates, William, *A Map of the County of Stafford from an Actual Survey.* 1775 (reprinted 1984 for The Staffordshire Record Society).

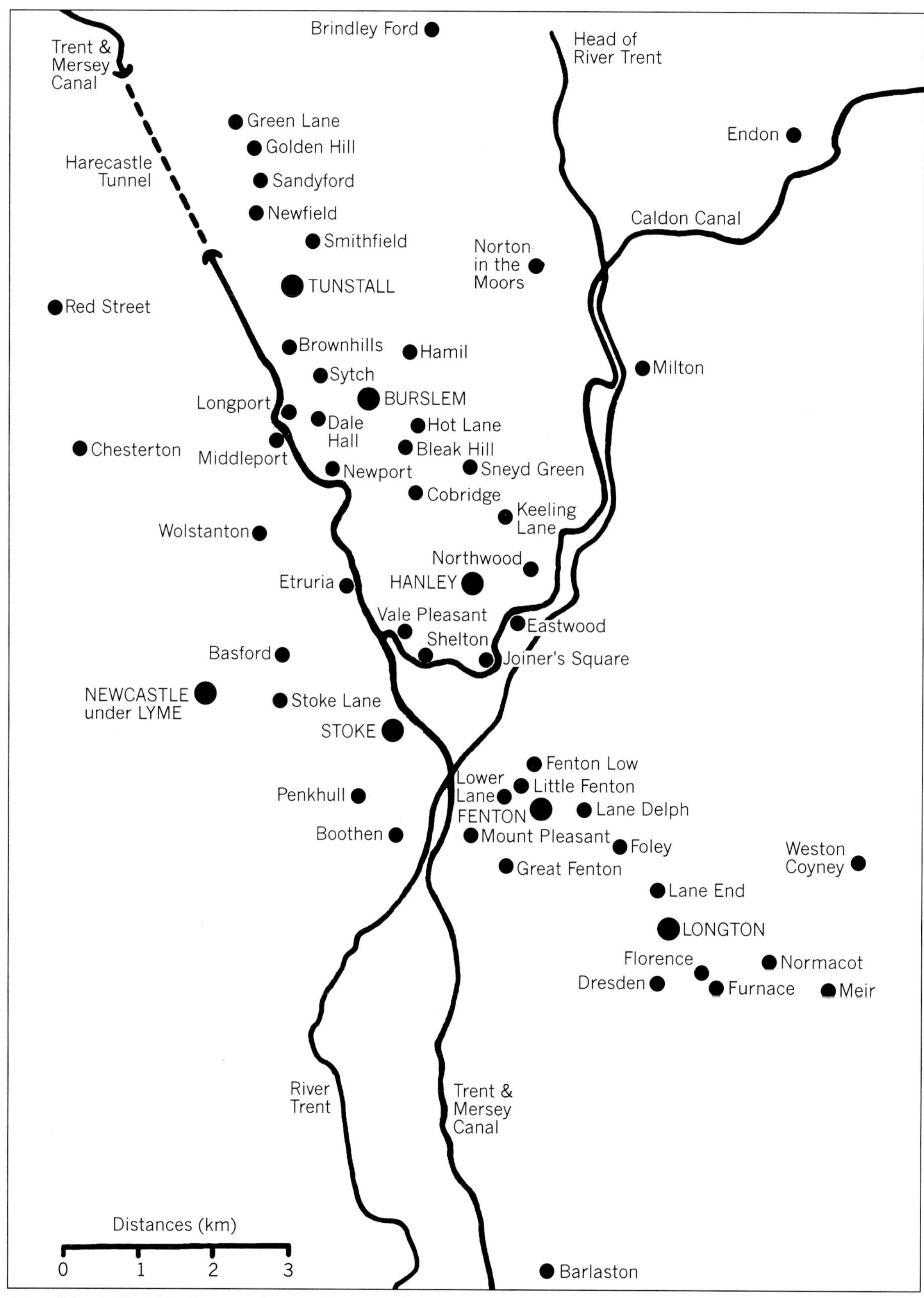

Map of the Staffordshire Potteries showing the principal towns and villages and most of the hamlets mentioned in the directories. See also the map from Allbut's 1802 Directory on page 266.

CHAPTER 1

INTRODUCTION

The study of English ceramics as a fascinating and absorbing hobby is not entirely a modern phenomenon. There were several famous collectors in the nineteenth century whose pioneering work laid a strong foundation for well-known museum collections, but they were wealthy people and collecting by the man or woman in the street is only a recent development. The early collectors had few reference books to guide them, but as the circle of collectors has grown wider, so the market for such books has expanded, and in the last two decades or so many notable standard reference works have been published.

As a general rule, the books available to collectors concentrate on the wares themselves, and it is only the larger, more prestigious manufacturers whose histories have been researched in depth. Famous names such as Wedgwood, Spode, Minton and Worcester all spring to mind, and it is no coincidence that for such famous factories documentary material has survived along with the firms themselves. Other well-known names such as Davenport, Mason, Rockingham and Ridgway also have books devoted to them, but available information on the myriad of smaller firms is sparse. The reasons are not hard to find. Even where material does exist the efforts necessary to locate and tap the sources cannot easily be justified except as a labour of love or by those with a particular interest. Audrey Dudson's history of the Dudson family firm is a notable and exceptional example.

There are many collectors who wish to discover more about their favourite pieces, however humble their origins. There are, of course, a few pioneering studies first published in the nineteenth century, notable amongst which are Simeon Shaw's *History of the Staffordshire Potteries,* John Ward's history of *The Borough of Stoke-upon-Trent,* and particularly Llewellynn Jewitt's more comprehensive *The Ceramic Art of Great Britain.* Fortunately, these have all been reprinted in recent years, but despite the level of interest there are virtually no modern equivalents. The one main exception is Geoffrey Godden's *Encyclopaedia of British Porcelain Manufacturers,* a pioneering study of great value, but restricted in scope to the makers of china and porcelain, probably less than a third of the potters in Staffordshire and even fewer elsewhere.

The only other major sources of information widely available are the books of pottery and porcelain marks. The most notable amongst these are John Cushion's *Handbook of Pottery and Porcelain Marks* and Geoffrey Godden's *Encyclopaedia of British Pottery and Porcelain Marks.* These are excellent works of reference, indispensable for all collectors. Mark books do, however, suffer from one obvious drawback in that they only list firms whose marked wares are known to the authors. While these books do cover by far the majority of marked wares, many collectors will have had the experience of unearthing some rarity with a mark which is not listed. In most cases the piece has remained a puzzle, sometimes prompting much discussion and speculation within publications by specialist organisations such as the Northern Ceramic Society or the Friends of Blue.

It is as an attempt to help in solving some of these puzzles that the present work has evolved. The limitations of mark books can best be overcome by attempting to record all potters, regardless of the known existence of marked wares. There are, of course, many sources of historical information which could be used to produce a truly comprehensive list of manufacturers, but they can be voluminous and tend to be stored away in newspaper archives, libraries, museums, record offices and other similar institutions which are not always easily accessible. Despite its potential value, such a truly comprehensive general survey would be a lifetime's work, and a more limited approach has been employed here.

Amongst the most valuable of the general sources to have survived are the national and provincial directories, which contain listings of firms and individuals, usually with their addresses, and sometimes with some short descriptive text. Their value has long been recognised, and their contents have repeatedly been tapped by researchers in their compilation of books and articles. However, while the knowledge that a firm is listed in a single directory can be useful, the true value of the directories is not realised without a systematic analysis of their contents. Although detailed searches have been made by researchers interested in a single firm, few have been truly complete since some of the surviving directories are little known and difficult to locate. In addition, accurate conclusions can only be drawn with a thorough knowledge of the limitations of directories, and some entries, while strictly correct, can easily be misinterpreted.

Charles Goss, the author of an early bibliography of the London Directories, stated that 'access to collections of directories is essential alike to the student of sociology and of topography, the antiquary, the historian, the biographer and the genealogist', and today we should add the collector to his list. Writing in 1932 he described how the directories were then becoming more appreciated, but also noted that 'early directories from their ephemeral character are the most elusive of books', and that there was an ever-increasing demand for 'particulars as to what directories have been published, and also for information concerning the whereabouts of sets for consecutive years'.

Goss also noted that 'the volumes have so long remained unrecorded and unanalysed', and to this day, no comprehensive study of the directories covering Staffordshire potters has previously been published. It is hoped that the current survey may fill a significant gap in available ceramics literature. The main value is, of course, not the long list of entries covering the major potters, but the record of the smaller, almost ephemeral firms. James Pigot, perhaps the greatest directory publisher of the first half of the nineteenth century, wrote in 1830 in the Address introducing one of his volumes, '...may not faithful directories of the present day be the means of preserving to after generations a local habitation and a name... that in future ages might, but for such means, cease to be recognized?' The wider dissemination of this information should make life easier for future researchers, and provide another valuable source of information for collectors, whatever their specialised interests.

SCOPE OF THIS SURVEY

Although it would be possible to put together a list of all British potters by reference to surviving directories, this study has been limited to manufacturers working in the Staffordshire Potteries between 1781 and 1900. The geographical restriction needs little justification since Staffordshire was, and is, the dominant centre of the British pottery industry. The sheer concentration of small firms within Staffordshire has never been matched elsewhere. A similar survey could be undertaken for other areas such as Tyneside, Wearside, South Wales, and Scotland, but most of these are already reasonably well served by existing reference books, and a survey of the directories would add little of real value. The start date of 1781 is that of the earliest known directory covering the Potteries, while the finishing date of 1900, although necessarily arbitrary, is a fair reflection of the current interest of the majority of collectors.

The area known as the Staffordshire Potteries is in the north of the county, to the east of Newcastle-under-Lyme. A detailed description can be found in Chapter 2, but the extent of such an area can never be rigidly defined. As far as this volume is concerned, information has been incorporated from all directories which cover the modern city of Stoke-on-Trent and its surroundings. Some peripheral areas of the Potteries are not well served by the directories and references to potters in such outlying areas are perforce rather sketchy. There were some potters in other areas of the county, particularly the south, but they were too few in number to justify inclusion here. They are listed in the Kelly's directories, which cover the whole county, and also in local directories not covered here. The towns and villages concerned are Audley, Biddulph, Bilston, Brierley Hill, Burton-on-Trent, Congleton, Dudley, Lichfield, Milwich, Rowley Regis, Rugeley, Smethwick, Stone, Stourbridge, Swadlincote, Tamworth, Tipton, Wednesbury, Willenhall and Wolverhampton.

Coverage has been restricted to manufacturers only. Related trades such as enamellers, printers, modellers, lusterers, ornamenters, gilders, and dealers are not generally included, although a few have been retained for completeness. Where such traders are listed, the entries will certainly not be comprehensive. The scope has been extended to all potters likely to be of interest to collectors and this includes the makers of decorative tiles, and even sanitary wares. Coarse ware potters – the makers of bricks, chimney pipes and coarse floor tiles – are not included, but once again a few will inevitably have survived. Note that the term terracotta could refer to either the coarse building material or relatively fine decorative wares.

THE DIRECTORIES

A book of this nature is not the place for detailed consideration of the evolution of directories or of their compilers and publishers. Any researcher interested in the history and development of directories can do no better than refer to the introductory sections in the three excellent bibliographies by Charles Goss, Jane Norton, and Gareth Shaw and Alison Tipper (see the bibliography for full details). These three books between them provide a comprehensive list of directories published before 1950, and they have proved invaluable in the compilation of this study.

Directories made their first appearance in England towards the end of the seventeenth century, but the serious development of provincial directories dates from about 1760. Thereafter, they proliferated, and by the second half of the nineteenth century virtually all major towns were covered. They can usefully be divided into three main types, the national directories which attempted to cover the whole country, county directories covering one or more of the English counties, and local directories covering a single city, town, or a particular area.

The Staffordshire Potteries made their first appearance in the great national directories which appeared at the end of the eighteenth century. The first was published by William Bailey in 1781, and subsequent publishers included Peter Barfoot and John Wilkes (from 1790), William Holden and Thomas Underhill (from 1805), and James Pigot and Isaac Slater (from 1814). As far as county directories are concerned, the only publishers to cover Staffordshire were William White (in 1834 and 1851), the famous Kelly firm (from 1845), and Harrison, Harrod & Co. (in 1861 and 1870). Local directories of such a specialised industrial area were inevitable and the first was produced by Chester & Mort as early as *c.*1796. Thereafter they appeared at irregular intervals throughout the period covered by this work. A detailed list of compilers and publishers can be found in Chapter 3.

It is perhaps surprising that specialised trade directories listing potters have not been mentioned. In general terms, such specialised directories did not appear much before the middle of the nineteenth century, but despite Shaw and Tipper's comment that they were being produced in reasonably large numbers after 1870, this does not appear to be the case for the pottery trades. The only specialist trade directory known to the author is *The Staffordshire Potters' Directory* for 1868, published by Unwin Brothers of London, and it appears that no other such publication appeared until the *Pottery Gazette's* reference book and directory, published annually from 1882. They have not been included here but would make a suitable companion to this volume.

The directories covered in this study are listed in full in Appendix I. In order to avoid needless repetition, they are referred to by an abbreviated title consisting of the date of publication (approximate if not dated) followed by the name of the first named compiler or publisher as credited on the title page (where two or more individuals are concerned, only the first name is used in the abbreviation). The directories vary considerably in their content, some listing all firms together in alphabetical order, while some are classified by trades, and others contain both types of list. In this study, the information has been extracted from classified lists where they exist. With one exception (1850 Kelly) it seems that the alphabetical lists add very little extra information, although serious researchers may be advised to check them. In the case of 1850 Kelly only, close examination shows that the classified list is rather restricted, omitting particularly the manufacturers of figures, ornaments and toys, so the alphabetical list has also been included here.

The directory listings are riddled with inconsistencies and there has been a great temptation to 'correct' apparent errors. However, this might have led to the loss of some small, apparently unimportant pieces of information, and this conflict has been resolved by reprinting the original listings in full in Appendix I, exactly as they appear, warts and all. Any interpretation of the listings has been restricted to the alphabetical list of manufacturers in Chapter 5, and even in that section it has been kept to an absolute minimum. This is predominantly a reference book for the serious collector, prepared to form his or her own judgment of this fascinating documentary material.

THE USE OF THIS VOLUME

The two main sections are the original directory listings, reprinted in Appendix I, and the alphabetical list of manufacturers assembled in Chapter 5. The latter will probably be the more useful starting point for collectors wishing to trace a manufacturer, and for researchers trying to trace the history of any particular firm. Some additional help is included in the form of an index of partnership surnames in Appendix II, listing all surnames with the names of partnerships in which they were involved. This should be of use in tracing the evolution of the smaller firms whose partners were continually changing.

In referencing the lists, remember that the directory compilers were fallible, mistakes were made in both names and addresses, and it is inevitable that some firms were omitted. It is also possible that the existence of some firms at the date the directory was published may be questionable. The compilers would have been working some months ahead of the publication date, and in some cases they may have updated previous lists without a completely new survey. If the date is of particular importance, Appendix I includes additional information for each directory, including dates from introductions, dedications, and prefaces. Where a month is listed, this may help in a more accurate assessment of the date of compilation. A few of the directories were not dated, and discussion of the dates adopted in this volume can also be found in Appendix I.

In most cases the classified lists and descriptions differentiate between china and earthenware, but this distinction can never be entirely reliable. A single reference to china, for example, in a list of other entries which all refer only to earthenware, should be treated with caution. This is particularly true in the case of figures, ornaments and toys, where the range of classifications is numerous and their titles are clearly imprecise. Some compilers, notably Frank Porter in 1887, seem to have used the words china and earthenware indiscriminately.

It is clear that the list of manufacturers is still not complete. As an example, two firms known to have marked their wares are Tams, Anderson & Tams and Jones & Son, both believed to have been working in the 1820s. Neither is listed here but they may have been short-lived, probably coinciding with a period when no directories were published, between 1822 and 1828. There are other gaps (see, for example, various marks shown on pages 44-46), notably in the late 1830s and the 1840s, but provided the information in this volume is used with due caution and along with other sources, it should provide much help in tracing the potters of Staffordshire.

CHAPTER 2

THE STAFFORDSHIRE POTTERIES

The area which has become known as the Staffordshire Potteries lies in the north of the county, to the east of Newcastle-under-Lyme. The various pottery towns and villages are now grouped together into the modern city of Stoke-on-Trent, which incorporates the six main towns of Tunstall, Burslem, Hanley, Stoke, Fenton and Longton.

The development as a contiguous area was recognisable from relatively early times. One writer said it 'may be looked upon as one continued town, the whole of which is surprisingly populous' (1798 Universal), while another noted how the area 'a considerable part of which by joining together, strikes the traveller as but one town', and continued with an opinion that 'in all probability, the various towns and villages will ere long be so intermixed with buildings as to form only one town and one name, they are already ranked under the general name of The Pottery' (1800 Allbutt).

The amalgamation of the towns was first formalised in 1832, when the Borough of Stoke-upon-Trent was enfranchised in the Reform Bill, and was virtually complete by the 1880s. Porter's directory of 1887, for example, states 'The name of The Staffordshire Potteries is given to an important district of the northern part of the shire. It includes four corporate towns, and two other townships of advanced growth' and goes on to list the six towns. In the eighteenth century these towns, and the many surrounding villages which they have now absorbed, were separate entities, and interpretation of the directories requires both some knowledge of the early place-names and an understanding of the growth and development of the towns, and also of the villages which have now become their suburbs.

Industrial concentration is, of course, quite common – 'men engaged in the same trade were ever gregarious, and from early days there has been a tendency to centralisation' (Goss, page 5) – but the degree to which it has arisen in the pottery industry is particularly marked. In 1948, for example, some 85% of pottery workers in the country were in the midlands, and almost the entire industry was located in the city of Stoke-on-Trent. The dependence of the area on the pottery industry was almost complete by the end of the eighteenth century – 'the staple, and almost only manufacture from one end to the other, is earthen-ware' (1798 Universal), and 'the manufacturing of earthen-wares is the general and nearly sole business' (1800 Allbutt).

The reason for the rise of the pottery industry in this particular area need not concern us in any detail here, but it is admirably covered by two quotes from the directories. In 1818 Parson – 'it has often been asked, Why the potters fixed themselves here, or the Potteries of this county continued to flourish more than those of any other part of the kingdom, or perhaps of the whole world? The answer to the question appears tolerably obvious – The abundant and almost inexhaustible supply of clay and coal upon the spot, the inland situation of this district, which contributed to render labour cheap, and some other circumstances that will be noticed hereafter, combined to fix and establish this important branch of commerce where it had been so successfully commenced. The coals here range from north to south the whole range of the Potteries.' And in 1834 White – 'the natural advantages, which have contributed to render this district the permanent and most extensive seat of the earthenware manufacture, are the abundance and variety of those essential mineral substances coal and clay. Here also the potters enjoy four of the chief natural benefits which can be connected with human existence, – air extremely salubrious; water of tolerable purity; the sun seldom obscured by fogs; and an entire freedom from damp: and owing to the hilly surface of the ground, the immense volumes of smoke which are generated here, are quickly dispersed; so that with these advantages, the Potteries may be considered as one of the pleasantest, as well as one of the busiest scenes of industry in this kingdom.'

Other early descriptions of the area clearly demonstrate the rate of growth. At the end of the eighteenth century manufacture was described as 'daily rising in estimation' and 'the increase of trade from the exertions of the manufacturers has been rapid' (1796 Chester). Just half a century later it was described as an 'opulent and interesting district' and 'the most eligible seat for the ingenious and useful manufactures that have so long made it conspicuous, and raised it to an enviable commercial eminence' (1850 Slater).

Statistics concerning the rapid growth are not hard to find. In 1834 William White referred to an increase in population, 'during the last thirty years, from 27,000 to about 60,000 souls'. His second directory of 1851 gives an updated estimate – 'during the last fifty years, from 27,659 to upwards of 80,000 souls'. His initial figure is supported elsewhere – 'the number of persons employed in the potting trade, is estimated at from 25 to 30,000' (1818 Pigot). White's increase to 80,000 was by no means the end, just twenty years later we are told that 'Stoke-upon-Trent is a parliamentary borough with a population of above 101,200' (1870 Harrod).

But the growth of the industry had its bad sides which are reflected throughout the period. As early as 1796, for example, 'as with most other places, where the increase of trade has been rapid, much remains to be done. Hitherto the attention of the public has been here chiefly engaged with the improvements of the manufacture, the great source of wealth, while regularity of building, excellent roads to accommodate the traveller, with several other things that could be mentioned, have not yet been so fully attended to as might be wished' (1796 Chester). And just four years later, 'The Pottery may with propriety be styled "The Seat of Industry." Whilst the strong and active are engaged in the more laborious and difficult branches of manufacture, children of five or six years, and decrepit old age, tottering on the brink of another world, find employ suitable to their strength and abilities' (1800 Allbutt). While this was then clearly seen as beneficial, similar conditions would not be tolerated today.

Disease was an integral part of life, and in 1850 a description of Longton rather offhandedly refers to the fact that 'rheumatism abounds, as also scrofula and the Derbyshire neck' (1850 Kelly). The horrors of pollution are graphically described in White's historical description in his 1834 directory, referring to salt glazing in the second quarter of the eighteenth century – 'there were twenty pottery ovens in Burslem, all of which cast in their salt glazing at the same time, generally on the Saturday morning, from nine to twelve o'clock. This occasioned such immense volumes of smoke, as literally to envelope the whole neighbourhood for several hours, so that persons not unfrequently mistook their way, or ran against each other, during the continuance of this process'. Pollution was not reduced with the decline of salt glazing, and the simple statistic that ten tons of coal were used for every one ton of clay reflects the huge volumes of smoke which continued to be created until the coal was replaced during the present century by gas and electricity for firing the kilns. The extent of smoke pollution can still graphically be seen in photographs dating from the early twentieth century.

The geographical extent of the area is described clearly in several of the directories – 'at this place [Golden-Hill] the Pottery commences, and continues to Lane-End, to the termination of which it is nearly eight miles, and may be looked upon as one continued town' (1798 Universal); 'about a mile from the borders of Cheshire, the Staffordshire Potteries commence, at a small village called Green-lane, from whence to the other extremity of the Pottery at Lane-end is about ten miles' (1800 Allbutt); and 'this opulent and interesting district extends about ten miles in length and one mile and a half in breadth' (1850 Slater).

For today's collector, a knowledge of the area need not be extensive, and it is hoped that the map shown on page 10 will be sufficient to locate most of the places named in the directories. This has been assembled from many sources, too numerous to mention individually, but two particularly useful documents have been 'A Map of the County of Stafford' by William Yates published in 1775, and the 'Map of the Potteries' in Allbutt's directory of 1802. The towns and villages changed markedly as the area developed, notably the mergers of Longton and Lane End, and Hanley and Shelton, and the absorption of many of the smaller villages into the spreading towns. There are many variations in the place-names, e.g. Lane Delph and Lane Delf, Goldenhill and Golden Hill. There are also many spelling conflicts of little consequence, a typical example being Normacott and Normacot. As a general rule modern spellings have been preferred here, but no rigid rules have been considered necessary.

The following list of towns and villages covers most of the place names encountered in the directories. They are listed roughly in geographical order, running from north to south. The descriptions have been extracted almost entirely from the directories themselves, supplemented with a few quotes from Simeon Shaw's *History of the Staffordshire Potteries* (1829). Some of the quotes have been abridged, but great care has been exercised to avoid any loss of meaning

RED STREET

Although not always considered part of the Staffordshire Potteries, Red Street is covered by several of the earlier directories. Situated to the north, about two miles west of Tunstall, it was never an important centre – 'some earthen-ware is also manufactured at Red-street, but not in so extensive a degree as in most of the other places' (1800 Allbutt). It was, however, described as a populous village with 'several manufactories of earthenware. A considerable quantity of tiles are also made in the neighbourhood' (1818 Parson). It was also thought to be 'one of the oldest seats of the earthenware manufactory, and, perhaps derived its name from the red pottery anciently made here' (1834 White).

GOLDEN HILL AND GREEN LANE

Golden Hill was generally considered to be the northern extremity of the Potteries – 'and so to Golden-hill, which terminates the Pottery this way' (1796 Chester), and 'Golden Hill is a village at the northern extremity of the Potteries, where there are two small earthenware manufactories' (1834 White). The attractiveness of the name was often derided as inappropriate, being derived from the value of the coal deposits rather than the beauty of the place – 'one would suppose this from its name, to be a considerable and even splendid place; but it is the least so of any in the pottery: however, its valuable mines of coal, make ample amends for its other deficiencies; and from those mines the name was given to it. Its manufacture consists chiefly of coarse black, chequer'd, and portobello wares' (1800 Allbutt). The importance of the coal mines is stressed repeatedly. Golden Hill 'is chiefly remarkable for its valuable mines of coal, and the best general view of the Potteries, with the surrounding country' (1818 Parson), and 'one mile east of Tunstall, is the village and township of Golden Hill. Mines of coal and iron stone are worked in this neighbourhood extensively' (1841 Pigot).

Green Lane was just a small village 'composed of only a few cottages, and a small manufactory of black ware' (1800 Allbutt). Shaw considered it to be the northern extremity of Golden Hill 'having its name from its fertile and pleasing appearance'.

SANDYFORD, NEWFIELD, AND SMITHFIELD OR GREENFIELD

A group of small villages between Golden Hill and Tunstall, the most northerly of which was Sandyford. None were very large, Sandyford and Greenfield, for example, were described simply as 'two hamlets about half a mile N. of Tunstall' (1834 White). As with Golden Hill, these northern villages were also noted for the presence of coal. Newfield 'is well situated for manufacturing purposes, having abundance of coal' (1818 Parson), and Smithfield 'possesses many strata of good coal and coarse clay' (also 1818 Parson) and was considered 'an excellent situation for the manufacturing of earthen-wares, having several valuable strata of coal in it, as well as coarse-clay, which the potters use much of' (1798 Universal).

Smithfield was later renamed Greenfield for a reason described by Shaw writing in 1829 – 'the present name has been substituted for that which kept in remembrance the unhappy founder, Theophilus Smith; who, in a fit of jealousy attempted the life of his kind friend, Mr. Wainwright, and subsequently in goal *(sic)* perished by his own hand'.

TUNSTALL

Tunstall is the first of the six towns comprising the modern-day city of Stoke-on-Trent. It was originally an attractive little place, described as 'a pleasant village' (1798 Universal), and 'the pleasantest village in the pottery' (1800 Allbutt). Its growth into a pottery town was soon noticeable – 'there are several considerable manufactories at Tunstall, particularly of a superior kind of blue tile, the clay found here being favourable to the purpose' (1818 Parson), and 'Tunstall is a considerable village. In this township abounds coal, iron stone, marl and fine cannel coal; and the manufactories of earthenware are very extensive here' (1828 Pigot).

As the more northerly villages declined in importance Tunstall became 'the most northerly town in the Staffordshire Potteries, arisen during the present century, from the rank of a small village to that of a respectable town' (1834 White), and by

1887 it was still 'a growing township which has recently been described [as] "plucky little Tunstall". In the popular mind Tunstall is the terminus of the Potteries' (1887 Porter). Its importance as a mining and manufacturing town was continually noted – 'earthenware is manufactured here to a great extent. There are also iron works. A large quantity of coal and ironstone is raised in the neighbourhood for the use of the various manufactures carried on here' (1861 Harrison).

BROWNHILLS

Just to the south, between Tunstall and Burslem, was Brownhills, 'a pleasant village on the Liverpool and Manchester road through the Potteries. There is a manufactory of considerable magnitude, noted for its excellent blue tiles, quarries and conduit pipes, &c. which are quite vitrified, and of a beautiful dark colour. The many various strata of clay got here, which are of excellent quality, and in great abundance, seem particularly adapted for making these articles' (1828 Pigot). Brownhills was steadily absorbed into Burslem, soon being listed as just one of 'the villages in the parish [which] may be considered as populous suburbs of the town' (1834 White), and as 'a pleasant hamlet, in the township of Burslem' (1835 Pigot). The area was particularly important as a source of one type of clay – 'it is chiefly to be noticed for the various strata of clay, of excellent quality, obtained here in great abundance, and principally employed in the manufacture of tiles' (1835 Pigot). This tile production was mentioned repeatedly.

LONGPORT AND NEWPORT

The village of Longport, in the valley about a mile west of Burslem, owed both its name and its status to the Trent and Mersey Canal, opened in 1777. The canal followed a course to the west of most of the pottery towns, and the wharves at Longport, Etruria and Stoke were of considerable importance. The name arose soon after the canal was built – 'this place was formerly called Long-bridge, from a kind of bridge which ran about a hundred yards parallel with the water, on the removal of which the inhabitants about twenty years ago, changed its name to that of Long-port' (1800 Allbutt). The presence of the canal is repeatedly stressed – 'the canal runs through it, and several large manufactories stand on its banks' (1796 Chester), and 'the canal passes this place, on which is a public wharf belonging to the Staffordshire Canal Company' (1798 Universal).

By 1834 Longport was effectively absorbed by Burslem, being just one of 'the villages in the parish [which] may be considered as populous suburbs of the town' (1834 White). Unlike some of the other suburbs, it never entirely lost its identity, and retained its importance when the railway was laid alongside the canal – 'Longport is a manufacturing district, within the parish and township of Burslem, situated in a valley, on the banks of the Trent and Mersey canal, where are several wharfs. The North Staffordshire Railway Company have a station here, which is also the nearest for Burslem and Tunstall' (1850 Slater).

Newport was a much smaller village to the south. Its size was put in context in 1800, being described as 'the residence of Mr Walter Daniel, whose elegant seat and manufactory, compose the whole of this place. It is situated on the canal between Long-port and Etruria' (1800 Allbutt). It was mentioned only as part of Longport in 1850 Slater.

BURSLEM

Burslem, the second of the six towns comprising the modern-day city Stoke-on-Trent, is frequently described as the 'Mother of The Potteries' (1887 Porter and elsewhere). At the end of the eighteenth century it was already a thriving pottery town, described as 'the old seat of the Pottery' (1796 Chester), and rather quaintly as 'a market town, having a neat market-house with a clock on the top' (1798 Universal). Its antiquity as a pottery centre is repeatedly stated – 'the ancient seat of the Pottery, where doubtless, earthenwares of one kind or other, have been made many centuries. Its manufactories are numerous and extensive' (1800 Allbutt), and 'this extensive and populous town claims the honour of being the Mother of the Staffordshire Potteries. Burslem is undoubtedly the ancient seat of the Pottery, where earthenwares have been made many centuries' (1818 Parson).

The polluting effects of salt glazing in Burslem have already been quoted, but it had other, more constructive claims to fame – 'Burslem is remarkable as being the place where the first clod of that great national undertaking, the Trent and Mersey Canal, was cut by the late Josiah Wedgwood, Esq.' (1818 Parson). It was generally considered an attractive town, with frequent references to its layout being 'admirably arranged', with 'streets wide and regular'.

Burslem's growth and development was considerable. 'Until the year 1807, it was a member of the parish of Stoke-upon-Trent' (1834 White), but by 1834 it was noted that many of 'the villages in the parish may be considered as populous suburbs of the town' (also 1834 White). These included Brownhills, Cobridge, Dale Hall, Longport, Sneyd and Hot Lane. The dominance of the pottery industry is frequently noted. Of the population given as 8,625 in 1811, 'it was computed that about nine-tenths were employed in, or connected with, the pottery business' (1818 Parson). A particularly complete list of the industries in the town reads – 'the long existing manufacture of china and earthenware is the great trade of the parish, in its several varieties of porcelain, china figures, blackware, lustre, ironstone, Parian brooches and shirt studs. Crates are made. There are flint mills and colour works; likewise steam boiler works, brick-yards, tileries, fire brick kilns, ropery, curriery, foundry, cooperage, corn mill, sago factory, &c. Coal and ironstone are also raised in considerable quantities' (1850 Kelly).

COBRIDGE

Cobridge lies between Burslem and Hanley, and was described variously as 'a neat village' (1796 Chester), 'a populous village, containing several respectable manufacturies' (1800 Allbutt), and 'a large village, a prosperous and increasing place' (1818 Parson). The status of Cobridge seems to have been continually changing – 'part in Stoke, and part in Burslem parish' (1800 Allbutt), 'partly in the township of Shelton, but mostly in the parish of Burslem' (1834 White), and 'about one mile from Shelton' (1850 Slater). Although it never lost its identity, Cobridge rapidly became simply one of 'the villages in the parish [of Burslem which] may be considered as populous suburbs of the town' (1834 White). As late as 1850 it was still important enough to justify a note as containing 'several porcelain and earthenware manufactories, and its vicinity abounds with coal and ironstone' (1850 Slater).

HANLEY AND SHELTON

Hanley is the third of the six towns comprising the modern-day city of Stoke-on-Trent, and was always one of the more prominent of the pottery towns. It grew from simply 'a market town' (1798 Universal) to 'a large modern town' (1818 Parson), and ultimately, together with Shelton, to a 'densely populated and well built market town, the largest in the district called the Potteries' (1834 White). Even as early as 1800 it had been 'in point of size the next to Burslem' (1800 Allbutt).

Early descriptions of Hanley emphasize its position and prestige – 'Hanley is nearly the centre of the pottery, with a number of very respectable manufacturers' (1796 Chester), and 'no part of the Pottery can boast of more respectable manufacturies than this place and its vicinity. It is nearly the centre of the Pottery' (1800 Allbutt). The sheer volume of the town's trade was often commented on – 'the exportation of earthenware to Liverpool, Hull, the metropolis, &c. is of such an extent that a company is established for the sole purpose of carrying that article' on the Grand Trunk Canal (1841 Pigot). One particularly complete description of the local industries points out that 'the town owes its prosperity to the manufacture of china and earthenware, and extensive mines of coal and ironstone, which abound in the neighbourhood. Among the trades are porcelain, earthenware, china toys and figures, Parian figures, works for colours, enamelling, potters tissue, crates, hair pencils, &c. There are iron foundries, copperas and chemical works, Britannia metal works, organ loft, barge yard, &c.' (1850 Kelly).

Shelton was somewhat smaller, albeit 'a village of considerable extent' (1796 Chester), but no less prestigious with frequent reference to 'several very respectable manufactories' (1796 Chester), and 'some of the oldest and most respectable manufacturers' (1818 Parson). The village had one particular claim to fame – 'We must not forget to mention, that here an excellent porcelain is made, under the firm of Hollins, Warburton, & Co. – it is carried on under a patent obtained by Mr. Champion, of Bristol, in the discovery of which he spent a large fortune, and sold the exclusive right to the above gentlemen. Some other manufacturers in the country have brought this article to great perfection; and there is little doubt it will be rendered here in large quantities, so as to rival the finest productions of the East' (1796 Chester).

Shelton was so close to Hanley that its existence as a separate town was always under threat – 'now generally included with Hanley' (1818 Parson), and 'Hanley and Shelton, though two distinct liberties or townships, now form one densely populated and well built market town' (1834 White). Although officially united with Hanley by Act of Parliament in 1812, Shelton's separate identity was maintained for many years. It was not until 1851 that 'at a public meeting held here in February, 1851, it was resolved that in future the whole town should be called Hanley' (1851 White). However, despite many subsequent statements such as 'Hanley and Shelton now form a united market town, the central and most populous of the Pottery towns' (1861 Harrison), the name Shelton did (and does) still survive.

By 1870 Hanley itself had become 'a municipal borough' (1870 Harrod), and its status within the Potteries continued unabated – 'the largest town of the group is Hanley [which] has not inaptly been styled the Metropolis of the Potteries. [It] receives its significant title from the vast amount of business enacted within its area' (1887 Porter). Today Hanley has developed into the commercial centre of the city of Stoke-on-Trent.

ETRURIA AND VALE PLEASANT

Etruria was originally developed as the site of an extensive new pottery by Josiah Wedgwood, opened in 1769. Its name 'was given to it by Mr. Wedgwood, in memory of an ancient state in Italy, once celebrated for the exquisite taste of its Pottery; the remaining specimens of which have served greatly to improve the beauty of the modern articles' (1800 Allbutt). The village was in a crucial position adjacent to both road and canal – 'the village is one neat, regular street, in the turnpike-road leading from Newcastle to Cobridge [and] in a beautiful valley by the side of the Grand Trunk canal' (1796 Chester). The canal project was important to Wedgwood and his factory was itself much admired – 'his very large manufactory is built with great taste, and admirably disposed for the business for which it is designed' (also 1796 Chester).

Quite apart from its association with the notable Wedgwood works, Etruria was 'a considerable village, chiefly inhabited by potters' (1818 Parson), and the wharves on the canal also served the other pottery towns, sited further to the east. The canal had been opened in 1777, and it was at Etruria that there was a junction with the Caldon (or Cauldon) Canal, opened early in 1779, which served as a branch running past Shelton and Hanley to Froghall.

Just below Etruria 'at the lower end of Shelton' lay Vale Pleasant. 'Here is a public and extensive wharf, the centre one of the Pottery. The beauty of this place, together with its vicinity, give rise to the above appellation' (1800 Allbutt). Etruria and Vale Pleasant were both effectively absorbed by Shelton – 'in this township are the potteries and the beautiful villa of Etruria; the works form a considerable hamlet' (1850 Slater). Shelton in turn was merged into Hanley as described above.

STOKE-UPON-TRENT

Stoke is the fourth of the six towns comprising the modern-day city of Stoke-on-Trent. Stoke-upon-Trent itself was originally just 'a pleasant, rural village' although 'the manufactories here are in general large, and some very handsomely built' (1796 Chester). It was 'intended for a market town, as there is a new market-house building' (1798 Universal), and by 1800 was the parish town of the Potteries. 'It is a pleasant rural place, and contains some handsome buildings. It has many earthenware manufacturies, some of which are upon an extensive scale; and from its contiguity to a wharf upon the canal, (which runs through the town) is conveniently situated for trade' (1800 Allbutt). Stoke was one of only three towns actually located on the Trent and Mersey, or Grand Trunk Canal, but it also had other claims to fame – 'the first steam-engine for grinding burned flint for the use of the potters, was established at Stoke' (1818 Parson). By this time it had 'recently been constituted a market town' (1818 Pigot).

Although in size by no means the largest of the pottery towns, by 1850 Stoke was 'considered the central town of the Potteries' (1850 Kelly). The same description referred to its importance in the production of tiles and the presence of particularly prestigious manufacturers – 'the employment carried on in this extensive parish, as its usual name, 'the Potteries,' implies, is chiefly the manufacture of china, earthenware, and ornamental and encaustic tiles, of which this is the principal seat in England, and though the number of china or other manufactories is not great, they are amongst the most important in the district' (1850 Kelly). Communications were enhanced with the arrival of the railway – 'it has visibly increased in consequence, from being a main station on a great railway line – the

North Staffordshire. The first sod of this line was cut 23rd of September, 1846, and it was opened for traffic 17th April 1848' (1850 Slater).

The town first achieved prominence as the centre of the Borough of Stoke-upon-Trent, which was enfranchised in the Reform Bill of 1832. Today the name is retained for the modern city of Stoke-on-Trent, although Stoke itself is but one of its six towns and the commercial centre is at Hanley.

LOWER LANE, FENTON, LANE DELPH AND FOLEY

Today Fenton is the fifth of the six towns comprising the city of Stoke-on-Trent, but the road between Stoke and Lane End was originally comprised of several distinct villages – 'Lower-lane, Lane-delf & Lane End conclude the Pottery beyond Stoke. As you pass from Stoke to Lower-lane, on the right hand, at Lower-lane, is Fenton. About half a mile from hence, you arrive at Lane-delph, a small but populous village. The above places contain a number of respectable manufacturies' (1800 Allbutt). In 1818 they were of relatively little consequence – 'Fenton and Lower Lane and Lane Delph present nothing remarkable, and indeed they may be properly incorporated with Lane-End, of which place they form a kind of suburbs' (1818 Parson).

The name Fenton itself covered several smaller hamlets, and variations encountered include Fenton Low, Great Fenton, Little Fenton, Fenton Culvert and Fenton Vivian. Referring to the last two, William White wrote 'the two Fentons extend from Stoke to Lane-End, and include the populous and adjacent villages of Great and Little Fenton, and Lane-Delph', and 'Fenton and Lane Delph form one continued line of streets and buildings extending from Stoke to Lane-End, a distance of two miles, and are comprised in the liberties and manors of Fenton-Culvert and Fenton-Vivian' (1834 White). He also included an interesting geographical description, 'Great Fenton is 1½ miles S.E.; Little Fenton half a mile N.E.; and Foley 1½ mile E. of Stoke. In these villages are many large potteries'. Some confusion was often revealed between the various names, in 1850 for example, both 'Fenton Culvert, or Great Fenton' and 'Fenton Vivian, or Little Fenton' were described as 'townships in the borough of Stoke-upon-Trent' (1850 Kelly). However, other references were more concise – 'Fenton is situated between Stoke and Longton, and contains some considerable pottery works, and mines of coal and ironstone' (1850 Slater).

Lane Delph and Foley both lay between Fenton and Lane End. Neither were large, Lane Delph being 'a small but populous village' (1800 Allbutt), and 'the Foley has only a few Houses, and three Manufactories in it' (Shaw). Lane Delph was both the largest and the oldest – 'Lane Delph, the most populous part of the district, is one of the oldest seats of the earthenware manufacture' (1834 White). However, by 1850 even Lane Delph was virtually absorbed by Fenton – 'Lane Delph is within the Fenton townships' (1850 Kelly), and thereafter references are few, restricted to notes such as 'Fenton includes the hamlets of Lane Delph [and] Foley' (1861 Harrison).

LONGTON AND LANE END

Longton is the most southerly of the six towns comprising the modern-day city of Stoke-on-Trent. It was formed from two separate townships, called Lane End and Longton, of which the former was originally the most prominent – 'Lane End is one extremity of the Pottery, with many flourishing manufactories' (1796

Chester). Originally just 'a market town' (1798 Universal), it grew very rapidly at the start of the nineteenth century to become 'a modern and populous town, risen in a few years to a respectable degree of opulence. Large quantities of earthenware are manufactured in the extensive potteries' (1818 Parson).

It was not long before references to Longton started to appear – 'Lane End, a populous and thriving market-town, with Longton, forms an extensive township' (1828 Pigot), and 'Lane-End and Longton are two townships or liberties, forming one populous market town, at the south-east end of the Potteries' (1834 White). William White went on to remark that 'eight tenths of the town is in the former liberty [Longton]. This modern and populous town has risen to its present consequence during the last sixty years, from the rank of a humble village, remarkable for the irregularity and meanness of its buildings'.

The name Lane End rapidly faded from use – 'Longton, formerly called Lane End, is one of the pottery towns' (1850 Kelly), and more specifically – 'Longton and Lane-End, now commonly called Longton, though, until about ten years ago, the town was popularly called Lane-End' (1851 White). By 1870 the ascendancy of Longton was complete 'Longton is a municipal borough' (1870 Harrod). As with the other pottery towns, both china and earthenware were produced by many small manufacturers, although Longton was certainly noted particularly for china.

OTHER PLACENAMES

The above list of names is by no means comprehensive. There are other places on the periphery of the Potteries such as Barlaston (site of the new Wedgwood factory opened in 1940), and many other tiny villages or districts which were absorbed into the main towns. Examples include Dale Hall (between Longport and Burslem), The Sytch, The Hamil, Hadderidge, and Furlong (all suburbs of Burslem), Hot Lane and Bleak Hill (between Burslem and Cobridge), Sneyd Green and Milton (to the east of Burslem), Booden Brook, Keeling Lane, Northwood and Eastwood (all around Hanley), Stoke Lane (to the west of Stoke on the road to Newcastle), and Normacot, Meir, Furnace and Dresden (all on the south-eastern end of Longton).

CHAPTER 3

THE DIRECTORIES COMPILERS AND PUBLISHERS

The emergence and evolution of directories as a general class has already been discussed in Chapter One but an understanding of the subject matter of this work can be enhanced by more specific evaluation of the directories covering the Potteries. Even in this book, where the primary consideration is the content of the directories, some background notes suitable for the non-historian may be considered pertinent.

The area known as the Staffordshire Potteries was an important, albeit specialised, industrial centre and the commercial value of accurate and comprehensive directories quickly became apparent. Publishers were not slow to recognise the potential financial returns, and despite a high proportion of failures, there was considerable competition between them. Some sixteen distinct publishers issued directories covering the area within our period, and while six of them produced effectively only a single edition, two of them managed nine and Kelly's ran to fourteen. As such, introductory notes which may enable readers to put the directories and their compilers and publishers into historical perspective are given below. Unfortunately, while both Norton and Shaw & Tipper include much valuable introductory material, neither of them give histories covering other than the major, and predominantly earlier publishers. Their listings have, however, proved invaluable in the compilation of this section and they deserve great credit for their pioneering work.

In the short histories which follow, the compilers and publishers are listed in chronological order of their first directory to include either Staffordshire or the Potteries. Full details of any directory mentioned may be found in Appendix I, which also includes comments pertinent to any one individual directory forming part of a general series. The dates given below are those of directories included in this volume. Many of the publishers covered other areas either before or after the periods quoted.

WILLIAM BAILEY (1781-1784)

William Bailey was the first person to seriously attempt the production of a national directory. His first ventures were a *Northern Directory* published at Warrington in 1781, and a *Western and Midland Directory*, published at Birmingham in 1783. These were followed by his *British Directory* in four volumes, published at London during 1784. All three of these include sections on the Potteries, and while Bailey subsequently published other directories, covering Bristol (in 1787), Liverpool (also 1787) and London (as late as 1790), there was no further coverage of Staffordshire.

The three directories which cover the Potteries all feature alphabetical listings of traders and manufacturers, but appear to concentrate particularly on pottery manufacturers. In this respect the 1783 edition seems to be little more than a repeat of the information from 1781. The 1784 edition is particularly interesting, with individual descriptions for each potter, later pirated by William Tunnicliff (see below).

WILLIAM TUNNICLIFF (1787-1789)

William Tunnicliff described himself as a land surveyor and published at least three Topographical Surveys, of which the first, published at Nantwich in 1787 covers Staffordshire along with Cheshire and Lancashire. Much of the text is descriptive, concentrating on country seats, but a directory section is included, with a particularly comprehensive list of Staffordshire potters. The book was expanded with the addition of Somerset, Gloucestershire and Worcestershire for an edition published at Bath in 1789, but the original pages were simply reprinted. He went on to publish a survey of some southern counties in 1791 but did no further work on Staffordshire.

Tunnicliff's 1787 list of potters has often been quoted in ceramics literature but close examination shows that it is pirated verbatim from Bailey's *British Directory* of 1784 (see above) and is thus at least three years out of date. It is clear that his contribution to the history of the Potteries has been greatly overestimated.

CHESTER & MORT (*c.*1796)

Little is known about Chester and Mort, publishers of the first local directory of the Staffordshire Potteries in about 1796. They are listed as simply 'printers and stationers' at Hanley in their own directory and Norton states that John Mort was a bookseller at Newcastle-under-Lyme, but no other references to them have yet been located. It is possible that John Mort was a member of the family which later became publishers of the *Staffordshire Advertiser.*

The directory itself is undated, and although Norton lists it as 1810, apparently based on a pencilled note in a copy at the William Salt Library, it is clearly of much earlier origin. Careful examination of its content suggests a date of about 1796 or 1797, both of which have been quoted in ceramics literature. Evidence to support the 1796 date has now been found in the *Staffordshire Advertiser* dated 16th March 1796, which reported that Chester & Mort had bought the Hanley business of a Mr. Straphan, and that they hoped to publish the *Pottery Directory* within a few weeks. It is this early date which makes it of great interest to ceramics historians. It is not classified, but consists of an alphabetical listing of inhabitants, grouped under the main towns and villages.

PETER BARFOOT AND JOHN WILKES (*c.*1798)

Norton devotes three pages to the history of one of the most important early national directories. Peter Barfoot was a country gentleman who lived at Midlington Place near Southampton and John Wilkes was a printer at Winchester, later to become proprietor of the *Hampshire Chronicle.* They were granted a Royal Patent on 28 August 1789 to produce a national directory, and it appeared as *The Universal British Directory of Trade, Commerce, and Manufacture,* in five volumes, between 1790 and 1798. Whether Barfoot was much involved in the project beyond a financial contribution is open to doubt, but Wilkes was certainly the active partner, and his methods of compilation were often extremely dubious. Norton describes examples of piracy and several cases where information is the same as that found in local directories, which may or may not have been used by agreement with the other publisher.

The directory was produced in parts over a period of nine years, and earlier volumes were reprinted to make sets, usually with little or no correction. The information contained is not easy to date, since Volume 1 can be found dated 1790, 1791 and 1793, and the other volumes are all undated, but Norton gives some useful guidance. The section which covers the Potteries in Volume 4 cannot have been compiled earlier than 3 January 1795, since it contains a reference to 'the late Mr. Wedgwood'. One copy of this volume has been inspected with the date 'post-1797' inscribed in pencil on the title page, and Norton lists it as 1798.

The question of piracy does not appear to apply to the section covering the Potteries, titled 'Account of the Potteries, or Manufactories of Staffordshire-Ware, in the Neighbourhood of Newcastle'. The entries consist of alphabetical listings of 'principal inhabitants', predominantly traders, for each town and village.

THOMAS ALLBUT (1800-1822)

The Allbut family made their debut as directory publishers in 1800 with *A View of the Staffordshire Potteries* by T. Allbutt of Burslem (the slight variation in the spelling of the surname appears to be of little significance). This book consisted of a historical description of the Potteries, followed by a directory of gentlemen, tradesmen and shopkeepers, but not potters. Despite the presence of the directory section it is not listed by Norton. It was reprinted with a new title referring to it as a directory in 1802 by J. Allbut & Son, then of Hanley, with the important addition of a detailed map showing the location of all the potteries and listing their owners. This was followed in 1822 by another directory of Newcastle and the Potteries, this time published by T. Allbut.

Thomas Allbut was a printer, bookseller, stationer and druggist, and he seems also to have had some involvement with Parson & Bradshaw's directory of 1818 since he is listed as one of its sellers on the title page. His business was in the High Street at Hanley, and by 1828 Thomas Allbut junior was responsible for publishing the *Pottery Gazette*. Soon after this date the paper was merged with James Amphlett's *Pottery Mercury* to become the *Staffordshire Mercury and Pottery Gazette*. The Allbut's involvement with the newspaper was maintained until the early 1840s but they did not publish any further directories. The firm continued as booksellers and stationers at Market Place, Hanley, in a succession of partnerships including Allbut & Kennedy, Thomas Allbut & Son (the son's name was Edwin), Allbut, Son & Hobson, and Allbut & Daniel (who were in existence until at least 1892 and possibly longer).

The format of the 1822 directory differs from the earlier two volumes. It consists mainly of a lengthy alphabetical listing of 'nobility, gentry, merchants, and inhabitants in general', and is not classified. It does, however, include 'a list of china, earthenware, &c. manufacturers' at the back of the volume, and it is that list which has been used here.

WILLIAM HOLDEN AND THOMAS UNDERHILL (1805-1816)

William Holden began publishing a series of *Triennial Directories* in 1799, originally covering only London. His efforts were expanded in 1805 with a fourth edition which incorporated some eighty-four other towns, including a section covering the Potteries. This directory was reprinted, unchanged except for the title page, in

1808, but a new updated edition appeared in 1809. Thereafter the Potteries also appeared in an *Annual London and Country Directory* of 1811. These Holden directories all list traders in the Potteries in a single alphabetical list, but pottery manufacturers are notably dominant.

In 1814 Holden published a classified directory of the textile trades only (described as Class 5), intended to be the first of a series covering different trades. William Holden died shortly afterwards but his successor, Thomas Underhill, proceeded to issue three other volumes covering Merchants, Shippers and Bankers (Class 1), Agents, Brokers and Brewers (Class 2), and Metal Trades (Class 3), all issued during 1816. Holden's name was retained in the title of the first two of these. For some reason, potters appeared in the volume covering the metal trades, in a section titled 'Potteries and Newcastle, Staffordshire'. They are listed in a sub-section titled 'Staffordshire Potteries', which appears to comprise manufacturers only.

The death of Holden seems to have been a blow from which the business never recovered. Apart from the London directory, the last edition of which appeared in 1822, the three classes published in 1816 marked the end of the Holden-Underhill attempt to produce a series of national directories.

WILLIAM PARSON AND THOMAS BRADSHAW (1818)

William Parson was a bookseller and stationer in Manchester, and is believed to have worked originally for James Pigot, although the first directory with which he can be directly associated was one of Leeds published by Edward Baines in 1817. In the following year he collaborated with Thomas Bradshaw in publishing a *Staffordshire General & Commercial Directory* which was issued originally in four parts but also as a combined volume. Norton states that Parson and Bradshaw probably purchased rights to a directory of Lancashire, also in 1818, with the idea that these two directories could form the basis of a complete *Directory of the English Counties.* Certainly this title is known on reprints of the Lancashire directory, but no other parts have been found and the project was presumably abandoned.

The partnership between Parson and Bradshaw appears to have been shortlived. Parson was subsequently involved in compiling directories of Yorkshire and Lancashire for Baines, in 1822 and 1824 respectively. He went on to compile a directory of Hull in 1826, marking the start of an important association with William White which continued until c.1830-31 (see below). Thomas Bradshaw went on to compile directories of Belfast (1819) and Gloucestershire (1820).

Parson and Bradshaw's Staffordshire directory is not classified but consists of a lengthy alphabetical list of 'merchants, manufacturers, and inhabitants in general'. It does, however, include 'a list of the earthenware manufacturers, in the Potteries, &c.' which has been used in this work. The directory was sold, amongst others, by Thomas Allbut of Hanley, a printer, bookseller, stationer and druggist, who in 1822 went on to compile a similar directory of Newcastle and the Potteries.

JAMES PIGOT AND ISAAC SLATER (1818-1862)

James Pigot was arguably the greatest of the directory publishers in the first half of the nineteenth century. Based in Fountain Street, Manchester, the first directory published under his own name, covering Manchester and Salford, appeared in 1811 although he had previously been associated with similar directories published by R. & W. Dean. The two firms subsequently cooperated on Manchester directories until 1824. The first national directory with which Pigot appears to have been associated was titled *The Commercial Directory* for 1814–15, although his name does not appear in the imprint until the subsequent edition 'for 1816–17'. Neither of these includes the Potteries, which were first included in *The Commercial Directory* for 1818–19–20 which was published jointly by Pigot and the Deans. Thereafter Pigot's operation expanded rapidly, with the first London office opened in 1823.

Norton classifies the various directories into five major surveys of the United Kingdom carried out between 1820 and 1853, and there were at least two subsequent surveys beyond Norton's dateline of 1855. Pigot himself died in 1843 but the operation was carried on by his then partner, Isaac Slater, until absorbed by Kelly's in 1892, although the firm later concentrated only on the northern counties. The directory titles varied in the earlier years, but later became standardised as Pigot and Co.'s or Slater's (late Pigot & Co.) *Royal National and Commercial Directory and Topography* of the counties included.

A fascinating insight to the approach used by Pigot in the compilation of his directories can be seen in the following advertisement which appeared on the front page of the *Staffordshire Advertiser* issued on Saturday, 12 January 1828:

> *Pigot and Co.'s National Mercantile Directory, and Merchants', Bankers' and Traders' Guide, for all England, and North and South Wales, illustrated by Historical and Topographical Delineations, and Embellished with a variety of elegant new County and other Maps.*
>
> Messrs. Pigot and Co. most respectfully inform the Public, that they have commenced the compilation of an improved *Mercantile Directory and Commercial Guide*; being the second of a series of Three Volumes, each of which will be complete in itself. The present Volume will comprise upwards of 600 Cities, Towns, Seaports and Villages, in the Counties of Cheshire, Cumberland, Derbyshire, Durham, Lancashire, Leicestershire, Lincolnshire, Northumberland, Nottinghamshire, Rutlandshire, Shropshire, Staffordshire, Warwickshire, Westmoreland, Worcestershire, and Yorkshire, with a new Map of each County, together with all the Counties in North Wales, and a large Sheet Map of England and Wales. This Volume will comprehend the Names, Addresses, &c, of every class of Persons, whether Mercantile or Professional, in any way connected by their pursuits with the commerce of the country. Each will be arranged under a distinct Alphabetical Classification. The entire will be compiled from the personal applications of the Proprietors' Assistants, who are now taking a survey, and collecting the Names and other information throughout the above Counties; and will take the liberty to wait on the Residents in every Town individually, for the purpose of receiving the Name, pursuit, and Address, in a correct form for insertion; and at the same time most respectfully to solicit the honour of that patronage so essential towards this extensive undertaking; but no money will be received from any Subscriber till the Work is delivered.
>
> Full particulars will be seen in the Prospectus, that will be generally distributed in every Town; and the information that will be diffused throughout the Work cannot fail of being of importance to the Merchant, Manufacturer, Trader, and every man of business, as well as to the Gentleman, the curious Tourist, and general Traveller.
>
> Offices, 24, Basing-lane, Cheapside, London; and 16, Fountain-street, Manchester.

The directory referred to is *Pigot and Co.'s National Commercial Directory, for 1828–9* (abbreviated to 1828 Pigot in this volume).

The Potteries appeared as a separate section within the Staffordshire pages of the Pigot and Slater directories, and following their first appearance in 1818 as mentioned above, new lists appeared in 1822, 1828, *c.*1830, 1835, 1841, 1850 and 1862, and also in a local directory of somewhat different format of *c.*1852. The firm issued several different editions of each directory, usually with different combinations of counties, and these can often be extremely confusing. Apart from the dates listed above, Staffordshire has been recorded also in editions dated 1839, 1842 and 1844, but these are all simply reprints of the immediately preceding edition. Norton lists an appearance in 1829, stating that it is simply a reprint of the 1828 pages, but this is not the case, and for reasons explained in the Appendix – Original Directory Listings, this edition has been listed here as *c.*1830. Researchers are advised to treat separate copies of individual counties with some caution; several have been examined catalogued as having dates other than those listed above, 1832 and 1834 for example, but without exception they have been found to be wrongly catalogued printings separated from larger volumes.

All the Pigot and Slater directories are classified within the section for the Potteries, which from 1850 onwards also incorporates an alphabetical list. In the earlier editions the only two relevant categories are china manufacturers and earthenware manufacturers. The number of classifications increased as new editions were issued, but Pigot never got carried away in the same way as Kelly's, and in the last edition to cover Staffordshire in 1862, there were still only seven relevant categories.

WILLIAM WHITE (1834-1851)

William White became one of the great directory publishers of the mid-nineteenth century. His first involvement seems to have been as an assistant to William Parson in a directory of Yorkshire published by Edward Baines in 1822. Parson had previously worked with Thomas Bradshaw on a directory of Staffordshire (see above). This cooperation developed into a partnership, with two directories edited by Parson and published by William White & Co., apparently from Leeds, in 1826. These covered Kingston-upon-Hull and the surrounding district, and Lincolnshire, and were followed by three more jointly produced directories of Durham and Northumberland (1827), Cumberland and Westmorland (1829), and Leeds and York (1830).

By 1831 White had moved to to Sheffield which was to become the base of his considerable directory business. He continued to produce directories of the northern and midland towns including Hull (from 1831), Sheffield (from 1833), Leeds (from 1842), York (from 1867), Birmingham and the Hardware District (from 1869), Nottingham (1885), Grimsby (1895), and towns in Northamptonshire (1896). William White is, however, particularly noted for his series of *History, Gazetteer and Directory* of various counties, predominantly in the midlands and the north, which include Nottinghamshire (from 1832), Staffordshire (from 1834), Norfolk (from 1836), Yorkshire (from 1837), Lincolnshire (from 1842), Suffolk (from 1844), Leicestershire and Rutland (from 1846), Lancashire (1847), Essex (from 1848), Devon (from 1850), and Hampshire and the Isle of Wight (from 1859). Most of these counties were covered at least twice, and there were five editions each of Norfolk and Suffolk and six of Lincolnshire. William

White's operation was eventually absorbed by Kelly & Co. at the end of the nineteenth century, although they continued to retain his name for some years.

There were two editions of the *History, Gazetteer and Directory of Staffordshire,* dating from 1834 and 1851. They both include lengthy histories of the Potteries followed by directories consisting of classified lists of trades and professions for the main towns and villages. The relevant categories vary slightly, but are all combinations of china, earthenware, and toy or ornament manufacturers.

ISAAC COTTRILL (1836–1839)

Isaac Cottrill was appointed Police Officer for Newcastle-under-Lyme, probably early in 1835. He must have been an organised man, since he arranged for street names to be clearly painted and for houses to be numbered, and as part of his duties he assembled a comprehensive list of householders. This formed the basis of his first *Police Directory* published in 1836, followed by a second, updated edition, in 1839. These two directories are included here for completeness since they both contain alphabetical lists covering a small part of Stoke-upon-Trent which had been transferred to the Borough of Newcastle. The lists consist only of forty names in 1836 and fifty names in 1839, and while the latter include two potters, they were probably only workers rather than pottery owners.

KELLY & CO. (1845–1900 *et seq.*)

The famous directory publishing firm of Kelly's had its origins in 1835 or 1836 when Frederick Kelly, an inspector in the Post Office, purchased the rights to *The Post Office London Directory* from another official named B. Critchett. He continued to publish the directory, and in 1839 set the operation up as a business with his brother. The format of the original London directory was modified from 1840, and in 1845 the firm branched out with directories of the Home Counties and areas around Birmingham. These were rapidly followed by other counties, too numerous to list here, the last English county being added in 1871. The organisation went on not only to become by far the most important publisher of British directories, but also to absorb other large competitors such as Isaac Slater (successor to James Pigot) and William White. The imprint was originally W. Kelly & Co. of Old Boswell Court, Temple Bar, but the initial was dropped by 1852 and there were several London address changes after the mid-1860s. The firm became a limited company by 1891, and by 1897 the style was Kelly's Directories Ltd.

Staffordshire was one of the first counties to be covered, making its initial appearance along with Warwickshire in 1845, albeit extending only to the southern areas around Birmingham. Full coverage began in 1850 in a combined volume with Birmingham and Worcestershire, and from 1854 the format settled down to a combined volume covering Birmingham with the three counties of Staffordshire, Warwickshire and Worcestershire. This was issued every four years from 1860 onwards, although the 1864 edition actually appeared early, during 1863. It was treated as a continuous series by Kelly's, 1845 being considered the first edition and, at the end of our period here, 1900 being the fourteenth edition. One deviation from the pattern appeared with an edition dated 1878, but it was never numbered in Kelly's sequence and as far as Staffordshire is concerned it is purely a reprint of the 1876 pages.

From 1860 onwards, the Staffordshire section was also issued as a separate volume, and there were occasional excursions with other combinations such as

Staffordshire and Shropshire in 1896. The title was always the *Post Office Directory* until 1876. From 1880 it became *Kelly's Directory*. As far as the Potteries is concerned there was one addition to the series before it had really settled into a pattern, another directory of Birmingham being issued in 1856 including the Hardware and Pottery districts. A similar format was also issued later, although without the Potteries, so that only one edition from that series need be included here. Although the four-yearly volumes cover the whole of the county, the entries show that there were very few potters operating outside the actual area of the Potteries.

The Kelly's directories all include alphabetical lists for each main town or village within the county, but the main interest for this work lies in the assembled classified trades listings. For the earlier editions these cover all the counties included in the appropriate volume, but from 1860 the counties were entirely separate, no doubt to facilitate the separate printings mentioned above. The classifications appear to be comprehensive in including all the potters from the alphabetical sections, but the 1850 edition is somewhat deficient in this respect, so for that edition only this volume includes also extracts from the alphabetical lists. The most fascinating (and frustrating) aspect of the Kelly's series is the large number of classifications employed. This reached a height in the 1864 edition which incorporates no less than forty-seven different classifications covering potters, and that excludes the coarse wares such as bricks and tiles. While every effort has been made to locate all such classifications for inclusion in this work, it is quite possible that one or two might have squeezed through the net.

J. WILLIAMS (1846)

The Williams family produced a series of local directories in the 1840s covering towns or counties as widely spaced as Cornwall and Northumberland. The earliest appears to be that of Newcastle published in 1844 and the latest was Hertfordshire (oddly including some Kentish towns) in 1850. Others cover Bolton, Huddersfield, Leeds, Rochdale and Stockport (all in 1845), Chester, Leamington Spa and Warwick, and Liverpool (1846), Cornwall, and Devonport and Plymouth (1847), and the South Eastern Coast and the Isle of Thanet (both in 1849). The firm's final publication of this type appears to have been a manufacturer's trade directory issued in 1864.

The titles nearly all start either *Williams's Directory* or *Williams's Commercial Directory* and the publisher is given sometimes as J. Williams and sometimes as J. Williams senior. The place of publication varies considerably, often being the town in question or the nearest city, but exceptions are London (1845, 1849, 1850), Manchester (1846) and Liverpool (1847). Some sections are repeated in more than one directory.

Stafford and the Potteries were covered in a single directory published by J. Williams senior in May 1846, although the pages can also be found printed in the directory of Chester and surrounding districts which was issued in the same year. The directory consists purely of alphabetical listings of traders and important inhabitants for each of the main towns and their surrounding villages. A unique feature is the inclusion of many individuals with a note of the firms in which they were partners. For the pottery manufacturers, this information has also been incorporated within the present work.

HARRISON, HARROD & CO. AND J.G. HARROD (1861–1870)

This firm appears to have started publishing directories from London in 1859 when the style was simply Harrison & Harrod. Their first directory covered Bristol and two neighbouring counties in South Wales, and was followed in 1860 with a directory of Derbyshire. By 1861 the style had become Harrison, Harrod & Co. and the first of two Staffordshire directories appeared, followed in 1862 by a directory of Devon and Cornwall. Shortly thereafter the style changed to J.G. Harrod & Co. and a series of county directories was produced, generally titled *J. G. Harrod & Co.'s Postal and Commercial Directory* of the area in question. These covered mainly the southern and eastern counties but also included the midland counties of Derbyshire and Leicestershire. Staffordshire was the most northerly county they covered, and the second edition appeared in 1870. An office in Norwich is first mentioned in 1870, and subsequent directories were published from Norwich rather than London. Their last recorded directory was dated 1880.

The two Staffordshire directories are similar in layout, with a single non-classified trade list for each town or village. The first edition of 1861 included Dudley in Worcestershire, and was also issued bound together with Shropshire. It is possible that the second edition of 1870 was similarly used in a combined volume, this time with the addition of Derbyshire, Leicestershire and Rutland.

JONES & PROUD (1864)

The firm of Jones & Proud advertised themselves as steam printers in Fetter Lane, London, and issued a series of *Mercantile Directories* in the mid-1860s. They described them as being for 'home, foreign, and colonial circulation' and in their Address in the edition covering the Potteries, issued in 1864, they explained that 'the manufacturing and commercial interests of this country have taken rapid strides of recent years, and notwithstanding their present magnitude, improvements and new inventions almost daily appear. The step we have taken – the production of a series of Directories, at a cheap rate for unlimited circulation, has, by our special selection of all the important Manufacturing Districts, proved of immense benefit to the mercantile community, thus serving a want long deeply felt, – is of the highest importance.'

The firm's involvement with directories appears to have begun as printers of a directory of Leeds, published by Simpkin, Marshall & Co. in 1863, although the title appeared as *Jones's Mercantile Directory*. This was followed in the same year by three further directories which were similarly titled but published by Jones & Proud themselves. These covered the areas around Bradford, Halifax, and Hull, and the series subsequently continued with the Potteries (1864), the Black Country (also 1864), and Birmingham (1865).

The volume covering the Potteries is organised with commercial directories for each main town, followed by the combined classified trades listings which have been used in this work. The Address referred to plans for a new issue 'when the necessity shall arise' but no further edition seems to have appeared.

JOHN KEATES (1865-1892)

In the 1861 directory by Harrison, Harrod & Co. John Keates is listed as a printer and publisher of the *Staffordshire Sentinel,* at Cheapside, Hanley. The latter activity appears to have been short-lived since the proprietor of the newspaper is listed as Thomas Andrew Potter, still at Cheapside, in both 1862 Slater and 1864 Jones. In

1862 Slater, a partnership of Keates & Adams is listed as booksellers and stationers (and also printers), still at Cheapside.

The first Keates directory appeared in 1865 under the imprint of Keates & Ford, printers, stationers, and bookbinders at 38 & 40 Cheapside, Hanley. This was followed by a second edition in 1867. The third edition, in 1869 was by John Keates alone, and the imprint remained J. Keates until an 1879 edition which was by J. Keates & Co. with a new address at 10 Brunswick Street, still in Hanley. Thereafter the style became just Keates & Co. A total of nine directories appeared at somewhat irregular intervals, the last being issued in 1892. They all follow a similar format, with trade classifications grouped under the six main towns. Unlike Kelly's, Keates was sparing in his classifications, and the only ones relevant are potters and various types of tile manufacturers.

FRANK PORTER AND ROCKLIFF BROTHERS (1887)

Little is known of Frank Porter, compiler of the 1887 *Postal Directory for the Potteries with Newcastle & District*, but the publishers, Rockliff Brothers of Liverpool, were active directory publishers for a short period. They appear first with three directories of Welsh counties dating from 1886, and a directory covering the area around Crewe in 1887. Following the Potteries volume was a directory of Shropshire in 1888 and a local directory of Liverpool suburbs in 1889. They also published a directory of the cycle trades in 1896, after which their involvement seems to have been confined to printing. Most of their directories are titled *Postal Directory* of, or for, the area in question. Their style appears inconsistently as either just Rockliff Brothers or as Rockliff Brothers Ltd.

The introduction in Porter's 1887 Potteries and Newcastle directory reads 'probably no district of equal enterprise and commercial standing has fewer works of this kind devoted to its interest than that which is so widely known as the Staffordshire Potteries'. The layout is similar in concept to the Keates series, with trade classifications grouped under the six main towns. The only major relevant category is earthenware manufacturers, except in the section covering Stoke-upon-Trent where it is titled manufacturers of china and earthenware, but there are also a few minor categories.

CHAPTER 4

POTTERS' MARKS

There are five main ways in which a pot can be marked. Three of them involve marking in the clay, these being incised marks, impressed marks and moulded marks; the other two are marks applied on to the fired pot, and these are painted marks and printed marks.

- Incised marks are created by scratching into the body of the clay before it is fired. They are individually applied and thus were not widely used by the manufacturers who predominate in this volume, except for small workmen's marks.
- Impressed marks are applied to the unfired clay while it is still in its wet or plastic state and involve the use of a die or stamp prepared with the desired lettering or design. Although still applied by hand, this is a relatively quick operation and was widely used. By their very nature, impressed marks will refer to the pot itself and not its decoration, which would be applied later. There is a limit to the complexity of design which could be satisfactorily impressed, so they tend to be simpler in form than the widely used printed marks (see below).
- Moulded marks make use of a mould to form the mark in the wet clay, either as an integral part of any mould used to form the pot itself or as a separate sprig mould. The latter would be used to form a thin impression in wet clay which could then be applied to the pot itself by means of liquid clay or slip. They are most commonly found on the various forms of dry-bodied stonewares or other moulded wares.
- Painted marks, as their name implies, are painted on to the pot, usually at the decorating stage. As with incised marks they are individually created but they are not uncommon on high-quality decorated wares which were themselves hand-painted.
- Printed marks are applied after the pot has been biscuit fired, and sometimes later. They are inevitably common on wares with printed decoration, but the relative ease with which they could be applied made them ideal for automation. The detail which they were capable of reproducing made them by far the most common mark from the mid-nineteenth century onwards.

Makers' marks, however formed, are always of interest. In most cases the maker will be easily identifiable but this is not always the case. For example, a simple surname such as "Adams", "Stevenson" or "Wedgwood" could apply to any potter with that surname. Initial marks are not always unique, so for example "C. & E." could apply to Cork & Edge or Cartwright & Edwards. Some further consideration of other aspects of the mark might help lead to an acceptable attribution. It is for reasons such as this that the form or style of any mark may be of further help.

Marks are rare before the middle of the eighteenth century and were not used by many potters before 1800. Thereafter they become more common, particularly with the widespread adoption of printed decoration. It should, however, be remembered that a significant number of the lesser manufacturers would never have marked their wares because they were mass-producing wares of lower quality and had little marketing reason to promote their output with marks. On the other hand, the major manufacturers had significant reputations to maintain and the most prestigious among them such as Spode and Wedgwood would tend to mark extensively. It is known that Wedgwood was marking his wares by the late 1760s and he decided to mark virtually all products from about 1772.

The earliest form of mark used by Wedgwood, and soon by others, was a simple impressed name. For some reason which remains unclear, marks which contain lower case letters tend to be earlier than those which are entirely upper case. Thus "Wedgwood" is normally earlier than "WEDGWOOD", "Spode" is usually earlier than "SPODE", and "Davenport" is earlier than "DAVENPORT". Such lower case marks seem to date predominantly to the years before 1815. By this time, upper case marks tended to be the norm.

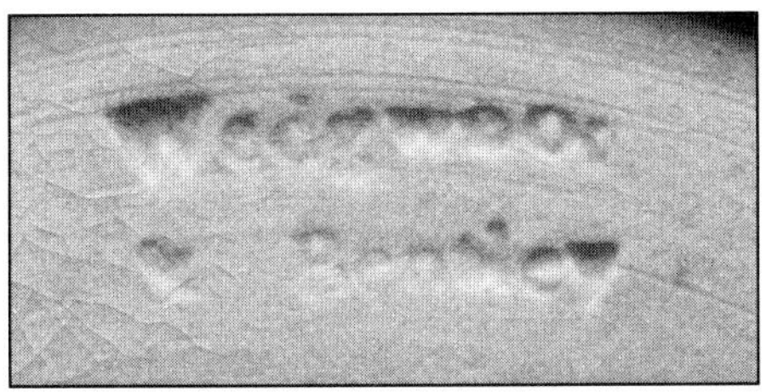

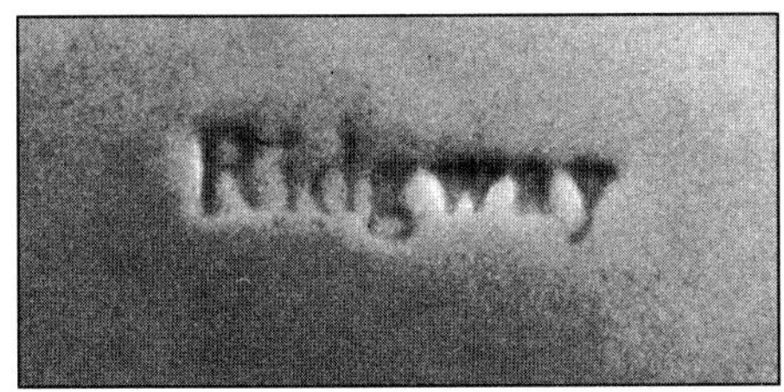

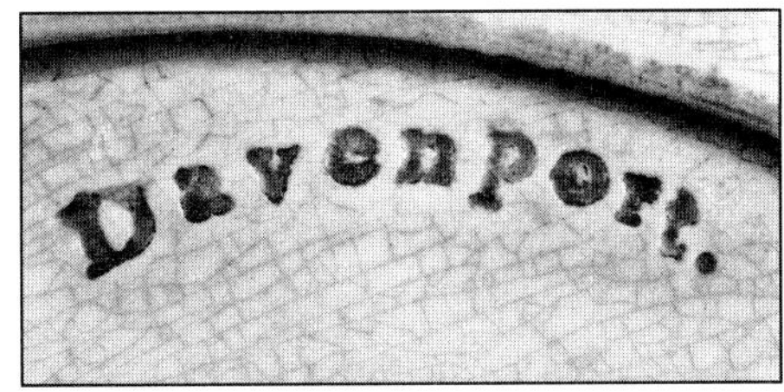

1. Four early impressed name marks utilising lower case letters, these examples from Wedgwood & Bentley, Spode, Ridgway and Davenport. The famous Wedgwood & Bentley partnership predates the directories.

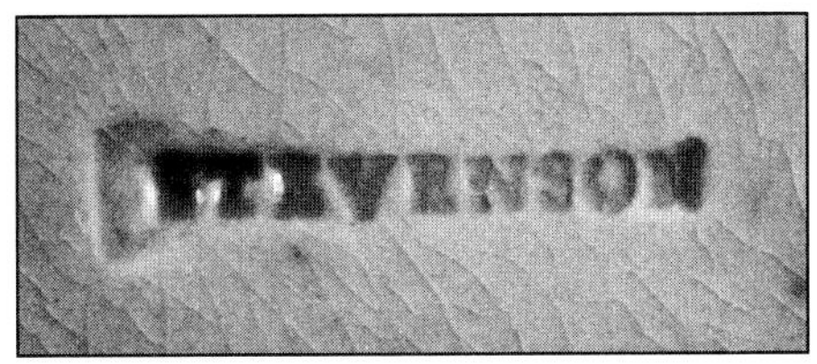

2. Four impressed name marks utilising only upper case letters, these examples from David Wilson, Samuel Hollins, John Rogers & Son, and one of the Stevenson firms.

3. Three impressed marks with additional detail in the form of a ship, a crown and an American eagle. The ship mark is traditionally attributed to Andrew Stevenson.

The use of a simple impressed name started to change around 1810, when some potters started to embellish the mark, either with additional wording or with some design feature such as a crown or an eagle. Thereafter, impressed marks did become more ornate, although the detail they could reproduce was limited and further detail tended to be reserved for printed marks.

Printed marks started to appear as transfer-printing and generally became more widespread from about 1810 onwards. Initially a printed mark would consist of just the potter's name, as with the first impressed marks, but in the early days they often appeared alongside an impressed mark, the two being applied at different stages in the manufacturing process. Again, examples using lower case letters tend to be early. The flexibility offered by transfer-printing, particularly the opportunity to make marks more ornate and informative, was soon recognised, and the potters

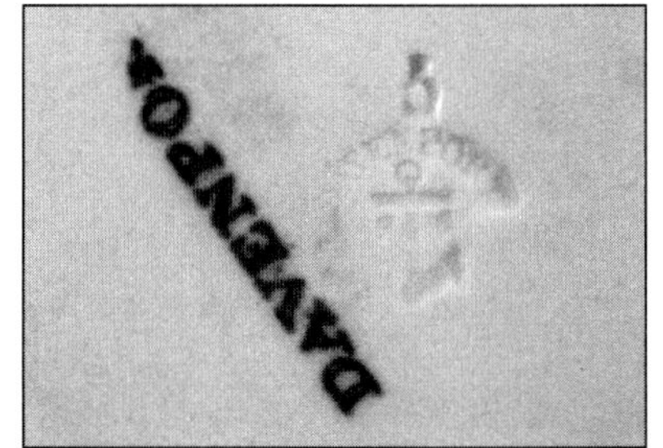

4. Three printed upper case name marks, these examples for Shorthose & Co., Spode (with matching impressed mark), and Davenport (together with impressed anchor mark).

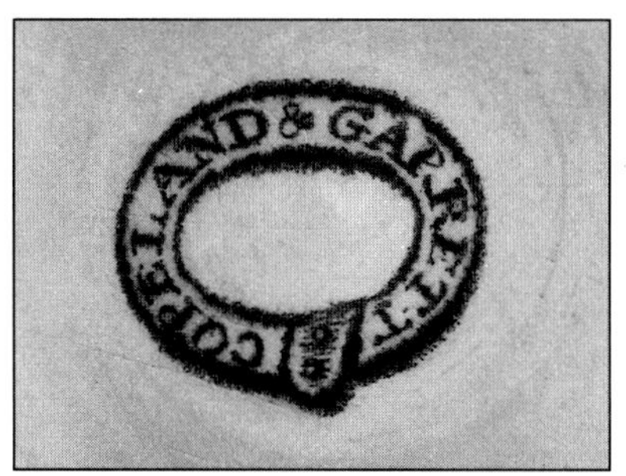

5. Three printed marks with additional detail in the form of a crown, a belt or garter, and a flower spray. The crown mark with "Stone China" is traditionally attributed to Hicks, Meigh & Johnson.

began to introduce decorative forms such as floral or scroll cartouches, crowns, belts and garters. These devices were all commonly used from the 1820s onwards, and indeed, remained in use throughout the 19th century. There is, however, a noticeable change of style from the striking flamboyance of the earlier marks to a much more staid and formal style as the century progressed. Recognising these style changes can be of great help in dating wares.

Perhaps one of the stranger fashions to emerge was the use of initials to indicate the manufacturer. This appears to have started at the very end of the 18th century, one maker of early blue-printed wares impressing his initials I.H., but it grew to prominence with the adoption of printed marks around 1820 or so and was then widespread throughout the remainder of the century. Unfortunately, it has left many puzzles in its wake since the initials used are often not unique. It becomes necessary to take into account other factors such as style or type of the pot or style of the mark before an acceptable attribution can be made. A range of such marks are illustrated in the next chapter, but their attribution to individual manufacturers has been by the author, who does not claim to be infallible! It is worth noting that single initials can rarely be attributed with any certainty. The possible exception is a cursive initial M which was used by Minton, but others such as A, B, G etc., generally remain unattributed.

6. Two impressed marks with maker's initials. The initials I.H. are found on late-18th century blue-printed wares and are traditionally ascribed to Joshua Heath although no potter of this name appears in the directories. The initials W. & B. are attributed to Wood & Brettell.

Initial marks employed by the Staffordshire potters often include an extra initial representing the town, specifically B for Burslem, C for Cobridge, F for Fenton, H for Hanley, L for Longton, LE for Lane End, T for Tunstall, and occasionally DH for Dale Hall. Staffordshire was by no means the only pottery centre to use initial marks, so initials which do not correspond to any firm in these listings might not be of Staffordshire origin. Remember, however, that the Staffordshire knot device

7. Four printed marks incorporating maker's initials. These are all unidentified although G. & E. probably relates to a short-lived but unlisted partnership of Goodwin & Ellis.

8. Two marks incorporating the Staffordshire knot. The first features the initials of Chetham & Robinson; the second is from wares attributed to Goodwins & Harris.

9. Two initial marks of non-Staffordshire origin. The initials P. & A. relate to Pountney & Allies of Bristol, whose impressed mark also appears in this case. Despite the trade name "English Porcelain" on the second example, the initials L.M. & Co. are those of Leboeuf, Milliet & Cie. from Creil in France.

often found in marks would not have been used elsewhere. Initial marks were also used in Bristol, Yorkshire, the North East, Scotland, Wales, and even on the Continent.

Another innovation was the widespread adoption of pattern titles. These date mainly from the introduction of transfer-printed views, mostly copied from travel books of the period, starting around 1810-15. The name of the individual view would be printed in the mark, although some potters chose to use a series title such as "British Views" rather than title each individually. Some used both individual and series titles. The use of titles soon spread to patterns other than

10. Four cartouche marks incorporating pattern titles: the first two from John & Richard Riley and Elkin, Knight & Co., the third used by Ralph Stevenson, and the fourth unattributed.

11. The first recorded use of the word "Patent" by John Turner on his stone china; this example is hand-painted but printed versions also exist.

views, and from 1842 when a Copyright Act prevented the potters from copying prints from books, imaginary "views" were created by the engravers, all rather romantic in style, and given whatever title came to mind. Thus titles such as "Andalusia" bear little, if any, relation to the place named. One good example of this is a moulded jug made by William Brownfield with the title "Nile" rather incongruously used for a Greek key design

The potters of the early 19th century were beginning to appreciate the power of marketing and this, of course, was one of the reasons for marking wares with their names. However, another approach was to try to promote wares by the use of trade names. Perhaps the earliest of these was "Turner's Patent", introduced by John Turner of Lane End in 1800, but other potters were probably goaded into similar action by the undoubted success of the Mason firm's introduction of their "Patent Ironstone China". Thus "Patent" indicating something special, "Ironstone"

12. Three marks incorporating the standard phrases "Ironstone China" or the simpler "Stone China".

13. Three marks with other trade names. Both "Opaque China" and "Semi-China" were widely used but the phrase "Florentine China" is less common and probably relates to Samuel Alcock & Co.

14. A printed mark incorporating the particularly inaccurate trade name of "Semi-Porcelain", the body in this case being standard earthenware.

representing strength, and "China" suggesting quality. A flood of such trade names paralleled the widespread adoption of various forms of stone china, largely after 1825 or so. But even before this became fashionable some potters adopted names for their standard earthenware bodies, particularly "Semi-China" and "Opaque China", and in a few cases the totally incorrect use of "Stone China".

Other trade names encountered can be more accurate. A good example is "Patent Mosaic", which was introduced by Richard Boote to describe some decorative processes he patented in 1843, and which were adopted by his own firm T. & R. Boote and several others.

Another marketing ploy was to use the word "Warranted", sometimes alone but more often as "Warranted Staffordshire". This seems to date mostly from the 1820s although later examples can also be found.

15. Two similar marks from T. & R. Boote and Cork & Edge, both incorporating the royal arms with the trade description "Patent Mosaic". The Boote mark properly relates to the manufacturing process used; the Cork & Edge example appears to be a pirated copy.

16. Three marks incorporating the assurance "Warranted": impressed and printed marks from Ralph & James Clews; an unattributed ornate printed mark including the trade name "Stone China"; and another printed mark featuring the pre-Victorian royal arms and the unidentified initials C.R. & S.

17. A promotional mark used by an unidentified potter, a clear case of one-upmanship, rather self-defeating without the potter's name.

18. Three typical pre-Victorian royal arms marks, these examples attributed to Hicks & Meigh, Stephen Folch, and Goodwins & Harris.

The use of the royal coat-of-arms might be seen as indicating some form of royal patronage, but it seems to have been widely used in the 19th century with little apparent justification. The style of the mark can, however, prove useful in dating wares. One key is the presence or absence of a small escutcheon (or shield) at the centre of the mark. This was dispensed with when Victoria ascended the throne, so wares with the royal arms including the escutcheon will be pre-Victorian (allowing for some short changeover period). Those without the escutcheon cannot pre-date 1837. Early versions of the royal arms can be very ornate, often with the additional Prince of Wales' feathers. Later versions tend to be quite formal and geometrical in shape. On a related topic, the use of the word "Royal" in a company title did not occur in Staffordshire before the 20th century, although a few trade names such as "Royal Stone China" date from the 1820s.

There are several other indicators which can help to date a mark. Amongst the most obvious are the registration diamond which was in use from 1842 to 1883, and its replacement with a system of "Registered Numbers" which ran sequentially from 1884. Reference to a limited company must post-date 1860, and use of the phrase "Trade Mark" indicates a date subsequent to the Trade Mark Act of 1862.

Before the introduction of registered designs, potters and other manufacturers

19. Another pre-Victorian royal arms mark, this example also boasting the phrase "Royal Stone China" and with initials for Ralph Stevenson & Williams (not listed in the directories).

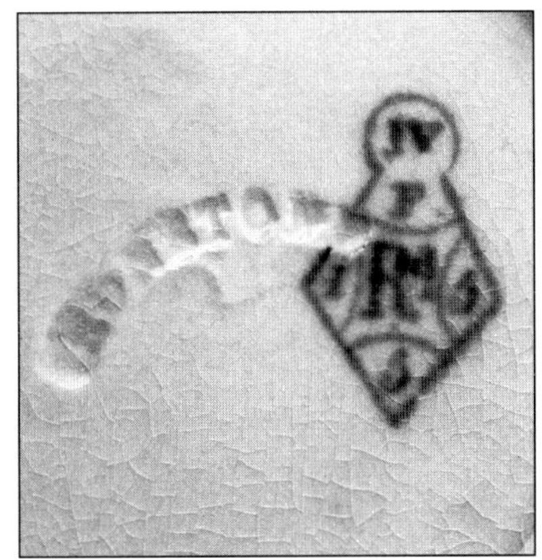

20. Two typical Victorian registration diamond marks, these from Mellor, Venables & Co., together with the impressed body name "Ironstone", and Beech & Hancock, with the helpful addition of their name and address.

had little protection against design piracy. There was, however, one earlier act which did provide some measure of protection for certain types of ware. An act of 1798 allowed designers protection against copying for fourteen years for any design based on a cast object decorated with human or animal figures. It was clearly aimed at sculptors, but the provisions did offer somewhat wider coverage, and several potters made use of the procedure to protect figures, jugs and other moulded wares. In order to claim protection, the wares had to be clearly marked "Published by" with the name and address of the manufacturer and the date of publication. Remember, however, that the same design may have been in production for some years, so the date refers to the year of introduction, not necessarily the year of manufacture.

Some potters made use of marks to date their wares, and the larger firms such as Copeland, Minton and Wedgwood used their own systems for this purpose. However, several other potters used date codes, usually consisting of a number or letter for the month over the last two numerals for the year (in the 19th century). Thus "2"or "F" over "64", for example, will indicate February 1864. The earliest use of this system appears to have been by Henshall & Co. around 1820, but such marks more usually relate to the second half of the 19th century.

21. Two typical publication marks. The first is from a Staffordshire jug although the mark relates to the Sheffield firm which manufactured the fitted Britannia metal lid. The second is from a china figure of the Dickens' character Kate Nickleby; the short-lived Ridgway & Robey partnership is not listed in the directories.

22. Impressed mark for Lakin & Poole. This partnership is not listed in the directories but was related to Poole, Shrigley & Lakin.

23. Impressed mark for John Dale from an earthenware figure. Dale is not listed in the directories but is known to have been making figures in Burslem around 1825.

24. Impressed mark of the surname Tittensor, again from an earthenware figure. No potter of this name is listed in the directories but Charles Tittensor is known to have been making figures in Shelton in the period around 1820.

25. Printed mark for Riddle & Bryan, noted within the decoration on a copper lustre jug. This partnership is not listed in the directories but is thought to pre-date Riddle & Lightfoot who are listed between 1841 and 1851.

A wide selection of potters' marks are illustrated in the following chapter, but despite the comprehensive nature of the list, marks can still be found for which no corresponding firm appears. Examples shown here include Ridgway & Robey, conveniently as part of a publication mark dated June 1839, and the Society of Operative Potters, a fascinating early attempt at union involvement in manufacturing, thought to date from around 1830. The directories did a great job of listing firms in operation when the survey was taken, but inevitably there will have been a few omissions. In addition, new directories and new surveys were not

26. Applied mark for G.R. Booth & Co. from a sprig-moulded stoneware jug. This firm does not appear in the directories but the 1839 publication date suggests that it may have been related to Booth, Robins & Co. of Hanley listed in 1841.

27. Impressed mark for Turpin & Co. from a blue-printed earthenware plate. No firm of this name appears in the directories and it is not necessarily of Staffordshire origin.

carried out every year, and some short-lived firms will have existed between surveys and hence are not recorded in the published directories.

There are also several forms of mark which do not relate to pottery manufacturers, amongst which may be mentioned the signatures of engravers and the names of retailers. Engravers' or printers' signatures are sometimes found on printed wares from the late eighteenth century, known examples including Robinson & Abbey, Thomas Fletcher of Shelton and Radford of Stoke. Such marks are, however, uncommon and they became even less common in the early nineteenth century. Retailers' marks are occasionally found on pottery and porcelain although such marks tend to relate to traders from larger cities or towns and relatively few are known from Staffordshire. Neither engravers nor retailers have beeen included in the survey covered by this volume.

28 (above). Printed mark for the "Operatives Manufactory" of Burslem, almost certainly related to the "Society of Operative Potters" featured in the following illustration.

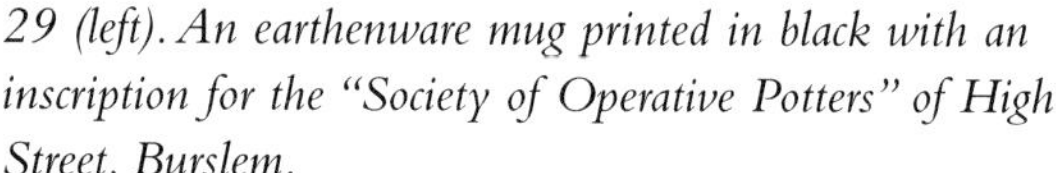

29 (left). An earthenware mug printed in black with an inscription for the "Society of Operative Potters" of High Street, Burslem.

30. An engraver's name Wear found within the pattern on blue-printed earthenwares. This and similar marks for Bentley, Wear & Bourne are probably from the 1820s.

CHAPTER 5

ALPHABETICAL LIST OF MANUFACTURERS

This list of manufacturers has been systematically assembled from the original directory entries, over 11,000 in total, reproduced in Appendix I. For each manufacturer, the firm's address is given, followed by a chronological list of the directory entries, including the date and name of the directory, an abbreviation indicating the classification under which the entry may be found, and any relevant descriptive text. Information such as private addresses, warehouses and showrooms have been assembled at the end of the section for the manufacturer in question. Some of the latest directory entries include details such as telegraphic addresses and telephone numbers, purely of administrative interest, which have not been repeated here.

Many of the later directories also include advertisements, most of which are reproduced adjacent to the relevant entry. Some of the compilers incorporated cross-references to the advertisements they printed, but several advertisements indicated in this way could not be found. Clearly some of the cross-references must be incorrect, but advertisement pages are often missing from surviving directories, and it may be necessary to examine more than one copy to find any advertisement of particular interest.

There are many inconsistencies in the original entries, and in the preparation of this list some interpretation has been inevitable, but in order to retain as much information as possible for researchers, this has been kept to a minimum. Where exact accuracy may be significant, reference can always be made to the original listings in Appendix I. Obvious spelling mistakes and printers' errors have been corrected without comment, but in all other cases, variations which may be significant have been noted with appropriate cross-references. Any conflicts which exist are similarly noted and cross-referenced.

NAMES

One particular problem is caused by the system of inverting names used by nearly all the compilers to facilitate their alphabetical lists. Several different methods of punctuation were used, and there are even inconsistencies within individual directories. In some cases it is not absolutely clear what was intended, particularly with names such as Harvey and Thomas, which are valid both as first names and surnames. As far as possible, assumptions have been avoided.

Another problem occurs with names which may be spelt phonetically in various ways. Simple examples are Steel vs. Steele, Clark vs. Clarke, Tomkinson vs. Tompkinson, and Bridgwood vs. Bridgewood. An excellent example of more complexity is Baggaley, Baggearley, Baggerley, Bagguley, Bagilly, Bagley, and Baguley. It is impossible to formulate a satisfactory rule to cover such situations, so all variations are listed as they appear, and in cases where it seems safe to assemble the entries together, the most common name has been preferred for the main entry and other variants are cross-referenced. It is emphasised that even the preferred name could be incorrect – there would probably not have been a 'right' or 'wrong' way in the eighteenth and nineteenth centuries. Plural names such as Balls and Goodwins occur, and since these may indicate multiple partners from the same family, they have generally been retained without comment.

Separate entries are given for each trading style such as & Co., Ltd., & Son, & Sons, etc. It must be emphasised that the compilers appear to have been imprecise in their use of such styles, but the temptation to make wholesale 'corrections' here has been resisted. Readers are encouraged to draw their own conclusions. One point to note is that some companies may deliberately have utilised various trading styles. Where a suffix & Co. was used, the first names or initials were often dropped. The entry Aynsley & Co., for example, could relate to either H. Aynsley & Co. or John Aynsley & Co. In such cases, the address or addresses are usually sufficient to identify which firm is intended, but the styles are listed separately here in order to retain any possible significance they may hold. Readers are recommended to search through the list for all possible variants, not forgetting that Appendix I should prove useful for tracing entries which appear to be 'missing'.

First names are given in full where they are known, but once again caution has been used in assembling the entries. Where two potters are listed, one with first names and the other with matching initials, they have only been assembled if the dates and addresses are consistent. Where the first names are quoted in full, they appear as such in at least one directory, but it is emphasised that the firm may not always have used the full names in their trading style.

ADDRESSES

Where a potter or firm operated at more than one address at different periods, the addresses are listed separately, or in combination if appropriate, within the appropriate section. Directory entries are repeated under each relevant address where necessary. Where two potters existed with identical names, they should be clearly identifiable by comparison of the dates and addresses. The addresses are listed in various ways in the directories, and the same address can easily appear in two apparently unrelated forms, using different street names for example, depending on the individual compilers. While it would have been possible to amalgamate addresses (and partnerships) which might be the same, the usefulness of this list may have been diminished, and the temptation has been resisted.

The names of the factories are a useful pointer to the identification of any address, but often they were not included and some names were not unique. The titles 'Pottery' and 'Works', and even 'Potteries', appear to have been used almost indiscriminately. As with the potters' names, there are many examples where alternate spellings can be found, such as Sylvester vs. Silvester, Normacot vs. Normacott, and particularly several variants of Ranelagh. It is felt that any attempt to enforce consistency throughout this list would be both unnecessary and unrewarding, and all original spellings have been retained except where required for consistency within each potter's entry. This has normally been achieved by using the most common spelling from the directory entries in question, although modern usage has been adopted in a few cases.

ALPHABETICAL ORDER

This list is in alphabetical order of the surname of the potter or first named partner. Entries with the same surname are listed in the following order:

Name or surname only
Name or surname with suffixes (Brothers, & Co., Ltd., & Son, & Sons)
One surname with initials (or first names), with suffixes where appropriate
Partnerships with two or more surnames, with suffixes where appropriate

ABBREVIATIONS

The following abbreviations are used to indicate the directory classifications:

CEM	China and Earthenware Manufacturers
CETM	China and Earthenware Toy Manufacturers
CETOM	China and Earthenware Toy and Ornament Manufacturers
CFM	China Figure Manufacturers
CM	China Manufacturers
COM	China Ornament Manufacturers
CTM	China Toy Manufacturers
EFM	Earthenware Figure Manufacturers
EM	Earthenware Manufacturers
ETM	Earthenware Toy Manufacturers
JM	Jet Ware Manufacturers
JRM	Jet and Rockingham Ware Manufacturers
LM	Lustre Manufacturers
MM	Majolica Manufacturers
OFM	Ornamental Figure Manufacturers
P	Potters
PFM	Parian Figure Manufacturers
PM	Parian Manufacturers
RM	Rockingham Ware Manufacturers
SM	Stoneware Manufacturers
TCM	Terra Cotta Manufacturers
TM	Toy Manufacturers
TOCM	Toy and Ornamental China Manufacturers

OTHER ABBREVIATIONS ARE:

A	A cross-reference to an advertisement appears in the directory
NC	Not classified
SC	Specialist classification (followed by the classification title in parentheses)

THE FOLLOWING SUFFIXES ARE USED TO INDICATE SPECIFIC TOWNS OR VILLAGES

-B	Burslem
-Bar	Barlaston
-C	Cobridge
-E	Etruria
-F	Fenton
-G	Golden Hill
-H	Hanley
-L	Longton
-LD	Lane Delph
-LE	Lane End
-LL	Lower Lane
-Lp	Longport
-N	Newcastle-under-Lyme
-Nf	Newfield
-R	Red Street
-S	Stoke-on-Trent
-Sf	Smithfield
-Sh	Shelton
-T	Tunstall
-V	Vale Pleasant

Abberley, James
(i) Waterloo Works, Longton
1870 Harrod NC-L (earthenware manufacturer for home and foreign markets)
(ii) Market Lane, Longton
1873 Keates P-L (china and earthenware)

Abington, Leonard J.
See: Ridgway, W. Son & Co.

Abraham, Robert Frederick
34 Victoria Street, Northwood, Hanley
1864 Jones CEM

Ackerley & Hassall
Commerce Street, Longton
1861 Harrison NC-L (china manufacturers)

Ackwood, Dimmock & Co.
See: Hackwood, Dimmock & Co.

Adams, Benjamin
Tunstall
1811 Holden NC (china & earthenware-manufacturer)
1816 Underhill P
1818 Parson EM-G-T-R
1818 Pigot EM

Benjamin Adams. Impressed mark from a small blue-printed dish.

Adams, Edward
High Street, Longton
1879 Keates P-L (china)

Adams, Harvey, & Co.
(i) Sutherland Road, Longton
1870 Harrod NC-L (manufacturers of china and earthenware suitable for home and export trade)
1872 Kelly CM
1873 Keates P-L (china and earthenware)
1875 Keates P-L (china and earthenware)
1876 Kelly CM
1879 Keates P-L (china and earthenware)
1880 Kelly CM
1882 Keates P-L (china and earthenware)
1884 Kelly CM
(ii) High Street, Longton
1872 Kelly CM
The firm is listed as Harvey, Adams & Co. in 1872 Kelly. A London office at 5 Bartlett's Buildings, Holborn, is listed in 1870 Harrod. A London agent is listed as James Gelson at 30 Holborn in 1880 Kelly.

Adams, J.
Tunstall
1809 Holden NC (china & earthenware-manufacturer)

Adams, John
(i) Victoria Works, High Street, Longton
1865 Keates P-L (china)
1868 Kelly CM
1870 Harrod NC-L (china manufacturers)
1872 Kelly CM
1873 Keates P-L (china)
(ii) Park Place, Longton
1868 Kelly CM
1872 Kelly CM
(iii) Dale Hall, Burslem
1869 Keates P-B (earthenware)
1870 Harrod NC-B (earthenware manufacturer)
(iv) Stafford Street, Longton
1889 Keates P-L (china, home and export)
(v) 275 Uttoxeter Road, Longton
1889 Keates P-L
The firm is noted as being in the hands of executors in 1868 Kelly, 1870 Harrod, 1872 Kelly, and 1873 Keates.

Adams, John, & Co.
Victoria Works, Broad Street and St. James's Street, Hanley
1865 Keates A; P-H (parian and majolica)
1867 Keates P-H (parian and majolica)
1868 Kelly EM
1869 Keates P-H (parian and majolica)
1870 Harrod NC-H (manufacturers of Wedgewood ware, majolica, green glaze, &c., for home and foreign markets)
1872 Kelly EM
1873 Keates P-H (parian and majolica)
London showrooms at 30 Ely Place are listed in 1870 Harrod. The advertisement in 1865 Keates describes the firm as potters and 'manufacturers of jasper, majolica, green glaze, Rockingham and stone ware'.

John Adams & Co. Impressed mark from a green-glazed earthenware dessert plate.

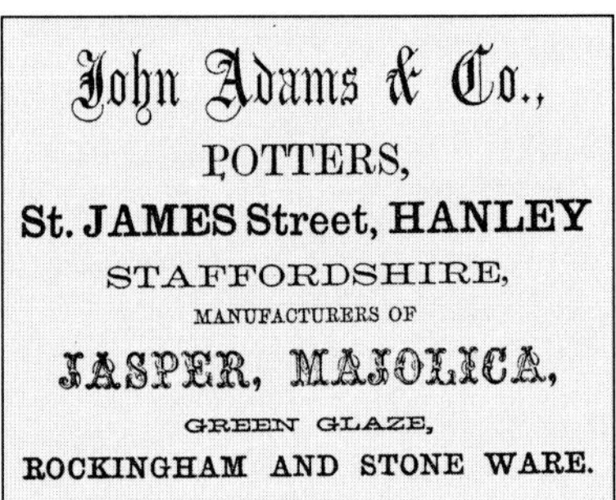
John Adams & Co.,
POTTERS,
St. JAMES Street, HANLEY
STAFFORDSHIRE,
MANUFACTURERS OF
JASPER, MAJOLICA,
GREEN GLAZE,
ROCKINGHAM AND STONE WARE.

John Adams & Co. Advertisement from 1865 Keates.

Adams, Joseph
28 Brook Street, Hanley
1887 Porter EM-H

Adams, Lewis
See: Adams, William, & Sons

Adams, R.S., & Co.
Chadwick Street, Longton
1889 Keates A; P-L
No copy of the advertisement in 1889 Keates could be located.

Adams, Richard Stanley
Anchor Works, Anchor Road, Longton
1887 Porter EM-L
1888 Kelly EM

Adams, Thomas
(i) Fenton Road, Hanley
1880 Kelly PM
(ii) Trent Works, Eastwood Vale, Hanley

1882 Keates P-H (parian)
Adams succeeded Stanway, Horne & Adams and was in turn succeeded by Edwards & Son (1887 Porter advertisement).

Adams, Thomas, & Co.
Greenfields and Newfield, Tunstall
1869 Keates P-T (earthenware)

Adams, William
(i) Cobridge
1796 Chester NC-C (manufacturer of earthenware)
1798 Universal NC-C (manufacturer of Staffordshire-ware)
1802 Allbut EM (map location 60)
1805 Holden NC (china and earthenware manufactory)
1809 Holden NC (china & earthenware-manufacturer)
1811 Holden NC (china & earthenware-manufacturer)
(ii) Golden Hill
1796 Chester NC-T-Lp (manufacturer of earthenware)
(iii) Tunstall
1798 Universal NC-T (earthenware manufacturer)
1802 Allbut EM (map location 11)
(iv) Stoke
1818 Parson EM-S-E
1818 Pigot EM
1822 Allbut CEM (earthenware manufacturer)
1822 Pigot EM
(v) Newcastle Street, Stoke
1828 Pigot CM; EM
(vi) High Street, Stoke
1830 Pigot CM; EM
(vii) Greenfield, Tunstall
1856 Kelly CEM
1860 Kelly EM
1862 Slater EM
1863 Kelly EM
1864 Jones EM
1865 Keates P-T (earthenware)
1872 Kelly EM
1876 Kelly EM
(viii) Newfield, Tunstall
1860 Kelly EM (two entries)
1861 Harrison NC-T (earthenware manufacturer)
1862 Slater EM
1863 Kelly EM (two entries)
1864 Jones EM
1865 Keates P-T (earthenware)
1867 Keates P-T (earthenware)
1868 Kelly EM
1869 Keates P-T (earthenware)
1870 Harrod NC-T (earthenware manufacturer, and grinder of potter's materials)
1873 Keates P-T (earthenware)
1875 Keates P-T (earthenware)
1879 Keates P-T (earthen.)
The entry at the Greenfield address is listed as William Adams senior in 1864 Jones. Most entries at the Newfield address are listed as William Adams junior between 1860 and 1868.

William Adams. Impressed mark from a sprigged stoneware jug with a silver mount hallmarked 1807.

Adams, William, & Co.
(i) Burslem
1781 Bailey NC (potters)
1783 Bailey NC (potters)
1784 Bailey NC-B (manufacturers of cream coloured ware, and china glazed ware painted)
(ii) Greenfield, Tunstall
1846 Williams NC-T (earthenware manufacturers)
1892 Keates P-T (earthenware)
1900 Kelly EM

William Adams & Co. Printed and impressed marks from a blue-printed earthenware mug. Marks with a claimed date of establishment are usually 20th century but Adams are believed to have used this form at very end of the 19th century.

William Adams & Co. Impressed and printed marks from a sprigged stoneware jug. Again, marks with a claimed date of establishment are usually 20th century but Adams are believed to have used this form at very end of the 19th century.

Adams, William, & Son
Church Street, Stoke
1851 White CEM-S

Adams, William, & Sons
(i) Church Street, Stoke
1834 White CM-S; EM-S
1835 Pigot CM; EM
1841 Pigot CM
1846 Williams NC-S (earthenware & china manuf.)
1850 Kelly CEM; NC-S (earthenware manufacturers)
1850 Slater EM
1852 Slater EM
1854 Kelly CEM
1856 Kelly CEM
1861 Harrison NC-S (earthenware manufacturers)
1862 Slater EM
(ii) Greenfield, Tunstall
1834 White EM-T
1835 Pigot EM
1841 Pigot EM
1850 Slater EM
1851 White EM-T
1852 Slater CM (and parian marble); EM
1854 Kelly CEM
(iii) High Street, Longton
1841 Pigot EM
(iv) High Street, Stoke
1852 Slater CM (and parian marble)

One partner is listed individually as Lewis Adams of Watlands, Stoke, in 1846 Williams. A London office at 25A Hatton Garden is listed in 1854 Kelly.

William Adams & Sons. Printed mark from a hand-painted china plate.

Adams, William & Thomas
Greenfield, Tunstall
1867 Keates P-T (earthenware)
1868 Kelly EM
1869 Keates P-T (earthenware)
1870 Harrod NC-T (earthenware and china manufacturers for home and foreign markets)
1872 Kelly EM
1873 Keates P-T (earthenware)
1875 Keates P-T (earthenware)
1876 Kelly EM
1879 Keates P-T (earthenware)
1880 Kelly EM
1882 Keates P-T (earthenware)
1884 Kelly EM
1887 Porter EM-T
1888 Kelly EM
1889 Keates P-T (earthenware)
1892 Kelly EM
1896 Kelly EM

William & Thomas Adams. Printed mark from a green and blue printed earthenware soup plate. The indistinct registration diamond appears to date from 1882.

Adams & Bromley
(i) Victoria Works, Broad Street, Hanley
1875 Keates P-H (jasper and majolica)
1876 Kelly MM
1879 Keates P-H (jasper and majolica)
1880 Kelly MM
1882 Keates P-H (jasper and majolica)
1884 Kelly MM
1887 Porter EM-H
1888 Kelly MM
1889 Keates P-H (jasper and majolica)
(ii) Castlefields Works, Newcastle Road, Stoke
1892 Kelly SC (Encaustic Tile Manufacturers)

Adams & Bromley. Impressed mark from a sprigged stoneware jug.

Adams & Cooper
High Street, Longton
1852 Slater CM
1854 Kelly CEM
1856 Kelly CEM
1860 Kelly CM-General
1861 Harrison NC-L (china manufacturers)
1862 Slater CM
1863 Kelly CM-General; CM-Tea, Breakfast, and Dessert Services
1864 Jones CEM
1865 Keates P-L (china)
1867 Keates P-L (china)
1868 Kelly CM
1869 Keates P-L (china)
1870 Harrod NC-L (china manufacturers)
1872 Kelly CM
1873 Keates P-L (china)
1875 Keates P-L (china)
1876 Kelly CM

Adams & Scrivener
The Pottery, Sutherland Road, Longton
1863 Kelly CM-Fancy Ware; CM-General; CM-Tea, Breakfast, and Dessert Services; CM-White & Finished
1864 Jones CEM
1865 Keates P-L (china)

Adams, Scrivener & Co.
Sutherland Road, Longton
1867 Keates P-L (china)
1868 Kelly CM
1869 Keates A; P-L (china & earthen.)
The advertisement in 1869 Keates describes the firm as 'manufacturers of china, earthenware, stoneware, etc.' and lists a London office at 5 Bartlett's Buildings, Holborn.

ADAMS, SCRIVENER, & Co.,
MANUFACTURERS OF
China, Earthenware, Stoneware,
ETC.,
LONGTON, STAFFORDSHIRE POTTERIES.
LONDON OFFICES—5, Bartlett's Buildings, Holborn, E.C.

Adams, Scrivener & Co. Advertisement from 1869 Keates.

Adams & Sleigh
17 Queen Street, Burslem
1882 Keates P-B

Adderley, William Alsager
Daisy Bank Works, Longton
1876 Kelly CM; EM
1879 Keates P-L (china and earthenware)
1880 Kelly CM; EM
1882 Keates P-L (china and earthenware)
1884 Kelly CM; EM
1888 Kelly CM; EM
1889 Keates P-L (china and earthenware)
1892 Keates P-L (china & earthenware)
1892 Kelly CM

Adderley, William Alsager, & Co.
Daisy Bank Pottery, Longton
1887 Porter EM-L
1896 Kelly CM; EM
1900 Kelly CM; EM

Adderley & Lawson
Salisbury Works, Edensor Road, Longton
1882 Keates P-L (china)
1884 Kelly CM
1887 Porter EM-L
1888 Kelly CM
1889 Keates P-L (china)
1892 Keates P-L (china)
1892 Kelly CM

Adderley, Shaw & Goldstraw
Daisy Bank Works, Longton
1863 Kelly P (chimney pot)

Adderley & Tams
Sutherland Works, High Street, Longton
1887 Porter EM-L

Aidney, John, & Co.
High Street, Longton
1879 Keates P-L (china)

Aidney, Griffiths & Co.
(i) High Street, Longton
1880 Kelly EM
(ii) Edensor Road, Longton
1882 Keates P-L (china)
1884 Kelly CM
1888 Kelly CM
1889 Keates P-L (china)

Alcock, George
See: Hill Pottery Co. Ltd.

Alcock, Henry, & Co.
(i) Cobridge Works
1863 Kelly EM
1864 Jones EM (ironstone and china)
1865 Keates P-B (china and earthenware)
1867 Keates P-B (earthenware)
1868 Kelly EM
1869 Keates P-B (earthenware)
1870 Harrod NC-B (manufacturers of white granite, for United States)
1872 Kelly EM
1873 Keates P-B (earthenware)
1875 Keates P-B (earthenware)
1876 Kelly EM
1879 Keates P-B (earthenware)
1882 Keates P-B (earthenware)
1889 Keates P-B (earthenware)
1892 Keates P-B (earthenware)
(ii) Waterloo Road, Cobridge
1880 Kelly EM
1884 Kelly EM
1887 Porter EM-B
1888 Kelly EM
1892 Kelly EM
1896 Kelly EM
1900 Kelly EM

Alcock, John
Cobridge
1852 Slater EM
1854 Kelly CEM
1856 Kelly CEM
1860 Kelly EM
1861 Harrison NC-B (earthenware manufacturer)

Alcock, John & George
Cobridge
1841 Pigot EM (improved Indian iron stone)
1846 Williams NC-C-F-E (earthenware manufacturers); NC-B (earthenware manufacturers)
The partners are listed individually as Mr. George Alcock and Mr. John Alcock (of the banking firm of Joseph, John and George Alcock), both of the Limes, in 1846 Williams.

John & George Alcock. Impressed mark from a large ironstone pot pourri vase.

Alcock, John & Samuel
Cobridge
1850 Slater EM

Alcock, Richard
Central Pottery, Market Place, Burslem
1870 Harrod NC-B (earthenware manufacturer)
1872 Kelly EM
1873 Keates P-B (earthenware)
1875 Keates P-B (earthenware)
1876 Kelly EM
1879 Keates P-B (earthenware)
1882 Keates P-B (earthenware)
1880 Kelly EM

Alcock, Samuel, & Co.
(i) Cobridge
1828 Pigot CM
1830 Pigot CM
1841 Pigot CM
1850 Slater CM; EM
1852 Slater CM
(ii) Hill Pottery, Liverpool Road, Burslem
1834 White EM-B (china mfrs. also)
1835 Pigot EM
1841 Pigot EM (& Indian iron stone)
1846 Williams NC-B
1850 Kelly NC-B (china & earthenware manufacturers); CEM
1850 Slater CM; EM
1851 White CEM-B (both)
1852 Slater CM
1854 Kelly CEM; PM
1856 Kelly CEM; PM
1860 Kelly CM-General; EM
The partners are listed individually as Samuel Alcock of Cobridge and Charles Keeling of White House, near Newcastle, in 1846 Williams. A London office at 89 Hatton Garden is listed in the four directories between 1851 and 1856.

Samuel Alcock & Co. Ornate printed publication mark from a Crimean War "Royal Patriotic Jug".

Samuel Alcock & Co. Printed publication mark from a parian figure of Wellington.

Samuel Alcock & Co. Printed royal arms mark from a relief-moulded jug. The registration diamond dates from 1847.

Alcock, Thomas
High Street, Burslem
1828 Pigot EM

Alcock & Diggory
(i) Central Pottery, Burslem
1868 Kelly EM
1869 Keates P-B (earthen.)
(ii) Burslem China Works, Burslem
1870 Harrod NC-B
(manufacturers of china, for the home and foreign trade)
An advertisement in 1869 Keates describes the firm simply as 'manufacturers of china' and gives the address as Burslem China Works.

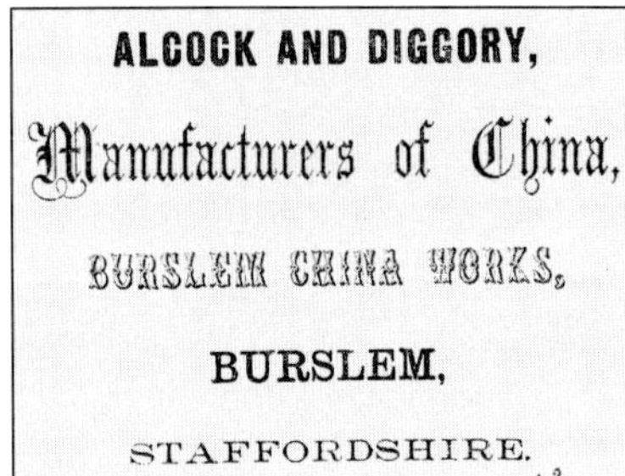

Alcock & Diggory. Advertisement from 1869 Keates.

Alcock & Forshaw
Railway Tileries, Fenton
1876 Kelly SC (Sanitary Ware Manufacturers)

Alcock, Mason & Co.
High Street, Lane End
1828 Pigot CM

Alcock & Williamson
St. Martin's Lane, Longton
1864 Jones LM

Allcock, Thomas Edward
Lane End
1798 Universal NC-LE
(manufacturer of Staffordshire-ware)

Allcock & Ward
Lane End
1796 Chester NC-LE-LD-LL
(manufacturers of earthenware)

Allen, H.W.
See: Asbury, Edward, & Co.

Allen, Henry
Wellington Street, Burslem
1882 Keates P-B (creel steps)

Allen, Herbert George
Broad Street, Hanley
1862 Slater CM
1863 Kelly CM-General
1865 Keates P-H (china)
1867 Keates P-H (china)

Allen, S.
See: Cartlidge & Allen

Allen, Sampson Henry
Jubilee Works, Mount Pleasant, High Street, Longton
1889 Keates A; P-L (china & earthenware)
1892 Keates P-L (china & earthenware)
1892 Kelly CM
1896 Kelly CM
The advertisement in 1889 Keates describes Allen as a 'china manufacturer and decorator of all kinds of earthenware'.

JUBILEE WORKS,
MOUNT PLEASANT, HIGH STREET
LONGTON, STAFFORDSHIRE.
S. H. ALLEN,
China Manufacturer
AND
DECORATOR OF ALL KINDS OF EARTHENWARE.

Sampson Henry Allen. Advertisement from 1889 Keates.

Allen, W.L.
See: Hammersley & Asbury
See: Hammersley, Freeman & Co.

Allerton Brothers
High Street, Longton
1870 Harrod NC-L (china and earthenware manufacturers)

Allerton, Charles, & Co.
High Street, Longton
1876 Kelly CM

Allerton, Charles, & Son
Park Works, High Street, Longton
1860 Kelly EM
1863 Kelly CM-General; CM-Tea, Breakfast, and Dessert Services
1864 Jones A; CEM; LM
1865 Keates A; P-L (china, earthenware, and gold and silver lustre)
1867 Keates P-L (china, earthenware, and gold and silver lustre)
1880 Kelly CM; EM; LM (gold & silver)
The advertisement in 1864 Jones is in the name of Charles Allerton & Sons (note the plural), late Allerton, Brough & Green, and claims 1831 as the date of establishment. The description reads 'manufacturers of decorated china & earthenware, gold, silver & orange lustre, Egyptian black, fancy stone and other colored bodies, &c., suitable for home & foreign markets'. Despite the cross-reference, no advertisement could be located in 1865 Keates.

Allerton, Charles, & Sons
Park Works, High Street, Longton
1861 Harrison NC-L (china and earthenware manufacturers)
1862 Slater CM; EM
1863 Kelly EM; LM
1868 Kelly CM
1869 Keates A; P-L (china, earthenware, and gold and silver lustre)
1872 Kelly CM
1873 Keates P-L (china, earthenware, and gold and silver lustre)
1875 Keates P-L (china, earthenware, and gold and silver lustre)
1879 Keates P-L (china, earthenware, and gold and silver lustre)
1882 Keates P-L (china, earthenware, and gold and silver lustre)
1884 Kelly CM; EM; LM (gold & silver)
1887 Porter EM-L
1888 Kelly CM; EM; LM (gold & silver)
1889 Keates P-L (china, earthenware, and gold and silver lustre)
1892 Keates P-L (china &c.)
1892 Kelly CM; EM; LM
1896 Kelly CM; EM
1900 Kelly CM; EM
An advertisement in 1864 Jones is in the name of Charles Allerton & Sons

although the entry is for Charles Allerton & Son (qv). The advertisement in 1869 Keates describes the firm as 'manufacturers of decorated china and earthenware, gold, silver, and orange lustre, Egyptian black, fancy stone and other coloured bodies, &c., &c., suitable for the home and foreign markets'. It also lists their predecessors as Allerton, Brough & Green and claims that they were established in 1831.

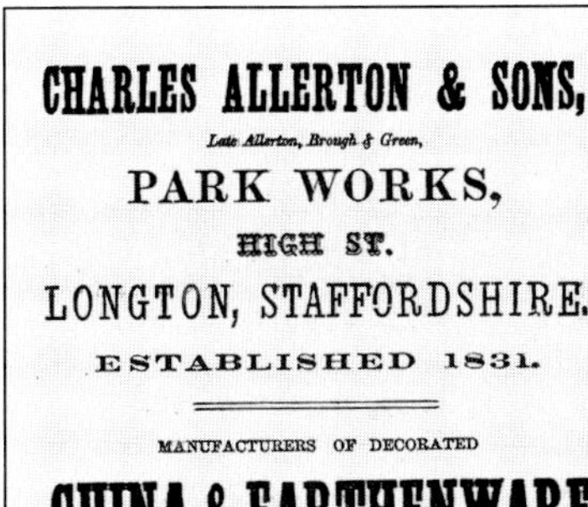

Charles Allerton & Sons. Advertisement from 1864 Jones.

CHAS. ALLERTON AND SONS
(LATE ALLERTON, BROUGH, & GREEN.)
PARK WORKS,
LONGTON, STAFFORDSHIRE,
ESTABLISHED 1831.
MANUFACTURERS OF
DECORATED CHINA
AND EARTHENWARE,
Gold, Silver, and Orange Lustre,
EGYPTIAN BLACK,
Fancy Stone and other Coloured Bodies,
&c. ,&c.
SUITABLE FOR THE HOME AND FOREIGN MARKETS.

Charles Allerton & Sons. Advertisement from 1869 Keates.

Allerton, Charles W.
Victoria Works, Longton
1887 Porter EM-L

Allerton, Brough & Green
(i) Park Works, High Street, Longton
1834 White CM-LE-L (lustre mfrs.)
1835 Pigot CM
1841 Pigot CM; EM
1846 Williams NC-L-LE (earthenware, china, and lustre manufacturers)
1850 Kelly NC-L (manufacturers of burnished gold, china, Egyptian black, lustre & earthenware)
1850 Slater CM; EM
1851 White CEM-L
1852 Slater CM; EM
1854 Kelly CEM
1856 Kelly CEM
(ii) Church Street, Stoke
1841 Pigot CM
The partners are listed individually as Charles Allerton of Sutherland Road, Benjamin S. Brough of Vauxhall Cottage, Stafford Street, and William Green of Sutherland Road in 1846 Williams. The firm was succeeded by Charles Allerton & Sons (1869 Keates advertisement).

Allerton & Lowe
High Street, Longton
1834 White EM-LE-L (and lustre)

Allin & Furnival
Miles Bank, Shelton
1841 Pigot EM

Allman, Henry, & Co.
Silvester Works, Silvester Square, Burslem
1862 Slater EM (& of lustre, Egyptian black and Rockingham ware)

Allman, Broughton & Co.
Wedgwood Place, Burslem
1862 Slater EM
1863 Kelly EM
1864 Jones EM
1865 Keates P-B (earthenware)
1867 Keates P-B (earthenware)

Alum & Bryant
Heathcote Road, Longton
1892 Kelly EM

Amison, Charles
(i) Wedgwood Pottery, Anchor Road, Longton
1889 Keates P-L (china)
1892 Keates P-L (china)
(ii) Wedgwood Street, Sandford Hill, Longton
1896 Kelly CM
1900 Kelly CM

Amison, Joseph
(i) Mount Pleasant, High Street, Longton
1882 Keates P-L (china)
1887 Porter EM-L
1888 Kelly CM
(ii) Chatfield Works, Longton
1884 Kelly CM

Amison & Edwards
Russell Street, Longton
1870 Harrod NC-L (earthenware manufacturers)
1872 Kelly EM
1873 Keates P-L

Amison & Lawson
Salisbury Works, Edensor Road, Longton
1879 Keates A; P-L (china)
1880 Kelly CM (manufacturers of all kinds of plain & decorated china in breakfast, tea, dessert, toilet & trinket services for the home, American & Australian markets)
A London agent is listed as J.K. Kendall at 3 Bucklersbury, Cheapside, in 1880 Kelly. The advertisement in 1879 Keates describes the firm as 'china manufacturers, dealers in stone and metal covered teapots and jugs'.

AMISON & LAWSON,
China Manufacturers,
DEALERS IN
STONE AND METAL COVERED TEAPOTS AND JUGS,
SALISBURY WORKS,
EDENSOR ROAD,
LONGTON.

Amison & Lawson. Advertisement from 1879 Keates.

Anderson, Robert
See: Bradbury, Anderson & Betteney

Anderson, William, & Co.
St. Martin's Lane, Longton
1880 Kelly CM
1892 Kelly CM

Anderson & Betteney
(i) Flint Street, Longton
1851 White NC-L (china manfrs.)
(ii) Stafford Street, Longton
1852 Slater CM
1854 Kelly CEM
1856 Kelly CEM
The third partner's surname is listed as Betteny in the three later directories.

Anderson & Betteny
See: Anderson & Betteney

Anderson & Copestake
St. Martin's Lane, Longton
1882 Keates P-L (china)
1884 Kelly CM
1887 Porter EM-L
1888 Kelly CM
1889 Keates P-L (china)
1892 Keates P-L (china)
The partnership is listed as Anderton & Copestake in the three Keates directories. The address is listed as St. Martin's Works, Market Street, in 1887 Porter.

Anderton & Copestake
See: Anderson & Copestake

Andrews, Edward
Clayhills Pottery, Tunstall
1892 Keates P-T

Arkinstall & George
Burslem
1802 Allbut EM (map location 50)

Arrowsmith, Thomas
Moorland Road, Burslem
1884 Kelly SC (Spur & Stilt Makers for Pottery Manufacturers)
1889 Keates P-B (spur and stilt manufacturer)
1892 Keates P-B (spur and stilt manufacturer)

Arrowsmith, Thomas, & Son
Moorland Road, Burslem
1888 Kelly SC (Spur & Stilt Makers for Pottery Manufacturers)
1892 Kelly SC (Stilt & Spur Manufacturers)
An advertisement in 1892 Keates gives the address as Wedgwood and Moorland Road Works, Burslem, and describes the firm as 'manufacturers of stilt spurs, thimbles, tile bats, tile boxes, pins, &c.'

THOMAS ARROWSMITH & SON,
MANUFACTURERS OF
STILT SPURS, THIMBLES, TILE BATS,
TILE BOXES, PINS, &c.,
Wedgwood and Moorland Road Works,
BURSLEM.
Telephone 333.

Thomas Arrowsmith & Son. Advertisement from 1892 Keates.

Arrowsmith, Thomas, & Sons
Moorland Road, Burslem
1896 Kelly SC (Stilt & Spur Manufacturers)
1900 Kelly SC (Stilt & Spur Manufacturers)

Art Pottery Co. (The)
Anchor Works, Brewery Street, Hanley
1892 Kelly A; EM
1896 Kelly EM
1900 Kelly EM
The advertisement in 1892 Kelly describes the firm as 'manufacturers of art pottery, toilet ware, &c.' and quotes their speciality as vases.

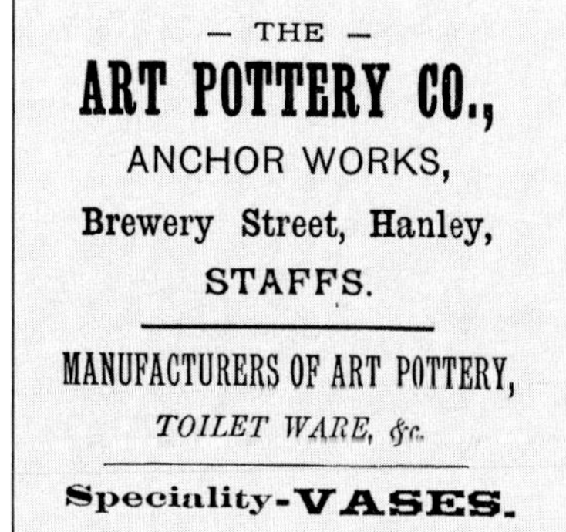

The Art Pottery Co. Advertisement from 1892 Kelly.

Art Tile Co.
Bryan Street, Hanley
1887 Porter EM-H

Asbury, Edward, & Co.
Sutherland Road, Longton
1875 Keates A; P-L (china)
1876 Kelly CM
1879 Keates P-L (china)
1880 Kelly CM
1882 Keates P-L (china)
1884 Kelly CM
1887 Porter EM-L
1888 Kelly CM
1889 Keates P-L (china)
1892 Keates P-L (china)
1892 Kelly CM
1896 Kelly CM
1900 Kelly CM
The surname is listed as Ashbury in 1888 Kelly. The advertisement in 1875 Keates describes the firm as 'manufacturers of china, tea, breakfast, and dessert services, also trinkets for the toilet table. Dealers in lustre & stone teapots & jugs, &c. Price lists, patterns, &c., sent on application'. It lists a London agent as Mr. H.W. Allen at 14 Bartlett's Buildings, Holborn, and states that the firm's predecessors were Hammersley & Asbury.

EDWARD ASBURY & Co.,
Late Hammersley and Asbury,
SUTHERLAND ROAD, LONGTON,
MANUFACTURERS OF
CHINA, TEA, BREAKFAST,
AND
DESSERT SERVICES,
ALSO,
TRINKETS FOR THE TOILET TABLE.
DEALERS IN
Lustre & Stone Teapots & Jugs, &c.
Price Lists, Patterns, &c., sent on application.
London Agent—Mr. H. W. ALLEN, 14, Bartlett's Buildings, Holborn.

Edward Asbury & Co. Advertisement from 1875 Keates.

Ash, George
Broad Street, Hanley
1865 Keates A; P-H (parian and majolica)
1867 Keates A; P-H (parian and majolica)
1868 Kelly MM; PM
1869 Keates A; P-H (parian and majolica)
1870 Harrod NC-H (manufacturer of parian statuettes, ornamental vases, &c.)
1873 Keates A; P-H (parian and majolica)
1875 Keates A; P-H (parian and majolica)
1876 Kelly PM
1879 Keates A; P-H (parian and majolica)
1880 Kelly PM
The advertisements in the Keates series of directories are all similar. They describe Ash as a manufacturer of 'parian statuettes, vases, decorated

GEO. ASH,
MANUFACTURER OF
PARIAN STATUETTES,
VASES,
DECORATED WITH PAINTED EGYPTIAN CHARACTERS
MODERN FLOWERS, &C.
MAJOLICA, STONE WARE,
AND COLOURED BODIES,
BROAD STREET, HANLEY,
STAFFORDSHIRE.

George Ash. Advertisement from 1865 Keates.

GEO. ASH,
MANUFACTURER OF
MAJOLICA, PARIAN,
STONE WARE,
AND
COLOURED BODIES.
BROAD STREET, HANLEY,
STAFFORDSHIRE.

George Ash. Advertisement from 1867 Keates.

GEORGE ASH,
MANUFACTURER OF
PARIAN STATUETTES,
ORNAMENTAL VASES, ETC.
BROAD STREET, HANLEY.

George Ash. Advertisement from 1869 Keates.

GEORGE ASH,
MANUFACTURER OF
Majolica, Parian Statuettes
ORNAMENTAL VASES, &C.
BROAD-ST., HANLEY

George Ash. Advertisement from 1873 Keates.

GEORGE ASH,
MANUFACTURER OF
Majolica, Parian, & China Statuettes,
ORNAMENTAL VASES, &c.,
BROAD STREET, HANLEY.

George Ash. Advertisement from 1875 Keates.

GEORGE ASH,
MANUFACTURER OF
ORNAMENTAL CHINA,
PARIAN AND MAJOLICA,
BROAD STREET, HANLEY,
STAFFORDSHIRE

George Ash. Advertisement from 1879 Keates.

with painted Egyptian characters, modern flowers, &c., majolica, stone ware, and coloured bodies' (1865), 'majolica, parian, stone ware, and coloured bodies' (1867), 'parian statuettes, ornamental vases, etc.' (1869), 'majolica, parian statuettes, ornamental vases, &c.' (1873), 'majolica, parian, & china statuettes, ornamental vases, &c.' (1875), and 'ornamental china, parian and majolica' (1879).

Ash, George, & Co.
Broad Street, Hanley
1872 Kelly MM; PM

Ashbury, E., & Co.
See: Asbury, Edward, & Co.

Ashwell & Co.
Anchor Lane, Lane End
1835 Pigot EM

Ashwell, John, & Co.
Anchor Lane, Lane End
1841 Pigot EM
1846 Williams NC-L-LE (earthenware manufacturers)

Ashworth, George L., & Brothers
Broad Street, Hanley
1861 Harrison NC-H-Sh (china and earthenware manufacturers)
1862 Slater CM (ironstone); EM
1863 Kelly CM-General; EM
1864 Jones EM
1865 Keates P-H (earthenware)
1867 Keates P-H (earthenware)
1868 Kelly CM
1869 Keates P-H (earthenware)
1870 Harrod NC-H (manufacturers of earthenware and ironstone china, specially adapted for ship purposes, hotels, &c., sole makers of Mason's patent ironstone china, both patterns and shapes, chemical goods, insulators, and other goods for telegraphic purposes, and sanitary ware for home and foreign markets)
1872 Kelly CM; EM
1873 Keates P-H (earthenware)
1875 Keates P-H (china and earthenware)
1876 Kelly CM; EM
1879 Keates P-H (china and earthenware)
1880 Kelly A; CM; EM
1882 Keates P-H (china and earthenware)
1884 Kelly CM; EM
1887 Porter EM-H
1888 Kelly CM; EM
1889 Keates P-H (china and ironstone earthenware)
1892 Keates P-H (china and ironstone earthenware)
1892 Kelly EM
1896 Kelly EM
1900 Kelly EM

The firm succeeded Morley & Ashworth (1863 Kelly). The proprietor is listed as J.S. Goddard in 1889 Keates and 1892 Keates. The advertisement in 1880 Kelly describes the firm as 'manufacturers of real ironstone-china, earthenware & ivory ware of every description'. It goes on to offer 'Mason's patent ironstone-china patterns and shapes' with 'samples and prices on application'. A London office is given as 13 & 14, Union Bank Buildings, Holborn Circus.

Geo. L. Ashworth & Bros.,
HANLEY, STAFFORDSHIRE POTTERIES,
MANUFACTURERS OF
Real Ironstone—China, Earthenware & Ivory Ware
OF EVERY DESCRIPTION.
MASON'S PATENT IRONSTONE—CHINA PATTERNS AND SHAPES.
SAMPLES AND PRICES ON APPLICATION.
LONDON OFFICES:—13 and 14, UNION BANK BUILDINGS, HOLBORN CIRCUS, E.C.

George L. Ashworth & Brothers. Advertisement from 1880 Kelly.

George L. Ashworth & Brothers. Printed mark from a blue-printed earthenware vegetable dish.

DIOMED
CASTING HIS SPEAR
AGAINST MARS

George L. Ashworth & Brothers. Impressed mark with printed pattern title from an earthenware jug.

George L. Ashworth & Brothers. Printed mark from a multicolour-printed dessert plate.

George L. Ashworth & Brothers. Printed mark from a colourful ironstone dinner plate which also bears an impressed maker's mark.

Ashworth, Taylor
Havelock Place, Shelton or Hanley
1861 Harrison NC-H-Sh (earthenware manufacturer)
See also: Old Hall Earthenware Co. Ltd.

Astbury, Richard
Lane Delph
1796 Chester NC-LE-LD-LL (manufacturer of earthenware)
1798 Universal NC-LD (manufacturer of Staffordshire-ware)

Austin & Co.

Richard Astbury. Impressed mark from a blue-painted earthenware dessert plate.

Canova Works, Stafford Street, Longton
1869 Keates A; P-L (parian)
1870 Harrod NC-L (parian manufacturers)
The advertisement in 1869 Keates describes the firm as 'manufacturers & decorators of superior parian jugs, vases, flower-holders, busts, figures, &c.'

CANOVA WORKS, STAFFORD ST., LONGTON
MESSRS. AUSTIN & Co.,
MANUFACTURERS & DECORATORS OF
SUPERIOR PARIAN JUGS, VASES,
FLOWER-HOLDERS, BUSTS, FIGURES, &c.

Austin & Co. Advertisement from 1869 Keates.

Ayland, Josiah Albert
Copeland Street, Stoke
1863 Kelly PM

Aynesley, John
See: Aynsley, John

Aynsley & Co.
(i) Market Place, Longton
1860 Kelly CM-White & Finished
1861 Harrison NC-L (china manufacturers)
(ii) Portland Works, Sutherland Road, Longton
1862 Slater CM
(iii) Chancery Lane & Sutherland Road, Longton
1876 Kelly EM

Aynsley, H., & Co.
(i) Commerce Street, Longton
1873 Keates A; P-L (earthenware)
1875 Keates P-L (earthenware)
1879 Keates A; P-L (earthenware)
1882 Keates P-L (earthenware)
1887 Porter EM-L
1889 Keates P-L (earthenware)
1892 Keates P-L (earthenware)
1892 Kelly EM
1896 Kelly EM
1900 Kelly EM
(ii) Chancery Lane, Longton
1880 Kelly EM (manufacturers for home & export)
1884 Kelly EM
1888 Kelly EM
The advertisements in 1873 Keates and 1879 Keates, and another in 1875 Keates, all describe the firm as 'manufacturers of lustre, black, drab, turquoise and printed wares, stone mortars, &c.'

H. AYNSLEY & Co.,
MANUFACTURERS OF
LUSTRE, BLACK, DRAB,
Torquoise and Printed Wares,
STONE MORTARS, &c.,
COMMERCE STREET, LONGTON
STAFFORDSHIRE.

H. Aynsley & Co. Advertisement from 1873 Keates. Similar advertisements appeared in 1875 Keates and 1879 Keates.

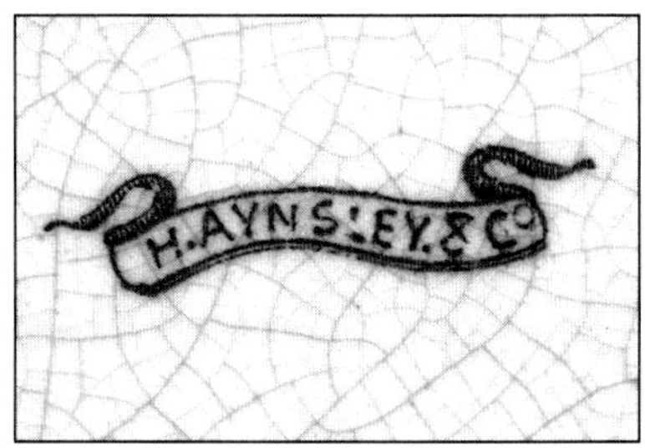

H. Aynsley & Co. Printed mark from a brown-printed and coloured plate commemorating the 1897 Diamond Jubilee.

Aynsley, John
(i) Lane End
1796 Chester NC-LE-LD-LL (manufacturer of earthenware)
1802 Allbut EM (map location 121)
(ii) Portland Works, Sutherland Road, Longton
1863 Kelly CM-General
1864 Jones CEM
1865 Keates P-L (china)
1867 Keates P-L (china)
1868 Kelly CM
1869 Keates P-L (china)
1870 Harrod NC-L (china manufacturer)
1873 Keates P-L (china)
1875 Keates P-L (china)
1876 Kelly CM

The potter's surname is listed as Aynesley in 1802 Allbut.

Aynsley, John, & Co.
Sutherland Road, Longton
1872 Kelly CM

Aynsley, John, & Son
Sutherland Road, Longton
1879 Keates P-L (china)
1888 Kelly CM

Aynsley, John, & Sons
Portland Works, Sutherland Road, Longton
1880 Kelly CM
1882 Keates P-L (china)
1884 Kelly CM
1889 Keates P-L (china)
1892 Keates P-L (china)
1892 Kelly CM
1896 Kelly CM
1900 Kelly CM

Aynsley, Cooper & Co.
Market Street, Longton
1856 Kelly CEM

B

Bacchus, William
Fenton
1781 Bailey NC (potter)
1783 Bailey NC (potter)
1784 Bailey NC-F (manufacturer of Queen's ware in all its various branches)

Bachhoffner, C.
See: Marsden Tile Co. Ltd.

Baddeley, Elizabeth (Mrs.)
(i) St. Martin's Lane, Longton
1864 Jones SC (Earthenware Rustic and Terra Cotta Figure Manufacturers)
(ii) 3 Commerce Street, Longton
1864 Jones SC (Earthenware Rustic and Terra Cotta Figure Manufacturers)
1865 Keates P-L (rustic & terra cotta)
1867 Keates P-L (rustic and terra cotta)
1868 Kelly TCM
1869 Keates P-L (rustic & terra cotta)
1870 Harrod NC-L (rustic and terra-cotta works)
1872 Kelly TCM (rustic)
1873 Keates P-L (rustic & terra cotta)
1875 Keates P-L (rustic & terra cotta)

Baddeley, James Henry
(i) Upper Hanley
1841 Pigot TOCM
(ii) East Wood Vale, Shelton
1861 Harrison NC-H-Sh (earthenware manufacturer)
(iii) Gloucester Street, Hanley
1862 Slater EM (rustic)
1863 Kelly CM-Horticultural & Rustic Ware
1864 Jones SC (Earthenware Rustic and Terra Cotta Figure Manufacturers)
1865 Keates P-H (rustic ware)
1867 Keates A; P-H (rustic ware)
(iv) 34 Barker Street, Longton
1869 Keates P-L (rustic and terra cotta)
1873 Keates P-L (rustic and terra cotta)
1875 Keates P-L (rustic and terra cotta)
The advertisement in 1867 Keates describes Baddeley as the 'original rustic ware manufacturer' and lists his products as 'tobacco jars, fern stands, garden seats and vases, mignonette stands, &c., &c.' Another advertisement in 1869 Keates describes him as 'the original rustic terra cotta manufacturer'.

J. H. BADDELEY,
ORIGINAL
Rustic Ware Manufacturer,
GLOUCESTER STREET, HANLEY.
Tobacco Jars, Fern Stands, Garden Seats and Vases, Mignonette Stands, &c., &c.

James Henry Baddeley. Advertisement from 1867 Keates.

JAMES HENRY BADDELEY,
THE ORIGINAL
Rustic Terra Cotta Manufacturer,
34, BARKER STREET,
LONGTON, STAFFORDSHIRE POTTERIES.

James Henry Baddeley. Advertisement from 1869 Keates.

Baddeley, John & Edward
Shelton
1784 Bailey NC-Sh (potters)
1796 Chester NC-H-Sh (manufacturers of earthenware)
1802 Allbut EM (map location 88)
1805 Holden NC (earthenware manufacturers)

Baddeley, Lucy (Mrs.)
(i) Drury Works, Normacott Road, Longton
1879 Keates P-L (rustic and terra cotta)
1880 Kelly MM
(ii) 4 Vauxhall Street, Longton
1880 Kelly MM

Baddeley, Lucy (Mrs.), & Co.
Drury Works, 5 Normacott Road, Longton
1882 Keates P-L (rustic & terra cotta)

Baddeley, Ralph
Shelton
1781 Bailey NC (potter)
1783 Bailey NC (potter)
1796 Chester NC-H-Sh (manufacturer of earthenware)

Baddeley, Ralph & John
Shelton
1798 Universal NC-Sh (manufacturers of Staffordshire-ware)
The potter's surname is listed as Badley in 1798 Universal.

Baddeley, Thomas
(i) Hill Street, Burslem
1800 Allbutt NC-B (toy manufacturer)
(ii) Slack Lane, Miles Bank, Hanley
1822 Allbut CEM (enameller & lusterer)
1822 Pigot EM
The potter's surname is listed as Badley in 1822 Pigot

Baddeley, W.
(i) Market Street, Longton
1854 Kelly TM
(ii) King Street, Longton
1856 Kelly TM

Baddeley, William
(i) Hanley
1802 Allbut EM (map location 85)

1809 Holden NC (Egyptian-black-manufacturer)
1811 Holden NC (Egyptian-black-manufacturer)
(ii) Shelton
1805 Holden NC (Egyptian black manufacturers)
(iii) Eastwood, Hanley
1818 Parson EM-H-Sh
1822 Allbut CEM (fancy and ornamental earthenware manufacturer)
1822 Pigot EM
(iv) Market Lane, Shelton
1841 Pigot EM (& toy)
(v) 3 Commerce Street, Longton
1860 Kelly P
1860 Kelly TM (stone)
1861 Harrison NC-L (tobacco pots, fancy pipes, &c., &c.)
1862 Slater EM (rustic)
1863 Kelly P
(vi) Drury Works, Normacott Road, Longton
1864 Jones SC (Earthenware Rustic and Terra Cotta Figure Manufacturers)
1865 Keates P-L (rustic and terra cotta)
1867 Keates P-L (rustic and terra cotta)
1869 Keates P-L (rustic and terra cotta)
1873 Keates P-L (rustic and terra cotta)
1875 Keates P-L (rustic and terra cotta)
(vii) High Street, Longton
1870 Harrod NC-L (rustic ware manufacturer)
The potter's surname is listed as Baddely in 1818 Parson.

Baddeley & Heath
Liverpool Road, Burslem
1876 Kelly EM (engravers)

Baddely, William
See: Baddeley, William

Badley, Ralph & John
See: Baddeley, Ralph & John

Badley, Thomas
See Baddeley, Thomas

Baggaley, Abraham
Golden Hill
1802 Allbut EM (map location 5)

Baggaley, Jacob
Hill Works, Liverpool Road, Burslem
1880 Kelly CM; EM
1882 Keates P-B (earthenware & china)
1884 Kelly CM; EM

Baggaley, Thomas
Tunstall
1796 Chester NC-T-Lp (manufacturer of earthenware)
1802 Allbut EM (map location 9)
See also: Baggeley, Thomas

Baggaley & Vodrey
Tunstall
1796 Chester NC-T-Lp (manufacturers of earthenware)

Baggearley & Ball
See: Baggerley & Ball

Baggeley, George
See: Baguley, George

Baggeley, Thomas
Lane Delph
1809 Holden NC (china-manufacturer)
1811 Holden NC (china-manufacturer)
1818 Parson EM-LE
1818 Pigot CM
The surname is listed as Baggaley in 1818 Parson and Bagley in 1818 Pigot.

Baggelley & Taylor
Lane Delph
1822 Pigot CM

Baggerley & Ball
High Street, Lane End
1828 Pigot CM
1830 Pigot CM
1834 White CM-LE-L
1835 Pigot CM
The first partner's name is listed as Baggearley in 1834 White and as Bagguley in 1835 Pigot.

Baggerley & Balls
High Street, Lane End
1822 Pigot CM

Bagguley & Ball
See: Baggerley & Ball

Bagley, Thomas
See: Baggeley, Thomas.

Baggerley & Ball. Printed mark from a blue-printed and coloured earthenware jug. Note that these initials could relate to other partnerships but are traditionally ascribed to Baggerley & Ball.

Bagley, William
Burslem
1784 Bailey NC-B (potter)

Bagnall, Sampson
(i) Hanley
1784 Bailey NC-H (potter)
(ii) Lane Delph
1796 Chester NC-LE-LD-LL (manufacturer of earthenware)
1798 Universal NC-LD (manufacturer of Staffordshire-ware)

Bagnall & Boon
Shelton
1796 Chester NC-H-Sh (manufacturers of earthenware)

Bagnall & Hull
Lane Delph
1802 Allbut EM (map location 108)

Bagshaw, Samuel
Basford, Newcastle
1818 Parson EM-N

Bagshaw & Alier
Burslem
1809 Holden NC (earthenware-manufacturers)

Bagshaw & Leigh
Burslem
1811 Holden NC (earthenware-manufacturers)

Bagshaw & Maier
Burslem
1802 Allbut EM (map location 46)
1805 Holden NC (earthenware manufacturers)
The partnership is listed as Bagshaw & Meir in 1805 Holden.

Bagshaw & Meir
See: Bagshaw & Maier.

Bagshaw, Taylor & Maier
Burslem
1796 Chester NC-B
(manufacturers of earthenware)

Bagster, John Denton
High Street, Hanley
1828 Pigot EM

John Denton Bagster. Printed mark from a hand-painted china dessert plate.

Baguley, George
(i) Wharf Lane, Shelton
1841 Pigot TOCM
(ii) High Street, Hanley
1850 Kelly NC-H
(manufacturer of parian marble figures)
1850 Slater TOCM (parian marble)
1851 White CETOM-H-Sh (parian)
1852 Slater A; PM; TOCM
1854 Kelly PM
(iii) Victoria Works, Broad Street, Hanley
1862 Slater CM (porcelain)
1863 Kelly CM-General
1864 Jones CEM
1865 Keates A; P-H (china)
1867 Keates P-H (china)
The surname is listed as Baggeley in 1851 White and the address as Upper Hanley in 1850 Slater. The advertisement in 1852 Slater refers to 'parian models and classical sculpture by George Baguley' and lists the wares as 'parian and stone jugs, vases, &c. in white or tinted bodies, unique in design and quality, for the home or foreign markets, as ice, molasses or hot water jugs, with Britannia metal covers, &c.' The advertisement in 1865 Keates describes Baguley as a 'manufacturer of porcelain in all its branches' and states that his predecessors were Lockett, Baguley & Cooper.

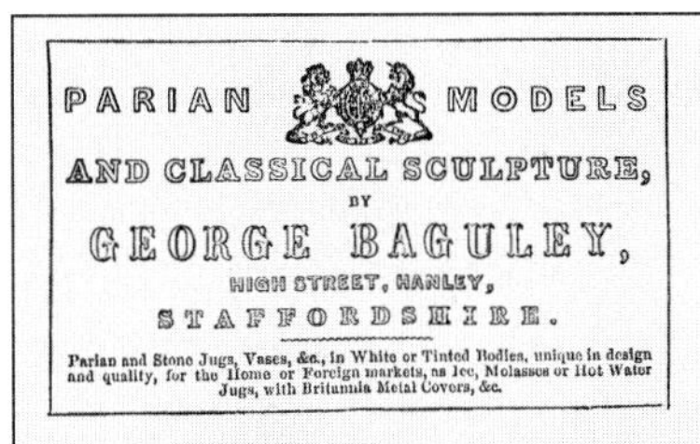

George Baguley. Advertisement from 1852 Slater.

G. BAGULEY,
(Late Locket, Baguley, and Cooper),
Manufacturer of Porcelain in all its Branches,
Victoria Works,
HANLEY, STAFFORDSHIRE.

George Baguley. Advertisement from 1865 Keates.

Bailey & Co. Advertisement from 1869 Keates.

Bailey & Co.
Brewery Street Works, Hope Street, Hanley
1870 Harrod NC-H
(manufacturers of parian statuettes, ornamental vases, china, stone, &c.)
An advertisement appears in 1869 Keates although there is no entry in the firm's name. It describes them as 'manufacturers of parian statuettes, ornamental vases, china, stone, etc.' London showrooms are listed at 12 Ely Place, Holborn, both in the advertisement and in 1870 Harrod. See also: Bailey, John, & Co.

Bailey, C.F.
See: Burslem Pottery Co.

Bailey, John
(i) Stafford Street, Longton
1851 White CEM-L
1852 Slater EM
1854 Kelly CEM
1856 Kelly CEM
(ii) 96 Bryan Street, Hanley
1860 Kelly PFM; PM
1862 Slater PM (& ornamental vase and statuary)
(iii) Hanley
1892 Keates P-H
1896 Kelly EM
The John Bailey at Stafford Street was previously a partner in Bailey & Batkin (1851 White), and his house is listed as Shooter's Hill in 1851 White and 1856 Kelly. The firm was succeeded by Wathen & Hudden (1860 Kelly). The Hanley address is listed as Bucknall Old Road in 1892 Keates but Bucknall New Road in 1896 Kelly.

Bailey, John, & Co.
(i) Elm Street, Hanley
1865 Keates P-H (parian)
(ii) Brewery Street, Hanley
1868 Kelly PM
1869 Keates A; P-H (parian manufacturers)
1870 Harrod NC-H (parian manufacturers)
The firm is noted as being in the hands of John Bailey's executors in 1869 Keates and 1870 Harrod. No advertisement appears in the firm's name in 1869 Keates and the cross-reference must relate to the advertisement in the name of Bailey & Co. (qv).

Bailey, L.
Penkhull, Stoke-upon-Trent
1860 Kelly P

Bailey, Robert
Swan Works, Elm Street, Hanley
1884 Kelly EM

Bailey, Robert, & Co.
Bryan Street, Hanley
1854 Kelly CEM

Bailey, William
Lane End
1816 Underhill P

Bailey, William & David
Flint Street, Lane End
1828 Pigot CM; EM
1830 Pigot CM; EM

William & David Bailey. Printed mark from a transfer-printed china saucer.

Bailey & Ball
Stafford Street, Longton
1846 Williams NC-L-LE (china and lustre manufacturers)
1850 Kelly NC-L (china & earthenware manfrs.); CEM
1850 Slater CM; EM
The partners are listed individually as John Bailey of Shooter's Hill and Joseph Ball in 1846 Williams

Bailey & Batkin
Flint Street, Lane End
1822 Allbut CEM (gilders and lusterers)
The first partner is identified as John Bailey in 1851 White.

Bailey & Bevington
Elm Street, Hanley
1867 Keates A; P-H (parian)
1869 Keates A; P-H (parian)
The advertisement in 1867 Keates describes the firm as 'manufacturers of parian statuettes, ornamental vases, china, stone, granite, &c.' and lists London showrooms at 19 Thavies Inn, Holborn. Despite the cross-reference, no advertisement could be located in 1869 Keates.

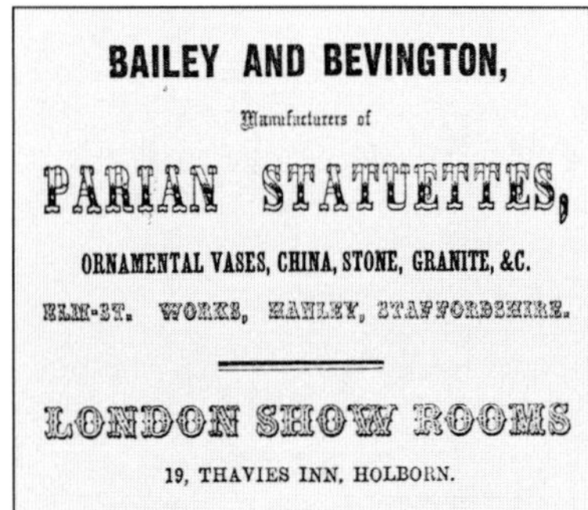
BAILEY AND BEVINGTON,
Manufacturers of
PARIAN STATUETTES,
ORNAMENTAL VASES, CHINA, STONE, GRANITE, &C.
ELM-ST. WORKS, HANLEY, STAFFORDSHIRE.
LONDON SHOW ROOMS
19, THAVIES INN, HOLBORN.

Bailey & Bevington. Advertisement from 1867 Keates.

Bailey & Cooper
London Road, Stoke
1900 Kelly EM

Bailey, Goodwin & Robey
High Street, Longton
1841 Pigot CM

Bailey, Hackney & Co.
King Street Works, Hanley
1889 Keates P-H

Bailey & Harvey
Flint Street, Longton
1834 White CM-LE-L (lustre mfrs.); EM-LE-L
1835 Pigot CM; EM
The partnership is listed as Baileys' & Harveys' in 1835 Pigot.

Bailey, Murrells & Co.
Elm Street Works, Market Street, Hanley
1863 Kelly MM
1864 Jones A; PM
The advertisement in 1864 Jones describes the firm as 'manufacturers of ornamental parian, statuettes, &c.' and lists a London office at 11 South Street, Finsbury Square.

BAILEY, MURRELLS, & Co.,
MANUFACTURERS OF
ORNAMENTAL PARIAN, STATUETTES, &c.
ELM STREET WORKS, MARKET STREET,
HANLEY, STAFFORDSHIRE.
LONDON HOUSE, 11, SOUTH STREET, FINSBURY SQUARE.

Bailey, Murrells & Co. Advertisement from 1864 Jones.

Bailey, Williams & Co.
Wellington Works, Newport Street, Burslem
1880 Kelly EM

Baileys' & Harveys'
See: Bailey & Harvey

Baker & Co.
(i) High Street, Fenton
1869 Keates P-F (earthenware)
1870 Harrod NC-F (earthenware manufacturers)
1872 Kelly EM
1873 Keates P-F (earthenware)
1875 Keates P-F (earthenware)
1876 Kelly EM
1879 Keates P-F (earthenware)
1880 Kelly EM
1882 Keates P-F (earthenware)
1884 Kelly EM
1888 Kelly EM
1889 Keates P-F (earthenware)
1892 Keates P-F (earthenware)
1892 Kelly EM
(ii) Fountain Square, Fenton
1887 Porter EM-F

Baker & Co. Ltd.
Fenton
1896 Kelly EM
1900 Kelly EM

Baker, Charles G.
Sylvester Pottery, Burslem
1875 Keates P-B (earthen.)

Baker, J.
Shelton Road, Stoke
1868 Kelly TCM

Baker, James
(i) Brewery Street, Hanley
1882 Keates P-H (earthenware)
(ii) Stoke Road, Shelton, Hanley
1887 Porter EM-H
1888 Kelly EM; JM; P; TCM
1889 Keates P-H (earthenware)
(iii) Kingsfield, Newcastle
1892 Kelly P
1896 Kelly P
1900 Kelly P

Baker, Samuel
Lower Lane
1802 Allbut EM (map locations 114 and 115)

Baker, William, & Co.
(i) High Street, Fenton
1841 Pigot EM
1850 Kelly CEM; NC-S (earthenware manufacturers)
1850 Slater CM; EM
1852 Slater CM; EM
1854 Kelly CEM
1856 Kelly CEM
1861 Harrison NC-F (earthenware manufactory)
1862 Slater EM
1863 Kelly EM
1864 Jones EM
1865 Keates P-F (earthenware)
1867 Keates P-F (earthenware)
1868 Kelly EM
(ii) Queen Street, Fenton
1851 White CEM-F (only earthenware)

Baker, William & George
Fenton
1846 Williams NC-C-F-E (earthenware manufacturers)

Baker & Chetwynd
Sylvester Pottery, Burslem
1870 Harrod NC-B (manufacturers of ironstone china, earthenware, &c., for foreign markets only)
1872 Kelly EM
1873 Keates P-B (earthenware)

Baker & Roycroft
Fountain Place Pottery, Burslem
1888 Kelly EM

Baker & Rycroft
Liverpool Road, Burslem
1887 Porter EM-B

Bale & Co.
Castle Field Pottery, off Newcastle Road, Hanley
1875 Keates P-H (porous and general earthenware)
1876 Kelly EM
1879 Keates P-H (porous & general earthenware)

Bale, Thomas S.
See: Ridgway, John, & Co.

Balfour & Co.
(i) Oldfield Terra Cotta Works, Lane End Works, Longton
1884 Kelly TCM
(ii) Lane End Works, Fenton Culvert
1888 Kelly SC (Encaustic Tile Manufacturers)

Ball, Charles
Burslem
1796 Chester NC-B (manufacturer of earthenware)

Ball, J., & Co.
Stoke Road, Shelton, Hanley
1892 Kelly EM

Ball, Joseph
See: Bailey and Ball

Ball, Joseph jun.
Anchor Road and 100 Caroline Street, Longton
1887 Porter EM-L

Ball, Richard
Burslem
1802 Allbut EM (map location 51)

Ball, William
Drury Works, Normacot Road, Longton
1889 Keates P-L

Ball & Baggaley
High Street, Lane End
1822 Allbut CEM (china manufacts.)

Bamford, John
Nelson Place, Hanley
1850 Slater TOCM
1851 White CETOM-H-Sh
1852 Slater TOCM
1854 Kelly CFM
1860 Kelly CFM
1861 Harrison NC-H-Sh (figure manufacturer)
1862 Slater TOCM
1864 Jones CFM
1865 Keates P-H (china and parian figure)
1867 Keates P-H (jug and figure)
1868 Kelly EM
1869 Keates P-H (jug & figure)
1870 Harrod NC-H (jug and figure manufacturer)
1872 Kelly EM
1873 Keates P-H (jug & figure)
1875 Keates P-H (jug and teapot)
1876 Kelly EM
1879 Keates P-H (jug & teapot)
1880 Kelly EM
Bamford's private residence is listed as Harley Street in 1870 Harrod.

Banks & Co.
Boston Works, High Street, Hanley
1887 Porter EM-H

Banks, E.
Boston Works, High Street, Hanley
1888 Kelly EM; MM

Banks, Edward
Broad Street Works, Hanley
1889 Keates P-H

Banks, Thomas
Copeland Street, Stoke
1862 Slater PM

Banks & Hodkinson
George Street, Hanley
1862 Slater PM

Banks & Thorley
(i) New Street, Hanley
1875 Keates P-H (majolica)
1876 Kelly PM
(ii) Boston Works, High Street, Hanley
1879 Keates P-H (majolica)
1880 Kelly EM; MM
1882 Keates P-H (majolica)
1884 Kelly EM; MM
An advertisement in 1882 Keates describes the firm as 'manufacturers of earthenware, porous goods, majolica, jet, & stone wares'. It lists London showrooms at 9 Bartlett's Buildings, Holborn Circus, with Edwin Fox as agent, and states that their predecessors were Davenport, Banks & Co.

BANKS & THORLEY
(LATE DAVENPORT, BANKS, & Co.),
Manufacturers of Earthenware,
POROUS GOODS, MAJOLICA, JET, & STONE WARES,
BOSTON WORKS, HIGH STREET, HANLEY.
London Show Rooms—9, Bartlett's Buildings, Holborn Circus.
Agent—EDWIN FOX.
4

Banks & Thorley. Advertisement from 1882 Keates.

Banner & Co.
Waterloo Road, Burslem
1900 Kelly SC (Sanitary Ware Manufacturers)

Barber, Joseph
Albert Street, Burslem
1887 Porter EM-B
1888 Kelly JM; RM
1889 Keates P-B (Rockingham and jet manufacturer)
1892 Kelly JRM
1896 Kelly JRM
1900 Kelly JRM

Barcroft, J.
Parliament Row, Hanley
1854 Kelly TM

Barker Brothers
(i) Gold Street, Longton
1876 Kelly EM
1879 Keates P-L (earthenware)
1880 Kelly EM
(ii) Barker Street, off High Street,

Longton
1882 Keates P-L (earthenware)
1884 Kelly EM
1888 Kelly EM
1889 Keates P-L (earthenware)
1892 Keates P-L (earthenware)
1892 Kelly EM
1896 Kelly EM
1900 Kelly EM
(iii) Meir Works, High Street, Longton
1887 Porter EM-L

Barker & Co.
Market Street, Burslem
1822 Allbut CEM
(earthenware manufacts.)

Barker, Charles
(i) Brook Street, Shelton
1822 Allbut CEM (lusterer and enameller)
(ii) Lower Lichfield Street, Hanley
1869 Keates P-H (parian)
1870 Harrod NC-H (parian manufacturer)

Barker, George
See: Cyples & Barker.

Barker, Henry K.
Fenton
1900 Kelly EM

Barker, John
(i) Lane End
1784 Bailey NC-LE
(manufacturer of cream coloured, china glaze, and blue wares)
(ii) Stoke
1839 Cottrill NC-S (potter)

Barker, John & James
Lane End
1811 Holden NC (earthenware-manufactory)
An Oxford office at Ship Lane is listed in 1811 Holden.

Barker, John & Joseph
High Street, Lane End
1822 Allbut CEM
(earthenware, shining black manufacturers, lusterers, and enamellers)
1822 Pigot EM
1828 Pigot CM; EM

Barker, Joseph
(i) Lane End
1798 Universal NC-LE
(manufacturer of Staffordshire-ware)
(ii) Stafford Street, Longton
1860 Kelly CM-General; PM
1861 Harrison NC-L (china and earthenware manufacturer)

Barker, Joseph & John
High Street, Lane End
1830 Pigot CM; EM

Barker, Richard
(i) Lane End
1784 Bailey NC-LE (potter)
1796 Chester NC-LE-LD-LL
(manufacturer of earthenware)
1798 Universal NC-LE
(manufacturer of Staffordshire-ware)
1802 Allbut EM (map location 126)
1805 Holden NC (earthenware manufacturer)
(ii) Flint Street, Lane End
1822 Allbut CEM
(earthenware manufact.)
1834 White EM-LE-L (lustre)
1835 Pigot EM

Richard Barker. Impressed mark from a blue-printed earthenware dessert plate.

Barker, Richard, John, & James
(i) Lane End
1809 Holden NC (earthenware-manufactory)
1816 Underhill P
(ii) Flint Street, Lane End
1818 Parson EM-LE
An Oxford office at Ship Lane is listed in 1809 Holden.

Barker, Samuel
Lane Delph
1796 Chester NC-LE-LD-LL
(manufacturer of earthenware)
1798 Universal NC-LD
(manufacturer of Staffordshire-ware)

Barker, T.
Stafford Street, Longton
1854 Kelly CEM (gilder)

Barker, Thomas
(i) Lane Delph
1781 Bailey NC (potter)
1783 Bailey NC (potter)
(ii) Lane End
1798 Universal NC-LE
(manufacturer of Staffordshire-ware)
(iii) Flint Street, Longton
1834 White CM-LE-L
(enamelled and burnished gold)

Barker, William
(i) Lane End
1784 Bailey NC-LE (potter)
(ii) Fenton
1818 Pigot CM
See also: Barker & Till
See also: Yale, Barker & Hall

William Barker & Son. Printed mark from a blue-printed earthenware soup plate.

Barker, William, & Son
(i) Sytch, Burslem
1851 White CEM-B (only earthenware)
(ii) Hill Works, Liverpool Road, Burslem
1851 White CEM-B (only earthenware)
1854 Kelly CEM
1856 Kelly CEM

Barker, W.S.
Sylvester Square, Burslem
1860 Kelly EM

Barker, William Thomas
Sylvester Square, Burslem
1860 Kelly CM-General
1861 Harrison NC-B (china decorator)

Barker, Batty & Read
Lane Delph, Fenton
1892 Keates P-F (earthenware)

1892 Kelly EM
1896 Kelly EM

Barker & Hall
Viaduct Works, Caroline Street, Longton
1852 Slater EM
1854 Kelly CEM

Barker & Hill
(i) Caroline Street, Longton
1856 Kelly CEM
(ii) King Street, Longton
1864 Jones CEM
1868 Kelly CM
1869 Keates P-L (china)
1870 Harrod NC-L (china and earthenware manufacturers, and merchants)
1872 Kelly CM
1873 Keates P-L (china)
1882 Keates P-L (china)
(iii) Stafford Street, Longton
1868 Kelly CM

Barker & Kent
King Street, Fenton
1889 Keates P-F (earthenware)

Barker, Sutton & Till
(i) High Street, Burslem
1830 Pigot EM
(ii) Sytch Pottery, Liverpool Road, Burslem
1834 White EM-B
1835 Pigot EM
1841 Pigot EM
The first partner's surname is listed as Barton in 1835 Pigot.

Barker & Till
Sytch Pottery, Burslem
1846 Williams NC-B (earthenware manufacturers)
1850 Kelly NC-B (manufacturers of earthenware); CEM
1850 Slater EM
The partners are listed individually as William Barker and Thomas Till in 1846 Williams.

Barkers & Kent
Foley Potteries, King Street, Fenton
1892 Keates P-F (earthenware)
1892 Kelly EM
1896 Kelly EM

Barkers & Kent Ltd.
Foley Potteries, Fenton
1900 Kelly EM

Barlow & Co.
Church Street Works, Longton
1887 Porter EM-L

Barlow & Son
Commerce Street, Longton
1888 Kelly EM
1892 Kelly EM

Barlow, Albert B.
Market Street, Longton
1879 Keates P-L (china)

Barlow, Alfred
Cyples' Old Pottery, Market Street, Longton
1876 Kelly CM

Barlow, Charles
(i) Lower Mollart Street, Hanley
1880 Kelly CM; EM (manufacturer of china & earthenware)
1889 Keates P-H (china and earthenware decorator and dealer)
1892 Keates P-H (china & earthenware decorator and dealer)
(ii) Smithfield Works, Hanley
1887 Porter EM-H

Barlow, James
Miles Bank, Hanley
1828 Pigot CM

Barlow, James, & Co.
Slack Lane, Miles Bank, Hanley
1822 Allbut CEM (china manufacts.)
1830 Pigot CM
1834 White CM-H-Sh
1835 Pigot CM

Barlow, Thomas
Cyples' Old Pottery, Market Street, Longton
1850 Kelly NC-L (Egyptian black & china manfr.)
1850 Slater CM (and of lustered Egyptian black); EM (and of lustered Egyptian black)
1851 White CEM-L
1852 Slater CM (and of lustered Egyptian black); EM (and of lustered Egyptian black)
1854 Kelly CEM
1856 Kelly CEM
1860 Kelly CM-General
1861 Harrison NC-L (china manufacturer)
1862 Slater CM
1863 Kelly CM-General
1864 Jones CEM
1865 Keates P-L (china)
1867 Keates P-L (china)
1868 Kelly CM
1869 Keates P-L (china)
1870 Harrod NC-L (china manufacturers)
1872 Kelly CM
1873 Keates P-L (china)
1875 Keates P-L (china)
1880 Kelly CM
Thomas Barlow succeeded Cyples & Co. (1850 Slater, 1852 Slater, 1854 Kelly). The firm is noted as being in the hands of executors in 1870 Harrod. A London office at 10 Dyers' Buildings, Holborn is listed in 1880 Kelly. An advertisement in 1861 Harrison describes Barlow simply as a 'china manufacturer'.

THOMAS BARLOW,
CHINA MANUFACTURER,
CYPLE'S OLD POTTERY
LONGTON,
STAFFORDSHIRE.

Thomas Barlow. Advertisement from 1861 Harrison.

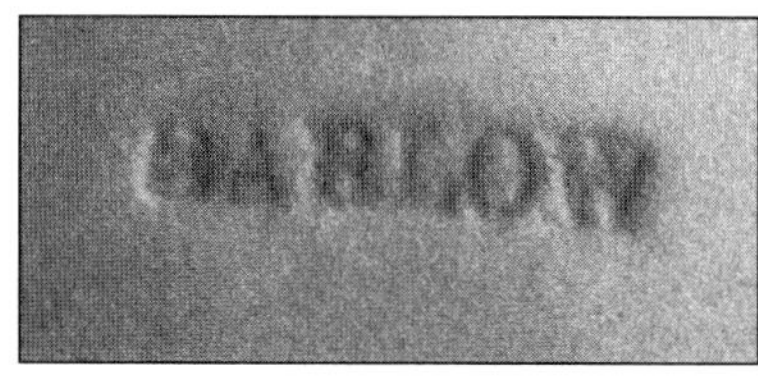

Thomas Barlow. Impressed mark from a china plate.

Barlow, Thomas Waterhouse
(i) Queen Street, Fenton
1851 White CEM-F (only earthenware)
(ii) Coronation Works, Commerce Street, Longton
1860 Kelly EM
1861 Harrison NC-L (earthenware manufacturer)
1862 Slater EM
1863 Kelly CM-General; EM
1864 Jones EM
1865 Keates P-L (earthenware)
1867 Keates P-L (earthenware)
1868 Kelly EM
1869 Keates P-L (earthen.)
1870 Harrod NC-L (earthenware manufacturer)

1872 Kelly EM
1873 Keates P-L (earthen.)
1875 Keates P-L (earthen.)
1876 Kelly EM
1879 Keates P-L (earthen.)
1880 Kelly EM

Barlow, Thomas W., & Son
Coronation Works, Commerce Street, Longton
1882 Keates P-L (earthenware)
1884 Kelly EM
1887 Porter EM-L
1889 Keates P-L (earthenware)
1892 Keates P-L (earthenware)
1896 Kelly EM
1900 Kelly EM

Barlow & Ford
Bridge Street, Lane End
1818 Pigot EM
1822 Allbut CEM (earthenware manufacts.)
1822 Pigot EM
1828 Pigot EM

Barnes, George
(i) Lane End
1802 Allbut EM (map location 137)
(ii) Hog's Lane, Lane End
1822 Allbut CEM (Egyptian black manufact.)

Barnes, George & William
Lane End
1805 Holden NC (earthenware manufacturer)

Barnett, William
17 Dimsdale Street, Burslem
1887 Porter EM-B (potters' manager)

Barrow & Co.
Market Street, Fenton
1852 Slater CM
1854 Kelly CEM
1856 Kelly CEM

Barton, Alexander
Bagnall, Longton
1841 Pigot TOCM

Barton, Sutton & Till
See: Barker, Sutton & Till.

Basford, James Powell
Dalehall, Burslem
1873 Keates SC-B (Encaustic and Geometric Tile Pavement Manufacturers); SC-B (Tile - Floor - Makers)
1875 Keates SC-B (Encaustic and Geometric Tile Pavement Manufacturers); SC-B (Floor Tile Works); SC-B (Tile - Floor - Makers)
1879 Keates SC-B (Encaustic and Geometric Tile Pavement Manufacturers); SC-B (Floor Tile Works); SC-B (Tile - Floor - Makers)
1882 Keates SC-B (Floor Tile Works)

Basford Brothers
Dalehall, Burslem
1873 Keates SC-B (Floor Tile Works)

Basford & Brothers
Dalehall, Burslem
1869 Keates SC-B (Tile - Floor - Makers)

Bates & Son
Albert Works, High Street, Longton
1892 Keates P-L (china)

Bates, Frederick
Weston Coyney, Longton
1869 Keates P-L (flower pots, &c.)
1873 Keates P-L (flower pots, &c.)
1875 Keates P-L (flower pots, &c.)

Bates, Thomas
Sutherland Road, Longton
1892 Kelly CM
See also: Waine & Bates

Bates, Thomas, & Son
Albert Works, High Street, Longton
1892 Kelly CM

Bates & Bennett
Sneyd Street, Cobridge, Burslem
1868 Kelly EM
1869 Keates P-B
1870 Harrod NC-B (earthenware manufacturers)
1872 Kelly EM
1873 Keates P-B
1875 Keates P-B
1876 Kelly EM
1879 Keates P-B (earthenware)
1880 Kelly EM
1882 Keates P-B (earthenware)
1884 Kelly EM
1887 Porter EM-B
1888 Kelly EM
1889 Keates P-B (earthenware)

Bates, Brown-Westhead & Moore
Cauldon Place, Hanley
1860 Kelly CM-General; EM; SC (Porcelain Statuary Manufacturers); SC (Sanitary Vessel Manufacturers)
1861 Harrison NC-H-Sh (earthenware manufacturers)
The partnership is listed as Bates, Brown, Westhead & Moore in both directories. A London office at 107 Hatton Garden is listed in 1860 Kelly.

Bates, Dewsberry & Co.
Mayer Street, Hanley
1896 Kelly SC (Encaustic Tile Manufacturers)
1900 Kelly SC (Encaustic Tile Manufacturers)

Bates, Elliot & Co.
Dale Hall, Burslem
1870 Harrod NC-B (manufacturers of earthenware for home and foreign markets, consisting of dinner, tea, toilet, and dessert ware, punchbowls, sanitary, photographic, druggist, electrical, galvanic, and perfumery ware, porcelain slates, artists' ware, sign-board letters, jet ware, &c.)
1872 Kelly EM
1873 Keates P-B (earthenware)
1875 Keates P-B (earthenware)
The second partner's surname is listed as Elliott in 1870 Harrod and 1873 Keates.

Bates, Gildea & Walker
Dale Hall, Burslem
1879 Keates P-B (earthenware)
1880 Kelly EM
A London office at 30 Holborn is listed in 1879 Keates.

Bates, Walker & Co.
Dale Hall, Burslem
1876 Kelly EM

Bath, William
Queen Street, Burslem
1834 White EM-B (coarse)

Bathwell, T. & E.
Chapel Bank, Burslem
1818 Parson EM-B-Lp-C

Bathwell, Thomas
Burslem
1816 Underhill P

Bathwell, Thomas, & Co.
Red Lion Square, Burslem
1818 Pigot EM

Bathwell, William & Thomas
Burslem
1805 Holden NC (earthenware manufacturers)
1811 Holden NC (earthenware-manufacturers)
1809 Holden NC (earthenware-manufacturers)

Bathwell & Goodfellow
Tunstall
1822 Allbut CEM (earthenware manufacts.)
1822 Pigot EM

Bathwell & Goodfellow. Impressed mark from a blue-printed earthenware plate.

Batkin, Dale & Deakin
Waterloo Place, Lane End
1822 Allbut CEM (earthenware manufacts.)
1822 Pigot EM

Batkin & Deakin
Waterloo, Flint Street, Lane End
1818 Parson EM-LE

Batkin, Thomas & Deakin
Waterloo Place, Lane End
1818 Pigot EM

Batkin, Walker & Broadhurst
Church Street, Longton
1841 Pigot EM

Baudelet, A.
Clayton Street, Longton
1892 Kelly EM (artistic)

Baxter, Rowley & Tams
High Street, Longton
1882 Keates P-L (china)
1884 Kelly CM

Bayley, William
Sheaf Works, Normacott Road, Longton
1882 Keates P-L (majolica)

Beach & Adams
See: Beech & Adams

Beach, James
See: Beech, James

Beard, Arthur
Pittshill, Tunstall
1887 Porter EM-T

Beardmer & Carr
See: Beardmore & Carr.

Beardmore, Henry
High Street, Longton
1846 Williams NC-L-LE (china manufacturer)

Beardmore, Sampson
Old Established Pottery, 17 High Street, Longton
1846 Williams NC-L-LE (earthenware manufacturer)
Beardmore was succeeded by George Townsend (1850 Slater, 1852 Slater).

Beardmore, Thomas
Coronation Works, Heathcote Road, Longton
1864 Jones A; EM
1865 Keates P-L (earthenware)
The advertisement in 1864 Jones describes Beardmore as a 'manufacturer of all kinds of earthenware, coloured bodies, &c.'

THOMAS BEARDMORE,
HEATHCOTE ROAD,
LONGTON, STAFFORDSHIRE.
MANUFACTURER OF ALL KINDS OF
EARTHENWARE,
COLOURED BODIES, &c.

Thomas Beardmore. Advertisement from 1864 Jones.

Beardmore & Birks
High Street, Longton
1834 White EM-LE-L
1835 Pigot EM
1841 Pigot EM

Beardmore, Birks & Blood
High Street, Longton
1851 White CEM-L
1852 Slater CM; EM
1854 Kelly CEM

Beardmore & Carr
High Street, Lane End
1818 Parson EM-LE
1818 Pigot EM
1822 Allbut CEM (earthenware manufacts.)
1822 Pigot EM
The first partner's name is listed as Beardmer in 1818 and 1822 Pigot.

Beardmore & Dawson
Commerce Street, Longton
1863 Kelly EM

Bebbington, J.
New Street, Hanley
1868 Kelly MM; SM

Beck, Blair & Co.
Beaconsfield Pottery, Anchor Road, Longton
1879 Keates P-L (china)

Becket, Robert
Lane End
1805 Holden NC (earthenware manufacturer)

Bednall & Heath
(i) Tinker's Clough, Hanley
1879 Keates P-H (earthenware)
1880 Kelly EM
1882 Keates P-H (earthenware)
(ii) Wellington Pottery, Nelson Place or Commercial Road, Hanley
1884 Kelly EM
1887 Porter EM-H
1888 Kelly EM
1889 Keates P-H (earthenware)
1892 Keates P-H (earthenware)
1892 Kelly EM
1896 Kelly EM
1900 Kelly EM

Bedson & Rhodes
Burslem
1796 Chester NC-B
(manufacturers of earthenware)

Beech & Son
Sutherland Road, Longton
1887 Porter EM-L

Beech, Frederick, & Co.
Lincoln Works, Sneyd Green, Burslem
1882 Keates P-B (earthenware)
1889 Keates P-B (earthenware)

Beech, James
(i) St. John's Street, Burslem
1818 Pigot EM
(ii) Sandyford, Tunstall
1834 White EM-T
1841 Pigot EM
(iii) Liverpool Road, Tunstall
1835 Pigot EM
(iv) High Street, Longton
1850 Kelly CEM; NC-L (china manufacturer)
1852 Slater CM
1854 Kelly CEM
1856 Kelly CEM
(v) Queen Street, Burslem
1865 Keates P-B (china and parian toy and fancy)
(vi) Swan Bank, High Street, Tunstall
1880 Kelly EM
1882 Keates P-T (earthenware)
1884 Kelly EM
1887 Porter EM-T
1888 Kelly EM
The surname is listed as Beach in 1887 Porter.

James Beech. Printed mark from brown-printed earthenware dinner wares.

Beech, James, & Son
(i) Albert & Sutherland Works, High Street, Longton
1860 Kelly CM-Tea, Breakfast & Dessert Services; COM; SC (China Porcelain Manufacturers); SC (Jug Manufacturers)
1861 Harrison NC-L (china manufacturers)
1863 Kelly CM-General; CM-Tea, Breakfast, and Dessert Services; COM; SC (China Porcelain Manufacturers); SC (Jug Manufacturers)
1870 Harrod NC-L (china manufacturers for home and foreign markets)
(ii) High Street, Longton
1862 Slater CM
1864 Jones CEM
1865 Keates P-L (china)
1867 Keates P-L (china)
1869 Keates P-L (china)
1873 Keates P-L (china)
1875 Keates P-L (china)
(iii) Sutherland Road, Longton
1869 Keates P-L (china)
1873 Keates P-L (china)
1875 Keates P-L (china)
1879 Keates P-L (china)
1880 Kelly CM
(manufacturers for home & export of superior china in tea, breakfast, dessert services &c.; also flint stone & potters' colour grinders)
1882 Keates P-L (china)
1889 Keates P-L (china)
1892 Keates P-L (china)
(iv) Albert Mills, Longton
1880 Kelly CM
(manufacturers for home & export of superior china in tea, breakfast, dessert services &c.; also flint stone & potters' colour grinders)
The proprietor is listed as Stephen Mear in 1879 Keates and 1882 Keates.

Beech, James, & Sons
(i) Albert & Sutherland Works, Longton
1868 Kelly CM; COM; SC (China Porcelain Manufacturers); SC (Jug Manufacturers)
1872 Kelly CM
1876 Kelly CM
(ii) Albert Works, Sutherland Road, Longton
1884 Kelly CM
1888 Kelly CM
1892 Kelly CM

Beech, Jane (Mrs.)
Bell Works, Queen Street, Burslem
1867 Keates P-B (toy and fancy)
1870 Harrod NC-B
(manufacturer of water-closets, china, and earthenware, toys, &c.)
1868 Kelly CFM
1869 Keates P-B (earthen.)
1872 Kelly CFM
1873 Keates P-B (earthen.)

Beech, Thomas
Brunswick Street, Shelton
1834 White CETM-H-Sh

Beech, William
(i) Bell Works, Queen Street, Burslem
1841 Pigot TOCM
1846 Williams NC-B (china manufacturer)
1850 Kelly CEM; NC-B (china manufacturer)
1850 Slater TOCM
1851 White CETM-B
1856 Kelly CEM
1860 Kelly CM-General
1861 Harrison NC-B (earthenware manufacturer)
1862 Slater TOCM
1863 Kelly CM-General; PM
1864 Jones A; CEM; PM
(ii) Waterloo Road, Burslem
1846 Williams NC-B (china figure manufacturer)
1850 Kelly NC-B (china figure manufacturer)
1851 White CETM-B
(iii) Albert Street, Burslem
1869 Keates P-B (earthenware)
The advertisement in 1864 Jones describes Beech as a 'parian & ornamental china manufacturer' and promises 'export orders promptly executed'.

WILLIAM BEECH,
PARIAN & ORNAMENTAL CHINA
MANUFACTURER,
QUEEN STREET, BURSLEM,
Staffordshire Potteries.
EXPORT ORDERS PROMPTLY EXECUTED.

William Beech. Advertisement from 1864 Jones.

Beech & Adams
John Street, Stoke
1889 Keates P-S (art and

general, home and export)
1892 Kelly SC (Art Pottery Manufacturers)
The first partner's name is listed as Beach in 1892 Kelly.

Beech & Brock
Bell Works, Queen Street, Burslem
1852 Slater CM (ornamental); TOCM
1854 Kelly PM (Ornamental Figure Makers)

Beech, Cooper, Sill & Co.
See: Beech, Cooper, Till & Co.

Beech, Cooper, Till & Co.
New Street, Longton
1872 Kelly EM
1873 Keates P-L (china and earthenware)
The third partner's name is listed as Sill in 1872 Kelly.

Beech & Goodall
Sylvester Pottery, Burslem
1892 Keates P-B (jet)

Beech & Hancock
(i) Church Bank, Tunstall
1860 Kelly EM
1861 Harrison NC-T (earthenware manufacturers)
(ii) Swan Pottery, Swan Bank, High Street, Tunstall
1862 Slater EM
1863 Kelly EM
1864 Jones EM
1865 Keates P-T (earthenware)
1867 Keates P-T (earthenware)
1868 Kelly EM
1869 Keates P-T
1870 Harrod NC-T (earthenware manufacturers)
1872 Kelly EM
1873 Keates P-T (earthenware)
1875 Keates P-T (earthenware)
1876 Kelly EM
The potters' residence is listed as Wolstanton in 1869 Keates and 1873 Keates.

Beech, Hancock & Co.
Swan Bank, Burslem
1851 White NC-B (earthenware manufacturers)
1852 Slater EM
1854 Kelly CEM
1856 Kelly CEM

Beech, Hancock & Co. Printed mark from a relief-moulded stoneware jug.

Beech & Morgan
Waterloo Works, Hanley
1880 Kelly EM

Beech & Podmore
(i) Bell Works, Queen Street, Burslem
1875 Keates P-B (figure and toy)
(ii) Wellington Street, Cobridge
1876 Kelly CM
1880 Kelly CM

Beech, Unwin & Co.
Green Dock Works, New Street, Longton
1870 Harrod NC-L (manufacturers of ornamental earthenware, stone bodies, &c., suitable for home and foreign markets)

Bell & Co.
Stoke Road, Hanley
1892 Keates P-H

Bell, Richard
Market Street, Longton
1862 Slater CM

Bell, Sarah
Stoke
1784 Bailey NC-S (potter)

Bell & Wolfe
Stoke
1781 Bailey NC (potters)
1783 Bailey NC (potters)

Bennett, George, & Co.
Victoria Works, Lonsdale Street, Stoke
1896 Kelly EM
1900 Kelly EM
The address is listed as Longsdale Street in 1896 Kelly.

Bennett, J.
Rectory Road, Hanley
1887 Porter EM-H

Bennett, John
Sneyd Pottery, Albert Street, Burslem
1863 Kelly EM
1864 Jones SC (Earthenware Rustic and Terra Cotta Figure Manufacturers)

Bennett, John, & Co.
Pelham Street, Hanley
1896 Kelly EM
1900 Kelly EM

Bennett, Joseph
Wharf Lane, Sheaf Street, Hanley
1873 Keates P-H (earthenware)
1875 Keates P-H (earthenware)
1876 Kelly EM
1879 Keates P-H (earthenware)
1880 Kelly EM
1882 Keates P-H (earthenware)
1884 Kelly EM
1888 Kelly EM

Bennett, Joseph, & Co.
Queen Street, Burslem
1822 Pigot EM

Bennett, William
(i) Broad Street, Shelton
1841 Pigot TOCM
(ii) Sneyd Potteries, Albert Street, Burslem
1867 Keates P-B (earthenware)
1870 Harrod NC-B (earthenware manufacturer)
(iii) Brook Street, Hanley
1876 Kelly EM
1879 Keates P-H (granite)
(iv) Cleveland Works, Victoria Road, Hanley
1882 Keates P-H (granite)
1884 Kelly EM
1887 Porter EM-H
1888 Kelly EM
1889 Keates P-H (earthenware)
1892 Keates P-H (earthenware)
1892 Kelly EM
1896 Kelly EM
1900 Kelly EM
Bennett's private residence is listed as

Podmore Street, Burslem in 1870 Harrod.

Bennett, William, & Co.
Burslem
1816 Underhill P

Bennett, Hurd & Co.
Eagle Pottery, Nile Street, Burslem
1865 Keates P-B (earthenware)

Bennett & Rathbone
Wharf Lane, Hanley
1867 Keates P-H (earthenware)
1869 Keates P-H (earthenware)
1870 Harrod NC-H (earthenware manufacturers)

Bennion & Co.
Swan Works, High Street, Stoke
1892 Keates P-S (earthenware)

Bennion, George
Albert Works, High Street, Longton
1889 Keates P-L (china & earthenware)

Bennison & Co.
High Street, Stoke
1892 Kelly EM

Bennison, Arthur
Lichfield Street, Hanley
1875 Keates P-H (Rockingham ware)

Benson, Bailey
See: Benson & Bailey

Benson & Bailey
(i) Normacott Road, Longton
1884 Kelly MM
(ii) Moorland Road, Burslem
1887 Porter EM-B
1888 Kelly EM; JM; MM
1892 Kelly JRM; MM
The firm is listed as Benson, Bailey in 1888 Kelly.

Bentley, Noah
55 Bryan Street, Hanley
1865 Keates P-H (parian)
1867 Keates P-H (parian)

Bentley, Thomas, & Co.
Church Street, Longton
1862 Slater CM
1863 Kelly CM-General
1864 Jones A; CEM
1865 Keates P-L (china)
1867 Keates P-L (china)
1868 Kelly CM
1869 Keates A; P-L (china)
1870 Harrod A; NC-L (china manufacturers for home and foreign markets)
1872 Kelly CM
1873 Keates P-L (china)
The advertisements in 1864 Jones and 1870 Harrod both describe the firm as 'manufacturers of china breakfast, dessert, and tea services', but in 1869 Keates they are simply 'china manufacturers'. All three advertisements state that their predecessors were Hilditch & Co.

THOS. BENTLEY & CO.,
(LATE HILDITCH AND CO.,)
MANUFACTURERS OF
China Breakfast, Dessert, and Tea Services,
CHURCH STREET, LONGTON,
STAFFORDSHIRE POTTERIES.

Thomas Bentley & Co. Advertisement from 1864 Jones.

THOMAS BENTLEY & Co.,
(LATE HILDITCH & Co.)
CHINA MANUFACTURERS,
CHURCH STREET, LONGTON,
STAFFORDSHIRE POTTERIES.

Thomas Bentley & Co. Advertisement from 1869 Keates.

THOMAS BENTLEY & CO.,
LATE HILDITCH & CO.,
MANUFACTURERS OF
CHINA BREAKFAST, DESSERT AND TEA SERVICES.
CHURCH STREET, LONGTON.
STAFFORDSHIRE POTTERIES.

Thomas Bentley & Co. Advertisement from 1870 Harrod.

Bentley & Copestake
Chancery Lane, Longton
1879 Keates A; P-L (china)
1880 Kelly CM
The advertisement in 1879 Keates describes the firm as 'china manufacturers for home and export'.

BENTLEY & COPESTAKE,
CHINA MANUFACTURERS
FOR HOME AND EXPORT,
CHANCERY LANE WORKS,
CHANCERY LANE,
LONGTON.

Bentley & Copestake. Advertisement from 1879 Keates.

Bentley, Lewis & Co.
Albion Street Longton
1892 Kelly EM

Bentley, Powis & Co.
William Street Works, Hanley
1887 Porter EM-H

Benton & Critchley
Style Works, Trent Walk, Hanley
1887 Porter EM-H

Beresford, T.
Heron Street, Fenton
1892 Keates P-F (china)

Berks, J. & W.
See: Birks, J. & W.

Berrisford, W., & Co.
Hanover Street, Hanley
1860 Kelly PM

Best & Varcoe
Nelson Place, Hanley
1865 Keates P-H (china & parian)

Bestwick, John
Gold Street, Longton
1900 Kelly EM

Beswick, James Wright
(i) Baltimore Works, Albion Street, Longton
1896 Kelly MM
1896 Kelly EM (specialities, figures, majolica, decorated toilet &c.)
(ii) High Street, Longton
1900 Kelly EM

Beswick, Robert
(i) Church Bank, Tunstall
1841 Pigot EM
1846 Williams NC-T
(earthenware manufacturer, coal owner, builder, &c.)
(ii) High Street, Tunstall
1850 Slater EM
1851 White EM-T
1852 Slater EM
1854 Kelly CEM
1856 Kelly CEM
Beswick's house is listed as Watergate Street in 1851 White.

Bettaney, George
See: Bettany, George

Bettaney, William
See: Bettany, William

Bettany, George
High Street, Lane End
1822 Allbut CEM (lusterer, &c.)
1828 Pigot CM
1830 Pigot CM; EM
The surname is listed as Bettaney in 1822 Allbut

Bettany, Thomas
See: Betteney, Thomas

Bettany, William
41 Hope Street, Hanley
1882 Keates P-H (china and earthenware)
1889 Keates P-H (china and earthenware)
1892 Keates P-H (china & earthenware)
The surname is listed as Bettaney in 1892 Keates

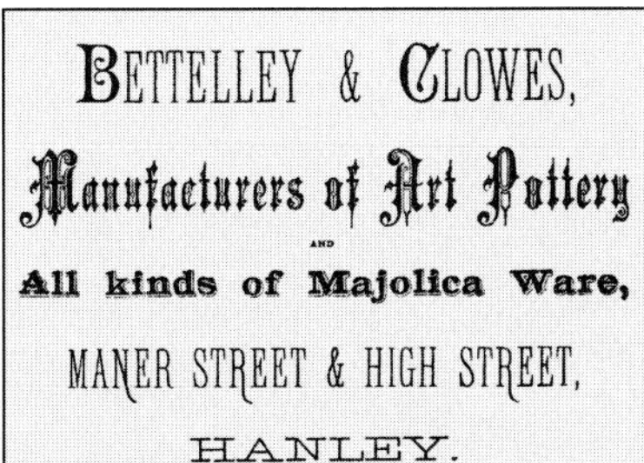

Bettelley & Clowes. Advertisement from 1887 Porter.

Betteley & Clowes
Mayer Street, Hanley
1887 Porter EM-H
An advertisement printed twice in 1887 Porter gives the firm's name as Bettelley & Clowes and describes them as 'manufacturers of art pottery and all kinds of majolica ware'. It also gives their address as Mayer Street and High Street, Hanley.

Bettelley, Joseph
Union Street, Hanley
1880 Kelly EM

Betteney, John, & Co.
Batavia Works, Stafford Street, Longton
1872 Kelly CM

Betteney, Thomas
Crown Works, Stafford Street, Longton
1860 Kelly CM-General
1861 Harrison NC-L (china manufacturer)
1862 Slater CM
1863 Kelly CM-General; CM-Tea, Breakfast, and Dessert Services; CM-White & Finished; SC (Jug Manufacturers)
1864 Jones CEM
1865 Keates P-L (china)
1867 Keates P-L (china)
1868 Kelly CM
1869 Keates P-L (china)
1870 Harrod NC-L (china manufacturer)
The surname is listed as Bettany in 1867 Keates and as Betteny in 1862 Slater, 1863 Kelly and 1864 Jones.

Betteney, William
Stafford Street, Longton
1873 Keates P-L (china & earthenware)

Betteny, Thomas
See: Betteney, Thomas.
See: Bradbury, Anderson & Betteney

Bevington & Son
(i) Marsh Street, Shelton
1856 Kelly PM
(ii) 10 and 11 Brunswick Street, Hanley
1864 Jones A; PM

Bevington, Ambrose
(i) Dresden Works, Birch Street, Hanley
1869 Keates P-H (china)
1870 Harrod NC-H (china decorator)
(ii) Great York Street, Hanley
1872 Kelly CM
1873 Keates P-H (china)
1876 Kelly CM
(iii) Clarence Street Works, Hanley
1875 Keates P-H (china and earthenware)
1879 Keates P-H (china and earthenware)
(iv) New Hall Works, York Street, Hanley
1889 Keates P-H (china and earthenware)

Bevington, Ambrose, & Co.
(i) New Hall Works, Great York Street, Hanley
1880 Kelly CM
1884 Kelly CM
1887 Porter EM-H
1888 Kelly EM
1892 Kelly EM
(ii) Clarence Street Works, Hanley
1882 Keates P-H (china and earthenware)
The address of the New Hall Works is listed as Marsh Street in 1887 Porter.

Bevington, J., & Co.
Brunswick Street, Hanley
1865 Keates P-H (china and parian)

Bevington, James
(i) New Street, Hanley
1880 Kelly EM
(ii) Cobden Works, High Street, Hanley
1882 Keates P-H
(iii) King Street Works, Hanley
1884 Kelly RM

Bevington, James & Thomas
(i) Marsh Street, Hanley
1865 Keates P-H (china and parian)
1867 Keates P-H (china and parian)
(ii) Burton Place, New Street, Hanley
1867 Keates P-H (china and parian)
1868 Kelly CM; PM
1869 Keates P-H (china and parian)
1870 Harrod NC-H (manufacturers of china, parian statuettes, &c., for home and foreign markets)
1872 Kelly CM
1873 Keates P-H (china &

earthenware)
1875 Keates P-H (china & earthenware)
1876 Kelly CM
(iii) Cannon Street, Hanley
1873 Keates P-H (china & earthenware)
1875 Keates P-H (china & earthenware)

Bevington, John
(i) 20 Clarence Street, Hanley
1860 Kelly CM-General; EM; PM
1861 Harrison NC-H-Sh (china, parian, and earthenware manufacturer)
1863 Kelly CM-General; EM; MM; PM

John Bevington. Advertisement from 1865 Keates.

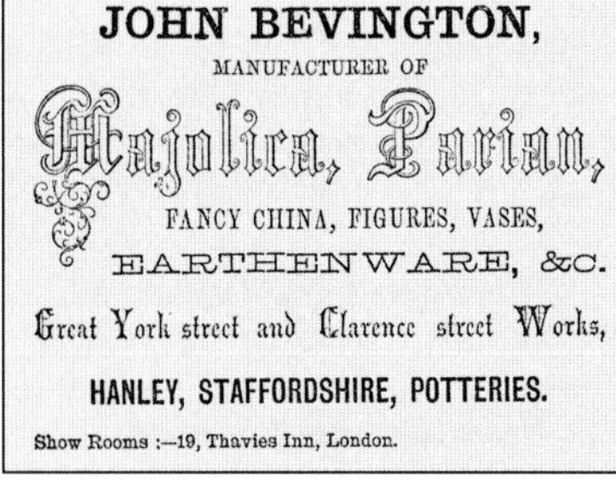

John Bevington. Advertisement from 1867 Keates.

John Bevington. Advertisement from 1869 Keates.

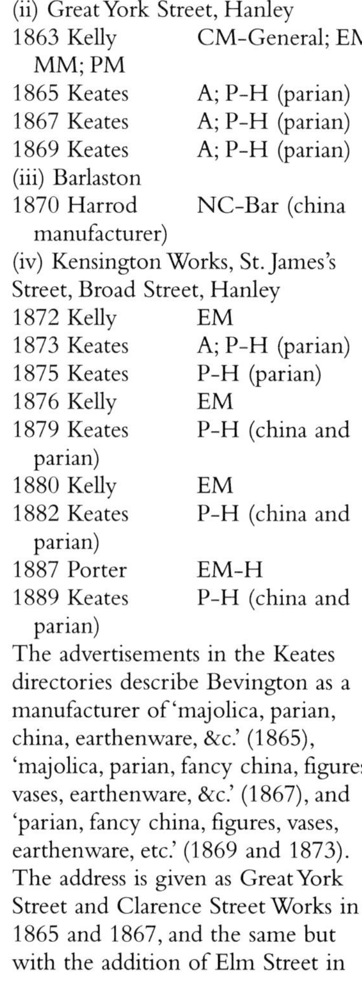

1864 Jones EM
(ii) Great York Street, Hanley
1863 Kelly CM-General; EM; MM; PM
1865 Keates A; P-H (parian)
1867 Keates A; P-H (parian)
1869 Keates A; P-H (parian)
(iii) Barlaston
1870 Harrod NC-Bar (china manufacturer)
(iv) Kensington Works, St. James's Street, Broad Street, Hanley
1872 Kelly EM
1873 Keates A; P-H (parian)
1875 Keates P-H (parian)
1876 Kelly EM
1879 Keates P-H (china and parian)
1880 Kelly EM
1882 Keates P-H (china and parian)
1887 Porter EM-H
1889 Keates P-H (china and parian)

The advertisements in the Keates directories describe Bevington as a manufacturer of 'majolica, parian, china, earthenware, &c.' (1865), 'majolica, parian, fancy china, figures, vases, earthenware, &c.' (1867), and 'parian, fancy china, figures, vases, earthenware, etc.' (1869 and 1873). The address is given as Great York Street and Clarence Street Works in 1865 and 1867, and the same but with the addition of Elm Street in 1869. The advertisements list London showrooms at 11 South Street, Finsbury Square (1865), 19 Thavies Inn (1867), and 12 Ely Place, Holborn (1869).

John Bevington. Advertisement from 1873 Keates.

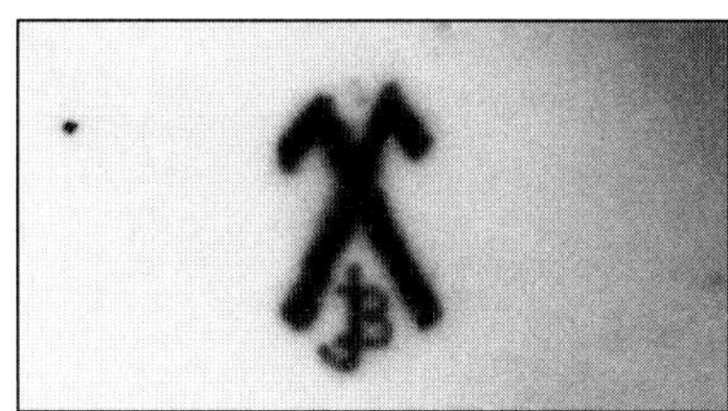

John Bevington. Printed monogram mark from a pair of ornate porcelain candelabra.

Bevington, John, & Co.
Elm Street, Hanley
1869 Keates P-H (parian)
1870 Harrod NC-H (china, parian, &c. manufacturers)

Bevington, S.
Mill Street, Hanley
1856 Kelly CEM

Bevington, Samuel
(i) Marsh Street, Shelton
1846 Williams NC-Sh (china figure manufacturer)
(ii) Brunswick Street, Shelton
1851 White CEM-H-Sh; CETOM-H-Sh
1852 Slater CM
1854 Kelly CEM
1861 Harrison NC-H-Sh (parian manufacturer)
(iii) 10 & 12 Brunswick Street and Marsh Street, Hanley
1863 Kelly EM; PFM; SC (China Porcelain Manufacturers); SC (Porcelain Manufacturers)
1864 Jones CEM (and parian)

An advertisement in 1864 Jones is in the name of Samuel Bevington & Son (qv).

S. BEVINGTON & SON,
MANUFACTURERS OF
PORCELAIN, PARIAN, STATUETTES,
AND EARTHENWARE,
10 & 11, BRUNSWICK STREET,
HANLEY, STAFFORDSHIRE POTTERIES.

Samuel Bevington & Son. Advertisement from 1864 Jones.

Bevington, Samuel, & Son
10 & 12 Brunswick Street and Marsh Street, Hanley
1862 Slater A; CM (and of porcelain & parian vases, parian statuettes, &c.); EM (and of porcelain, parian, &c.); PM (and of ornamental porcelain vase and parian statuary)

The advertisement in 1862 Slater describes the firm as a 'manufacturer of every description of china & earthenware, ornamental porcelain and parian vases, parian statuettes, &c.' Another advertisement appears in 1864 Jones although the directory entry is in the name of Samuel Bevington alone. It describes the firm as 'manufacturers of porcelain, parian, statuettes, and earthenware' and gives the address as 10 & 11 Brunswick Street.

SAMUEL BEVINGTON & SON,
10 & 12, Brunswick Street, and Marsh Stree
HANLEY, STAFFORDSHIRE POTTERIES,
MANUFACTURERS OF EVERY DESCRIPTION OF
CHINA & EARTHENWARE
Ornamental Porcelain and Parian Vases,
PARIAN STATUETTES, &c.

Samuel Bevington & Son. Advertisement from 1862 Slater.

Bevington, Thomas
(i) Burton Place, New Street, Hanley
1879 Keates P-H (china and earthenware)
1880 Kelly CM
1882 Keates P-H (china and earthenware)
1884 Kelly CM
1887 Porter EM-H
1888 Kelly CM
1889 Keates P-H (china and earthenware)
(ii) Mayer Street, Hanley
1892 Kelly EM

Bevington & Bradley
Elm Street and Clarence Street, Hanley
1868 Kelly PM

Bevington & Worthington
Clarence Street, Hanley
1862 Slater CM; EM; TOCM

Bill, Colclough & Co.
Flint Street, Longton (or Lane End)
1834 White EM-LE-L
1835 Pigot EM

Bill, Deakin & Procter
Great Charles Street, Longton (or Lane End)
1834 White EM-LE-L
1835 Pigot EM

Bill, Simpson & Co.
Flint Street, Lane End
1828 Pigot EM
1830 Pigot EM

Billings & Hammersley
Hanley
1802 Allbut EM (map location 81)

Billington & Co.
Copeland Street, Stoke
1875 Keates P-S

Billington, R.
(i) 96 Waterloo Road, Burslem
1884 Kelly EM
1888 Kelly EM
(ii) Gladstone Works, Commercial Street, Burslem
1889 Keates PB (manufacturer)
1892 Keates P-B

Billington, Richard
Eastwood Pottery, Joiner's Square, Hanley
1864 Jones PM

Billington, Richard., & Sons
Cobridge
1805 Holden NC (earthenware-manufacturers)
1809 Holden NC (earthenware manufacturers)
1811 Holden NC (earthenware-manufacturers)

Billington & Tompkinson
High Street and Stafford Street, Longton
1870 Harrod NC-L (china and earthenware manufacturers)

ERNEST BILTON,
Sole Manufacturer of the "NEW SAMIAN" EARTHENWARE.
Also Superior Jet and "Specialite" Rockingham, Terra Cotta, &c., &c.
Sole Manufacturer of the Patent "ARROW VALE" FLOWER-POTS, in all designs and prices.
Gordon Pottery, off Duke Street, FENTON.
(8 Minutes' Walk from Station, 3 Minutes Walk from Tramcar.)

Ernest Bilton. Advertisement from 1892 Keates.

Bilton, Ernest
China Street, Fenton
1889 Keates P-F
1892 Keates P-F
1896 Kelly EM
1900 Kelly EM
An advertisement for Ernest Bilton in 1892 Keates gives his address as Gordon Pottery, off Duke Street, Fenton, '8 minutes' walk from station, 3 minutes walk from tramcar'. It describes him as 'sole manufacturer of the "New Samian" earthenware. Also superior jet and "specialite" Rockingham, terra cotta, &c., &c. Sole manufacturer of the patent "Arrow Vale" flower-pots, in all designs and prices'.

Bilton, John, & Son
Glebe Buildings, Glebe Street, Stoke-on-Trent
1888 Kelly P

Birch, Edmund John
(i) Hanley
1802 Allbut EM (map location 66)
(ii) Shelton
1805 Holden NC (earthenware manufacturer)

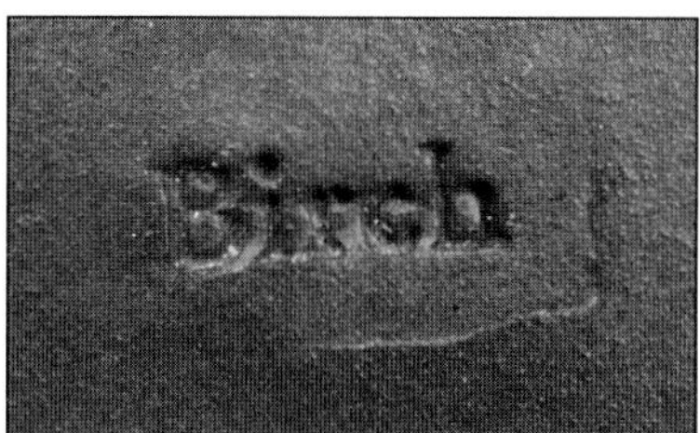

Edmund John Birch. Impressed mark from a black basalt jug.

Birch, Edmund John, & Co.
Hanley
1809 Holden NC (earthenware-manufacturers)
1811 Holden NC (earthenware-manufacturers)

Birch, Elijah
22 & 24 Clarence Street, Hanley
1888 Kelly SC (Encaustic Tile Manufacturers)
1892 Kelly SC (Encaustic Tile Manufacturers)

Birch, Elijah, & Co.
Broad Street, Hanley
1863 Kelly SC (Sanitary Vessel Manufacturers) (dealers)
1863 Kelly SM

Birch, Joseph
Hope Street, Shelton
1850 Slater TOCM
1851 White CETOM-H-Sh

Birch, Samuel
Burslem
1796 Chester NC-B (druggist and manufacturer of earthenware)

Birch Tile Co. Limited (The)
22 & 24 Clarence Street, Hanley
1896 Kelly SC (Encaustic Tile Manufacturers)
1900 Kelly SC (Encaustic Tile Manufacturers)

Birch & Whitehead
Hanley
1796 Chester NC-H-Sh (manufacturers of earthenware)

Birkin, Samuel
See: Blackhurst, Hulme & Birkin

Birks, Charles
(i) Market Street, Lane End
1822 Allbut CEM (lusterer and enameller)
(ii) High Street, Lane End
1822 Allbut CEM (china manufact.)
1828 Pigot CM
1830 Pigot CM; EM
1834 White CM-LE-L
1835 Pigot CM

Birks, J. & W.
Lane End
1802 Allbut EM (map location 135)
The surname is listed as Berks.

Birks, John & William, & Co.
Lane End
1805 Holden NC (Egyptian black manufacturers)

Birks, Joseph
Green Dock Works, Clayton Street, Longton
1863 Kelly CM-Tea, Breakfast, and Dessert Services

Birks, L.A., & Co.
The Vine Pottery, Boothen, Stoke
1896 Kelly EM

Birks, Samuel
Green Dock Works, Clayton Street, Longton
1863 Kelly CM-General
1864 Jones CEM

Birks, Thomas
High Street, Longton
1856 Kelly CEM
1860 Kelly CM-General; EM
1861 Harrison NC-L (china and earthenware manufacturer)
1862 Slater CM; EM
1863 Kelly CM-General
1864 Jones A; CEM; LM
1865 Keates P-L (china, earthenware, gold & silver lustre)
1867 Keates P-L (china, earthenware, gold and silver lustre)
1868 Kelly CM
1869 Keates P-L (china, earthenware, gold, and silver lustre)
1870 Harrod NC-L (china and earthenware manufacturer)
1872 Kelly CM
1873 Keates P-L (china, earthenware, gold and silver lustre)
The advertisement in 1864 Jones describes Birks as a 'manufacturer of china and earthenware, gold and silver lustre, Egyptian black, Rockingham, fancy-coloured bodies, stone ware, &c., suitable for home or abroad'.

THOMAS BIRKS,
HIGH STREET, LONGTON, POTTERIES,
STAFFORDSHIRE.
MANUFACTURER OF
CHINA AND EARTHENWARE,
Gold and Silver Lustre, Egyptian Black, Rockingham, Fancy-coloured Bodies, Stone Ware, &c., suitable for home or abroad.

Thomas Birks. Advertisement from 1864 Jones.

Birks, Thomas, & Co.
3 High Street, Longton
1875 Keates P-L (china, earthenware, gold and silver lustre)
1876 Kelly CM; EM

Birks Brothers & Seddon
Waterloo Road, Cobridge
1880 Kelly EM
1882 Keates P-B (earthenware)
1884 Kelly EM
The firm is listed as Birks Brother & Seddon in 1882 Keates.

Birks, Rawlin & Co.
The Vine Pottery, Boothen, Stoke
1900 Kelly EM

Birks & Seddon
Cobridge
1879 Keates P-B (earthenware)

Bishop & Stonier
(i) Stafford Street and High Street, Hanley
1892 Keates P-H
(ii) Stafford Street, Nelson Place and High Street, Hanley
1896 Kelly CM; EM
1900 Kelly CM; EM

Blacket, Elmore & Co.
Sneyd Street, Tunstall
1852 Slater EM

Blackhurst & Co.
Sandyford Pottery, Tunstall
1867 Keates P-T (earthenware)

Blackhurst, A.J.
Newfield Street, Tunstall
1896 Kelly EM

Blackhurst, Jabez
Sandyford, Tunstall
1872 Kelly EM
1873 Keates P-T (earthenware)
1875 Keates P-T (earthenware)
1876 Kelly EM
1879 Keates P-T (earthenware)
1880 Kelly EM

Blackhurst, R.
Paradise Street, Tunstall
1856 Kelly CEM

Blackhurst, Richard
High Street, Tunstall
1868 Kelly EM
1869 Keates P-T (earthenware)
1870 Harrod NC-T (earthenware manufacturer)
1872 Kelly EM
1873 Keates P-T (earthenware)
1875 Keates P-T (earthenware)
1876 Kelly EM
Blackhurst's residence is listed as Wesley Place in the three Keates directories.

Blackhurst & Bourne
Hadderidge Pottery, Bath Street, Burslem
1880 Kelly EM
1884 Kelly EM
1887 Porter EM-B
1888 Kelly EM
1889 Keates P-B (earthenware)
1892 Kelly EM

Blackhurst & Dunning
High Street, Tunstall
1860 Kelly EM
1861 Harrison NC-T (earthenware manufacturers)
1862 Slater EM
1863 Kelly EM
1864 Jones EM

1865 Keates P-T (earthenware)
1867 Keates P-T (earthenware)

Blackhurst & Hulme
51 High Street, Longton
1892 Keates P-L (china)
1892 Kelly CM
1896 Kelly CM
1900 Kelly CM

Blackhurst, Hulme & Birkin
Belgrave Works, High Street, Longton
1887 Porter EM-L
1888 Kelly CM
The partnership is listed as Blackhurst, Hulme & Berkin in 1887 Porter and as Blackhurst, Hume & Birkin in 1888 Kelly. The third partner is identified as Samuel Birkin in 1888 Kelly.

Blackhurst & Tunnicliffe
Hadderidge Pottery, Bath Street, Burslem
1879 Keates P-B (earthenware)
1882 Keates P-B (earthenware)

Blackshaw, J., & Co.
Providence Works, Copeland Street, Stoke
1870 Harrod NC-S (china and parian manufacturers)

Blackshaw, T. jun.
St. John's Square, Burslem
1854 Kelly CEM

Blackwell, Andrew
Cobridge
1809 Holden NC (earthenware-manufact.)

Blackwell, John
Cobridge
1781 Bailey NC (potter)
1783 Bailey NC (potter)
1784 Bailey NC-C (manufacturer of blue and white stone ware, cream and painted wares)
1798 Universal NC-C (manufacturer of Staffordshire-ware)
1805 Holden NC (china and earthenware manufacturer)
1811 Holden NC (earthenware-manufacturer)
1822 Allbut CEM (earthenware manufact.)
1822 Pigot EM

Blackwell, John & Andrew
Cobridge
1796 Chester NC-C (manufacturers of earthenware)
1802 Allbut EM (map location 59)

Blackwell, John & Robert
Cobridge
1816 Underhill P
1818 Parson EM-B-Lp-C
1818 Pigot EM

Blackwell, Joseph
Cobridge
1784 Bailey NC-C (manufacturer of blue and white stone ware, cream and painted wares)
1798 Universal NC-C (manufacturer of Staffordshire-ware)

Bladen & Molineux
See: Bladon & Mullineux

Bladon & Molyneux
See: Bladon & Mullineux

Bladon & Mullineux
Mayer Street, Hanley
1884 Kelly EM
1887 Porter EM-H
1888 Kelly EM
1889 Keates P-H
1892 Kelly EM
The partnership is listed as Bladen & Molineux in 1889 Keates and as Bladon & Molyneux in 1887 Porter.

Blair & Co.
Beaconsfield Pottery, Anchor Road, Longton
1880 Kelly CM (manufacturers for home & export)
1882 Keates P-L (china)
1884 Kelly CM (manufacturers for home & export)
1887 Porter EM-L
1888 Kelly CM (manufacturers for home & export)
1889 Keates P-L (china)
1892 Keates P-L (china)
1892 Kelly CM
1896 Kelly CM
1900 Kelly CM

Blood, Edwin
(i) High Street, Longton
1860 Kelly LM (silver)
1861 Harrison NC-L (manufacturer of silver lustres, &c.)
(ii) 62 High Street and Parkhall Street, Longton
1862 Slater EM (silver lustered)

Bloor, R.W.
See: Bloore, Ralph William

Bloore, Ralph William
North Road, Cobridge
1887 Porter EM-B
1889 Keates P-B
The surname is listed as Bloor in 1889 Keates.

Blote, Thomas & Richard
See: Boote, Thomas Latham & Richard

Boden, John
Tunstall
1818 Parson EM-G-T-R
1818 Pigot EM
1822 Allbut CEM (earthenware manufact. and gilder)
1822 Pigot EM

Bodley, E.F.
Scotia Works, Wedgwood Place, Burslem
1865 Keates P-B (earthenware)

Bodley, Edward Fisher, & Co.
(i) Scotia Works, Wedgwood Place or Scotia Road, Burslem
1867 Keates P-B (earthenware)
1868 Kelly EM
1869 Keates P-B (earthenware)
1870 Harrod NC-B (manufacturers of ironstone china for steam-ship and hotel use, also every description of first-class earthenware, suitable for the home, colonial, continental, and Indian markets)
1872 Kelly EM
1873 Keates P-B (earthenware)
1875 Keates P-B (earthenware)
1876 Kelly EM
1879 Keates P-B (earthenware)
1880 Kelly EM
(ii) Hill Pottery, Burslem
1872 Kelly EM
(iii) Market Place, Burslem
1873 Keates P-B (earthenware)

Bodley, Edward Fisher, & Son
New Bridge Pottery, Longport
1884 Kelly EM
1887 Porter EM-B
1888 Kelly EM
1889 Keates P-B
1892 Keates P-B

Bodley, Edward Fisher, & Sons
Longport
1892 Kelly EM
1896 Kelly EM

Bodley, Edwin James Drew
(i) Hill Pottery, Market Place, Burslem
1875 Keates P-B (china)
1876 Kelly CM
1879 Keates P-B (china)
1880 Kelly CM
1882 Keates P-B (china)
1884 Kelly CM; EM
1887 Porter EM-B
1888 Kelly CM
1889 Keates P-B (china)
1892 Kelly CM, EM
(ii) Crown Works, Burslem
1889 Keates P-B (china)
Bodley's initials are listed as Edwin F.D. in 1875 Keates. A London office at 3 & 5 Charterhouse Street is listed in 1884 Kelly, and at number 3 only in 1888 Kelly and 1892 Kelly.

Bodley & Harrold
Scotia Pottery, Scotia Road, Burslem
1863 Kelly EM
1864 Jones EM
(See right.)

Bodrey, Peter
Lane Delph
1798 Universal NC-LD (manufacturer of Staffordshire-ware)

Bold, Henry
(i) Waterloo Road, Burslem
1841 Pigot NC (pot step manufacturer for cotton manufacturers)
1850 Slater SC (Pot Step Manufacturers, for Cotton Spinners)
1852 Slater SC (Pot Step Manufacturers, for Cotton Spinners)
(ii) Lower Church Street Works, Burslem
1851 White CEM-B (only earthenware)
(iii) Commercial Street, Burslem
1852 Slater EM
(iv) 34 Chancery Lane, Longton
1860 Kelly SC (Pot Creel Maker)
1863 Kelly SC (China Letter Manufacturer) (rustic)
1862 Slater SC (Pot Step Manufacturers, for Cotton Spinners) (& mortice furniture)
1863 Kelly EM-Horticultural & Rustic Ware; P (rustic); SC (Shuttle Eyes Manufacturer)
1865 Keates P-L (rustic and terra cotta)
(v) 8 Commerce Street, Longton
1864 Jones EM-Miscellaneous (pot, step, worsted guide, and rustic flower-pot manufacturer)
(vi) Daisy Bank, Longton
1864 Jones EM-Miscellaneous (pot, step, worsted guide, and rustic flower-pot manufacturer)
1867 Keates P-L (rustic and terra cotta)
(vii) 18 High Street, Longton
1868 Kelly SC (Rustic Manufacturer)
1869 Keates P-L (porcelain and terra cotta)
1870 Harrod NC-L (manufacturer of porcelain gasaliers, centrepieces, &c.)
(viii) King Street, Hanley
1876 Kelly SC (Pot Step Maker)
(ix) 46 Lichfield Street, Hanley
1889 Keates P-H
Bold's house is listed as Cobridge in 1851 White.

Bodley & Harrold. Printed mark from an earthenware meat dish. The registration diamond dates from 1863.

Bold, J., & Co.
Church Works, Burslem
1854 Kelly CEM

Boon, Edward
Fenton
1784 Bailey NC-F (manufacturer of Queen's ware and blue painted)

Boon, John
Queen Street, Burslem
1818 Pigot EM

Boon, Joseph
(i) Hanley
1781 Bailey NC (potter)
1783 Bailey NC (potter)
1784 Bailey NC-H (potter)
(ii) Shelton
1809 Holden NC (earthenware-manufacturer)
The surname is listed as Boone in 1781 Bailey and 1783 Bailey.

Boon & Hicks
Shelton
1805 Holden NC (earthenware manufacturers)

Boon & Lovatt
Shelton
1811 Holden NC (earthenware-manufacs.)

Boon & Ridgway
Hanley
1802 Allbut EM (map location 77)

Boone, Joseph
See: Boon, Joseph

Boot, Jonathan
Cobridge
1800 Allbutt NC-C (modeller and toy manufacturer)

Boote, Thomas Latham & Richard
(i) Market Place, Burslem
1850 Slater EM

(ii) Waterloo Potteries, Waterloo Road, Burslem
1851 White CEM-B (both) (patentees of the royal mosaic, &c.)
1852 Slater EM (and stone, parian)
1854 Kelly CEM; PM
1856 Kelly CEM; PM
1860 Kelly EM
1861 Harrison NC-B (earthenware manufacturers)
1862 Slater A; EM
1863 Kelly EM
1865 Keates P-B (earthen.); SC-B (Tile - Floor - Makers)
1867 Keates P-B (earthen.); SC-B (Tile - Floor - Makers)
1868 Kelly SC (Encaustic & Geometric Tile Pavement Manufacturers – Patent)
1869 Keates P-B (earthen.); SC-B (Tile - Floor - Makers)
1870 Harrod NC-B (manufacturers of encaustic and plain flooring tiles of the hardest texture, and the finest colours (equal to enamel tints), which can be inlaid any depth, thereby ensuring durability, and at a much cheaper rate than hitherto charged, for churches, entrance halls, &c., &c.; white glazed tiles both for in and outdoor purposes, which will resist the severest weather; designs and estimates supplied without charge, and experienced pavers sent out to suit purchasers; prize encaustic tiles)
1873 Keates P-B (earthen.); SC-B (Encaustic and Geometric Tile Pavement Manufacturers); SC-B (Tile - Floor - Makers)
1875 Keates P-B (earthen); SC-B (Encaustic and Geometric Tile Pavement Manufacturers); SC-B (Tile - Floor - Makers)
1876 Kelly SC (Encaustic Tile Manufacturers)
1879 Keates P-B (earthen); SC-B (Encaustic and Geometric Tile Pavement Manufacturers); SC-B (Floor Tile Works); SC-B (Tile - Floor - Makers)
1880 Kelly SC (Encaustic Tile Manufacturers)
1882 Keates P-B (earthenware); SC-B (Encaustic and Geometric Tile Pavement Manufacturers); SC-B (Floor Tile Works)
1884 Kelly SC (Encaustic Tile Manufacturers)
1887 Porter EM-B
1888 Kelly SC (Encaustic Tile Manufacturers); P
1889 Keates P-B (earthenware); SC-B (Encaustic and Geometric Tile Pavement Manufacturers); SC-B (Floor Tile Works)
1892 Keates P-B (earthenware); SC-B (Encaustic and Geometric Tile Pavement Manufacturers); SC-B (Floor Tile Works)
1892 Kelly SC (Encaustic Tile Manufacturers)

The surname is misprinted as Blote in 1852 Slater. The address is listed as 43 and 32A Waterloo Road in 1882 Keates, 1889 Keates and 1892 Keates, and as Waterloo Potteries and Encaustic Tile Works in 1888 Kelly. The Bootes' house is listed as Central Cottage, Burslem, in 1851 White. The advertisement in 1862 Slater is for encaustic & ornamental flooring tiles. It states that 'T. and R. Boote are now manufacturing encaustic and highly decorative flooring tiles under their patent process, which enables them to supply the public at a considerable reduction in price', and offers 'patterns, prices, and estimates on application'.

ENCAUSTIC & ORNAMENTAL FLOORING TILES.
T. AND R. BOOTE
ARE NOW MANUFACTURING
ENCAUSTIC AND HIGHLY
Decorative Flooring Tiles
Under their Patent Process, which enables them to supply the Public at a considerable reduction in Price. Patterns, Prices, and Estimates on application to
T.&R. Boote, Waterloo Potteries Burslem, Staffordshire.

Thomas & Richard Boote. Advertisement from 1862 Slater.

Thomas & Richard Boote. Printed mark from an earthenware wash jug with inlaid figure decoration. The phrase "Patent Mosaic" refers to the decorative inlaying technique.

Thomas & Richard Boote. Another printed "Patent Mosaic" mark, this example with an eulogy for Robert Peel from a jug commemorating his death.

Thomas & Richard Boote. Printed mark from a blue-printed earthenware sauceboat.

Booth & Co.
Lane End
1802 Allbut EM (map location 127)

Booth, Messrs.
Lane End
1809 Holden NC (earthenware-manufac.)
1811 Holden NC (earthenware-manufacturers)
1816 Underhill P

Booth & Son
(i) Church Street, Lane End
1834 White CM-LE-L
1835 Pigot CM
(ii) Marsh Street, Hanley
1872 Kelly EM

Booth & Sons
Cliffgate-bank
1802 Allbut EM (map location 100)

Booth, Arthur
15 Sutherland Terrace, Longton
1887 Porter EM-L

Booth, E.
Stoke
1798 Universal NC-S (manufacturer of Staffordshire-ware)

Booth, Ephraim, & Sons
Stoke
1796 Chester NC-S (manufacturers of earthenware)

Booth, Henry
Nelson Place, Hanley
1869 Keates P-H (earthen.)
1870 Harrod NC-H (earthenware manufacturer)

Booth, Herbert
34 Berkley Street, Hanley
1887 Porter EM-H

Booth, Hugh
Stoke
1781 Bailey NC (potter)
1783 Bailey NC (potter)
1784 Bailey NC-S (manufacturer of china, china glaze, and Queen's ware in all its various branches)

Booth, Hugh & Joseph
Stoke
1805 Holden NC (earthenware manufacturer)

Booth, Joseph
Railway Works, Longton
1841 Pigot EM

Booth, Joseph & Thomas
(i) Lane End
1818 Parson EM-LE
1822 Allbut CEM (earthenware manufacts.)
(ii) Stafford Street, Lane End
1822 Pigot EM
(iii) Flint Street, Lane End
1828 Pigot EM
1830 Pigot EM

Booth, Richard
(i) Marsh Street, Shelton
1830 Pigot EM (toy only)
(ii) Brook Street, Shelton
1834 White CETM-H-Sh
1835 Pigot TOCM (fine)
1841 Pigot TOCM (fine)

Booth, Richard, & Son
Church Street, Lane End
1830 Pigot CM

Booth, Richard, & Sons
Church Street, Lane End
1828 Pigot CM

Thomas Booth. Moulded mark from a relief-moulded jug. The registration diamond dates from 1869.

Booth, Thomas
(i) Britannia Works, Lichfield Street, Hanley
1864 Jones EM (hot water pipes, &c.)
1870 Harrod NC-H (manufacturer of earthenware, stone, &c., druggists' sundries, Britannia metal mounted hot water jugs, molasses jugs, &c., for home and foreign markets)
(ii) Portland Street, Burslem
1865 Keates P-B (toy)
(iii) Waterloo Works, Hanley
1870 Harrod NC-H (manufacturer of earthenware, stone, &c., druggists' sundries, Britannia metal mounted hot water jugs, molasses jugs, &c., for home and foreign markets)
Although not listed as a potter in the directories, advertisements appear in both 1865 Keates and 1867 Keates for Thomas Booth at the Britannia Works, High Street, Hanley. They describe him as a 'manufacturer of Britannia metal goods, mounter and exporter of hot water jugs, molasses jugs, teapots, &c.' and promise 'the greatest assortments in the kingdom'. The 1867 advertisement adds that he was also an earthenware manufacturer at the Waterloo Works, Nelson Place, Hanley. Both advertisements claim that he was established in 1845.

ESTABLISHED, 1845.
THOMAS BOOTH,
MANUFACTURER OF
BRITANNIA METAL GOODS,
MOUNTER AND EXPORTER OF
Hot Water Jugs, Molasses Jugs, Teapots, &c.,
BRITANNIA WORKS,
HIGH STREET, HANLEY.
THE GREATEST ASORTMENTS IN THE KINGDOM.

Thomas Booth. Advertisement from 1865 Keates.

ESTABLISHED, 1845.
THOMAS BOOTH,
MANUFACTURER OF
BRITANNIA METAL GOODS,
MOUNTER AND EXPORTER OF
Hot Water Jugs, Molasses Jugs, Teapots, &c.,
BRITANNIA WORKS,
HIGH STREET, HANLEY,
AND
EARTHENWARE MANUFACTURER,
WATERLOO WORKS, NELSON PLACE.
THE GREATEST ASSORTMENTS IN THE KINGDOM.

Thomas Booth. Advertisement from 1867 Keates.

Thomas Booth. Engraved mark on a Britannia metal lid fitted to a relief-moulded jug manufactured by Charles Meigh.

THOMAS BOOTH & CO.
MOUNTERS
AND EXPORTERS OF
HOT WATER AND MOLASSES JUGS,
BRITANNIA WORKS,
LICHFIELD STREET, HANLEY.

Thomas Booth & Co. Advertisement from 1852 Slater.

Booth, Thomas, & Co.
(i) Britannia Works, Lichfield Street, Hanley

1854 Kelly CEM
(ii) Church Bank Pottery, Tunstall
1870 Harrod NC-T
(earthenware manufacturers)
1872 Kelly EM
Although not listed in the directory as a potter, an advertisement in 1852 Slater describes Thomas Booth & Co. of the Britannia Works as 'mounters, and exporters of hot water and molasses jugs'.

Booth, Thomas, & Son
Church Bank Pottery, High Street, Tunstall
1873 Keates P-T
1875 Keates P-T
1876 Kelly EM
Booth's residence is listed as Windmill Street in 1873 Keates and 1875 Keates.

Thomas Booth & Sons. Impressed mark from a rouletted stoneware jug.

Established 1845.
THOMAS BOOTH & SONS,
NEW HALL POTTERY, HANLEY,
Manufacturers of Earthenware
GENERALLY,
JASPER, STONE, MAJOLICA,
POROUS BOTTLES,
ACID-PROOF MORTARS AND PESTLES,
BRITANNIA METAL MOUNTED HOT WATER JUGS, TEAPOTS, &c.
Two Minutes Walk from Hanley Railway Station.

Thomas Booth & Sons. Advertisement from 1875 Keates. A very similar advertisement appeared in 1879 Keates.

Booth, Thomas, & Sons
(i) Britannia Works, High Street, Hanley
1872 Kelly EM; MM; SM
(ii) New Hall Pottery, Great York Street, Hanley
1872 Kelly EM; MM; SM
1876 Kelly EM; MM; SC
(Druggists' Stoneware Manufacturers)
(iii) Brook Street, Hanley
1873 Keates P-H
(earthenware)
1875 Keates P-H
(earthenware)
1879 Keates P-H
(earthenware)
Advertisements in 1875 Keates and 1879 Keates give the address as the New Hall Pottery, 'two minutes walk from Hanley railway station'. They describe the firm as 'manufacturers of earthenware generally, jasper, stone, majolica, porous bottles, acid-proof mortars and pestles, Britannia metal mounted hot water jugs, teapots, &c.' and claim that the firm was established in 1845.

Booth, Thomas Gimbert
Church Bank Pottery, High Street, Tunstall
1879 Keates P-T
1880 Kelly A; EM
1882 Keates P-T
Booth's names are listed as Thomas Gamber in 1879 Keates, and his residence is listed as Wolstanton in both 1879 Keates and 1882 Keates. The advertisement in 1880 Kelly describes him as a 'manufacturer of earthenware, also best ironstone china for hotels' and ships' use, suitable for home, foreign and colonial markets' and offered 'samples and prices on application'. London showrooms were given as 23 Ely Place, Holborn Circus with the contact as T.A. Green.

THOMAS GIMBERT BOOTH,
TUNSTALL, STAFFORDSHIRE,
MANUFACTURER OF
EARTHENWARE,
Also BEST IRONSTONE CHINA for Hotels' and Ships' Use.
SUITABLE FOR HOME, FOREIGN AND COLONIAL MARKETS.
London Show Rooms:—T. A. GREEN, 28, Ely Place, Holborn Circus.
SAMPLES AND PRICES ON APPLICATION.

Thomas Gimbert Booth. Advertisement from 1880 Kelly.

Booth, Thomas Gimbert & F.
(i) Church Bank Pottery, Tunstall
1884 Kelly EM
(ii) Church Bank Pottery, Tunstall, and Highgate Pottery, Brownhills
1887 Porter EM-T
1888 Kelly EM
1889 Keates P-T

Booth, William
Shelton
1805 Holden NC (Egyptian black manufacturer)

Booth, William, & Son
Waterloo Place, Hanley
1822 Pigot EM

Booth & Bentley
Hanley
1816 Underhill P

Booth & Bridgewood
Lane End
1805 Holden NC (earthenware manufacturers)

Booth & Dale
Shelton
1798 Universal NC-Sh
(manufacturers of Staffordshire-ware)

Booth & Marsh
Shelton
1796 Chester NC-H-Sh
(manufacturers of earthenware)
1802 Allbut EM (map location 64)

Booth (George), Robins & Co.
Waterloo Works, Hanley
1841 Pigot CM

Booths
Church Bank Pottery, Tunstall
1892 Keates P-T
1892 Kelly EM
1896 Kelly EM

Booths Ltd.
Church Bank Pottery, Tunstall
1900 Kelly EM

Borne, Ralph, & Co.
Lower Lane
1798 Universal NC-LL
(manufacturers of Staffordshire-ware)

Bott, Thomas, & Co.
Lane End
1809 Holden NC (earthenware-manufac.)
1811 Holden NC (earthenware-manufacturers)
1816 Underhill P

Boughey, Matthew
Willow Street Works, Daisy Bank, Longton
1887 Porter EM-L
1888 Kelly CM; SC
(Enamelled Goods Manufacturer)

1889 Keates P-L (earthenware)
1892 Keates P-L (earthenware)
1892 Kelly EM
1896 Kelly EM; SC
(Enamelled Letter Makers)
1900 Kelly EM; SC
(Enamelled Letter Makers)

Boughey & Goodwin
Stafford Street and Willow Street, Longton
1884 Kelly CM; EM

Boughey, Shore & Martin
Belgrave Works, High Street, Longton
1884 Kelly CM

Boughey & Wiltshaw
Market Street, Longton
1892 Keates P-L (china)
1892 Kelly CM

Boughton, R.T., & Co.
Fountain Place, Burslem
1865 Keates P-B (earthenware)
1867 Keates P-B (earthenware)

Boulton & Co.
(i) Tunstall
1888 Kelly SC (Encaustic Tile Manufacturers)
(ii) Mill Street Works, Longton
1892 Keates P-L (china)
(iii) Edensor Road, Longton
1892 Kelly CM
1896 Kelly CM
1900 Kelly CM

Boulton, C.
Market Square, Hanley
1854 Kelly TM

Boulton, Charles Bourne
Lamb Street, Hanley
1851 White CETOM-H-Sh

Boulton, John
Cliffe Bank Works, Stoke
1884 Kelly EM
1887 Porter CEM-S

Boulton, William
Navigation Road and Pleasant Street, Burslem
1884 Kelly A; SC (Encaustic Tile Manufacturers)
The advertisement in 1884 Kelly is for William Boulton of the Providence Foundry, Burslem, described as a 'manufacturer of patent pottery and encaustic tile machinery; patent clay presses & pumps' with no mention of pottery production. The firm's products were given as 'drying stoves heated by exhaust steam, or by the small bore high pressure hot water pipe system' with 'works fitted throughout at home and abroad', and offered 'testimonials on application'.

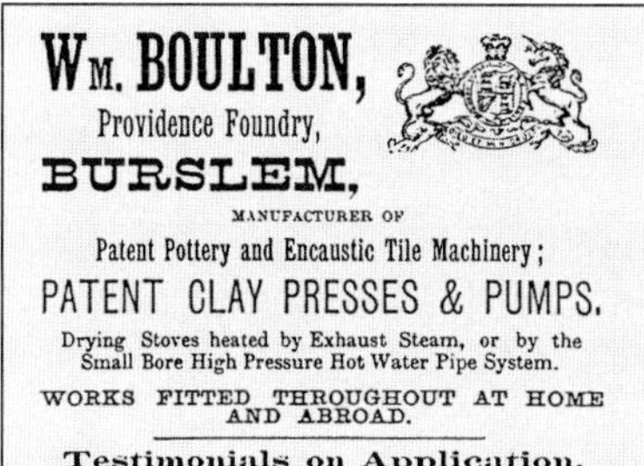

William Boulton. Advertisement from 1884 Kelly.

Boulton & Creyke
Avery Street, Hanley
1887 Porter EM-H

BOULTON & FLOYD,
MANUFACTURERS OF
Decorated Earthenware & Majolica
CLIFF BANK WORKS,
High Street and Lovatt Street, Stoke-upon-Trent.

Boulton & Floyd. Advertisement from 1889 Keates.

BOULTON & FLOYD,
MANUFACTURERS OF
Decorated Earthenware & Majolica,
CLIFF BANK WORKS,
Lovatt St. & Hall St., STOKE-UPON-TRENT.

Boulton & Floyd. Advertisement from 1892 Keates.

Boulton & Floyd
(i) Cliffe Bank Works, High Street, Stoke
1888 Kelly EM; MM
1889 Keates P-S (earthenware and majolica)
(ii) Hall Street, Stoke
1888 Kelly EM; MM
(iii) Hall Street and Lovatt Street, Stoke
1892 Keates A; P-S (earthenware and majolica)
1892 Kelly EM
1896 Kelly EM
1900 Kelly EM
An advertisement in 1889 Keates describes the firm as 'manufacturers of decorated earthenware & majolica' and gives the address as Cliff Bank Works, High Street and Lovatt Street. The advertisement in 1892 Keates is similar but gives the address as Cliff Bank Works, Lovatt Street and Hall Street.

Boulton, Machin & Tennant
Swan Bank Pottery, High Street, Tunstall
1889 Keates P-T
1892 Keates P-T
1892 Kelly EM
1896 Kelly EM

Boulton, Machin & Tennant. Printed mark from a transfer-printed and coloured earthenware dish.

Boulton, Machin & Tennant. Printed mark from a blue-printed earthenware meat dish.

Boulton & Worthington
Moorland Road, Burslem
1865 Keates SC-B (Tile - Floor - Makers)

Bourne & Co.
(i) Shelton
1802 Allbut EM (map location 65)
(ii) Cleveland Street, Shelton
1900 Kelly CM

Bourne, Charles
(i) Lane Delph
1805 Holden NC (earthenware manufacturer)
1809 Holden NC (manufac. of earthenware)
1811 Holden NC (manufacturer of earthenware)
(ii) Fenton
1816 Underhill P
(iii) Foley
1818 Parson EM-LE
1822 Allbut CEM (china and earthenware manufacturer)
1822 Pigot EM
1828 Pigot CM; EM
1830 Pigot CM; EM

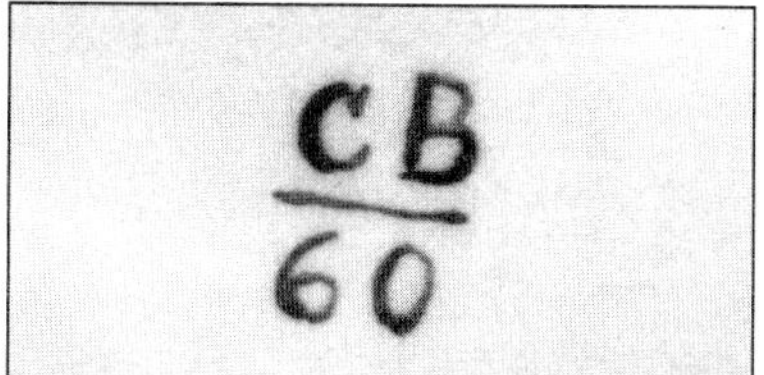

Charles Bourne. Hand-painted initial mark found on china wares.

Bourne, Edward
(i) Longport
1781 Bailey NC (potter)
1783 Bailey NC (potter)
(ii) Burslem
1796 Chester NC-B (manufacturer of earthenware)
1798 Universal NC-B (potter)
1802 Allbut EM (map location 35)
1805 Holden NC (earthenware manufacturer)
1809 Holden NC (earthenware-manufactr.)
1811 Holden NC (earthenware-manufacturer)
1816 Underhill P
Bourne is listed as Edward junior in 1796 Chester.

Bourne, Ezra
Newport Lane, Burslem
1869 Keates P-B (earthen.)
1870 Harrod NC-B (earthenware manufacturer)

Bourne, H.
Clough Street, Hanley
1892 Keates P-H (vase and toilet ware)

Bourne, John
Burslem
1784 Bailey NC-B (manufacturer of china glaze, blue painted, enamelled, and cream colour earthen ware)

Bourne, Ralph, & Co.
See: Borne, Ralph, & Co.

Bourne, Thomas William
See: Britannia China Co.

Bourne, William
(i) Burslem
1805 Holden NC (earthenware manufacturer)
1809 Holden NC (earthenware-manufacturer)
1811 Holden NC (earthenware-manufacturer)
(ii) Alma Place, High Street, Longton
1860 Kelly EM
1861 Harrison NC-L (earthenware manufacturer)
See also: Bowrne, William

Bourne, William, & Co.
Bell Works, Burslem
1818 Parson EM-B-Lp-C
1818 Pigot EM
The surname is listed as Bowrne in 1818 Pigot.

Bourne & Baker
(i) Lower Lane
1796 Chester NC-LE-LD-LL (manufacturers of earthenware)
(ii) Fenton
1802 Allbut EM (map location 106)

Bourne, Baker & Baker
Fenton
1834 White CEM-F-LD
1835 Pigot CM; EM

Bourne, Baker & Bourne
Fenton
1805 Holden NC (earthenware manufacturers)
1809 Holden NC (manufacturers of earthenware)
1811 Holden NC (manufacturers of earthenware)
1816 Underhill P
1818 Parson EM-LE
1818 Pigot EM
1822 Allbut CEM (china and earthenware manufacturers)
1822 Pigot EM
1828 Pigot EM
1830 Pigot EM
The second partner's name is listed as Barker in 1818 Pigot. A Liverpool address at Salthouse Dock is listed in 1809 Holden and 1811 Holden.

Bourne, Baker & Bourne or Bourne, Baker & Baker. Printed mark from earthenware dinner wares.

Bourne, Barker & Bourne
See: Bourne, Baker & Bourne

Bourne & Browne
King Street, Fenton
1861 Harrison NC-F (china manufacturers)
1862 Slater CM
The second partner's name is listed as Brown in 1862 Slater.

Bourne & Cormie
Queen Street, Burslem
1822 Allbut CEM (earthenware manufacturers)
1822 Pigot EM

Bourne & Leigh
Orme Street, Burslem
1892 Keates P-B (earthenware)

Bourne & Malkin
Burslem
1784 Bailey NC-B (manufacturers of china glazed, blue, and cream colour ware)

Bourne, Nixon & Co.
Tunstall
1828 Pigot EM
1830 Pigot EM

Bourne & Sheddadd
Swan Works, Elm Street, Hanley
1888 Kelly EM
1889 Keates P-H
1892 Kelly EM
The second partner's name is listed as Sherratt in 1889 Keates.

Bourne & Sherratt
See: Bourne & Sheddadd

Bowers, Frederick George
See: Bowers, George Frederick

Bowers, Frederick T.
Brownhills Pottery, between Burslem and Tunstall
1868 Kelly EM
1869 Keates P-T
1870 Harrod NC-B (china manufacturer); NC-T (manufacturer of improved porcelain, ironstone, earthenware, and white granite, in superior printed Japan and other dinner, dessert, toilette, tea, and breakfast ware, gilded and ornamented – awarded prize medal, London 1851, for home and foreign markets)

Bowers, George Frederick
Brownhills China Works, between

GEO. FREDK. BOWERS,
BROWNHILLS CHINA WORKS,
TUNSTALL, STAFFORDSHIRE POTTERIES,
MANUFACTURER OF
Improved Porcelain, Superior Printed, Japan, &c.,
Dinner, Dessert, Toilette, Tea & Breakfast Ware,
GILDED AND ORNAMENTED,
IN IRONSTONE, EARTHENWARE, AND WHITE GRANITE.
Also Flint, Stone and Potters' Colours Grinder.
THE TRADE AND MERCHANTS SUPPLIED.

George Frederick Bowers. Advertisement from 1864 Jones.

Burslem and Tunstall
1850 Kelly CEM; NC-B (china manufacturer)
1850 Slater CM
1851 White CEM-B (both)
1852 Slater CM; EM
1854 Kelly CEM
1856 Kelly CEM
1860 Kelly CM-General; EM
1861 Harrison NC-B (earthenware manufacturer and flint grinder)
1862 Slater CM; EM
1863 Kelly CM-General; EM
1864 Jones A; CEM (every variety)
1865 Keates P-T (china and earthenware)
The potter is listed as Frederick George Bowers in 1850 Kelly and his address as Brownhills Pottery and Mills in 1864 Jones. Bowers' house is listed as Brown Hills House in 1851 White. The advertisement in 1864 Jones describes him as a 'manufacturer of improved porcelain, superior printed, Japan, &c., dinner, dessert, toilette, tea & breakfast ware, gilded and ornamented, in ironstone, earthenware, and white granite'. It noted that Bowers was also a 'flint, stone and potters' colours grinder' with 'the trade and merchants supplied'.
See also: Brownhills China Works

Bowers, George Frederick, & Co.
China Works, Brownhills, Burslem
1846 Williams NC-B
The partners are listed individually as G.F. Bowers of Brownhills House and Edward Challinor of Tunstall in 1846 Williams.

George Frederick Bowers & Co. Printed mark.

Bowers, Challinor & Wooliscroft
Brownhills, Burslem
1851 White NC-B (china, &c., mfrs.)
1852 Slater EM (and architectural ornatures)
The third partner's name is listed as Wolliscroft in 1851 White.

Bowers & Lloyd
Navigation Road, Burslem
1846 Williams NC-B (earthenware manufacturers)
The partners are listed individually as John Bowers of Navigation Road and William Lloyd of King Street in 1846 Williams.

Bowler, W. & E.
New Street, Hanley
1872 Kelly EM

Bowrne, William
Foley
1818 Pigot EM

Box & Holdcroft
Cobridge
1816 Underhill P

Boyl & Co.
Fenton
1850 Kelly CEM
A Birmingham address at 108 Steelhouse Lane is listed in 1850 Kelly.

Boyle & Sons
High Street, Fenton
1850 Kelly CEM; NC-S (china & earthenware manufacturers)
1850 Slater CM; EM

Boyle, L., & Sons
Church Street, Stoke
1846 Williams NC-S (china & earthenware manuf.)

Boyle, Samuel, & Sons
Little Fenton
1851 White CEM-F
Boyle's house is listed as Seabridge, Fenton, in 1851 White.

Boyle, Zachariah, & Co.
Keeling's Lane, Hanley
1828 Pigot EM

Boyle, Zachariah, & Son
(i) Keeling's Lane, Hanley
1828 Pigot CM
(ii) Church Street, Stoke
1830 Pigot CM; EM
1834 White CM-S; EM-S
1835 Pigot CM; EM

Zachariah Boyle & Son. Printed mark from a blue-printed and enamelled earthenware jug.

Boyle, Zachariah, & Sons
Church Street, Stoke
1841 Pigot CM; EM

Bradbury & Sons
High Street, Longton
1882 Keates P-L (china)

Bradbury, James, & Co.
Clayton Pottery, Clayton Street, Longton
1889 Keates P-L (toilet, jugs, majolica, and jet)

Bradbury, Anderson & Betteney
(i) Crown Works, Stafford Street, Longton
1846 Williams NC-L-LE (china manftrs.)
1851 White CEM-L
(ii) Flint Street, Longton
1850 Kelly CEM; NC-L (china manfrs.)
1850 Slater CM
The third partner's surname is listed as Bettany in 1851 White and as Betteny in two cross references in 1846 Williams. The partners are listed as James Bradbury of High Street, Robert Anderson of Bridge Street, and Thomas Betteny of Furnace Spring in 1846 Williams.

Bradbury & Emery
Nelson Road, Hanley
1900 Kelly EM

Bradbury, Kellett & Co.
Heathcote Road, Longton
1882 Keates P-L (china)
1884 Kelly CM; EM

Bradbury, Mason & Bradbury
(i) Flint Street, Longton
1852 Slater CM
(ii) Crown Pottery, Stafford Street, Longton
1852 Slater EM
1854 Kelly CEM

Bradbury, Mason & Bradbury. Printed mark from a relief-moulded stoneware jug.

Bradely & Preece
See Bradley & Preece

Bradley, Frederick Douglas
(i) Elkin Works, Longton
1876 Kelly CM
(ii) Edensor Road, Longton
1879 Keates P-L (decorated china)
(iii) Clayton Street, Longton
1880 Kelly CM
1882 Keates P-L (decorated china)
1884 Kelly CM
(iv) Sutherland Road, Longton
1887 Porter EM-L
1888 Kelly CM
1892 Kelly CM
1896 Kelly CM

Bradley & Preece
(i) Hanover Street, Burslem
1896 Kelly EM
(ii) Waterloo Road, Burslem
1900 Kelly EM
The first partner is listed individually as Harry Preece in 1896 Kelly where his surname is misprinted once as Bradely.

Bradshaw, Joseph
Booden Brook, between Burslem and Hanley
1818 Parson EM-B-Lp-C; EM-H-Sh
1818 Pigot EM

Bradshaw, William
High Street, Lane End
1822 Allbut CEM (lusterer & enameller)
1822 Pigot CM; EM

Bradshaw & Binns
(i) Clarence Street, Hanley
1875 Keates P-H (china)
(ii) Hope Street, Hanley
1879 Keates P-H (china)

Bradshaw & Bourne
(i) Shelton
1809 Holden NC (earthenware-manufs.)
1811 Holden NC (earthenware-manufacturers)
(ii) Hanley
1816 Underhill P

Brain, Thomas
Church Street, Longton
1896 Kelly EM
1900 Kelly EM

Brall, Henry
54 Furlong Lane, Burslem
1882 Keates P-B (earthenware)

Brammall, Edwin
(i) Heathcote Works, Heathcote Road, Longton
1870 Harrod NC-L (china manufacturer for home and foreign markets)
1872 Kelly CM
1873 Keates P-L (china)
1875 Keates P-L (china)
(ii) Forrester Street, Anchor Road, Longton
1882 Keates P-L (china)

Brammall, William
Heathcote Works, Heathcote Road, Longton
1860 Kelly CM-General
1861 Harrison NC-L (china manufacturer)
1862 Slater CM
1863 Kelly CM-General
1864 Jones CEM

Brammall & Hamilton
St. John's Works, Church Street, Longton
1879 Keates P-L (china)
1880 Kelly CM

Brammall & Repton
Heathcote Works, Heathcote Road, Longton
1865 Keates P-L (china)
1867 Keates P-L (china)
1868 Kelly CM
1869 Keates P-L (china)

Brammar, Elizabeth
See: Brammer, Elizabeth

Brammer, Elizabeth
Daisy Bank, Lane End or Longton
1834 White EM-LE-L (toys)
1835 Pigot TOCM
1841 Pigot TOCM
The surname is listed as Brammar in 1841 Pigot.

Brammer, Thomas
Daisey Bank, Lane End
1830 Pigot EM (toy only)

Brammer, William
Trentham Road, Longton
1862 Slater PM

Brassington, Joseph Henry
Wharf Street, Stoke
1900 Kelly EM

Bratt, Joseph
Edward Street, Burslem
1882 Keates P-B

Bray & Harrison
Lane Delph
1796 Chester NC-LE-LD-LL (manufacturers of earthenware)
1798 Universal NC-LD (manufacturers of Staffordshire-ware)

Brayford & Gelson
(i) Fountain Place Works, Burslem
1889 Keates P-B (earthenware)
1892 Keates P-B (earthenware)
(ii) Park House Lane, Burslem
1892 Kelly EM

Breeze, Jesse
Greenfield, Tunstall
1816 Underhill P
1818 Parson EM-G-T-R
1818 Pigot EM
1822 Allbut CEM (earthenware manufact.)
1822 Pigot EM

Breeze, John
(i) Burslem
1796 Chester NC-B (manufacturer of earthenware)
(ii) Longport
1796 Chester NC-T-Lp (manufacturer of earthenware)
(iii) Smithfield
1802 Allbut EM (map location 12)

Breeze, John, & Co.
(i) Cobridge
1828 Pigot CM
(ii) Tunstall
1830 Pigot CM

Breeze, John, & Son
Greenfield, near Tunstall
1805 Holden NC (earthenware manufacturers)
1809 Holden NC (earthenware-manufacturers)
1811 Holden NC (earthenware-manufacturers)

Breeze, William
Shelton
1818 Pigot EM

Brewer & Co.
Stafford Street, Longton
1865 Keates P-L (rustic and lustre wares)

Brewer, F. & H., & Co.
Stafford Street, Longton
1864 Jones A; EM (all kinds of horticultural and fancy rustic wares, majolica and dessert wares, &c.); EM-Miscellaneous (manufacturers of all kinds of horticultural and fancy rustic ware and majolica); SC (Earthenware Rustic and Terra Cotta Figure Manufacturers)
The advertisement in 1864 Jones describes the firm as 'manufacturers of all kinds of horticultural and fancy rustic wares, green dessert services, filters, &c.', and repeats in French 'fabricants de faïence pour le jardinnage, et d'articles rustiques de toutes espèces, services ì dessert vertes, fontaines, &c.'

F. & H. Brewer & Co. Advertisement from 1864 Jones.

Brewer, Francis, & Son
(i) 3 St Martin's Lane, Longton
1862 Slater EM (rustic)
(ii) Stafford Street Works, Longton
1863 Kelly CM-Horticultural & Rustic Ware; COM (majolica); SC (China Vase Manufacturers); SC (Horticultural Goods Manufacturers – China)

Brick, Tile & Sanitary Ware Co.
Victoria Road, Shelton, Stoke
1900 Kelly SC (Sanitary Ware Manufacturers)

Bridgett & Bates
King Street China Works, Longton
1882 Keates P-L (china)
1884 Kelly CM (general china manufacturers for home & export)
1888 Kelly CM (general china manufacturers for home & export)
1889 Keates P-L (china)
1892 Keates P-L (china)
1892 Kelly CM (general china manufacturers for home & export)
1896 Kelly CM
1900 Kelly CM

Bridgett, Bates & Co.
King Street, Longton
1876 Kelly CM

Bridgett, Bates & Beech
King Street China Works, Longton
1875 Keates P-L (china)
1879 Keates P-L (china)
1880 Kelly CM (general china manufacturers for home & export)

Bridgewood, Jesse
See: Bridgwood, Jesse

Bridgewood, Sampson, & Son
See: Bridgwood, Sampson, & Son

Bridgewood, Samuel
See: Bridgwood, Samuel

Bridgwood, Davis
Heathcote Road, Longton
1869 Keates P-L (earthenware)
1870 Harrod NC-L (earthenware manufacturer)

Bridgwood, Jesse
(i) High Street, Tunstall
1841 Pigot SC (Palette and Colour Slab Manufacturers, for Artists)
1846 Williams NC-T (china slate manufacturer)
1850 Slater SC (Palette & Colour Slab Manufacturers – for Artists)
(ii) Church Works, Burslem
1851 White CEM-B (both)
1852 Slater EM (& artists' colour-slab and pallet manufactr, water-closet-pan and plug-bowl, and fancy iron-stone ware); SC (Palette and Colour Slab Manufacturers – for Artists)

1854 Kelly CEM
1856 Kelly CEM
The first name is listed as Jessie in 1846 Williams, and the surname as Bridgewood in 1851 White.

Bridgwood, Kitty
Lane End
1809 Holden NC (earthenware-manufac.)
1811 Holden NC (earthenware-manufac.)
1816 Underhill P

Bridgwood, Kitty, & Son
(i) Market Street, Lane End
1818 Parson EM-LE
(ii) High Street, Lane End
1818 Pigot EM
The first name is listed as Ketty in 1818 Pigot.

Bridgwood, Maria
Market Street, Lane End
1818 Parson EM-LE

Bridgwood, Richard
82 Stafford Street, Longton
1887 Porter EM-L
1889 Keates P-L (china and earthenware)
1892 Keates P-L (china and earthenware)

Bridgwood, S. jun.
Lane End
1809 Holden NC (earthenware-manufac.)
1811 Holden NC (earthenware-manuf.)
1816 Underhill P

Bridgwood, Sampson
(i) Market Street, Lane End
1822 Allbut CEM (china manufact.)
1828 Pigot CM
1830 Pigot CM
1834 White CM-LE-L
(ii) High Street, Lane End
1835 Pigot CM
(iii) Stafford Street, Longton
1841 Pigot CM
1846 Williams NC-L-LE (china manufacturer)
1850 Kelly CEM; NC-L (china manufacturer)
1850 Slater CM
1851 White CEM-L
Bridgwood's house is listed as High Street, Longton, in 1834 White and Spratslade in 1851 White.

Bridgwood, Sampson, & Son
(i) Stafford Street, Longton
1852 Slater CM
(ii) Stafford Street and Anchor Works, Longton
1854 Kelly CEM
1856 Kelly CEM
(iii) Anchor Pottery, Sutherland Road, Longton
1861 Harrison NC-L (china and earthenware manufacturers)
1862 Slater CM; EM
1864 Jones CEM
1865 Keates P-L (china, & earthenware)
1867 Keates P-L (china and earthenware)
1869 Keates P-L (china and earthenware)
1870 Harrod NC-L (manufacturers of china and earthenware for home and foreign markets, and grinders of all kinds of potters' materials, &c., &c.)
1873 Keates P-L (china and earthenware)
1875 Keates P-L (china and earthenware)
(iv) Anchor Pottery, Wharf Street, Longton
1879 Keates P-L (china and earthenware)
1882 Keates P-L (china and earthenware)
1887 Porter EM-L
1889 Keates P-L (earthenware and flint grinders)
1892 Keates P-L (earthenware and flint grinders)
(v) East Vale, Longton
1860 Kelly EM
1863 Kelly EM
1868 Kelly EM
1872 Kelly EM
1876 Kelly EM
1880 Kelly EM
1884 Kelly EM
1888 Kelly EM
1892 Kelly EM
1896 Kelly EM
1900 Kelly EM
Bridgwood's first name is listed as Simpson in 1861 Harrison and Samson in 1882 Keates. The surname is listed as Bridgewood in 1873 Keates, 1875 Keates and 1879 Keates, and the address as Anchor Pottery and Anchor Mills in 1870 Harrod. The firm is noted as being in the hands of executors in 1879 Keates and the manager is listed as Richard Gaskell of Sidmouth Road, Newcastle, in 1882 Keates.

Bridgwood, Samuel
(i) Lane End
1802 Allbut EM (map location 130)
1805 Holden NC (earthenware manufacturer)
(ii) Old Foley Pottery, Foley
1875 Keates P-F (earthenware); P-L (earthenware)
The surname is listed as Bridgewood in 1802 Allbut and 1875 Keates.

Bridgwood & Burgess
Market Street, Longton
1846 Williams NC-L-LE (china manufacturers)
The partners are listed individually as Samuel Bridgewood (sic), of Spratslade House, and John Burgess in 1846 Williams.

Bridgwood & Clarke
(i) Churchyard Works, Burslem
1860 Kelly EM
1861 Harrison NC-B (earthenware manufacturers)
1863 Kelly EM
1864 Jones EM; SC (China and Porcelain Door Furniture Manufacturers)
(ii) Phoenix Works, High Street, Tunstall
1862 Slater EM (stone and granite ware)
1863 Kelly EM
1864 Jones EM; SC (China and Porcelain Door Furniture Manufacturers)
The second partner's name is listed as Clark in 1862 Slater.

Bridgwood, Weston & Cokeler
Foley, Fenton
1851 White CEM-F

Brindley, James
(i) Stoke
1784 Bailey NC-S (potter)
(ii) Longport
1798 Universal NC-Lp (Staffordshire-ware manufacturer)

Brindley, John
(i) Longport
1781 Bailey NC (potter)
1783 Bailey NC (potter)
(ii) Norton-in-the-Moors
1852 Slater EM

Brindley, John, & Co.
Broad Street, Shelton
1828 Pigot EM

Brindley, Taylor
Fenton
1784 Bailey NC-F (potter)

Britannia China Co.
Edensor Road, Longton
1896 Kelly CM
1900 Kelly CM
The manager is listed as Thomas William Bourne in both directories.

British Anchor Pottery Co.
Anchor Road, Longton
1887 Porter EM-L

British Anchor Pottery Co. Ltd.
Anchor Road, Longton
1888 Kelly EM
1889 Keates P-L
1892 Keates P-L
1892 Kelly EM
1896 Kelly EM
1900 Kelly EM

British Anchor Pottery Co. Ltd. Printed mark from an 1887 jubilee earthenware plate.

Brittell, John
Burslem
1816 Underhill P

Broadhurst & Sons
Stafford Street, Longton
1856 Kelly CEM
1860 Kelly CM-General
1861 Harrison NC-L (china and earthenware manufacturers)

Broadhurst, James
(i) Crown Pottery, Stafford Street, Longton
1863 Kelly CM-White & Finished; EM; LM; SM
1864 Jones A; EM; LM
1865 Keates P-L (earthenware)
1867 Keates P-L (earthenware)
1868 Kelly EM
1869 Keates P-L (earthenware)
1870 Harrod NC-L (earthenware manufacturer)
(ii) Portland Pottery, Victoria Road, Fenton
1872 Kelly EM
1873 Keates P-F (earthenware)
1875 Keates P-F (earthenware)
1876 Kelly EM
1879 Keates P-F (earthenware)
1880 Kelly EM
1882 Keates P-F (earthenware)
1884 Kelly EM
1887 Porter EM-F
1888 Kelly EM
1889 Keates P-F (earthenware)
1892 Keates P-F (earthenware)
1892 Kelly EM
The address of the Portland Pottery is listed as Frederick Street (which is off Victoria Road) in 1887 Porter. The advertisement in 1864 Jones describes Broadhurst as a 'manufacturer of earthenware, gold & silver lustres, coloured and stone ware'.

JAMES BROADHURST,
MANUFACTURER OF
EARTHENWARE, GOLD & SILVER LUSTRES,
Coloured and Stone Ware,
CROWN POTTERY, STAFFORD STREET, LONGTON,
STAFFORDSHIRE POTTERIES.

James Broadhurst. Advertisement from 1864 Jones.

Broadhurst, James, & Sons
(i) Commerce Street and Crown Pottery, Stafford Street, Longton
1862 Slater EM (and of crown lustre, smeared black, &c.)
(ii) Portland Pottery, Fenton
1896 Kelly EM
1900 Kelly EM

Broadhurst, James & Samuel
(i) Gold Street, Longton
1860 Kelly EM
(ii) Commerce Street, Longton
1861 Harrison NC-L (earthenware manufacturers)

Broadhurst, Job
See: Broadhurst & Green

Broadhurst, Samuel
Gold Street Works, Gold Street, Longton
1862 Slater A; EM (and printer, enameller, lusterer, and gilder)
1863 Kelly EM
The advertisement in 1862 Slater describes Broadhurst as an 'earthenware manufacturer, printer, enameller, lusterer and gilder'.

SAMUEL BROADHURST,
EARTHENWARE MANUFACTURER,
PRINTER, ENAMELLER,
LUSTERER AND GILDER,
GOLD STREET WORKS, LONGTON,
STAFFORDSHIRE.

Samuel Broadhurst. Advertisement from 1862 Slater.

Broadhurst & Green
(i) New Street, Longton
1846 Williams NC-L-LE (earthenware manufctrs.)
(ii) Sutherland Road, Longton
1850 Kelly CEM; NC-L (earthenware, black & lustre manufacturers)
(iii) Anchor Works, Anchor Lane, Longton
1850 Slater EM
1851 White CEM-L (only earthenware)
The partners are listed individually as Job Broadhurst of Highfield Cottage and William Green of Green Dock in 1846 Williams.

Brock & Allen
Broad Street, Shelton, Hanley
1860 Kelly CM-General
1861 Harrison NC-H-Sh (parian manufacturers)

Bromley, John
Barker Street, Longton
1896 Kelly EM; JRM
1900 Kelly EM; JRM

Bromley & Shaw
Barker Street, Longton
1892 Kelly EM

Bromley, Turner & Hassall
Liverpool Road, Stoke
1862 Slater EM; PM

The third partner's surname is listed inconsistently as Hassall (EM) or Hassell (PM).

Brookes & Co.
Sitch, Burslem
1818 Pigot CM

Brookes, Elijah
Trent Walk, Hanley
1900 Kelly JRM

Brookes, Philip, & Co.
(i) Sitch, Burslem
1818 Parson EM-B-Lp-C
(ii) Clarence Street, Shelton
1851 White CEM-H-Sh

Brookfield Brothers
Market Lane, Longton
1892 Keates P-L (china and earthenware)

Brough Brothers
Gold Street Works, Gold Street, Longton
1865 Keates A; P-L (earthenware)
1868 Kelly EM
The advertisement in 1865 Keates is in the name of Brough Brothers & Co. (qv).

Brough Brothers. Printed mark from a blue-printed earthenware dinner plate.

Brough Brothers & Co.
Gold Street Works, Gold Street, Longton
1864 Jones EM
1867 Keates A; P-L (earthenware)
1869 Keates A; P-L (earthenware)
1870 Harrod NC-L (earthenware manufacturers)
The advertisement in 1867 Keates describes the firm simply as 'earthenware manufacturers' and the same advertisement appeared in 1865 Keates although the firm is listed in that directory as Brough Brothers (qv). The advertisement in 1869 Keates describes them as 'general earthenware manufacturers, for home and exportation'.

BROUGH BROTHERS, & CO.,
Earthenware Manufacturers,
GOLD STREET WORKS,
LONGTON,
STAFFORDSHIRE POTTERIES.

Brough Brothers & Co. Advertisement from 1865 Keates.

BROUGH, BROTHERS, & Co.,
Earthenware Manufacturers,
GOLD STREET WORKS,
LONGTON,
STAFFORDSHIRE POTTERIES.

Brough Brothers & Co. Advertisement from 1867 Keates.

BROUGH BROTHERS & COMPY.,
GENERAL
EARTHENWARE
MANUFACTURERS,
FOR HOME AND EXPORTATION,
GOLD STREET WORKS,
Longton, Staffordshire.

Brough Brothers & Co. Advertisement from 1869 Keates.

Brough & Son
Silverdale Tileries, Newcastle
1887 Porter NC-N (manufacturers of metalic (sic) blue bricks and tiles)
1888 Kelly A; SC (Sanitary Ware Manufacturers)
An advertisement in 1887 Porter offers 'superior pressed roofing tiles: red, blue, brindled, Broseley; paving tiles: best pressed, red, black, blue, buff; garden border tiles; ridge tiles; metallic blue bricks, facing and paving; manger bricks. &c. &c.' The advertisement in 1888 Kelly describes the firm as 'manufacturers of all kinds of roofing tiles, plain and ornamental' and list the products as 'metallic blue bricks, ridge tiles, facing, paving, and channel bricks, window-sill bricks, coping bricks; superior pressed paving tiles, in red, blue, black, and buff colors; garden

BROUGH & SON,
MANUFACTURERS OF
Blue Bricks, Tiles, Pipes, &c.
ROOFING, RIDGE, AND FLOORING TILES,
FACING, PAVING, AND CHANNEL BRICKS.
TERRA COTTA CHIMNEY TOPS, FIRE BRICKS, ETC.,
SILVERDALE TILERIES, NEWCASTLE,
STAFFORDSHIRE.

Brough & Son. Advertisement from 1867 Keates.

BROUGH & SON,
Silverdale Tileries
NEWCASTLE, STAFFORDSHIRE.
Superior Pressed ROOFING TILES:
RED, BLUE, BRINDLED, BROSELEY.
PAVING TILES
BEST PRESSED, RED, BLACK, BLUE, BUFF
GARDEN BORDER TILES.
RIDGE TILES.
METALLIC BLUE BRICKS
FACING AND PAVING.
MANGER BRICKS.
&c. &c.

Brough & Son. Advertisement from 1887 Porter.

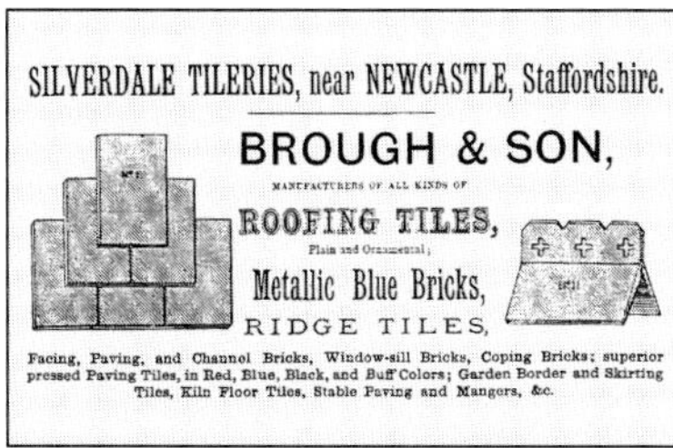

Brough & Son. Advertisement from 1884 Kelly. The same advertisement appeared in 1888 Kelly.

border and skirting tiles, kiln floor tiles, stable paving and mangers, &c.' An identical advertisement appeared in 1884 Kelly, where the firm is listed as William Brough & Son (qv). Another advertisement appears in 1867 Keates and describes the firm as 'manufacturers of blue bricks, tiles, pipes, &c., roofing, ridge, and flooring tiles, facing, paving, and channel bricks, terra cotta chimney tops, fire bricks, etc.'

Brough, Benjamin Hyde
Waterloo Works, Stafford Street, Longton
1892 Keates P-L (earthenware)
1892 Kelly EM

Brough, Benjamin S.
See: Allerton, Brough & Green

Brough, John Walley
Wharf Street, Stoke
1900 Kelly EM; MM

Brough, Thomas
Green Dock, Lane End
1816 Underhill P
1818 Parson EM-LE
1818 Pigot EM
1822 Pigot EM

Brough, William, & Co.
St. Martin's Lane, Longton
1879 Keates P-L (china)

Brough, William, & Son
Silverdale Tileries, near Newcastle-under-Lyme
1880 Kelly SC (Sanitary Ware Manufacturers)
1884 Kelly A; SC (Sanitary Ware Manufacturers)
The advertisement in 1884 Kelly describes Brough & Son as 'manufacturers of all kinds of roofing tiles, plain and ornamental' and list the products as 'metallic blue bricks, ridge tiles, facing, paving, and channel bricks, window-sill bricks, coping bricks; superior pressed paving tiles, in red, blue, black, and buff colors; garden border and skirting tiles, kiln floor tiles, stable paving and mangers, &c.' An identical advertisement appeared in 1888 Kelly, where the firm is listed simply as Brough & Son (qv).

Brough & Blackhurst
Waterloo Works, Stafford Street, Longton
1872 Kelly EM
1873 Keates P-L (earthenware)
1875 Keates P-L (earthenware)
1876 Kelly EM
1879 Keates P-L (earthenware)
1880 Kelly EM
1882 Keates P-L (earthenware)
1884 Kelly EM
1887 Porter EM-L
1888 Kelly EM
1889 Keates P-L (earthenware)

Brough & Jones
Wharf Street Pottery, Stoke
1887 Porter CEM-S
1888 Kelly EM; MM
1889 Keates P-S (earthenware)
1892 Kelly EM; MM
1896 Kelly EM; MM

Brough, Joynson & Co.
Bourne's Bank Pottery, Burslem
1860 Kelly EM
1861 Harrison NC-B (earthenware manufacturers)
1862 Slater EM
1863 Kelly EM
1864 Jones EM
1865 Keates P-B (earthenware)
1867 Keates P-B (earthenware)

Brougham, Thomas
Sandyford, Tunstall
1860 Kelly EM
1861 Harrison NC-T (earthenware manufacturer)

Brougham & Mayer
(i) Newfield, Tunstall
1852 Slater EM
(ii) Sandyford, Tunstall
1854 Kelly CEM
1856 Kelly CEM

Brown & Co.
Church Street Pottery, Longton
1875 Keates P-L (china)
1876 Kelly EM
1879 Keates P-L (china)
1880 Kelly EM
1882 Keates P-L (china)
1884 Kelly CM

Brown, H.
See: Edwards & Brown

Brown, Henry, & Co.
High Street, Lane End
1828 Pigot EM (toy only)

Brown, John
Market Lane, Hanley
1822 Allbut CEM (coarse ware manufact.)

Brown, Robert
See: Wedgwood, Josiah, & Sons

Brown, Sarah
Hanley
1822 Allbut CEM (earthenware manufact. & enameller)

Brown, Sarah, & Co.
George Street, Hanley
1822 Pigot EM

Brown, William
Trent Pottery, Peel Street, Burslem
1862 Slater EM

Brown, William Southwell, & Co.
Copeland Street, Stoke
1872 Kelly CM

Brown, Westhead & Moore
See: Brown-Westhead (T.C.), Moore & Co.

Browne, J., & Co.
Burslem
1809 Holden NC (earthenware-manufrs.)

Browne & Cartledge
Burslem
1811 Holden NC (earthenware-manufs.)

Brownfield, George
Keeling, Lane End
1818 Pigot EM

Brownfield, R. & J.
Hanley
1816 Underhill P

Brownfield, William
(i) Waterloo Road, Cobridge
1851 White CEM-H-Sh; CEM-B (both)
1852 Slater EM (& iron-stone)
1854 Kelly CEM
1856 Kelly CEM

1860 Kelly EM
1861 Harrison NC-B (iron stone and earthenware manufacturer)
1862 Slater CM (ironstone)
1863 Kelly EM
1864 Jones EM
1865 Keates P-B (earthen.)
1867 Keates P-B (earthen.)
1868 Kelly EM
1869 Keates P-B (earthen.)
1870 Harrod NC-B (manufacturer of improved ironstone and earthenware for the home markets)
(ii) Barlaston
1870 Harrod NC-Bar (china and earthenware manufacturer)
Brownfield's house is listed as Old Hall Street, Hanley in 1851 White.
See also: Wood & Brownfield

William Brownfield. Moulded mark from a stoneware relief-moulded jug. The registration diamond dates from 1871.

William Brownfield & Son. Printed mark from a black-printed ironstone soup plate. The registration diamond dates from 1875.

Brownfield, William, & Son
Waterloo Road, Cobridge
1872 Kelly EM
1873 Keates P-B (earthenware and china)
1875 Keates P-B (earthenware and china)
1889 Keates P-B (earthenware and china)
1892 Keates P-B (earthenware & china)

Brownfield, William, & Sons
Waterloo Road, Cobridge
1876 Kelly EM
1879 Keates P-B (earthenware and china)
1880 Kelly CM; EM
1882 Keates P-B (earthenware and china)
1884 Kelly CM; EM
1887 Porter EM-B
1888 Kelly EM
1892 Kelly CM; EM

William Brownfield & Sons. Printed mark from a brown-printed earthenware jug.

Brownfield, William & George
Keeling's Lane, Hanley
1818 Parson EM-H-Sh
1822 Allbut CEM (earthenware manufacts.)
1822 Pigot EM

Brownfields Guild-Pottery Society Ltd.
Cobridge
1896 Kelly EM
1900 Kelly EM

Brownhills China Works
Brownhills, Tunstall
1854 Kelly CEM
The manager is listed as G.F. Bowers in 1854 Kelly.

Brownhills Pottery Co.
Brownhills, between Burslem and Tunstall
1872 Kelly EM
1873 Keates P-B (earthenware); P-T
1875 Keates P-B (earthenware); P-T
1876 Kelly EM
1879 Keates P-B (earthenware); P-T
1880 Kelly CM (see EM); EM (manufacturers of decorated earthenware &c. for home & colonial markets)
1882 Keates P-B (earthenware); P-T
1884 Kelly EM (manufacturers of decorated earthenware &c. for home & colonial markets)
1887 Porter EM-B; EM-T
1888 Kelly CM; EM (manufacturers of decorated earthenware &c. for home & colonial markets)
1889 Keates P-B (earthenware); P-T
1892 Keates P-B (earthenware); P-T (earthenware)
1892 Kelly EM
1896 Kelly EM
The address is listed as Liverpool Road, Burslem in 1887 Porter. A London office at 34 Hatton Garden is listed in 1880 Kelly, 1884 Kelly and 1888 Kelly.

Brownhills Pottery Co. Impressed mark from a sprigged stoneware bowl, probably manufactured by Dudson.

Brownhills Pottery Co. Impressed mark from a sprigged stoneware bowl, probably manufactured by Dudson.

Browning & Lewis
Smithfield Works, Hanley
1900 Kelly CM; EM

Brown-Westhead & Co.
See: Brown-Westhead (T.C.), Moore & Co.

Brown-Westhead, Thomas C.
Barlaston
1870 Harrod NC-Bar (china and earthenware manufacturer)

Brown-Westhead (T.C.), Moore & Co.
(i) Cauldon Place Hanley
1862 Slater CM; EM
1863 Kelly CM-General; EM; SC (China Porcelain Manufacturers); SC (Porcelain Statuary Manufacturers); SC (Sanitary Vessel Manufacturers); SM
1864 Jones CEM
1865 Keates P-H (china, earthenware, parian, and majolica)
1867 Keates P-H (china, earthenware, parian and majolica)
1868 Kelly CM; EM; PFM; SC (China Porcelain Manfufacturers); SM
1869 Keates P-H (china, earthenware, parian and majolica)
1870 Harrod NC-H (china and earthenware manufacturers for home and foreign markets)
1872 Kelly CM; EM; PM; SC (Sanitary Ware Manufacturers); SM
(ii) Cauldon Place, and Victoria Works or Victoria Square, Hanley
1873 Keates P-H (china, earthenware, parian, and majolica)
1875 Keates P-H (china, earthenware, parian, and majolica)
1876 Kelly CM; EM; SC (Druggists' Stoneware Manufacturers)
1879 Keates P-H (china, earthenware, parian, and majolica)
1880 Kelly CM; EM; PM; SC (Sanitary Ware Manufacturers); SC (Stoneware Manufacturers for Druggists)
1882 Keates P-H (china, earthenware, parian, and majolica)
(iii) Cauldon Place, Hanley
1884 Kelly CM
1887 Porter EM-H
1888 Kelly CM
1889 Keates P-H (china, earthenware, parian, and majolica)
1892 Keates P-H (china sanitary, earthenware, parian, and majolica)
1892 Kelly CM
1896 Kelly CM
1900 Kelly CM
There is considerable variation in the style of this firm in directory listings, the main variants being Brown-Westhead & Co. in 1867 Keates and Brown, Westhead & Moore in 1887 Porter. Many minor variants have either no hyphen or without the initials T.C. and have not been recorded separately here. London offices are listed at 107 Hatton Garden (1863 Kelly, 1868 Kelly, 1870 Harrod, 1872 Kelly) and at Fitz Eylwin House, Holborn Viaduct (1872 Kelly, 1876 Kelly, 1880 Kelly). A German office at Grosse Reichen Strasse 38-B, Hamburg, is listed in 1870 Harrod.

T.C. Brown-Westhead, Moore & Co. Printed and impressed marks from a blue-printed earthenware plate. The registration diamond dates from 1879.

T.C. Brown-Westhead, Moore & Co. Printed and impressed marks from a mauve-printed earthenware dinner plate. The registration diamond dates from 1868.

Brunt, Ralph
King Street, Fenton
1850 Slater TOCM

Brunt, Thomas
Millfield Gate, Lane End
1835 Pigot TOCM
1841 Pigot TOCM

Brunt, William
Daisy Bank, Lane End or Longton
1834 White EM-LE-L (toys)
1835 Pigot TOCM
1841 Pigot TOCM

Bruze, Samuel
Longport
1798 Universal NC-Lp (Staffordshire-ware manufacturer)

Buckley & Co. Ltd.
Stafford Street, Longton
1896 Kelly SC (Sanitary Ware Manufacturers)

Buckley & Son
Navigation Road, Burslem
1892 Keates P-B (jet)

Buckley, H.
4 Victoria Place, Hanley
1892 Keates P-H (sanitary ware)

Buckley, James
Vine Street, Hanley
1865 Keates P-H (sanitary ware)
1867 Keates P-H (sanitary ware)
1868 Kelly SC (Sanitary Ware Manufacturers)
1869 Keates P-H (sanitary ware)
1870 Harrod NC-H (manufacturer of sanitary wares of every description)
1873 Keates P-H (sanitary ware)

ESTABLISHED 1856.
Albert Works, Victoria Road, Hanley.
J. BUCKLEY,
Earthenware Manufacturer,
SANITARY POTTER, &c.

Jane Buckley. Advertisement from 1889 Keates.

Buckley, Jane
4 Victoria Place, Hanley
1889 Keates A; P-H (sanitary ware)

The advertisement in 1889 Keates gives the address as Albert Works, Victoria Road, Hanley. It describes J. Buckley as an 'earthenware manufacturer, sanitary potter, &c.' and claims that the firm was established in 1856.

Buckley, John
(i) Clarence Street, Hanley
1860 Kelly EM
1861 Harrison NC-H-Sh (sanitary pottery)
(ii) Vine Street, Hanley
1862 Slater EM (sanitary); SC (Water-Closet Basin Manufacturers)
1863 Kelly EM (glazed); SC (Beer Machine Handle Maker); SC (Sanitary Vessel Manufacturers); SC (Water Closet Pan Manufacturer)
1864 Jones EM-Miscellaneous (beer machine handle maker, and sanitary earthenware manufacturer)
1875 Keates P-H (sanitary ware)
(iii) Albert Works, 4 Victoria Place, Hanley
1876 Kelly SC (Beer Engine Handle Maker); SC (Sanitary Ware Manufacturers); SC (Water Closet Makers)
1879 Keates P-H (sanitary ware)
1880 Kelly SC (Beer Engine Handle Maker); SC (Sanitary Ware Manufacturers), manufacturer of sanitary ware, water-closet pans & traps, urinals, ship & portable closets, closet pulls, beer handles &c.); SC (Water Closet Maker)
1882 Keates P-H (sanitary ware)
1884 Kelly SC (Sanitary Ware Manufacturers) (manufacturer of water-closet basins & traps, table tops, urinals, ship & portable closets &c. "Niagara Falls" basin & traps &c.); SC (Water Closet Makers)
1888 Kelly SC (Sanitary Ware Manufacturers) (manufacturer of water-closet basins & traps, table tops, urinals, ship & portable closets &c. "Niagara Falls" basin & traps &c.); SC (Water Closet Makers)
1892 Kelly SC (Sanitary Ware Manufacturers) (manufacturer of water-closet basins & traps, table tops, urinals, ship & portable closets &c. "Niagara Falls" basin & traps &c.)
The firm was succeeded by the Park Sanitary Co. (1896 Kelly).

Buckley, John, & Son
Navigation Road Pottery, Burslem
1892 Kelly JRM
1896 Kelly JRM

Buckley & Bent
Newcastle
1796 Chester NC-S (manufacturers of earthenware)

Buckley & Heath
High Street Pottery, Burslem
1889 Keates P-B (earthenware)

Buckley, Heath & Co.
High Street, Burslem
1887 Porter EM-B
1888 Kelly EM

Buckley, Heath & Greatbatch
High Street Pottery, Burslem
1892 Keates P-B (earthenware)

Buckley, Wood & Co.
High Street Pottery, Burslem
1875 Keates P-B (earthen.)
1876 Kelly EM
1879 Keates P-B (earthen.)
1880 Kelly EM
1882 Keates P-B (earthenware)
1884 Kelly EM

Bucknall, Ralph, & Son
Cobridge
1781 Bailey NC (potters)
1783 Bailey NC (potters)

Bucknell, Ralph & Joseph
Cobridge
1798 Universal NC-C (manufacturers of Staffordshire-ware)

Buller & Co.
Joiner's Square Works, Hanley
1861 Harrison NC-H-Sh (cock spur maker)
1870 Harrod NC-H (manufacturers of earthenware, thimble cockspurs, stilts, pins, cup rings, claws, and every sort of placing goods for potters' use, china, mortice, rim, and latch furniture, finger plates, shutter, drawer, and centre knobs, vitrified castor bowls, and every description of china for the brassfounders, cabinet, and metallic bedstead trades, &c., insulators, battery plates, cells, and all kinds of electric telegraph ware, mortars, pestles, &c.)
1872 Kelly SC (China & Porcelain Door Furniture Manufacturers); SC (Stone Mortar & Pestle Manufacturers)
1873 Keates P-H (spurs & stilts)
1875 Keates P-H (spurs and stilts)
1876 Kelly SC (Lock Furniture Makers – China); SC (Stone Mortar & Pestle Manufacturers)
1879 Keates P-H (spurs and stilts, and door furniture, &c.)
1880 Kelly SC (Door Furniture Makers – China)
1882 Keates P-H (spurs and stilts, and door furniture, &c.)
1884 Kelly SC (Door Furniture Makers – China)
1889 Keates P-H (spurs and stilts, and door furniture, &c.)
Birmingham depots are listed at 23 Congreve Street (1870 Harrod, 1872 Kelly) and Sherlock Street (1876 Kelly). London addresses are listed at 6 Martin's Lane, Cannon Street (1872 Kelly) and 132 Upper Thames Street (1876 Kelly).

Buller, Wentworth William
Joiner's Square, Hanley
1860 Kelly SC (Spur Makers) (patent cock spur & stilt)
The manager is listed as Thomas Forrester Walklet in 1860 Kelly. An address at Bovey Tracey, Devon, is listed in 1860 Kelly.

Buller, W.W., & Co.
Spur Street, Joiner's Square, Eastwood Vale, Hanley
1867 Keates P-H (spurs and stilts)
1869 Keates P-H (spurs and stilts)

Buller, Jobson & Co.
Joiner's Square, Hanley
1887 Porter EM-H
1892 Keates P-H (spurs & stilts, & door furniture, &c.)

Buller, Jobson & Co. Ltd.
Joiner's Square Works, Hanley
1888 Kelly SC (Door Furniture Makers – China)

Buller & Mugford
Joiner's Square, Eastwood Vale, Hanley
1862 Slater SC (Stilt and Spur Manufacturers – Patent)
1863 Kelly SC (Cock Spur Manufacturers) (patent)
The first partner was Wentworth William Buller. The firm is listed as Buller (Wentworth William) & Mugford in 1863 Kelly and as Wentworth, W., Buller & Mugford in 1862 Slater. The manager is listed as Charles A. Draycott in 1863 Kelly.

Buller, Mugford & Co. (W. W.)
Joiner's Square, Hanley
1864 Jones EM-Miscellaneous (patent cockspur, stilt, &c.)

Buller, Mugford & Draycott
Eastwood Vale, Hanley
1865 Keates P-H (spurs and stilts)

Bullers Ltd.
Joiner's Square Works, Hanley
1892 Kelly SC (Door Furniture Manufacturers – China)
1896 Kelly SC (Door Furniture Manufacturers – China)
1900 Kelly SC (Door Furniture Manufacturers – China)

Bullock, A., & Co.
Commercial Road, Hanley
1896 Kelly EM
1900 Kelly EM

Bullock, Alfred
Pelham Street, off Lichfield Street, and 42 Nelson Place, Hanley
1880 Kelly PM

Bullock, Charles
Britannia Works, Bagnall Street or High Street, Longton
1860 Kelly CM-General; COM
1861 Harrison NC-L (china manufacturer)
1862 Slater CM
1863 Kelly CM-General; CM-Tea, Breakfast, and Dessert Services; COM
1864 Jones CEM
1865 Keates P-L (china)

Bullock & Bennett
Pelham Street, Hanley
1892 Kelly EM

Bullock & Cornes
Pelham Street, off Lichfield Street, Hanley
1884 Kelly EM
1887 Porter EM-H
1888 Kelly EM
1892 Kelly EM

Burgess, Henry
Kilncroft Works, Sylvester Square or Chapel Lane, Burslem
1863 Kelly EM
1864 Jones EM
1865 Keates A; P-B (earthen.)
1868 Kelly EM
1869 Keates P-B (earthen.)
1870 Harrod NC-B (earthenware manufacturer)
1872 Kelly EM
1873 Keates P-B (earthen.)
1875 Keates P-B (earthenware)
1876 Kelly EM
1879 Keates P-B (earthenware)
1880 Kelly EM
1882 Keates P-B (earthenware)
1884 Kelly EM
1887 Porter EM-B
1888 Kelly EM
1889 Keates P-B (earthenware)
1892 Keates P-B (earthenware)
1892 Kelly EM
The advertisement in 1865 Keates describes Burgess as a 'manufacturer of white granite & stone ware, door furniture, decorated toilet sets and jugs, patent commode pans, &c.'

HENRY BURGESS,
MANUFACTURER OF
WHITE GRANITE & STONE WARE
DOOR FURNITURE,
DECORATED TOILET SETS AND JUGS,
PATENT COMMODE PANS, &c.,
KILN CROFT WORKS, BURSLEM, STAFFORDSHIRE POTTERIES.

Henry Burgess. Advertisement from 1865 Keates.

Burgess, Richard
See: Burgess & Gibson

Burgess & Gibson
Watergate Street, Tunstall
1846 Williams NC-T (earthenware manufacturers)
1850 Slater EM
1851 White EM-T
1852 Slater EM
1854 Kelly CEM
The partners are listed individually as Richard Burgess of Beswick Street and William Gibson of Audley Street in 1846 Williams.

Burgess, Leigh & Co. Printed mark from a black-printed earthenware tureen. The registration diamond dates from 1875.

Burgess & Leigh
(i) Central Pottery, Market Place, Burslem
1862 Slater EM
1863 Kelly EM
1864 Jones EM
1867 Keates P-B (earthen.)
(ii) Hill Pottery, Liverpool Road, Burslem
1880 Kelly EM (manufacturers of general earthenware for the home & foreign markets)
1882 Keates P-B (earthenware)
1884 Kelly EM
1887 Porter EM-B
1888 Kelly EM
(iii) Middleport Pottery, Burslem
1889 Keates P-B (earthenware)
1892 Keates P-B (earthenware)
1892 Kelly EM
1896 Kelly EM
1900 Kelly EM
This firm succeeded Samuel Alcock

& Co. at the Hill Pottery (1880 Kelly). London showrooms are listed at 6 Thavies Inn, Holborn Circus, in 1892 Kelly and at 60 Shoe Lane, Charterhouse Street, in 1896 Kelly.

Burgess, Leigh & Co.
Hill Pottery, Market Place or Liverpool Road, Burslem

1868 Kelly	EM
1869 Keates	P-B (earthen.)
1870 Harrod	NC-B (earthenware and china manufacturers for home and foreign markets)
1872 Kelly	EM
1873 Keates	P-B (earthen.)
1875 Keates	P-B (earthenware)
1876 Kelly	EM
1879 Keates	P-B (earthenware)

Burknall, Robert
Cobridge

1784 Bailey	NC-C (manufacturer of Queen's ware, blue painted, enamelled, printed, &c.)

Burrow, Arthur
Hanley

1798 Universal	NC-H (manufacturer of Staffordshire-ware)

Burrow, Joseph
Foley Works, Lane End

1818 Parson	EM-LE

Burrow, Joseph jun.
High Street, Lane End

1822 Pigot	EM
1828 Pigot	EM

Burslem Pottery Co.
Scotia Works, Wedgwood Place, Burslem

1892 Kelly	EM
1896 Kelly	EM
1900 Kelly	EM

The proprietor is listed as C.F. Bailey in 1892 Kelly.

Burton Brothers
Waterloo Works, Hanley

1887 Porter	EM-H
1888 Kelly	EM

Burton, George & Benjamin
(i) Waterloo Works, Nelson Place, Hanley

1884 Kelly	EM
1889 Keates	P-H

(ii) Registry Street, Stoke

1889 Keates	P-S (earthenware and figures)
1892 Keates	P-S (earthenware and figures)
1892 Kelly	EM
1896 Kelly	EM
1900 Kelly	EM

Samuel & John Burton. Printed mark from a blue-printed earthenware dinner plate.

Samuel & John Burton. Printed and impressed marks from a black-printed earthenware child's plate

Burton, Samuel & John
New Street, Shelton, Hanley

1834 White	EM-H-Sh
1835 Pigot	EM
1841 Pigot	EM

Burton & Morris
Bagnall Works, Bagnall Street, Longton

1879 Keates	P-L (china)
1884 Kelly	CM
1887 Porter	EM-L
1888 Kelly	CM

Burton, Morris & Co.
Bagnall Street, Longton

1876 Kelly	CM
1880 Kelly	CM
1882 Keates	P-L (china)
1889 Keates	P-L (china)
1892 Keates	P-L (china)

Although the directory contains no entry for the firm, there is an advertisement in 1873 Keates describing them simply as 'china manufacturers'.

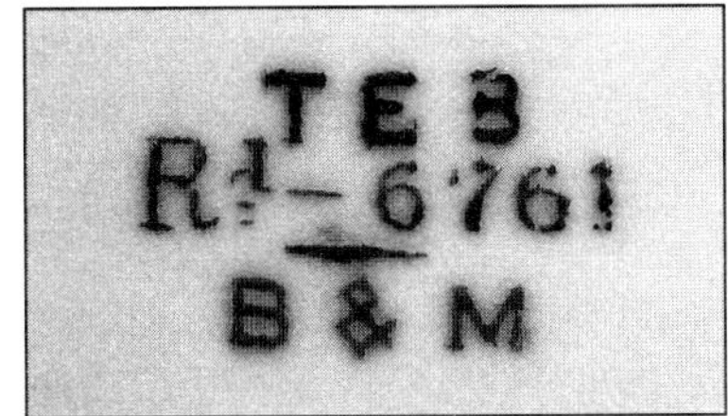

Burton & Morris. Printed mark from an overglaze-printed china saucer. The registration number dates from 1884.

BURTON, MORRIS, & Co.,
CHINA MANUFACTURERS,
BAGNALL WORKS,
BAGNALL STREET, LONGTON
STAFFORDSHIRE POTTERIES.

Burton, Morris & Co. Advertisement from 1873 Keates.

Burton, Wood & Co.
Mount Pleasant Works, High Street, Longton

1863 Kelly	CM-General; CM-Tea, Breakfast, and Dessert Services
1864 Jones	A; CEM
1865 Keates	P-L (china)

The advertisement in 1864 Jones describes the firm as 'manufacturers of all kinds of china, burnished & enameled (sic), suitable for home & foreign trade'.

MESSRS. BURTON, WOOD & Co.,
MOUNT PLEASANT WORKS,
HIGH STREET,
LONGTON, POTTERIES.
MANUFACTURERS OF
ALL KINDS OF CHINA,
BURNISHED & ENAMELED,
SUITABLE FOR
HOME & FOREIGN TRADE.

Burton, Wood & Co. Advertisement from 1864 Jones.

Butterfield, William & James
High Street, Tunstall

1856 Kelly CEM
1860 Kelly EM
1861 Harrison A; NC-T
The advertisement in 1861 Harrison describes the Butterfields as 'manufacturers of earthenware, comprising all kinds of printed and fancy printed common bodies, suitable for the East & West Indies, Australian, Russian, and North and South American Markets'.

WM. & JAS. BUTTERFIELD,
MANUFACTURERS OF
EARTHENWARE,
COMPRISING
All kinds of Printed and Fancy Printed Common Bodies,
SUITABLE FOR THE
EAST & WEST INDIES, AUSTRALIAN,
RUSSIAN,
AND
North and South AMERICAN Markets,
HIGH STREET POTTERY,
TUNSTALL, STAFFORDSHIRE.

William & James Butterfield. Advertisement from 1861 Harrison.

Byerley, J.
Fenton
1809 Holden NC (manufacturer of earthenware)
1816 Underhill P

C

Caldwell, Wood
See: Wood & Caldwell

Callinson, John
Golden Hill
1852 Slater SC (Saggar Maker) (and chimney pot)

Campbell Brick & Tile Co. (The)
London Road, Stoke
1875 Keates A; SC-S (Tile - Floor - Manufacturers)
1876 Kelly SC (Encaustic Tile Manufacturers) (manufacturers of encaustic geometrical & majolica tiles & mosaics)
1879 Keates SC-S (Tile - Floor - Manufacturers)
1880 Kelly SC (Encaustic Tile Manufacturers) (manufacturs. of encaustic, geometrical & majolica tiles & mosaics)
The manager is listed as Robert Minton Taylor in 1875 Keates and 1876 Kelly. London offices are listed at 27 Walbrook in 1876 Kelly and at 206 Great Portland Street in 1875 Keates (advertisement), 1876 Kelly and 1880 Kelly. The advertisement in 1875 Keates describes the firm as 'manufacturers of encaustic and geometrical tiles and mosaics, for churches, public buildings, halls, vestibules, conservatories, &c.; majolica, glazed, & other tiles, for hearths, fire-places, baths, walls, &c.; enamelled and earthenware tiles, from Minton's China Works'. The advertisement also lists their Dublin agents as Monsell, Mitchell & Co. of 73 Townsend Street.

THE CAMPBELL BRICK & TILE Co.,
STOKE-UPON-TRENT,
MANUFACTURERS OF
Encaustic and Geometrical Tiles and Mosaics,
For Churches, Public Buildings, Halls, Vestibules, Conservatories, &c.
MAJOLICA, GLAZED, & OTHER TILES,
For Hearths, Fire-places, Baths, Walls, &c.
Enamelled and Earthenware Tiles, from Minton's China Works.
ROBERT MINTON TAYLOR, Manager.
206, Gt. PORTLAND Street, W., LONDON.
Dublin Agents—MONSELL, MITCHELL, & Co., 73, Townsend Street

The Campbell Brick & Tile Co. Advertisement from 1875 Keates.

Campbell, O'Donnell & Co.
Stoke Road, Hanley
1887 Porter EM-H

Campbell, O'Donnell & Davies
Canning Street, Fenton
1887 Porter EM-F

Campbell Tile Works
Liverpool Road, Stoke
1887 Porter SC-S (Tile Manufacturers)

Campbell Tile Co.
London Road, Stoke
1882 Keates SC-S (Tile - Encaustic - Manufacturers); SC-S (Tile - Floor - Manufacturers)
1884 Kelly SC (Encaustic Tile Manufacturers) (manufacturers of encaustic, geometrical & majolica tiles & mosaics)
1888 Kelly SC (Encaustic Tile Manufacturers)
1889 Keates SC-S (Tile - Encaustic - Manufacturers); SC-S (Tile - Floor - Manufacturers)
1892 Keates SC-S (Tile - Encaustic - Manufacturers); SC-S (Tile - Floor - Manufacturers)
1892 Kelly SC (Encaustic Tile Manufacturers); SC (Mosaics Manufacturers)
1896 Kelly SC (Encaustic Tile Manufacturers); SC (Mosaics Manufacturers)
1900 Kelly SC (Encaustic Tile Manufacturers); SC (Mosaics Manufacturers)
A London office at 206 Great Portland Street is listed in 1884 Kelly.

Capper & Co.
Parkhall Street, Longton
1888 Kelly EM

Capper, John
Golden Hill
1796 Chester NC-T-Lp (manufacturer of earthenware)
1798 Universal NC-G (coarse-ware potter)

Capper, John & Thomas
Golden Hill
1802 Allbut EM (map location 2)

Carey & Son
Lane End
1818 Parson EM-LE

Carey, John, & Son
High Street, Lane End
1818 Pigot EM

Carey, John, & Sons
(i) Lane Delph
1822 Pigot EM
(ii) Lane Delph and Lane End
1822 Allbut CEM (earthenware manufacturers)
(iii) Anchor Street, Lane End
1828 Pigot CM; EM

Carey, Thomas & John
(i) Lane Delph
1830 Pigot EM
1834 White CEM-F-LD
(ii) Anchor Works, Anchor Street (or Lane), Lane End
1830 Pigot CM; EM
1834 White CM-LE-L; EM-LE-L
1835 Pigot CM
1834 White CEM-F-LD
1835 Pigot EM
1841 Pigot CM
(iii) Fenton and Longton
1841 Pigot EM

Thomas & John Carey. Moulded mark from a relief-moulded stoneware jug.

Thomas & John Carey. Printed and impressed marks from a blue-printed stone china dinner plate.

Carey Swan, T.
See: Malcolm, Frederick

Carlton Pottery Co.
20 Glebe Buildings, Stoke
1900 Kelly CM; EM

Carter, John
Milk Street, Hanley or Shelton
1851 White CETOM-H-Sh

Carter, W.
Mill Street, Hanley
1854 Kelly CEM (gilder)

Carter, William
High Street, Stoke
1870 Harrod NC-S (manufacturer)
Carter is listed simply as a manufacturer, he may not have been a potter.

Cartledge, F.
See: Cartlidge, F.

Cartledge, James
Golden Hill
1818 Parson EM-G-T-R

Cartledge, John
Market Street, Longton
1868 Kelly CM
1869 Keates P-L (china)
1870 Harrod NC-L (china manufacturer)
The surname is listed as Cartlidge in 1868 Kelly.

Cartledge, John, & Co.
Market Street, Longton
1864 Jones CEM
1865 Keates P-L (china)
1867 Keates P-L (china)

Cartledge, Richard
Golden Hill
1818 Parson EM-G-T-R
1818 Pigot EM (black ware)
1822 Allbut CEM (earthenware manufact.)
1822 Pigot EM
The surname is listed as Cartlidge in 1818 Pigot and 1822 Pigot.

Cartledge, W.E.
(i) Mayer Street, Hanley
1873 Keates P-H (stone & parian)
(ii) Bourne's Bank, Burslem
1875 Keates P-B
1876 Kelly EM
1879 Keates P-B (earthen.)
The surname is listed as Cartlidge in 1876 Kelly.
See also: Cartlidge, William Edward.

Cartledge & Beech
See: Cartlidge & Beech

Cartledge & Cork
Queen Street, Burslem
1822 Allbut CEM (earthenware manufacts.)

Cartledge & Stanway
Villa Pottery, Cobridge
1882 Keates P-B

Cartlich, Elija
Stoke
1839 Cottrill NC-S (potter)

Cartlich, Samuel & John
Tunstall
1796 Chester NC-T-Lp (manufacturers of earthenware)

Cartlich, Samuel & Thomas
Tunstall
1802 Allbut EM (map location 8)
1805 Holden NC (earthenware manufacturers)
1809 Holden NC (earthenware-manufactrs.)
1811 Holden NC (earthenware-manufr.)

Cartlick, Samuel & Thomas
Golden Hill
1798 Universal NC-G (earthenware-manufacturers)

Cartlidge, F.
Normacot Road, Longton
1889 Keates P-L (china)
1892 Keates P-L (china)
The surname is listed as Cartledge.

Cartlidge, F., & Co.
Normacot Road, Longton
1892 Kelly CM
1896 Kelly CM
1900 Kelly CM

Cartlidge, J.
See: Cartledge, John

Cartlidge, James
Burslem
1816 Underhill P

Cartlidge, Richard
See: Cartledge, Richard

Cartlidge, S. & J.
Burslem
1784 Bailey NC-B (potters)

Cartlidge, W.E.
Elder Road, Burslem
1887 Porter EM-B
See also: Cartledge, W.E.

Cartlidge, William
Sun Street, Hanley
1872 Kelly MM

Cartlidge, William Edward
(i) Silvester Works, Silvester Square, Burslem
1864 Jones A; EM-Miscellaneous (brown, black, and lustre earthenware)
1865 Keates P-B (black and lustre)
(ii) Villa Pottery, Cobridge, Burslem

1880 Kelly EM
1884 Kelly EM
1888 Kelly EM
1889 Keates P-B
1892 Kelly EM
The surname is listed as Cartledge in 1889 Keates. The advertisement in 1864 Jones describes Cartlidge as a 'manufacturer of brown, black, & lustre earthenware'.

W. E. CARTLIDGE,
MANUFACTURER OF
BROWN, BLACK, & LUSTRE
EARTHENWARE,
SYLVESTER WORKS,
BURSLEM.

William Edward Cartlidge. Advertisement from 1864 Jones.

Cartlidge & Allen
Mount Pleasant, Longton
1888 Kelly CM
The second partner is listed as S. Allen in 1888 Kelly.

Cartlidge & Beech
(i) Red Lion Square, Burslem
1818 Pigot EM (Egyptian black)
(ii) Knowle Street, Burslem
1818 Parson EM-B-Lp-C
1822 Allbut CEM (earthenware and Egyptian black manufacts.)
(iii) Hamill Street, Burslem
1822 Pigot EM
The first partner's name is listed as Cartledge in 1818 Parson.

Cartlidge & Matthews
Mount Pleasant Works, Hanley
1887 Porter EM-H

Cartlidge & Matthias
(i) Tinkersclough, Hanley
1888 Kelly EM
1889 Keates P-H
1892 Kelly EM
(ii) Broad Street, Hanley
1892 Keates P-H
(iii) Slippery Lane, Hanley
1896 Kelly EM
1900 Kelly EM

Cartwright & Edwards
(i) Weston Place, High Street, Longton
1860 Kelly EM
1861 Harrison NC-L (earthenware manufacturers)
1863 Kelly EM
1864 Jones EM
(ii) Lockett's Lane, Longton
1862 Slater EM
(iii) Russell Street, Longton
1865 Keates P-L (earthen.)
1867 Keates P-L (earthenware)
1868 Kelly EM
(iv) Borough Pottery, Trentham Road, Florence, Longton
1869 Keates P-L (earthenware)
1870 Harrod NC-L (ironstone, china, and earthenware manufacturers)
1872 Kelly EM
1873 Keates P-L (earthenware)
1875 Keates P-L (earthenware)
1876 Kelly EM
1879 Keates P-L (earthenware)
1880 Kelly EM
1882 Keates P-L (earthenware)
1884 Kelly EM
1887 Porter EM-L
1888 Kelly EM
1889 Keates P-L (earthenware)
1892 Keates P-L (earthenware)
1892 Kelly EM
1896 Kelly EM
1900 Kelly CM; EM

Cartwright & Edwards. Printed mark from a blue-printed earthenware plate.

Cartwright, M. & Thomas
Stafford Street, Longton
1864 Jones EM-Miscellaneous (telegraphic insulators mftrs.)

Cartwright, Moses
Cornhill Passage, Longton
1867 Keates P-L (insulators)

Cartwright, Thomas
(i) Sneyd Green, Burslem
1867 Keates P-B (earthen.)
(ii) 14 Rushton Road, Burslem
1882 Keates P-B (earthenware)

Cartwright, William
Lane Delph
1818 Pigot EM

Caufield, F., & Co.
High Street, Longton
1870 Harrod NC-L (china manufacturers)

Caulkin, Levi
Broad Street, Shelton
1846 Williams NC-Sh (pipe and toy manufacturer)
1851 White CETOM-H-Sh

Caulkner, Levi
Broad Street, Shelton
1841 Pigot TOCM

Ceramic Art Co.
Howard Place, Shelton, Hanley
1889 Keates P-H
1892 Keates P-H
1892 Kelly SC (Art Pottery Manufacturers)

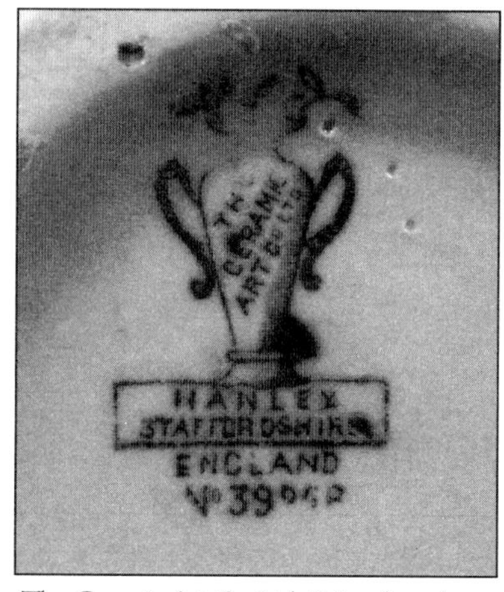

The Ceramic Art Co Ltd. Printed mark from a green-printed earthenware jug.

Ceramic Art Co. Ltd.
28 Howard Place, Shelton, Hanley
1896 Kelly SC (Art Pottery Manufacturers)
1900 Kelly SC (Art Pottery Manufacturers)
The manager is listed as J.W. Cooper in both directories.

The Ceramic Art Co. Ltd. Printed mark from a brown-printed and coloured covered soup tureen.

Challener (John), & Adams
Lower Lane
1798 Universal NC-LL (manufacturers of Staffordshire-ware)

Challiner, Edward
See: Challinor, Edward

Edward Challinor. Printed mark from a blue-printed earthenware wash jug.

Edward Challinor. Printed mark from a blue-printed meat dish.

Edward Challinor. Printed mark from a blue-printed earthenware feeding cup.

Challinor, C., & Co.
High Street, Fenton
1892 Keates P-F (earthenware)
1892 Kelly EM

Challinor, Charles
(i) High Street, Tunstall
1850 Slater EM
1851 White EM-T (Egyptian black)
1852 Slater EM
(ii) Trent Vale, Stoke
1870 Harrod NC-S (china manufacturer)

Challinor, Edmund
Brown Hills, Burslem
1851 White CEM-B (only earthenware)

Challinor, Edward
(i) Overhouse Works, Burslem
1822 Allbut CEM (earthenware manufacturer)
1822 Pigot EM
(ii) Pinnox Pottery, Great Woodland Street, Tunstall
1846 Williams NC-T (earthenware manufctr.)
1850 Slater EM
1852 Slater EM
1854 Kelly CEM
1856 Kelly CEM
1860 Kelly EM
(iii) Sandyford, Tunstall
1851 White EM-T
(iv) Amicable Street, Tunstall
1862 Slater EM
1864 Jones EM
1869 Keates P-T (earthen.)
(v) High Street, Tunstall
1851 White EM-T
1865 Keates P-T (earthenware)
1867 Keates P-T (earthenware)
1868 Kelly EM
1870 Harrod NC-T (manufacturer of water-closets, plug basins, &c.)
1872 Kelly EM
The surname is listed as Challiner in 1822 Allbut. Challinor's house is listed as Brown Hills, Tunstall, in 1851 White.
See also: Bowers, George Frederick, & Co.

Challinor, Edward, & Co.
(i) Sandyford, Tunstall
1850 Slater EM
1854 Kelly CEM
1856 Kelly CEM
(ii) Amicable Street, Tunstall
1851 White EM-T
(iii) New Road, Fenton
1852 Slater EM
1854 Kelly CEM
1856 Kelly CEM
1860 Kelly EM
1861 Harrison NC-F (patent iron stove (sic) and china manufactory)

Challinor, Edward & Charles
(i) Fenton Pottery, High Street, Fenton
1862 Slater CM (ironstone); EM
1863 Kelly EM
1864 Jones EM
1868 Kelly EM
1869 Keates P-F (earthenware)
1870 Harrod NC-F (earthenware and ironstone china manufacturers for foreign markets)
1872 Kelly EM
1873 Keates P-F (earthenware)
1875 Keates P-F (earthenware)
1876 Kelly EM
1879 Keates P-F (earthenware)
1880 Kelly EM
1882 Keates P-F (earthenware)
1884 Kelly EM
1888 Kelly EM
1889 Keates P-F (earthenware)
(ii) King Street, Fenton
1865 Keates P-F (earthenware)
1867 Keates P-F (earthenware)
(iii) Glebe Street, Stoke
1872 Kelly EM
1876 Kelly EM
1880 Kelly EM
1884 Kelly EM

Challinor & Mayor
Market Street, Fenton
1887 Porter EM-F

Chapman, D., & Sons
Sutherland Road, Longton
1896 Kelly CM
1900 Kelly CM

Chapman, David
Forrister Street, Anchor Road, Longton
1882 Keates P-L (china)
1884 Kelly CM
1888 Kelly CM
1892 Kelly CM

Chapman, David, & Sons
Forrister Street, Anchor Road, Longton
1889 Keates P-L (china)
1892 Keates P-L (china)

Chapman, Joseph
Atlas Works, Forrester Street, Longton
1887 Porter EM-L

Chaterley, Samuel
Hanley
1798 Universal NC-H (manufacturer of Staffordshire-ware)

Chatfield & Co.
Charles Street, Lane End
1822 Allbut CEM (earthenware manufacts.)

Chatfield, Henry
King Street, Longton
1865 Keates A; P-L (china)
Despite the cross-reference, no advertisement could be located in 1865 Keates.

Chatham & Wolley
See: Chetham & Woolley

Chatham & Woolley
See: Chetham & Woolley

Chatterley, Charles & Ephraim
Hanley
1781 Bailey NC (potters)
1783 Bailey NC (potters)
1784 Bailey NC-H (potters)

Chatterley, William
Hanley
1796 Chester NC-H-Sh (manufacturer of earthenware)

Chawser, J.W.
34 York Street, Hanley
1892 Keates P-H (modeller)

Cheap Tile Co.
Wolfe Street, Stoke
1892 Keates SC-S (Tile - Encaustic - Manufacturers); SC-S (Tile - Floor - Manufacturers)

Cheetham, J.R. & F.
See: Chetham, J.R. & F.

Cheetham, M., & Son
Commerce Street, Lane End
1818 Parson EM-LE

Cheetham & Robinson
See: Chetham & Robinson

Cheetham, Jonathan Lowe
See: Chetham, Jonathan Lowe

Chelenor & Adams
Fenton
1802 Allbut EM (map location 107)

Chesswas, Thomas Edensor
Market Place, Lane End or Longton
1834 White EM-LE-L
1835 Pigot EM

Chetham, Ann
No address listed.
1816 Underhill P

Chetham, Frederick, & Co.
Commerce Street, Longton
1870 Harrod NC-L (earthenware manufacturers)

J. R. & F. CHETHAM,
MANUFACTURERS OF
Lustre, Black, Drab, Torquoise & Printed Wares,
Stone Mortars, &c.,
LONGTON, STAFFORDSHIRE

J.R. & F. Chetham. Advertisement from 1864 Jones.

J. R. & F. CHETHAM,
MANUFACTURERS OF
LUSTRE, BLACK, DRAB,
Torquoise and Printed Wares,
STONE MORTARS, &c.,
COMMERCE STREET, LONGTON,
STAFFORDSHIRE.
RESIDENCE:-DRESDEN.

J.R. & F. Chetham. Advertisement from 1869 Keates.

Chetham, J.R. & F.
Commerce Street or Chancery Lane, Longton
1863 Kelly CM-General; LM; SC (Egyptian Black Ware Manufacturers); SC (Stone Mortar & Pestle Manufacturers); SM (druggists')
1864 Jones A; LM
1865 Keates P-L (earthenware and lustre)
1867 Keates P-L (earthenware, and lustre)
1868 Kelly LM; SC (Stone Mortar & Pestle Manufacturers); SM
1869 Keates A; P-L (earthenware)
The first partner's surname is listed as Cheetham in 1865 Keates and 1867 Keates. The advertisements in 1864 Jones and 1869 Keates describe the firm as 'manufacturers of lustre, black, drab, turquoise & printed wares, stone mortars, &c.' The latter also lists the Chethams' residence as Dresden.

Chetham, John, & Co.
Bridge Works, Church Street, Stoke
1870 Harrod NC-S (manufacturers of lustre black drab, turquoise and printed wares, stone mortars, &c., for home and foreign markets)

Chetham, Jonathan Lowe
Commerce Street, Longton
1841 Pigot CM; EM
1846 Williams NC-L-LE (china lustre & black mnfctr.)
1850 Kelly CEM; NC-L (manufacturers of china, lustre, black, pearl & printed wares, stone mortars, &c.)
1850 Slater CM; EM
1851 White CEM-L
1852 Slater CM; EM
1854 Kelly CEM
1856 Kelly CEM
1860 Kelly CM-General; LM; SC (Egyptian Black Ware Manufacturers); SC (Stone Mortar & Pestle Manufacturers)
1861 Harrison NC-L (manufacturer of lustre black and printed wares, &c.)
1862 Slater EM
The surname is listed as Cheetham in 1850 Slater. Chetham's house is listed as Blurton in 1851 White.

Chetham & Robinson
Commerce Street, Lane End
1822 Allbut CEM (china, earthenware, Egyptian black, &c. manufacts.)
1822 Pigot EM
1828 Pigot CM; EM

1830 Pigot CM; EM
1834 White CM-LE-L; EM-LE-L (lustre, Egyptian black, stone mortars, &c.)
1835 Pigot CM; EM
The first partner's name is listed as Cheetham in 1822 Allbut.

Chetham & Robinson. Printed mark from a black-printed and pink lustre-washed earthenware vase.

Chetham & Robinson. Printed mark from a blue-printed earthenware dinner plate.

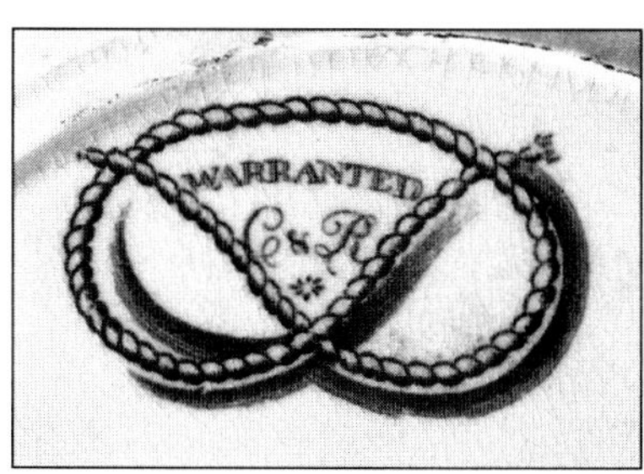

Chetham & Robinson. Printed mark from a blue-printed earthenware dessert plate.

Chetham & Woolley
Lane End
1796 Chester NC-LE-LD-LL (manufacturers of earthenware)
1798 Universal NC-LE (manufacturers of Staffordshire-ware)
1802 Allbut EM (map location 134)
1805 Holden NC (pearl and printed ware, Egyptian black, &c. manufacturers)
1809 Holden NC (pearl, printed ware, & Egyptian-black-manufacturers)
1811 Holden NC (pearl, printed ware, & Egyptian-black-manufacturers)
1816 Underhill P
The partnership is listed as Chatham & Wolley in 1798 Universal and Chatham & Woolley in 1796 Chester.

Chetwynd, Elijah
4A Mollart Street, Hanley
1889 Keates P-H (modeller)
1892 Keates P-H (modeller)

Child & Clive
Newfield, Tunstall
1809 Holden NC (earthenware-manufactrs.)
1811 Holden NC (earthenware-manufacs.)
1816 Underhill P
1818 Parson EM-G-T-R
1822 Allbut CEM (earthenware manufacts.)
1822 Pigot EM

Clare & Sons
Albert Street, Burslem
1900 Kelly JRM

Clare, Walter
(i) Podmore Street, Burslem
1882 Keates P-B (Rockingham)
1888 Kelly JM; RM
1889 Keates P-B (Rockingham)
1892 Keates P-B (Rockingham)
1892 Kelly JRM
1896 Kelly JRM
1900 Kelly JRM
(ii) Albert Street, Burslem
1889 Keates P-B (Rockingham)
1892 Keates P-B (Rockingham)

Clare & Chadwick
Albert Street, Burslem
1896 Kelly JRM

Clark, C.R., & Co.
Winton Works, Stoke
1888 Kelly EM
Although the directory contains no entry for the firm as potters, an advertisement in 1887 Porter includes the description 'manufacturers & merchants of earthenware for export'. This appears as part of the firm's full-page advertisement for their business of removals, hire goods, marquees, etc.

C. R. CLARK & CO.
MANUFACTURERS & MERCHANTS
OF
EARTHENWARE
FOR EXPORT.

C.R. Clark & Co. Advertisement from 1887 Porter.

Clark, E.R., & Co.
Winton Works, Stoke
1892 Kelly EM
1896 Kelly EM

Clark, Edward
Church Yard Works, Wood Street, Burslem
1882 Keates P-B
1884 Kelly EM
There is another entry in 1882 Keates for Edward Clarke (qv).

Clark, Joseph A.
See: Cope & Clark

Clarke, Edward
(i) High Street, Tunstall
1865 Keates P-T (earthenware)
1867 Keates P-T (earthenware)
1868 Kelly EM
1869 Keates P-T (earthenware)
1872 Kelly EM
1873 Keates P-T (earthenware)
1875 Keates P-T (earthenware)
1876 Kelly EM
(ii) Phoenix Works, Tunstall
1870 Harrod NC-T (earthenware manufacturer)
(iii) Longport, Burslem
1879 Keates P-B (earthenware)
(iv) Wood Street, Burslem
1882 Keates P-B (earthenware)
There is another entry in 1882 Keates for Edward Clark (qv).

Clarke, Richard B.
See: Furnival, Thomas, & Co.

Clementson Brothers
(i) Broad Street, Hanley
1868 Kelly EM
(ii) Phoenix Works, Broad Street, and Bell Works, George Street, Hanley
1867 Keates P-H (earthenware)
1869 Keates P-H (earthenware)
1870 Harrod NC-H (manufacturers of earthenware for foreign trade)
1872 Kelly EM
1873 Keates P-H (earthenware)
1875 Keates P-H (earthenware)
1876 Kelly EM
1879 Keates P-H (earthenware)
1880 Kelly EM
1882 Keates P-H (earthenware)
1884 Kelly EM
1887 Porter EM-H
1888 Kelly EM
1889 Keates P-H (earthenware)
1892 Keates P-H (earthenware)
1892 Kelly EM
1896 Kelly EM
1900 Kelly EM

Clementson, Joseph
(i) Broad Street, Shelton or Hanley
1841 Pigot EM
1854 Kelly CEM
1856 Kelly CEM
1860 Kelly EM
1861 Harrison NC-H-Sh (earthenware manufacturer)
1863 Kelly EM
1864 Jones EM
(ii) Phoenix Works, Broad Street or High Street, Shelton, Hanley
1846 Williams NC-Sh (earthenware manufacturer)
1850 Kelly CEM (two entries); NC-Sh (earthenware manufacturer)
1850 Slater EM
1851 White CEM-H-Sh
1852 Slater EM
1862 Slater EM
1865 Keates P-H (earthenware)
(iii) Bell Works, George Street, Hanley
1862 Slater EM
1865 Keates P-H (earthenware)
Clementson is listed at Chatterly House, Shelton, in 1850 Kelly and his house is listed as Old Hall Street, Hanley, in 1851 White.

Joseph Clementson. Printed mark from a blue-printed meat dish.

Clementson & Young
Broad Street, Shelton
1846 Williams NC-Sh (earthenware manufacturers)
The partners are listed individually as Francis Clementson of Cleveland House and Mr. Young of Cannon Street in 1846 Williams.

Clewer, R. & J.
See: Clews, Ralph & James

Ralph & James Clews. Printed and impressed marks from an ornate blue-printed dessert dish.

Clews, Ralph & James
Cobridge
1816 Underhill P
1818 Parson EM-B-Lp-C
1818 Pigot EM
1822 Allbut CEM (china and earthenware manufacts.)
1822 Pigot EM
1828 Pigot EM
1830 Pigot EM
1834 White EM-B
1835 Pigot EM
The surname is listed as Clewer in 1816 Underhill.

Ralph & James Clews. Printed and impressed marks from blue-printed stone china tea wares.

Clews, William
William Street, Hanley
1882 Keates P-H (earthenware)
1884 Kelly EM
1887 Porter EM-H

Cliff, William D.
See: Dimmock, John, & Co.

Cliff & Blore
North Road, Cobridge, Burslem
1884 Kelly EM

Clive, Stephen
Well Street, Tunstall
1875 Keates P-T (earthenware)

Clive, Stephen, & Co.
Well Street, Tunstall
1876 Kelly EM
1880 Kelly EM

Close & Co.
Church Street, Stoke
1868 Kelly EM

Close, J.P.
See: Close, John Theophilus

Close, J.T.
Brook Street and High Street, Stoke
1863 Kelly EM

Close, John Theophilus
Church Street, Stoke
1864 Jones EM (and lustre)
1865 Keates P-S (earthenware and lustre)
1867 Keates P-S (earthenware

and lustre)
1869 Keates P-S (earthenware)
Close is listed as J.P. Close in 1865 Keates and his residence is listed as Glebe Street in 1869 Keates.

Close, Valentine
Keeling's Lane, Hanley
1802 Allbut EM (map location 75)
1805 Holden NC (earthenware manufacturer)
1809 Holden NC (earthenware-manufacturer)
1811 Holden NC (earthenware-manufacturer)

Clowes, William, & Co.
Longport
1781 Bailey NC (potters)
1783 Bailey NC (potters)

Clowes & Williamson
Fenton
1784 Bailey NC-F (potters)

Clulow, Robert, & Co.
Lower Lane
1802 Allbut EM

Coalport China Co. Ltd.
8 Glebe Buildings, Stoke
1889 Keates P-S
1892 Kelly CM
The firm is identified as John Rose & Co. with John A. Service as their agent in 1889 Keates.

Cockson, Charles
Cobridge
1863 Kelly CM-General
1864 Jones A; CEM (plain and ornamental); EM
1865 Keates P-B (china)
The advertisement in 1864 Jones describes Cockson as a 'manufacturer of every description of plain and ornamental porcelaine (sic), suitable for the home, colonial, and foreign markets'.
See also: Harding & Cockson

CHARLES COCKSON,
MANUFACTURER OF EVERY DESCRIPTION OF
PLAIN AND ORNAMENTAL
PORCELAINE,
Suitable for the Home, Colonial, and Foreign Markets,
COBRIDGE, STAFFORDSHIRE.

Charles Cockson. Advertisement from 1864 Jones.

Cockson & Chetwynd
Cobridge
1873 Keates P-B (earthenware)
1875 Keates P-B (earthenware)

Cockson, Chetwynd & Co.
Cobridge, Burslem
1867 Keates A; P-B (earthenware)
1868 Kelly EM
1869 Keates P-B (earthenware)
1870 Harrod NC-B (earthenware manufacturers, for the American markets only)
1872 Kelly EM
The advertisement in 1867 Keates describes the firm as 'granite & earthenware manufacturers'.

COCKSON, CHETWYND, & Co.,
GRANITE & EARTHENWARE
MANUFACTURERS,
COBRIDGE, STAFFORDSHIRE.

Cockson, Chetwynd & Co. Advertisement from 1867 Keates.

Cockson & Harding
See: Cockson & Hardings

Cockson & Hardings
(i) Waterloo Road, Cobridge, Burslem
1860 Kelly CM-General
1861 Harrison A; NC-B (china manufacturers)
1862 Slater CM; EM
(ii) New Hall Works, Hanley
1860 Kelly CM-General; EM
1861 Harrison A; NC-B (china manufacturers)
(iii) Marsh Street, Hanley
1862 Slater CM; EM
The entry in 1861 Harrison is in the name of Cockson & Harding although the advertisement is for Cockson & Hardings, of the Cobridge China Works, and Newhall Pottery, Hanley. They are described as 'manufacturers of china and earthenwares, of great variety, in stone, Egyptian black, cane, drab, and other tinted bodies'. The advertisement lists 'printed & cream colour, tea, toilet, & table ware, particularly adapted for the continental markets', and also 'stone mortars, jars, and other articles, for medical fitters and for the perfumery trade'.

COCKSON & HARDINGS,
COBRIDGE CHINA WORKS,
AND
NEWHALL POTTERY,
HANLEY.
MANUFACTURERS OF
CHINA AND EARTHENWARES,
OF GREAT VARIETY, IN
STONE, EGYPTIAN BLACK, CANE, DRAB, AND OTHER TINTED BODIES.
Printed & Cream Colour, Tea, Toilet, & Table Ware,
PARTICULARLY ADAPTED FOR THE CONTINENTAL MARKETS.
Stone Mortars, Jars, and other Articles for Medical Fitters and for the Perfumery Trade.

Cockson & Hardings. Advertisement from 1861 Harrison.

Cockson & Hardings. Impressed mark from a blue-printed earthenware toy plate. The helpful addition of "late Hackwood" refers to Thomas Hackwood (qv).

Cockson & Seddon
Cobridge, Burslem
1876 Kelly EM

Coggins & Hill
St. James' Place, High Street, Longton
1892 Keates P-L (china)
1896 Kelly CM
1900 Kelly CM

COLCLOUGH & CO.
China and Earthenware
Decorators and Dealers,
CLAYTON STREET, LONGTON,
STAFFORDSHIRE.

Colclough & Co. Advertisement from 1887 Porter.

Colclough & Co.
(i) Clayton Street, Longton
1887 Porter EM-L
(ii) Anchor Works, Anchor Road, Longton
1892 Keates P-L (majolica)

1892 Kelly MM
1896 Kelly MM
(iii) Goddard Street, East Vale, Longton
1900 Kelly MM
An advertisement in 1887 Porter describes the firm as 'china and earthenware decorators and dealers'.

Colclough, Charles
Market Lane, Longton
1841 Pigot TOCM

Colclough, James
(i) Chapel Lane, Burslem
1834 White EM-B (ornamental)
(ii) Gold Street, Longton
1841 Pigot EM
(iii) Commerce Street, Longton
1850 Kelly CEM; NC-L (earthenware manufacturer)
1851 White CEM-L (only earthenware)
1854 Kelly CEM
1856 Kelly CEM
(iv) Commerce Street, Shelton
1850 Slater EM
1852 Slater EM
Colclough's house is listed as Green Dock in 1851 White.

Colclough & Lingard
(i) 32 High Street, Tunstall
1887 Porter EM-T
(ii) Britannia Black Works, High Street, Tunstall
1888 Kelly JM; RM
1889 Keates P-T
1892 Keates P-T
1892 Kelly JRM; SC (Black Ware Manufacturers) (Egyptian)
1896 Kelly JRM

Colclough, Mary
Pits Hill, Tunstall
1796 Chester NC-T-Lp (manufacturer of earthenware)

Colclough & Townsend
Lane Delph Pottery, High Street, Fenton
1846 Williams NC-C-F-E (earthenware, lustre & black manuftr.)
The partners are listed individually as Thomas Colclough and George Townsend in 1846 Williams.

Cole, Caleb, & Co.
Newfield
1798 Universal NC-Nf (earthenware manufacturers)
1802 Allbut EM (map location 10)

Cole, John & Caleb
Newfield
1796 Chester NC-T-Lp (manufacturers of earthenware)

Collingwood Brothers
Crown Works, Stafford Street, Longton
1887 Porter EM-L
1888 Kelly CM
1889 Keates P-L (china)
1892 Keates P-L (china)
1892 Kelly CM
1896 Kelly CM
1900 Kelly CM

Collingwood, Anthony
High Street, Longton
1850 Slater CM

Collingwood & Greatbatch
Crown Works, Stafford Street, Longton
1870 Harrod NC-L (china manufacturers for home and foreign markets)
1872 Kelly CM
1873 Keates P-L (china)
1875 Keates P-L (china)
1876 Kelly CM
1879 Keates P-L (china)
1880 Kelly CM
1882 Keates P-L (china)
1884 Kelly CM

Collinson, Charles
Fountain Place, Burslem
1870 Harrod NC-B (earthenware manufacturer)
See also: Holdcroft, Peter, & Co.

Collinson, Charles, & Co.
(i) Fountain Place, Burslem
1852 Slater EM
1854 Kelly CEM
1856 Kelly CEM; SC (Chemical Apparatus Manufacturers)
1860 Kelly EM; SC (Sanitary Vessel Manufacturers)
1861 Harrison NC-B (earthenware manufacturers)
1863 Kelly EM
1864 Jones EM-Miscellaneous (chemical apparatus and sanitary articles manufacturers)
1865 Keates P-B (chemical and sanitary articles)
1867 Keates P-B (chemical and sanitary articles)
(ii) Newcastle Street Pottery, Burslem
1862 Slater EM; SC (Water-Closet Basin Manufacturers)
1868 Kelly EM
1869 Keates P-B (earthenware)
1870 Harrod NC-B (earthenware manufacturers)
1872 Kelly EM
1873 Keates P-B (earthenware)
The firm is listed as G. Collinson & Co. in 1870 Harrod.

Charles Collinson & Co. Printed mark from a green-printed and coloured earthenware dinner service.

Charles Collinson & Co. Printed mark from another green printed and coloured earthenware dinner service.

Collinson, G., & Co.
See: Collinson, Charles, & Co.

Collinson, James
Golden Hill
1818 Parson EM-G-T-R
1818 Pigot EM (black ware)
1822 Allbut CEM (coarse ware manufacturer)
1822 Pigot EM
1828 Pigot EM
1830 Pigot EM
1835 Pigot EM

Collinson, John
(i) Tunstall
1796 Chester NC-T-Lp (manufacturer of earthenware)
(ii) Golden Hill
1798 Universal NC-G (coarse-ware potter)
1802 Allbut EM (map location 4)
(iii) Golden Hill
1834 White EM-B (crown *(sic)*); EM-T (brown); NC-G (brown earth. mfr.)
1841 Pigot EM (coarse)
1850 Slater EM (coarse)
1851 White EM-T (black); NC-G (blackware mfr)
1852 Slater EM (coarse)
1856 Kelly P
1860 Kelly P
1861 Harrison NC-G (garden potter)
The surname is listed as Collison in 1796 Chester and 1802 Allbut.

Collinson, William
Golden Hill
1863 Kelly P (garden)
1862 Slater EM (course (sic))
1864 Jones EM-Miscellaneous (garden pot)

Collison, John
See: Collinson, John

Collison, William & James
Golden Hill
1809 Holden NC (black-ware-manufacturers)
1811 Holden NC (black-ware-manufacturers)

Comer & Pratt
Lane Delph
1809 Holden NC (manufacturer of earthenware)
1811 Holden NC (manufacturers of earthenware)
1816 Underhill P

Cone, Thomas
High Street, Longton
1900 Kelly EM

Cone, Thomas, & Co.
Alma Works, High Street, Longton
1892 Keates P-L (earthenware)
1896 Kelly EM

Cook & Griffiths
See: Cooke & Griffiths

Cooke, Robert
Brewery Street Works, Hope Street, Hanley
1872 Kelly PM
1873 Keates A; P-H (parian)
1875 Keates P-H (parian)
1876 Kelly PM
1879 Keates P-H (parian)
The advertisement in 1873 Keates describes Cooke as a 'manufacturer of parian statuettes, etc., in great variety, suitable for home and exportation'. Another advertisement in 1875 Keates is the same except for the addition of stone ware. Both list London showrooms at Ely Place, Holborn, and note that Cooke was also a glass merchant at Fenton.

ROBERT COOKE,
MANUFACTURER OF
PARIAN STATUETTES,
Etc., in great variety, suitable
FOR HOME AND EXPORTATION,
BREWERY STREET WORKS
HOPE STREET, HANLEY.
London Show Rooms: 12, ELY PLACE, HOLBORN.
ALSO
GLASS MERCHANT,
See Fenton Advertisement.

Robert Cooke. Advertisement from 1873 Keates.

ROBERT COOKE,
MANUFACTURER OF
PARIAN STATUETTES,
STONE WARE, ETC.,
In great variety, suitable for Home and Exportation,
BREWERY STREET WORKS
HOPE STREET, HANLEY.
London Show Rooms:—12, ELY PLACE, HOLBORN
Also GLASS MERCHANT—See Fenton Advertisement.

Robert Cooke. Advertisement from 1875 Keates.

Cooke & Griffiths
Victoria Place, Flint Street, Longton
1850 Kelly CEM; NC-L (china manufacturers)
1850 Slater CM
1851 White CEM-L
The first partner's name is listed as Cook in 1850 Kelly.

Cooke & Hulse
(i) Victoria Place, Flint Street, Longton
1852 Slater CM
(ii) Stafford Street, Longton
1854 Kelly CEM
1856 Kelly CEM

Coomer, Sheridan & Hewit
Green Dock, Lane End
1805 Holden NC (earthenware manufacturers)

Cooper & Co.
Furlong Works, Burslem
1870 Harrod NC-B (earthenware manufacturers)

Cooper & Son
Viaduct Works, Caroline Street, Longton
1884 Kelly EM
1887 Porter EM-L
1888 Kelly EM

Cooper, A. (Mrs.)
Etruria Road, Hanley
1860 Kelly CFM; PFM

Cooper, J.W.
See: Ceramic Art Co. Ltd.

Cooper, John
(i) Boothen Road, Stoke
1841 Pigot EM
(ii) Clayton Street, Longton
1900 Kelly CM; EM

Cooper, John Thomas
(i) Furnace Pottery, Mill Street, Etruria Road, Shelton
1851 White NC-H-Sh (earthenware manufacturer)
1852 Slater CM; TOCM
1854 Kelly CFM (& parian)
(ii) High Street, Hanley
1850 Kelly NC-H (china toy manufacturer)
1851 White CETOM-H-Sh
Cooper's house is listed as Church Street in 1851 White.

Cooper, T., & Co.
High Street, Longton
1860 Kelly CTM

Cooper, Thomas
(i) High Street, Longton
1846 Williams NC-L-LE (china figure manufacturer)
1850 Kelly NC-L (china figure manufacturer)
1850 Slater TOCM

1851 White CEM-L; NC-L (china, &c., mfr.)
1852 Slater CM; TOCM
1854 Kelly PM
1856 Kelly CFM
1864 Jones CEM
(ii) Eagle Foundry, Shelton
1850 Slater TOCM
(iii) Royal Victoria Works, Broad Street, Hanley
1863 Kelly CM-General
1864 Jones EM
(iv) Victoria Square, Hanley
1865 Keates P-H (china and earthenware)
1867 Keates P-H (china and earthenware)
The firm is noted as being in the hands of executors in 1865 Keates and 1867 Keates.

Cooper, Thomas & Arthur
Wharf Lane, Hanley
1860 Kelly EM

Cooper, William
Boothen Road, Stoke
1841 Pigot CM

Cooper, William, & Co.
(i) High Street, Longton
1851 White, CEM-L
Cooper's house is listed as Furnace Road in 1851 White.
(ii) 32 Clayton Street, Longton
1889 Keates P-L (china & earthenware)
1892 Keates P-L (china and earthenware)

Cooper, William, & Sons
Viaduct Works, Caroline Street, Longton
1889 Keates P-L (earthenware)
1882 Keates P-L (earthenware)

Cooper & Birks
Bagnall Street, Longton
1852 Slater CM

Cooper & Cartledge
High Street, Longton
1862 Slater CM

Cooper & Cartlich
Market and High Street, Longton
1861 Harrison NC-L (china toy manufacturers)

Cooper & Cartlidge
High Street, Longton
1863 Kelly CTM

Cooper & Dethick
Viaduct Works, Caroline Street, Longton
1876 Kelly EM
1879 Keates P-L (earthenware)
1880 Kelly EM (manufacturers of earthenware, lustre china & printed ware)

Cooper & Dixon
Viaduct Works, Longton
1865 Keates P-L (earthenware)

Cooper & Keeling
Well Street, Tunstall
1865 Keates P-T (earthenware)

Cooper & Kent
New Street, Longton
1882 Keates P-L (china and earthenware)

Cooper & Moreton
Pyenest Street, Shelton, Hanley
1880 Kelly EM

Cooper, Moreton & Garside
St. Luke Street, Hanley
1879 Keates P-H (earthenware)

Cooper & Nixon
Viaduct Works, Caroline Street, Longton
1867 Keates P-L (earthenware)
1869 Keates P-L (earthenware)
1870 Harrod NC-L (earthenware manufacturers for home markets)
1873 Keates P-L (earthenware)
1875 Keates P-L (earthenware)

Cooper, Nixon & Co.
Caroline Street, Longton
1868 Kelly EM
1872 Kelly EM

Cooper & Smith
High Street, Longton
1850 Kelly CEM; NC-L (earthenware manufacturers); TOCM

Cooper, Till & Co.
New Street, Longton
1875 Keates P-L (china and earthenware)
1876 Kelly CM

Coopers & Co.
New Street, Longton
1879 Keates P-L (china and earthenware)

Coopers & Son
Edensor Works, Longton
1880 Kelly CM (china manufrs. for home & export)

Cope & Co.
High Street, Tunstall
1892 Keates P-T (jet)

Cope, J., & Son
Port Vale, Wolstanton, and Smallthorne
1868 Kelly A; P; TCM
The advertisement in 1868 Kelly gives the address as Port Vale Tileries, near Burslem, and describes the firm as 'manufacturers of all kinds of terra-metallic ridges, plain and ornamental roof and floor tiles, garden bordering, wall copings, blue and other coloured bricks of every description, orchid and garden pots, &c., &c.'

J. COPE AND SON,
PORT VALE TILERIES, NEAR BURSLEM, STAFFORDSHIRE,
MANUFACTURERS OF ALL KINDS OF
Terra-Metallic Ridges,
PLAIN AND ORNAMENTAL ROOF AND FLOOR TILES,
GARDEN BORDERING, WALL COPINGS,
BLUE AND OTHER COLOURED BRICKS OF EVERY DESCRIPTION,
Orchid and Garden Pots, &c., &c.

J. Cope & Son. Advertisement from 1868 Kelly.

Cope, James H., & Co.
Wellington Works, Stafford Street, Longton
1887 Porter EM-L
1888 Kelly CM
1889 Keates P-L (china)
1892 Keates P-L (china)
1892 Kelly CM
1896 Kelly CM
1900 Kelly CM

Cope, John Thomas
Broad Street Works, Hanley
1884 Kelly CM
1888 Kelly CM

Cope & Birks
(i) High Street, Longton
1852 Slater CM
(ii) Bagnall Street, Longton
1854 Kelly CEM

Cope & Clark
Russell Street, Longton or Lane End

1846 Williams NC-L-LE (china manufacturers)
The partners are listed individually as Edward Cope of Green Dock and Joseph A. Clark of High Street in 1846 Williams.

Cope & Dewsbury
Broad Street, Hanley
1887 Porter EM-H

Cope & Edwards
Market Street, Longton
1846 Williams NC-L-LE (china manufacturers)
1850 Kelly CEM; NC-L (china manufacturers)
1850 Slater CM
1851 White CEM-L
1852 Slater CM; EM
1854 Kelly CEM
1856 Kelly CEM
The partners are listed individually as Thomas Cope of Church Street and James Edwards of Mear Heath in 1846 Williams.

Copeland & Sons
High Street, Stoke
1869 Keates P-S (china, earthenware, and parian)
1873 Keates P-S (china, earthenware and parian)
1875 Keates P-S (china, earthenware, and parian)

Copeland, James
New Street, Hanley
1834 White CETM-H-Sh
1835 Pigot TOCM
1841 Pigot TOCM
1850 Kelly NC-H (figure manufacturer)
1850 Slater TOCM
1851 White CEM-H-Sh
1852 Slater TOCM
1854 Kelly CFM
1856 Kelly CFM
1860 Kelly CFM

Copeland, William Taylor
High Street, Stoke
1850 Kelly CEM; NC-S (china & earthenware manfr.)
1850 Slater CM; EM
1851 White CEM-S (also porcelain statuary, &c.)
1852 Slater CM (and porcelain statuary); EM
1854 Kelly CEM
1856 Kelly CEM
1860 Kelly CM-General; EM; SC (Porcelain Statuary Manufacturers)
1861 Harrison NC-S (earthenware manufacturer)
1862 Slater CM; EM
1863 Kelly CM-General; EM; SC (Porcelain Statuary Manufacturers)
1864 Jones CEM; CFM
1865 Keates P-S (china, earthenware, and parian)
1867 Keates P-S (china, earthenware, and parian)
Copeland is listed as an Alderman in 1865 Keates and 1867 Keates. A London office at 160 New Bond Street is listed in 1854 Kelly, 1856 Kelly, 1860 Kelly, 1863 Kelly, and 1864 Jones.
See also: Meli, Giovanni

William Taylor Copeland. Printed marks from a blue-printed earthenware dinner plate.

Copeland, William Taylor, & Sons
(i) High Street, Stoke
1868 Kelly CM; EM; SC (Porcelain Statuary Manufacturers)
1870 Harrod NC-S (porcelain, earthenware, and glass manufacturers for home and foreign markets)
1872 Kelly CFM
1876 Kelly CM; EM; MM; PM
1879 Keates P-S (china, earthenware and parian)
1880 Kelly CM; EM; PM
1882 Keates P-S (china, earthenware, and parian
1884 Kelly CM; EM; PM
1888 Kelly CM; EM
1889 Keates P-S (china, earthenware, and parian)
1892 Keates P-S (china, earthenware and parian)
1892 Kelly CM; EM; SC (Encaustic Tile Manufacturers)
1896 Kelly CM
1900 Kelly CM; EM; SC (Porcelain Manufacturers)
(ii) Church Street, Stoke
1887 Porter CEM-S
A London office at 160 New Bond Street is listed in 1868 Kelly, 1870 Harrod, 1872 Kelly, 1876 Kelly and 1880 Kelly. A London agency at 12 Charterhouse Street, Holborn, is listed in 1884 Kelly, 1888 Kelly, 1892 Kelly and 1896 Kelly.

Copeland & Garrett. Printed and colour-washed mark from a documentary china plaque dated 1834.

Copeland & Garrett. Printed marks from a green-printed earthenware soup plate.

Copeland & Garrett
(i) Church Street, Stoke
1835 Pigot CM; EM
(ii) High Street, Stoke
1834 White CM-S; EM-S
1841 Pigot CM; EM
1846 Williams NC-S (earthenware & china manuf.)
The partners are listed individually as William Taylor Copeland, M.P., of London, and Thomas Garrett of

Herne Hill, Surrey, in 1846 Williams. The second partner's surname is listed as Garratt in 1834 White. A London office at Portugal Street is listed in 1841 Pigot.

Copestake Brothers
Anchor Works, Anchor Road, Longton
1860 Kelly CM-General
1861 Harrison NC-L (manufacturers of china, &c.)
1862 Slater CM
1863 Kelly CM-General
1864 Jones CEM
1865 Keates P-L (china)
1867 Keates P-L (china)
1868 Kelly CM
1869 Keates P-L (china)
1870 Harrod NC-L (china manufacturers, for home and foreign markets)

Copestake & Co.
Alma Works, High Street, Longton
1872 Kelly CM

Copestake & Son
High Street, Lane End or Longton
1834 White CM-LE-L
1835 Pigot CM; EM

Copestake, A., & Co.
Alma Works, Longton
1876 Kelly CM

Copestake, George
Anchor Works, Market Street, Longton
1872 Kelly CM
1873 Keates P-L (china)
1875 Keates P-L (china)
1876 Kelly CM
1879 Keates P-L (china)
1880 Kelly CM
1882 Keates P-L (china)
1884 Kelly CM
1889 Keates P-L (china)
Copestake is listed as George junior in 1872 Kelly, 1876 Kelly, and 1880 Kelly.

Copestake, William
(i) Market Street, Lane End
1835 Pigot CM
1841 Pigot CM
(ii) High Street, Longton
1834 White CM-LE-L
1841 Pigot CM; EM
1846 Williams NC-L-LE (china manufactr., gilder, &c.)
1850 Kelly CEM (& gilder); NC-L (china manufacturer & gilder)
1850 Slater CM
1851 White CEM-L
1852 Slater CM
1854 Kelly CEM
1856 Kelly CEM
1860 Kelly CM-General
1861 Harrison NC-L (china manufacturer)
The potter at the High Street address is listed as William junior in 1841 Pigot, 1846 Williams, 1850 Slater, and 1851 White and his surname is listed as Copestick in 1856 Kelly. Houses are listed as Caroline Street, Lane End, in 1834 White and Sutherland Road, Longton, in 1851 White.

Copestake, William, & Co.
51 High Street, Longton
1864 Jones CEM

Copestake & Allin
Alma Works, High Street, Longton
1867 Keates P-L (china)
1868 Kelly CM
1869 Keates P-L (china)
1870 Harrod NC-L (china manufacturers)
1873 Keates P-L (china)
1875 Keates P-L (china)
1879 Keates P-L (china)

Copestake, Allin & Co.
Alma Works, High Street, Longton
1880 Kelly CM

Copestake & Bradbury
High Street, Longton
1860 Kelly CM-General
1861 Harrison NC-L (earthenware manufacturers)

Copestake, Shufflebotham & Allin
Alma Works, High Street, Longton
1862 Slater CM
1863 Kelly CM-General
1864 Jones A; CEM
1865 Keates P-L (china)
The partnership is listed as Copestake, Shufflebottom & Allen in 1862 Slater and 1865 Keates. The advertisement in 1864 Jones describes the firm as 'china manufacturers, enamelers (sic), gilders, decoraters (sic), and general finishers'.

COPESTAKE, SHUFFLEBOTHAM & ALLIN,
CHINA MANUFACTURERS,
ENAMELERS,
GILDERS, DECORATERS,
AND
GENERAL FINISHERS.
ALMA WORKS, HIGH STREET,
LONGTON.

Copestake, Shufflebotham & Allin. Advertisement from 1864 Jones.

Copestick, Daniel
Lane Delph
1830 Pigot EM (toy only)

Copestick, W.
See: Copestake, William

Copestick, Hassall & Gerard
Lane Delph
1828 Pigot EM

Corbett, Joseph
16 Market Place, Burslem
1860 Kelly EM
1861 Harrison NC-B (grocer and earthenware manufacturer)

Cork & Condliff
Queen Street, Burslem
1834 White EM-B (Egyptian black mfrs. only)
1841 Pigot EM (Egyptian black)
The second partner's name is listed as Condliffe in 1841 Pigot.

Cork & Edge
Queen Street, Burslem
1846 Williams NC-B (earthenware, lustre, and black manufacturers)
1850 Kelly NC-B (black, lustre & earthenware manfrs.)

Cork & Edge. Printed mark from a blue-printed earthenware Willow pattern dessert plate.

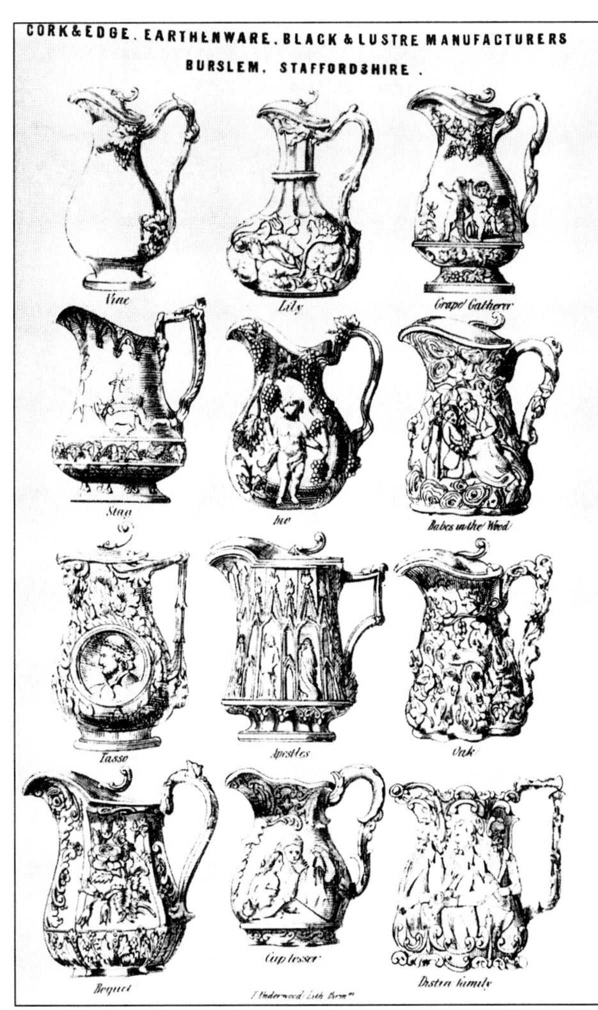

Cork & Edge. Two pages from a catalogue of the British section at the 1855 Paris Universal Exhibition, depicting various titled designs for relief-moulded jugs and teapots, both pages engraved by I. Underwood of Birmingham.

Cork & Edge. Printed mark from a stoneware relief-moulded jug.

1850 Kelly CEM (black)
1850 Slater EM
1851 White CEM-B (only earthenware) (black and lustre)
1852 Slater EM
1854 Kelly CEM

Cork & Edge. Printed mark from a blue-printed earthenware soup plate.

1856 Kelly CEM
1860 Kelly EM
The partners are listed individually as Benjamin Cork of Newport Road and Joseph Edge of St. John's Square in 1846 Williams.

Cork, Edge & Malkin
(i) New Wharf Potteries, Burslem
1860 Kelly EM
1861 Harrison A; NC-B (manufacturers of earthenware, black lustre, fancy coloured stone ware)
1863 Kelly EM
1864 Jones A; EM; EM-Miscellaneous (black, lustre, and fancy colored stone earthenware)
(ii) Queen Street, Burslem
1861 Harrison A; NC-B (manufacturers of earthenware, black lustre, fancy coloured stone ware)
1862 Slater EM
1863 Kelly EM
1864 Jones A; EM; EM-Miscellaneous (black, lustre, and fancy colored stone earthenware)

1865 Keates P-B (lustre & earthen.)
(iii) Navigation Road, Burslem
1862 Slater EM
1865 Keates P-B (lustre & earthen.)
1867 Keates P-B (earthen. & lustre)
(iv) Bourne's Bank, Burslem
1865 Keates P-B (lustre & earthen.)
(v) Newport, Burslem
1868 Kelly EM
1869 Keates P-B (earthen. & lustre)

The advertisements in 1861 Harrison and 1864 Jones describe the firm as 'manufacturers of earthenware, black lustre, and fancy coloured stone ware'.

Cork, Edge & Malkin. Printed mark from blue-printed toy earthenware dinner wares.

Cork, Edge & Malkin. Printed mark from a transfer-printed earthenware jug. The registration diamond dates from 1870. Note that the royal arms mark with initials D.W. is found on wares by various manufacturers and probably relates to an as yet unidentified retailer.

CORK, EDGE, & MALKIN,
MANUFACTURERS OF
EARTHENWARE.
BLACK LUSTRE,
AND
FANCY COLOURED STONE WARE,
QUEEN STREET
AND
NEW WHARF POTTERIES,
BURSLEM,
STAFFORDSHIRE.

Cork, Edge & Malkin. Advertisement from 1861 Harrison.

CORK, EDGE & MALKIN,
MANUFACTURERS OF EARTHENWARE,
BLACK, LUSTRE,
AND FANCY COLOURED STONE WARE,
QUEEN ST., & NEW WHARF POTTERIES,
BURSLEM,
STAFFORDSHIRE.

Cork, Edge & Malkin. Advertisement from 1864 Jones.

Cork, Edge & Shaw
High Street, Tunstall
1852 Slater EM (black tea-pot)
1854 Kelly CEM
1856 Kelly SC (Black Ware Manufacturers)

Cormie, John
(i) Sitch, Burslem
1818 Pigot EM
(ii) Queen Street, Burslem
1828 Pigot CM; EM
1830 Pigot CM; EM
(iii) Nile Street, Burslem
1834 White EM-B
1835 Pigot CM; EM

John Cormie. Printed mark from a blue-printed pot.

Corn Brothers
Albert Street, Tunstall
1900 Kelly SC (Encaustic Tile Manufacturers)

Corn, Edward
(i) Upper Hadderidge
1852 Slater EM
(ii) Navigation Road, Burslem
1854 Kelly CEM
1856 Kelly CEM
1860 Kelly EM
1861 Harrison NC-B (earthenware manufacturer)
1862 Slater EM
1864 Jones EM
1889 Keates P-B (earthenware)
(iii) Longport, Burslem
1892 Keates P-B (earthenware)

Corn, W.E.
See: Corn, William & Edward

Corn, William & Edward
(i) Navigation Road, Burslem
1863 Kelly EM
1865 Keates P-B (earthen.)
1867 Keates P-B (earthen.)
1868 Kelly EM
1869 Keates P-B (earthen.)
1870 Harrod NC-B (earthenware manufacturers)
1872 Kelly EM
1873 Keates P-B (earthen.)
1875 Keates P-B (earthen)
1876 Kelly EM
1879 Keates P-B (earthen)
1880 Kelly EM
1882 Keates P-B (earthenware)
1884 Kelly EM
1887 Porter EM-B
1888 Kelly EM
(ii) North Road, Burslem
1880 Kelly EM
1884 Kelly EM
(iii) Longport
1892 Kelly EM
1896 Kelly EM
1900 Kelly EM

The surname is listed as Corns in 1863 Kelly and the initials are listed as W.E. (not W. & E.) in 1875 Keates and 1879 Keates.

Corns & Co.
5 Club Buildings, Burslem
1864 Jones EM-Miscellaneous (creel cup and shuttle eye manufacturers)

Corns, James
5 Amicable Buildings, Burslem
1867 Keates P-B (creel steps)

Corns, W. & E.
See: Corn, William & Edward

Corns, Fenton & Co.
Amicable Buildings, Burslem
1865 Keates P-B (creel steps)

Cotton, Elijah
(i) Lichfield Street Works, Hanley
1880 Kelly EM
1882 Keates P-H (earthenware)
1884 Kelly EM
1889 Keates P-H (earthenware)
(ii) Nelson Pottery, Nelson Place or Nelson Road, Hanley
1887 Porter EM-H
1888 Kelly EM
1892 Kelly EM
1896 Kelly EM
1900 Kelly EM

Cotton, J.
Nelson Works, Hanley
1889 Keates P-H (earthenware)
1892 Keates P-H (earthenware)

Cotton, John
Peel Street Works, Northwood, Hanley
1884 Kelly EM

Cotton & Barlow
Commerce Street, Longton
1851 White CEM-L (only earthenware)
1852 Slater EM
1854 Kelly CEM
1856 Kelly CEM

Cotton & Rigby
Sylvester Square, Burslem
1876 Kelly EM

Cowap, Hughes & Co.
Cobridge
1822 Allbut CEM (earthenware manufacts.)
1822 Pigot EM

Cowie, John Edmund
Glebe Buildings, Stoke
1884 Kelly SC (Encaustic Tile Manufacturers)

Crown Staffordshire Porcelain Co.
Minerva Works, Fenton
Although listed as T.A. & S. Green, this trading style was used in an advertisement in 1889 Keates. The text reads 'Art porcelain. Vases and works of art in china. Tea, breakfast, and dessert ware, in Japan, Satsuma, and ivory decorations. The proprietors, T.A. & S. Green, desire it to be known that, although the above china is of the finest description, and the work not to be surpassed, the prices are such as to meet the requirements of the large middle-class body of the public; and they hope American and colonial friends will call and see the samples at their London rooms, 25 Ely Place, or at the works. Mr. T.A. Green always in London.'
See also: Green, Thomas Allen & Spencer

Crown Staffordshire Porcelain Co.,
MINERVA WORKS,
FENTON, STAFFS.
ART PORCELAIN.
VASES and Works of Art in CHINA.
Tea, Breakfast, and Desert Ware, in Japan, Satsuma, and Ivory Decorations.
The Proprietors, T. A. & S. GREEN, desire it to be known that, although the above China is of the finest description, and the work not to be surpassed, the Prices are such as to meet the requirements of the large Middle-class body of the Public; and they hope American and Colonial friends will call and see the samples at their LONDON ROOMS, 25, ELY PLACE, or at the Works.
Mr. T. A. GREEN always in London.

Crown Staffordshire Porcelain Co. Advertisement from 1889 Keates.

Crystal Porcelain Co.
Clarence Street, Hanley
1880 Kelly CM (manufacturers of crystal porcelain)

Crystal Porcelain Pottery Co. Ltd.
Elder Road, Cobridge
1882 Keates P-B
1884 Kelly EM
1889 Keates P-B

Crystal Porcelain Tile Co. (The)
London Road, Stoke, and Elder Road, Cobridge
1888 Kelly SC (Encaustic Tile Manufacturers)
The company is listed in association with Steele & Wood.

Crystal Porcelain Tile Co. Ltd. (The)
Elder Road, Cobridge
1892 Kelly SC (Encaustic Tile Manufacturers)
The company is listed in association with Steele & Wood.

Cumberlidge & Hines
Foley Pottery, Longton
1896 Kelly JRM
1900 Kelly JRM

Cumberlidge & Humphrey
See: Cumberlidge & Humphreys

Cumberlidge & Humphreys
(i) Well Street, Tunstall
1884 Kelly EM
(ii) Gordon Pottery, High Street, Tunstall
1887 Porter EM-T
1888 Kelly EM
1892 Kelly EM
1896 Kelly EM
The second partner's name is listed as Humphrey in 1887 Porter.

Cumberlidge, Humphreys & Hele
Gordon Pottery, Tunstall
1889 Keates P-T
1892 Keates P-T

Cumberlidge, Rathbone & Co.
Well Street, Tunstall
1882 Keates P-T

Curzon & Co.
Pyenest Street, Shelton
1896 Kelly CM; EM

Cutts, John
New Street, Hanley
1822 Allbut CEM (gilder and enameller)

Cyples & Co.
Thomas Barlow of Cyples' Old Pottery, Market Street, Longton, is listed as succeeding Cyples & Co. in 1850 Slater, 1852 Slater, and 1854 Kelly, but no firm with this trading style is listed in any directory.

Cyples, Jesse
Lane End
1805 Holden NC (Egyptian black manufacturer)
1809 Holden NC (earthenware-manufactr.)
1816 Underhill P

Cyples, Joseph
Lane End
1784 Bailey NC-LE (manufacturer of Egyptian black and pottery in general)

Cyples, Lydia
(i) Market Street, Lane End
1818 Parson EM-LE
1818 Pigot EM (Egyptian black)
1822 Allbut CEM (Egyptian black manufact.)
1822 Pigot EM
1828 Pigot CM (and Egyptian black)

1830 Pigot CM (and Egyptian black)
(ii) High Street, Longton
1834 White CM-LE-L (Egyptian black ware mfrs.)

Cyples, Mary
Lane End
1796 Chester NC-LE-LD-LL (manufacturer of earthenware)
1798 Universal NC-LE (manufacturer of Staffordshire-ware)
1802 Allbut EM (map location 132)
The surname is listed as Cyplis in 1798 Universal and as Syples in 1802 Allbut.

Cyples, R.
Church Street, Longton
1856 Kelly CEM

Cyples, Richard
(i) High Street, Longton
1846 Williams NC-L-LE (china lustre & black manufctrs.)
1850 Kelly CEM; NC-L (china & earthenware manufacturer)
(ii) Heathcote Road, Longton
1892 Kelly CM

Cyples, William & Richard
Market Street, Lane End
1835 Pigot EM (and Egyptian black)

Cyples & Barker
Market Street, Longton
1846 Williams NC-L-LE (china & black ware manftrs.)
The partners are listed individually as William Cyples of Stafford Street and George Barker of Daisy Bank in 1846 Williams.

Cyples, Barton & Cyples
Market Street, Longton
1841 Pigot CM; EM (lustre Egyptian black)

Cyples & Dakin
See: Cyples & Deakin

Cyples & Deakin
High Street, Longton
1850 Slater CM; EM
The second partner's name is listed as Dakin in one of the entries (CM).

Cyples & Ford
Heathcote Works, Heathcote Street (or Road), Longton
1889 Keates P-L (china)
1892 Keates P-L (china)
1892 Kelly CM

Cyplis, Mary
See: Cyples, Mary

D

Dale & Co.
Cobridge
1796 Chester NC-C (manufacturers of earthenware)

Dale, Joseph
See: Hopwood, William

Dale, William
Marsh Street, Shelton
1846 Williams NC-Sh (potter)
1850 Kelly NC-Sh (garden ornament maker)
1850 Slater TOCM (mould)
1851 White CETOM-H-Sh
1856 Kelly P

DALE, PAGE, AND Co.,
(LATE HILDITCH & HOPWOOD),
CHINA MANUFACTURERS,
LONGTON,
STAFFORDSHIRE POTTERIES.

Dale, Page & Co. Advertisement from 1869 Keates.

DALE, PAGE, & Co.,
(Late Hilditch & Hopwood,)
CHINA MANUFACTURERS,
CHURCH STREET, LONGTON;
STAFFORDSHIRE POTTERIES.

Dale, Page & Co. Advertisement from 1873 Keates. The same advertisement appeared in 1875 Keates.

Dale, Page & Co.
Church Street, Longton
1868 Kelly CM
1869 Keates A; P-L (china)

1870 Harrod NC-L (china manufacturers for home and foreign markets)
1872 Kelly CM
1873 Keates A; P-L (china)
1875 Keates A; P-L (china)
This firm succeeded Hopwood (1869 Keates, 1873 Keates, 1875 Keates).
The advertisements in the three Keates directories all describe the firm simply as 'china manufacturers' and state that their predecessors were Hilditch & Hopwood.

Dale, Page & Goodwin
New Town Pottery, High Street, Longton
1876 Kelly CM
1879 Keates P-L (china)
1880 Kelly CM (manufacturers of all kinds of plain & decorated china, also jet ware for home & exportation)
1882 Keates P-L (china & majolica)
1884 Kelly CM
1887 Porter EM-L
1888 Kelly CM
This firm succeeded Hilditch & Hopwood (1879 Keates, 1880 Kelly).

Dalehall Pottery Co. (The)
Dalehall, Burslem
1892 Keates P-B (earthenware)
1892 Kelly EM
The name is listed as two words, Dale Hall, in 1892 Kelly.

Daniel, Henry
Bedford Row, Shelton
1828 Pigot CM; EM

Daniel, Henry, & Co.
Bedford Row, Shelton
1830 Pigot CM; EM
1834 White EM-H-Sh (china mfrs. also)

Daniel, Henry & Richard
(i) New Road, Stoke
1828 Pigot CM; EM
(ii) Eldon Place (or Street), Stoke
1830 Pigot CM
1841 Pigot CM; EM
(iii) London Road, Stoke
1834 White CM-S; EM-S
1835 Pigot CM; EM
1841 Pigot CM
(iv) Shelton
1835 Pigot CM; EM
1841 Pigot CM
(v) Stoke
1846 Williams NC-S (china and earthenware manuf.)
Richard Daniel's address is listed as Oak Hill, Stoke, in 1846 Williams.

Henry & Richard Daniel. Hand-painted mark from a china saucer.

Henry & Richard Daniel. Hand-painted mark from a china dessert dish.

Daniel, J.
New Wharf Pottery, Burslem
1868 Kelly EM

Daniel, John
Burslem
1784 Bailey NC-B
(manufacturer of cream colour and red earthen ware)

Daniel, Levi
5 Queen Street, Burslem
1862 Slater EM (rustic)

Daniel, Richard
(i) Waterloo Pottery, Burslem
1841 Pigot CM; EM
(ii) Boothen Road, Stoke
1850 Slater CM
1852 Slater CM

Daniel, Richard, & Co.
Boothen Road, Stoke
1850 Kelly CEM; NC-S
(china manufacturers)
1851 White CEM-S
Richard Daniel's house is listed as 10 Glebe Street, Stoke, in 1851 White.

Daniel, T.
Pleasant Street, Burslem
1854 Kelly PM

Daniel, Thomas
Burslem
1781 Bailey NC (potter)
1783 Bailey NC (potter)
1784 Bailey NC-B (potter)

Daniel, Timothy
Burslem
1784 Bailey NC-B
(manufacturer of cream colour and red earthen ware)

Daniel, Walter
(i) Burslem
1781 Bailey NC (potter)
1783 Bailey NC (potter)
1784 Bailey NC-B
(manufacturer of cream colour and red earthen ware)
1798 Universal NC-B
(manufacturer of Staffordshire-ware)
(ii) Newport, Burslem
1796 Chester NC-B
(manufacturer of earthenware)
1802 Allbut EM (map location 24)

Daniel & Cork
(i) Navigation Road, Burslem
1867 Keates P-B (earthen.)
(ii) Freehold Villa, Burslem
1869 Keates P-B (earthen.)

Daniels, Whittingham & Walsh
Red Street
1862 Slater EM

Davenport & Co. Ltd.
Longport
1882 Keates P-B (china and earthenware)

Davenport, Messrs.
Longport Works, Burslem
1887 Porter EM-B

Davenport, Charles
Burslem
1802 Allbut EM (map location 38)

Davenport, Henry, & Co.
Longport
1870 Harrod NC-B (glass, china, and earthenware manufacturers)

Davenport, Henry & William, & Co.
Longport and Church Street, Stoke
1835 Pigot CM (& glass manufacturers); EM

Davenport, J. & J.
Newport
1818 Parson EM-B-Lp-C
1822 Allbut CEM (china and earthenware manufacturers)

Davenport, James
Longport
1798 Universal NC-Lp
(Staffordshire-ware manufacturer)

DAVENPORT'S PATENT.

INVENTOR and SOLE PATENTEE of COMPOUNDS for the MANUFACTURE of FIRE-BRICKS, SAGGARS, CEMENT, and all Articles intended to stand ntense Heat.

Manufacturer of Patent Fire-Resisting Compound Silicate Cement.

Works:—STOKE-UPON-TRENT.

This Invention is, without doubt, one of the most important of its class, pplying a want so much needed to meet the requirements of the day. For all actical purposes it is indistructible, economical in use, and adaptable for all anufacturers requiring high degrees of heat.

FIRE-BRICKS.

Fire-bricks can be manufactured under the patent almost anywhere—in all rts of the world—not necessarily in any fire brick-district—as the principal mponent part is silex or silica, in the form of sand or silicious rock, compounded d bound together chemically. Have stood the test of steel, iron, and gas anufacturers, and are admitted to be the best produced for fire-resisting purposes.

SAGGARS.

This invention is applicable and now in use for the manufacture of Saggars ith such success as must necessarily (from merit alone) become universally lopted. They are cheap in production, durable to a degree that is not yet nown, firm in wear, bear sudden transitions of heat and cold. Practically each ggar is a crucible and will only wear out.

CEMENT.

This Cement as manufactured by the Patentee prevents fusion in bricks. The nallest covering, say the thickness of a shilling, suffices. It is in use for steel, on, gas, brick makers, china and earthenware manufacturers, and in all instances ith satisfactory results. In analysis it is the nearest to asbestos that has therto been attained, to be useable in plastic form.

The Patentee is open to License the use of the Patent for all sections, excepting the Cement, which he (the Patentee) retains and manufactures.

All information required relative to either home or foreign patents will be pplied on application to the Patentee,

JOHN DAVENPORT, Stoke-upon-Trent.

7

John Davenport. Advertisement from 1889 Keates.

Davenport, John
(i) Longport
1796 Chester NC-T-Lp
(manufacturer of earthenware)
1802 Allbut EM (map location 19)
1805 Holden NC (china and earthenware manufacturer)

1809 Holden NC (china, glass, & earthenware-manufacturer)
(ii) 6 Penkhull Terrace, Stoke
1889 Keates A; P-S (patent compound silicate cement manufacturer)

The advertisement in 1889 Keates is a lengthy promotion for John Davenport's invention of 'compounds for the manufacture of fire-bricks, saggars, cement, and all articles intended to stand intense heat'. It describes Davenport himself as the 'manufacturer of patent fire-resisting compound silicate cement' and offers licenses for both home and foreign use of all sections of the patent 'excepting the cement, which he (the patentee) retains and manufactures'.

Davenport, John, & Co.
Longport
1811 Holden NC (china, glass, & earthenware-manufacturers)

John Davenport, Son & Co. Printed mark from green-printed earthenware dinner wares. Note the additional American importer's mark.

Davenport, John, Son & Co.
(i) Longport
1828 Pigot CM; EM
1830 Pigot CM (and glass manufacturers); EM
1834 White EM-B (china mfrs. also)
(ii) Newport
1834 White EM-B (china mfrs. also)
(iii) Eldon Place, Stoke
1834 White EM-B (china mfrs. also); EM-S

John Davenport, Son & Co. Printed mark from blue-printed earthenware dinner wares.

Davenport, John & James
Longport
1816 Underhill P
1818 Pigot CM; EM
1822 Allbut CEM (china and earthenware manufacturers, glass manufacturers, and manufacts. of lead and litherage)
1822 Pigot CM; EM (and flint and cut glass)

John & James Davenport. Impressed mark from a sprigged stoneware jug.

John & James Davenport or John Davenport (& Co.). Impressed mark.

John & James Davenport. Printed mark from a stone china tureen stand.

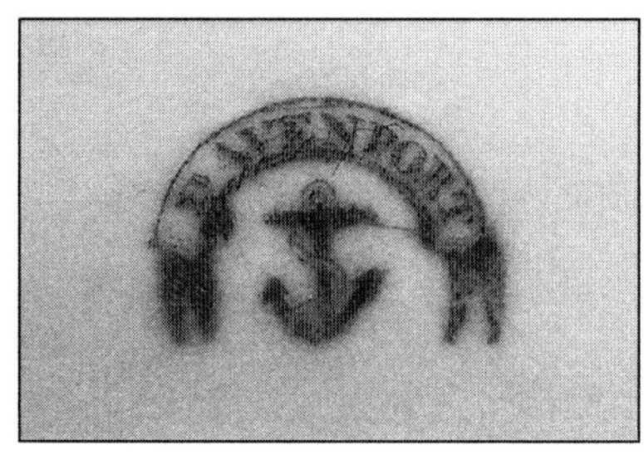

John & James Davenport. Printed mark from a china tea service.

Davenport, Thomas
Old Hall Street, Hanley
1822 Allbut CEM (gilder and painter)

Davenport, William
Stafford Street, Longton
1860 Kelly LM (silver)
1861 Harrison NC-L (lustre ware manufacturer)

Davenport succeeded J. Taylor (1860 Kelly)

Davenport, William, & Co.
(i) Church Street, Stoke
1841 Pigot CM (and flint glass manufacturers); EM
(ii) Newport
1850 Kelly CEM; NC-B (earthenware manufctrs.)
(iii) Longport
1841 Pigot CM (and flint glass manufacturers); EM
1846 Williams NC-Lp (earthenware, china, and glass manufacturers)
1850 Slater EM
1851 White CEM-B (both) (and glass manufacturers)
1852 Slater EM
1854 Kelly CEM
1856 Kelly CEM
1860 Kelly CM-General; E

WILLIAM DAVENPORT & CO.,

MANUFACTURERS OF

China, Earthenware & Glass,

LONGPORT, STAFFORDSHIRE.

Reproduction of the Old Dresden and Derby Patterns.

NEW AND REGISTERED SHAPES OF **DINNER AND TOILET WARE, TEA, BREAKFAST AND DESSERT SERVICES,** in Raised Gold, Gilt, Hand Painted, Enamelled, Printed and other Styles of Decoration.

IVORY OR QUEEN'S WARE, of Superior Tint and Quality, in the Newest and most Elegant Designs.

IRON STONE WARE, Plain and Decorated, in China Patterns, suitable for BARRACKS, CLUBS, HOTELS, and SHIPS' Uses.

WHITE GRANITE, in great variety, suitable for Home Trade, North and South America, and the Colonies.

TABLE GLASS—of very superior quality—of every description.

FOREIGN MARKETS.—Shippers supplied with Lustre, Japanned, Printed and Enamelled Earthenware, to which especial attention is paid to Design and Decoration.

SPECIALITÉ FOR MESS, HOTEL, AND SHIPS' WARE ORDERS.

London Offices and Show Rooms—32, Ely Place, E.C.
Liverpool „ „ „ 30, Canning Place.

William Davenport & Co. Advertisement from 1880 Kelly.

William Davenport & Co. Printed mark from a china jug with Imari-style decoration.

1861 Harrison NC-B (china and glass manufacturers)
1862 Slater CM; EM
1863 Kelly CM-General; EM
1864 Jones CEM (and glass)
1865 Keates P-B (china & earthenware)
1867 Keates P-B (china and earthenware)
1868 Kelly CM; EM
1869 Keates P-B (china & earthenware)
1870 Harrod NC-B (manufacturers of earthenware, china, and glass for home and foreign trade; wholesale warehouses)
1872 Kelly EM
1873 Keates P-B (china and earthenware)
1875 Keates P-B (china and earthen.)
1876 Kelly EM
1879 Keates P-B (china & earthen.)
1880 Kelly A; CM; EM
1884 Kelly CM

William Davenport's address is listed as Longport Hall in 1846 Williams. The Longport address is listed as Davenport Street in 1862 Slater, 1865 Keates, 1867 Keates, and 1869 Keates. London warehouses are listed at 82 Fleet Street (1852 Slater, 1860 Kelly, 1863 Kelly, 1868 Kelly, 1870 Harrod, 1872 Kelly, 1876 Kelly) and 32 Ely Place (1880 Kelly). A Liverpool warehouse is listed at 30 Canning Place (1860 Kelly, 1863 Kelly, 1868 Kelly, 1870 Harrod, 1872 Kelly, 1876 Kelly, 1880 Kelly).

The advertisement in 1880 Kelly describes the firm as 'manufacturers of china, earthenware & glass' and offers the following list of products:

- Reproduction of the Old Dresden and Derby Patterns.
- New and registered shapes of dinner and toilet ware, tea, breakfast and dessert services, in Raised Gold, Gilt, Hand Painted, Enamelled, Printed and other Styles of Decoration.
- Ivory or Queen's Ware, of Superior Tint and Quality, in the Newest and most Elegant Designs.
- Iron Stone Ware, Plain and Decorated, in China Patterns, suitable for Barracks, Clubs, Hotels, and Ships' Uses.
- White Granite, in great variety, suitable for Home Trade, North and South America, and the Colonies.
- Table Glass – of very superior quality – of every description.
- Foreign Markets. – Shippers supplied with Lustre, Japanned, Printed and Enamelled Earthenware, to which especial attention is paid to Design and Decoration.
- Specialité for mess, hotel, and ships' ware orders.

The advertisement also offers 'illustrated sheets & prices on application' and lists offices and showrooms in London at 32 Ely Place, and in Liverpool at 30 Canning Place.

Davenport, W., & Co. Ltd.
Longport, Burslem
1884 Kelly EM

Davenport & Banks
Castlefield Pottery, Etruria
1864 Jones A; PM
The advertisement in 1864 Jones is in the name of Davenport, Banks & Co. (qv).

Davenport, Banks & Co.
Castlefield Pottery, Bedford Street, between Etruria and Hanley
1862 Slater EM (porous &c.)
1863 Kelly CM-Antique; EM; SC (Chemical Ware Manufacturers); SC (Fancy Ware Manufacturers); SM (antique, mosaic & chemical porous)
1864 Jones A; EM (fancy and antique goods); NC (earthenware, and stone, and fancy ware manufacturers)
1865 Keates A; P-H (porous and fancy earthenware)
1867 Keates P-H (porous and fancy earthenware)
1868 Kelly EM
1869 Keates A; P-H (porous and fancy earthenware)
1870 Harrod NC-H

(manufacturers of porous general earthenware and fancy goods for home and export)
1872 Kelly EM
1873 Keates A; P-H (porus and fancy earthenware)
The advertisements in 1864 Jones and 1865 Keates both describe the firm as 'manufacturers of all kinds of porous earthenware, fancy and antique goods, paraffin lamps, chemical goods, &c.' The advertisement in 1869 Keates describes them as 'manufacturers of general earthenware, fancy goods in majolica, jet, & terra cotta, antiques, fancy jugs, dinner, tea, and toilet wares; chemical goods, porous water bottles, filters and spirit casks; suitable for home and export and exceptional goods, fittings, &c.' Despite the cross-reference, no advertisement could be located in 1873 Keates. The firm was succeeded by Banks & Thorley (1882 Keates advertisement).

DAVENPORT, BANKS, & Co.,
CASTLE FIELD POTTERY,
ETRURIA, near STOKE-UPON-TRENT, STAFFORDSHIRE.
MANUFACTURERS OF ALL KINDS OF
POROUS EARTHENWARE,
FANCY AND ANTIQUE GOODS,
PARAFFIN LAMPS, CHEMICAL GOODS, &c., &c.

Davenport, Banks & Co. Advertisement from 1864 Jones. A very similar advertisement appeared in 1865 Keates.

DAVENPORT, BANKS & Co.,
Castle Field Pottery. Etruria,
MANUFACTURERS OF GENERAL
Earthenware, Fancy Goods
In MAJOLICA, JET, & TERRA COTTA,
ANTIQUES, FANCY JUGS,
Dinner, Tea, and Toilet Wares.
CHEMICAL GOODS, POROUS WATER BOTTLES,
FILTERS AND SPIRIT CASKS.
Suitable for Home and Export and Exceptional Goods, Fittings, &c.

Davenport, Banks & Co. Advertisement from 1869 Keates.

Davies, John Heath
See: Davis, John Heath

Davis, J.H. & J.
Trent Pottery, Canal Side, Hanley
1872 Kelly CM; SC (Sanitary Ware Manufacturers)
1873 Keates P-H (earthenware)
1875 Keates P-H (earthenware)
1879 Keates P-H (earthenware)
1882 Keates P-H (earthenware)
London showrooms at 12 Thavie's Inn, Holborn, are listed in 1872 Kelly.

Davis, John Heath
Trent Pottery, Kirkham Street or Canal Side, Hanley
1876 Kelly EM
1880 Kelly EM
1884 Kelly EM
1887 Porter EM-H
1888 Kelly EM
1889 Keates P-H (earthenware and sanitary goods)
The surname is listed as Davies in 1876 Kelly, 1887 Porter, and 1888 Kelly.

Davison & Son
Bleak Hill Works, Burslem
1900 Kelly EM

Dawson
Lane End
1802 Allbut EM (map location 125)
No first name is listed.

Dawson, Daniel & William
Burslem
1798 Universal NC-B (manufacturers of Staffordshire-ware)

Dawson, James
(i) Lane Delph
1796 Chester NC-LE-LD-LL (manufacturer of earthenware)
(ii) Commerce Street, Longton
1867 Keates A; P-L (earthenware)
1868 Kelly EM
1869 Keates A; P-L (earthenware)
1870 Harrod NC-L (earthenware manufacturer)
1873 Keates A; P-L (earthenware)
(iii) Stafford Street, Longton
1875 Keates P-L (earthenware)
1876 Kelly EM
1879 Keates A; P-L (earthenware)
1880 Kelly EM
1882 Keates P-L (earthenware)
1884 Kelly EM
1887 Porter EM-L
1888 Kelly EM
1889 Keates P-L (earthenware)
The Keates advertisements in 1867, 1869 and 1873 all describe Dawson as an 'earthenware manufacturer, coloured bodies, etc., etc.' Another in 1875 Keates, together with the one in 1879, describes him simply as an 'earthenware manufacturer'.

JAMES DAWSON,
Earthenware Manufacturer,
COLOURED BODIES,
ETC., ETC.,
COMMERCE STREET,
LONGTON.

James Dawson. Advertisement from 1867 Keates. The same advertisement appeared in 1869 Keates and 1873 Keates.

JAMES DAWSON,
EARTHENWARE
MANUFACTURER,
STAFFORD STREET,
LONGTON,
STAFFORDSHIRE.

James Dawson. Advertisement from 1875 Keates. The same advertisement appeared in 1879 Keates.

Dawson, Joseph
Lane End
1798 Universal NC-LE (manufacturer of Staffordshire-ware)

Dawson, William
Burslem
1796 Chester NC-B (manufacturer of earthenware)
1802 Allbut EM (map location 31)

Day, George
Albion Works, High Street, Longton
1882 Keates P-L
1884 Kelly CM
1887 Porter EM-L
1888 Kelly CM
1889 Keates P-L (china and earthenware)

Day, George & Thomas
Albion Works, High Street, Longton
1880 Kelly CM

Day, Joseph, & Co.
High Street, Longton
1884 Kelly CM

Day, Thomas T.
High Street, Longton
1888 Kelly EM

Deakin & Son
Waterloo Manufactory, Stafford Street, Longton
1834 White CM-LE-L (ironstone); EM-LE-L (and ironstone china)
1835 Pigot EM
1841 Pigot CM (iron-stone); EM
1846 Williams NC-L-LE (earthenware manufacturers)
1850 Kelly CEM; NC-L (earthenware manufacturers)
1850 Slater EM
1852 Slater EM
1854 Kelly CEM
1856 Kelly CEM
1860 Kelly EM; LM; SC (Egyptian Black Ware Manufacturers)
1861 Harrison NC-L (earthenware and lustre manufacturers)
1862 Slater EM
The partners are listed individually as James Deakin of Hill Side, Mear, and John Deakin of Green Dock in 1846 Williams. The address is listed as Waterloo Works and Stafford Street in 1850 Slater, 1852 Slater, 1854 Kelly, and 1856 Kelly.

Deakin & Son. Printed mark from a blue-printed earthenware tea plate.

Deakin, James, & Son
Waterloo, Stafford Street, Longton
1851 White CEM-L

Deakin, William Oswald
Cromartie Works, Market Street, Longton
1887 Porter EM-L

Deakin & Bailey
Waterloo Factory, Lane End
1828 Pigot EM
1830 Pigot EM

Deakin & Bailey. Printed mark from a blue-printed earthenware plate.

Dean Brothers
Newcastle Street, Dale Hall, Burslem
1888 Kelly EM; JM
1889 Keates P-B

Dean, Lydia
Old Hall Street, Hanley
1841 Pigot TOCM

Dean, M.
Ranelagh Street, Hanley
1896 Kelly EM

Dean, Meshach
Hall Street, Burslem
1882 Keates P-B

Dean, Robert
Waterloo Road, Burslem
1869 Keates P-B (earthen.)
1870 Harrod NC-B (earthenware manufacturer)

Dean, Thomas
(i) Ducal Works, Newcastle Street, Burslem
1892 Keates P-B
1892 Kelly JRM
1896 Kelly JRM
(ii) High Street, Tunstall
1900 Kelly JRM (Rockingham ware)

Dean, Capper & Dean
Excelsior Works, New Street, Hanley
1882 Keates P-H (earthenware)
1884 Kelly EM

Dean, Lowe, Machin & Shorter
Parker Street, Hanley
1876 Kelly CM; EM; MM

Dean, M., & Rogers
Ranelagh Street, Hanley
1900 Kelly EM

Dean & Stokes
Sylvester Pottery, Nile Street, Burslem
1867 Keates P-B (earthenware)
1868 Kelly EM
1869 Keates P-B (earthenware)

Dean & Stokes. Printed mark from a flow-blue earthenware jug. Note that the initials could also relate to Deakin & Son or the unlisted partnership of Dimmock & Smith, but the use of flow blue suggests this later firm.

Deare Brothers
Ducal Works, Dale Hill (sic), Burslem
1887 Porter EM-B

Deaville & Co.
Bath Works, Hanley
1852 Slater EM (in pearl)

Decorative Art Tile Co.
200 & 202 Bryan Street, Hanley
1884 Kelly SC (Encaustic Tile Manufacturers)
1888 Kelly SC (Encaustic Tile Manufacturers)
1892 Kelly SC (Encaustic Tile Manufacturers)
The managing partner is listed as William Parrish in all three directories.

Decorative Art Tile Co. Ltd.
200 & 202 Bryan Street, Hanley
1896 Kelly SC (Encaustic Tile Manufacturers)
1900 Kelly SC (Encaustic Tile Manufacturers)
The managing director is listed as William Parrish in both directories.

Dennis, Joseph
Mount Pleasant Works, High Street, Longton
1900 Kelly MM

Derbyshire, William Henry, & Co.
Heathcote Works, Longton
1876 Kelly CM

Dewes & Copestake
Viaduct Works, Caroline Street, Longton
1896 Kelly CM; EM
1900 Kelly CM; EM

Dillon, Francis
Cobridge
1830 Pigot CM; EM
1834 White EM-B
1835 Pigot EM
1841 Pigot EM

Dillon, Francis & Nicholas
Cobridge
1816 Underhill P
1818 Parson EM-B-Lp-C
1818 Pigot EM
1822 Allbut CEM (earthenware manufacturers)
1822 Pigot EM
1828 Pigot CM; EM
The firm is listed as N. & F. Dillon in 1816 Underhill.

Dillon, N. & F.
See: Dillon, Francis & Nicholas

Dimmock, John
(i) Albion Street, Shelton
1851 White CEM-H-Sh
(ii) Stafford Street, Hanley
1865 Keates P-H (earthenware)
Dimmock's house is listed as Broom Street in 1851 White.

Dimmock, John, & Co.
Albion Works, Stafford Street, Hanley
1861 Harrison NC-H-Sh (earthenware manufacturers)
1862 Slater EM
1863 Kelly EM
1864 Jones EM
1867 Keates P-H (earthenware)
1868 Kelly EM
1869 Keates P-H (earthenware)
1870 Harrod NC-H (earthenware manufactures of every description, for home and export. Award, London, 1851, bronze medal; London, 1862, for general excellence)
1872 Kelly EM
1873 Keates P-H (earthenware)
1875 Keates P-H (earthenware)
1876 Kelly EM
1880 Kelly EM
1882 Keates P-H (earthenware)
1884 Kelly EM
1887 Porter EM-H
1888 Kelly EM
1889 Keates P-H (earthenware)
1892 Keates P-H (earthenware)
1892 Kelly EM
1896 Kelly EM
1900 Kelly EM
The proprietor is listed as William D. Cliff in 1892 Kelly, 1896 Kelly, and 1900 Kelly.

Dimmock, Thomas
(i) Cheapside, Shelton
1822 Allbut CEM (earthenware manufact.)
(ii) Albion Street, Shelton
1851 White CEM-H-Sh

Dimmock, Thomas, & Co.
(i) Cheapside, Shelton
1828 Pigot EM
(ii) Albion Street, Shelton
1834 White EM-H-Sh
1850 Slater EM
1851 White CEM-H-Sh
1852 Slater EM
See also: Dimmock, Thomas jun., & Co.

Thomas Dimmock & Co. Printed mark from a blue-printed earthenware soup plate.

Thomas Dimmock & Co. Printed mark from a grey-printed and coloured stone china tea plate. The registration diamond dates from 1844.

Dimmock, Thomas jun., & Co.
(i) James Street, Shelton
1822 Pigot EM
(ii) Tontine Street, Hanley
1828 Pigot EM
1834 White EM-H-Sh
1835 Pigot EM
1841 Pigot EM
(iii) Cheapside, Shelton
1830 Pigot EM
1835 Pigot EM
1841 Pigot EM
1850 Slater EM
1852 Slater EM
1854 Kelly CEM
(iv) Albion Street, Shelton
1846 Williams NC-Sh (china and earthenware manufacturers)
(v) Stafford Row or Stafford Street, Shelton, Hanley
1850 Kelly CEM; NC-Sh (earthenware manufs.)
1856 Kelly CEM
1860 Kelly EM
The partners are listed individually as Thomas Dimmock of Albion Street, Shelton, and John Wood of Dalehall, Burslem, in 1846 Williams.
See also: Dimmock, Thomas, & Co.

Dimmock, W.
3 Bath Terrace, Stoke
1889 Keates P-S

Dimmock & Wood
Albion Works, Stafford Street, Hanley
1879 Keates P-H (earthenware)

Dix & Tundley
Albert Street, Burslem
1864 Jones EM

Doherty & Bromley
High Street, Kidsgrove
1862 Slater EM (& stone, lustre, &c.); TOCM

Doulton & Co.
Nile Street Works, Burslem
1882 Keates P-B (earthenware)
1884 Kelly CM; EM
1887 Porter EM-B
1888 Kelly EM
1889 Keates P-B (earthenware)
1892 Keates P-B (earthenware)
1892 Kelly CM; EM; SC (Art Pottery Manufacturers)
1896 Kelly EM
1900 Kelly EM
London showrooms at Cornish House, 14 St. Andrew Street, Holborn Circus, are listed in 1892 Kelly.

Dowdeswell & Evans
Highfields Tileries, Wolstanton
1900 Kelly P

Downing & Co.
Wellington Works, Newport Street, Burslem
1870 Harrod NC-B (earthenware manufacturers)
1872 Kelly EM

Downing & Gilman
Newport Street, Burslem
1873 Keates P-B (earthenware)

Draycott, Charles A.
See: Buller & Mugford

Dresden Porcelain Co.
Blythe Works, High Street, Longton
1896 Kelly CM
1900 Kelly CM

Drewry & Son
Daisy Bank, Lane End
1822 Allbut CEM (china manufacts.)

Drewry & Son. Printed mark from a blue-printed creamer.

Drewry, Thomas
Daisy Bank, Lane End
1828 Pigot CM
1830 Pigot CM

Drewry, Thomas, & Son
Daisy Bank, Lane End
1818 Parson EM-LE
1822 Pigot CM

Drury Pottery Co.
Normacot Road, Longton
1892 Keates P-L

Dudson, J.
Broom Street, Hanley
1854 Kelly PM (Ornamental Figure Makers)

Dudson, James
(i) Hope Street, Shelton, Hanley
1846 Williams NC-Sh (china figure manufacturer)
1850 Kelly NC-Sh (ornamental china manufacturer, glass & earthenware colour maker)
1850 Slater TOCM
1851 White CETOM-H-Sh
1856 Kelly CEM
1860 Kelly CM-General
1862 Slater A; CM (& ironstone); EM (and metal mounted jugs); TOCM
1863 Kelly CFM; CM-General; EM; SC (Jug Manufacturers)
1864 Jones A; EM
1868 Kelly EM; SM
1870 Harrod NC-H (manufacturer of earthenware, improved ironstone china jugs, butters, teapots, candlesticks, colour manufacturer for china, earthenware, and glass, Britannia metal-mounted jugs, for home and foreign market)
1880 Kelly EM (manufacturer of earthenware, white & colored stone bodies in jugs, teapots &c.; britannia metal, covered ware &c)
1884 Kelly EM
1889 Keates P-H (earthenware, stone, and parian)
1892 Keates P-H (earthenware, stone, and parian)
(ii) Hanover Street, Hanley
1865 Keates P-H (earthenware and parian)
1867 Keates P-H (earthenware and parian)
1869 Keates A; P-H (earthenware and parian)
1872 Kelly EM
1873 Keates A; P-H (earthenware and parian)
1875 Keates P-H (earthenware and parian)
1876 Kelly EM
1879 Keates P-H (earthenware and parian)
1882 Keates P-H (earthenware and parian)
1884 Kelly EM
1888 Kelly EM
The advertisements in 1862 Slater and 1864 Jones both describe Dudson as a 'manufacturer of earthenware'. His specialities are
(Continued on next page)

JAMES DUDSON,
Manufacturer of Earthenware,
HOPE STREET, HANLEY,
STAFFORDSHIRE,
ORNAMENTAL CHINA FIGURES,
IMPROVED IRON STONE CHINA JUGS, BUTTERS,
TEA POTS AND CANDLESTICKS,
BRITANNIA METAL MOUNTED JUGS.
Colour Manufacturer for China, Earthenware, and Glass.

James Dudson. Advertisement from 1862 Slater.

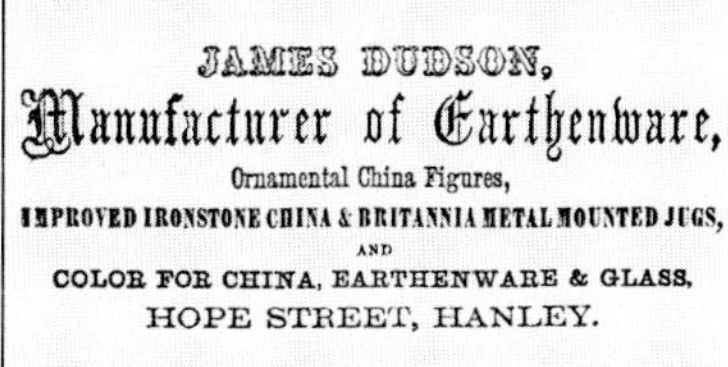

James Dudson. Advertisement from 1864 Jones.

JAMES DUDSON,
MANUFACTURER OF
Earthenware & Coloured Stone Bodies
IMPROVED IRONSTONE CHINA
AND
BRITANNIA METAL MOUNTED JUGS,
AND COLOURS
FOR CHINA, EARTHENWARE, & GLASS.
Works—Hope Street & Hanover Street, Hanley.

James Dudson. Advertisement from 1869 Keates.

JAMES DUDSON,
MANUFACTURER OF
Earthenware & Coloured Stone Bodies,
BRITANNIA METAL MOUNTED JUGS,
AND A
GENERAL VARIETY OF GOODS
SUITABLE FOR HOME & FOREIGN MARKETS.
WORKS:
HOPE Street & HANOVER Street,
HANLEY.

James Dudson. Advertisement from 1873 Keates.

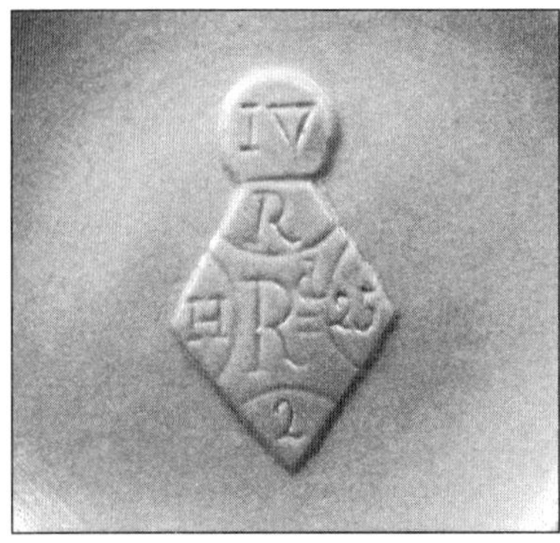

James Dudson. Impressed and moulded marks from a relief-moulded stoneware jug. The registration diamond dates from 1861.

Dudson, James. Impressed mark from a rouletted stoneware teapot.

given as 'ornamental china figures, improved iron stone china jugs, butters, tea pots and candlesticks, Britannia metal mounted jugs' in 1862, and as 'ornamental china figures, improved ironstone china & Britannia metal mounted jugs' in 1864. Both refer to him as a manufacturer of colours for china, earthenware, and glass. The two Keates advertisements of 1869 and 1873 give the address as Hope Street and Hanover Street and once again are similar, describing Dudson as a 'manufacturer of earthenware & coloured stone bodies, improved ironstone china and Britannia metal mounted jugs, and colours for china, earthenware, & glass' (1869) and as a 'manufacturer of earthenware & coloured stone bodies, Britannia metal mounted jugs, and a general variety of goods suitable for home & foreign markets' (1873).

Dudson, James Thomas
Hanover Street, Hanley
1892 Kelly EM
1896 Kelly EM
1900 Kelly EM

Dudson, Richard
Cannon Street, Shelton
1841 Pigot CM; TOCM

Dudson, Thomas
Hope Street, Shelton
1841 Pigot TOCM

Duke & Nephews
Hill Pottery, Burslem
1864 Jones CEM; PM

Duke (Sir J. bart. M.P.) Nephews
Hill Top Pottery, Burslem
1863 Kelly CM-General; EM

Dunn, Bennett & Co.
(i) Boothen Works, Brook Street, Hanley
1880 Kelly EM
1882 Keates P-H
1884 Kelly EM
(ii) Royal Victoria Works, Liverpool Road, Burslem
1887 Porter EM-B
1888 Kelly EM
1889 Keates P-B
1892 Keates P-B
1892 Kelly EM
1896 Kelly EM
1900 Kelly EM

Dunn, Bennett & Co. Printed mark from an ironstone soup plate. The registration diamond dates from 1883.

Dunn, William
266 Waterloo Road, Burslem
1882 Keates P-B

E

Eardley, Alfred Joseph
Dalehall, Burslem
1889 Keates P-B (floor and tile); SC-B (Encaustic and Geometric Tile Pavement Manufacturers)
1892 Keates P-B (floor and tile); SC-B (Encaustic and Geometric Tile Pavement Manufacturers)

Eardley, Herbert
(i) Oldhall Street, Hanley
1834 White EM-H-Sh (jugs & ornaments)
(ii) New Street, Hanley
1835 Pigot TOCM
1841 Pigot TOCM

Eardley, James
New Street, Hanley
1834 White CETM-H-Sh

Eardley & Hammersley
Church Bank Pottery, High Street, Tunstall

1862 Slater EM
1863 Kelly EM
1864 Jones EM
1865 Keates P-T (earthenware)

Eardley, Spear & Co.
Well Street, Tunstall
1873 Keates P-T (earthenware)

Eardly, William
63 Lichfield Street, Hanley
1887 Porter SC-H (Tile Manufacturer)

Eary, Thomas
King Street, Fenton
1846 Williams NC-C-F-E (earthenware &c., manfts.)
The firm is noted as being in the hands of executors.

Eccles, H.
Queen Anne Pottery, Shelton, Hanley
1892 Keates P-H

Edensor Pottery Co.
Edensor Road, Longton
1892 Keates P-L
1892 Kelly EM
1896 Kelly EM

Edensor Pottery Co. Ltd.
Edensor Road, Longton
1900 Kelly EM

Edge & Co.
High Street, Longton
1872 Kelly CM

Edge, Daniel
Waterloo Road, Burslem
1830 Pigot EM (toy only)
1834 White ETM-B (china toy mfrs.)
1835 Pigot TOCM (fine)
1841 Pigot TOCM (fine and earthenware)

Edge, Joseph
(i) Hamill, Burslem
1852 Slater EM
(ii) Elder House, Burslem
1882 Keates P-B (earthenware)

Edge, Timothy
(i) Marsh Street, Shelton, and Holehouse, Burslem
1822 Pigot EM (chimney pipe and flower pot)
(ii) Waterloo Road, Burslem
1850 Kelly NC-B (china figure manufacturer)
1850 Slater TOCM
1851 White CETM-B
1854 Kelly PM (Ornamental Figure Makers)

Edge, William
Primitive Works, Golden Hill
1828 Pigot EM
1830 Pigot EM
1834 White EM-B; EM-T; NC-G (earthenware mfr.)

Edge, William, & Co.
High Street, Longton
1873 Keates P-L (parian and majolica)

Edge, William & Samuel
Lane Delph
1841 Pigot EM
The partners are listed as William Edge of Church Street, Fenton, and Samuel Edge of Park Street, Fenton, in 1846 Williams.

Edge & Malkin
Newport Works, Burslem
1870 Harrod NC-B (manufacturers of earthenware and ironstone china, black lustre, fancy coloured stoneware, for home and foreign markets)
1887 Porter EM-B

Edge, Malkin & Co.
Newport Works, Burslem
1872 Kelly EM
1873 Keates P-B (earthenware and lustre)
1875 Keates P-B (earthenware and lustre)
1876 Kelly A; EM
1880 Kelly EM
1882 Keates P-B (earthenware)
1884 Kelly EM
1888 Kelly EM
1889 Keates P-B (earthenware)
1892 Keates P-B (earthenware)
1892 Kelly EM
1896 Kelly EM
1900 Kelly EM
Despite the cross-reference, no advertisement could be located in 1876 Kelly. The compilers may have been confused with Malkin, Edge & Co.

Edgerton, Beech & Birks
High Street, Longton
1850 Kelly CEM; NC-L (china, earthenware & black manufacturers)
1850 Slater CM; EM
1851 White CEM-L

Edgerton & Birks
(i) Little Lane, Longton
1854 Kelly CEM
(ii) Green Dock Works, Clayton Street, Longton
1856 Kelly CEM
1860 Kelly CM-General
1861 Harrison NC-L (china manufacturers, &c.)

Edward & Brown
High Street, Longton
1896 Kelly CM
1900 Kelly CM

Edwardes, J.
See: Edwards, John

Edwards Brothers
King Street, Fenton
1888 Kelly EM

Edwards & Son. Advertisement from 1887 Porter.

Edwards & Son
(i) Lower Hadderidge, Burslem
1865 Keates P-B (earthenware)
(ii) Newcastle Street, Burslem
1867 Keates P-B (earthen.)
(iii) Trent Works, Joiner's Square, Hanley
1887 Porter EM-H
1888 Kelly MM; PM
1889 Keates P-H (fancy goods)
1892 Keates P-H (fancy goods)
1892 Kelly MM; PM
1896 Kelly MM
(iv) Hanover Street, Burslem
1892 Keates P-B (earthenware)
(v) Hadderidge Pottery, Burslem

1896 Kelly EM
1900 Kelly EM
An advertisement in 1887 Porter describes the firm at the Trent Works as 'manufacturers of parian, salmon colour & majolica fancy goods, with mossed & raised flowers', and states that they succeeded Thomas Adams, formerly Stanway, Horne & Adams.

Edwards & Sons
King Street, Fenton
1889 Keates P-F (china and earthenware)
1892 Keates P-F (white granite)

Edwards, George
Sheridan Works, King Street, Longton
1873 Keates A; P-L (china)
1875 Keates P-L (china)
1876 Kelly CM
1879 Keates A; P-L (china)
1880 Kelly CM (manufacturer of superior china, suitable for the home & export trade)
1882 Keates P-L (china)
1884 Kelly CM (manufacturer of superior china, suitable for the home & export trade)
1887 Porter EM-L
1888 Kelly CM (manufacturer of superior china, suitable for the home & export trade)
1889 Keates P-L (china)
1892 Keates P-L (china)
1892 Kelly CM
1896 Kelly CM
1900 Kelly CM
The advertisements in 1873 Keates and 1879 Keates, together with a third in 1875 Keates, all describe Edwards as a 'manufacturer of white and decorative china, for home and foreign markets'.

GEO. EDWARDS,
MANUFACTURER OF
WHITE AND DECORATIVE CHINA,
FOR HOME AND FOREIGN MARKETS,
SHERIDAN WORKS,
LONGTON, STAFFORDSHIRE POTTERIES.

George Edwards. Advertisement from 1873 Keates. The same advertisement appeared in 1875 Keates and 1879 Keates.

Edwards, George, & Co.
(i) Cyple's Lane, Longton
1867 Keates P-L (china)
(ii) Sheridan Works, King Street, Longton
1868 Kelly CM
1872 Kelly CM
1869 Keates A; P-L (china)
1870 Harrod NC-L (manufacturers of white and decorative china for home and foreign markets)
The advertisement in 1869 Keates describes the firm as 'manufacturers of white and decorative china, for home & foreign markets'.

GEO. EDWARDS & CO.,
MANUFACTURERS OF
White and Decorative China,
FOR
HOME & FOREIGN MARKETS,
SHERIDAN WORKS, LONGTON,
STAFFORDSHIRE POTTERIES

George Edwards & Co. Advertisement from 1869 Keates.

Edwards, J.
(i) Fenton
1856 Kelly CEM
(ii) Normacot, Longton
1860 Kelly CM-General

Edwards, J., Ltd.
King Street, Fenton
1900 Kelly SC (Ironstone China Manufacturers)

Edwards, J.R., & Co.
Gordon Pottery, Anchor Road, Longton
1889 Keates P-L (china)
1892 Keates P-L (china)

Edwards, J. & B.
Fenton Road, Hanley
1884 Kelly EM
1888 Kelly EM; PM

Edwards, James
(i) Dale Hall, Burslem
1846 Williams NC-B (earthenware manufacturer)
1850 Kelly CEM; NC-B (earthenware manufacturer)
1850 Slater EM
1851 White CEM-B (only earthenware)
1852 Slater EM
(ii) Knowle Works, Hamill Street, Burslem
1850 Kelly CEM; NC-B (earthenware manufacturer)
1851 White CEM-B (only earthenware)
(iii) Market Street, Longton
1851 White CEM-L
1854 Kelly CEM
1860 Kelly CM-General
1861 Harrison NC-L (china manufacturer)
1862 Slater CM
Edwards' houses are listed as Dalchall in 1846 Williams and Lightwood in 1851 White.

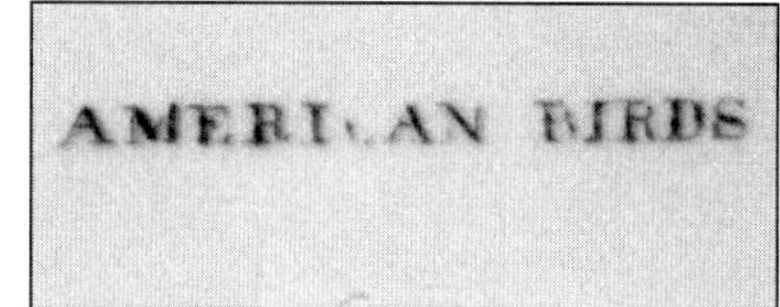

James Edwards & Son. Impressed and printed marks from a violet-printed ironstone dinner plate.

Edwards, James, & Son
(i) Knowle Pottery, Burslem
1852 Slater EM
(ii) Dale Hall Pottery, Burslem
1856 Kelly CEM
1860 Kelly EM
1861 Harrison NC-B (earthenware manufacturers)
1863 Kelly EM
1864 Jones EM
1868 Kelly EM
1869 Keates P-B (earthenware)
1870 Harrod NC-B (manufacturers of ironstone china, earthenware, electrical, chemical, galvanic, photographic appartus; fancy decorated table, toilet, and dessert ware, for home and foreign markets)
1872 Kelly EM
1873 Keates P-B (earthenware)
1875 Keates P-B (earthenware)
1876 Kelly EM
1879 Keates P-B (earthenware)

1880 Kelly EM
(iii) Market Street, Longton
1863 Kelly CM-General
1864 Jones CEM
1865 Keates P-L (china)
1867 Keates P-L (china)

Edwards, James & Richard
Knowle Pottery, Burslem
1850 Slater EM

Edwards, James & Thomas
Sylvester Square, Burslem
1841 Pigot EM

Edwards, John
(i) near Market Place, Longton
1850 Slater CM
(ii) Caroline Street, Longton
1852 Slater TOCM
(iii) King Street, Fenton
1865 Keates P-F (china and earthenware)
1867 Keates P-F (china and earthenware)
1868 Kelly SC (White Granite Manufacturer)
1869 Keates P-F (china and earthenware)
1870 Harrod NC-F (semi-porcelain manufacturer)
1872 Kelly SC (White Granite Manufacturer)
1876 Kelly SC (White Granite Manufacturer)
1880 Kelly CM
1882 Keates P-F (white granite)
1884 Kelly CM
1887 Porter EM-F
1888 Kelly CM
1892 Kelly SC (Ironstone China Manufacturers)
1896 Kelly SC (Ironstone China Manufacturer)
(iv) Hartwell Hills, Barlaston
1870 Harrod NC-Bar (china and earthenware manufacturer)
The surname is listed as Edwardes in 1896 Kelly.

Edwards, John, & Co.
King Street, Fenton
1875 Keates P-F (china and earthenware)
1879 Keates P-F (china and earthenware)
1882 Keates P-F (china and earthenware)

Edwards, John, & Son
King Street, Fenton
1873 Keates P-F (china and earthenware)

Edwards, John, & Sons
King Street, Fenton
1887 Porter SC-F (Spur and Stilt Manufacturers)
1888 Kelly SC (Spur & Stilt Makers for Pottery Manufacturers)
1892 Kelly SC (Stilt & Spur Manufacturers)
1896 Kelly SC (Stilt & Spur Manufacturers); SC (Spur Makers)
1900 Kelly SC (Stilt & Spur Manufacturers)

Edwards, John & James
King Street, Fenton
1861 Harrison NC-F (china and earthenware manufacturers)
1862 Slater CM; EM
1863 Kelly CM-General; CM-Tea, Breakfast, and Dessert Services; CM-White & Finished; SC (White Granite Manufacturers)
1864 Jones A; CEM (and white granite)
The advertisement in 1864 Jones describes the firm as 'manufacturers of decorated china, breakfast, dessert, & tea services, and white granite'.

JOHN & JAMES EDWARDS,
MANUFACTURERS OF
DECORATED CHINA,
BREAKFAST, DESSERT, & TEA SERVICES, and
WHITE GRANITE.
KING STREET, FENTON,
STAFFORDSHIRE POTTERIES.

John & James Edwards. Advertisement from 1864 Jones.

Edwards, R.J.
Gordon Pottery, Anchor Road, Longton
1887 Porter EM-L

Edwards, R.J., & Co.
(i) Forrister Street, Longton
1888 Kelly CM
(ii) Gordon Pottery, Anchor Road, Longton
1892 Kelly CM
1896 Kelly CM

Edwards, Richard
Newport Lane, Burslem
1862 Slater EM

Edwards, T. & B.
Fenton Road, Hanley
1884 Kelly PM

Edwards, Thomas
Swan Bank, Burslem
1846 Williams NC-B (potter)
Edwards' house is listed as Waterloo Road in 1846 Williams.

Edwards, William
(i) Lane Delph
1781 Bailey NC (potter)
1783 Bailey NC (potter)
(ii) Lane End
1784 Bailey NC-LE (potter)
(iii) High Street, Lane End
1830 Pigot EM
(iv) Russell Street, Longton
1875 Keates P-L (earthenware)
1879 Keates P-L (earthenware)
1880 Kelly EM
1882 Keates P-L (earthenware)
1884 Kelly EM
1887 Porter EM-L
1888 Kelly EM
(v) Lockett's Lane, Longton
1876 Kelly EM

Edwards, William Joseph
Russell Street Works, Warren Street, Longton
1896 Kelly EM
1900 Kelly EM

Edwards & Brown
Victoria Works, High Street, Longton
1882 Keates P-L (china)
1887 Porter EM-L
1888 Kelly CM
1889 Keates P-L (china)
1892 Keates P-L (china)
1892 Kelly CM
The second partner is listed as H. Brown in 1888 Kelly.

Edwards & Goodwin
Hanover Street Pottery, Burslem
1887 Porter EM-B
1888 Kelly EM
1892 Kelly EM

Edwards & Redfern
(i) Russell Street, Longton
1889 Keates P-L (earthenware)
(ii) Mount Pleasant, Longton
1892 Keates P-L (earthenware)

Elkin, Richard
High Street, Burslem
1834 White ETM-B

Elkin, Samuel
(i) Stafford Street and Mill Street, Longton
1860 Kelly EM; RM; SC (Egyptian Black Ware Manufacturers)
1861 Harrison NC-L (earthenware manufacturer)
1863 Kelly EM; RM; SC (Black Manufacturer – Egyptian)
(ii) Stafford Street, Longton
1862 Slater EM
1864 Jones EM
1865 Keates P-L (earthenware)
1867 Keates P-L (earthenware)
1868 Kelly EM
1869 Keates P-L (earthenware)
1870 Harrod NC-L (earthenware manufacturer)

George Elkin. Parian bust depicting George Elkin of the Foley Potteries. The relevant partnerships include Elkin, Knight & Bridgwood; Elkin, Knight & Elkin; Elkins & Co.; Knight, Elkin & Co.; and Knight, Elkin & Bridgwood.

Elkin, Knight & Bridgwood
Lane End
1828 Pigot EM

Elkin, Knight & Elkin
Church Street, Lane End
1822 Allbut CEM (earthenware manufacts.)
1822 Pigot EM

Elkin & Newbon
Stafford Street, Longton
1846 Williams NC-L-LE (earthenware manufacturers)

Elkin, Knight & Bridgwood. Printed mark from a blue-printed earthenware dinner plate.

Elkin, Knight & Bridgwood. Printed and impressed marks from blue-printed earthenware dinner wares. Note that the impressed style Elkin, Knight & Co. does not appear in the directories.

Elkin & Newbon. Printed mark from a blue-printed earthenware meat dish.

1850 Kelly CEM; NC-L (earthenware & black manufrs.)
1850 Slater EM
1852 Slater EM
1854 Kelly CEM
1856 Kelly CEM
The partners are listed individually as Samuel Elkin of Longton Road and Thomas Newbon of Green Dock in 1846 Williams. The second partner's surname is listed as Newborn in 1850 Slater.

Elkin & Newbons
Stafford Street, Longton
1851 White CEM-L (only earthenware)

Elkins, Knight & Bridgwood
Lane End
1830 Pigot EM

Elkins & Co.
See: Elkins, Knight & Bridgwood

Elkins & Co. Printed mark from a blue-printed earthenware dinner plate. The style Elkins & Co. would appear to relate to Elkins, Knight & Bridgwood but this firm used a variety of partnership styles, not all of which appear in the directories. Note also the additional retailer's or owner's mark.

Ellerton, E.
Golden Hill, Tunstall
1863 Kelly EM

Elliot, Liddle, & Son
(i) Longport, Burslem
1863 Kelly EM
1864 Jones EM
(ii) Dale Hall Works, Newcastle Street, Burslem
1864 Jones EM
1868 Kelly EM
1869 Keates P-B (earthenware)
The surname is listed as Elliott in 1864 Jones.

Elliott & Son
Dale Hall Works, Newcastle Street, Burslem
1862 Slater EM; PM
1865 Keates P-B (earthenware)
1867 Keates P-B (earthenware)

Elliott, Liddle, & Son
See: Elliot, Liddle, & Son

Elliott & Bate
Dale Hall Works, Newcastle Street, Burslem
1870 Harrod NC-B
(earthenware manufacturers)

Ellis, James
Pall Mall, Shelton
1830 Pigot EM (toy only)

Ellis, Moses
Tontine Street, Hanley
1822 Allbut CEM (lusterer and black printer)

Ellis, Thomas
Union Market Place, Lane End
1830 Pigot CM
1834 White CM-LE-L
1835 Pigot CM
Ellis's house is listed as Vauxhall, Longton, in 1834 White.

Ellis, Unwin & Mountford
Upper Hanley Works, High Street, Hanley
1860 Kelly EM
1861 Harrison NC-H-Sh
(earthenware manufacturers)
An advertisement in 1861 Harrison describes the firm simply as 'earthenware manufacturers'.

Ellis, Unwin, and Mountford,
EARTHENWARE
MANUFACTURERS,
UPPER HANLEY WORKS,
HANLEY,
STAFFORDSHIRE POTTERIES.

Ellis, Unwin & Mountford. Advertisement from 1861 Harrison.

Ellis, Unwin & Mountford. Printed mark from a grey-blue printed earthenware gravy dish.

Ellis, Unwin, Mountford & Taylor
High Street, Hanley
1862 Slater EM

Ellsmore, Thomas, & Son
See: Elsmore, Thomas, & Son

Elmore & Forster
See: Elsmore & Forster

Elsmore, Thomas
Brownhills, Burslem
1870 Harrod NC-B
(earthenware manufacturer)

Elsmore, Thomas, & Son
Clay Hills Pottery, Tunstall
1872 Kelly EM
1873 Keates P-T (earthenware)
1875 Keates P-T (earthenware)
1876 Kelly EM
1879 Keates P-T (earthenware)
1880 Kelly EM
1882 Keates P-T (earthenware)
The surname is listed as Ellsmore in 1873 Keates.

Elsmore & Forster
Clay Hills Pottery, Tunstall
1862 Slater EM
1863 Kelly EM
1864 Jones EM
1865 Keates P-T (earthenware)
1868 Kelly EM
The first partner's surname is listed as Elmore in 1868 Kelly.

Elsmore & Forster. Printed mark from an earthenware puzzle jug dated 1859.

Elsmore & Foster
Clay Hills Pottery, Tunstall
1860 Kelly EM
1861 Harrison NC-T
(earthenware manufacturers)
1867 Keates P-T (earthenware)
1869 Keates P-T (earthenware)
1870 Harrod NC-T
(earthenware manufacturers)

Elsmore, Foster & Co.
(i) Calver Street, Tunstall
1852 Slater EM
(ii) Tunstall
1854 Kelly CEM
(iii) Cross Street, Tunstall
1856 Kelly CEM

Emberton, James
(i) Brownhills, Burslem
1870 Harrod NC-B
(earthenware manufacturer)
1879 Keates P-B (earthenware)
(ii) Highgate Pottery, Tunstall
1884 Kelly EM

Emberton, Thomas
Brownhills, Burslem
1870 Harrod NC-B
(earthenware manufacturer)

Emberton, Thomas & James
Highgate Pottery, Tunstall
1870 Harrod NC-T
(manufacturers of plain and ornamental earthenware for home and foreign markets)

Emberton, Thomas I. & James
Highgate Pottery, Brownhills, Tunstall
1869 Keates P-T (earthenware)
1872 Kelly EM
1873 Keates P-T (earthenware)
1875 Keates P-T (earthenware)
1879 Keates P-T (earthenware)

Emberton, Thomas J.
Brownhills, Burslem
1879 Keates P-B (earthenware)

Emberton, Thomas James
Highgate Pottery, Brownhills, Tunstall
1882 Keates P-T (earthenware)

Emberton, Thomas J. & James
Highgate Pottery, Tunstall
1876 Kelly EM
1880 Kelly EM
(manufacturers of earthenware for the home trade, also lustre, japanned printed & enamelled earthenware, rice dishes &c. for the Indian & other foreign markets)

Emberton, William
Highgate Pottery, Brownhills, between Tunstall and Burslem
1851 White EM-T
1852 Slater EM
1854 Kelly CEM
1856 Kelly CEM
1860 Kelly EM

1861 Harrison NC-B (earthenware manufacturer)
1862 Slater EM
1863 Kelly EM
1864 Jones EM
1865 Keates P-T (earthenware for Ceylon, Bombay, and Calcutta markets)
1867 Keates P-T (earthenware)
1868 Kelly EM
1869 Keates P-B (earthen.)
Emberton's house is listed as Sneyd Street, Tunstall, in 1851 White.

Emberton, William, & Co.
Highgate Pottery, Brownhills, Burslem
1850 Kelly CEM; NC-B (earthenware manufrs.)
1850 Slater EM
1851 White CEM-B (only earthenware)

Emberton, Hancock & Co.
(i) High Street, Brownhills, Burslem
1846 Williams NC-B (earthenware manufacturers)
(ii) Tunstall
1846 Williams NC-T (earthenware mnftrs.)
The partners are listed individually as William Emberton of Lime Street, Tunstall, Redulphus Hancock of Liverpool Road, Burslem, and Thomas Johnson of Brownhills, Burslem, in 1846 Williams.

Emery, Francis Joseph
Bleak Hill Works, Bleak Street or Wood Street, Burslem
1879 Keates P-B (earthenware)
1880 Kelly EM
1882 Keates P-B (earthenware)
1884 Kelly EM
1887 Porter EM-B
1888 Kelly EM
1889 Keates P-B (earthenware)
1892 Keates P-B (earthenware)
1892 Kelly EM

Emery & Lea
(i) Market Place, Burslem
1863 Kelly CM-General
(ii) Crown Works, Burslem
1864 Jones CEM (and majolica)

Empire Porcelain Co. (The)
Stoke Road, Shelton
1896 Kelly CM; EM
1900 Kelly CM; EM

Enamel Porcelain Co.
Cannon Street, Hanley
1864 Jones EM

Enamel Porcelain Co. Ltd.
Burton Place, Old Hall Street, Hanley
1863 Kelly SC (Porcelain Manufacturers)
1864 Jones CEM

Espley, George
Chell Street, Hanley
1869 Keates P-H (spur)
1870 Harrod NC-H (spur manufacturer)

Evans, John
102 Hope Street, Hanley
1863 Kelly PM
1864 Jones PM

Evans, William L.
(i) Brunswick Street, Hanley
1869 Keates P-H (china and earthenware)
1870 Harrod NC-H (china and earthenware manufacturer)
(ii) Hall Field Works, Hanley
1875 Keates SC-H (Floor Tile Manufacturers)
1879 Keates SC-H (Floor Tile Manufacturers)

Evans & Booth
Knowles Works, Hamil Road, Burslem
1865 Keates P-B (earthen.)
1867 Keates P-B (earthenware)
1868 Kelly EM
1869 Keates P-B (earthen.)

Evans & Coyne
Brunswick Street, Hanley
1867 Keates P-H (china and earthenware)

Evans & Foulkes
Marsh Street, Hanley
1876 Kelly MM

Evans & Poulson
Eagle Foundry, Shelton
1850 Slater EM (and stone jug)

Evans, Poulson & Jackson
Eagle Foundry, Shelton
1850 Kelly CEM (stone jug); NC-Sh (stone jug manfrs.)

Evans & Tomkinson
Knowles Works, Burslem
1870 Harrod NC-B (earthenware manufacturers)
1872 Kelly EM

Everard, George
High Street, Longton
1850 Kelly CEM; NC-L (china lustre & earthenware manuf.)
1850 Slater CM; EM

Everard, Colclough & Townsend
Cornhill, Longton
1841 Pigot EM (& lustre & black)

Everard, Colclough & Townsend. Printed mark from a black-printed and pink lustre-washed earthenware jug.

Everard & Glover
Chancery Lane, Longton
1846 Williams NC-L-LE (china lustre & earthenware manufacturers)
The partners are listed individually as George Everard of Meir and James Glover of Sutherland Road in 1846 Williams.

Everett, E.P.
See: Lane End Works Ltd.

Everill, Henry
King Street, Hanley
1876 Kelly EM

F

Fanshaw & Hughes
Fenton
1882 Keates P-F (earthenware, china, jet and majolica)

Faulkner & Robinson
(i) George Street, Lane End
1828 Pigot CM
1830 Pigot CM
(ii) Great Charles Street, Longton
1834 White CM-LE-L (lustre mfrs.)
1835 Pigot CM

Fell & Co.
Union Place, Market Street, Longton
1887 Porter EM-L
1888 Kelly EM
1889 Keates P-L (earthenware)
1892 Keates P-L (earthenware)

Fell, John, & Co.
Adelaide Works, Longton
1884 Kelly JM; MM
A London address at 46 Fore Street is listed in 1884 Kelly.

Fell & Coy
Wharf Street, Stoke
1889 Keates P-S (earthenware)
This entry could be an abbreviation for Fell & Company.

Fenton, Alfred, & Sons
(i) Brook Street, Hanley
1888 Kelly EM
1889 Keates P-H (china and earthenware)
1892 Keates P-H (china and earthenware)
1892 Kelly EM
1896 Kelly EM
(ii) Clarence Street, Hanley
1888 Kelly EM
1892 Kelly EM
1896 Kelly EM
1900 Kelly EM

Fenton Pottery Company
King Street, Fenton
1851 White NC-F (china, &c., manufacturers)

Ferneyhough, John
(i) Dresden Works, Stafford Street, Longton
1876 Kelly CM
1879 Keates P-L (china)
1880 Kelly CM
1882 Keates P-L (china)
1884 Kelly CM
1887 Porter EM-L
1888 Kelly CM
1889 Keates P-L (china)
1892 Keates P-L (china)
(ii) Normacott Road, Longton
1879 Keates P-L (china)
1882 Keates P-L (china)
The surname is listed as Fernyhough in 1887 Porter.

Ferneyhough, John, & Co.
(i) Dresden Works, Stafford Street, Longton
1867 Keates P-L (china)
1868 Kelly CM
1869 Keates P-L (china)
1870 Harrod NC-L (china manufacturers)
1872 Kelly CM
1873 Keates P-L (china)
1875 Keates P-L (china)
(ii) Normacott Road, Longton
1875 Keates P-L (china)

Fernyhough, John
See: Ferneyhough, John

Fielding & Co.
(i) Railway Pottery, off Whieldon Road, Fenton
1880 Kelly EM; MM (manufacturers of majolica, terra cotta, porous ware, jet, green glaze, Rockingham earthenware & fancy goods)
1882 Keates P-F (majolica and earthenware)
1889 Keates P-F (majolica and earthenware)
1892 Keates P-F (earthenware)
(ii) Sutherland Street, Fenton
1887 Porter EM-F
This firm succeeded F. Hackney & Co. (1880 Kelly). A London agent is listed as M. Gray of Ely House, Charterhouse Street, Holborn Circus, in 1880 Kelly.

Fielding, A.
Trent Vale, Fenton
1892 Keates P-S

Fielding, S., & Co.
Railway Pottery, Stoke
1884 Kelly EM; MM
1888 Kelly EM; MM
1892 Kelly EM; MM
1896 Kelly EM; MM
1900 Kelly EM
London showrooms at Union Bank buildings, Holborn Circus, with F. Hope as agent, are listed in 1884 Kelly.

S. Fielding & Co. Printed mark from a printed and coloured pierced earthenware dessert plate.

Fielding, William
Cannon Street Works, Hanley
1892 Keates P-H
1892 Kelly EM
1896 Kelly EM
1900 Kelly EM

Finney & Co.
Victoria Works, Stafford Street, Longton
1865 Keates P-L (china)
1867 Keates P-L (china)

Finney, Joseph
(i) Victoria Works, Stafford Street, Longton
1860 Kelly CM-General; EM
1861 Harrison NC-L (china manufacturer)
1863 Kelly CM-General; EM
1864 Jones CEM
1868 Kelly CM
1869 Keates P-L (china)
1870 Harrod NC-L (china manufacturer)
1872 Kelly CM
1873 Keates P-L (china)
1875 Keates P-L (china)
1876 Kelly CM; EM
1879 Keates P-L (china)
1880 Kelly CM; EM
1882 Keates P-L (china)
1884 Kelly CM; EM
1887 Porter EM-L
1888 Kelly CM
1889 Keates P-L (china)
1892 Keates P-L (china)
1892 Kelly CM
1896 Kelly CM
1900 Kelly CM
(ii) Victoria Place, Longton

1862 Slater CM
(iii) Willow Cottage, Clayton Street, Longton
1887 Porter EM-L

Finney, William
Mount Pleasant Works, High Street, Longton
1896 Kelly EM

Finney & Sheldon
Anchor Pottery, Bourne's Bank, Burslem
1888 Kelly P

Flackett, Chetham & Toft
Church Street, Longton
1852 Slater CM; EM
1854 Kelly CEM

Flackett & Toft
Church Street, Longton
1856 Kelly CEM

Fletcher, Richard
Burslem
1798 Universal NC-B (manufacturer of Staffordshire-ware)

Fletcher, Thomas
Shelton
1798 Universal NC-Sh (manufacturer of Staffordshire-ware)

Floyd, Charles
See: Heath, Blackhurst & Co.

Floyd, Elizabeth
Cobridge
1841 Pigot TOCM

Floyd, Henry
Cobridge
1834 White CETM-H-Sh

Floyd, James
(i) Stafford Street, Longton
1846 Williams NC-L-LE (earthenware and china manufactr.)
(ii) Market Street, Fenton
1850 Slater CM; EM
1851 White CEM-F
1852 Slater CM; EM
(iii) Fenton
1850 Kelly CEM; NC-S (china & earthenware manufacturer)
1854 Kelly CEM
1856 Kelly CEM

Floyd & Savage
Foley, Longton
1841 Pigot CM

Floyd & Shubotham
Chadwick Lane, Lane End
1835 Pigot CM

Folch, Stephen
Church Street, Stoke
1822 Allbut CEM (iron stone china manufacturer)
1828 Pigot CM (stone); EM
The surname is listed as Fouche in 1822 Allbut.

Folch & Scott
Stoke
1822 Pigot CM

Ford & Co.
(i) Sandyford, Tunstall
1882 Keates P-T (earthenware)
1884 Kelly EM
1888 Kelly EM
1889 Keates P-T (earthenware)
(ii) Etruria Road, Hanley
1887 Porter SC-H (Spur and Stilt Manufacturers)

Ford & Son
Newcastle Street, Burslem
1889 Keates P-B
1892 Keates P-B

Ford & Sons
Newcastle Street, Burslem
1896 Kelly EM
1900 Kelly EM

Ford, Charles
(i) Parker Street, Shelton, Hanley
1850 Slater A; EM (manufacturer and patentee of the patent spur used by china and earthenware manufacturers in placing flat ware)
1851 White NC-H-Sh (patent spur manufacturer)
1852 Slater EM (manufacturer and patentee of the patent spur used by china and earthenware manufacturers in placing flat ware)
1854 Kelly SC (Spur Makers) (patent)
1856 Kelly SC (Spur Makers)
1861 Harrison NC-H-Sh (patent spur manufacturer)
1862 Slater SC (Stilt and Spur Manufacturers – Patent)
1864 Jones EM-Miscellaneous (patent spur and stilt)
1867 Keates P-H (spur)
1868 Kelly SC (Cock Spur Manufacturer)
1869 Keates P-H (spur)
1870 Harrod NC-H (spur and stilt manufacturer)
1872 Kelly SC (Spur Makers)
1873 Keates P-H (spur)
1875 Keates P-H (spur)
1876 Kelly SC (Spur and Stilt Makers for Pottery Manufacturers)
1879 Keates P-H (spur)
1882 Keates P-H (spur)
(ii) West Terrace, Hanley
1872 Kelly CM
(iii) Eastwood, Hanley
1873 Keates P-H (china)
(iv) Cannon Street, Hanley
1875 Keates P-H (china)
1876 Kelly CM
1879 Keates P-H (china)
1880 Kelly CM
1882 Keates P-H (china)
1884 Kelly CM
1887 Porter EM-H
1888 Kelly CM
1889 Keates P-H (china)
1892 Keates P-H (china)
1892 Kelly CM
1896 Kelly CM
1900 Kelly CM
The firm at Parker Street is noted as being in the hands of executors in 1879 Keates and 1882 Keates. The advertisement in 1850 Slater reads 'By Her Majesty's Royal Letters Patent. Charles Ford, engineer, iron & brass founder. Patentee and manufacturer of the patent spur for placing flat ware, used by china and earthenware manufacturers; also of patent paste boxes, gallipots, &c. and a variety of other articles used by

Charles Ford. Advertisement from 1850 Slater.

druggists, perfumers, &c. Licences granted under the patent for the manufacture of the paste boxes, gallipots, &c.' Another advertisement in 1882 Keates appears under the style Charles Ford & Co. (qv).

Ford, Charles, & Co.
(i) Parker Street, Hanley
1880 Kelly SC (Spur & Stilt Makers for Pottery Manufacturers)
1884 Kelly SC (Spur Makers); SC (Spur & Stilt Makers for Pottery Manufacturers)
1889 Keates P-H (spur and stilt)
1892 Keates P-H (spur and stilt)
1900 Kelly SC (Stilt & Spur Manufacturers)
(ii) Mill Street, Hanley
1896 Kelly SC (Stilt & Spur Manufacturers)
Although the directory entry is listed as simply Charles Ford, an advertisement in 1882 Keates, appears under the style of Charles Ford & Co. It mentions 'letters patent granted to Charles Ford, original inventor and patentee, 14th December, 1846' and describes the firm as 'manufacturers of cockspurs, stilts, pins, &c.', offering 'samples and prices on application'.

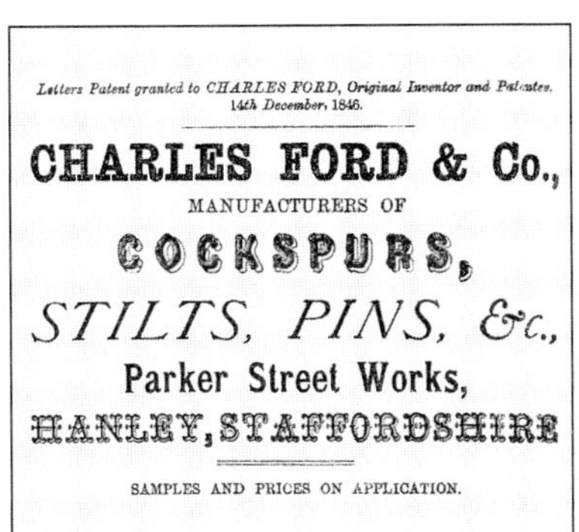

Charles Ford & Co. Advertisement from 1882 Keates.

Ford, Hugh
Green Dock, Lane End
1818 Parson EM-LE

Ford, Samuel, & Co.
Lincoln Pottery, Newport Lane, Burslem
1900 Kelly EM

Ford, Thomas
(i) Albion Place, Shelton
1852 Slater, PM
(ii) Cannon Street, Shelton, Hanley
1856 Kelly CEM
1860 Kelly CM-General
1861 Harrison NC-H-Sh (china manufacturer)
1862 Slater CM
1863 Kelly CM-General
1864 Jones CEM
1872 Kelly CM
1873 Keates P-H (china)

Ford, Thomas, & Co.
Sandyford Pottery, Tunstall
1887 Porter EM-T

Ford, Thomas, & Sons
Newcastle Street, Burslem
1892 Kelly EM

Ford, Thomas & Charles
Cannon Street, Hanley
1865 Keates P-H (china)
1867 Keates P-H (china)
1868 Kelly CM
1869 Keates P-H (china)
1870 Harrod NC-H (china manufacturers for the home trade)

Ford, William, & Co.
Lane End
1805 Holden NC (earthenware manufacturers)

Ford & Allerton
Lane Delph
1822 Allbut CEM (earthenware manufacturers)

Ford & Challinor
Sandyford, Tunstall
1870 Harrod NC-T (manufacturers of plain and ornamental earthenware for home and foreign markets)
1872 Kelly EM
1873 Keates P-T (earthenware)
1875 Keates P-T (earthenware)
1876 Kelly EM
1879 Keates P-T (earthen.)
1880 Kelly EM (manufacturers of plain & ornamental earthenware for home & foreign markets)

Ford, Challinor & Co.
Sandyford, Tunstall
1865 Keates P-T (earthenware)
1867 Keates P-T (earthenware)
1868 Kelly EM
1869 Keates P-T (earthenware)

Ford & Hull
Lane End
1809 Holden NC (manufac. of earthenware)
1811 Holden NC (manufacturers of earthenware)
1816 Underhill P

Ford, Lewis & Co.
Shelton Lane
1822 Allbut CEM (earthenware and shining black manufacturers)
1822 Pigot EM (shining black)

Ford & Riley
Newcastle Street, Burslem
1884 Kelly EM
1887 Porter EM-B
1888 Kelly EM

Ford, Whittingham & Co.
High Street, Burslem
1869 Keates P-B (earthenware)

Forester & Co.
Blythe Works, High Street, Longton
1892 Kelly CM

Forester & Sons
Phoenix Works, Church Street, Longton
1884 Kelly EM

Forester, G. & Thomas
Blyth Works, High Street, Longton
1889 Keates P-L (china)

Forester, Thomas
(i) Lane Delph
1796 Chester NC-LE-LD-LL (manufacturer of earthenware)
1802 Allbut EM (map location 112)
(ii) High Street, Longton
1880 Kelly EM
(iii) Church Street, Longton
1880 Kelly EM
1882 Keates P-L (majolica and earthenware)
The surname is listed as Forster in 1796 Chester.

Forester, Thomas, & Son
Mill Works and Phoenix Works, Church Street, Longton
1887 Porter EM-L (two entries)

Forester, Thomas, & Sons
Church Street, Longton
1888 Kelly MM
1889 Keates P-L (majolica and earthenware)

Thomas Forester & Sons. Printed mark from a violet-blue printed dessert plate.

Forester, Thomas, & Sons Ltd.
(i) Church Street, Longton
1892 Keates P-L (majolica and china)
(ii) Church Street and Stafford Street, Longton
1892 Kelly MM
1896 Kelly MM
1900 Kelly MM

Forester & Hulme
Sutherland Pottery, Fenton
1888 Kelly EM
1892 Kelly EM

Forrester, George
Market Place, Lane End
1805 Holden NC (earthenware manufacturer)
1809 Holden NC (earthenware-manufactory)
1811 Holden NC (earthenware-manufactory)
1816 Underhill P
1818 Parson EM-LE
1818 Pigot EM
1822 Allbut CEM (earthenware manufact.)
1822 Pigot EM
1828 Pigot EM
1830 Pigot EM
The surname is listed as Forrister in the four Pigot directories.

Forrester, John
(i) Lane End
1805 Holden NC (earthenware manufacturers)
1809 Holden NC (earthenware-manufacr.)
1811 Holden NC (earthenware-manufacr.)
1816 Underhill P
(ii) Podmore Street, Burslem
1867 Keates P-B (earthenware)
1868 Kelly EM

Forrester, Thomas William
Alma Works, Marsh Street, Hanley
1884 Kelly MM (dealer)

Forrester & Harvey
Lane End
1796 Chester NC-LE-LD-LL (manufacturers of earthenware)
1798 Universal NC-LE (manufacturers of Staffordshire-ware)
The first partner's surname is listed as Forster in 1796 Chester.

Forrester & Hulme
High Street, Fenton
1887 Porter EM-F
1892 Keates P-F (earthenware)

Forrester & Meredith
Lane End
1784 Bailey NC-LE (manufacturers of Queen's ware, Egyptian black, red china, and various other ware)

Forrister, George
See: Forrester, George

Forrister, Martin & John
Foley, Fenton
1851 White NC-F (china manufacturers)

Forrister, Copestake & Forrister
Foley, Fenton
1850 Kelly CEM; NC-S (china manufacturers)
1850 Slater CM
1851 White CEM-F
The second partner's name is listed as Copestick in 1850 Slater.

Forrister, Copestick & Forrister
See: Forrister, Copestake & Forrister

Forster, Thomas
See: Forester, Thomas

Forster & Harvey
See: Forrester & Harvey

Foster, Crutchley & Co.
3 Clarence Street, Hanley
1862 Slater PM

Fouche, Stephen
See: Folch, Stephen

Fox, Edwin
See: Banks & Thorley

Franter & Fieldsend
Normacot Road, Longton
1900 Kelly EM

Freakley, William, & Co.
Broad Street, Shelton
1852 Slater EM
1854 Kelly CEM

Freeman, W., & Co.
High Street, Longton
1875 Keates P-L (china)

Freeman, Walter
51 High Street, Longton
1876 Kelly CM
1879 Keates P-L (china)
1880 Kelly CM
1882 Keates P-L (china)

Freeman, Walter & Richard
High Street, Longton
1872 Kelly CM
1873 Keates P-L (china)

Frost, Bevington & Co.
Anchor Works, Brewery Street, Hanley
1889 Keates P-H

Furlong Works Co.
Newcastle Street, Burslem
1869 Keates P-B (earthenware)
1870 Harrod NC-B (earthenware manufacturers)

Furnival & Co.
Cobridge
1861 Harrison NC-B (earthenware manufacturers)
1865 Keates P-B (earthenware)
1867 Keates P-B (earthenware)
1869 Keates P-B (earthenware)

Furnival & Son
Waterloo Road, Burslem
1887 Porter EM-B

Furnival, J.
Cobridge
1854 Kelly CEM
1856 Kelly CEM

Furnival, J., & Co.
Cobridge

1860 Kelly EM
1863 Kelly EM
1864 Jones EM
1868 Kelly EM
1870 Harrod NC-B (general earthenware manufacturers for home and foreign markets)

Furnival, Jacob, & Co.
Cobridge
1846 Williams NC-C-F-E (manufacturers)
1850 Slater EM
1852 Slater EM
1862 Slater EM

Furnival, John, & Co.
Cobridge
1851 White CEM-B (only earthenware)

Furnival, Thomas, & Co.
Miles Bank, Hanley
1846 Williams NC-H (earthenware manuftrs.)
The partners are listed individually as Thomas Furnival of Miles Bank and Richard B. Clarke of Wheatley Place in 1846 Williams.

Furnival, Thomas, & Son
Cobridge
1872 Kelly EM
1873 Keates P-B (earthenware)
1875 Keates P-B (earthen.)
1879 Keates P-B (earthen.)
1882 Keates P-B (earthenware)
1889 Keates P-B (earthenware)
1892 Keates P-B (earthenware)

Thomas Furnival & Sons. Printed mark from a hand-painted earthenware jug.

Furnival, Thomas, & Sons
Cobridge
1880 Kelly EM (manufacturers of white granite & decorated earthenware for home and foreign markets)
1884 Kelly EM (manufacturers of white granite & decorated earthenware, for home & foreign markets)
1876 Kelly EM
1888 Kelly EM

Furnival, William
Old Hall Works, Old Hall Street, Hanley
1846 Williams NC-H (earthenware manufctr.)

Furnivals
Cobridge
1892 Kelly EM

Furnivals Ltd.
Cobridge
1896 Kelly EM
1900 Kelly EM (two entries)

G

Gallimore, Ambrose & Robert
High Street, Lane End or Longton
1834 White EM-LE-L (lustre)
1835 Pigot EM

Gallimore, Robert
(i) High Street, Longton
1841 Pigot CM (and lustre)
(ii) King Street, Fenton
1846 Williams NC-C-F-E (china manufacturer)
1850 Kelly CEM; NC-S (china earthenware manufacturer)
(iii) Foley, near Longton
1850 Slater CM

Gallimore, Thomas
Bourne's Bank, Burslem
1828 Pigot EM

Gardner, Robert
See: Garner, Robert

Garner, Joseph
Lane End
1784 Bailey NC-LE (potter)

Garner, Robert
(i) Lane End
1781 Bailey NC (potter)
1783 Bailey NC (potter)
1784 Bailey NC-LE (manufacturer of Queen's wares, and various other wares)
1796 Chester NC-LE-LD-LL (manufacturer of earthenware)
1798 Universal NC-LE (manufacturers of Staffordshire-ware)
1802 Allbut EM (map location 118)
1805 Holden NC (earthenware manufacturer)
1809 Holden NC (earthenware-manufacturer)
1811 Holden NC (earthenware-manufacturer)
1816 Underhill P
1818 Parson EM-LE
(ii) Church Street, Lane End
1818 Pigot EM
The surname is listed as Gardner in 1805 Holden.

Garrett, Thomas
See: Copeland & Garrett

Gaskell (James), Son & Co.
Crown Works, Market Place, Burslem
1875 Keates P-B (door furniture)
1876 Kelly EM
1879 Keates P-B (door furniture)
1880 Kelly EM

Gaskell, Richard
See: Bridgwood, Sampson, & Son

Gaskell & Grocott
Longport
1882 Keates P-B (door furniture)
1884 Kelly CM; SC (Door Furniture Makers – China)
1887 Porter EM-B
1888 Kelly CM; SC (Door Furniture Makers – China)
1892 Kelly CM; SC (Door Furniture Manufacturers – China)
1896 Kelly CM; SC (Door Furniture Manufacturers – China)
1900 Kelly SC (Door Furniture Manufacturers – China)

Gaskell, Kent & Parr
Novelty Works, Burslem
1887 Porter EM-B

Gater & Co.
Furlong Lane, Burslem
1884 Kelly EM
1888 Kelly EM
1892 Kelly EM

Gater, John
Dale Hall, Burslem

1872 Kelly EM
1873 Keates P-B (earthenware)

Gater, Thomas
Furlong Lane Pottery, Burslem
1887 Porter EM-B

Gater & Draycott
Newcastle Street, Burslem
1870 Harrod NC-B
(earthenware and cock-spur manufacturers)

Gater, Hall & Co.
(i) Furlong Lane, Burslem
1896 Kelly EM
(ii) Gordon Pottery, Tunstall
1900 Kelly EM

Gelson Brothers
High Street, Hanley
1868 Kelly EM
1869 Keates P-H
(earthenware)
1870 Harrod NC-H
(earthenware manufacturers for home and foreign markets)
1872 Kelly EM
1873 Keates P-H
(earthenware)
1875 Keates P-H
(earthenware)

Gelson, James
See: Adams, Harvey, & Co.

Gelson, Thomas, & Co.
High Street, Hanley
1876 Kelly EM

George Street Pottery Co.
George Street, Tunstall
1862 Slater EM

Gerrard, John
Bath Street, Hanley
1846 Williams NC-H
(manufacturer and flint grinder)
The entry lists Gerrard simply as a manufacturer, he may not have been a potter.

Gerrard, John, & Brothers
High Street, Longton or Lane End
1834 White CM-LE-L
1835 Pigot CM

Gerrard, Thomas
Thomas Gerard *(sic)* is listed by Godden as appearing in an 1822 directory but no mention could be found in 1822 Allbut or 1822 Pigot.

Thomas Gerrard. Commemorative panel from a hand-painted bone china vase.

Gerrard, William
High Street, Longton
1841 Pigot CM

Gerrard & Alker
Longport
1796 Chester NC-T-Lp
(manufacturers of earthenware)

Gerrard, Cope & Co.
High Street, Lane End
1828 Pigot CM

Gibbons, R.N.
See: Lincoln Works Pottery Co.

Gibbs & Hassall
Commerce Street, Longton
1860 Kelly CM-General; CM-Tea, Breakfast & Dessert Services
1861 Harrison NC-L (china manufacturers)

Gibson & Son
Moorland Road, Burslem
1889 Keates P-B
(Rockingham)
1892 Keates P-B
(Rockingham)

Gibson & Sons
Albany Works, Moorland Road, Burslem
1887 Porter EM-B
1888 Kelly JM; RM
1892 Kelly JRM
1896 Kelly JRM
1900 Kelly JRM

Gibson, John
High Street, Tunstall
1841 Pigot EM (Egyptian and lustre)
1846 Williams NC-T
(earthenware manufacturer)

Gibson, W.
Union Street, Burslem
1856 Kelly CEM

Gibson, William
See: Burgess & Gibson

Gibson & Hallam
St. Martin's Lane, Longton
1867 Keates P-L (china)
1868 Kelly CM
1869 Keates P-L (china)
1870 Harrod NC-L (china manufacturers)
1872 Kelly CM

Gibson, Lewis & Ludlow
Bourne's Bank, Burslem
1879 Keates P-B
(Rockingham)

Gibson, Sudlow & Co.
Bourne's Bank, Burslem
1880 Kelly RM
1882 Keates P-B
(Rockingham)

Gibson, Sudlow & Lewis
Bourne's Bank, Burslem
1876 Kelly RM

Gilbert, John
Burslem
1796 Chester NC-B
(manufacturer of earthenware)
1798 Universal NC-B
(manufacturer of Staffordshire-ware)
1802 Allbut EM (map location 41)

Gildea, James
Dale Hall Works, Burslem
1887 Porter EM-B
1888 Kelly EM

Gildea & Walker
Dale Hall, Burslem
1882 Keates P-B (earthenware)
1884 Kelly EM
1889 Keates P-B (earthenware)
The second partner is listed individually as John Walker in 1889

Keates. A London office at 30 Holborn is listed in all three directories.

Gilmore & Hawthorne
John Street, Stoke
1870 Harrod NC-S (door furniture manufacturers)

Gimson, J.
Fenton
1868 Kelly SC (Spur Makers)

Gimson, Joseph, & Co.
(i) Market Street, Fenton
1862 Slater SC (Stilt and Spur Manufacturers – Patent)
1864 Jones EM-Miscellaneous (patent placing pins, spurs, stilts, &c.)
1870 Harrod NC-F (manufacturers of patent spurs, stilts, &c.)
1872 Kelly SC (Spur Makers)
1873 Keates P-F (spur manufacturers)
1875 Keates P-F (spur manufacturers)
1876 Kelly SC (Spur and Stilt Makers for Pottery Manufacturers)
1879 Keates P-F (spur manufacturers)
1882 Keates P-F (spur manufacturers)
1887 Porter SC-F (Spur and Stilt Manufacturers)
1888 Kelly SC (Spur & Stilt Makers for Pottery Manufacturers)
1889 Keates P-F (spur manufacturer)
1892 Keates P-F (spur)
1892 Kelly SC (Stilt & Spur Manufacturers)
1896 Kelly SC (Spur Makers); SC (Stilt & Spur Manufacturers)
1900 Kelly SC (Stilt & Spur Manufacturers)
(ii) High Street, Fenton
1880 Kelly SC (Spur & Stilt Makers for Pottery Manufacturers)
1884 Kelly SC (Spur & Stilt Makers for Pottery Manufacturers)

Gimson, Baker & Challinor
(i) Market Street, Fenton
1865 Keates P-F (spur manufacturers)
1867 Keates P-F (spur manufacturers)
(ii) High Street, Fenton
1869 Keates P-F (spur manufacturers)

Gimson, Wallis, & Co.
Lane Delph
1889 Keates P-F (earthenware)
See also Wallis, Gimson & Co.

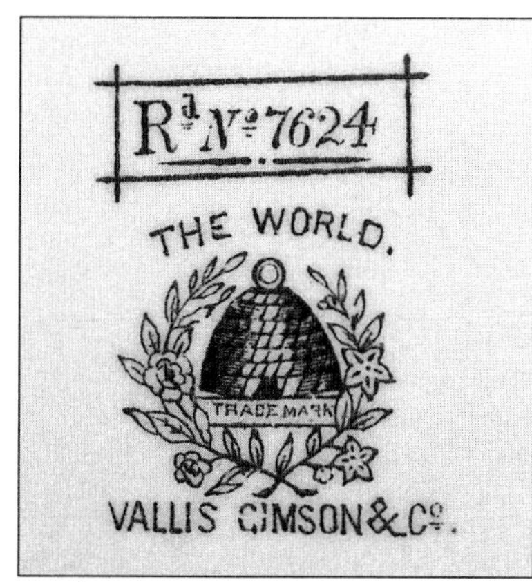

Wallis Gimson & Co. Printed mark from a brown-printed and coloured earthenware dinner plate. The registered number was issued in 1884.

Ginder, S.
(i) Lane Delph
1809 Holden NC (manufact. of earthenware)
1811 Holden NC (manufact. of earthenware)
(ii) Lane End
1816 Underhill P

Ginder, Samuel, & Co.
Lane Delph
1818 Parson EM-LE
1818 Pigot EM
1822 Allbut CEM (earthenware manufacts.)
1822 Pigot EM
1828 Pigot EM
1830 Pigot EM
1834 White CEM-F-LD (earthenware only)
1835 Pigot EM
1841 Pigot EM

Ginder & Hulse
Lane Delph
1828 Pigot EM
1830 Pigot EM

Glass & Sons
Hanley
1818 Pigot EM

Glass, J., & Son
Hanley
1816 Underhill P

Glass, John
(i) Hanley
1784 Bailey NC-H (potter)
1796 Chester NC-H-Sh (manufacturer of earthenware)
1798 Universal NC-H (manufacturer of Staffordshire-ware)
1802 Allbut EM (map location 78)
1805 Holden NC (earthenware manufacturer)
1809 Holden NC (manufacturer of earthenware)
1811 Holden NC (manufacturer of earthenware)
(ii) Market Street, Hanley
1822 Pigot EM
1828 Pigot EM
1830 Pigot EM
1834 White EM-H-Sh
1835 Pigot EM

John Glass. Impressed mark from a sprigged black basalt teapot.

Glass, John, & Sons
Market Street, Hanley
1818 Parson EM-H-Sh
1822 Allbut CEM (earthenware manufacts.)

Gleaves, William Thomas
(i) Albion Pottery, Etruria
1887 Porter CEM-S
(ii) Basford Bank, Basford, Stoke
1888 Kelly EM

Glover, James
See: Everard & Glover

Glover & Colclough
Chancery Lane, Longton
1850 Kelly CEM; NC-L (china & lustre manufactrs.)
1850 Slater CM; EM
1851 White CEM-L
1852 Slater CM; EM
1854 Kelly CEM

Goddard, J.S.
See: Ashworth, George L., & Brothers

Goddard, Thomas, & Co.
Commerce Street, Longton
1841 Pigot EM

Godwin, B. & S.
(i) Burslem
1809 Holden NC (earthenware-manufacturers)
1811 Holden NC (earthenware-manufacturers)
(ii) Cobridge
1818 Parson EM-B-Lp-C
The surname is listed as Goodwin in 1809 Holden and 1811 Holden.

Godwin, Benjamin
Cobridge
1796 Chester NC-C (manufacturer of earthenware)
1798 Universal NC-C (manufacturer of Staffordshire-ware)
1802 Allbut EM (map location 56)
1809 Holden NC (earthenware-manufactr.)
1811 Holden NC (earthenware-manufr.)
The surname is listed as Goodwin in 1798 Universal, 1809 Holden, and 1811 Holden.

Godwin, Benjamin, & Sons
Cobridge
1816 Underhill P
1818 Pigot EM
1822 Allbut CEM (earthenware manufacts.)
1822 Pigot EM
1828 Pigot EM
1830 Pigot EM

Godwin, Benjamin Clulow
Navigation Road, Burslem
1851 White CEM-B (only earthenware)

Godwin, Benjamin Endon
Cobridge
1834 White EM-B
1835 Pigot EM
1841 Pigot EM

Godwin, James
Cobridge
1846 Williams NC-C-F-E (earthenware manufacturer)
1850 Slater EM

Godwin, John
Sneyd Street, Cobridge, Burslem
1865 Keates P-B (earthen.)
1867 Keates P-B (earthenware)
See also: Godwin, John & Robert

Godwin, John & Richard
The partners are listed as John Godwin of Bleak Hill, Cobridge, and Richard Godwin of Cobridge in 1846 Williams. There is no entry for the firm itself but there is an entry for John & Robert Goodwin (sic).

Godwin, John & Robert
Cobridge
1834 White EM-B
1835 Pigot EM
1841 Pigot EM
1846 Williams NC-C-F-E (earthenware manfactrs.)
1850 Slater EM
1851 White CEM-B (only earthenware)
1852 Slater EM
1854 Kelly CEM
1856 Kelly CEM
1860 Kelly EM
1861 Harrison NC-B (earthenware manufacturers)
1862 Slater EM
1863 Kelly EM
1864 Jones EM
The surname is listed as Goodwin in 1846 Williams.

Godwin, John Mares & James
Cobridge
1841 Pigot EM

Godwin, Thomas
(i) Cobridge
1796 Chester NC-C (manufacturer of earthenware)
1798 Universal NC-C (manufacturer of Staffordshire-ware)
1802 Allbut EM (map location 55)
1805 Holden NC (earthenware manufacturer)
(ii) New Wharf, Burslem
1834 White EM-B
1850 Slater EM
1852 Slater EM
(iii) Canal Works, Navigation Road, Burslem
1841 Pigot EM
1846 Williams NC-B (earthenware manufacturer)
1850 Kelly CEM; NC-B (earthenware manufacturer)
1851 White CEM-B (only earthenware)
1854 Kelly CEM
The surname is listed as Goodwin in 1798 Universal and 1850 Kelly. Godwin's house is listed as Navigation Road in 1846 Williams.

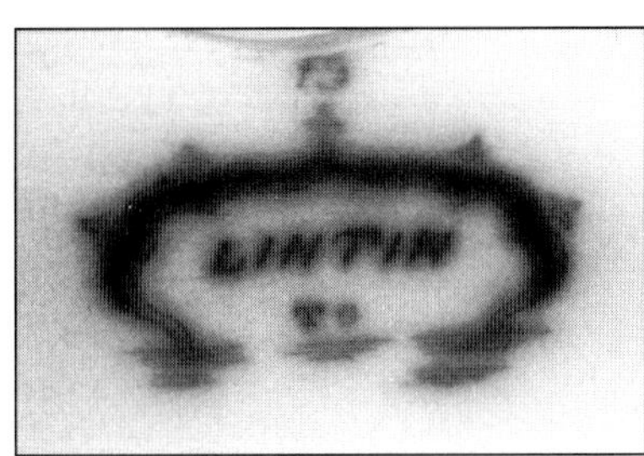

Thomas Godwin. Printed mark from a small flow-blue earthenware meat dish.

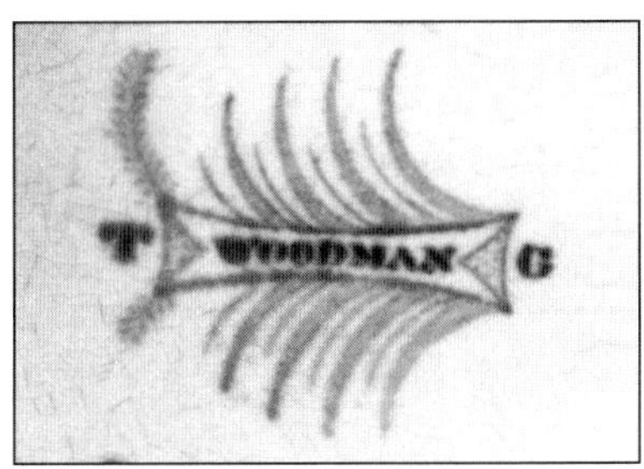

Thomas Godwin. Printed mark from blue-printed wares.

Thomas Godwin. Printed mark from blue-printed dinner wares.

Godwin, Thomas & Benjamin
(i) Cobridge
1781 Bailey NC (potters)
1783 Bailey NC (potter)
1784 Bailey NC-C (manufacturers of Queen's ware and china glazed blue)
(ii) Burslem
1809 Holden NC (earthenware-manufacs.)

1811 Holden NC (earthenware-manufacturers)
1816 Underhill P
(iii) New Wharf, Burslem
1818 Parson EM-B-Lp-C
1818 Pigot EM
1822 Allbut CEM (earthenware manufacts.)
1822 Pigot EM
1828 Pigot EM
1830 Pigot EM
The surname is listed as Goodwin in 1809 Holden and 1811 Holden.

Thomas & Benjamin Godwin. Printed mark from a blue-printed Willow pattern meat dish.

Thomas & Benjamin Godwin. Printed mark from a blue-printed earthenware soup plate.

Thomas & Benjamin Godwin. Impressed and printed marks from a blue-printed earthenware dessert plate.

Godwin, William
Market Place, Burslem
1834 White EM-B
1835 Pigot EM
The surname is listed as Goodwin in 1835 Pigot.

Godwin, Rathbone & Co.
Market Place, Burslem
1822 Pigot EM

Godwin, Rowley & Co.
Market Place, Burslem
1828 Pigot EM
1830 Pigot EM

Goode & Kenworthy
(i) High Street, Tunstall
1879 Keates P-T (earthen.)
1880 Kelly EM (manufacturers for home & foreign markets)
1882 Keates P-T (earthenware)
1884 Kelly EM (manufacturers for home & foreign markets)
1888 Kelly EM
(ii) Church Street Pottery, Tunstall
1887 Porter EM-T

Goode & Watton
High Street, Tunstall
1889 Keates P-T (earthenware)

Goodfellow & Co.
Port Vale, Longport
1892 Kelly SC (Encaustic Tile Manufacturers)

Goodfellow, Thomas
(i) Liverpool Road, Tunstall
1828 Pigot EM
1830 Pigot EM
(ii) Phoenix Pottery, Tunstall
1834 White EM-T
(iii) High Street, Tunstall
1835 Pigot EM
1841 Pigot EM
1846 Williams NC-T (earthenware manufacturer)
1850 Slater EM
1851 White EM-T
1852 Slater EM
1854 Kelly CEM
1856 Kelly CEM
1860 Kelly EM
1861 Harrison NC-T (earthenware manufacturer)
Goodfellow's house is listed as Calver House, Tunstall, in 1851 White. The firm is noted as being in the hands of executors in 1860 Kelly and 1861 Harrison.

Goodfellow & Bathwell
Upper House Works, Burslem
1818 Parson EM-B-Lp-C

Goodrun, William
Daisy Bank, Longton
1860 Kelly PM
1861 Harrison NC-L (parian manufacturer)
The surname is listed as Goodrum in 1860 Kelly.

Goodwin & Co.
High Street, Longton
1889 Keates P-L

Goodwin, B. & S.
See: Godwin, B. & S.

Goodwin, Benjamin
See: Godwin, Benjamin

Goodwin, Edmund
Shelton
1805 Holden NC (earthenware manufacturer)

Goodwin, Herbert
See: Hanley Porcelain Co. (The)

Goodwin, J.
Watergate Street, Tunstall
1856 Kelly CEM

Goodwin, John
(i) Boothenville, near Stoke
1805 Holden NC (china and earthen ware manufacturer)
(ii) Flint Street, Longton
1841 Pigot EM
1850 Slater EM
(iii) Commerce Street, Longton
1850 Kelly CEM; NC-L (earthenware manufacturer)
(iv) Crown Works, Stafford Street, Longton
1846 Williams NC-L-LE (earthenware mauuf. (sic))
1851 White CEM-L (only earthenware)
Goodwin's house is listed as City Road in 1851 White

Goodwin, John & Robert
See: Godwin, John & Robert

Goodwin, Joseph
Watergate Street, Tunstall
1860 Kelly EM
1861 Harrison NC-T
(earthenware manufacturer)

Goodwin, Robert
41 Newport Street, Burslem
1882 Keates P-B (flint grinder)

Goodwin, T. & B.
See: Godwin, Thomas & Benjamin

Goodwin, Thomas
See: Godwin, Thomas

Goodwin, William
See: Godwin, William

Goodwin & Bullock
Furnace Road, Longton
1852 Slater CM
1854 Kelly CEM
1856 Kelly CEM

Goodwin & Davison
Fountain Place Pottery, Burslem
1892 Kelly EM
1896 Kelly EM

Goodwin & Jarvis
Stoke
1805 Holden NC (china and earthenware manufacturers)

Goodwins, Bridgwood & Harris
Flint Street, Lane End
1830 Pigot EM

Goodwins, Bridgwood & Orton
High Street, Lane End
1828 Pigot EM

Goodwins, Bridgwood & Orton. Printed mark from a blue-printed plate which also bears an impressed mark for Goodwins & Harris.

Goodwins & Harris
Crown Potteries, Flint Street, Lane End or Longton
1834 White EM-LE-L
(ornamental, &c.)
1835 Pigot EM

Goodwins & Harris. Impressed mark from a blue-printed Willow pattern meat dish.

Goosetree, Daniel
Lane Delph
1818 Pigot CM

Gosling, Joseph
67 Hanover Street, Burslem
1896 Kelly SC (Encaustic Tile Manufacturers)

Goss, H.W.
Ashfield Cottage, Stoke
1860 Kelly PM

Goss, William Henry
(i) John Street, Liverpool Road, Stoke
1862 Slater CM; PM
1863 Kelly CM-General; PM; SC (Porcelain Manufacturers) (ivory)
1864 Jones CEM (statuettes, vases, tazzas, deserts, perfumers' goods, lamps, butters, jugs, &c., &c.); PM
1865 Keates P-S (parian)
1867 Keates P-S (parian and terra cotta)
1869 Keates P-S (parian and terra cotta)
(ii) London Road, Stoke
1872 Kelly CM; PM; TCM
1876 Kelly CM; PM; TCM
1879 Keates P-S (parian)
1882 Keates P-S (parian)
1884 Kelly CM
1887 Porter CEM-S
1888 Kelly CM
1889 Keates P-S (parian)
1892 Keates P-S (parian)
1892 Kelly SC (Ivory Porcelain Manufacturer)
1896 Kelly CM
1900 Kelly CM

Goss & Peake
John Street, Stoke
1868 Kelly PM

Gothard, John
See: Gothard, Thomas, & Co.

Gothard, Thomas
See: Gothard, Thomas, & Co.

Gothard, Thomas, & Co.
Union Street, Longton
1846 Williams NC-L-LE
(earthenware manufacturers)
The partners are listed individually as John Gothard and Thomas Gothard, both of Market Street, in 1846 Williams.

Gould, M.
Park Hall Street, Longton
1892 Kelly EM

Graham, John jun.
Burslem
1784 Bailey NC-B
(manufacturer of white stone earthen ware, enamelled white and cream colour)

Gratton & Co.
Victoria Works, Lonsdale Street, Stoke
1884 Kelly SC (Sanitary Ware Manufacturers); SC (Water Closet Makers)
See also: Victoria Sanitary Co.

Gray & Co.
William Street, Hanley
1896 Kelly EM

Gray, J.
William Street, Shelton
1900 Kelly EM

Gray, M.
See: Fielding & Co.

Gray & Jones
High Street, Hanley
1834 White CM-H-Sh
1835 Pigot CM

Gray & Wright
William Street, Hanley
1892 Kelly EM

Greatbach, William jun.
Stoke
1830 Pigot CM

Greatbatch, James
(i) Shelton
1796 Chester NC-H-Sh (manufacturer of earthenware)
1802 Allbut EM (map location 93)
1805 Holden NC (red potter)
(ii) Hanley
1809 Holden NC (red-potter)
1811 Holden NC (red-potter)
The surname is listed as Gridbach in 1805 Holden and as Gridbatch in 1809 Holden.

Greatbatch, William
Stoke Lane, Stoke
1835 Pigot EM

Green & Co.
Fenton
1860 Kelly CM-General

Green, F.A. & S.
Park Street, Fenton
1876 Kelly CM
1880 Kelly CM

Green, James
See: Worthington & Green

Green, John
(i) Burslem
1784 Bailey NC-B (potter)
(ii) Peel Pottery, Stafford Street, Longton
1873 Keates P-L (china)
1875 Keates P-L (china)
1876 Kelly CM
Green was succeeded by Thomas Hulse (1880 Kelly).

Green, M., & Co.
Minerva Works, Park Street, Fenton
1861 Harrison NC-F (china manufacturers)
1862 Slater CM
1863 Kelly CM-Fancy Ware; CM-General; CM-Tea, Breakfast, and Dessert Services; SC (Jug Manufacturers)
1864 Jones CEM
1865 Keates P-F (china)
1867 Keates P-F (china)
1868 Kelly CM
1869 Keates P-F (china)
1870 Harrod NC-F (manufacturers of tea, breakfast, dessert, and trinket services, &c., for home and foreign markets)
1872 Kelly CM
1873 Keates P-F (china)
1875 Keates P-F (china)
The first name is listed as Mary in 1865 Keates, 1867 Keates, and 1869 Keates. A London office at 20 Bartlett's Buildings, Holborn, is listed in 1863 Kelly.

Green, Spencer
Minerva Works, Park Street, Fenton
1882 Keates P-F (china)
1892 Keates P-F (china)

Green, T.A.
See: Booth, Thomas Gimbert
See: Crown Staffordshire Porcelain Co.
See: Green, Thomas Allen & Spencer
See: Lear, Samuel

Green, Thomas
(i) Church Yard, Burslem
1796 Chester NC-B (manufacturer of earthenware)
1802 Allbut EM (map location 53)
1805 Holden NC (earthenware manufacturer)
1809 Holden NC (earthenware-manufacturer)
1811 Holden NC (earthenware-manufacturer)
(ii) Minerva Works, Fenton
1850 Kelly CEM; NC-S (china manufacturer)
1850 Slater CM
1851 White CEM-F
1852 Slater A; CM
1854 Kelly CEM
1856 Kelly CEM
Green's house is listed as Stourbank House, Fenton, in 1851 White. The advertisement in 1852 Slater describes him as a 'manufacturer of china, &c., for the home or foreign markets'.

THOMAS GREEN,
Manufacturer of China, &c.
MINERVA WORKS,
FENTON,
STAFFORDSHIRE.
For the Home or Foreign Markets.

Thomas Green. Advertisement from 1852 Slater.

Green, Thomas, & Co.
Park Street, Fenton
1876 Kelly CM

Green, Thomas Allen & Spencer
Minerva Works, Park Street, Fenton
1879 Keates P-F (china)
1884 Kelly CM
1887 Porter EM-F
1888 Kelly CM
1889 Keates A; P-F (china)
1892 Kelly CM
1896 Kelly CM
The advertisement in 1889 Keates is in the name of the Crown Staffordshire Porcelain Co. (qv).

Crown Staffordshire Porcelain Co.,
MINERVA WORKS,
FENTON, STAFFS.
ART PORCELAIN.
VASES and Works of Art in CHINA.
Tea, Breakfast, and Desert Ware, in Japan, Satsuma, and Ivory Decorations.
The Proprietors, T. A. & S. GREEN, desire it to be known that, although the above China is of the finest description, and the work not to be surpassed, the Prices are such as to meet the requirements of the large Middle-class body of the Public; and they hope American and Colonial friends will call and see the samples at their LONDON ROOMS, 25, ELY PLACE, or at the Works.
Mr. T. A. GREEN always in London.

Thomas Allen & Spencer Green. Advertisement from 1889 Keates.

Green, William
Anchor Works, Market Street or Anchor Road, Longton
1852 Slater EM
1854 Kelly CEM
1856 Kelly CEM
The surname is listed as Greene in 1856 Kelly.
See also: Allerton, Brough & Green
See also: Broadhurst & Green

Green, Clark & Clay
Stafford Street, Longton
1882 Keates P-L (earthenware)

Green & Clay
Stafford Street, Longton
1884 Kelly EM
1887 Porter EM-L
1888 Kelly EM
1889 Keates P-L (earthenware)

Green & Richards
(i) Lane Delph
1834 White CEM-F-LD (china only)
1835 Pigot CM
(ii) Fenton
1841 Pigot CM

Green, Rouse & Co.
High Street, Longton
1882 Keates P-L (china)

Green & Worthington
Marsh Street, Shelton
1851 White CEM-H-Sh

Greene, William
See: Green, William

Grey, Alexander
William Street, Hanley
1892 Keates P-H (earthenware)

Gridbach, James
See: Greatbatch, James

Gridbatch, James
See: Greatbatch, James

Griffith, Edward
Burslem
1796 Chester NC-B
(manufacturer of earthenware)
1798 Universal NC-B
(manufacturer of Staffordshire-ware)

Griffiths, Thomas
(i) Furnace Road, Longton
1850 Kelly NC-L (figure manufacturer)
(ii) Flint Street, Longton
1850 Slater TOCM

Griffiths, Thomas, & Co.
Flint Street, Lane End
1828 Pigot EM
1830 Pigot EM

Grimwade Brothers
Winton Pottery, Stoke Road, Shelton, Hanley
1889 Keates P-H (earthenware)
1892 Keates P-H (earthenware)
1887 Porter EM-H
1888 Kelly EM
1892 Kelly EM
1896 Kelly EM
1900 Kelly EM

Grimwade (Mr.)
See: Trubshaw, Hand & Co.

Grindley, William Harry, & Co.
(i) Newfield Pottery, Tunstall
1880 Kelly A; EM
1882 Keates P-T (earthenware)
1884 Kelly EM

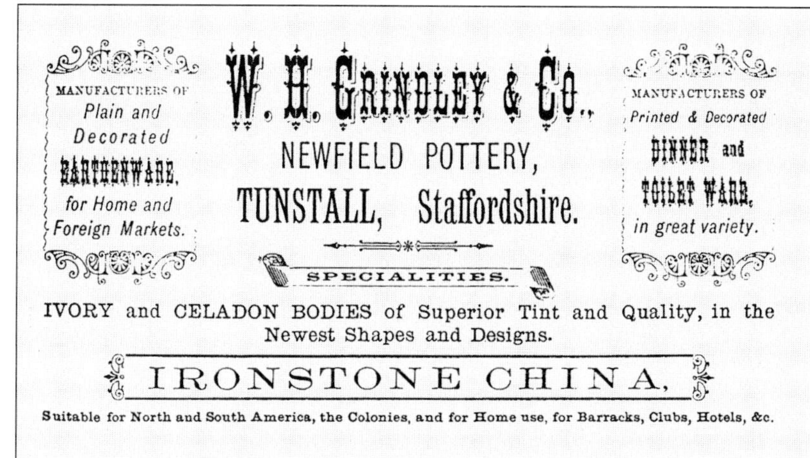

William Harry Grindley & Co. Advertisement from 1880 Kelly.

William Harry Grindley & Co. Printed mark from a flow-blue earthenware dinner service (the initials FB are unexplained).

(manufacturers of ironstone china & decorated earthenware suitable for the Canadian, United States, South American & Australian markets)
1887 Porter EM-T
1888 Kelly CM; EM
(manufacturers of ironstone china & decorated earthenware suitable for the Canadian, United States, South American, Cape & Australian markets)
1889 Keates P-T (earthenware)
(ii) Woodland Pottery, Woodland Street, Tunstall
1892 Keates P-T (earthenware)
1892 Kelly EM
1900 Kelly EM
The advertisement in 1880 Kelly reads 'Manufacturers of Plain and Decorated Earthenware for Home and Foreign Markets. Manufacturers of printed & decorated dinner and toilet ware in great variety. Specialities – ivory and celadon bodies of superior tint and quality, in the newest shapes and designs. Ironstone china, suitable for North and South America, the Colonies, and for home use, for barracks, clubs, hotels, &c.'

Grocott Brothers
Perry Street Works, Hanley
1888 Kelly EM

Grocott, John
Percy Street, Hanley
1889 Keates P-H

Grocott, Samuel
Liverpool Road, Tunstall
1828 Pigot EM (toy only)

Grocott & Dickenson
See: Grocott & Dickinson

Grocott & Dickinson
Longport
1889 Keates P-B (door furniture)
1892 Keates P-B (door furniture)
The second partner's name is listed as Dickenson in 1892 Keates.

Grose & Co.
Bridge Pottery, Church Street, Stoke
1867 Keates P-S (earthenware)
1868 Kelly EM
1869 Keates P-S (earthenware)

Grosvenor, John Boden
New Street, Hanley

1852 Slater A; EM; PM; TOCM

The advertisement in 1852 Slater describes Grosvenor as a 'manufacturer of earthenware, stone parian, &c.' and notes 'statuettes (classical & general) anatomically pourtrayed (sic). Stone, &c. ware adapted for home and foreign markets.'

JOHN B. GROSVENOR,
Manufacturer of
EARTHENWARE, STONE PARIAN,&c.
NEW STREET, HANLEY,
STAFFORDSHIRE POTTERIES.
N.B.—Statuettes (classical & general) anatomically pourtrayed.
Stone, &c. Ware adapted for Home and Foreign Markets.

John Boden Grosvenor. Advertisement from 1852 Slater.

Grove & Co.
Chancery Lane, Longton
1900 Kelly EM

Grove, F.M.
1887 Porter EM-L

Grove, Frederick W.
Palissy Works, Chancery Lane, Longton
1887 Porter EM-L
1888 Kelly EM

Grove, R.H.
(i) Barlaston
1860 Kelly CM-General; EM
1863 Kelly CM-General; EM
(ii) Palissy Works, Chancery Lane, Longton
1867 Keates A; P-L (rustic, lustre, china, and earthenware)
1868 Kelly CM; EM; SC (Beer Machine Handle Makers – China); SC (China & Porcelain Door Furniture Manufacturers)
1869 Keates P-L (rustic, lustre, china, and earthen.)

A London office at 71 Hatton Garden is listed in 1868 Kelly. The advertisement in 1867 Keates describes Grove as a 'merchant, and manufacturer of continental porcelain, lustre, earthenware, mortars and pestles, metal covered jugs, beer machine handles, barrels, mortice lock furniture, letters for signs, pomade boxes, garden labels, and all kinds of rustic and horticultural goods, for home consumption and exportation'.

R.H. Grove. Impressed mark from a pair of rustic stoneware tree-trunk vases.

Grove, Richard Henry
(i) Vine Street, Hanley
1860 Kelly CM-General; EM
1861 Harrison NC-H-Sh (china and earthenware manufacturer)
1862 Slater CM; EM (rustic)
(ii) Broad Street, Hanley
1882 Keates P-H (china and parian)

Grove & Oliver
Chancery Lane, Longton
1892 Kelly EM

Grove & Prouse
Chancery Lane, Longton
1896 Kelly EM

PALISSY WORKS, LONGTON,
STAFFORDSHIRE POTTERIES.
R. H. GROVE,
Merchant, and Manufacturer
OF CONTINENTAL PORCELAIN, LUSTRE, EARTHENWARE,
Mortars and Pestles, Metal Covered Jugs,
BEER MACHINE HANDLES, BARRELS,
Mortice-Lock Furniture, Letters for Signs, Pomade Boxes, Garden Labels, and all kinds of Rustic and Horticultural Goods,
For Home Consumption and Exportation.

R.H. Grove. Advertisement from 1867 Keates.

Grove & Robinson
Chancery Lane, Longton
1870 Harrod NC-L (lustre and china manufacturers)

Grove & Stark
Palissy Works, Chancery Lane, Longton
1872 Kelly EM
1873 Keates P-L (rustic, lustre, china and earthen.)
1875 Keates P-L (rustic, lustre, china and earthen)
1876 Kelly EM
1879 Keates P-L (rustic, lustre, china and earthenware)
1880 Kelly EM (manufacturers of printed & decorated earthenware, dinner & toilet sets in white & ivory bodies, porcelain, spirit barrels, beer machine handles &c)
1882 Keates P-L (rustic, lustre, china, and earthenware)
1884 Kelly EM

London agents are listed as Pattenden, Hurles & Co. of 20 Hatton Garden in 1880 Kelly.

Grove (F.), Wedgwood & Oliver
Palissy Works, Chancery Lane, Longton
1889 Keates P-L (rustic, lustre, china and earthenware)
1892 Keates P-L (rustic, lustre, china and earthenware)

Guest Brothers
High Street, Tunstall
1892 Kelly JRM

Guest, George
(i) Bleak Street, Burslem
1873 Keates P-B (Rockingham)
(ii) Soho Pottery, High Street, Tunstall
1875 Keates P-T (earthenware)
1876 Kelly EM
1879 Keates P-T (earthenware)
1880 Kelly EM
1882 Keates P-T (earthenware)
(iii) Albert Street, Tunstall
1887 Porter JM-T
1888 Kelly JM; RM
(iv) Albert or High Street Pottery, off High Street, Tunstall
1889 Keates P-T (earthenware)
1892 Keates P-T (earthenware)
(iv) 58 Liverpool Road, Burslem

1889 Keates P-B
1892 Keates P-B

Guest, George, & Son
Albert Street, Tunstall
1884 Kelly EM

Guest, J.
Kidsgrove
1863 Kelly EM

Guest, Thomas
Burslem
1802 Allbut EM (map location 40)

H

Hackney & Co.
Daisy Bank, Longton
1867 Keates A; P-L (parian)
The advertisement in 1867 Keates describes the firm as 'manufacturers of parian statuettes, vases, &c.'

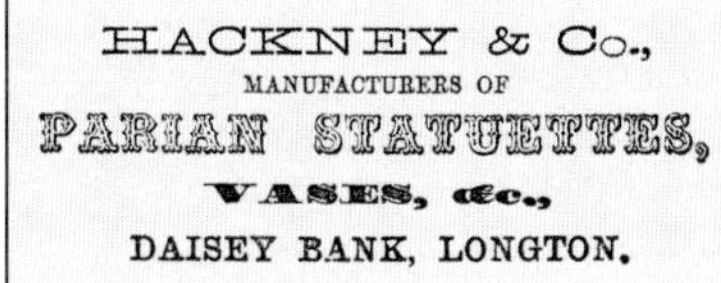

Hackney & Co. Advertisement from 1867 Keates.

Hackney, Albert G.
Slippery Lane, Hanley
1900 Kelly EM

Hackney, F., & Co.
Railway Pottery, off Whieldon Road, Fenton
This firm is recorded as being succeeded by Fielding & Co. in 1880 Kelly, but no manufacturer of this style is listed in any other directory.

Hackney, J.
18 High Street, Longton
1868 Kelly PM

Hackney, James S.
Victoria Place, Stafford Street, Longton
1869 Keates P-L (parian)
1870 Harrod NC-L (parian manufacturer)

Hackney, Nathan
Cobridge
1834 White EM-H-Sh

Hackney, Ralph
Peel Street, Stoke
1864 Jones CEM

Hackney, Greaves & Co.
Sheridan Works, King Street, Longton
1864 Jones CEM

Hackney, Greaves & Amison
Sheridan Works, Longton
1863 Kelly CM-Fancy Ware; CM-General; CM-Tea, Breakfast, and Dessert Services; SC (China Porcelain Manufacturers); SC (Porcelain Manufacturers)

Hackney, Kirkham & Co.
Sutherland Street, Fenton
1879 Keates P-F (earthenware)

Hackwood & Co.
Hanley
1816 Underhill P

Hackwood & Co. Impressed mark from sprig-decorated stonewares.

Hackwood & Son
New Hall Pottery, Shelton
1846 Williams NC-Sh
1850 Kelly NC-Sh (earthenware manufctrs.); CEM
The partners are listed individually as Thomas Hackwood of Hill Street and William Hackwood of Union Street in 1846 Williams.

Hackwood, Thomas
New Hall Works, Shelton
1851 White CEM-H-Sh
1852 Slater EM
1854 Kelly CEM
1856 Kelly CEM
Hackwood's house is listed as Union Street in 1851 White.

Hackwood, William
(i) Eastwood, Hanley
1828 Pigot EM
1830 Pigot EM
1834 White EM-H-Sh
1835 Pigot EM
1841 Pigot EM
(ii) Union Street, Shelton
1850 Kelly CEM
(iii) Hope Street, Shelton, Hanley
1852 Slater A; EM (and figure); TOCM
1854 Kelly CEM
The advertisement in 1852 Slater describes Hackwood simply as an 'earthenware & figure manufacturer'.

WILLIAM HACKWOOD,
EARTHENWARE & FIGURE
MANUFACTURER,
HOPE STREET,
HANLEY.

William Hackwood. Advertisement from 1852 Slater.

William Hackwood. A portrait of William Hackwood inscribed "Potter of Hanley, 1774-1849".

William Hackwood. Printed mark from a blue-printed earthemware meat dish.

Hackwood, William, & Son
New-hall Street, Shelton
1850 Slater EM

Hackwood, Dimmock & Co.
(i) Hanley
1809 Holden NC (earthenware-manufacturers)
1811 Holden NC (earthenware-manufacturers)
1818 Parson EM-H-Sh
1822 Allbut CEM (earthenware manufacts.)
(ii) Charles Street, Hanley
1818 Pigot EM
(iii) Eastwood, Hanley
1822 Pigot EM
The first partner's name is listed as Ackwood in 1818 Pigot.

Hadfield & Co.
King Street Works, King Street, Hanley
1880 Kelly RM
The directory lists an office in Market Street, Hanley.

Hales & Adams
Cobridge
1781 Bailey NC (potters)
1783 Bailey NC (potters)
1784 Bailey NC-C (potters)

Hall, Henry
(i) Church Street Works, Hanley
1870 Harrod NC-H (manufacturer of earthenware, stone, &c., Britannia metal mounted hot-water jugs, molasses jugs, for home and foreign markets)
(ii) New Hall Street, Hanley
1882 Keates P-H (earthenware and majolica)

Henry Hall. Engraved mark on a Britannia metal lid fitted to a relief-moulded jug manufactured by G.L. Ashworth & Bros.

Hall, Isaac
140 Hope Street, Hanley
1892 Keates P-H

Hall, John
Sitch, Burslem
1822 Allbut CEM (earthenware manufacturer)

John Hall. Printed mark from a blue-printed earthenware meat dish.

Hall, John, & Sons
Liverpool Road, Burslem
1828 Pigot EM
1830 Pigot EM

Hall, John & Ralph
(i) Burslem
1802 Allbut EM (map location 26)
1805 Holden NC (earthenware manufacturer)
1816 Underhill P
(ii) Burslem and Tunstall
1809 Holden NC (earthenware-manufacturers) (two entries)
1811 Holden NC (earthenware-manufacturers) (two entries)
1818 Parson EM-G-T-R; EM-B-Lp-C
1818 Pigot EM (two entries)
1822 Pigot EM
The Burslem address is listed as Sitch in 1818 Parson.

Hall, R.
Dale Hall, Longport
1854 Kelly CEM

Hall, Ralph
(i) Tunstall
1822 Allbut CEM (earthenware manufacturer)
1828 Pigot EM
1830 Pigot EM
(ii) High Street, Tunstall
1834 White EM-T
1835 Pigot EM
1850 Slater EM

Ralph Hall. Printed mark from a blue-printed earthenware dessert plate.

Hall, Ralph, & Co.
High Street, Tunstall
1841 Pigot EM
1846 Williams NC-T (earthenware manufacturers)
The partners are listed individually as Ralph Hall of High Street and James Holland of Hall Street in 1846 Williams.

Hall, Samuel
(i) Newhall Street, Shelton
1830 Pigot EM (toy only)
1834 White CETM-H-Sh
(ii) Marsh Street, Shelton
1841 Pigot TOCM
1846 Williams NC-Sh (china manufacturer)
1850 Kelly NC-Sh (china toy manufacturer)
1850 Slater TOCM
1854 Kelly PM (Ornamental Figure Makers)

Hall, Thomas
29 Church Street, Hanley
1889 Keates P-H

Hall, William
(i) Newcastle Road, Hanley
1876 Kelly MM
(ii) Wharf Lane, Hanley
1879 Keates P-H (majolica and earthenware)
1882 Keates P-H (majolica and earthenware)

Hall & Hulme
Havelock Works, Broad Street, Hanley
1887 Porter EM-H

1888 Kelly EM
1889 Keates P-H (earthenware and jet)

Hall & Hume
William Street, Hanley
1884 Kelly EM

Hall & Read
(i) Wellington Works, Newport Street, Burslem
1882 Keates P-B
(ii) Dresden Works, George Street, Hanley
1882 Keates P-H (earthenware)
(iii) Victoria Square, Hanley
1884 Kelly EM

Hall, Watkin & Co.
Union Street, Hanley
1880 Kelly EM

Hallam, Ephraim
Bourne's Bank, Burslem
1851 White CETM-B

Hallam, R.
Chaplin Works, Church Street, Longton
1889 Keates P-L (earthenware)

Hallam & Blair
Normacott Road, Longton
1887 Porter EM-L
1888 Kelly CM

Hallam & Brian
Heathcote Pottery, Heathcote Road, Longton
1892 Keates P-L

Hallam & Day
Mount Pleasant, High Street, Longton
1882 Keates P-L (china)

Hallam & Furber
Normacott Road, Longton
1884 Kelly CM

Hallam & Gibson
St. Martin's Lane, Longton
1870 Harrod NC-L (china manufacturers)

Hallam & Johnson
Mount Pleasant, High Street, Longton
1879 Keates P-L (china)
1880 Kelly CM

Hallam, Johnson & Co.
Mount Pleasant, High Street, Longton
1873 Keates P-L (china)
1875 Keates P-L (china)
1876 Kelly CM

Hallam & Shelley
Shelton
1796 Chester NC-H-Sh (manufacturers of earthenware)

Hallen & Co.
Wellington Street, Burslem
1865 Keates P-B (creel steps)

Hallen, Harding
(i) Newcastle Street, Burslem
1841 Pigot EM
(ii) Holehouse
1846 Williams NC-B (potter)
(iii) Wellington Street, Burslem
1850 Slater EM; SC (Pot Step Manufacturers, for Cotton Spinners)
1852 Slater EM (and earthenware gas-burner); SC (Pot Step Manufacturers, for Cotton Spinners)
1854 Kelly CEM
1867 Keates P-B (creel steps)
1868 Kelly SC (Creel Step Manufacturer)
1870 Harrod NC-B (pot-step and gas-burner manufacturer)
1872 Kelly SC (Creel Step Manufacturer); SC (Shuttle Eye Manufacturers)
1876 Kelly SC (Creel Step Manufacturer); SC (Shuttle Eye Manufacturers)
(iv) 29 Wellington Street, Burslem
1869 Keates P-B (creel steps)
1873 Keates P-B (creel steps)
1875 Keates P-B (creel steps)
1879 Keates P-B (creel steps)
(v) 31 Wellington Street, Burslem
1882 Keates P-B (creel steps)
1889 Keates P-B (creel steps)
1892 Keates P-B (creel steps)
Hallen's house is listed as Waterloo Road in 1846 Williams

Hallen, Harding & William Henry
(i) 29 Pitt Street, Burslem
1861 Harrison NC-B (creel step manufacturers)
1863 Kelly SC (Creel Step Manufacturers)
(ii) Wellington Street, Burslem
1862 Slater SC (Pot Step Manufacturers, for Cotton Spinners) (& gas burner & shuttle eye)
1864 Jones EM-Miscellaneous (pot creel step manfrs. for cotton mills)

Hallen, Henry
(i) Commercial Street, Burslem
1862 Slater SC (Pot Step Manufacturers, for Cotton Spinners)
(ii) Wellington Street, Burslem
1880 Kelly SC (Creel Step Manufacturers); SC (Shuttle Eye Manufacturers)
1884 Kelly SC (Creel Step Manufacturers); SC (Shuttle Eye Manufacturers)
1887 Porter EM-B
1888 Kelly SC (Creel Step Manufacturers)
1892 Kelly SC (Creel Step & Shuttle Eye Manufacturers); SC (Shuttle Eye Manufacturers)
1896 Kelly SC (Creel Step & Shuttle Eye Manufacturers)
1900 Kelly SC (Creel Step & Shuttle Eye Manufacturers)
The firm is noted as being in the hands of executors in 1896 Kelly and 1900 Kelly.

Hallen, Samuel
(i) Holehouse
1846 Williams NC-B (potter)
(ii) Sytch, Burslem
1851 White CEM-B (only earthenware)
1854 Kelly CEM
Hallen's house is listed as Bleakhill in 1846 Williams.

Hallen, William
(i) Liverpool Road, Burslem
1852 Slater SC (Pot Step Manufacturers, for Cotton Spinners)
(ii) Wellington Street, Burslem
1852 Slater EM (and pot-step)
1854 Kelly CEM
1856 Kelly SC (Creel Steps Maker)

Hallen, William Henry
29 Wellington Street, Burslem
1869 Keates P-B (creel steps)
1870 Harrod NC-B (creel-step maker)

Hamersley, John
See: Hammersley, John

Hamilton, Robert
Stoke
1818 Parson EM-S-E
1818 Pigot EM
1822 Allbut CEM (earthenware manufacturer)
1822 Pigot EM

Hamilton, Sampson
See: Hamilton & Moore

Hamilton, William
Sheaf Pottery, Normacott Road, Longton
1880 Kelly MM

Hamilton & Moore
Mount Pleasant Pottery, High Street, Longton
1841 Pigot CM
1846 Williams NC-L-LE (china manuf.)
1850 Kelly NC-L (china manufacturers); CEM
1850 Slater CM
1851 White CEM-L
1852 Slater CM
1854 Kelly CEM
1856 Kelly CEM
The partners are listed individually as Sampson Hamilton of Longton House, New Street, and Samuel Moore of Furnace, Longton, in 1846 Williams.

Hammersley Brothers
Nelson Place, Hanley
1884 Kelly EM; PM
1887 Porter EM-H
1888 Kelly EM; PM
1892 Kelly EM; PM
1896 Kelly EM; PM

Hammersley & Co.
Sutherland Road, Longton
1887 Porter EM-L
1888 Kelly CM
1889 Keates P-L (china)
1892 Keates P-L (china)
1892 Kelly CM
1896 Kelly CM
1900 Kelly CM
(See right)

Hammersley, John
(i) Cobridge
1796 Chester NC-C (manufacturer of earthenware)
1798 Universal NC-C (manufacturer of Staffordshire-ware)
(ii) Shelton
1802 Allbut EM (map location 87)
1805 Holden NC (course (sic) earthenware manufacturer)
The surname is listed as Hamersley in 1796 Chester.

Hammersley, Joseph & Robert
(i) New Street, Hanley
1876 Kelly CM
1879 Keates P-H (china & earthenware)
1880 Kelly CM
1882 Keates P-H (china and earthenware)
1884 Kelly CM
1888 Kelly CM
1889 Keates P-H (china and earthenware decorators)
1892 Keates P-H (china and earthenware decorators)
1892 Kelly CM
1896 Kelly CM
1900 Kelly CM
(ii) Nelson Place, Hanley
1882 Keates P-H (china and earthenware)

Hammersley, Ralph
(i) High Street, Tunstall
1860 Kelly EM; RM; SC (Egyptian Black Ware Manufacturers)
1861 Harrison NC-T (black earthenware manufacturer)
1862 Slater EM (Rockingham)
1863 Kelly RM
1864 Jones EM-Miscellaneous (Egyptian black and Rockingham teapots manfr.)

Hammersley & Co. Printed marks from a china plate hand-painted and signed by A. Colclough.

1865 Keates P-T (tea pot)
1867 Keates P-T (black earthenware)
1869 Keates P-T (Rockingham and Egyptian black)
1872 Kelly EM
1873 Keates P-T (Rockingham and Egyptian black)
1875 Keates P-T (Rockingham and Egyptian black)
1876 Kelly EM
1879 Keates P-T (Rockington *(sic)* and Egyptian black)
1880 Kelly EM
(ii) Church Bank Pottery, High Street, Tunstall
1868 Kelly EM
1869 Keates P-T (black earthenware)
(iii) Overhouse Pottery, Wedgwood Place, Burslem
1870 Harrod NC-B (earthenware manufacturer)
1872 Kelly EM
1873 Keates P-B (earthenware & ironstone china)
1875 Keates P-B (earthenware and ironstone china)
1876 Kelly EM
1879 Keates P-B (earthenware and ironstone china)
1880 Kelly EM
1882 Keates P-B (earthenware and ironstone china)
1889 Keates P-B (earthenware and ironstone china)
1892 Keates P-B (earthenware and ironstone china)

Ralph Hammersley. Printed mark from a blue-printed Willow pattern earthenware dessert plate.

Ralph Hammersley. Printed mark from a blue-printed earthenware plate.

Hammersley, Ralph, & Co.
Shelton
1822 Allbut CEM (enamellers and gilders)

Hammersley, Ralph, & Son
(i) High Street, Tunstall
1884 Kelly EM
(ii) Over House Pottery, Wedgwood Place, Burslem
1884 Kelly EM
1887 Porter EM-B
1888 Kelly EM
1892 Kelly EM
1896 Kelly EM
1900 Kelly EM

Hammersley, Robert M., & Co.
High Street Pottery, Tunstall
1880 Kelly EM
1882 Keates P-T (earthenware)
1889 Keates P-T (earthenware)

Hammersley, William
Lane End
1822 Allbut CEM (earthenware manufacturer)

Hammersley & Asbury
Sutherland Road, Longton
1872 Kelly CM
1873 Keates A; P-L (china)
The firm was succeeded by Edward Asbury & Co. (1875 Keates advertisement). The advertisement in 1873 Keates describes the firm as 'manufacturers of china tea, breakfast, and dessert services, also trinkets for the toilet table. Dealers in lustre & stone teapots & jugs, &c. H. & A. also make china specially adapted to the markets of Australia and South America'. It also lists their London agent as Mr. W.L. Allen at 11 Hatton Garden, Holborn.

HAMMERSLEY & ASBURY,
SUTHERLAND ROAD, LONGTON,
MANUFACTURERS OF
CHINA TEA, BREAKFAST,
AND
DESSERT SERVICES,
ALSO,
TRINKETS FOR THE TOILET TABLE.
DEALERS IN
Lustre & Stone Teapots & Jugs, &c.
H. & A. also make China specially adapted to the markets of Australia and South America.
London Agent—Mr. W. L. ALLEN, 11, Hatton Garden Holborn.

Hammersley & Asbury. Advertisement from 1873 Keates.

Hammersley & Freeman
Sutherland Road, Longton
1865 Keates P-L (china)
1867 Keates P-L (china)

Hammersley, Freeman & Co.
Prince of Wales Works, Sutherland Road, Longton
1868 Kelly CM
1869 Keates A; P-L (china)
1870 Harrod NC-L (china manufacturers for home and foreign markets)
The advertisement in 1869 Keates describes the firm as 'manufacturers of china tea, breakfast, and dessert services; also, trinkets for the toilet table. Dealers in lustre and stone teapots and jugs, &c., H.F. and Co. also make china specially adapted to the markets of Australia and South America'. It also lists their London agent as Mr. W.L. Allen at 105 Hatton Garden, Holborn.

HAMMERSLEY, FREEMAN, & CO.,
SUTHERLAND ROAD, LONGTON,
MANUFACTURERS OF
China Tea, Breakfast, and Dessert Services;
ALSO, TRINKETS FOR THE TOILET TABLE.
DEALERS IN LUSTRE AND STONE TEAPOTS AND JUGS, &c.,
H. F. and Co also make China specially adapted to the markets of Australia and South America.
London Agent—Mr. W. L. ALLEN, 105, Hatton Garden, Holborn.

Hammersley, Freeman & Co. Advertisement from 1869 Keates.

Hammond & Buckley
See: Hammonds & Buckley

Hammonds & Co.
Garfield Works, High Street, Longton
1884 Kelly EM
1888 Kelly EM

Hammonds, William
Victoria Works, High Street, Longton
1892 Kelly EM

Hammonds & Buckley
Victoria Works, High Street, Longton
1887 Porter EM-L
1889 Keates P-L (earthenware)
The first partner's name is listed as Hammond in 1889 Keates.

Hampson Brothers
Green Dock Works. New Street, Longton
1860 Kelly EM
1861 Harrison NC-L (earthenware manufacturers)
1862 Slater EM
1863 Kelly EM
1864 Jones A; EM
1865 Keates P-L (earthenware)
1867 Keates P-L (earthenware)
1868 Kelly EM
1869 Keates P-L (earthenware)
1870 Harrod NC-L (earthenware manufacturers)
The entry in 1861 Harrison is listed as Hampson & Brothers. The advertisement in 1864 Jones describes the firm as 'manufacturers of improved stone & earthenware, enamellers, gold, silver & brown lusterers, &c.'

HAMPSON BROTHERS,
MANUFACTURERS OF IMPROVED
STONE & EARTHENWARE,
Enamellers, Gold, Silver & Brown Lusterers, &c.,
GREEN DOCK WORKS,
LONGTON,
STAFFORDSHIRE POTTERIES.

Hampson Brothers. Advertisement from 1864 Jones.

Hampson, P.
Green Dock, Longton
1856 Kelly CEM

Hampson & Broadhurst
Green Dock Works, New Street, Longton
1850 Kelly CEM; NC-L (earthenware manufrs.)
1850 Slater EM
1851 White CEM-L (only earthenware)
1852 Slater EM
1854 Kelly CEM

Hancock & Son
Wolfe Street, Stoke
1892 Kelly EM

Hancock, Benjamin & Sampson
Church Street, Stoke
1876 Kelly EM
1880 Kelly EM

Hancock, Frederick, & Co.
Campbell Place Works, Stoke
1900 Kelly EM

Hancock, John
(i) Brownhills Pottery

1841 Pigot CM; EM
(ii) Brownhills Hall, Tunstall
1889 Keates P-T

Hancock, R., & Co.
High Street, Burslem
1850 Slater EM

Hancock, Redulphus
High Street, Burslem
1851 White CEM-B (only earthenware)
Hancock's house is listed as Sytch, Burslem, in 1851 White.
See also: Emberton, Hancock & Co.

Hancock, S., & Son
Wolfe Street, Stoke
1896 Kelly EM

Hancock, S., & Sons
Wolfe Street, Stoke
1892 Keates P-S (earthenware)
1900 Kelly EM

Sampson Hancock & Sons. Printed mark from a brown-printed and coloured earthenware plate.

Hancock, Sampson
(i) Victoria Street, Tunstall
1865 Keates P-T (earthen.)
1867 Keates P-T (earthen.)
(ii) High Street, Tunstall
1869 Keates P-T (earthenware)
1870 Harrod NC-T (earthenware manufacturer)
(iii) Bridge Works, Church Street, Stoke
1882 Keates P-S (earthenware)
1884 Kelly EM
1887 Porter CEM-S
1888 Kelly EM
1889 Keates P-S (earthenware)
The first name is listed as Samson in 1887 Porter.

Hancock, Leigh & Co.
Swan Bank or Swan Square, Burslem
1860 Kelly EM
1861 Harrison NC-B (earthenware manufacturers)
1862 Slater EM
The town is listed as Tunstall in 1862 Slater.

Hancock & Pearson
Cobridge
1851 White NC-B (earthenware manufacturers)

Hancock & Sheldon
Burslem
1816 Underhill P

Hancock & Whittingham
Swan Square, Burslem
1870 Harrod NC-B (earthenware manufacturers)

Hancock, Whittingham & Co.
(i) Queen Square, Burslem
1863 Kelly EM
1868 Kelly EM
1872 Kelly EM
(ii) Swan Bank Pottery, Waterloo Road or Chapel Square, Burslem
1864 Jones A; EM
1865 Keates P-B (earthenware)
1867 Keates P-B (earthenware)
1869 Keates P-B (earthenware)
1870 Harrod NC-B (earthenware manufacturers)
1873 Keates P-B (earthenware)
The second partner's name is listed as Whitingham in 1865 Keates. The advertisement in 1864 Jones describes the firm as 'plain and ornamental earthenware manufacturers'.

HANCOCK, WHITTINGHAM & Co.,
PLAIN AND ORNAMENTAL
Earthenware Manufacturers,
SWAN BANK POTTERY,
BURSLEM, STAFFORDSHIRE.

Hancock, Whittingham & Co. Advertisement from 1864 Jones.

Hancock & Whittington
Church Street, Stoke
1873 Keates P-S (earthenware)
1875 Keates P-S (earthenware)
1879 Keates P-S (earthenware)

Hand & Copestake
St. Martin's Lane, Market Street, Longton
1865 Keates A; P-L (china)
The advertisement in 1865 Keates describes the firm simply as 'china manufacturers'.

HAND & COPESTAKE,
CHINA MANUFACTURERS,
ST. MARTIN'S LANE,
MARKET STREET, LONGTON,
Potteries, Staffordshire.

Hand & Copestake. Advertisement from 1865 Keates.

Handley, James & William
(i) Chapel Street, Burslem
1822 Pigot EM
(ii) High Street, Shelton
1822 Allbut CEM (china manufacts.)
(iii) Kilncroft, Burslem
1822 Allbut CEM (earthenware manufacts)
1828 Pigot CM

James & William Handley. Printed mark from a blue-printed and coloured china cup.

Hanley China Co.
Burton Place, Hanley
1900 Kelly EM

Hanley Plain & Encaustic Tile Co. Ltd.
Havelock Works, Broad Street, Hanley
1876 Kelly SC (Encaustic Tile Manufacturers)
1879 Keates A; SC-H (Floor Tile Manufacturers)

Hanley Porcelain Co. (The)
Burton Place Works, Hanley
1892 Kelly CM
The manager is listed as Herbert Goodwin in 1892 Kelly.

Harding, Joseph
Navigation Road, Burslem

1850 Kelly CEM; NC-B (earthenware manufacturer)
1850 Slater EM
1851 White CEM-B (only earthenware)
Harding's house is listed as Wolstanton in 1851 White.

Joseph Harding. Printed mark from a blue-printed earthenware dinner plate.

Harding, W.
Furlong Pottery, Burslem
1856 Kelly CEM

Harding, William & George
Furlong Pottery, Navigation Road, Burslem
1851 White NC-B (china, &c., manufacturers)
1852 Slater EM
1854 Kelly CEM

William & George Harding. Printed mark from a blue-printed earthenware dinner plate.

Harding, William & Joseph
New Hall Pottery, Marsh Street, Hanley
1863 Kelly EM; RM; SC (Egyptian Black Ware Manufacturers); SM
1864 Jones EM
1865 Keates P-H (earthenware)
1867 Keates P-H (earthenware)
1868 Kelly EM
1869 Keates P-H (earthen.)

Harding, Wingfield
See: Harding & Cockson

Harding & Cockson
Cobridge
1834 White EM-B
1841 Pigot CM
1846 Williams NC-C-F-E (china manufacturers)
1850 Slater CM
1851 White CEM-B
1852 Slater CM
1854 Kelly CEM
1856 Kelly CEM
The partners are listed individually as Wingfield Harding of Booden Brook Cottage, Shelton, and Charles Cockson of Landscape House, Cobridge, in 1846 Williams. The entry in 1851 White has an indicator which is not explained; it could mean china only.

Harding, Cockson & Co.
Cobridge
1835 Pigot CM; EM
1841 Pigot EM

Harley, Thomas
Lane End
1805 Holden NC (enameller and earthenware manufacturer)

Harley & Seckerson
(i) Lane End
1809 Holden NC (earthenware-manufacturers)
1811 Holden NC (earthenware-manufacturers)
1816 Underhill P
1818 Parson EM-LE
(ii) High Street, Lane End
1818 Pigot EM
1822 Pigot EM
(iii) Market Street, Lane End
1822 Allbut CEM (earthenware manufacturers, lusterers, and enamellers)
The second partner's name is listed as Sackerson in 1816 Underhill.

Harris & Goodwins
Crown Works, Flint Street, Lane End or Longton
1834 White CM-LE-L (lustre mfrs.)
1835 Pigot CM

Harrison, Charles
(i) Queen Street, Longton
1887 Porter EM-L
(ii) Queen Street and Chadwick Street, Longton
1889 Keates P-L (china and earthenware)
1892 Keates P-L (china and earthenware)
An advertisement in 1887 Porter describes Harrison as a 'manufacturer of decorated china & earthenware, also, importer of Bohemian glass and other goods; wholesale and retail'. Advertisements in 1889 Keates and 1892 Keates both describe him simply as a 'china & earthenware manufacturer', but the address is given as the Bee Hive Works in 1892.

CHARLES HARRISON,
MANUFACTURER OF
Decorated China & Earthenware
ALSO,
Importer of Bohemian Glass
AND OTHER GOODS.
WHOLESALE AND RETAIL.
QUEEN STREET, LONGTON.

Charles Harrison. Advertisement from 1887 Porter.

CHARLES HARRISON,
CHINA & EARTHENWARE
MANUFACTURER,
QUEEN Street & CHADWICK Street,
LONGTON.

Charles Harrison. Advertisement from 1889 Keates.

CHARLES HARRISON,
China & Earthenware
MANUFACTURER,
BEE HIVE WORKS,
LONGTON.

Charles Harrison. Advertisement from 1892 Keates.

Harrison, David B., & Co.
(i) King's Field Pottery, Shelton Old Road, Stoke or Newcastle
1887 Porter CEM-S
1888 Kelly JM
(ii) Shelton New Road, Newcastle
1888 Kelly TCM

Harrison, George, & Co.
Lower Lane
1798 Universal NC-LL (manufacturers of Staffordshire-ware)

Harrison, John
(i) Stoke
1781 Bailey NC (potter)
1783 Bailey NC (potter)
1796 Chester NC-S (manufacturer of earthenware)
1798 Universal NC-S (manufacturer of Staffordshire-ware)
1802 Allbut EM (map location 99)
1809 Holden NC (earthenware-manufacturer)
1816 Underhill P
(ii) Longton Pottery
1830 Pigot EM
(iii) High Street, Tunstall, and Lane End
1841 Pigot TOCM
Harrison is listed as John junior in 1781 Bailey and 1783 Bailey. The address is listed as Cliffgate Bank in 1802 Allbut.

Harrison, W.
Burslem
1809 Holden NC (earthenware-manufacturer)

Harrison & Baker
(i) George Street, Newcastle
1876 Kelly TCM
(ii) Shelton New Road, Newcastle or Stoke
1876 Kelly TCM
1880 Kelly TCM
1884 Kelly TCM
(iii) King's Field Pottery, Newcastle
1880 Kelly JM
1884 Kelly JM

Harrison, Brough & Co.
Green Dock, Lane End
1805 Holden NC (earthenware manufacturers)
1809 Holden NC (earthenware-manufactories)
1811 Holden NC (earthenware-manufactories)
1816 Underhill P

Harrison & Hyatt
Lower Lane
1796 Chester NC-LE-LD-LL (manufacturers of earthenware)
1802 Allbut EM (map location 105)

Harrison, Neale & Co.
Elm Street, Hanley
1882 Keates P-H (china & earthenware)

Harrop & Co.
Dresden Works, Tinkersclough, Hanley
1892 Keates P-H (parian and china)

Harrop, John & Frederick
Dresden Works, Tinkersclough, Hanley
1889 Keates P-H (parian & china)

Harrop, William
Tinkersclough, Hanley
1875 Keates P-H (parian and earthenware)
1876 Kelly EM
1879 Keates P-H (parian and earthenware)

Harrop, William, & Co.
Dresden Works, Tinkersclough, Hanley
1880 Kelly EM (earthenware, stone & parian manufacturers &c)
1882 Keates P-H (parian & earthenware)
1884 Kelly EM; PM
1887 Porter EM-H
1888 Kelly EM
1892 Kelly EM

Harrop & Burgess
Tinkersclough, Hanley
1896 Kelly EM
1900 Kelly EM

Hartle, Singleton & Co.
Lane End
1805 Holden NC (earthenware manufacturers)
1809 Holden NC (earthenware-manufacturers)
1811 Holden NC (earthenware-manufacturers)
1816 Underhill P
The first partner's name is listed as Harte in 1805 Holden.

Hartley & Co.
High Street, Longton
1876 Kelly PM

Hartley, Joseph
Etruria
1870 Harrod NC-E (potter)

Hartshorne & Fernihough
Market Street, Longton
1854 Kelly CEM

Hartshorne, Fernihough & Adams
Market Street, Longton
1852 Slater CM

Harvey & Co.
Chancery Lane, Longton
1850 Kelly CEM

Harvey & Sons
Great Charles Street, Lane End
1818 Parson EM-LE
1822 Allbut CEM (earthenware manufacts.)

Harvey, Charles
Lane End
1802 Allbut EM (map locations 119 and 129)
See also: Harvey, Charles & William K.

Harvey, Charles, & Son
Charles Street, Lane End
1818 Pigot EM

Harvey, Charles, & Sons
Lane End
1805 Holden NC (earthenware manufacturers)
1809 Holden NC (earthenware-manufactory & flint-grinders)
1811 Holden NC (earthenware-manufactory & flint-grinders)
1816 Underhill P

Harvey, Charles & John
Lane End
1822 Pigot EM

Harvey, Charles & William K.
(i) Stafford Street, Longton
1841 Pigot CM; EM
1846 Williams NC-L-LE (china and earthenware manufacturers)
1850 Slater EM
1851 White CEM-L (only

earthenware)
(ii) Chancery Lane, Longton
1850 Kelly NC-L
(earthenware manufacturers)
(iii) Church Street, Longton
1851 White CEM-L (only earthenware)
The initial K. is listed as Kewright in 1841 Pigot and Kenwright in 1850 Kelly and 1850 Slater. The partners are also listed individually in 1846 Williams, with William's address given as Blurton. The firm was succeeded by Holland & Green (1860 Kelly).

Charles & William K. Harvey. Printed mark from a blue-printed earthenware plate. Note the initial H, one example has been noted with a separate impressed mark featuring the surname Harvey.

Harvey, Adams & Co.
See: Adams, Harvey, & Co.

Hassells, John
Shelton
1784 Bailey NC-Sh (potter)

Hawley & Co.
King Street, Foley, Fenton
1861 Harrison NC-F (china and earthenware manufacturers)
1862 Slater CM; EM
1864 Jones CEM
1865 Keates P-F (china and earthenware)
1867 Keates P-F (earthenware)
1869 Keates P-F (earthenware)
1870 Harrod NC-F (manufacturers of china and earthenware for home and foreign markets)
1873 Keates P-F (earthenware)
1875 Keates P-F (earthenware)
1876 Kelly EM
1879 Keates P-F (earthenware)
1880 Kelly EM
1882 Keates P-F (earthenware)
1884 Kelly EM
1887 Porter EM-F
1888 Kelly EM

Hawley, Elias, & Son.
Waterloo Road, Burslem
1828 Pigot EM

Hawley, John
(i) Great Charles Street, Lane End or Longton
1834 White EM-LE-L
1835 Pigot EM
(ii) Stafford Street, Longton
1841 Pigot EM
(iii) Foley Pottery, King Street, Fenton
1846 Williams NC-C-F-E (earthenware manufacturers)
1850 Kelly CEM; NC-S (china & earthenware manufacturer)
1850 Slater CM; EM
1851 White CEM-F
1852 Slater CM; EM
1854 Kelly CEM
1856 Kelly CEM
1860 Kelly EM
1863 Kelly EM
Hawley's house is listed as Daisy Bank in 1834 White, and just Longton in 1851 White.

Hawley, John, & Co.
Foley, Fenton
1851 White CEM-L (only earthenware)
1868 Kelly EM
Hawley's house is listed as Summer Row, Longton, in 1851 White.

Hawley, Joseph
Waterloo Road, Burslem
1830 Pigot EM
1834 White EM-B
1835 Pigot EM
1841 Pigot EM

Hawley & Brereton
Lichfield Pottery, Joiner's Square, Hanley
1889 Keates P-H

Hawley & Read
Waterloo Road, Burslem
1822 Allbut CEM (earthenware manufacturers)
1822 Pigot EM
The second partner's name is listed as Rhead in 1822 Allbut.

Hawley, Robert
Foley, Fenton
1872 Kelly EM

Hawley, Webberley & Co.
Garfield Works, High Street, Longton
1896 Kelly MM
1900 Kelly MM

Hawthorn, John
(i) Regent Street, Burslem
1852 Slater CM (china-lock furniture); EM (china door furniture, &c.)
1854 Kelly CEM
1856 Kelly CEM
(ii) Albert Street Works, Albert Street, Burslem
1860 Kelly CM-General; EM; SC (Beer Machine Handle Manufacturer); SC (China & Porcelain Door Furniture Manufacturers)
1861 Harrison NC-B (manufacturer of earthenware door and bell furniture)
1862 Slater CM (door furniture)
1863 Kelly CM-General; SC (Bell Furniture Manufacturers); SC (China & Porcelain Door Furniture Manufacturers); SC (China & Porcelain Handle Maker); SC (Knob Makers – Drawer, Hall & Door)
1864 Jones CEM (and patent knob)
1865 Keates P-B (earthen.)
1867 Keates P-B (earthen.)
(iii) Abbey Pottery, Cobridge
1880 Kelly EM
(iv) 118 Liverpool Road, Burslem
1882 Keates P-B
The surname is listed as Hawthorne in one of the entries in 1852 Slater (CM), and in 1861 Harrison, 1865 Keates, 1867 Keates, and 1882 Keates.

Hawthorn, John, & Son
Albert Street Works, Burslem
1869 Keates P-B (china, door, and bell furniture)
1870 Harrod NC-B (door and bell furniture manufacturers)
The surname is listed as Hawthorne in 1869 Keates.

Hawthorn, John, & Sons
Albert Street Works, Burslem
1868 Kelly EM

Hawthorne & Nash
Regent Street Works, Burslem
1851 White CEM-B (both)

Haywood, Howard & Richard
Brownhills Tileries, Burslem
1846 Williams NC-B
1850 Kelly NC-B

Haywood, John
Burslem
1816 Underhill P

Heap & Lownds
Amicable Street, Tunstall
1846 Williams NC-T (earthenware manufacturers)
The partners are listed individually as John Heap of High Street, Tunstall, and Thomas Lownds of Sandyford in 1846 Williams.

Heath & Son
Burslem
1796 Chester NC-B (manufacturers of earthenware)

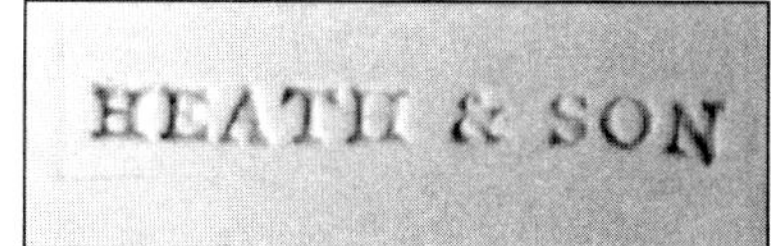

Heath & Son. Impressed mark from late 18th century stonewares.

Heath, Arthur, & Co.
Dale Hall, Burslem
1896 Kelly EM

Heath, J.
Burslem
1809 Holden NC (earthenware-manufacturer)
1811 Holden NC (earthenware-manufacturer)

Heath, John
(i) Old Sitch, Burslem
1818 Parson EM-B-Lp-C
1818 Pigot EM
1822 Allbut CEM (china and figure manufacturer)
1822 Pigot EM
(ii) Lower Hadderidge, Burslem
1865 Keates P-B (earthen.)

Heath, Joseph
(i) Newfield, Tunstall
1841 Pigot EM
(ii) High Street, Tunstall
1846 Williams NC-T (earthenware manufacturer)
1850 Slater EM
1851 White EM-T
1852 Slater EM
1854 Kelly CEM
1856 Kelly CEM
Heath's house is listed as Church Street in 1851 White.

Heath, Joseph, & Co.
Newfield, Tunstall
1828 Pigot EM
1830 Pigot EM
1834 White EM-T
1835 Pigot EM

Joseph Heath & Co. Printed mark from blue-printed earthenwares.

Heath, Lewis
Burslem
1796 Chester NC-B (manufacturer of earthenware)
1798 Universal NC-B (victualler, and manufacturer of Staffordshire-ware)
1802 Allbut EM (map location 39)

Heath, Nathan & John
Burslem
1802 Allbut EM (map location 30)

Heath, Thomas
(i) Shelton
1796 Chester NC-H-Sh (manufacturer of earthenware)
(ii) Burslem
1805 Holden NC (earthenware manufacturer)
1809 Holden NC (manufacturer of earthenware)
1811 Holden NC (manufacturer of earthenware)
1816 Underhill P
1822 Allbut CEM (earthenware manufacturer)
(iii) Hadderidge, Burslem
1818 Parson EM-B-Lp-C
1822 Pigot EM
1828 Pigot EM
1830 Pigot EM
1835 Pigot EM
(iv) near New Road, Burslem
1818 Pigot EM
(v) Beech Lane, Burslem
1834 White EM-B
(vi) High Street, Lane End
1835 Pigot CM; EM
(vii) Parkhall Street, Anchor Road, Longton
1884 Kelly MM
1882 Keates P-L (majolica and earthenware)
(viii) Baltimore Works, Albion Street, Longton
1887 Porter EM-L
1888 Kelly MM
1889 Keates P-L (majolica and earthenware)
1892 Keates P-L (majolica and earthenware)
(ix) Albion Works, High Street, Longton
1892 Kelly MM
1896 Kelly MM
1900 Kelly MM

Heath, Thomas & James
Podmore Street, Burslem
1879 Keates P-B (Rockingham)

Heath, William
High Street, Longton
1860 Kelly CTM

Heath & Bagnall
Shelton
1781 Bailey NC (potters)
1783 Bailey NC (potters)
1784 Bailey NC-Sh (potters)
The second partner's name is listed as Bagnell in 1784 Bailey.

Heath & Blackhurst
(i) Bath Street, Burslem
1865 Keates P-B (earthen.)
1867 Keates P-B (earthen.)
(ii) Hadderidge Pottery, Burslem
1868 Kelly EM
1870 Harrod NC-B (manufacturers of general earthenware, plain and decorated, for home and foreign markets)
1872 Kelly EM
1873 Keates P-B (earthenware)
1875 Keates P-B (earthenware)
1876 Kelly EM
(iii) Furlong Lane, Burslem
1869 Keates P-B (earthen.)

Heath, Blackhurst & Co.
(i) Bath Street, Burslem
1860 Kelly EM
1861 Harrison NC-B

(earthenware manufacturers)
(ii) Furlong Lane, Burslem
1862 Slater EM
(iii) Hadderidge Pottery, Burslem
1863 Kelly EM
1864 Jones EM
A London agent is listed as Charles Floyd of 2 Dorchester Place, New North Road, in 1860 Kelly. An advertisement in 1861 Harrison describes the firm simply as 'earthenware manufacturers'.

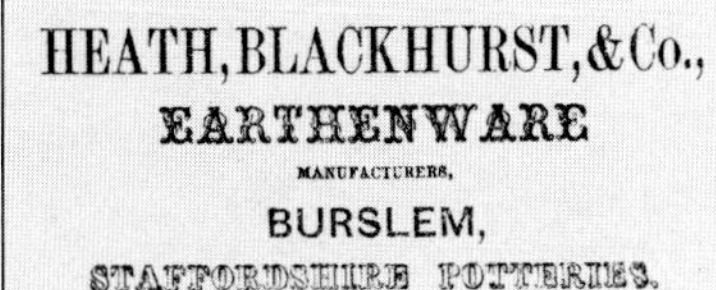

HEATH, BLACKHURST, & Co.,
EARTHENWARE
MANUFACTURERS,
BURSLEM,
STAFFORDSHIRE POTTERIES.

Heath, Blackhurst & Co. Advertisement from 1861 Harrison.

Heath, Boulton, Greenbanks & Co.
Watergate Street, Tunstall
1841 Pigot CM

Heath & Burton
St. Martin's Lane, Longton
1872 Kelly CM

Heath & Greatbatch
High Street, Burslem
1892 Kelly EM

Heath & Rigby
Waterloo Road, Burslem
1851 White CEM-B (only earthenware)

Heath & Shorthose
Hanley
1802 Allbut EM (map location 67)
1809 Holden NC (earthenware-manufactory)
1811 Holden NC (earthenware-manufactory)

Heath & Simpson
Hanley
1798 Universal NC-H (manufacturers of Staffordshire-ware)

Heath, Warburton & Co.
Hanley
1784 Bailey NC-H (china manufacturers)

Heathcote, Charles, & Co.
Lane End
1822 Allbut CEM (china and earthenware manufacturers)
1822 Pigot CM; EM

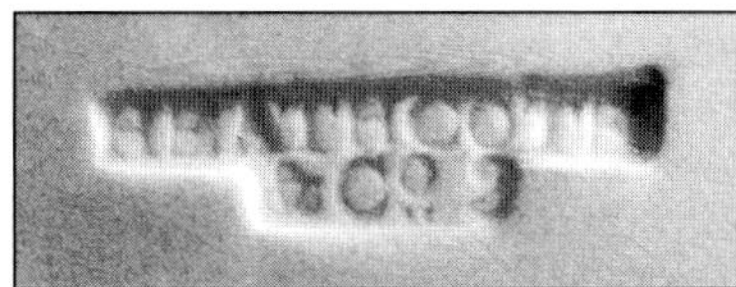

Heathcote & Co. Impressed mark from a blue-printed earthenware meat dish.

Heather, Frederick, & Co.
Kensington Works, Broad Street, Hanley
1868 Kelly CM
1870 Harrod NC-H (manufacturers of porcelain)

Hedge, Timothy
Burslem
1816 Underhill P

Henshall & Williamson
Longport
1805 Holden NC (earthenware manufacturers)
1809 Holden NC (earthenware-manufacturers in all its branches)
1811 Holden NC (earthenware-manufacturers in all its branches)
1816 Underhill P
1818 Pigot EM
1828 Pigot EM
1830 Pigot EM

Henshall, Williamson & Co.
Longport
1802 Allbut EM (map location 20)

Henshall, Williamson & Clowes
1796 Chester NC-T-Lp (manufacturers of earthenware)
1798 Universal NC-Lp (manufacturers of Staffordshire-ware)
The third partner's name is listed as Clewes in 1798 Universal.

Henshall & Williamsons
Longport
1818 Parson EM-B-Lp-C
1822 Allbut CEM (earthenware manufacts.)
1822 Pigot EM

Hett & Co.
Cannon Street, Shelton
1864 Jones EM

Hewit, John
Lane End
1802 Allbut EM (map location 122)

Hewit & Buckley
Booden Brook
1802 Allbut EM (map location 62)

Hewit & Comer
Lane End
1802 Allbut EM (map location 120)

Hewitt, John, & Son
Green Dock, Lane End
1818 Parson EM-LE
1818 Pigot EM
1822 Allbut CEM (earthenware manufact.)
1822 Pigot EM

Hibbert & Boughey
Market Street, Longton
1889 Keates P-L (china)

Hicks & Meigh
(i) Hanley
1809 Holden NC (earthenware-manufactrs.)
1811 Holden NC (earthenware-manufactrs.)
(ii) Shelton
1816 Underhill P
1818 Parson EM-H-Sh
1822 Pigot CM; EM

Hicks, Meigh & Johnson
(i) High Street, Shelton
1822 Allbut CEM (china and earthenware manufacturers)
1834 White EM-H-Sh (china mfrs. also)
1835 Pigot CM; EM
(ii) Broad Street, Shelton
1828 Pigot CM; EM
1830 Pigot CM; EM

Hicks, Meigh & Johnson. Printed mark from a green and pink printed earthenware dinner plate.

Hilditch & Co.
Church Street, Lane End
1834 White CM-LE-L (lustre mfrs.)
The firm was succeeded (presumably after Hilditch & Hopwood) by Thomas Bentley & Co. (advertisements in 1864 Jones, 1869 Keates, and 1870 Harrod).

Hilditch, Mary Ann
Peel Street
1862 Slater EM
The surname is actually listed as Hillditch, and no town is given.
See also: Hilditch & Hopwood

Hilditch, William, & Son
Lane End
1822 Pigot CM

Hilditch, William, & Sons
(i) Lane End
1822 Allbut CEM (china manufacts.)
(ii) Church Street, Lane End
1828 Pigot CM
1830 Pigot CM

William Hilditch & Son(s). Printed mark from a blue-printed china cup.

Hilditch, William & John
Church Street, Lane End
1835 Pigot CM

Hilditch & Hopwood
Church Street, Longton
1835 Pigot CM
1841 Pigot CM
1846 Williams NC-L-LE (china manufacturers)
1850 Kelly CEM; NC-L (china manufacturers)
1850 Slater CM
1851 White CEM-L
1852 Slater CM
1854 Kelly CEM
1856 Kelly CEM
The partners are listed individually as Mary Ann Hilditch of Furnace Road and William Hopwood of Church Street in 1846 Williams. The firm was succeeded by William Hopwood (1864 Jones advertisement), then by Dale, Page & Co. (advertisements in 1869 Keates, 1873 Keates, and 1875 Keates), and eventually by Dale, Page & Goodwin at the New Town Pottery, High Street, Longton (1879 Keates, 1880 Kelly).

Hilditch & Martin
Lane End
1818 Parson EM-LE

Hilditch & Morton
Lane End
1818 Pigot CM
The address is listed as 'near toll-bar'.

Hill & Co.
St. James' Works, High Street, Longton
1900 Kelly CM

Hill, George
12 Rushton Road, Burslem
1887 Porter EM-B

Hill, John
Wharf Street, Stoke
1861 Harrison NC-S (parian manufacturer)

Hill, Leveson
(i) Eldon Street, Stoke
1856 Kelly PM
(ii) 49 Wharf Street, Stoke
1860 Kelly PM
1862 Slater PM
1863 Kelly PM
1864 Jones A; PM
1865 Keates A; P-S (parian)
1867 Keates A; P-S (parian)
1868 Kelly PM
1869 Keates P-S (parian)
1870 Harrod NC-S (parian manufacturers)
The first name is listed as Levison in 1856 Kelly. All listings at the Wharf Street address indicate that the firm was in the hands of executors. The advertisements describe the firm as 'ornamental parian manufacturers' (1864 Jones), or 'manufacturers of parian, statuettes, &c., &c.' (1865 Keates and 1867 Keates). In 1867 the works are described as 'within two minutes walk of the railway station'. All three advertisements are in the name of the executors.

THE EXECUTORS OF LEVESON HILL,
ORNAMENTAL PARIAN
MANUFACTURERS,
Wharf Street, STOKE-UPON-TRENT,
STAFFORDSHIRE POTTERIES.

Leveson Hill. Advertisement from 1864 Jones.

THE EXECUTORS OF LEVESON HILL,
MANUFACTURERS OF
PARIAN, STATUETTES,
&c., &c.,
WHARF-ST., STOKE-UPON-TRENT,
STAFFORDSHIRE POTTERIES.

Leveson Hill. Advertisement from 1865 Keates.

THE EXECUTORS OF LEVESON HILL,
MANUFACTURERS OF
PARIAN, STATUETTES,
&c., &c.,
WHARF STREET,
STOKE-UPON-TRENT,
(Within two minutes walk of the Railway Station.)
STAFFORDSHIRE POTTERIES.

Leveson Hill. Advertisement from 1867 Keates.

Hill, M. (Mrs.)
High Street, Stoke
1860 Kelly PM

Hill Pottery (The)
Liverpool Road, Burslem
1862 Slater CM; EM; PM

Hill Pottery Co. Ltd.
Liverpool Road, Burslem
1865 Keates P-B (china, earthenware, majolica, parian)
1867 Keates P-B (china, earthenware, majolica, parian)
The manager is listed as George Alcock in both directories.

Hillditch, Mary Ann
See: Hilditch, Mary Ann

Hines Brothers
Heron Cross Pottery, Fenton
1887 Porter EM-F,
1892 Keates P-F (porcelain)
1900 Kelly EM
Although there is no entry in the directory, an advertisement in 1889

Keates describes the firm as 'manufacturers of opaque porcelaine (sic), in dinner, tea, breakfast, and toilet ware, for home & colonial markets'. It also lists London showrooms at 20 Thavies Inn, Holborn, and offers 'pattern sheets and price lists sent free on application'.

Hines Brothers. Advertisement from 1889 Keates.

Hobson & Co.
(i) Adelaide Works, Heathcote Road, Longton
1889 Keates P-L (majolica and earthenware)
1892 Keates P-L (majolica and earthenware)
1892 Kelly, EM; MM
(ii) Brewery (or Drewery) Works, Normacott Road, Longton
1896 Kelly SC (Sanitary Ware Manufacturers)
1900 Kelly SC (Sanitary Ware Manufacturers)

Hobson, Charles
Albert Street, Burslem
1865 Keates P-B (earthen.)
1867 Keates P-B (earthen.)
1868 Kelly EM
1869 Keates P-B (earthen.)
1870 Harrod NC-B (earthenware manufacturer)
1872 Kelly EM
1876 Kelly EM
1880 Kelly EM

Hobson, Charles, & Son
Albert Street, Burslem
1873 Keates P-B (earthenware)
1875 Keates P-B (earthenware)

Hobson, Ephraim
(i) Cobridge
1800 Allbutt NC-C (toy manufacturer)
1811 Holden NC (Egyptian-black & toy-manufacturer)
1818 Parson EM-B-Lp-C
(ii) Shelton
1809 Holden NC (Egyptian-black & toy-manufacturer)

Hobson, George & John
Albert Street, Burslem
1879 Keates P-B (earthenware)
1882 Keates P-B (earthenware)
1884 Kelly EM
1887 Porter EM-B
1888 Kelly EM
1889 Keates P-B (earthenware)
1892 Keates P-B (earthenware)
1892 Kelly EM
1896 Kelly EM
1900 Kelly EM
The firm is listed as John & George Hobson in the four Keates directories.

Hobson, John & George
See: Hobson, George & John

Hobson, T., & Co.
Cornhill, Longton
1863 Kelly EM

Hobson, Thomas, & Co.
Church Street, Longton
1864 Jones A; EM
1865 Keates P-L (earthenware)
The advertisement in 1864 Jones describes the firm simply as 'earthenware manufacturers, enamellers, lusterers, &c.'

Thomas Hobson & Co. Advertisement from 1864 Jones.

Hobson & Moston
Clayton Street, Longton
1868 Kelly CM

Hodgkinson, Elijah
(i) Mayer Street Works, High Street, Hanley
1867 Keates A; P-H (stone and parian)
1868 Kelly PM; SM
1869 Keates A; P-H (earthenware and parian)
1870 Harrod NC-H (earthenware, stone, and parian manufacturer)
1872 Kelly PM; SM
(ii) 26 Albion Place, Hanley
1869 Keates A; P-H (earthenware and parian)
The advertisements in 1867 Keates and 1869 Keates both describe Hodgkinson as a 'manufacturer of useful and ornamental stone, parian, &c.' An additional address is given as 4 Renalagh Street, Bethesda Street, in the 1867 advertisement.

ELIJAH HODGKINSON,
MANUFACTURER
OF USEFUL AND ORNAMENTAL
STONE, PARIAN, &c.
MAYER STREET WORKS, HIGH STREET,
HANLEY,
STAFFORDSHIRE POTTERIES.
4, RENALAGH STREET, BETHESDA STREET.

Elijah Hodgkinson. Advertisement from 1867 Keates.

ELIJAH HODGKINSON,
MANUFACTURER OF
USEFUL AND ORNAMENTAL STONE,
PARIAN. ETC.
Mayer Street Works, High Street, Hanley,
STAFFORDSHIRE POTTERIES.
26, ALBION PLACE, HANLEY.

Elijah Hodgkinson. Advertisement from 1869 Keates.

NEW STREET WORKS
WM. HODGKINSON,
Parian, Fancy Stone & Earthenware
MANUFACTURER,
NEW STREET, HANLEY, POTTERIES.

William Hodgkinson. Advertisement from 1867 Keates.

Hodgkinson, William
New Street, Hanley
1867 Keates A; P-H (parian and earthenware)
The advertisement in 1867 Keates

describes Hodgkinson as a 'parian, fancy stone & earthenware manufacturer'.

Hodson & Co.
High Street, Longton
1876 Kelly CM
1880 Kelly CM

Hodson, Richard
(i) Church Street, Longton
1850 Kelly CEM; NC-L (china manufacturer)
1851 White CEM-L
1852 Slater CM
1854 Kelly CEM
(ii) New Street, Longton
1860 Kelly CM-General
(iii) Chancery Lane, Longton
1860 Kelly CM-General
1861 Harrison NC-L (china manufacturer)
1862 Slater CM
1863 Kelly P (china)
1864 Jones CEM
1865 Keates P-L (china)
1867 Keates P-L (china)
1868 Kelly CM
1869 Keates P-L (china)
1872 Kelly CM
(iv) High Street, Longton
1873 Keates P-L (china)
1875 Keates P-L (china)
Hodson's house is listed as Bridge Street in 1851 White.

Hodson, Richard, & Co.
(i) Chancery Lane, Longton
1870 Harrod NC-L (china manufacturers)
(ii) High Street, Longton
1879 Keates P-L (china)
1882 Keates P-L (china)

Holcroft, Hill & Mellor
See: Holdcroft, Hill & Mellor

Holcroft & Wood
See: Holdcroft & Wood

Holdcott, John
Chapel Lane, Burslem
1850 Slater SC (Saggar Makers)

Holdcraft, Peter, & Co.
See: Holdcroft, Peter A., & Co.

Holdcroft & Co.
Queen Street Pottery, Burslem
1870 Harrod NC-B (earthenware manufacturers)

Holdcroft, J.P.
George Street, Tunstall
1896 Kelly EM
1900 Kelly EM

Holdcroft, Joseph
(i) St. Martin's Lane, Longton
1865 Keates A; P-L (silver lustre)
1867 Keates P-L (silver lustre)
1868 Kelly LM (silver)
1869 Keates P-L (silver lustre)
1870 Harrod NC-L (parian and lustre manufacturer)
1872 Kelly LM (silver)
1873 Keates P-L (silver lustre)
1875 Keates P-L (silver lustre)
(ii) Sutherland Pottery, Daisy Bank, Longton
1872 Kelly LM (silver)
1876 Kelly LM
1879 Keates P-L (silver lustre & majolica)
1880 Kelly MM (manufacturer of majolica statuettes, silvered goods &c. &c. in every variety)
1882 Keates P-L (silver lustre & majolica)
1884 Kelly MM
1887 Porter EM-L
1888 Kelly MM
1889 Keates P-L (silver lustre & majolica)
1892 Keates P-L (silver lustre and majolica)
1892 Kelly MM
1896 Kelly EM; MM
1900 Kelly EM; MM
The advertisement in 1865 Keates describes Holdcroft as a 'silver lustre manufacturer' and promises that 'all orders entrusted to his care will be punctually attended to'.

Joseph Holdcroft. Advertisement from 1865 Keates.

Holdcroft, Peter
See: Holdcroft, Peter A., & Co.

Holdcroft, Peter A., & Co.
Lower Works, Fountain Place, Burslem
1846 Williams NC-B (earthenware manufacturers)
1850 Kelly CEM; NC-B (earthenware manfrs.)
1851 White CEM-B (only earthenware)
The surname is listed as Holdcraft in 1850 Kelly. The partners are listed individually as Peter Holdcroft of Pleasant Street, Samuel Sherratt of Navigation Road, and Charles Collinson of Sytch in 1846 Williams.

Holdcroft, William
(i) 132 Liverpool Road, Burslem
1869 Keates P-B (earthen.)
1873 Keates P-B (earthenware)
1875 Keates P-B (earthenware)
1879 Keates P-B (earthenware)
(ii) George Street, Tunstall
1872 Kelly EM
1873 Keates P-T (earthenware)
1875 Keates P-T (earthenware)
1876 Kelly EM
1879 Keates P-T (earthenware)
1880 Kelly EM
1882 Keates P-T (earthenware)
1884 Kelly EM
1887 Porter EM-T
1888 Kelly EM
1889 Keates P-T (earthenware)
1892 Keates P-T (earthenware)
1892 Kelly EM
(iii) 116 Liverpool Road, Burslem
1882 Keates P-B (earthenware)
1889 Keates P-B (earthenware)
1892 Keates P-B (earthenware)

Holdcroft & Box
Cobridge
1818 Parson EM-B-Lp-C

Holdcroft, Hill & Mellor
(i) High Street, Burslem
1860 Kelly EM
1861 Harrison NC-B (earthenware manufacturers)
1862 Slater EM
1863 Kelly EM
1864 Jones EM
1865 Keates P-B (earthenware)
(ii) Queen Street, Burslem
1867 Keates P-B (earthenware)
1868 Kelly EM
1869 Keates P-B (earthenware)
The first partner's name is listed as Holcroft in 1860 Kelly and 1861 Harrison.

Holdcroft & Wood
George Street, Tunstall
1863 Kelly EM
1864 Jones EM
1865 Keates P-T (earthen.)
1867 Keates P-T (earthen.)
1868 Kelly EM
1869 Keates P-T (earthen.)
1870 Harrod NC-T (earthenware manufacturers for home and foreign markets)
The first partner's name is listed as Holcroft in 1870 Harrod.

Holden, John
Knowl Works, Burslem
1846 Williams NC-B (earthenware manufacturer)
Holden's house is listed as Furlong Place in 1846 Williams.

Holland & Co.
Burslem
1796 Chester NC-B (manufacturers of earthenware)
1802 Allbut EM (map location 25)

Holland, Ann
(i) Hill Top, Burslem
1818 Parson EM-B-Lp-C
(ii) Liverpool Road, Burslem
1822 Pigot EM
1834 White EM-B (shining black)
1835 Pigot EM (black)
1841 Pigot EM
1846 Williams NC-B (black works)
The first name is listed as Anne in 1818 Parson and 1846 Williams.

Holland, Ann, & Co.
(i) Burslem
1822 Allbut CEM (shining black manufacts.)
(ii) Liverpool Road, Burslem
1830 Pigot EM

Holland, J.
Tunstall
1854 Kelly CEM
The initial J stands for John.
(see marks on right.)

Holland, James
See: Hall, Ralph, & Co.

Holland, Thomas
(i) Burslem
1784 Bailey NC-B (manufacturer of black and red china ware and gilder)
1796 Chester NC-B (manufacturer of earthenware)
1802 Allbut EM (map location 37)
1809 Holden NC (earthenware-manufacturer)
1811 Holden NC (earthenware-manufacturer)
1816 Underhill P
(ii) Church Street, Burslem
1828 Pigot EM (toy only)
1830 Pigot EM (toy only)

Holland & Dobson
Burslem
1798 Universal NC-B (manufacturers of Staffordshire-ware and printers)

Holland & Green
(i) Stafford Street, Longton
1852 Slater EM
1860 Kelly CM-General; EM
1862 Slater EM
1863 Kelly CM-General
1864 Jones A; CEM
1865 Keates A; P-L (earthenware)
1867 Keates A; P-L (earthenware)
1868 Kelly EM
1869 Keates P-L (earthenware)
1870 Harrod NC-L (china and earthenware manufacturers for home and foreign markets)
1872 Kelly EM

John Holland. printed mark from a blue-printed earthenware tureen stand. The registration diamond dates from 1852.

1873 Keates P-L (earthenware)
1875 Keates P-L (earthenware)
1876 Kelly EM
1879 Keates P-L (earthenware)
1880 Kelly EM (for home & export)
(ii) High Street, Longton
1870 Harrod NC-L (china and earthenware manufacturers for home and foreign markets)
This firm succeeded C. & W.K. Harvey (1860 Kelly). The advertisements describe the firm as 'manufacturers of ironstone china, decorated and plain earthenware of all kinds' (1864 Jones), or 'white granite, decorated and plain earthenware manufacturers, of all kinds' (1865 Keates and 1867 Keates).

HOLLAND & GREEN,
MANUFACTURERS OF
IRONSTONE CHINA;
DECORATED AND PLAIN EARTHENWARE
OF ALL KINDS.
STAFFORD STREET, LONGTON,
STAFFORDSHIRE POTTERIES.

Holland & Green. Advertisement from 1864 Jones.

HOLLAND AND GREEN,
WHITE GRANITE,
Decorated & Plain Earthenware Manufacturers,
OF ALL KINDS,
STAFFORD STREET, LONGTON,
STAFFORDSHIRE POTTERIES.

Holland & Green. Advertisement from 1865 Keates. The same advertisement appeared in 1867 Keates.

Holland & Pearson
Liverpool Road, Burslem
1828 Pigot EM

Hollings & Co.
Brook Street, Shelton
1818 Parson EM-H-Sh

Hollings, Thomas & John
See: Hollins, Thomas & John

Hollings, Warburton & Co.
See: Hollins, Warburton & Co.

Hollins & Co.
5 Mayer Street, Hanley
1888 Kelly EM
1892 Kelly EM

Hollins, Henry
Queen Anne Pottery, Shelton, Hanley
1889 Keates P-H

Hollins, J., & Co.
Pallissy Pottery, Mayer Street, Hanley
1889 Keates A; P-H (jet & Rockingham)
The advertisement in 1889 Keates describes the firm as 'manufacturers of decorated jet, Rockingham, etc.' and gives their address as the Mayer Street Pottery. The main text promotes a novel teapot design and reads: 'Speciality in decorated jet teapots. Inventors and patentees of the "Eureka" teapot, which is an improvement over all teapots ever brought out in earthenware and china. It is a combination of teapot and tea brewing attachment; can be used with the brewer in until all that is healthy has been extracted, when the cylinder containing the spent leaves can be removed, thereby preventing tea tannin, which is injurious to health. The cover that fits the cylinder will also fit the teapot when it is removed, making it complete with or without the brewer.'

Hollins, Joseph, & Co.
King Street Jet and Rockingham Works, Hanley
1887 Porter EM-H
An advertisement in 1887 Porter describes the firm simply as 'Rockingham and jet manufacturers'.

JOSEPH HOLLINS & CO.
ROCKINGHAM
AND
Jet Manufacturers,
KING STREET WORKS,
HANLEY.

Joseph Hollins & Co. Advertisement from 1887 Porter.

Hollins, M.
See: Minton & Hollins

Hollins, Samuel
(i) Shelton
1781 Bailey NC (potter)
1783 Bailey NC (potter)
1784 Bailey NC-Sh (potter)
1796 Chester NC-H-Sh (manufacturer of earthenware)
(ii) Vale Pleasant
1798 Universal NC-V (manufacturer of Staffordshire-ware)
1802 Allbut EM (map location 95)

J. HOLLINS & Co.,
MANUFACTURERS OF
DECORATED JET, ROCKINGHAM, ETC.,
MAYER STREET POTTERY,
HANLEY, STAFF.
SPECIALITY IN DECORATED JET TEAPOTS.
INVENTORS AND PATENTEES OF THE "EUREKA" TEAPOT,
Which is an improvement over all Teapots ever brought out in Earthenware and China. It is a combination of Teapot and Tea Brewing Attachment; can be used with the brewer in until all that is healthy has been extracted, when the cylinder containing the spent leaves can be removed, thereby preventing tea tannin, which is injurious to health. The cover that fits the cylinder will also fit the teapot when it is removed, making it complete with or without the brewer.

J. Hollins & Co. Advertisement from 1889 Keates.

The surname is listed as Hollis in 1798 Universal.

Samuel Hollins. Impressed mark from a drab stoneware jug.

Hollins, Thomas jun., & Co.
Shelton
1809 Holden NC (earthenware-manufacturers)
1811 Holden NC (earthenware-manufacturers)

Hollins, Thomas & John
(i) Shelton
1796 Chester NC-H-Sh (manufacturers of earthenware)
(ii) Hanley
1798 Universal NC-H (manufacturers of Staffordshire-ware)
1802 Allbut EM (map location 74)
1805 Holden NC (earthenware manufacturers)
1809 Holden NC (earthenware-manufactory)
1811 Holden NC (earthenware-manufactory)
The surname is listed as Hollings in 1798 Universal.

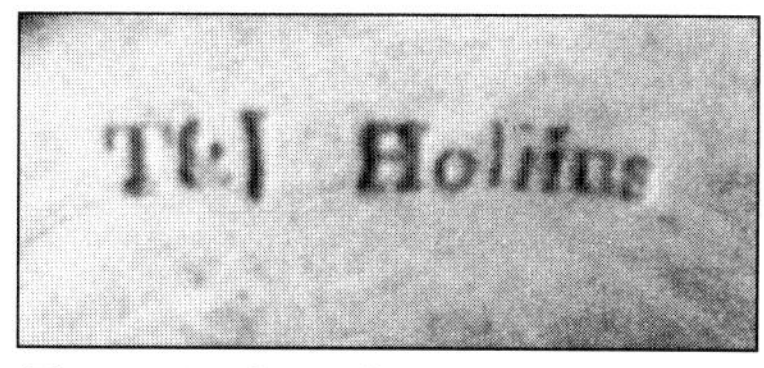

Thomas & John Hollins. Impressed mark from sprig-decorated stonewares.

Hollins, Thomas, John & Richard
(i) Hanley
1816 Underhill P
(ii) Upper Hanley
1818 Parson EM-H-Sh
(iii) Far (or Fare) Green, Hanley
1818 Pigot EM
1822 Pigot EM

Hollins, Daniels, Warburton & Co.
New Hall, Shelton
1828 Pigot EM

Hollins, Johnson & Co.
Palissy Pottery, Mayer Street, Hanley
1892 Keates A; P-H (jet and Rockingham)
The advertisement in 1892 Keates describes the firm as 'manufacturers of jet, Rockingham, speciality in earthenware, &c.' and mentions a 'special line in decorated teapots'.

Hollins, Johnson & Co. Advertisement from 1892 Keates.

Hollins, Warburton & Co.
(i) Shelton
1796 Chester NC-H-Sh (porcelain manufacturers)
1798 Universal NC-Sh (china manufacturers)
1802 Allbut EM (map location 63)
(ii) Hanley
1816 Underhill P
The first partner's name is listed as Hollings in 1798 Universal.

Hollins, Warburton, Daniel & Co.
(i) Shelton
1805 Holden NC (manufacturers of real china)
1809 Holden NC (manufacturers of real china)
1811 Holden NC (manufacturers of real china)
(ii) New Hall Street, Shelton
1822 Allbut CEM (china manufacturers)
1830 Pigot CM

Hollins, Warburton, Daniels & Co.
(i) Hanley
1818 Pigot CM
(ii) Shelton
1822 Pigot CM

Hollinshead & Griffiths
Chelsea Works, Moorland Road, Burslem
1889 Keates P-B
1892 Keates P-B
1892 Kelly CM; EM
1896 Kelly CM
1900 Kelly CM; EM

Hollinshead & Kirkham
(i) New Wharf Pottery, Navigation Street, Burslem
1875 Keates P-B
(ii) Woodland Pottery, Woodland Street, Tunstall
1876 Kelly EM
1879 Keates P-T (earthenware)
1880 Kelly EM
1882 Keates P-T (earthenware)
1884 Kelly CM; EM; JM; RM
1887 Porter EM-T
1888 Kelly EM
1889 Keates P-T
(iii) Unicorn Pottery, Amicable Street, Tunstall
1892 Keates P-T (earthenware)
1892 Kelly EM
1896 Kelly EM
1900 Kelly EM

Hollinson, James
Etruscan Pottery, High Street, Longton
Although no entry is listed in the directory, an advertisement in 1900 Kelly describes James Hollinson as 'late Hollinson & Goodall (Est. 1877)' and as a 'manufacturer of decorated toilet sets, dinner sets, tea sets, &c.' It also lists 'vases and flower pots in all shades and varieties' and gives as a speciality 'enamelled and gilt dinner sets'. Readers are urged 'Don't fail to send for our illustrated price lists, forwarded gratis'.

Hollinson & Goodall
23 High Street, Longton
1884 Kelly CM
1884 Kelly EM
1887 Porter EM-L
1892 Keates P-L (earthenware and china)
The firm was succeeded by James Hollinson (1900 Kelly). An advertisement in 1892 Keates gives the address as 28 High Street and describes the firm as 'manufacturers of china & earthenware, for home and colonies'. It also claims that they were established in 1877.

ESTABLISHED 1877.
Hollinson and Goodall,
MANUFACTURERS OF
CHINA & EARTHENWARE,
FOR HOME AND COLONIES,
28, HIGH STREET, LONGTON,
STAFFORDSHIRE.

Hollinson & Goodall. Advertisement from 1892 Keates

Hollis, Samuel
See: Hollins, Samuel

Holloway, John
73 Market Street, Hanley
1862 Slater CM
1864 Jones PM
1865 Keates P-H (parian)
1867 Keates P-H (parian)

Holmes & Son
Clayton Street, Longton
1900 Kelly EM

Holmes, Charles
High Street, Hanley
1873 Keates P-H (earthenware)
1875 Keates P-H (earthenware)
1876 Kelly EM

Holmes & Leese
Bourne's Bank, Burslem
1892 Keates P-B

JAMES . . . HOLLINSON, LATE HOLLINSON & GOODALL (Est. 1877).
ETRUSCAN POTTERY,
HIGH STREET, LONGTON, STAFFS.
MANUFACTURER OF Decorated Toilet Sets, Dinner Sets, Tea Sets, &c.
Vases and Flower Pots in all shades and varieties.
Speciality:—ENAMELLED and GILT DINNER SETS.
Don't fail to send for our Illustrated Price Lists, forwarded gratis.
[5] . . TELEGRAMS:—"JAMES HOLLINSON, LONGTON."

James Hollinson. Advertisement from 1900 Kelly.

Holmes, Plant & Co.
Silvester Pottery, Burslem
1887 Porter EM-B

Holmes, Plant & Madew
Sylvester Pottery, Nile Street, Burslem
1876 Kelly EM
1880 Kelly EM
1884 Kelly EM
1879 Keates P-B (earthenware)
1882 Keates P-B (earthenware)
The third partner's name is listed as Maydew in 1879 Keates and 1882 Keates.

Holmes, Plant & Whitehurst
Nelson Place, Hanley
1873 Keates P-H (door furniture)
1875 Keates P-H (door furniture)

Holmes, Stonier & Hollinshead
(i) Upper Hanley Works, Hanley
1879 Keates P-H (earthenware)
(ii) High Street, Hanley
1880 Kelly EM

Holt, John William
Clarence Works, High Street, Longton
1900 Kelly CM

Hood, G.
Church Works, Burslem
1854 Kelly CEM

Hood, George
(i) Tunstall
1822 Pigot EM (toy only)
1830 Pigot EM
(ii) Brownhills
1834 White EM-B (Egyptian black mfrs. only)
1835 Pigot EM
(iii) Navigation Road, Burslem
1841 Pigot EM
(iv) Nile Street, Burslem
1850 Slater TOCM
(v) Bourne's Bank, Burslem
1851 White CEM-B (only earthenware)
(vi) Commercial Street, Burslem
1852 Slater EM
(vii) Parker Street, Shelton, Hanley
1856 Kelly CEM
1860 Kelly EM
1861 Harrison NC-H-Sh (black and Rockingham earthstone manufacturer)
(viii) Wharf Lane, Hanley
1862 Slater EM
1863 Kelly EM
1864 Jones EM (brown)
Hood's house is listed as Queen Street in 1851 White.

Hope, F.
See: Fielding, S., & Co.

Hope & Carter. Printed mark from a brown printed earthenware soup plate. The registration diamond dates from 1867 but was taken out by Ford, Challinor & Co. Note that the initials D.W. are found on wares by various manufacturers and probably relate to an as yet unidentified retailer.

Hope & Carter
Fountain Place, Burslem
1862 Slater EM
1863 Kelly CM-General
1864 Jones EM
1865 Keates P-B (earthenware and ironstone)
1867 Keates P-B (earthen.)
1868 Kelly EM
1869 Keates P-B (earthen.)
1870 Harrod NC-B (earthenware manufacturers)
1872 Kelly EM
1873 Keates P-B (earthen.)
1875 Keates P-B (earthen.)
1876 Kelly EM
1879 Keates P-B (earthen.)
1880 Kelly EM

Hopkin, Peter
Market Place, Burslem
1834 White EM-B
1835 Pigot EM
The surname is listed as Hopkins in 1834 White.

Hopkin, Peter & Co.
Market Place, Burslem
1841 Pigot EM

Hopkins & Co.
Hose Street, Tunstall
1896 Kelly SC (Enamelled Tile Manufacturers)

Hopkins, Peter
See: Hopkin, Peter

Hopkinson, James
Ranelagh Street, Hanley
1887 Porter EM-H

Hopkinson, Richard & Edward
York Street, Shelton
1846 Williams NC-Sh (china manufacturers)
The partners are listed individually as Richard Hopkinson of Sheaf Street and Edward Hopkinson of Sun Street in 1846 Williams.

Hopkinson, William
148 Hope Street, Hanley
1862 Slater PM

Hopwood, William
Church Street, Longton
1860 Kelly CM-General
1861 Harrison NC-L (china manufacturer)
1862 Slater CM
1863 Kelly CM-General
1864 Jones A; CEM
1865 Keates P-L (china)
1867 Keates P-L (china)
The firm is noted as being in the hands of trustees in 1860 Kelly, 1861 Harrison, and 1863 Kelly, and in the hands of executors in 1862 Slater, 1864 Jones, 1865 Keates, and 1867 Keates. The manager is listed as Joseph Dale in 1862 Slater. The firm was succeeded by Dale, Page & Co. (1869 Keates, 1873 Keates, 1875

Keates). The advertisement in 1864 Jones appears in the name of 'the trustees of the late W. Hopwood (formerly Hilditch & Hopwood)'. It describes the firm simply as 'china manufacturers'.
See also: Hilditch and Hopwood

THE TRUSTEES OF THE LATE W. HOPWOOD,
(FORMERLY HILDITCH & HOPWOOD),
China Manufacturers,
LONGTON,
STAFFORDSHIRE POTTERIES.

William Hopwood. Advertisement from 1864 Jones.

Horn, John
Brimleyford
1802 Allbut EM (map location 15)

Howlett & Co.
Peel Street, Northwood, Hanley
1896 Kelly EM
1900 Kelly EM

Howlett, Joseph Redfern
Peel Street, Northwood, Hanley
1887 Porter EM-H
1888 Kelly EM
1892 Keates P-H
1892 Kelly EM

Howson, George
(i) Silvester Square, Burslem
1864 Jones EM
1865 Keates P-B (black and lustre)
(ii) Paxton Street, Hanley
1867 Keates P-H (sanitary ware)
1869 Keates P-H (sanitary ware)
1870 Harrod NC-H (sanitary ware manufacturer)
(iii) 9 Clifford Street, Eastwood Vale, Hanley
1873 Keates P-H (sanitary ware)
1875 Keates P-H (sanitary ware)
1876 Kelly SC (Sanitary Ware Manufacturers)
1879 Keates P-H (sanitary ware)
1880 Kelly SC (Sanitary Ware Manufacturers)
1882 Keates P-H (sanitary ware)
1884 Kelly SC (Sanitary Ware Manufacturers)
1887 Porter EM-H
1888 Kelly SC (Sanitary Ware Manufacturers)
1889 Keates P-H (sanitary ware)
1892 Keates P-H (sanitary ware)
(iv) Clifford and Ephraim Streets, Eastwood, Hanley
1892 Kelly SC (Sanitary Ware Manufacturers)
1896 Kelly SC (Sanitary Ware Manufacturers)

Howson, George, & Sons Ltd.
Clifford & Ephraim Streets, Eastwood, Hanley
1900 Kelly SC (Sanitary Ware Manufacturers)

Howson, W.
Eastwood Vale, Hanley
1868 Kelly SC (Sanitary Ware Manufacturers)

Hudden, John Thomas
(i) Stafford Street, Longton
1862 Slater A; EM
1863 Kelly EM
1864 Jones A; EM
1865 Keates P-L (earthenware)
1867 Keates P-L (earthenware)
1868 Kelly EM
1869 Keates P-L (earthenware)
1870 Harrod NC-L (earthenware manufacturer for home and foreign markets)
1872 Kelly EM
1876 Kelly EM
(ii) Anchor Works, Anchor Road, Longton
1873 Keates P-L (earthenware)
1875 Keates P-L (earthenware)
1879 Keates P-L (earthenware)
1882 Keates P-L (earthenware)
The advertisements in 1862 Slater and 1864 Jones both describe Hudden simply as an 'earthenware manufacturer'.

J. T. HUDDEN,
EARTHENWARE
MANUFACTURER,
STAFFORD ST., LONGTON,
Staffordshire Potteries.

John Thomas Hudden. Advertisement from 1862 Slater.

J. T. HUDDEN,
EARTHENWARE MANUFACTURER
STAFFORD STREET,
LONGTON.

John Thomas Hudden. Advertisement from 1864 Jones.

John Thomas Hudden. Printed mark from a blue-printed earthenware dessert plate.

Hudson Brothers
Stafford Street, Longton
1879 Keates P-L (china)

Hudson & Son
Stafford Street, Longton
1875 Keates P-L (earthenware)

WM. HUDSON,
CHINA MANUFACTURER
For Home and Foreign Markets,
ALMA WORKS,
HIGH STREET,
LONGTON.

William Hudson. Advertisement from 1889 Keates.

Hudson, William
(i) Alma Works, High Street, Longton
1889 Keates A; P-L (china)
1892 Kelly CM
(ii) Sutherland Works, Normacot Road, Longton
1892 Keates P-L (china)
1896 Kelly CM
1900 Kelly CM
The advertisement in 1889 Keates describes Hudson as a 'china manufacturer for home and foreign markets'.

Hudson, William, & Son
Stafford Street, Longton
1880 Kelly CM (china manufacturers for home & export)
1884 Kelly CM
1887 Porter EM-L
1888 Kelly CM

Hudson, William, & Sons
Stafford Street, Longton
1882 Keates P-L (china)

Hughes & Co.
Globe Pottery, Waterloo Road, Cobridge
1896 Kelly CM; EM

Hughes, Edward, & Co.
Opal China Works, Fenton
1889 Keates P-F
1892 Keates P-F
1892 Kelly CM
1896 Kelly CM
1900 Kelly CM

Hughes, Elijah
(i) Bleak Hill Pottery, Waterloo Road, Cobridge
1852 Slater EM
1854 Kelly CEM
1856 Kelly CEM
1860 Kelly EM
1861 Harrison NC-B (earthenware manufacturer)
1862 Slater EM
1863 Kelly EM
1864 Jones EM-Miscellaneous (granite-colored stone bodies in jugs, &c.)
(ii) Bleak Street, Burslem
1865 Keates P-B (earthenware)
1867 Keates P-B (earthenware)

Hughes, Elijah
See: Hughes, Stephen & Elijah

Hughes, John V.
Bleakhill Pottery, Cobridge
1864 Jones EM

Hughes, Peter & Thomas
Lane End
1805 Holden NC (earthenware manufacturers)
1809 Holden NC (earthenware-manufacts.)
1811 Holden NC (earthenware-manufacturers)
1816 Underhill P

Hughes, Samuel
Lane End
1796 Chester NC-LE-LD-LL (manufacturer of earthenware)
1802 Allbut EM (map location 124)

Hughes, Samuel, & Sons
Lane End
1798 Universal NC-LE (manufacturers of Staffordshire-ware)

Hughes, Stephen
Waterloo Road, Burslem
1852 Slater EM
1854 Kelly CEM
A Dublin address at New Row West is listed in 1852 Slater.
See also: Hughes, Stephen & Elijah

Hughes, Stephen, & Co.
Cobridge
1835 Pigot EM
1841 Pigot EM

Hughes, Stephen & Elijah
(i) Burslem
1846 Williams NC-B (earthenware & colour manufacturers)
(ii) Bleak Hill, Cobridge
1850 Slater EM
(iii) Grange Cottages, Cobridge
1851 White CEM-B (only earthenware)
The partners are listed individually as Stephen Hughes and Elijah Hughes, both of Waterloo Road, Burslem, in 1846 Williams.

Hughes, Thomas
(i) Lane Delph
1818 Parson EM-LE
1818 Pigot EM
(ii) Cobridge Villa
1830 Pigot EM
1834 White EM-B
(iii) Waterloo Road, Burslem
1856 Kelly CEM
1860 Kelly EM
1861 Harrison NC-B (earthenware manufacturer)
1862 Slater EM
1863 Kelly EM
1864 Jones EM
1865 Keates P-B (earthen.)
1867 Keates P-B (earthen.)
1868 Kelly EM
1869 Keates P-B (earthen.)
1870 Harrod NC-B (manufacturer of earthenware, merchant, &c.)
1873 Keates P-B (earthen.)
1875 Keates P-B (earthen.)
1879 Keates P-B (earthen)
(iv) 2A Waterloo Road, Burslem, and Top Bridge Works, Longport
1872 Kelly EM
1876 Kelly EM
1880 Kelly EM
1882 Keates P-B (earthenware and flint manufacturer)
(v) Top Bridge Works, Longport
1884 Kelly EM
1887 Porter EM-B
1888 Kelly EM
1889 Keates P-B (earthenware and flint manufacturer)
1892 Keates P-B (earthenware and flint manufacturer)
1892 Kelly EM
1896 Kelly EM
Hughes' house is listed as Waterloo Road, Burslem, in 1834 White.

Hughes, Thomas, & Son
Longport
1900 Kelly EM

Hughes & Robinson
Globe Pottery, Waterloo Road, Cobridge
1889 Keates P-B (earthenware)
1892 Keates P-B (earthenware)
1892 Kelly EM

Hughes & Taylor
Cobridge
1828 Pigot EM

Hull, Arthur John
Normacot Road, Longton
1900 Kelly CM; EM

Hulme, Henry
Kilncroft, Burslem
1879 Keates P-B (Rockingham)

Hulme, James
Flint Street, Longton
1841 Pigot CM

Hulme, John
New Street, Longton
1865 Keates A; P-L (rustic and terra cotta)
The advertisement in 1865 Keates describes Hulme as a 'modeller' and 'manufacturer of garden vases, seats, fountains, and rustic aquarium frames'. An additional note reads: 'Fitter up of aquariums. Collector of stock for the above if required.

Instructions given to purchasers for the proper management of the same.'

JOHN HULME,
MODELLER,
New Street, Longton,
MANUFACTURER OF GARDEN VASES,
SEATS, FOUNTAINS, AND RUSTIC AQUARIUM FRAMES.
N.B.—Fitter up of Aquariums. Collector of Stock for the above if required. Instructions given to purchasers for the proper management of the same.

John Hulme. Advertisement from 1865 Keates.

Hulme, John, & Sons
Great Charles Street, Lane End
1828 Pigot EM
1830 Pigot EM

Hulme, Thomas
(i) Central Pottery, 20 Market Place, Burslem
1856 Kelly CEM
1860 Kelly EM
1861 Harrison NC-B (earthenware manufacturer and pawnbroker)
(ii) 67 Bryan Street, Hanley
1896 Kelly P

Hulme, William Henry
Nelson Place, Hanley
1892 Kelly EM
1896 Kelly EM

Hulme & Booth
Market Place, Burslem
1851 White NC-B (earthenware mfrs.)
1852 Slater EM
1854 Kelly CEM

Hulme & Christie
Sutherland Pottery, Fenton
1896 Kelly EM
1900 Kelly EM

Hulme & Massey
Peel Works, Stafford Street, Longton
1882 Keates P-L (china)
1889 Keates P-L (china)

Hulse, T.
Stafford Street, Longton
1860 Kelly CM-General

Hulse, Thomas
Peel Pottery, Stafford Street, Longton
1879 Keates P-L (china)
1880 Kelly CM
1882 Keates P-L (china)
Hulse succeeded John Green (1880 Kelly).

Hulse, William
Pool Dole, Fenton
1864 Jones EM

Hulse & Adderley
Daisy Bank, Longton
1869 Keates P-L (china, earthenware, &c.)
1870 Harrod NC-L (earthenware and china manufacturers for home and foreign markets)
1872 Kelly CM; EM
1873 Keates P-L (china, earthenware, &c.)
1875 Keates P-L (china, earthenware, &c.)

Hulse, Jaquiss & Barlow
(i) Bridge Street, Lane End
1830 Pigot EM
(ii) Gold Street, Lane End or Longton
1834 White EM-LE-L
1835 Pigot EM

HULSE, NIXON, & ADDERLEY,
DAISY BANK MANUFACTORY,
LONGTON, STAFFORDSHIRE.
MANUFACTURERS OF
WHITE & DECORATED CHINA & EARTHENWARE,
FOR HOME, COLONIAL,
CONTINENTAL, SOUTH AMERICA, AFRICA, INDIA,
AND OTHER MARKETS.

Hulse, Nixon & Adderley. Advertisement from 1865 Keates. The same advertisement appeared in 1867 Keates

Hulse, Nixon & Adderley
Daisy Bank Works, Spring Gardens Road, Longton
1856 Kelly CEM
1860 Kelly CM-General; EM
1861 Harrison NC-L (china and earthenware manufacturers)
1862 Slater CM; EM (& lustre)
1863 Kelly CM-General; CM-Tea, Breakfast, and Dessert Services
1864 Jones CEM
1865 Keates A; P-L (china, earthenware, &c.)
1867 Keates A; P-L (china, earthenware, &c.)
1868 Kelly CM; EM
The advertisements in 1865 Keates and 1867 Keates both describe the firm as 'manufacturers of white & decorated china & earthenware, for home, colonial, continental, South America, Africa, India, and other markets'.

Hulse & Walters
Commerce Street, Longton
1870 Harrod NC-L (china manufacturers)

Hunt, Maria
66 Liverpool Road, Burslem
1887 Porter SC-B (Spur and Stilt Manufacturers)

Hurd, Thomas Mansfield
(i) Station Pottery, Burslem
1892 Keates P-B (jet)
1896 Kelly JRM
(ii) 12 Waterloo Road, Burslem
1896 Kelly P
1900 Kelly P
(iii) Commercial Street, Burslem
1900 Kelly JRM

Hurd, Thomas Mansfield, & Co.
(i) Nile Street, Burslem
1884 Kelly RM
1888 Kelly RM
(ii) Union Street Works, Burslem
1887 Porter EM-B
(iii) Sylvester Street, Burslem
1892 Kelly JRM

Hurd & Wood
Chapel Lane Works, Burslem
1882 Keates P-B (Rockingham)

Hytt & Harrison
Fenton
1805 Holden NC (earthenware manufacturers)

I

Ingleby, Thomas, & Co.
High Street, Tunstall
1834 White EM-T
1835 Pigot EM

Isaac & Son
Bleak Hill Works, Burslem
1875 Keates P-B

J

Jackson Brothers
Castle Field, Hanley
1887 Porter SC-H (Tile Manufacturer)

Jackson, Benjamin
Lane End
1796 Chester NC-LE-LD-LL (manufacturer of earthenware)

Jackson, Daniel, & Son
Clarence Street, Shelton
1851 White CEM-H-Sh

Jackson, Job & John
Church Pottery, Burslem
1830 Pigot EM
1834 White EM-B
1835 Pigot EM

Jackson, Joseph
Queen Street, Shelton
1834 White CETM-H-Sh

Jackson, Sarah
Lane End
1796 Chester NC-LE-LD-LL (manufacturer of earthenware)

Jackson, Thomas
Lane End
1796 Chester NC-LE-LD-LL (manufacturer of earthenware)
1798 Universal NC-LE (manufacturer of Staffordshire-ware)

Jackson, Thomas, & Co.
Lane End
1802 Allbut EM (map location 139)

Jackson & Brown
Grosvenor Works, King Street, Foley, Fenton
1863 Kelly CM-Fancy Ware; CM-General; CM-Tea, Breakfast, and Dessert Services; CM-White & Finished
1864 Jones CEM
1865 Keates P-F (china)

Jackson & Gosling
Grosvenor Works, Foley Place, King Street, Fenton
1867 Keates P-F (china)
1868 Kelly CM
1869 Keates P-F (china)
1870 Harrod NC-F (china manufacturers for home and foreign markets)
1872 Kelly CM
1873 Keates P-F (china)
1875 Keates P-F (china)
1876 Kelly CM
1879 Keates P-F (china)
1879 Keates P-L (china)
1880 Kelly CM
1882 Keates P-F (china)
1884 Kelly CM
1887 Porter EM-F
1888 Kelly CM
1889 Keates P-F (china)
1892 Keates P-F (china)
1892 Kelly CM
1896 Kelly CM
1900 Kelly CM

Jamieson, Robert
Victoria Works, Longton
1892 Kelly CM

Jarrott & Keeling
Hanley
1798 Universal NC-H (manufacturers of Staffordshire-ware)
The partners are listed as Edward Jarrott and James Keeling.

Jarvis, Janson & Co.
Burslem
1816 Underhill P

Jarvis & Love
near Church, Burslem
1818 Pigot CM; EM

Jarvis, Richard
Nile Street, Burslem
1818 Parson EM-B-Lp-C

Jarvis, William
Great Charles Street, Lane End
1822 Allbut CEM (lusterer and enameller)
1822 Pigot EM
1828 Pigot CM

Jeffery, Charles
60 Lower Lichfield Street, Hanley
1869 Keates P-H (spur)

Jeffries, William
Oldham Pottery, Leek New Road, Hanley
1889 Keates P-H (art ware)

Jelson, Brayford & Co.
Fountain Pottery, Burslem
1887 Porter EM-B

Jenkins, Porton & Co.
Copeland Street, Stoke
1876 Kelly CM

Jervis, William
(i) Great Charles Street, Lane End
1830 Pigot CM
(ii) Gold Street, Longton
1834 White EM-LE-L (lustre)
1835 Pigot EM
1841 Pigot EM (black Egyptian and lustre)

Jervis, Leese & Bradbury
Dresden Pottery, Chancery Lane, Longton
1860 Kelly CM-General; SC (Broseley Printed Ware Manufacturers)
1861 Harrison NC-L (china manufacturers, &c.)

Johnson Brothers
(i) Old Hall Street, Hanley
1884 Kelly EM
1887 Porter EM-H
1888 Kelly EM
(ii) Old Hall Street and Eastwood Road, Hanley
1889 Keates P-H (earthenware)
1892 Keates P-H (earthenware)
1892 Kelly EM

Johnson Brothers Ltd.
Scotia Road, Tunstall
1900 Kelly EM

Johnson Brothers (Hanley)
Trent and Charles Street Potteries, Hanley
1896 Kelly EM

Johnson Brothers (Hanley) Ltd.
Hanley, Imperial, Trent and Charles Street Potteries, Stoke
1900 Kelly EM; SC (Sanitary Ware Manufacturers)

Johnson, George
Sitch, Burslem
1818 Pigot EM

Johnson, John
High Street, Tunstall

1834 White EM-T (and Egyptian black)
1835 Pigot EM

Johnson, John Lorenzo
23 High Street, Longton
1875 Keates P-L (china)
1876 Kelly CM

Johnson, Phoebe
Miles Bank, Hanley
1828 Pigot EM
1834 White EM-H-Sh (china mfrs. also) (lustre)
1835 Pigot EM

Johnson, Phoebe, & Son
Miles Bank, Hanley
1830 Pigot CM; EM

Johnson, Ralph
(i) Burslem
1816 Underhill P
1822 Allbut CEM (earthenware manufacturer)
(ii) Church Street, Burslem
1818 Parson EM-B-Lp-C
1822 Pigot EM
(iii) Silvester Square, Burslem
1818 Pigot EM
(iv) Sitch, Burslem
1818 Pigot EM

Johnson, Reuben
Miles Bank, Hanley
1816 Underhill P
1818 Parson EM-H-Sh
1818 Pigot EM
1822 Allbut CEM (lusterer, enameller, and earthenware manufacturer)
1822 Pigot EM
The first name is listed as Reubin in 1818 Pigot.

Johnson, Richard
See: Johnson & Bridgwood

Johnson, Samuel
(i) King Street, Hanley
1882 Keates P-H (Rockingham and jet)
(ii) Newport Street, Burslem
1887 Porter EM-B
1888 Kelly JM; RM
1889 Keates P-B
1892 Keates P-B
1892 Kelly JRM
1896 Kelly JRM
(iii) Swan Square, Burslem
1892 Kelly JRM
1896 Kelly JRM
(iv) Hill Pottery, Burslem
1900 Kelly JRM

Johnson, Thomas
See: Emberton, Hancock & Co.

Johnson & Bridgwood
Lane End
1796 Chester NC-LE-LD-LL (manufacturers of earthenware)
1798 Universal NC-LE (manufacturers of Staffordshire-ware)
The partnership is listed as Johnson Rd. & Bridgewood in 1798 Universal.

Johnson & Brough
Lane End
1802 Allbut EM (map location 131)
1805 Holden NC (earthenware manufacturers)
1809 Holden NC (manufacturers of earthenware)
1811 Holden NC (manufacturers of earthenware)
1816 Underhill P

Johnson & Martin
Newport Street, Burslem
1884 Kelly JM; RM

Johnson & Plant
Heathcote Road (or Street), Longton
1880 Kelly CM
1882 Keates P-L (china)
1884 Kelly CM

Johnson & Poole
Edensor Road, Longton
1879 Keates P-L (china)
1880 Kelly CM

JONES & CO.
Manufacturers of all kinds of
EARTHENWARE,
MAJOLICA, &C.
NEW STREET, LONGTON,
STAFFORDSHIRE.

Jones & Co. Advertisement from 1887 Porter.

Jones & Co.
New Street, Longton
1889 Keates P-L
1892 Keates P-L
Although the directory entry is in the name of Thomas Jones & Co., an advertisement appears under the style Jones & Co. in 1887 Porter, describing the firm as 'manufacturers of all kinds of earthenware, majolica, &c.'

Jones, Alfred B.
Eagle Works, Station Square, Longton
1887 Porter EM-L
1889 Keates P-L
1892 Keates P-L
1892 Kelly CM

Jones, Elijah
(i) Hall Lane, Hanley
1828 Pigot EM
1830 Pigot EM
(ii) Cobridge Villa
1834 White EM-B
1835 Pigot EM

Elijah Jones. Printed mark from a blue-printed earthenware soup plate.

Elijah Jones. Printed mark from a blue-printed earthenware meat dish.

Jones, Frederick
(i) Stafford Street, Longton
1865 Keates P-L (earthenware)
1867 Keates P-L (earthenware)
(ii) Chadwick Street, Longton
1869 Keates P-L (earthenware)
1870 Harrod NC-L (earthenware manufacturer)

1880 Kelly EM
1884 Kelly EM

Jones, Frederick, & Co.
(i) Stafford Street, Longton
1868 Kelly EM
1873 Keates P-L (earthenware)
(ii) Chadwick Street, Longton
1868 Kelly EM
1872 Kelly EM
1873 Keates P-L (earthenware)
1875 Keates P-L (earthenware)
1876 Kelly EM

Jones, G.,
Barnfield House, Burslem
1854 Kelly CEM

George Jones. Moulded mark from a majolica dog dish.

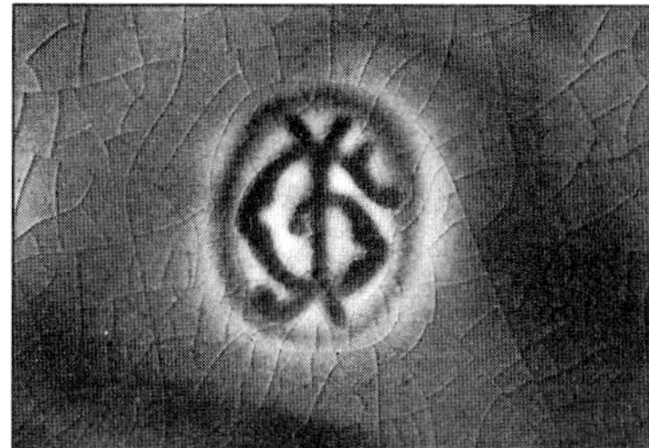

George Jones. Impressed mark from majolica wares.

Jones, George
(i) Glebe Street, Stoke
1863 Kelly EM
1864 Jones CEM
1867 Keates P-S (earthenware)
1868 Kelly EM
(ii) Bridge Works, Stoke
1864 Jones CEM
(iii) Wharf Street, Stoke
1864 Jones CEM
(iv) Trent Pottery, Church Street, Stoke
1864 Jones EM
1865 Keates P-S (china and earthenware)
1867 Keates P-S (earthenware)
1869 Keates P-S (earthenware)
(v) Trent Pottery, London Road, Stoke
1868 Kelly EM
1870 Harrod NC-S (manufacturer of earthenware, stone, china, and majolica)
1872 Kelly EM
1873 Keates P-S (earthenware)
1875 Keates P-S (earthenware)
1879 Keates P-S (earthenware)
George Jones' residence is listed as The Villas, Stoke, in 1869 Keates. The Glebe Street address is listed as a warehouse in 1864 Jones and as showrooms in 1867 Keates. The Wharf Street address is listed as a warehouse in 1864 Jones.

Jones, George, & Co.
High Street, Stoke
1862 Slater EM

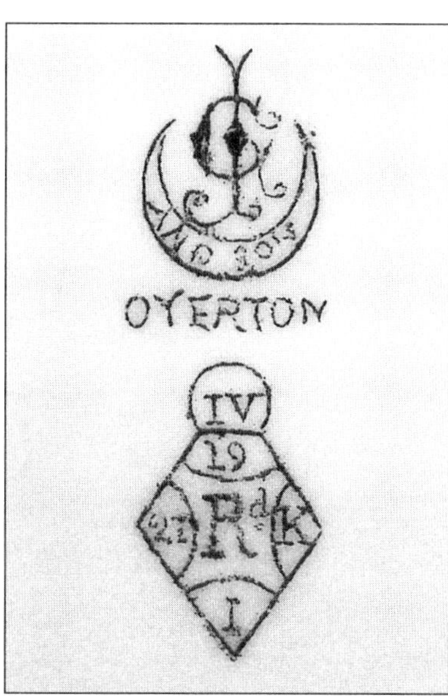

George Jones & Sons. Printed mark from a brown-printed and coloured earthenware plate. The registration diamond dates from 1883.

Jones, George, & Sons
Trent Potteries, London Road, Stoke
1876 Kelly EM
1880 Kelly EM
1884 Kelly EM
1887 Porter CEM-S
1888 Kelly CM; EM
1892 Kelly EM
1882 Keates P-S (earthenware)
1889 Keates P-S (earthenware and china)
1892 Keates P-S (earthenware and china)

Jones, George, & Sons Ltd.
Trent Potteries, London Road, Stoke
1896 Kelly CM; EM
1900 Kelly CM; EM

Jones, H., & Co.
Chadwick Street, Longton
1867 Keates P-L (earthen.)

Jones, Hannah
Market Place, Hanley
1830 Pigot EM (toy only)

Jones, Henry
See: Jones & Vigers

Jones, Josiah Ellis
(i) Portland Pottery, Church Street, Longton
1868 Kelly EM
1869 Keates P-L (china, lustre, and earthen.)
1870 Harrod NC-L (manufacturer of earthenware, ironstone, china, &c.)
1872 Kelly EM
(ii) Stafford Street, Longton
1869 Keates P-L (china, lustre, and earthen.)

Jones, Thomas
New Street, Longton
1888 Kelly EM
1892 Kelly EM
1896 Kelly EM

Jones, Thomas, & Co.
(i) Bedford Row, Shelton
1828 Pigot EM
(ii) New Street Works, Longton
1887 Porter EM-L
Although the directory entry is in the name of Thomas Jones & Co., an advertisement appears in 1887 Porter under the simple style Jones & Co. (qv). It describes the firm as 'manufacturers of all kinds of earthenware, majolica, &c.'

Jones, William
Market Street, Longton
1892 Keates P-L (china)
1892 Kelly CM
1896 Kelly CM
1900 Kelly CM

Jones & Ball
Tunstall
1822 Allbut CEM (gilders and enamellers)

Jones & Bromley
High Street, Longton
1884 Kelly EM

Jones & Ellis
Stafford Street, Longton
1863 Kelly EM
1864 Jones EM

Jones & Hopkins
Ranelagh Street, Hanley
1887 Porter EM-H

Jones & Hopkinson
Ranelagh Works, off Bethesda Street, Hanley
1879 Keates P-H (earthenware)
1880 Kelly EM
1882 Keates P-H (earthenware)
1884 Kelly EM

Jones, Hopkinson & Sherwin
(i) Ringold Works, Mollart Street, Hanley
1887 Porter EM-H
(ii) Renalagh Works, Renalagh Street, Hanley
1888 Kelly EM
1889 Keates P-H (earthenware)

Jones & Howson
Ebenezer Works, Market Street, Longton
1884 Kelly CM
1887 Porter EM-L
1888 Kelly CM
1889 Keates P-L (china)

Jones & Meakin
Cliff Bank, Stoke
1882 Keates P-S (terra cotta, majolica, and jet)

Jones, Shepherd & Co.
Portland Works, Church Street, Longton
1867 Keates A; P-L (earthenware) (manufacturers of all kinds of earthenware)
Despite the cross-reference, no advertisement could be located in 1867 Keates (two copies).

Jones & Thompson
Chadwick Street, Longton
1879 Keates P-L (earthenware)

Jones & Toplis
Bedford Row, Shelton
1830 Pigot EM

Jones & Vigers
Cobridge
1846 Williams NC-C-F-E (earthenware manufacturers)
The partners are listed individually as Henry Jones of Cobridge and Thomas Vigers of Shelton in 1846 Williams.

Jones & Walley
Villa Pottery, Cobridge
1841 Pigot EM

Jones & Walley. Applied publication mark from a relief-moulded stoneware jug.

K

Keates, J. E.
Market Place, Burslem
1854 Kelly PM

Keates, James Edward, & Co.
Market Place, Burslem
1851 White CEM-B (only earthenware) (parian statuette, & brooch.)

Keeling & Co
(i) Stoke Lane
1796 Chester NC-S (manufacturers of earthenware)
(ii) Swan Bank Pottery, Burslem
1887 Porter EM-B
1888 Kelly EM
(iii) Dale Hall Works, Newport Lane, Burslem
1889 Keates P-B
1892 Keates P-B
1892 Kelly EM
1896 Kelly EM
1900 Kelly EM

Keeling, Anthony
(i) Tunstall
1781 Bailey NC (potter)
1783 Bailey NC (potter)
1784 Bailey NC-B (manufacturer of Queen's ware in general, blue painted and enamelled Egyptian black)
(ii) Shelton
1784 Bailey NC-Sh (potter)
(iii) Well Street, Tunstall
1867 Keates P-T (earthenware)

Keeling, Anthony, & Son
Tunstall
1796 Chester NC-T-Lp (manufacturers of earthenware)

Keeling, Anthony, & Sons
Tunstall
1798 Universal NC-T (earthenware manufacturers)

Keeling, Anthony & Enoch
Tunstall
1802 Allbut EM (map location 17, two entries)
1805 Holden NC (china and earthenware manufacturers)
1809 Holden NC (china-manufacturers)
1811 Holden NC (china-manufacturers)

Keeling, Charles
(i) Albion Street, Shelton
1822 Allbut CEM (gilder and enameller)
(ii) Broad Street, Shelton
1822 Pigot CM
See also: Alcock, Samuel, & Co.

Keeling, Edward
Keeling's Lane, Hanley
1784 Bailey NC-H (potter)
1796 Chester NC-H-Sh (manufacturer of earthenware)
1798 Universal NC-H (manufacturer of Staffordshire-ware)

Keeling, Herbert
Church Street Works, Church Street, Longton

1889 Keates P-L (china, home and export)

Keeling, James
(i) Hanley
1796 Chester NC-H-Sh (manufacturer of earthenware)
1798 Universal NC-H (manufacturer of Staffordshire-ware)
1802 Allbut EM (map location 79)
1805 Holden NC (earthenware manufacturer)
1809 Holden NC (earthenware-manufacturer)
1811 Holden NC (earthenware-manufacturer)
1816 Underhill P
(ii) New Street, Hanley
1818 Parson EM-H-Sh
1818 Pigot EM
1822 Pigot EM
1828 Pigot EM
1830 Pigot EM
(iii) Cross Street, Hanley
1822 Allbut CEM (earthenware manufact.)

Keeling, Joseph
Keeling's Lane, Hanley
1802 Allbut EM (map location 76)
1805 Holden NC (earthenware manufacturer)

Keeling, Moses
Shelton
1798 Universal NC-Sh (manufacturer of Staffordshire-ware)

Keeling, Samuel
Bucknall Road
1835 Pigot EM

Keeling, Samuel, & Co.
Market Street, Hanley
1841 Pigot EM
1846 Williams NC-H (earthenware manufacturers)
1850 Kelly CEM; NC-H (earthenware manufacturers)
1850 Slater EM
The partners are listed individually as Samuel Keeling and John Shirley in 1846 Williams.

Keeling, Toft & Co.
(i) Hanley
1805 Holden NC (earthenware manufacturers)
1809 Holden NC (earthenware-manufacturers)
1811 Holden NC (earthenware-manufacturers)
1816 Underhill P
(ii) Charles Street, Hanley
1818 Pigot EM
1822 Pigot EM
(iii) Old Hall Street, Hanley
1822 Allbut CEM (earthenware and Egyptian black manufacts.)

Keeling, Toft & Co. Impressed mark from a sprigged black basalt jug.

Keeling & Walker
31 High Street, Longton
1868 Kelly EM
1869 Keates P-L (gold and silver, and earthenware manufacturers)
1870 Harrod NC-L (parian, china, and lustre manufacturers)
1872 Kelly EM

Keeling, Walker & Co.
(i) 31 High Street, Longton
1864 Jones LM
1865 Keates P-L (gold and silver lustre, and figure manftrs.)
(ii) 29 and 31 High Street, Longton
1867 Keates P-L (gold and silver lustre, and figure manufacturers)

Keeling, Walker & Cooper
31 High Street, Longton
1861 Harrison NC-L (figure, parian and earthenware manufacturers)
1862 Slater EM; TOCM; PM
1863 Kelly EM
1864 Jones EM
The town is listed as Hanley in 1862 Slater.

Keelings & Ogilvy
Tunstall
1809 Holden NC (china & earthenware-manufacturers)

Kellett, Proctor & Co.
Heathcote Pottery, Heathcote Road, Longton
1887 Porter EM-L
1888 Kelly EM
1889 Keates P-L
The first partner's name is listed as Kellets in 1888 Kelly and as Kellet in 1889 Keates.

Kelsher, Charles
High Street, Longton
1834 White EM-LE-L (yellow)

Kendall, J.K.
See: Amison & Lawson

Kennedy, W.S., & Co.
Waterloo Road, Burslem
1854 Kelly CEM

Kennedy, William Sadler
(i) Church Street, Burslem
1841 Pigot SC (Palette and Colour Slab Manufacturers, for Artists)
(ii) Washington Works, Waterloo Road, Burslem
1846 Williams NC-B (china manufacturer)
1850 Slater CM; EM; SC (Palette & Colour Slab Manufacturers – for Artists)
1851 White CEM-B (both) (door furniture, &c.)
1852 Slater CM (mortice-lock furniture); EM; SC (Palette and Colour Slab Manufacturers – for Artists)
Kennedy's second name is listed as Saddler in 1850 Slater (CM) and 1852 Slater (CM), and his house is listed as Camoys Cottages in 1846 Williams and Camoys Terrace in 1851 White. A London address at Pancrass Lane is listed in 1852 Slater.

Kensington Fine Art Pottery
Kensington Works, St. James Street, Hanley
1892 Keates P-H (parian and earthenware)

Kent, James
The Old Foley Pottery, Fenton
1900 Kelly EM

Kent, John
Market Place, Longton

1861 Harrison NC (china and earthenware merchant)
An advertisement in 1861 Harrison describes Kent as an 'exporter of china & earthenware', and not as a manufacturer. An advertisement for John Kent also appears in 1865 Keates describing him as an 'exporter of china & earthenware of every description'. It features a small engraving of a paddle steamer.

John Kent. Advertisement from 1861 Harrison.

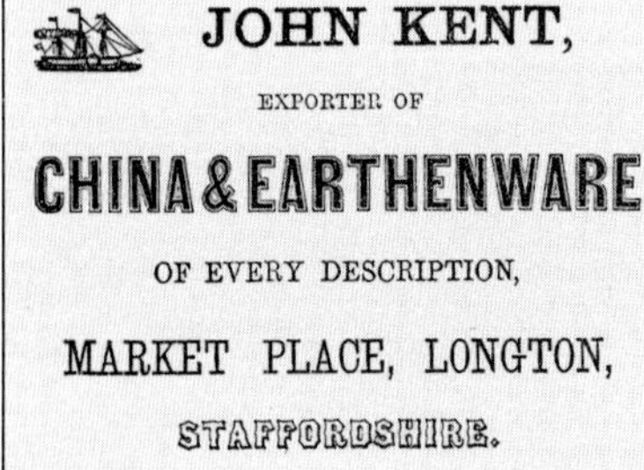

John Kent. Advertisement from 1865 Keates.

Kent, John, & Son
11 Market Street or Market Place, Longton
1868 Kelly CM
1870 Harrod NC-L (exporters of china and earthenware of every description for home and foreign markets)
1872 Kelly CM
1880 Kelly CM; EM
1882 Keates P-L (china & earthenware)
1884 Kelly CM; EM

Kent, John, & Sons
Market Place, Longton
1876 Kelly CM (home & export orders to any extent promptly executed); EM (home & export orders to any extent promptly executed)
The firm is listed as established in 1847 in 1876 Kelly.

Kent, Philip Joynson
Endon Edge Works, Endon, Stoke-on-Trent
1880 Kelly P
1884 Kelly P

Kent, Richard & John
Waterloo Road, Burslem
1846 Williams NC-B (potters)
Richard Kent is also listed individually at Waterloo Road in 1846 Williams.

Kent, William
(i) Wood Street, Burslem
1882 Keates P-B (figure maker)
(ii) Novelty Works, Wellington Street, Burslem
1889 Keates P-B (figure maker)
1892 Keates P-B (figure)
1892 Kelly CM (figure); SC (Brass Founders' China & Earthenware Figure Manufacturers)
1900 Kelly SC (Brass Founders' China Figure Manufacturer)
1896 Kelly SC (Brass Founders' China Figure Manufacturer)

Kent & Lovatt
New Street Pottery, Burslem
1887 Porter EM-B

Kent & Parr
Wellington Street, Burslem
1880 Kelly EM
1882 Keates P-B (figure makers)
1884 Kelly EM (figure)
1888 Kelly EM (figure)

Keys, Edward
High Street, Hanley
1841 Pigot TOCM

Keys, Samuel
John Street, Liverpool Road, Stoke
1850 Slater CM
1860 Kelly PM

Keys & Brewer
Wharf Street, Stoke
1856 Kelly P

Keys & Briggs
Copeland Street, Stoke
1860 Kelly PM
1862 Slater EM; PM
1863 Kelly MM; PM; SM

Keys & Mountford
John Street, Stoke
1851 White CEM-S (also porcelain statuary, &c.)
1852 Slater A; CM (and parian); TOCM (parian marble)
1854 Kelly PM
The advertisement in 1852 Slater gives the address as Liverpool Road, Stoke, and describes the firm as 'manufacturers of statuetts (sic), and ornaments of all kinds, wholesale and retail, in porcelain (or parian) statuary, for the home or foreign markets'.

Keys & Mountford. Advertisement from 1852 Slater.

William Kirkby & Co. Advertisement from 1884 Kelly.

Kirkby, William, & Co.
Sutherland Pottery, High Street, Fenton
1880 Kelly CM
1882 Keates P-F
1884 Kelly A; EM
The advertisement in 1884 Kelly offers 'general earthenware, for home,

colonial & foreign markets, specialities in fancy flowered goods', and 'special lines for Indian and South American markets'. It also features an engraving of the firm's mongoram trade mark.

Kirkham & Co.
Commercial Street, Burslem
1888 Kelly JM; RM

Kirkham, James, & Co.
Commercial Street Works, Burslem
1887 Porter EM-B

Kirkham, William
(i) London Road, Stoke
1863 Kelly EM; SM
1864 Jones EM
1865 Keates P-S (earthenware)
1867 Keates P-S (earthenware)
1868 Kelly EM; SC (Druggists' Sundries Manufacturer); SC (Stone Mortar & Pestle Manufacturers); TCM
1869 Keates P-S (earthenware)
1870 Harrod NC-S (earthenware manufacturer)
1872 Kelly EM; SC (Stone Mortar & Pestle Manufacturers); TCM
1873 Keates P-S (earthenware)
1875 Keates P-S (earthenware)
1876 Kelly EM; SC (Mortar & Pestle Manufacturer); TCM
1879 Keates P-S (earthenware)
1880 Kelly EM; TCM; SC (Mortar & Pestle Manufacturers)
1882 Keates P-S (earthenware)
1884 Kelly EM
1888 Kelly EM
1889 Keates P-S (earthenware and terra cotta)
1892 Keates P-S (earthenware and terra-cotta)
1892 Kelly EM
(ii) Kirkham Street, Stoke
1887 Porter CEM-S
Kirkham's residence is listed as The Villas, Stoke, in the Keates directories of 1869, 1873, 1875, 1879, and 1882. A London office at 13 Lime Street is listed in 1868 Kelly and 1872 Kelly.

Kirkhams
London Road, Stoke
1896 Kelly EM
1900 Kelly EM

Kirkland & Co.
Basford Bank, Stoke
1896 Kelly EM
1900 Kelly EM

Kirkland, Samuel
Basford Bank, Stoke
1892 Kelly EM

Knapper & Blackhurst
(i) Sandyford, Tunstall
1868 Kelly EM
1869 Keates P-T
1870 Harrod NC-T (earthenware manufacturers for home and foreign markets)
(ii) Newport Lane, Burslem
1884 Kelly EM

Knight, James K.
Fenton
1846 Williams NC-C-F-E (earthenware and iron stone manufacturer)

Knight, John
Market Street, Longton
1872 Kelly CM

Knight, John King
Foley Potteries, Fenton
1850 Kelly CEM; NC-S (earthenware manufacturer)
1850 Slater CM; EM (and of Egyptian black, iron-stone, stone ware, &c.)
1851 White CEM-F (only Earthenware)

JOSEPH KNIGHT,
(LATE KNIGHT AND ELKIN,)
ESTABLISHED 1820.
OLD FOLEY POTTERY,
NEAR LONGTON,
STAFFORDSHIRE.
MANUFACTURER OF
EARTHENWARE
FOR EXPORTATION.

Joseph Knight. Advertisement from 1864 Jones. The same advertisement appeared in 1865 Keates.

Knight, Joseph
(i) Old Foley Pottery, King Street, Fenton
1860 Kelly EM
1861 Harrison NC-F
1862 Slater EM (& of lustre, &c.)
1863 Kelly EM
1864 Jones A; EM; LM
1865 Keates A; P-F (earthenware)
1867 Keates P-F (earthenware)
1868 Kelly EM
(ii) Market Lane, Longton
1873 Keates P-L (china and earthenware)
(iii) Stafford Street, Longton
1880 Kelly EM
1882 Keates P-L (earthenware)
The advertisements in 1864 Jones and 1865 Keates both describe Knight as 'late Knight and Elkin, established 1820' and as a 'manufacturer of earthenware for exportation'.

Knight, Thomas & Joseph
Clay Hill, Tunstall
1816 Underhill P
1818 Parson EM-G-T-R
1818 Pigot EM

Knight & Bridgwood
Stafford Street, Longton
1884 Kelly CM; EM
The second partner's name is listed as Bridgewood in the CM entry.

Knight & Colclough
Market Street, Longton
1879 Keates P-L (china)
1880 Kelly CM

Knight & Elkin
Although no entries appear under this partnership name, advertisements for Joseph Knight in 1864 Jones and 1865 Keates both describe him as 'late Knight and Elkin, established 1820'.

Knight, Elkin & Co. Printed and impressed marks from a printed and coloured stone china plate.

Knight, Elkin & Co.
Foley Pottery, Longton

1835 Pigot CM; EM
1841 Pigot CM; EM

Knight, Elkin & Bridgwood
Foley
1834 White CEM-F-LD
The second partner's name is listed as Eltin.

Knight & Rowley
Market Street, Longton
1873 Keates A; P-L (china and earthenware)
1875 Keates A; P-L (china and earthenware)
1876 Kelly CM
The advertisements in 1873 Keates and 1875 Keates both describe the firm simply as 'china manufacturers'.

KNIGHT & ROWLEY,
CHINA MANUFACTURERS,
MARKET STREET WORKS,
LONGTON,
STAFFORDSHIRE POTTERIES.

Knight & Rowley. Advertisement from 1873 Keates. The same advertisement appeared in 1875 Keates.

Knight, Sproston & Knight
Tunstall
1809 Holden NC (earthenware-manufacturers)
1811 Holden NC (earthenware-manufacturers)

Knight & Wileman
Foley Potteries, Fenton
1852 Slater CM; EM
1854 Kelly CEM

L

Lambert & Stanley
High Street, Longton
1854 Kelly CEM

Lancaster, Frederick John
Shelton Works, Broad Street, Hanley
1892 Keates P-H
1892 Kelly EM

Lancaster, James
(i) Daisy Bank, Longton
1861 Harrison NC-L (parian works)
1863 Kelly PM
1864 Jones PM
1865 Keates P-L (parian)
(ii) 59 Stafford Street, Longton
1862 Slater PM
1863 Kelly PM
1864 Jones PM
1865 Keates P-L (parian)

Lancaster & Baker
Slippery Lane, Hanley
1896 Kelly EM

Lancaster & Barker
Dresden Works, Tinkersclough
1900 Kelly EM

Lancaster & Wright
William Street, Hanley
1889 Keates P-H

Lane End Works Ltd.
Fenton
1892 Kelly SC (Encaustic Tile Manufacturers)
The manager is listed as E.P. Everett.

Large, W. sen.
Lichfield Street, Hanley
1860 Kelly CM-General

Large, W., & Son
Parker Street, Shelton
1854 Kelly PM (Ornamental Figure Makers)

Large, W., Son & Co.
Marsh Street, Shelton
1852 Slater CM; EM

Lawler, William
Market Street, Shelton
1841 Pigot CM (dealer)

Lawrence, E., & Co.
Portland Mills, Church Street, Longton
1882 Keates P-L (china & earthenware)

T. LAWRENCE,
Earthenware Manufacturer,
TOILET WARE AND FANCY GOODS,
Wharf Street,
STOKE-ON-TRENT.

Thomas Lawrence. Advertisement from 1892 Keates.

Lawrence, Thomas
Wharf Street, Stoke
1892 Keates A; P-S (earthenware)
1892 Kelly EM
1896 Kelly EM
The advertisement in 1892 Keates describes Lawrence as an 'earthenware manufacturer, toilet ware and fancy goods'.

Lawton, Daniel
Chapel Lane, Burslem
1828 Pigot EM (toy only)
1830 Pigot EM (toy only)

Lawton, George
68 Furlong Lane, Burslem
1864 Jones EM-Miscellaneous (creel cup and shuttle eye)

Lawton, Henry
Clayton Street Works, Longton
1880 Kelly MM

Lawton, John W.
(i) 137 Waterloo Road, Burslem
1867 Keates P-B (creel steps)
(ii) North Road, Burslem
1873 Keates P-B (creel steps)
1875 Keates P-B (creel steps)
1879 Keates P-B (creel steps)

Lawton, Martin
Hope Street, Shelton
1850 Kelly NC-Sh (china toy manufacturer)
1850 Slater TOCM
1851 White CETOM-H-Sh
1852 Slater TOCM
1854 Kelly PM (Ornamental Figure Makers)

Lawton, Thomas
Hope Street, Shelton, Hanley
1841 Pigot TOCM
1852 Slater TOCM

Lawton, William
Oddfellows' Arms, Chapel Street, Fenton
1887 Porter EM-F

Lea & Co.
John Street, Stoke
1876 Kelly EM

Lea, James
High Street, Tunstall
1896 Kelly SC (Encaustic Tile Manufacturers)

Lea, W. Smith
Bethesda Street, Hanley
1892 Keates P-H

Lea, William Smith
New Street Pottery, Hanley
1864 Jones EM (manufacturer of earthenware, parian, brown and yellow ware, Egyptian black and stone)

Lea & Boulton
High Street, Tunstall
1900 Kelly SC (Art Tile Manufacturers); SC (Encaustic Tile Manufacturers)
The first partner's name is listed as Lee in the classification for Art Tile Manufacturers.

Lea, Boulton & Smith
Market Place, and Church Bank Pottery, Wood Street, Burslem
1865 Keates P-B (china)

Lea & Smith
Crown and Church Yard Pottery, Burslem
1869 Keates P-B (china and earthenware)
1870 Harrod NC-B (china and earthenware, lock furniture, finger plates, &c.)

Lea, Smith & Boulton
(i) Market Place and Wood Street, Burslem
1867 Keates P-B (china and earthenware)
(ii) Crown and Churchyard Manufactories, Burslem
1868 Kelly EM

Leader, Bainton
Smithfield
1798 Universal NC-Sf (potter)

Leader, Matthew
Portland Works, 174 Newcastle Street, Burslem
1868 Kelly EM
1869 Keates P-B
1872 Kelly EM
1873 Keates P-B

Leak, Elias
Church Street, Longton
1860 Kelly SC (Thimble Pillar Manufacturer)

Leak, Jonathan
20 Row, Burslem
1818 Parson EM-B-Lp-C
1818 Pigot EM (Egyptian)

Leak & Robinson
Church Street, Longton
1861 Harrison NC-L (stilt manufacturers)

Lear, James
High Street, Hanley
1876 Kelly EM

Lear, Samuel
High Street, Hanley
1880 Kelly CM (manufacturer of china & earthenware); EM
1882 Keates P-H (china, majolica and jasper)
1884 Kelly CM; EM
An advertisement in 1882 Keates gives Lear's address as High Street with the works in Mayer Street. It describes him as a 'manufacturer of plain & decorated china, earthenware, majolica, and jasper, suitable for the home and foreign markets', and notes that 'buyers' attention is particularly called to the superior quality of majolica and jasper: samples and prices upon application'. It also lists his London agent as Mr. T.A. Green at 25 Ely Place, Holborn.

Lee, Joseph
Mount Street, Tunstall
1864 Jones EM

Lee, William
Hall Street, Burslem
1870 Harrod NC-B (earthenware manufacturer)

Lee & Boulton
See: Lea & Boulton

Lees, Joseph
Hanley
1802 Allbut EM (map location 70)

Lees, William
(i) Keelings Lane, Hanley
1882 Keates P-H (parian)
(ii) Hawthorn Cottage, Hanley
1889 Keates P-H (parian)

Leese, William
High Street, Longton
1863 Kelly COM; SM (dealer)

Legg, Isaac
Furness or Furnace
1828 Pigot EM (coarse)
1830 Pigot EM (coarse)
1835 Pigot EM

Legge, I.
Normacot, Longton
1850 Kelly CEM
1854 Kelly CEM
1860 Kelly EM

Legge, John
Normacott Road, Furnace, Longton
1863 Kelly EM
1864 Jones EM-Miscellaneous (garden pot and chimney pipe)

Leib, Elizabeth
130 Hope Street, Hanley
1887 Porter EM-H

Leigh, Isaac
Burslem
1802 Allbut EM (map location 29)

SAMUEL LEAR,
MANUFACTURER OF PLAIN & DECORATED CHINA,
Earthenware, Majolica, and Jasper,
SUITABLE FOR THE HOME AND FOREIGN MARKETS,
High Street, HANLEY.
WORKS—MAYER STREET.
Buyers' attention is particularly called to the Superior Quality of Majolica and Jasper.
SAMPLES AND PRICES UPON APPLICATION.
London Agent—Mr. T. A. GREEN, 25, Ely Place, Holborn.

Samuel Lear. Advertisement from 1882 Keates.

Leigh, William
(i) 6 Newport Street, Burslem
1882 Keates P-B
(ii) Hill Pottery, Burslem
1884 Kelly EM
1888 Kelly EM

Leigh & Breeze
Hanley
1805 Holden NC (earthenware manufacturers)
1809 Holden NC (earthenware-manufacturers)

Leigh & Burgess
Market Place, Burslem
1865 Keates P-B (earthen.)

Lester & Smith
Clay Hills Pottery, Tunstall
1889 Keates P-T
1892 Kelly JRM
1896 Kelly JRM
1900 Kelly JRM

Lewis, C.
Penkhull, Stoke-upon-Trent
1860 Kelly P

Lightfoot, Arthur
See: Riddle & Lightfoot

Lilley, Burton & Morgan
Waterloo Mill, Charles Street, Hanley
1882 Keates P-H

Limer, Thomas
High Street, Longton
1852 Slater EM (dealer)

Lincoln Works Pottery Co.
Sneyd Sueet, Cobridge, Burslem
1880 Kelly EM
The manager is listed as R.N. Gibbons.

Lindop, John
Green Lane
1796 Chester NC-T-Lp (manufacturer of earthenware)
1802 Allbut EM (map location 1)

Lindop & Taylor
Longport
1805 Holden NC (earthenware manufacturers)
1811 Holden NC (earthenware-manufacturers)
1816 Underhill P

Lingard & Webster
Keile Street, Tunstall
1900 Kelly JRM (Rockingham ware)

Livesley, Ralph
See: Livesley, William & Ralph

Livesley, W., & Son
Cannon Street, Hanley
1868 Kelly EM

Livesley, William H.
Cannon Street, Hanley
1867 Keates P-H (earthenware, ornamental china figures, parian statuary, &c.)
1869 Keates P-H (china, figure, & earthenware manufacturer)
1870 Harrod NC-H (manufacturer of parian, earthenware, &c.)
See also: Livesley, William & Ralph

Livesley, William, & Co.
(i) Marsh Street, Shelton
1850 Kelly NC-Sh (ornamental china manufacturers)
1850 Slater TOCM
(ii) Old Hall Lane
1851 White CEM-H-Sh
Livesley's house is listed as Marsh Street in 1851 White.

Livesley, William & Ralph
Marsh Street, Shelton
1846 Williams NC-Sh (ornamental china manufacturers)
The partners are listed individually as William Livesley and Ralph Livesley, both of Marsh Street, in 1846 Williams.

Livesley & Davis
Trent Pottery, Hanley
1868 Kelly EM
1869 Keates P-H (earthen.)
1870 Harrod NC-H (manufacturers of earthenware for home and foreign markets, and all kinds of sanitary ware in great variety)
Offices at 5 College Place, New York, and Ely place, London, are listed in 1870 Harrod.

Livesley, Powell & Co.
(i) Miles Bank, Shelton, Hanley
1851 White NC-H-Sh (earthenware manufacturers)
1852 Slater EM; TOCM
1854 Kelly PM (Ornamental Figure Makers)
1856 Kelly PM
1860 Kelly EM
1861 Harrison NC-H-Sh (earthenware and china figure and parian statuary manufacturers)
1863 Kelly CFM; EM; PFM; SC (China Porcelain Manufacturers)
(ii) Old Hall Street, Hanley
1852 Slater EM; TOCM
1860 Kelly EM
1863 Kelly CFM; EM; PFM; SC (China Porcelain Manufacturers)
1864 Jones CFM; EM; PM
(iii) Stafford Street, Hanley
1862 Slater EM; PM
1864 Jones CFM; EM; PM
1865 Keates P-H (earthenware, china, and parian)
(iv) Parliament Row, Hanley
1864 Jones CFM; PM
1865 Keates P-H (earthenware, china, and parian)
The first partner's name is listed as Lovesley in 1864 Jones (CFM). An advertisement in 1861 Harrison describes the firm as 'manufacturers of earthenware, ornamental chin (sic) figures, parian statuary, &c.'

LIVESLEY, POWELL, & CO.,
MANUFACTURERS OF
EARTHENWARE,
ORNAMENTAL CHIN FIGURES,
PARIAN STATUARY, &c.,
HANLEY, STAFFORDSHIRE.

Livesley, Powell & Co. Advertisement from 1861 Harrison.

Livesley, Powell & Co. Impressed mark from a blue-printed earthenware toy plate.

Lloyd, Edward
Parker Street, Hanley
1872 Kelly CM; EM

Lloyd, F., & Son
Clarence Street, Shelton
1854 Kelly PM (Ornamental Figure Makers)

Lloyd, Francis
Hope Street, Shelton
1841 Pigot TOCM (& china dealer)

Lloyd, Francis & William, & Co.
Clarence Street, Shelton
1852 Slater CM; TOCM

Lloyd, G.
Marsh Street, Shelton
1856 Kelly PM

Lloyd, Jacob
Hanover Street, Shelton
1850 Kelly NC-Sh (china figure manufacturer)
1850 Slater TOCM
1852 Slater TOCM
1854 Kelly PM

Lloyd, John
(i) Marsh Street, Shelton
1834 White CETM-H-Sh
(ii) Parker Street, Shelton
1850 Kelly NC-Sh (china figure manufacturer)
1850 Slater TOCM

John Lloyd. Impressed mark from an earthenware figure of a spaniel.

Lloyd, Rebecca
Marsh Street, Shelton
1851 White NC-H-Sh (toy mfr.)

Lloyd, William
See: Bowers & Lloyd

Locker, John
Tunstall
1800 Allbutt NC-T (manufacturer of toys)

Locket, Timothy & John
See: Lockett, Timothy & John

Lockett & Son
King Street, Lane End
1835 Pigot EM (and Egyptian black)

Lockett, George
Great York Street, Shelton
1850 Slater EM

Lockett, George, & Co.
Lane End
1805 Holden NC (earthenware manufacturers)
1809 Holden NC (manufacturers of earthenware)
1811 Holden NC (manufacturers of earthenware)
1816 Underhill P

Lockett, J. & F.
See: Lockett, John & Thomas

Lockett, John
(i) Little Fenton
1851 White CEM-F
(ii) King Street and Market Street, Longton
1856 Kelly CEM (three entries)
1860 Kelly EM; LM (gold); SC (China Porcelain Manufacturers); SC (Egyptian Black Ware Manufacturers); SC (Stone Mortar & Pestle Manufacturers)
1861 Harrison NC-L (porcelain and earthenware manufacturer)
1864 Jones CEM; PM
1865 Keates P-L (china, earthenware, and lustre)
1868 Kelly CM; EM; SC (Stone Mortar & Pestle Manufacturers); SM
1869 Keates A; P-L (china, earthenware, and lustre)
1870 Harrod NC-L (china and earthenware manufacturer)
1872 Kelly CM; EM; SC (Stone Mortar & Pestle Manufacturers); SM
1873 Keates A; P-L (china, earthenware, and lustre)
1875 Keates A; P-L (china, earthenware, and lustre)
1876 Kelly EM
(iii) King Street and High Street, Longton
1862 Slater CM; EM
1867 Keates P-L (china, earthenware, and lustre)
(iv) Market Street, Longton
1863 Kelly SC (China Porcelain Manufacturers)
(v) King Street, Longton
1879 Keates P-L (china, earthenware, and lustre)
The potter is listed as John W. Lockett in 1869 Keates and 1870 Harrod. Lockett's house is listed as Fenton Hall in 1851 White. The firm is noted as being in the hands of executors in 1879 Keates. The advertisements in 1869 Keates, 1873 Keates and 1875 Keates are identically worded, describing Lockett as a 'manufacturer of stone mortars & pestles, funnels, evaporating dishes, and earthenware used by druggists; Egyptian black and black lustre teapots, and of turquoise, drab, sage, and white teapots, fluted; also of stone ware in jugs & teapots, &c., and of porcelain, gold lustre ware, and earthenware for export'.
See also: Lockett, John & Thomas

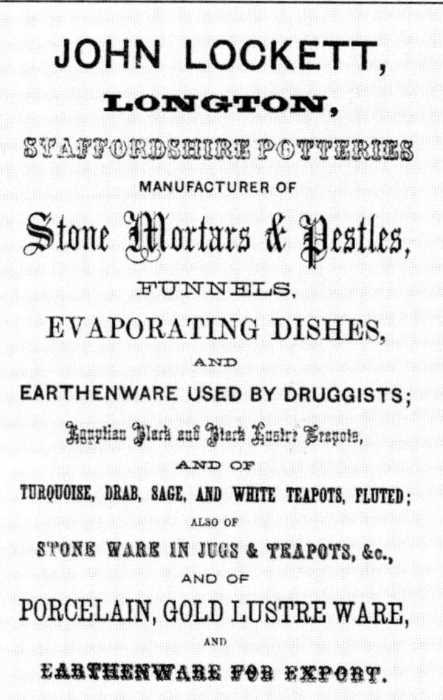

John Lockett. Advertisement from 1869 Keates. The same advertisement appeared in 1873 Keates and 1875 Keates.

Lockett, John, & Co.
(i) King Street, Lane End
1818 Parson EM-LE
(ii) King Street, Longton
1880 Kelly EM

1882 Keates P-L (china, earthenware and lustre)
1889 Keates P-L (china, earthenware and lustre)
1892 Keates P-L (china, earthenware, and lustre)
(iii) Chancery Lane, Longton
1884 Kelly EM
1887 Porter EM-L
1888 Kelly EM
1892 Kelly EM
1896 Kelly EM
1900 Kelly EM

Lockett, John, & Son
(i) King Street, Lane End
1828 Pigot EM
1830 Pigot EM
(i) Chapel Street, Longton
1834 White EM-LE-L (& Egyptian black, & stone)

Lockett, John & Thomas
(i) King Street, Longton
1841 Pigot CM; EM (and lustre Egyptian and pestle and mortar)
1850 Kelly CEM; NC-L (china & earthenware mnfrs.)
1850 Slater CM; EM
1852 Slater CM; EM
1854 Kelly CEM
(ii) Market Street, Longton
1846 Williams NC-L-LE (earthenware & china mnfctrs.)
1851 White CEM-L
1850 Slater CM; EM
1852 Slater CM; EM
1854 Kelly CEM
The partners are listed individually as John Lockett of Great Fenton and Thomas Lockett of Caroline Street in 1846 Williams. The partnership is listed as J. & F. Lockett in one entry (CEM) in 1850 Kelly.

Lockett, John & Timothy
See: Lockett, Timothy & John

Lockett, Thomas
Waterloo Road, Burslem
1850 Slater SC (Saggar Makers) (and chimney pot)

Lockett, Timothy & John
Burslem
1784 Bailey NC-B (white stone potters)
1796 Chester NC-B (manufacturers of earthenware)
1798 Universal NC-B (manufacturers of Staffordshire-ware)
The surname is listed as Locket in 1796 Chester and the partnership is listed as John & Timothy Lockett in 1798 Universal.

Lockett, Baguley & Cooper
Victoria Works, Broad Street, Shelton, Hanley
1856 Kelly PM
1860 Kelly CM-General; EM; PM; SC (Porcelain Statuary Manufacturers)
1861 Harrison NC-H-Sh (china, &c., manufacturers)
The firm was succeeded by George Baguley (1865 Keates advertisement).

Lockett & Cooper
Broad Street, Hanley
1862 Slater CM (porcelain); EM

Lockett & Hulme
King Street, Lane End
1822 Allbut CEM (china, earthenware, Egyptian black, &c. manufacturer)
1822 Pigot EM
The first partner is listed as John Lockett in 1822 Pigot.

Locketts, J. & G.
Lane End
1802 Allbut EM (map location 133)

Lomax, George
Miles Bank, Hanley
1841 Pigot CM

Loney, Samuel
Brewery Street, Hanley
1892 Keates P-H

Longton Porcelain Co.
Victoria Works, High Street, Longton
1892 Keates P-L
1896 Kelly CM
1900 Kelly CM; SC (Porcelain Manufacturers)

Love, Rushworth & Hobson
Cobridge
1834 White EM-B

Lovesley, Powell & Co.
See: Livesley, Powell & Co.

Lowe, Jonathan
Longton
1861 Harrison NC-L (china and lustre black manufacturer)

Lowe, Samuel, & Co.
Stafford Street, Longton
1892 Kelly EM

Lowe, Thomas
Gold Street, Longton
1870 Harrod NC-L (earthenware manufacturer)
1872 Kelly EM
1873 Keates P-L (earthenware)
1875 Keates P-L (earthenware)
The firm is noted as being in the hands of Mrs. Thomas Lowe in 1875 Keates.

Lowe, W. & J.
Church Street, Lane End
1818 Parson EM-LE

WILLIAM LOWE,
LATE TAMS & LOWE,
Manufacturer of China, Lustre,
BLACK, EGYPTIAN, DRAB,
TURQUOISE & PRINTED WARES, &c.
LONGTON, Staffordshire.

William Lowe. Advertisement from 1875 Keates.

WILLIAM LOWE
(LATE TAMS & LOWE),
Manufacturer of China and Earthenware,
Drab, Turquoise, Printed Ware, &c.,
SYDNEY WORKS,
HIGH STREET AND SUTHERLAND ROAD,
LONGTON, Staffordshire.

William Lowe. Advertisement from 1882 Keates.

Lowe, William
(i) High Street, Longton
1875 Keates A; P-L (earthenware)
1876 Kelly EM (manufacturer of drab turquoise, buff printed & gilt wares for home & export)
1879 Keates P-L (earthenware)
1880 Kelly CM (manufacturer of china, drab torquoise, buff printed & gilt wares for home & export); EM, manufacturer of china drab turquoise, buff printed & gilt wares for home & export)
(ii) Sydney Works, High Street and

Sutherland Road, Longton
1882 Keates P-L (earthenware)
1884 Kelly CM; EM
1887 Porter EM-L (two entries)
1888 Kelly CM
1889 Keates P-L (earthenware and china)
1892 Keates P-L (earthenware and china)
1892 Kelly CM
1896 Kelly EM
1900 Kelly CM; EM
The advertisement in 1875 Keates describes Lowe as a 'manufacturer of china, lustre, black, Egyptian, drab, turquoise & printed wares, &c.' A similar advertisement in 1882 Keates describes him as a 'manufacturer of china and earthenware, drab, turquoise, printed ware, &c.' Both advertisements state that the firm's predecessors were Tams & Lowe.

LOWE & ABBERLY,
Earthenware Manufacturers,
WATERLOO WORKS,
STAFFORD ST., LONGTON,
STAFFORDSHIRE POTTERIES.

Lowe & Abberley. Advertisement from 1864 Jones. Note the incorrect spelling of the second name, not repeated in the actual directory listing.

LOWE & ABBERLEY,
EARTHENWARE MANUFACTURERS,
WATERLOO WORKS,
STAFFORD STREET, LONGTON,
STAFFORDSHIRE POTTERIES.

Lowe & Abberley. Advertisement from 1865 Keates. The same advertisement appeared in 1867 Keates.

Lowe & Abberley
(i) Viaduct Works, Caroline Street, Longton
1862 Slater EM
1863 Kelly EM
(ii) Waterloo Works, Stafford Street, Longton
1864 Jones A; EM
1865 Keates A; P-L (earthenware, and lustre)
1867 Keates A; P-L (earthenware and lustre)
1868 Kelly EM; LM
1869 Keates A; P-L (earthenware)
The advertisements in 1864 Jones, 1865 Keates and 1867 Keates all describe the firm simply as 'earthenware manufacturers'. Despite the cross-reference, no advertisement could be located in 1869 Keates.

Lowe, Ratcliffe & Co.
Gold Street Works, Longton
1882 Keates P-L (earthenware)
1884 Kelly EM
1887 Porter EM-L
1888 Kelly EM
1889 Keates P-L (earthenware)

Lowndes & Beech
Sandyford, Tunstall
1822 Pigot EM
1828 Pigot EM
1830 Pigot EM
1822 Allbut CEM (earthenware manufacts.)
The first partner's name is listed as Lownds in 1822 Allbut.

Lucock, John
Lane Delph
1802 Allbut EM (map location 109)

Lythgoe, John
High Street, Burslem
1852 Slater EM
1854 Kelly CEM
1856 Kelly CEM

Lythgoe & Corn
High Street, Burslem
1851 White CEM-B (only earthenware)

M

Mace, John
Tunstall
1816 Underhill P

Mace, Matthew, & Co.
Shelton
1816 Underhill P

Machin & Co.
Nile Street, Burslem
1818 Pigot CM,
1822 Allbut CEM (china and earthenware manufacts.)
1822 Pigot CM
1830 Pigot CM; EM

Machin, A., & Co.
Longton
Although no entry for A. Machin & Co. has been located in the directory, an advertisement appears in 1900 Kelly giving the address as the Porcelain Art Pottery, Longton, and claiming 'established 1882'. The text reads 'The cheapest house in the trade, for decorated toilets, dinner and tea sets, jugs, vases, flower pots, &c., for home and export. Speciality: decorated toilets and jugs. Illustrated price lists and samples on application.'

Machin & Co. Printed mark from a hand-painted china tray.

A. MACHIN & CO.,
Porcelain Art Pottery,
Established 1882. LONGTON, STAFFS.
.... THE CHEAPEST HOUSE IN THE TRADE ....
For Decorated Toilets, Dinner and Tea Sets, Jugs, Vases, Flower Pots, &c., for Home and Export.
Speciality: Decorated Toilets and Jugs.
Illustrated Price Lists and Samples on Application. Telegraphic Address: "MACHIN & CO., LONGTON."

A. Machin & Co. Advertisement from 1900 Kelly.

Machin, John
(i) Holehouse, Burslem
1830 Pigot EM
(ii) Queen Street, Hanley
1850 Kelly CEM; NC-H (china manufacturer)
1850 Slater TOCM (earthenware)
The first name is listed as Machins in one entry in 1850 Kelly (CEM).

Machin, John & William
Marsh Street, Shelton
1841 Pigot CM (dealers); TOCM

Machin, Jonathan
(i) Tunstall
1796 Chester NC-T-Lp (manufacturer of earthenware)
(ii) Chell
1802 Allbut EM (map location 14)

Machin, Joseph
(i) Burslem
1802 Allbut EM (map location 49)
(ii) Waterloo Road, Burslem
1818 Parson EM-B-Lp-C
(iii) Burslem
1822 Allbut CEM (enameller and black printer)

Machin, Jos., & Co.
Nile Street, Burslem
1828 Pigot CM; EM

Machin, William
(i) Percy Street, Hanley
1875 Keates P-H (earthenware and figure)
1879 Keates P-H (earthenware & figure)
1880 Kelly EM
1882 Keates P-H (earthenware and figure)
1884 Kelly EM
(ii) 67 Bethesda Street, Hanley
1887 Porter EM-H
(iii) George Street, Hanley
1888 Kelly EM
1889 Keates P-H
1892 Keates P-H
1892 Kelly EM
1896 Kelly EM
1900 Kelly EM

Machin & Baggaley
Low Street, Burslem
1809 Holden NC (china-manufacturers)
1811 Holden NC (china-manufacrs.)
1816 Underhill P
1818 Parson EM-B-Lp-C
The second partner's name is listed as Bagilly in 1816 Underhill.

Machin & Potts
Waterloo Potteries, Burslem
1834 White EM-B (china mfrs. also)
1835 Pigot CM (and patentees and sole proprietors of the royal steam cylindrical printing apparatus); EM (and patentees and sole proprietors of the royal steam cylindrical printing apparatus)

Machin & Potts. Printed mark from a green-printed dessert dish.

Machin & Potts. Moulded publication mark from a relief-moulded and sprigged stoneware jug.

Machins, J.
See: Machin, John

Macintyre & Co.
Washington Works, Waterloo Road, Burslem
1867 Keates P-B (door furniture)
1869 Keates P-B (door furniture)
1873 Keates P-B (door furniture)
1875 Keates P-B (door furniture)
The name is listed as McIntyre in 1875 Keates.

Macintyre, James
Washington Works, Waterloo Road, Burslem
1856 Kelly CEM
1860 Kelly SC (China & Porcelain Door Furniture Manufacturers); SC (Stone Mortar & Pestle Manufacturers)
1861 Harrison NC-B (china and porcelain hall-door knob and finger-plate manufacturer)
1862 Slater CM (door furniture)
1863 Kelly SC (Bell Furniture Manufacturers) (lever); SC (China & Porcelain Door Furniture Manufacturers); SC (Jug Manufacturers); SC (Knob Makers – Drawer, Hall & Door); SC (Label Maker – Garden); SC (Letter Manufacturers); SC (Stone Mortar & Pestle Manufacturers)
1864 Jones SC (China and Porcelain Door Furniture Manufacturers)
1865 Keates P-B (door furniture)
The name is listed as Mackintyre in 1860 Kelly.

Macintyre, James, & Co.
Washington Works, Waterloo Road, Burslem
1868 Kelly CFM; CM; COM; EM; SC (China & Porcelain Door Furniture Manufacturers)
1870 Harrod NC-B (manufacturers of china, porcelain, mortice-lock and bell lever furniture, finger-plates, shutter, drawer, and hall-door knobs, mortars & pestles, metal-covered jugs, letters for signs, garden labels, artists' palettes, slabs, colour tiles, &c.)
1872 Kelly SC (Artists' Palette Manufacturers – China); SC (China & Porcelain Door Furniture Manufacturers); SC (Letter Manufacturers – China); SC (Lock Furniture Makers – China); SC (Stone Mortar & Pestle Manufacturers)

1876 Kelly, SC (Artists' China Palette Manufacturers); SC (China Letter Makers); SC (Lock Furniture Makers – China); SC (Stone Mortar & Pestle Manufacturers)
1880 Kelly SC (Artists' China Palette Manufacturers); SC (China Letter Makers); SC (Door Furniture Makers – China); SC (Lock Furniture Makers – China); SC (Mortar & Pestle Manufacturers)
1882 Keates P-B (china, porcelain and door furniture)
1884 Kelly CM; SC (Artists' China Palette Manufacturers); SC (China Letter Makers); SC (Door Furniture Makers – China); SC (Lock Furniture Makers – China); SC (Mortar & Pestle Manufacturers)
1887 Porter EM-B
1888 Kelly CM; SC (Door Furniture Makers – China); SC (Mortar & Pestle Manufacturers)
1889 Keates P-B (china, porcelain and door furniture)
1892 Keates P-B (china, porcelain and door furniture)
1892 Kelly CM; SC (China Letter & Name Plate Manufacturers); SC (Door Furniture Manufacturers – China); SC (Mortar & Pestle Manufacturers)
A London office at 23 Bartlett's Buildings is listed in 1888 Kelly and 1892 Kelly.

Macintyre, James, & Co. Ltd.
Washington Works, Burslem
1896 Kelly SC (China Letter & Name Plate Manufacturers); SC (Door Furniture Manufacturers – China); SC (Mortar & Pestle Manufacturers)
1900 Kelly SC (China Letter & Name Plate Manufacturers); SC (Door Furniture Manufacturers – China); SC (Mortar & Pestle Manufacturers)
A London office at 49 Holborn Viaduct is listed in 1896 Kelly.

Mackee, Andrew
Foley Works, Longton
1896 Kelly CM
1900 Kelly CM

Mackintyre, James
See: Macintyre, James

Maddock & Co.
Dale Hall Pottery, Taylor Street, Burslem
1876 Kelly EM
1880 Kelly EM
1882 Keates P-B (earthenware)
1884 Kelly EM
1887 Porter EM-B
1888 Kelly EM
1889 Keates P-B (earthenware)
1892 Keates P-B (earthenware)
1892 Kelly EM
1896 Kelly EM

Maddock & Son
Newcastle Street, Burslem
1862 Slater EM

Maddock, J. & J.
Dalehall Pottery, Burslem
1879 Keates P-B (earthen.)

Maddock, John
Newcastle Street, Burslem
1846 Williams NC-B (earthenware manufacturer)
1850 Kelly CEM; NC-B (earthenware manufacturer)
1850 Slater EM
1851 White CEM-B (only earthenware)
1852 Slater EM
1854 Kelly CEM
1856 Kelly CEM
Maddock's house is listed as Waterloo Road in 1846 Williams and as Stockton Brook in 1851 White.

John Maddock. Printed mark from a blue-printed earthenware meat dish. This attribution is generally accepted but may be considered suspect where a single initial is involved.

Maddock, John, & Son
Newcastle Street, Burslem
1860 Kelly EM
1861 Harrison NC-B (earthenware manufacturers)
1863 Kelly EM
1864 Jones EM-Miscellaneous (white granite)
1865 Keates P-B (earthenware)
1867 Keates P-B (earthenware)
1868 Kelly EM
1869 Keates P-B (earthenware)

Maddock, John, & Sons
Newcastle Street, Burslem
1876 Kelly EM
1880 Kelly EM
1884 Kelly EM
1888 Kelly EM
1892 Kelly EM
1870 Harrod NC-B (earthenware manufacturer for United States)
1872 Kelly EM
1873 Keates P-B (earthenware)
1875 Keates P-B (earthenware)
1887 Porter EM-B
1889 Keates P-B (earthenware)
1892 Keates P-B (earthenware)
1896 Kelly EM
1900 Kelly EM

Maddock, John & James
Newcastle Street, Burslem
1879 Keates P-B (earthenware)

Maddock & Gater
Dale Hall Pottery, Burslem
1875 Keates P-B (earthen.)

Maddock & Seddon
Newcastle Street, Burslem
1841 Pigot EM

Maddox, Ridge & Hughes
Chancery Lane, Longton
1882 Keates P-L (china)

Malcolm, Frederick
Boothen Road, Stoke
1860 Kelly EM
1861 Harrison NC-S (earthenware manufacturer)
An agent is listed as T. Carey Swan in 1860 Kelly.

Malcolm & Mountford
Dresden Pottery, Church Street, Stoke
1862 Slater CM; EM

MALKIN AND CO'S
PATENT ENCAUSTIC & GEOMETRIC TILE PAVEMENTS,
For Churches, Entrance Halls, Conservatories, Wall Decorations, &c.;
ALSO, WHITE GLAZED TILES, FOR BATHS, DAIRIES, ETC.
WORKS, BURSLEM, STAFFORDSHIRE POTTERIES.

M. & Co. are prepared to grant Licenses for the use of their Encaustic Tile Process. Terms on application to the Works, where designs for Floor Pavements may also be had.

Malkin & Co. Advertisement from 1868 Kelly.

MALKIN & CO.'S
PATENT
Encaustic & Geometric Tile Pavements
FOR CHURCHES, ENTRANCE HALLS, CONSERVATORIES, WALL DECORATIONS, ETC.
ALSO
WHITE GLAZED TILES, FOR BATHS, DAIRIES, ETC.
WORKS:
BURSLEM, Staffordshire Potteries.

M. & Co. are prepared to grant Licenses for the use of their Encaustic Tile process. Terms on application to the Works, where designs for Floor Pavements may also be had.

Malkin & Co. Advertisement from 1869 Keates.

Malkin & Co.
Patent Encaustic Tile Works, Burslem
1868 Kelly A; SC (Encaustic & Geometric Tile Pavement Manufacturers – Patent)
The advertisement in 1868 Kelly reads 'Malkin and Co's patent encaustic & geometric tile pavements, for churches, entrance halls, conservatories, wall decorations, &c.; also, white glazed tiles, for baths, dairies, etc. M. & Co. are prepared to grant licenses for the use of their encaustic tile process. Terms on application to the works, where designs for floor pavements may also be had.' An identical advertisement appears in 1869 Keates although the entry is in the name of J. Malkin & Co. (qv).

Malkin, Burnham
Burslem
1784 Bailey NC-B (potter)

Malkin, J., & Co.
Newport Lane, Burslem
1869 Keates A; SC-B (Tile - Floor - Makers)
The advertisement in 1869 Keates reads 'Malkin & Co.'s patent encaustic & geometric tile pavements for churches, entrance halls, conservatories, wall decorations, etc. Also white glazed tiles for baths, dairies, etc. M. & Co. are prepared to grant licenses for the use of their encaustic tile process. Terms on application to the works, where designs for floor pavements may also be had.'

Malkin, Ralph
Park Works, Market Street, Fenton
1865 Keates P-F (earthen.)
1867 Keates P-F (earthenware)
1868 Kelly EM
1869 Keates P-F (earthenware)
1870 Harrod NC-F (earthenware manufacturer)
1872 Kelly EM
1873 Keates P-F (earthenware)
1875 Keates P-F (earthenware)
1876 Kelly EM
1879 Keates P-F (earthenware)
1880 Kelly EM
1884 Kelly EM

Malkin, Ralph, & Sons
Park Works, Market Street, Fenton
1882 Keates P-F (earthenware)
1887 Porter EM-F
1888 Kelly EM
1889 Keates P-F (earthenware)
1892 Keates P-F (earthenware)
1892 Kelly EM

Malkin, Samuel
Lane End
1816 Underhill P

Malkin Tile Works Co. (The),
Newport Lane, Burslem
1900 Kelly SC (Encaustic Tile Manufacturers)

Malkin, Edge & Co.
Newport Works, Newport Lane, Burslem
1870 Harrod NC-B (patent encaustic and geometrical tile pavements for churches, entrance halls, conservatories, wall decorations, &c.; also white glazed tiles for baths, dairies, &c. M.E. & Co. are prepared to grant licenses for the use of their encaustic tile process; terms on application at the works, where designs for floor pavements may also be had)
1872 Kelly SC (Encaustic & Geometric Tile Pavement Manufacturers – Patent)
1873 Keates P-B (encaustic tile); SC-B (Encaustic and Geometric Tile Pavement Manufacturers); SC-B (Tile - Floor - Makers)
1875 Keates P-B (encaustic tile); SC-B (Encaustic and Geometric Tile Pavement Manufacturers); SC-B (Tile - Floor - Makers)
1876 Kelly A; SC (Encaustic Tile Manufacturers)
1879 Keates P-B (encaustic tile); SC-B (Encaustic and Geometric Tile Pavement Manufacturers); SC-B (Floor Tile Works); SC-B (Tile - Floor - Makers)
1880 Kelly A; SC (Encaustic Tile Manufacturers)
1882 Keates P-B (encaustic tile); SC-B (Encaustic and Geometric Tile Pavement Manufacturers); SC-B (Floor Tile Works)
1884 Kelly A; SC (Encaustic Tile Manufacturers)
1888 Kelly A; SC (Encaustic Tile Manufacturers)
1889 Keates P-B (encaustic tile); SC-B (Encaustic and Geometric Tile Pavement Manufacturers); SC-B (Floor Tile Works)
1892 Keates P-B (encaustic tile); SC-B (Encaustic and Geometric Tile Pavement Manufacturers); SC-B (Floor Tile Works)
1896 Kelly SC (Encaustic Tile Manufacturers)
The advertisements in the Kellys directories of 1876, 1880, 1884 and 1888 are all quite lengthy. The first, in 1876, promotes the firm's 'patent

MALKIN, EDGE, & CO.'S
PATENT
ENCAUSTIC & GEOMETRIC TILE PAVEMENTS,
For Churches, Entrance Halls, Conservatories, Wall Decorations, &c.
ALSO
WHITE, BUFF, RED, OLIVE, CELADON AND OTHER GLAZED TILES,
FOR BATHS, DAIRIES, WALLS, &C.
AND
Painted, Printed and Encaustic Glazed Tiles, for Hearths, Fireplaces, Jambs and Furniture.
WORKS:—
BURSLEM, STAFFORDSHIRE POTTERIES.
Extract from a Report of the Commissioners of the London International Exhibition, 1871, on Messrs. MALKIN, EDGE, & CO.'S PROCESS.
"This Patent Encaustic Tile Press, and the operation in making and inlaying the different colours in the Encaustic Tiles from pulverised clay, for all kinds of pavement, is very ingenious and complete. * * * This is certainly a great improvement upon the old method of making with clay in a plastic state; it is also a great saving in labour."

Malkin, Edge & Co. Advertisement from 1876 Kelly.

MALKIN, EDGE, & CO'S
PATENT
ENCAUSTIC & GEOMETRIC TILE PAVEMENTS,
For Churches, Entrance Halls, Conservatories, Wall Decorations, &c.
ALSO, WHITE GLAZED TILES, FOR BATHS, DAIRIES, ETC.
WORKS:—
BURSLEM, STAFFORDSHIRE POTTERIES.
M. E. & Co. are prepared to Grant Licenses for the Use of their Encaustic Tile Process.
TERMS ON APPLICATION AT THE WORKS, WHERE DESIGNS FOR FLOOR PAVEMENTS MAY ALSO BE HAD.
Extract from a Report of the Commissioners of the London International Exhibition, 1871, on Messrs. MALKIN, EDGE, & CO'S PROCESS.
"This Patent Encaustic Tile Press, and the operation in making and inlaying the different colours in the Encaustic Tiles from pulverised clay, for all kinds of pavement, is very ingenious and complete. * * * This is certainly a great improvement upon the old method of making with clay in a plastic state; it is also a great saving in labour."

Malkin, Edge & Co. Advertisement from 1880 Kelly.

MALKIN, EDGE & CO.'S
PATENT
ENCAUSTIC & GEOMETRIC TILE PAVEMENTS,
For Churches, Entrance Halls, Conservatories, Wall Decorations, &c.
ALSO
WHITE, IVORY, RED, OLIVE, CELADON AND OTHER GLAZED TILES,
FOR BATHS, DAIRIES, WALLS, &c.
AND
ART-PAINTED, PRINTED AND ENCAUSTIC GLAZED TILES, FOR HEARTHS, FIREPLACES, JAMBS AND FURNITURE.
WORKS:—
BURSLEM, STAFFORDSHIRE POTTERIES.
M. E. & CO. have had Awarded for their Tiles a BRONZE MEDAL, at the Calcutta International Exhibition of 1884.

Malkin, Edge & Co. Advertisement from 1884 Kelly.

MALKIN, EDGE & CO.'S
PATENT
ENCAUSTIC & GEOMETRIC TILE PAVEMENTS,
For Churches, Entrance Halls, Conservatories, Wall Decorations, &c.
ALSO
WHITE, IVORY, RED, OLIVE, CELADON & OTHER GLAZED TILES,
FOR BATHS, DAIRIES, WALLS, &c.
AND
Art-Painted, Printed and Encaustic Glazed Tiles, for Hearths, Fireplaces, Jambs and Furniture.
WORKS:—
BURSLEM, STAFFORDSHIRE POTTERIES.
M. E. & CO. have had Awarded for their Tiles a BRONZE MEDAL, at the Calcutta International Exhibition of 1884.
London Office and Show Rooms: 29, SANDRINGHAM BUILDINGS, CHARING CROSS ROAD, W.C.

Malkin, Edge & Co. Advertisement from 1888 Kelly.

encaustic & geometric tile pavements, for churches, entrance halls, conservatories, wall decorations, &c. Also, white glazed tiles, for baths, dairies, etc.' and states that they were 'prepared to grant licenses for the use of their encaustic tile process', with 'terms on application at the works, where designs for floor pavements may also be had'. By 1880 the description was lengthened to include 'also white, buff, red, olive, celadon and other glazed tiles, for baths, dairies, walls, &c. and painted, printed and encaustic glazed tiles, for hearths, fireplaces, jambs and furniture'. In 1884 and 1888 buff was replaced by ivory, and the painted tiles had become 'art-painted'.
In 1876 and 1880 an extract from a report describing the firm's process by the Commissioners of the 1871 London International Exhibition was included, 'this patent encaustic tile press, and the operation in making and inlaying the different colours in the encaustic tiles from pulverised clay, for all kinds of pavement, is very ingenious and complete. This is certainly a great improvement upon the old method of making with clay in a plastic state; it is also a great saving in labour.'
In 1884 and 1888 the firm announced the award of their bronze medal at the 1884 Calcutta International Exhibition. A London office and showroom at 29 Sandringham Buildings, Charing Cross Road, is listed in 1888.

Malkin & Shirley
Vulcan Works, High Street, Hanley
1887 Porter EM-H

Malkin, Walker & Hulse
British Anchor Pottery, Anchor Road, Longton
1860 Kelly EM
1861 Harrison NC-L
(earthenware manufacturers, enamellers, lustrers, gilders, &c.)
1862 Slater EM
1863 Kelly EM
1864 Jones A; EM; LM
The advertisement in 1864 Jones describes the firm as 'earthenware manufacturers, enamellers, lusterers, gilders, &c.'

MALKIN, WALKER, & HULSE,
EARTHENWARE MANUFACTURERS,
Enamellers, Lusterers, Gilders, &c.,
BRITISH ANCHOR POTTERY
LONGTON, STAFFORDSHIRE.

Malkin, Walker & Hulse. Advertisement from 1864 Jones.

Mallard, John
Market Place, Burslem
1818 Pigot EM

Malpass, Charles
Mill Street, Tunstall
1873 Keates P-T (earthenware)

Mann & Co.
Cannon Street, Hanley
1860 Kelly CM-General; EM; PM; SC (Porcelain Statuary Manufacturers)

Mann, Evans & Co.
Cannon Street, Hanley
1862 Slater EM

Mansfield & Co.
Keeting's Lane
1816 Underhill P

Mansfield & Hackney
Cobridge
1822 Allbut CEM (earthenware manufacts.)
1822 Pigot EM
1828 Pigot EM
1830 Pigot EM

Mansfield, Pawley & Co.
Market Place, Hanley
1818 Parson EM-H-Sh

Mantry, Adam
Shelton
1818 Pigot EM

Mare, John
Hanley
1796 Chester NC-H-Sh (manufacturer of earthenware)
1798 Universal NC-H (manufacturer of Staffordshire-ware)
1802 Allbut EM (map location 68)
1805 Holden NC (earthenware manufacturer)

Mare, J. & Matthew
Hanley
1809 Holden NC (earthenware-manufactrs.)
1811 Holden NC (earthenware-manufacs.)

Mare, John & Richard
Hanley
1781 Bailey NC (potters)
1783 Bailey NC (potters)
1784 Bailey NC-H (potters)

Mare, Matthew
Vale Pleasant, Shelton
1822 Pigot CM

Mare, Matthew, & Co.
(i) Vale Pleasant, Shelton
1818 Parson EM-H-Sh
(ii) Vale, Etruria Wharf
1822 Allbut CEM (china manufacts.)

Matthew Mare (& Co.). Printed mark from a blue-printed earthenware dinner plate also impressed "MARE".

Marple, Turner & Co.
(i) Upper Hanley Works
1851 White NC-H-Sh (earthenware mfrs.)
(ii) High Street, Hanley
1852 Slater EM
1854 Kelly CEM
1856 Kelly CEM
The second partner's name is listed as Turver in 1852 Slater.

Marsden Tile Co.
Dale Street, Burslem
1892 Keates SC-B (Floor Tile Works)

Marsden Tile Co. Ltd.
Burslem
1900 Kelly A; SC (Encaustic Tile Manufacturers), mfrs. of decorative & flooring tiles for all purposes; quotations on application)
The advertisement in 1900 Kelly offers 'tiles decorative and flooring, for all purposes, newest designs, best quality and finish'. It also lists London showrooms at 23 Farringdon Avenue, with C. Bachhoffner as their agent.

Marsh, J. & S.
Brownhills
1816 Underhill P

Marsh, Jacob
(i) Burslem
1802 Allbut EM (map location 32)
1805 Holden NC (earthenware manufacturer)
(ii) Lane Delph
1809 Holden NC (manufactr. of earthenware)
1811 Holden NC (manufac. of earthenware)
1816 Underhill P
1818 Parson EM-LE
1818 Pigot EM
(iii) Church Street, Lane End
1822 Allbut CEM (earthenware manufacturer)
1822 Pigot EM
1828 Pigot EM
1830 Pigot EM

Marsh, John Riley
Church Street, Lane End
1834 White CM-LE-L
1834 White EM-LE-L
1835 Pigot EM

Marsh, Joseph
Brownhills
1805 Holden NC (china manufacturer)
1809 Holden NC (earthenware-manufacturer)
1811 Holden NC (earthenware-manufacturer)

Marsh, S., & Co.
Waterloo Road, Burslem
1830 Pigot EM

Marsh, Samuel
Brownhills
1818 Parson EM-B-Lp-C

Marsden Tile Co. Ltd. Advertisement from 1900 Kelly.

Marsh, William
Gold Street, Longton
1841 Pigot TOCM (earthenware)

Marsh & Hall
Burslem
1796 Chester NC-B (manufacturers of earthenware)
1798 Universal NC-B (manufacturers of Staffordshire-ware)

Marsh & Haywood
Brownhills
1818 Parson EM-G-T-R
1818 Pigot CM; EM
1822 Allbut CEM (earthenware manufacts.)
1822 Pigot CM
1822 Pigot EM
1828 Pigot EM
1830 Pigot EM
1834 White EM-B
1835 Pigot EM
The second partner's name is listed as Heywood in 1818 Pigot and 1822 Allbut.

Marsh & Willatt
Silvester Square, Burslem
1834 White EM-B (Egyptian black mfrs. only)

Marsh & Willet
Burslem
1835 Pigot EM

Marsh & Willott
Keeling's Lane, Hanley
1822 Pigot EM

Martin, Ann (Mrs.)
Lane Delph
1796 Chester NC-LE-LD-LL (manufacturer of earthenware)
1798 Universal NC-LD (manufacturer of Staffordshire-ware)

Martin, E.
Marsh Street, Hanley
1868 Kelly EM (sanitary)

Martin, Thomas
St. Martin's Lane, Longton
1846 Williams NC-L-LE (china manufacturer)
1841 Pigot CM

Martin, William
(i) Market Place, Lane End
1828 Pigot CM
1830 Pigot CM
(ii) Market Street, Longton
1834 White CM-LE-L
(iii) St. Martin's Lane, Lane End
1835 Pigot CM
Martin's house is listed as Bridge Street in 1834 White.

Martin & Bailey
Lane End
1822 Allbut CEM (china manufacturers)

Martin, Shaw & Cope
St. Martin's Lane, Lane End
1822 Allbut CEM (china manufacts.)
1822 Pigot EM

Martin, Shaw & Cope. Printed mark from a blue-printed and enamelled bone china jug.

Maskery, Maria
Piccadilly, Shelton
1834 White CETM-H-Sh

Mason & Co.
Lane Delph
1802 Allbut EM (map location 111)
1828 Pigot CM; EM
1830 Pigot CM; EM

Mason, Charles James
(i) Fenton Works, Fenton
1846 Williams NC-C-F-E (earthenware & iron stone manufacturer)
1850 Slater CM (patentee, & manufacturer of patent ironstone china)
(ii) Mill Street, Longton
1851 White CEM-L (patentee of the ironstone china)
(iii) Daisy Bank, Longton
1854 Kelly CEM

Mason, Charles James, & Co.
(i) Fenton
1834 White CEM-F-LD (& patent ironstone china)
(ii) Lane Delph
1835 Pigot CM; EM

Charles James Mason & Co. Common printed mark from an ironstone dessert dish.

Mason, George & Charles
Lane Delph
1818 Parson EM-LE
1818 Pigot CM
1822 Allbut CEM (china, earthenware manufacts. and sole proprietors of the patent iron stone china)
1822 Pigot CM; EM

George & Charles Mason. Impressed mark from a blue-printed earthenware dish.

Mason, Miles
Lane Delph
1805 Holden NC (china manufacturer)
1822 Pigot EM

Miles Mason. Impressed mark from a blue-printed china plate.

Mason, Miles, & Son
Lane Delph
1809 Holden NC (china-manufactrs.) (two entries)
1811 Holden NC (china-manufacs.)
1816 Underhill P (two entries)

Mason, William
Lane Delph
1818 Parson EM-LE
1818 Pigot EM

Mason & Faraday
Fenton
1841 Pigot CM (and patentees of stone china); EM (and patentees of stone china)

Mason & Holt
Normacot Road, Longton
1861 Harrison NC-L (china manufacturers)

MASON, HOLT & CO.,
FURNACE ROAD,
LONGTON POTTERIES,
STAFFORDSHIRE.
MANUFACTURERS OF ALL KINDS OF
SUPERIOR PORCELAIN CHINA,
SUITABLE FOR
HOME AND ABROAD.

Mason, Holt & Co. Advertisement from 1864 Jones.

Mason, Holt & Co.
Normacot Road, Longton
1860 Kelly CM-Tea, Breakfast & Dessert Services
1860 Kelly COM; SC (China Porcelain Manufacturers)
1862 Slater CM
1863 Kelly CM-General
1864 Jones A; CEM
1865 Keates P-L (china)
1867 Keates P-L (china)
1868 Kelly CM
1869 Keates P-L (china)
1870 Harrod NC-L (manufacturers of improved porcelain china)
1872 Kelly CM
1873 Keates P-L (china)
1876 Kelly CM
1880 Kelly CM
The advertisement in 1864 Jones lists the address as Furnace Road, Longton, and describes the firm as 'manufacturers of all kinds of superior porcelain china, suitable for home and abroad'.

Massey & Son
13 Waterloo Road, Burslem
1864 Jones EM-Miscellaneous (stone in colour, lustre and parian ware)

Massey, David
30 Edmund Street, Hanley
1900 Kelly EM

Massey, E.
Heron Street, Fenton
1892 Keates P-F (opal china)

Massey, George
(i) Eagle Foundry, Shelton
1850 Kelly NC-Sh (china toy manufacturer)
(ii) 120 Hope Street, Hanley
1868 Kelly CFM
1869 Keates P-H
1870 Harrod NC-H (china and figure manufacturer)
(iii) Tinker's Clough, Hanley
1872 Kelly CFM
1873 Keates P-H (china)
(iv) Mayer Street, Hanley
1876 Kelly CM

Massey, J.S.
(i) 5 Princes Street, Chapel Lane, Burslem
1869 Keates P-B (earthen.)
(ii) Prince's Row, Burslem
1870 Harrod NC-B (earthenware manufacturer)

Massey, Jeremiah
Kilncroft, Burslem
1865 Keates P-B (teapot and figures)

Massey, John
Golden Hill
1805 Holden NC (Egyptian black manufacturer)
1809 Holden NC (black & red-ware manufacturers)
1811 Holden NC (black and red-ware manufacturer)

Massey, Mary (Mrs.)
(i) Mayer Street Works, Mayer Street, Hanley
1879 Keates P-H (earthenware)
1880 Kelly CM
(ii) Broad Street, Hanley
1882 Keates P-H (earthenware)

Massey, Nehemiah
(i) Newcastle Street, Burslem
1834 White EM-B (Egyptian black mfrs. only) (and lustre)
1835 Pigot EM
(ii) Burslem
1841 Pigot NC (black inkstand maker)
(iii) Russell Street, Burslem
1850 Slater EM
(iv) Kilncroft, Burslem
1851 White CEM-B, (only earthenware)
1867 Keates P-B (teapot and figures)
(v) Chapel Lane, Burslem
1852 Slater EM (lustre, black & Rockingham); SC (Pot Step Manufacturers, for Cotton Spinners) (& galvanic cells); SC (Saggar Maker) (chimney pot)
1860 Kelly EFM
(vi) 13 Waterloo Road, Burslem
1860 Kelly EFM
1861 Harrison NC-B (earthenware figure and parian manufacturer)
Massey's house is listed as Waterloo road in 1851 White, and his name is listed as both Nehemia and Nehemieh in 1852 Slater.

Massey, Nehemiah & Thomas
13 Waterloo Road, Burslem
1862 Slater TOCM; PM
1863 Kelly PFM; SM

Massey, Richard
(i) Castle Street, Burslem
1818 Parson EM-B-Lp-C
(ii) Burslem
1822 Allbut CEM (lusterer and enameller)
(iii) Newcastle Street, Burslem
1822 Pigot EM
1828 Pigot EM
1830 Pigot EM
(iv) Cannon Street, Shelton
1841 Pigot CM; TOCM

Massey, Richard & T.
Burslem
1816 Underhill P

Massey, S. & T.
Nile Street, Burslem
1818 Parson EM-B-Lp-C

Massey, Samuel
Burslem
1818 Pigot EM

1822 Allbut CEM (lusterer and enameller)
The address is listed as 'back of Methodist Chapel' in 1818 Pigot.

Massey, T.
(i) 13 Waterloo Road, Burslem
1863 Kelly RM
(ii) Chapel Lane, Burslem
1868 Kelly RM

Massey, Thomas W.
Kiln Croft, Burslem
1870 Harrod NC-B (earthenware manufacturer)

Massey, W.S.
Chapel Lane, Burslem
1860 Kelly TCM
1863 Kelly TCM

Massey, Wildblood & Co.
Stafford Street, Longton
1884 Kelly CM

Mathers & Ball
See: Matthes & Ball

Mathes & Balls
High Street, Lane End
1818 Pigot CM

Matthes & Ball
Lane End
1805 Holden NC (black glaze stone ware and gilt work manufacturers)
1809 Holden NC (earthenware-manufacturers & china-gilders)
1811 Holden NC (earthenware-manufacturers & china-gilders)
1816 Underhill P
1818 Parson EM-LE
The first partner's name is listed as Mathers in 1811 Holden and 1818 Parson.

Matthew, John, & Son
Milton, Stoke
1900 Kelly SM

Mawdesley & Co.
(i) Well Street Pottery, Tunstall
1862 Slater EM
1864 Jones EM
(ii) Cross Street, Tunstall
1863 Kelly EM
The name is listed as Mawdsley in 1862 Slater and an initial J. is listed in 1863 Kelly.

May, John Aubyn
(i) John Street, Tunstall
1851 White EM-T
(ii) Hamil Road, Burslem
1856 Kelly CEM
1860 Kelly EM
1861 Harrison NC-B (earthenware manufacturer)

May, Robert
Oldhall Street, Hanley
1834 White EM-H-Sh
1835 Pigot EM
May's house is listed as Union Street in 1834 White.

May (Job) & Walker
Hanley
1798 Universal NC-H (manufacturers of Staffordshire-ware)

Maybury, Alfred
Hope Street, Shelton
1851 White CETOM-H-Sh (brooch)

Mayer, Elijah
Hanley
1784 Bailey NC-H (enameller)
1796 Chester NC-H-Sh (manufacturer of earthenware)
1798 Universal NC-H (manufacturer of Staffordshire-ware)
1802 Allbut EM (map location 72)

Elijah Mayer. Impressed mark from a sprigged caneware bowl.

Mayer, Elijah, & Son
(i) Hanley
1805 Holden NC (china and earthenware manufacturers)
1809 Holden NC (china & earthenware-manufacturers)
1811 Holden NC (china & earthenware-manufacturers)
1816 Underhill P
1822 Allbut CEM (earthenware manufacts.)
(ii) High Street or Upper High Street, Hanley
1818 Parson EM-H-Sh
1822 Pigot EM
1828 Pigot EM (& drab china)
1830 Pigot EM (& drab china)
1834 White EM-H-Sh

Mayer, F. (Mrs.)
Brook Street, Shelton
1856 Kelly CEM

Mayer, John
(i) Hanley
1798 Universal NC-H (manufacturer of Staffordshire-ware)
(ii) Foley
1834 White CEM-F-LD
1835 Pigot CM; EM

Mayer, Jos
See: Mayer, Thomas, John, & Jos

Mayer, Joseph, & Co.
Old Church Street, Burslem
1841 Pigot EM

Mayer, Joseph, & Son
High Street, Hanley
1818 Pigot EM

Mayer, Samuel
(i) Piccadilly, Shelton
1830 Pigot EM (toy only)
1834 White CETM-H-Sh
(ii) Oldhall Street, Hanley
1835 Pigot TOCM (fine)
1841 Pigot CM; TOCM (fine)
(iii) Fountain Works, Fountain Place, Burslem
1846 Williams NC-B
Mayer's house is listed as Dalehall in 1846 Williams.

Mayer, Thomas
(i) Cliff Bank, Stoke
1828 Pigot CM; EM
1830 Pigot CM; EM
1834 White CM-S; EM-S
1835 Pigot CM; EM
(ii) Hope Street, Shelton
1834 White CETM-H-Sh (dlr.)
1841 Pigot TOCM (and china dealer)
(iii) Brook Street, Shelton
1846 Williams NC-Sh (china figure manufacturer)

1850 Kelly NC-Sh (china ornament manufacturer)
1850 Slater CM; TOCM
1852 Slater CM; TOCM
1854 Kelly CFM

Thomas Mayer. Printed mark from a green-printed earthenware dinner plate.

Thomas Mayer. Printed mark from a pink-printed earthenware plate.

Thomas Mayer. Printed and impressed marks from a blue-printed earthenware dessert plate.

Mayer, Thomas & John
Dale Hall
1841 Pigot EM

Mayer, Thomas, John, & Jos
(i) Longport
1846 Williams NC-Lp (ironstone and earthenware manufacturers)
(ii) Dale Hall, Burslem
1850 Kelly CEM; NC-B (iron stone, china & earthenware manufacturers)
1850 Slater CM; EM
(iii) Dale Hall Pottery, Longport, and Furlong Works, Burslem
1851 White CEM-B (both)
1852 Slater CM (stone china, ironstone, opaque, porcelain, parian, &c.); EM
1854 Kelly CEM
1856 Kelly CEM

The first and third partners are listed individually as Thomas Mayer and Jos Mayer, both of Longport, in 1846 Williams. The third partner is listed as Joseph in 1850 Kelly, 1850 Slater, and 1851 White. A London address is listed as 102 Leadenhall Street in 1852 Slater.

Thomas, John & Jos Mayer. Printed mark from a blue-printed earthenware plate.

Thomas, John & Jos Mayer. Printed mark from a relief-moulded stoneware jug.

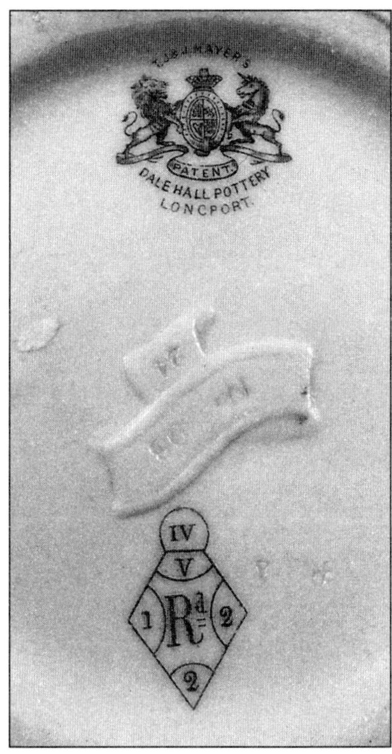

Thomas, John & Jos Mayer. Printed and moulded marks from a relief-moulded stoneware jug. The registration diamond dates from 1850.

Mayer & Elliot
Dale Hall Pottery, Burslem
1860 Kelly CM-General; EM; PM
1861 Harrison NC-B (earthenware manufacturers)

The second partner's name is listed as Elliott in one entry in 1860 Kelly (PM).

Mayer & Elliot. Printed mark from a printed and gilded earthenware jug.

Mayer & Newbold
(i) Market Place, Lane End
1818 Parson EM-LE
1818 Pigot EM
1822 Allbut CEM
(manufacturers and ornamenters of china and earthenware)
1822 Pigot CM
1828 Pigot CM; EM
(ii) Caroline Street, Lane End
1830 Pigot CM
(iii) Green Dock, Lane End
1830 Pigot EM
The first partner's name is listed as Mayor in 1818 Parson and 1822 Pigot, and the second partner's as Newbald in 1818 Pigot.

Mayor & Keeling
Charles Street, Hanley
1818 Parson EM-H-Sh
(commision dealers)

Mayor & Newbold
See: Mayer & Newbold

McIntyre & Co.
See: Macintyre & Co.

McNeal & Co.
Stafford Street, Longton
1896 Kelly EM
1900 Kelly EM

Meaken & Co.
See: Meakin & Co.

Meakin Brothers
Trent Pottery, Peel Street, Burslem
1865 Keates P-B (earthenware)
1867 Keates P-B (earthenware)
1869 Keates P-B (earthen.)
1873 Keates P-B (earthenware)

Meakin Brothers & Co.
Trent Pottery, Burslem
1868 Kelly EM
1870 Harrod NC-B
(earthenware manufacturers for foreign markets)
1872 Kelly EM

Meakin & Co.
Elder Road, Cobridge
1867 Keates P-B (earthenware)
1868 Kelly EM
1869 Keates P-B (earthen.)
1870 Harrod NC-B
(earthenware manufacturers for foreign markets)
1872 Kelly EM
1873 Keates P-B (earthenware)
1875 Keates P-B (earthenware)
1876 Kelly EM
The name is listed as Meaken in 1869 Keates.

Meakin, Alfred
(i) Royal Albert Pottery, Parsonage Street or Bank Street, Tunstall
1875 Keates P-T (earthenware)
1876 Kelly EM
1879 Keates P-T (earthen.)
1880 Kelly EM
1882 Keates P-T (earthen.)
1884 Kelly EM
1887 Porter EM-T
1888 Kelly EM
1889 Keates P-T (earthenware)
1892 Keates P-T (earthenware)
1892 Kelly EM
1896 Kelly EM
(ii) Wilkinson Street, Tunstall
1892 Kelly EM
1896 Kelly EM

Meakin, Alfred, Ltd.
Royal Albert Pottery, Parsonage Street and Wilkinson Street, Tunstall
1900 Kelly EM

Meakin, Charles
(i) Waterloo Road, Burslem
1870 Harrod NC-B
(earthenware manufacturer)
(ii) Furlong Lane, Burslem
1875 Keates P-B (earthen.)
1879 Keates P-B (earthen.)
1882 Keates P-B (earthenware)
(iii) Trent Pottery, Burslem
1876 Kelly EM
(iv) Elder Road, Cobridge
1879 Keates P-B (earthen.)
1880 Kelly EM
(v) Eastwood, Lichfield Street, Hanley
1882 Keates P-H (earthenware)
1884 Kelly EM
1887 Porter EM-H

Meakin, H.
Abbey Works, Sneyd Green, Burslem
1873 Keates P-B (earthenware)
1875 Keates P-B (earthenware)

Meakin, Harry
Lichfield Street, Hanley
1870 Harrod NC-H
(manufacturer)
The directory lists Meakin simply as a manufacturer, he may not have been a potter.

Meakin, Henry
(i) Sneyd Street, Cobridge, Burslem
1876 Kelly EM
(ii) Grove Street, Cobridge
1882 Keates P-B (earthenware)

Meakin, J. & G., Ltd.
Eastwood Works, Lichfield Street, and Eagle Pottery, Bucknall Road, Hanley
1896 Kelly EM
1900 Kelly EM

Meakin, J. & W.
Eagle Pottery, Bucknall Road, Hanley
1869 Keates P-H (earthenware)
1870 Harrod NC-H
(earthenware manufacturers)
The address is listed as near Bucknall New Road in 1869 Keates.

Meakin, James
(i) New Town Pottery, High Street, Longton
1846 Williams NC-L-LE
(earthenware and china manufacturer)
1850 Kelly CEM; NC-L
(china & earthenware manufacturer)
(ii) Cannon Street, Shelton
1850 Slater CM; EM
1851 White CEM-H-Sh
The surname is listed as Meaking in 1851 White.

Meakin, James & George
(i) Market Street, Hanley
1852 Slater EM
1854 Kelly CEM
1856 Kelly CEM
(ii) Eagle Pottery, Hanley
1862 Slater EM
(manufacturers of every description of earthenware, for export)
1863 Kelly EM
1864 Jones EM
1865 Keates P-H
(earthenware)
1867 Keates P-H
(earthenware)
1868 Kelly EM
1870 Harrod NC-H
(earthenware manufacturers for foreign markets)
1872 Kelly EM
1873 Keates P-H
(earthenware)

1875 Keates P-H (earthenware)
1876 Kelly EM
1879 Keates P-H (earthenware)
1880 Kelly EM
1882 Keates P-H (earthenware)
1884 Kelly EM
1887 Porter EM-H
1888 Kelly EM
1889 Keates P-H (earthenware)
1892 Keates P-H (earthenware)
1892 Kelly EM
(iii) 16 Glebe Street, Stoke
1868 Kelly EM
1870 Harrod NC-S (earthenware manufacturers and commission merchants)
1872 Kelly EM
1876 Kelly EM
1880 Kelly EM
1884 Kelly EM
1888 Kelly EM
(iv) St. Peter's Chambers (offices), Glebe Street, Stoke
1882 Keates P-S (earthenware)
1889 Keates P-S (earthenware)
(v) 31 Glebe Street, Stoke
1887 Porter CEM-S
(vi) Eastwood Works, Lichfield Street, Hanley
1889 Keates P-H (earthenware)
1892 Keates P-H (earthenware)
1892 Kelly EM
The firm is also listed as merchants in New York in 1870 Harrod. The address of the Eagle Pottery is listed variously as Bucknall Road, near Bucknall New Road, Ivy House Road, or Lichfield Street. The 16 Glebe Street address is listed as a branch office in 1870 Harrod.

Meakin, Lewis Henry
Cannon Street, Shelton
1852 Slater EM
1854 Kelly CEM

Meaking, James
See: Meakin, James

Mear, Stephen
See: Beech, James, & Son

Meigh, Charles
(i) Hill Street, Hanley
1835 Pigot EM
(ii) Old Hall Street, Hanley
1841 Pigot EM (and iron stone)
1846 Williams NC-H (earthenware manufacturer)
Meigh is also listed individually at Grove House, Shelton, in 1846 Williams.
See also: Meigh, Son & Pankhurst
See also: Old Hall Earthenware Co. Ltd.
See also: Old Hall Pottery Co. Ltd.

Charles Meigh. Printed mark from a relief-moulded stoneware mug, awarded a medal by the Society of Arts in 1847.

Charles Meigh. Applied registration mark from a relief-moulded stoneware jug.

Charles Meigh. Applied publication mark from a relief-moulded stoneware jug.

Charles Meigh & Son. Printed mark from a flow-blue earthenware dessert plate, also impressed "Opaque Porcelain".

Meigh, Charles, & Son
Old Hall Street, Hanley
1851 White CEM-H-Sh
1854 Kelly CEM
1856 Kelly CEM
1860 Kelly EM
1861 Harrison NC-H-Sh (earthenware manufacturers)

Meigh, Job
Hanley
1805 Holden NC (earthenware manufacturer)
1809 Holden NC (apaque *(sic)*, china, & earthenware-manufacturer)
1811 Holden NC (apaque *(sic)*, china, & earthenware-manufacturer)

Job Meigh. Portrait of Job Meigh by John Sherwin, dated 1821, inscribed "Job Meigh, died Feby. 6th 1817, aged 66".

Meigh, Job, & Son
Hill Street, Hanley
1818 Parson EM-H-Sh
1818 Pigot EM
1822 Allbut CEM
(earthenware manufacturers)
1822 Pigot EM
1828 Pigot EM
1830 Pigot EM
1834 White EM-H-Sh

Meigh, Job, & Sons
Hanley
1816 Underhill P

Meigh, W. & R.
Campbell Place, Stoke
1896 Kelly EM

Meigh & Forester
Melbourne Works, Church Street, Longton
1884 Kelly CM

Meigh, Son & Pankhurst
Old Hall Street, Hanley
1850 Kelly CEM; NC-H
(earthenware manufacturers)
1850 Slater EM
1852 Slater EM
The partnership is listed as 'Meigh, Charles, & Son, Pankhurst' in 1850 Slater and similarly in 1852 Slater.

Meigh & Walthall
Hanley
1796 Chester NC-H-Sh
(manufacturers of earthenware)
1798 Universal NC-H
(manufacturers of Staffordshire-ware)
1802 Allbut EM (map location 80)
The second partner's name is listed as Watthall in 1798 Universal.

Meir, Henry
Greengates, Tunstall
1851 White EM-T
1861 Harrison NC-T
(earthenware manufacturer)
1862 Slater EM (manufacturer of general earthenware and grinder of potters' materials)
Henry Meir succeeded John Meir & Son (1860 Kelly).

Meir, Henry, & Son
Greengates, Tunstall
1867 Keates P-T (earthen.)

Meir, J., & Co.
Greengates, Tunstall
1863 Kelly EM

Meir, John
(i) Tunstall
1818 Parson EM-G-T-R
1818 Pigot EM
1822 Pigot EM
1828 Pigot EM
1830 Pigot EM
1834 White EM-T
(ii) Greengates, Tunstall
1835 Pigot EM
(iii) Newport Lane, Burslem
1870 Harrod NC-B (potter)
The address is noted as 'near the Church' in 1834 White.

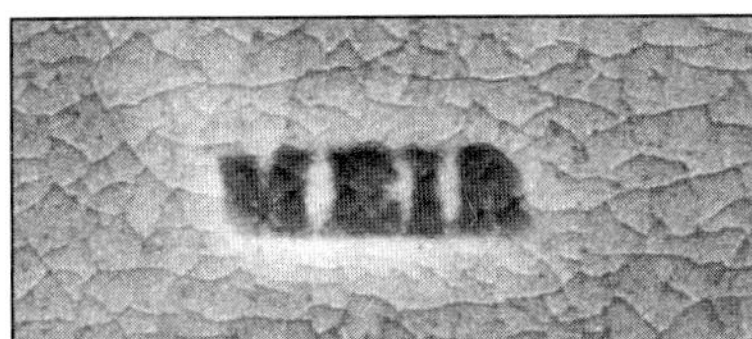

John Meir. Impressed mark from a blue-printed earthenware dinner plate.

Meir, John, & Son
Greengates, Tunstall
1846 Williams NC-T
(earthenware manufacturers)
1850 Slater EM
1852 Slater EM
1854 Kelly CEM
1856 Kelly CEM
1864 Jones EM
1865 Keates P-T (earthen.)
1868 Kelly EM
1869 Keates P-T (earthen.)
1870 Harrod NC-T
(earthenware manufacturers and flint-grinders, and home and foreign traders)
1872 Kelly EM
1873 Keates P-T (earthenware)
1875 Keates P-T (earthenware)
1876 Kelly EM
1879 Keates P-T (earthen.)
1880 Kelly EM
1882 Keates P-T (earthen.)
1884 Kelly EM
1887 Porter EM-T
1888 Kelly EM
1889 Keates P-T (earthenware)
1892 Keates P-T (earthenware)
1892 Kelly EM (& earthenware tiles)
1896 Kelly EM

Henry Meir is listed as late J. Meir & Son in 1860 Kelly.

John Meir & Son. Printed mark from a blue-printed earthenware Willow pattern plate.

John Meir & Son. Printed mark from a blue-printed earthenware soup plate.

Meir, John, & Sons
Greengates, Tunstall
1841 Pigot EM

Meli, Giovanni
(i) Liverpool Road, Stoke
1851 White NC-S (modeller)
(ii) Rome Street, Stoke
1860 Kelly PFM; PM
1861 Harrison NC-S (parian statue manufacturer)
1863 Kelly PFM
(iii) Glebe Street, Stoke
1862 Slater PM
1864 Jones A; PM (designer and modeller)
1865 Keates A; P-S (parian statuary)
The advertisements in 1864 Jones and 1865 Keates both give the address as 'near the Town Hall' and describe Meli as a 'designer & modeller, manufacturer of parian figures, ornaments, &c.' They also claim that he was 'modeller to the principal manufacturers in the Potteries, for the last twenty years, ten of which for Mr. Alderman Copeland'. Meli was succeeded by Robinson & Leadbeater (1867 Keates advertisement).
(See advertisement overleaf)

GIOVANNI MELI,
DESIGNER & MODELLER,
MANUFACTURER OF PARIAN FIGURES, ORNAMENTS, &c.
NEAR THE TOWN HALL,
STOKE - UPON - TRENT, Staffordshire.
Modeller to the principal Manufacturers in the Potteries, for the last twenty years, ten of which for Mr. Alderman Copeland.

Giovanni Meli. Advertisement from 1864 Jones. The same basic advertisement appeared in 1865 Keates.

Mellar, Reuben
See: Mellor, Reuben

Meller, Ann, & Co.
Hanley
1809 Holden NC (shining black-ware-manufacturers)

Meller, William
See: Mellor, William

Meller, Toft & Keeling
Hanley
1811 Holden NC (shining black-ware-manufacturers)

Mellor (Mrs.)
Hanley
1802 Allbut EM (map location 83)

Mellor, Charles
See: Mellor, Venables & Co.

Mellor, George
Fenton Wharf, Fenton
1882 Keates P-F (china and earthenware)

Mellor, George & Joshua
(i) Hamill Street, Burslem
1876 Kelly CM
(ii) Fenton Wharf, Stoke
1876 Kelly CM; EM
(iii) Hamilton Road, Burslem
1876 Kelly EM

Mellor, John
Near the Market Place, Burslem
1818 Parson EM-B-Lp-C

Mellor, Reuben
(i) 134 Normacott Road, Longton
1862 Slater PM
(ii) 66 Sutherland Road, Longton
1864 Jones PM (brooch and figure)
1865 Keates P-L (parian)
The surname is listed as Mellar in 1864 Jones.

Mellor, Samuel jun., & Co.
Broad Street, Hanley
1863 Kelly SC (Sanitary Vessel Manufacturers) (dealers); SM

Mellor, William
(i) Hanley
1784 Bailey NC-H (potter)
1796 Chester NC-H-Sh (manufacturer of earthenware)
1798 Universal NC-H (manufacturer of Staffordshire-ware)
(ii) Waterloo Works, Nelson Place, Hanley
1879 Keates P-H (earthenware)
The surname is listed as Miller in 1784 Bailey and as Meller in 1798 Universal.

Mellor & Birch
Broad Street and Cauldon Place Wharf, Hanley
1862 Slater A; SC (Water-Closet Basin Manufacturers)
The advertisement in 1862 Slater describes the firm as 'dealers in salt glazed stoneware sewerage pipes, terra cotta chimney tops, fire bricks, blue ware, Roman and Portland cements, plaster of Paris, &c., &c.' It also notes that they were agents to the County Fire and Provident Life Office and lists the Broad Street address as a depot and Cauldon Place as their wharf (on the Caldon canal).

MELLOR & BIRCH,
DEALERS IN
SALT GLAZED STONEWARE
SEWERAGE PIPES,
Terra Cotta Chimney Tops,
FIRE BRICKS, BLUE WARE, ROMAN AND PORTLAND CEMENTS, PLASTER OF PARIS, &c., &c.
Also AGENTS to the
County Fire and Provident Life Office.
DEPOT: BROAD STREET, HANLEY,
WHARF: CAULDON PLACE, HANLEY,
STAFFORDSHIRE.

Mellor & Birch. Advertisement from 1862 Slater.

Mellor & Taylor
Burslem
1805 Holden NC (earthenware manufacturers)
1809 Holden NC (earthenware-manufacts.)

Mellor, Taylor & Co.
(i) Bourne's Bank, Burslem
1880 Kelly EM
1882 Keates P-B (earthenware and white granite)
1884 Kelly EM
(ii) Waterloo Road, Burslem
1887 Porter EM-B
1888 Kelly EM
1889 Keates P-B (earthenware and white granite)
1892 Kelly EM
1896 Kelly EM
1900 Kelly EM

Mellor & Venables
Nile Street, Burslem
1850 Kelly CEM; NC-B (earthenware manufacturers)

Mellor, Venables & Co.
Nile Street Pottery, Nile Street, Burslem
1834 White ETM-B (china toy mfrs.)
1835 Pigot CM
1841 Pigot CM; EM
1846 Williams NC-B
1850 Slater CM; EM
1851 White CEM-B (only earthenware)
The partners are listed individually as Charles Mellor of Bleakhill, John Venables of Waterloo Road, and Thomas Pinder of Furlong Place in 1846 Williams.

Middleton, Joseph Henry
Bagnall Street, Longton
1889 Keates P-L (china)
1892 Keates P-L (china)
1892 Kelly CM
1896 Kelly CM
1900 Kelly CM

Middleton & Hudson
(i) Bagnall Street Works, Longton
1879 Keates P-L (china)
1880 Kelly CM
(manufacturers of china suitable for the Australian, New Zealand & American markets)
1882 Keates P-L (china)
1884 Kelly CM
1887 Porter EM-L
1888 Kelly CM
(ii) Alma Works, 100 High Street, Longton
1884 Kelly CM
1887 Porter EM-L
1888 Kelly CM

Mill, Edward
See: Mills, Edward

Miller, William
Paradise Street, Tunstall
1864 Jones CEM
See also: Mellor, William

Mills Brothers
Dresden Works, George Street, Shelton, Hanley
1864 Jones PM
1865 Keates P-H (parian)
1867 Keates A; P-H (parian)
1868 Kelly PM
1870 Harrod NC-H
(manufacturers of ornamental parian stone, &c.)
The advertisement in 1867 Keates describes the firm as 'manufacturers of ornamental parian figures and vases, stone jugs, &c., for home & export trade'. Both this advertisement and the entry in 1870 Harrod include the claim that they were established in 1836.

DRESDEN WORKS, GEORGE STREET, HANLEY,
ESTABLISHED 1836.
MILLS, BROTHERS,
Manufacturers of
Ornamental Parian Figures and Vases,
STONE JUGS, &c.,
FOR HOME & EXPORT TRADE.

Mills Brothers. Advertisement from 1867 Keates.

Mills & Son
182 Bryan Street, Hanley
1888 Kelly MM
1889 Keates P-H
1892 Kelly MM

Mills, Edward G.
George Street, Hanley
1869 Keates P-H (parian)
1870 Harrod NC-H (parian manufacturer)
1872 Kelly PM
1873 Keates P-H (parian)
1875 Keates P-H (parian)

Mills, Elizabeth (Mrs.)
Dresden Works, George Street, Shelton, Hanley
1852 Slater CM; EM; PM
1856 Kelly PM
1860 Kelly CM-General; PM
1863 Kelly CM-General

Mills, F.
61 Bethesda Street, Hanley
1889 Keates P-H
1892 Keates P-H

Mills, George
(i) Market Square, Hanley
1841 Pigot EM
(ii) Old Hall Street, Hanley
1846 Williams NC-H (toy manufacturer)
1850 Slater TOCM (earthenware)
(iii) Bethesda Street, Shelton
1846 Williams NC-Sh (earthenware manufactuier)

Mills, H.
Bryan Street, Hanley
1892 Keates P-H

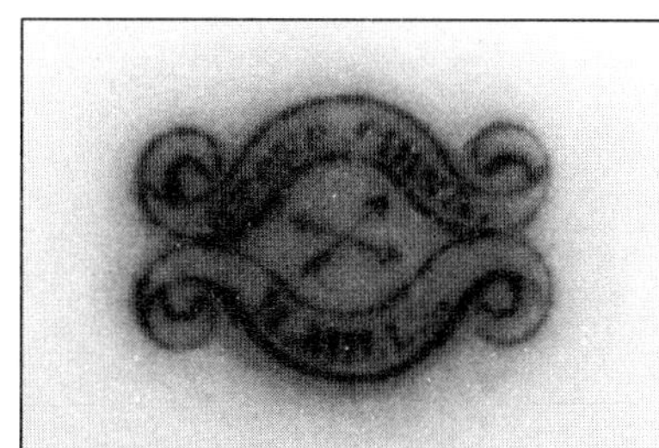

Henry Mills. Printed mark from a flow-blue earthenware tea plate.

Mills, Henry
(i) Hope Street, Shelton
1830 Pigot EM (toy only)
(ii) High Street, Shelton
1834 White CETM-H-Sh
1835 Pigot TOCM (fine)
1841 Pigot TOCM (fine)
(iii) George Street, Shelton
1841 Pigot CM
1846 Williams NC-Sh (china manufacturer)
1850 Slater CM; EM

Mills, J.
Mollart Street, Shelton
1854 Kelly CEM

Mills, J. & J.
Cannon Street, Hanley
1860 Kelly P

Mills, John
(i) 4 Clough Street, Shelton, Hanley
1841 Pigot EM (coarse and blue brick and crucible)
1850 Slater EM (coarse)
1852 Slater EM (coarse)
1860 Kelly EM
1862 Slater EM (coarse)
1864 Jones EM
1865 Keates P-H (brown ware)
1867 Keates P-H (brown ware)
1869 Keates P-H (brown ware)
1870 Harrod NC-H (brownware manufacturer)
(ii) Swan Square, Burslem
1841 Pigot TOCM
(iii) Herbert Street, Shelton
1850 Kelly CEM; NC-Sh (coarse ware manufacturer)

Mills, Josiah
George Street, Shelton
1852 Slater EM (coarse)

Mills, W.
George Street, Shelton
1854 Kelly PM (ornamental figure makers)

Mills, William
(i) Shelton
1798 Universal NC-Sh (manufacturer of Staffordshire-ware)
(ii) 1 George Street, Hanley
1872 Kelly PM
1876 Kelly PM
1879 Keates P-H (earthenware)
1880 Kelly PM

Mills & Fladley
Mill Street, Shelton
1835 Pigot EM

Mills & Perrot
Granville Pottery, Bryan Street, Hanley
1884 Kelly EM

Mills & Swann
George Street, Hanley
1862 Slater CM; EM; TOCM
The second partner's name is listed as Swan in one entry (TOCM).

Minshall, Elizabeth (Mrs.)
8 Boothenwood Terrace, Stoke
1889 Keates P-S (potters' clay press cloth maker)
1892 Keates P-S (potters' clay press cloth maker)

Minshall, Thomas
Brickfield House, London Road, Stoke
1860 Kelly TCM
1864 Jones EM-Miscellaneous (manufacturers of terra cotta and porcelain jet lamps, vases, vitrified jars, porous water bottles, butter coolers, filters, jugs, &c., &c.; also of terra-metallic bricks, tiles, ridges, quarries, &c., &c.)

Minshall & Tennant
Britannia Works, Bagnall Street, Longton
1865 Keates A; P-L (china)
The advertisement in 1865 Keates gives the address as Old Dresden Works, Bagnall Street, High Street, and describes the firm simply as 'manufacturers and decorators of china'. It also notes 'home and export trade attended to'.

MINSHALL & TENNANT,
Manufacturers and Decorators of China
OLD DRESDEN WORKS,
BAGNALL STREET, HIGH STREET
LONGTON.
N.B.—Home and Export Trade Attended to.

Minshall & Tennant. Advertisement from 1865 Keates.

Minton & Co.
Eldon Place, London Road, Stoke
1841 Pigot CM
1861 Harrison NC-S (china and earthenware manufacturers)
1862 Slater CM (and of patent agate buttons); EM
1864 Jones CEM; PM
1867 Keates P-S (china, earthenware, and parian)
1868 Kelly CM; EM; MM
1869 Keates P-S (china, earthenware, and parian)
1870 Harrod NC-S (manufacturers of china and earthenware tiles for flower-boxes, walls, hearths, &c.)
1872 Kelly CM; EM; MM; PM
1873 Keates P-S (china, earthenware, and parian)
1875 Keates P-S (china, earthenware, and parian)
1876 Kelly EM; PM; SC (Encaustic Tile Manufacturers)
A London office is listed at 50 Conduit Street in 1862 Slater and a London warehouse at 28 Walbrook in 1870 Harrod, 1872 Kelly, and 1876 Kelly.
See also: Minton, Hollins & Co.

Minton & Co. Printed and impressed marks from blue-printed dinner wares. The registration diamond dates from 1868.

Minton, Herbert, & Co.
Eldon Place, London Road, Stoke
1850 Kelly CEM; NC-S (china & earthenware ma.)
1850 Slater CM (& of patent agate buttons); EM
1852 Slater CM (& of patent agate buttons, and parian statuary); EM (and parian statuary); PM
1854 Kelly CEM
1856 Kelly CEM
1860 Kelly CM-General; EM
1863 Kelly CM-General
1863 Kelly EM; MM
1868 Kelly PM

Herbert Minton & Co. A prize medallion awarded to Herbert Minton & Co. for a jug and loving cup exhibited at the Society of Arts in 1847.

Minton, Thomas
(i) Stoke
1811 Holden NC (manufacturer of china & earthenware)
(i) New Road, Stoke
1828 Pigot CM; EM
1830 Pigot CM; EM
(ii) Eldon Place, Stoke
1834 White CM-S; EM-S
1835 Pigot CM; EM

Thomas Minton. Printed mark from a hand-painted bone china tray.

Minton, Thomas, & Co.
Eldon Place, Stoke
1841 Pigot EM

Thomas Minton (& Co.). Moulded mark from a relief-moulded stoneware jug.

Minton, Thomas, & Sons
Stoke
1818 Parson EM-S-E
1818 Pigot EM
1822 Allbut CEM (earthenware manufacts.)
1822 Pigot EM

Thomas Minton (& Sons). Printed and impressed marks from a blue-printed earthenware dinner plate.

Minton & Boyle
The partnership of Minton & Boyle does not appear in the directories due to the gap between 1835 Pigot and 1841 Pigot.

Minton & Boyle. Printed and impressed marks from a blue-printed earthenware dinner plate.

Minton & Hollins
Church Street, Stoke
1846 Williams NC-S (patent tyle manufacturers, &c.)
The partners are listed individually as Herbert Minton of Harts Hill and M. Hollins of Grove Hall in 1846 Williams.

Minton & Hollins. Printed mark from a blue-printed earthenware sauce tureen.

Minton & Hollins. Printed and impressed marks from a colourful stone china meat dish.

Minton, Hollins & Co.
(i) Eldon Place and Church Street, Stoke
1851 White CEM-S (also porcelain statuary, &c.) (and stone and parian wares, encaustic and mosaic pavements, &c.)
(ii) Church Street, Stoke
1856 Kelly SC (Encaustic, Venetian & Mosaic Pavement Manufacturers – Patent)
1867 Keates SC-S (Tile - Floor - Makers)
1868 Kelly SC (Encaustic & Geometric Tile Pavement Manufacturers – Patent)
1869 Keates P-S (encaustic tile); SC-S (Tile - Floor - Makers)
1870 Harrod NC-S (the old established manufacturers of encaustic and plain tiles for pavements, and of majolica and glazed tiles for all purposes of wall decoration. Exhibition awards – London 1851, council medal; Paris 1855, gold medal; London 1862, first-class medal; Paris 1867, gold medal)
1873 Keates P-S (encaustic tile); SC-S (Tile - Floor - Makers)
1875 Keates P-S (encaustic tile)
1879 Keates P-S (encaustic tile)
(iii) High Street, Stoke
1860 Kelly SC (Encaustic, Venetian & Mosaic Pavement Manufacturers)
1861 Harrison A; NC-S (earthenware manufacturers)
1863 Kelly SC (Encaustic, Venetian & Mosaic Pavement Manufacturers – Patent)
1864 Jones EM-Miscellaneous (patent encaustic, venetian, and mosaic pavements)
(iv) London Road, Stoke
1865 Keates P-S (china, earthenware, and parian)
(v) Patent Tile Works, Cliff Bank, Stoke
1872 Kelly SC (Encaustic & Geometric Tile Pavement Manufacturers – Patent)
1876 Kelly SC (Encaustic Tile Manufacturers)
1880 Kelly SC (Encaustic Tile Manufacturers)
1882 Keates P-S (encaustic tile)
1884 Kelly SC (Encaustic Tile Manufacturers)
1888 Kelly SC (Encaustic Tile Manufacturers)
1889 Keates P-S (encaustic tile)
1892 Keates P-S (encaustic tile)
1892 Kelly SC (Enamelled Tile Manufacturers); SC (Encaustic Tile Manufacturers)
1896 Kelly SC (Encaustic Tile Manufacturers); SC (Mosaics Manufacturers)
1900 Kelly MM (tiles); SC (Enamelled Tile Manufacturers); SC (Encaustic Tile Manufacturers); SC (Mosaics Manufacturers)
(vi) Shelton Old Road, Stoke
1873 Keates SC-S (Tile - Floor - Makers)
1875 Keates SC-S (Tile - Floor - Manufacturers)
1879 Keates SC-S (Tile - Floor - Manufacturers)
1882 Keates SC-S (Tile - Encaustic - Manufacturers); SC-S (Tile - Floor - Manufacturers)
1887 Porter SC-S (Tile Manufacturers)
1889 Keates SC-S (Tile - Encaustic - Manufacturers); SC-S (Tile - Floor - Manufacturers)
1892 Keates SC-S (Tile - Encaustic - Manufacturers); SC-S

(Tile - Floor - Manufacturers)
A London address at 9 Albion Place, Blackfriars, is listed in 1856 Kelly and 1860 Kelly. A Manchester house at Bridgewater Club Chambers, 110 King Street, is listed in 1870 Harrod and 1872 Kelly. Another London address at 50 Conduit Street, Regent Street, is listed in 1863 Kelly, 1864 Jones, 1868 Kelly, 1870 Harrod, 1872 Kelly, 1876 Kelly, 1888 Kelly, 1892 Kelly, 1896 Kelly, and 1900 Kelly, all but four of these references being in the name of Minton & Co. The firm is also listed as Minton & Co. in one of the entries in 1873 Keates. Despite the cross-reference, no advertisement could be located in 1861 Harrison (five copies).

Minton, Hollins & Wright
Church Street, Stoke
1850 Kelly NC-S
(manufacturers of patent mosaic pavements, & encaustic & venetian tiles)

Minton & Poulson
Stoke
1796 Chester NC-S
(manufacturers of earthenware)
1805 Holden NC (china and earthenware manufacturers)
1809 Holden NC (manufacturer of china & earthenware)
1816 Underhill P

Minton, Poulson & Co.
Stoke
1802 Allbut EM (map location 104)

Mintons
Eldon Place, London Road, Stoke
1879 Keates P-S (china, earthenware, and parian)
1880 Kelly CM; SC (Encaustic Tile Manufacturers)
1882 Keates P-S (china, earthenware, and parian)
1889 Keates P-S (china, earthenware, and parian)
A London address at 28 Walbrook is listed in 1880 Kelly.

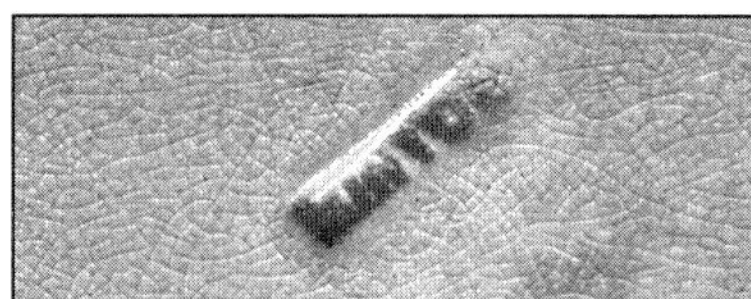

Mintons. Printed and impressed marks from a red-printed earthenware dinner plate. The registration diamond dates from 1878.

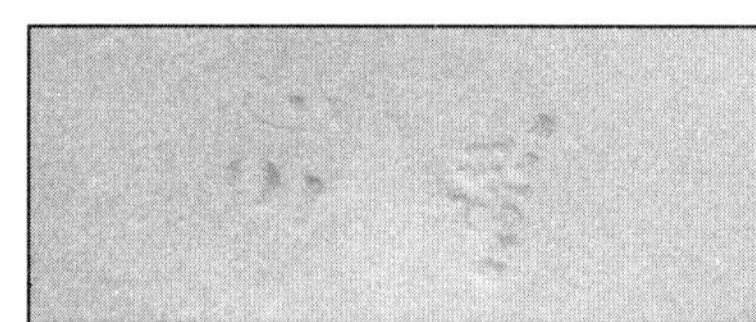

Mintons. Printed and impressed marks from a printed and coloured ironstone dinner plate.

Mintons Ltd.
Eldon Place, London Road, Stoke
1884 Kelly CM; EM; MM; PM; SC (Encaustic Tile Manufacturers)
1887 Porter CEM-S
1888 Kelly CM; EM; MM; PM; SC (Encaustic Tile Manufacturers)
1892 Keates P-S (china, earthenware, and parian)
1892 Kelly CM; EM; MM; PM; SC (Enamelled Tile Manufacturers)
1896 Kelly CM (china, majolica, parian, earthenware & enamelled tiles manufacturers); EM; MM; PM; SC (Enamelled Tile Manufacturers)
1900 Kelly CM (china, majolica, parian, earthenware & enamelled tiles manufacturers); EM; MM; PM; SC (Enamelled Tile Manufacturers)
London addresses are listed at 28 Walbrook in 1888 Kelly and 1892 Kelly, and at 25 Farringdon Avenue in 1896 Kelly.

Mintons Ltd. Printed mark used for 1897 Diamond Jubilee wares.

Minton's China Works
Stoke
1876 Kelly CM; EM; MM; SC (Tiles – Enamelled)
A London address is listed at 28 Walbrook in 1876 Kelly.

Mitchell, Anthony
Snow Hill, Hanley
1870 Harrod NC-H (figure-maker)

Mogridge, James T.
See: Plant, R.H., & Co.

Monsell, Mitchell & Co.
See: Campbell Brick & Tile Co. (The)

Moore Brothers
(i) Bleakhill Pottery, Cobridge, Burslem
1868 Kelly EM
1869 Keates P-B

1870 Harrod NC-B (ironstone china manufacturers)
1872 Kelly EM
(ii) St. Mary's Works, High Street, Longton
1873 Keates P-L (china)
1875 Keates P-L (china)
1876 Kelly CM
1879 Keates P-L (china)
1880 Kelly CM
1882 Keates P-L (china)
1884 Kelly CM
1887 Porter EM-L
1888 Kelly CM
1889 Keates A; P-L (china)
1892 Keates A; P-L (china)
1892 Kelly CM
1896 Kelly CM
1900 Kelly CM
The name is listed as Moor in 1876 Kelly and 1880 Kelly. The advertisement in 1889 Keates describes the firm as 'manufacturers of art porcelain, china, etc.' Despite the cross-reference, no advertisement could be located in 1892 Keates (two copies).

MOORE BROTHERS,
ST. MARY'S WORKS,
LONGTON, Staffs.,
Manufacturers of Art Porcelain
CHINA, ETC.

Moore Brothers. Advertisement from 1889 Keates.

Moore & Co.
(i) Old Foley Pottery, King Street, Fenton
1879 Keates P-F (earthenware); P-L (earthen.)
1880 Kelly EM
1882 Keates P-F (earthenware); P-L (earthen.)
1884 Kelly EM
1887 Porter EM-F
1888 Kelly EM
1889 Keates P-F (earthenware); P-L (earthenware)
1892 Keates P-F (earthenware); P-L (earthenware)
(ii) Victoria Square, Hanley
1900 Kelly EM

Moore & Son
(i) Mount Pleasant Works, Longton
1860 Kelly CM-General; CM-Tea, Breakfast & Dessert Services
1861 Harrison NC-L (china manufacturers)
(ii) St. Mary's Works, High Street, Longton
1865 Keates P-L (china)
1867 Keates P-L (china)
1868 Kelly CM
1870 Harrod NC-L (china manufacturers for home and foreign markets)
1872 Kelly CM

Moore, Edward T.
Waterloo Road, Burslem
1870 Harrod NC-B (earthenware manufacturer)

Moore, S.
Normacot, Longton
1860 Kelly CM-General

Moore, S., & Son
St. Mary's Works, High Street, Longton
1869 Keates P-L (china)

Moore, Samuel
St. Mary's Works, High Street or Mount Pleasant, Longton
1862 Slater CM
1863 Kelly CM-General; CM-Tea, Breakfast, and Dessert Services; COM (roman catholic); SC (China Vase Manufacturers) (roman catholic altar)
1864 Jones CEM
See also: Hamilton & Moore.

Moore, Leason & Co.
Old Foley Pottery, Fenton
1892 Kelly EM
1896 Kelly EM
The second partner's name is listed as Leeson in 1896 Kelly.

Moreton, John
Wellington Works, Wellington Street, Hanley
1882 Keates P-H (earthenware)

Moreton, Thomas
Eastwood, Hanley
1828 Pigot EM

Moreton & Baker
Elm Street, Hanley
1879 Keates P-H (earthenware)

Morgan, Wood & Co.
(i) Wedgwood Place Pottery, Burslem
1860 Kelly EM
1861 Harrison NC-B (earthenware manufacturers)
(ii) Liverpool Road, Burslem
1862 Slater EM
1863 Kelly EM
(iii) Hill or Hill Top Works, Burslem
1864 Jones EM
1868 Kelly EM
1869 Keates P-B (earthen.)
1870 Harrod NC-B (earthenware manufacturers)

Morley, Francis, & Co.
(i) High Street, Shelton
1850 Kelly CEM; NC-Sh (china, ironstone & earthenware manufacturers)
1850 Slater CM (ironstone china); EM
1851 White CEM-H-Sh
(ii) Broad Street, Shelton
1852 Slater CM (ironstone china); EM
1854 Kelly CEM
1856 Kelly CEM

Francis Morley & Co. Printed mark from a printed and enamelled tea plate.

Francis Morley & Co. Printed and impressed marks from an armorial ironstone china comport.

Morley, William
(i) Albion Street, Longton
1880 Kelly EM
1882 Keates P-L (earthenware)
(ii) Albert Road, Fenton
1884 Kelly EM
1888 Kelly EM
1892 Kelly EM
(iii) Salopian Works, Fenton
1887 Porter EM-F
(iv) Victoria Road, Fenton
1889 Keates P-F
1892 Keates P-F
1896 Kelly EM
1900 Kelly EM
The firm at Victoria Road is noted as being in the hands of executors in 1892 Keates.

Morley & Ashworth
Broad Street, Hanley
1860 Kelly CM-General; EM
The firm was succeeded by George L. Ashworth & Brothers (1863 Kelly).

Morris & Co.
(i) Lichfield Street, Hanley
1892 Keates P-H
(ii) Fenton Road, Hanley
1900 Kelly EM

Morris, A. & G.
Lichfield Street, Hanley
1889 Keates P-H

Morris, Daniel
Burslem
1796 Chester NC-B (manufacturer of earthenware)
1798 Universal NC-B (coarse-ware potter)

Morris, Thomas
(i) Marsh Street, Hanley
1818 Parson EM-H-Sh
(ii) Regent Works, Mount Pleasant, Longton
1892 Keates P-L (china)
1892 Kelly CM
1896 Kelly CM
1900 Kelly CM

Morris & Davis
Mount Pleasant, Longton
1900 Kelly CM

Mort, Barker & Chester
Burslem
1802 Allbut EM (map location 48)
1805 Holden NC (earthenware manufacturers)

Moseley, John
(i) Cobridge
1802 Allbut EM (map location 61)
1805 Holden NC (Egyptian black manufacturer)
1809 Holden NC (earthenware-manufacturer)
1811 Holden NC (earthenware & Egyptian-black-manufacturer)
1816 Underhill P
1818 Parson EM-B-Lp-C
(ii) Church Yard Works, Burslem
1818 Parson EM-B-Lp-C
1822 Allbut CEM (earthenware and Egyptian black manufact.)
1822 Pigot EM (& Egyptian black)
The surname is listed as Mozeley in 1802 Allbut.

John Moseley. Impressed mark from a black basalt teapot with Nelson and Trafalgar related decoration.

Moseley, John & William
Burslem
1809 Holden NC (Egyptian-black-manufacturers)

Moseley, William
Queen St. Black Works, Burslem
1811 Holden NC (Egyptian-black-manufr.)
1816 Underhill P
1818 Parson EM-B-Lp-C

Mosley, John
Queen Street, Burslem
1818 Pigot EM (Egyptian black)

Moss, Henshall
Red Street
1816 Underhill P
1822 Allbut CEM (earthenware manufacturer)

Moss, Richard
Red Street
1834 White EM-T; NC-R (earthenware & Egyptn. blk. mfr. & vict. Crown)
1835 Pigot EM (and Egyptian black)
1841 Pigot EM (and Egyptian black)

Moss, Thomas & Henshall
Red Street
1796 Chester NC-T-Lp (manufacturers of earthenware)
1818 Parson EM-G-T-R

Moss & Cartwright
Sneyd Green Pottery, Sneyd Street, Cobridge
1863 Kelly EM
1864 Jones EM
1865 Keates P-B (earthenware)

Moss & Henshall
Red Street
1802 Allbut EM (map location 6)

Moss & Hobson
Cornhill Works, Cornhill Passage, Longton
1860 Kelly EM; LM
1861 Harrison NC-L (earthenware manufacturers)
1862 Slater EM; PM

Ashford Works, Clayton Street, Longton,
(*Staffordshire Potteries.*)
JOSEPH EDWARD MOSTON,
(Late JAMES WILLIAMS,)
Manufacturer of Improved China,
(OF EVERY VARIETY.)

Joseph Edward Moston. Advertisement from 1869 Keates.

Moston, Joseph Edward
Ashford Works, Clayton Street, Longton
1869 Keates A; P-L (china)
1870 Harrod NC-L (china manufacturer)
1872 Kelly CM
The entry in 1869 Keates lists Moston's names as Edward Jos. whereas both 1870 Harrod and 1872 Kelly list his initials as J.E.B. The name preferred here is taken from

the advertisement in 1869 Keates which describes Moston as a 'manufacturer of improved china, of every variety' and states that he succeeded James Williams.

Mountford & Co.
Boothen Road, Stoke
1863 Kelly EM

Mountford, George
Market Street, Fenton
1862 Slater EM

Mountford, George Thomas
(i) Alexandra Pottery, Wharf Street, Stoke
1889 Keates P-S
(ii) Alexandra Pottery, Wolfe Street, Stoke
1892 Keates P-S
1892 Kelly EM
1896 Kelly EM

George Thomas Mountford. Printed mark from a brown-printed and coloured dessert plate. The registration number dates from 1888.

Mountford, J.
Liverpool Road and John Street, Stoke
1856 Kelly PM

Mountford & Thomas
Marlborough Works, Union Street, Hanley
1882 Keates P-H (majolica)
1884 Kelly EM
1887 Porter EM-H
1888 Kelly EM

Mozeley, John
See: Moseley, John

Muntford, John
Dresden Pottery, Stoke
1864 Jones EM

Myatt, Benjamin
Red Street
1818 Parson EM-G-T-R

Myatt, Benjamin & Joseph
High Street, Lane End
1818 Parson EM-LE
1818 Pigot EM

Myatt, Benjamin & Joseph, & Co.
High Street, Lane End
1822 Allbut CEM (china, earthenware manufacturers, lusterers and enamellers)
1822 Pigot EM

Myatt, John
Church Street, Lane End
1822 Pigot EM

Myatt, John, William & James
High Street, Lane End
1818 Pigot EM

Myatt, Joseph
(i) Lane End
1796 Chester NC-LE-LD-LL (manufacturer of earthenware)
(ii) Foley
1802 Allbut EM (map location 117)
(iii) High Street, Hanley or Shelton
1851 White CEM-H-Sh (yellow)

Myatt, Richard
Lane End
1781 Bailey NC (potter)
1783 Bailey NC (potter)
1798 Universal NC-LE (manufacturer of Staffordshire-ware)

Myatt & Hulse
Lane End
1822 Allbut CEM (earthenware manufacturers)

Myott, Son & Co.
Wolfe Street, Stoke
1900 Kelly EM

N

Neale, James
James Neale predated James Neale & Co. The style without "& Co." relates to the firm before the first directory appeared in 1781.

James Neale. Embossed mark from a sprigged black basalt vase.

Neale, James, & Co.
Hanley
1781 Bailey NC (potters)
1783 Bailey NC (potters)

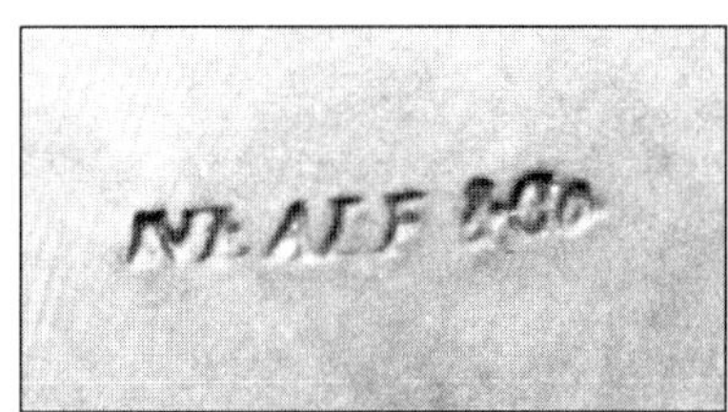

James Neale & Co. Impressed mark.

Neale, Harrison & Co.
Elm Street, Hanley
1875 Keates P-H (china and earthenware)
1879 Keates P-H (china and earthenware)

Neale, Marsh & White
Fenton
1896 Kelly JRM

Neale & White
Fountain Square, Fenton
1900 Kelly JRM

Neale & Wilson
Hanley
1784 Bailey NC-H (potters)

Neale & Wilson. Impressed mark from a hard-paste porcelain tray.

Neild, B.
Green Dock Pottery, Edensor Road, Longton
1889 Keates P-L (earthenware, majolica, and jet)
1892 Keates P-L (earthenware, majolica, and jet)

New Wharf Pottery Co.
Navigation Road, Burslem
1882 Keates P-B
1887 Porter EM-B
1888 Kelly P
1889 Keates P-B
1892 Keates P-B
1892 Kelly P
1896 Kelly P
1900 Kelly P
The managing partner is listed as Thomas F. Wood in all entries from 1888 Kelly onwards.

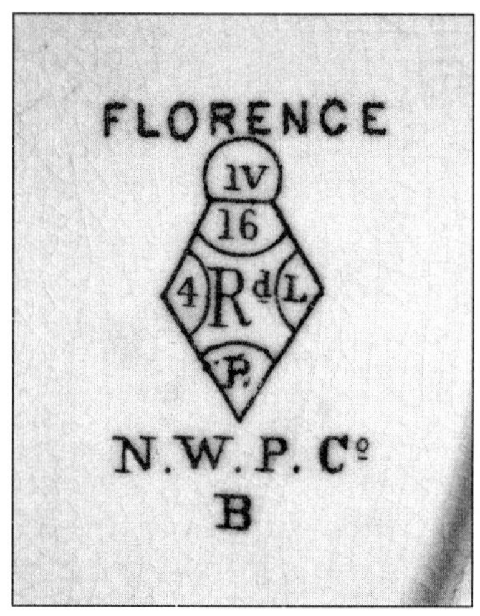

New Wharf Pottery Co. Printed mark from a green-printed earthenware dinner plate. The registration diamond dates from 1882 and relates to a design registered by the associated company Wood & Son.

Newberry, B.C.W.
Hanley
1816 Underhill P

Newbold, Richard
(i) Green Dock, Longton
1834 White CM-LE-L (Egyptian black ware mfrs.); EM-LE-L (lustre and black)
(ii) New Street, Lane End
1835 Pigot EM

Newbon, Thomas
See: Elkin & Newbon

Newbon & Beardmore
2 Commerce Street, Longton
1860 Kelly EM
1861 Harrison NC-L (earthenware manufacturers)
1862 Slater EM

Newbon & Dawson
Commerce Street, Longton
1864 Jones EM
1865 Keates A; P-L (earthenware)
The advertisement in 1865 Keates describes the firm as 'earthenware manufacturers, coloured bodies, etc., etc.'

NEWBON & DAWSON,
Earthenware Manufacturers,
COLOURED BODIES,
ETC., ETC.,
COMMERCE STREET,
LONGTON.

Newbon & Dawson. Advertisement from 1865 Keates.

Newport Wharf Pottery Co.
Navigation Road, Burslem
1884 Kelly EM
The managing partner is listed as Thomas F. Wood.

Nicholls, John
Weston Place, Longton
1851 White CEM-L
1854 Kelly CEM
Nicholls' house is listed as Furnace Road in 1851 White.

Nicholls, John, & Co.
Weston Place, Longton
1852 Slater CM; EM

Nixon, George
(i) Newfield View, Tunstall
1884 Kelly EM
1888 Kelly EM
(ii) Summer Bank Pottery, Newfield, Tunstall
1887 Porter JM-T
1889 Keates P-T (Rockingham, jet, &c.)

Nixon, J. (Mrs.)
Newfield Street, Tunstall
1892 Kelly EM

Nixon, James, & Co.
Cobridge
1835 Pigot EM

Nixon, Joseph
Market Lane, Longton
1876 Kelly PM

Nixon, Nathan
30 Caroline Street, Longton
1862 Slater PM (dealer)

Nixon & Boulton
Summer Bank Pottery, Newfield, Tunstall
1882 Keates P-T (Rockingham, jet, &c.)

Nixon & Walley
Tunstall
1818 Parson EM-G-T-R
1818 Pigot EM

Nutt, William
(i) Flint Street, Lane End
1818 Parson EM-LE
1830 Pigot EM
(ii) Great Charles Street, Lane End
1818 Pigot CM
1822 Pigot CM
(iii) Lane End
1822 Allbut CEM (china manufact. enameller, &c.)

O

Oakes, David
St. Martin's Lane, Longton
1863 Kelly PM
1864 Jones PM

Oakes, Clare & Chadwick
Sneyd Pottery, Albert Street, Burslem
1876 Kelly RM
1879 Keates P-B
1880 Kelly MM; RM
1882 Keates P-B (majolica and earthenware)
1884 Kelly MM; RM
1887 Porter EM-B
1888 Kelly MM; RM
1889 Keates P-B (majolica and earthenware)
1892 Keates P-B (majolica and earthenware)
1892 Kelly JRM
The second partner's name is listed as Clure in 1879 Keates and as Clarke in 1887 Porter.

Oakley & Co.
New Street, Longton
1884 Kelly EM

Oakley & Cope
New Street, Longton
1882 Keates P-L (majolica)

Oakley & Thacker
New Street, Longton
1880 Kelly EM

Oalsnam & Holdcroft
See: Oulsnam & Holdcroft

Ogden & Co.
Mayer Street, Hanley
1892 Keates P-H (stilt & thimble)

Ogden, Henry, & Co.
Mayer Street, Hanley
1896 Kelly SC (Stilt & Thimble Makers)
1900 Kelly SC (Stilt & Thimble Makers)

Old Hall Earthenware Co.
Hill Street, Hanley
1862 Slater EM; PM

Old Hall Earthenware Co. Ltd.
(i) Old Hall Street, Hanley
1863 Kelly CM-Fancy Ware; CM-General; CM-Tea, Breakfast, and Dessert Services; EM; PFM; SC (China Porcelain Manufacturers)
1865 Keates P-H
(ii) Old Hall Works, Hill Street, Hanley
1864 Jones EM
1868 Kelly CM; EM
1870 Harrod NC-H (manufacturers of earthenware, parian, and stoneware, for home and foreign markets) (two entries)
1872 Kelly EM
1873 Keates P-H (earthenware, parian, and china)
1875 Keates P-H (earthenware, parian, and china)
1876 Kelly EM
1879 Keates P-H (earthenware, parian, and china)
1880 Kelly EM
1882 Keates P-H (earthenware, parian, and china)
1884 Kelly EM
1888 Kelly EM
1889 Keates P-H (earthenware, parian and china)
1892 Keates P-H (earthenware, parian and china)
Charles Meigh is listed as managing director in 1870 Harrod and as manager in the five Keates directories between 1873 and 1889. Taylor Ashworth is listed as managing director in 1892 Keates.

Old Hall Porcelain Works Ltd.
(i) New Street, Hanley
1887 Porter EM-H
(ii) Hill Street, Hanley
1892 Kelly CM
1896 Kelly CM
1900 Kelly CM

Old Hall Pottery Co. Ltd.
(i) Old Hall Street, Hanley
1867 Keates P-H (earthenware, parian and china)
(ii) Hill Street, Hanley
1869 Keates P-H (earthenware, parian and china)
The manager is listed as C. Meigh in both directories.

Oldham & Co.
Ranelagh Street, Hanley
1872 Kelly EM
1876 Kelly EM

Oldham, James
Ranelagh Works, Ranelagh Street and Bethesda Street, Hanley
1860 Kelly CM-General; EM
1861 Harrison NC-H-Sh (mosaical and ornamental stone manufacturer)
1863 Kelly EM
1865 Keates P-H (door furniture & stoneware)
1867 Keates A; P-H (earthenware and stoneware)
1868 Kelly EM
1873 Keates P-H
An advertisement in 1861 Harrison describes Oldham as a 'mosaic & ornamental stoneware & earthenware manufacturer'. The advertisement in 1867 Keates describes him as a 'manufacturer of earthenware, mosaic and ornamental stone, parian vases & figures, lustres, &c.' An entry which may also relate to James Oldham appears in 1869 Keates under the name of Renalagh Works (qv).

JAMES OLDHAM,
MOSAIC & ORNAMENTAL
STONEWARE & EARTHENWARE
MANUFACTURER,
BETHESDA STREET & RANELAGH STREET,
HANLEY.

James Oldham. Advertisement from 1861 Harrison.

JAMES OLDHAM,
MANUFACTURER OF EARTHENWARE,
MOSAIC AND ORNAMENTAL STONE,
PARIAN VASES & FIGURES,
LUSTRES, &c.,
RENALAGH WORKS,
Renalagh Street, Bethesda Street,
HANLEY,
STAFFORDSHIRE POTTERIES.

James Oldham. Advertisement from 1867 Keates.

Oldham, James, & Co.
Ranelagh Street and Bethesda Street, Hanley
1862 Slater A; EM; PM
1864 Jones EM; PM
1870 Harrod NC-H (manufacturers of general earthenware, mosaic and ornamental stone, parian, &c.)
1875 Keates P-H (earthenware)
The advertisement in 1862 Slater describes the firm as 'mosaic and ornamental stone, parian, and earthenware manufacturers'.

J. OLDHAM & CO.
Mosaic and Ornamental Stone, Parian, and
EARTHENWARE MANUFACTURERS,
BETHESDA STREET, RANELAGH STREET,
Hanley, Staffordshire.

James Oldham & Co. Advertisement from 1862 Slater.

Oliver
Cobridge
1818 Pigot EM
No first name is listed.

Oliver, E.J.
212 Waterloo Road, Burslem
1889 Keates P-B
1892 Keates P-B

Oliver & Bourne
Cobridge
1816 Underhill P
1818 Parson EM-B-Lp-C
The second partner's name is listed as Burne in 1816 Underhill.

Ollivant, John
Edward Street, Burslem
1870 Harrod NC-B (potter)

Oswell, Nevitt
Wheatsheaf Street, Shelton
1852 Slater PM (broach (sic) and wicker baskets)

Oulsman, Thomas, & Sons
Furlong Works, Burslem
1887 Porter EM-B

Oulsnam, William, & Son
Furlong Works, Burslem
1872 Kelly EM
1873 Keates P-B (earthenware)
1875 Keates P-B (earthenware)
1876 Kelly EM
1879 Keates P-B (earthenware)
1882 Keates P-B (earthenware)
The surname is listed as Ouslman in 1872 Kelly.

Oulsnam, William Emerson
High Street, Tunstall
1862 Slater EM
1863 Kelly EM
1864 Jones EM
1865 Keates P-T (earthenware)
1867 Keates P-T (earthenware)
1868 Kelly EM
1869 Keates P-T (earthenware)
1870 Harrod NC-T (earthenware manufacturer)
Oulsnam is also listed as a cratemaker at Greenfields, Tunstall, in 1870 Harrod.

Oulsnam, William E., & Son
Furlong Works, Burslem
1889 Keates P-B (earthenware)
1892 Keates P-B (earthenware)

Oulsnam, William E., & Sons
Furlong Works, Burslem
1880 Kelly EM
1884 Kelly EM
1888 Kelly EM
1892 Kelly EM
The surname is listed as Ouslnam in 1884 Kelly, 1888 Kelly, and 1892 Kelly.

Oulsnam & Holdcroft
High Street, Tunstall
1860 Kelly EM
1861 Harrison NC-T (earthenware manufacturers)
The first partner's name is listed as Oalsnam in 1861 Harrison.

Oulsnam, Holdcroft & Co.
High Street, Tunstall
1852 Slater EM
1854 Kelly CEM
1856 Kelly CEM

Oulsnan, William
Newcastle Street, Burslem
1870 Harrod NC-B (earthenware manufacturer)

Ouslman, William, & Son
See: Oulsnam, William, & Son

Ouslnam, William E., & Sons
See: Oulsnam, William E., & Sons

Owen, Raby & Co.
Dalehall, Burslem
1884 Kelly EM

P

Palmer, Thomas
Lane End
1816 Underhill P

Pankhurst & Co.
Old Hall Street, Hanley
1863 Kelly EM
1868 Kelly EM

Pankhurst, James William
(i) Old Hall Street, Hanley
1851 White CEM-H-Sh
(ii) 2 Commerce Street, Longton
1862 Slater EM
(iii) Charles Street Manufactory, Hanley
1861 Harrison NC-H-Sh (earthenware manufacturer)
1864 Jones EM
Pankhurst's house is listed as 2 Wheatley Place in 1851 White. His surname is listed as Parkhurst in 1861 Harrison.

Pankhurst, James William, & Co.
(i) Old Hall Street, Hanley
1852 Slater EM
1854 Kelly CEM
1856 Kelly CEM
1860 Kelly EM
1865 Keates P-H (white granite earthenware)
1867 Keates P-H (white granite earthenware)
1869 Keates P-H (white granite earthenware)
1872 Kelly EM
1873 Keates P-H (white granite earthenware)
1875 Keates P-H (white granite earthenware)
1876 Kelly EM
1879 Keates P-H (white granite earthenware)
1880 Kelly EM
1882 Keates P-H (white granite earthenware)
(ii) Charles Street Works, Hanley
1870 Harrod NC-H (white granite manufacturers for the United States)

James William Pankhurst & Co. Moulded mark from a relief-moulded stoneware jug.

James William Pankhurst & Co. Printed mark from a blue-printed earthenware dish.

Park Hall Pottery Co.
Park Hall Street, Longton
1900 Kelly EM

Park Sanitary Co. (The)
Albert Pottery, Victoria Road, Hanley
1896 Kelly SC (Sanitary Ware Manufacturers)
The firm succeeded J. Buckley (1896 Kelly).

Parker & Brindley
Golden Hill
1822 Allbut CEM
(earthenware manufact.)

Parker, Thomas
Golden Hill
1822 Pigot EM

Parkhurst, J.W.
See: Pankhurst, James William

Parkins, Rathbone & Co.
Broad Street, Hanley
1892 Keates P-H

Parr Brothers
Podmore Street, Burslem
1861 Harrison NC-B (marble manufacturers)

Parr, Edward
Podmore Street Works, Waterloo Road, Burslem
1863 Kelly TM
1864 Jones EM-Miscellaneous (tea-pots, marbles, parlour balls, &c.)

Parr, Edwin
30 Church Street, Burslem
1860 Kelly TM (marble)
1861 Harrison NC-B (marble toy maker)

Parr, J., & Co.
Sandyford Pottery, Tunstall
1888 Kelly JM; RM

Parr, John
(i) 6 Podmore Street, Burslem
1860 Kelly TM (earthenware & marble)
1861 Harrison NC-B (marble toy maker)
(ii) Kiln Croft Works, Burslem
1863 Kelly TM (earthenware)
1864 Jones EM-Miscellaneous (toy and marble)
(iii) 78 Waterloo Road, Burslem
1863 Kelly TM (earthenware)
(iv) Wellington Street, Burslem
1870 Harrod NC-B (marble and nest-egg manufacturer)
1873 Keates P-B (nest egg)
1875 Keates P-B (nest egg)
1879 Keates P-B (nest egg)
(v) Adelaide Street Works, Burslem
1882 Keates P-B (nest egg)
Parr's private residence is listed as Pitt Street in 1870 Harrod.

Parr, Joseph
Sandyford, Tunstall
1887 Porter JM-T

Parr, Richard jun.
Church Street, Burslem
1828 Pigot EM (toy only)
1835 Pigot EM

Parr, Thomas
34 Church Street, Burslem
1856 Kelly TM
1860 Kelly TM (marble)
1861 Harrison NC-B (marble toy maker)
1863 Kelly TM
1864 Jones EM-Miscellaneous (toy and marble)
1870 Harrod NC-B (marble toy manufacturer)

Parr, W.
30 Church Street, Burslem
1863 Kelly TM

Parr, William
Waterloo Road, Burslem
1860 Kelly TM (earthenware marble)
1861 Harrison NC-B (marble toy maker)

Parrish, William
See: Decorative Art Tile Co.
See: Decorative Art Tile Co. Ltd.

Parrys Brothers
Sandyford
1816 Underhill P

Passenger & Co.
Hanley
1809 Holden NC (earthenware-manufactrs.)

Patent Fire Resisting Cement Co.
Brewery Street and Bryan Street, Hanley
1889 Keates P-H

Pattenden, Hurles & Co.
See: Grove & Stark

Pattison, James
High Street, Lane End
1818 Parson EM-LE
1818 Pigot EM (toy)
1822 Pigot EM (toy)
1828 Pigot EM (toy only)
1830 Pigot EM (toy only)

Payne Brothers
Podmore Street, Burslem
1869 Keates P-B (Rockingham)
1870 Harrod NC-B (Rockingham ware manufacturers)

Peake & Co.
(i) Wharf Lane, Hanley
1892 Keates P-H (Rockingham & earthenware)
(ii) Rectory Road, Hanley
1892 Kelly EM

Peake, J. & J.
Snow Hill, Shelton
1851 White CEM-H-Sh

Peake, Joseph
Etruria Vale, Hanley
1882 Keates P-H (Rockingham and earthenware)
1884 Kelly EM
1887 Porter EM-H
1888 Kelly EM
1889 Keates P-H (Rockingham and earthenware)
1892 Keates P-H (Rockingham & earthenware)
1892 Kelly EM
1896 Kelly EM
The address is listed as Bridgewater Arms in 1887 Porter.

Peake, Joseph, & Co.
Brook Street, Shelton
1835 Pigot EM (black)

Peake, Sarah Ann (Mrs.)
Rectory Road, Shelton
1896 Kelly EM
1900 Kelly EM

Peake, Samuel, & Co.
Brook Street, Shelton
1834 White EM-H-Sh (black & chimney pipe)

Peake, Thomas
(i) Tunstall
1830 Pigot EM (ornaments and vessels for gentlemen's gardens)
1835 Pigot EM
(ii) The Tileries, Tunstall
1870 Harrod NC-T (manufacturer of terra-metalic tiles,
pipes, &c., tileries, colliery, and ironstone works)
1880 Kelly TCM
1884 Kelly TCM

1888 Kelly SC (Encaustic Tile Manufacturers); TCM
1892 Kelly TCM

Peake, Thomas, & Co.
Tunstall
1828 Pigot EM (ornaments and vessels for gentlemen's gardens)

Pearce, William
High Street, Stoke
1900 Kelly EM

Pearl Pottery Co.
Brook Street, Hanley
1896 Kelly EM
1900 Kelly EM

Pearson, Edward
(i) Liverpool Road, Burslem
1850 Kelly CEM; NC-B (china black & earthenware mfr.)
1850 Slater EM
1851 White CEM-B (only earthenware)
(ii) Cobridge
1852 Slater EM
1854 Kelly CEM
1856 Kelly CEM
1860 Kelly EM
1864 Jones EM
(iii) Hill Works, Burslem
1861 Harrison NC-B (iron, stone, china, and earthenware manufacturer)
(iv) Sneyd Green or Sneyd Street, Cobridge, Burslem
1862 Slater EM
1863 Kelly EM
1865 Keates P-B (earthenware and ironstone)
1867 Keates P-B (earthenware)
1868 Kelly EM
1869 Keates P-B (earthen.)
1872 Kelly EM
1873 Keates P-B (earthen.)

Pearson, John
Newcastle Street, Burslem
1834 White EM-B
1835 Pigot EM

Pearson Pottery Co.
Brook Street and Clarence Street, Hanley
1900 Kelly, EM

Pedley, B. & J.
Hope Street, Shelton
1856 Kelly PM

Pennington, Charles
32 Old Hall Street, Hanley
1864 Jones EM

Pennington, John
Mayer Street, Hanley
1887 Porter EM-H
1888 Kelly MM
1889 Keates P-H

Penson, Frederick William
Vine Street, Stoke
1896 Kelly TCM

Peover, Ann
High Street, Hanley
1822 Allbut CEM (china manufact.)
1822 Pigot CM

Peover, Frederick
(i) High Street, Hanley
1818 Parson EM-H-Sh
(ii) Edmund Street, Hanley
1818 Pigot CM

Ann or Frederick Peover. Impressed mark from a hand-painted bone china plate.

Perkins & Co.
Royal Victoria Works, Hanley
1892 Kelly JRM

Perkins, Knight & Locker
High Street, Longton
1882 Keates P-L (earthenware)

Perry & Broadhurst
Fenton
1851 White CEM-F (lustre and black wares)

Perry, Samuel
Hanley
1784 Bailey NC-H (potter)

Perry, Samuel, & Co.
Hanley
1781 Bailey NC (potters)
1783 Bailey NC (potters)

Philips, Thomas
Lane End
1781 Bailey NC (potter)
1783 Bailey NC (potter)

Phillips, Edward
(i) York Street, Shelton
1852 Slater A; CM (and ormula ornaments)
(ii) Cannon Street, Hanley
1856 Kelly CEM
1860 Kelly CM-General; LM
1861 Harrison NC-H-Sh (glass and china manufacturer)
1862 Slater CM
The advertisement in 1852 Slater describes Phillips as a 'manufacturer of glass chandeliers, lustres, girandoles, gilt and enamelled china, ormolu ornaments, &c.'

EDWARD PHILLIPS,
Manufacturer of
GLASS CHANDELIERS,
LUSTRES, GIRANDOLES,
GILT AND ENAMELLED CHINA,
ORMOLU ORNAMENTS, &c.
YORK STREET,
SHELTON, STAFFORDSHIRE.
D 2 9

Edward Phillips. Advertisement from 1852 Slater.

Phillips, Edward & George
Longport
1822 Allbut CEM (earthenware manufacts.)
1828 Pigot EM
1830 Pigot EM
1834 White EM-B
1835 Pigot EM

Edward & George Phillips. Impressed mark from a blue-printed earthenware plate.

Phillips, George
Longport
1841 Pigot EM
1846 Williams NC-Lp (earthenware manufacturer)

Phillips, John Ball
See: Phillips, Thomas, & Son

Phillips, Thomas, & Son
Furlong Pottery, Burslem
1846 Williams NC-B (earthenware manufacturers)
The partners are listed individually as Thomas Phillips of High Street, Newcastle, and John Ball Phillips of Lower Hadderidge, Burslem, in 1846 Williams.

Phillips, William & John
Lane End
1796 Chester NC-LE-LD-LL (manufacturers of earthenware)
1802 Allbut EM (map location 123)

Phillips, William
Lane End
1798 Universal NC-LE (manufacturer of Staffordshire-ware)

Phillips & Bagster
High Street, Hanley
1822 Allbut CEM (earthenware manufacts.)
1822 Pigot EM

Pickance & Daniel
Cobridge
1781 Bailey NC (potters)
1783 Bailey NC (potters)

Pickard & Salt
Marsh Street, Longton
1864 Jones EM

Pinder, Thomas
(i) Swan Bank Works, Swan Square, Burslem
1850 Kelly CEM; NC-B (ironstone china & earthenware manufacturer)
1850 Slater CM; EM
1851 White CEM-B (both) (ironstone ware)
(ii) Fountain Place, Burslem
1852 Slater CM
Pinder's house is listed as Grange Terrace in 1851 White.

Pinder, Thomas
See: Mellor, Venables & Co.

Pinder, Bourne & Co
Nile Street, Burslem
1862 Slater EM
1863 Kelly CM-General
1864 Jones EM
1865 Keates P-B (earthenware and ironstone)
1867 Keates P-B (earthenware)
1868 Kelly EM
1869 Keates P-B (earthenware)
1870 Harrod NC-B (manufacturers of ironstone, china, and earthenware)
1872 Kelly EM
1873 Keates P-B (earthenware)
1875 Keates P-B (earthenware)
1876 Kelly EM
1879 Keates P-B (earthenware)
1880 Kelly A; EM; SC (Sanitary Ware Manufacturers)
The advertisement in 1880 Kelly announces 'the only silver medal and highest honour for fine earthenware, Paris exhibition, 1878' and describes the firm as 'manufacturers of every class of earthenware, for home & foreign markets'. It lists 'artistic pottery in ivory, céladon, jet, terra cotta, and gros bleu; sanitary and telegraphic ware of all kinds' and claims that 'their dinner, dessert, and toilet services in ivory and celadon are unequalled'. Two London offices are listed, at 23 Great Winchester Street (for export) and at 22 Thavies Inn, Holborn (for home). The advertisement finishes with the statement that 'P.B. & Co. having just doubled their producing power can execute orders very promptly'.

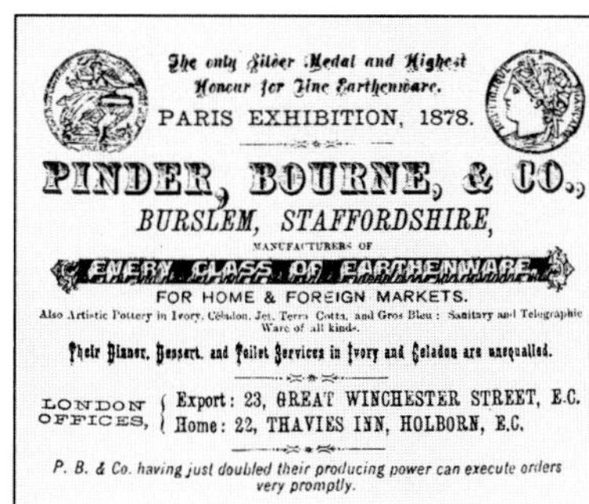

Pinder, Bourne & Co. Advertisement from 1880 Kelly.

Pinder, Bourne & Hope
(i) Fountain Place, Burslem
1851 White NC-B (china, &c., manufacturers)
1852 Slater EM (and ironstone)
1854 Kelly CEM
1856 Kelly CEM
1860 Kelly CM-General; EM
1861 Harrison NC-B (earthenware manufacturers)
(ii) Nile Street, Burslem
1860 Kelly CM-General; EM

Pitcairns Ltd.
Pinnox, Tunstall
1896 Kelly EM
1900 Kelly EM

Plant Brothers
(i) Newcastle Street, Burslem
1887 Porter EM-B
(ii) Crown Pottery, Dale Hall, Burslem
1888 Kelly EM
1892 Kelly EM; SC (Brass Founders' China & Earthenware Figure Manufacturers); SC (Door Furniture Manufacturers – China); SC (Ironstone China Manufacturers)
1896 Kelly EM
1900 Kelly EM
(iii) Bagnall Street, Longton
1892 Kelly CM
1896 Kelly CM
1900 Kelly CM

Plant, James
Registry Street, Stoke
1882 Keates P-S (stone and earthenware)
1884 Kelly EM
1888 Kelly EM
An advertisement in 1882 Keates describes Plant as a 'manufacturer of stone and earthenware and decorated goods, for home and export'.

JAMES PLANT,
MANUFACTURER OF
STONE AND EARTHENWARE
And DECORATED GOODS,
(FOR HOME AND EXPORT.)
Registry Street Works, Stoke-on-Trent.

James Plant. Advertisement from 1882 Keates.

Plant, James jun.
Brewery Street Works (off Hope Street), Hanley
1880 Kelly EM (stone & earthenware manufacturer); SM

Plant, James, & Co.
Stoke Pottery, Stoke

1892 Keates P-S (stone and earthenware)
1892 Kelly EM
1896 Kelly EM
1900 Kelly EM

Plant, James & Ralph
Stoke Pottery, Stoke
1889 Keates P-S (stone and earthenware)

Plant, John
Lane End
1798 Universal NC-LE (manufacturer of Staffordshire-ware)

Plant, John, & Co.
Stafford Street, Longton
1882 Keates P-L (decorating)

Plant, R., & Sons
Sneyd Green, Cobridge, Burslem
1860 Kelly EM
1861 Harrison NC-B (earthenware manufacturers)

R.H. Plant & Co. Advertisement from 1889 Keates. The same basic advertisement appeared in 1892 Keates.

Plant, R.H., & Co.
(i) Carlisle Works, High Street, Longton
1882 Keates P-L (china)
1884 Kelly CM
1888 Kelly CM
1889 Keates P-L (china)
1892 Keates P-L (china)
1892 Kelly CM
1896 Kelly CM
(ii) Forrester Street, Longton
1900 Kelly CM
Identical advertisements appear in 1889 Keates and 1892 Keates describing the firm as 'china manufacturers'. They offer 'specialities in tea and breakfast ware (entirely new shapes and designs) for home and foreign markets. Special hotel shapes. Illustrated sheets and price lists on application.' Both advertisements feature a possible trade mark of a winged crown over a Staffordshire knot with the firm's initials. They also list a London agent as James T. Mogridge with showrooms at 10 Bartlett's Buildings.

Plant, Ralph
Sylvester Pottery, Burslem
1884 Kelly EM

Plant, Ralph, & Sons
Warwick Works, Chadwick Street, Longton
1896 Kelly EM
1900 Kelly EM

Plant, Richard H.
Carlisle Works, Longton
1887 Porter EM-L

Plant, William, & Co.
The Foley, Fenton
1852 Slater CM; EM

Plant & Gardener
Bourne's Bank, Burslem
1867 Keates P-B (earthen.)

Plant & Gardiner
Sneyd Green, Burslem
1868 Kelly EM

Plant & Gilmore
New Hall Works, York Street, Hanley
1896 Kelly EM
1900 Kelly EM

Plant & Hallam
Fenton
1854 Kelly CEM

Plant & Johnson
Heathcote Works, Longton
1879 Keates P-L (china)
1882 Keates P-L (china)

Plant & Taylor
Chadwick Street, Longton
1892 Keates P-L (earthenware)
1892 Kelly EM

Platt, Ambrose
6 Moorland Road, Burslem
1887 Porter EM-B
An advertisement in 1887 Porter describes Platt as a 'manufacturer of specialities in earthenware, also letters for plate-glass windows, sign boards, &c.' with a 'special line in cruets'.

Ambrose Platt. Advertisement from 1887 Porter.

Platt & Bridgwood
High Street, Lane End
1818 Pigot EM
1822 Allbut CEM (earthenware manufacts.)
1822 Pigot EM

Platt & Wild
Sheaf Street and George Street, Hanley
1860 Kelly PM

Podmore, Thomas
See: Podmore, Walker and Co.

Podmore, Thomas, & Co.
Tunstall
1830 Pigot EM

Podmore, Walker & Co.
(i) Upper Pot Works, Tunstall
1834 White EM-T
(ii) Well Street, Tunstall
1835 Pigot EM
1841 Pigot EM
1846 Williams NC-T (earthenware manufacturers)
(iii) Old Bank
1841 Pigot EM
(iv) High Street, Tunstall
1851 White EM-T

1852 Slater EM
(v) Amicable Street, Tunstall
1851 White EM-T
1856 Kelly CEM
(vi) Swan Bank, Tunstall
1854 Kelly CEM
1856 Kelly CEM
The partners are listed individually as Thomas Podmore of Paradise Street and Thomas Walker of Wesley Place in 1846 Williams.

Podmore, Walker & Co. Printed mark from a brown-printed earthenware plate.

Pointon & Co.
(i) Well Street Pottery, Tunstall
1872 Kelly EM
(ii) Norfolk Works, Norfolk Street, Hanley
1887 Porter EM-H
1889 Keates P-H
1892 Keates P-H

Pointon & Co. (Ltd.). Printed and painted marks from a hand-painted bone china dessert plate.

Pointon & Co. Ltd.
Norfolk Works, Norfolk Street, Shelton, Hanley
1884 Kelly CM
1888 Kelly CM
1892 Kelly CM
1896 Kelly CM
1900 Kelly CM

Pointon, William
(i) Overhouse Works, Greenhead, Burslem
1828 Pigot EM
1830 Pigot EM
1834 White EM-B (china mfrs. also)
1841 Pigot EM
1846 Williams NC-B (earthenware manufacturer)
1850 Slater EM
1851 White CEM-B (both)
1852 Slater EM
1854 Kelly CEM
(ii) Market Place, Burslem
1850 Kelly CEM; NC-B (earthenware manufacturer)
(iii) High Street, Burslem
1856 Kelly CEM
Pointon's house is listed as High Street, Burslem, in 1846 Williams.

Pointon, William, & Co.
Greenhead, Burslem
1835 Pigot EM

Pointon, William B.
Parker Street, Hanley
1867 Keates P-H (earthenware)
1869 Keates P-H (earthenware)
1870 Harrod NC-H (earthenware manufacturer)

Pointon & Stubbs
Swan Street, Hanley
1822 Allbut CEM (painters and gilders)

Poole & Son
John Street, Stoke
1880 Kelly EM
1882 Keates P-S (parian, china, terra cotta, and majolica)
1884 Kelly EM

Poole, George
Ridding Lane, Hanley
1800 Allbutt NC-H (manufacturer of toys)

Poole, John
North Road, Cobridge
1892 Kelly EM

Poole, Richard
Shelton
1796 Chester NC-H-Sh (manufacturer of earthenware)
1798 Universal NC-Sh (manufacturer of Staffordshire-ware)

Poole, Thomas
(i) 45 Whieldon Road, Fenton
1882 Keates P-F (china)
(ii) Cobden Works, Edensor Road (or New Street), Longton
1882 Keates P-L (china & majolica)
1884 Kelly CM
1887 Porter EM-L
1888 Kelly CM
1889 Keates P-L (china and majolica)
1892 Keates P-L (china and majolica)
1892 Kelly CM
1896 Kelly CM
1900 Kelly CM

Poole & Shrigley
Burslem
1796 Chester NC-B (manufacturers of earthenware)

Poole, Shrigley & Lakin
Burslem
1798 Universal NC-B (manufacturers of earthen-ware)
The third partner's name is listed as Laking.

Poole, Stanway & Wood
(i) Copeland Street, Stoke
1875 Keates P-S (parian, earthenware, and china)
1876 Kelly CM
(ii) Liverpool Road, Stoke
1875 Keates P-S (parian, earthenware, and china)

Poole & Sutherland
(i) Heathcote Road, Longton
1860 Kelly RM; SC (Egyptian Black Ware Manufacturers)
1861 Harrison NC-L (Rockingham and black earthenware manufacturers)
1862 Slater EM
(ii) Cornhill Passage, Stafford Street, Longton
1860 Kelly RM; SC (Egyptian Black Ware Manufacturers)
1863 Kelly RM; SC

(Egyptian Black Ware Manufacturers)
1864 Jones CEM

Poole, Sutherland & Hallam
Cornhill Passage, Longton
1865 Keates P-L (gold and silver lustre, parian, &c.)
1867 Keates P-L (gold and silver lustre, parian, &c.)
1868 Kelly EM
1869 Keates P-L (earthenware, rustic and gold and silver lustre, parian, &c.)
1870 Harrod NC-L (earthenware and rustic manufacturers)

Poole & Unwin
Cornhill Works, Cornhill Passage, Longton
1872 Kelly EM
1873 Keates P-L (earthenware, rustic and gold and silver lustre, parian, &c.)
1875 Keates P-L (earthenware, rustic and gold and silver lustre, &c.)
1876 Kelly EM

Pope, J.
Sheaf Street, Shelton
1854 Kelly CEM

Pope, James
14 Wharf Lane, Shelton
1852 Slater A; EM (stone); PM; TOCM (parian marble)
The advertisement in 1852 Slater describes Pope simply as a 'stone & parian manufacturer'.

JAMES POPE,
STONE & PARIAN
MANUFACTURER,
14, WHARF LANE,
SHELTON.

James Pope. Advertisement from 1852 Slater.

Pope, James, & Co.
Brian Street, Shelton
1850 Kelly NC-Sh (stone ware manufacturers)

Pope, John
Brian Street, Shelton
1851 White CEM-H-Sh (stone ware)

Pope, John & James & Charles
Brian Street, Shelton
1850 Slater EM (and stone mortars, pestles, apothecaries' jars, &c.)

Pope, L.J., & Co.
(i) Sneyd Street, Cobridge
1872 Kelly EM
1876 Kelly EM
(ii) Lincoln Works, Sneyd Green, Burslem
1873 Keates P-B (earthenware)
1875 Keates P-B (earthenware)
1879 Keates P-B (earthenware)

Pope, Ralph
Shelton
1805 Holden NC (coarse ware potter)

Pope, Stephen
Shelton
1796 Chester NC-H-Sh (manufacturer of earthenware)

Pope, Thomas
Shelton
1796 Chester NC-H-Sh (manufacturer of earthenware)
1802 Allbut EM (map location 92)

Pope & Shaw
Hanover Street, Shelton
1861 Harrison NC-H-Sh (manufacturers of creels, cups, &c.)

Portland Pottery
Fenton
1882 Keates P-F (earthenware)

Potts, William Wainwright
Waterloo Road, Burslem
1846 Williams NC-B (patentee of the royal cylindrical printing)

Poulson
See: Poulson, Wm.

Poulson, George
(i) Cobridge
1805 Holden NC (china and earthenware manufacture)
(ii) Stoke
1809 Holden NC (china & earthenware-manufacturer)
1816 Underhill P

Poulson, Thomas
Stoke
1811 Holden NC (china & earthenware-manufacturer)

Poulson, William
Chancery Lane, Lane End
1818 Parson EM-LE
1818 Pigot EM
The entry in 1818 Pigot is incomplete, with no first name listed.

Poulson & Dale
Dale Street, Stoke
1818 Parson EM-S-E
1818 Pigot CM

Powell & Bishop
(i) Parliament Row, Hanley
1867 Keates P-H (earthenware)
1869 Keates P-H (earthenware)
1872 Kelly EM
1876 Kelly EM
(ii) Stafford Street, Hanley
1867 Keates P-H (earthenware)
1868 Kelly EM
1869 Keates P-H (earthenware)
1872 Kelly EM
1873 Keates P-H (china and earthenware)
1875 Keates P-H (china and earthenware)
1876 Kelly EM
(iii) High Street, Hanley
1868 Kelly EM
1869 Keates P-H (earthenware)
1870 Harrod NC-H (manufacturers of plain and ornamental china and earthenware, for home, American, and continental markets)
1872 Kelly EM
1873 Keates P-H (china and earthenware)
1875 Keates P-H (china and earthenware)
1876 Kelly EM
(iv) Hanley
1884 Kelly CM

Powell, Bishop & Co.
High Street and Stafford Street, Hanley
1879 Keates P-H (china & earthenware)

Powell, Bishop & Stonier
(i) Stafford Street, Hanley

1880 Kelly EM
1882 Keates P-H (china and earthenware)
1884 Kelly EM
1887 Porter EM-H
1888 Kelly EM
1889 Keates P-H (china and earthenware)
1892 Keates P-H (china and earthenware)
1892 Kelly CM; EM
(ii) High Street, Hanley
1880 Kelly EM
1882 Keates P-H (china and earthenware)
1884 Kelly EM
1887 Porter EM-H
1888 Kelly EM
1889 Keates P-H (china and earthenware)
1892 Keates P-H (china and earthenware)
1892 Kelly CM; EM
(iii) Nelson Place, Hanley
1880 Kelly EM
1889 Keates P-H (china and earthenware)
1892 Keates P-H (china and earthenware)
(iv) Botteslow Street, Hanley
1887 Porter EM-H
(v) Hanley
1888 Kelly CM

Powell, Bishop & Stonier. Printed mark from a grey-printed green earthenware tea plate. The registration diamond dates from 1880.

Powes, Henry & Charles
Sandiford, Golden Hill
1818 Pigot EM
1822 Pigot EM

Powis, Charles
Sandiford
1822 Allbut CEM (earthenware manufacturer)

Powis, H., & Co.
Sandiford
1818 Parson EM-G-T-R

Pratt & Co.
Lane Delph, Fenton
1876 Kelly EM
1880 Kelly EM

Pratt, Ellin
Lane Delph
1805 Holden NC (earthenware manufacturer)

Pratt, Felix, & Co.
Fenton
1846 Williams NC-C-F-E (earthenware manufacturers)

Felix Pratt. Portrait of Felix Pratt on a china plaque, believed to have been made in about 1888 for presentation to employees and friends.

Pratt, Felix Edwards
Brook Street, Stoke
1846 Williams NC-S (earthenware manufacturer)

Pratt, Felix & Richard
(i) Fenton
1818 Parson EM-LE
1818 Pigot EM
1822 Pigot EM
1828 Pigot EM
1830 Pigot EM
1834 White CEM-F-LD
1835 Pigot EM
1850 Kelly CEM; NC-S (earthenware manufacturers)
(ii) Lane Delph
1822 Allbut CEM (earthenware manufacts.)
(iii) High Street, Fenton
1887 Porter EM-F

Pratt, Felix & Richard, & Co.
(i) High Street or High Street East, Fenton
1841 Pigot CM; EM
1850 Slater CM; EM
1851 White CEM-F (only earthenware)
1852 Slater CM; EM
1862 Slater EM
1864 Jones EM
1867 Keates P-F (earthenware)
1869 Keates P-F (earthenware and terra cotta)
1873 Keates P-F (earthenware and terra cotta)
1875 Keates P-F (earthenware and terra cotta)
1876 Kelly EM
1879 Keates P-F (earthenware and terra cotta)
1882 Keates P-F (earthenware and terra cotta)
1884 Kelly EM
1888 Kelly EM
1889 Keates P-F (earthenware and terra cotta)
1892 Keates P-F (earthenware and terra cotta)
1892 Kelly EM
1896 Kelly EM
1900 Kelly EM
(ii) Fenton
1854 Kelly CEM
1856 Kelly CEM
1860 Kelly EM
1861 Harrison NC-F (earthenware manufacturers)
1863 Kelly EM
1868 Kelly EM
1870 Harrod NC-F (manufacturers of druggists' sundries, uniquely-decorated and general earthenware; awarded Soc. of Arts silver medal, 1848, and first-class medal International Exhibition, Paris, 1855)
1872 Kelly EM
1880 Kelly EM (manufacturers in great variety of uniquely ornamented earthenware, cream colour, pearl white, printed, enamelled, green glaze, Rockingham, porous, stone, terra cotta & druggists' ware, suitable for the home & foreign markets)
(iii) Lower Fenton

1865 Keates P-F (earthen.)
1867 Keates P-F (earthenware)
1869 Keates P-F (earthenware and terra cotta)
1873 Keates P-F (earthenware and terra cotta)
1875 Keates P-F (earthenware and terra cotta)
1879 Keates P-F (earthenware and terra cotta)
1882 Keates P-F (earthenware and terra cotta)
(iv) Market Street, Fenton
1865 Keates P-F (earthen.)

Felix & Richard Pratt & Co. Printed mark from a multicolour-printed dessert plate.

Felix & Richard Pratt & Co. Printed mark from a large multicolour-printed dish.

Pratt, John
Lane Delph
1805 Holden NC (earthenware manufacturer)
1809 Holden NC (manufacturer of earthenware)
1811 Holden NC (manufacr. of earthenware)
1816 Underhill P
1818 Parson EM-LE
1818 Pigot EM
1822 Pigot EM
1828 Pigot EM
1830 Pigot EM
1834 White CEM-F-LD (earthenware only)
1835 Pigot EM

Pratt, John jun.
See: Pratt, John, & Co. Ltd.

Pratt, John, & Co.
(i) Lane Delph
1851 White CEM-F (only earthenware)
1854 Kelly CEM
1856 Kelly CEM
1860 Kelly CM-General; EM
1863 Kelly EM
1864 Jones EM
1868 Kelly EM
1869 Keates P-F (earthenware)
1870 Harrod NC-F (earthenware manufacturers)
(ii) Park Street, Fenton
1861 Harrison NC-F (earthenware manufacturers)
1862 Slater EM
1865 Keates P-F (earthenware)
1867 Keates P-F (earthenware)
1873 Keates P-F (earthenware)
1875 Keates P-F (earthenware)
A London address at 19 Crosby Hall Chambers is listed in 1868 Kelly.

Pratt, John, & Co. Ltd.
Lane Delph
1872 Kelly EM
The secretary is given as John Pratt junior and a London address at 19 Crosby Hall Chambers is listed in 1872 Kelly.

Pratt, John & William
Lane Delph
1841 Pigot EM
1846 Williams NC-C-F-E (earthenware manufacturer)
1850 Kelly CEM; NC-S (earthenware manfrs.)
1850 Slater EM
1852 Slater EM

Pratt, P.
Brook Street, Stoke (house)
1861 Harrison NC-S (earthenware manufacturer)

Pratt, Samuel
Sheaf Street, Shelton
1861 Harrison NC-H-Sh (parian manufacturer)

Pratt, William
Lane Delph
1781 Bailey NC (potter)
1783 Bailey NC (potters)
1796 Chester NC-LE-LD-LL (manufacturer of earthenware)
1802 Allbut EM (map location 110)

Pratt, Hassall & Gerrard
(i) Lane Delph
1822 Allbut CEM (china manufacts.)
1822 Pigot EM
1828 Pigot CM
1830 Pigot CM
1834 White CM-LE-L
(ii) High Street, Longton
1834 White CM-LE-L
The second partner is listed as Hassell in 1822 Pigot and the third partner as Gerard in 1822 Allbut.

Pratt & Simpson
Lane Delph Pottery, Park Street, Fenton
1879 Keates P-F (earthenware)
1880 Kelly CM; EM
1882 Keates P-F (earthenware)

Pratt, Weston & Co.
Lane Delph
1818 Pigot CM

Preece, Harry
See: Bradley & Preece

Procter, Albert Henry
Edensor Road, Longton
1892 Kelly EM

Procter, George, & Co.
Gladstone Pottery, High Street, Longton
1892 Kelly CM; EM
1896 Kelly CM; EM
1900 Kelly CM; EM

Procter, John
(i) City Road, Longton or Lane End
1846 Williams NC-L-LE (earthenware manufacturer)
(ii) Madeley Street, Tunstall
1873 Keates P-T (earthenware)
1875 Keates P-T (earthenware)
1879 Keates P-T (earthenware)
(iii) Heathcote Pottery, Heathcote Road, Longton
1880 Kelly EM

Procter, John, & Son
Edensor Road, Longton
1896 Kelly EM
1900 Kelly EM

Procter, John & Henry
Heathcote Pottery, Longton
1876 Kelly EM

Procter, John & Henry, & Co.
(i) New Town Pottery, High Street, Longton
1856 Kelly CEM
1860 Kelly EM; RM
1861 Harrison NC-L (earthenware manufacturers)
1862 Slater EM
1864 Jones A; EM
1867 Keates P-L (earthenware)
1868 Kelly EM
1869 Keates P-L (earthenware)
1870 Harrod NC-L (earthenware, &c., manufacturers)
1872 Kelly EM
1873 Keates P-L (earthenware)
1875 Keates P-L (earthenware)
(ii) Stafford Street, Longton
1863 Kelly EM
(iii) Heathcote Road, Longton
1879 Keates P-L (earthenware)
The initials are listed as T. & H. in 1861 Harrison. The surname is listed as Proctor in 1862 Slater, 1867 Keates, 1869 Keates, 1875 Keates, and 1879 Keates. The advertisement in 1864 Jones also gives the surname as Proctor and describes the firm as 'manufacturers of earthenware, Rockingham gold lustre, coloured bodies, and a variety of articles suitable for home and foreign trade'.

J. & H. PROCTOR & Co.,
MANUFACTURERS OF
EARTHENWARE,
ROCKINGHAM GOLD LUSTRE,
COLOURED BODIES,
And a variety of Articles suitable for Home and Foreign Trade.
Manufactory: HIGH STEET, LONGTON, POTTERIES,
STAFFORDSHIRE.

John & Henry Proctor & Co. Advertisement from 1864 Jones.

Procter, T. & H., & Co.
See: Procter, John & Henry, & Co.

Procter & Collingwood
Furnace Road, Longton
1850 Kelly CEM; NC-L (china manufacturers)

Procter, Mayer & Woolley
Gladstone Pottery, High Street, Longton
1884 Kelly CM
1887 Porter EM-L
1888 Kelly CM
1889 Keates P-L (china)
1892 Keates P-L (china)
The third partner's name is listed as Wooley in 1892 Keates.

Proctor, George
Green Dock, Longton
1841 Pigot EM

Proctor, John
Furnace Road, Longton or Lane End
1846 Williams NC-L-LE (china manufacturer)

Proctor, John & Henry, & Co.
See: Procter, John & Henry, & Co.

Pugh, Edward John
Granville Pottery, High Street, Longton
1889 Keates P-L
1892 Kelly EM

Pugh, Edward John, & Co.
(i) 31 High Street, Longton
1882 Keates P-L
1884 Kelly EM
1888 Kelly EM
(ii) Market Street, Longton
1887 Porter EM-L

Pugh & Glover
(i) Waterloo Works, Nelson Place, Hanley
1875 Keates, P-H
(ii) Dresden Mills, Hanley
1876 Kelly, EM
(iii) Pelham Street Works, Pelham Street, Hanley
1879 Keates P-H
1880 Kelly EM
1882 Keates P-H (earthenware & majolica)
1884 Kelly EM

Pugh & Hackney
Pelham Street Works, Hanley
1887 Porter EM-H
1888 Kelly EM
1889 Keates P-H (earthenware)
1892 Kelly EM

Pugh & Shubotham
Fountain Square, High Street, Fenton
1900 Kelly EM

Pye & Booth
Lane End
1822 Allbut CEM (earthenware manufacts.)

Q

Quick, J.J., & Co. Ltd.
Clarence Street, Hanley
1884 Kelly EM
1888 Kelly EM

Quick, Joseph J., & Co.
Clarence Street, Hanley
1887 Porter EM-H

R

Radford, Samuel
(i) Newmarket Works, Chancery Lane, Longton
1879 Keates P-L (china)
1880 Kelly CM (china manufacturer for home & export)
1882 Keates P-L (china)
(ii) High Street, Fenton
1884 Kelly CM
1887 Porter EM-F
1888 Kelly EM
1889 Keates P-F (china)
1892 Keates P-F (china)
1892 Kelly CM
1896 Kelly CM
1900 Kelly CM

Radford & Amison
Chancery Lane, Longton
1876 Kelly CM

Radford, Amison & Perkins
Chancery Lane, Longton
1875 Keates P-L (china)

Radford & Ward
Newmarket Works, Chancery Lane, Longton
1884 Kelly CM
1887 Porter EM-L
1888 Kelly CM
1889 Keates P-L (china)
1892 Keates P-L (china)
1892 Kelly CM

Ranaleigh Works
Ranaleigh Street, Hanley
1870 Harrod NC-H (earthen and stoneware manufactory)
See also: Renalagh Works

Randall, T.
Broad Street, Shelton
1856 Kelly CEM

Randall, Thomas Martin
High Street, Shelton
1841 Pigot TOCM
1850 Kelly CEM; NC-Sh (china manufacturer)
1850 Slater CM

Randall, Thomas Martin, & Son
High Street, Shelton
1852 Slater CM
1854 Kelly CEM

Ratcliff, Humphrey
Black Works, Hartshill, Stoke
1834 White EM-S
See also: Ratcliffe, Humphrey

Ratcliff & Willett
Broad Street, Shelton
1830 Pigot EM

Ratcliffe & Co.
Gold Court, Longton
1892 Keates P-L (china)
1892 Kelly EM
1896 Kelly EM

Ratcliffe (Mrs.)
Stoke Lane
1802 Allbut EM (map location 98)

Ratcliffe, Humphrey
Stoke Road or Stoke Lane
1822 Allbut CEM (earthenware manufact.)
1830 Pigot EM (coarse)
The surname is listed as Ratcliff in 1830 Pigot.

Ratcliffe, William
High Street, Hanley
1834 White EM-H-Sh
1835 Pigot EM

Rathbone & Co.
George Street, Hanley
1834 White CM-H-Sh

Rathbone, James
Wharf Street and Queen Street, Burslem
1870 Harrod NC-B (earthenware manufacturer)

Rathbone, R.
(i) Sylvester Street, Burslem
1884 Kelly RM
(ii) Victoria Square, Hanley
1896 Kelly EM

Rathbone, Samuel & John
Amicable Street, Tunstall
1828 Pigot CM
1830 Pigot CM
1834 White EM-T (and china)
1835 Pigot EM

Rathbone, T., & Co.
Newfield Pottery, Tunstall
1900 Kelly EM

Rathbone, W. & R.
Sylvester Street, Burslem
1888 Kelly JM; RM
1892 Kelly JRM

Rathbone, W.S. & I.
Tunstall
1818 Parson EM-G-T-R

Rathbone, W.S. & J.
Tunstall
1818 Pigot CM
1822 Pigot CM

Rathbone, W.S. & T.
Tunstall
1822 Allbut CEM (china manufacts.)

Rathbone, William
(i) Tunstall
1809 Holden NC (earthenware-manufactr.)
1811 Holden NC (earthenware-manufacr.)
(ii) 50 Price Street, Burslem
1887 Porter EM-B

Rathbone, William, & Co.
Sylvester Street (or Square), Burslem
1880 Kelly RM
1882 Keates P-B (Rockingham and jet)
1889 Keates P-B (Rockingham and jet)
1892 Keates P-B (Rockingham and jet)

Rathbone, Hill & Co.
Queen Street Pottery, Burslem
1872 Kelly EM
1873 Keates P-B (earthenware)
1875 Keates P-B (earthenware)
1879 Keates P-B (earthenware)

Rathbone, Smith & Co.
Soho Pottery, High Street, Tunstall
1884 Kelly EM
1887 Porter EM-T
1888 Kelly EM
1889 Keates P-T
1892 Keates P-T
1892 Kelly EM
1896 Kelly EM

Ravenscroft & Co.
Joiner's Square, Hanley
1892 Keates P-H

Ray, Moses
Gower Street, Longton
1851 White CEM-L

Ray, Richard
High Street, Longton
1850 Slater CM; EM
1851 White CEM-L
See also: Ray & Wynne

Ray & Ball
High Street, Longton
1850 Kelly CEM; NC-L (china & earthenware manufacturers)

Ray, Ray & Bentley
High Street, Longton
1852 Slater CM
1854 Kelly CEM

Ray & Tideswell
Daisy Bank, Lane End or Longton
1834 White CM-LE-L
1835 Pigot CM

Ray & Wynne
(i) Daisy Bank, Longton
1841 Pigot CM
(ii) Stafford Street, Longton
1846 Williams NC-L-LE (china & earthenware manufacturer)
The partners are listed individually as Richard Ray of Daisy Bank and Thomas Wynne of Eddenson (presumably a misprint for Edensor) Place in 1846 Williams.

Read & Clementson
High Street, Shelton
1834 White EM-H-Sh
1835 Pigot EM

Read & Goodfellow
See: Rhead & Goodfellow

Read & Platt
Market Place, Burslem
1828 Pigot EM
1830 Pigot EM

Redfern & Drakeford
(i) High Street, Longton
1892 Keates P-L (china)
(ii) Mount Pleasant, Longton
1892 Kelly CM
1896 Kelly CM
1900 Kelly CM

Reeve, John
Commerce Street, Longton
1880 Kelly CM

Reeves, James
Victoria Works, Market Street (or High Street), Fenton
1870 Harrod NC-F (earthenware manufacturer)
1872 Kelly EM
1873 Keates P-F (earthenware)
1875 Keates P-F (earthenware)
1876 Kelly EM
1879 Keates P-F (earthenware)
1880 Kelly EM
1882 Keates P-F (earthenware)
1884 Kelly EM
1887 Porter EM-F
1888 Kelly EM
1889 Keates P-F (earthenware)
1892 Keates P-F (earthenware)
1892 Kelly EM
1896 Kelly EM
1900 Kelly EM
The manager is listed as Mr J.B. Wathen in 1870 Harrod. The firm is noted as being in the hands of executors in 1892 Keates.

Reeves, Joseph
Gold Street, Longton
1834 White EM-LE-L (marbles and nurs)

Renalagh Works
Renalagh Street, Hanley
1869 Keates A; P-H (earthenware & stone ware)
Despite the cross-reference, no advertisement could be located in 1869 Keates. The directory entry is not in alphabetical order, and its position suggests that it may relate to James Oldham (qv) who potted at the Ranelagh Works, Ranelagh Street and Bethesda Street, in Hanley. The spelling of Ranelagh varies considerably in the directories.
See also: Ranaleigh Works

Reynolds & Rhead
Normacot Road, Longton
1887 Porter EM-L

Rhead & Goodfellow
Burslem
1802 Allbut EM (map location 34)
1805 Holden NC (earthenware manufacturers)
1809 Holden NC (earthenware-manuf.)
1811 Holden NC (earthenware manuf.)
1816 Underhill P
1818 Pigot EM
The first partner's name is listed as Read in 1802 Allbut, 1809 Holden and 1811 Holden, and as Rhud in 1816 Underhill.

Rhoads & Bedson
Burslem
1798 Universal NC-B (manufacturers of Staffordshire-ware)

Rhodes & Co.
Bourne's Bank, Burslem
1884 Kelly EM

Rhodes, John
(i) King Street, Tunstall
1873 Keates P-T (earthenware)
(ii) Swan Bank, Burslem
1884 Kelly EM

Rhud & Goodfellow
See: Rhead & Goodfellow

Riddile & Lightfoot
See: Riddle & Lightfoot

Riddle, James
(i) Commerce Street, Longton
1851 White NC-L (china mfr.)
(ii) Union Square (or Union Market Place), Longton
1852 Slater CM
1854 Kelly CEM

Riddle & Lightfoot
(i) Union Square (or Union Market Place), Longton
1841 Pigot CM; EM (and lustre Egyptian)
1846 Williams NC-L-LE (earthenware &c., manufts.)
1850 Slater CM; EM
1851 White CEM-L
(ii) Market Street, Longton
1850 Kelly CEM; NC-L (china manufacturers)
The partners are listed individually as James Riddle of Barker Street and Arthur Lightfoot of High Street in 1846 Williams. The first surname is listed as Riddile in one entry in 1850 Kelly (CEM).

Ridge & Sons
Chancery Lane, Longton
1884 Kelly CM
1887 Porter EM-L
1888 Kelly CM
1889 Keates P-L (china)

Ridge, William A.
(i) Market Street, Longton
1887 Porter EM-L (two entries)
(ii) Albert Works, High Street, Longton
1887 Porter EM-L
1888 Kelly EM

Ridge, Meigh & Co.
Church Street, Longton
1876 Kelly CM
1879 Keates P-L (china)
1880 Kelly CM
1882 Keates P-L (china)
The firm is listed as Ridgemeigh & Co. in 1876 Kelly.

Ridge & Nicklin
Chancery Lane, Longton
1892 Kelly CM

Ridgemeigh & Co.
See: Ridge, Meigh & Co.

Ridgeway, George
Copeland Street, Stoke
1872 Kelly EM

Ridgeway, George, & Co.
Shelton
1798 Universal NC-Sh (factor)

Ridgway, Messrs., Ltd.
Bedford Works, Hanley
1887 Porter EM-H

Ridgway, E. & A.
See: Ridgway & Abington

Ridgway, Edward John
(i) High Street, Hanley
1861 Harrison NC-H-Sh (earthenware manufacturer)
1862 Slater EM

1863 Kelly EM
1864 Jones EM
1865 Keates P-H (earthenware)
(ii) Vale Road, Bedford Place, Hanley
1867 Keates P-H (earthenware)
1869 Keates P-H (earthenware)
(iii) Bedford Works, Hanley
1868 Kelly EM
1870 Harrod NC-H (earthenware, &c., manufacturer)
See also: Ridgway, William, Son & Co.

Ridgway, Edward John, & Son
Bedford Works, Hanley
1872 Kelly EM

Ridgway, George
Shelton
1805 Holden NC (china and earthenware manufacturers)
1809 Holden NC (earthenware-manufacturer)
1811 Holden NC (earthenware manuf.)

Ridgway, Job
Cauldon Place, Shelton
1805 Holden NC (china and earthenware manufacturer)
1809 Holden NC (china & earthenware-manufacturer)

Ridgway, Job, & Sons
Cauldon Place, Shelton
1811 Holden NC (china & earthenware manufacturers)

Ridgway, Job & George
Shelton
1802 Allbut EM (map location 86)

Ridgway, John
Cauldon Place, Shelton
1834 White EM-H-Sh (china mfrs. also)
1835 Pigot CM; EM

John Ridgway. Printed mark from a hand-painted bone china dessert plate.

John Ridgway. Printed mark from a printed and coloured earthenware dinner service.

John Ridgway. Printed mark from a green-printed and enamelled dessert plate.

John Ridgway. Printed mark from a blue-printed earthenware meat dish.

John Ridgway. Printed mark from a fine hand-painted bone china dish.

Ridgway, John, & Co.
(i) Shelton
1822 Allbut CEM (earthenware manufacts.)
(ii) Albion Street, Shelton
1822 Pigot EM
1828 Pigot EM (fine)
1830 Pigot EM (fine)
(iii) High Street, Shelton
1828 Pigot CM
1830 Pigot CM
(iv) Cauldon Place, Shelton
1841 Pigot CM; EM
1846 Williams NC-Sh (china and earthenware manufacturers)
1850 Kelly CEM; NC-Sh (manufacturers of porcelain, stone china & all kinds of earthenware)
1850 Slater CM; EM
1851 White CEM-H-Sh
1852 Slater CM; EM
1854 Kelly CEM
The partners are listed individually as John Ridgway and Thomas S. Bale in 1846 Williams

John Ridgway & Co. Paper label on an armorial bone china plate.

Ridgway, John, & Son
(i) Albion Street, Shelton
1818 Pigot EM
(ii) Cauldon Place, Shelton
1818 Pigot CM

Ridgway, John & William
(i) Shelton
1816 Underhill P
1818 Parson EM-H-Sh
(ii) Cauldon Place, Shelton
1822 Allbut CEM (china and earthenware manufacts.)
1822 Pigot CM; EM

1828 Pigot (fine) CM (stone); EM
1830 Pigot (fine) CM (stone); EM

John & William Ridgway. Printed mark from a blue-printed earthenware dinner plate.

John & William Ridgway. Printed mark from a blue-printed earthenware dessert dish.

William Ridgway. Printed mark from a blue-printed earthenware dinner plate.

Ridgway, William
(i) Albion Street, Shelton
1834 White EM-H-Sh
(ii) High Street, Shelton
1835 Pigot CM; EM
1841 Pigot EM
1850 Kelly CEM; NC-Sh (earthenware manufacturer)
1850 Slater EM
1851 White CEM-H-Sh
(iii) Broad Street, Shelton
1852 Slater EM
1854 Kelly CEM
Ridgway's house is listed as Wheatley Cottage in 1851 White.

Ridgway, William, & Co.
High Street, Hanley
1834 White EM-H-Sh
1835 Pigot CM; EM

William Ridgway & Co. Documentary painted mark from a hand-painted earthenware dinner plate.

William Ridgway & Co. Impressed mark from a pair of plain stoneware candlesticks.

William Ridgway & Co. Impressed publication mark from a relief-moulded stoneware jug.

William Ridgway & Co. Printed mark from a blue-printed earthenware dessert dish.

Ridgway, William, Son & Co.
High Street, Hanley
1841 Pigot EM
1846 Williams (manufacturers) NC-H
The partners are listed individually as William Ridgway of Northwood, Hanley, Edward J. Ridgway of Bank House, Albion Street, Shelton, and Leonard J. Abington of High Street, Hanley, in 1846 Williams

Ridgway, William Henry
Patent Floor Tile Works, Canal Side, Hanley
1869 Keates A; SC-H (Floor Tile Manufacturer)
1873 Keates A; SC-H (Floor Tile Manufacturer)
The advertisements offer 'plain floor tiles, encaustic tiles, made by newly-patented process' (1869 Keates) and promote the 'patent encaustic and geometrical floor tile works' (1873 Keates). The 1873 advertisement lists a London agent as Mr. A.J. Satham at 14 South Wharf, Paddington.

W. H. RIDGWAY,
PATENT "FLOOR" TILE WORKS
HANLEY, STAFFORDSHIRE.
PLAIN FLOOR TILES,
ENCAUSTIC TILES,
MADE BY NEWLY-PATENTED PROCESS.

William Henry Ridgway. Advertisement from 1869 Keates.

W. H. RIDGWAY,
Patent Encaustic and Geometrical
FLOOR TILE WORKS,
HANLEY, STOKE-UPON-TRENT.
LONDON AGENT:
MR. A. J. SATHAM,
14, SOUTH WHARF, PADDINGTON, W.

William Henry Ridgway. Advertisement from 1873 Keates.

Ridgway & Abington
(i) Church Bank, Hanley
1850 Kelly CEM; NC-H (earthenware manfactrs.)
(ii) High Street, Hanley
1850 Slater EM
1851 White CEM-H-Sh (fancy)
1852 Slater CM; EM
1854 Kelly CEM
1856 Kelly CEM
1860 Kelly EM
The firm is listed as Edward Ridgway & Abington in 1850 Slater and 1852 Slater and as E. & A. Ridgway in 1854 Kelly.

Ridgway & Abington. Moulded publication mark from a relief-moulded stoneware jug.

Ridgway (John), Bates & Co.
Cauldon Place, Shelton
1856 Kelly CEM; PM

Ridgway, Morley, Wear & Co.
Broad Street, Shelton
1841 Pigot CM (stone); EM

Ridgway, Morley, Wear & Co. Printed mark from a blue-printed earthenware plate.

Ridgway, Morley, Wear & Co. Printed mark from the underside of a blue-printed plate originally fitted with a Britannia metal hot-water container.

Ridgway, Smith & Ridgway
Shelton
1796 Chester NC-H-Sh (manufacturers of earthenware)

Ridgway, Sparks & Ridgway
Bedford Works, Bedford Place, Hanley
1873 Keates P-H (earthenware)
1875 Keates P-H (earthenware)
1876 Kelly EM (manufacturers of all kinds of earthenware for home & export, also of jasper, porous jet goods & stone ware)
1879 Keates P-H (earthenware)
London showrooms at 8 Thavie's Inn are listed in 1876 Kelly.

Ridgway, Sparks & Ridgway. Printed mark from a blue-printed sardine dish.

Ridgway, Wooliscroft & Co.
Encaustic Tile Works, Eastwood, Hanley
1875 Keates SC-H (Floor Tile Manufacturers)

Ridgway, Wooliscroft & Co. Ltd.
Encaustic Tile Works, Eastwood, Hanley
1879 Keates SC-H (Floor Tile Manufacturers)

Ridgway, Woolliscrofts & Co. Ltd.
Patent Tile Works, Hanley
1880 Kelly SC (Encaustic Tile Manufacturers) (encaustic & hearth tile manufacturers)

Ridgways
Bedford Works, Bedford Road, Shelton, Hanley
1880 Kelly EM
1882 Keates P-H (earthenware)
1884 Kelly EM
1888 Kelly EM
1889 Keates P-H (stone, parian, and earthenware)
1892 Keates P-H (stone, parian, & earthenware)
1892 Kelly EM
1896 Kelly EM
1900 Kelly EM

Rigby, Elijah jun.
Providence Pottery, Chell Street, Hanley
1884 Kelly EM
1887 Porter EM-H
1888 Kelly EM
1889 Keates P-H
1892 Keates P-H
1892 Kelly EM
Rigby is listed as Elijah junior in all entries except 1887 Porter.

Rigby, James
Milton
1880 Kelly EM
1884 Kelly SM
1888 Kelly SM
1892 Kelly SM
1896 Kelly SM

Rigby & Stevenson
High Street, Hanley
1896 Kelly EM
1900 Kelly EM

Riles & Bathwell
Red Street
1802 Allbut EM (map location 7)

Riley, John & Richard
(i) Burslem
1802 Allbut EM (map location 47)
1805 Holden NC (china glaze earthenware manufacturers)
1809 Holden NC (china &

earthenware-manufacturers)
1811 Holden NC (china & earthenware-manufacturers)
1816 Underhill P
1818 Pigot CM; EM
(ii) Hill Works, Liverpool Road, Burslem
1818 Parson EM-B-Lp-C
1822 Allbut CEM (china and earthenware manufacts.)
1822 Pigot CM; EM (and black lustre)
1828 Pigot CM; EM
The surname is listed as Rilley in 1805 Holden

John & Richard Riley. Printed mark from a blue-printed earthenware dinner plate.

Rilley, John & Richard
See: Riley, John & Richard

Rivers, William, & Co.
Bedford Row, Shelton
1818 Pigot EM
1822 Pigot CM; EM

Rivers & Clews
Shelton
1818 Parson EM-H-Sh
1822 Allbut CEM (china and earthenware manufacts.)

Roberts, Darius
Leek Road, Bucknall, Milton
1896 Kelly EM
1900 Kelly EM

Roberts, Darrus
Bath Street, Hanley
1892 Kelly EM
1896 Kelly EM
1900 Kelly EM

Roberts, James
Park Hall Street, Longton
1896 Kelly EM

Roberts & Cotton
Clayton Pottery, Stafford Street, Longton
1892 Keates P-L (earthenware)

Robey, William, & Co.
Furnace
1822 Pigot EM (coarse)

Robinson & Co.
(i) Navigation Road, Burslem
1873 Keates P-B (earthen.)
1875 Keates P-B (earthen)
(ii) The Foley, King Street, Fenton
1873 Keates P-F (china); P-L (china)
1875 Keates P-L (china)
1876 Kelly CM
1879 Keates P-L (china)
1880 Kelly CM
1882 Keates P-L (china)
(iii) Knowles Works, Burslem
1879 Keates P-B (earthen.)
(iv) Sutherland Road, Longton
1880 Kelly CM
1884 Kelly CM

ROBINSON & SON,
CHINA MANUFACTURERS,
WELLINGTON WORKS,
STAFFORD STREET,
LONGTON, POTTERIES.
SHOW ROOMS:
22, ELY PLACE, HOLBORN, LONDON.

Robinson & Son. Advertisement from 1865 Keates.

ESTABLISHED 1850
ROBINSON & SON,
CHINA MANUFACTURERS,
FOLEY WORKS,
LONGTON, Staffordshire.
HOME AND EXPORT.

Robinson & Son. Advertisement from 1889 Keates. The same advertisement appeared in 1892 Keates.

Robinson & Son
(i) Wellington Works, Stafford Street, Longton
1864 Jones CEM
1865 Keates A; P-L (china)
1867 Keates P-L (china)
1868 Kelly CM
1869 Keates P-L (china)
(ii) Foley Works, King Street, Fenton
1884 Kelly CM
1888 Kelly CM
1889 Keates P-F (china)
1889 Keates A; P-L (china)
1892 Keates P-F (china)
1892 Keates A; P-L (china)
1892 Kelly CM
1896 Kelly CM
1900 Kelly CM
The advertisement in 1865 Keates describes Robinson & Son as 'china manufacturers' with London showrooms at 22 Ely Place, Holborn. The advertisements in 1889 Keates and 1892 Keates both describe the firm as 'china manufacturers' for 'home and export' and claim that they were established in 1850.

Robinson & Sons
(i) Burslem
1796 Chester NC-B (manufacturers of earthenware)
1798 Universal NC-B (manufacturers of Staffordshire-ware)
1802 Allbut EM (map location 33)
(ii) Foley Works, Fenton
1887 Porter EM-F

Robinson, John
(i) Burslem
1784 Bailey NC-B (enameller and printer of cream colour and china glazed ware)
(ii) High Street, Lane End
1818 Parson EM-LE
(iii) George Street, Lane End
1818 Parson EM-LE
(iv) Hill Works, Burslem
1822 Allbut CEM (earthenware manufact.)
1822 Pigot EM
(v) Liverpool Road, Burslem
1870 Harrod NC-B (potter)

Robinson, John, & Sons
Burslem
1805 Holden NC (earthenware manufacturers)
1809 Holden NC (manufactrs. of earthenware)
1811 Holden NC (manufacturers of earthenware)

Robinson, John & Christopher
Hill Top or Hill Works, Burslem
1816 Underhill P

1818 Parson EM-B-Lp-C
1818 Pigot EM

Robinson, Joseph
(i) Knowle Works, Hamil Road, Burslem
1876 Kelly, EM
1880 Kelly EM
1882 Keates P-B (earthenware)
1884 Kelly EM
1888 Kelly EM
1889 Keates P-B (earthenware)
1892 Keates P-B (earthenware)
1892 Kelly EM
1896 Kelly EM
(ii) Moorland Road, Burslem
1887 Porter EM-B

Joseph Robinson. Printed mark from a blue-printed earthenware soup plate.

Robinson, Noah
Shelton
1828 Pigot EM
1830 Pigot EM

Noah Robinson. Impressed mark from a blue-printed earthenware dinner plate.

Robinson, William
Hartwell, Barlaston
1870 Harrod NC-Bar (china manufacturer)

Robinson, William, & Co.
King Street, Foley, Fenton
1875 Keates P-F (china)
1879 Keates P-F (china)
1882 Keates P-F (china)

Robinson & Chapman
Royal Porcelain Works, Longton
1872 Kelly CM
1875 Keates P-L (china)
1876 Kelly CM
1879 Keates P-L (china)
1880 Kelly CM

Robinson, Chapman & Co.
Forrister Street, Longton
1873 Keates P-L (china)

Robinson & Cooper
Stafford Street, Longton
1863 Kelly CM-General

Robinson & Dale
City Road, Longton
1841 Pigot EM

Robinson, Goodwin & Co.
High Street, Lane End
1822 Allbut CEM (earthenware and Egyptian black manufacturers)
1822 Pigot EM

Robinson & Hudson
Foley Works, King Street, Fenton
1868 Kelly CM
1869 Keates P-F (china)
1870 Harrod NC-F (china manufacturers)
1872 Kelly CM
An advertisement for Robinson & Hudson appears in 1864 Jones although the directory entry lists the firm as Robinson, Hudson & Co. (qv).

ROBINSON & HUDSON,
MANUFACTURERS OF
Burnished & Enamelled China,
OF EVERY DESCRIPTION.
FOLEY WORKS, near LONGTON,
POTTERIES.

Robinson & Hudson. Advertisement from 1864 Jones.

Robinson, Hudson & Co.
Foley Works, King Street, Fenton
1864 Jones A; CEM
1865 Keates P-F (china)
1867 Keates P-F (china)
The advertisement in 1864 Jones is under the style of Robinson & Hudson, and describes them as 'manufacturers of burnished & enamelled china, of every description'.

Robinson, Kirkham & Co.
(i) Wedgwood Place, Burslem
1868 Kelly EM
1869 Keates P-B (earthen.)
(ii) New Wharf Pottery, Burslem
1870 Harrod NC-B (general earthenware manufacturers for home and foreign markets)
1872 Kelly EM

Robinson & Leadbeater
(i) Glebe Street, Stoke
1867 Keates A; P-S (parian statuary)
1868 Kelly PM
1869 Keates P-S (parian statuary)
(ii) Glebe Street and 49 Wharf Street, Stoke
1870 Harrod A; NC-S (manufacturers of parian, statuary ornaments, &c., new subjects by eminent artists constantly being added for home and foreign markets)
1872 Kelly PM
1873 Keates P-S (parian statuary
1875 Keates A; P-S (parian statuary)
1876 Kelly PM
1879 Keates A; P-S (parian statuary)
1880 Kelly PM
(iii) Wolfe Street, Stoke
1882 Keates P-S (parian statuary)
1884 Kelly PM
1887 Porter CEM-S
1888 Kelly PM
1889 Keates A; P-S (parian statuary)
1892 Keates A; P-S (parian statuary)

ROBINSON & LEADBEATER,
(Successor to Giovanni Meli.)
MANUFACTURER OF
PARIAN STATUARY, &c.
Near the Town Hall, Stoke-upon-Trent,
STAFFORDSHIRE POTTERIES.
New Subjects by Eminent Artists Constantly Being Added.

Robinson & Leadbeater. Advertisement from 1867 Keates

ROBINSON & LEADBEATER,
MANUFACTURERS OF
Parian Statuary Ornaments,
ETC., ETC.,
FOR HOME & FOREIGN MARKETS.
NEW SUBJECTS IN PARIAN BY EMINENT ARTISTS ARE BEING CONSTANTLY ADDED.
WORKS:—
GLEBE STREET, & WHARF STREET,
STOKE-UPON-TRENT.

Robinson & Leadbeater. Advertisement from 1870 Harrod.

ROBINSON & LEADBEATER,
MANUFACTURERS OF
PARIAN STATUARY, &c.,
GLEBE STREET & WHARF STREET,
STOKE-UPON-TRENT.

Robinson & Leadbeater. Advertisement from 1873 Keates. The same advertisement appeared in 1875 Keates.

ROBINSON & LEADBEATER,
MANUFACTURERS OF
Parian and China Statuary, &c.,
GLEBE STREET & WHARF STREET,
STOKE-UPON-TRENT.

Robinson & Leadbeater. Advertisement from 1879 Keates.

ROBINSON & LEADBEATER,
MANUFACTURERS OF
Parian + Statuary, + &c.,
WOLFE STREET,
STOKE-UPON-TRENT.

Robinson & Leadbeater. Advertisement from 1882 Keates. The same advertisement appeared in 1889 Keates.

ESTABLISHED 1850.
ROBINSON & LEADBEATER,
MANUFACTURERS OF
Parian Statuary, etc.,
WOLFE STREET,
STOKE-UPON-TRENT.

Robinson & Leadbeater. Advertisement from 1892 Keates. Note the addition of the date of establishment.

ESTABLISHED 1850.

ROBINSON & LEADBEATER,
STOKE-UPON-TRENT,
Staffordshire, England.
MANUFACTURERS OF
Parian + Statuary,
FANCY GOODS, &c.
Price Lists and Photographs on application by the Trade.

Robinson & Leadbeater. Advertisement from 1900 Kelly.

1892 Kelly PM
1896 Kelly PM
1900 Kelly A; PM (parian statuary & fancy goods manfrs.; price lists & photos on application); SC (Statuary Manufacturers – Parian)

The advertisement in 1867 Keates gives the address as near the Town Hall and states that the firm were successors to Giovanni Meli. It describes them as a 'manufacturer of parian statuary, &c. New subjects by eminent artists constantly being added.' Most advertisements describe the firm simply as 'manufacturers of parian statuary, &c.' (1873 Keates, 1875 Keates, 1882 Keates, 1889 Keates, and 1892 Keates) but variants include 'manufacturers of parian statuary ornaments, etc., etc., for home & foreign markets. New subjects in parian by eminent artists are being constantly added.' (1870 Harrod); 'manufacturers of parian and china statuary, &c.' (1879 Keates); and 'manufacturers of parian statuary, fancy goods, &c.' with 'price lists and photographs on application by the trade', illustrated by a figure of a King in battle (1900 Kelly). The advertisements in 1892 Keates and 1900 Kelly both claim that the firm was established in 1850.

Robinson & Repton
Wellington Works, Stafford Street, Longton
1879 Keates A; P-L (china)

The advertisement in 1879 Keates describes the firm simply as 'china manufacturers'.

ROBINSON & REPTON,
CHINA MANUFACTURERS,
WELLINGTON WORKS,
STAFFORD STREET,
LONGTON.

Robinson & Repton. Advertisement from 1879 Keates.

Robinson, Repton & Robinson
Wellington Works, Stafford Street, Longton
1870 Harrod NC-L (china manufacturers)
1872 Kelly CM
1873 Keates P-L china)
1875 Keates P-L (china)
1876 Kelly CM

The second partner's name is listed as Ripton in 1872 Kelly.

Robinson & Smith
Cobridge
1781 Bailey NC (potters)
1783 Bailey NC (potters)
1784 Bailey NC-C (potters)
1798 Universal NC-C (manufacturers of Staffordshire-ware)

Robinson, Stubbs & Co.
Foley Works, near Longton
1862 Slater CM

Robinson, Stubbs & Hudson
The Foley, Fenton
1852 Slater CM
1854 Kelly CEM
1856 Kelly CEM
1860 Kelly CM-General
1861 Harrison NC-F
(manufacturers of every description of enamelled and burnished gold china)
1863 Kelly CM-General

Robinson & Wood
(i) Vale Lane, Shelton
1834 White EM-H-Sh
(ii) Broad Street, Shelton
1835 Pigot EM

Robinson & Wood. Printed mark from blue-printed earthenware dinner wares.

Robinson & Wood. Printed mark from an earthenware plate.

Robinson & Wood. Printed mark from a blue-printed earthenware tea plate.

Robinson, Wood & Brownfield
Robinson, Wood & Brownfield succeeded Robinson & Wood and became Wood & Brownfield. The short-lived partnership was too late for 1835 Pigot and too early for 1841 Pigot.

Robinson, Wood & Brownfield. Printed mark from a brown-printed and coloured earthenware dessert plate.

Robinsons & Smith
Cobridge
1796 Chester NC-C
(manufacturers of earthenware)

Roe & Son
Bow Street, Hanley
1862 Slater PM

Roe, Henry, & Son
Bow Street, High Street, Hanley
1860 Kelly PM
1863 Kelly PM
1864 Jones PM
1861 Harrison NC-H-Sh (parian manufacturers)

Rogers, John
Longport
1816 Underhill P

John Rogers & Son. Impressed mark from a sprigged earthenware jug.

Rogers, John, & Son
(i) Longport
1818 Parson EM-B-Lp-C
1818 Pigot EM
1822 Allbut CEM
(earthenware manufacts.)
1822 Pigot EM
1835 Pigot CM; EM
1841 Pigot CM; EM
(ii) Dale Hall, Longport
1828 Pigot EM
1830 Pigot EM
1834 White EM-B

John Rogers & Son. Printed mark from a blue-printed earthenware dinner plate also impressed "ROGERS".

Rogers, John & George
(i) Burslem
1784 Bailey NC-B
(manufacturers of china glazed blue painted wares, and cream coloured)
(ii) Longport
1796 Chester NC-T-Lp
(manufacturers of earthenware)
1798 Universal NC-Lp
(manufacturers of Staffordshire-ware)
1802 Allbut EM (map location 23, two entries)
1805 Holden NC (china earthenware manufacturer)
1809 Holden NC (china & earthenware-manufacturers)
1811 Holden NC (china & earthenware manufacturers)

Rogers, Spencer
Dale Hall
1818 Parson EM-B-Lp-C

Rose, John, & Co.
Glebe Street, Stoke
1882 Keates P-S (porcelain, &c.)
1884 Kelly CM
1889 Keates P-S (porcelain, &c.)
The firm is also listed as the Coalport China Co. (John Rose &

Co.) Ltd. in 1889 Keates with John A. Service as their agent at 8 Glebe Buildings, Stoke.

Rowley, Josiah
Stoke
1796 Chester NC-S
(manufacturer of earthenware)
1798 Universal NC-S
(manufacturer of Staffordshire-ware)

Rowley & Jervis
Park Place Works, High Street, Longton
1892 Kelly EM

Rowley, Moston & Co.
Clayton Street, Longton
1865 Keates P-L (china)

Rowley & Newton
Park Place Works, High Street, Longton
1896 Kelly EM

Rowley & Newton Ltd.
Gordon Pottery, Anchor Road and Park Place Works, High Street, Longton
1900 Kelly CM; EM

Rowley, Thomas
(i) Amicable Street, Tunstall
1834 White EM-T
1835 Pigot EM
1841 Pigot EM
(ii) High Street, Tunstall
1846 Williams NC-T
(earthenware manufacturer)
1850 Slater EM
1851 White EM-T
The firm is noted as being in the hands of executors in 1851 White.

Royle, Edward
Market Street, Lane End
1822 Pigot CM

Rushton, James
Chadwick Street, Longton
1896 Kelly EM
1900 Kelly EM

Ryles & Walsh
Burslem
1809 Holden NC (earthenware-manufacts.)
1811 Holden NC (earthenware-manuf.)

S

Sadler & Co.
(i) Moorland Road, Burslem
1889 Keates P-B (earthenware)
1892 Keates P-B (earthenware)
(ii) Reginald Street, Burslem
1896 Kelly JRM
1900 Kelly JRM

Sadler & Son
Reginald Street, Burslem
1892 Kelly JRM

Sadler, Edward William
Well Street Pottery, Well Street, Tunstall
1896 Kelly EM
1900 Kelly EM

Sadler, J., & Sons
Newport Street, Burslem
1900 Kelly JRM

Sadler, William
Well Street Pottery, Well Street, Tunstall
1892 Keates P-T (china decorator)

Sale, John
Bryan Street, Hanley
1867 Keates P-H (parian)

Sale, William
Bryan Street, Hanley
1865 Keates A; P-H (parian)
The advertisement in 1865 Keates is for 'Mr. Sale, manufacturer of white & coloured parian figures, jugs, flower pots, &c., works, end of Bryan Street, Hanley'.

MR. SALE,
MANUFACTURER OF
White & Coloured Parian Figures,
JUGS, FLOWER POTS, &c.,
WORKS, END OF BRYAN STREET,
HANLEY.

William Sale. Advertisement from 1865 Keates.

Salisbury & Wildblood
Church Street, Stoke
1870 Harrod NC-S
(earthenware manufacturers)

Salt Brothers
Brownhills, Tunstall
1900 Kelly EM

Salt, Charles
(i) Trinity Street, Shelton, Hanley
1852 Slater EM (and parian statuary); PM
1854 Kelly CFM
1861 Harrison NC-H-Sh (parian manufacturer)
(ii) Bethesda Street, Hanley
1862 Slater PM
1863 Kelly PM
An advertisement in 1861 Harrison describes Salt as an 'ornamental parian manufacturer' and notes 'jugs, vases, baskets, brooches, statue figures, etc., in the newest and richest designs'. The address is given as 12 Trinity Street with the manufactory at Bethesda Street.

C. SALT,
ORNAMENTAL PARIAN
MANUFACTURER,
12, TRINITY ST., HANLEY,
STAFFORDSHIRE.
N.B.—Jugs, Vases, Baskets, Brooches, Statue Figures, etc., in the newest and richest designs.
MANUFACTORY:—BETHESDA STREET.

Charles Salt. Advertisement from 1861 Harrison.

Salt, Jeremiah
78 Waterloo Road, Burslem
1888 Kelly JM; RM

Salt, John, & Co.
Etruscan Works, Marsh Street, Longton
1865 Keates A; P-L
The advertisement in 1865 Keates is for W.J. Salt & Co., described as 'manufacturers of mosaic, terra cotta, Etruscan ware, door furniture, jet black, fancy, and dry bodies, etc.' It promises 'home & colonial trade attended to' and offers 'butter and wine coolers, lamp stands on an improved scale, to prevent parafin (sic) oil penetrating'.

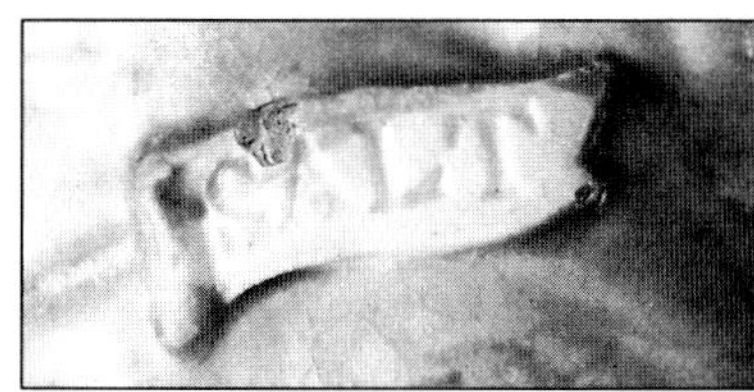

Ralph Salt. Impressed mark from an earthenware figure titled "Bird's Nest".

Salt, Ralph
(i) Miles Bank, Hanley
1822 Allbut CEM (lusterer

and enameller)
(ii) Marsh Street, Shelton
1828 Pigot EM (toy only)
1830 Pigot EM (toy only)
1834 White CETM-H-Sh
(figures & porcelain tablets)
1835 Pigot TOCM (fine)
1841 Pigot TOCM (fine)

Salt, Thomas
Fountain Works, Burslem
1846 Williams NC-B
(earthenware manufacturer)
Salt's house is listed as Newcastle Street, Burslem, in 1846 Williams.

Salt, W.J., & Co.
See: Salt, John, & Co.

W. J. SALT & Co.,
ETRUSCAN WORKS,
MARSH STREET, LONGTON,
MANUFACTURERS OF
Mosaic, Terra Cotta, Etruscan Ware
DOOR FURNITURE,
JET BLACK, FANCY, AND DRY BODIES, ETC.
Home & Colonial Trade attended to.
BUTTER AND WINE COOLERS, LAMP STANDS ON AN IMPROVED SCALE, TO PREVENT PARAFIN OIL PENETRATING.

W.J. Salt & Co. Advertisement from 1865 Keates.

Salt & Hopkinson
Bethesda Street, Shelton
1856 Kelly PM

Sambrook, T.C., & Co.
Furlong Works, Burslem
1868 Kelly EM

Sandland, William
Lichfield Street, Hanley
1896 Kelly EM
1900 Kelly EM

Sandland, Bennett & Co.
Victoria Works, Lonsdale Street, Stoke
1887 Porter CEM-S
1888 Kelly EM
1889 Keates P-S (earthenware)
1892 Keates A; P-S
(earthenware)
1892 Kelly EM
The advertisement in 1892 Keates describes the firm as 'earthenware manufacturers of useful & ornamental goods'.

SANDLAND, BENNETT & Co.,
Earthenware Manufacturers
OF
USEFUL & ORNAMENTAL GOODS
VICTORIA WORKS,
STOKE-ON-TRENT.

Sandland, Bennett & Co. Advertisement from 1892 Keates.

Sanforth, Samuel
Burslem
1822 Allbut CEM (stone bottle manufacturer)

Sanitary Pottery Co. Ltd.
Longport
1900 Kelly EM

Sant & Co.
Sneyd Street, Cobridge, Burslem
1892 Keates P-B (earthenware)
1892 Kelly EM

Sant, Jeremiah
(i) 98 Waterloo Road, Burslem
1876 Kelly EM (decorator)
(ii) 78 Waterloo Road, Burslem
1887 Porter EM-B
1889 Keates P-B (jet and Rockingham)
1892 Keates P-B (jet and Rockingham)
(iii) Adelaide Street, Burslem
1892 Kelly JRM

Sant & Vodrey
(i) Abbey Pottery, Cobridge
1887 Porter EM-B
1888 Kelly EM
(ii) Sneyd Street, Burslem
1889 Keates P-B (earthenware)

Satham, A.J.
See: Ridgway, William Henry

Saul, Edmund
Etruria
1862 Slater PM
1864 Jones PM

Scarrat, William
High Street, Longton
1869 Keates P-L (earthenware)

Scarratt & Baldwin
Fenton
1861 Harrison NC-F
(earthenware manufacturers)

Scott, Floyd & Co.
Caddick's Lane, Lane End or Longton
1834 White CM-LE-L

Scrivener, R.G., & Co.
Norfolk Street, Hanley
1870 Harrod NC-H
(manufacturers of decorated china earthenware, &c., for home and foreign markets)
1872 Kelly CM
1875 Keates P-H (china)
1876 Kelly CM
1879 Keates P-H (china)
1880 Kelly CM
1882 Keates P-H (china)

Seabridge, James
(i) High Street, Lane End
1830 Pigot CM
1834 White CM-LE-L
1835 Pigot CM
(ii) Church Street, Longport
1841 Pigot CM
(iii) Church Street, Lane End
1846 Williams NC-L-LE (china manufacturer)
Seabridge's house is listed as Anchor Lane, Longton, in 1834 White.

Seddon, Joshua
Commercial Street, Burslem
1850 Slater EM
See also: Seddon & Wildblood

Seddon & Wildblood
Church Yard Manufactory, Burslem
1846 Williams NC-B
(earthenware manufacturers)
The partners are listed individually as Joshua Seddon of Barnfield House and William Wildblood of Navigation Road in 1846 Williams.

Selman, J.
High Street, Tunstall
1854 Kelly TM (clay)
1856 Kelly TM (clay)

Selman, J. & W.
Gritten Street, Brownhills, Tunstall
1864 Jones A; EM-Miscellaneous (toy)
1865 Keates P-T (toy)
The advertisement in 1864 Jones describes the firm as 'bronze and earthenware toy manufacturers' and promises 'all orders punctually attended to'

J. & W. SELMAN,
Bronze and Earthenware Toy Manufacturers,
BROWNHILLS,
TUNSTALL, STAFFORDSHIRE.
ALL ORDERS PUNCTUALLY ATTENDED TO.

J. & W. Selman. Advertisement from 1864 Jones.

Service, John A.
See: Coalport China Co. Ltd.
See: Rose, John, & Co.

Sharpe, W.H.
Canning Street, Fenton
1896 Kelly JRM
1900 Kelly JRM

Sharratt, Obadiah
See: Sherratt, Obadiah

Shaw
See: Shaw, Thomas

Shaw & Son
(i) Bourne's Bank, Burslem
1889 Keates P-B (earthenware)
(ii) Sandyford, Tunstall
1892 Kelly EM
1896 Kelly EM
1900 Kelly EM

Shaw, Anthony
(i) Cross Street, Tunstall
1851 White EM-T
(ii) Newfield, Tunstall
1852 Slater EM
1854 Kelly CEM
1856 Kelly CEM
(iii) Newport Works, Newport Lane, Burslem
1860 Kelly EM
1861 Harrison NC-B (earthenware manufacturer)
1863 Kelly EM
1864 Jones EM
1868 Kelly EM
(iv) Newport Lane, Burslem
1862 Slater EM
1865 Keates P-B (earthen.)
1867 Keates P-B (earthen.)
1869 Keates P-B (earthen.)
1873 Keates P-B (earthen.)
1875 Keates P-B (earthen)
1892 Keates P-B (earthenware)
(v) Mersey Works, Newport Lane, Burslem
1870 Harrod NC-B (earthenware manufacturer)
1872 Kelly EM
1876 Kelly EM
1879 Keates P-B (earthen.)
1880 Kelly EM
1882 Keates P-B (earthenware)
1889 Keates P-B, earthenware)

Anthony Shaw. Printed mark from a blue-printed earthenware soup plate. The registration diamond dates from 1853.

Shaw, Anthony, & Son
(i) Mersey Works, Burslem
1884 Kelly EM
1888 Kelly EM
1892 Kelly EM
1896 Kelly EM
1900 Kelly EM
(ii) Prospect Street, Burslem
1887 Porter EM-B

Shaw, Emos
Chancery Lane, Lane End
1835 Pigot CM

Shaw, George & Thomas
Lane End
1805 Holden NC (earthenware manufacturers)

Shaw, James
Albion Street, Longton
1896 Kelly CM
1900 Kelly CM

Shaw, John
Green Dock, Lane End
1828 Pigot CM; EM
1830 Pigot EM

Shaw, John & Jesse
Green Dock, Lane End
1834 White EM-LE-L
1835 Pigot EM

Shaw, Kitty
(i) Market Place, Lane End
1830 Pigot CM
(ii) Chancery Lane, Longton
1834 White CM-LE-L
Shaw's house is listed as Steele's Nook, Longton, in 1834 White

Shaw, Robert
Bourne's Bank Works, Burslem
1887 Porter EM-B

Shaw, Thomas
Lane End
1796 Chester NC-LE-LD-LL (manufacturer of earthenware)
1798 Universal NC-LE (manufacturer of Staffordshire-ware)
1802 Allbut EM (map location 142)
1809 Holden NC (earthenware-manufacturer)
1811 Holden NC (earthenware manuf.)
1816 Underhill P
No first name is listed in the entry in 1802 Allbut.

Shaw, Goldstraw & Swift
Clayton Street, Daisy Bank, Longton
1869 Keates P-L (fire brick and sanitary tube)
1873 Keates P-L (fire brick and sanitary tube)
1875 Keates P-L (fire brick and sanitary tube)

Shaw, Griffiths & Co.
Stafford Street, Lane End
1822 Allbut CEM (earthenware manufacts.)
1822 Pigot EM

Shaw & Ridge
(i) Albion Street, Longton
1884 Kelly EM
(ii) Bank Pottery, Bourne Street, Burslem
1888 Kelly EM

Shaw & Swift
Clayton Street, Daisy Bank, Longton
1879 Keates P-L (fire brick and sanitary tube)
1882 Keates P-L (fire brick and sanitary tube)

Sheaf Pottery Co.
(i) Normacott Road, Longton
1896 Kelly EM
(ii) Commerce Street, Longton
1900 Kelly EM

Shelley
Lower-lane
1802 Allbut EM (map location 113)
No first name is listed in the entry.

Shelley, Michael
Lane End
1781 Bailey NC (potter)
1783 Bailey NC (potter)
1784 Bailey NC-LE (potter)
The surname is listed as Shelly in 1783 Bailey.

Shelley, Thomas
Lane End
1781 Bailey NC (potter)
1783 Bailey NC (potter)
1784 Bailey NC-LE (potter)
1796 Chester NC-LE-LD-LL (manufacturer of earthenware)
1802 Allbut EM (map location 140)
The surname is listed as Shelly in 1783 Bailey.

Shelley & Adams
Stafford Street, Longton
1862 Slater CM; TOCM
The first partner's name is listed as Shelly in one entry (TOCM).

Shelley, Booth & Co.
Lane End
1818 Parson EM-LE

Shelley & Hartshorne
Dresden Works, Stafford Street, Longton
1860 Kelly CM-General; EM
1861 Harrison NC-L (china manufacturers)

Shelly, Michael
See: Shelley, Michael

Shelly, Thomas
See: Shelley, Thomas

Shelly & Adams
See: Shelley & Adams

Shenton, Herbert
Hope Works, Union Street, Hanley
1884 Kelly EM
1888 Kelly EM
1889 Keates P-H
1892 Keates P-H
1892 Kelly EM
1896 Kelly EM

Shepherd & Co.
(i) Market Lane, Longton
1864 Jones CEM
(ii) Eagle Works, Stafford Street, Longton
1867 Keates P-L (china and earthenware; decorated china and earthenware manufacturers)
1869 Keates P-L (china and earthenware)
1870 Harrod NC-L (china and earthenware manufacturers)

Shepherd, A., & Co.
Eagle Works, Stafford Street, Longton
1864 Jones A; CEM
1868 Kelly CM
The advertisement in 1864 Jones qives the address as Eagle Place and describes the firm as 'china, glass, and earthenware exporters; enamellers, gilders, lusterers, &c.' It also notes 'an extensive assortment suitable for foreign markets always in stock'.

Sheridan, J.H.
Union Market Place, Lane End
1818 Parson EM-LE

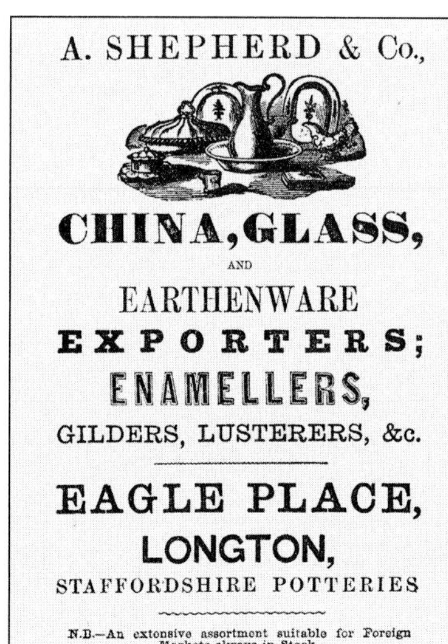

A. Shepherd & Co. Advertisement from 1864 Jones.

Sheridan & Hewitt
Lane End
1809 Holden NC (earthenware-manufacturers)
1811 Holden NC (earthenware-manufacturers)

Sheridan & Hyatt
Lane End
1809 Holden NC (Egyptian-black-manufacturers)
1811 Holden NC (Egyptian-black-manufacturers)
1816 Underhill P

Sherratt, Hamlet
Waterloo Road, Burslem
1846 Williams NC-B (figure manufacturer)
1850 Slater TOCM
1852 Slater TOCM
1854 Kelly PM (ornamental figure makers)
1856 Kelly TM

Sherratt, Martha (Mrs.)
Waterloo Road, Burslem
1850 Kelly NC-B (china figure manufactr.)
1851 White CETM-B
The surname is listed as Sperratt in 1850 Kelly.

Sherratt, Obadiah
(i) Hot Lane, Burslem
1828 Pigot EM (toy only)
(ii) Waterloo Road, Burslem
1830 Pigot EM (toy only)
1834 White ETM-B
1835 Pigot TOCM
1841 Pigot TOCM (& earthenware)
The surname is listed as Skerratt in 1828 Pigot and 1830 Pigot, and as Sharratt in 1834 White.

Sherratt, Samuel
See: Holdcroft, Peter, & Co.

Sherwin & Cotton
(i) Vine Street, Hanley
1880 Kelly SC (Encaustic Tile Manufacturers)
1882 Keates P-H (encaustic tiles); SC-H (Floor Tile Manufacturers)
1884 Kelly SC (Encaustic Tile Manufacturers)
1887 Porter SC-H (Tile Manufacturer)
1889 Keates P-H (encaustic tiles)

1892 Keates P-H (encaustic tiles)
1892 Kelly MM; SC (Encaustic Tile Manufacturers) (barbotine & majolica)
(ii) Vine Street and Cooper Street, Hanley
1896 Kelly SC (Sanitary Ware Manufacturers)
1900 Kelly SC (Sanitary Ware Manufacturers)

Sherwin, David
Renalagh Works, Hanley
1892 Keates P-H
1892 Kelly EM

Shingler & Co.
Albert Works, Liverpool Road, Stoke
1887 Porter CEM-S
1888 Kelly EM
1889 Keates A; P-S (earthenware)
1892 Keates P-S (earthenware)
1892 Kelly EM
The advertisement in 1889 Keates describes the firm as 'earthenware manufacturers, decorators, &c.'

SHINGLER & CO.,
Earthenware Manufacturers
DECORATORS, &c.,
LIVERPOOL ROAD,
STOKE-ON-TRENT.

Shingler & Co. Advertisement from 1889 Keates.

Shirley, Benjamin
See: Shirley, Thomas & Benjamin

Shirley, Cephas
Hanley
1818 Pigot, EM

Shirley, Elijah
(i) Silvester Square, Burslem
1882 Keates P-B (stilt and spur)
(ii) Moorland Road, Burslem
1884 Kelly SC (Spur & Stilt Makers for Pottery Manufacturers)
1887 Porter SC-B (Spur and Stilt Manufacturers)
1888 Kelly SC (Spur & Stilt Makers for Pottery Manufacturers)

Shirley, Jesse
Hanley
1811 Holden NC (earthenware-manufacturer)

Shirley, John
See: Keeling, Samuel, & Co.

Shirley, Thomas
Lane End
1798 Universal NC-LE (manufacturer of Staffordshire-ware)

Shirley, Thomas & Benjamin
Stafford Street, Longton
1846 Williams NC-L-LE (china manufacturers)
The partners are listed individually as Thomas Shirley of Wood Lane and Benjamin Shirley of Green Dock in 1846 Williams.

Shirley, W. & J.
Hanley and Shelton
1816 Underhill P

Shirley, William
Shelton
1809 Holden NC (earthenware-manufacturer)
1811 Holden NC (earthenware-manufacturer)

SHIRLEY & FREEMAN,
MANUFACTURERS OF
PORCELAIN CHINA,
PRINCE OF WALES' WORKS,
Longton, Staffordshire Potteries.
HOME AND EXPORT ORDERS PROMPTLY EXECUTED.

Shirley & Freeman. Advertisement from 1864 Jones.

Shirley & Freeman
(i) Chancery Lane, Longton
1860 Kelly CM-General
(ii) Sheridan Works, King Street, Longton
1861 Harrison NC-L (china manufacturers)
(iii) Cyples Lane, Market Street, Longton
1862 Slater CM
(iv) Prince of Wales' Works, Sutherland Road, Longton
1863 Kelly CM-General; CM-Tea, Breakfast, and Dessert Services
1864 Jones A; CEM
The advertisement in 1864 Jones describes the firm as 'manufacturers of porcelain china' and promises 'home and export orders promptly executed'.

Shirley, Lindop & Co.
Longport
1802 Allbut EM (map location 22)

Shone & Co.
See: Shore & Co.

Shore & Co.
Edensor Works, New Street, Longton
1889 Keates P-L (china)
1892 Keates P-L (china)
The firm is listed as Shone & Co. in 1889 Keates.

Shore, John, & Co.
Edensor Works, New Street, Longton
1887 Porter EM-L
1888 Kelly CM
1892 Kelly CM
1896 Kelly CM
1900 Kelly CM

Shorter & Boulton
Copeland Street, Stoke
1880 Kelly CM
1882 Keates P-S (majolica & earthenware)
1884 Kelly MM
1887 Porter CEM-S
1888 Kelly MM
1889 Keates P-S (majolica & earthenware)
1892 Keates P-S (majolica & earthenware)
1892 Kelly MM
1896 Kelly MM
1900 Kelly MM

Shorter & Heath
Hanley
1798 Universal NC-H (manufacturers of Staffordshire-ware)

Shorthose, John, & Co.
Hanley
1822 Allbut CEM (earthenware manufacts.)

Shorthose & Heath
Hanley
1796 Chester NC-H-Sh (manufacturers of earthenware)

1798 Universal NC-H (manufacturers of Staffordshire-ware)

Shorthose & Heaths, junrs.
Hanley
1805 Holden NC (earthenware manufacturers for exportation)
1809 Holden NC (earthenware-manufacturers for exportation)
1811 Holden NC (earthenware-manufacturers for exportation)

Shorthouse, John
Tontine Street, Hanley
1818 Parson EM-H-Sh

Shorthouse, John, & Co.
(i) Hanley
1816 Underhill P
(ii) Hill Street, Hanley
1818 Pigot EM
(iii) Tontine Street, Hanley
1822 Pigot EM

Shubotham, George
See: Shubotham & Webberley

Shubotham, Hannah & Mary (Misses)
Gold Street, Longton
1851 White CEM-L (only earthenware)
1852 Slater EM
1854 Kelly CEM
1856 Kelly CEM
The Shubothams' house is listed as Green Dock in 1851 White.

Shubotham & Webberley
St. James' Place, High Street, Longton
1846 Williams NC-L-LE (china manufacturers)
1850 Kelly CEM; NC-L (china manufacturers)
1850 Slater CM
The partners are listed individually as George Shubotham of High Street and William Webberley of Furnace Road in 1846 Williams.

Silvester, Frederick, & Co.
Castle Hill Works, Newcastle
1888 Kelly P
1892 Kelly P

Simkin, Hugh
(i) High Street, Lane End
1828 Pigot CM
1830 Pigot CM
(ii) Market Street, Lane End
1835 Pigot CM

Simkin, Woller
Lane End
1818 Pigot CM

Simkin & Waller
Lane End
1818 Parson EM-LE

Simms, George
22 Bedford Road, Hanley
1887 Porter EM-H

Simpkin, Hugh
(i) Flint Street, Lane End
1822 Pigot CM
(ii) High Street, Longton
1834 White CM-LE-L (lustre mfrs.)
Simpkin's house is listed as New Street in 1834 White.

Simpkin, Hugh, & Son
Lane End
1822 Allbut CEM (china manufacts.)

Simpson, Broom Thomas
See: Simpson, Thomas Broom

Simpson, Charles
Golden Hill
1811 Holden NC (china-ware manufr.)
1816 Underhill P

Simpson, John
Flint Street, Lane End
1834 White EM-LE-L
1835 Pigot EM
Simpson's house is listed as Gold Street, Longton, in 1834 White.

Simpson, Nicholas
Boden Brook, Shelton
1822 Allbut CEM (earthenware manufact.)
1822 Pigot EM

Simpson, Thomas Alfred
(i) Swan Works, Elm Street, Hanley
1880 Kelly EM
1882 Keates P-H (china)
(ii) High Street, Stoke
1884 Kelly SC (Encaustic Tile Manufacturers)
1892 Kelly SC (Encaustic Tile Manufacturers)
1900 Kelly SC (Encaustic Tile Manufacturers)
(iii) Cliff Bank Works, Stoke
1887 Porter SC-S (Tile Manufacturers)
1889 Keates SC-S (Tile - Encaustic - Manufacturers)
1892 Keates SC-S (Tile - Encaustic - Manufacturers)

Simpson, Thomas Broom
Hanley
1796 Chester NC-H-Sh (manufacturer of earthenware)
1798 Universal NC-H (manufacturer of Staffordshire-ware)
The potter is listed as Simpson, Broom Thomas, in 1798 Universal.

Simpson & Nicholls
Flint Street, Longton
1841 Pigot EM

Simpson & Wright
Shelton
1802 Allbut EM (map location 90)

Sims, Richard
16 Sheaf Street, Hanley
1864 Jones EM

Singleton, Benjamin, & Co.
Lane End
1816 Underhill P

Skelson & Son
Stafford Street, Longton
1892 Keates P-L (earthenware)

Skelson, William
Normacott Road, Longton
1879 Keates P-L (china and earthenware)

SKELSON AND PLANT,
MANUFACTURERS OF ALL KINDS OF
ENAMELLED GILT & CHINA,
NEW MARKET WORKS,
CHANCERY LANE, LONGTON,
STAFFORDSHIRE

Skelson & Plant. Advertisement from 1867 Keates.

Skelson & Plant
(i) New Market Works, Chancery Lane, Longton
1868 Kelly CM
1869 Keates P-L (china)

1870 Harrod NC-L (china and earthenware manufacturers)
1872 Kelly CM
(ii) Heathcote Road, Longton
1870 Harrod NC-L (china and earthenware manufacturers)
1872 Kelly CM
1873 Keates P-L (china & earthenware)
1875 Keates P-L (china & earthenware)
1876 Kelly CM
(iii) Normacott Road, Longton
1873 Keates P-L (china & earthenware)
1875 Keates P-L (china & earthenware)
1880 Kelly CM
1882 Keates P-L (china and earthenware)
1884 Kelly CM
1887 Porter EM-L
1888 Kelly CM
1889 Keates P-L (china and earthenware)
1892 Kelly CM
The second partner's name is listed as Platt in 1887 Porter. Although no entry appears in the directory, an advertisement in 1867 Keates describes the firm as 'manufacturers of all kinds of enamelled gilt & china'.

Skerratt, Obadiah
See: Sherratt, Obadiah

Slade, T., & Co.
Tunstall
1816 Underhill P

Smith & Co.
(i) Hill Pottery, Cliff Bank, Stoke
1882 Keates P-S (jet & Rockingham)
1892 Keates P-S (jet and Rockingham)
(ii) High Street, Stoke
1884 Kelly EM
1888 Kelly EM; JM; MM
1892 Kelly EM; JRM; MM
1896 Kelly EM; JRM; MM
(iii) Albert Works, Shelton
1900 Kelly, EM

Smith, Ambrose, & Co.
Burslem
1784 Bailey NC-B (manufacturers of cream coloured ware, and china glazed ware painted blue)

Smith, J. & H.
Cliff Bank, Stoke
1887 Porter CEM-S

Smith, James
Stoke
1805 Holden NC (earthenware manufacturer)

Smith, John
141 or 144 Hope Street, Hanley
1863 Kelly PM
1864 Jones PM (manufacturer of parian twig baskets and brooches)
1865 Keates P-H (toy)
1867 Keates P-H (parian)
1869 Keates P-H (parian)
1870 Harrod NC-H (parian manufacturer)

Smith, John & Joseph
Burslem
1784 Bailey NC-B (potters)

Smith, Joseph
Tunstall
1796 Chester NC-T-Lp (manufacturer of earthenware)
1798 Universal NC-T (earthenware manufacturer)

SAMPSON SMITH,
SUTHERLAND WORKS,
BARKER STREET, HIGH STREET,
LONGTON.
MANUFACTURER OF ALL KINDS OF
BURNISHED AND ENAMELLED
CHINA,
GOLD AND SILVER LUSTRES,
AND
FIGURES IN GREAT VARIETY.

Sampson Smith. Advertisement from 1864 Jones.

Smith, Sampson
Sutherland Works, Barker Street, High Street, Longton
1851 White NC-L (figure mfr.)
1852 Slater CM; TOCM
1854 Kelly PM (ornamental figure makers); TM
1856 Kelly TM (china)
1860 Kelly CFM; CM-General; CM-Tea, Breakfast & Dessert Services; SC (Jug Manufacturers) (fancy)
1861 Harrison NC-L (china manufacturer)
1862 Slater CM; TOCM
1863 Kelly CM-General
1864 Jones A; CEM; CFM; LM
1865 Keates P-L (china, gold and silver lustre)
1867 Keates P-L (china and gold and silver lustre)
1868 Kelly CM; LM
1869 Keates P-L (china and gold and silver lustre and figure)
1870 Harrod NC-L (china and figure manufacturer)
1872 Kelly CM
1873 Keates P-L (china and gold and silver lustre and figure)
1875 Keates P-L (china and gold and silver lustre and figure)
1876 Kelly CM
1879 Keates P-L (china and gold and silver lustre and figure)
1880 Kelly CM
1882 Keates P-L (china & gold & silver lustre & figure)
1884 Kelly CM
1888 Kelly CM
1889 Keates P-L (china & gold and silver lustre and figure)
1892 Keates P-L (china & gold & silver lustre and figure)
1892 Kelly CM
1896 Kelly CM
1900 Kelly CM
The firm is noted as being in the hands of executors in 1879 Keates. Smith's first name is listed as Samson in 1882 Keates. The advertisement in 1864 Jones describes Smith as a 'manufacturer of all kinds of burnished and enamelled china, gold and silver lustres, and figures in great variety'.

Smith, Theophilus
Smithfield
1796 Chester NC-T-Lp (manufacturer of earthenware)
1798 Universal NC-Sf (manufacturer of earthen-ware and merchant)

Theophilus Smith. Impressed mark from a blue-printed earthenware dinner plate.

Smith, Thomas, & Co.
Burslem
1781 Bailey NC (potters)
1783 Bailey NC (potters)

Smith, W.T.H., & Co.
Longport
1900 Kelly EM

Smith, William
Hope Street, Hanley
1860 Kelly PM

Smith, William, & Son
Albert Street, Burslem
1862 Slater EM
1863 Kelly EM

Smith, William H.
Fenton Park, Fenton
1860 Kelly EM
1862 Slater CM; EM

Smith & Billington
Cobridge
1802 Allbut EM (map location 57)

Smith & Ford
Lincoln Pottery, Newport Lane, Burslem
1896 Kelly EM

Smith, Ford & Jones
Lincoln Pottery, Newport Lane, Burslem
1892 Kelly EM

Smith & Frost
Anchor Works, Brewery Street, Hanley
1887 Porter EM-H
1888 Kelly EM

Smith & Jarvis
Stoke
1802 Allbut EM (map location 103)

Smith (William) & Ridgway
Hanley
1798 Universal NC-H (manufacturers of Staffordshire-ware)

Smith & Steel
Tunstall
1802 Allbut EM (map location 16)
1805 Holden NC (earthenware manufacturers)
The second partner's name is listed as Steele in 1805 Holden.

Snape, Samuel
Garshall Green, near Stone
1864 Jones A; EM-Miscellaneous (horticultural potter)
The advertisement in 1864 Jones is headed 'Horticultural Pottery' and describes Snape as a 'manufacturer of flower pots, round and square seed pans, rhubarb and seakale pots'. It states 'a good stock on hand' and promises 'orders carefully attended to'.

HORTICULTURAL POTTERY,
Garshall Green, near
STONE, STAFFORDSHIRE.
SAMUEL SNAPE,
MANUFACTURER OF FLOWER POTS,
ROUND AND SQUARE SEED PANS,
RHUBARB AND SEAKALE POTS.
A Good Stock on hand. Orders carefully attended to.

Samuel Snape. Advertisement from 1864 Jones.

Sneyd, Thomas
Miles Bank, Hanley
1846 Williams NC-H (earthenware manufacturer)

Snow, Henry
(i) Commercial Buildings, Stoke
1852 Slater TOCM
(ii) St. Martin's Lane, Market Street, Longton
1864 Jones LM

Snow, Henry, & Co.
Union Street, Stoke, and St. Ann's Street, Shelton
1852 Slater PM

Snow, J. & J.
Liverpool Road, Stoke
1882 Keates P-S (terra cotta and majolica)
1884 Kelly TCM

Snow, John & James
Pyenest Street Works, Hanley
1882 Keates P-H (terra cotta)

Snow, John & Jonathan
24 or 26 Howard Place, Hanley
1892 Kelly EM
1896 Kelly EM
1900 Kelly EM

Snow, Jonathan & John
(i) Pyenest Street Works, Hanley
1887 Porter EM-H
1889 Keates P-H (terra cotta, jet and majolica)
1892 Keates P-H (terra cotta, jet, and majolica)
(ii) 178 Howard Place, Hanley
1888 Kelly EM
1889 Keates P-H (terra cotta, jet and majolica)
1892 Keates P-H (terra cotta, jet, and majolica)

Snow & Littler
Liverpool Road, Stoke
1880 Kelly TCM

Sparkes, George
Hanley
1818 Pigot EM

Spencer & Hines
Edensor Road, Longton
1880 Kelly CM (manufacturers of decorated china & earthenware, spirit barrels, tea sets, jugs, toilet wares & general goods suitable for home & exportation)

Spencer & Stanway
Edensor Road, Longton
1884 Kelly CM (manufacturers of decorated china & earthenware, spirit barrels, tea sets, jugs, toilet wares & general goods suitable for home & exportation)

Sperratt, Martha
See: Sherratt, Martha (Mrs.)

Spode, Josiah
Stoke
1781 Bailey NC (potter)
1783 Bailey NC (potter)
1784 Bailey NC-S (potter)
1796 Chester NC-S (manufacturer of earthenware)
1798 Universal NC-S (manufacturer of Staffordshire-ware and Register-office keeper)
1802 Allbut EM (map location 101)
1805 Holden NC (china and earthenware manufacturer)
1809 Holden NC (potter & English porcelain-manufacturer to the Prince of Wales)
1811 Holden NC (potter &

English porcelain manufacturer to the Prince of Wales)
1816 Underhill P
1818 Parson EM-S-E
1818 Pigot CM; EM
1822 Allbut CEM (china and earthenware manufact.)
1822 Pigot CM; EM
1828 Pigot CM; EM
1830 Pigot CM; EM
The Stoke address is listed as Newcastle Street in 1828 Pigot and High Street in 1830 Pigot. A London address at Portugal Street is listed in 1809 Holden and 1811 Holden.

Josiah Spode. Printed mark used on fine Felspar Porcelain.

Josiah Spode. Printed mark from a fine gilt and enamelled Felspar Porcelain covered sugar basin.

Josiah Spode. Printed mark from a blue-printed earthenware sauce tureen.

Spode, Samuel
Folly (or Folley) House, Lane End
1796 Chester NC-LE-LD-LL (manufacturer of earthenware)
1798 Universal NC-LE (manufacturer of Staffordshire-ware)
1802 Allbut EM (map location 116)
1805 Holden NC (earthenware manufacturer)
1809 Holden NC (earthenware-manufacturer)
1811 Holden NC (earthenware-manufacturer)
1816 Underhill P

Stanley & Co.
Hanley
1796 Chester NC-H-Sh (manufacturers of earthenware)

Stanley, John
Hanley
1802 Allbut EM (map location 84)

Stanley, William
(i) Burslem
1805 Holden NC (earthenware manufacturer)
1809 Holden NC (earthenware-manufacturer)
1811 Holden NC (earthenware manufactr.)
1816 Underhill P
(ii) Knowle Works, Burslem
1818 Parson EM-B-Lp-C
1818 Pigot EM

Stanley, William & John
Burslem
1802 Allbut EM (map location 45)

Stanley & Lambert
High Street, Longton
1851 White CEM-L (only earthenware)
1852 Slater EM

Stannaway, John
New Street, Wolstanton
1864 Jones EM

Stanway, J.
Copeland Street and Liverpool Road, Stoke
1879 Keates P-S (parian, earthenware, and china)

Stanway, Levi
Sneyd Green, Burslem
1887 Porter EM-B

Stanway & Fellwright
Sneyd Street, Cobridge
1884 Kelly MM

Stanway & Horne
(i) Joiner's Square, Hanley
1861 Harrison NC-H-Sh (parian and stone manufacturers)
1862 Slater PM
(ii) Eastwood Vale, Hanley
1863 Kelly PM
The second partner's name is listed as Thorne in 1861 Harrison.

Stanway, Horne & Co.
Eastvale, Lichfield Street, Hanley
1864 Jones A; PM
The advertisement in 1864 Jones gives the address as Joiner's Square, Eastwood Vale and describes the firm as 'manufacturers of parian & stone ware'. It offers 'a large stock always kept on hand, ready for exportation'.

STANWAY, HORNE, & Co.,
MANUFACTURERS OF
PARIAN & STONE WARE,
JOINERS' SQUARE, EASTWOOD VALE,
HANLEY, STAFFORDSHIRE POTTERIES.
A large Stock always kept on hand, ready for exportation.

Stanway, Horne & Co. Advertisement from 1864 Jones.

Stanway, Horne & Adams
(i) Trent Works, Eastwood Vale, Hanley
1865 Keates P-H (parian)
1867 Keates P-H (parian)
1869 Keates P-H (parian)
1873 Keates P-H (parian)
1875 Keates P-H (parian)
1879 Keates P-H (parian)
(ii) Lower Lichfield Street, Hanley
1868 Kelly PM
1872 Kelly PM
(iii) Trent Works, Joiner's Square, Hanley
1870 Harrod NC-H (manufacturers of parian and stoneware, pearl and orange lustre, terra cotta, jet, and best parian statuary for home and foreign markets)
(iv) Fenton Road, Hanley
1876 Kelly PM

The third partner's name is listed as Adam in 1872 Kelly. The firm was succeeded in turn by Thomas Adams and Edwards & Son (1887 Porter advertisement).

Stanway & Tellwright
Sneyd Street, Cobridge
1884 Kelly EM

Stanway & Thorne
See: Stanway & Horne

Star China Co.
Gregory Street, Longton
1900 Kelly CM

Steel, Daniel
(i) Burslem
1796 Chester NC-B (manufacturer of earthenware)
1802 Allbut EM (map location 43)
1805 Holden NC (earthenware manufacturer)
(ii) St. John's Street, Burslem
1818 Parson EM-B-Lp-C
(iii) Nile Street, Burslem
1822 Allbut CEM (jasper and ornamental earthenware manufact.)
The surname is listed as Steele in 1805 Holden.

Daniel Steel. Impressed mark from a jasper portrait medallion of Admiral Howe.

Steel, Daniel, & Son
Bourne's Bank, Burslem
1828 Pigot EM (jasper & stone)
1830 Pigot EM (jasper & stone)

Steel, Daniel, & Sons
Hole House, Burslem
1822 Pigot EM

Steel, Edward
See: Steele, Edward

Steel, Henry
Marsh Street, Shelton
1841 Pigot NC (ornamental jasper manufacturer)

Steel, John, & Co.
Tunstall
1822 Allbut CEM (china manufacts.)

Steele, Alfred
Market Street, Longton
1846 Williams NC-L-LE (china manufacturer)

Steele, Daniel
See: Steel, Daniel

Steele, Edward
Cannon Street Works, Hanley
1875 Keates P-H (earthenware)
1876 Kelly EM
1879 Keates P-H (earthenware)
1880 Kelly EM (manufacturer of earthenware, majolica, & parian statuettes); PM
1882 Keates P-H (earthenware)
1884 Kelly EM (manufacturer of earthenware, majolica & parian statuettes); PM
1887 Porter EM-H
1888 Kelly EM (manufacturer of earthenware, majolica & parian statuettes); PM
1889 Keates P-H (earthenware, parian statuette and majolica)
The surname is listed as Steel in 1880 Kelly, 1884 Kelly, 1888 Kelly, and 1889 Keates.

Steele, John & Thomas
Newfield, Tunstall
1822 Pigot CM

Steele, William
Burslem
1809 Holden NC (earthenware-manufacturer)

Steele & Wood
(i) Eastwood, Hanley
1875 Keates SC-H (Floor Tile Manufacturers) (glazed encaustic hearth tiles)
(ii) London Road, Stoke
1880 Kelly SC (Encaustic Tile Manufacturers)
1882 Keates SC-S (Tile - Encaustic - Manufacturers)
1884 Kelly SC (Encaustic Tile Manufacturers)
1887 Porter SC-S (Tile Manufacturers)
1888 Kelly SC (Encaustic Tile Manufacturers)
1889 Keates SC-S (Tile - Encaustic - Manufacturers)
(iii) Elder Road, Cobridge, Burslem
1887 Porter EM-B
1888 Kelly SC (Encaustic Tile Manufacturers)
1889 Keates SC-B (Encaustic and Geometric Tile Pavement Manufacturers) (Porcelain Tile)
1892 Keates SC-B (Encaustic and Geometric Tile Pavement Manufacturers) (Porcelain Tile)
1892 Kelly SC (Encaustic Tile Manufacturers)
The firm is identified as The Crystal Porcelain Tile Co. in 1888 Kelly and The Crystal Porcelain Tile Co. Ltd. in 1892 Kelly.

Stephenson, John
Bethesda Street, Shelton
1850 Kelly NC-Sh (china ornament manufacturer)
1850 Slater TOCM
1851 White CETOM-H-Sh
1852 Slater TOCM
1854 Kelly CFM

Stephenson, Ralph, & Son
See: Stevenson, Ralph, & Son

Sterrup, Thomas
See: Stirrup, Thomas

Stevenson, Andrew
Cobridge
1811 Holden NC (earthenware-manuf.)
1818 Parson EM-B-Lp-C
1818 Pigot EM
1822 Allbut CEM (china & earthenware manufact.)
1822 Pigot EM
1828 Pigot EM

Stevenson, Charles, & Son
Burslem
1784 Bailey NC-B (manufacturers of cream coloured ware, blue painted, &c.)

Stevenson, J. & A.
Cobridge
1809 Holden NC (earthenware-manuf.)

Stevenson, Ralph
Cobridge
1811 Holden NC (earthenware manufr.)
1816 Underhill P
1818 Parson EM-B-Lp-C
1818 Pigot EM
1822 Allbut CEM (earthenware manufact.)
1822 Pigot EM
1828 Pigot EM
1830 Pigot EM

Ralph Stevenson. Printed mark from a blue-printed earthenware plate.

Stevenson, Ralph, & Son
Cobridge
1834 White EM-B (china mfrs. also)
1835 Pigot CM
The surname is listed as Stephenson in 1834 White.

Stevenson, Ralph, & Sons
Cobridge
1835 Pigot EM

Stevenson & Bucknall
Cobridge
1811 Holden NC (earthenware manufacs.)
1816 Underhill P

Stevenson & Dale
Cobridge
1802 Allbut EM (map location 58)

Stevenson & Godwin
Cobridge
1805 Holden NC (earthenware manufacturers)
1809 Holden NC (earthenware-manufacturers)

Steventon Brothers
Well Street Pottery, Tunstall
1888 Kelly EM
1889 Keates P-T (and decorators)

Stirrup, Thomas
(i) Lane End
1796 Chester NC-LE-LD-LL (manufacturer of earthenware)
1798 Universal NC-LE (manufacturer of Staffordshire-ware)
1802 Allbut EM (map location 128)
1805 Holden NC (earthenware manufacturer)
1809 Holden NC (manufacturer of earthenware)
1811 Holden NC (manufactr. of earthenware)
1816 Underhill P
(ii) Flint Street, Lane End
1818 Parson EM-LE
The surname is listed as Sterrup in 1798 Universal.

Stirrup & Beardmore
Lane End
1809 Holden NC (manufactrs. of earthenware)
1811 Holden NC (manufacturers, of earthenware)
1816 Underhill P

Stonier, Hollinshead & Co.
High Street, Hanley
1889 Keates P-H
1892 Keates P-H
1892 Kelly EM

Stonier, Hollinshead & Oliver
High Street, Hanley
1884 Kelly EM
1887 Porter EM-H
1888 Kelly EM

Street, John
Marsh Street, Shelton
1846 Williams NC-Sh (china figure manufacturer)

Stretton, Samuel
Lane Delph
1828 Pigot EM (toy only)

Stubbs, Benjamin
Longport
1818 Parson EM-B-Lp-C
1822 Pigot EM

Stubbs, Joseph
Longport
1822 Allbut CEM (earthenware manufact.)
1834 White EM-B
1835 Pigot EM

Stubbs, Joshua
31 High Street, Longton
1887 Porter EM-L
1888 Kelly EM

Stubbs, William
(i) Waterloo Works, Hanley
1850 Kelly CEM; NC-H (china manufacturer)
1850 Slater CM; TOCM
(ii) High Street, Hanley
1852 Slater CM; EM
1854 Kelly CFM
1856 Kelly CEM
1860 Kelly CM-General; EM
1861 Harrison NC-H-Sh (china and earthenware manufacturer)
(iii) Albion Pottery, Shelton or Hanley
1861 Harrison NC-H-Sh (earthenware manufacturer)
(iv) High Street and Eastwood Pottery, Eastwood Vale, Hanley
1862 Slater CM (& manufacturer of earthenware, Egyptian black, stone ware, lustre, parian & figures); EM (and manufacturer of china, parian, Egyptian black, stone ware, lustre, &c.); PM (and manufacturer of china, earthenware, Egyptian black, stoneware, lustre, &c.); TOCM
1864 Jones CEM
1865 Keates P-H (china, earthenware, and parian)
1867 Keates P-H (china, earthenware, lustre and parian)
1869 Keates P-H (china, earthenware, lustre & parian)
(v) Eastwood Pottery, Eastwood Vale, Hanley
1863 Kelly CFM; CM-Fancy Ware; CM-General; COM; EM; LM; PM; SC (Egyptian Black Ware Manufacturers); SM
1868 Kelly EM
1870 Harrod NC-H (china and earthenware manufacturer)

1872 Kelly EM
1873 Keates P-H (china and earthenware)
1875 Keates P-H (china and earthenware)
1876 Kelly EM
1879 Keates P-H (china and earthenware)
1880 Kelly EM
1882 Keates P-H (china and earthenware)
1884 Kelly EM
1887 Porter EM-H
1888 Kelly EM
1889 Keates P-H (china and earthenware)
1892 Keates P-H (china and earthenware)
1892 Kelly EM

An advertisement in 1861 Harrison describes Stubbs as a 'useful and ornamental china manufacturer' at High Street, Hanley, and as an 'earthenware manufacturer' at the Albion Pottery, Eastwood, Hanley. It also states 'manufacturer of toys, metal top jugs, teapots and mustards, earthenware, gilt, stone, and enamelled jugs in every variety, butter tubs, toast racks, pillar and bedroom candlesticks, flower pots, black, lustre, &c.'

Stubbs, William
See: Stubbs & Walker

WILLIAM STUBBS,
USEFUL AND ORNAMENTAL
CHINA MANUFACTURER,
HIGH STREET, HANLEY,
AND
EARTHENWARE MANUFACTURER,
ALBION POTTERY, EASTWOOD, HANLEY.
Manufacturer of Toys, Metal Top Jugs, Teapots and Mustards, Earthenware, Gilt, Stone, and Enamelled Jugs in every variety, Butter Tubs, Toast Racks, Pillar and Bedroom Candlesticks, Flower Pots, black, lustre, &c.

William Stubbs. Advertisement from 1861 Harrison.

Stubbs & Bird
(i) Waterloo Works, Well Street, Hanley
1851 White CETOM-H-Sh
(ii) High Street, Hanley or Shelton
1851 White NC-H-Sh (china, &c., manufacturers)

Stubbs & Bridgwood
Heathcote Road, Longton
1868 Kelly EM

Stubbs, Hackney & Tomkinson
High Street, Longton
1864 Jones A; CEM
The third partner's name is listed as Tompkinson in the entry but Tomkinson in the advertisement, which describes the firm as 'manufacturers of enamelled & gilt china'.

STUBBS, HACKNEY & TOMKINSON,
MANUFACTURERS OF
ENAMELLED & GILT CHINA,
HIGH STREET,
LONGTON, STAFFORDSHIRE.

Stubbs, Hackney & Tomkinson. Advertisement from 1864 Jones.

Stubbs & Hall
31 High Street, Longton
1889 Keates P-L (earthenware)
1892 Keates P-L (earthenware)
1892 Kelly EM

Stubbs & Holgart
Newcastle Street, Burslem
1892 Keates SC-B (Floor Tile Works)

Stubbs & Kent
Longport
1828 Pigot EM
1830 Pigot EM

STUBBS AND PLANT,
MANUFACTURERS OF EVERY DESCRIPTION OF
ENAMELLED & BURNISHED GOLD
CHINA,
NEW MARKET WORKS,
CHANCERY LANE,
LONGTON POTTERIES,
STAFFORDSHIRE.

Stubbs & Plant. Advertisement from 1864 Jones. The same basic advertisement appeared in 1867 Keates.

Stubbs & Plant
New Market Works, Chancery Lane, Longton
1864 Jones A; CEM
1865 Keates P-L (china)

The advertisement in 1864 Jones describes the firm as 'manufacturers of every description of enamelled & burnished gold china'. Although there is no entry in the directory, a similar advertisement also appears in 1867 Keates.

Stubbs & Taylor
Longport
1816 Underhill P

Stubbs, Tomkinson & Billington
High Street, Longton
1865 Keates P-L (china and parian)
1867 Keates P-L (china and parian)
The second partner is listed as Tomlinson in 1867 Keates. The third partner is listed as Millington in 1865 Keates.

Stubbs & Walker
Waterloo Works, Hanley
1846 Williams NC-H (china manufacturers)
The partners are listed individually as William Stubbs of Market Street and William Walker of Hope Street, Shelton, in 1846 Williams.

Sturgess, William Henry
(i) Edensor Road, Longton
1880 Kelly CM (china & earthenware for home & export – quotations on application)
(ii) New Street, Longton
1882 Keates P-L (china &c.)
Offices are listed at 18 Market Lane, Longton, in 1882 Keates.

Sudlow, R., & Sons
Adelaide Street, Burslem
1896 Kelly EM
1900 Kelly EM

Sudlow, Robert
Bourne's Bank, Burslem
1884 Kelly JM; RM
1887 Porter EM-B
1888 Kelly JM; RM
1889 Keates P-B (earthenware)
1892 Keates P-B (earthenware)
1892 Kelly JRM

Sunderland, John
Market Lane, Longton
1864 Jones PM

Sutherland & Sons
Park Hall Street, Anchor Road, Longton
1865 Keates P-L (parian and terra cotta)
1867 Keates P-L (parian & terra cotta)
1868 Kelly PFM
1869 Keates A; P-L (parian, ivory, rustic, & terra cotta)
1870 Harrod NC-L (manufacturers of ornamental, parian, rustic, and belbeck pearl ware, ivory, enamelled, flowered, risen, and plain gilt, &c., for home and foreign markets)
1872 Kelly MM; PM
1873 Keates A; P-L (parian, ivory, rustic, and terra cotta)
1875 Keates A; P-L (parian, ivory, rustic, and terra cotta)
The advertisements in 1869 Keates, 1873 Keates, and 1875 Keates all give the style as D. Sutherland & Sons. The firm is described as 'manufacturers of parian, ivory, terra cotta and rustic ware' (1869), and as 'manufacturers of parian, ivory, majolica, mother of pearl and rustic ware' (1873 and 1875).

Sutherland, D., & Sons
See: Sutherland & Sons

D. SUTHERLAND & SONS,
MANUFACTURERS OF
Parian, Ivory, Terra Cotta
AND RUSTIC WARE,
Park Hall St., Longton, Staffordshire

D. Sutherland & Sons. Advertisement from 1869 Keates.

D. SUTHERLAND & SONS,
MANUFACTURERS OF
PARIAN, IVORY, MAJOLICA,
MOTHER OF PEARL AND RUSTIC WARE,
PARK HALL STREET, LONGTON,
STAFFORDSHIRE.

D. Sutherland & Sons. Advertisement from 1873 Keates. The same advertisement appeared in 1875 Keates.

Sutherland, D. & T.
Caroline Street, Longton
1863 Kelly PFM

Sutherland, Daniel
(i) 17 Caroline Street, Longton
1862 Slater PM; TOCM
(ii) 18 Caroline Street, and Parkhall Street, Anchor Road, Longton
1864 Jones PM; SC (Earthenware Rustic and Terra Cotta Figure Manufacturers) (manufacturer of useful and ornamental parian, terra cotta, rustic, oak, and fir tobacco boxes, garden pots, spills, &c. Proprietor of the Temperance hotel)
Sutherland's house is listed as 18 Caroline Street with the works at Parkhall Street in 1864 Jones.

Sutherland, Hugh
Park Hall Street, Anchor Road, Longton
1879 Keates A; P-L (parian, ivory, rustic, and terra cotta)
1880 Kelly MM (manufacturer of useful & ornamental majolica in every variety)
The advertisement in 1879 Keates gives the style as H. Sutherland & Sons, and describes the firm as 'manufacturers of parian, ivory, majolica, and rustic ware'.

Sutherland, H., & Sons
See: Sutherland, Hugh

H. SUTHERLAND & SONS,
MANUFACTURERS OF
PARIAN, IVORY, MAJOLICA,
AND RUSTIC WARE,
PARKHALL STREET, LONGTON,
STAFFORDSHIRE.

H. Sutherland & Sons. Advertisement from 1879 Keates.

Sutherland, Thomas
Cromartie Works, Market Lane, Longton
1889 Keates P-L (china, earthenware, &c.)
1892 Keates P-L (china and earthenware)

Sutherland, Cyples & Co.
Heathcote Works, Heathcote Road, Longton
1887 Porter EM-L
1888 Kelly CM

Swan, Ebenezer
Amicable Street, Tunstall
1888 Kelly EM

Swan, T. Carey
See: Malcolm, Frederick

Swan & Paulson
Amicable Street, Tunstall
1884 Kelly EM

Swan Pottery Co.
High Street, Stoke
1896 Kelly EM

Swann, E.
(i) Globe Pottery, High Street, Tunstall
1887 Porter EM-T
1889 Keates P-T
(ii) Amicable Street, Tunstall
1892 Kelly EM

Swetman, William & George
Moorland Road, Burslem
1841 Pigot EM (Egyptian black)

Swettenham, Thomas
Nile Street, Burslem
1828 Pigot EM

Swift, John
St. Martin's Lane, Longton
1860 Kelly P
1861 Harrison NC-L (tobacco pot manufacturer)

Swift & Elkin
Stafford Street, Longton
1841 Pigot EM

Syples, Mary
See: Cyples, Mary

T

Talbot, Elizabeth
Market Street, Longton
1861 Harrison NC-L (silver lustre manufacturer)

Tams, Jesse
Cannon Street, Shelton
1841 Pigot EM

Tams, John
Crown Pottery, 57 Stafford Street, Longton

1875 Keates	P-L (earthenware)
1876 Kelly	EM; P
1879 Keates	A; P-L (earthenware)
1880 Kelly	EM
1882 Keates	P-L (earthenware)
1884 Kelly	EM
1887 Porter	EM-L
1888 Kelly	EM
1889 Keates	A; P-L (earthenware)
1892 Keates	A; P-L (earthenware)
1892 Kelly	EM
1896 Kelly	EM
1900 Kelly	EM

An advertisement in 1875 Keates is the same as the one in 1879 Keates, both describing Tams as a 'manufacturer of gilt & ground-laid toilet and dinner ware, spirit barrels, &c., lustre, Egyptian black, drab, turquoise and printed wares, &c.' A long advertisement appears in both 1882 Keates and 1892 Keates. It reads: 'Important !! By Royal letters patent. The Excelsior Government stamped earthenware measure. This measure is universally admitted to be the best and most reliable Government stamped earthenware measure in the market, and as such has received the special approbation of the Standards Department of the Board of Trade and of the district authorities at the Courts of Quarter Sessions. It can therefore be used in any part of the United Kingdom as a legal standard measure, in accordance with the provisions of the Act of Parliament by which it is rendered compulsory that jugs and mugs used as measures, must be Government stamped. N.B. – Each measure is tested and stamped by the Government Inspector before leaving the manufactory, and is therefore ready for immediate use. Manufactured only by the patentee and sole proprietor, John Tams, Crown Pottery, Longton, Staffordshire, from whom quotations for the above, as also price list for general goods, may be had post free upon application.' The text is illustrated by an engraving of a stamped one pint tankard. No copy of the advertisement in 1889 Keates could be located.

John Tams. Printed mark from a brown-printed earthenware dinner plate. The registration number dates from 1884.

CROWN POTTERY,
STAFFORD STREET, LONGTON, STAFFORDSHIRE
JOHN TAMS,
MANUFACTURER OF GILT & GROUND-LAID TOILET AND DINNER WARE, SPIRIT BARRELS, &c.
LUSTRE, EGYPTIAN BLACK, DRAB,
TURQUOISE AND PRINTED WARES, &c.

John Tams. Advertisement from 1875 Keates. The same advertisement appeared in 1879 Keates.

IMPORTANT !!
BY ROYAL LETTERS PATENT.
The Excelsior Government Stamped Earthenware Measure.
This Measure is universally admitted to be the best and most reliable Government Stamped Earthenware Measure in the Market, and as such has received the special approbation of
THE STANDARDS DEPARTMENT OF THE BOARD OF TRADE
AND OF THE
DISTRICT AUTHORITIES AT THE COURTS OF QUARTER SESSIONS.
It can therefore be used in any part of the United Kingdom as a *Legal Standard Measure*, in accordance with the Act of Parliament by which it is rendered compulsory that jugs and mugs, used as measures, must be Government stamped.

N.B.—Each Measure is Tested and Stamped by the Government Inspector before leaving the Manufactory, and is therefore ready for immediate use.
Manufactured only by the Patentee and Sole Proprietor,
JOHN TAMS,
CROWN POTTERY, LONGTON,
STAFFORDSHIRE,
From whom Quotations for the above, as also Price List for General Goods, may be had Post Free upon application.

John Tams. Advertisement from 1882 Keates. The same basic advertisement appeared in 1892 Keates.

Tams & Chatfield
Sheridan Works, Longton

Although there is no entry in the directory, an advertisement in 1865 Keates describes Tams & Chatfield as 'manufacturers of improved porcelain china, tea, breakfast & dessert services, for home & abroad'.

TAMS AND CHATFIELD,
Sheridan Works,
LONGTON, STAFFORDSHIRE,
MANUFACTURERS OF
IMPROVED PORCELAIN CHINA,
Tea, Breakfast & Dessert Services, for Home & Abroad.

Tams & Chatfield. Advertisement from 1865 Keates.

TAMS & LOWE,
MANUFACTURERS OF
Lustre, Egyptian, Black, Drab,
TURQUOISE & PRINTED WARES,
STONE MORTARS, &c.,
HIGH STREET,
LONGTON, STAFFORDSHIRE.

Tams & Lowe. Advertisement from 1865 Keates.

TAMS & LOWE,
MANUFACTURERS OF
Lustre, Egyptian, Black, Drab,
TURQUOISE & PRINTED WARES,
STONE MORTARS, &c.
ENAMELLERS, GROUNDLAYERS & GILDERS
HIGH STREET,
LONGTON, STAFFORDSHIRE.

Tams & Lowe. Advertisement from 1867 Keates. The same advertisement appeared in 1869 Keates.

Tams & Lowe
High Street, Longton

1865 Keates	A; P-L (earthenware)
1867 Keates	A; P-L (earthenware)
1868 Kelly	EM; SC (Beer

Machine Handle Makers – China); SC (Stone Mortar & Pestle Manufacturers)
1869 Keates A; P-L (earthenware)
1870 Harrod NC-L (earthenware manufacturers)
1872 Kelly EM; SC (Beer Machine Handle Makers – China); SC (Stone Mortar & Pestle Manufacturers)
1873 Keates P-L (earthenware)
The firm was succeeded by William Lowe (advertisements in 1875 Keates and 1882 Keates). The advertisements in 1865 Keates, 1867 Keates, and 1869 Keates all describe the firm as 'manufacturers of lustre, Egyptian, black, drab, turquoise & printed wares, stone mortars, &c.' The description 'enamellers, groundlayers & gilders' is added in both 1867 and 1869.

Taylor Brothers
Market Street, Hanley
1864 Jones EM
1865 Keates P-H (earthenware)
1867 Keates P-H (earthenware)
1868 Kelly EM
1869 Keates P-H (earthenware)
1870 Harrod NC-H (earthenware manufacturers for the South American, United States, and India markets)

Taylor Brothers & Co.
Market Street, Hanley
1860 Kelly EM; PM
1861 Harrison NC-H-Sh (earthenware manufacturers)
1862 Slater EM
1863 Kelly EM

Taylor & Co.
(i) Fenton
1870 Harrod NC-F (spur and stilt manufacturers)
(ii) Church Street, Longton
1889 Keates P-L (patent stilt and spur)
1892 Keates P-L (patent stilt and spur)
1896 Kelly SC (Spur Makers); SC (Stilt & Spur Manufacturers)
1900 Kelly SC (Spur Makers); SC (Stilt & Spur Manufacturers)

Taylor, G. jun.
Shelton
1809 Holden NC (earthenware-manufacturer)
1811 Holden NC (earthenware manufactr.)

Taylor, George
Hanley
1784 Bailey NC-H (potter)
1796 Chester NC-H-Sh (manufacturer of earthenware)
1798 Universal NC-H (manufacturer of Staffordshire-ware)
1802 Allbut EM (map location 73)
1805 Holden NC (earthenware manufacturer)
1809 Holden NC (earthenware-manufacturer)
1811 Holden NC (earthenware manufacturer)

George Taylor. Impressed mark from a moulded creamware teapot.

Taylor, James
Waterloo Road, Burslem
1851 White CEM-B, (only earthenware)
Taylor's house is listed as Bleak Hill in 1851 White.
See also: Vernon, James, & Co.

Taylor, John
Market Street, Longton
1851 White CEM-L
Taylor's house is listed as Caverswall in 1851 White. He was succeeded by William Davenport (1860 Kelly).

Taylor, John, & Co.
Burslem
1802 Allbut EM

Taylor, Robert Minton
See: Campbell Brick & Tile Company (The)

Taylor, Robert Minton, & Co.
High Street, Fenton
1869 Keates P-F (tile); SC-F (Tile - Ornamental - Manufacturers)
1870 Harrod NC-F (manufacturers of ornamental and all kinds of encaustic tiles)
1873 Keates P-F (tile); SC-F (Tile - Ornamental - Manufacturers)

Taylor, T. & J.
High Street, Hanley
1818 Parson EM-H-Sh

Taylor, Theophilus & James
Hanley
1816 Underhill P

Taylor, Thomas
High Street, Hanley
1822 Allbut CEM (earthenware manufact.)
1822 Pigot EM
1828 Pigot EM
1830 Pigot EM

Taylor, Thomas & James
High Street, Hanley
1818 Pigot EM

Taylor, W. & J.
Waterloo Road, Burslem
1856 Kelly CEM

Taylor, William
(i) Hogg's Lane, Lane End
1828 Pigot CM
1830 Pigot CM
(ii) Bourne's Bank, Burslem
1851 White CEM-B, (only earthenware)
1852 Slater EM
1854 Kelly CEM
(iii) Brook Street, Hanley
1860 Kelly EM
1861 Harrison NC-H-Sh (earthenware manufacturer)
1862 Slater EM
1863 Kelly EM (granite)
1864 Jones EM
1865 Keates P-H (earthenware)
1867 Keates P-H (earthenware)
1868 Kelly EM
1869 Keates P-H (earthenware)
1870 Harrod NC-H (earthenware manufacturer)
1872 Kelly EM

1873 Keates P-H (granite)
Taylor's house is listed as Waterloo Road in 1851 White.

Taylor, William, & Co.
(i) Cobridge
1834 White EM-H-Sh
(ii) Church Street, Longton
1865 Keates P-L (stilt and spur)
1867 Keates P-L (stilt and spur)
1868 Kelly SC (Spur Makers) (stilton (sic))
1869 Keates P-L (patent stilt and spur)
1870 Harrod NC-L (patent spurs and stilt manufacturers)
1872 Kelly SC (Spur Makers)
1873 Keates P-L (patent stilt and spur)
1875 Keates P-L (patent stilt and spur)
1876 Kelly SC (Spur and Stilt Makers for Pottery Manufacturers)
1879 Keates P-L (patent stilt and spur)
1880 Kelly SC (Spur & Stilt Makers for Pottery Manufacturers)
1882 Keates P-L (patent stilt and spur)
1884 Kelly SC (Spur & Stilt Makers for Pottery Manufacturers)
1888 Kelly SC (Spur & Stilt Makers for Pottery Manufacturers)
1892 Kelly SC (Stilt & Spur Manufacturers)

Taylor & Forester
Melbourne Works, Church Street, Longton
1887 Porter EM-L
1888 Kelly CM

Taylor, Hudson & Middleton
Chancery Lane, Longton
1870 Harrod NC-L (china manufacturers)
1872 Kelly CM
1873 Keates P-L (china)
1875 Keates P-L (china)
1876 Kelly CM

Taylor & Kent
Florence Works, High Street, Longton
1876 Kelly CM (for home & export)
1879 Keates P-L (china)
1880 Kelly CM (for home & export)
1882 Keates P-L (china)
1884 Kelly CM
1887 Porter EM-L
1888 Kelly CM
1889 Keates A; P-L (china)
1892 Keates P-L (china)
1892 Kelly CM
1896 Kelly CM
1900 Kelly CM
The advertisement in 1889 Keates describes the firm as simply 'china manufacturers' but adds 'manufacturers for the following markets:– England, Ireland, Scotland, Wales, Australia, New Zealand, The Cape, India, Canada, America'.

Taylor & Kent. Advertisement from 1889 Keates.

Taylor & Plant
Sneyd Green, near Burslem
1862 Slater EM

Taylor & Pope
Shelton
1784 Bailey NC-Sh (potters)

Taylor, Tunnicliff & Co.
(i) Havelock Works, Broad Street, Hanley
1868 Kelly CM; SC (Artists' Palette Manufacturers – China); SC (Beer Machine Handle Makers – China); SC (China & Porcelain Door Furniture Manufacturers)
1869 Keates P-H (door furniture)
1870 Harrod NC-H (manufacturers of china and porcelain, mortice, lock, and bell-lever furniture, finger-plates, shutter, drawer, and hall-door knobs, castor-bowls, door and kettle grips, beer-machine and tea-bell handles, and every description of porcelain articles for brassfounders, plumbers, &c., barometers, scales, slides, &c.)
1872 Kelly SC (Beer Machine Handle Makers – China); SC (China & Porcelain Door Furniture Manufacturers); SC (Inkstand Manufacturers – Fancy China); SC (Lock Furniture Makers – China)
1873 Keates P-H (door furniture)
1875 Keates P-H (door furniture)
(ii) Eastwood, Hanley
1876 Kelly SC (Inkstand Manufacturers); SC (Lock Furniture Makers China)
1879 Keates A; P-H (door furniture)
1880 Kelly CM (manufacturers of china mortice lock furniture, finger plates, fancy inkstands, stationers' goods & every description of china for brass founders, plumbers, silversmiths, lamp & chandelier manufacturers, scale plates & weights, artists' palettes, color tiles &c. plateaux in every color for painting); EM; SC (Door Furniture Makers – China); SC (Inkstand Manufacturers); SC (Lock Furniture Makers – China)
1882 Keates P-H (door furniture)
1884 Kelly CM (manufacturers of china mortice lock furniture, finger plates, fancy inkstands, stationers' goods & every description of china for brass founders, plumbers, silversmiths, lamp & chandelier manufacturers, scale plates & weights, artists' palettes, color tiles &c. plateaux in every color for painting); EM; SC (Door Furniture Makers – China); SC (Lock Furniture Makers – China)
1887 Porter EM-H
1888 Kelly CM (manufacturers of china mortice lock furniture, finger plates, fancy inkstands, stationers' goods & every description of china for brass founders, plumbers, silversmiths, lamp & chandelier manufacturers, scale plates & weights, artists' palettes, color tiles &c. plateaux in every color for painting)
1889 Keates A; P-H (door furniture, and china fitting, etc.)
1892 Keates A; P-H (door furniture and china fitting, etc.)
1892 Kelly CM (china, glass

& earthenware manufrs.); SC (Door Furniture Manufacturers – China) (China lock furniture manfrs.); SC (Electrical China Manufacturers) (switch cases, ceiling roses, cut outs, fuse blocks &c. &c.); SC (Lock Furniture Manufacturers), china lock furniture manufactrs.)
1896 Kelly CM (china, glass & earthenware manufacturers); SC (Door Furniture Manufacturers – China); SC (Electrical China Manufacturers) (switch cases, ceiling roses, cut outs, fuse blocks &c. &c.); SC (Lock Furniture Manufacturers)
1900 Kelly SC (Door Furniture Manufacturers – China)
The second partner's name is listed as Tunnicliffe in 1869 Keates, 1873 Keates, 1887 Porter, 1889 Keates, 1892 Keates, and one of the entries in 1892 Kelly. Similar advertisements appear in four of the Keates directories. The descriptions read: 'manufacturers of door furniture, china fittings for brassfounders, plumbers, &c., and every description of china used in connection with metal work' (1879); 'manufacturers of door furniture, &c., china fittings for brassfounders & plumbers; lamp & chandelier manufacturers; artists' palettes colour tiles, &c.; stationers' sundries; breakfast and dinner cruets, biscuits, marmalades, &c., for silversmiths' (1882); 'manufacturers of specialities in china of every description for electro-platers, lamp & chandelier makers, brassfounders, plumbers, japanners, door furniture, &c. Ornamental vases, scale plates and weights, name and number plates in raised figures. Artists' and stationers' sundries, guage dials, thermometer scales, &c.' (1889); and 'manufacturers of specialities in china of every description for electro-platers, lamp & chandelier makers, brassfounders, plumbers, japanners, door furniture, and all kinds of porcelain parts for electric lighting, scale plates and weights, name and number plates in raised figures. Artists' and stationers' sundries, &c.' (1892).

TAYLOR, TUNNICLIFF & CO.,
EASTWOOD, HANLEY,
MANUFACTURERS OF
DOOR FURNITURE,
China Fittings for Brassfounders, Plumbers, &c.,
And every description of China used in connection with Metal Work.

Taylor, Tunnicliff & Co. Advertisement from 1879 Keates.

TAYLOR, TUNNICLIFF & Co.,
EASTWOOD, HANLEY,
MANUFACTURERS OF
DOOR FURNITURE, &c.;
China Fittings for Brassfounders & Plumbers;
LAMP & CHANDELIER MANUFACTURERS;
ARTISTS' PALETTES COLOUR TILES, &c.;
STATIONERS' SUNDRIES;
Breakfast and Dinner Cruets, Biscuits, Marmalades, &c., for Silversmiths.

Taylor, Tunnicliff & Co. Advertisement from 1882 Keates.

TAYLOR, TUNNICLIFF & Co.,
EASTWOOD, HANLEY,
MANUFACTURERS OF
SPECIALITIES IN CHINA
OF EVERY DESCRIPTION
FOR
Electro-Platers, Lamp & Chandelier Makers, Brassfounders, Plumbers, Japanners, Door Furniture, &c.
ORNAMENTAL VASES,
SCALE PLATES AND WEIGHTS,
Name and Number Plates in Raised Figures.
ARTISTS' AND STATIONERS' SUNDRIES,
GUAGE DIALS, THERMOMETER SCALES, &c.

Taylor, Tunnicliff & Co. Advertisement from 1889 Keates.

TAYLOR, TUNNICLIFFE & Co.,
EASTWOOD, HANLEY,
MANUFACTURERS OF

Specialities in China,
OF EVERY DESCRIPTION
FOR
ELECTRO-PLATERS, LAMP & CHANDELIER MAKERS, BRASS-FOUNDERS, PLUMBERS, JAPANNERS, DOOR FURNITURE,
AND ALL KINDS OF PORCELAIN PARTS FOR
ELECTRIC LIGHTING,
SCALE PLATES AND WEIGHTS,
Name and Number Plates in Raised Figures.
Artists' and Stationers' Sundries, &c.

Taylor, Tunnicliff & Co. Advertisement from 1892 Keates. Note the alternative spelling of the Tunnicliff name.

Taylor, Tunnicliff & Co. Printed mark from a pair of covered spirit jars. The registration number dates from 1893.

Taylor, Tunnicliff & Co. Ltd.
Eastwood, Hanley
1900 Kelly CM (china, lock & door furniture, electrical china, artists' colormen's sundries &c.); SC (Electrical China Manufacturers) (switch cases, ceiling roses, cut outs, fuse blocks &c. &c.)

Taylor, Waine & Bates
(i) High Street, Longton
1879 Keates P-L (china)
1880 Kelly CM
1882 Keates P-L (china)
(ii) Sutherland Road, Longton
1884 Kelly CM
The second partner's name is listed as Wain in 1882 Keates.

Tellwright, William
Tunstall
1805 Holden NC (earthenware manufacturer)

Telwright & Co.
Burslem
1802 Allbut EM (map location 36)

Thomas & Co.
Union Street, Hanley
1889 Keates P-H
1892 Keates P-H

Thomas, Uriah
Marlborough Works, Union Street, Burslem
1882 Keates P-B

Thomas, Uriah, & Co.
Union Street, Hanley
1892 Kelly EM
1896 Kelly EM
1900 Kelly EM

Thomas, Brooks, Chesters & Co.
Wellington Works, Newport Street, Burslem
1879 Keates P-B (Rockingham ware)

Thomas, Rathbone, Oakley & Co.
Wellington Works, Newport Street, Burslem
1875 Keates P-B (Rockingham ware)
1876 Kelly RM

Till & Sons
Sytch Pottery, Liverpool Road, Burslem
1864 Jones EM
1865 Keates P-B (earthen.)
1867 Keates P-B (earthen.)
1869 Keates P-B (earthen.)
1870 Harrod NC-B (ironstone, china, and earthenware manufacturers, for home and foreign markets)
1873 Keates P-B (earthen.)
1875 Keates P-B (earthen.)
1879 Keates P-B (earthen.)
1882 Keates P-B (earthenware)
1887 Porter EM-B
1889 Keates P-B (earthenware)
1892 Keates P-B (earthenware)

Till, Edward
Smithfield
1798 Universal NC-Sf (toy-maker)

Till, Emma
Salem Street, Etruria
1865 Keates P-H (parian figure)

Till, Thomas
Sytch, Burslem
1851 White CEM-B (only earthenware)
Till's house is listed as Liverpool Road in 1851 White.
See also: Barker & Till

Till, Thomas, & Son
Sytch Pottery, Liverpool Road, Burslem
1852 Slater EM
1854 Kelly CEM
1856 Kelly CEM
1860 Kelly EM
1861 Harrison NC-B (earthenware manufacturers)

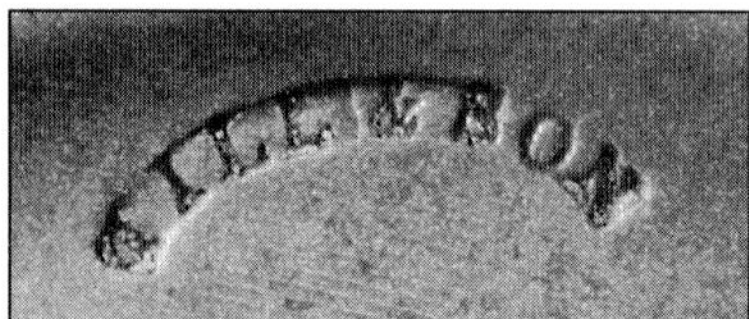

Thomas Till & Son. Impressed and moulded marks from a relief-moulded stoneware jug. The registration diamond dates from 1852.

Thomas Till & Son. Printed mark from a black-printed and relief-moulded stoneware jug. The registration diamond dates from 1852.

Till, Thomas, & Sons
Sytch Pottery, Liverpool Road, Burslem
1862 Slater EM
1863 Kelly CM-General; EM
1876 Kelly EM
1880 Kelly EM
1884 Kelly EM
1888 Kelly EM
1892 Kelly EM
1896 Kelly EM
1900 Kelly EM

Till, Bullock & Smith
Waterloo Works, Nelson's Place, Hanley
1862 Slater EM (and stone ware)

Till, Filcher & Co.
Waterloo Pottery, Nelson Place, Hanley
1864 Jones EM (manufacturers of jasper, mosaic, water coolers, jet glaze garden pots, and general stone ware); EM-Miscellaneous (manufacturers of jasper, mosaic, water coolers, jet glaze, garden pots, and general stone ware); PM

Timmis, Charles, & Co.
Sheaf Works, Normacot Road, Longton
1889 Keates A; P-L (tile)
The advertisement in 1889 Keates describes the firm as 'manufacturers of printed, hand-painted, majolica embossed tiles, etc., suitable for grates, hearths, walls, furniture, etc., white glazed tiles'.

CHARLES TIMMIS & Co.,
MANUFACTURERS OF
Printed, Hand-Painted, Majolica
Embossed Tiles, etc.,
SUITABLE FOR GRATES, HEARTHS, WALLS, FURNITURE, ETC.,
WHITE GLAZED TILES,
SHEAF WORKS, LONGTON.

Charles Timmis & Co. Advertisement from 1889 Keates.

Timmis, Henry
Market Place, Burslem
1850 Kelly NC-B (manufactr. of parian brooches & shirt pins)
1852 Slater PM
1854 Kelly PM (ornamental figure makers)
1856 Kelly PM

Timmis & Watkins
Sheaf Works, Normacott Road, Longton
1892 Kelly SC (Encaustic Tile Manufacturers)

Tinsley, George, & Co.
Queen Street Pottery, Burslem
1880 Kelly EM (manufacturers of earthenware, ivory, jet & red body ware; a large assortment of fancy vases &c.)

Tinsley & Bourne
(i) Bourne's Bank, Burslem
1868 Kelly EM
1869 Keates P-B (earthen.)
(ii) Queen Street, Burslem
1876 Kelly EM

Tinsley, Bourne & Co.
(i) Bourne's Bank, Burslem
1870 Harrod NC-B
(earthenware manufacturers)
1872 Kelly EM
1873 Keates P-B (earthenware)
1875 Keates P-B (earthenware)
(ii) Queen Street, Burslem
1879 Keates P-B (earthenware)
1882 Keates P-B (earthenware)

Tipper & Co.
(i) Flint Street, Longton
1850 Kelly CEM; NC-L
(china manufacturers)
1850 Slater CM
1852 Slater CM
(ii) Stafford Street, Longton
1854 Kelly CEM
1860 Kelly CM-General; EM

Tipper, Mary (Mrs.), & Co.
Stafford Street, Longton
1851 White CEM-L
1856 Kelly CEM
1861 Harrison NC-L
(manufacturers of china and earthenware)

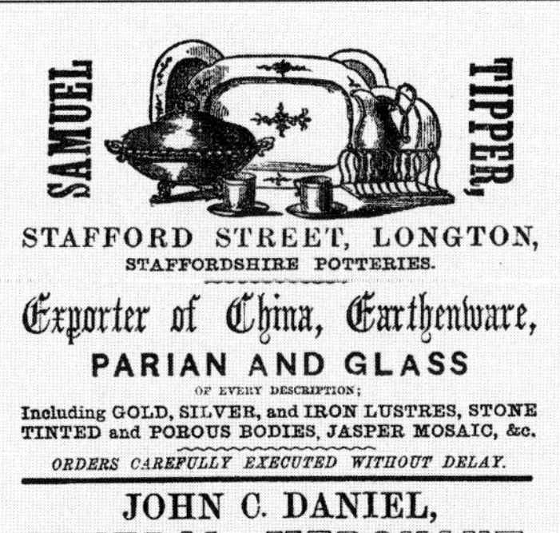

Samuel Tipper. Advertisement from 1864 Jones.

Tipper, Samuel
Stafford Street, Longton
1864 Jones A; CEM
The advertisement in 1864 Jones describes Tipper as an 'exporter of china, earthenware, parian and glass of every description; including gold, silver, and iron lustres, stone tinted and porous bodies, jasper mosaic, &c.' promising 'orders carefully executed without delay'.

Toft, Charles
Swan Works, High Street, Stoke
1887 Porter CEM-S
1888 Kelly EM
1889 Keates P-S

Toft, William
Church Street, Longton
1860 Kelly EM
1861 Harrison NC-L
(earthenware manufacturer)

Toft & Cope
High Street, Stoke
1884 Kelly EM

Toft & May
Old Hall Street, Hanley
1828 Pigot EM
1830 Pigot EM

Toft & May. Impressed mark from a blue-printed earthenware plate.

Tomkinson & Co.
Clarence Street, Shelton
1856 Kelly CEM

Tomkinson & Son
Hamill Road, Burslem
1873 Keates P-B (earthenware)

Tomkinson, Charles
Britannia Works, High Street, Longton
1887 Porter EM-L

Tomkinson, Samuel
Queen Street and Church Street, Burslem
1818 Parson EM-B-Lp-C
1818 Pigot EM
1822 Allbut CEM
(earthenware manufact.)
1822 Pigot EM

Tomkinson, T., & Co.
Clarence Street, Hanley
1869 Keates P-H (ironstone and earthenware)

Tomkinson & Phillips
Clarence Street, Hanley
1868 Kelly EM

Tompkinson, Edward John
Flaxman Pottery, Sutherland Road, Longton
1896 Kelly EM
1900 Kelly EM

Tompkinson, G.
62 High Street, Longton
1882 Keates P-L (china)

Tompkinson & Billington
51 High Street, Longton
1868 Kelly CM

Tompkinson, Billington & Co.
High Street, Longton
1870 Harrod NC-L (china manufacturers)

Tompkinson, Billington & Son
51 High Street, Longton
1869 Keates P-L (china)

Townsend, George
(i) Old Established Pottery, 17 High Street, Longton
1850 Kelly NC-L (lustre, black & earthenware manufacturer)
1850 Slater CM; EM (& of Egyptian black); TOCM
1851 White CEM-L
1852 Slater CM; EM (& of Egyptian black); TOCM
1854 Kelly CEM; PM (ornamental figure makers); TM
1856 Kelly CEM; TM (china)
1860 Kelly EM
1861 Harrison NC-L
(earthenware manufacturer)
1862 Slater EM; TOCM
1863 Kelly EM
1864 Jones CEM
(ii) Chadwick Street, Longton
1862 Slater EM
(iii) Stafford Street, Longton

1867 Keates P-L (china & earthenware)
Townsend succeeded Sampson Beardmore (1850 Slater, 1852 Slater).
See also: Colclough & Townsend

Tranter & Machin
Stafford Street, Longton
1892 Kelly CM
1896 Kelly CM

Troutbeck, E.T.
Sandyford, Tunstall
1846 Williams NC-T (earthenware manufacturer)

Trubshaw, Hand & Co.
Albert Works, High Street, Longton
1879 Keates P-L (china)
1880 Kelly CM
1882 Keates P-L (china)
1884 Kelly CM
(ii) Market Street, Longton
1882 Keates P-L (china)
A London agent is listed as Mr. Grimwade of Union Bank Buildings, Holborn, in 1880 Kelly.

Tundley, Rhodes & Pinder
Swan Bank Works, Burslem
1875 Keates P-B (earthen.)
1879 Keates P-B (earthen.)

Tundley, Rhodes & Procter
Swan Bank Works, Burslem
1876 Kelly EM
1880 Kelly EM
1882 Keates P-B (earthen.)
The third partner's name is listed as Proctor in 1882 Keates.

Tunicliff, Michael
See: Tunnicliff, Michael

Tunnicliff, Michael
(i) Tunstall
1828 Pigot EM (toy only)
1830 Pigot EM (toy only)
(ii) High Street, Tunstall
1834 White EM-T (china and earthenware figures)
1835 Pigot TOCM
(iii) Tunstall and Longton
1841 Pigot TOCM
(iv) Bleak Hill, Burslem
1850 Slater TOCM
The surname is listed as Tunnicliffe in 1828 Pigot and 1830 Pigot, and as Tuniclifff in 1835 Pigot and 1841 Pigot.

Tunnicliffe, James
25 Normacot Road, Longton
1887 Porter EM-L

Tunnicliffe, Michael
See: Tunnicliff, Michael

Tunstall, Thomas
(i) Tunstall
1796 Chester NC-T-Lp (manufacturer of earthenware)
(ii) Golden Hill
1798 Universal NC-G (earthenware manufacturer)
1802 Allbut EM (map location 3)
1805 Holden NC (banded ware manufacturer)
1809 Holden NC (red-ware-manufactory)

Turner & Co.
(i) King Street, Fenton
1872 Kelly EM
(ii) Mayer Street, Hanley
1875 Keates P-H (earthenware)

Turner, E., & Co.
Old Foley Pottery, Fenton
1873 Keates P-F (china and earthenware)
1873 Keates A; P-L (china & earthenware)
The advertisement in 1873 Keates describes the firm as 'manufacturers of enamelled earthenware, &c.'

E. TURNER & Co.,
MANUFACTURERS OF
ENAMELLED EARTHENWARE, &c.,
OLD FOLEY POTTERY,
LONGTON,
STAFFORDSHIRE POTTERIES.

E. Turner & Co. Advertisement from 1873 Keates.

Turner, George W., & Sons
(i) Victoria Works, High Street, Tunstall
1873 Keates P-T (earthenware)
1875 Keates P-T (earthenware)
1876 Kelly EM
1879 Keates P-T (earthenware)
1880 Kelly EM
1882 Keates P-T (earthenware)
1884 Kelly EM
(ii) Soho Mills, Tunstall
1876 Kelly EM
(iii) Alexander (or Alexandra) Works, Scotia Road, Tunstall
1887 Porter EM-T
1888 Kelly EM
1889 Keates P-T (earthenware)
1892 Keates P-T (earthenware)
1892 Kelly EM

Turner, John
(i) Lane End
1781 Bailey NC (potter)
1783 Bailey NC (potter)
(ii) Fenton
1784 Bailey NC-F (potter)

John Turner. Impressed mark from a sprigged stoneware bowl.

John Turner. Impressed mark from a sprigged stoneware jug.

Turner, John & William
Lane End
1798 Universal NC-LE (manufacturers of Staffordshire-ware)

John & William Turner. Hand-painted mark from an enamelled stone china dish.

John & William Turner. Printed mark from a stone china dinner plate.

Turner, William
(i) Folly, Lane End
1809 Holden NC (manufacturer of earthenware)
1811 Holden NC (manufacturer of earthenware)
1816 Underhill P
(ii) High Street, Lane End
1828 Pigot EM
1830 Pigot EM (Egyptian black)
(iii) Chapel Lane, Burslem
1834 White EM-B (sagars (sic) and quarry)

Turner, William, & Co.
Sneyd Pottery, Albert Street, Burslem
1869 Keates P-B (Rockingham & earthen.)
1870 Harrod NC-B (Rockingham and earthenware manufacturers)

Turner, William & John
Lane End
1796 Chester NC-LE-LD-LL (manufacturers of earthenware)
1802 Allbut EM (map locations 136 and 138)

Turner & Abbott
Lane End
1784 Bailey NC-LE (potters to the Prince of Wales)

Turner, Bromley & Hassall
Albert Works, Bryanstone Place, Stoke
1863 Kelly CM-General; EM; PM; TCM

Turner, Goddard & Co.
Royal Albert Pottery, Parsonage Street, Tunstall
1868 Kelly EM
1869 Keates P-T
1870 Harrod NC-T (earthenware manufacturers)
1872 Kelly EM
1873 Keates P-T

Turner & Hassall
Albert Works, Liverpool Road, Stoke
1864 Jones CEM; PM

Turner, Hassall & Peake
Copeland Street and Liverpool Road, Stoke
1865 Keates P-S (parian, earthenware and china)
1867 Keates P-S (parian, earthenware, and china)
1868 Kelly CM; EM; PM
1869 Keates P-S (parian, earthenware, and china)
The second partner's name is listed as Hassell in 1868 Kelly.

Turner, Hassall, Peake & Poole
Albert and Copeland Street Works, Stoke
1870 Harrod NC-S (manufacturers of parian, china, majolica, terra-cotta, and stone)

Turner, Hassall & Poole
Copeland Street, & Albert Works, Liverpool Road, Stoke
1872 Kelly CM; EM; MM; PM; TCM
The second partner's name is listed as Hassell.

Turner, Hassell & Peake
See: Turner, Hassall & Peake

Turner, Hassell & Poole
See: Turner, Hassall & Poole

Turner & Poole
(i) Liverpool Road, Stoke
1869 Keates P-S (terra cotta & parian)
1873 Keates P-S (terra cotta and parian)
(ii) Copeland Street and Liverpool Road, Stoke
1873 Keates P-S (parian, earthenware, and china)

Turner & Tomkinson
(i) Newfield, Tunstall
1860 Kelly EM
1861 Harrison NC-T (earthenware manufacturers)
(ii) Victoria Works, High Street, Tunstall
1862 Slater EM
1863 Kelly EM
1864 Jones EM
1865 Keates P-T (earthenware)
1867 Keates P-T (earthenware)
1868 Kelly EM
1869 Keates P-T (earthenware)
1870 Harrod NC-T (earthenware and ironstone china manufacturers)
1872 Kelly EM
A London office at Eley Place, Holborn, is listed in 1870 Harrod.

Turner & Wood
Copeland Street Works, Stoke
1880 Kelly PM
1882 Keates P-S (china and majolica)
1884 Kelly CM; EM; MM; PM; TCM

Turners, Glover & Simpson
Lane End
1805 Holden NC (china and earthenware manufacturers)

Turton, James
97 Hope Street, Shelton, Hanley
1852 Slater PM; TOCM

Turton & Gregg
(i) Miles Bank, Hanley
1851 White NC-H-Sh (parian figure mfrs.)
(ii) George Street, Shelton
1854 Kelly PM

Twambler, John
Shelton
1798 Universal NC-Sh (manufacturer of Staffordshire-ware)

Twemlow, G.
Shelton
1784 Bailey NC-Sh (potter)

Twemlow, George & Thomas
Shelton
1781 Bailey NC (potters)
1783 Bailey NC (potters)

Twemlow, John
Shelton
1796 Chester NC-H-Sh (manufacturer of earthenware)

Twigg & Mills
King Street, Hanley
1879 Keates P-H (earthenware)

Twyford, Christopher
New Street, Hanley
1860 Kelly EM,
1861 Harrison NC-H-Sh (parian manufacturer)
1862 Slater EM; PM; SC (Water-Closet Basin Manufacturers)
1864 Jones PM
1865 Keates P-H (sanitary ware)
1867 Keates P-H (sanitary ware)

1868 Kelly SC (Sanitary Ware Manufacturers)
1869 Keates P-H (sanitary ware)
1870 Harrod NC-H (sanitary ware manufacturer)

Twyford, Thomas
(i) Bath Street, Hanley
1860 Kelly EM
1861 Harrison NC-H-Sh (manufacturer of water closets, pan bason (sic) and blue maker)
1862 Slater A; SC (Water-Closet Basin Manufacturers)
1863 Kelly EM
1864 Jones NC
1865 Keates A; P-H (earthenware and sanitary ware)
1867 Keates A; P-H (earthenware and sanitary ware)
1868 Kelly SC (Sanitary Ware Manufacturers)
1869 Keates P-H (earthenware and sanitary ware)
1870 Harrod NC-H (manufacturer of water-closet basins, plug basins, urinals, &c.)
1872 Kelly SC (Sanitary Ware Manufacturers)
1873 Keates P-H (earthenware and sanitary ware)
1875 Keates P-H (earthenware and sanitary ware)
1876 Kelly SC (Sanitary Ware Manufacturers)
1879 Keates P-H (earthenware and sanitary ware)
1880 Kelly SC (Sanitary Ware Manufacturers)
1882 Keates P-H (plumbers and sanitary ware)
1884 Kelly A; SC (Beer Engine Handle Makers); SC (Sanitary Ware Manufacturers); SC (Water Closet Makers)
1887 Porter EM-H
(ii) Abbey, Bucknall
1879 Keates P-H (earthenware and sanitary ware)
1884 Kelly A; SC (Sanitary Ware Manufacturers)
1887 Porter EM-H
1888 Kelly A; SC (Sanitary Ware Manufacturers)
(iii) Cliffe Vale, Hanley
1888 Kelly A; SC (Beer Machine Handle Maker); SC (Sanitary Ware Manufacturers)
1892 Kelly EM
1896 Kelly EM

The firm is noted as being in the hands of trustees in 1873 Keates, 1875 Keates, 1879 Keates, and 1880 Kelly. A London depot at the Maiden Lane station of the London and North-Western Railway is listed in 1870 Harrod. The advertisement in 1862 Slater describes Twyford as a 'manufacturer of water-closet basins, plug basins, &c.' The advertisement in 1865 Keates adds 'urinals, and lavatories', and in 1867 Keates there is a further addition of 'spirit barrels, & beer pump handles, &c.'
There are long advertisements in 1884 Kelly and 1888 Kelly. In 1884 the heading is 'Sanitary Earthenware' and the text reads 'Manufacturer of every description of lavatory basins, plug basins, tip-up basins, urinals, closet basins, &c., &c., white, printed, gilt and decorated. Sole maker of the "National," "Alliance" and "Crown" closet basins. Simple, cleanly, effective. Tested and approved of, and now generally fitted up in H.M. Dockyards and Barracks, and in the military and naval hospitals; and recommended by the medical profession, leading architects, sanitarians, and practical plumbers, for general use in dwelling-houses,

SANITARY EARTHENWARE.

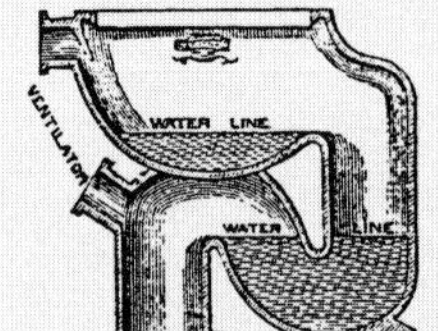

THOMAS TWYFORD,
HANLEY, STAFFORDSHIRE,
Manufacturer of every description of
LAVATORY BASINS, PLUG BASINS, TIP-UP BASINS, URINALS, CLOSET BASINS, &c., &c., White, Printed, Gilt and Decorated.
SOLE MAKER OF THE
"NATIONAL," "ALLIANCE" & "CROWN" CLOSET BASINS.
SIMPLE, CLEANLY, EFFECTIVE;
Tested and approved of, and now generally fitted up in H.M. Dockyards and Barracks, and in the Military and Naval Hospitals; and recommended by the Medical Profession, leading Architects, Sanitarians, and Practical Plumbers, for general use in Dwelling-houses, Hotels, Factories, Railway Stations, Hospitals, &c., &c., &c.
Special attention is given to the Modelling & Production of Architects' & Sanitary Engineers' own designs.

Thomas Twyford. Advertisement from 1884 Kelly.

THE PERFECTION OF CLEANLINESS, UTILITY, AND SIMPLICITY.
TWYFORD'S 'UNITAS,'

COMBINING
W.C. BASIN & TRAP, URINAL AND SLOP SINK.
No Wood Fittings are required except a hinged seat, which, being raised, the Basin can be used as a Urinal or a Slop Sink, the "wetting" so objectionable in Closets having permanent seats being avoided. Free access can thus be had to all parts of the Basin and Trap, so that everything about the Closet can be easily kept clean.
Made in Fine Earthenware, Plain or Decorated, and in Strong Fire Clay.
The flushing arrangements are so perfect that with a flush of two gallons of water, it is guaranteed that all the soil and paper will be completely removed from the Basin and through the Trap, the whole of the inside being thoroughly washed, and with the aid of the Patent "After Flush" Chamber, the full quantity of water required to receive the soil is left in the bottom of the Basin.
For Prices and Catalogues apply to
TWYFORD, HANLEY, STAFFORDSHIRE.

Thomas Twyford. Advertisement from 1888 Kelly.

hotels, factories, railway stations, hospitals, &c., &c., &c. Special attention is given to the modelling & production of architects' & sanitary engineers' own designs.'

In 1888 the advertisement features the firm's "Unitas" model, shown by an engraving and with the following lengthy text – 'The perfection of cleanliness, utility, and simplicity. Twyford's "Unitas," combining W.C. basin & trap, urinal and slop sink. No wood fittings are required except a hinged seat, which, being raised, the basin can be used as a urinal or a slop sink, the "wetting" so objectionable in closets having permanent seats being avoided. Free access can thus be had to all parts of the basin and trap, so that everything about the closet can be easily kept clean. Made in fine earthenware, plain or decorated, and in strong fire clay. The flushing arrangements are so perfect that with a flush of two gallons of water, it is guaranteed that all the soil and paper will be completely removed from the basin and through the trap, the whole of the inside being thoroughly washed, and with the patent "after flush" chamber, the full quantity of water required to receive the soil is left in the bottom of the basin. For prices and catalogues apply to Twyford, Hanley, Staffordshire.'

THOMAS TWYFORD,
MANUFACTURER OF
WATER-CLOSET BASINS,
PLUG BASINS, &c.,
BATH STREET, HANLEY,
STAFFORDSHIRE.

Thomas Twyford. Advertisement from 1862 Slater.

BATH-ST., HANLEY,
STAFFORDSHIRE.
THOMAS TWYFORD,
MANUFACTURER OF
WATER CLOSET BASINS
PLUG BASINS,
URINALS, AND LAVATORIES.
All Letters to THOMAS TWYFORD.

Thomas Twyford. Advertisement from 1865 Keates.

THOMAS TWYFORD,
MANUFACTURER OF
WATER CLOSET BASINS
PLUG BASINS,
URINALS, AND LAVATORIES,
Spirit Barrels, & Beer Pump Handles, &c.
All Letters to Mr. THOMAS TWYFORD, Bath street, Hanley.

Thomas Twyford. Advertisement from 1867 Keates.

Twyford, Thomas W.
Cliffe Vale, Hanley
1888 Kelly A; SC (Water Closet Makers)

Twyford, Thomas & Christopher
New Street, Hanley
1856 Kelly CEM

Twyford, W.
Cliffe Vale Pottery, Newcastle Road, Hanley
1889 Keates P-H (sanitary ware)
1892 Keates P-H (sanitary ware)

Twyfords Ltd.
Cliffe Vale Potteries, Shelton
1900 Kelly EM; SC (Sanitary Ware Manufacturers)

U

Unett, John
High Street, Lane End
1818 Parson EM-LE

Unett & Brammer
Lane End
1805 Holden NC (earthenware manufacturers)

Unwin, Joseph
Cornhill Works, Cornhill Passage or Market Lane, Longton
1879 Keates P-L (earthenware and lustre)
1880 Kelly EM
1882 Keates P-L (earthenware and lustre)
1884 Kelly EM
1887 Porter EM-L
1888 Kelly EM
1889 Keates P-L (earthenware and lustre)

Unwin, Joseph, & Co.
Cornhill Passage, Longton
1892 Kelly EM
1896 Kelly EM
1900 Kelly EM

Unwin & Holmes
Upper Hanley Works, High Street, Hanley
1868 Kelly EM
1869 Keates P-H (earthenware)
1870 Harrod NC-H (parian and earthenware manufacturers)
1872 Kelly EM

Unwin, Holmes & Worthington
High Street, Hanley
1865 Keates A; P-H (earthenware)
1867 Keates P-H (earthenware)
The advertisement in 1865 Keates describes the firm as 'manufacturers of earthenware, stone & coloured bodies'.

UNWIN, HOLMES, & WORTHINGTON,
Manufacturers of Earthenware,
STONE & COLOURED BODIES,
HIGH STREET, HANLEY.

Unwin, Holmes & Worthington. Advertisement from 1865 Keates.

Unwin, Mountford & Taylor
Upper Hanley Works, High Street, Hanley
1863 Kelly EM
1864 Jones EM; PM

Upper Hanley Pottery Co. (The)
High Street, Hanley
1896 Kelly EM
1900 Kelly EM

V

Vawdrey, Daniel
Golden Hill
1818 Parson EM-G-T-R
1822 Allbut CEM (red ware manufact.)

Venables, Henry
(i) Etruria Road, Hanley
1862 Slater EM; TOCM (& antique figures)

1863 Kelly SC (Jasper Makers)
1864 Jones CEM (Etruscan, jasper)
(ii) Mill Street, Hanley
1865 Keates P-H (terra cotta and parian)
1867 Keates P-H (porous and Etruscan)

Venables, J., & Co.
Nile Works, Burslem
1854 Kelly CEM

Venables, John
See: Mellor, Venables & Co.

Venables, John, & Co.
(i) Trent Pottery, Burslem
1860 Kelly EM
(ii) Waterloo Works, Waterloo Road, Burslem
1860 Kelly EM
1861 Harrison NC-B (china and earthenware manufacturers and patentees)
A London address at 19 Bishopsgate Street Within is listed in 1860 Kelly.

Venables & Baines
Nile Street, Burslem
1851 White NC-B (china, &c., manufacturers)

Venables, Mann & Co.
Nile Street, Burslem
1852 Slater CM; EM
1856 Kelly CEM

Venables & Morris
New Hall Street, Shelton
1830 Pigot EM (toy only)

Vernon, C.A., & Co.
Cobridge
1896 Kelly EM

Vernon, George, & Co.
Chapel Square, Burslem
1822 Pigot EM

Vernon, James
(i) Scotia Potteries, Scotia Road, Burslem
1860 Kelly EM
1861 Harrison NC-B (earthenware manufacturer)
1862 Slater EM
(ii) Waterloo Works, Waterloo Road, Burslem
1863 Kelly EM
1865 Keates P-B (earthen.)
1867 Keates P-B (earthen.)
1868 Kelly EM
1869 Keates P-B (earthen.)
1870 Harrod NC-B (earthenware manufacturer and potter's valuer)
1872 Kelly EM
1873 Keates P-B (earthen.)
(iii) Wellington Street, Burslem
1864 Jones EM
(iv) Hill Pottery, Burslem
1892 Keates P-B (earthenware)

Vernon, James, & Co.
(i) Church Yard and High Street, Burslem
1841 Pigot EM
(ii) Waterloo Works, Waterloo Road, Burslem
1846 Williams NC-B (earthenware manufacturers)
1850 Kelly CEM; NC-B (earthenware manufactrs.)
1851 White CEM-B (only earthenware)
1850 Slater EM
1852 Slater EM
1854 Kelly CEM
The partners are listed individually as James Vernon and James Taylor, both of Waterloo Road, in 1846 Williams. Vernon's house is listed as Bleak Hill in 1851 White.

Vernon, James, & Son
Waterloo Pottery, Waterloo Road, Burslem
1875 Keates P-B (earthenware)
1876 Kelly EM
1879 Keates P-B (earthenware)

Vernon, James & George
(i) Waterloo Pottery, Waterloo Road, Burslem
1880 Kelly EM
1882 Keates P-B (earthenware)
1884 Kelly EM
1887 Porter EM-B
1888 Kelly EM
1889 Keates P-B (earthenware)
(ii) African Works, High Street, Burslem
1892 Kelly EM

Vernon's Patent China & Glass Co. Ltd.
Wharf Street, Stoke
1884 Kelly CM

Victoria Pottery Co. (The)
(i) Lonsdale Street, Stoke
1882 Keates P-S (earthenware)
1889 Keates P-S (earthenware)
(ii) Broad Street, Hanley
1896 Kelly EM
1900 Kelly EM

Victoria Sanitary Co.
Victoria Works, Stoke
1884 Kelly SC (Sanitary Ware Manufacturers)
The proprietors are listed as Gratton & Co.

Vigers, Thomas
See: Jones & Vigers

Vodrey, Daniel
Golden Hill
1798 Universal NC-G (coarse-ware potter)

Vodril, Joseph
Golden Hill
1818 Pigot EM (black ware)
1822 Pigot EM

W

Wade & Co.
High Street, Burslem
1869 Keates P-B (teapot and toy)
1870 Harrod NC-B (Rockingham ware manufacturers)
1887 Porter EM-B
1888 Kelly RM
1889 Keates P-B (Rockingham stone and jet decorators)
1892 Keates P-B (Rockingham, stone and jet decorators)
1892 Kelly JRM
1896 Kelly JRM
1900 Kelly JRM

Wade & Sons
Hall Street, Burslem
1882 Keates P-B (shuttle eye and creel step)
1884 Kelly SC (Creel Step Manufacturers); SC (Shuttle Eye Manufacturers)
1888 Kelly SC (Creel Step Manufacturers); SC (Shuttle Eye Manufacturers)
1889 Keates P-B (shuttle eye and creel step)

1892 Keates P-B (shuttle eye and creel step)
1892 Kelly SC (Creel Step & Shuttle Eye Manufacturers); SC (Shuttle Eye Manufacturers)
1896 Kelly SC (Creel Step & Shuttle Eye Manufacturers)
The name is misprinted as Wade & Song in one entry in 1884 Kelly.

Wade, J. & W., & Co.
Flaxman Art Tile Works, High Street, Burslem
1892 Kelly SC (Enamelled Tile Manufacturers) (& glazed, printed & embossed)
1896 Kelly SC (Art Tile Manufacturers)
1900 Kelly SC (Art Tile Manufacturers)

Wade, John
(i) High Street, Burslem
1882 Keates P-B (earthenware)
(ii) 52 Hall Street, Burslem
1889 Keates P-B (earthenware)
1892 Keates P-B (earthenware)

Wade, John, & Co.
High Street, Burslem
1868 Kelly RM
1872 Kelly RM

Wade & Colclough
(i) High Street, Burslem
1870 Harrod NC-B (toy manufacturers)
1873 Keates P-B (Rockingham)
1876 Kelly RM
1880 Kelly RM
(ii) Bourne's Bank, Burslem
1875 Keates P-B (Rockingham)
1879 Keates P-B (Rockingham)

Wade, Colclough & Lingard
High Street, Burslem
1882 Keates P-B (Rockingham stone and jet decorators)
1884 Kelly RM

Wade & Myatt
Hall Street, Burslem
1868 Kelly SC (Shuttle Eye Manufacturers)
1869 Keates P-B (shuttle eye)
1870 Harrod NC-B (shuffle-eye (sic) manufacturers)
1872 Kelly SC (Shuttle Eye Manufacturers)
1873 Keates P-B (shuttle eye)
1875 Keates P-B (shuttle eye and creel step)
1876 Kelly SC (Shuttle Eye Manufacturers)
1879 Keates P-B (shuttle eye and creel step)
1880 Kelly SC (Creel Step Manufacturers); SC (Shuttle Eye Manufacturers) (manufacturers of all kinds of porcelain used in silk & cotton machinery)

Wade & Song
See: Wade & Sons

Wagstaff & Brunt
(i) Edensor Road, Longton
1884 Kelly CM; EM
(ii) King Street Pottery, Longton
1887 Porter EM-L
1889 Keates P-L (china and earthenware)
1892 Keates P-L (china and earthenware
1892 Kelly CM
1896 Kelly CM
The first partner's name is listed as Wagstaffe in 1892 Keates.

Waine, Charles
Sutherland Road, Longton
1892 Keates P-L (china)
1892 Kelly CM
1896 Kelly CM
1900 Kelly CM

Waine, E. & H.
Normacot Works, Normacot Road, Longton
1889 Keates P-L (china, earthenware, &c.)
1892 Keates P-L (china, earthenware, &c.)

Waine & Bates
Sutherland Road, Longton
1887 Porter EM-L
1888 Kelly CM
1889 Keates P-L (china)
The second partner is listed as Thomas Bates in 1888 Kelly.

Wakefield, George
63 William Street, Hanley
1887 Porter EM-H

Wakefield, Thomas
Botany Bay, Northwood, Hanley
1884 Kelly SC (Jagger (sic) Manufacturer)
1888 Kelly SC (Sagger Manufacturer)
1892 Kelly SC (Sagger Manufacturer)
1896 Kelly SC (Sagger Manufacturer)
1900 Kelly SC (Sagg (sic) Manufacturer)

Wakefield, Thomas, & Co.
Botany Bay, Northwood, Hanley
1889 Keates P-H (saggar)
1892 Keates P-H (saggar)

Walkelate, Mark
See: Walklate, Mark

Walker, John
(i) Low Street, Burslem
1800 Allbutt NC-B (toy manufacturer)
(ii) 31 High Street, Longton
1873 Keates P-L (earthenware)
1875 Keates P-L (earthenware)
1876 Kelly EM
1879 Keates P-L (earthenware)
1880 Kelly EM
(iii) Dalehall, Burslem
1889 Keates P-B (Gildea & Walker, earthenware)

Walker, Thomas
(i) Sandyford, Tunstall
1846 Williams NC-T (earthenware manufacturer)
1850 Slater EM
(ii) Newfield, Tunstall
1851 White EM-T; NC-G (earthenware manufacturer)
Walker's house is listed as Wesley Place in 1851 White.
See also: Podmore, Walker & Co.

Walker, Thomas Henry
Church Street, Lane End
1846 Williams NC-L-LE (earthenware & black manfr.)

Thomas Henry Walker. Printed mark from a blue-printed Willow pattern stone china meat dish.

Walker, William
See: Stubbs & Walker

Walker, Bateman & Co.
British Anchor Pottery, Anchor Road, Longton
1865 Keates P-L (earthenware)

Walker & Carter
(i) British Anchor Pottery, Anchor Road, Longton
1868 Kelly EM
1869 Keates P-L (earthenware)
(ii) British Anchor Potteries, Stoke
1870 Harrod NC-S (manufacturers of earthenware, stone, china, &c., for home and foreign markets)
(iii) Church Street, Stoke
1872 Kelly EM
1873 Keates P-S (earthenware)
1875 Keates P-S (earthenware)
1876 Kelly EM
1879 Keates P-S (earthenware)
1880 Kelly EM
1882 Keates P-S (earthenware)
1884 Kelly EM
(iv) Anchor Works, Church Street, Stoke
1887 Porter CEM-S

Walker, Carter & Co.
British Anchor Pottery, Anchor Road, Longton
1867 Keates P-L (earthenware)

Walker & Finney
Victoria Works, Victoria Place, Longton
1852 Slater CM
1856 Kelly CEM

Walker, Podmore & Co.
Amicable Street, Old Bank, and Newfield, Tunstall
1850 Slater EM
1852 Slater EM

Walker & Salt
High Street, Tunstall
1869 Keates P-T (china)
1873 Keates P-T (china)

Walkett, William H.
See: Walklet, William H.

Walklate, Hannah & Richard
(i) Lane End
1809 Holden NC (manufacturers of earthenware)
1811 Holden NC (manufacturers of earthenware)
1816 Underhill P
(ii) High Street, Lane End
1818 Parson EM-LE
1818 Pigot EM

Walklate, Mark
Lane End
1784 Bailey NC-LE (potter)
1796 Chester NC-LE-LD-LL (manufacturer of earthenware)
1798 Universal NC-LE
1802 Allbut EM (map location 144)
The surname is listed as Walklete in 1784 Bailey and 1802 Allbut, and as Walkelate in 1798 Universal.

Walklate, Mark, & Son
Lane End
1805 Holden NC (earthenware manufacturers)

Walklet, Thomas Forrester
See: Buller, Wentworth William

Walklet, William H.
14 Church Street, Hanley
1862 Slater A; CM (and Britannia metal mounted jugs, wholesale & for exportation); EM (and Britannia metal mounted jugs wholesale & for exportation)
The surname is misprinted as Walkett in one entry (EM). The advertisement in 1862 Slater describes Walklet as a 'mounter in every variety of china, stone, earthenware, hot water jugs, &c., wholesale and for exportation', with the address given as Britannia Metal Works, Church Street, Hanley.

WILLIAM H. WALKLET,
MOUNTER IN EVERY VARIETY OF CHINA, STONE, EARTHENWARE,
HOT WATER JUGS, &c.
WHOLESALE AND FOR EXPORTATION,
BRITANNIA METAL WORKS,
Church Street, Hanley, Staffordshire Potteries.

William H. Walklet. Advertisement from 1862 Slater.

Walklete, Mark
See: Walklate, Mark

Wallace & Co.
Railway Stilt and Spur Works, Fenton
1892 Keates P-F

Walley, E., & Son
Cobridge
1860 Kelly EM
1861 Harrison NC-B (earthenware manufacturers)

Edward & William Walley. Impressed and sprigged mark from a relief-moulded stoneware jug. The registration diamond dates from 1858. This style probably relates to the directory entries for E. Walley & Son.

Walley, Edward
(i) Villa Pottery, Cobridge
1846 Williams NC-C-F-E (manufacturer)
1850 Slater EM
1851 White CEM-B (only earthenware)
1852 Slater EM (and stone & fancy bodies)
1854 Kelly CEM
1856 Kelly CEM
(ii) Clifton Terrace, Waterloo Road, Burslem
1863 Kelly P (consulting)
Walley's house is listed as Hanley in 1846 Williams and 1851 White. The surname is listed as Whalley in 1846 Williams.

Edward Walley. Printed mark from a relief-moulded stoneware pot.

Walley, George
(i) Tunstall
1822 Allbut CEM
(earthenware manufact.)
1822 Pigot EM
(ii) Flint Street, Longton
1841 Pigot EM

Walley, J.
Market Street, Tunstall
1854 Kelly CEM

Walley, John
(i) High Street, Burslem
1850 Slater TOCM
1852 Slater EM (Rockingham ware); TOCM
1856 Kelly RM
1860 Kelly EM
1861 Harrison NC-B
(earthenware manufacturer)
1862 Slater EM
(Rockingham)
1864 Jones EM-Miscellaneous (Rockingham teapot and fancy toy)
1865 Keates P-B (teapot and toy)
1867 Keates P-B (teapot and toy)
(ii) Hope Street, Hanley
1852 Slater TOCM
1861 Harrison NC-H-Sh
(earthenware merchant and manufacturer)
1863 Kelly CM-General; PM
(iii) 118 Hope Street, Hanley
1862 Slater TOCM

Walley, William
(i) Marsh Street, Shelton
1841 Pigot EM (black cane and lustre)
(ii) Nile Street, Burslem
1868 Kelly RM
1869 Keates P-B
(Rockingham)
1870 Harrod NC-B
(Rockingham ware manufacturer)
1872 Kelly RM
1873 Keates P-B
(Rockingham)
1875 Keates P-B
(Rockingham)
1876 Kelly RM
1879 Keates P-B
(Rockingham)
1880 Kelly RM
1882 Keates P-B
(Rockingham)
(iii) 66 Newcastle Street, Burslem
1873 Keates P-B (earthenware)

Wallis, Gimson & Co.
Lane Delph Pottery, Park Street, Fenton
1884 Kelly EM
1887 Porter EM-F
1888 Kelly EM

Walsh, William
(i) Burslem
1816 Underhill P
1822 Allbut CEM
(earthenware manufat.)
(ii) Furlong, Burslem
1818 Parson EM-B-Lp-C
(iii) Newcastle Street, Burslem
1822 Pigot EM

Walsh & Ryles
Burslem
1809 Holden NC (earthenware-manufactrs.)
1811 Holden NC (earthenware manufacturers)

Walters, A. & G.
Commerce Street, Longton
1889 Keates P-L (china)

Walters, Peter A.
Commerce Street, Longton
1876 Kelly CM

Walters, Thomas
(i) Talbot Works, Commerce Street, Longton
1875 Keates P-L (china)
1879 Keates P-L (china)
1880 Kelly CM
1882 Keates P-L (china)
1884 Kelly CM
1888 Kelly CM
1892 Keates P-L (china)
1892 Kelly CM
1896 Kelly CM; EM
(ii) Stafford Street, Longton
1900 Kelly CM; EM

Walters & Hulse
Commerce Street, Longton
1868 Kelly CM
1869 Keates P-L (china)
1872 Kelly CM
1873 Keates P-L (china)

Walton, Ann
Brunswick Street, Shelton
1861 Harrison NC-H-Sh (china gilder and parian figure manufacturer)

Walton, James
Brunswick Street, Shelton, Hanley
1846 Williams NC-Sh (china figure manufacturer)
1850 Kelly NC-Sh (china toy manufacturer)
1850 Slater TOCM
1851 White CETOM-H-Sh
1852 Slater PM; TOCM
1854 Kelly PM (ornamental figure makers)
1860 Kelly PM

Walton, John
(i) Hadderage, Burslem
1818 Parson EM-B-Lp-C
(ii) Burslem
1822 Allbut CEM (Egyptian black and figure manufact.)
(iii) Navigation Road, Burslem
1818 Pigot EM
1822 Pigot EM
1828 Pigot EM
1830 Pigot EM
1834 White EM-B (Egyptian black mfrs. only)
1834 White ETM-B
1835 Pigot EM
(iv) Waterloo Road, Burslem
1835 Pigot TOCM

John Walton. Impressed mark from an earthenware figure of "St Paul".

Walton, Joshua
(i) Piccadilly, Shelton
1830 Pigot EM (toy only)
1834 White CETM-H-Sh
1835 Pigot TOCM (fine)
1841 Pigot TOCM (fine)
(ii) Brunswick Street, Shelton
1851 White CETOM-H-Sh

Walton, William
Hope Street, Shelton
1846 Williams NC-Sh (china figure manufacturer)

Warburton, Jacob
Cobridge
1781 Bailey NC (potter)
1783 Bailey NC (potter)
1784 Bailey NC-C (potter)
1796 Chester NC-C (manufacturer of earthenware)
1798 Universal NC-C (manufacturer of Staffordshire-ware)

Warburton, James
Hot Lane, Burslem
1818 Parson EM-B-Lp-C

Warburton, John
(i) Cobridge
1802 Allbut EM (map location 54, two entries)
1809 Holden NC (earthenware-manuf.)
1811 Holden NC (earthenware manuf.)
1816 Underhill P
1822 Allbut CEM (earthenware manufact.)
1822 Pigot EM
(ii) Hot Lane, Burslem
1818 Parson EM-B-Lp-C

Warburton, Joseph
Stoke
1781 Bailey NC (potter)
1783 Bailey NC (potter)

Warburton, Mary
Hot Lane, Burslem
1830 Pigot EM (coarse)

Warburton, Peter
Cobridge
1805 Holden NC (earthenware manufacturer)
1809 Holden NC (earthenware-manuf.)
1811 Holden NC (earthenware manuf.)

Ward & Co.
Stoke
1818 Parson EM-S-E

Ward, Frederick W.
179 High Street, Fenton
1887 Porter EM-F

Ward, Thomas, & Co.
(i) Stoke
1822 Allbut CEM (earthenware manufacts.)
(ii) Newcastle Street, Stoke
1828 Pigot EM
(iii) High Street, Stoke
1830 Pigot EM

Ward, William
Lane End
1802 Allbut EM (map location 141)

Ward & Davenport
Cliff Bank, Stoke
1818 Pigot EM
1822 Pigot EM

WARDLE & Co.,
William Street Pottery
HANLEY,
MANUFACTURERS OF USEFUL & ORNAMENTAL
PARIAN AND MAJOLICA
Statuettes, Vases, Centres, Ornaments, &c.,
Of every description, Enamelled and Plain.

Wardle & Co. Advertisement from 1873 Keates. The same advertisement appeared in 1875 Keates.

WARDLE & Co.,
William Street Pottery, Hanley,
MANUFACTURERS OF USEFUL AND ORNAMENTAL
MAJOLICA,
VASES, CENTRES, ORNAMENTS, &c.,
Of every description, Enamelled and Plain,
FOR HOME AND FOREIGN MARKETS

Wardle & Co. Advertisement from 1879 Keates.

WARDLE & CO.,
Washington Works, Victoria Road, HANLEY,
MANUFACTURERS OF USEFUL AND ORNAMENTAL
MAJOLICA,
VASES, CENTRES, ORNAMENTS, &c.,
Of every description, Enamelled and Plain,
FOR HOME AND FOREIGN MARKETS

Wardle & Co. Advertisement from 1882 Keates.

Wardle & Co.
(i) William Street Pottery, Hanley
1873 Keates A; P-H (parian and majolica)
1875 Keates P-H (parian and majolica)
1876 Kelly MM
1879 Keates P-H (parian and majolica)
1880 Kelly MM
1882 Keates P-H (parian and majolica)
(ii) Washington Works or Victoria Works, Victoria Road, Hanley
1882 Keates P-H (parian and majolica)
1884 Kelly MM
1887 Porter EM-H
1888 Kelly MM
1892 Keates P-H (art pottery and majolica)
1892 Kelly MM
1896 Kelly MM
1900 Kelly MM
The advertisement in 1873 Keates describes the firm as 'manufacturers of useful and ornamental parian and majolica, statuettes, vases, centres, ornaments, &c., of every description, enamelled and plain'. The same text appeared in 1875 Keates, and again in 1879 Keates but with the words 'parian' and 'statuettes' dropped and a note 'for home and foreign markets' added. This was repeated in 1882 Keates with the new address, Washington Works, Victoria Road, Hanley.

Wardle, J.
Hope Street, Shelton
1854 Kelly PM (ornamental figure makers)
1856 Kelly PM

Wardle, James
William Street Pottery, Hanley
1865 Keates A; P-H (parian and majolica)
1867 Keates A; P-H (parian and majolica)
1868 Kelly MM; PM
1869 Keates A; P-H (parian and majolica)
1870 Harrod NC-H (parian and belbeck china manufacturer for home and foreign markets)
The advertisements in the three Keates directories are similar, describing Wardle as a: 'manufacturer of majolica ware, china, coloured stone bodies, parian statuettes, vases, centres, and ornaments of every description, enamelled and plain. Lincoln, Cobden, and other busts. N.B. – Manufacturer of majolica and other colours.' (1865); 'manufacturer of majolica ware, china figures, coloured stone bodies, parian statuettes, vases, centres, and ornaments of every description, enamelled and plain. N.B. – Parian

jugs warranted to stand hot water, mounted or plain.' (1867); and 'manufacturer of parian statuettes, vases, centres, & ornaments of every description, enamelled and plain. N.B. – Parian jugs to stand hot water, mounted or plain.' (1869).

JAMES WARDLE,
WILLIAM STREET POTTERY;
HANLEY,
Manufacturer of Majolica Ware,
CHINA, COLOURED STONE BODIES,
PARIAN STATUETTES, VASES, CENTRES,
AND ORNAMENTS OF EVERY DESCRIPTION,
ENAMELLED AND PLAIN.
LINCOLN, COBDEN, AND OTHER BUSTS.
N.B—Manufacturer of Majolica and other Colours.

James Wardle. Advertisement from 1865 Keates.

JAMES WARDLE,
WILLIAM STREET, POTTERY,
HANLEY,
Manufacturer of Majolica Ware,
CHINA FIGURES, COLOURED STONE BODIES,
PARIAN STATUETTES, VASES, CENTRES,
AND ORNAMENTS OF EVERY DESCRIPTION,
ENAMELLED AND PLAIN
N.B.—Parian Jugs warranted to stand Hot Water, Mounted or Plain

James Wardle. Advertisement from 1867 Keates.

JAMES WARDLE,
WILLIAM STREET POTTERY, HANLEY.
MANUFACTURER OF
PARIAN STATUETTES,
VASES, CENTRES, & ORNAMENTS OF EVERY DESCRIPTION
ENAMELLED AND PLAIN.
N.B.—Parian Jugs warranted to stand Hot Water, Mounted or Plain.

James Wardle. Advertisement from 1869 Keates.

Wardle & Ash
(i) James Street, Hanley
1860 Kelly PM
1861 Harrison NC-H-Sh (parian manufacturers)
1862 Slater PM
(ii) Broad Street, Hanley
1863 Kelly PM (stone & colored bodies)
1864 Jones PM

Warner & Co.
New Street, Hanley
1872 Kelly SC (Sanitary Ware Manufacturers)

Warrellow, Joseph
See: Warrilow, Joseph

Warren, James
Park Place, High Street, Longton
1841 Pigot CM
1850 Kelly CEM; NC-L (china manufacturer)
1850 Slater CM
1851 White CEM-L
Warren's house is listed as Millfield Gt. in 1851 White.

Warren & Adams
(i) Victoria Works, High Street, Longton
1852 Slater CM
1864 Jones CEM
(ii) Park Place, High Street, Longton
1852 Slater CM
1854 Kelly CEM
1862 Slater CM
1864 Jones CEM
(iii) High Street, Longton
1856 Kelly CEM
1860 Kelly CM-General
1861 Harrison NC-L (china manufacturers)
1863 Kelly CM-General

Warrillow, Joseph
See: Warrilow, Joseph

Warrillow & Cope
See: Warrilow & Cope

Warrilow & Sons
Sutherland Road, Longton
1892 Kelly CM
1896 Kelly CM
1900 Kelly CM

Warrilow, George
(i) Park Place Works, High Street, Longton
1887 Porter EM-L
1888 Kelly CM
(ii) Queen's Pottery, Sutherland Road, Longton
1889 Keates P-L (china)
1892 Keates P-L (china)

Warrilow, Joseph
Hanley
1796 Chester NC-H-Sh (manufacturer of earthenware)
1798 Universal NC-H (manufacturer of Staffordshire-ware)
1805 Holden NC (earthenware manufacturer)
1809 Holden NC (earthenware-manufacturer)
1811 Holden NC (earthenware-manufacturer)
The surname is listed as Warrellow in 1798 Universal, and as Warrillow in 1796 Chester.

Warrilow & Cope
Wellington Works, Stafford Street, Longton
1880 Kelly CM
1882 Keates P-L (china and majolica)
1884 Kelly CM
The first partner's name is listed as Warrillow in 1882 Keates.

Warrington & Co.
Brewery Street, Hope Street, Hanley
1861 Harrison NC-H-Sh (parian manufacturers)
1862 Slater EM; PM

Warrington, W., & Co.
Brewery Street, Hanley
1863 Kelly PM

Warrington, William
(i) East Wood Vale, Hanley
1861 Harrison NC-H-Sh (beer retailer and grocer, parian stone manufacturer)
(ii) Brewery Street, Hanley
1864 Jones PM
1865 Keates P-H (parian)
1867 Keates P-H (parian)

Wathem, J. & B.
Victoria Works, Fenton
1861 Harrison NC-F (earthenware manufacturers)

Wathen & Co.
See: Wathen, James B.

WATHEN & Co.,
VICTORIA WORKS, FENTON,
STAFFORDSHIRE POTTERIES.
MANUFACTURERS OF
DECORATED & PLAIN EARTHENWARE
OF ALL KINDS;
GILT, ENAMELLED, LUSTRE, & DOUBLE PRINTED

Wathen & Co. Advertisement from 1864 Jones.

Wathen, B.
Victoria Works, Market Street, Fenton
1865 Keates P-F (earthenware)

Wathen, James B.
Victoria Works, Market Street, Fenton
1864 Jones A; EM
1867 Keates P-F (earthenware)
1868 Kelly EM
1869 Keates P-F (earthenware)
The surname is listed as Wathens in 1869 Keates. The advertisement in 1864 Jones gives the style as Wathen & Co. and describes the firm as 'manufacturers of decorated & plain earthenware of all kinds; gilt, enamelled, lustre, & double printed'.
See also: Reeves, James

Wathen & Hebb
Foley Works, Longton
1856 Kelly CEM

Wathen & Hudden
(i) Fenton
1860 Kelly EM
(ii) Stafford Street, Longton
1860 Kelly EM; LM
1861 Harrison NC-L (earthenware manufacturers)
This firm succeeded John Bailey (1860 Kelly).

Wathen & Lichfield
Victoria Works, Market Street, Fenton
1862 Slater EM
1863 Kelly EM

Wathens, James B.
See: Wathen, James B.

Watts & Co.
High Street, Fenton
1876 Kelly EM (finishers)

Watts & Tompkinson
High Street, Longton
1880 Kelly EM (finishers)

Wayte & Ridge
Waterloo Place Works, Heathcote Road, Longton
1864 Jones A; CEM; PM
There are two advertisements in 1864 Jones. The shorter one is in English and simply describes the firm as 'manufacturers of parian, china, lustre, &c.' The longer one is in French and reads 'Porcelaines, faiences, poteries, lustres, gres, biscuits, et tous produits des manufactures de porcelaines Anglaises. Mm. Wayte & Ridge, manufacturiers et commissionaires, désirant augmenter les relations qu'ils ont déjà sur le Continents ont toujours des articles variés et de bon gout; le choix de formes et de dessins nouveaux rend leur fabrication remarquable et leur a déjà valu un succes signale; la qualité et le bon marché de leur merchandise leur en assure encore un plus grand. Les bonnes conditions dans lesquelles ils se trouvent leur permet de ne redouter aucune concurrence. Des prix courants sont envoyes à toutes les personnes qui en font la demande à M. Wayte à Paris. On est prié d'ecrire chez Messrs. Arthur & Cie., 10 Rue Castiglione, à Paris, ou l'agent peut etre vu, ou à leur maison en Angleterre à l'adresse ci-dessous', followed by the firm's address.

Wayte & Ridge. Advertisement from 1864 Jones.

Weatherby & Sons
High Street, Hanley
1892 Keates P-H

Weatherby, J.H., & Sons
High Street, Hanley
1896 Kelly EM
1900 Kelly EM

Webb & Co.
Peel Street Pottery, Stafford Street, Longton
1869 Keates P-L (china)
1870 Harrod NC-L (china manufacturers for home and foreign markets)

Webb, Samuel, & Co.
Stafford Street, Longton
1868 Kelly CM
1872 Kelly CM

Webb & Walters
(i) St. Martin's Lane, Longton
1862 Slater CM
1863 Kelly CM-General
(ii) Stafford Street, Longton
1864 Jones LM
1865 Keates P-L (china, gold and silver lustre)
1867 Keates P-L (china, gold, and silver lustre)

Webberley, William
St. James' Place, High Street, Longton
1851 White CEM-L
1852 Slater CM
1854 Kelly CEM
1856 Kelly CEM
1860 Kelly CM-General; CM-Tea, Breakfast & Dessert Services; COM; SC (China Porcelain Manufacturers); SC (Jug Manufacturers) (fancy)
1861 Harrison NC-L (china manufacturer)
1862 Slater CM
1864 Jones A; CEM
1865 Keates A; P-L (china)
1867 Keates P-L (china)
1868 Kelly CM
1869 Keates A; P-L (china)
1870 Harrod NC-L (china manufacturer)
1872 Kelly CM
1873 Keates P-L (china)
1875 Keates P-L (china)
1876 Kelly CM
1879 Keates P-L (china)
1880 Kelly CM
1882 Keates P-L (china)
1884 Kelly CM
1887 Porter EM-L
1888 Kelly CM
1889 Keates P-L (china)
1892 Kelly CM
Webberley's house is listed as Terrace Buildings in 1851 White. The surname is listed as Webberly in 1892 Kelly and in the advertisement in

1864 Jones. The advertisements in 1864 Jones and 1865 Keates, and another in 1867 Keates all describe Webberley as a 'manufacturer of all kinds of improved china', with a note 'ground bone for potters' purposes always on hand'. The advertisement in 1869 Keates describes him simply as a 'china manufacturer'.
See also: Shubotham & Webberley

WILLIAM WEBBERLY,
MANUFACTURER OF ALL KINDS OF
IMPROVED CHINA,
ST. JAMES'S PLACE,
HIGH STREET, LONGTON,
STAFFORDSHIRE POTTERIES.
N.B.—Ground Bone for Potters' purposes always on hand.

William Webberley. Advertisement from 1864 Jones. The same advertisement but with the surname correctly spelled Webberley appeared in 1865 Keates and 1867 Keates.

WILLIAM WEBBERLEY,
CHINA MANUFACTURER
ST. JAMES' PLACE,
LONGTON, STAFFORDSHIRE.

William Webberley. Advertisement from 1869 Keates.

Wedgewood, J.
See: Wedgwood, Josiah

Wedgewood, Joseph
See: Wedgwood, Josiah

Wedgewood, Thomas
See: Wedgwood, Thomas

Wedgwood & Co.
(i) Burslem
1796 Chester NC-B
(manufacturer of earthenware)
(ii) Rotten Row, High Street, Burslem
1818 Pigot EM
(iii) Swan Bank, Tunstall
1860 Kelly CM-General; EM
(iv) Unicorn Works, Amicable Street, Tunstall
1860 Kelly CM-General; EM
1861 Harrison NC-T
(earthenware manufacturers)
1863 Kelly CM-General
1865 Keates P-T (earthenware)
1887 Porter EM-T
(v) Commerce Street, Longton
1865 Keates P-L (china)
(vi) Unicorn Works, also Pinnox Works, Great Woodland Street, Tunstall
1862 Slater EM
1864 Jones EM
1867 Keates P-T (earthenware)
1868 Kelly EM
1869 Keates P-T (earthenware)
1870 Harrod NC-T
(manufacturers of earthenware, for home, American, and continental markets)
1872 Kelly EM
1873 Keates P-T (earthenware)
1875 Keates P-T (earthenware)

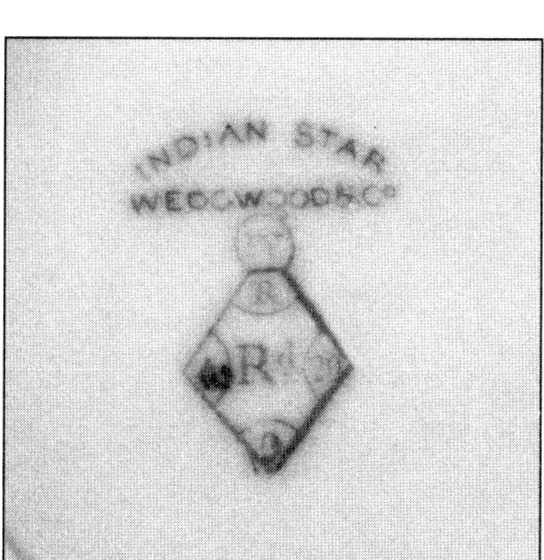

Wedgwood & Co. Printed mark from a transfer-printed vegetable dish. The registration diamond dates from 1861.

Wedgwood & Co. Printed mark from a brown-printed and coloured soap dish. The registration diamond dates from 1881.

1876 Kelly EM
1879 Keates P-T (earthenware)
1880 Kelly EM
1882 Keates P-T (earthenware)
1884 Kelly EM
1888 Kelly EM
(vii) High Street, Brownhills, Tunstall
1889 Keates P-T (earthenware)
1892 Keates P-T (earthenware)
1892 Kelly EM
1896 Kelly EM
1900 Kelly EM

Wedgwood & Co. Printed mark from a blue-printed earthenware plate. Note that they became a limited company in about 1900. The claim "The Original Manufacturer" relates to the commonly used "Asiatic Pheasants" design.

Wedgwood & Co. Printed mark from a green-printed earthenware gravy boat.

Wedgwood & Sons
Etruria
1856 Kelly CEM

Wedgwood, Francis
See: Wedgwood, Josiah, & Sons

Wedgwood, Francis, Godfry, Clement, & Lawrence
Barlaston
1870 Harrod NC-Bar
(earthenware manufacturers)

Wedgwood, J., & Co.
Burslem
1796 Chester NC-B
(manufacturers of earthenware)

Wedgwood, John
Tunstall
1846 Williams NC-T
(earthenware manfctr.)
Wedgwood's house is listed as Burslem.

Wedgwood, Joseph, & Sons
See: Wedgwood, Josiah, & Sons

Josiah Wedgwood & Sons. Advertisement from 1888 Kelly.

Wedgwood, Josiah
Etruria
1781 Bailey NC (potter to her Majesty)
1783 Bailey NC (potter to her Majesty)
1811 Holden NC (potter to her Majesty)
1816 Underhill P
1818 Parson EM-S-E
1818 Pigot EM
1822 Allbut CEM
(earthenware manufact.)
1822 Pigot EM
The potter is listed as Joseph Wedgewood in 1781 Bailey and the surname is also listed as Wedgewood in 1783 Bailey. A London address at St. James's Square is listed in 1811 Holden.

Wedgwood, Josiah, & Son
Etruria
1828 Pigot EM
1830 Pigot EM
1864 Jones PM
1887 Porter EM-H

Wedgwood, Josiah, & Sons
Etruria
1834 White EM-H-Sh
1835 Pigot EM
1841 Pigot EM
1846 Williams NC-C-F-E
(earthenware manufacturers)
1850 Kelly CEM
1850 Slater EM
1851 White CEM-H-Sh
1852 Slater EM
1854 Kelly CEM
1860 Kelly EM
1861 Harrison NC-E
(earthenware manufacturers)
1862 Slater EM
1863 Kelly EM; MM; PM; SC (Chemical Ware Manufacturers); SC (Jasper Makers); SM
1864 Jones EM; EM-Miscellaneous (parian, jasper, and majolica)
1865 Keates P-H (china and earthenware)
1867 Keates P-H (china and earthenware)
1868 Kelly EM
1869 Keates P-H (china and earthenware)
1870 Harrod NC-E
(manufacturers of earthenware, parian, majolica, chemical goods, porous ware for electric telegraph batteries, mortar and pestal stoneware, jasper, &c., for home and foreign markets); NC-H (manufacturers of earthenware, majolica, chemical goods, porous ware for electric telegraph batteries, mortars and pestles, stoneware, jasper, &c., for home and foreign markets)
1872 Kelly EM; MM; PM; SC (Chemical Ware Manufacturers); SM
1873 Keates P-H
(earthenware)
1875 Keates P-H
(earthenware)
1876 Kelly CM; EM
1879 Keates P-H
(earthenware)
1880 Kelly EM
1882 Keates P-H
(earthenware)
1884 Kelly EM
1888 Kelly A; EM; MM; SC (Encaustic Tile Manufacturers); SM
1889 Keates P-H (earthenware, &c.)
1892 Keates P-H (earthenware, etc.)
1892 Kelly EM; MM; SC (Encaustic Tile Manufacturers); SC (Jasper Manufacturers); SM
1896 Kelly EM
The partners are listed individually as Francis Wedgwood of Etruria Hall and Robert Brown of Shelton in 1846 Williams, although the firm is given in error as Joseph Wedgwood & Sons. The advertisement in 1888 Kelly describes the firm as 'manufacturers of tiles' and gives the varieties as 'encaustic and plain for floors; white, printed, coloured bodies, enamelled, coloured glazes and impressed for walls and hearths. Art and other tiles, for jambs, stoves and furniture decoration. Embossed tiles in great variety. Samples with estimates on application.' It lists London showrooms at St. Andrew's Buildings, Holborn Circus.

Wedgwood, Josiah, & Sons Ltd.
Etruria Pottery, Etruria
1896 Kelly MM; SC (Jasper Manufacturers); SM
1900 Kelly CM; EM; MM; SC (Encaustic Tile Manufacturers); SC (Jasper Manufacturers); SM

Wedgwood, Josiah & Thomas
Fenton
1784 Bailey NC-F (potters)

Wedgwood, Ralph, & Co.
Burslem
1798 Universal NC-B
(manufacturers of Staffordshire-ware)

Wedgwood, Thomas
(i) Burslem
1781 Bailey NC (potter)
1783 Bailey NC (potter)

1796 Chester NC-B
(manufacturer of earthenware)
1798 Universal NC-B
(manufacturer of Staffordshire-ware)
1802 Allbut EM (map location 42)
1809 Holden NC (earthenware-manufacturer)
1811 Holden NC (earthenware manufact.)
1822 Allbut CEM
(earthenware manufact.)
(ii) Big House, Burslem
1784 Bailey NC-B
(manufacturer of cream coloured ware, and china glazed ware, painted with blue, &c.)
1805 Holden NC (earthenware manufacturer)
(iii) Over House, Burslem
1784 Bailey NC-B
(manufacturer of cream coloured ware, and china glazed ware, painted with blue, &c.)
1805 Holden NC
(iv) Rotten Row, High Street, Burslem
1822 Pigot EM
(v) 22 Nile Street and works at Union Street, Burslem
1864 Jones EM
The surname is listed as Wedgewood in 1781 Bailey and 1783 Bailey.

Wedgwood, W., & Son
William Street, Hanley
1892 Kelly JRM
1896 Kelly JRM

Wedgwood & Ackerley
Commerce Street, Longton
1863 Kelly CM-General
1864 Jones CEM

Wedgwood & Brierly
Etruria
1798 Universal NC-E
(manufacturers of Staffordshire-ware)

Wedgwood & Byerley
Etruria
1796 Chester NC-C
(manufacturers of earthenware)
1802 Allbut EM (map location 96)
1805 Holden NC (potters to her Majesty)
1809 Holden NC (potters to her Majesty)
1816 Underhill P
The first partner is listed as Josiah Wedgwood in 1805 Holden, 1809 Holden, and 1816 Underhill. A London address at St. James's Square and a Dublin address at Sackville Street are listed in 1809 Holden.

Wedgwood & Johnson
High Street, Burslem
1818 Parson EM-B-Lp-C

Wedgwood & Walker
Tunstall
1863 Kelly EM

Welch, James B.
(i) Excelsior Works, New Street, Hanley
1887 Porter EM-H
1888 Kelly EM
1889 Keates P-H
1892 Kelly JRM
(ii) Broad Street, Hanley
1892 Keates P-H

Wenger, A.
Parker Street, Hanley
1882 Keates P-H
(earthenware)
1889 Keates P-H
(earthenware)
1892 Keates P-H
(earthenware)

Wentworth (W.), Buller & Mugford
See: Buller & Mugford

George Weston. Printed mark from a blue-printed Willow pattern stone china plate.

Weston, George
(i) Lane End
1802 Allbut EM (map location 143)
1822 Allbut CEM (china and earthenware manufact.)
(ii) High Street, Lane End
1818 Parson EM-LE
1818 Pigot EM
1822 Pigot EM
1828 Pigot CM; EM
1830 Pigot EM

Weston, George, & Co.
Lane End
1805 Holden NC (earthenware manufacturers)
1809 Holden NC
(manufacturers of earthenware)
1811 Holden NC
(manufacturers of earthenware)
1816 Underhill P

Weston, John
Shelton
1798 Universal NC-Sh
(manufacturer of Staffordshire-ware)

Weston, Sarah
High Street, Lane End
1822 Allbut CEM (lusterer and enameller)
1822 Pigot EM

Weston, Colclough & Bridgwood
Church Street, Longton
1851 White NC-L (china & earthenware mfrs.)

Weston & Hull
Lane End
1796 Chester NC-LE-LD-LL
(manufacturers of earthenware)
1798 Universal NC-LE
(manufacturers of Staffordshire-ware)

Whalley, Edward
See: Walley, Edward

Whitaker & Co.
See: Whittaker & Co.

Whitehall, Joseph
Nile Street, Burslem
1870 Harrod NC-B
(spurmaker)

Whitehead, Charles Christopher
Hanley
1798 Universal NC-H
(manufacturer of Staffordshire-ware)

Whitehead, Charles
Shelton
1818 Parson EM-H-Sh
The firm is listed as being in the hands of executors in 1818 Parson.

Whitehead, Charles & James
See: Whitehead, James & Charles

Whitehead, Christopher
Shelton
1805 Holden NC (earthenware manufacturer)

Whitehead, Christopher Charles
Shelton
1784 Bailey NC-Sh (potter)

Whitehead, Dorothy
(i) Hanley
1796 Chester NC-H-Sh (manufacturer of earthenware)
(ii) Shelton
1802 Allbut EM (map location 94)

Whitehead, James
(i) Old Hall Street, Hanley
1818 Parson EM-H-Sh (commission dealer)
(ii) Hill Street, Hanley
1818 Pigot EM
(iii) Charles Street, Hanley
1822 Pigot EM

Whitehead, James & Charles
Hanley
1796 Chester NC-H-Sh (manufacturers of earthenware)
1798 Universal NC-H (manufacturers of Staffordshire-ware)
1802 Allbut EM (map location 82)
1805 Holden NC (earthenware manufacturers)
1809 Holden NC (earthenware-manufs.)
The firm is listed as Charles & James Whitehead in 1805 Holden

Whittaker & Co.
Hallfield Pottery, Grafton Street or Festing Street, Hanley
1887 Porter EM-H
1888 Kelly EM
1889 Keates P-H (earthenware)
1892 Keates P-H (earthenware)
1892 Kelly EM
1896 Kelly EM
The surname is listed as Whitaker in 1887 Porter.

Whittaker, Edge & Co.
Hallfield Pottery, Grafton Street, Hanley
1882 Keates P-H (earthenware)
1884 Kelly EM

Whittam, Joseph
Fairfield Pottery, Slippery Lane or Broad Street, Hanley
1889 Keates P-H
1892 Keates P-H
1892 Kelly EM
The first name is listed as Josh. in 1892 Keates.

Whittam & Mear
Newcastle Street, Burslem
1887 Porter EM-B

Whittingham & Ford
High Street, Burslem
1870 Harrod NC-B (earthenware manufacturers)
The first partner's name is listed as Wittingham in 1870 Harrod.

Whittingham, Ford & Co.
High Street, Burslem
1868 Kelly EM
1872 Kelly EM
1873 Keates P-B (earthenware)

Whittingham, Ford & Riley
Newcastle Street, Burslem
1876 Kelly EM
1879 Keates P-B (earthenware)
1880 Kelly EM
1882 Keates P-B (earthenware)
The first partner's name is misprinted as Whittinghan in 1882 Keates.

Wigley, G.
Queen Street, Burslem
1868 Kelly EM

Wigley, George
Sylvester Square, Burslem
1867 Keates P-B (creel steps)
1869 Keates P-B (creel steps)
1870 Harrod NC-B (brick and marl works, manufacturer of creel cups, worsted guards, shuttle eyes, pot weights, &c.)

Wigley, William Henry
Sylvester Square, Burslem
1867 Keates P-B (black and lustre)
1868 Kelly RM
1869 Keates P-B (black and lustre)
1870 Harrod NC-B (earthenware manufacturer)

Wigley & Sherley
See: Wigley & Shirley

Wigley & Shirley
(i) Moorland Road, Burslem
1872 Kelly SC (Spur Makers)
1876 Kelly SC (Spur and Stilt Makers for Pottery Manufacturers)
1880 Kelly SC (Spur & Stilt Makers for Pottery Manufacturers)
(ii) Sylvester Square, Burslem
1873 Keates P-B (spur)
1875 Keates P-B (spur)
1879 Keates P-B (spur)
The second partner's name is listed as Sherley in 1876 Kelly and 1880 Kelly.

Wigley & Skiffley
Gallimore Square, Burslem
1870 Harrod NC-B (spurmakers)

Wild, Thomas, & Co.
Albert Works, High Street, Longton
1900 Kelly CM

Wildblood, Richard Vernon
Peel Works, Stafford Street, Longton
1887 Porter EM-L
1888 Kelly CM

Wildblood, William
See: Seddon & Wildblood

Wildblood & Heath
Peel Works, Stafford Street, Longton
1889 Keates P-L (china)
1892 Keates P-L (china)
1892 Kelly CM
1896 Kelly CM

Wildblood, Heath & Sons
Stafford Street, Longton
1900 Kelly CM

Wildblood & Ledgar
Heathcote Road, Longton
1896 Kelly EM
1900 Kelly EM

Wileman & Co.
Foley Potteries, Fenton
1872 Kelly CM
1876 Kelly CM
1880 Kelly CM
1884 Kelly CM
1887 Porter EM-F
1888 Kelly CM
1892 Kelly CM
1896 Kelly CM
1900 Kelly CM

Wileman, C. & J.
The Foley Pottery, Fenton
1865 Keates P-F (china and earthen.)

Wileman, Charles John
Foley, Fenton
1869 Keates P-F (china)

Wileman, Henry
Foley Works, King Street, Fenton
1856 Kelly CEM
1860 Kelly EM
1861 Harrison NC-F (earthenware, &c., manufacturer)
1862 Slater CM; EM
1863 Kelly CM-General
1864 Jones CEM

Wileman, J. & C.
The Foley Pottery, Fenton
1867 Keates P-F (china and earthenware)
1868 Kelly EM

James Francis Wileman. Printed mark from a blue-printed earthenware dinner plate.

Wileman, James Francis
Foley Works, King Street, Fenton
1869 Keates P-F (earthen.)
1870 Harrod NC-F (earthenware, china, and granite manufacturer)
1872 Kelly EM
1873 Keates P-F (earthenware)
1875 Keates P-F (earthenware)
1876 Kelly EM
1879 Keates P-F (earthenware)
1880 Kelly EM
1882 Keates P-F (earthenware)
1884 Kelly EM
1887 Porter EM-F
1888 Kelly EM
1889 Keates P-F (earthenware)
1892 Kelly EM

Wileman, James P.
King Street, Fenton
1892 Keates P-F (earthenware)

Wileman & Shelley
Foley Pottery, King Street, Fenton
1873 Keates P-F (china)
1875 Keates P-F (china)
1879 Keates P-F (china)
1882 Keates P-F (china)
1889 Keates P-F (china)
1892 Keates P-F (china)

Wilkinson & Sons
Havelock Works, Broad Street, Hanley
1863 Kelly CM-General; PM; SC (China Porcelain Manufacturers)
1864 Jones A; CEM; PM
1865 Keates P-H (china and parian)
1867 Keates P-H (china and parian)
The advertisement in 1864 Jones announces the firm's honourable mention at the 1862 International Exhibition, 'the only one given for parian'. The text reads 'Messrs. Wilkinson & Sons, china and parian manufacturers, beg most respectfully to invite an inspection of their new show rooms, where they display the most varied assortment of vases, hot water jugs, &c., which for pureness of design, excellency of material, perfection of workmanship, and cheapness, cannot be surpassed. Messrs. W. & Sons, have recently begun to manufacture porcelain vases in the following permeant (sic) colours:– peach, lavender, lilac, mauve, celwyn, and the latest blue produced, viz., the Alexandra; which they decorate in a most tasteful manner with raised flowers and grapes, and gild them in a style quite original; these they feel certain will ensure the admiration and patronage of all who see them.'

HONOURABLE MENTION,
INTERNATIONAL EXHIBITION, 1862.
(The only one given for Parian.)

MESSRS. WILKINSON & SONS,
CHINA AND PARIAN
MANUFACTURERS,

Beg most respectfully to invite an inspection of their new Show Rooms, where they display the most varied assortment of Vases, Hot Water Jugs, &c., which for pureness of design, excellency of material, perfection of workmanship, and cheapness, cannot be surpassed.

Messrs. W. & Sons, have recently begun to manufacture Porcelain Vases in the following permeant colours:—Peach, Lavender, Lilac, Mauve, Celwyn, and the latest Blue produced, viz., the Alexandra; which they decorate in a most tasteful manner with raised flowers and grapes, and gild them in a style quite original; these they feel certain will ensure the admiration and patronage of all who see them.

HAVELOCK WORKS, BROAD ST.,
HANLEY.

Wilkinson & Sons. Advertisement from 1864 Jones.

Wilkinson, A.J., Ltd.
Royal Staffordshire Pottery, Burslem
1896 Kelly EM
1900 Kelly EM

Wilkinson, Arthur James
(i) Central Pottery, Market Place, Burslem
1884 Kelly EM
1887 Porter EM-B
1888 Kelly EM
1889 Keates P-B (earthenware)
1892 Keates P-B (earthenware)
1892 Kelly EM
(ii) Lower Works, Wood Street, Burslem
1889 Keates P-B (earthenware)
1892 Keates P-B (earthenware)
1892 Kelly EM

Wilkinson & Hulme
Central Pottery, Market Place, Burslem
1882 Keates P-B (earthenware)

Wilkinson & Rickhuss
50 Broad Street, Hanley
1860 Kelly PM
1861 Harrison NC-H-Sh (parian and china manufacturers)
1862 Slater CM; PM

Wilkinson, Rickhuss & Toft
Broad Street, Shelton
1856 Kelly PM

Williams & Co.
Clayton Street, Longton
1867 Keates P-L (china)
See also: Williams, James

Williams, James
Ashford Works, Clayton Street, Longton
An advertisement for Joseph Edward Moston in 1869 Keates states that he succeeded James Williams, but no record of any potter of this name could be located in the directories. The reference may relate to Williams & Co. (qv).

Williams, Thomas
(i) Sylvester Square, Burslem
1863 Kelly EM (brown, black & lustre)
(ii) Hall Street, Burslem
1870 Harrod NC-B (earthenware manufacturer)

Williams, Oakes & Co.
Albert Street, Burslem
1875 Keates P-B (Rockingham)

Williams, Turner & Co.
Albert Street, Burslem
1872 Kelly RM
1873 Keates P-B (Rockingham)

Williamson & Son
Bridge Pottery, Heathcote Road, Longton
1882 Keates P-L (china)
1889 Keates P-L (china and earthenware)
1892 Keates P-L (china & earthenware)

Williamson, H.M., & Co.
St. Martin's Lane, Market Street, Longton
An advertisement in 1865 Keates describes H.M. Williamson & Co. as 'decorators of china & earthenware in all its branches' and promises 'all orders entrusted to their care punctually attended to'. They are not listed as manufacturers.

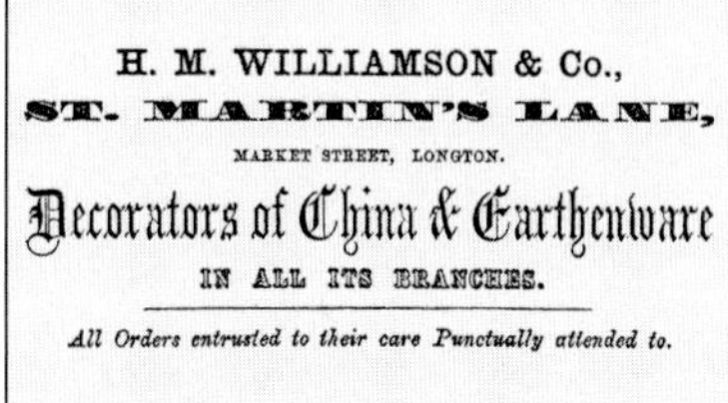

H.M. Williamson & Co. Advertisement from 1865 Keates.

Williamson, H.M., & Son
Waterloo Street, Longton
Advertisements appear in 1873 Keates and 1875 Keates for H.M. Williamson & Son, 'manufacturers of gilt china and earthenware', but no firm of this style is listed in the two directories or elsewhere.

H. M. WILLIAMSON & SON,
MANUFACTURERS OF
GILT CHINA AND EARTHENWARE,
WATERLOO STREET,
LONGTON.

H.M. Williamson & Son. Advertisement from 1873 Keates. The same advertisement appeared in 1875 Keates.

Williamson, Henry M., & Sons
Bridge Pottery, Heathcote Road, Longton
1880 Kelly CM (manufacturers of china for home & exports; special shapes for the American & Australian trade)
1887 Porter EM-L
1888 Kelly CM
1892 Kelly CM
1896 Kelly CM
1900 Kelly CM

Williamson, Thomas
Albert Street, Burslem
1870 Harrod NC-B (earthenware manufacturer)

Williamson & Son & Copestake
Bridge Works, Heathcote Road, Longton
1879 Keates P-L (china)

Williamson & Henshall
Longport
1802 Allbut EM (map location 21)

Williamson, Turner & Co.
Old Foley Pottery, Fenton
1869 Keates P-F
1869 Keates P-L (china and earthenware)
1870 Harrod NC-F (china and earthenware manufac.)

Willshaw & Sadler
Moorland Road, Burslem
1887 Porter EM-B

Wilshaw & Wood
See: Wiltshaw & Wood

Wilson, David
Hanley
1802 Allbut EM (map location 71)
1805 Holden NC (china and earthenware manufacturer)
1809 Holden NC (china & earthenware-manufacturer)
1811 Holden NC (china & earthenware manufacturer)

David Wilson (& Son). Impressed mark from a sprigged earthenware dish.

Wilson, David, & Son
High Street, Hanley
1816 Underhill P
1818 Pigot EM

Wilson, David, & Sons
High Street, Hanley
1818 Parson EM-H-Sh
The firm is noted as being in the hands of assignees.

Wilson, James
(i) Etruscan Works, High Street, Longton
1879 Keates P-L (parian)
1880 Kelly PM
1882 Keates P-L (parian)
(ii) Gregory Street, Longton
1884 Kelly CM; PM
1887 Porter EM-L
1888 Kelly CM
1889 Keates P-L (parian figure, &c.)
1892 Keates P-L (parian figure &c.)
1892 Kelly SC (China Parian Manufacturer)
1896 Kelly SC (China Parian Manufacturer)

Wilson, Robert
Hanley

1796 Chester NC-H-Sh (manufacturer of earthenware)
1798 Universal NC-H (manufacturer of Staffordshire-ware)

Wilson, S.T.
41 Duke Street, Fenton
1900 Kelly EM

Wilson & Breeze
Hanley
1811 Holden NC (earthenware-manufs.)
1816 Underhill P

Wilson & Green
Burslem
1809 Holden NC (earthenware-manufac.)
1811 Holden NC (earthenware manufacturers)

Wiltshaw, S.T., & Co.
Market Street, Longton
1896 Kelly CM

Wiltshaw & Robinson
Copeland Street, Stoke
1892 Keates P-S (earthenware)
1892 Kelly EM
1896 Kelly EM
1900 Kelly EM

Wiltshaw & Wood
Albert Street, Burslem
1873 Keates P-B (door furniture)
The first partner's name is actually listed as Wilshaw.

Wiltshaw, Wood & Co.
Albert Street Works, Burslem
1870 Harrod NC-B (manufacturers of mortice-lock furniture, finger-plates, shutter and hall-door knobs, drawer knobs, beer engine and other handles, castor bowls, bedstead vases, and rosettes, jug-stands, door-labels, &c.)
1872 Kelly SC (Beer Machine Handle Makers – China); SC (China & Porcelain Door Furniture Manufacturers)

Winkle, Frederick, & Co.
Colonial Pottery, Stoke
1892 Keates P-S (opaque porcelain)
1892 Kelly EM
1896 Kelly EM
1900 Kelly EM

Winkle & Wood
(i) Pearl Pottery, Marsh Street, Hanley
1887 Porter EM-H
(ii) Brook Street, Hanley
1888 Kelly EM
(iii) Colonial Pottery, Stoke
1889 Keates A; P-S (opaque porcelain)
The advertisement in 1889 Keates is listed as being inside the back cover but no copy could be located with the original binding.

Withinshaw, W.E.
(i) Crown Works and Lyndhurst Street, Burslem
1873 Keates P-B (earthenware)
(ii) Commercial Street, Burslem
1875 Keates P-B (earthenware)

Wittingham & Ford
See: Whittingham & Ford

Wittinshaw, William Edward
Church Street, Burslem
1876 Kelly EM

Wolf, Thomas
See: Wolfe, Thomas

Wolfe, Thomas
(i) Stoke
1781 Bailey NC (potter)
1783 Bailey NC (potter)
1784 Bailey NC-S (manufacturer of Queen's ware in general, blue, printed and Egyptian black, cane, &c.)
1796 Chester NC-S (manufacturer of earthenware)
1798 Universal NC-S (manufacturer of Staffordshire-ware)
1818 Parson EM-S-E
1818 Pigot CM; EM
(ii) Lower Lane
1796 Chester NC-LE-LD-LL (manufacturer of earthenware)
Wolfe is listed as Thomas junior in 1781 Bailey and 1783 Bailey. The surname is listed as Woolfe in 1784 Bailey and as Wolf in 1818 Parson.

Wolfe & Hamilton
Stoke
1802 Allbut EM (map location 102)
1805 Holden NC (china and earthenware manufacturers)
1809 Holden NC (manufacturers of china & earthenware)
1811 Holden NC (manufacturers of china & earthenware)
1816 Underhill P
A Liverpool address at 42 Old Dock is listed in 1809 Holden and 1811 Holden.

Wood Brothers
Chapel Lane, Burslem
1872 Kelly RM
1873 Keates P-B (Rockingham)

Wood & Co.
(i) Pinnox Works, Great Woodland Street, Tunstall
1865 Keates P-T (earthenware)
(ii) Mount Pleasant, High Street, Longton
1867 Keates P-L (china)
1869 Keates P-L (china)
1870 Harrod NC-L (china manufacturers, home and export)
(iii) Bagnall Street, Longton
1869 Keates P-L (china)
(iv) Albert Street, Burslem
1875 Keates P-B (earthenware)
(v) New Wharf Pottery, Navigation Road, Burslem
1879 Keates P-B (earthenware)
1882 Keates P-B (earthenware)
1889 Keates P-B (earthenware)
1892 Keates P-B (earthenware)
(vi) Boothen Road Tile Works, Stoke
1887 Porter SC-S (Tile Manufacturers)
1889 Keates SC-S (Tile - Encaustic - Manufacturers); SC-S (Tile - Floor - Manufacturers)
1892 Keates SC-S (Tile - Encaustic - Manufacturers); SC-S (Tile - Floor - Manufacturers)
1892 Kelly SC (Encaustic Tile Manufacturers)

Wood & Son
Trent Pottery, Furlong Lane, Burslem
1880 Kelly EM
1882 Keates P-B (earthenware)
1888 Kelly EM
1889 Keates P-B (earthenware)
1892 Keates P-B (earthenware)

1892 Kelly EM
1896 Kelly EM
1900 Kelly EM

Wood, Son & Co.
Villa Pottery, Cobridge
1869 Keates P-B (earthen.)
1870 Harrod NC-B (earthenware manufacturers for United States)
1872 Kelly EM
1873 Keates P-B (earthenware)
1875 Keates P-B (earthenware)
1876 Kelly EM
1879 Keates P-B (earthenware)

Wood, Abraham
Waterloo Road, Burslem
1841 Pigot TOCM

Wood, Ambrose
Regent House, Regent Road, Hanley
1884 Kelly SC (Encaustic Tile Manufacturers) (merchants)
1888 Kelly SC (Encaustic Tile Manufacturers)

Wood, Ambrose, & Co.
Waterloo Road, Burslem
1841 Pigot EM (Egyptian black, &c.)

Wood, Edmund Thomas Wedgwood
Woodland Pottery, Woodland Street, Tunstall
1860 Kelly EM
1861 Harrison NC-T (earthenware manufacturer)
1862 Slater EM
1863 Kelly EM
1864 Jones EM
1865 Keates P-T (earthenware)
1867 Keates P-T (earthenware)
1868 Kelly EM
1869 Keates P-T (earthenware)
1870 Harrod NC-T (earthenware manufacturer for United States)
1872 Kelly EM
1873 Keates P-T (earthenware)
1875 Keates P-T (earthenware)

Wood, Enoch
Fountain Place, Burslem
1846 Williams NC-B

Wood, Enoch, & Sons
Fountain Place, Burslem
1822 Allbut CEM (china and earthenware manufacts.)
1822 Pigot CM; EM
1828 Pigot EM
1830 Pigot EM
1834 White EM-B (china mfrs. also)
1835 Pigot EM (and borax)

Enoch Wood & Sons. Impressed and printed marks from a blue-printed earthenware dinner plate.

Enoch Wood & Sons. Printed mark from a blue-printed earthenware tea plate.

Wood, Enoch & Edward
Fountain Place, Burslem
1841 Pigot CM; EM

Wood, Enoch & Ralph
Burslem
1784 Bailey NC-B (manufacturers of all kinds of useful and ornamental earthen ware, Egyptian black, cane, and various other colours, also black figures, seals and cyphers)

Wood, Ephraim
(i) Hole House, Burslem
1818 Parson EM-B-Lp-C
(ii) Burslem
1822 Allbut CEM (figure maker and enameller)
(iii) Wood's Bank, Burslem
1828 Pigot EM (toy only)
(iv) St. John's Square, Burslem
1830 Pigot EM (toy only)

Wood, George
(i) Marsh Street, Shelton
1850 Kelly NC-Sh (china toy manufacturer)
1850 Slater TOCM
(ii) Hope Street, Shelton
1851 White CETOM-H-Sh
1854 Kelly PM (ornamental figure makers)
(iii) Bryan Street, Hanley
1852 Slater PM
(iv) Slippery Lane, Broad Street, Hanley
1864 Jones PM

Wood, Henry James
(i) Chapel Lane, Burslem
1884 Kelly JM; RM
1887 Porter EM-B
(ii) Alexandra Works, Navigation Road, Burslem
1888 Kelly JM; RM
1889 Keates P-B (manufacturer)
1892 Keates P-B
1892 Kelly JRM
1896 Kelly JRM
1900 Kelly JRM

Wood, J., & Co.
Mount Pleasant, Longton
1868 Kelly CM

Wood, Jacob
Waterloo Road, Burslem
1852 Slater SC (Saggar Maker) (chimney pot)

Wood, John
(i) Burslem
1781 Bailey NC (potter)
1783 Bailey NC (potter)
1784 Bailey NC-B (potter)
1798 Universal NC-B (manufacturer of Staffordshire-

ware)
(ii) Brownhills
1796 Chester NC-T-Lp (manufacturer of earthenware)
1802 Allbut EM (map location 18)
1805 Holden NC (earthenware manufacturer)
1809 Holden NC (earthenware-manufacturer)
1811 Holden NC (earthenware manufacturer)
1816 Underhill P
(iii) Tunstall
1818 Pigot EM

Wood, John
See: Dimmock & Co.
See: Wood & Brownfield

Wood, John Wedg
(i) Hadderidge Bank, Burslem
1841 Pigot EM
(ii) Woodland Street, Tunstall
1850 Slater EM
1851 White EM-T
1852 Slater EM
1854 Kelly CEM
1856 Kelly CEM
(iii) Brownhills
1851 White CEM-B (both)
The second name is listed as Wedge in 1841 Pigot. Wood's house is listed as Big House, Burslem, in 1851 White.

Wood, Josiah
Burslem
1784 Bailey NC-B (manufacturer of fine black, glazed, variegated and cream coloured ware and blue)

Wood, Ralph
Burslem
1796 Chester NC-B (manufacturer of earthenware)
1798 Universal NC-B (manufacturer of Staffordshire-ware)
1802 Allbut EM (map location 27)

Wood, Samuel
Hanley
1818 Pigot EM

Wood, Thomas
(i) Paradise Street, Tunstall
1865 Keates P-T (earthenware)
(ii) Queen Street, Burslem
1889 Keates P-B (manufacturer)

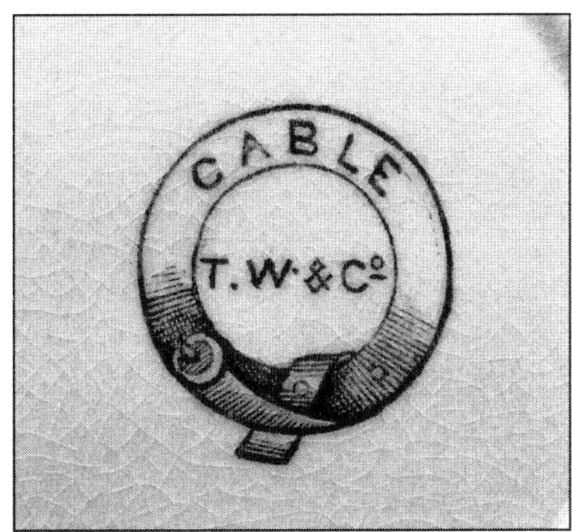

Thomas Wood & Co. Printed mark from brown-printed earthenware teawares made for a Primitive Methodist Chapel near Andover.

Wood, Thomas, & Co.
Queen Street, Burslem
1887 Porter EM-B
1888 Kelly EM

Wood, Thomas, & Son
Queen Street, Burslem
1892 Keates P-B

Wood, Thomas, & Sons
Queen Street, Burslem
1892 Kelly EM
1896 Kelly EM

Wood, Thomas F.
See: New Wharf Pottery Co.
See: Newport Wharf Pottery Co.

Wood, William
George Street, Shelton
1852 Slater EM (yellow)

Wood, William, & Co.
(i) Burslem
1802 Allbut EM (map location 52)
(ii) Albert Street Works, Albert Street, Burslem
1876 Kelly EM
1879 Keates P-B (door furniture)
1880 Kelly SC (Lock Furniture Makers – China)
1882 Keates P-B (door furniture)
1884 Kelly EM; SC (Lock Furniture Makers – China)
1887 Porter EM-B
1888 Kelly EM; SC (Door Furniture Makers – China)
1889 Keates P-B (door furniture)
1892 Keates P-B (door furniture)
1892 Kelly EM
1896 Kelly EM
1900 Kelly EM
An advertisement in 1882 Keates describes the firm as 'manufacturers of china mortice lock furniture, finger plates, shutter, drawer, and hall door knobs, door labels, sewing machine, scoop, coal vase, & other handles, bedstead knobs, castor bowls, inkstands and wells, match pots, umbrella and walking stick knobs and handles, lemon squeezers, and all kinds of ware used by brassfounders, japanners, electro-platers, &c., &c.' and boasts 'first awards and medals at the Sydney and Adelaide Exhibition, and two second awards at the Melbourne Exhibition'.
Another long advertisement appears in 1889 Keates and 1892 Keates describing the firm as 'manufacturers of china mortice, rim, and latch

ALBERT STREET WORKS,
BURSLEM,
STAFFORDSHIRE POTTERIES.
WILLIAM WOOD & Co.,
MANUFACTURERS OF
China Mortice Lock Furniture, Finger Plates,
Shutter, Drawer, and Hall Door Knobs, Door Labels
Sewing Machine, Scoop, Coal Vase, & other Handles,
Bedstead Knobs, Castor Bowls,
Inkstands and Wells, Match Pots, Umbrella and Walking
Stick Knobs and Handles,
Lemon Squeezers, and all kinds of Ware used by Brass-
founders, Japanners, Electro-Platers, &c., &c.
First Awards and Medals at the Sydney and Adelaide Exhibition, and two
Second Awards at the Melbourne Exhibition.

William Wood & Co. Advertisement from 1882 Keates.

William Wood & Co.,
ALBERT STREET WORKS, BURSLEM
MANUFACTURERS OF
CHINA
Mortice, Rim, and Latch Furniture
(Wood's, Wilks', Duce's, Pitt's, Mace's, and other Patents),
Door Plates, Shutter and Hall Door Knobs, Number Plates,
Scoop and Perambulator Handles, and all sorts of China
Articles used by Brassfounders, Electroplaters, Japanners;
also Switches, Ceiling Rose Suspenders, &c., used by
Electricians;
also Stationers' and Druggists' China Sundries;
also Tiles for Hearths, Stoves, &c.

William Wood & Co. Advertisement from 1892 Keates. The same advertisement had also appeared in 1892 Keates.

furniture (Wood's, Wilks', Duce's, Pitt's, Mace's, and other patents), door plates, shutter and hall door knobs, number plates, scoop and perambulator handles, and all sorts of china articles used by brassfounders, electroplaters, japanners; also switches, ceiling rose suspenders, &c., used by electricians; also stationers' and druggists' china sundries; also tiles for hearths, stoves, &c.'

Wood & Baggaley
Hill Works, Burslem
1870 Harrod NC-B (earthenware manufacturers)
1872 Kelly EM
1873 Keates P-B (earthenware)
1875 Keates P-B (earthenware)
1876 Kelly EM
1879 Keates P-B (earthenware)
1882 Keates P-B (earthenware)

Wood (Thomas), & Barker
Queen Street, Burslem
1900 Kelly EM

Wood & Bennett
Brook Street, Hanley
1892 Kelly EM

Wood & Blood
High Street, Lane End
1828 Pigot EM

Wood & Brettell
Brownhills, Burslem
1818 Parson EM-G-T-R
1818 Pigot EM
1822 Allbut CEM (earthenware manufacts.)
1822 Pigot EM
The second partner's name is listed as Brittell in 1818 Parson.

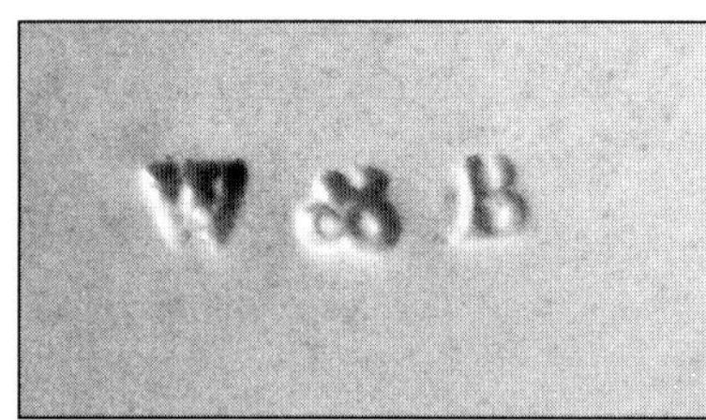

Wood & Brettell. Impressed mark from a blue-printed earthenware dinner plate.

Wood & Brittell
See: Wood & Brettell

Wood & Brownfield
Cobridge
1841 Pigot EM (and improved iron stone)
1846 Williams NC-C-F-E (manufacturers)
1850 Slater EM
The partners are listed individually as John Wood of Cobridge and William Brownfield of Market Street, Hanley, in 1846 Williams.

Wood & Brownfield. Printed mark from a blue-printed stone china dinner plate.

Wood & Brownfield. Impressed publication mark from a relief-moulded stoneware jug.

Wood & Caldwell
(i) Burslem
1796 Chester NC-B (manufacturers of earthenware)
1798 Universal NC-B (manufacturer of Staffordshire-ware)
1802 Allbut EM (map location 28)
1805 Holden NC (china and earthenware manufacturers)
1809 Holden NC (china & earthenware-manufacturers)
1811 Holden NC (china & earthenware manufacturers)
1816 Underhill P
(ii) Fountain Place, Burslem
1818 Parson EM-B-Lp-C
(iii) High Street, Burslem
1818 Pigot CM; EM
The firm is listed as Caldwell, Wood in 1798 Universal.

Wood & Challinor
(i) Brownhills
1828 Pigot EM
1830 Pigot EM
(ii) Woodland, Tunstall
1834 White EM-T
(iii) Tunstall
1835 Pigot EM
1841 Pigot EM

Wood & Challinor. Printed mark from a blue-printed earthenware soup plate.

Wood, Challinor & Co.
(i) Well Street Pottery, Tunstall
1860 Kelly EM
1861 Harrison NC-T (earthenware manufacturers)
(ii) Sandyford, Tunstall
1862 Slater EM
1863 Kelly EM
1864 Jones EM

Wood & Clarke
Church Works, Burslem
1872 Kelly EM

Wood, Hines & Winkle
Pearl Pottery, Brook Street, Hanley
1884 Kelly EM

Wood, Hines & Winkles
Brook Street, Hanley
1882 Keates P-H (earthenware)

Wood & Hulme
Garfield Pottery Works, Waterloo Road, Burslem
1882 Keates P-B

1884 Kelly EM
1887 Porter EM-B
1888 Kelly EM
1889 Keates P-B
1892 Keates P-B
1892 Kelly EM
1896 Kelly EM
1900 Kelly EM

Wood, Morgan & Co.
Liverpool Road, Burslem
1865 Keates P-B (earthen.)
1867 Keates P-B (earthenware)

Wood & Pigott
Well Street, Tunstall
1869 Keates P-T
1870 Harrod NC-T (earthenware manufacturers)
The second partner's name is listed as Piggott in 1870 Harrod.

Wood, Rathbone & Co.
Cobridge
1868 Kelly EM

Woodall & Hulme
Washington Works, Waterloo Road, Burslem
1879 Keates P-B (china, porcelain, and door furniture)

Woodward, William
Marsh Street, Shelton
1834 White CETM-H-Sh
1835 Pigot TOCM (fine)

Woolfe, Thomas
See: Wolfe, Thomas

Wooliscroft, G.
See: Woolliscroft, G.

Wooliscroft, G., & Co.
See: Woolliscroft, G., & Co.

Wooliscroft, George
See: Woolliscroft, George

Woolley, J.
Stafford Street, Longton
1854 Kelly TM

Woolliscroft & Co.
Sandyford, Tunstall
1861 Harrison NC-T (earthenware manufacturers)

Woolliscroft, G.
Amicable Street, Tunstall
1854 Kelly CEM
The surname is listed as Wooliscroft in 1854 Kelly.

Woolliscroft, G., & Co.
Sandyford, Tunstall
1856 Kelly CEM
1860 Kelly EM
1863 Kelly EM
The surname is listed as Wooliscroft in 1856 Kelly.

Woolliscroft, George
(i) Well Street, Tunstall
1851 White EM-T
(ii) High Street, Tunstall
1852 Slater EM
(iii) Sandyford Potteries, Tunstall
1864 Jones EM
(iv) Etruscan Street, Etruria
1887 Porter SC-H (Tile Manufacturer)
The surname is listed as Wooliscroft in 1852 Slater.

Woolliscroft, George, & Son
(i) Chesterton
1876 Kelly SC (Encaustic Tile Manufacturers)
(ii) Canal Tileries, Etruria
1880 Kelly SC (Encaustic Tile Manufacturers)
(iii) Patent Tile Works, Canal Side, Eastwood, Hanley
1882 Keates SC-H (Floor Tile Manufacturers)
1884 Kelly SC (Encaustic Tile Manufacturers)
(iv) Patent Tile Works, Nelson Place, Joiner's Square, Hanley
1888 Kelly SC (Encaustic Tile Manufacturers)
1892 Kelly SC (Encaustic Tile Manufacturers)
A long advertisement in 1882 Keates describes the firm as 'manufacturers of blue bricks, roof, ridge, and floor tiles, and all kinds of Staffordshire goods' and lists three works, at Chesterton Tileries; Canal Tileries, Etruria; and Encaustic Tile Works, Hanley. It includes a paragraph about bricks, tiles and stone, and also promotes 'tesselated glazed hearth and wall tiles'.

Woolliscroft, George, & Son Ltd.
(i) Patent Tile Works, Nelson Place, Joiner's Square, Hanley
1896 Kelly SC (Encaustic Tile Manufacturers)
(ii) Melville Street, Hanley
1900 Kelly A; SC (Ecclesiastical Decoration Manufacturers); SC (Enamelled Tile Manufacturers); SC (Encaustic Tile Manufacturers); SC (Ironstone Adamant Tile Manufacturers)
Despite the cross-reference, no advertisement could be located in 1900 Kelly (three copies).

Woolliscroft & Galley
Sandyford, Tunstall
1862 Slater EM

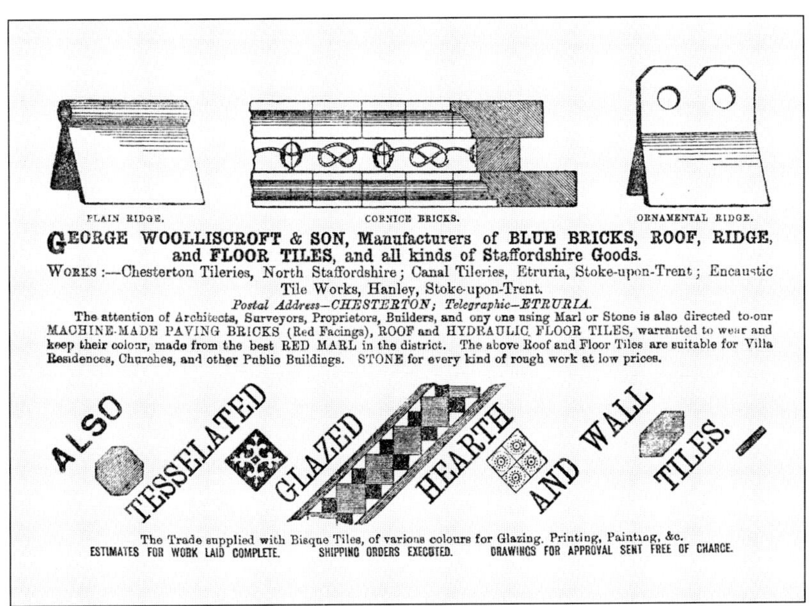

George Woolliscroft & Son. Advertisement from 1882 Keates.

Worthington & Son
(i) 20 Clarence Street, Hanley
1863 Kelly EM
1864 Jones EM
1865 Keates A; P-H (earthenware and majolica)
1887 Porter EM-H
(ii) Brook Street, Hanley
1867 Keates A; P-H (figures)
1868 Kelly EM
1869 Keates A; P-H (earthenware)
1870 Harrod NC-H (manufacturers of toilet ware figures, stoneware, dinner ware, &c., in great varieties, for home and foreign markets)
1872 Kelly EM
1873 Keates A; P-H (earthenware)
1875 Keates A; P-H (earthenware)
1876 Kelly EM
1879 Keates P-H (earthenware)
1880 Kelly EM
1882 Keates P-H (earthenware and china figures)
1884 Kelly EM
1887 Porter EM-H

The directory entry in 1869 Keates lists the firm as Worthington & Sons although the advertisement is for Worthington & Son. The advertisement in 1865 Keates describes the firm as 'manufacturers of majolica, ornamental toilet ware, etc. Ships supplied with every description of pottery, crests, &c.' The next advertisement, in both 1867 Keates and 1869 Keates, describes them as 'manufacturers of toilet ware, in great variety, ornamental china figures, and stoneware and coloured bodies'. The last advertisement, in both 1873 Keates and 1875 Keates, describes them simply as 'earthenware manufacturers'.

WORTHINGTON & SON,
MANUFACTURERS of MAJOLICA,
ORNAMENTAL TOILET WARE, ETC.
Ships supplied with every description of Pottery, Crests, &c.
CLARENCE STREET, HANLEY.

Worthington & Son. Advertisement from 1865 Keates.

MESSRS. WORTHINGTON & SON,
MANUFACTURERS OF
TOILET WARE,
IN GREAT VARIETY,
ORNAMENTAL CHINA FIGURES,
AND STONEWARE & COLOURED BODIES,
Brook Street Works, Hanley.

Worthington & Son. Advertisement from 1867 Keates. The same basic advertisement appeared in 1869 Keates.

WORTHINGTON & SON,
EARTHENWARE MANUFACTURERS,
BROOK STREET WORKS,
HANLEY.

Worthington & Son. Advertisement from 1873 Keates. The same basic advertisement appeared in 1875 Keates.

Worthington & Sons
See: Worthinton & Son

Worthington, Thomas
See: Worthington & Green

Worthington & Green
(i) Brook Street Works, Shelton, Hanley
1846 Williams NC-Sh (ornamental china manfrs.)
1850 Slater CM; EM
1854 Kelly PM (ornamental figure makers)
1861 Harrison NC-H-Sh (parian, china, and earthenware manufacturers)
1862 Slater CM; EM; PM; TOCM
1864 Jones A; EM
1865 Keates A; P-H (figures)
(ii) Booden Brook, Shelton
1850 Kelly NC-Sh (china figure manfctrs.)
1852 Slater CM; EM
1856 Kelly CFM
1860 Kelly CFM; CM-General
1863 Kelly CFM
(iii) Marsh Street, Shelton

The partners are listed individually as Thomas Worthington of Mill Street, Shelton, and James Green of John Street, Shelton, in 1846 Williams. The advertisements in 1864 Jones and 1865 Keates both describe the firm as 'manufacturers of toilet ware, in great variety, ornamental china figures, and stoneware and coloured bodies'.

MESSRS. WORTHINGTON & GREEN,
MANUFACTURERS OF
TOILET WARE,
IN GREAT VARIETY,
ORNAMENTAL CHINA FIGURES,
AND STONEWARE & COLOURED BODIES,
Brook Street, Works, Hanley

Worthington & Green. Advertisement from 1865 Keates. The same basic advertisement had also appeared in 1864 Jones.

Worthington & Harrop
(i) Mount Pleasant, Shelton
1856 Kelly CEM
1861 Harrison NC-H-Sh (parian manufacturer)
(ii) Tinkersclough, Hanley
1860 Kelly CFM; PM
1862 Slater PM
1863 Kelly CFM
1864 Jones PM
1865 Keates A; P-H (parian)
1867 Keates A; P-H (parian)
1868 Kelly PFM
1869 Keates P-H (parian)
1872 Kelly PM
(iii) Dresden Works, Tinkersclough, Hanley
1870 Harrod NC-H (manufacturers of parian figures, vases, and stoneware, for home and foreign markets)
1873 Keates A; P-H (parian)

The second partner's name is listed as Harop in 1856 Kelly. The advertisements in the Keates directories all describe the firm simply as 'parian manufacturers'. They give the address just as Tinkersclough in 1865 and 1867; as Mount Pleasant Works, Tinkersclough, in 1869; and as Dresden Works, Tinkersclough, in 1873.

WORTHINGTON & HARROP,
Parian Manufacturers,
TINKERSCLOUGH, HANLEY.

Worthington & Harrop. Advertisement from 1865 Keates. The same advertisement appeared in 1867 Keates.

WORTHINGTON & HARROP,
Parian Manufacturers,
Mount Pleasant Works,
TINKERSCLOUGH, HANLEY.

Worthington & Harrop. Advertisement from 1869 Keates. Note the addition of the works' name.

WORTHINGTON & HARROP,
Parian Manufacturers,
DRESDEN WORKS,
TINKERSCLOUGH, HANLEY.

Worthington & Harrop. Advertisement from 1873 Keates. Note the changed works' name.

Worthington, Ridgway & Harrop
Mount Pleasant, Tinkersclough, Hanley
1869 Keates A; P-H (china)
The advertisement in 1869 Keates describes the firm simply as 'china manufacturers', and gives their address as Dresden Works, Hanley.

WORTHINGTON, RIDGWAY & HARROP
CHINA
MANUFACTURERS,
DRESDEN WORKS,
HANLEY, STAFFORDSHIRE.

Worthington, Ridgway & Harrop. Advertisement from 1869 Keates.

Worthy, Mathias
Cobridge
1834 White ETM-B

Wright & Co.
William Street, Hanley
1888 Kelly EM

Wright, Thomas
(i) Hanley
1784 Bailey NC-H (potter)
1822 Allbut CEM (coarse ware manufact.)
(ii) Upper Green, Hanley
1818 Pigot EM
(iii) Upper High Street, Hanley
1822 Pigot EM

Wright, William
Upper High Street, Hanley
1828 Pigot EM (coarse)
1830 Pigot EM (coarse)

Wright, Burgess & Taylor
Amicable Street, Tunstall
1841 Pigot CM; EM

Wright & Rigby
Providence Pottery, Providence Place, Hanley
1882 Keates P-H (earthenware)

Wright & Simpson
New Street, Hanley
1850 Kelly NC-H (china figure manufacturers)
1850 Slater TOCM

Wyme, T.
See: Wynne, Thomas

Wynce, Thomas
See: Wynne, Thomas

Wynne, Thomas
(i) Flint Street, Longton
1850 Kelly CEM; NC-L (earthenware manufacturer)
1850 Slater EM
1852 Slater EM
(ii) Stafford Street, Longton
1851 White CEM-L (only earthenware)
1854 Kelly CEM
The potter's surname is listed as Wyme (CEM) and Wynce (NC-L) in 1850 Kelly. Wynne's house is listed as Edensor Place in 1851 White.
See also: Ray & Wynne

Y

Yale, W.
Liverpool Road, Stoke
1892 Keates A; P-S (porcelain slab and tile decorator); SC-S (Tile - Encaustic - Manufacturers) (slab & tile decorator)
The advertisement in 1892 Keates describes Yale as a 'decorator of porcelain slabs, &c., in sizes suitable for pictures, walls, fireplaces, stoves, hearths and cabinets' and offers 'high class work painted under and on glaze'.

W. Yale,
DECORATOR OF PORCELAIN SLABS, &c.,
In sizes suitable for Pictures, Walls, Fireplaces, Stoves, Hearths and Cabinets.
HIGH CLASS WORK PAINTED UNDER AND ON GLAZE.
LIVERPOOL ROAD, STOKE-ON-TRENT.

W. Yale. Advertisement from 1892 Keates.

Yale & Barker
Victoria Place, Longton
1841 Pigot EM

Yale, Barker & Hall
(i) Anchor Works, Longton
1846 Williams NC-L-LE (china and earthenware manufacturers)
(ii) Caroline Street, Longton
1850 Kelly NC-L (china & earthenware manufacturers); CEM
1850 Slater CM; EM
1852 Slater EM
(iii) Viaduct and Caroline Street Works, Longton
1851 White CEM-L
Two of the partners are listed individually as William Barker of Caroline Street and George Yale of Green Dock House in 1846 Williams.

Yates, John
(i) Shelton
1781 Bailey NC (potter)
1783 Bailey NC (potter)
1784 Bailey NC-Sh (potter)
1809 Holden NC (earthenware-manufacturer)
1811 Holden NC (earthenware manufacturer)
1816 Underhill P
1818 Pigot EM
1822 Allbut CEM (china and earthenware manufact.)
(ii) Hanley
1784 Bailey NC-H (potter)
(iii) Keeling's Lane, Hanley
1796 Chester NC-H-Sh (manufacturer of earthenware)
(iv) Broad Street, Shelton
1818 Parson EM-H-Sh

1822 Pigot EM
1828 Pigot CM; EM
1830 Pigot CM; EM
1834 White EM-H-Sh (china mfrs. also)
1835 Pigot CM; EM
The surname is listed as Yeates in 1818 Pigot.

Yates, John & William
Shelton
1796 Chester NC-H-Sh (manufacturers of earthenware)
1802 Allbut EM (map location 91)
1805 Holden NC (earthenware manufacturers)

Yates, William
Shelton
1798 Universal NC-Sh (manufacturer of Staffordshireware)

Yates & Bamford
Cobridge
1896 Kelly EM
1900 Kelly EM

Yates & May
Broad Street, Shelton
1841 Pigot EM

Yates & Shelley
Hanley
1802 Allbut EM (map location 69)

Yates, Sherwen & Co.
Shelton
1816 Underhill P

Yearsley, George
Market Lane, Longton
1860 Kelly PFM; PM
1861 Harrison NC-L (modeller, &c.)
1862 Slater PM
1863 Kelly PFM
1864 Jones PM
1865 Keates P-L (parian)
1867 Keates P-L (parian)
1868 Kelly PFM
1869 Keates P-L (parian and patentee of the gold astrakan trimming for decorating parian goods)
1870 Harrod NC-L (modeller, parian figure manufacturer)
1872 Kelly PM
1873 Keates P-L (parian and patentee of the gold astrakan trimming for decorating parian goods)
The address is listed as 14 Market Lane in 1862 Slater.

Yearsley, George, & Co.
Market Lane, Longton
1875 Keates P-L (parian and patentee of the gold astrakan trimming for decorating parian goods)

Yearsley, Mary Ann (Mrs.)
(i) Market Lane, Longton
1876 Kelly PM
1879 Keates P-L (parian and patentee of the gold astrakan trimming for decorating parian goods)
1880 Kelly PM
1882 Keates P-L (parian and patentee of the gold Astrakan trimming for decorating parian goods)
1887 Porter EM-L
(ii) 12 & 14 Market Lane, Longton
1884 Kelly PM
1888 Kelly PM
(iii) 14 & 16 Market Lane, Longton
1889 Keates P-L (parian, china, and earthenware)

Yeates, John
See: Yates, John

Young (Mr.)
See: Clementson and Young

APPENDIX I

ORIGINAL DIRECTORY LISTINGS

The directories covered in this work are listed in chronological order. For each directory, the abbreviated title is followed by the full title and details of the imprint (including author, compiler and publisher) exactly as they appear on the original title page. No attempt has been made to list the printers who are generally only of academic interest. The page or reference numbers in Goss, Norton, and Shaw & Tipper are given where relevant. When appropriate, this information is followed by discussion of the date of the directory, ranging from simple statements of any exact dates which may appear on the title page or elsewhere in the volume, through to explanations of estimated dates.

General comments on the content of the directory are then followed by exact copies of relevant sections. The temptation to incorporate corrections has been resisted in this chapter, however obvious they may appear. The originals contain many errors in alphabetical order, in the spelling of names, both of people and places, and in punctuation, quite apart from simple typographical errors. All such corrections, together with related interpretation, have been reserved for the alphabetical list of manufacturers in Chapter 5. It is important to note that many of the publishers were not local and would not be familiar with the names and places listed.

As a general rule, the lists reproduced here include only manufacturers based in the Potteries, and are in the form either of classification listings or extracts from longer alphabetical lists where appropriate. Each of the headings is followed by its page numbers in the original directory. Entries which are not relevant to this work have generally been omitted. Such omissions include importers and dealers, pottery trades other than manufacturing, and manufacturers outside the Potteries. In classified lists there are often cross-references such as 'Earthenware Manufacturers – see China and Earthenware Manufacturers' or 'Parian Manufacturers - see Potters'. These are felt to be of little consequence and have not been included here.

A few directories are listed for completeness only (1787 and 1789 Tunnicliff, 1808 Holden, 1836 Cottrill, 1842 and 1844 Pigot, 1845 and 1878 Kelly). This is normally because they are only reprints of earlier issues, but may be because they include no relevant entries. In these cases, the preliminary details are still given in full and explanations of their relevance are given, but no detailed lists are reproduced.

In the original directories some entries are given prominence by either capital letters or by typesetting in bold characters. There appears to be no consistent reason for such prominence, and in some cases it may have been promoted as an option by the publisher at some special charge. All such entries are indicated here by the use of capital letters. A few abbreviations also occur, examples being:

P.R. Private residence
T.A. Telegraphic address
T.N. Telephone number

Additional guidance is given, where necessary, in the section for each individual directory.

1781 Bailey

Bailey's Northern Directory, or, Merchant's and Tradesman's Useful Companion, For the Year 1781, W. Bailey, Warrington (Goss p.62, Norton 1).

This directory is not classified. The following list of potters has been extracted from the section for 'Newcastle under Line, and Neighbourhood' (pages 255-257).

Adams William and Co. potters, Burslem
Baddeley Ralph, potter, Shelton
Bacchus William, potter, Fenton
Barker Thomas, potter, Lane delf
Bell and Wolfe, potters. Stoke
Blackwell John, potter, Cobridge
Booth Hugh, potter, Stoke
Boone Joseph, potter, Hanley
Bourne Edward, potter, Longport
Brindley John, potter, Longport
Bucknall Ralph and Son, potters, Cobridge
Chatterley Charles and Ephraim, potters, Hanley
Clowes William and Co. potters, Longport
Daniel Walter, potter, Burslem
Daniel Thomas,. Potter, Burslem
Edwards William, potter, Lane delf
Garner Robert, potter, Lane end
Godwin Thomas and Benj. potters, Cobridge
Hales and Adams, potters, ditto
Harrison John, jun. potter, Stoke
Heath and Bagnall, potters, Shelton
Hollins Samuel, potter, Shelton
Keeling Anthony, potter, Tunstall
Mare John and Richard, potters, Hanley
Myatt Richard, potter, Lane end
Neale James and Co: potters, Hanley
Philips Thomas, potter, Lane end
Perry Samuel and Co. potters, Hanley
Pratt William, potter, Lane delf
Pickance and Daniel, potters, Cobridge
Robinson and Smith, potters, Cobridge
Shelley Thomas, potter, Lane end
Shelley Michael, potter, Lane end
Spode Josiah, potter, Stoke
Smith Thomas and Co. potters, Burslem
Turner John, potter, Lane end
Twemlow Geo. & Thomas, potters, Shelton
Wedgewood Joseph Esq. potter to her Majesty, Etruria
Wedgewood Thomas, potter, Burslem
Warburton Joseph, potter, Stoke
Warburton Jacob, potter, Cobridge
Wolfe Thomas, jun. potter, Stoke
Wood John, potter, Burslem
Yates John, potter, Shelton

1783 Bailey

Bailey's Western and Midland Directory; or, Merchant's and Tradesman's Useful Companion, For the Year, 1783, W. Bailey, Birmingham (Goss p.64, Norton 2). Dated MDCCLXXXIII on the title page.

The potters listed in this directory are the same as in 1781 Bailey with only minor changes to the typesetting. In view of the fact that alterations in the relevant section are limited to attorneys and a few other traders, and that there were a large number of changes in the subsequent edition (1784 Bailey), it seems probable that no new survey was carried out.

The directory is not classified. The following list of potters has been extracted from the section for 'Newcastle-under-Line, Staffordshire, and Neighbouring Potteries' (pages 283-285).

Adams, William, and Co. Potters, Burslem
Baddeley, Ralph, ditto, Shelton
Bacchus, William, Potter, Fenton
Barker, Thomas, ditto, Lane Delf
Bell and Wolfe, Potters, Stoke
Blackwell, John, Potter, Cobridge
Booth, Hugh, ditto, Stoke
Boone, Joseph, ditto, Hanley
Bourne, Edward, Potter, Longport
Brindley John, Potter, Longport
Bucknall, Ralph, and Son, Potters, Cobridge
Chatterley, Charles and Ephraim, Potters, Hanley
Clowes, William, and Co. ditto, Longport
Daniel, Walter, ditto, Burslem
Daniel, Thomas, ditto, ditto
Edwards, William, ditto, Lane Delf
Garner, Robert, Potter, Lane End
Godwin, Thomas and Benjamin, ditto, Cobridge
Hales and Adams, ditto, ditto
Harrison, John, jun. Potter, Stoke
Heath and Bagnall, ditto, Shelton
Hollins, Samuel, Potter, Shelton
Keeling, Anthony, Potter, Tunstall
Mare, John and Richard, Potters, Hanley
Myatt, Richard, ditto, Lane End
Neale, James, and Co. ditto, Hanley
Philips, Thomas, ditto, Lane End
Perry, Samuel, and Co. ditto, Hanley
Pratt, William, ditto, Lane Delf
Pickance and Daniel, ditto, Cobridge
Robinson and Smith, Potters, Cobridge
Shelly, Thomas, Potter, Lane End
Shelly, Michael, ditto, ditto
Spode, Josiah, ditto, Stoke

Smith, Thomas, and Co. Potters, Burslem
Turner, John, Potter, Lane End
Twemlow, George, and Thomas, ditto, Shelton
Wedgewood, J. Esq. ditto, to her Majesty, Etruria
Wedgewood, Thomas, ditto, Burslem
Warburton, Joseph, Potter, Stoke
Warburton, Jacob, ditto, Cobridge
Wolfe, Thomas, jun. ditto, Stoke
Wood, John, ditto Burslem
Yates, John, ditto, Shelton

1784 Bailey

Bailey's British Directory; or, Merchant's and Trader's Useful Companion, For the Year 1784, in Four Volumes. Volume the Second. The Western Directory, The First Edition, William Bailey, 53 Basinghall Street, London (Goss p.65, Norton 3). Dated MDCCLXXXIV on the title page. The complete directory consists of four volumes. The dedication 'to the Public' in Volume 1 is dated 4 June 1784, and refers to the publication of Volume 2 'without fail, the beginning of July'. The dedications in both Volume 2 and Volume 4 are not dated. The title pages of Volumes 1 and 2 refer to William Bailey as the author. Volume 4 was printed by W. Bailey & Co.

This directory is not classified but consists of alphabetical lists of traders for the various towns and villages in a section titled 'Potteries, in Staffordshire' (pages 390-393 in Volume 2). The following lists of potters have been extracted for the towns or villages as shown.

Burslem, near Newcastle, Staffordshire (pages 390-391)
ADAMS, William, and Co. Manufacturers of cream coloured Ware, and China glazed Ware painted
Bagley, William, Potter
Bourne, John, Manufacturer of China glaze, blue painted, enamelled, and cream colour Earthen Ware
Bourne and Malkin, Manufacturers of China glazed, blue, and cream colour Ware
Cartlidge, S. and J. Potters
Daniel, Thomas, Potter
Daniel, John, Manufacturer of cream colour and red Earthen Ware
Daniel, Timothy, Manufacturer of cream colour and red Earthen Ware
Daniel, Walter, Manufacturer of cream colour and red Earthen Ware
Graham, John, Jun. Manufacturer of white stone Earthen Ware, enamelled white and cream colour
Green, John, Potter
Holland, Thomas, Manufacturer of black and red China Ware and Gilder
Keeling, Anthony, Manufacturer of Queen's Ware in general, blue painted and enamelled Egyptian Black, Tunstal, near Burslem
Lockett, Timothy, and John, White Stone Potters, Burslem
Malkin, Burnham, Potter, Burslem
Robinson, John, Enameller and Printer of Cream colour and China glazed Ware, Burslem
Rogers, John, and George, Manufacturers of China glazed Blue painted Wares, and Cream coloured, Burslem
Smith, Ambrose, and Co. Manufacturers of Cream coloured Ware, and China glazed Ware painted Blue, Burslem
Smith, John, and Joseph, Potters, Burslem
Stevenson, Charles, and Son, Manufacturers of Cream coloured Ware, Blue painted, &c. Burslem
Wedgwood, Thomas, Manufacturer of Cream coloured Ware, and China glazed Ware, painted with Blue, &c. Big House
Wedgwood, Thomas, Manufacturer of Cream coloured Ware, and China glazed Ware, painted with Blue, &c. Over House
Wood, John, Potter, Burslem
Wood, Enoch, and Ralph, Manufacturers of all kinds of useful and ornamental Earthen Ware, Egyptian Black, Cane, and various other Colours, also Black Figures, Seals and Cyphers, Burslem
Wood, Josiah, Manufacturer of fine Black, glazed, variegated and Cream coloured Ware and Blue

Cobridge, near Newcastle, Staffordshire (page 391)
BLACKWELL, Joseph, Manufacturer of Blue and White Stone Ware, Cream and painted Wares
Blackwell, John, Manufacturer of Blue and White Stone Ware, Cream and painted Wares
Burknall, Robert, Manufacturer of Queen's Ware, Blue painted, enamelled, printed, &c.
Godwin, Thomas, and Benjamin, Manufacturers of Queen's Ware and China glazed Blue
Hales and Adams, Potters
Robinson and Smith, Potters
Warburton, Jacob, Potter

Handley, near Newcastle, Staffordshire (page391)
Bagnall, Sampson, Potter
Boon, Joseph, Potter
Chatterley, C. and E. Potters
Glass, John, Potter
Heath, Warburton, and Co. China Manufacturers
Keeling, Edward, Potter
Mare, John, and Richard, Potters
Mayer, Elijah, Enameller
Miller, William, Potter
Neale and Wilson, Potters
Perry, Samuel, Potter
Taylor, George, Potter
Wright, Thomas, Potter
Yates, John, Potter

Shelton, near Newcastle, Staffordshire (page 392)
Baddeley, J. and E. Potters
Hassells, John, Potter
Heath and Bagnell, Potters
Hollins, Samuel, Potter
Keeling, Anthony, Potter
Taylor and Pope, Potters
Twemlow, G. Potter
Whitehead, Christopher Charles, Potter
Yates, John, Potter

Stoke, near Newcastle, Staffordshire (page 392)
Bell, Sarah, Potter
Booth, Hugh, Manufacturer of China, China glaze, and Queen's Ware in all its various Branches
Brindley, James, Potter
Spode, Josiah, Potter
Woolfe, Thomas, Manufacturer of Queen's Ware in general, Blue, printed and Egyptian Black, Cane, &c.

Fenton, near Newcastle, Staffordshire (page 392)
Bacchus, William, Manufacturer of Queen's Ware in all its various Branches
Boon, Edward, Manufacturer of Queen's Ware and Blue painted
Brindley, Taylor, Potter
Clowes and Williamson, Potters
Turner, John, Potter
Wedgwood, Josiah, and Thomas, Potters

Lane End, near Newcastle, Staffordshire (pages 392-393)
Barker, John, Manufacturer of Cream coloured, China glaze, and Blue Wares
Barker, William, Potter
Barker, Richard, Potter
Cyples, Joseph, Manufacturer of Egyptian Black and Pottery in general
Edwards, William, Potter
Forrester and Meredith, Manufacturers of Queen's Ware, Egyptian Black, Red China, and various other Ware
Garner, Joseph, Potter
Garner, Robert, Manufacturer of Queen's Wares, and various other Wares
Shelley, Michael, Potter
Shelley, Thomas, Potter
Turner and Abbott, Potters to the Prince of Wales
Walklete, Mark, Potter

1787 Tunnicliff

A Topographical Survey of the Counties of Stafford, Chester, and Lancaster, By William Tunnicliff, Land-Surveyor, Nantwich (Norton 6). Dated MDCCLXXXVII on the title page.

This directory is not classified but consists of alphabetical lists of potters for the various towns and villages in a section titled 'Manufacturers of Pottery Ware, near Newcastle, in Staffordshire' (pages 35-40). The section is subdivided under Burslem (pages 35-37), Cobridge (page 37), Handley (pages 37-38), Shelton (page 38), Stoke (pages 38-39), Fenton (page 39), and Lane End (pages 39-40). Close examination of the lists show that they have been pirated verbatim from 1784 Bailey (see above). In order to avoid misleading data in this work the entries are neither repeated here nor included in the alphabetical list. The Staffordshire pages were reissued, unchanged, in an expanded 1789 edition (see 1789 Tunnicliff below).

1789 Tunnicliff

A Topographical Survey of the Counties of Somerset, Gloucester, Worcester, Stafford, Chester, and Lancaster, By William Tunnicliff, Land-Surveyor, Bath (Norton 7). Dated MDCCLXXXIX on the title page and December 1788 in the Dedication.

The Staffordshire pages in this volume are purely reprints from the 1787 edition (see above). The comment concerning piracy from 1784 Bailey still applies and once again, in order to avoid misleading data in this work, the entries are neither repeated here nor included in the alphabetical list.

1796 Chester

The Staffordshire Pottery Directory, Printed and Sold by Chester and Mort, Hanley and Newcastle (Norton 643). There has been some doubt about the date of this directory, being listed as 1810 by Norton but as either 1796 or 1797 by various other authorities. The text cannot have been compiled earlier than 3 January 1795, since it contains a reference to 'the late Mr. Wedgwood'. Evidence that it was published in 1796 has been found in the *Staffordshire Advertiser* for 26 March, where it was reported that Chester & Mort hoped to publish their Pottery Directory within a few weeks. Some of the descriptive text has similarities with 1800 Allbutt, and may have been written by the same hand.

This directory is not classified but contains 'An Historical Sketch of the Pottery, and its Environs', followed by an 'Alphabetical List of the Names and Places of Abode of the Principal Inhabitants, &c. in the Staffordshire Potteries' (pages

25-61). The list is subdivided into various towns and villages, and an 'Advertisement' on page 2 of the volume points out that 'the Reader is requested to observe, that whenever the term Manufacturer occurs in the List of Names, a Manufacturer of Earthen Ware is always to be understood'. Accordingly, the following lists of potters have been extracted from the sections for the towns or villages shown.

Hanley, Shelton, &c. (pages 27-36)
Baddeley Ralph, manufacturer, Shelton
Bagnall and Boon, manufacturers, Shelton
Birch and Whitehead, manufacturers, Hanley
Baddeley John and Edward, manufacturers Shelton
Booth and Marsh, manufacturers, Shelton
Chatterley William, manufacturer, Hanley
Greatbatch James, manufacturer, Shelton
Glass John, manufacturer, Hanley
Hallam and Shelley, manufacturers, Shelton
Hollins Samuel, manufacturer, Shelton
Hollins, Warburton & Co. porcelain manufacturers, Shelton
Heath Thomas, manufacturer, Shelton
Hollins Thomas & John, manufacturers, Shelton
Keeling James, manufacturer, Hanley
Keeling Edward, manufacturer, Keeling's-Lane, Hanley
Mare John, manufacturer, Hanley
Mayer Elijah, manufacturer, Hanley
Mellor William, manufacturer, Hanley
Meigh and Walthall, manufacturers, Hanley
Poole Richard, manufacturer Shelton
Pope Thomas, manufacturer, Shelton
Pope Stephen, manufacturer, Shelton
Ridgway, Smith & Ridgway, manufacturers, Shelton
Stanley and Co. manufacturers, Hanley
Simpson Thomas Broom, manufacturer, Hanley
Shorthose and Heath, manufacturers, Hanley
Taylor George, manufacturer, Hanley
Twemlow John, manufacturer, Shelton
Warrillow Joseph, manufacturer, Hanley
Whitehead Dorothy, manufacturer, Hanley
Whitehead James and Charles, manufacturers, Hanley
Wilson Robert, manufacturer, Hanley
Yates John, manufacturer, Keeling's-lane, Hanley
Yates John and William, manufacturers, Shelton

Burslem (pages 36-43)
Bagshaw, Taylor and Maier, manufacturers, Burslem
Ball Charles, manufacturer, Burslem
Birch Samuel, druggist and manufacturer, Burslem
Bourne Edward, jun. manufacturer, Burslem
Breeze John, manufacturer, Burslem
Bedson and Rhodes, manufacturers, Burslem
Dawson William, manufacturer, Burslem
Daniel Walter, manufacturer, New-Port
Griffith Edward, manufacturer, Burslem
Green Thomas, manufacturer, Burslem
Gilbert John, manufacturer, Burslem
Heath and Son, manufacturers, Burslem
Holland and Co. manufacturers, Burslem
Heath Lewis, manufacturer, Burslem
Holland Thomas, manufacturer, Burslem
Locket Timothy and John, manufacturers, Burslem
Morris Daniel, manufacturer, Burslem
Marsh and Hall, manufacturers, Burslem
Poole and Shrigley, manufacturers, Burslem
Robinson and Sons, manufacturers, Burslem
Steel Daniel, manufacturer, Burslem
Wedgwood J. and Co. manufacturers, Burslem
Wedgwood Thomas, manufacturer, Burslem
Wedgwood and Co. manufacturer, Burslem
Wood Ralph, manufacturer, Burslem
Wood and Caldwell, manufacturers, Burslem

Cobridge and Neighbourhood (pages 43-46)
ADAMS William, manufacturer, Cobridge
Blackwell John and Andrew, manufacturers, Cobridge
Dale and Co. manufacturers, Cobridge
Godwin Benjamin, manufacturer, Cobridge
Godwin Thomas, manufacturer, Cobridge
Hamersley John, manufacturer, Cobridge
Robinsons and Smith, manufacturers, Cobridge
Wedgwood and Byerley, manufacturers, Etruria
Warburton Jacob, manufacturer, Cobridge

Tunstall, Longport, &c. (pages 46-49)
Adams William, manufacturer, Golden-hill
Baggaley and Vodrey, manufacturers, Tunstall
Baggaley Thomas, manufacturer, Tunstall
Breeze John, manufacturer, Longport
Capper John, manufacturer, Golden-hill
Cartlich Samuel and John, manufacturers, Tunstall
Collison John, manufacturer, Tunstall
Cole John and Caleb, manufacturers, Newfield
Colclough Mary, manufacturer, Pits-hill
Davenport John, manufacturer, Longport
Gerrard and Alker, manufacturers, Longport
Henshall Williamson & Clowes, manufacturers, Longport
Keeling Anthony and Son, manufacturers, Tunstall
Lindop John, manufacturer, Green-lane
Machin Jonathan, manufacturer, Tunstall
Moss Thomas & Henshall, manufacturers, Red-street
Rogers John and George, manufacturers, Longport
Smith Joseph, manufacturer, Tunstall
Smith Theophilus, manufacturer, Smithfield
Tunstall Thomas, manufacturer, Tunstall
Wood John, manufacturer, Brown-hills

Stoke, Penkhull, &c. (pages 49-53)
Booth Ephraim and Sons, manufacturers, Stoke
Buckley and Bent, manufacturers, Newcastle
Harrison John, manufacturer, Stoke
Keeling and Co. manufacturers, Stoke-lane
Minton and Poulson, manufacturers, Stoke

Rowley Josiah, manufacturer, Stoke
Spode Josiah, manufacturer, Stoke
Wolfe Thomas, manufacturer, Stoke

Lane-End, Folly, Lane-Delph, Lower-Lane, &c. (pages 53-61)
Allcock and Ward, manufacturers, Lane-end
Astbury Richard, manufacturer, Lane-delph
Aynsley John, manufacturer, Lane-end
Bagnall Sampson, manufacturer, Lane-delph
Barker Samuel, manufacturer, Lane-delph
Barker Richard, manufacturer, Lane-end
Bourne and Baker, manufacturers, Lower-Lane
Bray and Harrison, manufacturers, Lane-delph
Chatham and Woolley, manufacturers, Lane-end
Cyples Mary, manufacturer, Lane-end
Dawson James, manufacturer, Lane-delph
Forster Thomas, manufacturer, Lane-delph
Forster and Harvey, manufacturers, Lane-end
Garner Robert, manufacturer, Lane-end
Harrison and Hyatt, manufacturers, Lower-lane
Hughes Samuel, manufacturer, Lane-end
Jackson Benjamin, manufacturer, Lane-end
Jackson Sarah, manufacturer, Lane-end
Jackson Thomas, manufacturer, Lane-end
Johnson and Bridgwood, manufacturers, Lane-end
Martin Ann, manufacturer, Lane-delph
Myatt Joseph, manufacturer, Lane-end
Philips William and John, manufacturers, Lane-end
Pratt William, manufacturer, Lane-delph
Shaw Thomas, manufacturer, Lane-end
Shelley Thomas, manufacturer, Lane-end
Spode Samuel, manufacturer, Folly
Stirrup Thomas, manufacturer, Lane-end
Turner William and John, manufacturers, Lane-end
Walklate Mark, manufacturer, Lane-end
Weston and Hull, manufacturers, Lane-end
Wolfe Thomas, manufacturer, Lower-lane

1798 Universal

The Universal British Directory of Trade, Commerce, and Manufacture, Volume the Fourth, Peter Barfoot & John Wilkes (of Midlington Place, Hants.), London (Goss p.83, Norton 18). This directory consists of five volumes, the fourth of which is believed to date from 1798. The title page notes simply 'London' and 'Printed for the Patentees, at the British Directory Office, Ave Maria Lane'. One copy examined had a pencil note 'post 1797' on the title page. The section covering the Potteries cannot have been compiled earlier than 3 January 1795, since it contains a reference to 'the late Mr. Wedgwood'. The earlier volumes were reprinted to make up sets and in view of the fact that the first volume can be found dated 1790, 1791 or 1793, there has previously been some understandable confusion.

This directory is not classified but consists of alphabetical lists of 'Traders, &c.' for various towns and villages in a section titled 'Account of the Potteries, or Manufactories of Staffordshire-Ware, in the Neighbourhood of Newcastle' (pages 104-111). The following lists of potters have been extracted for the towns or villages as shown.

Golden-Hill (page 104)
Capper John, Coarse-ware Potter
Cartlick Samuel and Thomas, Earthenware-manufacturers
Collinson John, Coarse-ware Potter
Tunstall Thomas, Earthen-ware Manufacturer
Vodrey Daniel, Coarse-ware Potter

New-field (page 104)
Cole Caleb and Co. Earthen-ware Manufacturers

Tunstall (page 105)
Adams William, Earthen-ware Manufacturer
Keeling Anthony and Sons, Earthen-ware Manufacturers
Smith Joseph, Earthen-ware Manufacturer

Smith-field (page 105)
Leader Bainton, Potter
Smith Theophilus, Manufacturer of Earthen-ware and Merchant
Till Edward, Toy-maker

Long-port (page 105)
Bruze Samuel, Staffordshire-ware Manufacturer
Brindley James, Ditto
Davenport James, Ditto
Henshall, Williamson, and Clewes, Manufacturers of Staffordshire-ware
Rogers John and George, Ditto

Burslem (pages 105-107)
Bourne Edward, Potter
Caldwell Wood, Manufacturer of Staffordshire-ware
Daniel Walter, Manufacturer of Staffordshire-ware
Dawson Daniel and William, Manufacturers of Staffordshire-ware
Fletcher Rich. Manufacturer of Staffordshire-ware
Gilbert John, Manufacturer of Staffordshire-ware
Griffith Edward, Manufacturer of Staffordshire-ware
Heath Lewis, Victualler, and Manufacturer of Staffordshire-ware
Holland and Dobson, Manufacturers of Staffordshire-ware and Printers
Lockett John and Timothy, Manufacturers of Staffordshire-ware
Marsh and Hall, Manufacturers of Staffordshire-ware
Morris Daniel, Coarse-ware Potter
Poole, Shrigley, and Laking, Manufacturers of Earthen-ware
Rhoads and Bedson, Manufacturers of Staffordshire-ware

Robinson and Sons, Manufacturers of Staffordshire-ware
Wedgwood Thomas, Manufacturer of Staffordshire-ware
Wedgwood Ralph and Co. Manufacturers of Staffordshire-ware
Wood John, Manufacturer of Staffordshire-ware
Wood Ralph, Manufacturer of Staffordshire-ware

Cobridge (page 107)
Adams William, Manufacturer of Staffordshire-ware
Blackwell John, Manufacturer of Staffordshire-ware
Blackwell Joseph, Ditto
Bucknell Ralph and Joseph, Manufacturers of Staffordshire-ware
Goodwin Benjamin, Manufacturer of Staffordshire-ware
Goodwin Thomas, Ditto
Hammersley John, Ditto
Robinson and Smith, Manufacturers of Staffordshire-ware
Warburton Jacob, Manufacturer of Staffordshire-ware

Etruria (page 107)
Wedgwood and Brierly, Manufacturers of Staffordshire-ware

Hanley (pages 107-109)
Burrow Arthur, Manufacturer of Staffordshire-ware
Chaterley Samuel, Manufacturer of Staffordshire-ware
Glass John, Manufacturer of Staffordshire-ware
Heath and Simpson, Manufacturers of Staffordshire-ware
Hollings Thomas and John, Manufacturers of Staffordshire-ware
Jarrott Edward and Keeling Jas. Manufacturers of Staffordshire-ware
Keeling Edward, Manufacturer of Staffordshire-ware
Keeling James, Manufacturer of Staffordshire-ware
Mare John, Manufacturer of Staffordshire-ware
May Job and Walker, Manufacturers of Staffordshire-ware
Mayer John, Manufacturer of Staffordshire-ware
Mayer Elijah, Manufacturer of Staffordshire-ware
Meigh and Watthall, Manufacturers of Staffordshire-ware
Meller William, Manufacturer of Staffordshire-ware
Shorter and Heath, Manufacturers of Staffordshire-ware
Shorthose and Heath, Manufacturers of Staffordshire-ware
Simpson Broom Thomas, Manufacturer of Staffordshire-ware
Smith William and Ridgway, Manufacturers of Staffordshire-ware
Taylor George, Manufacturer of Staffordshire-ware
Warrellow Joseph, Manufacturer of Staffordshire-ware
Whitehead Cha. Christ. Manufacturer of Staffordshire-ware
Whitehead James & Cha. Ditto
Wilson Robert, Manufacturer of Staffordshire-ware

Sheldon (page 109)
Badley Ralph and John, Manufacturers of Staffordshire-ware
Booth and Dale, Manufacturers of Staffordshire-ware
Fletcher Thomas, Manufacturer of Staffordshire-ware
Hollings, Warburton, and Co. China-manufacturers
Keeling Moses, Manufacturer of Staffordshire-ware
Mills William, Manufacturer of Staffordshire-ware
Poole Richard, Manufacturer of Staffordshire-ware
Ridgeway George and Co. Ditto [Factor]
Twambler John, Manufacturer of Staffordshire-ware
Weston John, Manufacturer of Staffordshire-ware
Yates William, Manufacturer of Staffordshire-ware

Vale-Pleasant (page 109)
Hollis Samuel, Manufacturer of Staffordshire-ware

Stoke (pages 109-110)
Booth E. Manufacturer of Staffordshire-ware
Harrison John, Manufacturer of Staffordshire-ware
Rowley Josiah, Manufacturer of Staffordshire-ware
Spode Josiah, Manufacturer of Staffordshire-ware and Register-office Keeper
Wolfe Thomas, Manufacturer of Staffordshire-ware

Lower-Lane (page 110)
Borne Ralph and Co. Manufacturers of Staffordshire-ware
Challener John and Adams, Manufacturers of Staffordshire-ware
Harrison George and Co. Ditto

Lane-Delph (page 110)
Astbury Richard, Manufacturer of Staffordshire-ware
Bagnall Sampson, Manufacturer of Staffordshire-ware
Barker Samuel, Ditto
Bodrey Peter, Manufacturer of Staffordshire-ware
Bray and Harrison, Ditto
Martin Mrs. Manufacturer of Staffordshire-ware

Lane-End (pages 110-111)
Allcock Tho. Edw., Manufacturer of Staffordshire-ware
Barker Thomas, Manufacturer of Staffordshire-ware
Barker Joseph, Ditto
Barker Richard, Ditto
Chatham and Wolley, Manufacturers of Staffordshire-ware
Cyplis Mary, Manufacturer of Staffordshire-ware
Dawson Joseph, Manufacturer of Staffordshire-ware
Forrester and Harvey, Manufacturers of Staffordshire-ware
Garner Robert, Ditto
Hughes Samuel and Sons, Manufacturers of Staffordshire-ware
Jackson Thomas, Manufacturer of Staffordshire-ware
Johnson Rd. and Bridgewood, Manufacturers of Staffordshire-ware
Myatt Richard, Manufacturer of Staffordshire-ware
Phillips William, Manufacturer of Staffordshire-ware
Plant John, Ditto
Shaw Thomas, Manufacturer of Staffordshire-ware
Shirley Thomas, Manufacturer of Staffordshire-ware
Spode Samuel, Manufacturer of Staffordshire-ware
Sterrup Thomas, Manufacturer of Staffordshire-ware
Turner John and William, Manufacturers of Staffordshire-ware
Walkelate, Mark [no trade given]
Weston and Hull, Manufacturers of Staffordshire-ware

1800 Allbutt

A View of the Staffordshire Potteries, Printed for and sold by T. Allbutt, Burslem. Dated 1800 on the title page.

This volume consists of a descriptive chapter 'The History of the Staffordshire Potteries', followed by 'A Directory Containing an Alphabetical List of the Names and Places of Abode of the Gentlemen, Tradesmen, Shop-Keepers, &c. &c. in the Staffordshire Potteries'. The directory, which is sub-divided into various towns and villages, is not classified and does not include any potters except for the six manufacturers of toys listed below. The entire book was reprinted with additions and minor corrections by J. Allbut & Son as *The Staffordshire Pottery Directory* in 1802 (qv). Some of the descriptive text has marked similarities with 1796 Chester, and may have been either pirated or written by the same hand.

Golden-Hill, Tunstall, Longport, &c.
Locker John, manufacturer of toys, Tunstall

Burslem
Baddeley Thomas, toy manufacturer, Hill-street
Walker John, toy manufacturer, Low-street

Cobridge, Etruria, &c.
Boot Jonathan, modeller and toy manufacturer, Cobridge
Hobson Ephraim, toy manufacturer, Cobridge

Hanley
Poole George, manufacturer of toys, Ridding-lane

1802 Allbut

The Staffordshire Pottery Directory, Printed by J. Allbut and Son. Hanley (Norton 642). Dated 1802 on the title page. Publication was announced in the *Staffordshire Advertiser* dated 27 March 1802.

This volume is essentially just a reprint of 1800 Allbutt with a few minor corrections in the directory section, which still contains only the six manufacturers of toys (not repeated here). The important additional feature is a detailed map of the Potteries together with a key list of the potters titled 'Names and Residences of the Earthenware Manufacturers'. The numbers show the locations of the potteries on the map.

1	JOHN LINDOP,	Green-lane
2	John and Thomas Capper,	Golden-hill
3	Thomas Tunstall,	ditto
4	John Collison,	ditto
5	Abraham Baggaley,	ditto
6	Moss and Henshall,	Red-street
7	Riles and Bathwell,	ditto
8	Samuel and Thomas Cartlich,	Tunstall
9	Thomas Baggaley,	ditto
10	Caleb Cole and Co.	New-field
11	William Adams,	Tunstall
12	John Breeze,	Smith-field
13	Unoccupied	Pits-hill
14	Jonathan Machin,	Chell
15	John Horn,	Brimleyford
16	Smith and Steel,	Tunstall
17	A. and E. Keeling,	ditto
17	A. and E. Keeling,	ditto
18	John Wood,	Brown-hills
19	John Davenport,	Long-port
20	Henshall, Williamson and Co.	ditto
21	Williamson and Henshall,	ditto
22	Shirley, Lindop and Co.	ditto
23	John and George Rogers,	ditto
23	John and George Rogers,	ditto
24	Walter Daniel,	New-port
25	Holland and Co.	Burslem
26	John and Ralph Hall,	ditto
27	Ralph Wood,	ditto
28	Wood and Caldwell,	ditto
29	Isaac Leigh,	Burslem
30	Nathan and John Heath,	ditto
*	John Taylor and Co.	ditto
31	William Dawson,	ditto
32	Jacob Marsh,	ditto
33	Robinson and Sons,	ditto
34	Read and Goodfellow,	ditto
35	Edward Bourne,	ditto
36	Telwright and Co.	ditto
37	Thomas Holland,	ditto
38	Charles Davenport,	ditto
39	Lewis Heath,	ditto
40	Thomas Guest,	ditto
41	John Gilbert,	ditto
42	Thomas Wedgwood,	ditto
43	Daniel Steel,	ditto
44,	Unoccupied	ditto
45	William and John Stanley,	ditto
46	Bagshaw and Maier,	ditto
47	J. and R. Riley,	ditto
48	Mort, Barker and Chester,	ditto
49	Joseph Machin,	ditto
50	Arkinstall and George,	ditto
51	Richard Ball,	ditto
52	William Wood and Co.	ditto
53	Thomas Green,	ditto
54	John Warburton,	Cobridge
54	John Warburton,	Cobridge
55	Thomas Godwin,	ditto
56	Benjamin Godwin,	ditto
57	Smith and Billington,	Cobridge
58	Stevenson and Dale,	ditto

59	J. and A. Blackwell,	ditto
60	William Adams,	ditto
61	John Mozeley,	ditto
62	Hewit and Buckley,	Booden Brook
63	Hollins, Warburton, and Co.	Shelton
64	Booth and Marsh,	ditto
65	Bourne and Co.	ditto
66	E.J. Birch,	Hanley
67	Heath and Shorthose,	ditto
68	John Mare,	ditto
69	Yates & Shelley,	ditto
70	Joseph Lees,	ditto
71	David Wilson,	ditto
72	Elijah Mayer,	ditto
73	George Taylor,	ditto
74	T. and J. Hollins,	ditto
75	Valentine Close	ditto
76	Joseph Keeling,	ditto
77	Boon and Ridgway,	ditto
78	John Glass,	ditto
79	James Keeling	ditto
80	Meigh and Walthall,	ditto
81	Billings and Hammersley,	ditto
82	James and Charles Whitehead,	ditto
83	Mrs. Mellor,	ditto
84	John Stanley,	ditto
85	William Baddeley,	ditto
86	Job and George Ridgway,	Shelton
87	John Hammersley,	Shelton
88	J. and E. Baddeley,	ditto
89	Unoccupied,	ditto
90	Simpson and Wright,	ditto
91	John and William Yates,	ditto
92	Thomas Pope,	ditto
93	James Greatbatch,	ditto
94	Dorothy Whitehead,	ditto
95	Samuel Hollins,	Vale-pleasant
96	Wedgwood and Byerley	Etruria
97	Unoccupied,	Stoke-lane
98	Mrs. Ratcliffe,	ditto
99	John Harrison,	Cliffgate-bank
100	Booth and Sons,	ditto
101	Josiah Spode Esq.	Stoke
102	Wolfe and Hamilton,	ditto
103	Smith and Jarvis,	ditto
104	Minton, Poulson and Co.	ditto
105	Harrison and Hyatt,	Lower-lane
†	Robert Clulow and Co.	ditto
106	Bourne and Baker,	Fenton
107	Chelenor and Adams,	ditto
108	Bagnall and Hull,	Lane-delph
109	John Lucock,	ditto
110	William Pratt,	ditto
111	Mason & Co.	ditto
112	Thomas Forester,	ditto
113	——— Shelley,	Lower-lane
114	Samuel Baker	ditto
115	Samuel Baker	ditto
116	Samuel Spode,	Folley
117	Joseph Myatt,	ditto
118	Robert Garner,	Lane-end
119	Charles Harvey,	ditto
120	Hewit and Comer,	ditto
121	John Aynesley,	ditto
122	John Hewit,	ditto
123	W. and J. Phillips,	ditto
124	Samuel Hughes,	ditto
125	——— Dawson,	ditto
126	Richard Barker,	ditto
127	Booth & Co.	ditto
128	Thomas Stirrup,	ditto
129	Charles Harvey,	ditto
130	Samuel Bridgewood,	ditto
131	Johnson and Brough,	ditto
132	Mary Syples,	ditto
133	J. and G. Locketts,	ditto
134	Chetham and Woolley,	ditto
135	J. and W. Berks,	ditto
136	William and John Turner,	ditto
137	George Barnes,	ditto
138	William and John Turner,	ditto
139	Thomas Jackson and Co.	ditto
140	Thomas Shelley,	ditto
141	William Ward,	ditto
142	——— Shaw,	ditto
143	George Weston,	ditto
144	Mark Walklete,	ditto

Note that two potteries each are shown for A. & E. Keeling (17), John & George Rogers (23), John Warburton (54), and Samuel Baker (114 and 115).

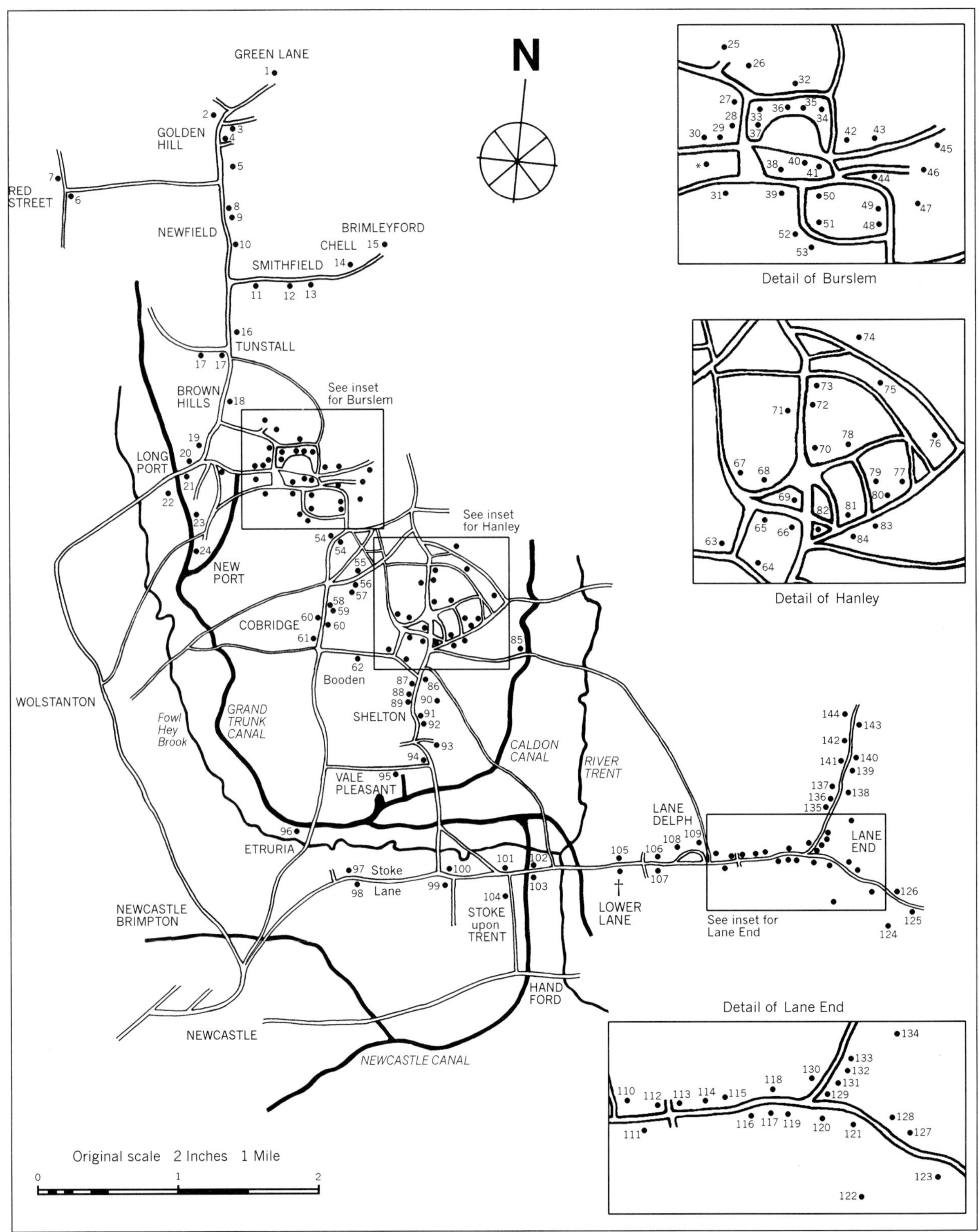

"A Map of the Potteries, Staffordshire", extracted from Allbut's 1802 Directory. The original map is approximately twice this size but no example suitable for reproduction could be located. This copy has been based on the best available example (in the Birmingham Reference Library) and shows the locations of all the numbered manufactories in Allbut's list, with the addition of larger scale insets of Burslem, Hanley and Lane End for clarity. The original map features other information not relevant to this work, including wharfs, churches, chapels, market halls, toll gates etc

1805 Holden

Holden's Triennial Directory, Fourth edition, for 1805, 1806, 1807. Second Volume, W. Holden, No. 8, Corner of Northampton Buildings, Rosoman Street, Clerkenwell, London (Goss p.92, Norton 21). This directory consists of two volumes and the Address in Volume 1 includes a note that the Addenda 'will be published in April, 1805'. The date 1805 also appears on the title page of Volume 2.

This directory is not classified. The following list of potters has been extracted from the section titled 'Potteries, Staffordshire' (pages 250-252).

ADAMS Wm. china and earthenware manufactory, Cobridge
Baddeley John and Edward, earthenware manufacturers, Shelton
Baddeley Wm. Egyptian black manufacturers, Shelton
Bagshaw and Meir, earthenware manufacturers, Burslem
Barker Rich. earthenware manufacturer, Lane end
Barnes Geo. and Wm. earthenware manufacturer, Lane end
Bathwell Wm. and Tho., earthenware manufacturers, Burslem
Blackwell John, china and earthenware manufacturer, Cobridge
Becket Robt. earthenware manufacturer, Lane end
Billington Rich. and Sons, earthenware manufacturers, Cobridge
Birch Edmund John, earthenware manufacturer, Shelton
Birks John and Wm. and Co. Egyptian black manufacturers, Lane end
Boon and Hicks, earthenware manufacturers, Shelton
Booth and Bridgewood, earthenware manufacturers, Lane end
Booth Hugh and Joseph, earthenware manufacturer, Stoke upon Trent
Booth Wm. Egyptian black manufacturer, Shelton
Bourne Wm. earthenware manufacturer, Burslem
Bourne Edward, earthenware manufacturer, Burslem
Bourne, Baker and Bourne, earthenware manufacturers, Fenton Potteries
Bourne Charles, earthenware manufacturer, Lane Delph
Breeze John and Son, earthenware manufacturers, Tunstall
Bridgwood Sam. earthenware manufacturer, Lane end
Cartlich Sam and Tho. earthenware manufacturers, Tunstall
Chetham and Woolley, pearl and printed ware, Egyptian black, &c. manufacturers, Lane end
Close Valentine, earthenware manufacturer, Keelings la.
Coomer, Sheridan and Hewit, earthenware manufacturers, Green Dock, Lane end
Cyples Jesse, Egyptian black manufacturer, Lane end
Davenport John, china and earthenware manufacturer, Longport
Ford Wm. and Co. earthenware manufacturers, Lane end
Forrester John, earthenware manufacturers, Lane end
Forrester Geo. earthenware manufacturer, Lane end
Gardner Robt. earthenware manufacturer, Lane end
Glass John, earthenware manufacturer, Hanley
Godwin Tho. earthenware manufacturer, Cobridge
Goodwin and Jarvis, china and earthenware manufacturers, Stoke upon Trent
Goodwin Edmund, earthenware manufacturer, Shelton
Goodwin John, china and earthen ware manufacturer, Boothenville, near Stoke upon Trent
Green Tho. earthenware manufacturer, Burslem Church yard
Gridbach James, red potter, Shelton
Hall John and Ralph, earthenware manufacturer, Burslem
Hammersley John, course earthenware manufacturer, Shelton
Harley Tho. enameller and earthenware manufacturer, Lane End
Harrison, Brough and Co. earthenware manufacturers, Green Dock, Lane end
Harte, Singleton and Co. earthenware manufacturers, Lane end
Harvey Charles and Sons, earthenware manufacturers, Lane end
Heath Tho. earthenware manufacturer, Burslem
Henshall and Williamson, earthenware manufacturers, Longport
Hollins, Warburton, Daniel, and Co. manufacturers of real china, Shelton
Hollins Tho. and John, earthenware manufacturers, Hanley
Hughes Peter and Tho. earthenware manufacturers
Hytt and Harrison, earthenware manufacturers, Fenton
Johnson and Brough, earthenware manufacturers, Lane end
Keeling Joseph, earthenware manufacturer, Keeling's la.
Keeling Anthony and Enoch, china and earthenware manufacturers, Tunstall
Keeling James, earthenware manufacturer, Hanley
Keeling, Toft and Co. earthenware manufacturers, Hanley
Leigh and Breeze, earthenware manufacturers, Hanley
Lindop and Taylor, earthenware manufacturers, Longport
Lockett Geo. and Co. earthenware manufacturers, Lane end
Mare John, earthenware manufacturer, Hanley
Marsh Jacob, earthenware manufacturer, Burslem
Marsh Joseph, china manufacturer, Brownhill
Mason Miles, china manufacturer, Lane delph
Massey John, Egyptian black manufacturer, Golden hill
Matthes and Ball, black glaze stone ware and gilt work manufacturers, Lane end
Mayer Elijah and Son, china and earthenware manufacturers, Hanley
Meigh Job, earthenware manufacturer, Hanley
Mellor and Taylor, earthenware manufacturers, Burslem
Minton and Poulson, china and earthenware manufacturers, Stoke upon Trent
Mort, Barker and Chester, earthenware manufacturers, Burslem
Moseley John, Egyptian black manufacturer, Cobridge
Pope Ralph, coarse ware potter, Shelton

Poulson Geo. china and earthenware manufacture, Cobridge
Pratt John, earthenware manufacturer, Lane Delph
Pratt Ellin, earthenware manufacturer, Lane Delph
Rhead and Goodfellow, earthenware manufacturers, Burslem
Ridgway Geo. china and earthenware manufacturers, Shelton
Ridgway Job, china and earthenware manufacturer, Cauldon pl. Shelton
Rilley John and Rich. china glaze earthenware manufacturers, Burslem
Robinson John and Sons, earthenware manufacturers, Burslem
Rogers John and Geo. china earthenware manufacturer, Longport
Shaw Geo. and Tho. earthenware manufacturers, Lane end
Shorthose and Heaths, junrs. earthenware manufacturers for exportation, Hanley
Smith & Steele, earthenware manufacturers, Tunstall
Smith James, earthenware manufacturer, Stoke upon Trent
Spode Josiah, china and earthenware manufacturer, Stoke upon Trent
Spode Sam. earthenware manufacturer, Folley house
Stanley Wm. earthenware manufacturer, Burslem
Steele Dan. earthenware manufacturer, Burslem
Stevenson and Godwin, earthenware manufacturers, Cobridge
Stirrup Tho. earthenware manufacturer, Lane end
Taylor G earthenware manufacturer, Hanley
Tellwright Wm. earthenware manufacturer, Tunstall
Tunstall Tho. banded ware manufacturer, Golden hill
Turners, Glover and Simpson, china and earthenware manufacturers, Lane end
Unett and Brammer, earthenware manufacturers, Lane end
Walklate Mark and Son, earthenware manufacturers, Lane end
Warburton Peter, earthenware manufacturer, Cobridge
Warrilow Jos. earthenware manufacturer, Hanley
Wedgwood Josiah and Byerley, potters to her Majesty, Etruria
Wedgwood Tho. earthenware manufacturer, Bighouse, Burslem
Wedgwood Tho. esq. Overhouse, Burslem
Weston Geo. and Co. earthenware manufacturers, Lane end
Whitehead Charles and James, earthenware manufacturers, Hanley
Whitehead Christopher, earthenware manufacturer, Shelton
Wilson David, china and earthenware manufacturer, Hanley
Wolfe and Hamilton, china and earthenware manufacturers, Stoke upon Trent
Wood and Caldwell, china and earthenware manufacturers, Burslem
Wood John, earthenware manufacturer, Brown hills
Yates John and Wm. earthenware manufacturers, Shelton

1808 Holden

Holden's Triennial Directory, Fourth Edition, Including the Year 1808, W. Holden, 122 Newgate Street, London (Goss p.95, Norton 22).

This directory is purely a reprint of 1805 Holden with a new title page. Even the Address is unchanged, including the note that the Addenda 'will be published in April, 1805'. In order to avoid misleading data in this work the entries are neither repeated here nor included in the alphabetical list.

1809 Holden

Holden's Triennial Directory, (Fifth Edition,) for 1809, 1810, 1811. Second Volume, William Holden, 122 Newgate Street, London (Goss p.95, Norton 23). This directory consists of two volumes, neither of which are dated other than in the title.

This directory is not classified. The following list of potters has been extracted from the section titled 'Potteries and Newcastle' (pages 367-371).

ADAMS Wm. china & earthenware-manufacturer, Cobridge
Adams J. china & earthenware-manufacturer, Tunstall
Baddeley Wm. Egyptian-black-manufacturer, Hanley
Baggeley Thos. china-manufacturer, Lane-delph
Bagshaw & Alier, earthenware-manufacturers, Burslem
Barker Rd. John & Js. earthenware-manufactory, Lane-end, & Ship-lane, Oxford
Bathwell Wm. & Thos. earthenware-manufacturers, Burslem
Billington Rd. & Sons, earthenware-manufacturers, Cobridge
Birch Edmund, John, & Co. earthenware-manufacturers, Hanley
Blackwell And. earthenware-manufact. Cobridge
Boon Joseph, earthenware-manufacturer, Shelton
Booth Messrs. earthenware-manufac. Lane-end
Bott Thos. & Co. earthenware-manufac. Lane-end
Bourne, Baker, & Bourne, manufacturers of earthenware, Fenton-potteries, & Salthouse-dock, Liverpool
Bourne Wm. earthenware-manufacturer, Burslem
Bourne C. manufac. of earthenware, Lane-delph
Bourne Edw. earthenware-manufactr. Burslem
Bradshaw & Bourne, earthenware-manufs. Shelton
Breeze John & Son, earthenware-manufacturers, Greenfield, near Tunstall
Bridgwood Kitty, earthenware-manufac. Lane-end
Bridgwood S. jun. earthenware-manufac. Lane-end
Browne J. & Co. earthenware-manufrs. Burslem
Byerley J. manufacturer of earthenware, Fenton
Cartlich S. & T. earthenware-manufactrs. Tunstall
Chetham & Woolley, pearl, printed ware, & Egyptian-black-

manufacturers, Lane-end
Child & Clive, earthenware-manufactrs. Tunstall
Close Valen. earthenware-manufacturer, Hanley
Collison Wm. & Js. black-ware-manufacturers, Golden-hill
Comer & Pratt, manufacturer of earthenware, Lane-delph
Cyples Jesse, earthenware-manufactr. Lane-end
Davenport John, china, glass, & earthenware-manufacturer, Longport
Ford & Hull, manufac. of earthenware, Lane-end
Forrester John, earthenware-manufacr. Lane-end
Forrester G. earthenware-manufactory, Lane-end
Garner Rt. earthenware-manufacturer, Lane-end
Ginder S. manufact. of earthenware, Lane-delph
Glass J. manufacturer of earthenware, Hanley
Goodwin B. & S. earthenware-manufacturers, Burslem
Goodwin T. & B. earthenware-manufacs. Burslem
Goodwin Ben. earthenware-manufactr. Cobridge
Green T. earthenware-manufacturer, Burslem
Gridbatch Js. red-potter, Hanley
Hackwood, Dimmock, & Co. earthenware-manufacturers, Hanley
Hall J. & R. earthenware-manufacturers, Burslem
Hall J. & R. earthenware-manufacturers, Tunstall
Harley & Seckerson, earthenware-manufacturers, Lane-end
Harrison, Brough, & Co. earthenware-manufactories, Lane-end
Harrison J. earthenware-manufacturer, Stoke
Harrison W. earthenware-manufacturer, Burslem
Hartle, Singleton, & Co. earthenware-manufacturers, Lane-end
Harvey Chs. & Sons, earthenware-manufactory & flint-grinders, Lane-end
Heath & Shorthose, earthenware-manufactory, Hanley
Heath J. earthenware-manufacturer, Burslem
Heath T. manufacturer of earthenware, Burslem
Henshall & Williamson, earthenware-manufacturers in all its branches, Longport
Hicks & Meigh, earthenware-manufactrs. Hanley
Hobson Ephraim, Egyptian-black & toy-manufacturer, Shelton
Holland T. earthenware-manufacturer, Burslem
Hollins, Warburton, Daniel, & Co. manufacturers of real china, Shelton
Hollins T. & J. earthenware-manufactory, Hanley
Hollins Thos. jun. & Co. earthenware-manufacturers, Shelton
Hughes Peter & Thos. earthenware-manufacts. Lane-end
Johnson & Brough, manufacturers of earthenware, Lane-end
Keelings & Ogilvy, china & earthenware-manufacturers, Tunstall
Keeling Js. earthenware-manufacturer, Hanley
Keeling Anthony & Enoch, china-manufacturers, Tunstall
Keeling, Toft, & Co. earthenware-manufacturers, Hanley
Knight, Sproston, & Knight, earthenware-manufacturers, Tunstall
Leigh & Breeze, earthenware-manufacturers, Hanley
Lindop & Taylor, earthenware-manufacturers, Longport
Lockett George & Co. manufacturers of earthenware, Lane-end
Machin & Baggaley, china-manufacturers, Burslem
Mare J. & Mat. earthenware-manufactrs. Hanley
Marsh J. manufactr. of earthenware, Lane-delph
Marsh J. earthenware-manufacturer, Brown-hills
Mason M. & Son, china-manufactrs. Lane-delph
Massey John, black & red-ware manufacturers, Golden-hill
Matthes & Ball, earthenware-manufacturers & china gilders, Lane-end
Mayer Elijah & Son, china & earthenware-manufacturers, Hanley
Meigh Job, apaque, china, & earthenware-manufacturer, Hanley
Meller Ann & Co. shining black-ware-manufacturers, Hanley
Mellor & Taylor, earthenware-manufacts. Burslem
Miles Mason & Son, china-manufactr. Lane-delph
Minton & Poulson, manufacturer of china & earthenware, Stoke
Moseley John & Wm. Egyptian-black-manufacturers, Burslem
Moseley J. earthenware-manufacturer, Cobridge
Passenger & Co. earthenware-manufactrs. Hanley
Poulson George, china & earthenware-manufacturer, Stoke
Pratt J. manufacturer of earthenware, Lane-delph
Rathbone Wm. earthenware-manufactr. Tunstall
Read & Goodfellow, earthenware-manuf. Burslem
Ridgway Job, china & earthenware-manufacturer, Caulden-place, Shelton
Ridgway G. earthenware-manufacturer, Shelton
Riley John & Rd. china & earthenware-manufacturers, Burslem
Robinson J. & Sons, manufactrs. of earthenware, Burslem
Rogers John & George, china & earthenware-manufacturers, Longport
Ryles & Walsh, earthenware-manufacts. Burslem
Shaw T. earthenware-manufacturer, Lane-end
Sheridan & Hyatt, Egyptian-black-manufacturers, Lane-end
Sheridan & Hewitt, Earthenware-manufacturers, Lane-end
Shirley Wm. earthenware-manufacturer, Shelton
Shorthose & Heaths, junrs. earthenware-manufacturers for exportation, Hanley
Spode Josiah, potter & English porcelain-manufacturer to the Prince of Wales, Stoke-pottery, & Portugal-st. London
Spode Samuel, earthenware-manufacturer, Folly house, Lane-end
Stanley Wm. earthenware-manufacturer, Burslem
Steele Wm. earthenware-manufacturer, Burslem
Stevenson & Godwin, earthenware-manufacturers, Cobridge
Stevenson J. & A. earthenware-manuf. Cobridge
Stirrup & Beardmore, manufactrs. of earthenware, Lane-end
Stirrup T. manufacturer of earthenware, Lane-end
Taylor G. jun. earthenware-manufacturer, Shelton
Taylor G. earthenware-manufacturer, Hanley
Turner Wm. manufacturer of earthenware, Folly, Lane-end
Tunstall Thos. red-ware-manufactory, Golden-hill
Warburton Peter, earthenware-manuf. Cobridge
Warburton John, earthenware-manuf. Cobridge
Walklate Hannah & Rich. manufacturers of earthenware, Lane-end

Walsh & Ryles, earthenware-manufactrs. Burslem
Warrilow J. earthenware-manufacturer, Hanley
Wedgwood Josiah & Byerley, potters to her Majesty, Etruria, St. James's-square, London, & Sackville-st. Dublin
Wedgwood T. earthenware-manufacturer, Burslem
Weston G. & Co. manufacturers of earthenware, Lane-end
Whitehead J. & C. earthenware-manufs. Hanley
Wilson & Green, earthenware-manufac. Burslem
Wilson David, china & earthenware-manufacturer, Hanley
Wolfe & Hamilton, manufacturers of china & earthenware, Stoke-pottery, & 42, Old-dock, Liverpool
Wood & Caldwell, china & earthenware-manufacturers, Burslem
Wood J. earthenware-manufacturer, Brown-hills
Yates J. earthenware-manufacturer, Shelton

1811 Holden

Holden's Annual London and Country Directory, of the United Kingdom and Wales, in Three Volumes, for the Year 1811. Second Volume, Published by W. Holden, 122 Newgate Street, London (Goss p.97, Norton 24). This directory consists of two volumes and is dated 1811 on the title page of Volume 2. In the Advertisement in Volume 1 Holden refers to 'the lateness in the year of the production of his work'.

This directory is not classified. The following list of potters has been extracted from the section titled 'Potteries and Newcastle' (four un-numbered pages in the second volume).

ADAMS Wm. china & earthenware-manufacturer, Cobridge
Adams Benjamin, china & earthenware-manufacturer, Tunstall
Baddeley Wm. Egyptian-black-manufacturer, Hanley
Baggeley Thos. china-manufacturer, Lane-delph
Bagshaw & Leigh, earthenware-manufacturers, Burslem
Barker John & Jas. earthenware-manufactory, Lane-end, & Ship-lane, Oxford
Bathwell Wm. & Thomas, earthenware-manufacturers, Burslem
Billington, Rich. & Sons, earthenware-manufacturers, Cobridge
Birch Edmund, John, & Co. earthenware-manufacturers, Hanley
Blackwell John, earthenware-manufacturer, Cobridge
Boon & Lovatt, earthenware-manufacs. Shelton
Booth Messrs. earthenware-manufacturers, Lane-end
Bott Thomas & Co. earthenware-manufacturers, Lane-end
Bourne, Baker, & Bourne, manufacturers of earthenware, Fenton-potteries, & Salthouse-dock, Liverpool
Bourne Wm. earthenware-manufacturer, Burslem
Bourne C. manufacturer of earthenware, Lane-delph
Bourne Edw. earthenware-manufacturer, Burslem
Bradshaw & Bourne, earthenware-manufacturers, Shelton
Breeze John & Son, earthenware-manufacturers, Greenfield, near Tunstall
Bridgwood Kitty, earthenware-manufac. Lane-end
Bridgwood S. jun. earthenware-manuf. Lane-end
Browne & Cartledge, earthenware-manufs. Burslem
Cartlich S. & T. earthenware-manufr. Tunstall
Chetham & Woolley, pearl, printed ware, & Egyptian-black-manufacturers, Lane-end
Child & Clive, earthenware-manufacs. Tunstall
Close Valen. earthenware-manufacturer, Hanley
Collison Wm. & Jas. black-ware-manufacturers, Golden-hill
Comer & Pratt, manufacturers of earthenware, Lane-delph
Davenport John & Co. china, glass, & earthenware-manufacturers, Longport
Ford & Hull, manufacturers of earthenware, Lane-end
Forrester John, earthenware-manufacr. Lane-end
Forrester G. earthenware-manufactory, Lane-end
Garner Rt. earthenware-manufacturer, Lane-end
Ginder S. manufact. of earthenware, Lane-delph
Glass J. manufacturer of earthenware, Hanley
Goodwin B. & S. earthenware-manufacturers, Burslem
Goodwin T. & B. earthenware-manufacturers, Burslem
Goodwin Benj. earthenware-manufr. Cobridge
Greatbatch Jas. red-potter, Hanley
Green T. earthenware-manufacturer, Burslem
Hackwood, Dimmock, & Co. earthenware-manufacturers, Hanley
Hall J. & R. earthenware-manufacturers, Burslem
Hall J. & R. earthenware-manufacturers, Tunstall
Harley & Seckerson, earthenware-manufacturers, Lane-end
Harrison, Brough, & Co. earthenware-manufactories, Lane-end
Hartle, Singleton, & Co. earthenware-manufacturers, Lane-end
Harvey Chas. & Sons, earthenware-manufactory & flint-grinders, Lane-end
Heath & Shorthose, earthenware-manufactory, Hanley
Heath J. earthenware-manufacturer, Burslem
Heath T. manufacturer of earthenware, Burslem
Henshall & Williamson, earthenware-manufacturers in all its branches, Longport
Hicks & Meigh, earthenware-manufactrs. Hanley
Hobson Ephraim, Egyptian-black & toy-manufacturer, Cobridge
Holland T. earthenware-manufacturer, Burslem
Hollins, Warburton, Daniel, & Co. manufacturers of real china, Shelton
Hollins T. & J. earthenware-manufactory, Hanley
Hollins Thos. jun. & Co. earthenware-manufacturers, Shelton
Hughes Peter & Thos. earthenware-manufacturers, Lane-end
Johnson & Brough, manufacturers of earthenware, Lane-end
Keeling Jas. earthenware-manufacturer, Hanley
Keeling Anthony & Enoch, china-manufacturers, Tunstall
Keeling, Toft, & Co. earthenware-manufacturers, Hanley

Knight, Sproston, & Knight, earthenware-manufacturers, Tunstall
Wilson & Breeze, earthenware-manufs. Hanley
Lindop & Taylor, earthenware-manufacturers, Longport
Lockett George & Co. manufacturers of earthenware, Lane-end
Machin & Baggaley, china-manufacrs. Burslem
Mare J. & Mat. earthenware-manufacs. Hanley
Marsh J. manufac. of earthenware, Lane-delph
Marsh J. earthenware-manufacturer, Brown-hills
Mason M. & Son, china-manufacs. Lane-delph
Massey John, black and red-ware manufacturer, Golden-hill
Mathers & Ball, earthenware-manufacturers & china-gilders, Lane-end
Mayer Elijah & Son, china & earthenware-manufacturers, Hanley
Meigh Job, apaque, china, & earthenware-manufacturer, Hanley
Meller, Toft, & Keeling, shining black-ware-manufacturers, Hanley
Minton Thos. manufacturer of china & earthenware, Stoke
Moseley Wm. Egyptian-black-manufr. Burslem
Moseley J. earthenware & Egyptian-black-manufacturer, Cobridge
Poulson Thos. china & earthenware-manufacturer, Stoke
Pratt J. manufacr. of earthenware, Lane-delph
Rathbone Wm. earthenware-manufacr. Tunstall
Read & Goodfellow, earthenware manuf. Burslem
Ridgway Job & sons, china & earthenware manufacturers, Caulden-place, Shelton
Ridgway G. earthenware manuf. Shelton
Riley John & Rd. china & earthenware-manufacturers, Burslem
Robinson J. & Sons, manufacturers of earthenware, Burslem
Rogers John & Geo. china & earthenware manufacturers, Longport
Ryles & Walsh, earthenware-manuf. Burslem
Shaw T. earthenware manuf. Lane-end
Sheridan & Hyatt, Egyptian-black-manufacturers, Lane-end
Sheridan & Hewitt, earthenware-manufacturers, Lane-end
Shirley Jesse, earthenware-manufacturer, Hanley
Shirley Wm. earthenware-manufacturer, Shelton
Shorthose & Heaths, junrs. earthenware-manufacturers for exportation, Hanley
Simpson C. china-ware manufr. Golden-hill
Spode Josiah, potter & English porcelain manufacturer to the Prince of Wales, Stoke-pottery, & Portugal-st. London
Spode Sam. earthenware-manufacturer, Folly-house, Lane-end
Stanley Wm. earthenware manufactr. Burslem
Stevenson Ralph, earthenware manufr. Cobridge
Stevenson A. earthenware-manuf. Cobridge
Stevenson & Bucknall, earthenware manufacs. Cobridge
Stirrup & Beardmore, manufacturers, of earthenware, Lane-end
Stirrup T. manufactr. of earthenware, Lane-end
Taylor G. jun. earthenware manufactr. Shelton
Taylor G. earthenware manufacturer, Hanley
Turner Wm. manufacturer of earthenware, Folly Lane-end
Warburton Peter, earthenware manuf. Cobridge
Warburton John, earthenware manuf. Cobridge
Walklate Hannah & Rich. manufacturers of earthenware, Lane-end
Walsh & Ryles, earthenware manufacturers Burslem
Warrilow J. earthenware-manufacturer, Hanley
Wedgwood Josiah, potter to her Majesty, Etruria, St. James's-square, London
Wedgwood T. earthenware manufact. Burslem
Weston G. & Co. manufacturers of earthenware, Lane-end
Wilson & Green, earthenware manufacturers Burslem
Wilson David, china & earthenware manufacturer, Hanley
Wolfe & Hamilton, manufacturers of china & earthenware, Stoke pottery, & Old-dock, Liverpool
Wood & Caldwell, china & earthenware manufacturers, Burslem
Wood J. earthenware manufacturer, Brown hills
Yates J. earthenware manufacturer, Shelton

1816 Underhill

Biennial Directory. Class Third, First Edition, for the Years 1816 & 1817, Thomas Underhill, 11 Coleman Street, London (Goss p.101, Norton 28).

This is one of four classified directories issued by Thomas Underhill and his predecessor William Holden, this volume covering their Class 3, or 'Iron, Brass, Copper, and Metal Trades, &c.' The following list of potters appears under the title 'Staffordshire Potteries' (pages 215-216) within a section on the 'Potteries and Newcastle, Staffordshire' (page 215).

Adams Benjamin, Tunstall
Bailey William, Lane end
Barker Richard, John and James, Lane end
Bathwell Thomas, Burslem
Bennett Wm. and Co. Burslem
Blackwell J. and R. Cowbridge
Booth and Bentley, Hanley
Booth Messrs. Lane end
Bott Thomas and Co. Lane end
Bourne, Baker and Bourne, Fenton
Bourne Charles, Fenton
Bourne Edward, Burslem
Box and Holdcroft, Cobridge
Bradshaw and Bourne, Hanley
Breeze Jesse, Tunstall
Bridgwood Kitty, Lane end
Bridgwood S. jun. Lane end
Brittell John, Burslem

Brough Thomas, Lane end
Brownfield R. and J. Hanley
Byerley J. Fenton
Cartlidge James, Burslem
Chetham Ann
Chetham and Woolley, Lane end
Child and Clive, Newfield
Clewer R. and J. Cobridge
Comer and Pratt, Lane Delph
Cyples Jesse, Lane end
Davenport J. and J. Longport
Dillon N. and F. Cowbridge
Ford and Hull, Lane end
Forrester G. Lane end
Forrester Joen, Lane end
Garner Robert, Lane end
Ginder S. Lane end
Glass J. and Son, Hanley
Godwin Benjamin and Sons, Cobridge
Godwin Thomas and Benjamin, Burslem
Hackwood and Co. Hanley
Hall J. and R. Burslem
Harley and Sackerson, Lane end
Harrison, Brough and Co. Lane end
Harvey Charles and Sons, Lane end
Hancock and Sheldon, Burslem
Harrison J. Stoke
Hartle, Singleton and Co. Lane end
Haywood John, Burslem
Heath Thomas, Burslem
Hedge Timothy, Burslem
Henshall and Williamson, Longport
Hicks and Meigh, Shelton
Holland Thomas, Burslem
Hollins T. J. and R. Hanley
Hollins, Warburton and Co. Hanley
Hughes Peter and Thomas, Lane end
Jarvis, Janson and Co. Burslem
Johnson and Brough, Lane end
Johnson Ralph, Burslem
Johnson Reuben, Hanley
Keeling James, Hanley
Keeling, Toft and Co. Hanley
Knight T. and J. Tunstall
Lindop and Taylor, Longport
Lockett George and Co. Lane end
Mace John, Tunstall
Mace Matthew and Co. Shelton
Machin and Bagilly, Burslem
Malkin Samuel, Lane end
Mansfield and Co. Keeting's lane
Marsh J. Lane Delph
Marsh J. and S. Brownhill
Mason M. and Son, Lane Delph
Massey Richard and T. Burslem
Matthes and Ball, Lane end
Mayer Elijah and Son, Hanley
Meigh Job and Sons, Hanley
Miles, Mason and Son, Lane Delph
Minton and Poulson, Stoke
Moseley John, Cobridge
Moseley Wm. Burslem
Moss H. Red street
Newberry B.C.W. Hanley
Oliver and Burne, Cobridge
Palmer Thomas, Lane end
Parrys Brothers, Sandyford
Poulson George, Stoke
Pratt J. Lane Delph
Rhud and Goodfellow, Burslem
Ridgway J. and W. Shelton
Riley John and Richard, Burslem
Robinson John and Christopher, Burslem
Rogers John, Longport
Shaw T. Lane end
Sheridan and Hyatt, Lane end
Shirley W. and J. Hanley and Shelton
Shorthouse John and Co. Hanley
Simpson Charles, Golden hill
Singleton Benjamin and Co. Lane end
Slade T. and Co. Tunstall
Spode Josiah, Stoke
Spode Samuel, Lane end
Stanley William, Burslem
Stevenson and Bucknall, Cobridge
Stevenson Ralph, Cobridge
Stirrup and Beardmore, Lane end
Stirrup T. Lane end
Stubbs and Taylor, Longport
Taylor Theophilus and James, Hanley
Turner William, Lane end
Walklate Hannah and Richard, Lane end
Walsh William, Burslem
Warburton John, Cowbridge
Wedgwood J. Esq. Etruria
Wedgwood Josiah and Byerley
Weston G. and Co. Lane end
Wilson and Breeze, Hanley
Wilson D. and Son, Hanley
Wolfe and Hamilton, Stoke
Wood and Caldwell, Burslem
Wood J. Brownhill
Yates, Sherwen and Co. Shelton
Yates John, Shelton

1818 Parson

Staffordshire General & Commercial Directory, for 1818, Part First, containing the Borough of Newcastle-under-Line, The Potteries, and the Town of Leek, &c., Compiled by Messrs. W. Parson and T. Bradshaw, Manchester (Norton 644, Norton 645). Dated 30 March 1818 in the Address of Part 1. This directory was published in four parts, with the Potteries in the first. A combined edition with all four parts was issued as the *Staffordshire General & Commercial Directory,* with an Address dated 21 October 1818.

This directory is not classified, the main section consisting of 'An Alphabetical List of the Merchants, Manufacturers, and Inhabitants in General'. It does, however, contain 'A List of the Earthenware Manufacturers in the Potteries, &c.' (pages 128-129), subdivided into the towns and villages shown.

Newcastle (page 128)
Bagshaw Samuel, Basford

Golden-Hill, Tunstall, Red-street, &c. (page 128)
Adams Benjamin, Tunstall
Boden John, Tunstall
Breeze Jesse, Green field
Cartledge Richard, Golden hill
Cartledge James, Golden hill
Child and Clive, New field
Collinson James, Golden hill
Hall J. and R. Tunstall and Burslem
Knight T. and J. Clay hill
Marsh & Haywood, Brown hills
Meir John, Tunstall
Moss T. and H. Red street
Myatt Benjamin, Red street
Nixon and Walley, Tunstall
Powis H. and Co. Sandiford
Rathbone W. S. & I. Tunstall
Vawdrey Daniel, Golden hill
Wood & Brittell, Brown hills

Burslem, Longport, Cobridge, &c. (page 128)
Bathwell T. & E. Chapel bank
Blackwell J. & R. Cobridge
Bourne W. & Co. Bell works
Bradshaw Jos. Booden brook
Brookes Philip and Co. Sitch
Cartledge and Beech, Knowle
Clews R. & J. Cobridge
Davenport J. and J. Newport
Dillon F. and N. Cobridge
Godwin B. and S. Cobridge
Godwin T. and B. New Basin
Goodfellow and Bathwell Upper House Works
Hall J. & R. Sitch & Tunstall
Heath John, Sitch
Heath Thomas, Hadderage
Henshall and Williamsons, Longport
Hobson Ephraim, Cobridge
Holdcroft and Box, Cobridge
Holland Anne, Hill top
Jarvis Richard, Nile street
Johnson Ralph, Church street
Leak Jonathan, 20 Row
Machin and Baggaley, Low st.
Machin Joseph, Waterloo road
Marsh Samuel, Brown hills
Massey Richard, Castle street
Massey S. and T. Nile street
Mellor John, near the Market place
Moseley John, Cobridge
Moseley John, Church yard
Moseley William, Queen st. Black Works
Oliver and Bourne, Cobridge
Riley J. and R. Hill works
Robinson J. and C. Hill top
Rogers John & Son, Longport
Rogers Spencer, Dale Hall
Stanley Wm. Knowle works
Steel Daniel, St. John's street
Stevenson Ralph, Cobridge
Stevenson Andrew, Cobridge
Stubbs Benjamin, Longport
Tomkinson Samuel, Church st
Walsh William, Furlong
Walton John, Hadderage
Warburton James, Hot lane
Warburton John, Hot lane
Wedgwood & Johnson, High st
Wood and Caldwell, Fountain place
Wood Ephraim, Hole house

Hanley and Shelton (pages 128-129)
Baddely William, Eastwood
Bradshaw Joseph, Booden Bk.
Brownfield W. and G. Keeling's lane
Glass John and Sons, Market-street
Hackwood, Dimmock, and Co. Hanley
Hicks and Meigh, Shelton
Hollins T. J. and R. Upper Hanley
Hollings and Co. Brook street, Shelton
Johnson Reuben, Miles bank
Keeling James, New st. Hanley
Mansfield, Pawley, & Co. Market-place
Mare Matthew and Co. Vale Pleasant
Mayer E. and Son, High street Hanley
Mayor & Keeling, (commision dealers) Charles street
Meigh Job & Son, Hill street, Hanley
Morris Thomas, Marsh street
Peover Frederick, High street

Ridgway J. and W. Shelton
Rivers and Clews, Shelton
Shorthouse John, Tontine st.
Taylor T. and J. High-street, Hanley
Whitehead Charles, (executors of) Shelton
Whitehead James, (commission dealer) Old Hall street,
Wilson D. and Sons, (assignees of) High street
Yates John, Broad st. Shelton

Stoke and Etruria (page 129)
Adams William, Stoke
Hamilton Robert, Stoke
Minton T. and Sons, Stoke
Poulson and Dale, Stoke
Spode Josiah, Esq. Stoke
Ward and Co. Stoke
Wedgwood Josiah, Esq. Etruria
Wolf Thomas, Stoke

Lane-End, &c. (page 129)
Baggaley Thomas, Lane delph
Barker R. J. & J. Flint street
Batkin and Deakin, Waterloo, Flint street.
Beardmore & Carr, Lane end
Booth J. and T. Lane end
Bourne, Baker, and Bourne, Fenton
Bourne Charles, Foley
Burrow Joseph, Foley works
Bridgwood Maria, Market st
Bridgwood Kitty and Son, Market street
Brough Thomas, Green dock
Carey and Son, Lane end
Cheetham M. and Son, Commerce street
Cyples Lydia, Market street
Drury T. & Son, Daisy Bank
Ford Hugh, Green dock
Forrester George, Market-pl.
Garner Robert, Lane end
Ginder S. and Co. Lane delph
Harley & Seckerson, Lane end
Harvey & Sons, Great Charles street
Hewitt J. & Son, Green dock
Hilditch and Martin, Lane end
Hughes Thomas, Lane delph
Lockett John and Co. King st
Lowe W. and J. Church street
Marsh Jacob, Lane delph
Mason William, Lane delph
Mason George and Charles, Lane delph
Mathers and Ball, Lane end
Mayor and Newbold, Market place
Myatt Benj. & Jos. Lane end
Nutt William, Flint street
Pattison James, High street
Poulson Wm. Chancery lane
Pratt F. and R. Fenton
Pratt John, Lane delph
Robinson John, High street
Robinson John, George street
Shelley, Booth & Co. Lane end
Sheridan J.H. Union Market pl
Simkin and Waller, Lane end
Stirrup Thomas, Flint street
Unett John, High street
Walklate H. & R. High street
Weston George, High street

1818 Pigot

The Commercial Directory, for 1818-19-20, Published by James Pigot, Fountain Street, and R. & W. Dean, Market Street, Manchester (Norton 31). Dated 1818 on the title page and 3 August 1818 in the Preface.

As with all the Pigot and Slater series, this directory is classified within a separate section for 'The Potteries' (pages 356-361). There are only two relevant categories.

China Manufacturers (page 357)
Bagley Thomas, Lane Delph
Barker William, Fenton
Brookes and Co. Sitch, Burslem
Davenport John and James, Longport
Goosetree Daniel, Lane Delph
Hilditch & Morton, near toll-bar, Lane-end
Hollins, Warburton, Daniels & Co. Hanley
Jarvis and Love, Burslem
Machin and Co. Nile-street, Burslem
Mason George and Charles, Lane Delph
Marsh and Heywood, Brownhill Potteries, Burslem
Mathes & Balls, High-street, Lane-end
Nutt William, Great Charles-st. Lane-end
Peover Frederick, Edmund-st. Hanley
Poulson and Dale, Dale-street, Stoke
Pratt, Weston, and Co. Lane Delph
Rathbone W. S. and J. Tunstall
Ridgway J. & Son, Caulden-place, Shelton
Riley John and Richard, Burslem
Simkin Woller, Lane-end
Spode Josiah, Stoke
Wolfe Thomas, Stoke
Wood and Caldwell, High-street, Burslem

Earthenware Manufacturers (page 358)
Ackwood, Dimmock and Co. Charles-street, Hanley
Adams William, Stoke
Adams Benjamin, Tunstall
Barlow and Ford, Bridge-street, Lane-end
Batkin, Thomas and Deakin, Waterloo-place, Lane-end
Bathwell Thomas, and Co. Red Lion-sq. Burslem
Beardmer and Carr, High-street, Lane-end
Beech James, St. John's-street, Burslem

Blackwell John and Robert, Cobridge
Boden John, Tunstall
Boon John, Qeen-street, Burslem
Bourne, Barker, and Bourne, Fenton
Bowrne Wm. and Co. Burslem
Bowrne William, Foley
Bradshaw Joseph, Booden-street, Hanley
Breeze William, Shelton
Breeze Jesse, Tunstall
Bridgwood, Ketty & Son, High-st Lane-end
Brough Thomas, Green-dock, Lane-end
Brownfield George, Keeling, Lane-end
Carey John, and Son, High-st Lane-end
Cartlidge and Beech (Egyptian black) Red Lion-square, Burslem
Cartlidge Richard, (black ware) Golden-hill
Cartwright William, Lane Delph
Clews Ralph and James, Cobridge
Collinson James (black ware) Golden-hill
Cormie John, Sitch, Burslem
Cyples Lydia (Egyptian black) Market-st. Lane-end
Davenport John and James, Longport
Dillon Francis and Nicholas, Cobridge
Forrister George, Market-place, Lane-end
Garner Robert, Church-street, Lane-end
Ginder Samuel, and Co. Lane Delph
Glass and Sons, Hanley
Godwin T. and B. New Wharf, Burslem
Godwin Benjamin, and Sons, Cobridge
Hall John and Ralph, Tunstall
Hall John and Ralph, Burslem-bank
Hamilton Robert, Stoke
Harley and Seckerson, High-st. Lane-end
Harvey Charles & Son, Charles-st. Lane-end
Heath John, Old Sitch, Burslem
Heath Thomas, near New Road, Burslem
Henshall and Williamson, Longport
Hewitt John & Son, Green-dock, Lane-end
Hollins Thosmas, John and Richard, Fare-green, Hanley
Hughes Thomas, Lane Delph
Jarvis and Love, near Church, Burslem
Johnson Ralph, Silvester-square, Burslem
Johnson Reubin, Hanley
Johnson George, Sitch, Burslem
Johnson Ralph, Sitch, Burslem
Keeling, Toft & Co. Charles-st. Hanley
Keeling James, New-street, Hanley
Knight Thomas and Joseph, Tunstall
Leak Jonathan, (Egyptian) Burslem
Mallard John, Market-place, Burslem
Mantry Adam, Shelton
Marsh and Heywood, Brown-hill
Marsh Jacob, Lane Delph
Massey Samuel, Back of Methodist Chapel, Burslem
Mason William, Lane Delph
Mayer & Newbald, Market-place, Lane-end
Mayer Joseph & Son, High-street, Hanley
Meir John, Tunstall
Meigh Job and Son, Hill-street, Hanley
Minton Thomas & Sons, Stoke
Mosley John, (Egyptian black) Queen-st. Burslem
Myatt B. and J. High-street, Lane-end
Myatt John, Wm. & Jas. High-st. Lane-end
Nixon and Walley, Tunstall
Oliver ———, Cobridge
Pattison James, (toy) Lane-end
Platt and Bridgwood, High-st. Lane-end
Poulson ———, Lane-end
Powes Henry & Chas. Sandiford, Golden-hill
Pratt Felix and Richard, Fenton
Pratt John, Lane Delph
Rhead and Goodfellow, Burslem
Ridgway John & Son, Albion-st. Shelton
Riley John and Richard, Burslem
Rivers Wm. and Co. Shelton
Robinson John & Christopher, Hill-works, Burslem
Rogers John and Son, Longport
Shirley Cephas, Hanley
Shorthouse John and Co. Hill-st. Hanley
Sparkes George, Hanley
Spode Josiah, Stoke
Stanley Wm. Knowle-street, Burslem
Stevenson Ralph, Cobridge
Stevenson Andrew, Cobridge
Taylor Thomas and James, High-st Hanley
Tomkinson Samuel, Queen-st. Church-st. Burslem
Vodril Joseph (black ware) Golden Hill
Walklate Hannah and Richard, High-street, Lane-end
Walton John, Navigation-road, Burslem
Ward and Davenport, Cliff-bank, Stoke
Wedgwood Josiah, Etruria
Wedgwood and Co. Rotten-row, High-st. Burslem
Weston George, High-street, Lane-end
Whitehead James, Hill-street, Hanley
Wilson David, and Son, High-st. Hanley
Wolfe Thomas, Stoke
Wood Samuel, Hanley
Wood and Caldwell, High-street, Burslem
Wood John, Tunstall
Wood and Brettell, Brownhills, Burslem
Wright Thomas Upper-green, Hanley
Yeates John, Shelton

1822 Allbut

The Newcastle and Pottery General and Commercial Directory, for 1822-23, Printed and Sold by T. Allbut, Hanley (Norton 646).

This directory is not classified, the main section consisting of 'An Alphabetical Arrangement of the Names and Residences of the Nobility, Gentry, Merchants, and Inhabitants in General'. It does, however, contain 'A List of China, Earthenware, &c. Manufacturers' (pages 125-128). Note that despite being titled 'manufacturers' the list includes several enamellers, lusterers, gilders and similar tradesmen. They have been retained below for completeness.

ADAMS William, earthenware manufacturer, Stoke
Baddeley Thomas, enameller & lusterer, Slack' lane, Hanley
——— William, fancy and ornamental earthenware manufacturer, Eastwood, Hanley
Bailey and Batkin, gilders and lusterers, Flint st. Lane-end
Ball and Baggaley, china manufacts. High st. Lane-end
Barker and Co. earthenware manufacts. Market st. Burslem
——— Charles, lusterer and enameller Brook st. Shelton
——— Richard, earthenware manufact. Flint st. Lane-end
——— J. and J., earthenware, shining black manufacturers, lusterers, and enamellers, High street, Lane-end
Barlow James, and Co. china manufacts. Miles bk. Hanley
——— & Ford, earthenware manufacts. Bridge st. Lane-end
Barnes Geo. Egyptian black manufact. Hog's ln. Lane-end
Bathwell and Goodfellow, earthenware manufacts. Tunstall
Batkin, Dale, & Deakin, earthenware manufacts. Lane-end
Beardmore and Carr, earthenware manufacts. Lane-end
Bettaney George, lusterer, &c. High street, Lane-end
Birks Chas. lusterer and enameller, Market st. Lane-end
—— Chas. china manufact. High street, Lane-end
Blackwell John, earthenware manufact. Cobridge
Boden John, earthenware manufact. and gilder, Tunstall
Booth Jos. & Thos. earthenware manufacts. Lane-end
Bourne and Cormie, earthenware manufacturers, Burslem
———, Baker, and Bourne, china and earthenware manufacturers, Fenton
——— Charles, china and earthenware manufacturer, Foley
Bradshaw William, lusterer & enameller, High st. Lane-end
Breeze Jesse, earthenware manufact. Green-field, Tunstall
Bridgwood Sampson, china manufact. Market st. Lane-end
Brown Sarah, earthenware manufact. & enameller, Hanley
——— John, coarse ware manufact. Market lane, Hanley
Brownfield W. & G. earthenware manufacts. Keeling's lane, Hanley
CAREY John and Sons, earthenware manufacturers, Lane-delph and Lane-end
Cartledge Richard, earthenware manufact. Golden hill
——— & Cork, earthenware manufacts. Queen st. Burslem
Cartlidge and Beech, earthenware and Egyptian black manufacts. Knowl street, Burslem
Challiner Edward, earthenware manufacturer, Burslem
Chatfield & Co. earthenware manufacts. Charles st. Lane-end
Cheetham and Robinson, china, earthenware, Egyptian black, &c. manufacts. Commerce st. Lane-end
Child and Clive, earthenware manufacts. Newfield, Tunstall
Clews R. & J. china and earthenware manufacts. Cobridge
Collinson James, coarse ware manufacturer, Golden hill
Cowap, Hughes, & Co. earthenware manufacts. Cobridge
Cutts John, gilder and enameller, New street, Hanley
Cyples Lydia, Egyptian black manufact. Lane-end
DAVENPORT J. and J. china and earthenware manufacturers, Longport and Newport, glass manufacturers, and manufacts. of lead and litherage, Longport
——— Thomas, gilder and painter, Old Hall st. Hanley
Dillon F. and N. earthenware manufacturers, Cobridge
Dimmock Thos. earthenware manufact. Cheapside, Shelton
Drewry and Son. china manufacts. Daisy bank, Lane-end
ELKIN, Knight, & Elkin, earthenware manufacts. Lane-end
Ellis Moses, lusterer and black printer, Tontine st. Hanley
FORD Lewis, and Co. earthenware and shining black manufacturers, Shelton lane
—— and Allerton, earthenware manufacturers, Lane-delph
Forrester George, earthenware manufact. Lane-end
Fouche Stephen, iron stone china manufacturer, Stoke
GINDER Samuel, & Co. earthenware manufacts. Lane-delph
Glass John and Sons, earthenware manufacts. Hanley
Godwin Ben. and Sons, earthenware manufacts. Cobridge
——— Thos. & Ben. earthenware manufacts. Burslem
HACKWOOD, Dimmock, & Co. earthenware manufacts. Hanley
Hall Ralph, earthenware manufacturer, Tunstall
—— John, earthenware manufacturer, Sitch, Burslem
Hamilton Robert, earthenware manufacturer, Stoke
Hammersley Ralph and Co. enamellers and gilders, Shelton
——— William, earthenware manufacturer, Lane-end
Handley J. and W. earthenware manufacts. Kilcroft, Burslem, and china manufacts. High street, Shelton
Harley and Seckerson, earthenware manufacturers, lusterers, and enamellers, Market street, Lane-end
Harvey and Sons, earthenware manufacts. Lane-end
Hawley and Rhead, earthenware manufacturers, Burslem
Heath John, china and figure manufacturer, Sitch, Burslem
——— Thomas, earthenware manufacturer, Burslem
Heathcote Charles, and Co. china and earthenware manufacturers, Lane-end
Henshall & Williamsons, earthenware manufacts. Longport
Hewitt John, and Son, earthenware manufact. Lane-end
Hicks, Meigh, and Johnson, china and earthenware manufacturers, High street, Shelton
Hilditch William, and Sons, china manufacts. Lane-end
Hollins, Warburton, Daniel, and Co. china manufacturers, New Hall, New Hall street, Shelton
Holland Ann, & Co. shining black manufacts. Burslem

JARVIS William, lusterer and enameller, Charles st. Lane-end
Johnson Ralph, earthenware manufacturer, Burslem
——— Reuben, lusterer, enameller, and earthenware manufacturer, Miles bank, Hanley
Jones and Ball, gilders and enamellers, Tunstall
KEELING James, earthenware manufact. Cross st. Hanley
——— Toft, and Co. earthenware and Egyptian black manufacts. Old Hall street, Hanley
——— Charles, gilder and enameller, Albion st. Shelton
LOCKETT and Hulme, china, earthenware, Egyptian black, &c. manufacturer, King street, Lane-end
Lownds and Beech, earthenware manufacts. Sandiford
MACHIN and Co. china and earthenware manufacts. Burslem
——— Joseph, enameller and black printer, Burslem
Mansfield and Hackney, earthenware manufacts. Cobridge
Marsh and Heywood, earthenware manufacts. Brown hills
——— Jacob, earthenware manufacturer, Lane-end
Mare Matthew, & Co. china manufacts. Vale, Etruria wharf
Martin, Shaw, and Cope, china manufacts. Lane-end
——— and Bailey, china manufacturers, Lane-end
Mason George and Charles, china, earthenware manufacts. and sole proprietors of the patent iron stone china, Lane-\ delph
Massey Richard, lusterer and enameller, Burslem
——— Samuel, lusterer and enameller, Burslem
Mayer Elijah and Son, earthenware manufacts. Hanley
——— and Newbold, manufacturers and ornamenters of china and earthenware, Market place, Lane-end
Meigh Job and Son, earthenware manufacturers, Hanley
Minton Thomas and Sons, earthenware manufacts. Stoke
Moseley John, earthenware and Egyptian black manufact. Church yard works, Burslem
Moss Henshall, earthenware manufacturer, Red street
Myatt and Hulse, earthenware manufacturers, Lane-end
—— Benjamin, Joseph, & Co. china, earthenware manufacturers, lusterers and enamellers, Lane-end
NUTT William, china manufact. enameller, &c. Lane-end
PARKER and Brindley, earthenware manufact. Golden hill
Peover Ann, china manufact. High street, Hanley
Philips Edward & George, earthenware manufacts. Longport
——— and Bagster, earthenware manufacts. Hanley
Platt and Bridgwood, earthenware manufacts. Lane-end
Pointon and Stubbs, painters and gilders, Swan st. Hanley
Powis Charles, earthenware manufacturer, Sandiford
Pratt Felix & Richard, earthenware manufacts. Lane-delph
——, Hassall, & Gerard, china manufacts. Lane-delph
Pye and Booth, earthenware manufacts. Lane-end
RATHBONE W. S. & T. china manufacts. Tunstall
Ratcliffe Humphrey, earthenware manufact. Stoke lane
Ridgway John and Co. earthenware manufacts. Shelton
——— John and William, china and earthenware manufacts. Cauldon place, Shelton
Riley John and Richard, china and earthenware manufacts. Hill works, Burslem
Rivers & Clews, china and earthenware manufacts. Shelton
Robinson John, earthenware manufact. Hill, Burslem
Robinson, Goodwin, and Co. earthenware and Egyptian black manufacturers, High street, Lane-end
Rogers John and Son, earthenware manufacts. Longport
SALT Ralph, lusterer and enameller, Miles bank, Hanley
Sanforth Samuel, stone bottle manufacturer, Burslem
Shaw, Griffiths, and Co. earthenware manufacts. Lane-end
Shorthose John, and Co. earthenware manufacts. Hanley
Simpson Nicholas, earthenware manufact. Shelton
Simpkin Hugh and Son, china manufacts. Lane-end
Spode Josiah, Esq. china and earthenware manufact. Stoke
Steel John, and Co. china manufacts. Tunstall
——— Daniel, jasper and ornamental earthenware manufact. Nile street, Burslem
Stevenson Andrew, china & earthenware manufact. Cobridge
——— Ralph, earthenware manufact. Cobridge
Stubbs Joseph, earthenware manufact. Longport
TAYLOR Thomas, earthenware manufact. Hanley
Tomkinson Samuel, earthenware manufact. Burslem
VAWDREY Daniel, red ware manufact., Golden hill
Walley George, earthenware manufact. Tunstall
Walsh William, earthenware manufat. Burslem
Walton John, Egyptian black and figure manufact. Burslem
Warburton John, Earthenware manufact. Cobridge
Ward Thomas, and Co. earthenware manufacts. Stoke
Wedgwood Thomas, earthenware manufact. Burslem
——— Josiah, Esq. earthenware manufact. Etruria
Weston George, china and earthenware manufact. Lane-end
——— Sarah, lusterer and enameller, High st. Lane-end
Wood and Brettell, earthenware manufacts. Brown hills
Wood Ephraim, figure maker and enameller, Burslem
Wood Enoch and Sons, china and earthenware manufacts. Fountain place, Burslem
Wright Thomas, coarse ware manufact. Hanley
YATES John, china and earthenware manufact. Shelton

1822 Pigot

Pigot and Co.'s London & Provincial New Commercial Directory, for 1822-3, Published by J. Pigot and Co., Fountain Street, Manchester (Goss p.109, Norton 35). Dated 24 June 1822 in the Address.

As with all the Pigot and Slater series, this directory is classified within a separate section for 'The Potteries' (pages 474-480). There are only two relevant categories.

China Manufacturers (page 476)
Baggelley and Taylor, Lane-delph
Baggerley and Balls, High-street, Lane-end
Bradshaw Wm. High-st. Lane-end
Davenport Jas. & John, Longport
Drewry Thos & Son, Daisy-bank, Lane-end
Folch and Scott, Stoke
Heathcote Charles & Co. Lane-end

Hicks and Meigh, Shelton
Hilditch Wm. and Son, Lane-end
Hollins, Warburton, Daniels & Co. Shelton
Keeling Chas. Broad-st. Shelton
Machin and Co. Nile-st. Burslem
Mare Mattw. Vale-pleasant, Shelton
Marsh and Haywood, Brownhill-potteries, Burslem
Mason Geo. and Chas. Lane-delph
Mayor and Newbold, Market-place, Lane-end
Nutt Wm. gt. Charles-st. Lane-end
Peover Ann, High-street, Hanley
Rathbone W. S. and J. Tunstall
Ridgway John and Wm. Caulden-place, Shelton
Riley John and Richard, Liverpool-road, Burslem
Rivers Wm. and Co. Bedford-row, Shelton
Royle Edward, Market-st. Lane-end
Simpkin Hugh, Flint-st. Lane-end
Spode Josiah, Stoke
Steele John & Thomas, New-field, Tunstall
Wood Enoch and Sons, Burslem

Earthenware Manufacturers (pages 476-477)
Adams Wm. Stoke
Baddeley Wm. Eastwood, Hanley
Badley Thos. Miles-bank, Hanley
Barker John and Joseph, High-st. Lane-end
Barlow & Ford, Bridge-st. Lane-end
Bathwell and Goodfellow, Tunstall
Batkin, Dale & Deakin, Waterloo-place, Lane-end
Beardmer and Carr, High-street, Lane-end
Bennett Joseph and Co. Queen-st. Burslem
Blackwell John, Cobridge
Boden John, Tunstall
Booth Wm. and Son, Waterloo place, Hanley
Booth Joseph and Thos. Stafford-street, Lane-end
Bourne, Baker and Bourne, Fenton
Bourne & Cormie, Queen-st. Burslem
Bourne Charles, Foley
Bradshaw Wm. High-st. Lane-end
Breeze Jesse, Tunstall
Brough Thos. Green-dock, Lane-end
Brown Sarah and Co. George-st. Hanley
Brownfield Wm. and George, Keelings-lane, Hanley
Burrow Joseph, junr. High-street, Lane-end
Carey John and Sons, Lane-delph
Cartlidge and Beech, Hamill-st. Burslem
Cartlidge Richard, Golden-hill
Challinor Edwd. Overhouse-works, Burslem
Chetham and Robinson, Commercial-street, Lane-end
Child & Clive, New-field, Tunstall
Clews Ralph and James, Cobridge
Collinson James, Golden-hill
Cowap, Hughes & Co. Cobridge
Cyples Lydia, Market-st. Lane-end
Davenport John and James, (and flint and cut glass) Longport
Dillon Francis & Nicholas, Cobridge
Dimmock Thomas, junr. and Co. James-street, Shelton
Edge Timothy, (chimney pipe and flower pot) Marsh-st. Shelton, and Holehouse, Burslem
Elkin, Knight and Elkin, Church-street, Lane-end
Ford, Lewis & Co. (shining black) Shelton
Forrister Geo. Market-pl. Lane-end
Ginder Samuel and Co. Lane-delph
Glass John, Market-st. Hanley
Godwin T. and B. New-wharf, Burslem
Godwin Benj. and Sons, Cobridge
Godwin, Rathbone & Co. Market-place, Burslem
Hackwood, Dimmock and Co. Eastwood, Hanley
Hall John and Ralph, Tunstall and Burslem
Hamilton Robert, Stoke
Handley James and Wm. Chapel-street, Burslem
Harley & Seckerson, High-st Lane-end
Harvey Charles and John, Lane-end
Hawley and Read, Waterloo-road, Burslem
Heath John, Old-sitch, Burslem
Heath Thos. Hadderidge, Burslem
Heathcote Chas. and Co. Lane-end
Henshall & Williamsons, Long-port
Hewitt John and Son, Longton, Lane End
Hicks and Meigh, Shelton
Holland Ann, Liverpool-rd. Burslem
Hollins Thomas, John, & Richard, Far-green, Hanley
Hood George, (toy only) Tunstall
Jarvis Wm. Gt. Charles-st. Lane-end
Johnson Rbn. Miles-bank, Hanley
Johnson Ralph, Church-st. Burslem
Keeling Toft and Co. Charles-st. Hanley
Keeling James, New-st. Hanley
Lockett John, & Hulme, King-street, Lane-end
Lowndes and Beech, Sandiford, Golden-hill
Mansfield & Hackney, Cobridge
Marsh & Haywood, Brown-hill
Marsh Jacob, Lane-end
Marsh and Willott, Keeling's-lane, Hanley
Martin Shaw and Cope, St. Martin's-lane, Lane-end
Mason Geo. and Chas. Lane-delph
Mason Miles, Lane-delph
Massey Richd. Newcastle-st. Burslem
Mayer Elijah & Son, High-st. Hanley
Meir John, Tunstall
Meigh Job & Son, Hill-st. Hanley
Minton Thomas and Sons, Stoke
Moseley John, (& Egyptian black) Church-pottery, Burslem
Myatt John, Church-st. Lane-end
Myatt B. & J. & Co. High-st. Lane-end
Parker Thos. Golden-hill
Pattison Jas. (toy) High-st. Lane-end
Phillips & Bagster, High-st. Hanley
Platt & Bridgwood, High-st. Lane-end
Powes Henry & Charles, Sandiford, Golden-hill
Pratt Felix & Richard, Fenton
Pratt, Hassell & Gerrard, Lane-delph
Pratt John, Lane-delph
Ridgway John & William, Caulden-place, Shelton
Ridgway J. & Co. Albion-st. Shelton
Riley John and Richard, (and black lustre) Liverpool-road, Burslem

Rivers Wm. & Co. Bedford-ro. Shelton
Robey Wm. & Co. (coarse) Furnace
Robinson, Goodwin & Co. High-st. Lane-end
Robinson John, Hill-works, Burslem
Rogers John & Son, Long-port
Shaw Griffiths and Co. Stafford-st. Lane-end
Shorthouse John & Co. Tontine-st. Hanley
Simpson Nich. Boden-brook, Shelton
Spode Josiah, Stoke
Steel Daniel & Sons, Hole-house, Burslem
Stevenson Ralph, Cobridge
Stevenson Andrew, Cobridge
Stubbs Benjamin, Long-port
Taylor Thomas, High-st. Hanley
Tomkinson Samuel, Church-street, Queen-street, Burslem
Vernon Geo. & Co. Chapel-sq. Burslm
Vodril Joseph, Golden-hill
Walley George, Tunstall
Walsh Wm. Newcastle-st. Burslem
Walton John, Navigation-rd. Burslm
Warburton John, Cobridge
Ward & Davenport, Cliff-bank, Stoke
Wedgwood Josiah, Etruria
Wedgwood Thos. Rotten-row, High-street, Burslem
Weston Geo. High-st. Lane-end
Weston Sarah, High-st. Lane-end
Whitehead Jas. Charles-st. Hanley
Wood Enoch & Sons, Burslem
Wood & Brettell, Brownhill, Burslm
Wright Thos. up. High-st. Hanley
Yates John, Broad-st. Shelton

1828 Pigot

Pigot and Co.'s National Commercial Directory, for 1828-9, Published by J. Pigot & Co., 24 Basing Lane, London, and 18 Fountain Street, Manchester (Goss p.119, Norton 47). Address not dated.

As with all the Pigot and Slater series, this directory is classified within a separate section for 'The Potteries' (pages 722-730). There are only two relevant categories.

China Manufacturers (page 725)
Adams Wm. Newcastle st. Stoke
Alcock, Mason & Co. High st, Lane E
Alcock Samuel & Co. Cobridge
Baggerley & Ball, High st, Lane End
Bailey Wm. & David, Flint st, Lane E
Barker Jno. & Jos. High st, Lane E
Barlow James, Miles bank, Hanley
Bettany Geo. High st, Lane End
Birks Chas. High st, Lane End
Booth Rd. & Sons, Church st, Lane E
Bourne Charles, Foley
Boyle Zach. & Son, Keeling's lane, Hanley
Breeze John & Co. Cobridge
Bridgwood Samp. Market st, Lane E
Carey Jno & Sons, Anchor st, Lane E
Chetham & Robinson, Commerce st, Lane End
Cormie John, Queen st, Burslem
Cyples Lydia (and Egyptian black) Market st, Lane End
Daniel Henry, Bedford row, Shelton
Daniel Hy. & Rd. New road, Stoke
Davenport Jno. Son & Co. Longport
Dillon Fras. & Nicholas, Cobridge
Drewry Ts. Daisy bank, Lane End
Faulkner & Robinson, George st, Lane End
Folch Stephen (stone) Church st, Stoke
Gerrard, Cope & Co. High st, Lane E
Handley James & Willm. Killcroft, Burslem
Hicks, Meigh & Johnson, Broad st, Shelton
Hilditch Wm. & Sons, Church st, Lane End
Jarvis Wm. Great Charles st, Lane End
Machin Jos. & Co. Nile st, Burslem
Martin Wm. Market pl, Lane End
Mason & Co. Lane Delph
Mayer & Newbold, Market pl, Lane End
Mayer Thomas, Cliff bank, Stoke
Minton Thos. New road, Stoke
Pratt, Hassall & Gerrard, Lane Delph
Rathbone Saml. & John, Tunstall
Ridgway Jno. & Co. High st, Shelton
Ridgway Jno. & Wm. (stone) Cauldon place
Riley Jno. & Richd. Liverpool road, Burslem
Shaw Jno. Green dock, Lane End
Simkin Hugh, High st, Lane End
Spode Josiah, Newcastle st, Stoke
Taylor William, Hogg's lane, Lane E
Weston Geo. High st, Lane End
Yates John, Broad st, Shelton

Earthenware Manufacturers (page 726)
Marked thus * are Toy only.
Adams Wm. Newcastle st, Stoke
Alcock Thos. High st, Burslem
Bagster Jno. Denton, High st, Hanley
Bailey Wm. & Dav. Flint st, Lane E
Barker Jn. & Jos. High st, Lane End
Barlow & Ford, Bridge st, Lane E
Bill, Simpson & Co. Flint st, Lane E
Booth Jos. & Thos. Flint st, Lane End
Bourne, Baker & Bourne, Fenton
Bourne Charles, Foley
Bourne, Nixon & Co. Tunstall
Boyle Zach. & Co. Keeling's la, Hanley
Brindley Jno. & Co. Broad st, Sheltn
* Brown Hy. & Co. High st, Lane End
Burrow Jos. jun. High st, Lane End

Carey Jno. & Sons, Anchor st, Lane E
Chetham and Robinson, Commerce street, Lane End
Clews Ralph & James, Cobridge
Collinson Jas. Golden hill
Copestick, Hassall & Gerard, Lane Delph
Cormie John, Queen st, Burslem
Daniel Henry, Bedford row, Shelton
Daniel Hen. & Rd. New road, Stoke
Davenport Jno. Son & Co. Longport
Deakin & Bailey, WATERLOO FACTORY, Lane End
Dillon Fras. & Nicholas, Cobridge
Dimmock Ts. & Co. Cheapside, Sheltn
Dimmock Thos. jun. & Co. Tontine street, Hanley
Edge William, PRIMITIVE WORKS, Golden hill
Elkin, Knight & Bridgwood, Lane E
Folch Stephen, Church st, Stoke
Forrister Geo. Marker pl, Lane End
Gallimore Ts. Bourne's bank, Burslm
Ginder and Hulse, Lane Delph
Ginder Saml. & Co. Lane Delph
Glass John, Market st, Hanley
Godwin Benj. and Sons, Cobridge
Godwin, Rowley & Co. Market pl, Burslem
Godwin Thos. & Benj. New wharf, Burslem
Goodfellow Ts. Liverpool rd, Tunstal
Goodwins, Bridgwood and Orton, High street, Lane End
Griffiths Ths. & Co. Flint st, Lane End
* Grocott Sml. Liverpool rd, Tunstall
Hackwood Wm. Eastwood, Hanley
Hall Jn. & Sons, Liverpool rd, Burslm
Hall Ralph, Tunstall
Hawley Elias & Son, Waterloo road, Burslem
Heath Jos. & Co. Newfield, Tunstall
Heath Thos. Haderidge, Burslem
Henshall & Williamson, Longport
Hicks, Meigh & Johnson, Broad st, Shelton
Holland & Pearson, Liverpool road, Burslem
* Holland Thos. Church st, Burslem
Hollins, Daniels, Warburton & Co. New hall, Shelton
Hughes & Taylor, Cobrigde
Hulme Jn. & Sons, Gt Charles st, Lane End
Johnson Phoebe, Miles bank, Hanley
Jones Elijah, Hall lane, Hanley
Jones Ts. & Co. Bedford row, Shelton
Keeling Jas. New st, Hanley
* Lawton Dnl. Chapel lane, Burslem
Legg Isaac (coarse) Furness
Lockett Jno. & Son, King st, Lane End
Lowndes & Beech, Sandy ford, Tunstl
Machin Jos. & Co. Nile st, Burslem
Mansfield and Hackney, Cobridge
Marsh & Haywood, Brownhills
Marsh Jacob, Church st, Lane End
Mason and Co. Lane Delph
Massey Rd. Newcastle st, Burslem
Mayer & Newbold, Market pl, Lane E
Mayer Elijah & Son (& drab china) Upper High st, Hanley
Mayer Thos. Cliff bank, Stoke
Meigh Job & Son, Hill st, Hanley
Meir John, Tunstall
Minton Thos. New road, Stoke
Moreton Thos. Eastwood, Hanley
* Parr Rich. jun. Church st, Burslem
* Pattison Jas. High st, Lane End
Peake Thos. & Co. (ornaments and vessels for gentlemen's gardens) Tunstall
Phillips Edwd. & Geo. Longport
Pointon Wm. Overhouse, Burslem
Pratt Felix & Rd. FENTON POTTERY
Pratt John, Lane Delph
Read & Platt, Market pl, Burslem
Ridgway John and Co. (fine) Albion st, Shelton
Ridgway John & Wm. (fine) Cauldon pl, Shelton
Riley Jn. & Rd. Liverpool rd, Burslem
Robinson Noah, Shelton
Rogers Jno. & Son. Dale hall, Longport
* Salt Ralph, Marsh st, Shelton
Shaw John, Green dock, Lane End
* Skerratt Obad. Hot lane, Burslem
Spode Josiah, Newcastle st, Stoke
Steel Daniel & Son (jasper & stone) Bourne's bank, Burslem
Stevenson Andrew, Cobridge
Stevenson Ralph, Cobridge
* Stretton Saml. Lane Delph
Stubbs & Kent, Longport
Swettenham Thos. Nile st, Burslem
Taylor Thos. High st, Hanley
Toft & May, Oldhall st, Hanley
* Tunnicliffe Michael, Tunstall
Turner Wm. High st, Lane End
Walton Jno. Navigation rd, Burslem
Ward Thos. & Co. Newcastle st, Stoke
Wedgwood Josiah & Son, Etruria
Weston Geo. High st, Lane End
Wood & Blood, High st, Lane End
Wood & Challinor, Brownhills
Wood Enoch and Sons, Fountain place, Burslem
* Wood Ephraim, Wood's bank, Burslem
Wright Wm. (coarse) Upper High street, Hanley
Yates John, Broad st, Shelton

1830 Pigot

Pigot and Co.'s New Commercial Directory, for Staffordshire, Warwickshire, Worcestershire, Shropshire & North Wales, Published by J. Pigot & Co., 17 Basing Lane, London, and 18 Fountain Street, Manchester (Norton 52). This volume is not dated, and while Norton lists it as 1829, she suggests that it is just a reprint of 1828 Pigot whereas examination shows that it has definitely been updated. The only original located is in the William Salt Library at Stafford, and their copy has been rebound and contains no Address (often dated in Pigot directories). Photocopies in the Stoke library are catalogued as 1830-31. The only clue to an accurate date is that Pigot's London address is given as No. 17 Basing Lane on the title page. In the Post Office London Directories, Pigot was listed at No. 24 until 1829, No. 17 during 1830 and 1831 only, and then at No.1 until his later move to Fleet Street. Taking this into account, it was felt that a date of 1830 would be most appropriate for the purposes of this work. Should further information subsequently become available, this date may need to be reconsidered.

As with all the Pigot and Slater series, this directory is classified within a separate section for 'The Potteries' (pages 720-730). There are only two relevant categories.

China Manufacturers (page 724)
Adams William, High st, Stoke
Alcock Samuel & Co. Cobridge
Baggerley & Ball, High st, Lane End
Bailey Wm. & David, Flint st, Lane E.
Barker Jos. & Jno. High st, Lane E.
Barlow Jas. & Co. Slack's la. Sheltn
Bettany George, High st, Lane End
Birks Charles, High st, Lane End
Booth Rd. & Son, Church st, Lane E.
Bourne Charles, Foley
Boyle Zachariah & Son, Stoke
Breeze John & Co. Tunstall
Bridgwood Sampson, Market st, Lane End
Carey Thomas & John, Anchor st, Lane End
Chetham and Robinson, Commerce street, Lane End
Cormie John, Queen st, Burslem
Cyples Lydia (and Egyptian black) Market street, Lane End
Daniel Henry and Co. Bedford row, Shelton
Daniel Henry and Richard, Eldon st, Stoke
Davenport John, Son and Co. (and glass manufacturers) Longport
Dillon Francis, Cobridge
Drewry Thomas, Daisy bank, Lane End
Ellis Ths. Union Market pl, Lane E.
Faulkner and Robinson, George st, Lane End
Greatbach William, jun. Stoke
Hicks, Meigh & Johnson, Broad st, Shelton
Hilditch Wm. and Sons, Church st, Lane End
Hollins, Warburton, Daniel & Co. New hall street, Shelton
Jervis Wm. Gt. Charles st, Lane E.
Johnson Phoebe & Son, Miles bank, Shelton
Machin & Co. Nile st, Burslem
Martin Wm. Market pl, Lane End
Mason and Co. Lane Delph
Mayer and Newbold, Caroline st, Lane End
Mayer Thomas, Cliff bank, Stoke
Minton Thomas, New road, Stoke
Pratt, Hassall & Gerrard, Lane Delph
Rathbone Saml. & John, Tunstall
Ridgway Jno. & Co. High st, Shelton
Ridgway Jno. & Wm. (stone) Cauldon place
Seabridge James, High st, Lane End
Shaw Kitty, Market pl, Lane End
Simkin Hugh, High st, Lane End
Spode Josiah, High st, Stoke
Taylor William, Hogg's la, Lane E.
Yates John, Broad st, Shelton

Earthenware Manufacturers (pages 725-726)
Marked thus * are Toy only
Adams William, High st. Stoke
Bailey Wm. & Dav. Flint st. Lane End
Barker Jos. & Jno. High st. Lane End
Barker, Sutton and Till, High st. Burslem
Bettany George, High st. Lane End
Bill, Simpson & Co. Flint st. Lane End
Birks Charles, High st. Lane End
Booth Jos. & Thos. Flint st. Lane End
* Booth Richard, Marsh st. Shelton
Bourne, Baker and Bourne, Fenton
Bourne Charles, Foley
Bourne, Nixon and Co. Tunstall
Boyle Zachariah and Son, Stoke
* Brammer Ths. Daisey bank, Lane E
Carey Thomas and John, Anchor st. Lane end, and Lane Delph
Chetham and Robinson, Commerce street, Lane end
Clews Ralph and James, Cobridge
Collinson James, Golden hill
* Copestick Daniel, Lane Delph
Cormie John, Queen st. Burslem
Daniel Henry & Co. Bedford row, Shelton
Davenport Jno. Son & Co. Longport
Deakin & Bailey, WATERLOO FACTORY, Lane End
Dillon Francis, Cobridge
Dimmock Thomas, jun. and Co. Cheapside, Shelton
* Edge, Danl. Waterloo road, Burslem
Edge William, PRIMITIVE WORKS, Golden hill
Edwards Wm. High st. Lane End
Elkins', Knight & Bridgwood, Lane E
* Ellis James, Pall mall, Shelton
Forrister Geo. Market pl. Lane End
Ginder and Hulse, Lane Delph
Ginder Samuel & Co. Lane Delph
Glass John, Market st. Hanley

Godwin Benj. and Sons, Cobridge
Godwin, Rowley & Co. Market pl. Burslem
Godwin Thos. & Benj. New wharf, Burslem
Goodwins, Bridgwood and Harris, Flint st. Lane End
Goodfellow Ts. Liverpool rd. Tunstal
Griffiths Ths. & Co. Flint st, Lane E.
Hackwood William, Hanley
Hall Jn. & Sons, Liverpool rd. Burslm
Hall Ralph, Tunstall
* Hall Saml. New Hall st. Shelton
Harrison John, Longton pottery
Hawley Jos. Waterloo road, Burslem
Heath Jos. & Co. Newfield, Tunstall
Heath Thomas, Haderidge, Burslem
Henshall & Williamson, Longport
Hicks, Meigh & Johnson, Broad st. Shelton
Holland Ann & Co. Liverpool road, Burslem
* Holland Thos. Church st. Burslem
Hood George, Tunstall
Hughes Thomas, Cobrige
Hulme Jn. & Sons, Gt. Charles st. Lane End
Hulse, Jaquiss and Barlow, Bridge st. Lane End
Jackson Job and John, Church pottery, Burslem
Johnson Phoebe and Son, Miles bank, Hanley
Jones & Toplis, Bedford rw, Shelton
Jones Elijah, Hanley
* Jones Hannah, Market pl. Hanley
Keeling James, New st. Hanley
* Lawton Dnl. Chapel lane, Burslem
Legg Isaac (coarse) Furness
Lockett Jno. & Son, King st. Lane End
Lowndes & Beech, Sandyford, Tunstl
Machin and Co. Nile st. Burslem
Machin John, Holehouse, Burslem
Mansfield and Hackney, Cobridge
Marsh and Haywood, Brownhills
Marsh Jacob, Church st. Lane End
Marsh S. & Co. Waterloo rd. Burslem
Mason and Co. Lane Delph
Massey Richd. Newcastle st. Burslm
Mayer and Newbold, Green dock, Lane End
Mayer Elijah & Son, (& drab china) Upper High st. Hanley
* Mayer Samuel, Piccadiily, Shelton
Mayer Thomas, Cliff bank, Stoke
Meigh Job and Son, Hill st. Hanley
Meir John, Tunstall
* Mills Henry, Hope st. Shelton
Minton Thomas, New road, Stoke
Nutt William, Flint st. Lane End
* Pattison Jas. High st, Lane End
Peake Thomas, (ornaments and vessels for gentlemen's gardens) Tunstall
Phillips Edwd. & Geo. Longport
Podmore Thos. & Co. Tunstall
Pointon Wm. Green Head, Burslem
Pratt Felix & Rd. FENTON POTTERY
Pratt John, Lane Delph
Ratcliff & Willett, Broad st, Shelton
Ratcliff Humphy (coarse) Stoke rd
Read & Platt, Market pl, Burslem
Ridgway John & Co. (fine) Albion st, Shelton
Ridgway John & Wm. (fine) Cauldon plaec, Shelton
Robinson Noah, Shelton
Rogers Jno. & Son, Dale hall, Longprt
* Salt Ralph, Marsh st, Shelton
Shaw John, Green dock, Lane End
* Skerratt Obd. Waterloo rd. Burslm
Spode Josiah, High st, Stoke
Steel Daniel & Son (jasper & stone) Bourne's bank, Burslem
Stevenson Ralph, Cobridge
Stubbs & Kent, Longport
Taylor Thos. High st, Hanley
Toft & May, Hanley
* Tunnicliffe Michael, Tunstall
Turner Wm. (Egyptian black) High st, Lane End
* Venables & Morris, New Hall st, Shelton
Walton Jno. Navigation rd, Burslem
* Walton Joshua, Piccadilly, Shelton
Warburton Mary, (coarse) Hot lane, Burslem
Ward Thos. & Co. High st, Stoke
Wedgwood Josiah & Son, Etruria
Weston Geo. High st, Lane End
Wood & Challinor, Brownhills
Wood Enoch & Sons, Fountain pl, Burslem
* Wood Ephraim, St. John's square, Burslem
Wright Wm. (coarse) Upper High st, Hanley
Yates John, Broad st, Shelton

1834 White

History, Gazetteer, and Directory, of Staffordshire, By William White, Sheffield (Norton 647). Dated 1834 on the title page and 12 May 1834 in the Preface. Publication was announced for the following week in the *Staffordshire Advertiser* dated 17 May 1834.

This directory includes a lengthy history of the Potteries followed by sections containing classified lists for the main towns and alphabetical lists for the smaller villages. The pottery categories vary slightly, but are all combinations of china, earthenware, and toy manufacturers. There are thirteen relevant categories for the towns and villages as shown.

Stoke-upon-Trent Directory – China Manufacturers (page 555)
Adams Wm. & Sons, Church st.
Boyle Zach. & Son, Church st.
Copeland & Garratt, High street
Daniel Henry & Rd. London road

Mayer Thomas, Cliff bank
Minton Thomas, Eldon place

Stoke-upon-Trent Directory – Earthenware Manufacturers (page 555)

Adams Wm. & Sons, Church st.
Boyle Zach. & Son, Church st.
Copeland & Garratt, High street
Daniel Hy. & Rd. London road
Davenport John, Son, & Co. Eldon place
Mayer Thomas, Cliff bank
Minton Thomas, Eldon place
Ratcliff Humphrey, Black works, Hartshill

Hanley & Shelton Directory – China Manufacturers (page 563)

See also Earthenware mfrs.
Barlow James & Co. Miles' bank
Gray & Jones, High street
Rathbone & Co. George street

Hanley & Shelton Directory – China & Earthenware Toy Manufacturers (page 563)

Beech Thomas, Brunswick street
Booth Richard, Brook street
Copeland James, New street
Eardley James, New street
Floyd Henry, Cobridge
Hall Samuel, Newhall street
Jackson Joseph, Queen street, S.
Lloyd John, Marsh street,
Maskery Maria, Piccadilly
Mayer Samuel, Piccadilly
Mayer Thomas, (dlr.) Hope st.
Mills Henry, High street, S.
Salt Ralph, (figures & porcelain tablets,) Marsh street
Walton Joshua, Piccadilly
Woodward Wm. Marsh street

Hanley & Shelton Directory – Earthenware Manufacturers (page 564)

Marked * are China mfrs. also.
Burton Samuel & John, New street
* Daniel Hy. & Co. Bedford row
Dimmock Thos. & Co. Albion st.
Dimmock Thomas, jun. and Co., Tontine street
Eardley Herbert, (jugs & ornaments,) Oldhall street
Glass John, Market street
Hackney Nathan, Cobridge
Hackwood Wm. Eastwood
* Hicks, Meigh, and Johnson, High street
* Johnson Phoebe (lustre,) Miles' bank
May Rt. Oldhall st.; h. Union st.
Mayer Elijah & Son, High street
Meigh Job and Son, Hill street
Peake Samuel and Co. (black & chimney pipe,) Brook street
Ratcliffe Wm. High street
Read & Clementson, High street
* Ridgway John, Cauldon place
Ridgway Wm. Albion street
Ridgway Wm. & Co. High street
Robinson & Wood, Vale lane
Taylor Wm. & Co. Cobridge
Wedgwood Josiah and Sons, Etruria
* Yates John, Broad street

Lane-End and Longton – China Manufacturers (pages 572-573)

Those marked * are lustre, and + Egyptian black ware mfrs. See also Earthenware mfrs.
* Allerton, Brough, and Green, High street
Baggearley and Ball, High street
* Bailey and Harvey, Flint st.
Barker Thomas, (enamelled and burnished gold) Flint street
Birks Charles, High street
Booth and Son, Church street
Bridgwood Sampson, Market st.; house, High street
Carey Thomas and John, Anchor works, L.
Chetham and Robinson, Commerce street
Copestake and Son, High street
Copestake Wm. High street; house Caroline street
+ Cyples Lydia, High street
Deakin and Son, (ironstone) Waterloo manufactory
Ellis Thomas, Union market; house, Vauxhall
* Faulkner and Robinson, Great Charles street
Gerrard John & Brothers, High st.
* Harris and Goodwins, Crown Works, Flint street
* Hilditch and Co. Church street
Martin Wm. Market street; house, Bridge street
Marsh John Riley, Church street
+ Newbold Richard, Green dock
Pratt, Hassall, and Gerrard, High street, and Lane delph
Ray and Tideswell, Daisy bank
Scott, Floyd, & Co., Caddick's ln.
Seabridge James, High street; house, Anchor lane
Shaw Kitty, Chancery lane; h. Steele's nook
* Simpkin Hugh, High street; house, New street

Lane-End and Longton – Earthenware Manufacturers (pages 573-574)

See also China manfrs.
Allerton and Lowe, (and lustre) High street
Bailey and Harvey, Flint street
Barker Rd. (lustre) Flint street
Beardmore and Birks, High st.
Bill, Deakin, and Procter, Great Charles street
Bill, Colclough, and Co. Flint st.
Brammer Eliz. (toys) Daisy bank
Brunt Wm. (Toys) Daisy bank
Carey Thomas and John, Anchor Works
Chesswas Thomas Edensor, Market place
Chetham and Robinson, (lustre, Egyptian black, stone mortars, &c) Commerce street
Deakin and Son, (and ironstone china) Waterloo manufactory
Gallimore Ambrose and Robert, (lustre) High street

Goodwins & Harris, (ornamental, &c) Crown Potteries, Flint st.
Hawley John, Great Charles st.; house, Daisy bank
Hulse, Jaquiss, and Barlow, Gold Street
Jervis Wm. (lustre) Gold street
Kelsher Chas. (yellow) High st.
Lockett John and Son, (& Egyptian black, & stone) Chapel st.
Marsh John Riley, Church st. L.
Newbold Richard, (lustre and black) Green dock
Reeves Joseph, (marbles and nurs) Gold street
Shaw John & Jesse, Green dock
Simpson John, Flint street; h. Gold street

Fenton Township, including Lane Delph, &c. – China & Earthenware Manufacturers (page 578)

Those marked 1 reside at Bassilow, 2 Fenton, 3 Foley, 4 Great Fenton, 5 Lane Delph, 6 Pool Dole, and 7 Sidiway. Those marked * mfr. Earthenware only, & + China only.
2 Bourne, Baker and Baker
5 Carey Thos. & Jno. and Lane end
5 * Ginder Sl. & Co.
5 + Green & Richards
3 Knight, Eltin, and Bridgwood
2 Mason Charles Jas. and Co. (& patent ironstone china)
3 Mayer John
2 Pratt Felix & Rd.
5 * Pratt John

Burslem Town and Parish Directory – Earthenware Manufacturers (page 584)

Marked * are Egyptian black mfrs. only, and + are China mfrs. also.
+ Alcock Samuel & Co. Hill pottery
Barker, Sutton, and Till, Sitch pottery
Bath Wm. (coarse) Queen street
Clews Ralph and Jas. Cobridge
Colclough James, (ornamental) Chapel lane
Collinson John, (crown) Golden hill
* Cork and Condliff, Queen st.
Cormie John, Nile street
+ Davenport John, Son and Co. Longport, Newport, and Stoke
Dillon Francis, Cobridge
Edge Wm. Golden hill
Godwin Benjamin E. Cobridge
Godwin John & Robt. Cobridge
Godwin Thomas, New wharf
Godwin Wm. Market place
Harding and Cockson, Cobridge
Hawley Joseph, Waterloo road
Heath Thomas, Beech lane
Holland Ann, (shining black) Liverpool road
* Hood, George, Brown hills
Hopkins Peter, Market place
Hughes Thomas Cobridge villa; house, Waterloo road
Jackson Job and John, Church pottery
Jones Elijah, Cobridge villa
Love, Rushworth, and Hobson, Cobridge
+ Machin and Potts, Waterloo pottery
Marsh & Haywood, Brown hills
* Marsh & Willatt, Silvester sq.
* Massey Nehemiah, (and lustre) Newcastle street
Pearson John, Newcastle street
Phillips Edw. and Geo. Longport
+ Pointon Wm. Overhouse works
Rogers John and Son, Dale hall
+ Stephenson Ralph and Son, Cobridge
Stubbs Joseph, Longport
Turner Wm. (sagars and quarry) Chapel lane
* Walton John, Navigation road
+ Wood Enoch and Sons, Fountain place

Burslem Town and Parish Directory – Earthenware Toy Manufacturers (page 584)

Those marked * are china toy mfrs.
* Edge Daniel, Waterloo road
Elkin Richard, High street
* Mellor, Venables, & Co. Nile st.
Sharratt Obadiah, Waterloo road
Walton John, Navigation road
Worthy Mathias, Cobridge

Tunstall – Earthenware Manufacturers (pages 589-590)

Adams Wm. and Sons, Greenfield
Beech James, Sandyford
Collinson John, (brown) Golden hill
Edge Wm. Golden hill
Goodfellows Ts. Phoenix pottery
Hall Ralph, High street
Heath Joseph and Co. Newfield
Ingleby Thos. & Co. High street
Johnson John, (and Egyptian black,) High street
Moss Richard, Red st. Chesterton
Meir John, near the Church
Podmore, Walker, and Co. Upper pot works
Rathbone S. and J. (and china,) Amicable street
Rowley Thomas. Amicable st.
Tunnicliff Michael, (china and earthenware figures,) High st.
Wood and Challinor, Woodland

Chesterton (pages 591-592)

Marked * are in Red street.
* Moss Richard, earthenware & Egyptn. blk. mfr. & vict. Crown

Oldcott & Golden Hill (page 592)

Marked * are at Golden hill.
* Collinson Jno. brown earth. mfr.
* Edge Wm. earthenware mfr.

1835 Pigot

Pigot and Co.'s National Commercial Directory, Published by J. Pigot & Co., Basing Lane, London, and Fountain Street, Manchester (Norton 62). Dated 1835 on the title page and May 1835 in the Address.

As with all the Pigot and Slater series, this directory is classified within a separate section for 'The Potteries' (pages 425-436). There are three relevant categories.

China Manufacturers (pages 429-430)

See also Earthenware Manufacturers, and also Toy and Ornamental China Manufacturers

Adams Wm. & Sons, Church st, Stke
Allerton, Brough and Green, High street, Lane End
Bagguley & Ball, High st, Lane End
Baileys' & Harveys', Flint st, Lane End
Barlow James and Co. Slack lane, Hanley
Birks Charles, High st, Lane End
Booth & Son, Church st, Lane End
Bourne, Baker & Baker, Fenton
Boyle Zachariah and Son, Church street, Stoke
Bridgwood Sampson, High st, Lane End
Carey Thomas and John, Anchor lane, Lane End
Chetham and Robinson, Commerce street, Lane End
Copeland and Garrett, Church st, Stoke
Copestake and Son, High st, Lane End
Copestake William, Market street, Lane End
Cormie John, Nile st, Burslem
Daniel Henry and Richard, London road, Stoke, and Shelton
Davenport Henry & William & Co. (& glass manufacturers) Longport, and Church St, Stoke
Ellis Thomas, Union Market place, Lane End
Faulkner and Robinson, Charles st, Lane End
Floyd and Shubotham, Chadwick lane, Lane End
Gerrard John & Brothers, High st, Lane End
Gray and Jones, High st, Hanley
Green and Richards, Lane Delph
Harding, Cockson & Co. Cobridge
Harris and Goodwins, Flint street, Lane End
Heath Thomas, High st, Lane End
Hicks, Meigh and Johnson, High street, Shelton
Hilditch and Hopwood, Church street, Lane End
Hilditch William and John, Church street, Lane End
Knight, Elkin and Co. FOLEY POTTERY
Machin and Potts (and patentees and sole proprietors of the royal steam cylindrical printing apparatus) WATERLOO POTTERIES, Burslem
Martin William, St. Martin's lane, Lane End
Mason Charles James & Co. Lane Delph
Mayer John, Foley
Mayer Thomas, Cliff bank, Stoke
Mellor, Venables and Co. Nile st, Burslem
Minton Thomas, Eldon place, Stoke
Ray and Tideswell, Daisy bank, Lane End
Ridgway John, Cauldon place, Shelton
Ridgway William, High st, Shelton
Ridgway Wm. & Co. High st, Hanley
Rogers John and Son, Longport
Seabridge Jas. High st, Lane End
Shaw Emos, Chancery la, Lane End
Simkin Hugh, Market st, Lane End
Stevenson Ralph & Son, Cobridge
Yates John, Broad st, Shelton

Earthenware Manufacturers (pages 430-431)

See also China Manufacturers; & also Toy and Ornamental China Manufacturers

Adams William and Sons, Church street, Stoke, and Tunstall
Alcock Samuel and Co. Liverpool road, Burslem
Ashwell & Co. Anchor la, Lane End
Baileys' & Harveys', Flint st, Lane E.
Barker Richard, Flint st, Lane End
Barton, Sutton & Till, Liverpool road, Burslem
Beardmore and Birks, High street, Lane End
Beech James, Liverpool rd, Tunstall
Bill, Colclough & Co. Flint street, Lane End
Bill, Deakin & Procter, Gt. Charles st, Lane End
Bourne, Baker & Baker, Fenton
Boyle Zach. & Son, Church st, Stoke
Burton Saml. & Jno. New st, Hanley
Carey Thos. & John, Anchor lane, Lane End
Chesswas Thomas Edensor, Market place, Lane End
Chetham & Robinson, Commerce st, Lane End
Clews Ralph & James, Cobridge
Collinson James, Golden hill
Copeland & Garrett, Church st, Stoke
Copestake & Son, High st, Lane End
Cormie John, Nile st, Burslem
Cyples William and Richard (and Egyptian black) Market st, Lane E.
Daniel Henry & Richard, London road, Stoke, and Shelton
Davenport Henry & William & Co. Longport, and Church st, Stoke
Deakin & Son, WATERLOO MANUFACTORY, Lane End
Dillon Francis, Cobridge
Dimmock Thomas, jun. & Co. Tontine street, Hanley, and Shelton
Gallimore Ambrose and Robert, High street, Lane End
Ginder Samuel & Co. Lane Delph
Glass John, Market street, Hanley
Godwin Benjamin, Cobridge
Godwin John & Robert, Cobridge
Goodfellow Thos. High st, Tunstall
Goodwin Wm. Market pl, Burslem
Goodwins & Harris, Flint st, Lane E.
Greatbatch William, Stoke la, Stoke
Hackwood Wm. Eastwood, Hanley
Hall Ralph, High st, Tunstall
Harding, Cockson & Co. Cobridge

Hawley Jno. Gt. Charles st, Lane End
Hawley Jos. Waterloo road, Burslem
Heath Joseph and Co. Newfield, Tunstall
Heath Thos., Hadderidge, Burslem
Heath Thomas, High st, Lane End
Hicks, Meigh and Johnson, High street, Shelton
Holland Ann (black) Liverpool road, Burslem
Hood George, Brownhills
Hopkin Peter, Market pl, Burslem
Hughes Stephen and Co. Cobridge
Hulse, Jaquiss and Barlow, Gold street, Lane End
Ingleby Thos. & Co. High st, Tunstall
Jackson Job and John, CHURCH POTTERY, Burslem
Jervis William, Gold st, Lane End
Johnson John, High st, Tunstall
Johnson Phoebe, Miles bank, Hanley
Jones Elijah, Cobridge
Keeling Samuel, Bucknall road
Knight, Elkin & Co. FOLEY POTTERY
Legg Isaac, Furnace
Lockett & Son (and Egyptian black) King street, Lane End
Machin and Potts (and patentees and sole proprietors of the royal steam cylindrical printing apparatus) WATERLOO POTTERIES, Burslem
Marsh and Haywood, Brownhills
Marsh & Willet, Burslem
Marsh John Riley, Church st, Lane End
Mason Charles James and Co. Lane Delph
Massey Nehemiah, Newcastle st, Burslem
May Robert, Oldhall st, Hanley
Mayer John, Foley
Mayer Thomas, Cliff bank, Stoke
Meigh Charles, Hill st, Hanley
Meir John, Green gates, Tunstall
Mills and Fladley, Mill st, Shelton
Minton Thos. Eldon place, Stoke
Moss Richard (and Egyptian black) Red street, Wolstanton
Newbold Richd. New st, Lane End
Nixon James and Co. Cobridge
Parr Richd. jun. Church st, Burslem
Peake Joseph and Co. (black) Brook street, Shelton
Peake Thomas, Tunstall
Pearson Jno. Newcastle st, Burslem
Phillips Edward & Geo. Longport
Podmore, Walker and Co. Well st, Tunstall
Pointon William and Co. Greenhead, Burslem
Pratt Felix and Richard, Fenton
Pratt John, Lane Delph
Ratcliffe William, High st, Hanley
Rathbone Samuel & John, Tunstall
Read & Clementson, High st, Sheltn
Ridgway John, Cauldon pl, Shelton
Ridgway William, High st, Shelton
Ridgway Wm. & Co. High st, Hanley
Robinson & Wood, Broad st, Shelton
Rogers John and Son, Longport
Rowley Thos. Amicable st, Tunstall
Shaw John and Jesse, Green dock, Lane End
Simpson John, Flint st, Lane End
Stevenson Ralph & Sons, Cobridge
Stubbs Joseph, Longport
Walton Jno. Navigation rw, Burslem
Wedgwood Josiah & Sons, Etruria
Wood and Challinor, Tunstall
Wood Enoch and Sons (and borax) Fountain place, Burslem
Yates John, Broad st, Shelton

Toy & Ornamental China Manufacturers (page 435)
Booth Richd. (fine) Brook st, Shelton
Brammer Eliz. Daisy bank, Lane End
Brunt Thos. Millfield gate, Lane End
Brunt Wm. Daisy bank, Lane End
Copeland James, New st, Hanley
Eardley Herbert, New st, Hanley
Edge Daniel (fine) Waterloo road, Burslem
Mayer Samuel (fine) Oldhall street, Hanley
Mills Henry (fine) High st, Shelton
Salt Ralph (fine) Marsh st, Shelton
Sherratt Obadiah, Waterloo road, Burslem
Tunicliff Michael, High st, Tunstall
Walton John, Waterloo rd, Burslem
Walton Joshua (fine) Piccadilly, Shelton
Woodward William (fine) Marsh st, Shelton

1836 Cottrill

Cottrill's Police Directory of the Borough of Newcastle-under-Lyme for 1836, (Isaac Cottrill) Newcastle-under-Lyme (Norton 651). Dated January 1836 in the Address.

This directory is included here for completeness since it includes a commercial list for 'Part of the Parish of Stoke-upon-Trent, added to the Borough by the Boundary Act' (page 67). The list, however, consists of only 40 names, none of which are potters.

1839 Cottrill

Cottrill's Police Directory of the Borough of Newcastle-under-Lyme, for the Year 1839, (Isaac Cottrill) Newcastle-under-Lyme (Norton 652). Dated MDCCCXXXIX on the title page and January 1839 in the Address.

This directory is included here since it contains a commercial list for a small 'portion of the Parish of Stoke-upon-Trent . . attached to the Borough . . by the Municipal Act of Parliament' (pages 66-67). The list consists of 50 names, and unlike the earlier 1836 edition, includes two potters. They are reported here for completeness, although they are probably only workmen rather than pottery owners.

Barker John, potter
Cartlich Elija, potter

1841 Pigot

Pigot and Co.'s Royal National and Commercial Directory and Topography, Published by J. Pigot & Co., Fleet Street, London, and Fountain Street, Manchester (Norton 71). Dated December 1841 on the title page and in the Address. There are two editions of this directory, one with nine counties and the other with only six. Staffordshire is included in both, and the same section was also reprinted in four 1842 editions (qv).

As with all the Pigot and Slater series, this directory is classified within a separate section for 'The Potteries' (pages 38-55). There are five relevant categories.

China Manufacturers (page 44)
Adams William & Sons, Church st, Stoke
Alcock Samuel & Co. Cobridge
Allerton, Brough & Green, High st, Longton, and Church st, Stoke
Bailey, Goodwin & Robey, High st, Longton
Booth George, Robins & Co. WATERLOO WORKS, Hanley
Boyle Zachariah & Sons, Church st, Stoke
Bridgwood Sampson, Stafford street, Longton
Carey Thos. & John, Anchor lane, Lane end
Chetham Jonathan Lowe, Longton
Cooper William, Boothen road, Stoke
Copeland & Garrett, High st, Stoke, and London
Copestake William, Market st, Lane End
Copestake William, jun. High street, Longton
Cyples, Barton & Cyples, Market st, Longton
Daniel Henry & Richard, London rd, and Eldon place, Stoke, & Shelton
Daniel Richard, WATERLOO POTTERY, Burslem
Davenport William & Co. (and flint glass manufacturers) Longport, & Church st, Stoke
Deakin & Son (iron-stone) WATERLOO WORKS, Stafford st, Longton
Dudson Richard, Cannon st, Shelton
Floyd & Savage, Foley, Longton
Gallimore Robt. (and lustre) High st, Longton
Gerrard William, High st, Longton
Green & Richards, Fenton
Hamilton & Moore, Mount pleasant, Longton
Hancock John, BROWNHILLS POTTERY
Harding & Cockson, Cobridge
Harvey Charles & William Kewright, Stafford st, Longton
Heath, Boulton, Greenbanks & Co. Watergate st, Tunstall
Hilditch & Hopwood, Church street, Longton
Hulme James, Flint st, Longton
Knight, Elkin & Co. FOLEY POTTERY, Longton
Lawler William (dealer) Market st, Shelton
Lockett John & Thomas, King st, Longton
Lomax George, Miles bank, Hanley
Machin John and William (dealers) Marsh st, Shelton
Martin Thos. St. Martin's lane, Longton
Mason & Faraday (and patentees of stone china) Fenton
Massey Richard, Cannon st, Shelton
Mayer Samuel, Oldhall st, Hanley
Mellor, Venables & Co. Nile st, Burslm
Mills Henry, George st, Shelton
Minton & Co. Eldon place, Stoke
Pratt Felix & Richard & Co. High st, Fenton
Ray & Wynne, Daisy bank, Longton
Riddle & Lightfoot, Union square, Longton
Ridgway John & Co. Cauldon place, Shelton
Ridgway, Morley, Wear and Co. (stone) Broad street, Shelton
Rogers John & Son, Longport
Seabridge Jas. Church st, Longport
Warren James, High st, Longton
Wood Enoch & Edward, Fountain place, Burslem
Wright, Burgess & Taylor, Amicable st, Tunstall

Earthenware Manufacturers (pages 45-46)
Adams William and Sons, GREENFIELD POTTERY, Tunstall, and High st. Longton
Alcock John and George (improved Indian iron stone) Cobridge
Alcock Samuel and Co. (& Indian iron stone) HILL POTTERY, Burslem
Allerton, Brough & Green, High st, Longton
Allin & Furnival, Miles bank, Shelton
Ashwell John & Co. Anchor lane, Lane End
Baddeley William (& toy) Market lane, Shelton

Baker Wm. & Co. High st, Fenton
Barker, Sutton & Till, SYTCH POTTERY, Burslem
Batkin, Walker & Broadhurst, Church st, Longton
Beardmore and Birks, High street, Longton
Beech James, Sandyford, Tunstall
Beswick Robt. Church bank, Tunstall
Booth Joseph, RAILWAY WORKS, Longton
Boyle Zachariah & Sons, Church st, Stoke
Burton Samuel & John, New st, Hanley
Carey Thomas & John, Fenton and Longton
Chetham Jonathan Lowe, Commerce street, Longton
Clementson Joseph, Broad street, Shelton
Colclough James, Gold st, Longton
Collinson John (coarse) Golden Hill
Cooper John, Boothen road, Stoke
Copeland & Garrett, High st, Stoke, and Portugal Street, London
Copestake Wm. jun. High st, Longton
Cork & Condliffe (Egyptian black) Queen street, Burslem
Cyples, Barton & Cyples (lustre Egyptian black) Market st, Longton
Daniel Henry & Richard, Eldon place, Longton
Daniel Richard, Waterloo, Burslem
Davenport William & Co. Longport, and Church street, Stoke
Deakin & Son, WATERLOO MANUFACTORY, Longton
Dillon Francis, Cobridge
Dimmock Thomas, jun. & Co. Tontine street, Hanley, and Shelton
Edge Wm. & Samuel, Lane Delph
Edwards James & Thomas, Sylvester square, Burslem
Everard, Colclough & Townsend (& lustre & black) Cornhill, Longton
Gibson John (Egyptian and lustre) High street, Tunstall
Ginder Samuel & Co. Lane Delph
Goddard Thomas & Co. Commerce street, Longton
Godwin Benjamin Endon, Cobridge
Godwin John & Robert, Cobridge
Godwin John Mares & James, Cobridge
Godwin Thomas, Navigation road, Burslem
Goodfellow Thomas, High street, Tunstall
Goodwin John, Flint st, Longton
Hackwood Wm. Eastwood, Hanley
Hall Ralph & Co. High st. Tunstall
Hallen Harding, Newcastle street, Burslem
Hancock John, BROWNHILL'S POTTERY
Harding, Cockson & Co. Cobridge
Harvey Charles & William Kewright, Stafford street, Longton
Hawley John, Stafford st, Longton
Hawley Jos. Waterloo road, Burslem
Heath Joseph, Newfield, Tunstall
Holland Ann, Liverpool rd. Burslem
Hood George, Navigation road, Burslem
Hopkin Peter & Co. Market place, Burslem
Hughes Stephen & Co. Cobridge
Jervis William (black Egyptian and lustre) Gold street, Longton
Jones & Walley, VILLA POTTERY, Cobridge
Keeling Samuel & Co. Market st, Hanley
Knight, Elkin & Co. FOLEY POTTERY, Longton
Lockett John & Thomas (and lustre Egyptian and pestle and mortar) King st, Longton
Maddock & Seddon, Newcastle st, Burslem
Mason & Faraday (and patentees of stone china) Fenton
Mayer Joseph & Co. Old Church st, Burslem
Mayer Thomas & John, Dale hall
Meigh Charles (and iron stone) Old Hall st, Hanley
Meir John & Sons, Green gates, Tunstall
Mellor, Venables & Co. Nile st, Burslem
Mills George, Market square, Hanley
Mills John (coarse and blue brick and crucible) Clough st, Shelton
Minton Thos. & Co. Eldon place, Stoke
Moss Richard (and Egyptian black) Red st, Wolstanton
Phillips George, Longport
Podmore, Walker & Co. Old bank, and Well st, Tunstall
Pointon Wm. Greenhead, Burslem
Pratt Felix & Richard & Co. Fenton
Pratt John & William, Lane Delph
Proctor Geo. Green dock, Longton
Riddle & Lightfoot (and lustre Egyptian) Union square, Longton
Ridgway John & Co. Cauldon place, Shelton
Ridgway, Morley, Wear & Co. Broad st, Shelton
Ridgway William, High st, Shelton
Ridgway William, Son & Co. High st, Hanley
Robinson & Dale, City road, Longton
Rogers John & Son, Longport
Rowley Thos. Amicable st, Tunstall
Simpson & Nicholls, Flint st, Longton
Swetman William & Geo. (Egyptian black) Moorland road, Burslem
Swift & Elkin, Stafford st, Longton
Tams Jesse, Cannon st, Shelton
Vernon James & Co. Church yard, and High st, Burslem
Walley George, Flint st, Longton
Walley Wm. (black cane and lustre) Marsh st, Shelton
Wedgwood Josiah & Sons, Etruria
Wood Ambrose & Co. (Egyptian black, &c.) Waterloo rd, Burslem
Wood & Brownfield (and improved iron stone) Cobridge
Wood & Challinor, Tunstall
Wood Enoch & Edward, Fountain place, Burslem
Wood John Wedge, Hadderidge bank, Burslem
Wright, Burgess & Taylor, Amicable st, Tunstall
Yale & Barker, Victoria place, Longton
Yates & May, Broad st, Shelton

Palette and Colour Slab Manufacturers, for Artists (page 49)
Bridgwood Jesse, High st, Tunstall
Kennedy William Sadler, Church street, Burslem

Toy & Ornamental China Manufacturers (page 53)
Baddeley Jas. Henry, Upper Hanley
Baguley George, Wharf lane, Shelton

Barton Alexander, Bagnall, Longton
Beech William, Queen st, Burslem
Bennett William, Broad st, Shelton
Booth Richd. (fine) Brook st, Shelton
Brammar Eliz. Daisy bank, Lane End
Brunt Thos. Millfield gate, Lane End
Brunt William, Daisy bank, Lane End
Caulkner Levi, Broad st. Shelton
Colclough Chas. Market Lane, Longtn
Copeland James, New st, Hanley
Dean Lydia, Old hall st. Hanley
Dudson Richard, Cannon st Shelton
Dudson Thomas, Hope st, Shelton
Eardley Herbert, New st, Hanley
Edge Daniel (fine and earthenware) Waterloo road, Burslem
Floyd Elizabeth, Cobridge
Hall Samuel, Marsh st, Shelton
Harrison John, High st, Tunstall, and Lane End
Keys Edward, High st, Hanley
Lawton Thomas, Hope st, Shelton
Lloyd Francis (& china dealer) Hope st, Shelton
Machin John & William, Marsh st, Shelton
Marsh William (earthenware) Gold street, Longton
Massey Richard, Cannon st, Shelton
Mayer Saml. (fine) Old hall st, Hanley
Mayer Thomas (and china dealer) Hope st, Shelton
Mills Henry (fine) High st, Shelton
Mills John, Swan square, Burslem
Randall Thos. Martin, High st, Sheltn
Salt Ralph (fine) Marsh st, Shelton
Sherratt Obadiah (& earthenware) Waterloo road, Burslem
Tunicliff Michael, Tunstall & Longton
Walton Joshua (fine) Piccadilly, Shltn
Wood Abraham, Waterloo rd, Burslm

Miscellaneous (page 54)
Bold Henry, pot step manufacturer for cotton manufacturers, Burslem
Massey Nehemiah, black inkstand maker, Burslem
Steel Henry, ornamental jasper manufacturer, Marsh st, Shelton

1842 Pigot

Pigot and Co.'s Royal National and Commercial Directory and Topography, Published by J. Pigot & Co., Fleet Street, London, and Fountain Street, Manchester (Norton 72, Norton 74, Norton 75). Four editions of this directory including Staffordshire appeared during 1842. They are dated January 1842 on the title page, or March 1842, July 1842, or September 1842 on both the title page and in the Address.

These editions are all purely reprints of 1841 Pigot (qv), and in order to avoid misleading data in this work the entries are neither repeated here nor included in the alphabetical list.

1844 Pigot

Pigot and Co.'s Royal National and Commercial Directory and Topography, Published by J. Pigot & Co., Fleet Street, London, and Fountain Street, Manchester (Norton 80). Norton records an undated copy of this directory in the Bodleian Library and states that it contains purely reprints from 1841 and 1842 Pigot (qv). Her date appears to be based on another Pigot directory of the same year.

As a reprint, this directory is included here purely for completeness. In order to avoid misleading data in this work the entries are neither repeated here nor included in the alphabetical list.

1845 Kelly

Post Office Directory of Birmingham, Warwickshire, and Part of Staffordshire, Printed and Published by W. Kelly & Co., 19 & 20 Old Boswell Court, Temple Bar, London (Norton 109). Dated September 1845 in the Preface.

This directory is listed here for completeness only. The 'part of Staffordshire' referred to in the title is the area around Birmingham, and does not extend to the Potteries. Its significance lies in the fact that it was effectively the first edition of what was to become Kelly's series of directories covering the whole of Staffordshire. The Potteries made their first appearance in the second edition in 1850.

1846 Williams

Williams's Commercial Directory for Stafford and the Potteries, Published by J. Williams sen., Manchester (Norton 649). Dated May 1846 on the title page. The pages relating to the Potteries were also printed in another Williams directory covering Chester and surrounding districts (Norton 141).

This directory is not classified but consists of alphabetical lists of traders for the various Pottery towns and nearby villages. The lists are particularly interesting in that they include many individual partners giving their firms and, in some cases, their private addresses. The following lists of potters have been extracted from the sections for the towns or villages as shown.

Hanley Directory (pages 1-8)
Abington Leonard J. (Ridgway, W. Son & Co.), High street
Brownfield William (Wood & B.), Market street
Clarke Richard B. (Furnival Thomas & Co.), Wheatley place
Furnival William, earthenware manufctr., Old Hall Works, Old Hall street
Furnival Thomas & Co., earthenware manuftrs., Miles Bank
Furnival Thomas (F.T. and Co.), Miles Bank
Gerrard John, manufacturer and flint grinder, Bath street
Keeling Samuel & Co., earthenware manufacturers, Market st
Keeling Samuel (S.K. and Co.), Market street
Meigh Charles, earthenware manufacturer, Old Hall street
Mills George, toy manufacturer, Old Hall street
Ridgway William (R.W., Son & Co.), Northwood
Ridgway Wm., Son and Co., manufacturers, High street
Shirley John (Samuel Keeling and Co.), Market street
Sneyd Thomas, earthenware manufacturer, Miles bank
Stubbs William (S. and Walker), Market street
Stubbs and Walker, china manufacturers, Waterloo works

Burslem Directory (pages 1-20)
Alcock Samuel and Co., Hill Pottery, Liverpool road
Alcock Samuel, (A.S. and Co.) Cobridge
Alcock John and George, earthenware manufacturers, (and of the firm Alcock Joseph, J. and G.) Limes
Barker William (B. and Till,) Sytch
Barker & Till, earthenware manufacturers, Sytch pottery, Sytch
Beech William, china figure manufacturer, Waterloo road
Beech William, china manufacturer, Bell works, Queen street
Bowers & Lloyd, earthenware manufacturers, Navigation road
Bowers Geo. Fred. & Co., china works, Brownhills
Bowers, G.F. (B.G.F. & Co.), Brownhills house
Bowers John, (B. & Lloyd,) Navigation road
Challinor Edward, (Bowers G.F. & Co.) Tunstall
Collinson Charles, (Holdcroft Peter & Co.) Sytch
Cork & Edge, earthenware, lustre, and black manufacturers, Queen street
Cork Benjamin, (C. & Edge) Newport road
Edge Joseph, (Cork & E.) St. John's square
Edwards James, earthenware manufacturer, Dalehall; house, Dalehall
Edwards Thomas, potter, Swan bank; house, Waterloo road
Emberton, Hancock, & Co. earthenware manufacturers, high-street, Brownhills
Godwin Thomas, earthenware manufacturer, Canal works, Navigation road; house, Navigation road
Hallen Samuel, potter, Holehouse; house, Bleakhill
Hallen Harding, potter, Holehouse; house, Waterloo-road
Hancock Redulphus, (Emberton H. & Co.) Liverpool road
Haywood Howard & Richard, Brownhills Tileries
Holdcroft Peter & Co. earthenware manufacturers, Lower Works, Fountain place
Holdcroft Peter, (H.P. & Co.) Pleasant street
Holden John, earthenware manufacturer, Knowl works; house, Furlong place
Holland Anne, black works, Liverpool road
Hughes Stephen & Elijah, earthenware & colour manufacturers
Hughes Stephen, (H.S. & Elijah) Waterloo road
Hughes Elijah, (H. Stephen & Co.) Waterloo road
Johnson Thomas, (Emberton, Hancock & Co.) Brownhills
Keeling Charles, (Alcock Samuel & Co.) White house, near Newcastle
Kennedy William Sadler, china manufacturer, Waterloo road; house, Camoys cottages, Waterloo road
Kent Richard, (K.R. & John) Waterloo road
Kent Richard and John, potters, Waterloo road
Lloyd William (Bowers & L.) King street
Maddock John, earthenware manufacturer, Newcastle street; house, Waterloo road
Mayer Samuel, Fountain works, Fountain place; house, Dalehall
Mellor Charles, (M. Venables & Co.) Bleakhill
Mellor, Venables & Co, Nile street pottery, Nile street
Phillips John Ball, (P.T. & Son) Lower Hadderidge
Phillips Thomas & Son, earthenware manufacturers, Furlong pottery
Phillips Thomas, (P.T. & Son) High street, Newcastle
Pinder Thomas, (Mellor, Venables & Co.) Furlong place
Pointon William, earthenware manufacturer, Overhouse works, Greenhead; house, High street
Potts William Wainwright, patentee of the royal cylindrical printing, Waterloo road
Salt Thomas, earthenware manufacturer, Fountain works; house, Newcastle street
Seddon Joshua, (S. & Wildblood) Barnfield house
Seddon & Wildblood, earthenware manufacturers, Church yard manufactory
Sherratt Hamlet, figure manufacturer, Waterloo road
Sherratt Samuel, (Holdcroft P. & Co.) Navigation road
Taylor James, (Vernon J. & Co.) Waterloo road
Till Thomas, (Barker & T.) Sytch

Venables John, (Mellor & Co.) Waterloo road
Vernon James, (V.J. & Co.) Waterloo road
Vernon James & Co. earthenware manufacturers, Waterloo works, Waterloo road
Wildblood William, (Seddon & W.) Navigation road
Wood Mr. Enoch, Fountain place
Wood John, (Dimmock & Co. of Shelton,) earthenware manufacturer, Dalehall

Burslem Directory – Places Adjacent – Longport (pages 17-18)

Davenport William & Co. earthenware, china, and glass manufacturers
Davenport Mr. William, Longport hall
Mayer Thomas, John, & Jos, ironstone and earthenware manufacturers
Mayer Thomas, (M.T. John and Jos,)
Mayer Jos, (Mayer Thomas, John, & J.)
Phillips George, earthenware manufacturer

Shelton Directory (pages 1-9)

Bale Thomas S. (Ridgway John and Co.), Cauldon place
Bevington Samuel, china figure manufacturer, Marsh street
Brown Robert (Wedgwood Joseph and Sons), Shelton
Caulkin Levi, pipe and toy manufacturer, Broad street
Clementson Francis (C. & Young), Cleveland House
Clementson Joseph, earthenware manufacturer, High street
Clementson & Young, earthenware manufacturers, Broad street
Dale William, potter, Marsh street
Dimmock Thomas (D. Thomas, jun. & Co.), Albion street
Dimmock Thomas, jun. & Co., china and earthenware manufacturers, Albion street
Dudson James, china figure manufacturer, Hope street
Green James (Worthington & G.), John street
Hackwood and Son, New Hall Pottery
Hackwood Thos. (Hackwood & Son), Hill street
Hackwood William (Hackwood and Son), Union street
Hall Samuel, china manufacturer, Marsh street
Hopkinson Richd. & Edwd., china manufacturers, York street
Hopkinson Edward (H. Richard & E.), Sun street
Hopkinson Richard (H., R & Edward), Sheaf street
Livesley W. & R., ornamental china manufacturers, Marsh st
Livesley Ralph (L. William and R.), Marsh street
Livesley William (L.W. & Ralph), Marsh street
Mayer Thomas, china figure mannfacturer, Brook street
Meigh Mr. Charles, Grove House
Mills George, earthenware manufacturer, Bethesda street
Mills H., china manufacturer, George street
Ridgway John and Co., china and earthenware manufacturers, Cauldon place
Ridgway John (R. John and Co.), Cauldon place
Ridgway Edward J. (R. and Co.), Bank House, Albion st
Street John, china figure manufacturer, Marsh street
Walker William (Stubbs & W.), Hope street
Walton James, china figure manufacturer, Brunswick street
Walton William, china figure manufacturer, Hope street
Worthington & Green, ornamental china manfrs., Brook street
Worthington Thomas (W. and Green), Mill street
Young Mr. (Clementson and Y.), Cannon street

Places adjacent to Hanley and Shelton, viz., Cobridge, Fenton, Etruria, &c. (pages 10-12)

Alcock John & George, earthenware manufacturers, Cobridge
Alcock Mr. George, Limes
Alcock Mr. John, Limes
Baker William & George, earthenware manufacturers, Fenton
Brownfield William (Wood & B.), Market street, Hanley
Cockson Charles (Harding & Co.), Landscape house, Cobridge
Colclough & Townsend, earthenware, lustre & black manuftr., Lane Delph Pottery, High street, Fenton
Colclough Thomas, (C. and Townsend), High street, Fenton
Edge Samuel (E. William and S.), Park street, Fenton
Edge William (E.W. and Samuel), Church street, Fenton
Executors of the late Thomas Eary, earthenware &c., manfts., King street, Fenton
Furnival Jacob & Co., manufacturers, Cobridge
Gallimore Robert, china manufacturer, King street, Fenton
Godwin James, earthenware manufacturer, Cobridge
Godwin John (J. & Richard Godwin), Bleak hill, Cobridge
Goodwin John & Robert, earthenware manfactrs., Cobridge
Godwin Richard (John & R.), Cobridge
Harding Wingfield (H. and Cockson), Booden Brook Cottage, Shelton
Harding and Cockson, china manufacturers, Cobridge
Hawley John, earthenware manufacturers, Foley Pottery, King street, Fenton
Jones Henry (J. and Vigers), Cobridge
Jones and Vigers, earthenware manufacturers, Cobridge
Knight James K., earthenware and iron stone manufacturer, Fenton
Mason Charles James, earthenware & iron stone manufacturer, Fenton Works
Pratt Felix and Co., earthenware manufacturers, Fenton
Pratt John and William, earthenware manufacturer, Lane Delph Pottery, Fenton
Vigers Thomas, (Jones and V.), Shelton
Wedgwood Jos. & Sons, earthenware manufacturers, Etruria
Wedgwood Francis (W. Joseph & Sons), house, Etruria hall
Whalley Edward, manufacturer, Cobridge; house, Hanley
Wood John (W. and Brownfield), Cobridge
Wood and Brownfield, manufacturers, Cobridge

Stoke Directory (pages 1-6)

Adams Lewis (A. Wm. & Sons), Watlands
Adams W. and Sons, earthenware & china manuf., Church st
Boyle L. & Sons, china & earthenware manuf., Church street
Copeland & Garrett, earthenware & china manuf., High street
Copeland William Taylor, M.P. (C. & Garrett), London
Daniel H. & R., china and earthenware manuf., Stoke

Daniel Richard (D. Henry and R.), Oak hill
Garrett Thomas, (Copeland and G.), Herne Hill, Surrey
Hollins M. (Minton and H.), Grove Hall
Minton & Hollins, patent tyle manufacturers, &c., Church st
Minton Herbart, (M. and Hollins), Harts hill
Pratt Felix Edwards, earthenware manufacturer, Brook street

Longton and Lane End Directory (pages 7-16)
Allerton, Brough & Green, Park Works, earthenware, china, and lustre manufacturers, High street
Allerton Charles (A., Brough & Green), Sutherland road
Anderson Robert (Bradbury, A. & Betteny), Bridge street
Ashwell John & Co., earthenware manufacturers, Anchor rd
Bailey and Ball, china and lustre manufacturers, Stafford st
Bailey John (B. and Ball), Shooter's hill
Ball Joseph (Bailey and B.), Stafford street
Barker George (Ceyples and B.), Daisy Bank
Barker William (Yale, B. & Hall), Caroline street
Beardmore Henry, china manufacturer, High street
Beardmore Sampson, earthenware manufacturer, High street
Betteny Thos. (Bradbury, Anderson & B.), Furnace Spring
Bradbury, Anderson and Betteney, china manftrs., Stafford st
Bradbury James (B,. Anderson & Betteney), High street
Bridgwood and Burgess, china manufacturers, Market street
Bridgwood Sampson, china manufacturer, Stafford street
Bridgewood Samuel (B. & Burgess), Spratslade House
Broadhurst and Green, earthenware manufctrs., New street
Broadhurst Job (B. & Green), Highfield cottage
Brough Benjamin S. (Allerton, B. & Green), Vauxhall cottage, Stafford treet
Burgess John (Bridgwood & B.), china manufactr., Market st
Chetham J.L., china lustre & black mnfctr., Commerce street
Clark Joseph A. (Cope and Co.), High street
Cooper Thomas, china figure manufacturer, High street
Cope and Clark, china manufacturers, Russell street
Cope Edward (C. & Clark), Green Dock
Cope and Edwards, china manufacturers, Market street
Cope Thomas (C. and Edwards), Church street
Copestake Wm., jun., china manufactr., gilder, &c., High st
Cyples & Barker, china & black ware manftrs., Market street
Cyples William (C. and Barker), Stafford street
Cyples Richard, china lustre & black manufctrs., High street
Deakin and Son, earthenware manufacturers, Stafford street
Deakin John (Deakin and Son), Green Dock
Deakin James (Deakin and Son), Hill Side Mear
Edwards James (Cope and E.), Mear Heath
Elkin and Newbon, earthenware mannfacturers, Stafford street
Elkin Samuel (E. and Newbon), Longton road
Everard George (E. and Glover), Meir
Everard & Glover, china lustre & earthenware manufacturers, Chancery lane
Floyd James, earthenware and china manufactr., Stafford st
Glover James (Everard and G.), Sutherland road
Goodwin J., earthenware mauuf., Crown Works, Stafford st
Gothard John (G. Thos. & Co.), Market street
Gothard Thomas (G.T. & Co.), Market street, Longton
Gothard Thomas & Co., earthenware manufacturers, Union st
Green William (Allerton, Brough & G.), Sutherland road
Green Wm. (Broadhurst & G.), earthenware manufacturer, Green Dock
Hamilton Sampson, (H. & Moore), Longton House, New st
Hamilton and Moore, china manuf., Mount pleasant pottery, High street
Harvey C., (H.C. & W.K.), china & earthenware manufactr
Harvey C. and W.K., china and earthenware manufacturers, Stafford street
Harvey William K., (H.C. & W.K.), Blurton
Hilditch & Hopwood, china manufacturers, Church street
Hilditch Mary Ann (H. and Hopwood), Furnace road
Hopwood William (Hilditch and H.), Church street
Lightfoot Arthur (Riddle & L), High street
Lockett John & Thos., earthenware & china mnfctrs., Market street
Lockett John (L.J. & Thomas), Great Fenton
Lockett Thomas (S., John & T.), Caroline street
Martin Thomas, china manufacturer, Martin's lane
Meakin James, earthenware and china manufacturer, New Town Pottery, High street
Moore Samuel (Hamilton & M.), Furnace
Newbon Thomas (Elkin and N.), Green Dock
Proctor John, china manufacturer, Furnace Road
Procter John, earthenware manufacturer, City road
Ray & Wynne, china & earthenware manufacturer, Stafford st
Ray Richard (R. and Wynne), Daisy bank
Riddle and Lightfoot, earthenware &c., manufts., Union sq
Riddle James (R. and Lightfoot), Barker street
Seabridge James, china manufacturer, Church street
Shirley T. and B., china manufacturers, Stafford street
Shirley Benjamin (S. Thos. & B.), Green Dock
Shirley Thomas (S.T. & Benjamin), Wood lane
Shubotham George (S. and Webberley), High street
Shubotham and Webberley, china manufacturers, High street
Steele Alfred, china manufacturer, Market street
Townsend George (Colclough & T.), High street
Walker Thomas Henry, earthenware & black manfr., Church st
Webberley William (Shubotham and W.), Furnace road
Wynne Thomas (Ray and W.), Eddenson place
Yale, Barker and Hall, china and earthenware manufacturers, Anchor Works
Yale George (Y. Barker and Hall), Green Dock House

Tunstall Directory (pages 18-24)
Adams Wm. & Co., earthenware manufacturers, Greenfield
Beswick Robt., earthenware manufacturer, coal owner, builder, &c., Church bank
Bridgwood Jessie, china slate manufacturer, Tunstall
Burgess & Gibson, earthenware manufacturers, Watergate st
Burgess Richard (B. and Gibson), Beswick street
Challinor Edw., earthenware manufctr., Great Woodland st.
Emberton Wm. (E. Hancock and Co.), Lime street
Emberton, Hancock & Co., earthenware mnftrs., Tunstall

Gibson John, earthenware manufacturer, High street
Gibson William (Burgess & G.), Audley street
Goodfellow Thomas, earthenware manufacturer, High street
Hall Ralph (H. and Co.), High street
Hall Ralph and Co., earthenware manufacturers, High street
Hancock R. (Emberton, H. and Co.), Burslem
Heap John (H. and Lownds), High street
Heap and Lownds, earthenware manufacturers, Amicable st
Heath Joseph, earthenware manufacturer, High street
Holland James (Hall & Co.), Hall street
Lownds Thomas (Heap & L.), Sandy Ford
Meir John & Son, earthenware manufacturers, Greengate
Podmore Thomas (P. Walker and Co.), Paradise street
Podmore, Walker & Co., earthenware manufacturers, Well st
Rowley Thomas, earthenware manufacturer, High street
Troutbeck E.T., earthenware manufacturer, Sandyford
Walker Thos. (Podmore W. and Co.), Wesley place
Walker Thomas, earthenware manufacturer, Sandyford
Wedgwood John, earthenware manfctr., Tunstall; h. Burslem

1850 Kelly

Post Office Directory of Birmingham, with Staffordshire and Worcestershire, Printed and Published by W. Kelly & Co., 19 & 20 Old Boswell Court, Temple Bar, London (Norton 116, Shaw & Tipper 1, Shaw & Tipper 1222). Dated January 1850 in the Preface.

As with all the Kelly's series, this directory contains alphabetical lists of traders for the various towns and villages and also classified lists, in this case for the two counties combined. This was the publisher's first coverage of the Potteries and since the classified lists are not as comprehensive as in later editions, extracts from the alphabetical listings for the Pottery towns are also shown here. Note that Tunstall is not included in either alphabetical or classified listings. There is only one category relevant to potters.

Burslem (pages 222-224)
Alcock Samuel & Co. china & earthenware manufacturers, Hill pottery
Barker & Till, manufacturers of earthenware, Lytch pottery
Beech William, china manufacturer, Queen street
Beech William, china figure manufacturer, Waterloo road
Bowers Frederick George, china manufacturer, Brown hills
Cork & Edge, black, lustre & earthenware manfrs. Queen st
Davenport William & Co. earthenware manufctrs. Newport
Edge Timothy, china figure manufacturer, Waterloo road
Edwards James, earthenware manufacturer, Deal hall
Edwards James, earthenware manufacturer, Knowle works
Emberton William & Co. earthenware manufrs. Brown hills
Goodwin Thomas, earthenware manufacturer, Navigation rd
Harding Joseph, earthenware manufacturer, Navigation rd
Haywood Howard & Richard, Brown hills tileries
Holdcraft Peter A. & Co. earthenware manfrs. Fountain pl
Maddock John, earthenware manufacturer, Newcastle st
Mayer Thomas John & Joseph, iron stone, china & earthen ware manufacturers, Dale hall
Mellor & Venables, earthenware manufacturers, Nile street
Pearson Edwd. china black & earthenware mfr. Liverpool rd
Pinder Thomas, ironstone china & earthenware manufacturer, Swan square
Pointon William, earthenware manufacturer, Market place
Sperratt Mrs. Martha, china figure manufactr. Waterloo rd
Timmis Henry, manufactr. of Parian brooches & shirt pins, Market place
Vernon James & Co. earthenware manufactrs. Waterloo road
Copeland James, figure manufacturer, New street
Keeling Samuel & Co. earthenware manufacturers, Market st
Machin John, china manufacturer, Queen street
Meigh, Son & Pankhurst, earthenware manufacturers, Old Hall street
Ridgway & Abington, earthenware manfactrs. Church bank
Stubbs William, china manufacturer, Waterloo works
Wright & Simpson, china figure manufacturers, New street

Hanley (pages 258-260)
Baguley George, manufacturer of Parian marble figures, High street
Cooper John, china toy manufacturer, High street

Shelton (pages 260-262)
Clementson Joseph, earthenware manufr. Chatterly house
Clementson Joseph, earthenware manufacturer, Phoenix works, High street
Dale William, garden ornament maker, Marsh street
Dimmock Thos. jun. & Co. earthenware manufs. Stafford row
Dudson James, ornamental china manufacturer, glass & earthenware colour maker, Hope street
Evans, Poulson & Jackson, stone jug manfrs. Eagle foundry
Hackwood & Son, earthenware manufctrs. New hall pottery
Hall Samuel, china toy manufacturer, Marsh street
Lawton Martin, china toy manufacturer, Hope street
Livesley William & Co. ornamental china manufacturers, Marsh street
Lloyd John, china figure manufacturer, Parker street
Lloyd Jacob, china figure manufacturer, Hanover street
Massey George, china toy manufacturer, Eagle foundry
Mayer Thomas, china ornament manufacturer, Brook st
Mills John, coarse ware manufacturer, Herbert street
Morley Francis & Co. china, ironstone & earthenware manufacturers, High street
Pope James & Co. stone ware manufacturers, Brian street
Randall Thomas Martin, china manufacturer, High street
Ridgway John & Co. manufacturers of porcelain, stone china & all kinds of earthenware, Cauldon place

Ridgway William, earthenware manufacturer, High street
Stephenson John, china ornament manufacturer, Bethesda street
Walton James, china toy manufacturer, Brunswick street
Wood George, china toy manufacturer, Marsh street
Worthington & Green, china figure manfctrs. Boothen brook

Longton, formerly called Lane End (pages 282-284)
Allerton, Brough & Green, manufacturers of burnished gold, china, egyptian black, lustre & earthenware, High street
Bailey & Ball, china & earthenware manfrs. Stafford street
Barlow Thomas, egyptian black & china manfr. Market st
Beech James, china manufacturer, High street
Bradbury, Anderson & Betteney, china manfrs. Flint street
Bridgwood Sampson, china manufacturer, Stafford street
Broadhurst & Green, earthenware, black & lustre manufacturers, Sutherland road
Chetham Jonathan Lowe, manufacturers of china, lustre, black, pearl & printed wares, stone mortars, &c. Commerce st
Colclough James, earthenware manufacturer, Commerce st
Cook & Griffiths, china manufacturers, Flint street
Cooper & Smith, earthenware manufacturers, High street
Cooper Thomas, china figure manufacturer, High street
Cope & Edwards, china manufacturers, Market street
Copestake William, china manufacturer & gilder, High st
Cyples Richard, china & earthenware manufacturer, High st
Deakin & Son, earthenware manufacturers, Stafford street
Edgerton, Beech & Birks, china, earthenware & black manufacturers, High street
Elkin & Newbon, earthenware & black manufrs. Stafford st
Everard George, china lustre & earthenware manuf. High st
Glover & Colclough, china & lustre manufactrs. Chancery la
Goodwin John, earthenware manufacturer, Commerce st
Griffiths Thomas, figure manufacturer, Furnace road
Hamilton & Moore, china manufacturers, High street
Hampson & Broadhurst, earthenware manufrs. New street
Harvey Charles & William Kenwright, earthenware manufacturers, Chancery lane
Hilditch & Hopwood, china manufacturers, Church street
Hodson Richard, china manufacturer, Church street
Lockett John & Thomas, china & earthenware mnfrs. King st
Meakin James, china & earthenware manufacturer, High st
Procter & Collingwood, china manufacturers, Furnace road
Ray & Ball, china & earthenware manufacturers, High st
Riddle & Lightfoot, china manufacturers, Market street
Shubotham & Webberley, china manufacturers, High street
Tipper & Co. china manufacturers, Flint street
Townsend George, lustre, black & earthenware manufacturer, High street
Warren James, china manufacturer, Park place
Wynce Thomas, earthenware manufacturer, Flint street
Yale, Barker & Hall, china & earthenware manufacturers, Caroline street

Stoke-upon-Trent (pages 318-321)
Adams Wm. & Sons, earthenware manufacturers, Church st
Baker William & Co. earthenware manufacturers, Fenton
Boyle & Sons, china & earthenware manufacturers, Fenton
Copeland Wm. Taylor, china & earthenware manfr. High st
Daniel Richard & Co. china manufacturers, Boothen road
Floyd James, china & earthenware manufacturer, Fenton
Forrister, Copestake & Forrister, china manufacturers, Fenton
Gallimore Robert, china earthenware manufacturer, Fenton
Green, Thomas, china manufacturer, Minervia works, Fenton
Hawley John, china & earthenware manufacturer, Fenton
Knight John King, earthenware manufacturer, Fenton
Minton Herbert & Co. china & earthenware ma. London rd
Minton, Hollins & Wright, manufacturers of patent mosaic pavements, & encaustic & venetian tiles, Church st. Stoke
Pratt Felix & Richard, earthenware manufacturers, Fenton
Pratt John & Wm. earthenware manfrs. Lane Delph potteries

China & Earthenware Manufacturers (page 566)
Adams W. & Sons, Church st. Stoke-on-Tr
Alcock S. & Co. Hill pottery, Burslem
Bailey & Ball, Stafford street, Longton
Baker William & Co. Fenton, Stoke-upon-Trent
Barker & Till, Sytch pottery, Burslem
Beech J. High street, Longton
Beech W. Queen street, Burslem
Bowers F.G. Brown hills, Burslem
Boyle & Co. 108 Steelhouse lane, Birmingham, & at Fenton
Boyle & Sons, Fenton, Stoke-on-Trent
Bradbury, Anderson & Betteney, Flint street, Longton
Bridgwood S. Stafford street, Longton
Broadhurst & Green, Sutherland road, Longton
Chetham J. L. Commerce st Longton
Clementson J. High street, Shelton
Clementson Joseph, Phoenix works, High street, Shelton
Colclough J. Commerce street, Longton
Cook & Griffiths, Flint street, Longton
Cooper & Smith, High street, Longton
Cope & Edwards, Market st. Longton
Copeland William Taylor, High street, Stoke-upon-Trent
Copestake W. (& gilder), High st. Longton
Cork & Edge (black), Queen st. Burslem
Cyples R. High street, Longton
Daniel R. & Co. Boothen rd. Stok-on-Tr
Davenport W. & Co. Newport, Burslem
Deakin & Son, Stafford street, Longton
Dimmock T. jun. & Co. Stafford rw. Shelton
Edgerton, Beech & Birks, High st. Longtn
Edwards J. Deal hall, Burslem
Edwards J. Knowle works, Burslem
Elkin & Newbon, Stafford st. Longton
Emberton W. & Co. Brown hills, Burslem
Evans, Poulson & Jackson (stone jug), Eagle foundry, Shelton
Everard G. High street, Longton
Floyd J. Fenton, Stoke-upon-Trent
Forrister, Copestake & Forrister, Fenton, Stoke-upon-Trent
Gallimore R. Fenton, Stoke-upon-Trent
Glover & Colclough, Chancery la. Longton
Goodwin J. Commerce street, Longton
Goodwin T. Navigation road, Burslem

Green T. Fenton, Stoke-upon-Trent
Hackwood & Son, Newhall pottry. Shelton
Hackwood W. Union street, Shelton
Hamilton & Moore, High street, Longton
Hampson & Broadhurst, New st. Longtn
Harding J. Navigation road, Burslem
Harvey & Co. Chancery lane, Longton
Hawley J. Fenton, Stoke-upon-Trent
Hilditch & Hopwood, Church st. Longtn
Hodson R. Church street, Longton
Holdcraft P. & Co. Fountain pl. Burslem
Keeling S. & Co. Market street, Hanley
Knight J.K. Fenton, Stoke-upon-Trent
Legge I. Normacott, Longton
Lockett J. & F. King street, Longton
Machins J. Queen street, Hanley
Maddock J. Newcastle street, Burslem
Mayer T. J. & J. Dale hall, Burslem
Meakin J. High street, Longton
Meigh, Son, & Pankhurst, Old Hall street, Hanley
Mellor & Venebles, Nile street, Burslem
Mills J. Herbert street, Shelton
Minton H. & Co. London rd. Stok-on-Tr
Morley Francis & Co. High st. Shelton
Pearson E. Liverpool road, Burslem
Pinder T. Swan square, Burslem
Pointon W. Market place, Burslem
Pratt F. & R. Fenton, Stoke-upon-Trent
Pratt John & William, Lane Delph Potteries, Fenton, Stoke-upon-Trent
Procter & Collingwood, Furnace rd. Lngtn
Randall T.M. High street, Shelton
Ray & Ball, High street, Longton
Riddile & Lightfoot, Market st. Longton
Ridgway & Abington, Church bnk. Hanley
Ridgway J. & Co. Cauldon pl. Shelton
Ridgway W. High street, Shelton
Stubbs W. Waterloo works, Hanley
Tipper & Co. Flint street, Longton
Vernon J. & Co. Waterloo rd. Burslem
Shubotham & Webberley, High st. Lngtn
Warren J. Park place, Longton
Wedgwood J. & Sons, Etruria wks. Etruria
Wyme T. Flint street, Longton
Yale, Barker & Hall, Caroline st. Lngtn

1851 White

History, Gazetteer, and Directory of Staffordshire (Second Edition), By William White, Sheffield (Norton 650, Shaw & Tipper 1223). Dated 1851 on the title page and 28 July 1851 in the Preface. Publication was predicted for about the end of July in the *Staffordshire Advertiser* dated 7 June 1851.

This directory includes a lengthy history of the Potteries followed by sections containing classified lists for the main towns and alphabetical lists for the smaller villages. There are also appendices with some additional names. The pottery categories vary slightly, but are all combinations of china, earthenware, and toy or ornament manufacturers. There are fourteen relevant categories for the towns and villages as shown.

Stoke-upon-Trent Directory – China and Earthenware Manufacturers (page 240)
(* also Porcelain Statuary, &c.)
Adams Wm. & Son, Church street
* Copeland Wm. Taylor, High street
Daniel Richard & Co., Boothen rd; h 10 Glebe street
* Keys & Mountford, John street
* Minton, Hollins & Co., (and stone and parian wares, encaustic and mosaic pavements, &c.,) Eldon pl. and Church street

Fenton Directory – China & Earthenware Manufacturers (page 244)
Those marked 2 are in Little Fenton; 3 in Foley, and the others in Great Fenton, or where specified. (* only Earthenware)
* Baker William and Co. Queen st
* Barlow Thos. Waterhouse, Queen st
2 Boyle Saml. & Sons; h. Seabridge
3 Bridgwood, Weston, and Cokeler
Floyd James, Market street
3 Forrister, Copestake, and Forrister
Green Thos., Minerva China Works; h. Stourbank House
Hawley John, Foley; h. Longton
* Knight John King, Foley Potteries
2 Lockett John; h. Fenton Hall
Perry and Broadhurst (lustre and black wares)
2 * Pratt F. & R. and Co. High street
* Pratt John & Co. Lane Delph

Hanley and Shelton Directory – China and Earthenware Manufacturers (page 252)
Bevington Samuel, Brunswick st
Brookes Pp. & Co., Clarence st
Brownfield Wm. Cobridge; h Old hall street
Clementson Jph., Phoenix Works; h Old hall street
Copeland James, New street
Dimmock Thos. & Co., Albion st
Dimmock Thomas, Albion street
Dimmock John, Albion st; h Broom st
Green & Worthington, Marsh street
Hackwood Thos., Newhall Works; h Union street
Jackson Danl. & Son, Clarence st
Livesley Wm. & Co., Old hall lane; h Marsh street
Meaking James, Cannon street
Meigh Chas. & Son, Old hall street

Morley Fras. & Co,, High street
Myatt Jph. (yellow) High street
Pankhurst Jas. Wm., Old hall st; h 2, Wheatley place
Peake J. and J., Snow hill
Pope John, (stone ware) Brian st
Ridgway Jno. & Co., Cauldon place
Ridgway & Abington, (fancy,) High st
Ridgway Wm. High street; h Wheatley Cottage
Wedgwood Josiah & Sons, Etruria

Hanley and Shelton Directory – China & Earthenware Toy & Ornament Manufacturers (page 252)
(The foregoing also make Ornaments.)
Baggeley Geo. (parian,) High st
Bamford John, Nelson place
Bevington Samuel, Brunswick st
Birch Joseph, Hope street
Boulton Chas. Bourne, Lamb street
Carter John, Milk street
Caulkin Levi, Broad street
Cooper John Thos., High street; h Church street
Dale William, Marsh street
Dudson James, Hope street
Lawton Martin, Hope street
Maybury Alfred, (brooch,) Hope st
Stephenson John, Bethesda street
Stubbs and Bird, Waterloo Works, Well street
Walton James, Brunswick street
Walton Joshua, Brunswick street
Wood George, Hope street

Longton Directory – China and Earthenware Manufacturers (page 263)
(Marked * only Earthenware Mfrs.)
Allerton, Brough, and Green, Park Works, High street
Bailey John (late B. and Batkin,) Stafford street; h Shooter's hill
Barlow Thomas, Market street
Beardmore, Birks, & Blood, High st
Bradbury, Anderson, and Bettany, Crown Works, Stafford street
Bridgwood Sampson, Stafford street; house Spratslade
* Broadhurst & Green, Anchor lane
Chetham Jonathan Lowe, Commerce street; house Blurton
* Colclough James, Commerce street; house Green dock
Cooke and Griffiths, Victoria place
Cooper Wm. & Co., High street house Furnace road
Cooper Thomas, High street
Cope and Edwards, Market street
Copestake Wm. jun. High street; h Sutherland road
* Cotton and Barlow, Commerce st
Deakin Jas. & Son, Waterloo, Stafford st
Edgerton, Beech, and Birks, High st
Edwards J., Market st; h Lightwood
* Elkin and Newbons, Stafford street
Glover and Colclough, Chancery lane
* Goodwin Jno., Stafford st; h City rd
Hamilton and Moore, High street
* Hampson and Broadhurst, Green dock works, New street
* Harvey Charles and Wm. K., Stafford street and Church street
* Hawley John and Co. Foley; house Summer row
Hilditch and Hopwood, Church st
Hodson Rd., Church st; h Bridge st
Lockett John and Thos., Market st
Mason Chas. Jas. (patentee of the ironstone china,) Mill street
Nicholls John, Weston place; house Furnace road
Ray Moses, Gower street
Ray Richard, High street
Riddle and Lightfoot, Union square
* Shubotham Hannah and Mary, Gold street; house Green dock
* Stanley and Lambert, High street
Taylor Jno., Market st; h Caverswall
Tipper Mary and Co., Stafford st
Townsend George, High street
Warren Jas., High st; h Millfield gt
Webberley William, St James' place Works; house Terrace buildings
* Wynne Thomas, Stafford street h Edensor place
Yale, Barker, and Hall, Viaduct and Caroline street Works

Burslem Town and Parish Directory – China and Earthenware Manufacturers (page 279)
(Marked thus † are both, and the rest only Earthenware Mfrs.) [Note: the symbol * which appears against Harding and Cockson is not explained by White.]
† Alcock Saml. & Co., Hill Pottery, and London
Barker Wm. and Son, Hill Works, and Sytch
Bold Henry, Lower Church st. Works; house Cobridge
† Boote Thos. Latham & Rd. (patentees of the royal mosaic, &c.) Waterloo Pottery; h Central Cottage, Waterloo road
† Bowers Geo. F., Brown hills China Works; h Brown hills House
† Bridgewood Jesse, Church Works
† Brownfield Wm., Cobridge; house Hanley
Challinor, Edmund, Brown hills
Cork and Edge, (black and lustre,) Queen street
† Davenport Wm. & Co., (and glass manufacturers,) Longport
Edwards James, Knowle Works, Hamill street, and Dale hall
Emberton Wm. & Co., Highgate Pottery, Brownhills
Furnival John & Co., Cobridge
Godwin Benj. Clulow, Navigation rd
Godwin John and Robert, Cobridge
Godwin Thomas, Navigation road
Hallen Samuel, Sytch
Hancock Redulphus, High st; house Sytch
* Harding and Cockson, Cobridge
Harding Jph., Navigation road; h Wolstanton
† Hawthorne & Nash, Regent st wks.
Heath and Rigby, Waterloo road
Holdcroft Peter and Co., Fountain pl
Hood George, Bourne's bank; hs Queen street
Hughes Stephen and Elijah, Grange Cottages, Cobridge

Keates Jas. Edw. & Co. (parian statuette, & brooch,) Market place
† Kennedy Wm. Sadler, (door furniture, &c.) Washington Works, Waterloo rd; h Camoys terrace
Lythgoe and Corn, High street
Maddock John, Newcastle st; house Stockton brook
Massey Nehemiah, Kilncroft; house Waterloo road
† Mayer Thos., John, and Joseph, Furlong works and Dale hall Pottery
Mellor, Venables and Co., Nile street Pottery
Pearson Edward, Liverpool road
† Pinder Thomas, (ironstone ware,) Swan bank; h Grange terrace
† Pointon Wm., Overhouse Works
Taylor James, Waterloo road; hs Bleak hill
Taylor Wm., Bourne's bank; house Waterloo road
Till Thomas, Sytch; h Liverpool rd
Vernon James & Co., Waterloo rd; house, Bleak hill
Walley Edward, Cobridge; h Hanley
† Wood John Wedg, Brown hills; h Big House

Burslem Town and Parish Directory – China &c. Toy Manufacturers (page 279)
(The foregoing also manfr. Toys.)
Beech Wm., Waterloo rd; Queen st
Edge Timothy, Waterloo road
Hallam Ephraim, Bourne's bank
Sherratt Martha, Waterloo road

Tunstall Directory – Earthenware, &c. Manufacturers (page 294)
Adams Wm. and Sons, Greenfield
Beswick Rt., High st; h Watergt. st
Burgess and Gibson, Watergate st
Challinor Chas. (Egyptian black,) High street
Challinor Edward, High street
Challinor Edw., Sandyford; house Brown hills
Challinor Edw. and Co., Amicable st
Collinson John, (black,) Golden hill
Emberton Wm., Highgate; h Sneyd st
Goodfellows Thos., High st; house Calver House
Heath Jph., High st; h Church st
May John Aubyn, John street
Meir Henry, Greengate
Podmore, Walker, and Co., High st. and Amicable street
Rowley Thos. (Exors. of,) High st
Shaw Anthony, Cross street
Walker Thos., Newfield; h Wesley pl
Wood John Wedg, Woodland st; h Burslem
Woolliscroft George, Well street

Oldcott and Golden Hill (page 298)
Marked ★ are at Golden Hill
★ Collinson John, blackware mfr
Walker Thos., earthenware manufacturer, Newfield

Longton Appendix (page 13)
Anderson & Betteney, china manfrs., Flint street
Cooper Thos., china, &c., mfr., High st
Riddle Jas., china mfr., Commerce st
Smith Sampson, figure mfr., High st
Weston, Colclough & Bridgwood, china & earthenware mfrs., Church st

Stoke-upon-Trent Appendix (page 13)
Meli Giovanni, modeller, Lpool. rd

Burslem Appendix (page 808)
Beech, Hancock, & Co., earthenware manufacturers, Swan bank
Bowers, Challinor, and Wolliscroft, china, &c., mfrs., Brownhills
Harding Wm. & George, china, &c., manufacturers, Furlong Works
Hancock and Pearson, earthenware manufacturers, Cobridge
Hulme & Booth, earthenware mfrs., Market place
Pinder, Bourne, & Hope, china, &c., manufacturers, Fountain place
Venables & Baines, china, &c., manufacturers, Nile street

Fenton Appendix (page 808)
Fenton Pottery Company, china, &c., manufacturers, King street
Forrister Martin & John, china manufacturers, Foley

Hanley & Shelton Appendix (pages 808-809)
Cooper John Thomas, earthenware manufacturer, Mill street
Ford Charles, patent spur manufacturer, Shelton
Livesley, Powell, & Co., earthenware manufacturers, Miles bank
Lloyd Rebecca, toy mfr., Marsh st
Marple, Turner, & Co., earthenware mfrs., Upper Hanley Works
Stubbs & Bird, china, &c., manufacturers, High street
Turton & Gregg, Parian figure mfrs. Miles bank

1852 Slater

Slater's Classified Directory of the Extensive and Important Manufacturing District 15 miles round Birmingham, Including also Worcester & the Potteries, Printed and Published by Isaac Slater, Fountain Street and Portland Street, Manchester (Norton 695, Shaw & Tipper 1427). This directory is not dated but both Norton and Shaw & Tipper give 1852. A copy at Birmingham is catalogued as c.1850, another at Wolverhampton has c.1851 pencilled on the title page and written on the spine, and a photocopy at Stoke is catalogued as c.1852-3. None of these copies contains any Preface or Address.

As with all the Pigot and Slater series, this directory is classified within a separate section for 'The Potteries' (pages 422-474). A note in the text points out that 'the letters B. F. H. L. S. T. signify respectively the Towns, &c. of Burslem, Fenton, Hanley, Longton, Shelton, and Tunstall'. There are seven relevant categories.

China Manufacturers (pages 436-437)
See also Earthenware Manufacturers; and also Toy and Ornamental Manufacturers
Adams & Cooper, High st. Longton
Adams Wm. & Sons (and Parian marble), High st. Stoke & Greenfield, Tunstall
Alcock Samuel & Co. Hill Pottery, Burslem, & at Cobridge, & 89 Hatton Garden, London
Allerton, Brough & Green, High st. L
Anderson & Betteny, Stafford st. L
Baker William & Co. High st. Fenton
Barlow Thomas (late Cyples & Co. – and of lustered Egyptian black), Cyples' Old Pottery, Market st. L
Barrow & Co. Market st. Fenton
Beardmore, Birks & Blood, High st. L
Beech & Brock (ornamental), Queen st. Burslem
Beech James, High st. Longton
Bevington Samuel, Brunswick street, Shelton
Bowers George Frederick, Brownhills, B
Bradbury, Mason & Bradbury, Flint st. Longton
Bridgwood Sampson & Son, Stafford st. L
Chetham Johnathan Lowe, Commerce st, Longton
Cooke & Hulse, Victoria place, Flint street, Longton
Cooper & Birks, Bagnall st. Longton
Cooper John, Furnace Pottery, Mill st. Etruria road
Cooper Thomas, High st. Longton
Cope & Birks, High st. Longton
Cope & Edwards, Market st. L
Copeland, William Taylor (and porcelain statuary); High st. Stoke
Copestake William, High st. L
Daniel Richard, Boothen road, Stoke
Flackett, Chetham & Toft, Church st L
Floyd James, Market st. Fenton
Glover & Colclough, Chancery la. L
Goodwin & Bullock, Furnace rd. L
Green Thomas, MINERVA WORKS, Fenton – (See advertisement)
Hamilton & Moore, High st. L
Harding & Cockson, Cobridge
Hartshorne, Fernihough & Adams, Market st. Longton
Hawley John, Foley, near Longton
Hawthorne John, (china-lock furniture) Regent st, Burslem
Hilditch & Hopwood, Church st. L
Hodson Richard, Church st. L
Kennedy William Saddler, mortice-lock furniture, Waterloo road, B & Pancrass lane, London
Keys & Mountford (and Parian), John st. Stoke – (See advertisement)
Knight & Wileman, Foley Potteries, F
Large W. Son & Co. Marsh st. S
Lloyd Francis & William & Co. Clarence st. Shelton
Lockett John & Thomas, King st. and Market st. Longton
Mayer Thomas, Brook st. Shelton
Mayer Thomas & John & Jos., stone china, ironstone, opaque, porcelain, Parian, &c., Dale hall, and FURLONG WORKS, Burslem, 102 Leadenhall st. London
Mills Elizabeth, George st. Shelton
Minton Herbert & Co. (& of patent agate buttons, and Parian statuary), Eldon place, Stoke
Morley Francis & Co. (ironstone china), Broad st
Nicholls John & Co. Weston pl. L
Phillips Edward (and ormula ornaments) York st, Shelton – (See advertisement)
Pinder Thomas, Fountain Place, Works, Burslem
Plant William & Co. The Foley, F.
Pratt Felix & Richard & Co., High street, Fenton
Randall Thomas Martin & Son, High st. S
Ray, Ray & Bentley, High st. L
Riddle James, Union Market pl. L
Ridgway Edward and Abington, High st. Hanley
Ridgway John & Co., Cauldon place, S
Robinson, Stubbs & Hudson, the Foley, Fenton
Smith Sampson, High st. Longton
Stubbs William, High st. H
Tipper & Co. Flint st. L
Townsend George (late Sampson Beardmore), OLD ESTABLISHED POTTERY, High st. Longton
Venables, Mann & Co. Nile st. B
Walker & Finney, Victoria place, L
Warren & Adams, VICTORIA WORKS and Park place, High st. L
Webberley William, High st. L
Worthington & Green, Booden brook and Marsh st. S

Earthenware Manufacturers (pages 440-442)
See also China Manufacturers; and also Toy and Ornamental China Manufacturers.
Adams William & Sons, Church st, Stoke, and Greenfield, Tunstall
Alcock John, Cobridge
Allerton, Brough & Green, High st, L
Bailey John, Stafford st, Longton
Baker William & Co. High st, Fenton
Barker & Hall, Caroline st, Longton
Barlow Thomas (late Cyples & Co., and of lustered Egyptian black), Cyples' Old Pottery, Market st, L
Beardmore, Birks & Blood, High street, Longton
Beech, Hancock & Co. Swan bank, Burslem
Beswick Robert, High st, Tunstall
Blacket, Elmore & Co. Sneyd st, T.
Blote Thomas & Richard (and stone, Parian), Waterloo Pottery, B.
Bold Henry, Commercial st, B.
Bowers, Challinor & Wooliscroft, (and architectural ornatures), Brownhills, Burslem
Bowers George Frederick, Brownhills, B
Bradbury, Mason & Bradbury, Stafford street, Longton
Bridgwood Jesse (& artists' colour-slab and pallet manufactr, water-closet-pan and plug-bowl, and fancy iron-stone ware), CHURCH WORKS, Burslem
Brindley John, Norton-in-the-Moors
Brougham & Mayer, Newfield, T.
Brownfield William (& iron-stone), Cobridge

Burgess & Gibson, Watergate st, T.
Challinor Charles, High st, Tunstall
Challinor Edward, Pinnox Pottery, Great Woodland st, Tunstall
Challinor Edward & Co. New rd, F
Chetham Jonathan Lowe, Commerce street, Longton
Clementson Joseph, Phoenix Works, High street, Shelton
Colclough James, Commerce st, S.
Collinson Charles & Co. Fountain place, Burslem
Collinson John (coarse), Golden Hill
Cope & Edwards, Market st, L.
Copeland Wm. Taylor, High st, Stoke
Cork & Edge, Queen st, Burslem
Cork Edge & Shaw (black tea-pot), High street, Tunstall
Corn Edward, Upper Hadderidge
Cotton & Barlow, Commerce st, L
Davenport William & Co. Longport, and 82 Fleet street, London
Deakin & Son, Waterloo Works, and Stafford st, Longton
Deaville & Co. (in pearl), Bath Works, Hanley
Dimmock Thos. & Co. Albion st, S.
Dimmock Thomas Junior & Co., Cheapside, Hanley
Edge Joseph, Hamill, Burslem
Edwards James, Dale hall, Burslem
Edwards James & Son, Knowle Pottery, Burslem
Elkin & Newbon, Stafford st, L.
Elsmore, Foster & Co. Calver st, T
Emberton William, Brownhills, B.
Flackett, Chetham & Toft, Church street, Longton
Floyd James, Market st, Fenton
Ford Charles (manufacturer and patentee of the patent spur used by china and earthenware manufacturers in placing flat ware), Parker street, Shelton
Freakley William & Co. Broad st, S
Furnival Jacob & Co. Cobridge
Glover & Colclough, Chancery la, L
Godwin John & Robert, Cobridge
Godwin Thomas, New wharf, B.
Goodfellow Thomas, High st, T.
Green William, Anchor Works, Market street, Longton
Grosvenor John Boden, New st, H.
Hackwood Thomas, New Hall Works, Shelton
Hackwood William (and figure), Hope st, Hanley – (See advert.)
Hallen Harding (and earthenware gas-burner), Wellington st, B.
Hallen William (and pot-step), Wellington street, Burslem
Hampson & Broadhurst, New st, L
Harding William & George, Navigation road, Burslem
Hawley John, Foley, near Longton
Hawthorn John (china door furniture, &c.), Regent st, Burslem
Heath Joseph, High st, Tunstall
Holland & Green, Stafford st, L.
Hood George, Commercial st, B.
Hughes Elijah, Bleak hill, Cobridge
Hughes Stephen, Waterloo road, Burslem & New row West, Dublin
Hulme & Booth, Market place, B.
Kennedy William Sadler, Waterloo road, Burslem
Knight & Wileman, Foley Potteries, Fenton
Large W. Son & Co. Marsh st, S.
Limer Thomas (dealer), High st, L.
Livesley, Powell & Co. Miles bank and Oldhall Works, Hanley
Lockett John & Thomas, King st, and Market street, Longton
Lythgoe John, High st, Burslem
Maddock John, Newcastle st, B.
Marple, Turver & Co. High st, H.
Massey Nehemieh (lustre, black & Rockingham), Chapel lane, B.
Mayer Thomas and John and Jos., Dale hall and Furlong Works, B., and 102 Leadenhall st, London
Meakin James & George, Market street, Hanley
Meakin Lewis Henry, Cannon st, S.
Meigh Charles & Son, Pankhurst, Oldhall street, Hanley
Meir John & Son, Greengaten, T.
Mills Elizabeth, George st, Shelton
Mills John (coarse), Clough st, S.
Mills Josiah (coarse), George st, S.
Minton Herbert & Co. (and Parian statuary), Eldon place, Stoke
Morley Francis & Co. Broad st. S.
Nicholls John & Co. Weston pl. L.
Oulsnam, Holdcroft & Co. High st, T
Pankhurst J.W. & Co. Oldhall st. H
Pearson Edward, Cobridge
Pinder, Bourne & Hope (and ironstone), Fountain place, Burslem
Plant William & Co. the Foley, F.
Podmore, Walker & Co. High st. T
Pointon William, Green head, B.
Pope James (stone), 14 Wharf la. S.
Pratt Felix & Richard & Co. High street, Fenton
Pratt John & William, Lane Delph
Ridgway Edward & Abington, High street, Hanley
Ridgway John & Co. Cauldon place, S.
Ridgway William, Broad st, Shelton
Salt Charles (and Parian statuary), Trinity street, Hanley
Shaw Anthony, Newfield, Tunstall
Shubotham H. & M. Gold st. L.
Stanley & Lambert, High st, L.
Stubbs William, High st, Hanley
Taylor William, Bourne's bank, B.
Till Thomas & Son, Liverpool rd. B
Townsend George (late Sampson Beardmore – & of Egyptian black), OLD ESTABLISHED POTTERY, High street, Longton
Venables, Mann & Co. Nile st. B.
Vernon Jas. & Co. Waterloo road. B.
Walker, Podmore & Co. Amicable street, Old bank, & Newfield, T.
Walley Edward (and stone & fancy bodies), Villa Pottery, Cobridge
Walley John (Rockingham ware), High street, Burslem
Wedgwood Josiah & Sons, Etruria

Wood John Wedg, Woodland st. T.
Wood Wm. (yellow), George st, S.
Wooliscroft George, High st, T.
Worthington & Green, Booden brook, and Marsh st, Shelton
Wynne Thomas, Flint st, Longton
Yale, Barker & Hall, Caroline st, L.

Palette and Colour Slab Manufacturers – for Artists (page 453)
Bridgwood Jesse, CHURCH WORKS, Burslem
Kennedy William Sadler, Waterloo road, Burslem

Parian Manufacturers (pages 453-454)
Baguley George, High st, Hanley – (See advertisement.)
Ford Thomas, Albion pl, Shelton
Grosvenor John Boden, New street, Hanley – (See advertisement)
Mills Elizabeth, George st, Shelton
Minton Herbert & Co. Eldon pl, Stoke
Oswell, Nevitt (broach and wicker baskets), Wheatsheaf st, Shelton
Timmis Henry, Market place, B.
Pope James, 14 Wharf lane, Shelton – (See advertisement)
Salt Charles, Trinity street, Shelton
Snow Henry & Co. Union street, Stoke, and St. Ann's st, Shelton
Turton James, Hope st, Hanley
Walton James, Brunswick st, S.
Wood George, Bryan st, Hanley

Pot Step Manufacturers for Cotton Spinners (page 454)
Bold Henry, Waterloo rd, Burslem
Hallen Harding, Wellington st, B.
Hallen William, Liverpool road, B.
Massey Nehemia (& galvanic cells), Chapel lane, Burslem

Saggar Maker (page 455)
Callinson John, (and chimney pot), Golden Hill
Massey Nehemia, (chimney pot), Chapel lane, Burslem
Wood Jacob, (chimney pot), Waterloo road, Burslem

Toy & Ornamental China Manufacturers (page 468)
See also China Manufacturers and also Earthenware Manufacturers.
Baguley George, High st, Hanley
Bamford John, Nelson place, H.
Beech & Brock, Queen st, Burslem
Cooper John, FURNACE POTTERY, Mill street, Shelton
Cooper Thomas, High st, Longton
Copeland James, New st, Hanley
Edwards John, Caroline st, Longton
Grosvenor John Boden, New st, H.
Hackwood William, Hope st. Hanley – (See advertisement.)
Keys & Mountford (Parian marble), John street, Stoke – (See advertisement.)
Lawton Martin, Hope st, Shelton
Lawton Thomas, Hope st, Hanley
Livesley, Powell & Co. Miles bank, and Old Hall Works, Hanley
Lloyd Francis & William & Co., Clarence st, Shelton
Lloyd Jacob, Hanover st, Shelton
Mayer Thomas, Brook st, Shelton
Pope James (Parian marble), 14 Wharf lane, Shelton
Sherratt Hamlet, Waterloo road, B.
Smith Sampson, High st, Longton
Snow Hy. Commercial buildgs. Stke
Stephenson John, Bethesda st, S.
Townsend George (late Sampson Beardmore), OLD ESTABLISHED POTTERY, High st, Longton
Turton James, 97 Hope st, S.
Walley John, Hope st, Hanley
Walley John, High st, Burslem
Walton James, Brunswick st, S.

1854 Kelly

Post Office Directory of Birmingham, with Warwickshire, Worcestershire, and Staffordshire, Printed and Published by Kelly & Co., 19 & 20 Old Boswell Court, Temple Bar, London (Norton 121, Shaw & Tipper 6, Shaw & Tipper 1222). Dated 1854 on the title page and January 1854 in the Preface. It is noted as the Third Edition in the Preface.

As with all the Kelly's series, this directory contains alphabetical lists for the various towns and villages and also classified lists, in this case for the three counties combined. Only the classified lists are included here. The range of categories is not extensive in this early edition, there are only five relevant to this work.

China & Earthenware Manufacturers (pages 524-525)
Adams & Cooper, High street, Longton
Adams William & Sons, Church street, Stoke-upon-Trent; Greenfield, Tunstall; & 25A, Hatton garden, London
Alcock S. & Co. Hill pottery, Burslem, & 89 Hatton garden, London
Alcock J. Cobridge, Burslem
Allerton, Brough & Green, High st. Longtn
Anderson & Betteny, Stafford st. Longtn
Bailey Robert & Co. Bryan st. Hanley
Bailey J. Stafford street, Longton
Baker W. & Co. Fenton, Stoke-on-Trnt
Barker & Hall, Viaduct works, Longton
Barker W. & Son, Hill works, Burslem
Barker T. (gilder), Stafford st. Longton
Barlow T. (late Cyples & Co.), Market street, Longton
Barrow & Co. Fenton, Stoke-upon-Trent
Beardmore, Birks & Blood, High street, Longton

Beech, Hancock & Co. Swan bk. Burslm
Beech J. High street, Longton
Beswick R. Tunstall, Newcastle
Bevington S. Brunswick street, Shelton
Blackshaw T. jun. St. John's sq. Burslm
Bold J. & Co. Church works, Burslem
Boote T. & R. Waterloo road, Burslem
Booth T. & Co. Lichfield street, Hanley
Bowers G.F. Brownhills china works, Tunstall
Bradbury, Mason & Bradbury, Crown pottery, Stafford street, Longton
Bridgwood Sampson & Son, Anchor works, & Stafford street, Longton
Bridgwood J. Church works, Burslem
Brougham & Mayer, Sandyford, Tunstall
Brownfield W. Cobridge, Burslem
Brownhills China Works (G.F. Bowers, man.), Brownhills, Tunstall
Burgess & Gibson, Tunstall, Newcastle
Carter W. (gilder), Mill street, Hanley
Challinor Edward & Co. Sandyford, Tunstall, Newcastle; & at Fenton, Longton
Challinor E. Tunstall, Newcastle
Chetham J.L. Commerce st. Longton
Clementson J. Broad street, Shelton
Colclough J. Commerce street, Longton
Collinson C. & Co. Fountain pl. Burslem
Cooke & Hulse, Stafford street, Longton
Cope & Birks, Bagnall street, Longton
Cope & Edwards, Market st. Longton
Copeland W.T. Stoke-upon-Trent, & New Bond street, London
Copestake W. High street, Longton
Cork & Edge, Queen st. pottery, Burslem
Cork, Edge & Shaw, Tunstall, Newcstle
Corn E. Navigation road, Burslem
Cotton & Barlow, Commerce st. Longtn
Davenport W. & Co. Longport
Deakin & Son, Waterloo works, & Stafford street, Longton
Dimmock T. jun. & Co. Cheapside, Shltn
Edgerton & Birks, Little lane, Longton
Edwards J. Market street, Longton
Elkin & Newbon, Stafford st. Longton
Elsmore, Foster & Co. Tunstall, Newcstl
Emberton W. Brownhills, Tunstall
Flackett, Chetham & Toft, Church st. Longton
Floyd J. Fenton, Stoke-upon-Trent
Freakley W. & Co. Broad st. Shelton
Furnival J. Cobridge, Burslem
Glover & Colclough, Chancery la. Longton
Godwin J. & R. Cobridge, Burslem
Godwin T. Navigation road, Burslem
Goodfellow Thomas, High st. Tunstall, Newcastle
Goodwin & Bullock, Furnace rd. Longton
Green T. Fenton, Stoke-upon-Trent
Green W. Anchor road, Longton
Hackwood T. Newhall works, Shelton
Hackwood W. Hope street, Shelton
Hall R. Dale hall, Longport
Hallen H. Wellington street, Burslem
Hallen S. Sytch, Burslem
Hallen W. Wellington street, Burslem
Hamilton & Moore, High street, Longton
Hampson & Broadhurst, New st. Longtn
Harding & Cockson, Cobridge, Burslem
Harding W. & G. Furlong pottery, Burslem
Hartshorne & Fernihough, Mrkt. st. Lngtn
Hawley J. Fenton, Stoke-on-Trent
Hawthorn J. Regent street, Burslem
Heath J. High st. Tunstall, Newcastle
Hilditch & Hopwood, Church st. Longton
Hodson R. Church street, Longton
Holland J. Tunstall, Newcastle
Hood G. Church works, Burslem
Hughes E. Cobridge, Burslem
Hughes S. Waterloo road, Burslem
Hulme & Booth, Market place, Burslem
Jones G. Barnfield house, Burslem
Kennedy W.S. & Co. Waterloo rd. Burslem
Knight & Wileman, Fenton, Stke.-on-Trnt
Lambert & Stanley, High street, Longton
Legge I. Normacot, Longton
Lockett J. & T. King st. & Market st. Lngtn
Lythgoe J. High street, Burslem
Maddock J. Newcastle street, Burslem
Marple, Turner & Co. High street, Hanley
Mason C.J. Daisy bank, Longton
Mayer T., J. & J. Dale hall pottery, Longport, & Furlong works, Burslem
Meakin J. & G. Market street, Hanley
Meakin L.H. Cannon street, Shelton
Meigh C. & Son, Oldhall street, Hanley
Meir J. & Son, Tunstall, Newcastle
Mills J. Mollart street, Shelton
Minton H. & Co. Eldon pl. Stoke.-on-Trent
Morley F. & Co. Broad street, Shelton
Nicholls J. Weston place, Longton
Oulsnam, Holdcroft & Co. High st. Tunstl
Pankhurst J.W. & Co. Old Hall st. Hanley
Pearson E. Cobridge, Burslem
Pinder, Bourne & Hope, Fountn. pl. Brslm
Plant & Hallam, Fenton, Stoke-on-Trent
Podmore, Walker & Co. Swan bk. Tnstall
Pointon W. Green head, Burslem
Pope J. Sheaf street, Shelton
Pratt F. & R. & Co. Fenton, Stoke-on-Trent
Pratt John & Co. Lane Delph, Stoke-upon-Trent
Randall T.M. & Son, High st. Shelton
Ray, Ray & Bentley, High st. Longton
Riddle J. Union square, Longton
Ridgway E. & A. High street, Hanley
Ridgway J. & Co. Cauldon pl. Shelton
Ridgway W. Broad street, Shelton
Robinson, Stubbs, & Hudson, Fenton, Stoke-upon-Trent
Shaw A. Newfield, Tunstall, Newcastle
Shubotham H. & M. Gold st. Longton

Taylor W. Bournes bank, Burslem
Till T. & Son, Sytch pottery, Burslem
Tipper & Co. Stafford street, Longton
Townsend G. High street, Longton
Venables J. & Co. Nile works, Burslem
Vernon J. & Co. Waterloo rd. Burslem
Walley E. Cobridge, Burslem
Walley J. Market st. Tunstall, Newcastle
Warren & Adams, Park pl. High st. Lngtn
Webberley W. High street, Longton
Wedgwood J. & Sons, Etruria, Newcastle-under-Lyme
Wood J.W. Tunstall, Newcastle
Wooliscroft G. Amicable st. Tunstl. Nwcsl
Wynne T. Stafford street, Longton

China Figure Manufacturers (page 525)
See also Parian Manufacturers.
Bamford J. Nelson place, Hanley
Cooper J. (& parian), Etruria rd. Sheltn
Copeland J. New street, Hanley
Mayer T. Brook street, Shelton
Salt C. Trinity street, Shelton
Stephenson J. Bethesda street, Shelton
Stubbs W. High street, Hanley

Parian Manufacturers (page 604)
See also China Figure Makers.
Marked thus * are Ornamental Figure Makers.
Alcock Samuel & Co. Hill pottery, Burslem, & 89 Hatton garden, London
Baguley G. High street, Hanley
* Beech & Brock, Bell works, Burslem
Boote T. & R. Waterloo road, Burslem
Cooper T. High street, Longton
Daniel T. Pleasant street, Burslem
* Dudson J. Broom street, Hanley
* Edge T. Waterloo road, Burslem
* Hall S. Marsh street, Shelton
Keates J.E. Market place, Burslem
Keys & Mountford, John st. Stk.-on-Trnt
* Large W. & Son, Parker st. Shelton
* Lawton M. Hope street, Shelton
* Livesley, Powell & Co. Miles' bnk. Sheltn
* Lloyd F. & Son, Clarence st. Shelton
Lloyd J. Hanover street, Hanley
* Mills W. George street, Shelton
* Sherratt H. Waterloo road, Burslem
* Smith S. High street, Longton
* Timmis H. Market place, Burslem
* Townsend G. High street, Longton
Turton & Gregg, George street, Shelton
* Walton J. Brunswick street, Shelton
* Wardle J. Hope street, Shelton
* Wood G. Hope street, Shelton
* Worthington & Green, Brook street, & Marsh street, Shelton

Spur Makers (page 657)
Ford C. (patent), Parker st. Shelton

Toy Makers & Dealers (page 670)
Baddeley W. Market street, Longton
Barcroft J. Parliament row, Hanley
Boulton C. Market square, Hanley
Selman J. (clay), High st. Tunstl. Nwcstl
Smith S. High street, Longton
Townsend G. High street, Longton
Woolley J. Stafford street, Longton

1856 Kelly

Post Office Directory of Birmingham, with the Principal Towns in the Hardware and Pottery Districts, Printed and Published by Kelly & Co., 18-21 Old Boswell Court, St. Clement's, Strand, London (Shaw & Tipper 1432). Dated 1856 on the title page and September 1856 in the Preface. It is noted as the Fourth Edition in the Preface but this may be misleading since 1860 Kelly is the true fourth edition of the series covering Staffordshire.

As with all the Kelly's series, this directory contains both alphabetical lists, in this case for the various pottery towns and villages, and classified lists, in this case for the Hardware and Pottery districts combined. Only the classified lists are included here. The range of categories is extensive and there are eleven relevant to this work.

Black Ware Manufacturers (page 514)
Cork, Edge & Shaw, High st. Tunstall

Chemical Apparatus Manufacturers (page 526)
Collinson Charles & Co. Fountain place, Burslem

China & Earthenware Manufacturers (pages 527-528)
Adams & Cooper, High street, Longton
Adams William & Sons, Church street, Stoke-upon-Trent
Adams W. Greenfield, Tunstall
Alcock S. & Co. Hill pottery, Burslem & at 89 Hatton garden, London
Alcock J. Cobridge, Burslem
Allerton, Brough & Green, High st. Lngtn
Anderson & Betteny, Stafford st. Longton
Aynsley, Cooper & Co. Market st. Longton
Bailey John, Stafford street, & Shooter's hills, Longton
Baker W. & Co. Fenton, Stoke-up.-Trnt
Barker & Hill, Caroline st. Longton
Barker W. & Son, Liverpool rd. Burslem
Barlow T. Market street, Longton
Barrow & Co. Fenton, Stoke-up.-Trent
Beech, Hancock & Co. Swan bank, Burslem
Beech J. High street, Longton

Beech W. Bell works, Burslem
Beswick R. High street, Tunstall
Bevington S. Mill street, Hanley
Birks T. High street, Longton
Blackhurst R. Paradise street, Tunstall
Boote T. & R. Waterloo road, Burslem
Bowers G.F. Brownhills, Tunstall
Bridgwood S. & Son, Anchor works & Stafford street, Longton
Bridgwood J. Church works, Burslem
Broadhurst & Sons, Stafford st. Longton
Brougham & Mayer, Sandyford, Tunstall
Brownfield W. Cobridge, Burslem
Butterfield W. & J. High st. Tunstall
Challinor E. & Co. Fenton, Stoke-upon-Trent
Challinor E. & Co. Sandyford, Tunstall
Challinor E. Pinnox pottery, Tunstall
Chetham J.L. Commerce st. Longton
Clementson J. Broad street, Shelton
Colclough J. Commerce st. Longton
Collinson Charles & Co. Fountain place, Burslem
Cooke & Hulse, Stafford st. Longton
Cope & Edwards, Market st. Longton
Copeland W.T. High street, Stoke-upon-Trent, & 160 New Bond street, London
Copestick W. High street, Longton
Cork & Edge, Queen st. pottery, Burslem
Corn E. Navigation road, Burslem
Cotton & Barlow, Commerce st. Longton
Cyples R. Church street, Longton
Davenport William & Co. Longport, Burslem
Deakin & Son, Waterloo works & Stafford street, Longton
Dimmock T. jun. & Co. Stafford street, Shelton
Dudson J. Hope street, Shelton
Edgerton & Birks, Clayton st. Longton
Edwards J. & Son, Dale hall, Burslem
Edwards J. Fenton, Stoke-upon-Trent
Elkin & Newbon, Stafford st. Longton
Elsmore, Foster & Co. Cross st. Tunstall
Emberton W. Highgate, Tunstall
Flackett & Toft, Church st. Longton
Floyd J. Fenton, Stoke-upon-Trent
Ford T. Cannon street, Shelton
Furnival J. Cobridge, Burslem
Gibson W. Union street, Burslem
Godwin J. & R. Cobridge, Burslem
Goodfellow T. High street, Tunstall
Goodwin & Bullock, Furnace rd. Longtn
Goodwin J. Watergate street, Tunstall
Green T. Fenton, Stoke-upon-Trent
Greene William, Anchor works, Longton
Hackwood T. Newhall works, Shelton
Hamilton & Moore, High st. Longton
Hampson P. Green dock, Longton
Harding & Cockson, Cobridge china works, Burslem
Harding W. Furlong pottery, Burslem
Hawley J. Foley potteries, Fenton, Stoke-upon-Trent
Hawthorn J. Regent street, Burslem
Heath J. High street, Tunstall
Hilditch & Hopwood, Church st. Longtn
Hood G. Parker street, Shelton
Hughes E. Cobridge, Burslem
Hughes T. Waterloo road, Burslem
Hulme T. Central works, Burslem
Hulse, Nixon & Adderley, Daisy bank, Longton
Lockett J. King st. & Market st. Longton
Lockett J. King street, Longton
Lockett J. Market street, Longton
Lythgoe J. High street, Burslem
Macintyre J. Waterloo road, Burslem
Maddock J. Newcastle street, Burslem
Marple, Turner & Co. High st. Hanley
May J. Hamill pottery, Burslem
Mayer T., J. & J. Dale hall pottery & Furlong works, Burslem
Mayer Mrs. F. Brook street, Shelton
Meakin James & George, Market street, Hanley
Meigh C. & Son, Oldhall street, Hanley
Meir J. & Son, Greengates pottery, Tunstl
Minton Herbert & Co. Eldon place, Stoke-upon-Trent
Morley Francis & Co. Broad street, Shelton
Oulsnam, Holdcroft & Co. High street, Tunstall
Pankhurst J.W. & Co. Oldhall st. Hanley
Pearson E. Cobridge, Burslem
Phillips E. Cannon street, Shelton
Pinder, Bourne & Hope, Fountain place, Burslem
Podmore, Walker & Co. Amicable street & Swan bank, Tunstall
Pointon W. High street, Burslem
Pratt F., R. & Co. Fenton, Stoke-upon-Trnt
Pratt John & Co. Lane delph potteries, Stoke-upon-Trent
Procter J. & H. & Co. High st. Longton
Randall T. Broad street, Shelton
Ridgway (John), Bates & Co. Cauldon place, Shelton
Ridgway & Abington, High st. Hanley
Robinson, Stubbs & Hudson, Fenton, Stoke-upon-Trent
Shaw A. Newfield, Tunstall
Shubotham Misses H. & M. Gold street, Longton
Stubbs W. High street, Hanley
Taylor W. & J. Waterloo road, Burslem
Till T. & Son, Sytch pottery, Liverpool road, Burslem
Tipper Mrs. M. & Co. Stafford st. Longtn
Tomkinson & Co. Clarence st. Shelton
Townsend George, High street, Longton
Twyford Thomas & Christopher, New street, Hanley
Venables, Mann & Co. Nile st. Burslem
Walker & Finney, Victoria works, Longtn
Walley E. Cobridge, Burslem
Warren & Adams, High street, Longton
Wathen & Hebb, Foley works, Longton, Stoke-upon-Trent
Webberley W. High street, Longton
Wedgwood & Sons, Etruria, Stoke-upon-Trent
Wileman H. Fenton, Stoke-upon-Trent
Wood J. W. Woodland street, Tunstall
Wooliscroft G. & Co. Sandyford, Tunstall
Worthington & Harop, Mount Pleasant, Shelton

China Figure Makers (page 528)
See also Parian Manufacturers.
Cooper T. High street, Longton
Copeland J. New street, Hanley
Worthington & Green, Booden brook, Shelton

Creel Steps Maker (page 533)
Hallen W. Wellington street, Burslem

Encaustic, Venetian & Mosaic Pavement Manufacturers – Patent (page 535)
Minton, Hollins & Co. Church street, Stoke-upon-Trent, & 9 Albion place, Blackfriars, London

Parian Manufacturers (page 559)
See also China Figure Makers.
Alcock S. & Co. Hill pottery, Burslem; & at 89 Hatton garden, London
Bevington & Son, Marsh st. Shelton
Boote T. & R. Waterloo road, Burslem
Hill Levison, Eldon street, Stoke-upon-Trent
Livesley, Powell & Co. Miles' bank, Sheltn
Lloyd G. Marsh street, Shelton
Lockett, Baguley & Cooper, Broad street, Shelton
Mills Mrs. E. George street, Shelton
Mountford J. Liverpool road & John street, Stoke-upon-Trent
Pedley B. & J. Hope street, Shelton
Ridgway John, Bates & Co. Cauldon place, Shelton
Salt & Hopkinson, Bethesda st. Shelton
Timmis H. Market place, Burslem
Wardle J. Hope street, Shelton
Wilkinson, Rickhuss & Toft, Broad street, Shelton

Potters (page 562)
Collinson J. Golden hill, Stoke-on-Trent
Dale W. Marsh street, Shelton
Keys & Brewer, Wharf street, Stoke-upon-Trent

Rockingham Ware Manufacturer (page 573)
Walley J. High street, Burslem

Spur Makers (page 585)
Ford C. Parker street, Shelton

Toy Makers & Dealers (page 591)
Baddeley W. King street, Longton
Parr T. Church street, Burslem
Selman J. (clay), High street, Tunstall
Sherratt H. Waterloo road, Burslem
Smith S. (china), High street, Longton
Townsend George (china), High street, Longton

1860 Kelly

Post Office Directory of Birmingham, with Warwickshire, Worcestershire, and Staffordshire (also *Post Office Directory of Staffordshire*), Printed and Published by Kelly & Co., 18-21 Old Boswell Court, St. Clement's, Strand, London WC (Shaw & Tipper 6, Shaw & Tipper 1222). Dated 1860 on the title page and September 1860 in the Preface and in a Caution. It is noted as the Fourth Edition in the Preface.

As with all the Kelly's series, this directory contains alphabetical lists for the various towns and villages and also classified lists for each county. Only the classified lists are included here. The range of categories is extensive and there are twenty-eight relevant to this work.

Beer Machine Handle Manufacturer (page 773)
Hawthorn J. Albert st. works, Burslem

Broseley Printed Ware Manufacturers (page 792)
Jervis, Leese & Bradbury, Dresden Pottery, Chancery lane, Longton

China Figure Manufacturers (page 802)
Bamford J. Nelson place, Hanley
Cooper Mrs. A. Etruria road, Hanley
Copeland J. New street, Hanley
Smith Sampson, Sutherland works, Barker street, Longton
Worthington & Green, Booden brook, Hanley
Worthington & Harrop, Tinker's clough, Hanley

China Manufacturers – General (pages 802-803)
Adams & Cooper, High street, Longton
Alcock S. & Co. Hill pottery, Hill top, Burslem
Barker Joseph, Stafford street, Longton
Barker William Thomas, Sylvester square, Burslem
Barlow Thomas, Cyples's Old pottery, Market street, Longton
Bates, Brown, Westhead & Moore, Cauldon place, Hanley; & 107 Hatton garden, London EC
Beech W. Queen street, Burslem
Betteney T. Stafford street, Longton
Bevington John, works, Clarence street, Hanley
Birks Thomas, High street, Longton
Bowers George Frederick, Brown hills, Burslem
Brammall W. Heathcote works, Longton
Broadhurst & Sons, Stafford st. Longton
Brock & Allen, Broad street, Hanley
Bullock C. Bagnall street, Longton
Chetham Jonathan Lowe, Longton
Cockson & Hardings, Cobridge, Burslem; & New Hall pottery, Hanley, Stoke-upon-Trent
Copeland William Taylor, High street, Stoke-upon-Trent; &

160 New Bond street, London W
Copestake & Bradbury, High st. Longton
Copestake Bros. Anchor works, Longton
Copestake W. High street, Longton
Davenport W. & Co. Longport, Burslem; warehouses at 82 Fleet street, London, & 30 Canning place, Liverpool
Dudson J. Hope street
Edgerton & Birks, Green Dock works, Clayton street, Longton
Edwards J. Market street, Longton
Edwards J. Normacot, Longton
Finney Joseph, Victoria works, Longton
Ford T. Cannon street, Hanley
Gibbs & Hassall, Commerce st. Longton
Green & Co. Fenton, Stoke-upon-Trent
Grove R.H. Barlaston, Stoke-on-Trent
Grove Richard Henry, Vine st. Hanley
Hawthorn J. Albert st. works, Burslem
Hodson R. Chancery la. & New st. Longtn
Holland & Green (late C. & W.K. Harvey), Stafford street, Longton
Hopwood W. (trustees of), Church street, Longton
Hulse, Nixon & Adderley, Daisy bank works, Longton
Hulse T. Stafford street, Longton
Jervis, Leese & Bradbury, Dresden pottery, Chancery-lane, Longton
Large W. sen. Lichfield street, Hanley
Lockett, Baguley & Cooper, Hanley
Mann & Co. Cannon street, Hanley
Mayer & Elliot, Dale hall pottery, Burslem
Mills Mrs. Elizabeth, Dresden works, George street, Hanley
Minton Herbert & Co. Eldon place, Stoke-upon-Trent
Moore & Son, Mount Pleasant works, Longton
Moore S. Normacot, Longton
Morley & Ashworth, Broad st. Hanley
Oldham James, Bethesda street, Hanley
Phillips E. Cannon street, Hanley
Pinder, Bourne & Hope, Fountain place & Nile street, Burslem, Stafford
Pratt John & Co. Lane Delph, Fenton, Stoke-upon-Trent
Robinson, Stubbs & Hudson, Fenton, Stoke-upon-Trent
Shelley & Hartshorne, Stafford st. Longton
Shirley & Freeman, Chancery la. Longton
Smith Sampson, Sutherland works, Barker street, Longton
Stubbs William, High street, Hanley
Tipper & Co. Stafford street, Longton
Warren & Adams, High street, Longton
Wedgwood & Co. Amicable street & Swan bank, Tunstall
Webberley W. St. James's place, Longton
Worthington & Green, Booden brook, Hanley

China Manufacturers – Tea, Breakfast & Dessert Services (page 803)
Beech James & Son, Albert & Sutherland works, Longton
Gibbs & Hassall, Commerce st. Longton
Mason, Holt & Co. Normacot rd. Longton
Moore & Son, Mount Pleasant works, Longton
Smith Sampson, Sutherland works, Barker street, Longton
Webberley W. St. James's pl. Longton

China Manufacturers – White & Finished (page 803)
Aynsley & Co. Market place, Longton

China Ornament Manufacturers (page 803)
Beech James & Son, Albert & Sutherland works, Longton
Bullock Charles, Bagnall street, Longton
Mason, Holt & Co. Normacot rd. Longton
Webberley W. St. James's pl. Longton

China Porcelain Manufacturers (page 803)
Beech, James & Son, Albert & Sutherland works, Longton
Lockett John, King street & Market street, Longton
Mason, Holt & Co. Normacot rd. Longton
Webberley William, St. James's place, Longton

China & Porcelain Door Furniture Manufacturers (page 803)
Hawthorn J. Albert st. works, Burslem
Mackintyre James, Washington works, Waterloo road, Burslem

China Toy Makers (page 803)
Cooper T. & Co. High street, Longton
Heath William, High street, Longton

Earthenware Manufacturers (pages 813-814)
Adams William, Greenfield & Newfields collieries, Tunstall
Adams W. jun. Newfield, Tunstall
Alcock S. & Co. Hill pttery. Hill top, Brslm
Alcock J. Cobridge, Stoke-upon-Trent
Allerton C. & Son, High street, Longton
Barker W.S. Sylvester sq. Burslem, Staffd
Barlow Thomas Waterhouse, Coronation works, Commerce street, Longton
Bates, Brown, Westhead & Moore, Cauldon place, Hanley, & 107 Hatton garden, London EC
Beech & Hancock, Church bank, Tunstall
Bevington John; works, Clarence street, Hanley
Birks Thomas, High street, Longton
Blackhurst & Dunning, High st. Tunstall
Boote T. & R. Waterloo road, Burslem
Bourne W. High street, Longton
Bridgwood & Clarke, Churchyard works, Burslem
Bowers G.F. Brown hills, Burslem, Staffrd
Bridgwood S. & Son, East vale, Longton
Broadhurst James & Samuel, Gold street, Longton
Brough, Joynson & Co. Bourne's bank pottery, Burslem
Brougham T. Sandyford, Tunstall
Brownfield W. Cobridge, Stoke-on-Trent
Buckley John, works, Clarence st. Hanley
Butterfield William & James, High street, Tunstall
Cartwright & Edwards, Weston place, High street, Longton
Challinor E. & Co. Fenton, Stoke-on-Trent
Challinor E. Pinnox pottery, Tunstall

Clementson J. Broad street, Hanley
Cockson & Hardings, New Hall works, Hanley
Collinson Charles & Co. Fountain place, Burslem
Cooper Thomas & Arthur; works, Wharf lane, Hanley
Copeland William Taylor, High street, Stoke-on-Trent, & 160 New Bond street, London W
Corbett J. 16 Market place, Burslem
Cork & Edge, Queen street, Burslem
Cork, Edge & Malkin, New wharf pottery, Burslem
Corn E. Navigation road, Burslem
Davenport W. & Co. Longport, Burslem; warehouses at 82 Fleet street, London, & 30 Canning pl. Liverpool
Deakin & Son, Waterloo works, Longton
Dimmock T. jun. & Co. Stafford st. Hanley
Edwards J. & Son, Dale hall pottery, Burslem, Stafford
Elkin Samuel, works, Stafford street, & Mill street, Longton
Ellis, Unwin & Mountford, High st. Hanley
Elsmore & Foster, Clay hills pottery, Tunstall
Emberton W. High gate, Brown hills, Burslem
Finney Joseph, Victoria works, Longton
Furnival J. & Co. Cobridge, Stoke-on-Trnt
Godwin J. & R. Cobridge, Stoke-on-Trent
Goodfellow Thomas (exors. of the late), High street, Tunstall
Goodwin Joseph, Watergate st. Tunstall
Grove R.H. Barlaston, Stoke-on-Trent
Grove Richard Henry, Vine st. Hanley
Hammersley R. High street, Tunstall
Hampson Brothers, Green dock works, Longton
Hancock, Leigh & Co. Swan sq. Burslem
Hawley J. Fenton, Stoke-upon-Trent
Hawthorn J. Albert st. works, Burslem
Heath, Blackhurst & Co. Burslem (Charles Floyd, agent, 2 Dorchester place, New North road, London N)
Holcroft, Hill & Mellor, High st. Burslem
Holland & Green (late C. & W.K. Harvey), Stafford street, Longton
Hood G. Parker street, Hanley
Hughes E. Bleak hill, Cobridge, Stoke-upon-Trent
Hughes T. Waterloo road, Burslem
Hulme T. Central pottery, 20 Market place, Burslem
Hulse, Nixon & Adderley, Daisy bank works, Longton
Knight Joseph, Old Foley pottery, Fenton, Stoke-upon-Trent
Legge I. Normacot, Longton
Livesley, Powell & Co. Old Hall street & Miles bank, Hanley
Lockett, Baguley & Cooper, Victoria works, Hanley
Lockett John, King street & Market street, Longton
Maddock J. & Son, Newcastle st. Burslem
Malcolm F. (T. Carey Swan, agent), Boothen road, Stoke-upon-Trent
Malkin, Walker & Hulse, Anchor road, Longton
Mann & Co. Cannon street, Hanley
May John Aubyn, Hamil road, Burslem
Mayer & Elliot, Dale hall pottery, Burslm
Meigh C. & Son, Old Hall street, Hanley
Meir H. (late J. Meir & Son), Green gates pottery, Tunstall
Mills J. Clough street, Hanley
Minton H. & Co. Eldon pl. Stoke-on-Trnt
Morgan, Wood & Co. Wedgwood place pottery, Burslem
Morley & Ashworth, Broad st. Hanley
Moss & Hobson, Cornhill works, Longton
Newbon & Beardmore, Commerce street, Longton
Oldham James, Bethesda st. Hanley
Oulsnam & Holdcroft, High st. Tunstall
Pankhurst J.W. & Co. Old Hall street, Hanley
Pearson E. Cobridge, Stoke-upon-Trent
Pinder, Bourne & Hope, Fountain place & Nile street, Burslem, Stafford
Plant R. & Sons, Sneyd green, Cobridge, Stafford
Pratt F. & R. & Co. Fenton, Stoke-on-Trnt
Pratt John & Co. Lane Delph, Fenton, Stoke-upon-Trent
Procter J. & H. & Co. New town pottery, Longton
Ridgway & Abington, High st. Hanley
Shaw A. Newport works, Burslem, Staffrd
Shelley & Hartshorne, Stafford st. Longtn
Smith W.H. Fenton, Stoke-on-Trent
Stubbs William, High street, Hanley
Taylor Brothers & Co. Market street, Hanley
Taylor W. Brook street, Hanley
Till T. & Son, Liverpool road, Burslem
Tipper & Co. Stafford street, Longton
Toft W. Church street, Longton
Townsend G. High street, Longton
Turner & Tomkinson, Newfield, Tunstall
Twyford C. New street, Hanley
Twyford Thomas, Bath street pottery, Hanley
Venables J. & Co. Trent pottery & Waterloo works, Waterloo road, Burslem, & 19 Bishopsgate st. within, London EC
Vernon J. Scotia potteries, Burslem
Walley E. & Son, Cobridge, Burslem, Stoke-upon-Trent
Walley J. High street, Burslem
Wathen & Hudden, Fenton, Stke-on-Trnt
Wathen & Hudden (late John Bailey), Stafford street, Longton
Wedgwood & Co. Amicable street & Swan bank, Tunstall
Wedgwood J. & Sons, Etruria, Stoke-upon-Trent
Wileman H. Fenton, Stoke-upon-Trent
Wood, Challinor & Co. Well street pottery, Tunstall
Wood E.T.W. Woodland pottery, Tunstl
Woolliscroft G. & Co. Sandyford, Tunstall

Earthenware Figure Manufacturer (page 814)
Massey N. Chapel lane & 13 Waterloo road, Burslem

Egyptian Black Ware Manufacturers (page 814)
Chetham Jonathan, Commerce street, Longton
Deakin & Son, Waterloo works, Longton
Elkin Samuel; works, Stafford street & Mill street, Longton
Hammersley R. High street, Tunstall
Lockett John, King street & Market street, Longton
Poole & Sutherland, Heathcote road & Cornhill passage, Longton

Encaustic, Venetian & Mosaic Pavement Manufacturers (page 814)
Minton, Hollins & Co. High street, Stoke-upon-Trent, & 9 Albion place, Blackfriars, London S

Jug Manufacturers (page 853)
Beech James & Son, Albert & Sutherland works, Longton
Smith Sampson (fancy), Sutherland works, Barker street, Longton
Webberley William (fancy), St. James's place, Longton

Lustre Manufacturers (page 856)
Blood Edwin (silver), High st. Longton
Chetham Jonathan Lowe, Commerce street, Longton
Davenport W. (late J. Taylor), (silver), Stafford street, Longton
Deakin & Son, Waterloo works, Longton
Lockett John (gold), King street & Market street, Longton
Moss & Hobson, Cornhill works, Longton
Phillips Edward, Cannon street, Hanley
Wathen & Hudden (late John Bailey), Stafford street, Longton

Parian Figure Manufacturers (page 864)
See also China Figure Manufacturers.
Bailey John, Bryan street, Hanley
Cooper Mrs. A. Etruria road, Hanley
Meli Giovanni, Rome st. Stoke-on-Trent
Yearsley George, Market lane, Longton

Parian Manufacturers (page 864)
Bailey John, Bryan street, Hanley
Barker Joseph, Stafford street, Longton
Berrisford W. & Co. Hanover st. Hanley
Bevington John; works, Clarence street, Hanley
Goodrum W. Daisy bank, Longton
Goss H.W. Ashfield cottage, Stoke-upon-Trent
Hill L. (exors. of), Wharf street, Stoke-upon-Trent
Hill Mrs. M. High street, Stoke-on-Trent
Keys & Briggs, Stoke-upon-Trent
Keys Samuel, John street, Liverpool road, Stoke-upon-Trent
Lockett, Baguley & Cooper, Victoria works, Hanley
Mann & Co. Cannon street, Hanley
Mayer & Elliott, Dale hall pottery, Burslem
Meli Giovanni, Rome st. Stoke-on-Trent
Mills Mrs. Elizabeth, Dresden works, George street, Hanley
Platt & Wild, Sheaf street & George street, Hanley
Roe H. & Son, Bow street, Hanley
Smith William, Hope street, Hanley
Taylor Brothers & Co. Market st. Hanley
Walton J. Brunswick street, Hanley
Wardle & Ash, James street, Hanley
Wilkinson & Rickhuss, Broad st. Hanley
Worthington & Harrop, Tinker's clough, Hanley
Yearsley George, Market lane, Longton

Porcelain Statuary Manufacturers (page 866)
Bates, Brown, Westhead & Moore, Cauldon place, Hanley, & 107 Hatton garden, London
Copeland William Taylor, High street, Stoke-upon-Trent, & 160 New Bond street, London W
Lockett, Baguley & Cooper, Victoria works, Hanley
Mann & Co. Cannon street, Hanley

Pot Creel Maker (page 867)
Bold H. Chancery lane, Longton

Potters (page 867)
See also Drain Pipe Makers; Earthenware Manufacturers, also Stone Ware Manufacturers.
Baddeley William, Commerce street, Longton
Bailey L. Penkhull, Stoke-upon-Trent
Collinson John, Golden hill, Tunstall
Lewis C. Penkhull, Stoke-upon-Trent
Mills J. & J. Cannon street, Hanley
Swift J. St. Martin's lane, Longton

Rockingham Ware Manufacturers (page 882)
Elkin Samuel; works, Stafford street & Mill street, Longton
Hammersley R. High street, Tunstall
Poole & Sutherland, Heathcote road & Cornhill passage, Longton
Procter J. & H. & Co. New town pottery, Longton

Sanitary Vessel Manufacturers (page 883)
Bates, Brown, Westhead & Moore, Cauldon place, Henley, & 107 Hatton garden, London EC
Collinson C. & Co. Fountain pl. Burslem

Spur Makers (page 897)
Buller Wentworth William (patent cock spur & stilt), (Thomas Forrester Walklet, manager); works, Joiner's sq. Hanley, & Bovey Tracey, Devon

Stone Mortar & Pestle Manufacturers (page 899)
Chetham Jonathan Lowe, Commerce street, Longton
Lockett John, King street & Market street, Longton
Mackintyre J. Washington works, Waterloo road, Burslem

Terra Cotta Manufacturers (page 905)
Massey W.S. Chapel lane, Burslem
Minshall Thomas, Brickfield house, Stoke-upon-Trent

Thimble Pillar Manufacturer (page 905)
(For placing Ware in Glost Ovens for China or Earthenware)
Leak Elias, works, Church st. Longton

Toy Makers (page 906)
Baddeley William (stone), Commerce street, Longton
Parr E. (marble), 30 Church st. Burslem
Parr J. (earthenware & marble), 6 Podmore street, Burslem
Parr T. (marble), 34 Church st. Burslem
Parr W. (earthenware marble), Waterloo road, Burslem

1861 Harrison

Harrison, Harrod, and Co.'s Directory and Gazetteer of Staffordshire, with Dudley, in Worcestershire, Harrison, Harrod & Co., London (Shaw & Tipper 1224). Dated 1861 on the title page and January 1861 in the Preface. Another edition was issued as *Harrison, Harrod, and Co.'s Directory and Gazetteer of Staffordshire and Shropshire, with Dudley, in Worcestershire,* dated April 1861 in the Preface.

This directory is not classified but contains descriptive text followed by alphabetical lists of traders for the various towns and villages. Some of the text is clearly derived from earlier Kelly's directories. The following lists of potters have been extracted from the sections for the towns or villages as shown.

Longton – Traders, &c. (pages 362-370)

Ackerley and Hassall, china manufacturers, Commerce street
Adams and Cooper, china manufacturers, High street
Allerton, Charles and Sons, china and earthenware manufacturers, High street
Aynsley and Company, china manufacturers, Market place
Baddeley, William, tobacco pots, fancy pipes, &c., &c., Commerce street
Barlow, Thomas, china manufacturer, Cyples's Old Pottery, Market street
Barlow, Thomas W., earthenware manufacturer, Coronation Works
Barker, Joseph, china and earthenware manufacturer, Stafford street
Beech, James and Son, china manufacturers, Albert and Sutherland Works
Betteney, Thomas, china manufacturer, Stafford street
Birks, Thomas, china and earthenware manufacturer, High street
Blood, Edwin, manufacturer of silver lustres, &c., High street
Bourne, William, earthenware manufacturer, Alma place
Brammall, William, china manufacturer, Heathcote Works
Bridgwood, Simpson and Son, china and earthenware manufacturers, Anchor factory
Broadhurst and Sons, china and earthenware manufacturers, Stafford street
Broadhurst, James and Samuel, earthenware manufacturers, Commerce street
Bullock, Charles, china manufacturer, High street
Cartwright and Edwards, earthenware manufacturers, Weston place, High st.
Chetham, Jonathan L., manufacturer of lustre black and printed wares, &c., Commerce street
Cooper and Cartlich, china toy manufacturers, Market and High street
Copestake and Bradbury, earthenware manufacturers, High street
Copestake, Brothers, manufacturers of china, &c., Anchor Works
Copestake, William, china manufacturer, High street
Davenport, William, lustre ware manufacturer, Stafford street
Deakin, and Son, earthenware and lustre manufacturers, Waterloo Works, Stafford street
Edgerton and Birks, china manufacturers, &c., Green Dock Works
Edwards, James, china manufacturer, Market street
Elkin, Samuel, earthenware manufacturer, Stafford street and Mill street
Finney, Joseph, china manufacturer, Victoria Works
Gibbs and Hassall, china manufacturers, Commerce street
Goodrun, William, Parian manufacturer, Daisy Bank
Hampson and Brothers, earthenware manufacturers, Green Dock Works
Hodson, Richard, china manufacturer, Chancery lane
Hopwood, William, Trustees of, china manufacturer, Church street
Hulse, Nixon, and Adderley, china and earthenware manufacturers, Daisy Bank
Jervis, Leese, and Bradbury, china manufacturers, &c., Dresden Pottery, Chancery lane
Keeling, Walker, and Cooper, figure, parian and earthenware manufacturers, High street
Kent, John, china and earthenware merchant, Market place
Lancaster, James, Parian Works, Daisy Bank
Leak and Robinson, stilt manufacturers, Church street
Lockett, John, porcelain and earthenware manufacturer, King street and Market st.
Lowe, Jonathan, china and lustre black manufacturer, Longton
Malkin, Walker, and Hulse, earthenware manufacturers, enamellers, lustrers, gilders, &c., British Anchor Pottery
Mason and Holt, china manufacturers, Normacot road
Moore and Son, china manufacturers, Mount Pleasant Works
Moss and Hobson, earthenware manufacturers, Cornhill Works
Newbon and Beardmore, earthenware manufacturers, Commerce street
Poole and Sutherland, Rockingham and black earthenware manufacturers, Heathcote road
Procter, T. and H. and Co., earthenware manufacturers, New Town Pottery
Shelley and Hartshorne, china manufacturers, Dresden Works, Stafford street
Shirley and Freeman, china manufacturers, Sheridan Works, King street
Smith, Sampson, china manufacturer, Barker street
Swift, John, tobacco pot manufacturer, St. Martin's lane
Talbot, Elizabeth, silver lustre manufacturer, Market street
Tipper, M. and Co., manufacturers of china and earthenware, Stafford street
Toft, William, earthenware manufacturer, Church street
Townsend, George, earthenware manufacturer, High street

Warren and Adams, china manufacturers, High street
Wathen and Hudden, earthenware manufacturers, Stafford street
Webberley, William, china manufacturer, High street
Yearsley, George, modeller, &c., Market lane

Fenton – Traders, &c. (pages 372-373)
Baker, William and Co., earthenware manufactory
Bourne and Browne, china manufacturers
Challinor, Edward and Co., patent iron stove and china manufactory
Edwards, John and James, china and earthenware manufacturers
Green, M. and Co., china manufacturers
Hawley and Co., china and earthenware manufacturers, Foley Potteries
Knight, Joseph, Foley Old Pottery
Pratt, F. and R. and Co., earthenware manufacturers
Pratt, John and Co., earthenware manufacturers
Robinson, Stubbs, and Hudson, manufacturers of every description of enamelled and burnished gold china, Foley Works
Scarratt and Baldwin, earthenware manufacturers
Wathem, J. and B., earthenware manufacturers, Victoria Works
Wileman, Henry, earthenware, &c., manufacturer, Foley

Stoke-upon-Trent – Traders, &c. (pages 396-399)
Adams, William, and Sons, earthenware manufacturers, Church street, Stoke-upon-Trent
Copeland, William Taylor, earthenware manufacturer, High street
Hill, John, Parian manufacturer, Wharf st.
Malcolm, Frederick, earthenware manufacturer, Boothen road
Meli, Giovanni, Parian statue manufacturer Rome street
Minton and Co., china and earthenware manufacturers, Stoke-upon-Trent
Minton, Hollins, and Co., earthenware manufacturers, (see advt.) Stoke-upon-Trent
Pratt, P., earthenware manufacturer; h., Brook street

Etruria – Traders, &c. (pages 412-413)
Wedgwood, Josiah and Sons, earthenware manufacturers

Burslem – Traders, &c. (pages 424-433)
Alcock, John, earthenware manufacturer, Cobridge
Barker, W.T., china decorator, Silvester square
Beech, William, earthenware manufacturer, Queen street
Boote, T. and R., earthenware manufacturers, Waterloo road
Bowers, George F., earthenware manufacturer and flint grinder, Brownhills
Bridgwood and Clarke, earthenware manufacturers, Churchyard Works
Brough, Joynson and Co., earthenware manufacturers, Bourne's Bank Pottery
Brownfield, William, iron stone and earthenware manufacturer, Cobridge
Cockson and Harding, china manufacturers, Cobridge (see advt.)
Collinson, Charles, and Co., earthenware manufacturers, Fountain place
Corbett, Joseph, grocer and earthenware manufacturer, Market place
Cork, Edge, and Malkin, manufacturers of earthenware, black lustre, fancy coloured stone ware, Queen street and New Wharf Potteries (see advt.)
Corn, Edward, earthenware manufacturer, Navigation road
Davenport, William, and Co., china and glass manufacturers, Longport
Edwards, James, and Son, earthenware manufacturers, Dale hall
Emberton, William, earthenware manufacturer, Brownhills
Furnival and Co., earthenware manufacturers, Cobridge
Godwin, John and Robert, earthenware manufacturers, Cobridge
Hallen, H. and W.H., creel step manufacturers, Pitt street
Hancock, Leigh, and Co., earthenware manufacturers, Swan Bank
Hawthorne, John, manufacturer of earthenware door and bell furniture, Albert street
Heath, Blackhurst, and Co., earthenware manufacturers, Bath street
Holcroft, Hill, and Mellor, earthenware manufacturers, High street
Hughes, Elijah, earthenware manufacturer, Bleak hill Pottery
Hughes, Thomas, earthenware manufacturer, Waterloo road
Hulme, Thomas, earthenware manufacturer and pawnbroker, Market place
Macintyre, James, china and porcelain hall-door knob and finger-plate manufacturer, Washington Works
Maddock, John, and Son, earthenware manufacturers, Newcastle street
Massey, Nehemiah, earthenware figure and Parian manufacturer, Waterloo road
May, John A., earthenware manufacturer, Hamil road
Mayer and Elliot, earthenware manufacturers, Dale Hall Pottery
Morgan, Wood, and Co., earthenware manufacturers, Wedgewood place Pottery
Parr, Brothers, marble manufacturers, Podmore street
Parr, Edwin, marble toy maker, Church street
Parr, John, marble toy maker, Podmore street
Parr, Thomas, marble toy maker, Church street
Parr, William, marble toy maker, Waterloo road
Pearson, Edward, iron, stone, china, and earthenware manufacturer, Hill Works
Pinder, Bourne, and Hope, earthenware manufacturers, Fountain place Pottery
Plant, R., and Sons, earthenware manufacturers, Sneyd green
Shaw, Anthony, earthenware manufacturer, Newport Works
Till, Thomas, and Son, earthenware manufecturers, Liverpool road
Venables, John and Comp., China and earthenware manufecturers and patentees, Waterloo road

Vernon, James, earthenware manufacturer, Scotia Pottery
Walley, E., and Son, earthenware manufacturers, Cobridge
Walley, John, earthenware manufacturer, High street

Golden Hill – Traders, &c. (page 438)
Collinson, John, garden potter

Hanley and Shelton – Traders, &c. (pages 444-453)
Ashworth and Brothers, George L., china and earthenware manufacturers, Broad street
Ashworth, Taylor, earthenware manufacturer, Havelock place
Baddeley, James Henry, earthenware manufacturer, East Wood Vale
Bamford, John, figure manufacturer, Nelson place
Bates, Brown, Westhead, and Moore, earthenware manufacturers, Cauldon place
Bevington, John, china, Parian, and earthenware manufacturer, Clarence street
Bevington, Samuel, Parian manufacturer, Brunswick street
Brock and Allen, Parian manufacturers, Broad street, Shelton
Buckley, John, sanitary pottery, Clarance street Works
Buller and Co., cock spur maker, Joiner square
Clementson, Joseph, earthenware manufacturer, Broad street
Dimmock, John, and Co., earthenware manufacturers, Stafford street
Ellis, Unwin, and Mountford, earthenware manufacturers, Upper Hanley Works
Ford, Thomas, china manufacturer, Canon street
Ford, Charles, patent spur manufacturer, Parker street
Grove, R.H., china and earthenware manufacturer, Vine street
Hood, George, black and Rockingham earthstone manufacturer, Parcer street
Livesley, Powell, and Co., earthenware and china figure and Parian statuary manufacturers, Miles Bank
Lockett, Baguley, and Cooper, china, &c., manufacturers, Broad street
Meigh, Charles, and Son, earthenware manufacturers, Old Hall street
Oldham, James, mosaical and ornamental stone manufacturer, Bethesda street and Ranelagh street
Parkhurst, J.W., earthenware manufacturer, Charles street
Philips, Edward, glass and china manufacturer, Canon street
Pope and Shaw, Messrs., manufacturers of creels, cups, &c., Hanover street
Pratt, Samuel, Parian manufacturer, Sheaf street
Ridgway, Edward John, earthenware manufacturer, High street
Roe, Henry, and Son, Messrs., Parian manufacturers, Bow street, High street
Salt, Charles, Parian manufacturer, Trinity street
Stanway and Thorne, Parian and stone manufacturers, Joiner's square
Stubbs, William, earthenware manufacturer, Albion pottery
Stubbs, William, china and earthenware manufacturer, High street
Taylor, Brothers and Co., earthenware manufacturers, Market street
Taylor, William, earthenware manufacturer, Brook street
Twyford, Christopher, Parian manufacturer, New street
Twyford, Thomas, manufacturer of water closets, pan bason and blue maker, Bath street
Walley, John, earthenware merchant and manufacturer, Hope street
Walton, Ann, china gilder and Parian figure manufacturer, Brunswick street
Wardle and Ash, Parian manufacturers, James street
Warrington, William, beer retailer and grocer, Parian stone manufacturer, East Wood vale
Warrington and Co., Messrs., Parian manufacturers, Brewery street, Hope st.
Wilkinson and Rickhuss, Parian and china manufacturers, Broad street
Worthington and Green, Parian, china, and earthenware manufacturers, Brook street, Hanley
Worthington, Harrop, Parian manufacturer, Mount Pleasant

Tunstall – Traders, &c. (pages 455-460)
Adams, William, jun., earthenware manufacturer, Newfield
Beech and Hancock, earthenware manufacturers, Church Bank
Blackhurst and Dunning, earthenware manufacturers, High street
Brougham, Thomas, earthenware manufacturer, Sandyford
Butterfield, William and James, High street Pottery (see advt.)
Elsmore and Foster, earthenware manufacturers, Tileries
Goodfellow, Thomas, (executors of) earthenware manufacturer, High street
Goodwin, Joseph, earthenware manufacturer, Watergate street
Hammersley, Ralph, black earthenware manufacturer, High street
Meir, Henry, earthenware manufacturer, Greengates pottery
Oalsnam and Holdcroft, earthenware manufacturers, High street
Turner and Tomkinson, earthenware manufacturers, Newfield
Wedgwood and Co., earthenware manufacturers, Amicable street
Wood, Challinor, and Co., earthenware manufacturers, Well street
Wood, E.T.W., earthenware manufacturer, Woodland Pottery
Woolliscroft and Co., earthenware manufacturers, Sandypond

1862 Slater

Slater's (late Pigot & Co.) Royal National Commercial Directory and Topography, Printed and Published by Isaac Slater, 36 Portland Street, Manchester, and Falcon Court, Fleet Street, London (Shaw & Tipper 42). Dated 1862 on the title page and July 1862 in the Address. Shaw & Tipper give the date as 1863 but they may not have seen the complete volume.

As with all the Pigot and Slater series, this directory is classified within a separate section for 'The Potteries' (pages 57-124). A note in the text points out that 'the letters B., F., H., L., S., T., signify respectively the Towns, &c. of Burslem, Fenton, Hanley, Longton, Stoke and Tunstall'. There are seven relevant categories.

China Manufacturers (page 102)
See also Earthenware Manufacturers; and also Toy and Ornamental China Manufacturers
Adams & Cooper, High st. Longton
Allen Herbert Geo. Broad st. Hanley
Allerton Charles & Sons, High st.
Ashworth George. L. & Brothers (ironstone), Broad st. Hanley
Aynsley & Co. Portland works, Sutherland road, Longton
Baguley George (porcelain), Broad st. Hanley
Barlow Thomas, Cyples' Old Pottery, Market st. Longton
Beech James & Son, High st. Longtn
Bell Richard, Market st. Longton
Bentley Thomas & Co. Church st. L
Betteny Thomas, Crown Works, Stafford st. Longton
Bevington & Worthington, Clarence st. Hanley
Bevington Samuel & Son (and of porcelain & parian vases, parian statuettes, &c.), 10 & 12 Brunswick st. & Marsh st. Hanley – See advt
Birks Thomas. High st. Longton
Bowers Geo. Frederick, Brownhills, T
Bourne & Brown, King st. Fenton
Brammall William, Heathcote rd. L
Bridgwood Sampson & Son, Anchor Pottery, Longton
Brown-Westhead T.C. Moore & Co. Cauldon place, Hanley
Brownfield William (ironstone), Waterloo road, Cobridge
Bullock Charles, Bagnall st. Longton
Challinor Edward & Charles (ironstone), High st. Fenton
Cockson & Hardings, Waterloo rd. Burslem, & Marsh st. Hanley
Cooper & Cartledge, High st. Longton
Copeland Wm. Taylor, High st. Stoke
Copestake Brothers, Anchor rd. L
Copestake, Shufflebottom & Allen, High st. Longton
Davenport William & Co. Davenport st. Longport
Dudson James (& ironstone), Hope st. Hanley – See advertisement
Edwards James, Market st. Longton
Edwards John & James, King st. F
Finney Joseph, Victoria pl. Longton
Ford Thomas, Cannon st. Hanley
Goss William, John st. Stoke
Green M. & Co. Park st. Fenton
Grove Richard Henry, Vine st. H
Hawley & Co. Foley, nr Longton
Hawthorn John (door furniture), Albert st. Burslem
Hodson Richard, Chancery lane, L
Holloway John, 73 Market st. H
Hopwood William (Exors. of the late), Church st. Longton – Joseph Dale, manager
Hulse, Nixon & Adderley, DAISY BANK POTTERY, Spring-gardens road, Longton
Lockett & Cooper (porcelain), Broad st. Hanley
Lockett John, King st. & High st. L
Macintyre James (door furniture), Waterloo road, Burslem
Malcolm & Mountford, Dresden Pottery, Church st. Stoke
Mason, Holt & Co. Normacott rd. L
Mills & Swann, George st. Hanley
Minton & Co. (and of patent agate buttons), Eldon pl. London road, Stoke, & 50 Conduit st. London W
Moore Samuel, High ss. Longton
Phillips Edward, Cannon st. Hanley
Robinson, Stubbs & Co. Foley Works, near Longton
Shelley & Adams, Stafford st Longton
Shirley & Freeman, Cyples lane, Market st. Longton
Smith Sampson, Barker st. Longton
Smith William H. Fenton park, F
Stubbs William (& manufacturer of earthenware, Egyptian black, stone ware, lustre, parian & figures), High st. & EASTWOOD POTTERY, Hanley
THE HILL POTTERY, Liverpool rd. B
Walklet William H. (and Britannia metal mounted jugs, wholesale & for exportation), 14 Church st. Hanley – See advetisement
Warren & Adams, Park pl. High st. L
Webb & Walters, St. Martin's la. L
Webberley William, High st. Longtn
Wileman Henry, King st. Fenton
Wilkinson & Rickhuss, 50 Broad st. H
Worthington & Green, Brook st. H

Earthenware Manufacturers (pages 104-105)
See also China Manufacturers; and also Toy and Ornamental China Manufacturers
Adams Wm. & Sons, Church st. S
Adams William, Greenfield, Tunstall
Adams William, jun. Newfield, T
Allerton Charles & Sons, High st L
Allman, Broughton & Co. Wedgwood place, Burslem
Allman Henry & Co. (& of lustre, Egyptian black and Rockingham ware), SILVESTER WORKS, Silvester square, Burslem
Ashworth George L. & Brothers, Broad st. Hanley
Baddeley James Henry (rustic), Gloucester st. Hanley
Baddeley William (rustic), 3 Commerce st. Longton
Baker William & Co. High st. Fenton

Barlow T.W. Commerce st. Longton
Beech & Hancock, High st. Tunstall
Bevington & Worthington, Clarence st. Hanley
Bevington Samuel & Son (and of porcelain, parian, &c.), 10 and 12 Brunswick st. and Marsh st. Hanley – See advertisement
Birks Thomas, High st. Longton
Blackhurst & Dunning, High st. T
Blood Edwin (silver lustered), 62 High st. and Parkhall st. Longton
Boote T. & R. Waterloo rd. Burslem – See advertisement
Bowers George F. Brownhills, T
Brewer Francis & Son (rustic), 3 St. Martin's lane, Longton
Bridgwood & Clark (stone and granite ware), High st. Tunstall
Bridgwood Sampson & Son, Anchor Pottery, Longton
Broadhurst James & Sons (and of crown lustre, smeared black, &c.), CROWN POTTERY, Stafford st. and Commerce st. Longton
Broadhurst Samuel (and printer, enameller, lusterer, and gilder), GOLD STREET WORKS, Gold st. Longton – See advertisement
Bromley, Turner & Hassall, Liverpool road, Stoke
Brough, Joynson & Co. Bourne's Bank Works, Burslem
Brown, – Westhead, T.C. Moore and Company, Cauldon place, Hanley
Brown Wm. Trent Pottery Peel st. B
Buckley John (sanitary), Vine st. H
Burgess & Leigh, Market place, B
Cartwright & Edwards, Lockett's lane, Longton
Challinor Edward, Amicable st, T
Challinor Edwd. & Chas. High st. F
Chetham Jonathan Lowe, Commerce st. Longton
Clementson Joseph, PHOENIX & BELL WORKS, Broad st. Hanley
Cockson & Hardings, Waterloo road, Burslem and Marsh st. Hanley
Collinson Charles & Co. Newcastle st. Burslem
Collinson Wm. (course), Goldenhill
Copeland Wm. Taylor, High st. Stoke
Cork, Edge & Malkin, Queen st. & Navigation road, Burslem
Corn Edward, Navigation road, B
Daniel Levi (rustic), 5 Queen st. B
Daniels, Whittingham & Walsh, Red st. near Harecastle
Davenport, Banks & Co. (porous &c.), Castle Field Pottery, Etruria
Davenport Wm. & Co. Davenport st. L
Deakin & Son, Stafford st. Longton
Dimmock John & Co. Stafford st. H
Doherty & Bromley (& stone, lustre, &c.), High st. Kidsgrove
Dudson James (and metal mounted jugs), Hope st. Hanley – See advt.
Eardley & Hammersley, High st. T
Edwards John & James, King st. F
Edwards Richard, Newport lane, B
Elkin Samuel, Stafford st. Longton
Elliott & Son, Dale Hall Works, B
Ellis, Unwin, Mountford & Taylor, High st. Hanley
Elsmore & Forster, Clay hills, T
Emberton Wm. Highgate Pottery, T
Furnival Jacob & Co. Cobridge
George Street Pottery Company, George st. Tunstall
Godwin John & Robert, Cobridge
Grove Richard Henry (rustic), Vine st. Hanley
Hammersley Ralph (rockingham), High st. Tunstall
Hampson Brothers, New st. Longton
Hancock, Leigh & Co. Swan sq. T
Hawley & Co. Foley, near Longton
Heath, Blackhurst & Co. Furlong la. B
Hillditch Mary Ann, Peel st.
Holdcroft, Hill & Mellor, High st. B
Holland & Green, Stafford st. L
Hood George, Wharf lane, Hanley
Hope & Carter, Fountain Works, B
Hudden John Thomas, Stafford st. Longton – See advertisement
Hughes Elijah. Bleak Hill, Cobridge
Hughes Thomas, Waterloo road, B
Hulse, Nixon & Adderley (& lustre), DAISY BANK POTTERY, Spring gardens road, Longton
Jones George & Co. High st. Stoke
Keeling, Walker & Cooper, High st. H
Knight Joseph (& of lustre, &c.), OLD FOLEY POTTERIES, near L
Keys & Briggs, Copeland st. Stoke
Livesley, Powell & Co. Stafford st. H
Lockett & Cooper, Broad st. Hanley
Lockett John, King st. & High st. L
Lowe & Abberley, Viaduct Works, Caroline st. Longton
Maddock & Son, Newcastle st. B
Malcolm & Mountford, Dresden Pottery, Church st. Stoke
Malkin, Walker & Hulse, Anchor road, Longton
Mann, Evans & Co. Cannon st. H
Mawdsley & Co. Well st. Tunstall
Meakin James & George (manufacturers of every description of earthenware, for export), EAGLE POTTERY, Hanley
Meir Henry (manufacturer of general earthenware and grinder of potters' materials), Greengates, T
Mills John (coarse), Clough st. H
Mills & Swann, George st. Hanley
Minton & Co. Eldon pl. London rd. and 50 Conduit st. London, W
Morgan, Wood & Co. Liverpool rd. B
Moss & Hobson, Cornhill passage, L
Mountford George, Market st. F
Newbon & Beardmore, 2 Commerce st. Longton
OLD HALL EARTHENWARE CO. Hill st. Hanley
Oldham James & Co. Bethesda st. Ranelagh st. Hanley – See advt
Oulsnam Wm. E. High st. Tunstall
Owners of the Hill Pottery, Liverpool road, Burslem
Pankhurst James W. 2 Commerce st L
Pearson Edwd. Sneyd green, Cobridge
Pinder, Bourne & Co, Nile st. Works, B
Poole & Sutherland, Heathcote rd, L
Pratt Felix & Richard & Co. High street, Fenton

Pratt John & Co. Park st. Fenton
Proctor John & Henry & Co. High street, Longton
Ridgway Edward John, High st. H
Shaw Anthony, Newport lane, B
Smith William H. Fenton Park, F
Smith William & Son, Albert st. B
Stubbs William (and manufacturer of china, parian, Egyptian black, stone ware, lustre, &c.), HIGH STREET & EASTWOOD POTTERY, Hanley
Taylor Brothers & Co. Market st. H
Taylor & Plant, Sneyd green, nr. B
Taylor William, Brook st. Hanley
Till, Bullock & Smith (and stone ware), Waterloo Works, Nelson's place, Hanley
Till Thomas & Sons, Sytch Pottery, Liverpool road, Burslem
Townsend George, High st. and Chadwick st. Longton
Turner & Tomkinson, High st. T
Twyford Christopher, New st. H
Venables Henry, Etruria road, L
Vernon James, Scotia rd. Burslem
Walkett William H. (and Britannia metal mounted jugs wholesale & for exportation), 14 Church st. Hanley – See advertisement
Walley Jno. (rockingham), High st. B
Warrington & Co. Brewery st. H
Wathen & Lichfield, VICTORIA WORKS, Market st. Fenton
Wedgwood & Co. Pinnox Works, Woodland st. and Unicorn Works, Amicable st. Tunstall
Wedgwood Josiah & Sons, Etruria
Wileman Henry, King st. Fenton
Wood Challinor & Co. Sandyford, T
Wood Edmund Thomas Wedgwood, Woodland st. Tunstall
Woolliscroft & Galley, Sandyford, T
Worthington & Green, Brook st. H

Parian Manufacturers (page 112)
Bailey John (& ornamental vase and statuary), 96 Bryan st. Hanley
Banks & Hodkinson, George st. H
Banks Thomas, Copeland st. Stoke
Bevington Samuel & Son (and of ornamental porcelain vase and parian statuary), 10 & 12 Brunswick st. and Marsh st. Hanley – See advertisement
Brammer William, Trentham rd. L
Bromley, Turner & Hassell, Liverpool rd. Stoke
Elliott & Son, Dale Hall Works, B
Foster, Crutchley & Co. 3 Clarence st. Hanley
Goss William H. John st. Stoke
Hill Leveson (executors of the late), Wharf st. Stoke
Hopkinson William, 148 Hope st. H
Keeling, Walker & Cooper, High st. L
Keys & Briggs, Copeland st. Stoke
Lancaster James, Stafford st. L
Livesley, Powell & Co. Stafford st. H
Massey Nehemiah & Thomas, 13 Waterloo road, Burslem
Meli Giovanni, Glebe st. Stoke
Mellor Reuben, 134 Normacott rd. L
Nixon Nathan (dealer), 30 Caroline st. Longton
Moss & Hobson, Cornhill passage, L
OLD HALL EARTHENWARE CO. Hill st. Hanley
Oldham James & Co. Bethesda st Ranelagh st. Hanley – See advt.
OWNERS OF THE HILL POTTERY, Liverpool road, Burslem
Roe & Son, Bow st. Hanley
Salt Charles, Bethesda st. Hanley
Saul Edmund, Etruria
Stanway & Horne, Joiner's square, H
Stubbs William (and manufacturer of china, earthenware, egyptian black, stoneware, lustre, &c. High st. and EAST WOOD POTTERY, H
Sutherland Daniel, 17 Caroline st. L
Twyford Christopher, New st. H
Wardle & Ash, James st. Hanley
Warrington & Co. Brewery st. HH
Wilkinson & Rickhuss, 50 Broad st. H
Worthington & Green, Brook st.
Worthington and Harrop, Tinkers clough, Hanley
Yearsley George, 14 Market lane, L

Pot Step Manufacturers for Cotton Spinners (page112)
Bold Henry (& mortice furniture), 34 Chancery lane, Longton
Hallen Harding & William Henry (& gas burner & shuttle eye), Wellington st. Burslem
Hallen Henry, Commercial st. B

Stilt and Spur Manufacturers – Patent (page 116)
Ford Charles, Parker st. Hanley
Gimson Joseph & Co. Market st. F
Wentworth, W. Buller & Mugford, JOINER SQUARE WORKS, Eastwood Vale, Hanley

Toy & Ornamental China Manufacturers (page 121)
See also China Manufacturers, and also Earthenware Manufacturers
Bamford John, Nelson place, H.
Beech Wm. Queen st. Burslem
Bevington & Worthington, Clarence st. Hanley
Doherty & Bromley, High street, Kidsgrove
Dudson James, Hope st. Hanley – See advertisement
Keeling, Walker & Cooper, High st. L
Massey Nehemiah & Thomas, 13 Waterloo road, Burslem
Mills & Swan, George st. Hanley
Shelly & Adams, Stafford st. L
Smith Sampson, Barker st. Longton
Stubbs William, High street, and EASTWOOD POTTERY, Hanley
Sutherland Daniel, 17 Caroline st. L
Townsend George, High st. Longton
Venables Henry (& antique figures), Etruria road, Hanley
Walley John, 118 Hope st. Hanley
Worthington & Green, Brook st. H

Water-Closet Basin Manufacturers (page 121)
Buckley John, Vine st. Hanley
Collinson Charles & Co. Newcastle st. Burslem
Mellor and Birch (dealers), Broad street and Cauldon place wharf, Hanley – See advertisement
Twyford Christopher, New st. H
Twyford Thomas, Bath st. Hanley – See advertisement

1863 Kelly

The Post Office Directory of Birmingham, Staffordshire, Warwickshire, and Worcestershire, for 1864 (also *The Post Office Directory of Staffordshire)*, Printed and Published by Kelly & Co., Old Boswell Court, St. Clement's, Strand, London WC (Shaw & Tipper 6, Shaw & Tipper 1222). Dated MDCCCLXIII on the title page and September 1863 in the Preface. It is noted as the Fifth Edition in the Preface. Although the assembled edition is titled 'for 1864', both the title page and the Preface are dated 1863, and the earlier date has been used in order to avoid misleading data in this work.

As with all the Kelly's series, this directory contains alphabetical lists for the various towns and villages and also classified lists for each county. Only the classified lists are included here. The range of categories is extensive and there are forty-seven relevant to this work.

Beer Machine Handle Maker (page 709)
Buckley John, Vine Street works, Hanley

Bell Furniture Manufacturers (page 719)
Hawthorn John, Albert Street works, Albert street, Burslem
Macintyre James (lever), Washington works, Waterloo road, Burslem

Black Manufacturer – Egyptian (page 719)
Elkin S. Stafford st. & Mill st. Longton

Chemical Ware Manufacturers (page 739)
Davenport, Banks & Co. Castle Field pottery, Etruria, Stoke-upon-Trent
Wedgwood Josiah & Sons, Etruria pottery, Etruria, Stoke-upon-Trent

China Figure Manufacturers (page 740)
Dudson James, Hope street, Hanley
Livesley, Powell & Co. Old Hall street, & Miles Bank, Hanley
Stubbs William, Eastwood pottery, Hanley
Worthington & Green, Booden brook, Hanley
Worthington & Harrop, Tinker's clough, Hanley

China Letter Manufacturer (page 741)
Bold H. (rustic), Chancery la. Longton

China Manufacturers – Antique (page 741)
Davenport, Banks & Co. Castle Field pottery, Etruria, Stoke-upon-Trent

China Manufacturers – Fancy Ware (page 741)
See also China Manufacturers – General.
Adams & Scrivener, The Pottery, Sutherland road, Longton
Green M. & Co. Minerva works, Fenton, Stoke-upon-Trent; London office, 20 Bartlett's buildings, Holborn EC
Hackney, Greaves & Amison, Sheridan works, Longton
Jackson & Brown, Grosvenor works, Foley, Longton
Old Hall Earthenware Co. (limited), Old Hall street, Hanley
Stubbs William, Eastwood pottery, Hanley

China Manufacturers – General (page 741)
Adams & Cooper, High street, Longton
Adams & Scrivener, The Pottery, Sutherland road, Longton
Allen H.G. Broad street, Hanley
Allerton Charles & Son, Park works, Longton
Ashworth George L. & Brothers (late Morley & Ashworth), Broad st. Hanley
Aynsley J. Sutherland road, Longton
Baguley G. Hanley
Barlow T. Cyples's Old pottery, Market street, Longton
Barlow T.W. Commerce st. Longton
Beech James & Son, Albert & Sutherland works, Longton
Beech W. Queen street, Burslem
Bentley T. & Co. Church street, Longton
Betteny Thomas, Crown works, Stafford street, Longton
Bevington John, Works, Great York street, & Clarence street, Hanley
Birks Samuel, Green Dock works, Clayton street, Longton
Birks T. High street, Longton
Bowers George Frederick, Brownhills, Burslem
Brammall W. Heathcote works, Longton
Brown Westhead (T.C.), Moore & Co. Cauldon place, Hanley; & 107 Hatton garden, London EC
Bullock Charles, Bagnall st. Longton
Burton, Wood & Co. Mount Pleasant, Longton
Chetham J.R. & F. Commerce st. Longton
Cockson Charles, Cobridge, Burslem
Cooper T. Hanley
Copeland William Taylor, High street, Stoke-upon-Trent; & 160 New Bond street, London W
Copestake Bros. Anchor works, Longton
Copestake, Shufflebotham & Allin, High street, Longton
Davenport W. & Co. Longport, Burslem; warehouses, 82 Fleet street, London EC, & 30 Canning place, Liverpool
Dudson James, Hope street, Hanley
Duke (Sir J. bart. M.P.) Nephews, Hill Top pottery, Burslem
Edwards J. & Son, Market st. Longton
Edwards John & James, King street, Fenton, Stoke-upon-Trent
Emery & Lea, Market place, Burslem

Finney Joseph, Victoria works, Longton
Ford T. Cannon street, Hanley
Goss William Henry, John street, Liverpool road, Stoke-upon-Trent
Green M. & Co. Minerva works, Fenton, Stoke-upon-Trent; London office, 20 Bartlett's buildings, Holborn EC
Grove R.H. Barlaston, Stone
Hackney, Greaves & Amison, Sheridan works, Longton
Hawthorn John, Albert Street works, Albert street, Burslem
Holland & Green, Stafford st. Longton
Hope & Carter, Fountain place, Burslem
Hopwood W. (trustees of), Church street, Longton
Hulse, Nixon & Adderley, Daisy Bank works, Longton
Jackson & Brown, Grosvenor works, Foley, Longton
Mason, Holt & Co. Normacot road, Longton
Mills Mrs. E. George street, Hanley
Minton Herbert & Co. Eldon place, Stoke-upon-Trent
Moore Samuel, St. Mary's works, Mount Pleasant, Longton
Old Hall Earthenware Co. (limited), Old Hall street, Hanley
Pinder, Bourne & Co. Nile Street works, Nile street, Burslem
Robinson & Cooper, Stafford st. Longton
Robinson, Stubbs & Hudson, Foley, Longton
Shirley & Freeman, Prince of Wales's works, Sutherland road, Longton
Smith S. Barker street, Longton
Stubbs Wm. Eastwood pottery, Hanley
Till T. & Sons, Sytch pottery, Liverpool road, Burslem
Turner, Bromley & Hassall, Albert works, Bryanstone place, Stoke-upon-Trent
Walley John, Hope street, Hanley
Warren & Adams, High street, Longton
Webb & Walters, St. Martin's la. Longton
Wedgwood & Ackerley, Commerce street, Longton
Wedgwood & Co. Amicable st. Tunstall
Wileman H. Foley, Longton
Wilkinson & Sons, Havelock works, Broad street, Hanley

China Manufacturers – Horticultural & Rustic Ware (page 741)
Baddeley J. Gloucester st. John st. Hanly
Brewer F. & Son, Stafford Street works, Longton

China Manufacturers – Tea, Breakfast, and Dessert Services (page 741)
Adams & Cooper, High street, Longton
Adams & Scrivener, The Pottery, Sutherland road, Longton
Allerton Charles & Son, Park works, Longton
Beech James & Son, Albert & Sutherland works, Longton
Betteny Thomas, Crown works, Stafford street, Longton
Birks Joseph, Green Dock works, Clayton street, Longton
Bullock Charles, Bagnall st. Longton
Burton, Wood & Co. Mount Pleasant, Longton
Edwards John & James, King street, Fenton, Stoke-upon-Trent
Green M. & Co. Minerva works, Fenton, Stoke-upon-Trent; & London office, 20 Bartlett's buildings, Holborn EC
Hackney, Greaves & Amison, Sheridan works, Longton
Hulse, Nixon & Adderley, Daisy Bank works, Longton
Jackson & Brown, Grosvenor works, Foley, Longton
Moore Samuel, St. Mary's works, Mount Pleasant, Longton
Old Hall Earthenware Company (limited), Old Hall street, Hanley
Shirley & Freeman, Prince of Wales's works, Sutherland road, Longton

China Manufacturers – White & Finished (page 741)
Adams & Scrivener, The Pottery, Sutherland road, Longton
Betteny Thomas, Crown works, Stafford street, Longton
Broadhurst James, Crown pottery, Stafford street, Longton
Edwards John & James, King street, Fenton, Stoke-upon-Trent
Jackson & Brown, Grosvenor works, Foley, Longton

China Ornament Manufacturers (pages 741-742)
Beech James & Son, Albert & Sutherland works, Longton
Brewer F. & Son (majolica), Stafford Street works, Longton
Bullock Charles, Bagnall st. Longton
Leese William, High street, Longton
Moore Samuel (roman catholic), St. Mary's works, Mount Pleasant, Longton
Stubbs William, Eastwood pottery, Hanley

China Porcelain Manufacturers (page 742)
Beech James & Son, Albert & Sutherland works, Longton
Bevington Samuel, Brunswick street & Marsh street, Hanley
Brown Westhead (T.C.), Moore & Co. Cauldon place, Hanley; & 107 Hatton garden, London EC
Hackney, Greaves & Amison, Sheridan works, Longton
Livesley, Powell & Co. Old Hall street & Miles bank, Hanley
Lockett J. Market street, Longton
Old Hall Earthenware Company (limited), Old Hall street, Hanley
Wilkinson & Sons, Havelock works, Broad street, Hanley

China & Porcelain Door Furniture Manufacturers (page 742)
Hawthorn John, Albert Street works, Albert street, Burslem
Macintyre James, Washington works, Waterloo road, Burslem

China & Porcelain Handle Maker (page 742)
Hawthorn John, Albert Street works, Albert street, Burslem

China Toy Makers (page 742)
Cooper & Cartlidge, High st. Longton

China Vase Manufacturers (page 742)
Brewer F. & Son, Stafford Street works, Longton
Moore Samuel (roman catholic altar), St. Mary's works, Mount Pleasant, Longton

Cock Spur Manufacturers (page 746)
Buller (Wentworth William) & Mugford (patent) (Charles A. Draycott, manager); works, Joiner sq. Hanley

Creel Step Manufacturers (page 749)
Hallen H. & W.H. 29 Pitt st. Burslem

Earthenware Manufacturers (pages 752-753)
Adams W. Greenfield & Newfields collieries, Tunstall, Stoke-upon-Trent
Adams W. jun. Newfield, Tunstall, Stoke-upon-Trent
Alcock H. & Co. Cobridge, Burslem
Allerton Charles & Sons, Park works, Longton
Allman, Broughton & Co. Wedgwood place, Burslem
Ashworth George L. & Brothers (late Morley & Ashworth), Broad street, Hanley
Baker W. & Co. Fenton, Stoke-upon-Trent
Barlow Thomas Waterhouse, Coronation works, Commerce street, Longton
Beardmore & Dawson, Commerce street, Longton
Beech & Hancock, Swan bank, High street, Tunstall, Stoke-upon-Trent
Bennett J. Sneyd pottery, Albert street, Burslem
Bevington John, works, Great York street & Clarence street, Hanley
Bevington Samuel, Brunswick street & Marsh street, Hanley
Blackhurst & Dunning, High street, Tunstall, Stoke-upon-Trent
Bodley & Harrold, Scotia pottery, Scotia road, Burslem
Boote T. & R. Waterloo road, Burslem
Bowers George Frederick, Brownhills, Burslem
Bridgwood & Clarke, Churchyard works, Burslem; & Phoenix works, High street, Tunstall
Bridgwood S. & Son, East vale, Longton
Broadhurst James, Crown pottery, Stafford street, Longton
Broadhurst S. Gold street, Longton
Brough, Joynson & Co. Bourne's bank, Burslem
Brownfield W. Cobridge, Burslem
Brown Westhead (T.C.), Moore & Co. Cauldon place, Hanley; & 107 Hatton garden, London EC
Buckley John (glazed), Vine Street works, Hanley
Burgess & Leigh, Central pottery, Market place, Burslem
Burgess H. Kilncroft pottery, Sylvester square, Burslem
Cartwright & Edwards, Weston place, High street, Longton
Challinor Edward & Charles, Fenton, Stoke-upon-Trent
Clementson J. Broad street, Hanley
Close J.T. Brook street & High street, Stoke-upon-Trent
Collinson C. & Co. Fountain pl. Burslem
Copeland William Taylor, High street, Stoke-upon-Trent; & 160 New Bond street, London W
Cork, Edge & Malkin, New Wharf pottery & Queen street, Burslem
Corns W. & E. Navigation rd. Burslem
Davenport, Banks & Co. Castle Field pottery, Etruria, Stoke-upon-Trent
Davenport W. & Co. Longport, Burslem; warehouses, 82 Fleet street, London EC, & 30 Canning place, Liverpool
Dimmock John & Co. Stafford street, Hanley
Dudson James, Hope street, Hanley
Duke (Sir J. bart. M.P.) Nephews, Hill Top pottery, Burslem
Eardley & Hammersley, Church Bank pottery, Tunstall, Stoke-upon-Trent
Edwards J. & Son, Dale Hall pottery, Burslem
Elkin S. works, Stafford street & Mill street, Longton
Ellerton E. Golden hill, Tunstall, Stoke-upon-Trent
Elliot L. & Son, Longport, Burslem
Elsmore & Forster, Clay Hills pottery, Tunstall, Stoke-upon-Trent
Emberton W. Highgate pottery, Brownhills, Tunstall, Stoke-upon-Trent
Finney Joseph, Victoria works, Longton
Furnival J. & Co. Cobridge, Burslem
Godwin J. & R. Cobridge, Burslem
Grove R.H. Barlaston, Stone
Guest J. Kidsgrove, Stoke-upon-Trent
Hampson Brothers, Green Dock works, Longton
Hancock, Whittingham & Co. Queen square, Burslem
Harding William & Joseph, New Hall pottery, Hanley
Hawley J. Fenton, Stoke-upon-Trent
Heath, Blackhurst & Co. Hadderidge pottery, Burslem
Hobson T. & Co. Cornhill, Longton
Holdcroft, Hill & Mellor, High street, Burslem
Holdcroft & Wood, George street, Tunstall, Stoke-upon-Trent
Hood G. Wharf lane, Hanley
Hudden J.T. Longton
Hughes E. Bleak hill, Waterloo road, Burslem
Hughes T. Waterloo road, Burslem
Jones & Ellis, Stafford street, Longton
Jones G. Glebe street, Stoke-upon-Trent
Keeling, Walker & Cooper, High street, Longton
Kirkham W. London road, Stoke-upon-Trent
Knight J. Foley, Longton
Legge J. Normacot, Longton
Livesley, Powell & Co. Old Hall street & Miles bank, Hanley
Lowe & Abberley, Viaduct works, Caroline street, Longton
Maddock J. & Son, Newcastle street, Burslem
Malkin, Walker & Hulse, British Anchor pottery, Longton
Mawdesley (J.) & Co. Cross street, Tunstall, Stoke-upon-Trent
Meakin J. & G. Eagle pottery, Hanley
Meir J. & Co. Greengates pottery, Tunstall, Stoke-upon-Trent
Minton Herbert & Co. Eldon place, Stoke-upon-Trent
Morgan, Wood & Co. Liverpool road, Burslem
Moss & Cartwright, Sneyd street, Cobridge, Burslem
Mountford & Co. Boothen road, Stoke-upon-Trent
Old Hall Earthenware Company (limited), Old Hall street, Hanley
Oldham J. Bethesda street, Hanley
Oulsnam W.E. High street, Tunstall, Stoke-upon-Trent
Pankhurst & Co. Old Hall st. Hanley
Pearson E. Sneyd st. Cobridge, Burslem
Pratt F. & R. & Co. Fenton, Stoke-upon-Trent
Pratt John & Co. Lane Delph, Fenton, Stoke-upon-Trent
Procter J. & H. & Co. Stafford street, Longton
Ridgway E.J. High street, Hanley
Shaw A. Newport works, Burslem
Smith W. & Son, Albert street, Burslem
Stubbs William, Eastwood pottery, Hanley
Taylor Bros. & Co. Market st. Hanley
Taylor William (granite); works, Brook street, Hanley
Till T. & Sons, Sytch pottery, Liverpool road, Burslem
Townsend G. High street, Longton

Turner, Bromley & Hassall, Albert works, Bryanstone Place, Stoke-upon-Trent
Turner & Tomkinson, Victoria works, Tunstall, Stoke-upon-Trent
Twyford T. Bath street, Hanley
Unwin, Mountford & Taylor, Upper Hanley works, Hanley
Vernon J. Waterloo works, Waterloo road, Burslem
Wathen & Lichfield, Fenton, Stoke-upon-Trent
Wedgwood Josiah & Sons, Etruria pottery, Etruria, Stoke-upon-Trent
Wedgwood & Walker, Tunstall, Stoke-upon-Trent
Williams Thomas (brown, black & lustre), Sylvester square, Burslem
Wood, Challinor & Co. Sandyford, Tunstall, Stoke-upon-Trent
Wood E.T.W. Woodland pottery, Tunstall, Stoke-upon-Trent
Woolliscroft G. & Co. Sandyford, Tunstall, Stoke-upon-Trent
Worthington & Son, Clarence street, Hanley

Earthenware Manufacturer (Horticultural & Rustic Ware) (page 753)
Bold Henry, Chancery lane, Longton

Egyptian Black Ware Manufacturers (page 753)
Chetham J.R. & F. Commerce street, Longton
Harding William & Joseph, New Hall pottery, Hanley
Poole & Sutherland, Cornhill, Longton
Stubbs William, Eastwood pottery, Hanley

Encaustic, Venetian & Mosaic Pavement Manufacturers – Patent (page 753)
Minton, Hollins & Co. High street, Stoke-upon-Trent; & 50 Conduit st. Regent street, London W

Fancy Ware Manufacturers (page 754)
See also China Manufacturers – Fancy Ware.
Davenport, Banks & Co. Castle Field pottery, Etruria, Stoke-upon-Trent

Horticultural Goods Manufacturers – China (page 789)
Brewer F. & Son, Stafford Street works, Longton

Jasper Makers (page 794)
Venables H. Etruria road, Hanley
Wedgwood Josiah & Sons, Etruria pottery, Etruria, Stoke-upon-Trent

Jug Manufacturers (page 794)
Beech James & Son, Albert & Sutherland works, Longton
Betteny Thomas, Crown works, Stafford street, Longton
Dudson James, Hope street, Hanley
Green M. & Co. Minerva works, Fenton, Stoke-upon-Trent; & London office, 20 Bartlett's buildings, Holborn EC
Macintyre James, Washington works, Waterloo road, Burslem

Knob Makers – Drawer, Hall & Door (page 794)
Hawthorn John, Albert Street works, Albert street, Burslem
Macintyre James, Washington works, Waterloo road, Burslem

Label Maker – Garden (page 794)
Macintyre James, Washington works, Waterloo road, Burslem

Letter Manufacturers (page 795)
Macintyre James, Washington works, Waterloo road, Burslem

Lustre Manufacturers (page 798)
Allerton Charles & Sons, Park works, Longton
Broadhurst James, Crown pottery, Stafford street, Longton
Chetham J.R. & F. Commerce street, Longton
Stubbs Wm. Eastwood pottery, Hanley

Majolica Manufacturers (page 798)
Bailey, Murrells & Co. Elm st. Hanley
Bevington John; works, Great York street & Clarence street, Hanley
Keys & Briggs, Copeland street, Stoke-upon-Trent
Minton, Herbert & Co. Eldon place, Stoke-upon-Trent
Wedgwood Josiah & Sons, Etruria pottery, Etruria, Stoke-upon-Trent

Parian Figure Makers (page 806)
Bevington Samuel, Brunswick street & Marsh street, Hanley
Livesley, Powell & Co. Old Hall street & Miles bank, Hanley
Massey Nehemiah & Thomas, 13 Waterloo road, Burslem
Meli G. Rome street, Stoke-upon-Trent
Old Hall Earthenware Co. (limited), Old Hall street, Hanley
Sutherland D. & T. Caroline st. Longton
Yearsley G. Market lane, Longton

Parian Manufacturers (page 806)
Ayland Josiah Albert, Copeland street, Stoke-upon-Trent
Beech W. Queen street, Burslem
Bevington J. Great York street & Clarence street, Hanley
Evans John, Hope street, Hanley
Goss William Henry, John street, Liverpool road, Stoke-upon-Trent
Hill L. (exors. of) Wharf street, Stoke-upon-Trent
Keys & Briggs, Copeland street, Stoke-upon-Trent
Lancaster James, Stafford street & Daisy bank, Longton
Oakes D. St. Martin's lane, Longton
Roe H. & Son, Bow street, Hanley
Salt C. Bethesda street, Hanley
Smith J. Hope street, Hanley
Stanway & Horne, Eastwood vale, Hanley
Stubbs William, Eastwood pottery, Hanley
Turner, Bromley & Hassall, Bryanstone place, Stoke-upon-Trent
Walley John, Hope street, Hanley
Wardle & Ash (stone & colored bodies), Broad street, Hanley
Warrington W. & Co. Brewery st. Hanley
Wedgwood Josiah & Sons, Etruria pottery, Etruria, Stoke-upon-Trent
Wilkinson & Sons, Havelock works, Broad street, Hanley

Porcelain Manufacturers (page 809)
Bevington Samuel, Brunswick street & Marsh street, Hanley
Goss William Henry (ivory), John street, Liverpool rd. Stoke-upon-Trent

Hackney, Greaves & Amison, Sheridan works, Longton
The Enamel Porcelain Co. (limited), Old Hall street, Hanley

Porcelain Statuary Manufacturers (page 809)
Brown Westhead (T.C.), Moore & Co. Cauldon place, Hanley; & 107 Hatton garden, London EC
Copeland William Taylor, High street, Stoke-upon-Trent; & 160 New Bond street, London W

Potters (page 809)
Adderley, Shaw & Goldstraw (chimney pot), Daisy Bank works, Longton
Baddeley W. Commerce street, Longton
Bold Henry (rustic), Chancery lane, Longton
Collinson W. (garden), Golden hill, Tunstall, Stoke-upon-Trent
Hodson R. (china), Chancery la. Longtn
Walley Edward (consulting), Clifton terrace, Waterloo road, Burslem

Rockingham Ware Manufacturers (page 826)
Elkin S. works, Stafford street & Mill street, Longton
Hammersley R. High street, Tunstall, Stoke-upon-Trent
Harding William & Joseph, New Hall pottery, Hanley
Massey T. 13 Waterloo road, Burslem
Poole & Sutherland, Cornhill, Longton

Sanitary Vessel Manufacturers (page 828)
Birch Elijah & Co. (dealers), Broad street, Hanley
Brown Westhead (T.C.), Moore & Co. Cauldon place, Hanley
Buckley John, Vine Street works, Hanley
Mellor S. jun. & Co. (dealers), Broad street, Hanley

Shuttle Eyes Manufacturer (page 840)
Bold Henry, Chancery lane, Longton

Stone Mortar & Pestle Manufacturers (page 847)
Chetham J.R. & F. Commerce street, Longton
Macintyre James, Washington works, Waterloo road, Burslem

Stone Ware Manufacturers (page 847)
Birch Elijah & Co. Broad street, Hanley
Broadhurst James, Crown pottery, Stafford street, Longton
Brown Westhead (T.C.), Moore & Co. Cauldon place, Hanley; & 107 Hatton garden, London EC.
Chetham J.R. & F. (druggists'), Commerce street, Longton
Davenport, Banks & Co. (antique, mosaic & chemical porous), Castle Field pottery, Etruria, Stoke-upon-Trent
Harding William & Joseph, New Hall pottery, Hanley
Keys & Briggs, Copeland street, Stoke-upon-Trent
Kirkham W. London rd. Stoke-upon-Trnt
Leese Wm. (dealer), High st. Longton
Massey Nehemiah & Thomas, 13 Waterloo road, Burslem
Mellor Samuel, jun. & Co. Broad street, Hanley
Stubbs Wm. Eastwood pottery, Hanley
Wedgwood Josiah & Sons, Etruria pottery, Etruria, Stoke-upon-Trent

Terra Cotta Manufacturers (page 852)
Massey W.S. Chapel lane, Burslem
Turner, Bromley & Hassall, Albert works, Bryanstone place, Stoke-upon-Trent

Toy Makers (page 854)
Parr E. Podmore street, Burslem
Parr J. (earthenware), Kilncroft bank & 78 Waterloo road, Burslem
Parr T. 34 Church street, Burslem
Parr W. 30 Church street, Burslem

Water Closet Pan Manufacturer (page 856)
Buckley John, Vine St. works, Hanley

White Granite Manufacturers (page 858)
Edwards John & James, King street, Fenton, Stoke-upon-Trent

1864 Jones

Jones's Mercantile Directory of the Pottery District of Staffordshire, Printed and Published by Jones & Proud, 7 & 8 Rolls Buildings, Fetter Lane, London (Shaw & Tipper 1225). Dated 1864 on the title page and February 1864 in the Address. Publication was announced in the *Staffordshire Advertiser* dated 5 March 1864, and it was reviewed in the issue dated 26 March.

This directory consists of separate alphabetical sections for each town in the area plus an assembled trades directory. There are nine relevant categories.

China and Earthenware Manufacturers (pages 170-171)
See also Earthenware Manufacturers.
Abraham Robert Frederick, 34 Victoria st, Northwood, Hanley
Adams & Cooper, High st, Longton
Adams & Scrivener, The Pottery, Sutherland rd, Longton
ALLERTON C. & SON, High st, Longton – (see Advertisement)
Aynsley John, Sutherland rd, Longton
Baguley George, Victoria works, Broad st, Hanley
Barker & Hill, King st, Longton
Barlow Thomas, Market st, Longton

Beech James & Son, High st, Longton
BEECH WILLIAM, Queen st, Burslem – (see Advertisement)
BENTLEY THOMAS & Co., Church st, Longton – (see Advertisement)
Betteney Thomas, Crown works, Stafford st, Longton
Bevington Samuel (and parian), 10 & 12 Brunswick st, and Marsh st, Hanley
Birks Saml., Green dock works, Longton
BIRKS THOMAS, High st, Longton – (see Advertisement)
Bowers Geo. Frederick (every variety), Brownhills pottery & mills, Tunstall – (see Advertisement)
Brammall William, Heathcote works, Longton
BRIDGWOOD SAMPSON & SON, Anchor works, Longton
Brown-Westhead, Moore, & Co., Cauldon place, Hanley
Burton, Wood, & Co., Mount Pleasant, High st, Longton – (see Advt.)
Bullock Charles, Britannia works, Bagnall st, Longton
Cartledge J. & Co., Market st, Longton
COCKSON CHARLES (plain and ornamental), Cobridge, Burslem – (see Advertisement)
Cooper Thomas, High st, Longton
Copeland Wm. Taylor, High st, Stoke-upon-Trent; and 160 New Bond st, London, W.
Copestake Brothers, Anchor rd, Longton
COPESTAKE, SHUFFLEBOTHAM & ALLIN, High st, Longton – (see Advertisement)
Copestake Wm. & Co., 51 High st, Longton
Davenport William & Co. (and glass), Longport, Burslem
DUKE & NEPHEWS, Hill pottery, Burslem
Edwards Jas. & Son, Market st, Longton
EDWARDS JOHN & JAMES (and white granite), King st, Fenton, Stoke-upon-Trent – (see Advertisement)
Emery & Lea (and majolica), Crown works, Burslem
Enamel Porcelain Company (limited), Burton place, Hanley
Finney Joseph, Victoria works, Stafford st, Longton
Ford Thomas, Cannon st, Shelton
GOSS WILLIAM HENRY, John st, Stoke-upon-Trent. Statuettes, vases, tazzas, deserts, perfumers' goods, lamps, butters, jugs, &c., &c.
Green M. & Co., Minerva china works, Fenton, Stoke-upon-Trent
HACKNEY, GREAVES & Co., Sheridan works, King st, Longton
Hackney Ralph, Peel st, Stoke-upon-Trent
HAWLEY & Co., Foley, Fenton, Stoke-upon-Trent
Hawthorn John (and patent knob), Albert street works, Burslem
Hodson Richard, Chancery ln, Longton
HOLLAND & GREEN, Stafford street, Longton – (see Advertisement)
HOPWOOD W. (executors of the late), Church st, Longton – (see Advt.)
Hulse, Nixon, & Adderley, Daisy bank, Longton
JACKSON & BROWN, The Foley, Fenton, near Longton
Jones Geo., Bridge works; warehouses, Wharf st & Glebe st, Stoke-upon-Trent
Lockett Jno., Market st & King st, Longton
MASON, HOLT & Co., Normacott rd, Longton – (see Advertisement)
Miller William, Paradise st, Tunstall
MINTON & Co., Stoke-upon-Trent
Moore Samuel, St. Mary's works, High st, Longton
POOLE & SUTHERLAND, Cornhill works, Cornhill passage, Stafford st, Longton
ROBINSON, HUDSON & Co., Foley, Fenton, near Longton – (see Advt.)
Robinson & Son, Wellington works, Stafford st, Longton
Shepherd A. & Co., Eagle works, Longton – (see Advertisement)
Shepherd & Co., Market lane, Longton
SHIRLEY & FREEMAN, Prince of Wales' works, Sutherland rd, Longton – (see Advertisement)
SMITH SAMPSON, Sutherland works, Barker st, Longton – (see Advt.)
STUBBS & PLANT, Chancery lane, Longton – (see Advertisement)
STUBBS, HACKNEY, & TOMPKINSON, High st, Longton – (see Advertisement)
Stubbs Wm., High st & Eastwood, Hanley
Tipper Samuel, Stafford st, Longton – (see Advertisement)
Townsend George, 17 High st, Longton
TURNER & HASSALL, Albert works, Liverpool rd, Stoke-upon-Trent
Venables Henry (etruscan, jasper), Etruria rd, Hanley
WAYTE & RIDGE, Waterloo pl works, Heathcote rd, Longton – (see Advt.)
WARREN & ADAMS, Pash pl, and Victoria works, High st, Longton
WEBBERLEY WILLIAM, St. James's pl, High st, Longton – (see Advt.)
WEDGWOOD & ACKERLEY, Commerce st, Longton
Wileman Henry, Foley works, Fenton
WILKINSON & SONS, Broad st, Hanley – (see Advertisement)

China (Gold and Silver Lustre) Manufacturers (page 171)

Alcock & Williamson, St. Martin's lane, Longton
ALLERTON C. & SON, High st, Longton – (see Advertisement)
BIRKS THOMAS, High st, Longton – (see Advertisement)
BROADHURST JAMES, Crown pottery, Stafford st, Longton – (see Advt.)
CHETHAM J. R. & F., Commerce st, Longton – (see Advertisement)
Keeling, Walker & Co., 31 High st, Longton
Knight Joseph, Foley, Fenton, Stoke-upon-Trent
Malkin, Walker, & Hulse, British Anchor pottery, Longton
SMITH SAMPSON, Barker st, High st, Longton – (see Advertisement)
Snow Henry, St. Martin's lane, Market st, Longton
Webb & Walters, Stafford st, Longton

China Figure Manufacturers (page 171)
Bamford John, Nelson Place, Hanley
Copeland William Taylor, High st, Stoke-upon-Trent; and 160 New Bond st, London, W.
Lovesley, Powell & Co., Old Hall st, and Parliament row; and Stafford st, Hanley
SMITH SAMPSON, Sutherland works, Longton – (see Advertisement)

China and Porcelain Door Furniture Manufacturers (page 171)
Bridgwood & Clarke, Burslem; and High st, Tunstall
Macintyre James, Washington works, Waterloo rd, Burslem

Earthenware Manufacturers (page 180-181)
See also China Manufacturers; Parian Manufacturers; & Earthenware Manufacturers (Miscellaneous)
ADAMS WILLIAM, SEN., Greenfield colliery, Tunstall
ADAMS WILLIAM, JUN., Newfield pottery, Tunstall
Alcock Henry & Co., (ironstone and china), Cobridge, Burslem
Allman, Broughton & Co., Wedgwood place pottery, Burslem
Ashworth George L. & Brothers, Broad st, Hanley
Baker William & Co., High st, Fenton
Barlow Thomas Waterhouse, Commerce st, Longton
BEARDMORE THOMAS, Heathcote rd, Longton – (see Advertisement)
BEECH & HANCOCK, Swan works, High st, Tunstall
Bevington John, 20 Clarence st, Hanley
Blackhurst & Dunning, High st, Tunstall
BODLEY & HARROLD, Scotia pottery, Burslem
Booth Thomas (hot water pipes, &c.), Britannia works, Lichfield st, Hanley
BREWER F. & H. & Co., Stafford st, Longton. All kinds of horticultural and fancy rustic wares, majolica and dessert wares, &c. – (see Advt.)
Bridgwood & Clarke, High st, Tunstall; and Burslem
BROADHURST JAMES, Crown pottery, Longton – (see Advt.)
Brough Brothers & Co., Gold street works, Longton
Brough, Joynson & Co., Bourne's bank pottery, Burslem
Brownfield William, Cobridge, Burslem
Burgess Henry, Kilncroft works, Burslem
Burgess & Leigh, Central pottery, Burslem
Cartwright & Edwards, High st, Longton
Challinor Edward, Amicable st, Tunstall
Challinor Edward & Charles, Fenton, Stoke-upon-Trent
Clementson Joseph, Broad st, Hanley
Close John Theophilus (and lustre), Church st, Stoke-upon-Trent
Cockson Charles, Cobridge – (see Advt.)
Cooper Thomas, Royal Victoria works, Broad st, Hanley
CORK, EDGE & MALKIN, Queen st, and New wharf potteries, Burslem – (see Advertisement)
Corn Edward, Navigation road pottery, Burslem
DAVENPORT, BANKS & Co. (fancy and antique goods), Castlefield pottery, near Stoke-upon-Trent – (see Advertisement.)
Dimmock John & Co., Albion works, Hanley
Dix & Tundley, Albert st, Burslem
DUDSON JAMES, Hope st, Hanley – (see Advertisement)
EARDLEY & HAMMERSLEY, Church bank pottery, High st, Tunstall
Edwards James & Son, Dalehall, Burslem
Elkin Samuel, Stafford st, Longton
ELLIOTT LIDDLE, & SON, Dalehall potteries, Burslem; and Longport
ELSMORE & FORSTER, Clay hills pottery, Tunstall
Emberton William, Highgate pottery, Tunstall
Enamel Porcelain Co., Cannon st, Hanley
Furnival J. & Co., Cobridge, Burslem
Godwin John & Robert, Cobridge, Burslem
HAMPSON BROTHERS, Green dock works, Longton – (see Advt.)
HANCOCK, WHITTINGHAM & Co., Swan bank pottery, Burslem – (see Advertisement)
Harding W. & J., New Hall pottery, Hanley
HEATH, BLACKHURST & Co., Hadderidge potteries, Burslem
Hett & Co., Cannon st, Shelton
HOBSON THOMAS & Co., Church st, Longton – (see Advertisement)
HOLDCROFT, HILL & MELLOR, High street pottery, Burslem
Holdcroft & Wood, George street pottery, Tunstall
Hood Geo., (brown) Wharf lane, Hanley
Hope & Carter, Fountain place, Burslem
Howson George, Silvester sq, Burslem
HUDDEN J.T., Stafford st, Longton – (see Advertisement)
Hughes John V., Bleakhill pottery, Cobridge, Burslem
Hughes Thomas, Waterloo rd, Burslem
Hulse William, Pool dole, Fenton, Stoke-upon-Trent
Jones George, Church st, Stoke-upon-Trent
Jones & Ellis, Stafford st, Longton
Keeling, Walker & Cooper, 31 High st, Longton
Kirkham William, London rd, Stoke-upon-Trent
KNIGHT JOSEPH, Old Foley pottery, Fenton near Longton – (see Advt.)
LEA WILLIAM SMITH, New Street pottery, Hanley. Manufacturer of earthenware, parian, brown and yellow ware, Egyptian black and stone
Lee Joseph, Mount st, Tunstall
Livesley, Powell & Co., Stafford st; and Old Hall st, Hanley
LOWE & ABBERLEY, Waterloo works, Stafford st, Longton – (see Advertisement)
MALKIN, WALKER & HULSE, British anchor pottery, Longton – (see Advertisement)
MAWDESLEY & Co., Well street pottery, Tunstall
MEAKIN J. & G., Eagle pottery, Hanley
MEIR JOHN & SON, Green gate pottery, Tunstall
Mills John, 4 Clough st, Hanley
Morgan, Wood & Co., Hill works, Burslem
MOSS & CARTWRIGHT, Sneyd green pottery, Cobridge, Burslem

Muntford John, Dresden pottery, Stoke-upon-Trent
Newbon & Dawson, Commerce st, Longton
Old Hall Earthenware Co. (limited), Hill st, Hanley
Oldham James & Co., Ranalgh st, Hanley
OULSNAM WILLIAM EMERSON, High st, Tunstall
Pankhurst James William, Charles street manufactory, Hanley
Pearson Edward, Cobridge, Burslem
Pennington Charles, 32 Old Hall st, Hanley
Pickard & Salt, Marsh st, Longton
Pinder, Bourne & Co., Nile street works, Burslem
Pratt F. & R. & Co., High st, Fenton
Pratt John & Co., Lane Delph, Fenton, Stoke-upon-Trent
PROCTER J. & H. & Co., High st, Longton – (see Advertisement)
Ridgway Edward John, High st, Hanley
Shaw Anthony, Newport works, Burslem
Sims Richard, 16 Sheaf st, Hanley
Stannaway John, New st, Wolstanton
Taylor Brothers, Market st, Hanley
Taylor William, Brook st, Hanley
TILL, FILCHER & Co., Waterloo pottery, Nelson pl, Hanley. Manufacturers of jasper, mosaic, water coolers, jet glaze garden pots, and general stone ware
Till & Sons, Sytch pottery, Burslem
Turner & Tomkinson, Victoria works, High st, Tunstall
Unwin, Mountford & Taylor, High st, Hanley
Vernon James, Wellington st, Burslem
WATHEN JAMES B., Victoria works, Market st, Fenton, Stoke-upon-Trent – (see Advertisement)
WEDGWOOD & Co., Pinnox; and Amicable st works, Tunstall
WEDGWOOD JOSIAH & SONS, Etruria, Stoke-upon-Trent
Wedgwood Thos., 22 Nile st; works, Union st, Burslem
WOOD, CHALLINOR & Co., Sandyford pottery, Tunstall
Wood Edmund Thomas Wedgwood, Woodland pottery, Tunstall
Woolliscroft George, Sandyford potteries, Tunstall
WORTHINGTON & GREEN, Brook street works, Hanley – (see Advt.)
Worthington & Son, 20 Clarence st, Hanley

Earthenware (Miscellaneous) Manufacturers
(pages 181-182)

See China Manufacturers; also Earthenware Manufacturers
Bold Henry (pot, step, worsted guide, and rustic flower-pot manufacturer), 8 Commerce st, and Daisy bank, Longton
BREWER F. & H. & Co., Stafford st, Longton. Manufacturers of all kinds of horticultural and fancy rustic ware and majolica – (see Advertisement)
Buckley John (beer machine handle maker, and sanitary earthenware manufacturer), Vine st, Hanley
BULLER, MUGFORD & Co. (W.W.) (patent cockspur, stilt, &c.), Joiner's square, Hanley
Cartwright M. & Thos. (telegraphic insulators mftrs), Stafford st, Longton
CARTLIDGE WM. ED. (brown, black, and lustre earthenware), Silvester works, Burslem – (see Advertisement)
Collinson Charles & Co. (chemical apparatus and sanitary articles manufacturers), Fountain place, Burslem
Collinson Wm. (garden pot), Golden hill
CORK, EDGE & MALKIN (black, lustre, and fancy colored stone earthenware), Queen st, and New wharf potteries, Burslem – (see Advt.)
Corns & Co. (creel cup and shuttle eye manufacturers), 5 Club bldgs, Burslem
Ford Charles (patent spur and stilt), Parker st, Hanley
Gimson J. & Co. (patent placing pins, spurs, stilts, &c.), Market st, Fenton
Hallen H. & W. (pot creel step manfrs, for cotton mills), Wellington street works, Burslem
Hammersley Ralph (Egyptian black and Rockingham teapots manfr), High st, Tunstall
Hughes Elijah (granite-colored stone bodies in jugs, &c.), Bleak hill pottery, Cobridge, Burslem
Lawton George (creel cup and shuttle eye), 68 Furlong lane, Burslem
Legge John (garden pot and chimney pipe), Normacott road furnace, Longton
Maddock John & Son (white granite), Newcastle st, Burslem
MASSEY & SON (stone in colour, lustre and parian ware), 13 Waterloo rd, Burslem
MINSHALL THOMAS, Brickfield house, London rd, Stoke-upon-Trent. Manufacturer of terra cotta and porcelain jet lamps, vases, vitrified jars, porous water bottles, butter coolers, filters, jugs, &c., &c.; also of terra-metallic bricks, tiles, ridges, quarries, &c., &c.
MINTON, HOLLINS & Co. (patent encaustic, venetian, and mosaic pavements), High st, Stoke-upon-Trent; and 50 Conduit st, Regent st, London
PARR EDWARD (tea-pots, marbles, parlour balls, &c.), Podmore street works, Waterloo rd, Burslem
Parr John (toy and marble), Kiln croft works, Burslem
Parr Thomas (toy and marble), 34 Church st, Burslem
SELMAN J. & W. (toy), Gritten st, Brownhill, Tunstall – (see Advt.)
SNAPE SAMUEL (horticultural potter), Garshall green, near Stone – (see Advertisement)
TILL, FILCHER & Co., Waterloo pottery, Nelson place, Hanley. Manufacturers of jasper, mosaic, water çoolers, jet glaze, garden pots, and general stone ware
WALLEY JOHN (Rockingham teapot and fancy toy), High st, Burslem
Wedgwood Josiah & Sons (parian, jasper, and majolica), Etruria, viâ Stoke-upon-Trent

Earthenware (Rustic and Terra Cotta Figure) Manufacturers (page 182)

Baddeley Elizabeth, St. Martin's lane, and 3 Commerce st, Longton
Baddeley Jas. Henry, Gloster st, Shelton
BADDELEY WILLIAM, Normacott rd, Longton
Bennett John, Sneyd pottery, Albert st, Burslem

BREWER F. & H. & Co., Stafford st, Longton – (see Advertisement)
Sutherland Danl., – house, 18 Caroline st; and works, Parkhall st, Anchor rd, Longton. Manufacturer of useful and ornamental parian, terra cotta, rustic, oak, and fir tobacco boxes, garden pots, spills, &c. Proprietor of the Temperance hotel

Parian Manufacturers (pages 217-218)
Bailey, Murrells & Co., Elm st, Market st, Hanley – (see Advertisement)
BEECH WILLIAM, Queen st, Burslem – (see Advertisement)
BEVINGTON & SON, 10 and 11 Brunswick st, Hanley – (see Advt.)
Billington Richard, Eastwood pottery, Joiner's sq, Hanley
Davenport & Banks, Castlefield pottery, Etruria, near Stoke-upon-Trent – (see Advertisement)
DUKE & NEPHEWS, Hill pottery, Burslem
Evans John, 102 Hope st, Hanley
Goss William Henry, John st, Liverpool rd, Stoke-upon-Trent
HILL LEVESON (executors of), Wharf st, Stoke-upon-Trent – (see Advertisement)
Holloway John, 73 Market st, Hanley
Lancaster James, Daisy bank, and 59 Stafford st, Longton
Lockett John, King st and Market st, Longton
Livesley, Powell & Co., Old Hall st and Parliament row, and Stafford st, Hanley
MELI GIOVANNI (designer and modeller), Glebe st, Stoke-upon-Trent – (see Advertisement)
MELLAR REUBEN (brooch and figure), 66 Sutherland rd, Longton
Mills Brothers, George st, Shelton
MINTON & Co., Stoke-upon-Trent
Oakes David, St. Martin's lane, Longton
Oldham James & Co., Ranalgh st, Hanley
Roe Henry & Son, Bow st, High st, Hanley
Saul Edmund, Etruria
SMITH JOHN, 144 Hope st, Hanley. Manufacturer of pari an twig baskets and brooches
STANWAY, HORNE & Co., Eastvale, Lichfield st, Hanley – (see Advertisement)
Sunderland John, Market lane, Longton
Sutherland Daniel, 18 Caroline st, and Parkhall st, Anchor rd, Longton
Till, Filcher & Co., Waterloo pottery, Nelson place, Hanley
TURNER & HASSALL, Albert works, Liverpool rd, Stoke-upon-Trent
Twyford Christopher, New st, Hanley
Unwin, Mountford & Taylor, High st, Hanley
WARDLE & ASH, Broad st, Hanley
Warrington Wm., Brewery st, Hanley
WAYTE & RIDGE, Waterloo place works, Heathcote rd, Longton – (see Advertisement)
WEDGWOOD JOSIAH & SON, Etruria, Stoke-upon-Trent
Wilkinson & Sons, Broad st, Hanley – (see Advertisement)
Wood George, Slippery lane, Broad st, Hanley
Worthington & Harrop, Tinkersclough, Hanley
Yearsley George, Market lane, Longton

Names Received too late for Classification, Alterations, &c. (page 239)
Davenport, Banks & Co., earthenware, and stone, and fancy ware manufacturers, Castlefield pottery, Etruria, Hanley – (see Advertisement)
Twyford Thomas, Bath st, Hanley

1865 Keates

Keates & Ford's Annual Potteries and Newcastle Street and Trade Directory with Almanack, for 1865-6, Keates & Ford, Printers and Publishers, 38 & 40 Cheapside, Hanley (Shaw & Tipper 1232). Dated 30 October 1865 in the Preface.

As with all the Keates series, this directory is classified within separate sections for each of the six pottery towns and the only relevant categories are potters and various types of tile manufacturers. The list for Hanley excludes an importer, Schiegnitz and Kramer.

Burslem – Potters (pages 61-62)
Alcock Henry and Co. (china and earthenware), Cobridge Works
Allman, Broughton and Co. (earthenware), Wedgwood place
Beech James (china and parian toy and fancy), Queen street
Bennett, Hurd and Co. (earthenware), Eagle Pottery, Nile street
Bodley E.F. (earthenware), Scotia Works, Wedgwood place
Boote T. & R. (earthen.), Waterloo rd
Booth Thomas (toy), Portland street
Boughton R.T. and Co. (earthenware), Fountain place
Brough, Joynson and Co. (earthenware), Bourne's bank
Brownfield Wm. (earthen.), Cobridge
Burgess H. (earthen.), Kilncroft (see Advt)
Cartlidge Wm. Edwd. (black and lustre), Silvester square
Cockson Charles (china), Cobridge
Collinson Charles and Co. (chemical and sanitary articles), Fountain place
Cork, Edge & Malkin, (lustre & earthen.), Bourne's bnk., Navigation rd. & Queen st
Corn W. and E. (earthen.), Navigation rd
Corns, Fenton and Co. (creel steps), Amicable buildings
Davenport Wm. & Co. (china & earthenware), Davenport street, Longport
Edwards and Son (earthenware) Lower Hadderidge
Elliott and Son (earthenware), Dale Hall Works, Newcastle street
Evans and Booth (earthen.), Hamil road

Furnival and Co. (earthenware), Cobridge
Godwin John (earthen.), Sneyd st., Cobridge
Hallen & Co. (creel steps), Wellington st
Hancock, Whitingham and Co. (earthenware), Swan bank Works, Waterloo road
Hawthorne John (earthen.), Albert st
Heath John (earthen.), Lower Hadderidge
Heath and Blackhurst (earthen.), Bath st
Hill Pottery Company, Limited (china, earthenware, Majolica, Parian), Liverpool road; Alcock George, manager
Hobson Charles (earthen.), Albert street
Holdcroft, Hill and Mellor (earthenware), High street
Hope and Carter (earthenware and ironstone), Fountain place
Howson George (black and lustre), Silvester square
Hughes Elijah (earthenware), Bleak street
Hughes Thomas (earthen.), Waterloo rd
Lea, Boulton and Smith (china), Market place, and Church bank Pottery, Wood st
Leigh and Burgess (earthen.), Market pl
Macintyre James (door furniture), Washington Works, Waterloo road
Maddock John and Son (earthenware), Newcastle street
Massey Jeremiah (teapot and figures), Kilncroft
Meakin Brothers (earthenware), Peel st
Moss and Cartwright (earthenware), Sneyd green Pottery, Cobridge
Pearson Edward (earthenware and ironstone), Sneyd green, Cobridge
Pinder, Bourne and Co. (earthenware and ironstone), Nile street
Shaw Anthony (earthen.), Newport lane
Till and Sons (earthen.), Liverpool road
Vernon James (earthen.), Waterloo road
Walley John (teapot and toy), High st
Wood, Morgan & Co. (earthen.), L'pool rd

Burslem – Tile Floor Makers (page 63)
Boote T. and R., Waterloo road
Boulton & Worthington, Moorland road

Fenton – Potters (page 73)
Baker W. & Co., (earthenware,) High st
Challinor Edward and Charles, (earthenware,) King street
Edwards John, (china and earthenware) King street
Gimson, Baker, and Challinor, (spur manufacturers,) Market street
Green Mary and Co., (china,) Minerva works, Park st
Hawley & Co., (china and earthenware) King st, Foley
Jackson & Brown, (china,) King st, Foley
Knight Josh., (earthenware,) Old Foley Works, King street. (See advt.)
Malkin Ralph, (earthen,) Park Works, Market street
Pratt F. & R. & Co., (earthen,) Lower Fenton, Market street
Pratt John & Co., (earthenware,) Park st
Robinson, Hudson, and Co., (china,) King street
Wathen B., (earthenware,) Victoria Works, Market street
Wileman C. & J., (china and earthen,) the Foley Pottery

Hanley – Potters (pages115-116)
Adams John & Co. (parian and majolica), St. James street (see Advt.)
Allen H.G. (china), Broad street
Ash George (parian and majolica), Broad street (see Advt.)
Ashworth G.L. & Bros. (earthenware), Broad street
Baddeley James H. (rustic ware), Gloucester street, Bethesda street
Baguley George (china), Broad street, (see Advt.)
Bailey John & Co. (parian), Elm street
Bamford John (china and parian figure), Nelson place
Bentley Noah (parian), Bryan street
Best and Varcoe (china & parian), Nelson place
Bevington John (parian), Great York street (see Advt.)
Bevington J. & T. (china and parian), Marsh street
Bevington J. & Co. (china and parian), Brunswick street
Brown-Westhead, Moore, & Co. (china earthenware, parian, and majolica), Cauldon place
Buckley James (sanitary ware), Vine street
Buller, Mugford, & Draycott (spurs and stilts), Eastwood vale
Clementson Jos. (earthenware), Phoenix works, Broad street, and Bell works, George street
Cooper Thos., Executors of (china and earthenware), Victoria square
Davenport, Banks, & Co. (porous and fancy earthenware), Etruria (see Advt.)
Dimmock John (earthenware), Stafford st.
Dudson Jas. (earthenware and parian), Hanover street
Ford Thomas & Charles (china), Cannon street
Harding W. & J. (earthenware), Marsh street
Holloway John (parian), Market street
Livesley, Powell, & Co. (earthenware, china, and parian), Parliament row, and Stafford street
Meakin J. & G. (earthenware), Eagle Pottery, near Bucknall New road
Mills Bros. (parian), George street
Mills John (brown ware), Clough street
Old Hall Earthenware Co. (Limited), Old Hall street
Oldham James (door furniture & stoneware) Renalagh street
PANKHURST JAMES W. & Co., (white granite earthenware), Old Hall street
Ridgway Ed. John (earthenware), High st.
Sale Wm. (parian), Bryan st. (see Advt.)
Smith John (toy), Hope street
Stanway, Horne, & Adams (parian), Eastwood vale
Stubbs Wm. (china, earthenware, and parian), High street & Eastwood vale
Taylor, Bros. (earthenware), Market st.
Taylor William (earthenware), Brook st.
Till Emma (parian figure), Salem street, Etruria
Twyford Christopher (sanitary ware), New street
TWYFORD THOMAS (earthenware and sanitary ware), Bath street (see Advt.)
Unwin, Holmes, & Worthington (earthenware), High street (see Advt.)
Venables Henry (terra cotta and parian), Mill street
Wardle James (parian and majolica), William street (see Advt.)
Warrington William (parian), Brewery st.

Wedgwood Josiah and Sons (china and earthenware), Etruria
Wilkinson & Sons (china and parian), Broad street
Worthington and Green (figures), Brook street (see Advt.)
Worthington & Harrop (parian), Tinkersclough (see Advt).
Worthington & Son (earthenware and majolica), Clarence street (see Advt.)

Longton – Potters (pages 152-153)
Adams John (china), Victoria works, High street
Adams & Cooper (china), High st.
Adams & Scrivener (china), Sutherland rd.
ALLERTON CHARLES & SON (china, earthenware, and gold and silver lustre), Park works, High street (see Advt.)
Aynsley John (china), Sutherland road
Baddeley William (rustic and terra cotta), Drury court
Baddeley Elizabeth (rustic & terra cotta), Commerce street
Barlow Thomas (china), Market street
Barlow T.W. (earthenware), Commerce st.
Beardmore Thomas (earthenware), Coronation works, Heathcote road
Beech James & Son (china), High street
Bentley Thomas & Co. (china), Church st
Betteney Thomas (china), Crown works, Stafford street
Birks Thomas (china, earthenware, gold & silver lustre), High st.
Bold Henry (rustic and terra cotta), Chancery lane
Brammall & Repton (china), Heathcote rd.
Brewer and Co. (rustic and lustre wares), Stafford street
Bridgwood Sampson & Son (china, & earthenware), Anchor works
Broadhurst James (earthenware), Crown Pottery, Stafford street
Brough Brothers (earthenware), Gold street, (see Advt.)
Bullock Charles (china), Brittania works, High street
Burton, Wood & Co, (china), Mount pleasant
Cartledge John & Co. (china), Market st.
Cartwright & Edwards (earthen.), Russell st
CHATFIELD HENRY (china), King street (see Advt.)
Cheetham J.R. & F. (earthenware and lustre), Chancery lane
Cooper & Dixon (earthenware), Viaduct works
Copestake Bros. (china), Anchor road
Copestake, Shufflebottom, & Allen (china), High street
Edwards James & Son (china), Market st.
Elkin Samuel (earthenware), Stafford st.
FINNEY & CO. (china), Victoria works, Stafford street
Hammersley & Freeman (china), Sutherland road
Hampson Bros. (earthenware), Green Dock works, New street
Hand & Copestake (china), St. Martin's lane (see Advt.)
HOBSON THOMAS, & CO. (earthenware), Church street
Hodson Richard (china), Chancery lane
Holdcroft Joseph (silver lustre), St. Martin's lane (see Advt.)
HOLLAND & GREEN (earthenware), Stafford street (see Advt.)
HOPWOOD W. (executors of the late) (china), Church street
Hudden J.T. (earthenware), Stafford st.
Hulme John (rustic and terra cotta), New street (see Advt.)
HULSE, NIXON, & ADDERLEY (china), earthenware, &c) Daisy bank (see Advt.)
Jones Fred. (earthenware), Stafford street
Keeling, Walker, & Co. (gold and silver lustre, and figure manftrs.), High street
Lancaster James (parian), Stafford street, and Daisy bank
Lockett John, (china, earthenware, and lustre), King street, and Market street
LOWE & ABBERLEY, (earthenware, and lustre), Waterloo works, Stafford street (see Advt.)
Mason, Holt, & Co. (china), Normacott rd
Mellor Reuben (parian), Sutherland road
Minshall & Tennant (china), Brittania works, Bagnall street (see Advt.)
Moore & Son (china), St. Mary's works, High street
NEWBON & DAWSON (earthenware), Commerce street (see Advt.)
POOLE, SUTHERLAND, & HALLAM, (gold and silver lustre, parian, &c.), Cornhill passage
Robinson & Son (china), Wellington works, Stafford street (see Advt.)
Rowley, Moston, & Co. (china), Clayton st
Salt John and Co., Étruscan works, Marsh street (see Advt.)
Smith Sampson (china, gold and silver lustre), Sutherland works, Barker street
Stubbs & Plant (china), Chancery lane
Stubbs, Tomkinson, & Millington, (china and parian), High street
Sutherland & Sons, (parian and terra cotta), Park Hall street
Tams & Lowe (earthenware), High street see Advt.
Taylor William, and Co. (stilt and spur), Church street
WALKER, BATEMAN, AND CO., (earthenware), British Anchor Pottery, Anchor road
Webb and Walters, (china), gold and silver lustre) Stafford street
WEBBERLEY WILLIAM (china), St. James's works, High street (see Advt.)
WEDGWOOD AND CO. (china), Commerce street
Yearsley George (parian), Market lane

Stoke – Potters (page 206)
Close J.P., (earthenware and lustre), Church street
Copeland Alderman W.T. (china, earthenware, and parian), High street
GOSS WILLIAM HENRY (parian), John street
Hill Leveson, Executors of (parian), Wharf st. (see Advt.)
Jones George (china and earthenware), Church st.
KIRKHAM WILLIAM (earthenware), London road
Meli Giovanni (parian statuary), Glebe street (see Advt.)
Minton, Hollins, and Co. (china, earthenware, and parian), London road
TURNER, HASSALL, AND PEAKE (parian, earthenware and china), Copeland street and Liverpool road

Tunstall – Potters (page 224)
Adams Wm., jun. (earthenware), Newfield
Adams William (earthenware), Greenfield
Beech & Hancock (earthenware), Swan Pottery, High street

Blackhurst & Dunning (earthenware), High street
BOWERS GEORGE FREDERICK (china and earthenware), Brownhills
Challinor Edward (earthenware), High st.
Clarke Edward (earthenware) High street
Cooper & Keeling (earthenware), Well st.
Eardley & Hammersley earthenware), High street
Elsmore & Forster (earthenware), Clayhills, Pottery
Emberton William (earthenware for Ceylon, Bombay, and Calcutta markets), Brownhills
Ford, Challinor, & Co. (earthenware), Sandyford
Hammersley Ralph (tea pot), High street
Hancock Sampson (earthen.), Victoria st.
Holdcroft & Wood (earthen.), George st.
Meir John & Son (earthen.), Greengates
Oulsnam W.E. (earthenware), High st.
Selman J. & W. (toy), Brownhills
Turner & Tomkinson (earthenware), Victoria Works, High street
Wedgwood & Co. (earthenware), Unicorn Pottery, Amicable street
Wood & Co. (earthenware), Pinnox Works, Great Woodland street
Wood Edmund T.W. (earthenware) Woodland Pottery, Woodland street
Wood Thomas (earthenware), Paradise st

1867 Keates

Keates & Ford's Annual Directory of the Potteries and Newcastle, with Almanack, for 1867, Keates & Ford, Printers and Publishers, 38 & 40 Cheapside, Hanley (Shaw & Tipper 1232). Dated January 1867 in the Preface.

As with all the Keates series, this directory is classified within separate sections for each of the six pottery towns and the only relevant categories are potters and various types of tile manufacturers.

Burslem – Potters (pages 64-65)
Alcock Henry and Co. (earthenware), Cobridge Works
Allman, Broughton and Co. (earthenware), Wedgwood place
Beech Jane (toy and fancy), Queen street
Bennett William (earthenware), Albert st.
Bodley E.F. and Co. (earthenware), Scotia works, Wedgwood place
Boote T. and R. (earthen.), Waterloo road
Boughton R.T. and Co. (earthenware), Fountain place
Brough, Joynson, and Co. (earthenware), Bourne's bank
Brownfield Wm. (earthen.), Waterloo road
Burgess and Leigh (earthen.), Market pl.
Cartwright Thomas (earthen.), Sneyd grn.
Cockson, Chetwynd, & Co. (earthenware) (see Advt.)
Collinson Charles and Co. (chemical and sanitary articles), Fountain place
Cork, Edge & Malkin, (earthen. & lustre), Navigation road
Corn W. and E. (earthen.), Navigation rd.
Corns James (creel steps), 5 Amicable buildings
Daniel and Cork (earthen.), Navigation rd.
Davenport Wm. & Co. (china and earthenware), Davenport street
Dean and Stokes (earthenware), Nile street
Edwards and Son (earthen.), Newcastle st.
Elliott and Son (earthenware), Dale Hall Works, Newcastle street
Evans and Booth (earthenware), Hamil road
Forrester John (earthenware), Podmore st.
Furnival and Co. (earthenware), Cobridge
Godwin John (earthenware), Sneyd street
Hallen Harding (creel steps), Wellington st
Hancock, Whittingham, and Co. (earthenware), Swan bank Works, Chapel sq.
Hawthorne John (earthen.), Albert street
Heath and Blackhurst (earthen), Bath st.
Hill Pottery Company, Limited (china, earthenware, majolica, parian), Liverpool road; Alcock George, manager
Hobson Charles (earthen.), Albert street
Holdcroft, Hill, and Mellor (earthenware), Queen street
Hope and Carter (earthen.), Fountain pl.
Hughes Elijah (earthenware), Bleak st.
Hughes Thomas (earthen.), Waterloo road
Lawton John W. (creel steps), 137 Waterloo road
Lea, Smith, and Boulton (china and earthenware), Market place and Wood street
Macintyre & Co. (door furniture), Washington Works, Waterloo road
Maddock John and Son (earthenware), Newcastle street
Massey Nehemiah (teapot and figures), Kilncroft
Meakin Brothers (earthenware), Peel street
Meakin and Co. (earthenware), Cobridge
Pearson Edward (earthenware), Sneyd grn.
Pinder, Bourne, and Co. (earthenware), Nile street
Plant & Gardener (earthen.), Bourne's bank
Shaw Anthony (earthen.), Newport lane
Till and Sons (earthen.), Liverpool road
Vernon James (earthen.), Waterloo road
Walley John (teapot and toy), High street
Wigley Wm. Henry (black and lustre), Sylvester square
Wigley George (creel steps), Sylvester sq.
Wood, Morgan, & Co. (earthenware), Liverpool road

Burslem – Tile (Floor) Makers (page 66)
Boote T. and R., Waterloo road

Fenton – Potters (page 77)
Baker W. and Co. (earthenware), High st
Challinor Edward and Charles, (earthenware), King street
Edwards John (china and earthenware), King street
Gimson, Baker, and Challinor (spur manufacturers), Market street
Green Mary and Co. (china), Minerva works, Park street

Hawley and Co. (earthenware), King street, Foley
Jackson and Gosling (china), King street,
Knight Josh. (earthenware), Old Foley Works, King street
Malkin Ralph (earthenware), Park works, Market street
Pratt F. & R. & Co. (earthenware), Lower Fenton, High street
Pratt John & Co. (earthenware), Park st.
Robinson, Hudson, and Co. (china), King street, Foley
Wathen James B. (earthenware), Victoria works, Market street
Wileman J. and C. (china and earthenware), the Foley Pottery

Hanley – Potters (pages 125-126)
Adams John & Co. (parian and majolica), St. James's street
Allen H.G. (china), Broad street
Ash George (parian and majolica), Broad street (see Advt.)
Ashworth G.L. & Bros. (earthenware), Broad street
Baddeley James H. (rustic ware), Gloucester street (see Advt.)
Baguley George (china), Broad street
Bailey & Bevington (parian), Elm street (see Advt.)
Bamford John (jug and figure), Nelson place
Bentley Noah (parian), 55 Bryan street
Bennett & Rathbone (earthenware), Wharf lane
BEVINGTON JOHN (parian), Great York street (see Advt.)
Bevington J. & T. (china and parian), Marsh street and Burton place
Brown-Westhead & Co. (china, earthenware, parian and majolica), Cauldon place
Buckley James (sanitary ware), Vine st.
Buller W.W. & Co. (spurs and stilts), Eastwood vale
Clementson, Bros. (earthenware), Phoenix works, Broad street, and Bell works, George street
Cooper Thomas, Executors of (china and earthenware), Victoria square
Davenport, Banks, & Co. (porous and fancy earthenware), Castlefield pottery, Etruria
Dimmock John & Co. (earthenware), Stafford street
Dudson James (earthenware and parian), Hanover street
Evans & Coyne (china and earthenware), Brunswick street
Ford Charles (spur), Parker st
Ford Thomas and Charles (china), Cannon street
Harding W. and J. (earthenware), Marsh street
Hodgkinson Elijah (stone and parian), Mayer st. works, High street (see Advt.)
Hodgkinson William (parian and earthenware, New street (see Advt.)
Holloway John (parian), 73 Market st.
Howson Geo. (sanitary ware), Paxton st.
LIVESLEY WILLIAM (earthenware, ornamental china figures, parian statuary, &c.), Cannon street
Meakin J. and G. (earthenware), Eagle Pottery, near Bucknall new road
Mills, Bros. (parian), George st. (see Advt.)
Mills John (brown ware), 4 Clough street
Old Hall Pottery Co. Limited (earthenware, parian and china), Old Hall street; Meigh C., manager
Oldham James (earthenware and stoneware), Renalagh street (see Advt.)
Pankhurst Jas. W. and Co. (white granite earthenware), Old Hall street
Pointon William B. (earthenware), Parker street
Powell and Bishop (earthenware), Parliament row and Stafford street
Ridgway Edward J. (earthenware), Vale rd.
Sale John (parian), Bryan street
Smith John (parian), 141 Hope street
Stanway, Horne, and Adams (parian), Eastwood vale
Stubbs William (china, earthenware, lustre and parian), High street and Eastwood vale
Taylor, Bros. (earthenware), Market street
Taylor William (earthenware), Brook st.
Twyford Christopher (sanitary ware), New street
Twyford Thomas (earthenware and sanitary ware), Bath street (see Advt.)
Unwin, Holmes, & Worthington (earthenware), High street
Venables Henry (porous and etruscan), Mill street
Wardle James (parian and majolica), William street (see Advt.)
Warrington William (parian), Brewery st.
Wedgwood Josiah and Sons (china and earthenware), Etruria
Wilkinson & Sons (china and parian), Broad street
Worthington & Son (figures), Brook street (see Advt.)
Worthington & Harrop (parian), Tinker's clough (see Advt.)

Longton – Potters (pages 163-164)
Adams & Cooper (china), High street
Adams, Scrivener & Co., (china), Sutherland road
Allerton Charles & Son (china, earthenware, and gold and silver lustre), Park works, High street
Aynsley John (china), Sutherland road
Baddeley William (rustic and terra cotta), Drury court
Baddeley Elizabeth (rustic and terra cotta), 3 Commerce st.
Barlow Thomas (china), Market street
Barlow, T.W. (earthenware), Commerce st.
Beech James & Son (china), High street
Bentley Thos. & Co. (china), Church street
Bettany Thomas (china), Crown works, Stafford street
Birks Thomas (china, earthenware, gold and silver lustre), High street
Bold Henry (rustic and terra cotta), Daisy bank
Brammall and Repton (china), Heathcote road
Bridgwood Sampson and Son (china and earthenware), Anchor works, Sutherland road
Broadhurst James (earthenware), Crown Pottery, Stafford street
Brough, Brothers, & Co. (earthenware), Gold street (see Advt.)
Cartledge John & Co. (china), Market st.
Cartwright and Edwards (earthenware), Russell street
Cartwright Moses (insulators), Cornhill passage
Cheetham J.R. & F. (earthenware, and lustre), Chancery lane
Cooper and Nixon (earthenware), Viaduct works
Copestake, Brothers (china), Anchor road
Copestake and Allin (china), High street
Dawson James (earthenware), Commerce street (see Advt.)
Edwards James & Son (china), Market st.
Edwards Geo. & Co. (china), Cyple's lane
Elkin Samuel (earthenware), Stafford st.

FERNEYHOUGH JOHN & Co. (china), Dresden works, Stafford street
Finney & Co. (china), Victoria works, Stafford street
Gibson and Hallam (china), St. Martin's lane
Grove R.H. (rustic, lustre, china, and earthenware), Palissy works, Chancery lane (see Advt.)
Hackney & Co. (parian), Daisy bank (see Advt.)
Hammersley & Freeman (china), Sutherland road
Hampson, Brothers (earthenware), Green Dock works, New street
Hodson Richard (china), Chancery lane
Holdcroft Joseph (silver lustre), St. Martin's lane
Holland & Green (earthenware), Stafford street (see Advt.)
Hopwood W. (executors of the late), (china), Church street
Hudden J.T. (earthenware) Stafford st.
HULSE, NIXON, AND ADDERLEY (china, earthenware, &c.), Daisy bank (see Advt.)
Jones Fred. (earthenware), Stafford street
Jones H. & Co. (earthen.), Chadwick street
JONES, SHEPHERD, & CO. (earthenware), Portland works, Church street. Manufacturers of all kinds of earthenware (see Advt.)
Keeling, Walker, & Co. (gold and silver lustre, and figure manufacturers), 29 and 31 High street
Lockett John (china, earthenware, and lustre), King street and High street
LOWE & ABBERLEY (earthenware and lustre), Waterloo works, Stafford street (see Advt.)
Mason, Holt, & Co. (china), Normacott road
Moore and Son (china), St. Mary's works, High street
POOLE, SUTHERLAND, & HALLAM (gold and silver lustre, parian, &c.), Cornhill passage
PROCTOR J. & H. & Co. (earthenware), New Town works, High street
Robinson and Son (china), Wellington works, Stafford street
SHEPHERD & Co. (china and earthenware), Eagle Works, Stafford street. Decorated china and earthenware manufacturers
Smith Sampson (china and gold and silver lustre), Sutherland works, Barker street
Stubbs, Tomlinson, and Billington (china and parian), High street
Sutherland & Sons (parian & terra cotta), Parkhall street
Tams & Lowe (earthenware), High street (see Advt.)
Taylor William & Co. (stilt and spur), Church street
Townsend George (china & earthenware), Stafford street
WALKER, CARTER, & Co. (earthenware), British Anchor pottery, Anchor road
Webb and Walters (china, gold, and silver lustre), Stafford street
WEBBERLEY WILLIAM (china, St. James' works, High street
Williams & Co. (china), Clayton street
WOOD & Co. (china), Mount pleasant
Yearsley George (parian), Market lane

Stoke – Potters (page 220)
Close J.T. (earthenware and lustre), Church street
Copeland Alderman W.T. (china, earthenware, and parian), High street
Goss William Henry (parian and terra cotta), John street
Grose & Co. (earthenware), Church st.
Hill Leveson, Executors of (parian), Wharf street (see Advt.)
Jones George (earthenware), Trent Pottery, Church st.; show rooms, Glebe st.
Kirkham Wm. (earthenware), London rd.
Minton & Co. (china, earthenware, and parian), London road
Robinson & Leadbeater (parian statuary), Glebe street (see Advt.)
Turner, Hassall, & Peake (parian, earthenware, and china), Copeland street and Liverpool road

Stoke – Tile (Floor) Makers (page 221)
Minton, Hollins, & Co., Church street

Tunstall – Potters (page 242)
Adams Wm., jun. (earthenware), Newfield
Adams William & Thomas (earthenware), Green field
Beech & Hancock (earthenware), Swan Pottery, High street
Blackhurst & Dunning (earthenware), High street
Blackhurst & Co. (earthenware), Sandyford Pottery
Challinor Edward (earthenware), High st.
Clarke Edward (earthenware), High street High street Works
Elsmore & Foster (earthenware), Clayhills Pottery
Emberton Wm. (earthenware), Brownhills
Ford, Challinor, & Co. (earthenware), Sandyford
Hammersley Ralph (black earthenware),
Hancock Sampson (earthen.), Victoria st.
Holdcroft & Wood (earthen.), George st.
Keeling Anthony (earthenware) Well st.
Meir Henry & Son (earthen.), Greengates
Oulsnam W.E. (earthenware), High street
Turner & Tomkinson (earthenware), Victoria Works, High street
Wedgwood & Co. (earthenware), Unicorn Pottery, Amicable street; and Pinnox Works, Great Woodland street
Wood Edmund T.W. (earthenware), Woodland Pottery, Woodland street

1868 Kelly

The Post Office Directory of Birmingham, Staffordshire, Warwickshire, and Worcestershire (also *The Post Office Directory of Staffordshire*), Printed and Published by Kelly & Co., 12 Carey Street, Lincoln's Inn, London WC (Shaw & Tipper 6, Shaw & Tipper 1222). Dated MDCCCLXVIII on the title page and August 1868 in the Preface. It is noted as the Sixth Edition in the Preface.

As with all the Kelly's series, this directory contains alphabetical lists for the various towns and villages and also classified lists for each county. Only the classified lists are included here. The range of categories is extensive and there are twenty-eight relevant to this work.

Artists' Palette Manufacturers – China (page 808)
Taylor, Tunnicliff & Co. Havelock works, Broad street, Hanley

Beer Machine Handle Makers – China (page 812)
Grove R.H. Palissy works, Longton, Stoke-upon-Trent; & at 71 Hatton garden, London e.c
Tams & Lowe, High street, Longton, Stoke-upon-Trent
Taylor, Tunnicliff & Co. Havelock works, Broad street, Hanley

China Manufacturers (pages 848-849)
Adams & Cooper, High street, Longton, Stoke-upon-Trent
Adams, Scrivener & Co. Sutherland road, Longton, Stoke-upon-Trent
Adams J. (exors. of), Park place & Victoria works, Longton, Stoke-upon-Trent
Allerton C. & Sons, High street, Longton, Stoke-upon-Trent
Ashworth G.L. & Brothers, Broad street, Hanley
Aynsley J. Sutherland road, Longton, Stoke-upon-Trent
Barker & Hill, Stafford street & King street, Longton, Stoke-upon-Trent
Barlow T. Cyples' Old pottery, Market street, Longton, Stoke-upon-Trent
Beech James & Sons, Albert & Sutherland works, Longton, Stoke-upon-Trent
Bentley T. & Co. Church street, Longton, Stoke-upon-Trent
Betteney T. Stafford street, Longton, Stoke-upon-Trent
Bevington J. & T. Burton place, Hanley
Birks T. High street, Longton, Stoke-upon-Trent
Brammall & Repton, Heathcote street, Longton, Stoke-upon-Trent
Brown-Westhead (T.C.), Moore & Co. Cauldon place, Hanley; & 107 Hatton garden, London e.c
Cartlidge J. Market street, Longton, Stoke-upon-Trent
Copeland William Taylor & Sons, High street, Stoke-upon-Trent; & at 160 New Bond street, London w
Copestake & Allin, Alma works, Longton, Stoke-upon-Trent
Copestake Brothers, Anchor works, Longton, Stoke-upon-Trent
Dale, Page & Co. Church street, Longton, Stoke-upon-Trent
Davenport William & Co. Longport, Burslem; warehouses, 82 Fleet street, London e.c. & 30 Canning place, Liverpool
Edwards G. & Co. King street, Longton, Stoke-upon-Trent
Ferneyhough J. & Co. Dresden works, Stafford street, Longton, Stoke-upon-Trent
Finney J. Victoria works, Longton, Stoke-upon-Trent
Ford T. & C. Cannon street, Hanley
Gibson & Hallam, St. Martin's lane, Longton, Stoke-upon-Trent
Green M. & Co. Park street, Fenton, Stoke-upon-Trent
Grove R.H. Palissy works, Longton, Stoke-upon-Trent; & at 71 Hatton garden, London e.c
Hammersley, Freeman & Co. Sutherland road, Longton, Stoke-upon-Trent
Heather Frederick & Co. Kensington works, Broad street, Hanley
Hobson & Moston, Clayton street, Longton, Stoke-upon-Trent
Hodson R. Chancery lane, Longton, Stoke-upon-Trent
Hulse, Nixon & Adderley, Daisy Bank works, Longton, Stoke-upon-Trent
Jackson & Gosling, King street, Fenton, Stoke-upon-Trent
Kent J. & Son, Market street, Longton, Stoke-upon-Trent
Lockett John, King street & Market street, Longton, Stoke-upon-Trent
Macintyre James & Co. Washington works, Waterloo road, Burslem
Mason, Holt & Co. Normacott road, Longton, Stoke-upon-Trent
Minton & Co. Eldon place, Stoke-upon-Trent
Moore & Son, High street, Longton, Stoke-upon-Trent
Old Hall Earthenware Co. Limited, Hill street, Hanley
Robinson & Hudson, Foley, Fenton, Stoke-upon-Trent
Robinson & Son, Stafford street, Longton, Stoke-upon-Trent
Shepherd A. & Co. Eagle works, Stafford street, Longton, Stoke-upon-Trent
Skelson & Plant, Chancery lane, Longton, Stoke-upon-Trent
Smith S. Barker street, Longton, Stoke-upon-Trent
Taylor, Tunnicliff & Co. Havelock works, Broad street, Hanley
Tompkinson & Billington, 51 High street, Longton, Stoke-upon-Trent
Turner, Hassell & Peake, Copeland street, & Liverpool road, Stoke-upon-Trent
Walters & Hulse, Commerce street, Longton, Stoke-upon-Trent
Webb S. & Co. Stafford street, Longton, Stoke-upon-Trent
Webberley W. St. James's place, Longton, Stoke-upon-Trent
Wood J. & Co. Mount Pleasant, Longton, Stoke-upon-Trent

China Figure Manufacturers (page 849)
Beech Mrs. J. Queen street, Burslem
Macintyre J. & Co. Washington works, Waterloo road, Burslem
Massey G. 120 Hope street, Hanley

China Ornament Manufacturers (page 849)
Beech James & Sons, Albert & Sutherland works, Longton, Stoke-upon-Trent
Macintyre J. & Co. Washington works, Waterloo road, Burslem

China Porcelain Manufacturers (page 849)
Beech James & Sons, Albert & Sutherland works, Longton, Stoke-upon-Trent
Brown-Westhead (T.C.), Moore & Co. Cauldon place, Hanley; & 107 Hatton garden, London e.c

China & Porcelain Door Furniture Manufacturers (page 849)
Grove R.H. Palissy works, Longton, Stoke-upon-Trent; & at 71 Hatton garden, London e.c
Macintyre James & Co. Washington works, Waterloo road, Burslem
Taylor, Tunnicliff & Co. Havelock works, Broad street, Hanley

Cock Spur Manufacturer (page 854)
Ford C. Parker street, Hanley

Creel Step Manufacturer (page 857)
Hallen Harding, Wellington st. Burslem

Druggists' Sundries Manufacturer (page 861)
Kirkham William, London road, Stoke-upon-Trent; office, 13 Lime street, London e.c

Earthenware Manufacturers (page 862)
Adams J. & Co. Broad street, Hanley
Adams William & Thomas, Tunstall, Stoke-upon-Trent
Adams William, jun. Newfield, Tunstall, Stoke-upon-Trent
Alcock & Diggory, Central pottery, Burslem
Alcock H. & Co. Cobridge, Burslem
Baker W. & Co. Fenton, Stoke-upon-Trnt
Bamford J. Nelson place, Hanley
Barlow T.W. Commerce street, Longton, Stoke-upon-Trent
Bates & Bennett, Cobridge, Burslem
Beech & Hancock, Swan bank, Tunstall, Stoke-upon-Trent
Blackhurst R. High street, Tunstall, Stoke-upon-Trent
Bodley E.F. & Co. Scotia works, Burslem
Bowers F.T. Brownhills, Burslem
Bridgwood S. & Son, East vale, Longton, Stoke-upon-Trent
Broadhurst James, Crown pottery, Stafford street, Longton, Stoke-upon-Trent
Brough Brothers, Gold Street works, Longton, Stoke-upon-Trent
Brown-Westhead (T.C.), Moore & Co. Cauldon place, Hanley; & 107 Hatton garden, London e.c
Brownfield W. Cobridge, Burslem
Burgess, Leigh & Co. Hill pottery, Burslm
Burgess H. Kiln Croft works, Burslem
Cartwright & Edwards, Russell street, Longton, Stoke-upon-Trent
Challinor E. & C. High street, Fenton, Stoke-upon-Trent
Challinor E. High Street pottery, Tunstall, Stoke-upon-Trent
Clarke E. High street, Tunstall, Stoke-upon-Trent
Clementson Brothers, Broad st. Hanley
Close & Co. Church street, Stoke-upon-Trent
Cockson, Chetwynd & Co. Cobridge, Burslem
Collinson C. & Co. Newcastle st. Burslem
Cooper, Nixon & Co. Caroline street, Longton, Stoke-upon-Trent
Copeland William Taylor & Sons, High street, Stoke-upon-Trent; & at 160 New Bond street, London w.
Cork, Edge & Malkin, Newport, Burslem
Corn W. & E. Navigation Road Pottery, Burslem
Daniel J. New Wharf pottery, Burslem
Davenport, Banks & Co. Castle Field pottery, Hanley
Davenport William & Co. Longport, Burslem; warehouses, 82 Fleet street, London e.c.; & 30 Canning place, Liverpool
Dawson J. Commerce street, Longton, Stoke-upon-Trent
Dean & Stokes, Sylvester pottery, Burslm
Dimmock J. & Co. Stafford st. Hanley
Dudson James, Hope street, Hanley
Edwards J. & Son, Dale Hall pottery, Burslem
Elkin S. Stafford street, Longton, Stoke-upon-Trent
Elliot Liddle, & Son, Dale hall, Burslem
Elmore & Forster, Clay Hills pottery, Tunstall, Stoke-upon-Trent
Emberton W. Brownhills, Burslem
Emberton W. Highgate pottery, Tunstall, Stoke-upon-Trent
Evans & Booth, Knowles works, Burslem
Ford, Challinor & Co. Sandyford pottery, Tunstall, Stoke-upon-Trent
Forrester J. Podmore street, Burslem
Furnival J. & Co. Cobridge, Burslem
Gelson Brothers, High street, Hanley
Grose & Co. Church st. Stoke-upon-Trent
Grove R.H. Palissy works, Longton, Stoke-upon-Trent; & at 71 Hatton garden, London e.c
Hammersley R. Church Bank pottery, Tunstall, Stoke-upon-Trent
Hampson Brothers, Green Dock works, Longton, Stoke-upon-Trent
Hancock, Whittingham & Co. Queen square, Burslem
Harding W. & J. New Hall pottery, Hanley
Hawley J. & Co. Foley, Fenton, Stoke-upon-Trent
Hawthorn J. & Sons, Albert Street works, Burslem
Heath & Blackhurst, Hadderidge pottery, Burslem
Hobson C. Albert street, Burslem
Holdcroft, Hill & Mellor, Queen street, Burslem
Holdcroft & Wood, George street, Tunstall, Stoke-upon-Trent
Holland & Green, Stafford street, Longton, Stoke-upon-Trent
Hope & Carter, Fountain place, Burslem
Hudden J.T. Stafford street, Longton, Stoke-upon-Trent
Hughes T. Waterloo road, Burslem
Hulse, Nixon & Adderley, Daisy Bank works, Longton, Stoke-upon-Trent
Jones F. & Co. Chadwick street & Stafford street, Longton, Stoke-upon-Trent
Jones G. London road & Glebe street, Stoke-upon-Trent
Jones J.E. Church street, Longton, Stoke-upon-Trent
Keeling & Walker, 31 High street, Longton, Stoke-upon-Trent
Kirkham William, London road, Stoke-upon-Trent; & offices, 13 Lime street, London e.c
Knapper & Blackhurst, Sandyford, Tunstall, Stoke-upon-Trent
Knight J. Foley, Fenton, Stoke-upon-Trent
Lea, Smith & Boulton, Crown & Churchyard manufactories, Burslem
Leader M. Newcastle street, Burslem

Livesley & Davis, Trent pottery, Hanley
Livesley W. & Son, Cannon st. Hanley
Lockett John, King street & Market street, Longton, Stoke-upon-Trent
Lowe & Abberley, Waterloo works, Stafford street, Longton, Stoke-upon-Trent
Macintyre James & Co. Washington works, Waterloo road, Burslem
Maddock J. & Son, Newcastle st. Burslem
Malkin R. Fenton, Stoke-upon-Trent
Martin E. (sanitary), Marsh st. Hanley
Meakin Brothers & Co. Trent pottery, Burslem
Meakin & Co. Cobridge, Burslem
Meakin J. & G. Eagle pottery, Hanley
Meakin J. & G. 16 Glebe street, Stoke-upon-Trent
Meir John & Son, Greengate pottery, Tunstall, Stoke-upon-Trent
Minton & Co. Eldon pl. Stoke-upon-Trent
Moore Bros. Bleak hill, Cobridge, Burslm
Morgan, Wood & Co. Hill works, Burslem
Old Hall Earthenware Co.Limited, Hill street, Hanley
Oldham J. Ranelagh street, Hanley
Oulsnam W.E. High street, Tunstall, Stoke-upon-Trent
Pankhurst & Co. Old Hall st. Hanley
Pearson E. Sneyd st. Cobridge, Burslem
Pinder, Bourne & Co. Nile Street works, Burslem
Plant & Gardiner, Sneyd green, Burslem
Poole, Sutherland & Hallam, Cornhill passage, Longton, Stoke-upon-Trent
Powell & Bishop, Stafford street & High street, Hanley
Pratt F. & R. & Co. Fenton, Stoke-upon-Trent
Pratt John & Co. Lane Delph, Stoke-upon-Trent; & 19 Crosby Hall chambers, London e.c
Procter J. & H. & Co. High street, Longton, Stoke-upon-Trent
Ridgway E.J. Bedford works, Hanley
Robinson, Kirkham & Co. Wedgwood place, Burslem
Sambrook T.C. & Co. Furlong works, Burslem
Shaw A. Newport works, Burslem
Stubbs & Bridgwood, Heathcote road, Longton, Stoke-upon-Trent
Stubbs W. Eastwood pottery, Hanley
Tams & Lowe, High street, Longton, Stoke-upon-Trent
Taylor Brothers, Market street, Hanley
Taylor W. Brook street, Hanley
Tinsley & Bourne, Bourne's bank, Burslm
Tomkinson & Phillips, Clarence st. Hanly
Turner, Goddard & Co. Royal Albert pottery, Tunstall, Stoke-upon-Trent
Turner, Hassell & Peake, Copeland st. & Liverpool street, Stoke-upon-Trent
Turner & Tomkinson, Victoria works, Tunstall, Stoke-upon-Trent
Unwin & Holmes, Upper Hanley works, Hanley
Vernon J. Waterloo road, Burslem
Walker & Carter, British Anchor pottery, Longton, Stoke-upon-Trent
Wathen J.B. Market street, Fenton, Stoke-upon-Trent
Wedgwood & Co. Pinnox & Unicorn works, Tunstall, Stoke-upon-Trent
Wedgwood J. & Sons, Etruria, Stoke-upon-Trent
Whittingham, Ford & Co. High street, Burslem
Wigley G. Queen street, Burslem
Wileman J. & C. Fenton, Stoke-upon-Trent
Wood, Rathbone & Co. Cobridge, Burslem
Wood E.T.W. Woodland pottery, Tunstall, Stoke-upon-Trent
Worthington & Son, Brook st. Hanley

Encaustic & Geometric Tile Pavement Manufacturers – Patent (page 863)
Boote Thomas & Richard, Waterloo pottery, Burslem
Malkin & Co. Patent encaustic tile works, Burslem. See advertisement
Minton, Hollins & Co. Church street, Stoke-upon-Trent, & 50 Conduit street, London w

Jug Manufacturers (page 908)
Beech James & Sons, Albert & Sutherland works, Langton, Stoke-upon-Trent

Lustre Manufacturers (page 913)
Chetham J.R. & F. Commerce street, Longton, Stoke-upon-Trent
Holdcroft J. (silver), St. Martin's lane, Longton, Stoke-upon-Trent
Lowe & Abberley, Waterloo works, Stafford street, Longton, Stoke-upon-Trent
Smith S. Barker street, Longton, Stoke-upon-Trent

Majolica Manufacturers (page 913)
Ash G. Broad street, Hanley
Bebbington J. New street, Hanley
Minton & Co. Eldon place, Stoke-upon-Trent
Wardle J. William street, Hanley

Parian Manufacturers (page 921)
Ash G. Broad street, Hanley
Bailey J. & Co. Brewery street, Hanley
Bevington & Bradley, Elm street & Clarence street, Hanley
Bevington J. & T. Burton place, Hanley
Goss & Peake, John street, Stoke-upon-Trent
Hackney J. 18 High street, Longton, Stoke-upon-Trent
Hill L. (executors of), 49 Wharf street, Stoke-upon-Trent
Hodgkinson E. Mayer street, Hanley
Mills Brothers, George street, Hanley
Minton Herbert & Co. Eldon place, Stoke-upon-Trent
Robinson & Leadbeater, near Town hall, Stoke-upon-Trent
Stanway, Horne & Adams, Lower Lichfield street, Hanley
Turner, Hassell & Peake, Copeland street & Liverpool street, Stoke-upon-Trent
Wardle J. William street, Hanley

Parian Figure Makers (page 921)
Brown-Westhead (T.C.), Moore & Co. Cauldon place, Hanley; & 107 Hatton garden, London e.c

Sutherland & Sons, Park Hall street, Longton, Stoke-upon-Trent
Worthington & Harrop, Tinkersclough, Hanley
Yearsley G. Market lane, Longton, Stoke-upon-Trent

Porcelain Statuary Manufacturers (page 924)
Copeland William Taylor & Sons, High street, Stoke-upon-Trent; & at 160 New Bond street, London w

Potters (page 925)
Cope J. & Son, Port vale, Wolstanton, Stoke-upon-Trent, & at Smallthorne. See advertisement

Rockingham Ware Manufacturers (page 943)
Massey T. Chapel lane, Burslem
Wade J. & Co. High street, Burslem
Walley W. Nile street, Burslem
Wigley W.H. Sylvester square, Burslem

Rustic Manufacturer (page 943)
Bold H. 18 High street, Longton, Stoke-upon-Trent

Sanitary Ware Manufacturers (page 945)
Buckley J. Vine street, Hanley
Howson W. Eastwood vale, Hanley
Twyford C. New street, Hanley
Twyford T. Bath street, Hanley

Shuttle Eye Manufacturers (page 959)
Wade & Myatt, Hall street, Burslem

Spur Makers (pages 964-965)
Gimson J. Fenton, Stoke-upon-Trent

Taylor W. & Co. (stilton), Church street, Longton, Stoke-upon-Trent

Stone Mortar & Pestle Manufacturers (page 967)
Chetham J.R. & F. Commerce street, Longton, Stoke-upon-Trent
Kirkham William, London road, Stoke-upon-Trent; office, 13 Lime street, London e.c
Lockett John, King street & Market street, Longton, Stoke-upon-Trent
Tams & Lowe, High street, Longton, Stoke-upon-Trent

Stoneware Manufacturers (page 967)
Bebbington J. New street, Hanley
Brown-Westhead (T.C.), Moore & Co. Cauldon place, Hanley; & 107 Hatton garden, London e.c
Chetham J.R. & F. Commerce street, Longton, Stoke-upon-Trent
Dudson James, Hope street, Hanley
Hodgkinson E. Mayer street, Hanley
Lockett John, King street & Market street, Longton, Stoke-upon-Trent

Terra Cotta Manufacturers (page 972)
Baddeley Mrs. E. 3 Commerce street, Longton, Stoke-upon-Trent
Baker J. Shelton road, Stoke-upon-Trent
Cope J. & Son, Port vale, Wolstanton, Stoke-upon-Trent, & Smallthorne. See advertisement
Kirkham William, London road, Stoke-upon-Trent; & office, 13 Lime street, London e.c

White Granite Manufacturer (page 978)
Edwards J. King street, Fenton, Stoke-upon-Trent

1869 Keates

Keates's Directory of the Staffordshire Potteries and Newcastle. 1869-70, J. Keates, Printer and Publisher, 38 & 40 Cheapside, Hanley (Shaw & Tipper 1233).

As with all the Keates series, this directory is classified within separate sections for each of the six pottery towns and the only relevant categories are potters and various types of tile manufacturers.

Burslem – Potters (pages 61-62)
Adams John (earthenware) Dale hall
Alcock Henry and Co. (earthenware), Cobridge Works
Alcock & Diggory (earthen.), Central pottery
Bates and Bennett, Sneyd street
Beech Mrs. Jane (earthen.), Bell works Queen street
Beech Wm., (earthenware), Albert st.
Bodley E.F. & Co. (earthenware), Scotia works, Scotia road
Boote T. & R. (earthen.), Waterloo road
Bourne Ezra (earthen.), Newport lane
Brownfield Wm. (earthen.), Cobridge
Burgess, Leigh, and Co. (earthen.), Hill pottery, Market place
Burgess Hy., (earthen.), Kilncroft works
Cockson, Chetwynd, & Co. (earthenware), Cobridge
Collinson C. and Co. (earthenware), Newcastle street pottery
Cork, Edge & Malkin (earthen. & lustre), Newport
Corn W. and E. (earthen), Navigation rd.
Daniel & Cork (earthen.), Freehold villa
Davenport Wm. & Co. (china & earthenware), Davenport street, Longport
Dean Robt. (earthen.), Waterloo road
Dean and Stokes (earthenware), Nile st.
Edwards J. and Son (earthenware), Dale hall pottery
Elliot Liddle & Son (earthenware), Dale hall works, Newcastle street
Emberton Wm. (earthen.), Brownhills
Evans and Booth (earthen.), Knowles works, Hamill road
Furnival & Co. (earthenware), Cobridge
Ford, Whittingham, and Co. (earthenware), High street
Furlong Works Co. (earthenware), Newcastle street
Hallen Harding (creel steps), 29, Wellington street
Hallen Wm. Henry, (creel steps), 29, Wellington street
Hancock, Whittingham, and Co. earthenware), Swan bank works

Hawthorne John and Son (china, door, and bell furniture), Albert street
Heath & Blackhurst (earthen.), Furlong lane
Hobson Charles (earthen.), Albert street
Holdcroft Wm. (earthen.), 132, Liverpool road
Holdcroft, Hill and Mellor (earthenware), Queen street
Hope and Carter (earthen.), Fountain pl.
Hughes Thomas (earthen.), Waterloo rd.
Leader Matthew, Portland works, Newcastle street
Lea and Smith (china and earthenware), Crown and Church yard pottery
Macintyre & Co. (door furniture), Washington works, Waterloo road
Maddock John and Son (earthenware), Newcastle street
Massey J.S. (earthen.), 5, Princes street, Chapel lane
Meakin Brothers (earthen.), Trent pottery, Peel street
Meaken & Co. (earthen.), Elder road, Cobridge
Moore Bros., Bleak hill pottery
Morgan, Wood, and Co. (earthen.), Hill top works
Payne Bros. (rockingham), Podmore st.
Pearson Edward (earthen.), Sneyd green
Pinder, Bourne, and Co. (earthenware), Nile street works
Robinson, Kirkham, and Co. (earthen.), Wedgwood place
Shaw Anthony (earthen.), Newport lane
Till and Sons (earthen.), Liverpool road
Tinsley and Bourne (earthen.), Bourne's bank
Turner W. & Co. (rockingham & earthen.) Sneyd pottery, Albert street
Vernon James (earthen.), Waterloo road
Wade and Myatt (shuttle eye), Hall street
Walley Wm. (rockingham), Nile street
Wade & Co. (teapot and toy), High street
Wigley Wm. Henry (black and lustre), Sylvester square
Wigley George (creel steps), Sylvester sq.
Wood, Son, and Co. (earthen.), Villa Pottery, Cobridge

Burslem – Tile (Floor) Makers (page 63)
Basford and Brothers, Dalehall
Boote T. and R., Waterloo road
Malkin J. & Co., Newport lane (see Advt.)

Fenton – Potters (page 90)
Baker and Co. (earthenware), High st.
Challinor Edward and Charles (earthenware), Fenton pottery
Edwards John (china and earthenware), King street
Gimson, Baker, and Challinor (spur manufacturers, High street
Green Mary and Co. (china), Minerva works, Park street
Hawley and Co. (earthenware), King street, Foley
Jackson and Gosling (china), Grosvenor works, King street
Malkin Ralph (earthenware), Park works, Market street
Pratt F. and R. and Co. (earthenware and terra cotta), Lower Fenton, High st.
Pratt John and Co. (earthenware), Lane Delph pottery
Robinson and Hudson (china), King street, Foley
TAYLOR R. MINTON & CO. (tile), High street
Wathens James B. (earthenware), Victoria works, Market street
Wileman Chas. John (china), Foley
Wileman Jas. Francis (earthen.), Foley
Williamson, Turner, and Co., Old Foley pottery

Fenton – Tile (Ornamental) Manufacturers (page 90)
TAYLOR R. MINTON & CO., High st.

Hanley – Floor Tile Manufacturer (page 139)
Ridgway William Henry, Canal side, (see Advt.)

Hanley – Potters (pages 147-148)
Adams John & Co. (parian and majolica), Broad street and St. James's street
Ash George (parian and majolica), Broad street (see Advt.)
Ashworth G.L. and Bros. (earthenware), Broad street
Bailey and Bevington (parian), Elm street (see Advt.)
Bailey John (executors of) parian manufacturers, Brewery street (see Advt.)
Bamford John (jug & figure), Nelson pl.
Barker Chas. (parian), Lower Lichfield st.
Bennett and Rathbone (earthenware), Wharf lane
Bevington Ambrose (china), Birch street
Bevington John and Co. (parian), Elm st.
Bevington John (parian), Great York st. (see Advt.)
Bevington J. and T. (china and parian), Burton place, New street
Booth Henry, (earthen.) Nelson place
Brown-Westhead, Moore, and Co. (china, earthenware, parian and majolica), Cauldon place
Buckley James (sanitary ware), Vine st.
Buller W.W. and Co. (spurs and stilts), Spur street, Joiner's square
Clementson Bros. (earthenware), Phoenix works, Broad street, and Bell works, George street
Davenport, Banks, and Co. (porous and fancy earthenware), Castlefield pottery, Bedford street (see Advt.)
Dimmock John and Co. (earthenware), Stafford street
Dudson James (earthenware and parian), Hanover street (see Advt.)
Espley George (spur), Chell street
Evans William L. (china and earthenware), Brunswick street
Ford Charles (spur), Parker street
Ford Thomas and Charles (china), Cannon street
Gelson Bros. (earthenware), High street
Harding W. and J. (earthen.), New hall pottery, Marsh street
Hodgkinson Elijah (earthenware and parian), Albion place; works, High st. (see Advt.)
Howson Geo) (sanitary ware), Paxton st.
Jeffery Charles (spur) 60, Lower Lichfield street
Livesley & Davis, (earthen.) Trent Pottery
Livesley William, china, figure, & earthenware manufacturer, Cannon street
Massey George, 120, Hope street
Meakin J. and W. (earthenware), Eagle Pottery, near Bucknall new road
Mills Edward, (parian), George street
Mills John, (brown ware), 4 Clough st.
Old Hall Pottery Co. Limited (earthenware, parian and

china), Hill street; Meigh C., manager
Renalagh Works, (earthenware & stone ware), Renalagh street (see Advt)
Pankhurst Jas. W. and Co., (white granite earthenware), Old Hall street
Pointon Wm. B. (earthenware), Parker st.
Powell and Bishop (earthenware), High street, Parliament row & Stafford street
Ridgway Edward J., (earthenware), Vale road, Bedford place
Smith John (parian), 141, Hope street
Stanway, Horne, and Adams (parian) Eastwood vale
Stubbs William (china, earthenware, lustre & parian), High st. and Eastwood vale
Taylor Bros. (earthenware), Market st.
Taylor, Tunnicliffe, and Co. (door furniture), Broad street
Taylor William (earthenware) Brook st.
Tomkinson T. and Co. (ironstone and earthenware) Clarence street
Twyford Christopher (sanitary ware) New street
Twyford Thomas (earthenware and sanitary ware) Bath street
Unwin & Holmes (earthenware) High st.
Wardle James (parian and majolica), William street (see Advt.)
Wedgwood Josiah and Sons (china and earthenware), Etruria
Worthington, Ridgway, & Harrop, (china) Mt. pleasant, Tinkersclough (see Advt.)
Worthington and Sons (earthenware,) Brook st., (see Advt.)
Worthington & Harrop (parian), Tinkersclough

Longton – Potters (page 229-230)
Adams and Cooper (china), High street
Adams, Scrivener & Co. (china & earthen.), Sutherland road (see Advt.)
Allerton Charles & Sons (china, earthenware, and gold and silver lustre), Park works, High street (see Advt.)
Austin and Co. (parian), Canova works, Stafford street (see Advt.)
Aynsley John (china), Sutherland road
Baddeley Elizabeth (rustic & terra cotta), 3, Commerce street
Baddeley J.H. (rustic and terra cotta), 34, Barker street
Baddeley Wm. (rustic and terra cotta), Drury works, Normacott road
Barker and Hill (china), King street
Barlow Thomas (china), Market street
Barlow T.W. (earthen), Commerce st.
Bates Fredk. (flower pots, &c.), Weston coyney
Beech James & Son (china), High street and Sutherland road
Bentley Thos. & Co. (china), Church st. (see Advt.)
Betteney Thomas (china), Crown works, Stafford street
Birks Thomas (china, earthenware, gold, and silver lustre), High street
Bold Henry (porcelain and terra cotta), 18, High street
Brammall and Repton (china), Heathcote works, Heathcote road
Bridgwood Davis (earthenware), Heathcote road
Bridgwood Sampson and Son (china and earthenware), Anchor pottery, Sutherland road
Broadhurst James (earthenware), Crown pottery, Stafford street
Brough Brothers, and Co. (earthenware), Gold street (see Advt.)
Cartledge John (china), Market street
Cartwright and Edwards (earthenware), Borough pottery, Trentham road
Chetham J.R. and F. (earthenware), Commerce street (see Advt.)
Cooper and Nixon (earthenware), Viaduct works, Caroline street
Copestake, Brothers (china), Anchor road
Copestake and Allin (china), High street
Dale, Page & Co. (late Hopwood), (china), Church street (see Advt.)
Dawson James (earthenware), Commerce street (see Advt.)
Edwards Geo. and Co. (china), Sheridan works, King street, (see Advt.)
Elkin Samuel (earthenware), Stafford st.
Ferneyhough John and Co. (china), Dresden works, Stafford street
Finney Joseph (china), Victoria works, Stafford street
Gibson and Hallam (china), St. Martin's lane
Grove R.H. (rustic, lustre, china, and earthen.), Palissy works, Chancery lane
Hackney Jas. S. (parian), Victoria place, Stafford street
Hammersley, Freeman, and Co. (china), Sutherland road (see Advt.)
Hampson, Brothers (earthenware), Green Dock works, New street
Hodson Richard (china), Chancery lane
Holdcroft Joseph (silver lustre), St. Martin's lane
Holland & Green (earthenware), Stafford street
Hudden J.T. (earthenware), Stafford st.
Hulse & Adderley (china, earthenware, &c.), Daisy bank
Jones Fred. (earthenware), Chadwick st.
Jones J.E., (china, lustre, and earthen.), Portland pottery, Church st., & Stafford street
Keeling and Walker (gold and silver, and earthenware manufacturers), High st.
Lockett John W. (china, earthenware, and lustre), King street and Market street (see Advt.)
Lowe and Abberley (earthenware), Waterloo works, Stafford street (see Advt.)
Mason, Holt & Co. (china), Normacott rd.
Moore S. and Son (china), St. Mary's works, High street
Moston Ed. Jos. (china), Clayton street (see Advt.)
Poole, Sutherland, and Hallam (earthenware, rustic and gold and silver lustre, parian, &c.) Cornhill works, Cornhill passage
Proctor J. and H. and Co. (earthenware), New Town works, High street
Robinson and Son (china), Wellington works, Stafford street
Scarrat Wm. (earthenware), High street
Shaw, Goldstraw, & Swift (fire brick and sanitary tube), Clayton st., Daisy bank
Shepherd & Co. (china and earthenware), Eagle works, Stafford street
Skelson and Plant (china), Chancery lane

Smith Sampson (china and gold and silver lustre and figure), Sutherland works, Barker street
Sutherland & Sons (parian, ivory, rustic, & terra cotta), Parkhall st., Anchor road (see Advt.)
Tams & Lowe (earthenware), High street (see Advt.)
Taylor William & Co. (patent stilt and spur), Church street
Tompkinson, Billington, and Son (china), 51, High street
Walker & Carter, (earthenware), Anchor pottery, Anchor road
Walters & Hulse (china), Commerce st.
Webb and Co. (china), Peel pottery, Stafford street
Webberley William (china), St. James's works, High street (see Advt.)
Williamson, Turner, and Co. (china and earthenware), Foley pottery
Wood and Co. (china), Mount pleasant, Bagnall street, and High street
Yearsley George (parian and patentee of the gold astrakan trimming for decorating parian goods), Market lane

Stoke – Potters (page 328)
Close J.T. (earthenware), Church street; residence, Glebe street
Copeland and Sons (china, earthenware, and parian), High street
Goss William Henry (parian and terra cotta), John street
Grose and Co. (earthenware), Bridge pottery, Church street
Hill Leveson, Executors of (parian), Wharf street
Jones George (earthenware), Trent Pottery, Church street; res., The Villas
Kirkham Wm. (earthenware), London rd., residence, the Villas
Minton and Co. (china, earthenware, and parian), London road
Minton, Hollins & Co. (encaustic tile), Church street
Robinson & Leadbeater (parian statuary), Glebe street
Turner, Hassall, & Peake (parian, earthenware, and china), Copeland street and Liverpool road
Turner and Poole (terra cotta & parian), Liverpool road

Stoke – Tile (Floor) Makers (page 329)
Minton, Hollins, and Co., Church street

Tunstall – Potters (pages 361-362)
Adams Thomas and Co. (earthenware), Greenfields and Newfield
Adams William (earthenware), Newfield pottery
Adams William & Thomas (earthenware), Greenfield pottery
Beech & Hancock (earthenware), Swan pottery, High street; residence, Wolstanton
Blackhurst Richd. (earthenware), High street; res., Wesley place
Bowers Frederick T., Brownhills
Challinor Edwd. (earthen.), Amicable st.
Clarke Edward (earthenware), High street works, High street
Elsmore and Foster (earthenware), Clay hills pottery
Emberton Thomas I. & James (earthenware), High gate pottery, Brownhills
Ford, Challinor, and Co. (earthenware), Sandyford
Hammersley Ralph (rockingham and Egyptian black), High street
Hammersley Ralph (black earthenware), Church bank pottery, High street
Hancock Sampson (earthenware), High st.
Holdcroft & Wood (earthen.), George st.
Knapper & Blackhurst, Sandyford
Meir John & Son (earthen.), Greengates
Oulsnam W.E. (earthenware), High st.
Turner and Tomkinson (earthenware), Victoria works, High street
Turner, Goddard, and Co., Royal Albert pottery, Parsonage street
Walker and Salt (china), High street
Wedgwood & Co. (earthenware), Unicorn pottery, Amicable street; and Pinnox works, Great Woodland street
Wood Edmund T.W. (earthenware), Woodland pottery, Woodland street
Wood and Pigott, Well street

1870 Harrod

J.G. Harrod & Co.'s Postal and Commercial Directory of Staffordshire, Second Edition, J.G. Harrod & Co., London and Norwich (Shaw & Tipper 1226). Dated 1870 on the title page and September 1870 in the Preface. The 'second edition' is a reference to the previous directory by the publishers' predecessors Harrison, Harrod & Co. (see 1861 Harrison). It is believed that another edition was issued in 1870 containing Derbyshire, Leicestershire and Rutland in addition to Staffordshire but no copy has been located and the Staffordshire pages would almost certainly be identical.

This directory is not classified but consists of descriptive text followed by alphabetical lists of traders for the various towns and villages. Some of the descriptive text lists the major pottery firms with occasional descriptions. The following lists of potters have been extracted from the sections for the towns or villages as shown. The abbreviation P.R. stands for Private Residence.

Barlaston – General Trades, &c. (page 730)
Bevington John, china manufacturer
Brown-Westhead Thomas C., china and earthenware manufacturer
Brownfield Wm., china and earthenware manufacturer
Edwards John, china and earthenware manufacturer, Hartwell hills
Robinson William, china manufacturer, Hartwell
Wedgwood Francis, Godfry, Clement, & Lawrence, ware manufacturers

Burslem – General Trades, Professions, &c. (pages 768-782)
Adams John, earthenware manufacturer, Dalehall

ALCOCK & DIGGORY, manufacturers of china, for the home and foreign trade, Burslem china works
Alcock Henry & Co., manufacturers of white granite, for United States, Cobridge
Alcock Richard, earthenware manufacturer, Market place
BAKER & CHETWYND, manufacturers of ironstone china, earthenware, &c., for foreign markets only, Sylvester pottery
Bates & Bennett, earthenware manufacturers, Cobridge
BATES, ELLIOTT, & CO., manufacturers of earthenware for home and foreign markets, consisting of dinner, tea, toilet, and dessert ware, punchbowls, sanitary, photographic, druggist, electrical, galvanic, and perfumery ware, porcelain slates, artists' ware, sign-board letters, jet ware, &c., Dalehall
Beech Jane, manufacturer of water-closets, china, and earthenware, toys, &c., Bell works
Bennett William, earthenware manufacturer, Sneyd potteries – P.R. Podmore street
BODLEY EDWARD F. & CO., manufacturers of ironstone china for steam-ship and hotel use, also every description of first-class earthenware, suitable for the home, colonial, continental, and Indian markets, Scotia pottery
BOOTE T. & R., manufacturers of encaustic and plain flooring tiles of the hardest texture, and the finest colours (equal to enamel tints), which can be inlaid any depth, thereby ensuring durability, and at a much cheaper rate than hiterto charged, for churches, entrance halls, &c., &c.; white glazed tiles both for in and outdoor purposes, which will resist the severest weather; designs and estimates supplied without charge, and experienced pavers sent out to suit purchasers; prize encaustic tiles – Waterloo Potteries
Bourne Ezra, earthenware manufacturer, Newport lane
Bowers Frederick, china manufacturer, Brownhills
BROWNFIELD WILLIAM, manufacturer of improved ironstone and earthenware for the home markets, Cobridge
Burgess Henry, earthenware manufacturer, Kilncroft works
BURGESS, LEIGH, & CO., earthenware and china manufacturers for home and foreign markets, Hill pottery, Liverpool road
COCKSON, CHETWYND, & CO., earthenware manufacturers, for the American markets only, Cobridge
Collinson Charles, earthenware manufacturer, Fountain place
Collinson G. & Co., earthenware manufacturers, Newcastle street pottery
Cooper & Co., earthenware manufacturers, Furlong works
Corn W. & E., earthenware manufacturers, Navigation road
Davenport Henry & Co., glass, china, and earthenware manufacturers, Longport
DAVENPORT WILLIAM & CO., manufacturers of earthenware, china, and glass for home and foreign trade, Longport potteries; wholesale warehouses, 30 Canning place, Liverpool, and 82 Fleet street, London, E.C.
Dean Robert, earthenware manufacturer, Waterloo road
Downing & Co., earthenware manufacturers, Wellington works
EDGE & MALKIN, manufacturers of earthenware and iron stone china, black lustre, fancy coloured stoneware, for home and foreign markets, Newport works
EDWARDS JAMES & SON, manufacturers of ironstone china, earthenware, electrical, chemical, galvanic, photo graphic appartus; fancy decorated table, toilet, and dessert ware, for home and foreign markets – Dalehall pottery
Elliott & Bate, earthenware manufacturers, Dalehall works, Newcastle st.
Elsmore Thomas, earthenware manufacturer, Brownhills
Emberton James, earthenware manufacturer, Brownhills
Emberton Thomas, earthenware manufacturer, Brownhills
Evans & Tomkinson, earthenware manufacturers, Knowle works
Furlong Works Company, earthenware manufacturers, Newcastle street
FURNIVAL J. & CO., general earthenware manufacturers for home and foreign markets, Cobridge
Gater & Draycott, earthenware and cock-spur manufacturers, Newcastle street
HALLEN HARDING, pot-step and gas-burner manufacturer, Wellington street
Hallen William Henry, creel-step maker, Wellington street
Hammersley Ralph, earthenware manufacturer, Overhouse works
Hancock & Whittingham, earthenware manufacturers, Swan square
Hancock, Whittingham, & Co., earthenware manufacturers, Swan bank pottery
Hawthorn J. & Son, door and bell furniture manufacturers, Albert st. works
HEATH & BLACKHURST, manufacturers of general earthenware, plain and decorated, for home and foreign markets, Hadderidge pottery
Hobson Charles, earthenware manufacturer, Albert pottery
Holdcroft & Co., earthenware manufacturers, Queen street pottery
Hope & Carter, earthenware manufacturers, Fountain place works
Hughes Thomas, manufacturer of earthenware, merchant, &c., Waterloo road
Lea & Smith, china and earthenware, lock furniture, finger plates, &c., Crown works
Lee William, earthenware manufacturer, Hall street
MACINTYRE JAMES & CO., manufacturers of china, porcelain, mortice-lock and bell lever furniture, finger-plates, shutter, drawer, and hall-door knobs, mortars & pestles, metal-covered jugs, letters for signs, garden labels, artists' palettes, slabs, colour tiles, &c., Washington works
Maddock John & Sons, earthenware manufacturer for United States, Newcastle street pottery
MALKIN, EDGE, & CO., patent encaustic and geometrical tile pavements for churches, entrance halls, conservatories, wall decorations, &c.; also white glazed tiles for baths, dairies, &c. M.E. & Co. are prepared to grant licenses for the use of their encaustic tile process; terms on application at the works, where designs for floor pavements may also be had – Newport works
Massey J.S., earthenware manufacturer, Prince's row
Massey Thomas W., earthenware manufacturer, Kiln croft

MEAKIN & CO., earthenware manufacturers for foreign markets, Cobridge
MEAKIN, BROTHERS, & CO., earthenware manufacturers for foreign markets
Meakin Charles, earthenware manufacturer, Waterloo road
Meir John, potter, Newport lane
Moore Brothers, ironstone china manufacturers, Bleakhill pottery, Cobridge
Moore Edward T., earthenware manufacturer, Waterloo road
Morgan, Wood, & Co., earthenware manufacturers, Hill Top works
Ollivant John, potter, Edward street
Oulsnan William, earthenware manufacturer, Newcastle street
Parr John, marble and nest-egg manufacturer, Wellington street – P.R. Pitt st.
Parr Thomas, marble toy manufacturer, Church street
Payne, Brothers, Rockingham ware manufacturers, Podmore street
Pinder, Bourne, & Co., manufacturers of ironstone, china, and earthenware, Nile street
Rathbone James, earthenware manufacturer, Wharf street and Queen street
Robinson John, potter, Liverpool road
ROBINSON, KIRKHAM, & CO., general earthenware manufacturers for home and foreign markets, New Wharf pottery
Shaw Anthony, earthenware manufacturer, Mersey pottery, Newport lane
TILL & SONS, ironstone, china, and earthenware manufacturers, for home and foreign markets, Sytch pottery
Tinsley, Bourne, & Co., earthenware manufacturers, Bourne's Bank pottery
Turner William & Co., Rockingham and earthenware manufacturers, Albert st.
Vernon James, earthenware manufacturer and potter's valuer, Waterloo road
Wade & Co., Rockingham ware manufacturers, High street
Wade & Colclough, toy manufacturers, High street
Wade & Myatt, shuffle-eye manufacturers, Hall street
Walley William, Rockingham ware manufacturer, Nile street
Whitehall Joseph, spurmaker, Nile street
Wigley & Skiffley, spurmakers, Gallimore square
Wigley George, brick and marl works, manufacturer of creel cups, worsted guards, shuttle eyes, pot weights, &c., Sylvester square
Wigley William Henry, earthenware manufacturer, Sylvester street
Williams Thomas, earthenware manufacturer, Hall street
Williamson Thomas, earthenware manufacturer, Albert street
WILTSHAW, WOOD, & CO., manufacturers of mortice-lock furniture, finger-plates, shutter and hall-door knobs, drawer knobs, beer engine and other handles, castor bowls, bedstead vases, and rosettes, jug-stands, door-labels, &c., Albert street works
Wittingham & Ford, earthenware manufacturers, High street
Wood & Baggaley, earthenware manufacturers, Hill works
Wood, Son, & Co., earthenware manufacturers for United States, Villa pottery, Cobridge

Etruria – General Trades, &c. (pages 841-842)
Hartley Joseph, potter
WEDGWOOD J. & SONS, manufacturers of earthenware, parian, majolica, chemical goods, porous ware for electric telegraph batteries, mortar and pestal stoneware, jasper, &c., for home and foreign markets – Etruria potteries

Fenton – General Trades, &c. (pages 846-847)
BAKER & CO., earthenware manufacturers, High street
CHALLINOR E. & C., earthenware and ironstone china manufacturers for foreign markets, Fenton pottery
Edwards John, semi-porcelain manufacturer, King street works
GIMSON J. & CO., manufacturers of patent spurs, stilts, &c.
GREEN M. & CO., manufacturers of tea, breakfast, dessert, and trinket services, &c., for home and foreign markets, Minerva china works
HAWLEY & CO., manufacturers of china and earthenware for home and foreign markets, Foley potteries
JACKSON & GOSLING, china manufacturers for home and foreign markets, Grosvenor works
Malkin Ralph, earthenware manufacturer, Park works
PRATT F. & R. & CO., manufacturers of druggists' sundries, uniquely-decorated and general earthenware; awarded Soc. of Arts silver medal, 1848, and first-class medal International Exhibition, Paris, 1855 – Fenton potteries
Pratt John & Co., earthenware manufacturers, Lane Delph pottery
Reeves J., earthenware manufacturer, Victoria works – Mr J.B. Wathen, manager
Robinson & Hudson, china manufacturers, Foley works
TAYLOR R. MINTON & CO., manufacturers of ornamental and all kinds of encaustic tiles, High street
Taylor & Co., spur and stilt manufacturers
Wileman J.F., earthenware, china, and granite manufacturer, Foley potteries
Williamson, Turner, & Co., china and earthenware manufac., Foley Old pottery

Hanley – General Trades, Professions, &c. (pages 871-885)
ADAMS JOHN & CO., manufacturers of wedgewood ware, majolica, green glaze, &c., for home and foreign markets, Victoria works, Broad street; London show-rooms, 30 Ely place
ASH GEORGE, manufacturer of parian statuettes, ornamental vases, &c., Broad street
ASHWORTH GEORGE L. & BROTHERS, manufacturers of earthenware and ironstone china, specially adapted for ship purposes, hotels, &c., sole makers of Mason's patent ironstone china, both patterns and shapes, chemical goods, insulators, and other goods for telegraphic purposes, and sanitary ware for home and foreign markets, works, Broad street
BAILEY & CO., manufacturers of parian statuettes,

ornamental vases, china, stone, &c., Brewery Street works, Hope street; London show-rooms, Ely place, Holborn

Bailey John (executors of), parian manufacturers, Brewery street

Bamford John, jug and figure manufacturer, Nelson place – P.R. Harley street

Barker Charles, parian manufacturer, Lower Lichfield street

Bennett & Rathbone, earthenware manufacturers, Wharf lane

Bevington Ambrose, china decorator, Dresden works, Birch street

Bevington John & Co., china, parian, &c. manufacturers, Elm street

BEVINGTON JAMES & THOS., manufacturers of china, parian statuettes, &c., for home and foreign markets, Burton place works

Booth Henry, earthenware manufacturer, Nelson place

BOOTH THOMAS, manufacturer of earthenware, stone, &c., druggists' sundries, Britannia metal mounted hot water jugs, molasses jugs, &c., for home and foreign markets, Waterloo and Britannia works

BROWN-WESTHEAD, MOORE, & CO., china and earthenware manufacturers for home and foreign markets, Cauldon place; London offices and show-rooms, 107 Hatton gardens, and at Grosse Reichen strasse 38-B, Hamburg

BUCKLEY J., manufacturer of sanitary wares of every description, Vine street works

BULLER & CO., manufacturers of earthenware, thimble cockspurs, stilts, pins, cup rings, claws, and every sort of placing goods for potters' use, china, mortice, rim, and latch furniture, finger plates, shutter, drawer, and centre knobs, vitrified castor bowls, and every description of china for the brassfounders, cabinet, and metallic bedstead trades, &c., insulators, battery plates, cells, and all kinds of electric telegraph ware, mortars, pestles, &c., depot, 23 Congreve street, Birmingham

CLEMENTSON BROTHERS, manufacturers of earthen ware for foreign trade, Phoenix and Bell works

DAVENPORT, BANKS, & CO., manufacturers of porous general earthenware and fancy goods for home and export, Castlefield pottery

DIMMOCK JOHN & CO., earthenware manufactures of every description, for home and export. Award, London, 1851, bronze medal; London, 1862, for general excellence – Albion works

DUDSON JAMES, manufacturer of earthenware, improved ironstone china jugs, butters, teapots, candlesticks, colour manufacturer for china, earthenware, and glass, Britannia metal-mounted jugs, for home and foreign market – Hope street

Espley Geo., spur manufacturer, Chell st.

Evans W.L., china and earthenware manufacturer, Brunswick street

Ford Charles, spur and stilt manufacturer, Parker street

FORD THOMAS & CHARLES, china manufacturers for the home trade, Cannon street

GELSON BROTHERS, earthenware manufacturers for home and foreign markets, High street

HALL HENRY, manufacturer of earthenware, stone, &c., Britannia metal mounted hot-water jugs, molasses jugs, for home and foreign markets – Church street works

Heather F. & Co., manufacturers of porcelain, Kensington works

Hodgkinson E., earthenware, stone, and parian manufacturer, Mayer st. works

Howson George, sanitary ware manufacturer, Paxton street

LIVESLEY & DAVIS, manufacturers of earthenware for home and foreign markets, and all kinds of sanitary ware in great variety, Trent pottery – offices, 5 College place, New York, and Ely place, London

Livesley W.H., manufacturer of parian, earthenware, &c., Cannon st.

Massey George, china and figure manufacturer, Hope street

Meakin Harry, manufacturer, Lichfield st.

MEAKIN J. & G., earthenware manufacturers for foreign markets, Eagle pottery, and merchants, New York

Meakin J. & W., earthenware manufacturers, Eagle pottery, Bucknall road

MILLS BROTHERS (established 1836), manufacturers of ornamental parian stone, &c., Dresden works, George street

Mills E., parian manufacturer, George st.

Mills John, brownware manufacturer, 4 Cleugh street

Mitchell Anthony, figure-maker, Snow hill

OLD HALL EARTHENWARE COMPANY (Limited), manufacturers of earthenware, parian, and stoneware, for home and foreign markets – Charles Meigh, Esq., managing director, the Old Hall works, Hill st.

OLDHAM JAMES & CO., manufacturers of general earthenware, mosaic and ornamental stone, parian, &c., Ranalagh works

PANKHURST J.W. & COMPANY, white granite manufacturers for the United States, Charles street works

Pointon Wm. B., earthenware manufacturer, Parker street

POWELL & BISHOP, manufacturers of plain and ornamental china and earthenware, for home, American, and continental markets, High street

Ranaleigh Works, earthen and stoneware manufactory, Ranaleigh street

Ridgway Edward John, earthenware, &c., manufacturer, Bedford works

SCRIVENER R.G. & CO., manufacturers of decorated china earthenware, &c., for home and foreign markets, Norfolk street works

Smith J., parian manufacturer, Hope st.

STANWAY, HORNE, & ADAMS, manufacturers of parian and stoneware, pearl and orange lustre, terra cotta, jet, and best parian statuary for home and foreign markets – Trent works, Joiner's square

Stubbs William, china and earthenware manufacturer, Eastwood pottery

TAYLOR BROTHERS, earthenware manufacturers for the South American, United States, and India markets, Market street

TAYLOR, TUNNICLIFF, & CO., manufacturers of china

and porcelain, mortice, lock, and bell-lever furniture, finger-plates, shutter, drawer, and hall-door knobs, castor-bowls, door and kettle grips, beer-machine and tea-bell handles, and every description of porcelain articles for brassfounders, plumbers, &c., barometers, scales, slides, &c. – Havelock works, Broad street

Taylor William, earthenware manufacturer, Brook street

THE OLD HALL EARTHENWARE COMPANY (Limited), manufacturers of earthenware, parian, and stoneware for home and foreign markets – Charles Meigh, Esq., managing director, the Old Hall works, Hill st.

Twyford Christopher, sanitary ware manufacturer, New street

Twyford Thomas, manufacturer of water-closet basins, plug basins, urinals, &c., Bath street; London depot, London and North-Western Railway, Maiden lane station

Unwin & Holmes, parian and earthenware manufacturers, High street

WARDLE JAMES, parian and belbeck china manufacturer for home and foreign markets, William street

WEDGWOOD JOSIAH & SONS, manufacturers of earthenware, majolica, chemical goods, porous ware for electric telegraph batteries, mortars and pestles, stoneware, jasper, &c., for home and foreign markets, Etruria Potteries

WORTHINGTON & SON, manufacturers of toilet ware figures, stoneware, dinner ware, &c., in great varieties, for home and foreign markets, Brook street works

WORTHINGTON & HARROP, manufacturers of parian figures, vases, and stoneware, for home and foreign markets, Dresden Works, Tinkers' clough

Longton – General Trades, Professions, &c.
(pages 925-932)

ABBERLEY JAMES, earthenware manufacturer for home and foreign markets, Waterloo works

Adams & Cooper, china manufacturers, High street

ADAMS HARVEY & CO., manufacturers of china and earthenware suitable for home and export trade – works, Sutherland road; London offices, 5 Bartlett's buildings, Holborn

Adams John (Executors of), china manufacturers, High street

ALLERTON BROTHERS, china and earthenware manufacturers, High street

Amison & Edwards, earthenware manufacturers, Russell street

Austin & Co., parian manufacturers, Stafford street

Aynsley John, china manufacturer, Portland works, Sutherland road

Baddeley Elizabeth, rustic and terra-cotta works, Commerce street

Baddeley Wm., rustic ware manufacturer, High street

Barker & Hill, china and earthenware manufacturers, and merchants, King st.

Barlow Thomas (Executors of), china manufacturers, Market street

Barlow Thomas W., earthenware manufacturer, Commerce street

BEECH JAMES & SON, china manufacturers for home and foreign markets, Albert and Sutherland works, High street

BEECH, UNWIN, & CO., manufacturers of ornamental earthenware, stone bodies, &c., suitable for home and foreign markets, Green Dock works, New street

BENTLEY THOMAS & CO., china manufacturers for home and foreign markets, Church street (See Advt.)

Betteney Thomas, china manufacturer, Stafford street

Billington & Tompkinson, china and earthenware manufacturers, High street and Stafford street

Birks Thomas, china and earthenware manufacturer, High street

Bold Henry, manufacturer of porcelain gasaliers, centrepieces, &c., High st.

BRAMMALL EDWIN, china manufacturer for home and foreign markets, Heathcote works

BRIDGWOOD, SAMPSON, & SON, manufacturers of china and earthenware for home and foreign markets, and grinders of all kinds of potters' materials, &c., &c., Anchor pottery and Anchor mills

Bridgwood Davis, earthenware manufacturer, Heathcote road

Broadhurst James, earthenware manufacturer, Stafford street

Brough Brothers & Co., earthenware manufacturers, Gold street

Cartledge John, china manufacturer, Market street

Cartwright & Edwards, ironstone, china, and earthenware manufacturers, Borough pottery

Caufield F. & Co., china manufacturers, High street

CHETHAM FREDERICK & CO., earthenware manufacturers, Commerce street

COLLINGWOOD & GREATBATCH, china manufacturers for home and foreign markets, Crown works, Stafford street

Cooper & Nixon, earthenware manufacturers for home markets, Viaduct works

Copestake & Allin, china manufacturers, Alma works, High street

Copestake Brothers, china manufacturers, for home and foreign markets, Anchor works

DALE, PAGE, & CO., china manufacturers for home and foreign markets, Church street

Dawson James, earthenware manufacturer, Commerce street

EDWARDS GEORGE & CO., manufacturers of white and decorative china for home and foreign markets, Sheridan works

Elkin Samuel, earthenware manufacturer, Stafford street

Ferneyhough J. & Co., china manufacturers, Dresden works, Stafford street

Finney Joseph, china manufacturer, Victoria works

Gibson & Hallam, china manufacturers, St. Martin's lane

Grove & Robinson, lustre and china manufacturers, Chancery lane

Hackney James S., parian manufacturer Stafford street

Hallam & Gibson, china manufacturers, St. Martin's lane

HAMMERSLEY, FREEMAN, & CO., china manufacturers for home and foreign markets, Prince of Wales works, Sutherland road

Hampson Brothers, earthenware manufacturers, New street

Hodson Richard & Co., china manufacturers, Chancery lane
Holdcroft Joseph, parian and lustre manufacturer, St. Martin's lane
HOLLAND & GREEN, china and earthenware manufac turers for home and foreign markets, High street, and Stafford street
HUDDEN JOHN THOMAS, earthenware manufacturer for home and foreign markets, Stafford street
Hulse & Walters, china manufacturers, Commerce street
HULSE & ADDERLEY, earthenware and china manufacturers for home and foreign markets, Daisy bank pottery
Jones Frederick, earthenware manufacturer, Chadwick street
Jones J.E., manufacturer of earthenware, ironstone, china, &c., Portland pottery
Keeling & Walker, parian, china, and lustre manufacturers, High street
KENT JOHN & SON, exporters of china and earthenware of every description for home and foreign markets, Market place
Lockett John W., china and earthenware manufacturer, King st., and Market st.
Lowe Thomas, earthenware manufacturer, Gold street
Mason, Holt, & Co., manufacturers of improved porcelain china
MOORE & SON, china manufacturers for home and foreign markets, St Mary's works, High street
Moston J.E.B., china manufacturer, Clayton street
Poole, Sutherland, & Hallam, earthenware and rustic manufacturers, Cornhill
Procter J. & H. & Co., earthenware, &c., manufacturers, New town pottery
Robinson, Repton, & Robinson, china manufacturers, Wellington works, Stafford street
Shepherd & Co., china and earthenware manufacturers, Stafford street
Skelson & Plant, china and earthenware manufacturers, Chancery lane, and Heathcote road
Smith Sampson, china and figure manufacturer, Barker street
SUTHERLAND & SONS, manufacturers of ornamental, parian, rustic, and belbeck pearl ware, ivory, enamelled, flowered, risen, and plain gilt, &c., for home and foreign markets, Park Hall street
Tams & Lowe, earthenware manufacturers, High street
Taylor, Hudson, & Middleton, china manufacturers, Chancery lane
Taylor William & Co., patent spurs and stilt manufacturers, Church street
Tompkinson, Billington & Co., china manufacturers, High street
WEBB & CO., china manufacturers for home and foreign markets, Peel street pottery
Webberley William, china manufacturer, St. James place, High street
WOOD & CO., china manufacturers (home and export), Mount Pleasant, High street
Yearsley George, modeller, parian figure manufacturer, Market lane

Stoke-upon-Trent – General Trades, Professions, &c.
(pages 1005-1011)
Blackshaw J. & Co., china and parian manufacturers, Providence works, Copeland street
Carter William, manufacturer, High st.
Challinor Charles, china manufacturer, Trent vale
CHETHAM JOHN & COMPANY, manufacturers of lustre black drab, turquoise and printed wares, stone mortars, &c., for home and foreign markets, Bridge works, Church street
COPELAND W.T. & SONS, porcelain, earthenware, and glass manufacturers for home and foreign markets, High street, and 160 New Bond street, London, W.
Gilmore & Hawthorne, door furniture manufacturers, John street
Hill Leveson (Executors of), parian manufacturers, Wharf street
JONES GEORGE, manufacturer of earthenware, stone, china, and majolica, Trent potteries
Kirkham Wm., earthenware manufacturer, London road
MEAKIN J. & G., earthenware manufacturers and commission merchants – branch office, Glebe street
MINTON & CO., manufacturers of china and earthenware tiles for flower-boxes, walls, hearths, &c., London road, and London warehouse, 28 Wallbrook
MINTON, HOLLINS, & CO., patent tile works, the old established manufacturers of encaustic and plain tiles for pavements, and of majolica and glazed tiles for all purposes of wall decoration. Exhibition awards – London 1851, council medal; Paris 1855, gold medal; London 1862, first-class medal; Paris 1867, gold medal. London house, 50 Conduit street, Regent street, W. (Minton & Co.); Manchester house, Bridgewater Club Chambers, 110 King street
ROBINSON & LEADBEATER, manufacturers of parian, statuary ornaments, &c., new subjects by eminent artists constantly being added for home and foreign markets – works, Glebe street and Wharf street (See advertsiement)
Salisbury and Wildblood, earthenware manufacturers, Church street
Turner, Hassall, Peake, & Poole, manufacturers of parian, china, majolica, terra-cotta, and stone, Albert and Copeland street works
WALKER & CARTER, manufacturers of earthenware, stone, china, &c., for home and foreign markets, British Anchor potteries

Tunstall – General Trades, Professions, &c.
(pages 1040-1047)
Adams William, earthenware manufacturer, and grinder of potter's materials, Newfield works
ADAMS W. & T., earthenware and china manufacturers for home and foreign markets, Greenfields
Beech & Hancock, earthenware manufacturers, Swan bank pottery
Blackhurst Richard, earthenware manufacturer, High street
Booth Thomas & Co., earthenware manufacturers, Church bank pottery
BOWERS FREDERICK T., manufacturer of improved

porcelain, ironstone, earthenware, and white granite, in superior printed Japan and other dinner, dessert, toilette, tea, and breakfast ware, gilded and ornamented – awarded prize medal, London 1851, for home and foreign markets – Brown hills pottery
Challinor Edward, manufacturer of water-closets, plug basins, &c., High street
Clarke Edward, earthenware manufacturer, Phoenix works
Elsmore & Foster, earthenware manufacturers, Clay hills pottery
EMBERTON THOMAS & JAMES, manufacturers of plain and ornamental earthenware for home and foreign markets, Highgate pottery
FORD & CHALLINOR, manufacturers of plain and ornamental earthenware for home and foreign markets, Sandyford pottery
Hancock Sampson, earthenware manufacturer, High street
HOLCROFT & WOOD, earthenware manufacturers for home and foreign markets, George street pottery
KNAPPER & BLACKHURST, eathenware manufacturers for home and foreign markets, Sandyford pottery
MEIR JOHN & SON, earthenware manufacturers and flint-grinders, and home and foreign traders, Greengate pottery
Oulsnam W.E., earthenware manufacturer, High street, and cratemaker, Greenfields
Peake Thomas, manufacturer of terra-metalic tiles, pipes, &c., tileries, colliery, and ironstone works
Turner & Tomkinson, earthenware and ironstone china manufacturers, Victoria works – London office, Eley pl., Holborn
Turner Goddard & Co., earthenware manufacturers, Royal Albert pottery
WEDGWOOD & CO., manufacturers of earthenware, for home, American, and continental markets, Pinnox and Union works
Wood & Piggott, earthenware manufacturers, Well street
Wood Edmund Thomas Wedgwood, earthenware manufacturer for United States, Woodland pottery

1872 Kelly

The Post Office Directory of Birmingham, Staffordshire, Warwickshire, and Worcestershire (also *The Post Office Directory of Staffordshire),* Printed and Published by Kelly & Co., 51 Great Queen Street, Lincoln's Inn Fields, London WC (Shaw & Tipper 6, Shaw & Tipper 1222). Dated MDCCCLXXII on the title page and September 1872 in the Preface. It is noted as the Seventh Edition in the Preface.

As with all the Kelly's series, this directory contains alphabetical lists for the various towns and villages and also classified lists for each county. Only the classified lists are included here. The range of categories is extensive and there are twenty-three relevant to this work.

Artists' Palette Manufacturers – China (page 907)
Macintyre James & Co. Washington works, Waterloo road, Burslem

Beer Machine Handle Makers – China (page 911)
Taylor, Tunnicliff & Co. Havelock works, Broad street, Hanley
Tams & Lowe, High street, Longton
Wiltshaw, Wood & Co. Albert Street works, Burslem

Chemical Ware Manufacturers (page 947)
Wedgwood Josiah & Sons, Etruria pottery, Stoke-upon-Trent

China Manufacturers (page 947)
Adams & Cooper, High street, Longton
Adams, Harvey & Co. High st. Longton
Adams John (exors. of), Park place & Victoria works, Longton
Allerton C. & Sons, High st. Longton
Ashworth George L. & Brothers, Broad street, Hanley
Aynsley John & Co. Sutherland road, Longton
Barker & Hill, King street, Longton
Barlow Thomas, Cyples Old pottery, Market street, Longton
Beech James & Sons, Albert & Sutherland works, Longton
Bentley Thos. & Co. Church st. Longton
Betteney John & Co. Batavia works, Stafford street, Longton
Bevington J. & T. Burton place, Hanley
Bevington Ambrose, Gt. York st. Hanley
Birks Thomas, High street, Longton
Brammall E. Heathcote street, Longton
Brown William Southwell & Co. Copeland street, Stoke-upon-Trent
Brown-Westhead (T.C.), Moore & Co. Cauldon place, Hanley; & 107 Hatton garden & Fitz Eylwin house, Holborn viaduct, London e.c
Collingwood & Greatbatch, Stafford street, Longton
Copestake Geo. jun. Anchor wrks. Longton
Copestake & Co. Alma works, High street, Longton
Dale, Page & Co. Church st. Longton
Davis J. H. & J. Trent pottery, Hanley; show rooms, 12 Thavies inn, Holborn, London e.c
Edge & Co. High street, Longton
Edwards G. & Co. King street, Longton
Ferneyhough John & Co. Dresden works, Stafford street, Longton
Finney Joseph, Victoria works, Longton
Ford Charles, West terrace, Hanley
Ford Thomas, Cannon street, Hanley
Freeman Wltr. & Rd. High st. Longton
Gibson & Hallam, St. Martin's lane, Longton
Goss Wm. Hy. London rd. Stoke-on-Trent
Green M. & Co. Park street, Fenton, Stoke-upon-Trent

Hammersley & Asbury, Sutherland road, Longton
Harvey, Adams & Co. Sutherland road, Longton
Heath & Burton, St. Martin's lane, Longton
Hodson Richard, Chancery la. Longton
Hulse & Adderley, Daisy Bank works, Longton
Jackson & Gosling, King street, Fenton, Stoke-upon-Trent
Kent John & Son, Market st. Longton
Knight John, Market street, Longton
Lloyd Edward, Parker street, Hanley
Lockett John, King street & Market street, Longton
Mason, Holt & Co. Normacott road, Longton
Minton & Co. Eldon place, Stoke-upon-Trent; & 28 Walbrook, London e.c
Moore & Son, High street, Longton
Moston J.E. Clayton street, Longton
Robinson & Chapman, Royal works, Longton
Robinson & Hudson, Foley, Fenton, Stoke-upon-Trent
Robinson, Ripton, & Robinson, Stafford street, Longton
Scrivener R.G. & Co. Norfolk st. Hanley
Skelson & Plant, Chancery lane, Heathcote road, Longton
Smith Sampson, Barker street, Longton
Taylor, Hudson & Middleton, Chancery Lane works, Longton
Turner, Hassell & Poole, Copeland street & Albert works, Liverpool road, Stoke-upon-Trent
Walters & Hulse, Commerce st. Longton
Webb Samuel & Co. Stafford st. Longton
Webberley W. St. James's pl. Longton
Wileman & Co. Foley potteries, Fenton, Stoke-upon-Trent

China Figure Makers (page 947)
Beech Mrs. Jane, Queen street, Burslem
Massey George, Tinker's clough, Hanley
Copeland Wm. Taylor & Sons, High st. Stoke-upon-Trent; & at 160 New Bond street, London w.

China & Porcelain Door Furniture Manufacturers (page 947)
Buller & Co. Joiner's Square works, Hanley; & 23 Congreve street, Birmingham; & 6 Martin's Lane, Cannon street, London e.c
Macintyre James & Co. Washington works, Waterloo road, Burslem
Taylor, Tunnicliff & Co. Havelock works, Broad street, Hanley
Wiltshaw, Wood & Co. Albert street works, Burslem

Creel Step Manufacturer (page 957)
Hallen Harding, Wellington st. Burslem

Earthenware Manufacturers (page 962)
Adams John & Co. Broad street, Hanley
Adams William & Thomas, Tunstall
Adams William, Greenfield, Tunstall
Alcock Henry & Co. Cobridge, Burslem
Alcock Richard, Market place, Burslem
Amison & Edwards, Russell st. Longton
Ashworth Geo. L. & Bros. Broad st. Hanley
Baker & Chetwynd, Sylvester pottery, Burslem
Baker & Co. Fenton, Stoke-upon-Trent
Bamford John, Nelson place, Hanley
Barlow Thomas Waterhouse, Coronation works, Commerce street, Longton
Bates & Bennett, Cobridge, Burslem
Bates, Elliot & Co. Dale hall, Burslem
Beech, Cooper, Sill & Co. New street, Longton
Beech & Hancock, Swan bank, Tunstall
Bevington John, Broad street, Hanley
Blackhurst Jabez, Sandyford, Tunstall
Blackhurst Richard, High st. Tunstall
Bodley Edward Fisher & Co. Hill pottery & Scotia works, Burslem
Booth & Son, Marsh street, Hanley
Booth Thomas & Co. Church Bank pottery, Tunstall
Booth Thomas & Sons, Britannia works, High street, & New Hall works, Gt. York street, Hanley
Bowler W. & E. New street, Hanley
Bridgwood S. & Son, East vale, Longton
Broadhurst James, Portland pottery, Fenton, Stoke-upon-Trent
Brough & Blackhurst, Waterloo works, Longton
Brownfield W. & Son, Cobridge, Burslem
Brown-Westhead (T.C.), Moore & Co. Cauldon place, Hanley; & 107 Hatton garden & Fitz Eylwin House, Holborn viaduct, London e.c
Brownhills Pottery Company (The), Tunstall
Burgess, Leigh & Co. Hill pottery, Burslem
Burgess H. Kiln Croft works, Burslem
Cartwright & Edwards, Trentham street, Longton
Challinor Edward & Charles, High st. Fenton, & Glebe st. Stoke-upon-Trent
Challinor Edward, High Street pottery, Tunstall
Clarke Edward, High street, Tunstall
Clementson Brothers, Phoenix & Bell works, Hanley
Cockson, Chetwynd & Co. Cobridge, Burslem
Collinson Charles & Co. Newcastle street, Burslem
Cooper, Nixon & Co. Caroline st. Longton
Corn William & Edward, Navigation Road pottery, Burslem
Davenport, Banks & Co. Castle Field pottery, Hanley
Davenport William & Co. Longport, Burslem; warehouses, 82 Fleet st. London e.c. & 30 Canning pl. Liverpool
Dimmock J. & Co. Stafford st. Hanley
Downing & Co. Newport st. Burslem
Dudson James, Hanover street, Hanley
Edge, Malkin & Co. Newport works, Burslem
Edwards James & Son, Dale Hall pottery, Burslem
Elsmore Thomas & Son, Clay Hills pottery, Tunstall
Emberton T. I. & J., Highgate pottery, Tunstall
Evans & Tomkinson, Knowles works, Burslem
Ford & Challinor, Sandyford, Tunstall
Furnival T. & Son, Cobridge, Burslem
Gater John, Dale hall, Burslem
Gelson Brothers, High street, Hanley
Grove & Stark, Palissy works, Longton
Hammersley Ralph, High street, Tunstall, & at Wedgwood place, Burslem

Hancock, Whittingham & Co, Queen square, Burslem
Hawley Robert, Foley, Fenton, Stoke-upon-Trent
Heath & Blackhurst, Hadderidge pottery, Burslem
Hobson Charles, Albert street, Burslem
Holdcroft William, George st. Tunstall
Holland & Green, Stafford st. Longton
Hope & Carter, Fountain place, Burslem
Hudden J.T. Stafford street, Longton
Hughes Thomas, Waterloo road & Longport, Burslem
Hulse & Adderley, Daisy Bank works, Longton
Jones F. & Co. Chadwick st. Longton
Jones George, London road, Stoke-upon-Trent
Jones Josiah Ellis, Church st. Longton
Keeling & Walker, 31 High st. Longton
Kirkham Wm. London rd, Stoke-upon-Trent; office, 13 Lime st. London e.c
Leader M. 174 Newcastle st. Burslem
Lloyd Edward, Parker street, Hanley
Lockett Jhn. King st. & Market st. Longtn
Lowe Thomas, Gold street, Longton
Maddock John & Sons, Newcastle street, Burslem
Malkin R. Fenton, Stoke-upon-Trent
Meakin Brothers & Co. Trent pottery, Burslem
Meakin J. & G. Eagle pottery, Hanley
Meakin James & George, 16 Glebe street, Stoke-upon-Trent
Meakin & Co. Cobridge, Burslem
Meir John & Son, Greengate pottery, Tunstall
Minton & Co. Eldon place, Stoke-upon-Trent; & 28 Walbrook, London e.c
Moore Brothers, Bleak hill, Cobridge, Burslem
Old Hall Earthenware Company Limited, Hill street, Hanley
Oldham & Co. Ranelagh street, Hanley
Ouslman William & Son, Furlong works, Burslem
Pankhurst James Williams & Co. Old Hall street, Hanley
Pearson E. Sneyd st. Cobridge, Burslem
Pinder, Bourne & Co. Nile st. Burslem
Pointon & Co. Well street pottery, Tunstll
Poole & Unwin, Cornhill passage, Longtn
Pope L.J. & Co. Sneyd street, Cobridge, Burslem
Powell & Bishop, Stafford street, High street, & Parliament row, Hanley
Pratt Felix & Richard & Co. Fenton, Stoke-upon-Trent
Pratt John & Co. Limited (John Pratt, jun. secretary), Lane Delph, Stoke-upon-Trent; & 19 Crosby Hall chambers, London
Procter John & Henry & Co. High street, Longton
Rathbone, Hill & Co. Queen st. Burslem
Reeves James, Market street, Fenton, Stoke-upon-Trent
Ridgeway George, Copeland street, Stoke-upon-Trent
Ridgway Edward John & Son, Bedford works, Hanley
Robinson, Kirkham & Co. New Wharf pottery, Burslem
Shaw Anthony, Mersey works, Burslem
Stubbs Wm. Eastwood pottery, Hanley
Tams & Lowe, High street, Longton
Taylor William, Brook street, Hanley
Tinsley, Bourne & Co. Bourne's bank, Burslem
Turner, Goddard & Co. Royal Albert pottery, Tunstall
Turner, Hassell & Poole, Copeland street, & Albert works, Liverpool road, Stoke-upon-Trent
Turner & Tomkinson, Victoria works, Tunstall
Turner & Co. King street, Fenton, Stoke-upon-Trent
Unwin & Holmes, Upper Hanley works, Hanley
Vernon Jas. Waterloo pottery, Burslem
Walker & Carter, Church street, Stoke-upon-Trent
Wedgwood Josiah & Sons, Etruria pottery, Etruria, Stoke-upon-Trent
Wedgwood & Co. Pinnox & Unicorn works, Tunstall
Whittingham, Ford & Co. High street, Burslem
Wileman James F. Foley works, Fenton, Stoke-upon-Trent
Wood & Baggaley, Hill works, Burslem
Wood & Clarke, Church works, Burslem
Wood, Son & Co. Cobridge, Burslem
Wood Edmund Thomas Wedgwood, Woodland pottery, Tunstall
Worthington & Son, Brook st. Hanley

Encaustic & Geometric Tile Pavement Manufacturers – Patent (page 963)
Malkin, Edge & Co. Burslem
Minton, Hollins & Co. Patent tile works, Stoke-upon-Trent, & at 50 Conduit street, Regent street, London w; & Bridgewater Club chambers, 110 King street, Manchester

Inkstand Manufacturers – Fancy China (page 1007)
Taylor, Tunnicliff & Co. Havelock works, Broad street, Hanley

Letter Manufacturers – China (page 1015)
Macintyre James & Co. Washington works, Waterloo road, Burslem

Lock Furniture Makers – China (page 1018)
Macintyre James & Co. Washington works, Waterloo road, Burslem
Taylor, Tunnicliff & Co. Havelock works, Broad street, Hanley

Lustre Manufacturers (page 1018)
Holdcroft Joseph (silver), St. Martin's lane & Daisy bank, Longton

Majolica Manufacturers (pages 1018-1019)
Ash George & Co. Broad street, Hanley
Booth Thomas & Sons, Britannia works, High street; & New Hall works, Great York street, Hanley
Cartlidge William, Sun street, Hanley
Minton & Co. Eldon place, Stoke-upon-Trent; & 28 Walbrook, London e.c
Sutherland & Sons, Park Hall street, Longton
Turner, Hassell & Poole, Copeland street; & Albert works, Liverpool road, Stoke-upon-Trent
Wedgwood Josiah & Sons, Etruria pottery, Etruria, Stoke-upon-Trent

Parian Manufacturers (page 1028)
Ash George & Co. Broad street, Hanley

Brown-Westhead (T.C.), Moore & Co. Cauldon place, Hanley; & 107 Hatton garden & Fitz Eylwin house, Holborn viaduct, London e.c
Cooke Robert, Brewery street, Hanley
Goss W.H. London rd. Stoke-on-Trent
Hodgkinson Elijah, Mayor st. Hanley
Mill Edward, George street, Hanley
Mills William, 1 George street, Hanley
Minton & Co. Eldon place, Stoke-upon-Trent; & 28 Walbrook, London e.c
Robinson & Leadbeater, 49 Wharf street & Glebe street, Stoke-upon-Trent
Stanway, Horne & Adam, Lower Lichfield street, Hanley
Sutherland & Sons, Park Hall st. Longton
Turner, Hassell & Poole, Copeland street & Albert works, Liverpool road, Stoke-upon-Trent
Wedgwood Josiah & Sons, Etruria pottery, Etruria, Stoke-upon-Trent
Worthington & Harrop, Tinker's clough, Hanley
Yearsley George, Market lane, Longton

Rockingham Ware Manufacturers (page 1051)
Wade John & Co. High street, Burslem
Walley William, Nile street, Burslem
Williams, Turner & Co. Albert st. Burslem
Wood Brothers, Chapel lane, Burslem

Sanitary Ware Manufacturers (page 1053)
Brown-Westhead (T.C.), Moore & Co. Cauldon place, Hanley; & 107 Hatton garden & Fitz Eylwin house, Holborn viaduct, London e.c
Davis J.H. & J. Trent pottery, Hanley; show rooms, 12 Thavie's inn, Holborn, London w
Twyford Thomas, Bath street, Hanley
Warner & Co. New street, Hanley

Shuttle Eye Manufacturers (page 1070)
Hallen Harding, Wellington st. Burslem
Wade & Myatt, Hall street, Burslem

Spur Makers (page 1076)
Ford Charles, Parker street, Hanley
Gimson Joseph & Co. Fenton, Stoke-upon-Trent
Taylor Wm. & Co. Church street, Longton
Wigley & Shirley, Moorland rd. Burslem

Stone Mortar & Pestle Manufacturers (page 1078)
Buller & Co. Joiners' square works, Hanley & 23 Congreve street, Birmingham; & 6 Martin's lane, Cannon street, London e.c
Kirkham William, London road, Stoke-upon-Trent, office, 13 Lime street, London e.c
Lockett J. King st. & Market st. Longton
Macintyre James & Co. Washington works, Waterloo road, Burslem
Tams & Lowe, High street, Longton

Stoneware Manufacturers (page 1078)
Booth Thomas & Sons, Britannia works, High street & New Hall works, Great York street, Hanley
Brown-Westhead (T.C.), Moore & Co. Cauldon place, Hanley; & 107 Hatton garden & Fitz Eylwin house, Holborn viaduct, London e.c
Hodgkinson Elijah, Mayor st. Hanley
Lockett J. King st. & Mrkt. st. Longton
Wedgwood Josiah & Sons, Etruria pottery, Stoke-upon-Trent

Terra Cotta Manufacturers (page 1083)
Baddeley Mrs. Elizabeth (rustic), 3 Commerce street, Longton
Goss W.H. London rd. Stoke-upon-Trent
Kirkham Wm. London rd. Stoke-upon-Trent; office, 13 Lime st. London e.c
Turner, Hassell & Poole, Copeland street & Albert works, Stoke-upon-Trent

White Granite Manufacturer (page 1090)
Edwards John, King street, Fenton, Stoke-upon-Trent

1873 Keates

Keates's Gazetteer & Directory of the Staffordshire Potteries, Newcastle and District. 1873-4, J. Keates, Printer and Publisher, Cheapside, Hanley (Shaw & Tipper 1233).

As with all the Keates series, this directory is classified within separate sections for each of the six pottery towns and the only relevant categories are potters and various types of tile manufacturers.

Burslem – Encaustic and Geometric Tile Pavement Manufacturers (page 127)
Basford James Powell, Dalehall
Boote Thomas and Richard, Waterloo rd.
Malkin, Edge and Co., Newport lane

Burslem – Floor Tile Works (page 127)
Basford Brothers, Dalehall

Burslem – Potters (pages 132-133)
Alcock Henry and Co. (earthenware), Cobridge works
Alcock Richard (earthenware), Central pottery
Baker and Chetwynd (earthenware), Sylvester works
Bates, Elliott & Co. (earthenware) Dalehall
Bates and Bennett, Sneyd street
Beech Mrs. Jane (earthen.), Bell works, Queen street
Bodley E.F. & Co., (earthenware), Scotia works, Scotia road, and Market place
Boote T. & R. (earthen.), Waterloo road

Brownfield William and Son, (earthenware and china), Cobridge
Brownhills Pottery Co., (earthenware), Brownhills
Burgess, Leigh, and Co. (earthen.), Hill pottery, Market place
Burgess Hy., (earthen.), Kilncroft works
Cockson and Chetwynd, (earthenware), Cobridge
Collinson C. and Co. (earthenware), Newcastle street pottery
Corn W. and E. (earthen.), Navigation rd.
Davenport Wm. and Co., (china and earthenware,) Longport
Downing and Gilman (earthenware), Newport street
Edge, Malkin, and Co. (earthenware and lustre), Newport works
Edwards J. and Son (earthenware), Dalehall pottery
Furnival Thomas and Son (earthenware), Cobridge
Gater John (earthenware), Dalehall
Guest George (rockingham), Bleak street
Hallen Harding (creel steps), 29, Wellington street
Hammersley Ralph, earthenware & ironstone china), Overhouse pottery
Hancock, Whittingham, & Co., (earthenware), Swan bank works
Heath and Blackhurst (earthenware), Hadderidge pottery
Hobson Charles and Son (earthenware), Albert street
Holdcroft William (earthenware), 132, Liverpool road
Hope & Carter (earthen.), Fountain place
Hughes Thomas (earthen.), Waterloo rd.
Lawton John W. (creel steeps), North road
Leader Matthew, Portland works, Newcastle street
MacIntyre & Co. (door furniture), Washington works, Waterloo road
Maddock John and Sons (earthenware), Newcastle street
Malkin, Edge, and Co. (encaustic tile), Newport lane
Meakin Brothers (earthenware), Trent pottery, Peel street
Meakin and Co. (earthenware), Elder road, Cobridge
Meakin H. (earthenware), Abbey works, Sneyd green
Oulsnam William & Son (earthenware), Furlong works
Parr John (nest egg), Wellington street
Pearson Edward (earthen.), Sneyd green
Pinder, Bourne, and Co. (earthenware), Nile street works
Pope L.J. and Co. (earthenware), Sneyd green
Rathbone, Hill, and Co. (earthenware), Queen street pottery
Robinson & Co. (earthen.), Navigation rd.
Shaw Anthony (earthen.), Newport lane
Till and Sons (earthen.), Liverpool road
Tinsley, Bourne, and Co. (earthenware), Bourne's bank
Tomkinson and Son, (earthenware), Hamill road
Vernon James (earthen.), Waterloo road
Wade and Myatt (shuttle eye), Hall street
Wade & Colclough (rockingham), High st
Walley Wm. (rockingham), Nile street
Walley Wm. (earthenware), 66, Newcastle street
Whittingham, Ford, and Co., (earthenware), High street pottery
Wigley & Shirley (spur), Sylvester square
Williams, Turner, & Co. (rockingham), Albert street
Wilshaw and Wood (door furniture), Albert street
Withinshaw W.E. (earthenware), Crown works and Lyndhurst street
Wood and Baggaley, (earthenware), Hill works
Wood, Son, and Co., (earthenware), Villa pottery, Cobridge
Wood Brothers (rockingham), Chapel lane

Burslem – Tile (Floor) Makers (page 134)
Basford James Powell, Dalehall
Boote T. and R., Waterloo road
Malkin, Edge, and Co., Newport lane

Fenton – Potters (page 153)
Baker and Co. (earthenware), High street
Braodhurst James (earthenware), Victoria road
Challinor Edward and Charles (earthenware), Fenton pottery
Edwards John & Son (china and earthenware), King street
Gimson Joseph and Co., (spur manufacturers), Market street
Green M. & Co. (china), Minerva works, Park street
Hawley and Co. (earthenware), King street, Foley
Jackson and Gosling (china), Grosvenor works, Foley place
Malkin Ralph (earthenware), Park works, Market street
Pratt F. and R. and Co. (earthenware and terra cotta), Lower Fenton, High street
Pratt John and Co. (earthenware), Park street
Reeves James (earthenware), Victoria works, Market street
Robinson and Co., (china), King street), Foley
TAYLOR R. MINTON & CO. (tile), High street
Turner E. and Co. (china and earthenware), Old Foley pottery
Wileman and Shelley (china), Foley pottery
Wileman James F. (earthenware), Foley works

Fenton – Tile (Ornamental) Manufacturers (page 154)
TAYLOR R. MINTON & Co., High street

Hanley – Floor Tile Manufacturer (page 214)
Ridgway William Henry, Hanley, Stoke-upon-Trent (see advt.)

Hanley – Potters (page 223)
Adams John & Co. (parian and majolica), Broad street and St. James's street
Ash George (parian and majolica), Broad street (see advt)
Ashworth G.L. and Bros., (earthenware) Broad street
Bamford Jno. (jug & figure), Nelson place
Bennett J., (earthenware), Wharf lane Sheaf street
Bevington Ambrose (china), Great York st
Bevington John (parian), Broad street (see advt)
Bevington J. & T. (china & earthenware) Burton place, New st. and Cannon st.
Booth Thomas and Sons (earthenware) Brook street
Brown-Westhead, Moore, and Co. (china, earthenware, parian, and majolica), Cauldon place and Victoria square
Buckley James (sanitary ware), Vine st.
Buller & Co. (spurs & stilts), Joiner's sq.
Cartledge W.E. (stone & parian), Mayer street
Clementson Bros. (earthenware), Phoenix works, Broad street, and Bell works, George street
Cooke Robert (parian), Brewery street (see advt)

Davenport, Banks, and Co. (porus and fancy earthenware), Castlefield pottery, Bedford street (see advt)
Davis J.H. & J. (earthenware), Trent pottery
Dimmock John and Co. (earthenware), Stafford street
Dudson James (earthenware and parian), Hanover street (see advt)
Ford Charles (spur), Parker street
Ford Thomas (china), Cannon street
Ford Charles (china), Eastwood
Gelson Bros. (earthenware), High street
Holmes Charles, (earthenware), High st.
Holmes, Plant, and Whitehurst (door furniture), Nelson place
Howson George (sanitary ware), 9, Clifford street
Massey George (china), Tinkersclough
Meakin J. and G. (earthenware), Eagle Pottery, near Bucknall New road
Mills Edward (parian), George street
Oldham Jas. (earthenware), Renaleigh st.
Old Hall Earthenware Company Limited (earthenware, parian, and china), Hill street; Meigh C., manager
Pankhurst Jas. W. and Co. (white granite earthenware), Old Hall street
Powell & Bishop (china and earthenware), High street and Stafford street
Ridgway, Sparks, and Ridgway, (earthenware), Bedford place
Stanway, Horne, and Adams (parian) Eastwood vale
Stubbs William, (china and earthenware), Eastwood vale
Taylor, Tunnicliffe, and Co. (door furniture), Broad street
Taylor William (granite), Brook street
Twyford Thomas, Trustees of (earthenware and sanitary ware), Bath street
Wardle and Co. (parian and majolica), William street (see advt)
Wedgwood Josiah and Sons (earthenware) Etruria
Worthington and Son (earthenware), Brook street (see advt)
Worthington & Harrop (parian), Tinkersclough (see advt)

Longton – Potters (page 269-271)
Abberley James (china and earthenware), Market lane
Adams John (Exors. of), (china), High st
Adams Harvey & Co. (china and earthenware), Sutherland road
Adams and Cooper (china), High street
Allerton Charles & Sons (china, earthenware, and gold and silver lustre), Park works, High street
Amison and Edwards (earthenware), Russell street
Aynsley H. and Co. (earthenware), Commerce street (see advt)
Aynsley John (china), Sutherland road
Baddeley Elizabeth (rustic & terra cotta), 3 Commerce street
Baddeley J.H. (rustic and terra cotta), 34 Barker street
Baddeley Wm. (rustic and terra cotta), Drury works, Normacott road
Barker and Hill (china), King street
Barlow Thomas (china), Market street
Barlow T.W. (earthen.), Commerce street
Bates Frederick (flower pots, &c.), Weston coyney
Beech James & Son (china), High street and Sutherland road
Beech, Cooper, Till and Co. (china and earthenware), New street
Bentley Thomas and Co. (china), Church street
Betteney William (china & earthenware), Stafford street
Birks Thomas (china, earthenware, gold and silver lustre), High street
Brammall Edwin (china), Heathcote works, Heathcote road
Bridgewood Sampson & Son (china and earthenware), Anchor pottery, Sutherland road
Brough and Blackhurst (earthenware), Waterloo works, Stafford street
Cartwright and Edwards (earthenware), Borough pottery, Trentham road
Collingwood and Greatbatch (china), Crown works, Stafford street
Cooper and Nixon (earthenware), Viaduct works, Caroline street
Copestake George (china), Anchor works, Market street
Copestake and Allin (china), High street
Dale, Page & Co. (late Hopwood), (china), Church street (see advt)
Dawson James (earthenware), Commerce street (see advt)
Edge Wm. & Co. (parian and majolica), High street
Edwards George (china), Sheridan works, King street (see advt)
Ferneyhough John & Co. (china), Dresden works, Stafford street
Finney Joseph (china), Victoria works, Stafford street
Freeman W. and R. (china), High street
Green John (china), Stafford street
Grove and Stark (rustic, lustre, china and earthen.), Palissy works, Chancery lane
Hallam, Johnson & Co. (china), Mount pleasant, High street
Hammersley and Asbury (china), Sutherland road (see advt)
Hodson Richard (china), High street
Holdcroft Joseph (silver lustre), St. Martin's lane
Holland and Green (earthenware), Stafford street
Hudden J.T. (earthenware), Anchor works, Anchor road
Hulse and Adderley (china, earthenware, &c.), Daisy bank
Jones Fred. and Co. (earthenware), Chadwick street and Stafford street
Knight Joseph (china and earthenware), Market lane
Knight and Rowley (china and earthenware), Market street (see advt)
Lockett John (china, earthenware, and lustre), King st. & Market st. (see advt)
Lowe Thomas (earthenware), Gold street
Mason, Holt & Co. (china), Normacott rd.
Moore Bros. (china), St. Mary's works, High street
Poole and Unwin (earthenware, rustic and gold and silver lustre, parian, &c.), Cornhill works, Cornhill passage
Procter J. and H. and Co. (earthenware), New Town works, High street
Robinson & Co. (china), The Foley
Robinson, Chapman & Co. (china), Forrister street
Robinson, Repton, and Robinson (china), Wellington works, Stafford street
Shaw, Goldstraw, & Swift (fire brick and sanitary tube), Clayton st., Daisy bank

Skelson and Plant (china & earthenware), Heathcote road and Normacott road
Smith Sampson (china and gold and silver lustre and figure), Sutherland works, Barker street
Sutherland and Sons (parian, ivory, rustic, and terra cotta), Parkhall st., Anchor road (see advt)
Tams & Lowe (earthenware), High street
Taylor, Hudson, and Middleton (china), Chancery lane
Taylor William and Co. (patent stilt and spur), Church street
Turner E. and Co. (china & earthenware) Old Foley pottery (see advt)
Walker John (earthenware), High street
Walters & Hulse (china), Commerce st.
Webberley William (china), St James's works, High street
Yearsley George (parian and patentee of the gold astrakan trimming for decorating parian goods), Market lane

Stoke – Potters (page 358)
Copeland and Sons (china, earthenware and parian), High street
Hancock and Whittington (earthenware), Church street
Jones Geo. (earthenware), Trent pottery
Kirkham William (earthenware), London road; residence, The Villas
Minton and Co. (china, earthenware, and parian), London road
Minton, Hollins and Co. (encaustic tile), Church street
Robinson & Leadbeater (parian statuary), Wharf street
Turner and Poole (parian, earthenware, and china), Copeland street and Liverpool road
Turner and Poole (terra cotta and parian), Liverpool road
Walker and Carter (earthenware), Church street

Stoke – Tile (Floor) Makers (page 359)
Minton & Co., Church street
Minton Hollins and Co., Shelton old road

Tunstall – Potters (page 391)
Adams William (earthenware), Newfield pottery
Adams William & Thomas (earthenware), Greenfield pottery
Beech and Hancock (earthenware), Swan pottery, High street; res., Wolstanton
Blackhurst Richard (earthenware), High street; res., Wesley place
Booth Thomas and Son, High street; res., Windmill street
Brownhills Pottery Co., Brownhills
Clarke Edward (earthenware), High st.
Eardley, Spear, and Co. (earthenware), Well street
Ellsmore Thos. and Son (earthenware), Clayhills pottery
Emberton Thomas I. & James (earthenware), High gate pottery, Brownhills
Ford and Challinor (earthenware), Sandyford
Hammersley Ralph (rockingham and Egyptian black), High street
Holdcroft Willm. (earthenware), George st
Blackhurst Jabez (earthenware), Sandyford
Malpass Chas. (earthenware), Mill street
Meir John and Son (earthenware), Greengates
Procter John (earthenware), Madeley st.
Rhodes John (earthenware), King street
Turner George and Sons (earthenware), Victoria works, High street
Turner, Goddard, and Co., Royal Albert pottery, Parsonage street
Walker and Salt (china), High street
Wedgwood & Co. (earthenware), Unicorn pottery, Amicable street; and Pinnox works, Great Woodland street
Wood Edmund T.W. (earthenware), Woodland pottery, Woodland street

1875 Keates

Keates's Gazetteer & Directory of the Staffordshire Potteries, Newcastle and District. 1875-6, J. Keates, Printer and Publisher, Cheapside, Hanley (Shaw & Tipper 1233). Dated October 1875 in the Preface.

As with all the Keates series, this directory is classified within separate sections for each of the six pottery towns and the only relevant categories are potters and various types of tile manufacturers.

Burslem – Encaustic and Geometric Tile Pavement Manufacturers (page 133)
Basford James Powell, Dalehall
Boote Thomas and Richard, Waterloo rd.
Malkin, Edge and Co., Newport lane

Burslem – Floor Tile Works (page 133)
Basford James Powell, Dalehall

Burslem – Potters (pages 138-139)
Alcock Henry & Co. (earthenware), Cobridge works
Alcock Richard (earthenware), Central Pottery, Market place
Baker Charles G. (earthen.), Sylvester Pottery
Bates, Elliot & Co. (earthenware), Dalehall
Bates and Bennett, Sneyd street
Beech and Podmore (figure and toy), Bell Works, Queen street
Bodley Edwin F.D. (china), Hill Pottery
Bodley E.F. & Co. (earthenware), Scotia Works, Scotia road
Boote T. & R. (earthen), Waterloo road
Brownfield William & Son (earthenware and china), Cobridge
Brownhill Pottery Co. (earthenware), Brownhills
Burgess Leigh & Co. (earthenware), Hill Pottery, Market place
Burgess Henry (earthenware), Kilncroft works
Buckley, Wood & Co. (earthen.), High street Pottery
Cartledge W.E., Bourne's Bank

Cockson and Chetwynd (earthenware), Cobridge
Corn W.E. (earthen), Navigation road
Davenport Wm. & Co. (china and earthen.), Longport
Edge, Malkin & Co. (earthenware and lustre), Newport works
Edwards J. & Son (earthenware), Dale Hall Pottery
Furnival Thos. & Son (earthen.), Cobridge
Gaskell, Son & Co. (door furniture), Crown works, Market place
Hallen Harding (creel steps), 29, Wellington street
Hammersley Ralph (earthenware and ironstone china), Overhouse pottery
Heath and Blackhurst (earthenware), Hadderidge pottery
Hobson Charles & Son (earthenware), Albert street
Holdcroft William (earthenware), 132, Liverpool road
Hollinshead and Kirkham, New Wharf pottery, Navigation street
Hope & Carter (earthen.), Fountain place
Hughes Thos. (earthen.), Waterloo road
Isaac and Son, Bleak Hill works
Lawton John W. (creel steps), North road
McIntyre & Co. (door furniture), Washington works, Waterloo road
Maddock John and Sons (earthenware), Newcastle street
Maddock and Gater (earthen,), Dalehall pottery
Malkin, Edge, & Co. (encaustic tile), Newport lane
Meakin & Co. (earthenware), Elder road, Cobridge
Meakin H. (earthenware), Abbey works, Sneyd green
Meakin Charles (earthen.), Furlong lane
Oulsnam William and Son (earthenware), Furlong works
Parr John (nest egg), Wellington street
Pinder, Bourne, and Co. (earthenware), Nile street works
Pope L.J. and Co. (earthenware), Lincoln works, Sneyd green
Rathbone, Hill, and Co. (earthenware), Queen street pottery
Robinson & Co. (earthen), Navigation rd.
Shaw Anthony (earthen), Newport lane
Thomas, Rathbone, Oakley, & Co, (Rockingham ware), Wellington works, Newport street
Till and Sons (earthen.), Liverpool road
Tinsley, Bourne, and Co. (earthenware), Bourne's bank
Tundley, Rhodes, and Pinder (earthen.), Swan Bank works
Vernon James and Son (earthenware), Waterloo road
Wade and Myatt (shuttle eye and creel step), Hall street
Walley Wm. (rockingham), Nile street
Wade & Colclough (rockingham), Bourne's Bank
Wigley and Shirley (spur), Sylvester square
Williams, Oakes, and Co. (rockingham), Albert street
Withinshaw W.E. (earthenware), Commercial street
Wood & Co. (earthenware), Albert street
Wood and Baggaley (earthenware), Hill works
Wood, Son, and Co. (earthenware), Villa pottery, Cobridge

Burslem – Tile (Floor) Makers (page 140)
Basford James Powell, Dalehall
Boote T. and R., Waterloo road
Malkin, Edge, and Co., Newport lane

Fenton – Potters (pages 158-159)
Baker and Co. (earthenware), High street
Broadhurst James (earthenware), Victoria road
Bridgwood Samuel (earthenware), Old Foley pottery, Foley
Challinor Edward and Charles (earthenware), Fenton pottery, High street
Edwards John and Co. (china and earthenware), King street
Gimson Joseph and Co. (spur manufacturers), Market street
Green M. and Co. (china), Minerva works, Park street
Hawley and Co. (earthenware), King street, Foley
Jackson and Gosling (china), Grosvenor works, Foley place
Malkin Ralph (earthenware), Park works, Market street
Pratt F. and R. and Co. (earthenware and terra cotta), Lower Fenton and High street east
Pratt John and Co. (earthenware), Park street
Reeves James (earthenware), Victoria works, Market street
Robinson William and Co. (china), King street, Foley
Wileman and Shelley (china), Foley pottery
Wileman James F. (earthenware), Foley works

Hanley – Floor Tile Manufacturers (page 222)
Evans William L., Hall Field works
Ridgway, Wooliscroft, and Co., Encaustic Tile works, Eastwood, Hanley, Stoke-upon-Trent
Steele and Wood (glazed encaustic hearth tiles), Eastwood

Hanley – Potters (pages 232-233)
Adams and Bromley (jasper and majolica), Victoria works, Broad street
Ash George (parian and majolica), Broad street (see advt.)
Ashworth G.L. and Bros. (china and earthenware), Broad street
Bale and Co. (porous and general earthenware), Castle Field pottery, off Newcastle road
Bamford John (jug and teapot), Nelson place
Banks and Thorley (majolica), New street
Bennett J. (earthenware), Wharf lane, Sheaf street
Bennison Arthur (rockingham ware), Lichfield street
Bevington Ambrose (china and earthenware), Clarence street works
Bevington John (parian), St. James's street
Bevington J. & T. (china & earthenware), Burton place, New st. and Cannon st.
Booth Thomas and Sons (earthenware), Brook street
Bradshaw and Binns (china), Clarence st.
Brown-Westhead, Moore, and Co. (china, earthenware, parian, and majolica), Cauldon place and Victoria square
Buckley John (sanitary ware), Vine street
Buller and Co. (spurs and stilts), Joiner's square
Clementson Bros. (earthenware), Phoenix works, Broad street, and Bell works, George street
Cooke Robert (parian), Brewery street
Davis J.H. and J. (earthenware), Trent pottery
Dimmock John and Co. (earthenware), Albion works, Stafford street
Dudson James (earthenware and parian), Hanover street
Ford Charles (spur), Parker street
Ford Charles (china), Cannon street

Gelson Bros. (earthenware), High street
Harrop William (parian and earthenware), Tinkersclough
Holmes Charles (earthenware), High street
Holmes, Plant, and Whitehurst (door furniture), Nelson place
Howson George (sanitary ware), Eastwood vale
Machin William (earthenware and figure), Percy street
Meakin J. and G. (earthenware), Eagle pottery, near Bucknall New road
Mills Edward G. (parian), George street
Neale, Harrison and Co. (china and earthenware), Elm street
Oldham James and Co. (earthenware), Renalagh street
Old Hall Earthenware Company Limited (earthenware, parian, and china), Hill street; Meigh C., manager
Pankhurst Jas. W. and Co. (white granite earthenware), Old Hall street
Powell & Bishop (china and earthenware), High street and Stafford street
Pugh and Glover, Waterloo works, Nelson place
Ridgway, Sparks, and Ridgway, (earthenware), Bedford place
Scrivener R.G. and Co. (china), Norfolk street
Stanway, Horne, and Adams (parian), Eastwood vale
Steele Edward (earthenware), Cannon street works
Stubbs William (china and earthenware), Eastwood vale
Taylor, Tunnicliffe, and Co. (door furniture), Broad street
Turner and Co. (earthenware), Mayer street
Twyford Thomas, Trustees of (earthenware and sanitary ware), Bath street
Wardle and Co. (parian and majolica), William street
Wedgwood Josiah and Sons (earthenware), Etruria
Worthington and Son (earthenware), Brook street (see advt)

Longton – Potters (pages 281-282)
Adams Harvey & Co. (china and earthenware), Sutherland road
Adams and Cooper (china), High street
Allerton Charles & Sons (china, earthenware, and gold and silver lustre), Park works, High street
Asbury Edward and Co. (china), Sutherland road (see advt)
Aynsley H. and Co. (earthenware), Commerce street
Aynsley John (china), Sutherland road
Baddeley Elizabeth (rustic & terra cotta), 3, Commerce street
Baddeley J.H. (rustic and terra cotta), 34, Barker street
Baddeley Wm. (rustic and terra cotta), Drury works, Normacott road
Barlow Thomas (china), Market street
Barlow T.W. (earthen.), Commerce street
Bates Frederick (flower pots, &c.), Weston Coyney
Beech James & Son (china), High street, and Sutherland road
Birks Thomas and Co. (china, earthenware, gold and silver lustre), High st
Brammall Edwin (china), Heathcote works, Heathcote road
Bridgett, Bates, and Beech (china), King street
Bridgewood Sampson & Son (china and earthenware), Anchor pottery, Sutherland road
Bridgewood Samuel, (earthenware), Old Foley pottery
Brough and Blackhurst (earthenware), Waterloo works, Stafford street
Brown and Co. (china), Church street pottery
Cartwright and Edwards (earthenware) Borough pottery, Trentham road
Collingwood and Greatbatch (china), Crown works, Stafford street
Cooper and Nixon (earthenware), Viaduct works, Caroline street
Cooper, Till and Co. (china and earthenware), New street
Copestake George (china), Anchor works, Market street
Copestake and Allin (china), High street
Dale, Page & Co. (late Hopwood) (china), Church street (see advt)
Dawson James (earthenware), Stafford street
Edwards Wm. (earthenware), Russell st
Edwards George (china), Sheridan works, King street
Ferneyhough John & Co. (china), Dresden works, Stafford street, and Normacott road
Finney Joseph (china), Victoria works, Stafford street
Freeman W. and Co. (china), High st
Green John (china), Stafford street
Grove and Stark (rustic, lustre, china and earthen), Palissy works, Chancery lane
Hallam, Johnson & Co. (china), Mount Pleasant, High street
Hodson Richard (china), High street
Holdcroft Joseph (silver lustre), St. Martin's lane
Holland and Green (earthenware), Stafford street
Hudden J.T. (earthenware), Anchor works, Anchor road
Hudson and Son (earthenware), Stafford street
Hulse and Adderley (china, earthenware, &c.), Daisy bank
Jones Fred. and Co. (earthenware), Chadwick street
Johnson John Lorenzo (china), High st
Knight and Rowley (china and earthenware), Market street (see advt)
Lockett John (china, earthenware, and lustre), King st. & Market st. (see advt)
Lowe Mrs. Thos. (earthenware), Gold st
Lowe William (earthenware), High street (see advt)
Moore Bros. (china), St. Mary's works, High street
Poole and Unwin (earthenware, rustic and gold and silver lustre, &c.), Cornhill works, Cornhill Passage
Proctor J. and H. and Co. (earthenware), New Town works, High street
Radford, Amison, and Perkins (china), Chancery lane
Robinson and Co. (china), The Foley
Robinson and Chapman (china), Royal Porcelain works
Robinson, Repton, and Robinson (china), Wellington works, Stafford street
Shaw, Goldstraw, & Swift (fire brick and sanitary tube), Clayton st., Daisy bank
Skelson and Plant (china & earthenware), Heathcote road and Normacott road
Smith Sampson (china and gold and silver lustre and figure), Sutherland works, Barker street
Sutherland and Sons (parian, ivory, rustic, and terra cotta), Parkhall street, Anchor road (see advt)
Tams John (earthenware), Crown pottery, Stafford street
Taylor, Hudson, and Middleton (china), Chancery lane
Taylor Wm. and Co. (patent stilt and spur), Church street
Walker John (earthenware), High street

Walters Thomas (china), Commerce street
Webberley William (china), St. James's works, High street
Yearsley Geo. & Co. (parian and patentee of the gold astrakan trimming for decorating parian goods), Market lane

Stoke – Potters (page 374)
Billington and Co., Copeland street
Copeland and Sons (china, earthenware, and parian), High street
Hancock and Whittington (earthenware), Church street
Jones Geo. (earthenware), Trent pottery
Kirkham William (earthenware), London road; residence, The Villas
Minton and Co. (china, earthenware, and parian), London road
Minton, Hollins, and Co. (encaustic tile), Church street
Robinson & Leadbeater (parian statuary), Wharf street (see advt.)
Poole, Stanway, and Wood (parian, earthenware, and china), Copeland street and Liverpool road
Walker and Carter (earthenware), Church street

Stoke – Tile (Floor) Manufacturers (page 375)
Campbell Brick and Tile Company – R. Minton Taylor, manager (see advt.)
Minton, Hollins and Co., Shelton Old rd.

Tunstall – Potters (pages 411-412)
Adams William (earthenware), Newfield pottery
Adams William & Thomas (earthenware), Greenfield pottery
Beech and Hancock (earthenware), Swan pottery, High street
Blackhurst Richard (earthenware), High street; residence, Wesley place
Blackhurst Jabez (earthenware), Sandyford
Booth Thomas and Son, High street; residence, Windmill street
Brownhills Pottery Co., Brownhills
Clarke Edward (earthenware), High street
Clive Stephen (earthenware), Well street
Elsmore Thomas and Son (earthenware), Clayhills pottery
Emberton Thomas I. and James (earthenware), Highgate pottery, Brownhills
Ford and Challinor (earthenware), Sandyford
Guest George (earthenware), High street
Hammersley Ralph (Rockingham and Egyptian black), High street
Holdcroft Wm. (earthenware), George st.
Meakin Alfred (earthenware), Parsonage st
Meir John and Son (earthenware), Greengates
Procter John (earthenware), Madeley st.
Turner George W. and Sons (earthenware), Victoria Works, High street
Wedgwood & Co. (earthenware), Unicorn pottery, Amicable street; and Pinnox works, Great Woodland street
Wood Edmund T.W. (earthenware), Woodland pottery, Woodland street

1876 Kelly

The Post Office Directory of Birmingham, Staffordshire, Warwickshire, and Worcestershire (also *The Post Office Directory of Staffordshire*), Printed and Published by Kelly & Co., 51 Great Queen Street, Lincoln's Inn Fields, London WC (Shaw & Tipper 6, Shaw & Tipper 1222). Dated MDCCCLXXVI on the title page and November 1876 in the Preface. It is noted as the Eighth Edition in the Preface.

As with all the Kelly's series, this directory contains alphabetical lists for the various towns and villages and also classified lists for each county. Only the classified lists are included here. The range of categories is extensive and there are twenty-five relevant to this work.

Artists' China Palette Manufacturers (page 418)
Macintyre James & Co. Washington works, Waterloo road, Burslem

Beer Engine Handle Maker (page 422)
Buckley John, Albert works, Victoria place, Hanley

China Manufacturers (pages 455-456)
See also Earthenware Manufacturers.
Adams & Cooper, High street, Longton
Adams Harvey & Co. Sutherland road, Longton
Adderley William Alsager, Daisy Bank works, Longton
Allerton Chas. & Co. High st. Longton
Asbury E. & Co. Sutherland rd. Longton
Ashworth George L. & Brothers, Broad street, Hanley
Aynsley John, Sutherland road, Longton
Barlow Alfred, Cyples Old pottery, Market street, Longton
Beech James & Sons, Albert & Sutherland works, Longton
Beech & Podmore, Cobridge, Burslem
Bevington Jas. & Thos. Burton pl. Hanley
Bevington Ambrose, Gt. York st. Hanley
Birks Thomas & Co. 3 High st. Longton
Bodley Edwin J.D. Hill pottery, Burslem
Bradley Frederick Douglas, Elkin works, Longton
Bridgett, Bates & Co. King st. Longton
Brown-Westhead (T.C.), Moore & Co. Cauldon pl. & Victoria works, Hanley; & FitzEylwin house, Holborn viaduct, London e.c
Burton, Morris & Co. Bagnall st. Longton
Collingwood & Greatbatch, Stafford street, Longton
Cooper, Till & Co. New street, Longton
Copeland William Taylor & Sons, High street, Stoke-on-Trent; & at 160 New Bond street, London w
Copestake A. & Co. Alma works, Longton
Copestake G. jun. Anchor wrks. Longton
Dale, Page & Goodwin, New Town pottery, High street, Longton
Dean, Lowe, Machin & Shorter, Parker street, Hanley

Derbyshire William Henry & Co. Heathcote works, Longton
Edwards George, King street, Longton
Ferneyhough John, Stafford st. Longton
Finney Joseph, Victoria works, Longton
Ford Charles, Cannon street, Hanley
Freeman Walter, High street, Longton
Goss W.H. London rd. Stoke-on-Trent
Green F.A. & S. Park street, Fenton, Stoke-on-Trent
Green Thomas & Co. Park street, Fenton, Stoke-on-Trent
Green John, Stafford street, Longton
Hallam, Johnson & Co. Mount Pleasant, High street, Longton
Hammersley J. & R. New st. Hanley
Hodson & Co. High street, Longton
Jackson & Gosling, King street, Fenton, Stoke-on-Trent
Jenkins, Porton & Co. Copeland street, Stoke-on-Trent
Johnson John L. 23 High st. Longton
KENT JOHN & SONS, Market place, Longton, Stoke-on-Trent; (established 1847). Home & export orders to any extent promptly executed
Knight & Rowley, Market st. Longton
Mason, Holt & Co. Normacott rd. Longtn
Massey George, Mayer street, Hanley
Mellor George & Joshua, Hamill street, Burslem; & Fenton whf. Stke.on-Trnt
Minton's China Works, Stoke-on-Trent; & 28 Walbrook, London e.c
Moor Brothers, High street, Longton
Poole, Stanway & Wood, Copeland street, Stoke-on-Trent
Radford & Amison, Chancery la. Longton
Ridgemeigh & Co. Church st. Longton
Robinson & Chapman, Royal wks. Lngtn
Robinson, Repton & Robinson, Stafford street, Longton
Robinson & Co. Foley, Fenton, Stoke-on-Trent
Scrivener R.G. & Co. Norfolk st. Hanley
Skelson & Plant, Heathcote rd. Longton
Smith Sampson, Barker street, Longton
Taylor Hudson & Middleton, Chancery Lane works, Longton
Taylor & Kent, Florence works, High street, Longton; for home & export
Walters Peter A. Commerce st. Longton
Webberley Wm. St. James's pl. Longton
Wedgwood Josiah & Sons, Etruria pottery, Stoke-on-Trent
Wileman & Co. Foley potteries, Fenton, Stoke-on-Trent

China Letter Makers (page 456)
Macintyre James & Co. Washington works, Waterloo road, Burslem

Creel Step Manufacturer (page 466)
Hallen Harding, Wellington st. Burslem

Druggists' Stoneware Manufacturers (pagé 471)
Booth Thomas & Sons, New Hall pottery, Great York street, Hanley
Brown-Westhead (T.C.), Moore & Co. Cauldon place & Victoria works, Hanley; & FitzEylwin house, Holborn viaduct, London e.c

Earthenware Manufacturers (pages 471-472)
See also China Manufacturers.
Adams William & Thomas, Tunstall
Adams William, Greenfield, Tunstall
Adderley W.A. Daisy Bank works, Longtn
Alcock Henry & Co. Cobridge, Burslem
Alcock Richard, Market place, Burslem
Ashworth G.L. & Bros. Broad st. Hanley
Aynsley & Co. Chancery lane & Sutherland road, Longton
Baddeley & Heath (engravers), Liverpool road, Burslem
Baker & Co. Fenton, Stoke-on-Trent
Bale & Co. Newcastle road, Hanley
Bamford John, Nelson place, Hanley
Barker Brothers, Gold street, Longton
Barlow Thomas W. Commerce st. Longton
Bates & Bennett, Cobridge, Burslem
Bates Walker & Co. Dale hall, Burslem
Beech & Hancock, Swan bank, Tunstall
Bennett Joseph, Wharf lane, Hanley
Bennett William, Brook street, Hanley
Bevington John, Broad street, Hanley
Birks Thomas & Co. High st. Longton
Blackhurst Jabez, Sandyford, Tunstall
Blackhurst Richard, High st. Tunstall
Bodley E.F. & Co. Scotia wrks. Burslem
Booth Thomas & Son, Church Bank pottery, Tunstall
Booth Thomas & Sons, New Hall pottery, Great York street, Hanley
Bridgwood S. & Son, East vale, Longton
Broadhurst James, Portland pottery, Fenton, Stoke-on-Trent
Brough & Blackhurst, Waterloo works, Longton
Brown & Co. Church street, Longton
Brown-Westhead (T.C.), Moore & Co. Cauldon place & Victoria works, Hanley; & FitzEylwin house, Holborn viaduct, London e.c
Brownfield W. & Sons, Cobridge, Burslem
Brownhills Pottery Company (The), Tunstall
Buckley, Wood & Co. High Street pottery, Burslem
Burgess, Leigh & Co. Hill pottery, Burslem
Burgess Hy. Kiln Croft works, Burslem
Cartlidge W.E. Bourne's bank, Burslem
Cartwright & Edwards, Trentham road, Longton
Challinor Edward & Charles, High st. Fenton; & Glebe st. Stoke-on-Trent
Clarke Edward, High street, Tunstall
Clementson Brothers, Phoenix & Bell works, Hanley
Clive Stephen & Co. Well st. Tunstall
Cockson & Seddon, Cobridge, Burslem
Cooper & Dethick, Caroline st. Longton
Copeland William Taylor & Sons, High street, Stoke-on-Trent; & at 160 New Bond street, London w
Corn William & Edward, Navigation Road pottery, Burslem
Cotton & Rigby, Sylvester sq. Burslem
Davenport William & Co. Longport, Burslem; warehouses, 82 Fleet street, London e.c.; & 30 Canning pl. L'pool

Davies J.H. Trent pottery, Hanley
Dawson James, Stafford street, Longton
Dean, Lowe, Machin & Shorter, Parker street, Hanley
Dimmock John & Co. Stafford st. Hanley
Dudson James, Hanover street, Hanley
Edge, Malkin & Co. Newport works, Burslem. See advertisement
Edwards, James & Son, Dale Hall pottery, Burslem
Edwards Wm. Lockett's lane, Longton
Elsmore Thomas & Son, Clay Hills pottery, Tunstall
Emberton T.J. & J. Highgate pottery, Tunstall
Everill Henry, King street, Hanley
Finney Joseph, Victoria works, Longton
Ford & Challinor, Sandyford, Tunstall
Furnival Thos. & Sons, Cobridge, Burslem
Gaskell James, Son & Co. Crown works, Market place, Burslem
Gelson Thomas & Co. High st. Hanley
Grove & Stark, Palissy works, Longton
Guest George, Soho pottery, Tunstall
Hammersley Ralph, Wedgwood place, Burslem; & at High street, Tunstall
Hancock Benjamin & Sampson, Church street, Stoke-on-Trent
Harrop William, Tinkersclough, Hanley
Hawley & Co. Foley, Fenton, Stoke-on-Trent
Heath & Blackhurst, Hadderidge pottery, Burslem
Hobson Charles, Albert street, Burslem
Holdcroft William, George st. Tunstall
Holland & Green, Stafford st. Longton
Hollinshead & Kirkham, Woodland pottery, Tunstall
Holmes, Plant & Madew, Sylvester pottery, Burslem
Holmes Charles, High street, Hanley
Hope & Carter, Fountain pl. Burslem
Hudden John Thos. Stafford st. Longton
Hughes Thomas, Waterloo road & Longport, Burslem
Jones Fredk. & Co. Chadwick st. Longton
Jones George & Sons, London road, Stoke-on-Trent
Kent John & Sons, Market place, Longton, Stoke-on-Trent. (Established 1847.) Home & export orders to any extent promptly executed
Kirkham W. London rd. Stoke-on-Trent
Lea & Co. John street, Stoke-on-Trent
Lear James, High street, Hanley
Lockett Jhn., King st. & Market st. Longtn
Lowe William, High street, Longton; manufacturer of drab turquoise, buff printed & gilt wares for home & export
Maddock & Co. Dale Hall pottery, Burslm
Maddock J. & Sons, Newcastle st. Burslem
Malkin Ralph, Fenton, Stoke-on-Trent
Meakin & Co. Cobridge, Burslem
Meakin J. & G. Eagle pottery, Hanley
Meakin J. & G. 16 Glebe st. Stoke-on-Trent
Meakin Charles, Trent pottery, Burslem
Meakin Hy. Sneyd st. Cobridge, Burslem
Meakin A. Royal Albert pottery, Tunstall
Meir J. & Son, Greengate pottery, Tunstall
Mellor George & Joshua, Fenton wharf, Stoke-on-Trent, & Hamiltn. rd. Burslm
Minton's China Works, Stoke-on-Trent; & 28 Walbrook, London e.c
Minton & Co. Eldon place, Stoke-on-Trent; & 28 Walbrook, London e.c
Old Hall Earthenware Company Limited, Hill street, Hanley
Oldham & Co. Ranelagh street, Hanley
Oulsnam William & Son, Furlong works, Burslem
Pankhurst James William & Co. Old Hall street, Hanley
Pinder, Bourne & Co. Nile Street works, Burslem
Poole & Unwin, Cornhill passage, Longton
Pope L.J. & Co. Sneyd st. Cobridg. Burslm
Powell & Bishop, Stafford street, High street & Parliament row, Hanley
Pratt & Co. Lane Delph, Fenton, Stoke-on-Trent
Pratt Felix & Richard & Co. High street east, Fenton, Stoke-on-Trent
Procter John & Henry, Heathcote pottery, Longton
Pugh & Glover, Dresden mills, Hanley
Reeves J. Market st. Fentn. Stoke-on-Trnt
RIDGWAY, SPARKS & RIDGWAY, Bedford works, Stoke-on-Trent. London Showrooms, 8 Thavie's inn. Manufacturers of all kinds of earthenware for home & export, also of jasper, porous jet goods & stone ware
Robinson Jsph. Knowle works, Burslem
Sant Jeremiah (decorator), 98 Waterloo road, Burslem
Shaw Anthony, Mersey works, Burslem
Steele Edward, Cannon street, Hanley
Stubbs Wm. Eastwood pottery, Hanley
Tams John, Crown pottery, Stafford street, Longton
Till Thos. & Sons, Liverpool rd. Burslem
Tinsley & Bourne, Queen st. Burslem
Tundley, Rhodes & Procter, Swan bank, Burslem
Turner G.W. & Sons, Victoria works, & Soho mills, Tunstall
Vernon J. & Son, Watrloo. pottery, Burslm
Walker & Carter, Chrch. st. Stoke-on-Trnt
Walker John, 31 High street, Longton
Watts & Co. (finishers), High st. Fenton
Wedgwood & Co. Pinnox & Unicorn works, Tunstall
Wedgwood Josiah & Sons, Etruria pottery, Etruria, Stoke-on-Trent
Whittingham, Ford & Riley, Newcastle street, Burslem
Wileman James F. Foley works, Fenton, Stoke-on-Trent
Wittinshaw Wm. Ed. Church st. Burslem
Wood & Baggaley, Hill works, Burslem
Wood, Son & Co. Cobridge, Burslem
Wood W. & Co. Albert st. works, Burslem
Worthington & Son, Brook st. Hanley

Encaustic Tile Manufacturers (page 472)
Boote Thomas & Richard, Waterloo potteries, Burslem
CAMPBELL BRICK & TILE COMPANY (THE), Stoke-on-Trent; manufacturers of encaustic geometrical & majolica tiles & mosaics; Robert Minton Taylor, manager. – London houses, 206 Gt. Portland st. w. & 27 Walbrook e.c
Hanley Plain & Encaustic Tile Co. Limited, Havelock works, Hanley

Malkin, Edge & Co. Newport works, Burslem.
See advertisement
Minton, Hollins & Co.'s patent tile works, Stoke-on-Trent; & Minton & Co. 50 Conduit street, Regent st. London w
Minton & Co. Eldon place, Stoke-on-Trent; & 28 Walbrook, London e.c
Woolliscroft George & Son, Chesterton, Newcastle

Inkstand Manufacturers (page 516)
Taylor, Tunnicliff & Co. Eastwood works, Hanley

Lock Furniture Makers – China (page 527)
Buller & Co. Joiner's Square works, Hanley; Sherlock street, Birmingham; & 132 Upper Thames street, London e.c
Macintyre James & Co. Washington works, Waterloo road, Burslem
Taylor, Tunnicliff & Co. Eastwood works, Hanley

Lustre Manufacturers (page 528)
Holdcroft Joseph, Daisy bank, Longton

Majolica Manufacturers (page 528)
Adams & Bromley, Broad street, Hanley
Booth Thomas & Sons, New Hall pottery, Great York street, Hanley
Copeland William Taylor & Sons, High street, Stoke-upon-Trent; & 160 New Bond street, London w
Dean, Lowe, Machin & Shorter, Parker street, Hanley
Evans & Foulkes, Marsh street, Hanley
Hall William, Newcastle road, Hanley
Minton's China Works, Stoke-on-Trent; & 28 Walbrook, London e.c
Wardle & Co. William street, Hanley

Mortar & Pestle Manufacturer (page 533)
Kirkham Wm. London rd. Stoke-on-Trent

Parian Manufacturers (page 537)
Ash George, Broad street, Hanley
Banks & Thorley, New street, Hanley
Cooke Robert, Brewery street, Hanley
Copeland Wm. Taylor & Sons, High street, Stoke-on-Trent, & 160 New Bond street, London w
Goss Wm. H. London rd. Stoke-on-Trent
Hartley & Co. High street, Longton
Mills William, 1 George street, Hanley
Minton & Co. Eldon place, Stoke-on-Trent; & 28 Walbrook, London e.c
Nixon Joseph, Market lane, Longton
Robinson & Leadbeater, 49 Wharf street & Glebe street, Stoke-on-Trent
Stanway, Horne & Adams, Fenton road, Hanley
Yearsley Mrs. M.A. Market la. Longton

Pot Step Maker (page 541)
Bold Henry, King street, Hanley

Potters (page 541)
Tams John, Crown pottery, Stafford st. Longton

Rockingham Ware Manufacturers (page 559)
Gibson, Sudlow & Lewis, Bourne's bank, Burslem
Oakes, Clare & Chadwick, Albert street, Burslem
Thomas, Rathbone, Oakley & Co. Newport street, Burslem
Wade & Colclough, High st. Burslem
Walley William, Nile street, Burslem

Sanitary Ware Manufacturers (page 561)
Alcock & Forshaw, Railway tileries, Fenton, Stoke-on-Trent
Buckley John, Albert works, Victoria place, Hanley
Howson George, Eastwood, Hanley
Twyford Thomas, Bath street, Hanley

Shuttle Eye Manufacturers (page 577)
Hallen Harding, Wellington st. Burslem
Wade & Myatt, Hall street, Burslem

Spur and Stilt Makers for Pottery Manufacturers (page 583)
Ford Charles, Parker street, Hanley
Gimson J. & Co. Fenton, Stoke-on-Trent
Taylor Wm. & Co. Church st. Longton
Wigley & Sherley, Moorland rd. Burslem

Stone Mortar & Pestle Manufacturers (page 585)
Buller & Co. Joiners' Square works, Hanley; Sherlock street, Birmingham & 132 Up. Thames st. London e.c
Macintyre James & Co. Washington works, Waterloo road, Burslem

Terra Cotta Manufacturers (page 590)
Goss W.H. London rd. Stoke-on-Trent
Harrison & Baker, George street, Newcastle; & Sheltn. New rd. Stke.-on-Trnt
Kirkham W. London rd. Stoke-on-Trnt

Tiles – Enamelled (page 590)
Minton's China Works, Stoke-on-Trent; & 28 Walbrook, London e.c

Water Closet Makers (page 596)
Buckley John, Albert works, Victoria place, Hanley

White Granite Manufacturer (page 598)
Edwards J. King st. Fenton, Stk.-on-Trnt

1878 Kelly

The Post Office (or Kelly's) Directory of Birmingham, Staffordshire, Warwickshire, and Worcestershire. Kelly & Co., 51 Great Queen Street, Lincoln's Inn Fields, London WC. This directory is not listed by Shaw & Tipper but must be related to their number 1441.

This directory is listed here for completeness only. The only copy located is in the Central Library, Birmingham, and has no title page. While it is dated 1878 on the rebound spine, and contains an advert which is also dated 1878, the Staffordshire section appears to be purely a reprint of the 1876 directory, presumably issued with an updated Birmingham section. As such, in order to avoid misleading data in this work, the entries are neither repeated here nor included in the alphabetical list of manufacturers.

1879 Keates

Keates's Gazetteer & Directory of the Staffordshire Potteries, Newcastle and District. 1879, J. Keates & Co., Printers and Publishers, Hanley (Shaw & Tipper 1233). Dated April 1879 in the Preface.

As with all the Keates series, this directory is classified within separate sections for each of the six pottery towns and the only relevant categories are potters and various types of tile manufacturers.

Burslem – Encaustic and Geometric Tile Pavement Manufacturers (pages 138-139)
Basford James Powell, Dalehall
Boote Thomas & Richard, Waterloo road
Malkin, Edge and Co., Newport lane

Burslem – Floor Tile Works (page 139)
Basford James Powell, Dalehall
Boote Thomas and Richard, Waterloo rd.
Malkin, Edge, and Co., Newport lane

Burslem – Potters (pages 144-145)
Alcock Henry & Co. (earthenware), Cobridge works
Alcock Richard (earthenware), Central Pottery, Market place
Bates, Gildea and Walker (earthenware), Dalehall, Burslem, and 30, Holborn, London
Bates and Bennett (earthenware) Sneyd street
Birks and Seddon (earthenware), Cobridge
Blackhurst and Tunnicliffe, (earthenware) Hadderidge pottery
Bodley Edwin J.D,, (china) Hill Pottery
Bodley E.F. & Co. (earthenware) Scotia Works, Scotia road
Boote T. & R. (earthen) Waterloo road
Brownfield William & Sons (earthenware and china), Cobridge
Brownhill Pottery Co. (earthenware), Brownhills
Buckley, Wood & Co. (earthen.), High street Pottery
Burgess, Leigh & Co. (earthenware), Hill Pottery, Market place
Burgess Henry (earthenware), Kilncroft works
Cartledge W.E. (earthen.), Bourne's bank
Clarke Edward (earthenware), Longport
Corn W.E. (earthen), Navigation road
Davenport Wm. & Co. (china & earthen.), Longport
Edwards J. & Son (earthenware), Dalehall Pottery
Emery Francis J. (earthenware), Wood street
Emberton James (earthenware), Brownhills
Emberton Thomas J. (earthenware), Brownhills
Furnival Thos. & Son (earthen.), Cobridge
Gaskell, Son & Co. (door furniture), Crown works, Market place
Gibson, Lewis and Ludlow (rockingham), Bourne's bank
Hallen Harding (creel steps), 29, Wellington street
Hammersley Ralph (earthenware and ironstone china), Overhouse Pottery
Heath Thomas and James (rockingham), Podmoee street
Hobson John and George (earthenware), Albert street
Holdcroft William (earthenware) 132, Liverpool road
Holmes, Plant and Maydew (earthenware), Silvester Pottery
Hope & Carter (earthen.), Fountain place
Hughes Thos. (earthen), Waterloo road
Hulme Henry (rockingham) Kilncroft
Lawton John W. (creel steps), North road
Maddock John and James (earthenware), Newcastle street
Maddock J. & J., (earthen.), Dalehall Pottery
Malkin, Edge & Co. (encaustic tile), Newport lane
Meakin Charles (earthen.), Furlong lane and Cobridge
Oakes, Clure and Chadwick, Albert street
Oulsnam William and Son (earthenware) Furlong works
Parr John (nest egg), Wellington street
Pinder, Bourne and Co. (earthenware), Nile street works
Pope L.J. and Co. (earthenware), Lincoln works, Sneyd green
Rathbone, Hill and Co. (earthenware), Queen street pottery
Robinson & Co. (earthen.), Knowles works
Shaw Anthony (earthen.), Mersey Pottery, Newport lane
Thomas, Brooks, Chesters, & Co., (Rockingham ware) Wellington works, Newport street
Till and Sons (earthen.), Liverpool road
Tinsley, Bourne, and Co. (earthenware), Queen street
Tundley, Rhodes, and Pinder (earthen.), Swan Bank works
Vernon James and Son (earthenware), Waterloo road
Wade and Myatt (shuttle eye and creel step), Hall street
Walley Wm. (rockingham), Nile street
Wade and Colclough (rockingham) Bourne's bank
Whittingham, Ford and Riley (earthenware), Newcastle street
Wigley and Shirley (spur), Sylvester sq.
Wood and Co. (earthenware), Navigation road
Wood William & Co. (door furniture), Albert street
Wood and Baggaley (earthenware), Hill works
Wood, Son and Co. (earthenware), Villa pottery, Cobridge
Woodall and Hulme (china, porcelain, and door furniture) Washington Works, Waterloo road

Burslem – Tile (Floor) Makers (page 146)
Basford James Powell, Dalehall

Boote T. and R. Waterloo road
Malkin, Edge, & Co., Newport lane

Fenton – Potters (page 165)
Baker and Co. (earthenware), High street
Broadhurst James (earthenware), Victoria road
Challinor E. and C. (earthenware), Fenton pottery, High street
Edwards John and Co. (china and earthenware), King street
Gimson Josepn and Co. (spur manufacturers), Market street
Green Thomas Allen and Spencer (china), Minerva works, Park street
Hackney, Kirkham and Co. (earthenware), Sutherland street
Hawley and Co. (earthenware), King street, Foley
Jackson and Gosling (china), Grosvenor works, Foley place
Malkin Ralph (earthenware), Park works, Market street
Moore and Co. (earthenware), Old Foley Pottery, Foley
Pratt F. and R. and Co. (earthenware and terra cotta), Lower Fenton and High street East
Pratt and Simpson, (earthenware), Park street
Reeves James (earthenware), Victoria works, Market street
Robinson William and Co. (china), King street, Foley
Wileman and Shelley (china), Foley pottery
Wileman James F. (earthenware), Foley works

Hanley – Floor Tile Manufacturers (page 229)
Evans William L., Hall Field works
Hanley Plain & Encaustic Tile Company (Limited), Havelock works, Broad Street (see advt. page xliv.)
Ridgway, Wooliscroft, and Co. (Limited), Encaustic Tile works, Eastwood, Hanley, Stoke-upon-Trent

Hanley – Potters (pages 239-240)
Adams & Bromley (jasper and majolica), Victoria works, Broad street
Ash George (parian and majolica), Broad street (see advt., p. xlvii.)
Ashworth G.L. and Bros. (china and earthenware), Broad street
Bale & Co. (porous & general earthenware), Castle Field pottery, off Newcastle road
Bamford John (jug & teapot), Nelson place
Banks and Thorley (majolica), High st.
Bednall & Heath (earthenware), Tinkersclough
Bennett J. (earthenware), Wharf lane, Sheaf street
Bennett William (granite), Brook street
Bevington Ambrose (china and earthenware), Clarence street works
Bevington John (china and parian), St. James's street
Bevington Thomas (china and earthenware, Burton place
Booth Thomas and Sons (earthenware), Brook street
Bradshaw and Binns (china), Hope st.
Brown-Westhead, Moore and Co. (china, earthenware, parian, and majolica), Cauldon place and Victoria square
Buckley John (sanitary ware), 4 Victoria place
Buller and Co. (spurs and stilts, and door furniture, &c.), Joiners' square
Clementson Bros. (earthenware), Phoenix works, Broad street, and Bell works, George street
Cooke Robert (parian), Brewery street
Cooper, Moreton & Garside (earthenware), St. Luke street
Davis J.H. and J. (earthenware), Trent Pottery
Dimmock & Wood (earthenware), Albion works, Stafford street
Dudson James (earthenware and parian), Hanover street
Ford Charles (executors of), (spur), Parker street
Ford Charles (china), Cannon street
Hall Wm. (majolica and earthenware), Wharf lane
Hammersley J. and R. (china & earthenware), New street
Harrop William (parian and earthenware), Tinkersclough
Holmes, Stonier and Hollinshead (earthenware), Upper Hanley works
Howson George (sanitary ware), Eastwood vale
Jones & Hopkinson (earthenware), Renalagh works, off Bethesda street
Machin William (earthenware & figure), Percy street
Massey Mary (earthenware) Mayer street
Meakin J. and G. (earthenware), Eagle pottery, near Bucknall New road
Mellor William (earthenware), Waterloo works, Nelson place
Mills William (earthenware), George st.
Moreton und Baker (earthenware), Elm street
Neale, Harrison and Co. (china and earthenware), Elm street
Old Hall Earthenware Company, Limited (earthenware, parian, and china), Hill street; Meigh C., manager
Pankhurst James W. and Co. (white granite earthenware), Old Hall street
Powell, Bishop, and Co. (china & earthenware), High street and Stafford street
Pugh and Glover, Pelham street
Ridgway, Sparks, and Ridgway (earthenware), Bedford works
Scrivener R.G. and Co. (china), Norfolk street
Stanway, Horne, and Adams (parian), Trent works, Eastwood vale
Steele Edward (earthenware), Cannon street works
Stubbs William (china and earthenware), Eastwood vale
Taylor, Tunnicliff, and Co. (door furniture), Eastwood vale (see advt. page xlvii.)
Twigg and Mills (earthenware), King st.
Twyford Thomas (trustees of), earthenware and sanitary ware), Bath street and The Abbey
Wardle and Co. (parian and majolica), William street
Wedgwood Josiah & Sons (earthenware), Etruria
Worthington and Son (earthenware), Brook street

Longton – Potters (pages 290-291)
Adams Harvey & Co. (china and earthenware), Sutherland road
Adams Edward (china), High street
Adderley William A. (china and earthenware) Daisy bank
Aidney John and Co. (china), High street
Allerton Charles & Sons (china, earthenware, and gold and silver lustre), Park works, High street
Amison and Lawson (china), Edensor road (see advt. page lix.)
Asbury Edward and Co. (china), Sutherland road
Aynsley H. and Co. (earthenware), Commerce street (see advt. page lxiii.)

Aynsley John and Son (china), Sutherland road
Baddeley Mrs. (rustic and terra cotta), Drury works, Normacott road
Barker Brothers (earthenware), Gold st.
Barlow Albert B. (china), Market street
Barlow T.W. (earthen.), Commerce street
Beck, Blair and Co. (china), Beaconsfield pottery, Anchor road
Beech James & Son (china), Sutherland road; Stephen Mear, proprietor
Bentley and Copestake (china), Chancery lane (see advt. page lx.)
Bradley F.D. (decorated china), Edensor road
Brammall and Hamilton (china), Church street
Bridgett, Bates and Beech (china), King street
Bridgewood Sampson and Son, Exors. of (china and earthenware), Anchor pottery, Wharf street
Brough and Blackhurst (earthenware), Waterloo works, Stafford street
Brough Wm. & Co. (china), St. Martin's lane
Brown and Co. (china), Church street pottery
Burton & Morris (china), Bagnall street
Cartwright and Edwards (earthenware), Borough pottery, Trentham road
Collingwood and Greatbatch (china), Crown works, Stafford street
Cooper & Dethick (earthenware), Viaduct works, Caroline street
Coopers and Co. (china and earthenware), New street
Copestake George (china), Anchor works, Market street
Copestake and Allin (china), High street
Dale, Page & Goodwin (late Hilditch and Hopwood), (china), Newtown pottery, High street
Dawson James (earthenware), Stafford st. (se advt. page lx.)
Edwards William (earthenware), Russell street
Edwards George (china), Sheridan works, King street (see advt. page lxiii.)
Ferneyhough John (china), Dresden works, Stafford street, and Normacott road
Finney Joseph (china), Victoria works, Stafford street
Freeman W. (china), High street
Grove and Stark (rustic, lustre, china and earthenware), Palissy works, Chancery lane
Hallam and Johnson (china), Mount pleasant, High street
Hodson Richard and Co. (china), High street
Holdcroft Jos. (silver lustre & majolica), Daisy bank
Holland & Green (earthenware), Stafford street
Hudden J.T. (earthenware), Anchor works, Anchor road
Hudson Brothers (china), Stafford street
Hulse Thomas (china), Stafford street
Jackson and Gosling (china), Foley
Jones & Thompson (earthenware), Chadwick street
Johnson and Poole (china). Edensor road
Knight and Colclough (china), Market st.
Lockett John (Exors. of), (china, earthenware, and lustre), King street
Lowe William (earthenware), High street
Middleton & Hudson (china), Bagnall st.
Moore & Co. (earthen.), Old Foley pottery
Moore Bros. (china), St. Mary's works, High street
Plant & Johnson (china), Heathcote works
Proctor J. and H. and Co. (earthenware), Heathcote road
Radford Samuel (china), Chancery lane
Ridge, Meigh & Co. (china), Church st.
Robinson and Co. (china), The Foley
Robinson and Chapman (china), Royal Porcelain works
Robinson and Repton (china), Wellington works, Stafford st. (see advt. page lix.)
Shaw and Swift (fire brick and sanitary tube), Clayton street, Daisy bank
Skelson William (china and earthenware), Normacott road
Smith Sampson, Exors. of (china and gold and silver lustre and figure), Sutherland works, Barker street
Sutherland Hugh (parian, ivory, rustic, and terra cotta), Parkhall street, Anchor road (see advt., page lxiii.)
Tams John (earthenware), Crown pottery, Stafford street (see advt. page lviii.)
Taylor and Kent (china), High street
Taylor, Waine & Bates (china), High st.
Taylor Wm. & Co. (patent stilt and spur), Church street
Trubshaw, Hand & Co. (china), High st.
Unwin Joseph (earthenware and lustre), Cornhill passage
Walker John (earthenware), High street
Walters Thomas (china), Commerce street
Webberley William (china), St. James's works, High street
Williamson & Son & Copestake (china), Bridge works, Heathcote road
Wilson James (parian), High street
Yearsley Mrs. (parian and patentee of the gold astrakan trimming for decorating parian goods), Market lane

Stoke – Potters (pages 372-373)
Copeland W.T. & Sons (china, earthenware and parian), High street
Goss W.H. (parian), London road
Hancock and Whittington (earthenware), Church street
Jones Geo. (earthenware), Trent pottery
Kirkham William (earthenware), London road; residence, The Villas
Mintons (china, earthenware, and parian), London road
Minton, Hollins and Co. (encaustic tile), Church street
Robinson & Leadbeater (parian statuary), Wharf street (see advt. page lxxxvii.)
Stanway J. (parian, earthenware, and china), Copeland street & Liverpool rd.
Walker and Carter (earthenware), Church street

Stoke – Tile (Floor) Manufacturers (page 374)
Campbell Brick and Tile Company
Minton, Hollins and Co., Shelton old rd.

Tunstall – Potters (page 405)
Adams Wm. (earthen.), Newfield pottery
Adams William & Thomas (earthenware), Greenfield pottery
Blackhurst Jabez (earthenware), Sandyford
Booth Thomas Gamber, High street; residence, Wolstanton

Brownhills Pottery Co., Brownhills
Elsmore Thomas and Son (earthenware), Clayhills pottery
Emberton Thomas I. and James (earthenware), Highgate pottery, Brownhills
Ford and Challinor (earthen.), Sandyford
Goode & Kenworthy (earthen.), High st.
Guest George (earthenware), Soho pottery, High street
Hammersley Ralph (Rockington and Egyptian black), High street
Holdcroft Wm. (earthenware), George st.
Hollinshead and Kirkham (earthenware), Woodland pottery, Woodland street
Meakin Alfred (earthen.), Parsonage st.
Meir John & Son (earthen.), Greengates
Procter John (earthenware), Madeley st.
Turner George W. and Sons (earthenware), Victoria works, High street
Wedgwood & Co. (earthenware), Unicorn pottery, Amicable street; and Pinnox works, Great Woodland street

1880 Kelly

Kelly's Directory of Birmingham, Staffordshire, Warwickshire, and Worcestershire (also *Kelly's Directory of Staffordshire*), Kelly & Co., 51 Great Queen Street, Lincoln's Inn Fields, London WC (Shaw & Tipper 6, Shaw & Tipper 1222). Dated MDCCCLXXX on the title page and November 1880 in the Preface. It is noted as the Ninth Edition in the Preface.

As with all the Kelly's series, this directory contains alphabetical lists for the various towns and villages and also classified lists for each county. Only the classified lists are included here. The range of categories is extensive and there are twenty-four relevant to this work.

Artists' China Palette Manufacturers (page 469)
Macintyre James & Co. Washington works, Waterloo road, Burslem

Beer Engine Handle Maker (page 474)
Buckley John, Albert works, Victoria place, Handley

China Manufacturers (page 512)
See also Earthenware Manufacturers.
Adams, Harvey & Co. Sutherland road, Longton; London agent (James Gelson), 30 Holborn e.c
Adderley W.A. Daisy Bank works, Longtn
Allerton Charles & Son, Park works, High street, Longton
AMISQN & LAWSON, Salisbury works, Edensor road, Longton; manufacturers of all kinds of plain & decorated china in breakfast, tea, dessert, toilet & trinket services for the home, American & Australian markets; London agent, J.K. Kendall, 3 Bucklersbury, Cheapside, London e.c
Anderson William & Co. Saint Martin's lane, Longton
Asbury E. & Co. Sutherland rd. Longton
Ashworth George L. & Bros. Broad street, Hanley. See advertisement
Aynsley J. & Sons, Sutherland rd. Longton
Baggaley Jacob, Hill works, Burslem
Barlow Charles, Lower Mollart st. Hanley
Barlow Thomas, Market street, Longton; London office, 10 Dyers' buildings, Holborn e.c
BEECH JAMES & SON, manufacturers for home & export of superior china in tea, breakfast, dessert services &c.; also flint stone & potters' colour grinders, Sutherland road & Albert mills, Longton
Beech & Podmore, Wellington street, Cobridge, Burslem
Bentley & Copestake, Chancery la. Longtn
Bevington Ambrose & Co. Newhall works, Great York street, Hanley
Bevington Thomas, Burton place, Hanley
BLAIR & CO. Beaconsfield pottery, Anchor road, Longton; manufacturers for home & export
Bodley Edwin J.D. Hill pottery, Burslem
Bradley Fredk. D. Clayton st. Longton
Brammall & Hamilton, St. John's works, Church street, Longton
BRIDGETT, BATES & BEECH, King Street china works, Longton; general china manufacturers for home & export
Brown-Westhead (T.C.), Moore & Co. Cauldon place & Victoria works, Stoke-on-Trent; & Fitz Eylwin ho. Holborn viaduct, London e.c
Brownfield Wm. & Sons, Cobrdge. Burslm.
BROWNHILL'S POTTERY CO. Tunstall, Stoke-on-Trent. See Earthenware Manufacturers
Burton, Morris & Co. Bagnall st. Longton
Collingwood & Greatbatch, Stafford street, Longton
COOPERS & SON, Edensor works, Longton; china manufrs. for home & export
Copeland W.T. & Sons, High street, Stoke-on-Trent; & 160 New Bond street, London w
Copestake, Allin & Co. Alma works, High street, Longton
Copestake Geo. jun. Anchor wrks. Longtn
Crystal Porcelain Co. manufacturers of crystal porcelain, Clarence street, Hanley
DALE, PAGE & GOODWIN (late Hilditch & Hopwood), New Town pottery, High street, Longton; manufacturers of all kinds of plain & decorated china, also jet ware for home & exportation
Davenport William & Co. Longport, Burslem; 32 Ely place, London e.c; & 30 Canning pl. Liverpool. See advert
Day George & Thomas, Albion works, High street, Longton
EDWARDS GEORGE, Sheridan works, Longton; manufacturer of superior china, suitable for the home & export trade
Edwards John, King street, Fenton Culvert, Stoke-on-Trent
Ferneyhough John, Stafford st. Longton
Finney Joseph, Victoria works, Longton
Ford Charles, Cannon street, Hanley

Freeman Walter, 51 High st. Longton
Green F.A. & S. Park street, Fenton Culvert, Stoke-on-Trent
Hallam & Johnson, Mount Pleasant, High street, Longton
Hammersley Joseph & Robert, New street, Hanley
Hodson & Co. High street, Longton
HUDSON WILLIAM & SON, Stafford street, Longton; china manufacturers for home & export
Hulse Thomas (late John Green), Peel pottery, Stafford street, Longton
Jackson & Gosling, King street, Fenton Culvert, Stoke-on-Trent
Johnson & Plant, Heathcote rd. Longton
Johnson & Poole, Edensor road, Longtn
Kent John & Son, Market pl. Longton
Kirkby William & Co. Sutherland pottery, Fenton Culvert, Stke.-on-Trnt
Knight & Colclough, Market st. Longtn
Lear Samuel, High street, Hanley, manufacturer of china & earthenware
Lowe William, High street, Longton; manufacturer of china, drab torquoise, buff printed & gilt wares for home & export
Mason, Holt & Co. Normacott rd. Longton
Massey Mrs. Mary, Mayer Street works, Mayer street, Hanley
MIDDLETON & HUDSON, Bagnall St. works, Longton; manufacturers of china suitable for the Australian, New Zealand & American markets
Mintons, Eldon place, Stoke-on-Trent; & 28 Walbrook, London e.c
Moor Brothers, High street, Longton
Pratt & Simpson, Lane Delph pottery, Park street, Fenton Culvert, Stoke-on-Trent
RADFORD SAMUEL, New Market works, Longton; china manufacturer for home & export
Reeve John, Commerce street, Longton
Ridge, Meigh & Co. Church st. Longton
Robinson & Chapman, Royal works, Longton
Robinson & Co. Foley, Fenton Culvert, Stoke-on-Trent
Robinson & Co. Sutherland rd. Longton
Scrivener R.G. & Co. Norfolk st. Hanley
Shorter & Boulton, Copeland street, Stoke-on-Trent
Skelson & Plant, Normacott rd. Longton
Smith Sampson, Barker street, Longton
SPENCER & HINES, Edensor road, Longton; manufacturers of decorated china & earthenware, spirit barrels, tea sets, jugs, toilet wares & general goods suitable for home & exportation
Sturgess William Henry, Edensor road, Longton; china & earthenware for home & export – quotations on application
Taylor & Kent, Florence works, High street, Longton; for home & export
Taylor, Tunnicliff & Co. Eastwood, Hanley; manufacturers of china mortice lock furniture, finger plates, fancy inkstands, stationers' goods & every description of china for brass founders, plumbers, silversmiths, lamp & chandelier manu facturers, scale plates & weights, artists' palettes, color tiles &c. plateaux in every color for painting
Taylor, Waine & Bates, High st. Longtn
Trubshaw, Hand & Co. Albert works, High street, Longton; London agent, Mr. Grimwade, Union Bank buildings, Holborn e.c
Walters Thomas, Talbot works, Commerce street, Longton
Warrilow & Cope, Wellington works, Stafford street, Longton
Webberley Wm. St. James pl. Longton
Wileman & Co. Foley potteries, Fenton Culvert, Stoke-on-Trent
WILLIAMSON H.M. & SONS, Bridge pottery, Heathcote road, Longton; manufacturers of china for home & exports; special shapes for the American & Australian trade

China Letter Makers (page 512)
Macintyre James & Co. Washington works, Waterloo road, Burslem

Creel Step Manufacturers (page 524)
Hallen Henry, Wellington st. Burslem
Wade & Myatt, Hall street, Burslem

Door Furniture Makers – China (page 526)
Buller & Co. Joiner's Square wrks. Hanley
Macintyre James & Co. Washington works, Waterloo road, Burslem
Taylor, Tunnicliff & Co. Eastwd. Hanley

Earthenware Manufacturers (pages 530-531)
See also China Manufacturers.
Adams William & Thomas, Tunstall
Adderley Wm. A. Daisy Bank wrks. Lngtn
Aidney, Griffiths & Co. High st. Longton
Alcock Henry & Co. Waterloo road, Cobridge, Burslem
Alcock Richd. Market place, Burslem
Allerton Charles & Son, Park works, High street, Longton
Ashworth George L. & Brothers, Broad street, Hanley. See advertisement
AYNSLEY H. & CO. Chancery lane, Longton; manufacturers for home & export
Baggaley Jacob, Hill works, Burslem
Bailey, Williams & Co. Wellington works, Newport street, Burslem
Baker & Co. Fenton Culvrt. Stoke-on-Trnt
Bamford John, Nelson place, Hanley
Banks & Thorley, Boston works, High street, Hanley
Barker Brothers, Gold street, Longton
Barlow Charles, Lower Mollart street, Hanley; manufacturer of china & earthenware
Barlow Thos. W. Commerce st. Longton
Bates & Bennett, Sneyd st. Cobridge, Burslem
Bates, Gildea & Walker, Dale hall, Burslm
Bednall & Heath, Tinker's clough, Hanley
Beech & Morgan, Waterloo works, Hanley
Beech James, Swan bank, Tunstall
Bennett Joseph, Wharf lane, Hanley
Bettelley Joseph, Union street, Hanley

Bevington James, New street, Hanley
Bevington John, Broad street, Hanley
Birks Brothers & Seddon, Waterloo rd. Cobridge, Burslem
Blackhurst & Bourne, Hadderidge pottery, Burslem
Blackhurst Jabez, Sandyford, Tunstall
Bodley E.F. & Co. Scotia works, Burslem
Booth Thomas Gimbert, Church Bank pottery, Tunstall. See advertisement
Bridgwood, Sampson & Son, East vale, Longton
Broadhurst James, Portland pottery, Fenton Culvert, Stoke-on-Trent
Brough & Blackhurst, Waterloo works, Stafford street, Longton
Brown & Co. Church street, Longton
Brown-Westhead (T.C.), Moore & Co. Cauldon place & Victoria works, Stoke-on-Trent; & Fitz Eylwin house, Holborn viaduct, London e.c
Brownfield William & Sons, Cobridge, Burslem
BROWNHILL'S POTTERY CO. Tunstall, Stoke-on-Trent; manufacturers of decorated earthenware &c. for home & colonial markets; London, 34 Hatton garden e.c
Buckley, Wood & Co. High Street pottery, Burslem
BURGESS & LEIGH (late S. Alcock & Co.), Hill pottery, Burslem; manufacturers of general earthenware for the home & foreign markets
Burgess Henry, Kiln Croft works, Chapel lane, Burslem
Cartlidge William Edward, Villa pottery, Cobridge, Burslem
Cartwright & Edwards, Trentham road, Longton
Challinor Edwd. & Chas. High st. Fenton Culvert & Glebe st. Stoke-on-Trent
Clementson Brothers, Phoenix & Bell works, Broad street, Hanley
Clive Stephen & Co. Well st. Tunstall, Stoke-on-Trent
COOPER & DETHICK, Viaduct works, Caroline st. Longton; manufacturers of earthenware, lustre china & printed ware
Cooper & Moreton, Pyenest street, Shelton, Hanley
Copeland W.T. & Sons, High st. Stoke-on-Trent; & 160 New Bond street, London w
Corn William & Edward, Navigation rd. & North road, Burslem
Cotton Elijah, Lichfield St. works, Hanley
Davenport William & Co. Longport, Burslem; warehouses, 32 Ely place, London e.c; & 30 Canning place, Liverpool. See advertisement
Davis John Heath, Trent pottery, Kirkham street, Hanley
Dawson James, Stafford st. Longton
Dimmock John & Co. Stafford st. Hanley
Dudson James, Hope Street works, Hanley; manufacturer of earthenware, white & colored stone bodies in jugs, teapots &c.; britannia metal, covered ware &c
Dunn, Bennett & Co. Boothen works, Brook street, Hanley
Edge, Malkin & Co. Newport wrks. Brslm
Edwards Jas. & Son, Dalehall pttry. Brslm
Edwards William, Russell st. Longton
Elsmore Thomas & Son, Clay Hills pottery, Tunstall
EMBERTON THOMAS J. & JAMES, Highgate pottery, Tunstall, Stoke-on-Trent; manufacturers of earthenware for the home trade, also lustre, japanned printed & enamelled earthenware, rice dishes &c. for the Indian & other foreign markets
Emery F.J. Bleak Hl. wrks. Bleak st. Bslm
Fielding & Co. Railway pttry. Stke-on-Tnt
Finney Joseph, Victoria works, Longton
FORD & CHALLINOR, Sandyford pottery, Tunstall, Stoke-on-Trent; manufacturers of plain & ornamental earthenware for home & foreign markets
Forester T. High st. & Church st. Longton
FURNIVAL THOMAS & SONS, Cobridge, Stoke-on-Trent; manufacturers of white granite & decorated earthenware for home and foreign markets
Gaskell James, Son & Co. Crown works, Market place, Burslem
Goode & Kenworthy, High st. Tunstall, Stoke-on-Trent; manufacturers for home & foreign markets
GRINDLEY W.H. & CO. Newfield pottery, Tunstall, Stoke-on-Trent. See advertisement
GROVE & STARK, Palissy works, Longton; manufacturers of printed & decorated earthenware, dinner & toilet sets in white & ivory bodies, porcelain, spirit barrels, beer machine handles &c; Pattenden, Hurles & Co. agents, 20 Hatton garden, London e.c
Guest George, Soho pottery, Tunstall
Hall, Watkin & Co. Union st. Hanley
Hammersley Robert M. & Co. High Street pottery, Tunstall
Hammersley Ralph, High st. Tunstall & at Wedgwood place, Burslem
Hancock B. & S. Church st. Stoke-on-Trnt
Harrop William & Co. Dresden works, Hanley; earthenware, stone & parian manufacturers &c
Hawley & Co. Foley, Fenton Culvert, Stoke-on-Trent
Hawthorn J. Abbey pttry. Cobrdge. Brslm
Hobson Charles, Albert street, Burslem
Holdcroft William, George st. Tunstall
Holland & Green, Stafford st. Longton; for home & export
Hollinshead & Kirkham, Woodland pottery, Tunstall
Holmes, Plant & Madew, Sylvester pottery, Burslem
Holmes, Stonier & Hollinshead, High street, Hanley
Hope & Carter, Fountain pl. Burslem
Hughes Thomas, Waterloo rd. Burslem & Longport
Jones George & Sons, London road, Stoke-on-Trent
Jones & Hopkinson, Ranelagh wrks. Hnly
Jones Frederick, Chadwick st. Longton
Kent John & Son, 11 Market pl. Longton
Kent & Parr, Wellington st. Burslem
Kirkham W. London rd. Stoke-on-Trent
Knight Joseph, Stafford street, Longton
Lear Samuel, High street, Hanley
Lincoln Works Pottery Co. (R.N. Gibbons, manager), Sneyd street, Cobridge, Burslem,
Lockett John & Co. King st. Longton
Lowe William, High street, Longton; manufacturer of china drab turquoise, buff printed & gilt wares for home & export
Machin William, Percy st. works, Hanley
Maddock J. & Sons, Newcastle st. Burslem

Maddock & Co. Dale Hall pottery, Burslem
Malkin R. Fenton Culvrt. Stoke-on-Trnt
Meakin Jas. & Geo. 16 Glebe st. Stoke; & at Eagle pottery, Hanley
Meakin Alfred, Royal Albert pottery, Parsonage street, Tunstall
Meakin C. Elder rd. Cobridge, Burslem
Meir J. & Son, Greengate potteries, Tunstll
Mellor Taylor & Co. Bourne's bnk. Burslm
Moore & Co. Old Foley pottery, Longton
Morley William, Albion street, Longton
Oakley & Thacker, New street, Longton
Old Hall Earthenware Co. Limited, Hill street, Hanley
Oulsnam William E. & Sons, Furlong works, Burslem
Pankhurst J.W. & Co. Old Hall st. Hanley
Pinder Bourne & Co. Nile street, Burslem. See advertisement
Plant James junior, stone & earthenware manufacturer, Brewery Street works (off Hope street), Hanley
Poole & Son, John street, Stoke-on-Trent
Powell Bishop & Stonier, Stafford street, High street & Nelson place, Hanley
PRATT F. & R. & Co. Fenton potteries, Fenton, Stoke-on-Trent, manufacturers in great variety of uniquely ornamented earthenware, cream colour, pearl white, printed, enamelled, green glaze, Rockingham, porous, stone, terra cotta & druggists' ware, suitable for the home & foreign markets
Pratt & Simpson, Lane Delph pottery, Park st. Fenton Culvert, Stk.-on-Trnt
Pratt & Co. Lane Delph, Fenton Culvert, Stoke-on-Trent
Procter John, Heathcote pottery, Heathcote road, Longton
Pugh & Glover, Pelham street works, Pelham street, Hanley
Reeves James, Market street, Fenton Culvert, Stoke-on-Trent
Ridgways, Bedford works, Hanley
Rigby James, Milton, Stoke-on-Trent
Robinson J. Knwle. wks. Hamil rd. Burslm
Shaw Anthony, Mersey works, Burslem
Simpson T.A. Swan wrks. Elm st. Hanley
Steel Edward, manufacturer of earthenware, majolica, & parian statuettes, Cannon Street works, Hanley
Stubbs Wm. Eastwood pottery, Hanley
Tams John, Stafford street, Longton
Taylor, Tunnicliff & Co. Eastwood, Hanley
Till Thos. & Sons, Liverpool rd. Burslem
TINSLEY GEORGE & Co. Queen Street pottery, Burslem, manufacturers of earthenware, ivory, jet & red body ware; a large assortment of fancy vases &c
Tundley, Rhodes & Procter, Swan bank, Burslem
Turner G.W. & Sons, Victoria wks. Tunstll
Unwin Joseph, Cornhill works, Longton
Vernon J. & G. Waterloo wks. Burslem
Walker & Carter, Church st. Stk.-on-Trnt
Walker John, 31 High street, Longton
Watts & Tompkinson (finishers), High street, Longton
Wedgwood J. & Sons, Etruria pottery, Etruria, Stoke-on-Trent
Wedgwood & Co. Pinnox & Unicorn works, Tunstall
Whittingham, Ford & Riley, Newcastle street, Burslem
Wileman James F. Foley works, Fenton Culvert, Stoke-on-Trent
Wood & Son, Trnt. ptry. Furlng. la. Burslm
Worthington & Son, Brook st. Hanley

Encaustic Tile Manufacturers (page 532)
Boote Thomas & Richard, Waterloo potteries, Burslem
CAMPBELL BRICK & TILE CO. (THE), London road, Stoke-on-Trent; manufacturs. of encaustic, geometrical & majolica tiles & mosaics; London house, 206 Great Portland street w
Malkin, Edge & Co. Newport works, Burslem. See advertisement
Minton, Hollins & Co. Stoke-on-Trent
Mintons, Eldon place, Stoke-on-Trent
Ridgway, Woolliscrofts & Co. Limited, encaustic & hearth tile manufacturers, Patent tile works, Hanley
Sherwin & Cotton, Vine street, Hanley
Steele & Wood, London rd. Stoke-on-Trnt
Woolliscroft George & Son, Canal tileries, Etruria, Stoke-on-Trent

Inkstand Manufacturers (page 581)
Taylor, Tunnicliff & Co. Eastwood, Hanly

Jetware Manufacturers (page 587)
Harrison & Baker, King's Field pottery, Newcastle

Lock Furniture Makers – China (page 593)
Macintyre James & Co. Washington works, Waterloo road, Burslem
Taylor, Tunnicliff & Co. Eastwood, Hanly
Wood William & Co. Albert St. works, Burslem

Lustre Manufacturers (page 594)
Allerton Charles & Son (gold & silver), Park works, High street, Longton

Majolica Manufacturers (page 594)
Adams & Bromley, Broad st. Hanley
Baddeley Mrs. Lucy, Drury works, Normacott rd. & 4 Vauxhall st. Longtn
Banks & Thorley, Boston works, High street, Hanley
Fielding & Co. (late F. Hackney & Co.), Railway pottery, Stoke-on-Trent; manufacturers of majolica, terra cotta, porous ware, jet, green glaze, Rockingham earthenware & fancy goods, London agent, M. Gray, Ely ho. Charterhouse st. Holborn circus e.c
Hamilton William, Sheaf pottery, Normacott road, Longton
HOLDCROFT JOSEPH, Sutherland pottery, Daisy bank, Longton; manufacturer of majolica statuettes, silvered goods &c. &c. in every variety
Lawton Henry, Clayton Street works, Longton
Oakes, Clare & Chadwick, Albert street, Burslem
SUTHERLAND HUGH, Park Hall st. Longton; manufacturer of useful & ornamental majolica in every variety
Wardle & Co. William street, Hanley

Mortar & Pestle Manufacturers (page 600)
Kirkham Wm. London rd. Stoke-on-Trent
Macintyre James & Co. Washington works, Waterloo road, Burslem

Parian Manufacturers (page 605)
Adams Thomas, Fenton road, Hanley
Ash George, Broad street, Hanley
Brown-Westhead (T.C.), Moore & Co. Cauldon place & Victoria works, Stoke-on-Trent; & Fitz Eylwin house, Holborn viaduct, London e.c
Bullock Alfred, Pelham street, off Lichfield street & 42 Nelson place, Hanley
Copeland W.T. & Sons, High street, Stoke-on-Trent; & 160 New Bond street, London w
Mills William, 1 George street, Hanley
Robinson & Leadbeater, Wharf street & Glebe street, Stoke-on-Trent
Steel Edward, Cannon street, Hanley
Turner & Wood, Copeland Street works, Stoke-on-Trent
Wilson James, Etruscan works, High street, Longton
Yearsley Mrs. M.A. Market la. Longton

Potters (page 609)
Kent Philip Joynson, Endon Edge works, Endon, Stoke-on-Trent

Rockingham Ware Manufacturers (page 629)
Gibson, Sudlow & Co. Bourne's bank, Burslem
Hadfield & Co. King Street works, King street; office, Market street, Hanley
Oakes, Clare & Chadwick, Albert street, Burslem
Rathbone Wm. & Co. Sylvester st. Burslm
Wade & Colclough, High street, Burslm
Walley William, Nile street, Burslem

Sanitary Ware Manufacturers (page 631)
Brough Wm. & Son, Silverdale, Newcastle
Brown-Westhead (T.C.), Moore & Co. Cauldon place & Victoria wks. Stoke-on-Trent
Buckley John, manufacturer of sanitary ware, water-closet pans & traps, urinals, ship & portable closets, closet pulls, beer handles &c. Albert works, Victoria place, Hanley
Howson G. Clifford st. Eastwood, Hanley
Pinder, Bourne & Co. Nile st. Burslem. See advertisement
Twyford Thomas (the trustees of), Bath street, Hanley

Shuttle Eye Manufacturers (page 653)
Hallen Henry, Wellington st. Burslem
Wade & Myatt, Hall street, Burslem; manufacturers of all kinds of porcelain used in silk & cotton machinery

Spur & Stilt Makers for Pottery Manufacturers (page 660)
Ford Charles & Co. Parker street, Hanley
Gimson Joseph & Co. High street, Fenton Culvert, Stoke-on-Trent
Taylor William & Co. Church st. Longton
Wigley & Sherley, Moorland rd. Burslem

Stoneware Manufacturers (page 663)
Plant James, jun. Brewery st. Hanley

Stoneware Manufacturers for Druggists (page 663)
Brown-Westhead (T.C.), Moore & Co. Cauldon place & Victoria works, Stoke-on-Trent; & Fitz-Eylwin house, Holborn viaduct, London e.c

Terra Cotta Manufacturers (page 668)
Harrison & Baker, Shelton New rd. Nwcstl
Kirkham W. London rd. Stoke-on-Trent
Peake Thomas, The Tileries, Tunstall
Snow & Littler, Liverpool rd. Stk.-on-Tnt

Water Closet Maker (page 675)
Buckley John, Albert works, Victoria place, Hanley

1882 Keates

Keates's Gazetteer & Directory of the Staffordshire Potteries, Newcastle and District. 1882, Keates & Co., Printers and Publishers, Hanley (Shaw & Tipper 1233). Dated December 1882 in the Preface.

As with all the Keates series, this directory is classified within separate sections for each of the six pottery towns and the only relevant categories are potters and various types of tile manufacturers.

Burslem – Encaustic and Geometric Tile Pavement Manufacturers (page 155)
Boote Thomas & Richard, 32A, Waterloo rd.
Malkin, Edge & Co., Newport lane

Burslem – Floor Tile Works (page 155)
Basford James Powell, Dalehall
Boote Thomas and Richard, Waterloo rd.
Malkin, Edge & Co., Newport lane

Burslem – Potters (pages 160-161)
Adams and Sleigh, 17 Queen street
Alcock Henry & Co. (earthenware) Cobridge works
Alcock Richard (eartherware), Central Pottery, Market place
Allen Henry, (creel steps) Wellington st.
Bates and Bennett (earthenware), Sneyd street
Baggaley Jacob, (earthenware & china), Hill works, Liverpool road
Beech Frederick & Co. (earthenware), Lincoln works, Sneyd green

Birks Brother & Seddon, (earthenware), Waterloo road, Cobridge
Blackhurst and Tunnicliffe (earthenware), Hadderidge pottery, Bath street
Bodley Edwin J.D., (china), Hill pottery, Market place
Boote T. & R., (earthenware) 43 & 32A Waterloo road
Brall Hy. (earthenware), 54 Furlong lane
Bratt Joseph, Edward street
Brownfield William & Sons, (earthenware and china), Waterloo road, Cobridge
Brownhills Pottery Co. (earthenware), Brownhills
Buckley, Wood & Co. (earthenware) High street Pottery
Burgess and Leigh, (earthenware), Hill Pottery, Liverpool road
Burgess Henry (earthenware), Kilncroft works, Chapel lane
Cartledge and Stanway, Villa Pottery, Cobridge
Cartwright Thomas (earthenware), 14 Rushton road
Clark Edward, Church yard works, Wood street
Clarke Edward, (earthenware) Wood st.
Clare Walter (rockingham), Podmore st.
Corn W. & E. (earthenware), Navigation road
Crystal Porcelain Pottery Co. Limited Elder road
Davenport & Co. Limited, (china and earthenware), Longport
Dean Meshach, Hall street
Doulton & Co. (earthenware) Nile street, works
Dunn William, 266 Waterloo road
Edge Joseph (earthenware), Elder house
Edge, Malkin & Co. (earthenware), Newport works, Newport
Emery Francis J. (earthenware), Bleak hill works, Wood street
Furnival T. & Son (earthenware), Cobridge
Gaskell & Grocott (door furniture), Longport, near Station
Gibson, Sudlow, & Co. (rockingham), Bourne' bank
Gildea & Walker (earthenware) Dalehall, Burslem, and 30 Holborn, London
Goodwin Robert, Flint grinder, 41 Newport street
Hall & Read (Wellington works), Newport street
Hallen Harding (creel steps), 31 Wellington street
Hammersley Ralph (earthenware and ironstone china), Overhouse pottery, Wedgwood place
Hawthorne John, 118 Liverpool road
Hobson John and George (earthenware), Albert street
Holdcroft William (earthenware), 116 Liverpool road
Holmes, Plant and Maydew (earthenware), Silvester pottery, Nile street
Hughes Thomas (earthenware and flint manufacturer), Top Bridge works, Longport, and 2A Waterloo road
Hurd and Wood (rockingham), Chapel lane works
Kent and Parr (figure makers), Wellington street
Kent William (figure maker), Wood st.
Leigh William, 6 Newport street
Macintyre James & Co. (china, porcelian and door furniture), Washington works, Waterloo road
Maddock & Company (earthenware), Dalehall works, Taylor street
Malkin Edge & Co. (encaustic tile), Newport lane
Meakin Charles (earthenware), Furlong lane
Meakin Henry (earthenware), Grove street, Cobridge
Mellor, Taylor & Co. (earthenware and white granite), Bournes bank
New Wharf Pottery Co., Navigation road
Oakes, Clare & Chadwick (majolica and earthenware), Albert street
Oulsnam William and Son (earthenware), Furlong works
Parr John (nest egg), Adelaide st. works
Rathbone Wm. & Co. (rockingham and jet), Silvester square
Robinson Joseph, (earthenware), Knowle works, Hamil road
Shaw Anthony (earthenware), Mersey pottery, Newport lane
Shirley Elijah, (stilt and spur) silvester sq
Thomas Uriah, Marlborough works, Union street
Till and Sons (earthenware), Sytch pottery, Liverpool road
Tinsley, Bourne, & Co. (earthenware) Queen street
Tundley, Rhodes and Proctor, (earthen.), Swan bank works
Vernon James and George (earthenware) Waterloo pottery, Waterloo road
Wade and Sons, (shuttle eye and creel step), Hall street
Wade John, (earthenware), High street
Wade, Colclough & Lingard, (rockingham stone and jet decorators) High street
Walley Wm. (rockingham), Nile street
Whittinghan, Ford and Riley (earthenware), Newcastle street
Wilkinson & Hulme (earthenware), Central pottery, Market place
Wood and Hulme Garfield Pottery Works, Waterloo road
Wood and Son (earthenware), Furlong lane
Wood William & Co. (door furniture), Albert street works, Albert street
Wood and Baggaley (earthenware), Hill works
Wood and Co. (earthenware), New Wharf pottery, Navigation road

Fenton – Potters (page 184)
Baker and Co. (earthenware), High street
Broadhurst James (earthenware), Victoria road
Challinor E. and C. (earthenware), Fenton pottery, High street
Edwards John, (white granite), King street
Edwards John and Co. (china and earthenware), King street
Fanshaw & Hughes (earthenware, china, jet and majolica),
Fielding and Co. (majolica and earthenware), Railway pottery, off Whieldon road
Gimson Joseph and Co. (spur manufacturers), Market street
Green Spencer (china), Minerva works, Park street
Hawley and Co. (earthenware), King street, Foley
Jackson and Gosling (china), Grosvenor works, Foley place, King street
Kirkby William and Co. Sutherland pottery, High street
Malkin Ralph and Sons, (earthenware), Park works, Market street
Mellor George (china and earthenware), Fenton wharf
Moore and Co. (earthenware), Old Foley pottery, King street
Poole Thomas (china), 45 Whieldon rd
Portland pottery, (earthenware) Fenton
Pratt F. and R. and Co. (earthenware and terra cotta), Lower Fenton and High street, east

Pratt and Simpson (earthenware), Park street
Reeves James (earthenware), Victoria works, Market street
Robinson William and Co. (china), King street, Foley
Wileman and Shelley, (china), Foley pottery, King street
Wileman James F. (earthenware), Foley works, King street

Hanley – Floor Tile Manufacturers (page 252)
Sherwin and Cotton, Vine street
Woolliscroft Geo. and Son, Canal side, Eastwood

Hanley – Potters (pages 262-263)
Adams and Bromley (jasper and majolica), Victoria works, Broad street
Adams Thomas (parian), Trent works, Eastwood vale
Ashworth G.L. and Bros. (china and earthenware), Broad street
Baker James, (earthenware), Brewery st.
Banks and Thorley (majolica), High st.
Bednall & Heath (earthenware), Tinkersclough
Bennett J. (earthenware), Wharf lane, Sheaf street
Bennett William (granite), Victoria road
Bevington Ambrose & Co., (china and earthenware), Clarence street works
Bevington John (china and parian), Kensington works, St. James's street
Bevington Thomas, (china and earthenware), Burton place
Bevington James, Cobden works, High st
Bettany William (china and earthenware), 41 Hope street
Brown-Westhead, Moore and Co. (china, earthenware, parian, and majolica), Cauldon place, and Victoria square
Buckley John (sanitary ware), 4 Victoria place
Buller and Co. (spurs and stilts, and door furniture, &c), Joiners square
Clementson Bros. (earthenware), Phoenix works, Broad street, and Bell works, George street
Clews William (earthenware), William st.
Cotton Elijah (earthenware), Lichfield st.
Davis J.H. and J. (earthenware), Trent pottery, Canal side
Dean, Capper, and Dean (earthenware), Excelsior works, New street
Dimmock John & Co. (earthenware), Albion works, Stafford street
Dudson James (earthenware and parian), Hanover street
Dunn, Bennett & Co., Boothen works, Brook street
Ford Charles (executors of), (spur), Parker street
Ford Charles (china), Cannon street
Grove Richard Henry (china and parian), Broad street
Hall Henry (earthenware and majolica) New Hall street
Hall and Read (earthenware), Dresden works, George street
Hall William (majolica and earthenware), Wharf lane
Hammersley J. and R. (china and earthenware), New street and Nelson place
Harrison, Neale, & Co. (china & earthenware), Elm street
Harrop William & Co. (parian & earthenware), Tinkersclough
Howson George (sanitary ware), Eastwood vale
Johnson Samuel (rockingham and jet), King street
Jones & Hopkinson (earthenware), Renalagh works, off Bethesda street
Lear Samuel (china, majolica and jasper), High street
Lees William (parian), Keelings lane
Lilley, Burton and Morgan, Waterloo mill, Charles street
Machin William (earthenware and figure), Percy street
Massey Mary (earthenware), Broad street
Meakin Charles (earthenware), Eastwood
Meakin J. and G. (earthenware), Eagle pottery, Ivy house road
Moreton John (earthenware), Wellington works, Wellington street
Mountford and Thomas (majolica), Marlborough works, Union street
Old Hall Earthenware Company, Limited (earthenware, parian, and china), Hill street; Meigh C., Manager
Pankhurst James W. and Co. (white granite earthenware), Old Hall street
Peake Joseph (rockingham and earthenware), Etruria vale
Powell, Bishop, and Stonier (china and earthenware), High st. & Stafford st.
Pugh and Glover (earthenware & majolica), Pelham street
Ridgways (earthenware), Bedford works
Scrivener R.G. and Co. (china), Norfolk street
Sherwin and Cotton (encaustic tiles), Vine street
Simpson Thomas A. (china), Swan works, Elm street
Snow John and James (terra cotta), Pyenest street works
Steele Edward (earthenware), Cannon street works
Stubbs William, (china and earthenware), Eastwood vale
Taylor, Tunnicliff, and Co. (door furniture), Eastwood vale
Twyford Thomas (plumbers and sanitary ware), Bath street
Wardle and Co. (parian and majolica), William street, and Washington works, Victoria road
Wedgwood Josiah & Sons (earthenware) Etruria
Wenger A. (earthenware), Parker street
Whittaker, Edge, & Co. (earthenware), Grafton street
Wood, Hines, and Winkles (earthenware), Brook street
Worthington and Son (earthenware and china figures), Brook street
Wright and Rigby (earthenware), Providence pottery, Providence place

Longton – Potters (pages 310-311)
Adams Harvey & Co. (china and earthenware), Sutherland road
Adderley & Lawson (china), Salisbury works, Edensor road
Adderley William A., (china and earthenware), Daisy bank
Aidney, Griffiths & Co. (china), Edensor rd
Allerton Charles & Sons (china, earthenware, and gold and silver lustre), Park works, High street
Amison Joseph (china), Mount pleasant, High street
Anderton & Copestake (china), St. Martin's lane
Asbury Edward & Co. (china), Sutherland road
Aynsley H. and Co. (earthenware), Commerce street
Aynsley John & Sons (china), Portland works, Sutherland road
Baddeley Mrs. Lucy & Co. (rustic & terra cotta), Drury works, 5 Normacott road
Barker Brothers (earthenware), Barker street, off High street
Barker & Hill (china), King street
Barlow T.W. & Son (earthenware), Commerce street

Baxter, Rowley & Tams (china), High st
Bayley William (majolica), Sheaf works, Normacott road
Blair & Co. (china), Beaconsfield pottery, Anchor road
Beech James & Son (china), Sutherland road; Stephen Mear, proprietor
Bradbury and Sons (china), High street
Bradbury, Kellett and Co. (china), Heathcote road
Bradley F.D. (decorated china), Clayton street
Brammall Edwin (china), Forrester street, Anchor road
Bridgett and Bates (china), King street
Bridgwood Samson and Son, (china and earthenware), Anchor Pottery, Wharf street; manager, Richd. Gaskell, Sidmouth road, Newcastle
Brough and Blackhurst (earthenware), Waterloo works, Stafford street
Brown and Co. (china), Church street
Burton, Morris & Co. (china), Bagnall st.
Cartwright and Edwards (earthenware), Borough pottery, Trentham road
Chapman David (china), Forrister street, Anchor road
Collingwood and Greatbatch (china), Crown works, Stafford street
Cooper Wm. and Sons (earthenware), Viaduct works, Caroline street
Cooper & Kent (china and earthenware), New street
Copestake George (china), Anchor works, Market street
Dale, Page & Goodwin (china & majolica), Newtown pottery, High street
Dawson James (earthenware), Stafford st.
Day George, Albion works, High street
Edwards and Brown (china), High street
Edwards George (china), Sheridan works, King street
Edwards Wm. (earthenware), Russell st.
Ferneyhough John (china), Dresden works, Stafford street, and Normacott road
Finney Joseph (china), Victoria works, Stafford street
Forester Thomas (majolica and earthenware), Church street
Freeman W. (china), High street
Green, Clark, and Clay (earthenware) Stafford street
Green, Rouse and Co. (china), High st.
Grove and Stark (rustic, lustre, china, and earthenware), Palissy works, Chancery lane
Hallam & Day (china), Mount pleasant, High street
Heath Thos. (majolica and earthenware), Parkhall street, Anchor road
Hodson Richard & Co. (china), High st.
Holdcroft Jos. (silver lustre & majolica), Daisy bank
Hudden J.T. (earthenware), Anchor works, Anchor road
Hudson Wm. & Sons (china), Stafford st.
Hulme and Massey (china), Peel works, Stafford street
Hulse Thomas (china), Stafford street
Johnson & Plant (china), Heathcote works, Heathcote street
Kent John & Son (china & earthenware), Market place
Knight Joseph (earthenware), Stafford st.
Lawrence E. & Co. (china & earthenware), Portland mills, Church street
Lockett John & Co, (china, earthenware and lustre), King street
Lowe, Ratcliffe and Co. (earthenware), Gold street works
Lowe William (earthenware), High street, and Sutherland road
Maddox, Ridge & Hughes (china), Chancery lane
Middleton & Hudson (china), Bagnall st.
Moore & Co. (earthen.), Old Foley pottery
Moore Bros. (china), St. Mary's works, High street
Morley William (earthenware), Albion st.
Oakley & Cope (majolica), New street
Perkins, Knight & Locker (earthenware), High street
Plant & Johnson (china), Heathcote works
Plant John & Co. (decorating), Stafford st.
Plant R.H. & Co. (china), Carlisle works, High street
Poole Thos. (china & majolica), Cobden works
Pugh E.J. and Co., High street
Radford Samuel (china), Chancery lane
Ridge, Meigh & Co. (china), Church st.
Robinson and Co. (china), The Foley
Shaw and Swift (fire brick and sanitary tube), Clayton street, Daisy bank
Skelson and Plant (china and earthenware), Normacott road
Smith Samson (china & gold & silver lustre & figure), Sutherland works, Barker street
Sturgess W.H. (china &c.), works, New street; offices, 18 Market lane
Tams John (earthenware), Crown pottery, 57 Stafford street
Taylor and Kent (china), High street
Taylor, Wain & Bates (china), High st.
Taylor Wm. & Co. (patent stilt and spur), Church street
Tompkinson G. (china), 62 High street
Trubshaw, Hand & Co. (china), High st. and Market street
Unwin Joseph (earthenware and lustre), Cornhill passage
Walters Thomas (china), Commerce street
Warrillow & Cope (china and majolica), Stafford street
Webberley William (china), St. James's works, High street
Williamson and Son (china), Bridge works, Heathcote road
Wilson James (parian), High street
Yearsley Mrs. (parian and patentee of the gold Astrakan trimming for decorating parian goods), Market lane

Stoke – Potters (pages 406-408)
Copeland W.T. & Sons (china, earthenware, and parian), High street
Goss W.H. (parian), London road
Hancock S. (earthenware), Church street
Jones and Meakin (terra cotta, majolica, and jet), Cliff bank
Jones Geo. & Sons (earthenware), Trent pottery
Kirkham William (earthenware), London road; residence, The villas
Meakin J. and G. (earthenware); offices, St. Peter's chambers, Glebe street
Mintons (china, earthenware, and parian), London road
Minton, Hollins and Co. (encaustic tile), Cliff bank
Plant James (stone and earthenware), Registry street
Poole & Son (parian, china, terra cotta, and majolica), John street
Robinson & Leadbeater (parian statuary), Wolfe street
Rose John & Co. (porcelain, &c.), Glebe st

Shorter and Boulton (majolica & earthenware), Copeland street
Smith & Co. (jet & rockingham) Cliff bank
Snow J. & J. (terra cotta and majolica) Liverpool road
Turner and Wood (china and majalica), Copeland street
Victoria Pottery Co. (earthenware), Lonsdale street
Walker and Carter (earthenware), Church street

Stoke – Tile (Encaustic) Manufacturers (page 409)
Campbell Tile Company
Minton, Hollins & Co., Shelton old road
Steele and Wood, London road

Stoke – Tile (Floor) Manufacturers (page 409)
Campbell Tile Company
Minton, Hollins and Co., Shelton old rd.

Tunstall – Potters (page 442)
Adams William & Thomas (earthenware), Greenfields pottery
Beech James (earthenware), High st.
Booth Thomas Gimbert, High street; residence, Wolstanton
Brownhills Pottery Co., Brownhills
Cumberlidge, Rathbone and Co., Well st.
Elsmore Thomas and Son (earthenware), Clayhills pottery
Emberton Thomas James (earthenware), Highgate pottery, Brownhills
Ford and Co., (earthenware), Sandyford
Goode and Kenworthy (earthenware), High street
Grindley W.H. and Co. (earthenware), Newfields pottery
Guest Geo. (earthenware), Soho pottery, off High street
Hammersley R.M. & Co. (earthenware), High street
Holdcroft Wm. (earthenware), George st.
Hollinshead and Kirkham (earthenware), Woodland pottery, Woodland street
Meakin Alfred (earthen.), Parsonage st.
Meir John & Son (earthen.), Greengates
Nixon & Boulton (rockingham, jet, &c.), Summer bank pottery, Newfield
Turner George W. and Sons (earthenware), Victoria works, High street
Wedgwood & Co. (earthenware), Unicorn pottery, Amicable street; and Pinnox works, Great Woodland street

1884 Kelly

Kelly's Directory of Birmingham, Staffordshire, Warwickshire, and Worcestershire (also *Kelly's Directory of Staffordshire*), Kelly & Co., 51 Great Queen Street, Lincoln's Inn Fields, London WC (Shaw & Tipper 6, Shaw & Tipper 1222). Dated MDCCCLXXXIV on the title page and November 1884 in the Preface. It is noted as the Tenth Edition in the Preface.

As with all the Kelly's series, this directory contains alphabetical lists for the various towns and villages and also classified lists for each county. Only the classified lists are included here. The range of categories is extensive and there are twenty-four relevant to this work.

Artists' China Palette Manufacturers (page 483)
Macintyre James & Co. Washington works, Waterloo road, Burslem

Beer Engine Handle Makers (page 487)
Twyford T. Bath st. Hanley. See advt

China Manufacturers (pages 522-523)
See also Earthenware Manufacturers.
Adams, Harvey & Co. Sutherland road, Longton
Adderley & Lawson, Salisbury works, Edensor road, Longton
Adderley W.A. Daisy Bank wrks. Longtn
Aidney, Griffiths & Co. Edensor rd. Lngtn
Allerton Charles & Sons, Park works, High street, Longton
Amison Jsph. Chatfield works, Longton
Anderson & Copestake, Saint Martin's lane, Longton
Asbury E. & Co. Sutherland rd. Longtn
Ashworth G.L. & Bros. Broad st. Hanley
Aynsley J. & Sons, Sutherland rd. Longtn
Baggaley Jacob, Hill works, Burslem
Baxter, Rowley & Tams, High st. Longtn
Beech James & Sons, Albert works, Sutherland road, Longton
Bevington Ambrose & Co. New Hall works, Great York street, Hanley
Bevington Thomas, Burton pl. Hanley
BLAIR & CO. Beaconsfield pottery, Anchor road, Longton; manufacturers for home & export
Bodley Edwin J.D. Hill pottery, Burslem; & 3 & 5 Charterho. st. London e.c
Boughey & Goodwin, Stafford street; works, Willow street, Longton
Boughey, Shore & Martin, Belgrave works, High street, Longton
Bradbury, Kellett & Co. Heathcote road, Longton
Bradley Fredk. D. Clayton st. Longton
Bridgett & Bates, King Street china works, Longton; general china manufacturers for home & export
Brown & Co. Church street, Longton
Brown-Westhead, Moore & Co. Cauldon place, Hanley
Brownfield Wm. & Sons, Cobrdg. Burslm
Burton & Morris, Bagnall st. Longton
Chapman David, Forrister street, Anchor road, Longton
Collingwood & Greatbatch, Stafford street, Longton
Cope Jn. T. Broad Street works, Hanley
Copeland W.T. & Sons, High street, Stoke-on-Trent; London agency, 12 Charterhouse street, Holborn e.c
Copestake George, Anchor wrks. Longtn
Dale, Page & Goodwin, New Town pottery, High street, Longton
Davenport Wm. & Co. Longport, Burslm
Day Joseph & Co. High street, Longton
Day Geo. Albion works, High st. Longtn

Doulton & Co. Nile street, Burslem
EDWARDS GEORGE, Sheridan works, King street, Longton; manufacturer of superior china, suitable for the home & export trade
Edwards John, King street, Fenton Culvert, Stoke-on-Trent
Ferneyhough John, Stafford st. Longton
Finney Joseph, Victoria works, Longton
Ford Charles, Cannon street, Hanley
Gaskell & Grocott, Longport, Stoke-on-Trent
Goss Wm. H. London rd. Stoke-on-Trent
Green T.A. & S. Park street, Fenton Culvert, Stoke-on-Trent
Hallam & Furber, Normacott rd. Longtn
Hammersley J. & R. New st. Hanley
Hollinshead & Kirkham, Woodland pottery, Tunstall
Hollinson & Goodall, 23 High st. Longtn
Hudson Wm. & Son, Stafford st. Longtn
Jackson & Gosling, King street, Fenton Culvert, Stoke-on-Trent
Johnson & Plant, Heathcote rd. Longton
Jones & Howson, Market st. Longton
Kent John & Son, 11 Market street, Longton
Knight & Bridgewood, Staffd. st. Longtn
Lear Samuel, High street, Hanley
Lowe William, Sutherland road & High street, Longton
Macintyre James & Co. Washington works, Waterloo road, Burslem
Massey, Wildblood & Co. Stafford street, Longton
Meigh & Forester, Melbourne works, Church street, Longton
Middleton & Hudson, High street & Bagnall Street works, Longton
Mintons Lim. Eldon pl. Stoke-on-Trent
Moore Brothers, High street, Longton
Plant R.H. & Co. High street, Longton
Pointon & Co. Limited, Norfolk works, Norfolk street, Hanley
Poole Thomas, Edensor road, Longton
Powell & Bishop, Hanley
Procter, Mayer & Woolley, High street, Longton
Radford & Ward, Chancery la. Longton
Radford Samuel, High street, Fenton Culvert, Stoke-on-Trent
Ridge & Sons, Chancery lane, Longton
Robinson & Son, Foley, Fenton Culvert, Stoke-on-Trent
Robinson & Co. Sutherland rd. Longton
Rose John & Co. Glebe st. Stoke-on-Trent
Skelson & Plant, Normacott rd. Longtn
Smith Sampson, Barker street, Longton
SPENCER & STANWAY, Edensor road, Longton; manufac turers of decorated china & earthenware, spirit barrels, tea sets, jugs, toilet wares & general goods suitable for home & exportation
Taylor & Kent, Florence works, High street, Longton
Taylor, Tunnicliff & Co. Eastwood, Hanley; manufacturers of china mortice lock furniture, finger plates, fancy inkstands, stationers' goods & every description of china for brass founders, plumbers, silversmiths, lamp & chandelier manu facturers, scale plates & weights, artists' palettes, color tiles &c. plateaux in every color for painting
Taylor, Waine & Bates, Sutherland road, Longton
Trubshaw, Hand & Co. Albert works, High street, Longton
Turner & Wood, Copeland Street works, Stoke-on-Trent
Vernon's Patent China & Glass Co. Limited, Wharf street, Stoke-on-Trent
Wagstaff & Brunt, Edensor rd. Longton
Walters Thomas, Talbot works, Commerce street, Longton
Warrilow & Cope, Wellington works, Stafford street, Longton
Webberley Wm. St. James wrks. Longtn
Wileman & Co. Foley potteries, Fenton Culvert, Stoke-on-Trent
Wilson James, St. Gregory st. Longton

China Letter Makers (page 523)
Macintyre James & Co. Washington works, Waterloo road, Burslem

Creel Step Manufacturers (page 535)
Hallen Henry, Wellington st. Burslem
Wade & Song, Hall street, Burslem

Door Furniture Makers – China (page 538)
Buller & Co. Joiner's Square wrks. Hanley
Gaskell & Grocott, Longport, Burslem
Macintyre James & Co. Washington works, Waterloo road, Burslem
Taylor, Tunnicliff & Co. Eastwd. Hanley

Earthenware Manufacturers (pages 542-543)
Adams William & Thomas, Tunstall
Adderley Wm. A. Daisy Bank wrks. Lngtn
Alcock Henry & Co. Waterloo road, Cobridge, Burslem
Allerton Charles & Sons, Park works, High street, Longton
Ashworth Geo. L. & Bros. Broad st. Hanley
Aynsley H. & Co. Chancery la. Longton
Baggaley Jacob, Hill works, Burslem
Bailey Rbt. Swan wrks. Elm st. Hanley
Baker & Co. Fenton Culvrt. Stoke-on-Trnt
Banks & Thorley, Bstn. wks. Hgh. st. Hnly
Barker Bros. Barker street, Longton
Barlow Thomas W. & Son, Commerce street, Longton
Bates & Bennett, Sneyd st. Cobrdg. Burslm
Bednall & Heath, Wellington pottry. Hnly
Beech Jas. Swan bank, High st. Tunstall
Bennett Joseph, Wharf lane, Hanley
Bennett William, Victoria road, Hanley
Billington R. 96 Waterloo rd. Burslem
Birks Brothers & Seddon, Waterloo road, Cobridge, Burslem
Blackhurst & Bourne, Hadderidge pottery, Burslem
Bladon & Mullineux, Mayer st. Hanley
Bodley E.F. & Son, Longport
Bodley Edwin Jas. D. Hill pottery, Burslm
Booth T.G. & F. Church Bnk. pottry. Tnstll
Boughey & Goodwin, Stafford street; works, Willow street, Longton
Boulton Jn. Cliffe Bank wks. Stke-on-Trnt
Bradbury Kellett & Co. Heathcote road, Longton
Bridgwood Sampson & Son, East vale, Longton

Broadhurst James, Portland pottery, Fenton Culvert, Stoke-on-Trent
Brough & Blackhurst, Waterloo works, Stafford street, Longton
Brownfield Wm. & Sons, Cobridge, Burslm
BROWNHILLS POTTERY CO. Tunstall, Stoke-on-Trent; manufacturers of decorated earthenware &c. for home & colonial markets; London, 34 Hatton garden e.c
Buckley Wood & Co. High Street pottery, Burslem
Bullock & Cornes, Pelham street, off Lichfield street, Hanley
Burgess & Leigh, Hill pottery, Burslem
Burgess Henry, Kiln Croft works, Chapel lane, Burslem
Burton G. & B. Waterloo works, Hanley
Cartlidge William Edward, Villa pottery, Cobridge, Burslem
Cartwright & Edwards, Trentham road, Longton
Challinor Edwd. & Chas. High st. Fenton Culvert & Glebe st. Stoke-on-Trent
Clark Edward, Wood street, Burslem
Clementson Brothers, Phoenix & Bell works, Broad street, Hanley
Clews William, William street, Hanley
Cliff & Blore, North rd. Cobridge, Burslem
Cooper & Son, Caroline street, Longton
Copeland W.T. & Sons, High st. Stoke-on-Trent; London agency, 12 Charterhouse street, Holborn e.c
Corn William & Edward, Navigation road & North road, Burslem
Cotton Elijah, Lichfield St. works, Hanley
Cotton Jn. Peel St. wks. Northwood, Hanly
Crystal Porcelain Pottery Co. Lim. Elder road, Cobridge, Burslem, Stoke-on-Trent
Cumberlidge & Humphreys, Well street, Tunstall
Davenport W. & Co. Lim, Longprt. Burslm
Davis John Heath, Trent pottery, Kirkham street, Hanley
Dawson James, Stafford st. Longton
Dean, Capper & Dean, New st. Hanley
Dimmock J. & Co. Stafford st. Hanley
Doulton & Co. Nile street, Burslem
Dudson James, Hope street & Hanover street, Hanley
Dunn, Bennett & Co. Boothen works, Brook street, Hanley
Edge, Malkin & Co. Newport wrks. Brslm
Edwards J. & B. Fenton road, Hanley
Edwards William, Russell st. Longton
Emberton Jas. Highgate pottery, Tunstall
Emery F.J. Bleak Hl. wrks. Bleak st. Bslm
Fielding S. & Co. Railway pottery, Stoke-on-Trent
Finney Joseph, Victoria works, Longton
Ford & Riley, Newcastle st. Burslem
Ford & Co. Sandyford, Tunstall
Forester & Sons, Phoenix works, Church street, Longton
Furnival Thomas & Sons, Cobridge, Stoke-on-Trent; manufacturers of white granite & decorated earthenware, for home & foreign markets
Gater & Co. Furlong lane, Burslem
Gildea & Walker, Dale hall, Burslem; & 30 Holborn, London e.c
Goode & Kenworthy, High st. Tunstall, Stoke-on-Trent; manufacturers for home & foreign markets
Green & Clay, Stafford street, Longton
GRINDLEY W.H. & CO. Newfield pottery, Tunstall, Stoke-on-Trent; manufacturers of ironstone china & decorated earthenware suitable for the Canadian, United States, South American & Australian markets
Grove & Stark, Palissy works, Longton
Guest Geo. & Son, Albert st. Tunstall
Hall & Hume, William street, Hanley
Hall & Read, Victoria square, Hanley
Hammersley Brothers, Nelson pl. Hanley
Hammersley Ralph & Son, High st. Tunstall & at Wedgewood pl. Burslem
Hammonds & Co. Garfield works, High street, Longton
Hancock S. Church st. Stoke-on-Trent
Harrop W. & Co. Tinker's clough, Hanley
Hawley & Co. Foley, Fenton Culvert, Stoke-on-Trent
Hobson Geo. & John, Albert st. Burslem
Holdcroft William, George st. Tunstall
Hollinshead & Kirkham, Woodland pottery, Tunstall
Hollinson & Goodall, 23 High st. Longton
Holmes, Plant & Madew, Sylvester pottery, Burslem
Hughes Thomas, Longport, Burslem
Johnson Bros. Old Hall street, Hanley
Jones & Bromley, High street, Longton
Jones G. & Sons, London rd. Stoke-on-Tnt
Jones & Hopkinson, Ranelagh wrks. Hnly
Jones Frederick, Chadwick st. Longton
Kent John & Son, 11 Market st. Longton
Kent & Parr (figure), Wellington street, Burslem
Kirkby William & Co. Sutherland pottery, Fenton Culvert, Stoke-on-Trent. See advertisement
Kirkham W. London rd. Stoke-on-Trent
Knapper & Blackhurst, Newport la. Brslm
Knight & Bridgwood, Stafford st. Longton
Lear Samuel, High street, Hanley
Leigh William, Hill pottery, Burslem
Lockett Jn. & Co. Chancery la. Longton
Lowe Ratcliffe & Co. Gold st. Longton
Lowe Wm., Sutherlnd. rd. & High st. Lngtn
Machin William, Percy St. works, Hanley
Maddock & Co. Dale Hall pottery, Burslem
Maddock J. & Sons, Newcastle st. Burslem
Malkin R. Fenton Culvrt. Stoke-on-Trent
Meakin James & George, 16 Glebe street, Stoke; & at Eagle Pottery, Hanley
Meakin Alfred, Royal Albert pottery, Parsonage street, Tunstall
Meakin Charles, Lichfield st. Hanley
Meir J. & Son, Greengate potteries, Tunstll
Mellor Taylor & Co. Bourne's bnk. Burslm
Mills & Perrot, Granville pottery, Bryan street, Hanley
Mintons Lim. Eldon pl. Stoke-on-Trent
Moore & Co. Old Foley pottery, Longton
Morley William, Albert road, Fenton Culvert, Stoke-on-Trent
Mountford & Thomas, Union st. Hanley
Newport Wharf Pottery Co. (Thomas F. Wood, managing partner), Navigation road, Burslem

Nixon George, Newfield view, Tunstall
Oakley & Co. New street, Longton
Old Hall Earthenware Co. Limited, Hill street, Hanley
Ouslnam William E. & Sons, Furlong works, Burslem
Owen, Raby & Co. Dalehall, Burslem
Peake Joseph, Etruria Vale, Hanley
Plant James, Registry st. Stoke-on-Trent
Plant Ralph, Sylvester pottery, Burslem
Poole & Son, John street, Stoke-on-Trent
Powell, Bishop & Stonier, Stafford St.; & High street, Hanley
Pratt Felix & Richard & Co. High street east, Fenton Culvert, Stoke-on-Trent
Pugh Edwd. Jn. & Co. 31 High st. Longton
Pugh & Glover, Pelham Street works, Pelham street, Hanley
Quick J.J. & Co. Limited, Clarence street, Hanley
Rathbone, Smith & Co. Soho pottry. Tnstll
Revees James, Victoria works, Market street, Fenton, Stoke-on-Trent
Rhodes & Co. Bourne's bank, Burslem
Rhodes John, Swan bank, Burslem
Ridgways, Bedford wrks. Bdfrd. rd. Hnly
Rigby Elijah, jun. Chell street, Hanley
Robinson J. Knwle. wks. Hamil rd. Brslm
Shaw Anthony & Son, Mersey wks. Burslm
Shaw & Ridge, Albion street, Longton
Shenton Herbert, Hope works, Union street, Hanley
Smith & Co. High street, Stoke-on-Trnt
Stanway & Tellwright, Sneyd street, Cobridge, Burslem
Steel Edward, manufacturer of earthenware, majolica & parian statuettes, Cannon street works, Hanley
Stonier, Hollinshead & Oliver, High street, Hanley
Stubbs Wm. Eastwood pottery, Hanley
Swan & Paulson, Amicable st. Tunstall
Tams John, Stafford street, Longton
Taylor, Tunnicliff & Co. Eastwood, Hanley
Till Thos. & Sons, Liverpool rd. Burslem
Toft & Cope, High st. Stoke-on-Trent
Turner G.W. & Sons, Victoria wks. Tunstll
Turner & Wood, Copeland street works, Stoke-on-Trent
Unwin Joseph, Cornhill works, Longton
Vernon J. & G. Waterloo wks. Burslem
Wagstaff & Brunt, Edensor rd. Longton
Walker & Carter, Church st. Stk.-on-Trnt
Wallis Gimson & Co. Park street, Fenton Culvert, Stoke-on-Trent
Wedgwood J. & Sons, Etruria pottery, Etruria, Stoke-on-Trent
Wedgwood & Co. Pinnox & Unicorn works, Tunstall
Whittaker, Edge & Co. Hallfield pottery, Grafton street, Hanley
Wileman James F. Foley works, Fenton Culvert, Stoke-on-Trent
Wilkinson A. Central pottery, Burslem
Wood, Hines & Winkle, Pearl pottery, Brook street, Hanley
Wood & Hulme, Waterloo rd. Burslem
Wood William & Co. Albert Street works, Burslem
Worthington & Son, Brook st. Hanley

Encaustic Tile Manufacturers (page 543)
Boote Thomas & Richard, Waterloo potteries, Burslem
Boulton William, Navigation road & Pleasant street, Burslem. See advt
CAMPBELL TILE CO. (THE), London road, Stoke-on-Trent; manufacturers of encaustic, geometrical & majolica tiles & mosaics; London house, 206 Great Portland street w
Cowie John Edmund, Glebe buildings, Stoke-upon-Trent
Decorative (The) Art Tile Company (William Parrish, managing partner), 200 & 202, Bryan street, Hanley
Malkin, Edge & Co. Newport works, Burslem. See advertisement
Minton, Hollins & Co. Stoke-on-Trent
Mintons Lim. Eldon pl. Stoke-on-Trent
Sherwin & Cotton, Vine street, Hanley
Simpson T.A. High st. Stoke-on-Trent
Steele & Wood, London rd. Stoke-on-Trnt
Wood Ambrose (merchants), Regent house, Regent road, Hanley
Woolliscroft George & Son, Patent tile works, Canal side, Hanley

Jagger (sic) Manufacturer (page 598)
Wakefield Thomas, Botany Bay, Northwood, Hanley

Jet Ware Manufacturers (page 599)
Fell John & Co. Adelaide works, Longtn
Harrison & Baker, King's Field pottery, Newcastle
Hollinshead & Kirkham, Woodland pottery, Tunstall
Johnson & Martin, Newport st. Burslem
Sudlow Robert, Bourne's bank, Burslem
Wood Hy. James, Chapel lane, Burslem

Lock Furniture Makers – China (page 605)
Macintyre James & Co. Washington works, Waterloo road, Burslem
Taylor, Tunnicliff & Co. Eastwood, Hanley
Wood W. & Co. Albert St. works, Burslem

Lustre Manufacturers (page 606)
Allerton Charles & Sons (gold & silver), Park works, High street, Longton

Majolica Manufacturers (page 606)
Adams & Bromley, Broad st. Hanley
Banks & Thorley, Boston works, High street, Hanley
Benson & Bailey, Normacott rd. Longton
Fell John & Co. Adelaide works & 46 Fore street, London
Fielding S. & Co. Railway pottery, Stoke-on-Trent. London show rooms, Union Bank buildings, Holborn circus (F. Hope, agent)
Forrester Thomas Wm. (dealer) Alma works, Marsh street, Hanley
Heath Thomas, Parkhall street, Longton
Holdcroft Joseph, Daisy bank, Longton
Mintons Limited, Eldon pl. Stoke-on-Trnt
Oakes, Clare & Chadwick, Albert st. Brslm

Shorter & Boulton, Copeland street, Stoke-on-Trent
Stanway & Fellwright, Sneyd street, Cobridge, Burslem
Turner & Wood, Copeland Street works, Stoke-on-Trent
Wardle & Co. Victoria road, Hanley

Mortar & Pestle Manufacturers (page 612)
Macintyre James & Co. Washington works, Waterloo road, Burslem

Parian Manufacturers (page 617)
Copeland W.T. & Sons, High street, Stoke-on-Trent; London agency, 12 Charterhouse street, Holborn e.c
Edwards T. & B. Fenton road, Hanley
Hammersley Bros. Nelson pl. Hanley
Harrop W. & Co. Tinker's clough, Hanley
Mintons' Limited, Eldon place, Stoke-on-Trent
Robinson & Leadbeater, Wolfe street, Stoke-on-Trent
Steel Edward, Cannon street, Hanley
Turner & Wood, Copeland Street works, Stoke-on-Trent
Wilson James, St. Gregory st. Longton
Yearsley Mrs. M.A. 12 & 14 Market lane, Longton

Potters (page 621)
Kent Philip Joynson, Endon Edge works, Endon, Stoke-on-Trent

Rockingham Ware Manufacturers (page 639)
Bevington Jas. King St. works, Hanley
Hollinshead & Kirkham, Woodland pottery, Tunstall
Hurd Thomas Mansfield & Co. Nile street, Burslem
Johnson & Martin, Newport st. Burslem
Oakes, Clare & Chadwick, Albert street, Burslem
Rathbone R. Sylvester street, Burslem
Sudlow Robert, Bourne's bank, Burslem
Wade, Colclough & Lingard, High street, Burslem
Wood Henry James, Chapel la. Burslem

Sanitary Ware Manufacturers (page 641)
Brough William & Son, Silverdale, Newcastle. See advertisement
Buckley John, manufacturer of water-closet basins & traps, table tops, urinals, ship & portable closets &c. 'Niagara Falls' basin & traps &c. Albert works, Victoria place, Hanley
Gratton & Co. Victoria works, Lonsdale street, Stoke-on-Trent
Howson G. Clifford st. Eastwood, Hanley
Twyford Thomas, Abbey, Bucknall, Stoke-on-Trent & at Bath street, Hanley. See advertisement
Victoria Sanitary Co. (Gratton & Co. proprs.), Victoria wks. Stoke-on-Trnt

Shuttle Eye Manufacturers (page 662)
Hallen Henry, Wellington st. Burslem
Wade & Sons, Hall street, Burslem

Spur Makers (page 669)
Ford Charles & Co. Parker st. Hanley

Spur & Stilt Makers for Pottery Manufacturers (page 669)
Arrowsmith T. Moorland rd. Burslem
Ford Charles & Co. Parker street, Hanley
Gimson Joseph & Co. High street, Fenton Culvert, Stoke-on-Trent
Shirley Elijah, Moorland road, Burslem
Taylor William & Co. Church st. Longton

Stoneware Manufacturers (page 672)
Rigby James, Milton, Stoke-on-Trent

Terra Cotta Manufacturers (page 677)
Balfour & Co. Oldfield Terra Cotta works, Lane End works, Longton
Harrison & Baker, Shelton New rd. Nwcstl
Peake Thomas, The Tileries, Tunstall
Snow J. & J. Liverpool rd. Stk.-on-Trent
Turner & Wood, Copeland Street works, Stoke-on-Trent

Water Closet Makers (page 684)
Buckley John, Albert works, Victoria place, Hanley
Gratton & Co. Victoria works, Lonsdale street, Stoke-on-Trent
Twyford Thomas, Bath street, Hanley. See advertisement

1887 Porter

Postal Directory for the Potteries with Newcastle & District, Published for the Compiler, Frank Porter, New Brighton, by Rockliff Brothers Limited, 44 Castle Street, Liverpool (Shaw & Tipper 1242). Dated 1887 on the title page.

This directory is classified within areas which include the six main pottery towns. The major relevant category is Earthenware Manufacturers, except for Stoke where it is listed as Manufacturers of China and Earthenware, although there are a few other minor categories. The list for Burslem appears twice, the original (pages 119-121) being supplemented by an errata (page 118B). The list included here is the errata which incorporates some minor changes (while introducing a few obvious typographical errors) and was presumably more up to date.

Hanley – Earthenware Manufacturers (pages 33-35)
Adams and Bromley, Broad st
——— Joseph, 28 Brook st
Art Tile Company, Bryan st
Ashworth George L. and Brothers, Broad st
Baker James, Stoke rd
Banks and Co., Boston works, High st
Barlow Charles, Smithfield works

Bednall and Heath, Wellington pottery
Bennett J., Rectory rd
——— Wm., Cleveland works, Victoria rd
Bentley, Powis and Co., William Street works
Benton and Critchley, Style works, Trent walk
Betteley and Clowes, Mayer st
Bevington John, Broad st
——— Ambrose and Co., New Hall works, Marsh st
——— Thomas, Burton place
Bladon and Molyneux, Mayer Street works
Boulton and Creyke, Avery st
Booth Herbert, 34 Berkley st
Brown, Westhead and Moore, Cauldon place
Buller, Jobson and Co., Joiners' square
Bullock and Cornes, Pelham st
Burton Brothers, Waterloo Pottery
Campbell, O'Donnell and Co., Stoke rd
Cartlidge and Matthews, Mount Pleasant works
Clementson Brothers, Phoenix and Bell works
Clews Wm., William Street Pottery
Cope and Dewsbury, Broad st
Cotton Elijah, Nelson Pottery
Davies John H., Trent Pottery
Dimmock J. and Co., Albion works, Stafford st
Edwards and Son, Trent works
Ford Charles, Cannon st
Grimwade Brothers, Winton Pottery, Stoke road
Hall and Hulme, Havelock works, Broad st
Hammersley Brothers, Nelson place
Harrop Wm. and Co., Dresden works, Tinkers clough
Hollins Joseph and Co., King Street jet and Rockingham works
Hopkinson James, Ranelagh st
Howlett Joseph, Northwood Pottery
Howson George, Clifford st
Johnson Brothers, Oldhall st
Jones and Hopkins, Ranelagh st
Jones, Hopkinson and Sherwin, Ringold works, Mollart st
Leib Elizabeth, 130 Hope st
Machin Wm., 67 Bethesda st
Malkin and Shirley, Vulcan works, High st
Meakin Charles, Eastwood, Lichfield st
——— J. and G., Eagle Pottery
Mountford and Thomas, Marlborough works, Union st
Old Hall Porcelain Works, limited, New st
Peake Joseph, Bridgewater arms, Etruria vale
Pennington John, Mayer st
Pointon and Co., Norfolk works, Norfolk st
Powell, Bishop and Stonier, Botteslow st, Stafford st and High st
Pugh and Hackney, Pelham st works
Quick Joseph J. and Co., Clarence st works
Rigby Elijah, Providence Pottery
Ridgway Messrs., limited, Bedford works
Simms George, 22 Bedford rd
Smith and Frost, Anchor works, Brewery st
Snow Jonathan and John, Pyenest st works
Steele Edward, Cannon st works
Stonier, Hollinshead and Oliver, High st
Stubbs Wm., Eastwood Pottery
Taylor, Tunnicliffe and Co., Eastwood
Twyford Thomas, Bath st and Abbey works
Wakefield George, 63 William st
Wardle and Co., Victoria works, Victoria rd
Welch James B., Excelsior works, New st
Whitaker and Co., Hallfield Pottery
Winkle and Wood, Pearl Pottery, Marsh st
Wedgwood Josiah and Son, Etruria works
Worthington and Son, Brook st & Clarence street

Hanley – Spur and Stilt Manufacturers (page 48)
Ford and Co., Etruria rd

Hanley – Tile Manufacturer (page 49)
Sherwin and Cotton, Vine st
Eardly Wm., 63 Lichfield st
Jackson Brothers, Castle field
Woolliscroft George, Etruscan st, Etruria

Burslem Errata – Earthenware Manufacturers (page 118B)
Alcock Henry and Co., Waterloo rd
Baker and Rycroft, Liverpool rd
Barber Joseph, Albert st
Barnett Wm., potters' manager, 17 Dimsdale st
Bates and Bennett, Cobridge
Benson and Bailey, Moorland rd
Blackhurst and Bourne, Bath st
Bloore Ralph Wm., North rd
Bodley E.F. and Son, Longport
——— Edwin J.D., Market place
Boote Thomas and Richard, Waterloo rd
Brownfield Wm. and Sons, Cobridge
Brownhills Pottery Co., Liverpool rd
Buckley, Heath and Co., High st
Burgess Henry, Kilncroft works
——— and Leigh, Hill pottery
Cartlidge W.E., Elder rd
Corn Wm. and Edward, Navigation road pottery
Davenport Messrs., Longport works
Deare Brothers, Ducal works, Dale hill
Doulton and Co., Nile st works
Dunn, Bennett and Co., Royal Victoria pottery
Edge and Malkin, Newport works
Edwards and Goodwin, Hanover st pottery
Emery Francis J., Bleak hill works
Ford and Riley, Newcastle st
Furnival and Son, Waterloo rd
Gaskell and Grocott, Longport
——— Kent and Parr, Novelty works
Gater Thomas, Furlong lane pottery
Gildea James, Dale Hall works
Gibson and Sons, Moorland rd
Hallen Henry, Wellington st works
Hammersley Ralph and Son, Over House pottery
Hill George, 12 Rushton rd

Hobson George and John, Albert st
Holmes, Plant and Co., Silvester pottery
Hughes Thomas, Longport works
Hurd Thomas Mansfield and Co., Union st works
Jelson, Brayford and Co., Fountain pottery
Johnson Samuel, Newport st
Keeling and Co., Swan bank pottery
Kent and Lovatt, New st pottery
Kirkham James and Co., Commercial st works
Macintyre James and Co., Washington works, Waterloo rd
Maddock and Co., Dale Hall pottery
——— John and Sons, Newcastle st
Mellor, Taylor and Co., Waterloo rd
New Wharf Pottery Company
Oakes, Clarke and Chadwick, Albert st
Oulsman Thomas and Sons, Furlong works
Plant Brothers, Newcastle st
Platt Ambrose, 6 Moorland rd
Rathbone Wm., 50 Price st
Robinson Joseph, Moorland rd
Sant Jeremiah, 78 Waterloo rd
——— and Vodrey, Cobridge
Shaw Anthony and Son, Prospect st
——— Robert, Bourne's Bank works
Stanway Levi, Sneyd green
Steele and Wood, Elder rd
Sudlow Robert, Bourne's Park works
Till and Sons, Sylch pottery
Vernon James and George, Waterloo rd
Wade and Co., High st works
Whittam and Mear, Newcastle st
Wilkinson Arthur James, Market place
Willshaw and Sadler, Moorland rd
Wood Henry James, Chapel lane works
——— and Hulme, Waterloo rd
——— Thomas and Co., Queen st pottery
——— Wm. and Co., Albert st works

Burslem – Spur and Stilt Manufacturers (page 133)
Hunt Maria, 66 Liverpool rd
Shirley Elijah, Moorland rd

Fenton – Earthenware Manufacturers (page 171)
Baker and Co., Fountain square
Broadhurst James, Portland pottery, Frederick st
Campbell, O'Donnell and Davies, Canning street
Challinor and Mayor, Market st
Edwards John, King st
Fielding and Co., Sutherland st
Forrester and Hulme, High st
Green Thomas A. and Spencer, Minerva china works
Hawley and Co., Foley works
Hines Bros., Heron Cross pottery
Jackson and Gosling, Grosvenor works
Lawton Wm., Oddfellows' Arms, Chapel st
Malkin Ralph and Sons, Park works
Moore and Co., Old Foley pottery
Morley Wm., Salopian works
Pratt F. and R., High st
Radford Samuel, High st
Reeves James, Victoria works, High st
Robinson and Sons, Foley works
Wallis, Gimson and Co., Lane Delf pottery
Ward Frederick W., 179 High st
Wileman and Co., Foley china works
——— J.F., Foley potteries

Fenton – Spur and Stilt Manufacturers (page 175)
Edwards John and Sons, King st
Gimson J. and Co., Market st

Longton – Earthenware Manufacturers (pages 205-207)
Adams Richard Stanley, Anchor works, Anchor rd
Adderley Wm. Alsager & Co., Daisy bank
——— and Tams, Sutherland works, High st
——— and Lawson, Edensor rd
Allerton Charles and Sons, Park works, High st
Allerton Charles W., Victoria works
Amison Joseph, Mount pleasant, High st
Anderson and Copestake, St. Martin's works, Market st
Asbury Edward and Co., Sutherland rd
Aynsley H. and Co., Commerce st works
Ball Joseph, jun., Anchor rd
Ball Joseph, jun,, 100 Caroline st
Barlow Thomas and Son, Coronation works, Commerce st
Barlow and Co., Church st works
Barker Bros., Meir works, High st
Blackhurst, Hulme and Berkin, Belgrave works, High st
Beech and Son, Sutherland rd
Blair and Co., Beaconsfield pottery, Anchor street
Booth Arthur, 15 Sutherland ter
Boughey Matthew, Willow st works
Bradley Frederick D., Sutherland rd
Bridgwood Sampson and Son, Anchor pottery
——— Richard, 82 Stafford st
British Anchor Pottery Co., Anchor rd
Brough and Blackhurst, Waterloo works, Stafford st
Burton and Morris, Bagnall works, Bagnall street
Cartwright and Edwards, Borough pottery, Trentham rd
Chapman Joseph, Atlas works, Forrester st
Colclough and Co., Clayton st
Collingwood Bros., Crown works, Stafford st
Cope James H. and Co., Wellington works, Stafford st
Cooper and Son, Viaduct works, Caroline st
Dale, Page and Goodwin, New Town works
Dawson James, Stanley pottery, Stafford st
Day George, Albion works, High st
Deakin Wm. Oswald, Cromartie works, Market st
Edwards and Brown, Victoria works, High street
——— George, Sheridan works, King st
——— R.J., Gordon pottery, Anchor rd
——— Wm., Russell st
Fell and Co., Union place
Fernyhough John, Dresden works, Stafford street
Finney Joseph, Willow cot, Clayton st
——— Joseph, Victoria works, Willow st

Forester Thomas and Son, Phoenix works, Church st
——— Thomas and Son, Mill works and Phoenix works
Green and Clay, Stafford st
Grove F.M., Chancery lane
——— Fredk. W., Palissy works, Chancery lane
Hallam and Blair, Normacot rd
Hammersley and Co., Sutherland rd
Hammonds and Buckley, Victoria works, High st
Harrison Charles, Queen st
Heath Thomas, Baltimore works
Holdcroft Joseph, Sutherland Pottery, Daisy bank
Hollinson and Goodall, 23 High st
Hudson Wm. and Son, Stafford st
Jones Alfred B., Eagle works, Station square
——— Thomas and Co., New st works
——— and Howson, Ebenezer works, Market st
Kellett, Proctor and Co., Heathcote pottery
Lockett John and Co., Chancery lane
Lowe Wm., Sydney works, High st
——— —, Sydney works, Sutherland rd
——— Ratcliffe and Co., Gold street works
Middleton & Hudson, Bagnall street works
——— ———, Alma works, 100 High street
Moore Brothers, St. Mary's works
Plant Richard H., Carlisle works
Poole Thomas, Cobden works, New st
Procter, Mayer and Woolley, Gladstone works, High st
Pugh E.J. and Co., Market st
Radford and Ward, Newmarket works, Chancery lane
Reynolds and Rhead, Normacot rd
Ridge and Sons, Chancery lane
——— Wm. A., Market st
——— Wm. A., Albert works, High st and Market st works
Shore John and Co., Edensor works, New street
Skelson and Platt, Normacot rd
Stubbs Joshua, 31 High st
Sutherland, Cyples and Co., Heathcote works, Heathcote rd
Tams John, Crown pottery, Stafford st
Taylor and Forester, Melbourne works, Church st
——— and Kent, Florence works, High st
Tomkinson Charles, Britannia works, High street
Tunnicliffe James, 25 Normacot rd
Unwin Joseph, Cornhill works, Market lane
Wagstaff and Brunt, King st pottery
Waine and Bates, Sutherland rd
Warrilow George, Park Place works, High street
Webberley Wm., St. James works, High st
Wildblood Richard Vernon, Peel works, Stafford st
Williamson Henry M. and Sons, Bridge pottery, Heathcote rd
Wilson James, Gregory st
Yearsley Mary A., Market lane

Stoke – Manufacturers of China and Earthenware (page 281)
Boulton John, Cliff bank
Brough and Jones, Wharf st pottery
Copeland Wm. T. and Sons, Church st
Gleaves Wm. Thomas, Albion pottery, Etruria
Goss Wm. Henry, London rd
Hancock Samson, Bridge works, Church st
Harrison David B. and Co., Kingsfield pottery, Shelton Old rd
Jones George and Sons, Trent potteries
Kirkham Wm., Kirkham st
Meakin J. and G., 31 Glebe st
Mintons, Limited, London rd
Robinson and Leadbeater, Wolfe st
Sandland, Bennett and Co., Victoria works, Lonsdale st
Shingler and Co., Albert works, Liverpool rd
Shorter and Boulton, Copeland st
Smith J. and H., Cliff bank
Toft Charles, Swan works, High st
Walker and Carter, Anchor works, Church street

Stoke – Tile Manufacturers (page 283)
Campbell Tile Works, Liverpool rd
Minton Hollins and Co., Shelton Old rd
Simpson Thomas A., Cliff Bank works
Steele and Wood, London rd
Wood and Co., Boothen Road works

Tunstall – Earthenware Manufacturers (page 323)
Adams Wm. and Thomas, Greenfield pottery
Beach James, Swan bank
Beard Arthur, Pittshill
Booth T.G. and F., Church bank and Highgate potteries
Brownhills Pottery Co., Brownhills
Colclough and Lingard, 32 High st
Cumberlidge and Humphrey, Gordon pottery, High st
Ford, Thomas and Co., Sandyford pottery
Goode and Kenworthy, Church st pottery
Grindley Wm. Harry and Co., Newfield pottery
Holdcroft —, George st pottery
Hollinshead and Kirkham, Woodland st
Meakin Alfred, Royal Albert pottery, Bank street
Meir John and Son, Greengates
Rathbone, Smith and Co., Soho pottery, High st
Swann E., Globe pottery, High st
Turner G.W. and Sons, Scotia rd
Wedgwood and Co., Unicorn pottery

Tunstall – Jet Manufacturers (page 329)
Guest George, Albert st pottery
Nixon George, Summer bank pottery
Parr Joseph, Sandyford

Silverdale (page 451)
BROUGH & SON, manufacturers of metalic blue bricks and tiles, Silverdale Tileries

1888 Kelly

Kelly's Directory of Birmingham, Staffordshire, Warwickshire, and Worcestershire (also *Kelly's Directory of Staffordshire*), Kelly & Co., 51 Great Queen Street, Lincoln's Inn Fields, London WC (Shaw & Tipper 6, Shaw & Tipper 1222). Dated MDCCCLXXXVIII on the title page and August 1888 in the Preface. It is noted as the Eleventh Edition in the Preface.

As with all the Kelly's series, this directory contains alphabetical lists for the various towns and villages and also classified lists for each county. Only the classified lists are included here. The range of categories is extensive and there are twenty-one relevant to this work

Beer Machine Handle Maker (page 519)
Twyford Thomas, Cliffe vale, Hanley. See advertisement

China Manufacturers (pages 553-554)
See also Earthenware Manufacturers.
Adderley & Lawson, Salisbury works, Edensor road, Longton
Adderley W.A. Daisy Bank works, Longtn
Aidney, Griffiths & Co. Edensor road, Longton
Allen S. see Cartlidge & Allen, Longton
Allerton Charles & Sons, Park works, High street, Longton
Amison Jsph. Mount Pleasant, Longton
Anderson & Copestake, St. Martin's lane, Longton
Ashbury E. & Co. Sutherland rd. Longtn
Ashworth G.L. & Bros. Broad st. Hanley
Aynsley J. & Son, Sutherland rd. Longton
Bates Thos. see Waine & Bates, Longton
Beech James & Sons, Albert works, Sutherland road, Longton
Bevington Thomas, Burton pl. Hanley
Birkin Samuel, see Blackhurst, Hume & Birkin, Longton
Blackhurst, Hume & Birkin, High street, Longton
BLAIR & CO. Beaconsfield pottery, Anchor road, Longton; manufacturers for home & export
Bodley Edwin James Drew, Hill pottery, Burslem; & 3 Charterhouse street, London EC
Boughey Matth. Willow St. wrks. Longton
Bradley Fk. D. Sutherland rd. Longton
Bridgett & Bates, King Street china works, Longton; general china manufacturers for home & export
Brown-Westhead (T.C.), Moore & Co. Cauldon place, Hanley
Brown H. see Edwards & Brown, Longtn
Brownhills Pottery Co. (The), Tunstall
Burton & Morris, Bagnall st. Longton
Cartlidge & Allen, Mt. Pleasant, Longton
Chapman David, Forrister street, Anchor road, Longton
Collingwood Bros. Stafford st. Longton
Cope Jas. H. & Co. Stafford st. Longton
Cope Jn. Thos. Broad Street wrks. Hanley
Copeland W.T. & Sons, High st. Stoke; London agency, 12 Charterhouse st EC
Dale, Page & Goodwin, New Town pottery, High street, Longton
Day Geo. Albion wrks. High st. Longton
Edwards & Brown, High street, Longton
Edwards R.J. & Co. Forrister st. Longtn
Edwards George, Sheridan works, King street, Longton; manufacturer of superior china, suitable for the home & export trade
Edwards J. King st. Fenton culvert, Stoke
Ferneyhough John, Stafford st. Longton
Finney J. Victoria pl. Stafford st. Longton
Ford Charles, Cannon street, Hanley
Gaskell & Grocott, Longport, Wolstanton, Stoke-on-Trent
Goss William H. London road, Stoke
Green T.A. & S. Park street, Fenton culvert, Stoke-on-Trent
Grindley W.H. & Co. Newfield pttry. Tnstll
Hallam & Blair, Normacott rd. Longton
Hammersley Jsph. & Rt. New st. Hanley
Hammersley & Co. Sutherland rd. Longtn
Hudson Wm. & Son, Stafford st. Longton
Jackson & Gosling, King street, Fenton Culvert, Longton
Jones George & Sons, London rd. Stoke
Jones & Howson, Market street, Longton
Lowe W. Sutherland rd. & High st. Longtn
Macintyre Jas. & Co. Washington works, Burslem; & 23 Bartlett's bldgs. Londn
Middleton & Hudson, High street & Bagnall Street works, Longton
Mintons Limited, Eldon place, Stoke-on-Trent; & 28 Walbrook, London EC
Moore Brothers, High street, Longton
Plant R.H. & Co. High street, Longton
Pointon & Co. Limited, Norfolk works, Norfolk street, Hanley
Poole Thomas, Edensor road, Longton
Powell, Bishop & Stonier, Hanley
Procter, Mayer & Woolley, High street, Longton
Radford & Ward, Chancery la. Longton
Ridge & Sons, Chancery lane, Longton
Robinson & Son, Folcy, Fenton culvert, Longton
Shore J. & Co. New street, Longton
Skelson & Plant, Normacott rd. Longtn
Smith Sampson, Barker street, Longton
Sutherland, Cyples & Co. Heathcote rd. Longton
Taylor & Forester, Melbourne works, Church street, Longton
Taylor & Kent, Florence works, High street, Longton
Taylor, Tunnicliff & Co. Eastwood, Hanley; manufacturers of china mortice lock furniture, finger plates, fancy inkstands, stationers' goods & every description of china for brass founders, plumbers, silversmiths, lamp & chandelier manu facturers, scale plates & weights, artists' palettes, color tiles &c. plateaux in every color for painting
Waine & Bates, Sutherland rd. Longton
Walters Thomas, Commerce st. Longton
Warrilow George, High street, Longton
Webberley Wm. St. James' wrks. Longtn
Wildblood Richd. V. Stafford st. Longton
Wileman & Co. Foley potteries, Fenton culvert, Longton

Williamson H.M. & Sons, Bridge pottery, Heathcote road, Longton
Wilson James, Gregory street, Longton

Creel Step Manufacturers (page 566)
Hallen Henry, Wellington st. Burslem
Wade & Sons, Hall street, Burslem

Door Furniture Makers – China (page 569)
Buller Jobson & Co. Limited, Joiner's Square works, Hanley
Gaskell & Grocott, Longport, Burslem
Macintyre James & Co. Washington works, Burslem; or 23 Bartlett's buildings, London
Wood William & Co. Albert Street works, Burslem

Earthenware Manufacturers (page 573)
Adams William & Thomas, Tunstall
Adams Richd. S. Anchor rd. Longton
Adderley Wm. A. Daisy bank wrks. Longtn
Alcock Henry & Co. Waterloo road, Cobridge, Burslem
Allerton Charles & Sons, Park works, High street, Longton
Ashworth G.L. & Bros. Broad st. Hanley
Aynsley H. & Co. Chancery la. Longton
Baker & Roycroft, Fountain Place pottery, Burslem
Baker & Co. Fenton culvert, Stoke
Baker James, Stoke rd. Shelton, Hanley
Banks E. Boston works, High st. Hanley
Barker Brothers, Barker street, Longton
Barlow & Son, Commerce street, Longton
Bates & Bennett, Sneyd street, Cobridge, Burslem
Bednall & Heath, Wellington pottry. Hanly
Beech J. Swan bank, High st. Tunstall
Bennett Joseph, Wharf lane, Hanley
Bennett William, Victoria road, Hanley
Benson Bailey, Moorland road, Burslem
Bevington Ambrose & Co. New Hall works, Great York street, Hanley
Billington R. 96 Waterloo rd. Burslem
Blackhurst & Bourne, Hadderidge pottery, Burslem
Bladon & Mullineux, Mayer st. Hanley
Bodley Edwd. & Son, Longport, Burslem
Booth T.G. & F. Church Bank pottery & Highgate, Tunstall
Boulton & Floyd, Cliffe Bank works, High street & Hall st. Stoke-on-Trent
Bourne & Sheddadd, Swan works, Elm street, Hanley
Bridgwood S. & Son, East vale, Longton
British Anchor Pottery Co. Lim. Anchor road, Longton
Broadhurst James, Portland pottery, Fenton culvert, Stoke-on-Trent
Brough & Blackhurst, Waterloo works, Stafford street, Longton
Brough & Jones, Wharf st. pottery, Stoke
Brownfield W. & Sons, Cobridge, Burslem
BROWNHILLS POTTERY CO. Tunstall, Stoke-on-Trent; manufacturers of decorated earthenware &c. for home & colonial markets; London, 34 Hatton garden EC
Buckley, Heath & Co. High st. Burslem
Bullock & Cornes, Pelham street, off Lichfield street, Hanley
Burgess & Leigh, Hill pottery, Burslem
Burgess Henry, Kiln Croft works, Chapel lane, Burslem
Burton Brothers, Waterloo wrks. Hanley
Capper & Co. Parkhall street, Longton
Cartlidge & Matthias, Tinkers clough, Hanley
Cartlidge William Edward, Villa pottery, Cobridge, Burslem
Cartwright & Edwards, Trentham road, Longton
Challinor Edward & Charles, High street, Fenton culvert, Stoke-on-Trent
Clark C.R. & Co. Winton works, Stoke
Clementson Brothers, Phoenix & Bell works, Broad street, Hanley
Cooper & Son, Caroline street, Longton
Copeland W.T. & Sons, High street, Stoke-on-Trent; London agency, 12 Charterhouse street, Holborn EC
Corn Wm. & Ed. Navigation rd. Burslem
Cotton Elijah, Nelson place, Hanley
Cumberlidge & Humphreys, Gordon pottery, Tunstall
Davies John Heath, Trent pottery, Kirkham street, Hanley
Dawson James, Stafford street, Longton
Day Thomas T. High street, Longton
Dean Brothers, Dale hall, Burslem
Dimmock J. & Co. Stafford st. Hanley
Doulton & Co. Nile street, Burslem
Dudson James, Hanover street, Hanley
Dunn, Bennett & Co. Royal Victoria works, Burslem
Edge, Malkin & Co. Newport wrks. Burslm
Edwards Brothers, King street, Fenton culvert, Stoke-on-Trent
Edwards & Goodwin, Hanover street pottery, Burslem
Edwards J. & B. Fenton road, Hanley
Edwards William, Russell st. Longton
Emery Francis Joseph, Bleak Hill works, Bleak street, Burslem
Fell & Co. Union pl. Market st. Longton
Fenton Alfred & Sons, Brook street & Clarence street, Hanley
Fielding S. & Co. Railway pottery, Stoke
Ford & Riley, Newcastle street, Burslem
Ford & Co. Sandyford, Tunstall
Forester & Hulme, Sutherland pottery, Fenton culvert, Stoke-on-Trent
Furnival Thos. & Sons, Cobridge, Burslem
Gater & Co. Furlong lane, Burslem
Gildea James, Dale hall, Burslem
Gleaves W.T. Basford bank, Basford, Stoke
Goode & Kenworthy, High st. Tunstall
Green & Clay, Stafford street, Longton
Grimwade Brothers, Stoke rd. Hanley
GRINDLEY W.H. & Co. Newfield pottery, Tunstall, Stoke-on-Trent; manufacturers of ironstone china & decorated earthenware suitable for the Canadian, United States, South American, Cape & Australian markets
Grocott Bros. Perry st. works, Hanley
Grove F.W. Chancery lane, Longton
Hall & Hulme, Havelock works, Broad street, Hanley
Hammersley Bros. Nelson pl. Hanley
Hammersley Ralph & Son, Wedgwood place, Burslem
Hammonds & Co. Garfield works, High street, Longton

Hancock Sampson, Church street, Stoke
Harrop W. & Co. Tinkers clough, Hanley
Hawley & Co. Foley, Fenton culvert, Longton
Hobson Geo. & Jn. Albert st. Burslem
Holdcroft William, George st. Tunstall
Hollins & Co. 5 Mayer street, Hanley
Hollinshead & Kirkham, Woodland pottery, Tunstall
Howlett Joseph Redfern, Peel street works, Northwood, Hanley
Hughes Thomas, Longport, Burslem
Johnson Bros. Old Hall street, Hanley
Jones George & Sons, London rd. Stoke
Jones, Hopkinson & Sherwin, Renalagh works, Hanley
Jones Thomas, New street, Longton
Keeling & Co. Swan bank, Burslem
Kellets, Proctor & Co. Heathcote road, Longton
Kent & Parr (figure), Wellington street, Burslem
Kirkham William, London road, Stoke
Leigh William, Hill pottery, Burslem
Lockett Jn. & Co. Chancery la. Longton
Lowe, Ratcliffe & Co. Gold st. Longton
Machin William, George street, Hanley
Maddock J. & Sons, Newcastle st. Burslm
Maddock & Co. Dale Hall pottry. Burslm
Malkin R. & Sons, Fenton culvert, Stoke
Meakin James & George, 16 Glebe street, Stoke-on-Trent & Eagle pottery, Lichfield street, Hanley
Meakin Alfred, Royal Albert pottery, Parsonage street, Tunstall
Meir J. & Son, Greengate potteries, Tunstll
Mellor, Taylor & Co. Waterloo road, Burslem
Mintons Lim. Eldon pl. Stoke-on-Trent
Moore & Co. Old Foley pottery, Fenton culvert, Longton
Morley W. Albert rd. Fenton culvrt. Stoke
Mountford & Thomas, Union st. Hanley
Nixon George, Newfield view, Tunstall
Old Hall Earthenware Co. Limited, Hill street, Hanley
Ouslnam William E. & Sons, Furlong works, Burslem
Peake Joseph, Etruria vale, Hanley
Plant Brothers, Crown pottery, Dale hall, Burslem
Plant Jas. Registry st. Stoke-on-Trent
Powell, Bishop & Stonier, Stafford street & High street, Hanley
Pratt Felix & Richard & Co. High street east, Fenton culvert, Stoke-on-Trent
Pugh Edward J. & Co. High street, Longton
Pugh & Hackney, Pelham st. wrks. Hanley
Quick J.J. & Co. Lim. Clarence st. Hanley
Radford Samuel, Fenton culvert, Stoke
Rathbone, Smith & Co. Soho pottery, Tunstall
Reeves James, Victoria works, Market street, Fenton culvert, Stoke-on-Trent
Ridge William, High street, Longton
Ridgways, Bedford works, Bedford road, Hanley
Rigby Elijah, jun. Chell street, Hanley
Robinson Joseph, Knowl works, Hamil road, Burslem
Sandland, Bennett & Co. Victoria works, Lonsdale street, Stoke-on-Trent
Sant & Vodrey, Abbey pottery, Cobridge, Burslem
Shaw A. & Son, Mersey works, Burslem
Shaw & Ridge, Bank pottery, Bourne street, Burslem
Shenton Herbert, Union street, Hanley
Shingler & Co. Liverpool road, Stoke
Smith & Frost, Brewery street, Hanley
Smith & Co. High street, Stoke-on-Trent
Snow J. & J. 178 Howard place, Hanley
Steel Edward, manufacturer of earthenware, majolica & parian statuettes, Cannon street works, Hanley
Steventon Bros. Well st. pottery, Tunstall
Stonier, Hollinshead & Oliver, High street, Hanley
Stubbs Joshua, 31 High street, Longton
Stubbs Wm. Eastwood pottery, Hanley
Swan Ebenezer, Amicable st. Tunstall
Tams John, Stafford street, Longton
Till Thos. & Sons, Liverpool rd. Burslem
Toft Charles, High st. Stoke-on-Trent
Turner G.W. & Sons, Alexandra works, Tunstall
Unwin Joseph, Cornhill passage, Longtn
Vernon J. & G. Waterloo works, Burslem
Wallis, Gimson & Co. Fenton Culvert, Stoke-on-Trent
Wedgwood & Co. Pinnox & Unicorn works, Tunstall
Wedgwood Josiah & Sons, Etruria pottery, Etruria, Stoke-on-Trent
Welch J.B. New street, Hanley
Whittaker & Co. Hallfield pottery, Grafton street, Hanley
Wileman James F. Foley works, Fenton culvert, Longton
Wilkinson A. Central pottery, Burslem
Winkle & Wood, Brook street, Hanley
Wood & Hulme, Waterloo rd. Burslem
Wood & Son, Trent pottery, Furlong lane, Burslem
Wood Thomas & Co. Queen st. Burslem
Wood William & Co. Albert street works, Burslem
Wright & Co. William street, Hanley

Enamelled Goods Manufacturer (page 574)
Boughey M. Willow st. works, Longton

Encaustic Tile Manufacturers (page 574)
Balfour & Co. Lane End works, Fenton culvert, Stoke-on-Trent
Birch Elijah, 22 & 24 Clarence st. Hanley
Boote T. & R. Waterloo potteries & encaustic tile works, Burslem
Boulton & Co. Tunstall
Campbell Tile Co. (The), London rd. Stoke
Decorative Art Tile Co. (Wm. Parrish, managing partner), 200 & 202 Bryan street, Hanley
Malkin, Edge & Co. Newport works, Burslem. See advertisement
Minton, Hollins & Co. patent tile works, Stoke-on-Trent; & Minton & Co. 50 Conduit street, Regent st. London W
Mintons Limited, Eldon place, Stoke
Peake Thomas, The Tileries, Tunstall
Steele & Wood (The Crystal Porcelain Tile Co.), London rd. Stoke-on-Trent & Elder road, Cobridge, Burslem
Wedgwood Josiah & Sons, Etruria pottery, Etruria, Stoke-on-Trent

Wood A. Regent house, Regent rd. Hanley
Woolliscroft G. & Son, Patent Tile works, Nelson place, Joiners' square, Hanley

Jet Ware Manufacturers (page 627)
Baker James, Stoke rd. Shelton, Hanley
Benson Bailey, Moorland road, Burslem
Barber Joseph, Albert street, Burslem
Clare Walter, Podmore street, Burslem
Colclough & Lingard, Britannia Black works, High street, Tunstall
Dean Brothers, Dalehall, Burslem
Gibson & Sons, Albany works, Moorland road, Burslem
Guest George, Albert street, Tunstall
Harrison D.B. & Co. King's Field pottery, Newcastle-under-Lyme
Johnson Samuel, Newport st. Burslem
Kirkham & Co. Commercial st. Burslem
Parr J. & Co. Sandyford pottery, Tunstall
Rathbone W. & R. Sylvester st. Burslem
Salt Jeremiah, 78 Waterloo rd. Burslem
Smith & Co. High street, Stoke-on-Trent
Sudlow Robert, Bourne's bank, Burslem
Wood Henry James, Alexandra works, Navigation road, Burslem

Lustre Manufacturers (page 634)
Allerton Charles & Sons (gold & silver), Park works, High street, Longton

Majolica Manufacturers (page 634)
Adams & Bromley, Broad st. Hanley
Banks E. Boston works, High st. Hanley
Benson Bailey, Moorland rd. Burslem
Boulton & Floyd, Cliffe Bank works, High st. & Hall st. Stoke-on-Trent
Brough & Jones, Wharf St. pottery, Stoke
Edwards & Son, Trent works, Joiners' square, Hanley
Fielding S. & Co. Railway pottery, Stoke
Forester T. & Sons, Church st. Longton
Heath Thomas, Albion street, Longton
Holdcroft Joseph, Daisy bank, Longton
Mills & Son, 182 Bryan street, Hanley
Mintons Limited, Eldon place, Stoke
Oakes, Clare & Chadwick, Sneyd pottery, Albert street, Burslem
Pennington John, Mayer street, Hanley
Shorter & Boulton, Copeland st. Stoke
Smith & Co. High st. Stoke-on-Trent
Wardle & Co. Victoria road, Hanley
Wedgwood Josiah & Sons, Etruria pottery, Etruria, Stoke-on-Trent. See advert

Mortar & Pestle Manufacturers (page 640)
Macintyre Jas. & Co. Washington wrks. Burslem; or 23 Bartlett's bdgs. London

Parian Manufacturers (page 644)
Edwards J. & B. Fenton road, Hanley
Edwards & Son, Trent works, Joiners' square, Hanley
Hammersley Brothers, Nelson pl. Hanley
Mintons Lim. Eldon pl. Stoke-on-Trent
Robinson & Leadbeater, Wolfe st. Stoke
Steel Edward, Cannon street, Hanley
Yearsley Mrs. Mary Ann, 12 & 14 Market lane, Longton

Potters (page 648-649)
Baker James, Stoke rd. Shelton, Hanley
Bilton John & Son, Glebe buildings, Glebe street, Stoke-on-Trent
Boote T. & R. Waterloo potteries & encaustic tile works, Burslem
Finney & Sheldon, Anchor pottery, Bourne's bank, Burslem
New Wharf Pottery Co. (Thomas F. Wood, managing partner), Navigation road, Burslem
Silvester Fred. & Co. Castle Hill works, Newcastle-under-Lyme

Rockingham Ware Manufacturers (page 667)
Barber Joseph, Albert street, Burslem
Clare Walter, Podmore street, Burslem
Colclough & Lingard, Britannia Black works, High street, Tunstall
Gibson & Sons, Albany works, Moorland road, Burslem
Guest George, Albert street, Tunstall
Hurd Thos. M. & Co. Nile st. Burslem
Johnson Samuel, Newport st. Burslem
Kirkham & Co. Commercial st. Burslem
Oakes, Clare & Chadwick, Sneyd pottery, Albert street, Burslem
Parr J. & Co. Sandyford pottery, Tunstall
Rathbone W. & R. Sylvester st. Burslem
Salt Jeremiah, 78 Waterloo rd. Burslem
Sudlow Robert, Bourne's bank, Burslem
Wade & Co. High street, Burslem
Wood Henry James, Alexandra works, Navigation road, Burslem

Sagger Manufacturer (page 669)
Wakefield Thomas, Botany bay, Northwood, Hanley

Sanitary Ware Manufacturers (page 669)
Brough & Son, Silverdale, Newcastle-under-Lyme. See advert
Buckley John, manufacturer of water-closet basins & traps, table tops, urinals, ship & portable closets &c. 'Niagara Falls' basin & traps &c. Albert works, Victoria place, Hanley
Howson G. Clifford st. Eastwood, Hanley
Twyford Thomas, Cliffe vale, Hanley; & at Abbey Bucknall, Stoke-on-Trent. See advertisement

Shuttle Eye Manufacturer (page 690)
Wade & Sons, Hall street, Burslem

Spur & Stilt Makers for Pottery Manufacturers (page 697)
Arrowsmith Thomas & Son, Moorland road, Burslem
Edwards John & Sons, King street, Fenton Culvert, Stoke-on-Trent
Gimson Joseph & Co. Market street, Fenton Culvert, Stoke-on-Trent
Shirley Elijah, Moorland rd. Burslem
Taylor Wm. & Co. Church st. Longton

Stoneware Manufacturers (page 699)
Rigby James, Milton, Stoke-on-Trent

Wedgwood Josiah & Sons, Etruria pottery, Etruria, Stoke. See advert

Terra Cotta Manufacturers (page 705)
Baker Jas. Stoke road, Shelton, Hanley
Harrison D.B. & Co. Shelton New road, Newcastle
Peake Thomas, The Tileries, Tunstall

Water Closet Makers (page 710)
Buckley J. Albert wks. Victoria rd. Hanley
Twyford Thomas W. Cliffe vale, Hanley. See advertisement

1889 Keates

Keates's Gazetteer & Directory of the Staffordshire Potteries, Newcastle and District. 1889-90, Keates & Co., Printers and Publishers, Hanley (Shaw & Tipper 1233). Dated 1 October 1889 in the Preface.

As with all the Keates series, this directory is classified within separate sections for each of the six pottery towns and the only relevant categories are potters and various types of tile manufacturers.

Burslem – Encaustic and Geometric Tile Pavement Manufacturers (page 148)
Boote T. & R., Waterloo pottery, Waterloo road
Eardley Alfred J., Dalehall
Malkin, Edge & Co., Newport lane
Steele & Wood (Porcelain Tile), Elder rd.

Burslem – Floor Tile Works (page 148)
Boote Thomas & Richard, Waterloo rd.
Malkin, Edge & Co., Newport lane

Burslem – Potters (pages 155-156)
Alcock Henry and Co. (earthenware), Cobridge works
Arrowsmith Thomas (spur and stilt manufacturer), Moorland road
Barber Joseph (rockingham and jet manufacturer), Albert street
Bates & Bennett (earthenware), Sneyd st.
Beech Frederick and Co. (earthenware), Lincoln works, Sneyd green
Billington R. (manufacturer), Gladstone works, Commercial street
Blackhurst and Bourne (earthenware), Hadderidge pottery, Bath street
Bloor R.W., North road, Cobridge
Bodley E.F. and Son, New Bridge pottery, Longport
BODLEY EDWIN J.D. (china), Hill pottery, Market place, & Crown works
Boote T. and R. (earthenware), 43 and 32A Waterloo road
Brayford and Gelson (earthenware), Fountain place works
Brownfield William & Son (earthenware and china), Waterloo road, Cobridge
Brownhills Pottery Co. (earthenware), Brownhills
Buckley and Heath (earthenware), High street Pottery
Burgess & Leigh (earthenware), Middleport
Burgess Henry (earthenware), Kilncroft works, Chapel lane
Cartledge W.E., Villa pottery, Cobridge
Clare Walter (rockingham), Podmore st. and Albert street
Corn E. (earthenware), Navigation road
Crystal Porcelain Pottery Co. Limited, Elder road
Dean Brothers, Newcastle street
Doulton & Co. (earthenware), Nile street works
Dunn, Bennett, and Co., Royal Victoria Works, Liverpool road
Eardley Alfred Joseph (floor and tile), Dalehall
Edge, Malkin & Co. (earthenware), Newport works, Newport
Emery Francis J. (earthenware), Bleak hill works, Wood street
Ford and Son, Newcastle street
Furnival T. & Son (earthenware), Cobridge
Grocott and Dickinson (door furniture), Longport, near Station
Gibson and Son (rockingham), Moorland road
Gildea & Walker (earthenware), Dalehall, Burslem, and 30 Holborn, London
Guest George, 58 Liverpool road
Hallen Harding (creel steps), 31 Wellington street
Hammersley Ralph (earthenware and ironstone china), Overhouse pottery, Wedgwood place
HOBSON JOHN & GEO. (earthenware), Albert street
Holdcroft William (earthenware), 116 Liverpool road
Hollinshead and Griffiths, Chelsea works, Moorland road
Hughes Thomas (earthenware and flint manufacturer), Top Bridge works, Longport
Hughes and Robinson (earthenware), Cobridge
Johnson Samuel, Newport street
Keeling and Co., Newport lane
Kent William (figure maker), Wellington street
Macintyre Jas, and Co. (china, porcelain and door furniture), Washington works, Warerloo road

Maddock and Co. (earthenware), Dalehall works, Taylor street
Maddock John and Sons (earthenware), Newcastle street
Malkin, Edge and Co. (encaustic tile), Newport lane
Mellor, Taylor and Co. (earthenware and white granite), Waterloo road
New Wharf Pottery Co., Navigation road (Thos. F. Wood)
Oakes, Clare & Chadwick (majolica and earthenware), Albert street
Oliver E.J., 212 Waterloo road
Oulsnam William E. & Son (earthenware), Furlong works
Rathbone Wm. & Co. (rockingham and jet), Silvester square
Robinson Joseph (earthenware), Knowle works, Hamil road
Sadler and Co. (earthenware), Moorland road
Sant & Vodrey (earthenware), Sneyd st.
Sant, J. (jet and rockingham), 78, Waterloo road
Shaw Anthony (earthenware), Mersey pottery, Newport lane
Shaw & Son (earthenware), Bournes bank
Sudlow R. (earthenware), Bournes bank
Till & Sons (earthenware), Sytch pottery, Liverpool road
Vernon James and George (earthenware), Waterloo pottery, Waterloo road
Wade and Sons (shuttle eye and creel step), Hall street
Wade John (earthenware), 52 Hall street
Wade and Co. (rockingham stone and jet decorators), High street
Walker John (Gildea & Walker, earthenware), Dalehall
Wilkinson Arthur J. (earthenware), Central pottery, Market place, and Lower works, Wood street
Wood Thos. (manufacturer), Queen street pottery, Queen street
Wood H.J. (manufacturer), Alexandra pottery, Navigation road
Wood & Hulme, Garfield Pottery works, Waterloo road
Wood & Son (earthenware), Furlong lane
Wood William and Co. (door furniture), Albert street works, Albert street
Wood and Co. (earthenware), New Wharf pottery, Navigation road

Fenton – Potters (page 181)
BAKER & CO. (earthenware) High street
Barker and Kent (earthenware), King st.
Bilton E., China street
Broadhurst Jas. (earthenware), Victoria rd.
Challinor E. and C. (earthenware), Fenton pottery, High street
Edwards and Sons, (china and earthenware), King street
Fielding and Co. (majolica and earthenware), Railway pottery, off Whieldon rd.
GIMSON JOSEPH & CO. (spur manufacturer), Market street
Gimson Wallis and Co. (earthenware), Lane Delph
Green T.A. & S. (china), Minerva works, Park street (see advt.)
Hughes E. and Co., Opal china works
Jackson and Gosling (china), Grosvenor works, King street
MALKIN RALPH & SONS (earthenware), Park works, Market street
Moore and Co. (earthenware), Old Foley pottery, King street
Morley Wm., Victoria road
Pratt F. and R. and Co. (earthenware and terra cotta), High street east
Radford Samuel (china), High street
Reeves James (earthenware) Victoria works, Market street
Robinson and Son (china), King street
Wileman and Shelley (china), Foley pottery, King street
Wileman James (earthenware), Foley works, King street

Hanley – Potters (pages 282-283)
Adams & Bromley (jasper and majolica), Victoria works, Broad street
ASHWORTH G.L. & BROS., proprietor, J.S. Goddard (china and ironstone earthenware), Broad street
BAILEY, HACKNEY & Co., King street works
Baker James (earthenware), Stoke road
Banks Edward, Broad street works
Barlow Charles (china and earthenware decorator and dealer), Lower Mollart st.
Bednall & Heath (earthenware), Wellington pottery, Nelson place
Bennett William (earthenware), Cleveland works, Victoria road
Bevington Ambrose (china and earthenware), New Hall works, York street
Bevington John (china and parian), Kensington works, St. James's street
Bevington Thomas (china and earthenware), Burton place, New street
Bettany William (china and earthenware), 41 Hope street
Bladen and Molineux, Mayer street
Bold Henry, 46 Lichfield street
BOURNE & SHERRATT, Swan works, Elm street
Brown-Westhead, Moore, and Co. (china, earthenware, parian, and majolica), Cauldon place
BUCKLEY JANE (sanitary ware), 4 Victoria place (see advt.)
Burton G. & B, Waterloo works, Nelson pl.
Buller and Co. (spurs and stilts, and door furniture, &c.), Joiners' square
Cartlidge and Matthias, Tinkersclough
Ceramic Art Co., Howard place
Chetwynd Elijah (modeller), 4A Mollart st.
Clementson Bros. (earthenware), Phoenix works, Broad street, and Bell works, George street
COTTON J. (earthenware), Nelson works
Cotton Elijah (earthenware), Lichfield st.
Davis J.H. (earthenware and sanitary goods), Trent pottery, Canal side
Dimmock John and Co. (earthenware), Albion works, Stafford street
Dudson James (earthenware, stone, and parian), Hope street
EDWARDS & SON (fancy goods), Trent works, Joiners square
Fenton Alfred & Sons (china and earthenware), Brook street
Ford Charles (china), Cannon street
Ford Charles and Co. (spur and stilt), Parker street

Frost, Bevington, & Co., Anchor works, Brewery street
Grimwade Bros. (earthenware), Winton pottery, Stoke road
Grocott John., Percy street
Hall and Hulme (earthenware and jet), Havelock works, Broad street
Hall Thomas, 29 Church street
Hammersley Joseph and Robert (china and earthenware decorators), New st.
Harrop John and Fredk. (parian & china), Dresden works, Tinkersclough
HAWLEY & BRERETON, Lichfield pottery, Joiners' square
Hollins Henry, Queen Anne pottery, Shelton
HOLLINS J. & CO. (jet & rockingham), Pallissy pottery, Mayer st. (see advt.)
Howson George (sanitary ware), Eastwood vale
Jeffries Wm. (art ware), Oldham pottery, Leek new road
Johnson Bros. (earthenware), Old Hall street and Eastwood road
Jones, Hopkinson & Sherwin (earthenware), Renalagh works, Renalagh st.
Lancaster & Wright, William street
Lees Wm. (parian), Hawthorn cottage
Machin William, George street
Meakin J. and G. (earthenware), Eagle pottery, near Bucknall New road and Eastwood
Mills and Son, Bryan street
Mills F., 61 Bethesda street
Morris A. & G., Lichfield street
Old Hall Earthenware Company, Lim. (earthenware, parian and china), Hill street; Meigh C., manager
Patent Fire Resisting Cement Company, Brewery street and Bryan street
Peake Joseph (rockingham and earthenware), Etruria vale
Pennington John, Mayer street
Pointon and Co., Norfolk street
Powell, Bishop, and Stonier (china and earthenware), High street, Stafford street, and Nelson place
Pugh & Hackney (earthenware) Pelham street
Ridgways (stone, parian, and earthenware), Bedford works
Rigby E., junr. and Co., Providence pottery
Sherwin and Cotton (encaustic tiles), Vine street
Shenton Herbert, Union street
Snow Jonathan and John (terra cotta, jet and majolica), Pyenest st. works and Howard place
STEEL EDWARD (earthenware, parian statuette and majolica), Cannon st. works
Stonier, Hollinshead & Co., High st.
Stubbs Wm. (china and earthenware), Eastwood pottery
Taylor, Tunnicliffe & Co. (door furniture, and china fitting, etc.,) Eastwood (see advt.)
Thomas & Co., Union street
Twyford W. (sanitary ware), Cliffe vale pottery, Newcastle road
Wakefield Thos. & Co. (saggar), Botany Bay, Northwood
Wedgwood Josiah & Sons (earthenware, &c.), Etruria
Wenger A. (earthenware), Parker st.
Welch J.B., Excelsior works, New st.
Whittaker & Co. (earthenware), Hallfield works, Festing street
Whittam Joseph, Fairfield pottery, Slippery lane

Longton – Potters (pages 341-343)
ADAMS JOHN (china, home and export), Stafford street
ADAMS R.S. & Co., Chadwick street (see advt.)
Adams John, 275 Uttoxeter road
Adderley and Lawson (china), Salisbury works, Edensor road
Adderley William A. (china and earthenware), Daisy bank
Aidney, Griffiths & Co. (china), Edensor rd.
Allen Sampson Henry (china & earthenware), Jubilee works, High street (see advt.)
ALLERTON CHARLES & SONS (china, earthenware, and gold and silver lustre), Park works, High street
Amison Chas. (china), Wedgwood pottery, Anchor road
Anderton & Copestake (china), St. Martin's lane
Asbury Edward & Co. (china), Sutherland road
Aynsley H. & Co. (earthenware), Commerce street
Aynsley John & Sons (china), Portland works, Sutherland road
Ball William, Drury works, Normacot rd.
Barker Brothers (earthenware), Barker street, off High street
BARLOW T.W. & SON (earthenware), Commerce street
Blair & Co. (china), Beaconsfield pottery, Anchor road
BEECH JAMES & SON (china), Sutherland road
BENNION GEORGE (china & earthenware), Albert works, High street
BOUGHEY MATTHEW (earthenware), Willow street works, Daisy bank
BRADBURY JAMES & CO. (toilet, jugs, majolica, and jet), Clayton pottery, Clayton street
Bridgett and Bates (china), King street
Bridgwood Sampson & Son (earthenware and flint grinders), Anchor pottery, Wharf street
BRIDGWOOD RICHARD (china and earthenware), Stafford street
BRITISH ANCHOR POTTERY CO., LIMITED, Anchor road
Brough and Blackhurst (earthenware), Waterloo works, Stafford street
Burton, Morris & Co. (china), Bagnall st.
Cartledge F. (china), Normacot road
CARTWRIGHT & EDWARDS (earthenware), Borough pottery, Trentham road
Chapman David & Sons (china), Forrister street, Anchor road
Collingwood Bros. (china), Crown works, Stafford street
COOPER WM. & CO. (china & earthenware), 32 Clayton street
Cooper William & Sons (earthenware), Viaduct works, Caroline street
Cope James H. and Co. (china), Wellington works, Stafford street
Copestake George (china), Anchor works, Market street
CYPLES & FORD (china), Heathcote works, Heathcote street
Dawson James (earthenware), Stafford st.
Day George (china and earthenware), Albion works, High street

Edwards and Brown (china), High street
EDWARDS GEORGE (china), Sheridan works, King street
EDWARDS J.R. & CO. (china), Gordon pottery, Anchor road
EDWARDS & REDFERN (earthenware), Russell street
FELL & CO. (earthenware), Market st.
Ferneyhough Jno. (china), Dresden works, Stafford street
Finney Joseph (china), Victoria works, Stafford street
FORESTER THOMAS AND SONS (majolica and earthenware), Church street
FORESTER G. & THOMAS (china), Blyth works, High street
Goodwin and Co., High street
Green and Clay (earthenware), Stafford st.
GROVE F., WEDGWOOD & OLIVER (rustic, lustre, china and earthenware), Palissy works, Chancery lane
Hallam R. (earthenware), Chaplin works, Church street
HAMMERSLEY & CO. (china), Sutherland road
Hammond and Buckley (earthenware), Victoria works, High street
HARRISON CHARLES (china and earthenware), Queen street and Chadwick street
Heath Thos. (majolica and earthenware), Baltimore works. Albion street
Hibbert and Boughey (china), Market st.
HOBSON & CO. (majolica and earthenware), Adelaide works, Heathcote road
Holdcroft Jos. (silver lustre & majolica), Daisy bank
Hudson William (china), Alma works, High street (see advt.)
Hulme and Massey (china), Peel works, Stafford street
Jones Alfred B., Eagle works, Station sq.
Jones and Co., New street
Jones and Howson (china), Market street
KEELING HERBERT (china, home and export), Church street works, Church st.
Kellet, Proctor and Co., Heathcote pottery, Heathcote road
Lockett John & Co. (china, earthenware and lustre), King street
Lowe, Ratcliffe and Co. (earthenware), Gold street works
LOWE WM. (earthenware and china), High street and Sutherland road
MIDDLETON J.H. (china), Bagnall st.
Moore & Co. (earthenware), Old Foley pottery
Moore Bros. (china), St. Mary's works, High street (see advt.)
NEILD B. (earthenware, majolica, and jet), Green Dock pottery, Edensor road
PLANT R.H. & CO. (china), Carlisle works, High street
Poole Thos. (china and majolica), Cobden works, Edensor road
Procter, Mayer, and Woolley (china), Gladstone pottery, High street
PUGH E.J., Granville pottery, High street
RADFORD & WARD (china), Chancery lane
Ridge & Sons (china), Chancery lane
Robinson & Son (china), The Foley (see advt).
Shone & Co. (china), Edensor works, New street
Skelson & Plant (china and earthenware), Normacot road
Smith Sampson (china & gold and silver lustre and figure), Sutherland works, Barker street
STUBBS & HALL (earthenware), High street
SUTHERLAND THOS. (china, earthenware, &c.), Cromartie works, Market lane
Tams John (earthenware), Crown pottery, 57 Stafford street (see advt.)
Taylor and Kent (china), Florence works, High street (see advt.)
TAYLOR & CO. (patent stilt and spur), Church street
TIMMIS CHARLES & CO. (tile), Normacot road (see advt.)
Unwin Joseph (earthenware and lustre), Cornhill passage
WAINE E. & H. (china, earthenware, &c.), Normacot works, Normacot road
Waine and Bates (china), Sutherland road
Wagstaff and Brunt (china and earthenware), King street pottery, King street
Walters A. & G. (china), Commerce street
Warrilow George (china), Queen's pottery, Sutherland road
WEBBERLEY WILLIAM (china), St. James's works, High street
Wildblood and Heath (china), Peel works, Stafford street
Williamson & Son (china and earthenware), Bridge pottery, Heathcote road
Wilson James (parian figure, &c.), Gregory street
Yearsley Mrs. (parian, china, and earthenware), 14 & 16 Market lane

Stoke – Potters (pages 465-467)
BEECH AND ADAMS (art and general, home and export) John street
BOULTON & FLOYD (earthenware and majolica), Cliffe bank works
Brough and Jones (earthenware), Wharf street
BURTON G. and B. (earthenware and figures), Registry street
COALPORT CHINA CO. (John Rose and Co.), Limited, 8 Glebe Buildings; agent John A. Service
Copeland W.T. & Sons (china, earthenware, and parian), High street
DAVENPORT JOHN (patent compound silicate cement manufacturer), 6 Penkhull Terrace (see advt.)
Dimmock W., 3 Bath terrace
FELL & COY (earthenware), Wharf st.
Goss W.H. (parian), London road
Hancock S. (earthenware), Church street
JONES GEO. & SONS (earthenware and china), Trent pottery
Kirkham William (earthenware and terra cotta), London road
Meakin J. and G. (earthenware); offices, St. Peter's chambers, Glebe street
MINSHALL MRS. ELIZABETH (potters' clay press cloth maker, 8 Boothenwood terrace
Mintons (china, earthenware, and parian), London road
Minton, Hollins & Co. (encaustic tile), Cliff bank
Mountford G.T., Alexandra pottery, Wharf street
PLANT JAMES AND RALPH (stone and earthenware), Stoke pottery

ROBINSON & LEADBEATER (parian statuary), Wolfe street (see advt)
ROSE JOHN & CO. (porcelain, &c.), Glebe street
SANDLAND, BENNETT AND CO. (earthenware), Victoria works, Lonsdale street
SHINGLER & CO. (earthenware), Liverpool road (see advt.)
Shorter and Boulton (majolica & earthenware), Copeland street
Toft Charles, Swan works, High street
Victoria Pottery Co. (earthenware), Lonsdale street
WINKLE & WOOD (opaque porcelain), Colonial pottery (see advt.)

Stoke – Tile (Encaustic) Manufacturers (page 469)
Campbell Tile Company
Minton, Hollins, & Co., Shelton Old road
Simpson Thomas A., Cliff bank
STEELE & WOOD, London road
WOOD & CO., Boothen road

Stoke – Tile (Floor) Manufacturers (page 469)
Campbell Tile Company
Minton, Hollins and Co., Shelton Old rd.
WOOD & CO., Boothen road

Tunstall – Potters (page 503)
Adams Wm. and Thos. (earthenware), Greenfields pottery
Booth Thomas Gimbert and F., Church bank pottery and Highgate pottery, Brownhills
Boulton, Machin and Tennant, Swan bank pottery
Brownhills Pottery Co., Brownhills
Colclough and Lingard, britannia black works, High street
Cumberlidge, Humphreys and Hele, Gordon pottery
Ford and Co. (earthenware), Sandyford
Goode and Watton (earthenware), High street
Grindley W.H. and Co. (earthenware), Newfields pottery
Guest George (earthenware), Albert pottery, off High street
Hammersley R.M. and Co. (earthenware), High street
Hancock John, Brownhills hall
Holdcroft Wm. (earthenware), George street
Hollinshead and Kirkham (earthenware), Woodland pottery, Woodland street
Lester and Smith, Clayhills pottery
Meakin Alfd. (earthenware), Parsonage street
Meir John and Son (earthenware), Greengates
Nixon George (rockingham, jet, &c.), Summer bank pottery, Newfield
Rathbone, Smith & Co., Soho pottery, High street
Steventon Bros. (and decorators), Well street pottery
Swann E., High street
Turner George W. and Sons (earthenware), Alexander works, Scotia road
Wedgwood and Co. (earthenware), High street, Brownhills

1892 Keates

Keates's Gazetteer & Directory of the Staffordshire Potteries, Newcastle and District. 1892-93, Keates & Co., Printers and Publishers, Hanley (Shaw & Tipper 1233). Dated December 1892 in the Preface.

As with all the Keates series, this directory is classified within separate sections for each of the six pottery towns and the only relevant categories are potters and various types of tile manufacturers.

Burslem – Encaustic and Geometric Tile Pavement Manufacturers (page 169)
Boote T. & R., Waterloo pottery, Waterloo road
Eardley Alfred J., Dalehall
Malkin, Edge & Co., Newport lane
Steele & Wood (Porcelain Tile), Elder rd.

Burslem – Floor Tile Works (page 170)
Boote Thomas and Richard, Waterloo rd
Malkin, Edge & Co., Newport lane
MARSDEN TILE CO., Dale street
Stubbs and Holgart, Newcastle street

Burslem – Potters (pages 176-177)
Alcock Henry and Co. (earthenware), Cobridge works
Arrowsmith Thomas (spur and stilt manufacturer), Moorland road
Beech and Goodall (jet), Sylvester pottery
Billington R., Commercial street
Bodley E.F. and Son, Longport
Boote T. and R. (earthenware), 43 and 32A Waterloo road
Bourne and Leigh (earthenware), Orme street
Brayford and Gelson (earthenware), Fountain place works
Brownfield William & Son (earthenware & china), Waterloo rd., Cobridge
Brownhills Pottery Co. (earthenware), Brownhills
Buckley, Heath & Greatbatch (earthenware), High street pottery
Buckley and Son (jet), Navigation rd.
Burgess and Leigh (earthenware), Middleport
Burgess Henry (earthenware), Chapel lane
Clare Walter (rockingham), Podmore street and Albert street
Corn E. (earthenware), Longport
Dean Thos., Newcastle street
Doulton & Co. (earthenware) Nile street works
Dunn, Bennett and Co., Liverpool road
Eardley Alfred Joseph (floor and tile), Dalehall
Edge, Malkin & Co. (earthenware), Newport works
Edwards & Son (earthenware), Hanover street
Emery Francis J. (earthenware), Wood street
Ford and Son, Newcastle street
Furnival T. & Son (earthenware) Cobridge

Grocott & Dickenson (door furniture) Longport
Gibson and Son (rockingham), Moorland road
Dalehall Pottery Co. (earthenware), Dalehall
Guest George, 58 Liverpool road
Hallen Harding (creel steps), 31 Wellington street
Hammersley Ralph (earthenware and ironstone china), Wedgwood place
Holmes and Leese, Bourne's bank
Hobson John & Geo. (earthenware), Albert street
Holdcroft William (earthenware), 116 Liverpool road
Hollinshead and Griffiths, Chelsea works, Moorland road
Hughes Thomas (earthenware and flint manufacturer), Longport
Hughes and Robinson (earthenware), Cobridge
Hurd T.M. (jet) Station pottery
Johnson Samuel, Newport street
Keeling & Co., Newport lane
Kent William (figure), Wellington st.
Macintyre Jas. & Co. (china, porcelain and door furniture), Waterloo road
Maddock and Co. (earthenware), Dalehall works
Maddock John and Sons (earthenware), Newcastle street
Malkin, Edge & Co. (encaustic tile), Newport lane
New Wharf Pottery Co., Navigation road – Thos. F. Wood
Oakes, Clare & Chadwick (majolica and earthenware), Albert street
Oliver E.J., 212 Waterloo road
Oulsnam William E. & Son, (earthenware), Furlong works
Rathbone Wm. and Co. (rockingham and jet) Silvester square
Robinson Joseph (earthenware), Knowle works, Hamil road
Sadler and Co. (earthenware) Moorland road
Sant and Co. (earthenware) Sneyd st.
Sant J. (jet and rockingham), 78 Waterloo road
Shaw Anthony (earthenware), Newport lane
Sudlow R. (earthenware), Bournes bank
Till and Sons (earthenware) Sytch pottery, Liverpool road
Vernon James (earthenware), Hill pottery
Wade and Sons (shuttle eye and creel step), Hall street
Wade John (earthenware), 52 Hall street
Wade and Co. (rockingham, stone and jet decorators), High street
Wilkinson Arthur J. (earthenware) Market place, and Lower works, Wood street
Wood Thos. and Son, Queen street
Wood H.J., Navigation road
Wood and Hulme, Waterloo road
Wood and Son (earthenware), Furlong lane
Wood William & Co. (door furniture), Albert street works
Wood and Co. (earthenware), New Wharf pottery, Navigation road

Fenton – Potters (pages 204-205)
BAKER & Co., (earthenware) High st.
Barkers & Kent (earthenware) King st.
Barker, Batty and Read (earthenware), Lane delph
Beresford T., (china) Heron street
BILTON E., China street
Broadhurst James (earthenware) Victoria road
Challinor C. & Co., (earthenware), High street
Edwards and Sons (white granite), King street
Fielding and Co. (earthenware), off Whieldon road
Forrester and Hulme, (earthenware) High street
Gimson Joseph & Co., (spur), Market street
Green Spencer (china), Park street
Hines Bros., (porcelain) Heron cross
Hughes E. and Co., Opal china works
Jackson and Gosling (china), King st.
Malkin Ralph and Sons (earthenware), Market street
Massey E. (Opal china), Heron street
Moore & Co. (earthenware), King street
Morley Wm. (exors. of), Victoria road
Pratt F. and R. and Co., (earthenware and terra cotta) High street east
Radford Samuel (china) High street
Reeves James (exors. of), earthenware, Market street
ROBINSON & SON, (china), King street
Wallace & Co., Railway Stilt and Spur Works
Wileman & Shelley (china), King st.
Wileman James P. (earthenware), King street

Hanley – Potters (pages 298-300)
ASHWORTH G.L. & BROS., proprietor J.S. Goddard (china and ironstone earthenware), Broad street
BAILEY JOHN, Bucknall Old road
Barlow Charles, (china & earthenware decorator and dealer), Lower Mollart street
Bednall & Heath (earthenware) Wellington pottery Nelson place
Bell and Co., Stoke road
Bennett William, (earthenware) Cleveland works, Victoria road
Bettaney William, (china & earthenware) Hope street
Bishop and Stonier, Stafford street and High street
BOURNE H., (vase and toilet ware), Clough street
BROWN-WESTHEAD, MOORE, & Co., (china sanitary, earthenware, parian, and majolica), Cauldon place
BUCKLEY H., (sanitary ware), 4 Victoria place
Buller, Jobson, & Co., (spurs & stilts, & door furniture, &c.), Joiners square
CARTLIDGE & MATTHIAS, Broad street
Ceramic Art Co., Howard place
CHAWSER J.W., (modeller) 34 York street
Chetwynd Elijah, (modeller), 4a Mollart street
Clementson Bros. (earthenware), Phoenix works, Broad street and Bell works, George street
COTTON J., (earthenware), Nelson works
Dimmock John & Co., (earthenware,) Albion works, Stafford street
Dudson James (earthenware), stone, and parian), Hope street
ECCLES H., Queen Anne Pottery, Shelton
Edwards and Son (fancy goods), Trent works, Joiners square
Fenton Alf. and Sons (china and earthenware), Brook street
Fielding W., Cannon street
Ford Charles (china), Cannon street
Ford Charles and Co. (spur and stilt), Parker street
Grey Alexander (earthenware), William st.

Grimwade Bros. (earthenware), Winton pottery, Stoke road
Hall Isaac, 140 Hope street
Hammersley Joseph and Robert (china and earthenware decorators), New st.
HARROP & CO. (parian and china), Dresden works, Tinkersclough
Hollins, Johnson & Co. (jet and rockingham), Pallisy pottery, Mayer street (see advt.)
Howlett J., Peel street
Howson George (sanitary ware), Eastwood vale
Johnson Bros. (earthenware), Old Hall street and Eastwood road
Kensington Fine Art Pottery (parian and earthenware), Kensington works St. James street
Lea W. Smith, Bethesda street
Lancaster F., Shelton works, off Broad street
Loney Samuel, Brewery street
Machin William, George street
Meakin J. & G. (earthenware), Eagle Pottery, near Bucknall New road and Eastwood
Mills H., Bryan street
Mills F., 61 Bethesda street
Morris & Co., Lichfield street
Ogden & Co., (stilt & thimble), Mayer street
Old Hall Earthenware Company, Ltd. (earthenware, parian and china). Hill street; managing director, Taylor Ashworth
Parkins, Rathbone & Co., Broad st.
Peake Joseph (rockingham & earthenware), Etruria vale
Peake & Co., (rockingham & earthenware), Wharf lane
Pointon & Co., Norfolk street
Powell, Bishop, and Stonier (china and earthenware), High street, Stafford st., and Nelson place
Ravenscroft & Co., Joiners square
Ridgways (stone, parian, & earthenware), Bedford works
Rigby E., junr. & Co., Providence pottery
Shenton Herbert, Union street
Sherwin & Cotton (encaustic tiles), Vine street
Sherwin David, Renalagh street
Snow Jonathan and John (terra cotta, jet, and majolica), Pynest street works and Howard place
Stonier, Hollinshead and Co., High street
Stubbs Wm. (china and earthenware), Eastwood pottery
Taylor, Tunnicliffe & Co. (door furniture and china fitting, etc.), Eastwood (see advt.)
Thomas and Co., Union street
Twyford W. (sanitary ware), Cliffe vale pottery, Newcastle road
Wakefield Thos. & Co. (saggar), Botany Bay, Northwood
Wardle & Co. (art pottery and majolica), Victoria road
Weatherby and Sons, High street
Wedgwood Josiah and Sons (earthenware, etc.), Etruria
Welch J.B., Broad street
Wenger A. (earthenware), Parker street
Whittaker and Co. (earthenware), Hallfield works, Festing street
Whittam Josh., Fairfield pottery, Slippery lane

Longton – Potters (pages 351-353)
Adderley & Lawson (china) Salisbury works, Edensor road
Adderley William A. (china & earthenware), Daisy bank
Allen Sampson Henry (china & earthenware), Jubilee works, High street
Allerton Chas. & Sons, (china &c.), Park works, High street
Amison Chas. (china), Wedgwood pottery, Anchor road
Anderton and Copestake (china), St. Martin's lane
Asbury Edward & Co. (china), Sutherland road
Aynsley H. & Co., (earthenware) Commerce street
Aynsley John & Sons (china), Portland works, Sutherland road
Barker Brothers (earthenware), Barker street, off High street
Barlow T.W. & Son (earthenware), Commerce street
Bates & Son, (china), Albert works, High street
Beech James and Son (china), Sutherland road
Blackhurst & Hulme (china), High st.
Blair & Co. (china), Beaconsfield pottery, Anchor road
BOUGHEY MATTHEW (earthenware) Willow street, Daisy bank
BOUGHEY & WILTSHAW (china), Market street
Boulton & Co., (china), Mill street works
Bridgett & Bates (china) King street
Bridgwood Sampson & Son (earthenware and flint grinders), Anchor pottery, Wharf street
BRIDGWOOD RICHARD (china and earthenware), Stafford street
BRITISH ANCHOR POTTERY CO,, LIMITED, Anchor road
Brough B.H. (earthenware), Waterloo works, Stafford street
Brookfield Bros. (china and earthenware), Market lane
Burton, Morris & Co. (china), Bagnall st.
Cartledge F. (china), Normacot road
CARTWRIGHT & EDWARDS (earthenware), Borough pottery, Trentham road
Chapman David & Sons (china), Forrister street, Anchor road
Coggins & Hill (china), St James' place, High street
Colclough & Co. (majolica), Anchor works, Anchor road
Collingwood Bros. (china), Crown works, Stafford street
Cone T. & Co. (earthenware), Alma works, High street
Cooper Wm. & Co. (china and earthenware), 32 Clayton street
Cope James H. & Co. (china), Wellington works, Stafford street
CYPLES & FORD (china), Heathcote works, Heathcote street
Drury Pottery Co., Normacot road
Edensor Pottery Co., Edensor road
Edwards & Brown (china), High street
EDWARDS GEORGE (china), Sheridan works, King street
Edwards J.R. and Co. (china), Gordon pottery, Anchor road
Edwards and Redfern (earthenware), Mount pleasant
FELL & CO. (earthenware), Market st.
Ferneyhough J. (china), Dresden works, Stafford street
Finney Joseph (china), Victoria works, Stafford street
FORESTER THOMAS AND SONS, LTD. (majolica and china), Church st.

Grove F., Wedgwood and Oliver (rustic, lustre, china and earthenware), Palissy works, Chancery lane
Hallam and Brian, Heathcote pottery, Heathcote road
HAMMERSLEY & CO. (china), Sutherland road
Harrison Charles (china and earthenware) Queen street and Chadwick street
Heath Thos. (majolica and earthenware), Baltimore works, Albion street
Hobson and Co. (majolica and earthenware), Adelaide works,
Heathcote road
Holdcroft J. (silver lustre and majolica), Daisy bank
HOLLINSON & GOODALL (earthenware and china), 23 High street
Hudson Wm. (china), Sutherland works, Normacot road
Jones Alfred B., Eagle works, Station sq.
Jones and Co., New street
Jones Wm. (china), Market street
Lockett John & Co. (china, earthenware, and lustre), King street
LONGTON PORCELAIN CO., High st.
LOWE WM. (earthenware and china), High street and Sutherland road
Middleton J.H. (china), Bagnall street
Moore and Co. (earthenware), Old Foley pottery
Moore Bros. (china), St. Mary's works, High street (see advt.)
Morris Thos. (china), Regent works, Mount pleasant
NEILD B. (earthenware, majolica, and jet), Green Dock pottery, Edensor road
PLANT R.H. & CO. (china), Carlisle works, High street
Plant & Taylor (earthenware), Chadwick street
Poole Thos. (china and majolica), Cobden works, Edensor road
Procter, Mayer and Wooley (china), Gladstone pottery, High street
Radford and Ward (china), Chancery lane
Ratcliffe and Co. (china), Gold court
Redfern and Drakeford (china), High st.
Roberts and Cotton (earthenware), Clayton pottery, Stafford street
Robinson and Son (china), The Foley (see advt.)
Shore & Co., (china), Edensor works, New street
Skelson and Son (earthenware) Stafford street
Smith Sampson (china & gold & silver lustre and figure), Sutherland works, Barker street
Stubbs & Hall (earthenware), High st.
Sutherland Thos. (china and earthenware), Market lane
Tams John (earthenware), Crown pottery, 57 Stafford street (see advt.)
Taylor & Kent (china), Florence works, High street
Taylor & Co. (patent stilt and spur), Church street
WAINE E. & H. (china, earthenware, &c.), Normacot works, Normacot rd.
Waine Chas., (china), Sutherland road
Wagstaffe & Brunt (china and earthenware), King st. pottery, King st.
Walters Thos., (china), Commerce st.
Warrilow Geo. (china), Queen's pottery Sutherland road
Wildblood & Heath (china), Peel works Stafford street
Williamson & Son (china & earthenware), Bridge pottery, Heathcote rd.
Wilson Jas. (parian figure &c.), Gregory street

Stoke – Potters (pages 467-468)
Bennion and Co. (earthenware), Swan works, High street
Boulton and Floyd (earthenware and majolica), Lovatt and Hall st. works (see advt.)
BURTON G. and B. (earthenware and figures), Registry street
Copeland W.T. & Sons (china, earthenware and parian), High street
Fielding A. (Fenton), Trent vale
Goss W.H. (parian), London road
Hancock S. and Sons (earthenware), Wolfe street
JONES GEO. and Sons (earthenware and china), Trent potteries
Kirkham William (earthenware and terra-cotta), London road
LAWRENCE THOS. (earthenware), Wharf street (see advt.)
Minshall Mrs. Elizabeth (potters' clay press cloth maker) 8 Boothenwood ter.
Mintons, Ltd. (china, earthenware, and parian), London road
Minton, Hollins & Co. (encaustic tile), Patent Tile works, Cliff bank
Mountford G.T., Alexandra pottery, Wolfe street
PLANT JAMES & CO. (stone and earthenware), Stoke pottery
ROBINSON & LEADBEATER (parian statuary), Wolfe street (see advt.)
SANDLAND, BENNETT AND CO. (earthenware), Victoria works, Lonsdale street (see advt.)
Shingler & Co. (earthenware), Liverpool road
Shorter and Boulton (majolica & earthenware), Copeland street
Smith & Co. (jet and Rockingham), Hill pottery, Cliff bank
Wiltshaw and Robinson (earthenware), Copeland street works
WINKLE F. & CO. (opaque porcelain), Colonial pottery
YALE W. (porcelain slab and tile decorator), Liverpool road (see advt.)

Stoke – Tile (Encaustic) Manufacturers (page 470)
Campbell Tile Company, London road
Cheap Tile Co., Wolfe street
Minton, Hollins, & Co., Shelton old road
Simpson Thomas A., Cliff bank
WOOD & CO., Boothen road
YALE W. (slab & tile decorator), Liverpool road (see advt.)

Stoke – Tile (Floor) Manufacturers (page 471)
Campbell Tile Company, London road
Cheap Tile Company, Wolfe street
Minton, Hollins, & Co., Shelton old road
WOOD & CO., Boothen road

Tunstall – Potters (page 506)
Adams William and Co. (earthenware), Greenfields pottery
Andrews Edward, Clayhills pottery
Booths, Church bank pottery
Boulton, Machin and Tennant, Swan bank pottery
Brownhills Pottery Co. (earthenware), Brownhills
Colclough and Lingard, Britannia black works, High street
Cope and Co. (jet), High street
Cumberlidge, Humphreys and Hele, Gordon pottery
Grindley W.H. and Co. (earthenware), Woodland pottery
Guest George (earthenware), High street pottery, off High street
Holdcroft Wm. (earthenware), George st.
Hollinshead and Kirkham (earthenware), Unicorn pottery, Amicable street
Meakin Alfred (earthenware), Parsonage street
Meir John and Son (earthenware), Greengates
Rathbone, Smith and Co., Soho pottery, High street
Sadler Wm. (china decorator), Well street pottery, Well street
Turner George W. & Sons (earthenware), Alexander works, Scotia road
Wedgwood and Co. (earthenware), High street, Brownhills

1892 Kelly

Kelly's Directory of Birmingham, Staffordshire, Warwickshire, and Worcestershire (also *Kelly's Directory of Staffordshire*), Kelly & Co. Ltd., 51 Great Queen Street, Lincoln's Inn Fields, London WC (Shaw & Tipper 6, Shaw & Tipper 1222). Dated MDCCCXCII on the title page and May 1892 in the Preface. It is noted as the Twelfth Edition in the Preface.

As with all the Kelly's series, this directory contains alphabetical lists for the various towns and villages and also classified lists for each county. Only the classified lists are included here. The range of categories is extensive and there are twenty-nine relevant to this work.

Art Pottery Manufacturers (page 543)
Beach & Adams, John street, Stoke
Ceramic Art Co. Howard pl. Shelton, Hnley
Doulton & Co. Nile Street works, Burslem

Black Ware Manufacturers (page 559)
COLCLOUGH & LINGARD, (egyptian), Britannia Black works, High street, Tunstall, Stoke

Brass Founders' China & Earthenware Figure Manufacturers (page 567)
Kent William, Novelty works, Wellington street, Burslem
Plant Brothers, Crown pottery, Dale hall, Burslem

China Manufacturers (pages 583-584)
See also Earthenware Manufacturers.
Adderley & Lawson, Salisbury works, Edensor road, Longton
Adderley W.A. Daisy Bank works, Longtn
Allen S.H. Mount Pleasant, Longton
Allerton Charles & Sons, Park works, High street, Longton
Anderson W. & Co. St. Martin's la. Longton
Asbury E. & Co. Sutherland rd. Longton
Aynsley J. & Sons, Sutherland rd. Longtn
Bates Thomas & Son, Albert works, High street, Longton
Bates Thomas, Sutherland road, Longtn
Beech James & Sons, Albert works, Sutherland road, Longton
Blackhurst & Hulme, High st. Longton
Blair & Co. Beaconsfield pottery, Anchor road, Longton
Bodley E.J.D. Hill pottery, Burslem & 3 Charterhouse street, London EC
Boughey & Wiltshaw, Market st. Longton
Boulton & Co. Edensor road, Longton
Bradley F.D. Sutherland road, Longton
Bridgett & Bates, King Street china works, Longton; general china manufacturers for home & export
Brown Westhead T.C. Moore & Co. Cauldon place, Hanley
Brownfield W. & Sons, Cobridge, Burslm
Cartlidge F. & Co. Normacott rd. Longtn
Chapman David, Forrister street, Anchor road, Longton
Coalport China Co. Lim. Glebe bldgs. Stke
Collingwood Bros. Stafford st. Longton
Cope Jas. H. & Co. Stafford st. Longton
Copeland W.T. & Sons, High street, Stoke-upon-Trent; & London agency, 12 Charterhouse street, Holborn EC
Cyples & Ford, Heathcote road, Longton
Cyples Richard, Heathcote road, Longtn
Edwards & Brown, High street, Longton
EDWARDS R.J. & CO. Gordon pottery, Anchor road, Longton
Edwards George, Sheridan works, King street, Longton
Finney J. Victoria pl. Stafford st. Longton
Ford Charles, Cannon street, Hanley
Forester & Co. Blythe works, High street, Longton
Gaskell & Grocott, Longport, Stoke
Green T.A. & S. Park st. Fenton, Stoke
Hammersley Jsph. & Robt. New st. Hanley
Hammersley & Co. Sutherland rd. Longtn
Hanley Porcelain Co. (The) (Herbert Goodwin, manager), Burton Place works, Hanley
Hollinshead & Griffiths, Chelsea works, Moorland road, Burslem
Hudson William, High street, Longton
Hughes Edward & Co. Opal china works, Fenton, Stoke-on-Trent
Jackson & Gosling, King st. Fenton, Lngtn
Jamieson Robt. Victoria works, Longtn
JONES ALFRED B. Eagle works, Station square, Longton
Jones William, Market street, Longton
Kent William (figure), Novelty works, Wellington street, Burslem
Lowe W. Sutherland rd. & High st. Longtn
Macintyre James & Co. Washington works, Burslem & 23 Bartlett's buildings, London
Middleton Jsph. Hy. Bagnall st. Longton

Mintons Limited, Eldon place, Stoke-upon-Trent & 28 Walbrook, Londn EC
Moore Brothers, St. Mary's works, High street, Longton
Morris Thomas, Mount Pleasant, Longtn
Old Hall Porcelain Works Limited, Hill street, Hanley
Plant Brothers, Bagnall street, Longton
Plant R.H. & Co. High street, Longton
Pointon & Co. Limited, Norfolk works, Norfolk street, Hanley
Poole Thomas, Edensor road, Longton
Powell, Bishop & Stonier, Stafford street & High street, Hanlen
Procter George & Co. Gladstone pottery, High street, Longton
Radford & Ward, Chancery la. Longton
Radford Samuel, Fenton, Stoke
Redfern & Drakeford, Mount Pleasant, Longton
Ridge & Nicklin, Chancery la. Longton
Robinson & Son, Foley, Fenton, Longton
Shore J. & Co. New street, Longton
Skelson & Plant, Normacott rd. Longton
Smith Sampson, Barker street, Longton
Taylor & Kent, Florence works, High street, Longton
Taylor, Tunnicliff & Co. Eastwood, Hanley; china, glass & earthenware manufrs
Tranter & Machin, Stafford st. Longton
Wagstaff & Brunt, King Street pottery, Longton
Waine Charles, Sutherland rd. Longton
Walters Thomas, Commerce st. Longton
Warrilow & Sons, Sutherland rd. Longton
Webberly William, St. James' works, High street, Longton
Wildblood & Heath, Stafford st. Longtn
Wileman & Co. Foley potteries, Fenton, Longton
Williamson H.M. & Sons, Bridge pottery, Heathcote road, Longton

---

Doulton & Co. Nile Street works, Burslem, Stoke-on-Trent; London show rooms, Cornish house, 14 St. Andrew street, Holborn circus EC

China Parian Manufacturer (page 584)
Wilson James, Gregory street, Longton

China Letter & Name Plate Manufacturers (page 584)
Macintyre James & Co. Washington works, Burslem & 23 Bartlett's bldgs. London

Creel Step & Shuttle Eye Manufacturers (page 598)
Hallen Henry, Wellington street, Burslem
Wade & Sons, Hall street, Burslem

Door Furniture Manufacturers – China (page 600)
Bullers Lim. Joiner's Square wks. Hanley
Gaskell & Grocott, Longport, Burslem
Macintyre James & Co. Washington works, Burslem; & 23 Bartlett's buildings, London
Plant Brothers, Crown pottery, Dale Hall, Burslem
Taylor Tunnicliffe & Co. Eastwood, Hanley; China lock furniture manfrs

Earthenware Manufacturers (pages 604-605)
Adams W. & T. Greenfields, Tunstall, Stoke
Alcock H. & Co. Waterloo rd. Cobridge, Stke
Allerton Charles & Sons, Park works, High street, Longton
Alum & Bryant, Heathcote rd. Longton
Art Pottery Co. (The), Anchor works, Brewery street, Hanley. See advert
Ashworth George L. & Brothers, Broad street, Hanley
Aynsley H. & Co. Commerce st. Longton
Baker & Co. Fenton, Stoke-on-Trent
Ball J. & Co. Stoke road, Shelton, Hanley
Barker, Batty & Read, Fenton, Stoke
Barker Brothers, Barker street, Longton
Barkers & Kent, Foley potteries, Fenton, Longton
Barlow & Son, Commerce street, Longton
Baudelet A. (artistic), Clayton st. Longton
Bednall & Heath, Wellington pottery, Hanley
Bennett William, Victoria road, Hanley
Bennison & Co. High street, Stoke
Bentley, Lewis & Co. Albion st. Longton
Bevington Ambrose & Co. New Hall works, Great York street, Hanley
Bevington Thomas, Mayer street, Hanley
Blackhurst & Bourne, Hadderidge pottery, Burslem
Bladon & Mullineux, Mayer st. Hanley
Bodley Edwd. F. & Sons, Longport, Stoke
Bodley Edwin J.D. Hill pottery, Burslem
Booths, Church Bank pottery, Tunstall, Stoke-on-Trent
Boughey M. Willow Street wrks. Longton
Boulton & Floyd, Lovatt street & Hall street, Stoke-upon-Trent
Boulton, Machin & Tennant, Swan Bank pottery, High street, Tunstall, Stoke
Bourne & Sheddadd, Swan works, Elm street, Hanley
Brayford & Gelson, Park House la. Burslm
Bridgwood S. & Son, East vale, Longton
British Anchor Pottery Co. Limited, Anchor road, Longton
Broadhurst James, Portland pottery, Fenton, Stoke-on-Trent
Bromley & Shaw, Barker street, Longton
Brough & Jones, Wharf street, Stoke
Brough Benjamin Hyde, Waterloo works, Stafford street, Longton
Brownfield Wm. & Sons, Cobridge, Stoke
Brownhills Pottery Co. (The), Brownhills, Tunstall, Stoke-on-Trent
Bullock & Bennett, Pelham street, Hanley
Bullock & Cornes, Pelham street, off Lichfield street, Hanley
Burgess & Leigh, Middleport pottery, Burslem, Stoke; London show rooms, 6 Thavies inn, Holborn circus EC
Burgess Henry, Kiln Croft works, Chapel lane, Burslem
Burslem Pottery Co. (C.F. Bailey, propr.) Scotia works, Wedgwood pl. Burslem
Burton Geo. & Benj. Registry st. Stoke
Cartlidge & Matthias, Tinkersclough, Hnly

Cartlidge William Edward, Villa pottery, Cobridge, Burslem
Cartwright & Edwards, Trentham road, Longton
Challinor C. & Co. High st. Fenton, Stoke
Clark E.R. & Co. Winton works, Stoke
Clementson Brothers, Phoenix & Bell works, Broad street, Hanley
Copeland W.T. & Sons, High street, Stoke-on-Trent & London agency, 12 Charterhouse street, Holborn EC
Corn William & Edward, Longport, Stoke
Cotton Elijah, Nelson place, Hanley
Cumberlidge & Humphreys, Gordon pottery, Tunstall, Stoke-on-Trent
Dale Hall Pottery Co. (The), Dale hall, Burslem
Dimmock J. & Co. (William D. Cliff, proprietor), Stafford street, Hanley
Doulton & Co. Nile Street works, Burslem, Stoke-on-Trent;
London show rooms, Cornish house, 14 St. Andrew street, Holborn circus EC
Dudson Jas. Thos. Hanover st. Hanley
Dunn, Bennett & Co. Royal Victoria works, Burslem
EDENSOR POTTERY COMPANY, Edensor road, Longton
EDGE, MALKIN & CO. Newport works, Burslem, Stoke-on-Trent
Edwards & Goodwin, Hanover Street pottery, Burslem
Emery Francis Joseph, Bleak Hill works, Bleak street, Burslem
Fenton Alfred & Sons, Brook street & Clarence street, Hanley
Fielding S. & Co. Railway pottery, Stoke
Fielding Wm. Cannon Street wks. Hanley
Ford Thos. & Sons, Newcastle st. Burslem
Forester & Hulme, Sutherland pottery, Fenton, Stoke-on-Trent
FURNIVALS, Cobridge, Burslem, Stoke
Gater & Co. Furlong lane, Burslem
Goodwin & Davison, Fountain Place pottery, Burslem
Gould M. Park Hall street, Longton
Gray & Wright, William street, Hanley
Grimwade Brothers, Stoke road, Hanley
Grindley W.H. & Co. Woodland street, Tunstall, Stoke-on-Trent
Grove & Oliver, Chancery lane, Longton
Hammersley Brothers, Nelson pl. Hanley
Hammersley Ralph & Son, Wedgwood place, Burslem
Hammonds William, Victoria works, High street, Longton
Hancock & Son, Wolfe street, Stoke
Harrop W. & Co. Tinkersclough, Hanley
Heath & Greatbatch, High st. Burslem
Hobson Geo. & Jn. Albert st. Burslem
Hobson & Co. Heathcote road, Longton
Holdcroft W. George st. Tunstall, Stoke
Hollins & Co. 5 Mayer street, Hanley
Hollinshead & Griffiths, Chelsea works, Moorland road, Burslem
Hollinshead & Kirkham, Unicorn pottery, Tunstall, Stoke-on-Trent
Howlett Joseph Redfern, Peel street, Hanley; works, Northwood
Hughes & Robinson, Globe pottery, Waterloo road, Stoke-on-Trent
Hughes Thomas, Longport, Stoke
HULME WILLIAM HENRY, Nelson place, Hanley
Johnson Brothers, Old Hall street & Eastwood road, Hanley
Jones George & Sons, London rd. Stoke
Jones Thomas, New street, Longton
Keeling & Co. Dale Hall works, Newport lane, Burslem
Kirkham William, London road, Stoke
Kirkland Samuel, Basford bank, Stoke
Lancaster Frederick John, Shelton works, Broad street, Hanley
Lawrence Thomas, Wharf street, Stoke
Lockett John & Co. Chancery la. Longton
Lowe Samuel & Co. Stafford st. Longton
Machin William, George street, Hanley
Maddock J. & Sons, Newcastle st. Burslem
Maddock & Co. Dale Hall pottery, Burslem
Malkin R. & Sons, Market st. Fenton, Stoke
Meakin James & George, Eastwood wks. Lichfield street & Eagle pottery, Bucknall road, Hanley
Meakin A. Royal Albert pottery, Parsonage st. & Wilkinson st. Tunstall, Stoke
Meir John & Son (& earthenware tiles), Greengate potteries, Tunstall, Stoke
Mellor, Taylor & Co. Waterloo rd. Burslem
Mintons Limited, Eldon place, Stoke-upon-Trent & 28 Walbrook, London EC
Moore, Leason & Co. Old Foley pottery, Fenton, Longton
Morley Wm. Albert road, Fenton, Stoke
Mountford George Thos. Wolfe st. Stoke
Nixon Mrs. J. Newfield st. Tunstall, Stoke
Ouslnam W.E. & Sons, Furlong wks. Brslm
Peake & Co. Rectory road, Hanley
Peake Joseph, Etruria vale, Hanley
Plant Brothers, Crown pottery, Dalehall, Burslem
Plant James & Co. Stoke-on-Trent
Plant & Taylor, Chadwick st. Longton
Poole John, North road, Cobridge, Stoke
Powell, Bishop & Stonier, Stafford street & High street, Hanley
Pratt Felix & Richard & Co. High street east, Fenton, Stoke-on-Trent
Procter George & Co. Gladstone pottery, High street, Longton
Procter Albert Hy. Edensor rd. Longton
Pugh & Hackney, Pelham St. wks. Hanley
Pugh Edward John, High street, Longton
Ratcliffe & Company, Gold st. Longton
Rathbone, Smith & Co. Soho pottery, Tunstall, Stoke-on-Trent
Reeves James, Victoria works, Market street, Fenton, Stoke-on-Trent
Ridgways, Bedford wks. Bedfrd. rd. Hanly
Rigby Elijah, jun. Chell street, Hanley
Roberts Darrus, Bath street, Hanley
Robinson J. Knowl wks. Hamil rd. Burslm

Rowley & Jervis, Park Place works, High street, Longton
Sandland, Bennett & Co. Victoria works, Lonsdale street, Stoke-upon-Trent
Sant & Co. Cobridge, Stoke-on-Trent
Shaw Anthony & Son, Mersey wks. Burslem
Shaw & Son, Sandyford, Tunstall, Stoke
Shenton Herbert, Union street, Hanley
Sherwin David, Renalagh works, Hanley
Shingler & Co. Liverpool road, Stoke
Smith, Ford & Jones, Lincoln pottery, Newport lane, Burslem
Smith & Co. High street, Stoke-on-Trent
Snow Jn. & Jonathan, 24 Howard pl. Hanley
Stonier, Hollinshead & Co. High st. Hanley
Stubbs & Hall, 31 High street, Longton
Stubbs Wm. Eastwood pottery, Hanley
Swann E. Amicable st. Tunstall, Stoke
Tams John, Stafford street, Longton
Thomas Uriah & Co. Union st. Hanley
Till Thos. & Sons, Liverpool rd. Burslem
Turner G.W. & Sons, Alexandra works, Tunstall, Stoke-on-Trent
Twyford Thomas, Cliffe vale, Hanley
Unwin J. & Co. Cornhill passage, Longton
Vernon James & George, African works, High street, Burslem
Wedgwood Josiah & Sons, Etruria pottery, Etruria, Stoke-on-Trent
Wedgwood & Co. Brownhills, Tunstall, Stoke-on-Trent
Whittaker & Co. Hallfield pottery, Grafton street, Hanley
Whittam Joseph, Fairfield pottery, Broad street, Hanley
Wileman J.F. Foley wks. Fenton, Longton
Wilkinson Arthur James, Central pottery & Lower works, Burslem
Wiltshaw & Robinson, Copeland st. Stoke
Winkle Fdk. & Co. Colonial pottery, Stoke
Wood & Bennett, Brook street, Hanley
Wood & Hulme, Waterloo rd. Burslem
Wood & Son, Trent pottery, Furlong lane, Burslem
Wood Thos. & Sons, Queen st. Burslem
Wood W. & Co. Albert Street wks. Burslem

Electrical China Manufacturers (page 606)
TAYLOR, TUNNICLIFF & CO. Eastwood, Hanley; switch cases, ceiling roses, cut outs, fuse blocks &c. &c.

Enamelled Tile Manufacturers (page 606)
Mintons Limited, Eldon place, Stoke-on-Trent & 28 Walbrook, London EC
Minton, Hollins & Co.'s patent tile works, Stoke-upon-Trent, & Minton & Co. 50 Conduit st. Regent st. London W
Wade J. & W. & Co. (& glazed, printed & embossed), Flaxman art tile works, High street, Burslem

Encaustic Tile Manufacturers (page 606)
Adams & Bromley, Castlefields works, Newcastle road, Stoke
Birch Elijah, 22 & 24 Clarence st. Hanley
Boote T. & R. Waterloo road, Burslem
Campbell Tile Co. (The), London rd. Stoke
Copeland W.T. & Sons, High street, Stoke-on-Trent & London agency, 12 Charterhouse street, Holborn EC
Decorative Art Tile Co. (Wm. Parrish, managing partner), 200 & 202 Bryan street, Hanley
Goodfellow & Co. Port vale, Longport, Stke
Lane End Works Limited (E.P. Everett, manager), Fenton, Stoke-on-Trent
Minton, Hollins & Co.'s patent tile works, Stoke-on-Trent & 50 Conduit street, Regent street, London W
Sherwin & Cotton (barbotine & majolica), Vine street, Hanley
Simpson Thos. Alfd. High street, Stoke
Steele & Wood & The Crystal Porcelain Tile Co. Limited, Elder road, Cobridge, Stoke-on-Trent
Timmis & Watkins, Sheaf works, Normacott road, Longton
Wedgwood Josiah & Sons, Etruria pottery, Etruria, Stoke-on-Trent
Wood & Co. Boothen Rd, Tile wks. Stoke
Woolliscroft George & Son, Patent Tile works, Nelson pl. Joiner's sq. Hanley

Ironstone China Manufacturers (page 668)
Edwards John, King st. Fenton, Stoke
Plant Brothers, Crown pottery, Dale hall, Burslem

Ivory Porcelain Manufacturer (page 669)
Goss William H. London road, Stoke

Jasper Manufacturers (page 669)
Wedgwood Josiah & Sons, Etruria pottery, Etruria, Stoke-on-Trent

Jet & Rockingham Ware Manufacturers (page 669)
See also Earthenware Manufacturers.
Barber Joseph, Albert street, Burslem
Benson & Bailey, Moorland rd. Burslem
Buckley John & Son, Navigation Road pottery, Burslem
Clare Walter, Podmore street, Burslem
Colclough & Lingard, Britannia black works, High street, Tunstall, Stoke
Dean T. Ducal wrks. Newcastle st. Burslm
Gibson & Sons, Albany works, Moorland road, near the station, Burslem
Guest Bros. High street, Tunstall, Stoke
Hurd Thos. M. & Co. Sylvester st. Burslem
Johnson Samuel, Newport st. Burslem
Johnson Samuel, Swan square, Burslem
Lester & Smith, Clay Hills pottery, Tunstall, Stoke-on-Trent
Oakes, Clare & Chadwick, Sneyd pottery, Albert street, Burslem
Perkins & Co. Royal Victoria wks. Hanley
Rathbone W. & R. Sylvester st. Burslem
Sadler & Son, Reginald street, Burslem
Sant Jeremiah, Adelaide street, Burslem
Sudlow Robert, Bourne's bank, Burslem
Wade & Co. High street, Burslem
Smith & Co. High street, Stoke
Wedgwood W. & Son, William st. Hanley
Welch J.B. New street, Hanley

Wood Henry James, Alexandra works, Navigation road, Burslem

Lock Furniture Manufacturers (page 676)
Taylor, Tunnicliff & Co. Eastwood, Hanley, china lock furniture manufactrs

Lustre Manufacturers (page 676)
Allerton Charles & Sons, Park works, High street, Longton

Majolica Manufacturers (page 677)
Benson & Bailey, Moorland rd. Burslem
Brough & Jones, Wharf street, Stoke
Colclough & Co. Anchor road, Longton
Edwards & Son, Trent works, Joiner's square, Hanley
Fielding S. & Co. Railway pottery, Stoke
Forester T. & Sons, Limited, Church street & Stafford street, Longton
Heath Thos. Albion wks. High st. Longton
Hobson & Co. Heathcote road, Longton
Holdcroft Joseph, Daisy bank, Longton
Mills & Son, 182 Bryan street, Hanley
Mintons Limited, Eldon place, Stoke-on-Trent & 28 Walbrook, London EC
Sherwin & Cotton, Vine street, Hanley
Shorter & Boulton, Copeland st. Stoke
Smith & Co. High street, Stoke-on-Trent
Wardle & Co. Victoria road, Hanley
Wedgwood Josiah & Sons, Etruria pottery, Etruria, Stoke-on-Trent

Mortar & Pestle Manufacturers (page 683)
Macintyre James & Co. Washington works, Burslem & 23 Bartlett's buildings, London

Mosaics Manufacturers (page 683)
Campbell Tile Co. (The), London road, Stoke-upon-Trent

Parian Manufacturers (page 688)
Edwards & Son, Trent works, Joiner's square, Hanley
Hammersley Bros. Nelson place, Hanley
Mintons Limited, Eldon place, Stoke
Robinson & Leadbeater, Wolfe st. Stoke

Potters (page 693)
See also Art Potters.
Baker James, Kingsfield, Newcastle
New Wharf Pottery Co. (Thomas F. Wood, managing partner), Navigation road, Burslem
Silvester Fred. & Co. Castle Hill works, Newcastle-under-Lyme

Sagger Manufacturer (page 713)
Wakefield Thomas, Botany bay, Northwood, Hanley

Sanitary Ware Manufacturers (pages 713-714)
Buckley John, manufacturer of water-closet basins & traps, table tops, urinals, ship & portable closets &c. 'Niagara Falls' basin & traps &c. Albert works, Victoria place, Hanley
Howson George, Clifford & Ephraim street, Eastwood, Hanley

Shuttle Eye Manufacturers (page 737)
Hallen Henry, Wellington st. Burslem
Wade & Sons, Hall street, Burslem

Stilt & Spur Manufacturers (page 746)
Arrowsmith Thomas & Son, Moorland road, Burslem
Edwards John & Sons, King street, Fenton, Stoke-on-Trent
Gimson Joseph & Co. Market street, Fenton, Stoke-on-Trent
Taylor Wm. & Co. Church st. Longton

Stoneware Manufacturers (page 747)
Rigby James, Milton, Stoke-on-Trent
Wedgwood Josiah & Sons, Etruria pottery, Etruria, Stoke-upon-Trent

Terra Cotta Manufacturers (page 753)
Peake Thos. The Tileries, Tunstall, Stoke

1896 Kelly

Kelly's Directory of Birmingham, Staffordshire, Warwickshire and Worcestershire (also *Kelly's Directory of Staffordshire*; also Kelly's *Directory of Staffordshire and Shropshire*), Kelly & Co. Ltd., 182-184 High Holborn, London WC (Shaw & Tipper 6, Shaw & Tipper 1222). Dated MDCCCXCVI on the title page and February 1896 in the Preface. It is noted as the Thirteenth Edition in the Preface.

As with all the Kelly's series, this directory contains alphabetical lists for the various towns and villages and also classified lists for each county. Only the classified lists are included here. The range of categories is extensive and there are twenty-nine relevant to this work. The abbreviations T.A. and T.N. stand for Telegraphic Address and Telephone Number respectively. The letters S.O. are a Post Office delivery abbreviation for Sub-Office.

Art Pottery Manufacturers (page 592)
Ceramic Art Co. Limited (J.W. Cooper, man.), Howard pl. Shelton, Hanley

Art Tile Manufacturers (page 592)
Wade J. & W. & Co. High st. Burslem

Brass Founders' Chain (sic) Figure Manufacturer (page 618)

Kent Wm. Wellington st. Burslem

China Manufacturers (page 638)

See also Earthenware Manufacturers.

Adderley William & Co. Daisy Bank pottery, Longton
Allen S.H. Mount Pleasant, Longton
Allerton Charles & Sons, Park works, High street, Longton
Amison Charles, Wedgwood street, Sandford hill, Longton
Asbury E. & Co. Sutherland rd. Longtn
Aynsley J. & Sons, Sutherland rd. Lngtn
Bishop & Stonier, Stafford st. Nelson place & High street, Hanley
Blackhurst & Hulme, High st. Longton
Blair & Co. Beaconsfield pottery, Anchor road, Longton
Boulton & Co. Edensor road, Longton
Bradley Fred. D. Sutherland rd. Lngtn
Bridgett & Bates, King street, Longtn
Britannia China Co. (Thomas Wm. Bourne, manager), Edensor rd. Lgtn
Brown Westhead T.C. Moore & Co. Cauldon place, Hanley
Cartlidge F. & Co. Normacott rd. Lgtn
Chapman D. & Sons, Sutherland rd. Lgtn
Coggins & Hill, St. James' place, High street, Longton
Collingwood Brothers, Stafford st. Lgtn
Cope James H. & Co. Stafford st. Lgtn
Copeland W.T. & Sons, High street, Stoke-on-Trent; & London agency, 12 Charterhouse st. Holborn EC
Curzon & Co. Pyenest st. Shetlon, Stke
DEWES & COPESTAKE, Viaduct wrks. Caroline street, Longton
Dresden Porcelain Co. Blythe works, High street, Longton
Edward & Brown, High street, Longtn
Edwards R.J. & Co. Gordon pottery, Anchor road, Longton
Edwards George, Sheridan works, King street, Longton
Empire Porcelain Co. (The), Stoke rd. Shelton, Stoke
Finney J. Victoria pl. Stafford st. Lgtn
Ford Charles, Cannon street, Hanley
Gaskell & Grocott, Longport, Woolstanton, Stoke
Goss William H. London road, Stoke
Green T.A. & S. Park st. Fentn. Stoke
Hammersley J. & R. New st. Hanley
Hammersley & Co. Sutherland rd. Lngtn
Hollinshead & Griffiths, Chelsea works, Moorland road, Burslem
Hudson Wm. Normacott rd. Longton
Hughes E. & Co. Opal wrks. Fntn. Stke
Hughes & Co. Globe pottery, Waterloo road, Cobridge, Burslem
Jackson & Gosling, Foley, Longton
Jones George & Sons Limited, Trent Potteries, London road, Stoke
Jones William, Market st. Longton
Longton Porcelain Co. Victoria works, High street, Longton
Mackee Andrew, Foley works, Longton
Middleton Jsph. H. Bagnall st. Lngtn
MINTONS LIMITED, china, majolica, parian, earthenware & enamelled tiles manufacturers, Eldon place, Stoke. TA 'Mintons, Stoke'; TN 203; & 25 Farringdon avenue, London EC. TA 'Mintons, London'; TN 6877
Moore Brothers, St. Mary's works, High street, Longton
Morris Thomas, Mt. Pleasant, Longtn
Old Hall Porcelain Works Limited, Hill street, Hanley
Plant Bros. Bagnall street, Longton
Plant R.H. & Co. High st. Longton
Pointon & Co. Limited, Norfolk works, Norfolk street, Shelton, Stoke
Poole Thomas, Edensor rd. Longton
Procter George & Co. Gladstone pottery, High street, Longton
Radford Samuel, Fenton, Stoke
Redfern & Drakeford, Mt. Plsnt. Longtn
Robinson & Son, Foley, Longton
Shaw James, Albion street, Longton
Shore J. & Co. New street, Longton
Smith Sampson, Barker st. Longton
Taylor & Kent, Florence works, High street, Longton
Taylor, Tunnicliff & Co. Eastwood, Hanley; china, glass & earthenware manufacturers
Tranter & Machin, Stafford st. Longtn
Wagstaff & Brunt, King Street pottery, Longton
Waine Charles, Sutherland rd. Longtn
Walters Thos. Commerce st. Longton
Warrilow & Sons, Sutherland rd. Lgtn
Wildblood & Heath, Stafford st. Longtn
Wileman & Co. Foley potteries, Longtn
Williamson H.M. & Sons, Bridge pottery, Heathcote road, Longton
Wiltshaw S.T. & Co. Market st. Longtn

China Parian Manufacturer (page 638)

Wilson James, Gregory st. Longton

China Letter & Name Plate Manufacturers (page 639)

Macintyre James & Co. Limited, Washington works, Burslem

Creel Step & Shuttle Eye Manufacturers (page 656)

Hallen Henry (exors. of), Wellington street, Burslem
Wade & Sons, Hall street, Burslem

Door Furniture Manufacturers – China (page 659)

Bullers Limited, Joiner's Square works, Hanley
Gaskell & Grocott, Longport, Burslem, Stoke
Macintyre James & Co. Limited, Washington works, Burslem; & 49 Holborn viaduct, London
Taylor Tunnicliff & Co. Eastwood, Hnly

Earthenware Manufacturers (pages 667-668)

Adams W. & T. Greenfields, Tunstall
Adderley William A. & Co. Daisy Bank pottery, Longton
Alcock Henry & Co. Waterloo road, Cobridge, Burslem
Allerton Charles & Sons, Park works, High street, Longton
Art Pottery Co. (The), Brewery st. Hnly
Ashworth G.L. & Bros, Broad st. Hnly
Aynsley H. & Co. Commerce st. Longtn

Bailey Jn. Bucknall New rd. Hanley
Baker & Co. Limited, Fenton, Stoke
Barker Brothers, Barker st. Longton
Barker Batty & Read, Fenton, Stoke
Barkers & Kent, Foley potteries, Fenton, Longton
Barlow T.W. & Son, Commerce st. Longton
Bednall & Heath, Wellington pottery, Commercial road, Hanley
Bennett George & Co. Victoria works, Longsdale street, Stoke
Bennett John & Co. Pelham st. Hanley
Bennett William, Victoria rd. Hanley
Bilton Ernest, Fenton, Stoke
Beswick Jas. Wright, Baltimore works, Albion st. Longton; specialities, figures, majolica, decorated toilet &c
Birks L.A. & Co. The Vine Pottery, Boothen, Stoke
Bishop & Stonier, Stafford street, Nelson place & High street, Hanley
Blackhurst A.J. Newfield st. Tunstall
Bodley Edward, Fisher & Sons, Longport, Stoke
Booths, Church Bank pottry. Tunstall
Boulton & Floyd, Lovatt street & Hall street, Stoke
Boughey M. Willow St. wrks. Longton
Boulton, Machin & Tennant, Swan Bank pottery, High street, Tunstall
Bradely & Preece, Hanover st. Burslem
Brain Thomas, Church street, Longton
Bridgwood Sampson & Son, East vale, Longton
British Anchor Pottery Co. Limited, Anchor road, Longton
Broadhurst James & Sons, Portland pottery, Fenton, Stoke
Bromley John, Barker street, Longton
Brough & Jones, Wharf street, Stoke
Brownfields Guild-Pottery Society Lim. Cobridge, Burslem
Brownhills Pottery Co. (The), Brownhills, Tunstall
Bullock A. & Co. Commercial rd. Hanly
Burgess & Leigh, Middleport pottery, Burslem, Stoke; London show rooms, 60 Shoe la. corner Charterhouse st. EC
Burslem Pottery Co. Scotia wrks. Brslm
Burton Geo. & B. Registry st. Stoke
Cartlidge & Matthias, Slippery la. Hnly
Cartwright & Edwards, Trentham rd. Longton
Clark E.R. & Co. Winton works, Stoke
Clementson Brothers, Phoenix & Bell works, Broad street, Hanley
Cone Thomas & Co. High st. Longton
Corn William & Edward, Longprt. Stke
Cotton Elijah, Nelson road, Hanley
Cumberlidge & Humphreys, Gordon pottery, Tunstall
Curzon & Co. Pyenest st. Shelton, Stke
Dean M. Ranelagh street, Hanley
Dewes & Copestake, Viaduct works, Caroline street, Longton
Dimmock J. & Co. (Wm. D. Cliff, proprietor), Stafford street, Hanley
Doulton & Co. Nile Street works, Brslm
Dudson Jas. Thos. Hanover st. Hanley
Dunn, Bennett & Co. Royal Victoria works, Burslem
Edensor Pottery Company, Edensor road, Longton
EDGE, MALKIN & CO. Newport works, Burslem
Edwards & Son, Hadderidge pottery, Burslem
Edwards William Joseph, Russell St. works, Warren street, Longton
Empire Porcelain Co. (The), Stoke road, Shelton, Stoke
Fenton Alfred & Sons, Brook street & Clarence street, Hanley
Fielding S. & Co. Railway pottry. Stke
Fielding Wm. Cannon St. works, Hanly
Finney William, Mount Pleasant wrks. High street, Longton
Ford & Sons, Newcastle st. Burslem
FURNIVALS LIMITED, Cobridge, Burslem
Gater, Hall & Co. Furlong la. Burslm
Goodwin & Davison, Fountain Place pottery, Burslem
Gray & Co. William street, Hanley
Grimwade Brothers, Stoke road, Shelton, Hanley
Grindley W.H. & Co. Woodland st. Tunstall
Grove & Prouse, Chancery la. Longton
Hammersley Ralph & Son, Wedgwood place, Burslem
Hammersley Brothers, Nelson pl. Hanly
Hancock S. & Son, Wolfe street, Stoke
Harrop & Burgess, Tinkersclough, Hnly
Heath Arthr. & Co. Dale hall, Burslem
Hobson Geo. & Jn. Albert st. Burslem
Holdcroft J.P. George st. Tunstall
Holdcroft Joseph, Daisy bank, Longtn
Hollinshead & Kirkham, Unicorn pottery, Tunstall
Howlett & Co. Peel st. Northwood, Hnly
Hughes & Co. Globe pottery, Waterloo road, Cobridge, Burslem
Hulme & Christie, Sutherland pottery, Fenton, Stoke
Hughes Thomas, Longport, Stoke
HULME WILLIAM HENRY, Nelson pl. Hanley
Johnson Bros. Hanley, Trent & Charles Street potteries, Hanley
Jones George & Sons Limited, Trent potteries, London road, Stoke
Jones Thomas, New street, Longton
Keeling & Co. Dale hall, Burslem
Kirkhams, London road, Stoke
Kirkland & Co. Basford bank, Stoke
Lancaster & Baker, Slippery la. Hanley
Lawrence Thomas, Wharf street, Stoke
Lockett John & Co. Chancery la. Lngtn
Lowe William, Sutherland road & High street, Longton
Machin William, George street, Hanley
McNeal & Co. Stafford street, Longton
Maddock John & Sons, Newcastle st. Burslem
Maddock & Co. Dale Hall pottery, Brslm
Meakin J. & G. Limited, Eastwood works, Lichfield street; Eagle pottery, Bucknall road, Hanley
Meakin Alfred, Royal Albert pottery, Parsonage st. & Wilkinson st. Tunstll
Meigh W. & R. Campbell place, Stoke-on-Trent
Meir John & Son, Greengate potteries, Tunstall
Mellor, Taylor & Co. Waterloo road, Burslem
Mintons Limited, Eldon place, Stoke (TA 'Mintons, Stoke-on-Trent'; TN 203); & 25 Farringdon avenue, London EC (TA 'Mintons, London'; TN 6877

Moore, Leeson & Co. Old Foley pottery, Longton
Morley W. Victoria rd. Fenton, Stoke
Mountford George Thos. Wolfe st. Stke
Peake Joseph, Etruria vale, Hanley
Peake Mrs. Sarah Ann, Rectory road, Shelton, Stoke
Pearl Pottery Co. Brook st. Hanley
Pitcairns Limited, Pinnox, Tunstall
Plant Brothers, Crown pottery, Dale hall, Burslem
Plant & Gilmore, York street, Hanley
Plant James & Co. Stoke
Plant Ralph & Sons, Warwick works, Chadwick street, Longton
Pratt F. & R. & Co. High street east, Fenton, Stoke
Preece Harry, see Bradley & Preece, Burslem
Procter George & Co. Gladstone pottery, High street, Longton
Procter John & Son, Edensor rd. Lngtn
Ratcliffe & Co. Gold street, Longton
Rathbone, Smith & Co. Soho pottery, Tunstall
Rathbone R. Victoria square, Hanley
Reeves James, Victoria works, Market street, Fenton, Stoke
Ridgways, Bedford works, Bedford rd. Shelton, Stoke
Rigby & Stevenson, High st. Hanley
Roberts Darius, Leek road, Bucknall, Milton S.O
Roberts Darrus, Bath street, Hanley
Roberts James, Park Hall st. Longton
Robinson Joseph, Knowl works, Hamil road, Burslem
Rowley & Newton, Park place works, High street, Longton
Rushton James, Chadwick st. Longton
Sadler Edward William, Well Street pottery, Well street, Tunstall
Sandland William, Lichfield st. Hanley
Shaw A. & Son, Mersey works, Burslm
Shaw & Son, Sandyford, Tunstall
Sheaf Pottery Co. Normacott rd. Lngtn
Shenton Herbert, Union street, Hanly
Smith & Ford, Lincoln pottery, Newport lane, Burslem
Smith & Co. High street, Stoke
Snow John & J. 26 Howard pl. Hanley
Sudlow R. & Sons, Adelaide st. Burslem
Swan Pottery Co. High street, Stoke
Tams John, Stafford street, Longton
Thomas Uriah & Co. Union st. Hanley
Till T. & Sons, Liverpool rd. Burslem
Tompkinson Edward John, Flaxman pottery, Sutherland road, Longton
Twyford Thomas, Cliffe vale, Hanley
UNWIN JOSEPH & CO. Cornhill passage, Longton
Upper Hanley Pottery Co. (The), High street, Hanley
Vernon C.A. & Co. Cobridge, Burslem
Victoria Pottery Co. (The), Broad st. Hanley
Walters Thomas, Commerce st. Lngtn
Weatherby J.H. & Sons, High st. Hanley
Wedgwood Josiah & Sons, Etruria pottery, Etruria, Stoke
Wedgwood & Co. Brownhills, Tunstall
Whittaker & Co. Hallfield pottery, Grafton street, Hanley
Wildblood & Ledgar, Heathcote road, Longton
Wilkinson A.J. Lim, Royal Staffordshire pottery, Burslem
Wiltshaw & Robinson, Copeland st. Stke
Winkle F. & Co. Colonial pottery, Stoke
Wood & Hulme, Waterloo rd. Burslm
Wood & Son, Trent pottery, Furlong lane, Burslem
Wood Thomas & Sons, Queen st. Brslm
Wood W. & Co. Albert St. wrks. Brslm
Yates & Bamford, Cobridge, Burslem

Electrical China Manufacturers (page 668)
TAYLOR, TUNNICLIFF & CO. Eastwood, Hanley; switch cases, ceiling roses, cut outs, fuse blocks &c. &c.

Enamelled Letter Makers (page 669)
Boughey M. Willow Street works, Lngtn

Enamelled Tile Manufacturers (page 669)
Hopkins & Co. Hose street, Tunstall
Mintons Limited, Eldon place, Stoke; T.A. 'Mintons, Stoke-on-Trent'; T.N. 203; & 25 Farringdon avenue, London EC; T.A. 'Mintons, London'; T.N. 6877

Encaustic Tile Manufacturers (page 669)
Bates, Dewsberry & Co. Mayer st. Hnly
Birch Tile Co. Limited (The), 22 & 24 Clarence street, Hanley
Campbell Tile Co. (The), London rd. Stke
Decorative Art Tile Co. Limited (Wm. Parrish, managing director), 200 & 202 Bryan street, Hanley
Gosling Joseph, 67 Hanover st. Burslm
Lea James, High street, Tunstall
Malkin, Edge & Co. Newport wrks. Brslm
MINTON, HOLLINS & CO.'S PATENT TILE WORKS, Stoke-on-Trent; & Minton & Co. 50 Conduit street, Regent street, London W
Woolliscroft George & Son Limited, Patent Tile works, Nelson place, Joiner's square, Hanley

Ironstone China Manufacturer (page 735)
Edwardes J. King st. Fenton, Stoke

Jasper Manufacturers (page 736)
Wedgwood Josiah & Sons Limited, Etruria pottery, Etruria, Stoke

Jet & Rockingham Ware Manufacturers (page 736)
See also Earthenware Manufacturers.
Barber Joseph, Albert st. Burslem
Bromley John, Barker st. Longton
Buckley John & Son, Navigation Road pottery, Burslem
Clare & Chadwick, Albert st. Burslem
Clare Walter, Podmore st. Burslem
Colclough & Lingard, Britannia works, High street, Tunstall
Cumberlidge & Hines, Foley pottery, Longton
Dean Thomas, Ducal works, Newcastle street, Burslem
Gibson & Sons, Moorland rd. Burslem
Hurd Thomas Mansfield, Station pottery, Burslem
Johnson Samuel, Newport st. Burslem
Johnson Samuel, Swan sq. Burslem

Lester & Smith, Clay Hills pottery, Tunstall
Neale, Marsh & White, Fenton, Stoke
Sadler & Co. Reginald st. Burslem
Sharpe W.H. Canning st. Fenton Stoke
Smith & Co. High street, Stoke
Wade & Co. High street, Burslem
Wedgwood W. & Son, William st. Hnly
Wood Henry James, Alexandra works, Navigation road, Burslem

Lock Furniture Manufacturers (page 744)
Taylor, Tunnicliff & Co. Eastwood, Hanley

Majolica Manufacturers (page 745)
Beswick James Wright, Baltimore works, Albion street, Longton
Brough & Jones, Wharf street, Stoke
Colclough & Co. Anchor road, Longton
Edwards & Son, Trent works, Joiner's square, Hanley
Fielding S. & Co. Railway pottry. Stoke
Forester Thomas & Sons Limited, Church st. & Stafford st. Longton
Hawley, Webberley & Co. Garfield works, High street, Longton
Heath T. Albion works, High st. Longtn
Holdcroft Joseph, Daisy bank, Longton
Mintons Limited, Eldon place, Stoke; TA 'Mintons, Stoke'; TN 203; & 25 Farringdon avenue, London EC; TA 'Mintons, London'; TN 6,877
Shorter & Boulton, Copeland street, Stoke-on-Trent
Smith & Co. High street, Stoke
Wardle & Co. Victoria road, Hanley; TN 141
Wedgwood Josiah & Sons Limited, Etruria pottery, Etruria, Stoke

Mortar & Pestle Manufacturers (page 749)
Macintyre James & Co. Limited, Washington works, Burslem

Mosaics Manufacturers (page 749)
Campbell Tile Co. (The), London road, Stoke
Minton, Hollins & Co. Stoke-on-Trent

Parian Manufacturers (page 756)
Hammersley Bros. Nelson pl. Hanley
Mintons Limited, Eldon place, Stoke; T.A. 'Mintons, Stoke-on-Trent'; T.N. 203; & 25 Farringdon avenue, London EC; T.A. 'Mintons, London'; T.N. 6877
Robinson & Leadbeater, Wolfe street, Stoke-on-Trent

Potters (page 761)
See also Art Potters.
Baker James, Kingsfield, Newcastle
Hulme Thomas; office, 67 Bryan st. Hanley. TN 31
Hurd T.M. 12 Waterloo rd. Burslem
New Wharf Pottery Co. (Thomas F. Wood, managing partner), Navigation road, Burslem

Sagger Manufacturer (page 783)
Wakefield T. Botany bay, Nrthwd. Hnly

Sanitary Ware Manufacturers (page 783)
Buckley & Co. Lim. Stafford st. Lngtn
Hobson & Co. Brewery works, Normacott road, Longton
Howson George, Clifford & Ephraim streets, Eastwood, Hanley
Park Sanitary Co. (The) (late J. Buckley), Albert pottery, Victoria road, Hanley
Sherwin & Cotton, Vine street & Cooper street, Hanley

Spur Makers (page 818)
Edwards John & Sons, King street, Fenton, Stoke
Gimson J. & Co. Market st. Fenton, Stoke
Taylor & Co. Church st. Longton

Stilt & Spur Manufacturers (page 820)
Arrowsmith Thomas & Sons, Moorland road, Burslem
Edwards John & Sons, King street, Fenton, Stoke
Ford Charles & Co. Mill street, Hanley
Gimson J. & Co. Market st. Fentn. Stke
Taylor & Co. Church street, Longton

Stilt & Thimble Makers (page 820)
Ogden Henry & Co. Mayer st. Hanley

Stoneware Manufacturers (page 821)
Rigby James, Milton S.O
Wedgwood Josiah & Sons Limited, Etruria pottery, Etruria, Stoke

Terra Cotta Manufacturer (page 828)
Penson Fredk. Wm. Vine st. Stoke

1900 Kelly

Kelly's Directory of Birmingham, Staffordshire, Warwickshire and Worcestershire (also *Kelly's Directory of Staffordshire),* Kelly's Directories Ltd., 182-184 High Holborn, London WC (Shaw & Tipper 6, Shaw & Tipper 1222). Dated MDCCCC on the title page and March 1900 in the Preface. It is noted as the Fourteenth Edition in the Preface.

As with all the Kelly's series, this directory contains alphabetical lists for the various towns and villages and also classified lists for each county. Only the classified lists are included here. The range of categories is extensive and there are thirty relevant to this work. The abbreviations T.A. and T.N. stand for Telegraphic Address and Telephone Number respectively

Art Pottery Manufacturers (page 617)
Ceramic Art Co. Limited (J.W. Cooper, man), 28 Howard pl. Shelton, Stoke

Art Tile Manufacturers (page 617)
Lee & Boulton, High street, Tunstall
Wade J. & W. & Co. High st. Burslem

Brass Founders' China Figure Manufacturer (page 644)
Kent William, Novelty works, Wellington street, Burslem

China Manufacturers (page 664)
See also Earthenware Manufacturers.
Adderley William A. & Co. Daisy Bank pottery, Longton
Allerton Charles & Sons, Park works, High street, Longton
Amison Charles, Wedgwood street, Sandford hill, Longton
Asbury E. & Co. Sutherland rd. Longtn
Aynsley J. & Sons, Sutherland rd. Lngtn
Bishop & Stonier, Stafford st. Nelson place & High street, Hanley
Blackhurst & Hulme, 51 High street, Longton
Blair & Co. Beaconsfield pottery, Anchor road, Longton
Boulton & Co. Edensor road, Longton
Bourne & Co. Cleveland street, Shelton, Stoke-on-Trent
Bridgett & Bates, King street, Longtn
Britannia China Co. (Thomas Wm. Bourne, manager), Edensor rd. Lgtn
Brown-Westhead Moore & Co. Cauldon place, Shelton, Stoke
Browning & Lewis, Smithfield works, Hanley
Carlton Pottery Co. 20 Glebe bldgs. Stk
Cartlidge F. & Co. Normacot rd. Lngtn
Cartwright & Edwards, Trentham rd. Florence, Longton
Chapman D. & Sons, Sutherland rd. Lgtn
Coggins & Hill, St. James' place, High street, Longton
Collingwood Brothers, Stafford st. Lgtn
Cooper John, Clayton street, Longton
Cope James H. & Co. Stafford st. Lgtn
Copeland W.T. & Sons, High street, Stoke-on-Trent
Dewes & Copestake, Viaduct works, Caroline street, Longton
Dresden Porcelain Co. Blythe works, High street, Longton
Edward & Brown, High street, Longtn
Edwards George, Sheridan works, King street, Longton
Empire Porcelain Co. (The), Stoke rd. Shelton, Stoke
Finney J. Victoria pl. Stafford st. Lgtn
Ford Charles, Cannon street, Hanley
Goss William H. London road, Stoke
Hammersley J. & R. New st. Hanley
Hammersley & Co. Sutherland rd. Lngtn
Hill & Co. St. James' works, High street, Longton
Hollinshead & Griffiths, Chelsea works, Moorland road, Burslem
Holt John William, Clarence works, High street, Longton
Hudson Wm. Normacot rd. Longton
Hughes E. & Co. Opal wrks. Fntn. Stke
Hull Arth. Jn. Normacot rd. Longton
Jackson & Gosling, Foley, Longton
Jones George & Sons Limited, Trent Potteries, Stoke
Jones William, Market st. Longton
Longton Porcelain Co. Victoria works, High street, Longton
Lowe William, Sutherland road & High street, Longton
Mackee Andrew, Foley works, Longton
Middleton Jsph. H. Bagnall st. Lngtn
Mintons Limited, china, majolica, parian, earthenware & enamelled tiles manufacturers, Stoke
Moore Brothers, St. Mary's works, High street, Longton
Morris & Davis, Mt. Pleasant, Longtn
Morris Thomas, Mt. Pleasant, Longtn
Old Hall Porcelain Works Limited, Hill street, Hanley
Plant Bros. Bagnall street, Longton
Plant R.H. & Co. Forrester street, Longton
Pointon & Co. Limited, Norfolk works, Norfolk street, Shelton, Stoke
Poole Thomas, Edensor rd. Longton
Procter George & Co. Gladstone pottery, High street, Longton
Radford Samuel, Fenton, Stoke
Redfern & Drakeford, Mt. Plsnt. Longtn
Robinson & Son, Foley, Longton
Rowley & Newton Limited, Gordon pottery, Anchor road & Park Place works, High street, Longton
Shaw James, Albion street, Longton
Shore J. & Co. New street, Longton
Smith Sampson, Barker st. Longton
Star China Co. Gregory st. Longton
Taylor & Kent, Florence works, High street, Longton
Taylor, Tunnicliff & Co. Limited, Eastwood, Hanley; china, lock & door furniture, electrical chnina, artists' colormen's sundries &c
Waine Charles, Sutherland rd. Longtn
Walters Thomas, Stafford st. Longton
Warrilow & Sons, Sutherland rd. Lgtn
Wedgwood Josiah & Sons Limited, Etruria pottery, Etruria, Stoke
Wild Thomas & Co. Albert works, High street, Longton
Wildblood, Heath & Sons, Stafford st. Longton
Wileman & Co. Foley potteries, Longtn
Williamson H.M. & Sons, Bridge pottery, Heathcote road, Longton

China Letter & Name Plate Manufacturers (page 665)
Macintyre James & Co. Limited, Washington works, Burslem

Creel Step & Shuttle Eye Manufacturers (page 682)
Hallen Henry (exors. of), Wellington street, Burslem

Door Furniture Manufacturers – China (page 686)
Bullers Limited, Joiner's Square works, Hanley
Gaskell & Grocott, Longport, Burslem, Stoke
Macintyre James & Co. Limited, Washington works, Burslem
Taylor Tunnicliff & Co. Eastwood, Hnly

Earthenware Manufacturers (pages 694-695)
Adams W. & Co. Greenfields, Tunstll
Adderley William A. & Co. Daisy Bank pottery, Longton
Alcock Henry & Co. Waterloo road, Cobridge, Burslem
Allerton Charles & Sons, Park works, High street, Longton
Art Pottery Co. (The), Brewery st. Hnly
Ashworth G.L. & Bros. Broad st. Hnly
Aynsley H. & Co. Commerce st. Longtn
Bailey & Cooper, London road, Stoke
Baker & Co. Limited, Fenton, Stoke
Barker Brothers, Barker st. Longton
Barker Henry K. Fenton, Stoke

Barkers & Kent Limited, Foley potteries, Fenton, Longton
Barlow T.W. & Son, Commerce st. Longton
Bednall & Heath, Wellington pottery, Commercial road, Hanley
Bennett George & Co. Victoria works, Lonsdale street, Stoke
Bennett John & Co. Pelham st. Hanley
Bennett William, Victoria rd. Shelton
Bestwick John, Gold street, Longton
Beswick James W. High st. Longton
Bilton Ernest, Fenton, Stoke
Birks Rawlin & Co. The Vine Pottery, Boothen, Stoke
Bishop & Stonier, Stafford street, Nelson place & High street, Hanley
Booths Limited, Church Bank pottery, Tunstall
Boughey M. Willow St. wrks. Longton
Boulton & Floyd, Lovatt street & Hall street, Stoke
Bradbury & Emery, Nelson rd. Hanley
Bradley & Preece, Waterloo rd. Burslm
Brain Thomas, Church street, Longton
Brassington Joseph Hy. Wharf st. Stoke
Bridgwood Sampson & Son, East vale, Longton
British Anchor Pottery Co. Limited, Anchor road, Longton
Broadhurst James & Sons, Portland pottery, Fenton, Stoke
Bromley John, Barker street, Longton
Brough John Walley, Wharf st. Stoke
Brownfields Guild-Pottery Society Lim. Cobridge, Burslem
Browning & Lewis, Smithfield works, Hanley
Bullock A. & Co. Commercial rd. Hanly
Burgess & Leigh, Middleport pottery, Burslem
Burslem Pottery Co. Scotia wrks. Brslm
Burton Geo. & B. Registry st. Stoke
Carlton Pottery Co. 20 Glebe buildings, Stoke
Cartlidge & Matthias, Slippery la. Hnly
Cartwright & Edwards, Trentham rd. Florence, Longton
Clementson Brothers, Phoenix & Bell works, Broad street, Hanley
Cone Thomas, High street, Longton
Cooper John, Clayton street, Longton
Copeland W.T. & Sons, High street, Stoke-on-Trent
Corn William & Edward, Longprt. Stke
Cotton Elijah, Nelson road, Hanley
Davison & Son, Bleak Hill wks. Burslm
Dean M. & Rogers, Ranelagh st. Hnly
Dewes & Copestake, Viaduct works, Caroline street, Longton
Dimmock J. & Co. (Wm. D. Cliff, proprietor), Stafford street, Hanley
Doulton & Co. Nile Street works, Brslm
Dudson Jas. Thos. Hanover st. Hanley
Dunn, Bennett & Co. Royal Victoria works, Burslem
Edensor Pottery Company Limited, Edensor road, Longton
Edge, Malkin & Co. Newport works, Burslem
Edwards & Son, Hadderidge pottery, Burslem
Edwards William Joseph, Russell St. works, Warren street, Longton
Empire Porcelain Co. (The), Stoke road, Shelton, Stoke
Fenton A. & Sons, Clarence st. Hanley
Fielding S. & Co. Railway pottry. Stke
Fielding Wm. Cannon St. works, Hanly
Ford Samuel & Co. Lincoln pottery, Newport lane, Burslem
Ford & Sons, Newcastle st. Burslem
Franter & Fieldsend, Normacot road, Longton
Furnivals Limited, Cobridge, Burslm
FURNIVALS LIMITED, Cobridge, Burslem
Gater, Hall & Co. Gordon pottery, Tunstall
Gray J. William st. Shelton, Stoke
Grimwade Brothers, Stoke road, Shelton, Stoke
Grindley W.H. & Co. Woodland st. Tunstall
Grove & Co. Chancery la. Longton
Hackney Albt. G. Slippery la. Hanley
Hammersley Ralph & Son, Wedgwood place, Burslem
Hancock Fred. & Co. Campbell Place works, Stoke
Hancock S. & Sons, Wolfe st. Stoke
Hanley China Co. Burton pl. Hanley
Harrop & Burgess, Tinkersclough, Hnly
Hines Bros. Heron cross, Fenton, Stke
Hobson Geo. & Jn. Albert st. Burslem
Holdcroft J.P. George st. Tunstall
Holdcroft Joseph, Daisy bank, Longtn
Hollinshead & Griffiths, Chelsea works, Moorland road, Burslem
Hollinshead & Kirkham, Unicorn pottery, Tunstall
Holmes & Son, Clayton street, Longtn
Howlett & Co. Peel st. Northwood, Hnly
Hughes Thomas & Son, Longport, Stke
Hull Arth. Jn. Normacot rd. Longton
Hulme & Christie, Sutherland pottery, Fenton, Stoke
Johnson Bros. Lim. Scotia rd. Tunstall
Johnson Brothers (Hanley) Limited, Hanley, Imperial, Trent & Charles Street potteries, Stoke-on-Trent
Jones George & Sons Limited, Trent potteries, Stoke
Keeling & Co. Dale hall, Burslem
Kent James, The Old Foley pottery, Fenton, Stoke
Kirkhams, London road, Stoke
Kirkland & Co. Basford bank, Stoke
Lancaster & Barker, Dresden works, Tinkersclough
Lockett John & Co. Chancery la. Lngtn
Lowe William, Sutherland road & High street, Longton
Machin William, George street, Hanley
McNeal & Co. Stafford street, Longton
Maddock John & Sons, Newcastle st. Burslem
Massey David, 30 Edmund st. Hanley
Meakin Alfred Limited, Royal Albert pottery, Parsonage street & Wilkinson street, Tunstall
Meakin J. & G. Limited, Eastwood works, Lichfield street; Eagle pottery, Bucknall road, Hanley
Mellor, Taylor & Co. Waterloo road, Burslem
Mintons Limited, Stoke
Moore & Co. Victoria square, Hanley
Morley W. Victoria rd. Fenton, Stoke
Morris & Co. Fenton road, Hanley
Myott, Son & Co. Wolfe street, Stoke
Park Hall Pottery Co. Park Hall st. Longton
Peake Mrs. Sarah Ann, Rectory road, Shelton, Stoke
Pearce William, High street, Stoke
Pearl Pottery Co. Brook st. Hanley
Pearson Pottery Co. Brook street & Clarence street, Hanley

Pitcairns Limited, Pinnox, Tunstall
Plant Brothers, Crown pottery, Dalehall, Burslem
Plant & Gilmore, New Hall works, York street, Hanley
Plant James & Co. Stoke
Plant Ralph & Sons, Warwick works, Chadwick street, Longton
Pratt F. & R. & Co. High street east, Fenton, Stoke
Procter George & Co. Gladstone pottery, High street, Longton
Procter John & Son, Edensor rd. Lngtn
Pugh & Shubotham, Fountain square, High street, Fenton, Stoke
Rathbone T. & Co. Newfield pottery, Tunstall
Reeves James, Victoria works, Market street, Fenton, Stoke
Ridgways, Bedford works, Bedford rd. Shelton, Stoke
Rigby & Stevenson, High st. Hanley
Roberts Darius, Leek road, Bucknall, Milton, Stoke
Roberts Darrus, Bath street, Hanley
Rowley & Newton Limited, Gordon pottery, Anchor road & Park place works, High street, Longton
Rushton James, Chadwick st. Longton
Sadler Edward William, Well Street pottery, Well street, Tunstall
Salt Brothers, Brownhills, Tunstall
Sandland William, Lichfield st. Hanley
Sanitary Pottery Co. Limited, Longport, Stoke-on-Trent
Shaw A. & Son, Mersey works, Burslm
Shaw & Son, Sandyford, Tunstall
Sheaf Pottery Co. Commerce st. Lngtn
Smith W.T.H. & Co. Longport, Stoke
Smith & Co. Albert works, Shelton, Stoke
Snow John & J. 26 Howard place, Shelton, Stoke
Sudlow R. & Sons, Adelaide st. Burslem
Tams John, Stafford street, Longton
Thomas Uriah & Co. Union st. Hanley
Till T. & Sons, Liverpool rd. Burslem
Tompkinson Edward John, Flaxman pottery, Sutherland road, Longton
Twyfords Limited, Cliffe vale potteries, Shelton, Stoke
UNWIN JOSEPH & CO. Cornhill passage, Longton
Upper Hanley Pottery Co. (The), High street, Hanley
Victoria Pottery Co. (The), Broad st. Hanley
Walters Thomas, Stafford st. Longtn
Weatherby J.H. & Sons, High st. Hanley
Wedgwood Josiah & Sons Limited, Etruria pottery, Etruria, Stoke
Wedgwood & Co. Brownhills, Tunstall
Wildblood & Ledgar, Heathcote road, Longton
Wilkinson A.J. Lim. Royal Staffordshire pottery, Burslem
Wilson S.T. 41 Duke st. Fenton, Stke
Wiltshaw & Robinson, Copeland st. Stke
Winkle F. & Co. Colonial pottery, Stoke
Wood & Hulme, Waterloo rd. Burslm
Wood & Son, Trent pottery, Furlong lane, Burslem
Wood Thomas & Barker, Queen street, Burslem
Wood W. & Co. Albert St. wrks. Brslm
Yates & Bamford, Cobridge, Burslem

Ecclesiastical Decoration Manufacturers (page 695)
Woolliscroft Geo. & Son Lim. Hanley, Staffordshire: TA 'Woolliscroft, Hanley.' See advert

Electrical China Manufacturers (page 696)
TAYLOR, TUNNICLIFF & CO. LIMITED, Eastwood, Hanley; switch cases, ceiling roses, cut outs, fuse blocks &c. &c.

Enamelled Letter Makers (page 696)
Boughey M. Willow Street works, Lngtn

Enamelled Tile Manufacturers (page 696)
Minton, Hollins & Co. Stoke-on-Trent
Mintons Limited, Stoke
Woolliscroft George & Son Lim. Melville street, Hanley

Encaustic Tile Manufacturers (page 696)
Bates, Dewsberry & Co. Mayer st. Hnly
Birch Tile Co. Limited (The), 22 & 24 Clarence street, Hanley
Campbell Tile Co. (The), London rd. Stke
Corn Bros. Albert street, Tunstall
Decorative Art Tile Co. Limited (Wm. Parrish, managing director), 200 & 202 Bryan street, Hanley
Lea & Boulton, High street, Tunstall
Malkin (The) Tile works Co. Newport lane, Burslem
Marsden Tile Co. Lim. Burslem, mfrs. of decorative & flooring tiles for all purposes; quotations on application; TA 'Tiles, Burslem'; TN 3076. See advert
MINTON, HOLLINS & CO.'S PATENT TILE WORKS, Stoke-on-Trent; & Minton & Co. 50 Conduit street, Regent street, London W
Simpson T. Alfd. High street, Stoke
Wedgwood Josiah & Sons Limited, Etruria pottery, Etruria, Stoke
WOOLLISCROFT GEORGE & SON LIMITED, Melville street, Hanley, Staffs; TA 'Woolliscroft, Hanley.' See advert

Ironstone Adamant Tile Manufacturers (page 765)
Woolliscroft George & Son Limited, Hanley. See advert

Ironstone China Manufacturers (page 765)
Edwards J. Lim. King st. Fenton, Stk

Jasper Manufacturers (page 767)
Wedgwood Josiah & Sons Limited, Etruria pottery, Etruria, Stoke

Jet & Rockingham Ware Manufacturers (page 767)
See also Earthenware Manufacturers.
Barber Joseph, Albert st. Burslem
Bromley John, Barker st. Longton
Brookes Elijah, Trent walk, Hanley
Clare & Sons, Albert street, Burslem
Clare Walter, Podmore st. Burslem
Cumberlidge & Hines, Foley pottery, Longton

Dean Thomas (rockingham ware), High street, Tunstall
Gibson & Sons, Moorland rd. Burslem
Hurd T.M. Commercial st. Burslem
Johnson Saml. Hill pottery, Burslem
Lester & Smith, Clay Hills pottery, Tunstall
Lingard & Webster (rockingham ware), Keile street, Tunstall
Neale & White, Fountain square, Fenton, Stoke
Sadler J. & Sons, Newport st. Burslem
Sadler & Co. Reginald st. Burslem
Sharpe W.H. Canning st. Fenton, Stke
Wade & Co. High street, Burslem
Wood Henry James, Alexandra works, Navigation road, Burslem

Majolica Manufacturers (page 775)
Brough John Walley, Wharf st. Stoke
Colclough & Co. Goddard street, East vale, Longton
Dennis Joseph, Mount Pleasant works, High street, Longton
Forester Thomas & Sons Limited, Church st. & Stafford st. Longton
Hawley, Webberley & Co. Garfield works, High street, Longton
Heath T. Albion works, High st. Longtn
Holdcroft Joseph, Daisy bank, Longton
Minton, Hollins & Co. (tiles), Stoke-on-Trent
Mintons Limited, Stoke
Shorter & Boulton, Copeland st. Stoke
Wardle & Co. Victoria rd. Shltn. Stke
Wedgwood Josiah & Sons Limited, Etruria pottery, Etruria, Stoke

Mortar & Pestle Manufacturers (page 779)
Macintyre James & Co. Limited, Washington works, Burslem

Mosaics Manufacturers (page 779)
Campbell Tile Co. (The), London road, Stoke
Minton, Hollins & Co. Stoke-on-Trent

Parian Manufacturers (page 786)
Mintons Limited, Stoke
Robinson & Leadbeater, Wolfe street, Stoke-on-Trent; parian statuary & fancy goods manfrs.; price lists & photos on application; TA 'Leadbeater, Stoke-on-Trent.' See advt

Porcelain Manufacturers (page 791)
Copeland W.T. & Sons, High street, Stoke-on-Trent
Longton Porcelain Co. Victoria wrks. High street, Longton

Potters (page 792)
See also Art Potters.
Baker James, Kingsfield, Newcastle
Dowdeswell & Evans, Highfields Tileries, Wolstanton, Stoke
Hurd T.M. 12 Waterloo rd. Burslem
New Wharf pottery Co. (Thomas F. Wood, managing partner), Navigation road, Burslem

Sagg (*sic*) Manufacturer (page 815)
Wakefield T. Botany bay, Nrthwd. Hnly

Sanitary Ware Manufacturers (page 815)
Banner & Co. Waterloo rd. Burslem
Brick, Tile & Sanitary Ware Co. Victoria road, Shelton, Stoke
Hobson & Co. Drewery works, Normacot road, Longton
Howson George & Sons Lim. Clifford & Ephraim streets, Eastwood, Hanley
Johnson Brothers (Hanley) Lim. Hanley, Imperial, Trent & Charles St. potteries, Stoke
Sherwin & Cotton, Vine street & Cooper street, Hanley
Twyfords Limited, Cliffe Vale potteries, Shelton, Stoke

Spur Makers (page 851)
Taylor & Co. Church st. Longton

Statuary Manufacturers – Parian (page 853)
Robinson & Leadbeater, Wolfe street, Stoke-on-Trent. See advert

Stilt & Spur Manufacturers (page 854)
Arrowsmith Thomas & Sons, Moorland road, Burslem
Edwards John & Sons, King street, Fenton, Stoke
Ford Chas. & Co. Parker st. Hanley
Gimson J. & Co. Market st. Fentn. Stke
Taylor & Co. Church street, Longton

Stilt & Thimble Makers (page 854)
Ogden Henry & Co. Mayer st. Hanley

Stoneware Manufacturers (page 854)
Matthew Jn. & Son, Milton, Stoke
Wedgwood Josiah & Sons Limited, Etruria pottery, Etruria, Stoke

APPENDIX II

INDEX OF PARTNERSHIP SURNAMES

The following list includes all surnames which occur in partnership titles, other than the first-named partners which can be found directly in the alphabetical list of manufacturers in Chapter 5. Each surname is followed by a list of all the partnerships involved. Spelling and typographical variants are also included, cross-referenced to the partnership style adopted in Chapter 5.

INDEX

This is intended as a working index. Potters are only included if they are mentioned in the preliminary Chapters 1 to 4. They can be accessed directly in the alphabetical listing in Chapter 5, and thus to their directory appearances in Appendix 1. Places in Staffordshire are referenced to their main appearance in the text.